Current Biography Yearbook 2001

EDITOR
Clifford Thompson

PRODUCTION STAFF
Gray Young (Manager)
Tia Brown
Jacquelene Latif
Richard J. Stein
Sandra Watson

SENIOR EDITOR
Miriam Helbok

ASSISTANT EDITORS
Jeremy K. Brown
Christopher Luna
Mari Rich

CONTRIBUTING EDITOR
Kieran Dugan

STAFF WRITERS
Josha Hill
Patrick Kelly
Geoff Orens
Kate Stern

CONTRIBUTING WRITERS
Dimitri Cavalli
Terence J. Fitzgerald
Willie Gin
Peter G. Herman
Martha A. Hostetter
Christopher Mari
Gregory K. Robinson
Aaron Tassano
Selma Yampolsky

RESEARCHER
Verna J. Coleman

EDITORIAL ASSISTANT
Carolyn Ellis

THE H. W. WILSON COMPANY
NEW YORK   DUBLIN

SIXTY-SECOND ANNUAL CUMULATION—2001

PRINTED IN THE UNITED STATES OF AMERICA

International Standard Serial No. (0084-9499)

International Standard Book No. (0-8242-1016-6)

Library of Congress Catalog Card No. (40-27432)

Table of Contents

PREFACE

The aim of *Current Biography Yearbook 2001*, like that of the preceding volumes in this series of annual dictionaries of contemporary biography, now in its seventh decade of publication, is to provide reference librarians, students, and researchers with objective, accurate, and well-documented biographical articles about living leaders in all fields of human accomplishment the world over. Whenever feasible, obituary notices appear for persons whose biographies have been published in *Current Biography*.

Current Biography Yearbook 2001 carries on the policy of including new and updated biographical profiles that supersede earlier articles. Profiles have been made as accurate and objective as possible through careful researching of newspapers, magazines, the World Wide Web, authoritative reference books, and news releases of both government and private agencies. Immediately after they are published in the 11 monthly issues, articles are submitted to biographees to give them an opportunity to suggest additions and corrections in time for publication of the *Current Biography Yearbook*. To take account of major changes in the careers of biographees, articles are revised before they are included in the yearbook.

Classification by Profession—2001 and *2001 Index* are at the end of this volume. *Current Biography Cumulated Index 1940–2000* cumulates and supersedes all previous indexes. For the index to the 1991–2000 issues, see the 2000 yearbook.

For their assistance in preparing *Current Biography Yearbook 2001*, I thank the staff of *Current Biography* and other members of The H. W. Wilson Company's General Reference Department, and also the staffs of the company's Computer and Manufacturing departments.

Current Biography welcomes comments and suggestions. Please send your comments to: The Editor, *Current Biography*, The H. W. Wilson Company, 950 University Ave., Bronx, NY 10452; fax: 718-590-4566; E-mail: cthompson@hwwilson.com.

Clifford Thompson

List of Biographical Sketches

Current Biography Yearbook
2001

Current Biography Yearbook 2001

Abakanowicz, Magdalena

(ah-bah-kah-NO-vitch)

1930– Sculptor. Address: c/o Marlborough Gallery, 40 W. 57th St., New York, NY 10019

"Material is for me a tool, like an instrument, on which I play with my insides," the Polish sculptor Magdalena Abakanowicz told Michael Brenson for the *New York Times Magazine* (November 29, 1992). "It can be a violin, or piano, or a whole orchestra, but it does not change the music." During her 40-year career, Abakanowicz has "played" with fiber, burlap, wood, stone, and bronze to create sculptures that range from pebble-size to tree-scale. Her search for material for her art has led her to gather wood from the forests of Poland, mine stone from the deserts of Israel, and salvage old rope from a Warsaw dock; in contrast to her contemporary Richard Serra, an American sculptor who creates enormous geometric works out of factory-made steel, Abakanowicz emphasizes irregular forms and organic materials. Her work defies categorization; much of it evokes 20th-century experiences, but not in the way that Felix DeWel-

don's famous depiction of the American soldiers raising a flag at Iwo Jima memorializes a specific event. Her sculptures—of giant hands, trees, birds, skulls, and human figures—seem to conjure their own events. Since she first came to international attention, in 1965, by winning the top prize at the Saõ Paulo Biennale, in Brazil, she has had several major exhibits and has seen her work installed in art museums and galleries around the world.

Magdalena Abakanowicz was born into an aristocratic family in Falenty, Poland, in 1930. Her father was a descendant of Abaka-Khan, a great-grandson of Genghis Khan, the 13th-century Mongol chieftain whose empire ranged from Eastern Europe to the Sea of Japan. Her family lived on a country estate east of Warsaw, and Abakanowicz spent her childhood among servants and tutors and in solitary exploration of the ancient woods surrounding her home. As she recalled to Michael Brenson for *Art Journal* (Spring 1995), she was drawn to the mystery and grandeur of the forest, and remembers "learning about all that was alive" and feeling that "all was at one with me." In 1939 German army tanks rolled into the family park, changing Abakanowicz's world suddenly and irrevocably. "The house exposed us, it ceased to be a shelter. The forest also became alien. I no longer went there to talk to it as before," she wrote in her memoir, *Portrait X 20*, as quoted by Brenson in the *New York Times Magazine*. Abakanowicz lived through the Nazi occupation of Poland, the ill-fated Warsaw uprising of 1944, and the installation of a repressive Communist government in Poland. During World War II her family lost their property and wealth, and, in postwar Communist Poland, the former aristocrats became classified as enemies of the people.

By hiding her family background, Abakanowicz succeeded in winning acceptance to the Academy of Fine Arts in Warsaw, in 1950. Since she did not get into the sculpture program, she enrolled in the painting course, but she soon discovered that her nonrealistic drawings offended her teachers. In 1950s Poland, studying art meant adopting "socialist realism," the officially sanctioned theory and method of art favored by Joseph Stalin, the dictator of the Soviet Union, who believed that the purpose of art was to help build a Communist society. To avoid such restrictions, Abakanowicz gravitated toward weaving and tapestry, low-visibility arts that had long been associated with craft. "With my first work I wanted to get as far as possible from everything around me in art," she told Alan G. Artner for the *Chicago Tribune* (October 31, 1982). Weaving, she told Artner, was a "desert" that few other artists wanted to traverse.

While attending art school, Abakanowicz supported herself by donating blood, working small construction jobs, and coaching athletes. After she graduated, in 1954, she went to work at a factory, designing fabric for neckties. Like many Poles (families as well as unmarried people), she lived in a one-room apartment and had very little space to do artwork. Making art out of soft materials like fiber allowed her to create objects that could exist in multiple parts and be folded away easily. The materials were also readily available; Abakanowicz collected old natural-fiber ropes, untwined them, and then dyed the threads. At a time when tapestry was still the principal form of fiber art, and when weavers seldom aimed for more than decoration, Abakanowicz created weavings that were radically unconventional. Dense, dark, and shaggy, they were neither flat nor pictorial and would never be considered "craft." Dubbed by one critic "Abakans" after the artist's family name, these pieces were exhibited widely during the 1960s and early 1970s, so that the obscure art of weaving brought Abakanowicz international fame.

Monumental in scale and construction—they ranged from 10 to 16 feet tall and measured about five feet wide—the Abakans were suspended from the ceilings of galleries and resembled an airborne herd of shaggy buffalos. Likening them to cocoons, hollow tree trunks, or "mutilated torsos of giants," critics struggled to describe their strange energy and audacious body imagery. Through her innovative use of fiber, Abakanowicz had turned materials and techniques associated with crafts into high-powered, three-dimensional sculptures. "The 'Abakans' were guests either in exhibitions of weavings or sculpture, and I existed between categories because the work was neither here nor there," Abakanowicz told Artner. "This I rather enjoyed."

In the early 1970s Abakanowicz moved a step closer to traditional sculpture through a cycle of works based on the human form. With *Backs*, hunched torsos kneeling on the floor in rows, and *Seated Figures*, a line of figures perched on stools, Abakanowicz began to people the art world with the brown, headless, and hollow creatures that have become her trademark. To construct them, Abakanowicz made a plaster cast from a nude male model, then wrapped the cast in burlap sacks stiffened with vegetable glue. In her interview with Artner, Abakanowicz pointed out that these figural works evolved out of her weaving of old, natural-fiber rope. "I still use old material that has its own history. It is organic, meaning something that once grew and will finish by disintegrating." Some of the works have since been cast in bronze, imparting to them longer life and allowing them to be installed outdoors.

Iconic and provocative, all of Abakanowicz's figures are cast from the same mold but vary subtly in color, texture, and shape, and they suggest vastly different things to different viewers. Some liken the folds in the burlap to wrinkles, and the fragile surfaces to mummified human skin—evidence, however scant, of the figures' essential humanity and individuality. To others, the faceless and sexless crowds appear terrifying and anonymous, signaling the belief that the individual has become an anonymous cog, a far cry from what classical sculptors regarded as the ideal man or woman. Most powerfully, Abakanowicz's figures recall World War II images of prisoners lined up in concentration camps or in front of firing squads, or of the fascist gangs responsible for such atrocities. Writing for the London *Guardian* (February 14, 1982), one critic observed, "The Polish tragedy is inescapably present in [Abakanowicz's] tense, harrowing, expressive work. . . . She transmits an infinitely painful image of man through her sculptures of rope, twine, and patched and woven burlap." Although Abakanowicz resists strictly autobiographical interpretations of her work, she has spoken of the figures in relationship to the mangled victims she helped to nurse in 1944, as the Soviet army approached Nazi-occupied Warsaw, and as symbols of those whose childhoods, like her own, were curtailed by the war. Others, in discussing these works, have noted that as a teenager, Abakanowicz witnessed a Nazi soldier shoot off her mother's arm.

One of the constants in Abakanowicz's work is the group. In one installation, *Embryology*, nearly 800 burlap sacks of various sizes form a river of stones and boulders. Abakanowicz has said that her groupings translate a single art object into a larger statement about society. "If you have one sculpture, you can put it into your sitting room. If you have a group, you are forced to contemplate the place of man in our times," she told Alan Riding for the *New York Times* (July 1, 1999). At the same time, the multiple iterations also display difference. As Abakanowicz was quoted as saying in a press release issued by the Marlborough Gallery, in New York City, which represents her, a crowd provides evidence of nature's "abhorrence to exact repetition or inability to produce it, just as a human hand can not repeat its own gesture."

Abakanowicz also regards her art as a means of probing the mysteries of nature. Early on, it was a way for her to defy the Communist government's attempts to regulate artistic imagination. "In Poland it was almost forbidden to talk about mystery," she told Brenson during the *New York Times Magazine* interview. "I did." Her sculptures of heads, figures, and birds have often been compared to magical objects, with their rough-hewn construction and organic materials lending them a touch of the primeval. Like shamanistic objects, some of her sculptures seem endowed with their own life forces, so that burlap sacks become eggs, sculpted figures become silent armies, and even the abstract Abakans can be seen as cocoons or nests, harboring secrets of life. Her art, she says, takes place in the junctures between organic and inorganic, life and death, creation and destruction. "I reveal what is common to all of us," Abakanowicz has said, as quoted by Barbara Rose in *Vogue* (April 1988). Her art, she has explained, refers to "what is unnamed, what is forgotten, what is contained in our feelings and fears."

Because of the symbolic resonances of her work, Abakanowicz has insisted on exercising control over how and where the sculptures appear. She has personally organized more than 100 exhibitions of her work, which she terms "still ceremonies." When offered her choice of location within a famed sculpture garden in the Israel Museum, in Jerusalem—where such masters as Alberto Giacometti, Henry Moore, Pablo Picasso, and Joan Miró are represented—Abakanowicz surprised curators by asking instead for a place outside the museum walls, on the edge of a rocky cliff overlooking the city. She then created what in the art world is termed a "site-specific" piece, one that is the product of an artist's response to a given location. For the Jerusalem piece, Abakanowicz used translucent limestone from the Negev Desert, in Israel, cutting seven massive wheels of stone and then setting them in a row on the edge of the cliff, where they perch—perilously, in the eyes of some observers—above the ancient city. "The hill is as important as the stone is to the artwork," Abakanowicz was quoted as saying by a reporter for the *New York Times* (September 10, 1987). "The wheels are frozen in time, ready to run away with just a nudge from the wind." The sculpture, called *Negev*, invites a rapport with its environment. The stones' pinkish hues brighten and darken as the sun rises and sets. And, as Barbara Rose wrote, the crude shapes bring to mind the world's first wheel, the seven ancient gates of Jerusalem, and—because one wheel has a navel-like indentation—the notion of Jerusalem as *omphalos mundi*, the navel of the world. In 1999 Abakanowicz exhibited sculptures of human figures on the roof garden of the Metropolitan Museum of Art in New York. Silhouetted against the towers of the Manhattan skyline, the figures seemed neither vulnerable nor menacing to most viewers but, rather, appeared romantic, even heroic.

"In the evening, leaving my studio, I often have the impression the sculptures will begin to behave in their own way, not being under my control," Abakanowicz told *Current Biography*. Perhaps moved by that idea, in 1999 the sculptor for the first time depicted human figures in motion. The burlap forms of *Walking*, which consist of legs and the trunks of bodies, are depicted taking long strides forward. Abakanowicz also choreographed dances linked with the sculptures. An exhibition of her new work, including figures of adults and children walking, opened in Warsaw in December 2000 with a dance performed around the sculptures.

Abakanowicz has been a rigorous presence on the international art scene for 40 years. Unlike many Eastern-bloc artists, she never considered emigrating from Poland, although she faced many challenges as an artist there. Because she and her husband had no children, they had to live in a one-room apartment for many years. She also had to overcome many bureaucratic hurdles before gaining permission to leave Poland to attend art shows abroad. Now retired after 25 years as a professor at the Academy of Fine Arts in Poznan, Poland, Abakanowicz currently lives in a house on the outskirts of Warsaw. Her honors include being named both an officer and a chevalier of France's Order of Arts and Letters. Books about her and her work include *Magdalena Abakanowicz: Recent Sculpture* (1993), by Michael Brenson, *Magdalena Abakanowicz* (1994), by Barbara Rose, and *Magdalena Abakanowicz: Bronze Sculpture* (1996), by the artist and others. — M.A.H.

Suggested Reading: *Art Journal* p56+ Spring 1995; *Chicago Tribune* VI p21+ Oct. 31, 1982, with photos; *Christian Science Monitor* p16+ Mar. 15, 1993, with photos; *New York Times Magazine* p47+ Nov. 29, 1992, with photos; *Vogue* p354+ Apr. 1988, with photos

Selected Works: *Abakans*, 1966–75; *Heads*, 1975; *Backs*, 1976–82; *Embryology*, 1978–81; *War Games*, 1989–90; *Walking*, 1999

Abraham, Spencer

June 12, 1952– U.S. Secretary of Energy.
Address: U.S. Dept. of Energy, 1000
Independence Ave., S.W., Washington, DC 20585

On January 20, 2001, the day that George W. Bush was inaugurated as the nation's 43d president, former Michigan senator Spencer Abraham was sworn in as the secretary of the United States Department of Energy. Active in Republican Party politics since the early 1980s, Abraham served as Vice President Dan Quayle's deputy chief of staff from 1990 to 1991. He was elected to the U.S. Senate in 1994. According to *Politics in America 2000*, he is a "devout conservative of considerable intellect" who tends to shun "headlines in favor of working quietly behind the scenes." An active member of the Arab–American community throughout his career, Abraham was dedicated to issues related to immigration when he served in Congress. He was also known for his close ties to the pharmaceutical and insurance industries. The subjects of energy needs, sources, and supplies were not among his areas of expertise; indeed, as Carl M. Cannon pointed out in *Forbes* (September 10, 2001), "In his six years in the Senate, Abraham had little intersection with the issue of energy or

Courtesy of U.S. Department of Energy

Spencer Abraham

considerable influence during the administration of President Ronald Reagan. After he completed his law degree, in 1979, Abraham returned to Lansing, where he taught as a professor at the Thomas M. Cooley Law School for a few years.

Democrats controlled both houses of the Michigan state legislature when, in 1983, Abraham was elected chairman of the state Republican Party. He soon erased the organization's considerable debt and raised an additional $2.5 million. In the following year the GOP gained control of the state legislature for the first time in a decade—an achievement for which many felt that Abraham deserved much of the credit—and Michigan voters supported President Reagan's reelection bid with the largest margin of any industrial state. Abraham also played a key role in the victory of his friend John M. Engler over the incumbent James Blanchard in the race for governor of Michigan in 1990. That same year Abraham became Vice President Dan Quayle's deputy chief of staff, serving under William Kristol. Kristol described Abraham to Nicholas Confessore for the *American Prospect* (October 20, 2000, on-line) as "a classic staff guy, detail-oriented, you know, always making lists. He's not a classic glad–hander and mixer with people." He was also named chairman of the National Republican Congressional Committee.

Abraham hoped to be named chairman of the Republican National Committee in 1993, but the title went to Haley Barbour of Mississippi. Although Abraham was disappointed, his being passed over spurred him to run for the U.S. Senate in 1994, after Michigan senator Donald W. Riegle, a Democrat, announced his retirement. In the GOP primary, he narrowly defeated the radio host Ronna Romney (a daughter-in-law of the former Michigan governor George Romney). In the general election he faced Representative Bob Carr. Abraham ran on a platform of lower taxes, free trade, term limits, and "family values"; he also accused his rival of defending the tax increase in President Bill Clinton's budget and what he termed the excess spending in Clinton's crime bill. During the campaign Abraham distinguished himself through unexpected moves such as a visit to Focus Hope, a successful inner-city youth job-training program. He was hurt to some extent by one of his own political advertisements, which stated erroneously that Carr stood to receive millions from his government pension; the actual amount was in the thousands. Abraham pulled the ad but did not apologize for misinforming the public. On Election Day he won 52 percent of the vote, thus becoming the first Republican elected to the U.S. Senate from Michigan since 1978. Some commentators suggested that his victory was helped by the careful publicizing of his association with the governor of Michigan, John M. Engler.

the agency he now leads, save for cosponsoring legislation to abolish the department as recently as 1999." Family is extremely important to Abraham; as a senator, he made sure to set aside time for his three children, occasionally bringing them to work with him. "Having small children while you're in this job keeps you on a normal lifestyle," he has said, as quoted in *Politics in America 2000*. "You don't get too wrapped up in Washington. You have that other life, too."

The grandson of immigrants from Lebanon, Edmund Spencer Abraham was born in or near Lansing, Michigan, on June 12, 1952. His father worked in the automobile industry before opening a small store. Abraham was raised in Auburn Hills, Michigan, as a member of the Eastern Orthodox church. His political conservatism developed during his college years, when he began formulating his views on individual freedom and economic opportunity. Upon his graduation from Michigan State University, with a B.A. degree in political science and social science, in 1974, he began working for the Republican Party. Abraham managed Republican Clifford W. Taylor's unsuccessful 1974 and 1976 campaigns for a seat in the House of Representatives; in both races Taylor was defeated by the Democratic candidate, Bob Carr. In about 1976 Abraham entered Harvard Law School, in Cambridge, Massachusetts. As a student there he cofounded a right-wing law review called the *Harvard Journal of Law and Public Policy*, created as an alternative to the existing campus law publications. He also helped to develop the Washington, D.C.–based Federalist Society for Law & Public Policy Studies, a group of conservative and libertarian thinkers and lawyers who would later have

Abraham was among many other newly elected Republican members of Congress who intended to challenge what they considered the exorbitant expenditures of the federal government. During his campaign he had joined other GOP Senate candidates to sign a set of pledges known as the "Agenda for a Republican Majority," which resembled the "Contract with America," written chiefly by Newt Gingrich, who became the Speaker of the House in January 1994. The "Agenda for a Republican Majority" called for higher defense spending, tax cuts, welfare reform, and the enactment of tougher anticrime legislation. During the 104th Congress Abraham introduced a proposal to reduce legislators' salaries by 10 percent; he later called for a dismantling of the U.S. Department of Commerce. In addition, he served as an adviser to Senator Bob Dole during Dole's unsuccessful bid for the presidency in 1996. As a member of the 105th Congress, Abraham often advised Senate majority leader Trent Lott. In 1999 Abraham co-sponsored the Social Security Preservation Act, also known as the "Social Security lockbox," intended to prevent the government from borrowing from the Social Security surplus. Other notable actions in Abraham's Senate career included his co-sponsorship of the China Sanctions and Human Rights Advancement Act, which, among other provisions, would have placed sanctions on the government of Communist China for its many human-rights violations and banned two Chinese companies with known ties to the military from doing business in the United States for one year. He also organized the creation of a book of condolences following the death of Princess Diana of Great Britain, in 1997; nominated Rosa Parks for a Congressional Gold Medal for her role in the Montgomery, Alabama, bus boycott of 1955, one of the events that sparked the civil rights movement; and, along with more than 220 other members of Congress, sponsored the Made in the USA Label Defense Act of 1999, aimed at ensuring that all products bearing the "Made in the USA" label had actually been manufactured in this country. "If [a label] says 'Made in USA' the U.S. consumer has a right to expect that the entire product and all of its components was made by U.S. citizens," Abraham said in a Senate speech on April 29, 1999, as reported on the Web site of the Take Pride in America Coalition. "The standard is honest. It is clear. It provides value for all those who look for the label and for those who have earned the use of it. But in order to retain that value, the integrity of the 'Made in USA' label must be defended. We cannot and will not permit the 'Made in USA' label to be used misleadingly. It belongs to those American businesses and workers who follow the rules, pay the taxes, and work hard—often against the odds presented by unfair foreign competition—to continue to manufacture products here in America."

During the 105th Congress Abraham became the chairman of the Senate Judiciary Committee's Immigration Subcommittee, succeeding the retiring Wyoming senator Alan K. Simpson, who—like most of Abraham's Republican colleagues—had favored imposing stricter limits on immigration. Abraham successfully pushed through a bill that increased the number of visas (so-called H1-B visas) issued to highly skilled immigrants. After President Clinton threatened to veto the measure, on the grounds that it might hurt American workers, Abraham negotiated a compromise with Gene Sperling, chair of the president's National Economic Council.

In 2000 Debbie Stabenow, a former social worker and 15-year Democratic veteran of the Michigan state legislature, challenged Abraham for his Senate seat. Abraham's detractors included the Center for Responsive Politics, which describes itself as "a non-partisan, non-profit research group . . . that tracks money in politics, and its effect on elections and public policy"; according to that group, Abraham voted against the patients' bill of rights and legislation that would have held HMOs accountable when the deaths of patients could be traced to the decisions of HMO staff members. Other watchdog groups charged that a clear relationship existed between the campaign money Abraham received from pharmaceutical companies and his decision to vote against measures to make prescription drugs more affordable for Medicaid recipients. Others tried to link the generous support he received from commercial banks with his decision to vote against measures such as the prohibition of an ATM surcharge and the Community Reinvestment Act, designed to prevent banks from discriminating against minority-owned businesses seeking loans. After a bitter, expensive race, Stabenow won the election, with 49.5 percent of the vote—1.6 percent more than the total for Abraham.

Soon afterward President-elect George W. Bush picked Abraham to head the Department of Energy—a choice that struck some observers as odd, in light of the fact that three times during his Senate career he had sponsored legislation to abolish that very department. Environmental groups opposed his nomination, on the ground that during his tenure in Congress, he had voted to cut the Environmental Protection Agency's budget by 21 percent and to reduce environmental programs by $3.7 billion; he had also opposed clean-water programs and efforts to conduct research aimed at setting fuel-efficiency standards. Environmentalists were further outraged over his support of oil drilling in the Arctic National Wildlife Refuge, in Alaska. "He's the wrong man for the wrong job," Dave Dempsey of the Michigan Environmental Council declared to Curt Guyette for *Metro Times Detroit* (January 9, 2001, on-line). "He's shown throughout his career that he has absolutely no grasp of the wrenching changes that are coming in American energy use. He's a defender of the old guard that just wants to drill for oil to support gas-guzzlers." Other expressions of concern about Abraham's nomination had to do with his membership on the board of advisers for the Washington Legal Foundation, an organization that has opposed affirmative action, the Voting Rights Act, and various pieces of environmental legislation. Other groups criticized him for his support of the World Trade

Organization and the expansion of the North American Free Trade Agreement into 24 Latin American countries, which many have predicted will lead to the loss of many American jobs. Despite such opposition, the Senate confirmed Abraham by a voice vote, and he was sworn in as secretary of energy on January 20, 2001.

In March 2001 Abraham announced that the Bush administration would soon release a "comprehensive and balanced" energy plan. "I think it's important for the United States to be less at the mercy of foreign countries and their decision-making and politics, and more under our own control to address these problems," Abraham told an interviewer, according to *CNN.com* (March 19, 2001). He also said, "There's really only three things you can do about a difference between supply and demand. One is to conserve more. The second is to import more. And the third is to produce more. I think we want to focus more on conserving more and producing more rather than depending more on other countries."

In May 2001 Abraham, Education Secretary Rod Paige, and Health and Human Services Secretary Tommy G. Thompson reversed their decisions to attend a $23.9 million Republican fund-raising dinner, after campaign-finance-reform supporters and others charged that, by means of such events, the Bush administration was giving special access to individuals or groups that had donated money to the Republican Party. Abraham, Paige, and Thompson had been scheduled to hold policy seminars in conjunction with the dinner, which was sponsored by the Inner Circle, a group made up of donors of $1,000 or more to the GOP.

In the midst of the power crisis that gripped California in the spring of 2001 and included rolling blackouts and huge increases in the prices of natural gas and electricity, the Bush administration rejected requests made by the state's governor, Gray Davis, that the federal government institute temporary price controls to stabilize energy costs. In an op-ed article in the *New York Times* (June 9, 2001), Abraham maintained that such a strategy would encourage suppliers to take their business elsewhere and would also lead to a cessation of the construction of new power plants, the financing of which is based on market prices. He also wrote out that less than 50 percent of the companies that sell power to Western states fall under the jurisdiction of the federal government, and to place price controls only on those companies would be unfair. Additionally, he reported, the Federal Energy Regulation Commission had ordered that $125 million be refunded to customers who had been overcharged. "We will help in any way," Abraham wrote, "but we will not be a party to making the situation worse."

In his September 2001 interview with Carl M. Cannon for *Forbes*, Abraham agreed that the continuing exponential increase in the use of technology associated with the Internet will require a concomitant increase in the production of energy.

(Cannon noted that at various times Abraham himself had cited studies in which the energy consultants Mark P. Mills and Peter Huber had found that at present, in Cannon's words, "between 8 and 13 percent of all the electric power consumed in this country is used to power computers, servers, telecommunications, and other devices related to the Internet.") "The best thing we can do to ensure there is energy for the high technology sector is to ensure an expedited and certain regulatory system that will allow developers to construct plants in a timely fashion," Abraham told Cannon. "They must be able to quickly respond to market signals that indicate the need for more stable power sources. In addition, we need the market to provide flexible products, ones that can suit the working patterns of the new economy businesses. Finally, we need to create the environment where willing entrepreneurs are eager to risk their capital on new products and innovative ideas."

Associates of his have noted Abraham's near-photographic memory and his skill with numbers. In his leisure time he enjoys reading and playing golf. He and his wife, Jane, who have three children, maintain homes in Michigan and Virginia. — C.L.

Suggested Reading: *Nation* p20+ Mar. 6, 2000; *National Review* p30+ Sep. 25, 2000; *New York Times* A p2 Jan. 3, 2001; *Politics in America 2000*

Arnesen, Liv

(AR-neh-sen, leeve)

June 1, 1953– Explorer; educator; writer.
Address: Yourexpedition, 119 N. Fourth St., Suite 406, Minneapolis, MN 55401

At the age of 12, Liv Arnesen, a polar explorer and educator, knew that she wanted to travel to Antarctica, the fifth-largest—and the most barren and brutally cold—of Earth's seven continents. She had read *Endurance* (1959), Alfred Lansing's account of Sir Ernest Shackleton's 1914–16 attempt to cross Antarctica, which is asymmetrically centered around the South Pole. She was proud that Roald Amundsen, a Norwegian like herself, had been the first explorer to reach the South Pole, during a 1911–12 expedition. In addition, she loved the outdoors and didn't mind snowy, freezing weather. "We spent all our holidays in the mountains, especially in the wintertime," she explained to Kyle Noone for *myprimetime.com* (2000). "I really loved to be out there in the snow covered trees, the wide open spaces and the beautiful light." As an adult Arnesen became a teacher, spending her summer vacations as a leader of trips to the Arctic. In the 1990s she completed several spectacular feats of endurance that involved cross-country skiing over

Courtesy of yourexpedition.com

Liv Arnesen

remarkable distances with little or no support. Late in 1994 she became the first woman to ski solo to the South Pole, thus realizing a childhood dream. In 2000–01 Arnesen teamed with Ann Bancroft, an American Arctic and Antarctic explorer, to traverse Antarctica on skis. They are the first women to have done so.

Liv Arnesen was born on June 1, 1953 in Bærum, Norway, near Oslo. Her father, Finn Chr. Arnesen, worked in construction, and her mother, Berit Arnesen, was an accountant; both were avid cross-country skiers and transmitted their enthusiasm for the sport to their daughter and son. Before she reached her teens, Arnesen had read accounts of Amundsen's and Shackleton's trips to the South Pole and developed a longing to go there herself. "I think it wasn't so much the South Pole that attracted me," she confessed to William Plummer and Lydia Denworth for *People* (March 13, 1995), "as it was that long ski trip." In high school Arnesen participated in competitive cross-country skiing and orienteering events.

After graduating from the University of Oslo, with degrees in history and literature, in 1979, Arnesen became a high-school teacher and cross-country skiing coach. She also earned counseling credentials and worked in drug-rehabilitation programs during a year off from classroom teaching. During summer breaks she led expeditions for Svalbard Polar Travel, an adventure-vacation outfit; her groups skied and explored glaciers above the Arctic Circle. In time she became the marketing director for her summer employer. Inspired by Carl Emil Petersen, who skied solo across Greenland in 1983, she decided to undertake the same journey. "I began to think that I didn't have to just read

about it," she told Plummer and Denworth. In 1991, accompanied by three friends, she tried to cross the Greenland ice cap, but the trip ended in failure. She succeeded in her next attempt, made the next year with Julie Maske, a polar-travel guide. Unaccompanied by a dog-sled team or equipment carriers, she and Maske skied for 24 days and covered several hundred miles. They were the first women to complete an unsupported crossing of the Greenland ice cap.

Her appetite whetted for an even greater challenge, Arnesen decided to chase her childhood dream of skiing to the South Pole. She found corporate sponsorship, primarily from Italian companies, to cover the cost of such a trip, and then began to train intensively. Her wintertime routine consisted of cross-country skiing while carrying a heavy backpack and dragging a sled. In the summer she jogged along unpaved roads while pulling 100 pounds of automobile tires. "People thought I was crazy when they met me in the woods," she told Plummer and Denworth. Aiming to ski at the height of the Antarctic summer, she departed from Hercules Inlet, on the Antarctic coast along the Weddell Sea, on November 5, 1994.

Like her trip across the Greenland ice cap, this venture was unsupported; unlike the Greenland trip, she did not have a companion. She skied solo for 50 days, pulling a 50-pound storage sled, called a pulka, stocked with 200 pounds of equipment and provisions. She gradually lengthened her daily skiing schedule from six hours to 11 and averaged 15 miles a day over the course of her 750-mile journey to the South Pole. Although she "tried not to think about home," as she told Plummer and Denworth, loneliness was not a major problem for Arnesen, whose husband and children in Norway awaited coded messages from her transmitter. She did, however, have to deal with physical hardships. Prominent among them were the fierce winds and driving snow, which sometimes created whiteouts in which visibility dropped to almost zero, forcing her to stop skiing. The topography presented other problems. "The terrain wasn't flat. It was like a stormy ocean," she explained to Plummer and Denworth. She also experienced the unforeseen: one day, walking without her skis on a ridge, she slipped into a crevasse that had been hidden beneath a layer of snow and almost plunged to her death. "I sank suddenly through to the hip. My heart almost stopped, but the backpack and sled prevented me from falling all the way down into the blue depth," she recalled to Plummer and Denworth.

Although her clothing kept her well-insulated, Arnesen developed frostbite about 10 days before she reached the South Pole. "On Dec. 14, it was very, very cold," she explained to Malcolm W. Browne for the *New York Times* (January 6, 1995). "For 10 hours I had been skiing over sastrugi—ice ridges—which is very tiring. I thought I should rest for a day, but changed my mind and started out. The frost began covering my snow goggles, and to see I kept taking off my glove to scratch the ice off with my fingernails. It was then that I got frostbite." (Within a few months the affected finger had healed almost completely.)

To her surprise, Arnesen felt emotional as she approached the domed, U.S.-run Amundsen-Scott Station, on Christmas Eve, 1994. "I was thinking it would be anticlimactic because it was this big station with bulldozers, cars, planes and so on. But the last few meters, up to the point where a sign says 'Geographic South Pole,' I was really moved," she told Plummer and Denworth. She was also surprised by the warmth of the Americans at the facility—as were three other Norwegian skiers who arrived there four days later—since station personnel are not required to admit visitors. "The skiers were uncertain what kind of welcome they would get on their arrival at the United States base," Malcolm W. Browne wrote, explaining that "relations between the polar program officials of the National Science Foundation and nonofficial expeditions, tour groups and unauthorized visitors have been uneasy, if not downright hostile." During the next two weeks, while waiting to be airlifted out, Arnesen camped in her tent outside the station and bartered her dishwashing and cooking skills for meals and companionship inside it. Having her hands in hot water while dishwashing helped minimize permanent frostbite damage to her hands. Upon her return to Oslo, Arnesen got a hero's welcome. Her book about her experience—in English, its title means "Good Girls Do Not Ski to the South Pole"— was published in Norwegian in 1995; to date it has not been translated into English. Not wanting to risk boring readers with a day-by-day chronicle, she wove into the text an inspirational message for women and girls: "Live your own life, make your own choices," as she phrased it to Plummer and Denworth.

Arnesen's next adventure came to a premature end. While attempting to scale the north face of the world's highest peak—the 29,035-foot Mount Everest, in Nepal—she suffered an attack of altitude sickness; because of her insufficient intake of oxygen, abnormal amounts of fluid accumulated in her brain (a condition called edema). Going further would have endangered her health, so after she climbed to an altitude of about 22,300 feet, she turned back. After her Everest climb Arnesen started her own business in Norway, drawing on both her adventurous travels and her experiences as an educator. Called White Horizons, the company offers motivational lectures and confidence-building initiatives for adults and children.

In 1998 Arnesen met Ann Bancroft, an American explorer and teacher who had traveled to both the North and South Poles. "It was like they had found each other," Einar Glestad, Arnesen's husband, said to Jerry Zgoda for the *Minneapolis-St. Paul Star Tribune* (February 25, 2001). Describing themselves as "soul sisters," Arnesen and Bancroft began planning a joint U.S.-Norway expedition to Antarctica. The women proposed skiing across the entire continent, starting from Queen Maud Land, which lies along the Atlantic Ocean, crossing the continent at the end of the Shackleton Glacier, and ending at McMurdo Station, which is on the Ross Ice Shelf, in the Ross Sea, an arm of the Pacific Ocean. They estimated that the trip, more than 2,300 miles, would take 100 days. They intended not only to ski but to parasail; depending on wind speed, a parasail—a rectangular sail controlled by dozens of lines—could propel them at an average velocity of about six miles per hour. With the help of consultants in public relations and marketing, Arnesen and Bancroft founded a company called yourexpedition, with the aim of getting corporate sponsorships. (Volvo, Pfizer, Motorola, Apple Computer, and others contributed toward the project.) As teachers, both women regarded their expedition as an opportunity to teach others; in reports posted on *yourexpedition.com*, they wrote about their preparations, and they promised to send daily reports from Antarctica about their experiences and thoughts, as a way of engaging students' interest in aspects of of science, health, and geography. The idea appealed to other teachers, hundreds of whom signed up to follow the expedition with their classes. The Girls Scouts of the USA, too, made plans to use the trip as a teaching tool for their troops. Arnesen was pleased with the response she and Bancroft got. "My motivation for going back [to Antarctica] is mixed," she wrote for *yourexpedition.com* before she departed. "I still have this longing for the great wide open spaces, but after my last expedition I also learned from numbers of lectures in schools what a privilege it was to have a story to tell about the fulfillment of a dream."

For several months Arnesen and Bancroft trained separately for the expedition in their respective countries. Both maintained regular routines of running, weight and strength training, and skiing, and both gained extra pounds as a safeguard against burning muscle during the journey. (For the same reason, they planned to eat foods extremely high in fat during their journey.) Training together for a while in Canada and Norway, they practiced skiing, parasailing, pulling heavily loaded sleds, and executing emergency rescues, and they tested various equipment. Anticipating temperatures of 35 degrees below zero and lower, 100-mile-an-hour winds, and feelings of isolation, they also tried to strengthen themselves psychologically. "We're going to have to be very cautious every second," Arnesen told Kyle Noone. "I think that is the most important thing for us; having the concentration, being in the moment."

In October 2000 Arnesen and Bancroft held a send-off celebration with schoolchildren in South Africa. A tense waiting period followed, as their departure was delayed for three weeks, because the weather at the Antarctic airstrip on which they were scheduled to land was too rough for a safe touchdown. On November 13, 2000 the women arrived at Blue One Runway, in Queen Maud Land, where they loaded each sled with about 200 pounds of food and supplies for skiing, parasailing, climbing, cooking, navigating, sheltering themselves, and communicating with others by radio, telephone, and computer. After ascending the 10,940-foot-high Sygyn Glacier, which took two weeks, they headed across the frozen desert that constitutes the polar plateau. During windy weeks they would travel more than 200 miles; when there was little or no wind, they would cover fewer than 40. "Neither of us is a negative person," Arnesen told Jerry Zgoda. "After the first week without wind [in mid-December], we said, 'My, this is unusual.' After the second week we realized it was a special summer. Yes, it was really depressing, but we don't dig down into it. We tried to remember the beauty that we saw each day." Their slowed pace jeopardized their goal of completing the journey by mid-February 2001, before the Antarctic autumn, when being airlifted out or picked up by ship would become impossible.

In the middle of the sunlit night of January 16, 2001, Arnesen and Bancroft reached the South Pole. With a little over a month remaining before the anticipated freezing of the Antarctic seas, the women still had just under 1,000 miles to cover. Nonetheless, they paused briefly at the Amundsen-Scott Station at the South Pole to bathe and change their clothes and to enjoy a meal other than chocolate (their hourly snack while skiing) or something freeze-dried. The weather was good as they departed from the South Pole, but they soon encountered difficult terrain: the 10,200-foot Titan Dome and the Shackleton Glacier, part of which they nicknamed "Hell" because of its ubiquitous spikes of blue ice, which damaged Arnesen's sled and some of their hiking equipment. After traversing the glacier, the women briefly celebrated crossing Antarctica's land mass. Then they set out across the Ross Ice Shelf and headed for McMurdo Station. After they had traveled 30 miles the wind disappeared, and they realized that they might not be able to complete the remaining 470 miles in the 10 days until their cutoff date. On February 17, 2001 an airplane picked them up and took them to the McMurdo Station, on the edge of the Ross Ice Shelf. The next day they took a helicopter to a waiting ship, which brought them to Australia. Both were disappointed. Arnesen knew that the journey was not technically complete, because "crossing the continent is all the way to McMurdo," as she told Jerry Zgoda, but she said that she would not attempt the journey again. "We're not going to die here like Shackleton did," Bancroft explained in their post-expedition interview with Zgoda. "There is value to ending like this because you can teach kids that you don't always get [all] the pieces of the dream. The important ones are those that you do get." Arnesen described their experience to Zgoda as a "mental trip." "A lot of people mentally collapse. Our weather was much more mild than we expected, but the trip was mentally harder than we ever anticipated," she said.

Currently, Arnesen and Bancroft are dedicating their efforts to a venture called Bancroft Arnesen Explore. An offshoot of yourexpedition, the company promotes exploration and trips for women and girls; in the first of its excursions, 16 teenagers planned to scale a peak in the Peruvian Andes in May 2001. Arnesen and Bancroft have hinted that they may undertake a new trip together themselves, perhaps kayaking off the coast of Antarctica or crossing a desert.

Arnesen lives in Norway with her three daughters and her husband, Einar Glestad. In addition to the outdoors, she enjoys reading, listening to music, and going to the theater. — K.S.

Suggested Reading: *Minneapolis-St. Paul Star Tribune* (on-line) Feb. 25, 2001, with photos; *New York Times* A p1 Jan. 6, 1995; *People* p109+ Mar. 13, 1995, with photos; *Time for Kids* (on-line) Jan. 12, 2001

Selected Books: *Snille piker gar ikke til Sydpolen (Good Girls Do Not Ski to the South Pole)*, 1995

Steve Granitz/Retna Ltd.

Austin, "Stone Cold" Steve

Dec. 18, 1964– Professional wrestler. Address: c/o World Wrestling Federation, 1241 E. Main St., Stamford, CT 06902

In his onstage persona—that of a belligerent, beer-guzzling thug, inspired in part by an HBO program on serial killers—"Stone Cold" Steve Austin has entertained millions of wrestling fans across the nation. Not only has he become one of the biggest names in the World Wrestling Federation, with an estimated annual income of between $5 million and $10 million; he has also pushed the limits of acceptable behavior in the ring. "He was the first guy to come on TV and be uncontrollable, to use the word 'ass,' to flip the bird," said Mark Nulty, a lifelong wrestling fan and curator of the Web site *wrestlingclassics.com*, as quoted by Steve Spong in *Texas Monthly* (September 1999).

Austin is dismissive of those who claim that professional wrestling is a farce. "To me," he told an interviewer for *Sport* (October 1998), "those people are extremely narrow-minded, uptight and insecure. I bust my ass every night and I challenge anybody in the world to get on the road with me, for 250 days a year, and do what I do every single night: living out of a suitcase, hotels, catching planes, renting cars. It's a drag. For anybody that can sit there on a high-horse and knock what I do, they can just piss off. This is wrestling. It's tongue in cheek. Take it for what it is."

Steve Austin was born Steven Williams on December 18, 1964 in Austin, Texas. He grew up with his two brothers in Edna, a town in southern Texas. A natural athlete, Austin played fullback and linebacker for his high-school football team. He was talented enough to win a football scholarship to Wharton County Junior College, southwest of Houston, and later, to the University of North Texas, in Denton. At North Texas, where he studied physical education, Austin played linebacker on the school football team. In 1987, in the middle of his senior year and after the conclusion of football season, Austin, bored with school, dropped out. To support himself he took a job loading trucks at a freight terminal. In his free time he would hang around the Sportatorium, a Dallas venue that often staged wrestling matches. With his powerful build and love of the spotlight, Austin often imagined himself administering "pile drivers" and chokeholds in the ring.

One day while working at the freight dock, Austin spotted a television advertisement for Chris Adams's wrestling school in Dallas. He signed up immediately, and quickly mastered the basics of holding and throwing an opponent. He also learned the importance of cultivating a professional ringside manner, by working the crowd and showering one's foe with abuse. In 1989 Austin became the first graduate of Chris Adams's academy; soon thereafter, in his professional debut, he defeated a faux Frenchman billed as Frogman Lablanc.

In 1991, after two years of paying his professional dues on the small-time local wrestling scene, Austin relocated to Memphis, Tennessee. There, he was hired by Ted Turner's World Championship Wrestling (WCW)—a new league then regarded by many in Vince McMahon's older and more established World Wrestling Federation (WWF) as a gimmicky upstart. It was at this time that Austin adopted his current surname, largely to avoid con-

fusion with another wrestler named Steve Williams. With his incarnation as "Stone Cold" Steve Austin still several years in the future, he appeared as "Stunning" Steve Austin, a dandyish beefcake sporting a luxuriant blonde mane. Austin achieved his greatest renown in the WCW as a member of the "Hollywood Blonds" tag team, alongside the late Brian Pillman. Together, the two captured the 1993 WCW tag team title.

Austin remained with the WCW through 1995, when he was fired by Eric Bishoff, the head of the WCW. One reason was the number of injuries he had sustained, which included a severely torn triceps resulting from a 1995 bout in Japan. According to some sources, WCW officials were also concerned about Austin's declining marketability. The WCW's action angered Austin, but rather than merely feeling embittered, he linked up with another upstart wrestling league, the Atlanta-based Extreme Championship Wrestling (ECW). While nursing his injuries, Austin worked as a ringside ECW commentator—a job that gave him the opportunity to forge his professional persona anew. "That was the best thing that ever happened to me," Austin told Spong. "For the first three months I was rehabbing, and I couldn't do anything but interview. I didn't have a character. I gave basically real deal-style interviews, shooting the truth from the ECW platform." The ECW—which placed a high premium on sleaze—encouraged Austin to vent his bile at his former employer. He did so, and thus his new, frankly antisocial persona gradually began to take shape.

In late 1995 the WWF, apparently impressed with the wrestler's flair for no-holds-barred ranting, hired Austin. After a brief but fairly unsuccessful incarnation as the "Ringmaster," Austin chanced upon the idea for the "Stone Cold" character while viewing a cable TV program about serial killers; according to Spong, the name occurred to Austin after Jeannie Clarke, the wrestler's English wife, seeing that the program was monopolizing his attention, told him, "Drink your tea before it gets stone cold." Austin even developed a signature move to help distinguish his new persona: the "Stone Cold Stunner."

While Austin has said that he originally conceived "Stone Cold" as a "heel"—the wrestling term for a character who serves as a magnet for audience abuse—he found to his surprise that crowds sided with him. Fans loved it when he threatened to serve his opponents a cup of shut-the-hell-up, or when he promised to open up a can of whoop-ass. His popularity grew steadily until it attained critical mass during a 1996 match called "King of the Ring." The contest pitted Austin against a Bible-spouting snake handler known as Jake the Snake. After defeating the Snake, Austin delivered a line that has since become legendary in the annals of wrestling history: "Jake," he declared, according to Spong, "you can thump your Bible and say your prayers, and you see where it got you. You can have your psalms and your John 3:16. Austin 3:16

says that I just whipped your ass!" A slew of currently available "Austin 3:16" merchandise—including shot glasses, T-shirts, and giant foam hands with only the middle finger extended—commemorates the event. (Other popular "Stone Cold" T-shirts feature the mottos "100% Pure Whoop Ass," "100% Pure Rattlesnake," and "100% Pure Hell Raiser.") Sales of "Stone Cold" merchandise, which reportedly topped $250 million in 1998, constitute a substantial source of revenue for both Austin and the WWF.

Ever since his defeat of Jake the Snake, Austin has remained one of the most popular figures in the WWF, with five championship titles to his name.

The father of two girls, Stephanie and Cassidy (who were nine and four, respectively, in 2001), he disagrees with those who maintain that wrestling exerts a negative influence on children. "I don't expect the TV or anybody else to raise my kids," he told Spong.

Austin makes his home in Boerne, Texas. — P.K.

Suggested Reading: *Newsweek* p60+ Nov. 23, 1998, with photos; *People* p114+ Dec. 28, 1998, with photo; *Texas Monthly* p124+ Sep. 1999, with photo

Darla Khazei/AP

Bailey, Glenda

Nov. 16, 1958– Editor in chief of Harper's Bazaar. *Address:* Harper's Bazaar, *1700 Broadway, New York, NY 10019*

"I was born to be an editor and have loved it since I became one at 27," Glenda Bailey told Tanya Jensen for *Fashion Wire Daily* (April 4, 2001, on-line). "The joy of being an editor is making the most of very talented people." On May 31, 2001 the Hearst Corp. named Bailey editor in chief of its venerable monthly magazine *Harper's Bazaar*. A native of Great Britain, she came to the job after serving for four years as editor in chief of the U.S. edition of *Marie Claire*, also a Hearst publication. While at the helm of the U.S. *Marie Claire*, she orchestrated an 80 percent increase in the magazine's circulation, with both the August and December 2000 is-

sues surpassing the coveted one-million mark in sales. She thus built *Marie Claire* into the number-one fashion publication on newsstands in the U.S. Bailey's résumé also includes the launch, in 1988, of *Marie Claire*'s British edition, at which she held the title of editor in chief for nearly eight years. "Glenda is the ultimate editor," Anna Marie Solowij, a former *Marie Claire* beauty editor, told Caroline Roux for the London *Guardian* (June 6, 2001). "She's incredibly careful in how she makes her decisions. She's not a writer and she's not a stylist. Maybe that's her talent. She takes people on to do those jobs and trusts them to do the work, and inspires huge loyalty for that. Then she watches over the whole thing."

Glenda Adrianne Bailey was born into a working-class family on November 16, 1958 in the town of Derby (pronounced "DAR-bee") in central England. Her father, John, worked as a forklift operator; her mother, Constance, was a shop assistant. The Baileys rented a small, two-bedroom house in Derby, in which Glenda Bailey shared a bedroom with her sister. As reported by David Handelman for *Adweek* (March 5, 2001), Bailey "began a life-long love affair with magazines" when she was eight years old. Her interest in fashion apparently took hold not long afterward; according to Handelman, at 12 she started working on Saturdays and putting away money to purchase clothes. Among the magazines she read in her youth, Bailey told Handelman, she was "addicted" to the British girls' publication *Jackie*, which featured outline drawings of the latest fashion trends for young readers to color in. Later, Bailey became enamored of *Honey* and *19* and then the British edition of *Vogue*.

After receiving a public education at the Noel Baker School in Derby, Bailey moved to Blackpool, on England's northwest coast, and enrolled in a course in the foundations of fashion. There, at age 18, she met her eventual life partner, Stephen Sumner. After completing the course she and Sumner entered the prestigious Kingston Polytechnic (now Kingston University), in Kingston-upon-Thames, a London suburb, to study fashion design. During her first year at Kingston, Bailey suffered the loss of her mother to breast cancer. She also became increasingly aware that, as she told Handelman, she "was not going to become the next Karl Lagerfeld," a reference to the successful avant-garde fashion designer. During her third year at Kingston, she secured a summer internship at IPC Magazines Ltd., Britain's largest consumer-magazine publishing company. Having enjoyed writing a few short fashion-related articles for various IPC publications, Bailey chose women's fashion magazines as the subject of her senior thesis at Kingston.

After she earned a B.A. degree in fashion, Bailey worked briefly at an Italian knitwear company and then at a London-based, fashion-forecasting trade magazine called *Design Directions*. For a short while in 1986, she edited *Honey*. Meanwhile, 18 months after her graduation, Bailey's father was diagnosed with cancer. His illness led her to leave her job at *Design Directions* and return to Derby, where she helped care for him in his last days. Recalling how her father's death affected her, she told Handelman, "There's nothing like losing everything to really clear your mind as to what you really want."

After her father died Bailey immediately returned to London, where she contacted Malcolm Abraham, the publisher of *Jackie*, and Colin Reeves-Smith, who held the title of group publisher at IPC, and persuaded them to finance the launch of a new fashion magazine, to be called *Folio*. The first issue of *Folio* sold a total of 90,000 copies, a huge number for a brand-new title. Seeing the impressive sales of its next two issues, IPC entertained the possibility of adding *Folio* to its entourage of permanent monthly titles. Meanwhile, at about the time that the third issue appeared on newsstands, Bailey had become ill with pneumonia. While convalescing in bed she learned that a rival British publishing company was vying for the rights to produce a British edition of the French magazine *Marie Claire*. "I thought, that is the magazine of my dreams!" she recalled to Jan Moir for the London *Guardian* (September 7, 1994). "I leapt out of bed and went to a garden party that night with my IPC managing director, Colin Reeves-Smith, and we danced together to 'I Can't Get No Satisfaction.' And I said: 'Colin, I want *Marie Claire*.' And he said: 'Well go and get it then.'" The next day Bailey telephoned a representative of Comary, the French company that owned *Marie Claire*, and declared, "I'm either going to be your greatest asset or your worst enemy. Please come talk to me because I love *Marie Claire*."

Thus it happened that in 1988, after meeting with Comary's president and CEO, Evelyne Prouvost-Berry, the 30-year-old Bailey became the launch editor, and then editor in chief, of the British edition of *Marie Claire*. According to an unsigned article in the London *Observer Review* (January 21, 1996), she "*loved* the French *Marie Claire* because unlike the other women's glossies its primary motor of fashion was fronted by serious arti-

cles of reportage. It was a blend that Glenda was desperate to feed to the British audience." At the time the most successful women's fashion magazine was *Cosmopolitan*. Bailey believed that *Marie Claire*, with its mixture of affordable-fashions coverage and thoughtful reportage, would successfully compete with *Cosmo*, as it is widely known. For the *Observer Review* article, Sally Brampton, the launch editor of British *Elle*, expressed the view that *Marie Claire* had captured the mood of a decade: "The public mentality changed [and] *Marie Claire* and the values it embodied took off." In 1989 Bailey was named Women's Magazine Editor of the Year, and two years later British *Marie Claire* was awarded Consumer Magazine of the Year honors.

Unlike most other editors and their magazines, Bailey and *Marie Claire* became connected in the public consciousness. A large part of this recognition can be traced to a televised documentary entitled *Absolutely Marie Claire*, which revealed Bailey's enthusiasm and passion for her work and followed her in the office and on trips to promote the magazine. She became even more widely known through her appearances in a series of American Express commercials. By the end of her tenure at British *Marie Claire*, Bailey had garnered 11 awards, including four for Consumer Magazine of the Year. In addition, in 1992 her magazine won an Amnesty International Press Award for a *Marie Claire* report exposing the murders of children in Brazilian slums. Of the five articles short-listed for that award, four came from *Marie Claire*. Bailey told Jan Moir that of all the honors she and the magazine earned, she felt most proud of the one from Amnesty International. "I was thrilled. A fashion magazine winning an Amnesty award. It was unheard of." By 1994 the magazine's circulation had reached more than 398,000, outselling the British editions of *Vogue*, *Harper's & Queen*, *Tatler*, and *Elle*. *Marie Claire* was also creeping up on a faltering *Cosmopolitan*.

In 1996 Bailey left Great Britain for New York, to take the reins of the recently launched U.S. edition of *Marie Claire*. In doing so she joined a group of other British female editors who had gotten jobs in the Big Apple, among them Anna Wintour (who edits American *Vogue*); Liz Tilberis (who edited *Harper's Bazaar* from 1992 until her death, in 1999); and Tina Brown (*Vanity Fair*, the *New Yorker*, and, currently, *Talk*). Explaining the presence of British women in such high-profile editorial jobs in the U.S., Bailey told Nadine Brozan for the *New York Times* (September 17, 1996), "I think it is because we [British editors] are given opportunities so early in our careers. . . . Britain is a lot smaller country so people are willing to take risks because the stakes are not so high, and we have more responsibility earlier."

To prepare for her new job, Bailey traveled throughout the U.S., talking to women in many walks of life. She announced plans to include hard-nosed journalism along with fashion coverage in *Marie Claire*, thereby straying from the sexual sensationalism that had flavored the magazine until then. In an interview for *Mediaweek* (December 8, 1997), Bailey said, "Quite a few very experienced editors have said, 'Glenda, the American woman is not interested in world affairs.' I told them I had never heard such a patronizing load of rubbish. My readers love fashion and beauty, but they're also interested in other women's lives in other cultures. Some of our stories don't have happy endings, but my readers want to know." In 1997 Lara Marlowe won an Amnesty International Press Award for the 1996 *Marie Claire* article "Where Girls Are Killed for Going to School," an investigative report about the murders of young Muslim women in Algeria.

Serious news articles notwithstanding, Bailey never strayed far from the world of fashion. She also added to her magazine's distinctiveness by publishing articles that provided unusual insights into the lives of celebrities. Bailey, whose circle of celebrated acquaintances is wide, told Tanya Jensen for *fashionavenue.com* (April 7, 2001), "We have always had great celebrity relationships; they become a part of the extended family. I think it's because we push them. . . . It sets us apart—I am sick of reading the same old interviews." The March 2000 issue of *Marie Claire*, for example, contained pictures of the actress and model Brooke Shields in the Arctic, posing in an igloo that she had helped build. The article included excerpts from a journal Shields kept while living in the igloo for a few days with a friend. On several occasions Bailey has invited celebrities to guest-edit her magazine; all of them have agreed to do so free of charge. The first was the actress Gwyneth Paltrow, who worked on the January 1998 issue. The resulting stir boosted advertising pages in that issue by 33 percent over the previous one, and newsstand sales by 36 percent. Subsequent guest editors have included the actresses Susan Sarandon and Demi Moore.

During Bailey's five years as editor in chief of the U.S. *Marie Claire*, its circulation grew by 80 percent, to an average of 948,000 copies per issue (20 percent more than what Hearst had anticipated), thus making it the number-one fashion title at newsstands in the U.S. In her last year alone, advertising revenues rose 19 percent, to $88.8 million. Offering her recipe for success, Bailey told David Handelman, "It's about having fun, being entertained, being surprised—and not taking ourselves too seriously." In 2000 *Adweek* named Bailey its Editor of the Year.

On May 31, 2001 the Hearst Corp. asked Bailey to take over the position of editor in chief at *Harper's Bazaar*, which was founded in 1867. Hearst had forced Katherine Betts to leave the post the day before, one year before her three-year contract was to expire. The ouster of Betts, who had succeeded the late Liz Tilberis amid much fanfare, followed a 7.5 percent decline in *Harper's Bazaar*'s circulation. Betts was held responsible for the drop; according to Caroline Roux in the London *Guardian*

(June 6, 2001), "in the process of trying to make [the magazine] hipper," Betts had "managed simply to please fewer people." Quoting an unnamed New York fashion editor, Roux wrote, "Under [Tilberis], *Bazaar* was a sacred cow. But Hearst really wants a cash cow. Bailey has created in *Marie Claire* a magazine that moves off the newsstands, and they want her to do that again."

According to Roux, "Bailey doesn't just inspire loyalty: she demands it." But "for all her scariness," she "has one rather endearing and unique selling point: she will never quite look or maybe even be the part. With her massive mane of naturally curly reddish hair and uneven features and big bone structure, she is the physical polar opposite of the hyper-controlled plastic presence of Anna Wintour, editor of American *Vogue*. And with her closely maintained regional accent and spontaneous outbursts of enthusiasm, she exudes a sort of realness not usually associated with the upper echelons of the publishing world." "For all she admires the celebrity lifestyle . . . , she still has some normal life," a friend of Bailey's told Roux. "It's difficult to maintain that, and it's what makes her successful. It allows her to tap into what readers want, and then she gives them a lot more than they expect."

Bailey lives in New York with her partner, Stephen Sumner. — J.H.

Suggested Reading: *Adweek* SR p38+ Mar. 5, 2001, with photos; *fashionavenue.com* Apr. 7, 2001, with photo; *Houston Chronicle* p30 Sep. 24, 1997, with photo; (London) *Guardian* II p8 Sep. 7, 1994, II p4 June 6, 2001, with photo; (London) *Observer Review* p5 Jan. 21, 1996; *Mediaweek* p30 Dec. 8, 1997; *New York Observer* p1 June 11, 2001; *New York Times* A p20 Sep. 17, 1996, IX p1 June 10, 2001, with photos; *Wall Street Journal* B p12 Sep. 10, 1996, B p1 Feb. 22, 1999

Baker, Dusty

June 15, 1949– Manager of the San Francisco Giants. Address: San Francisco Giants, Pacific Bell Park, 24 Willie Mays Plaza, San Francisco, CA 94107

"My whole career—my life, really—has been a dream," Dusty Baker, the manager of the San Francisco Giants, told Steve Rushin for *Sports Illustrated* (August 23, 1999). Baker overcame racism and the disapproval of his father to become one of the few men who has found success in major-league baseball both as a player and a manager. In his 19 seasons as a player, when he was an outfielder for the Atlanta Braves and then the Los Angeles Dodgers, Baker's batting power often intimidated opposing pitchers. As manager of the Giants for the

Tom Hauck/Retna Ltd.

Dusty Baker

past eight years, he has enjoyed five winning seasons and made two trips to the post-season. Many sportswriters have praised Baker as one of the best managers in baseball, citing his hands-on approach to managing and his success in motivating his players. Baker, who signed a two-year contract extension in October 2000, hopes to become the first manager of the San Francisco Giants to win a World Series.

The oldest of five children, Johnnie B. Baker Jr. was born on June 15, 1949 in Riverside, California. His father, Johnnie Sr., worked as a civilian sheet-metal technician for the air force and frequently took odd jobs during evenings and nights to earn extra money for the family. Baker's mother, Christine, nicknamed Johnnie Jr. "Dusty" because he often came home dirty after playing with his friends. Baker's parents separated in 1967 and eventually divorced.

In the early 1960s the family moved to Carmichael, a suburb of Sacramento, California, where Baker attended Del Campo High School. He excelled at sports, running track and playing football, baseball, and basketball, the last of which he loved the most. After graduating from high school, in 1967, he enlisted in the marines as a reservist and also enrolled at American River Junior College, in Sacramento. In the summer of 1967, Baker had to decide between attending Santa Clara University, in California, which offered him a basketball scholarship, and signing with the Atlanta Braves organization, which recognized his talent as a baseball player and offered him a $15,000 signing bonus. In August Baker and his mother flew to Los Angeles, where the Braves were playing the Dodgers, to discuss the offer with the team's representatives. At

one point Baker's mother encountered Hank Aaron, the Braves' veteran outfielder and future home-run king, and asked him to promise her that he would look after her son if he signed with the Braves. At the time, many places in the South were still racially segregated, and African-American players, including Aaron, often experienced racism there. Aaron agreed to Mrs. Baker's request, and Dusty Baker signed a contract with the Braves in the Dodgers' parking lot.

Baker made his decision without the knowledge or consent of his father, whose dream was that his son would attend college. Believing that his son was making a mistake, Johnnie Baker Sr. immediately took legal action to nullify the contract. Although the action was unsuccessful, a legal settlement was reached that placed the $15,000 signing bonus in a trust fund for Dusty Baker and stipulated that the Braves would also pay for his tuition if he ever decided to attend college. Angered by his father's actions, Dusty Baker stopped speaking to him and, in an effort to prove him wrong, became even more determined to succeed in major-league baseball. By 1974, however, father and son had reconciled.

True to his word, Hank Aaron looked after Baker, and the pair developed a close friendship. At the time, the Braves' minor-league teams were all based in the South. Baker, who had experienced a degree of racism back in Carmichael, was angered by what he now encountered. "I didn't like people calling me 'boy,'" he told Ron Kroichick, a reporter for the *San Francisco Chronicle* (August 11, 2000). "I didn't like having to stay in my place, because I didn't think I had a 'place.'" Aaron, drawing from his own experiences battling racism, counseled Baker to stay out of trouble by avoiding places that were still racially segregated and by stopping himself from lashing out at racists—which was often his first instinct. Although Baker was still angry, he took Aaron's advice. Looking back, Baker believed that Aaron was right, telling Kroichick, "Hank taught me so much, I'll be forever grateful. He kept me from either getting in trouble or getting my head beat up."

In 1968 Dusty Baker made his major-league debut with the Braves, playing in only six games. Over the next several years, he played mainly in the minor leagues, where he established himself as an excellent hitter and outfielder, and joined the Braves for a few games whenever the rosters were expanded.

In 1972 Baker began playing full-time for the Braves, joining his mentor and friend Hank Aaron. That year Baker hit an impressive .321 (the third-highest average in the National League for the season) and contributed 27 doubles, 17 home runs, and 76 RBIs. The next year Baker's batting average dropped to .288, but he slugged 21 home runs and reached a career-high 99 RBIs. For Baker, the highlight of his years with the Braves came on April 8, 1974, when he watched Aaron hit his 715th career home run, which broke Babe Ruth's record.

In November 1975, after four full seasons in the major leagues, Baker was traded to the Los Angeles Dodgers. In his first season with the team, Baker played poorly, batting .242 and hitting only four home runs. The next year, however, he improved, reaching a career-high 30 home runs and raising his batting average to .291. The Dodgers also enjoyed a great season in 1977, finishing in first place in the National League West Division and defeating the Philadelphia Phillies in four games to win the pennant. In the second game of that series, Baker hit a grand-slam home run off the veteran pitcher Jim Lonborg. Baker, who also hit .357 and drove in eight RBIs, was named the series' Most Valuable Player (MVP). In the World Series the Dodgers faced their arch-rivals, the New York Yankees, for the first time since 1963. Although Baker played well, hitting a long, three-run home run in Game 3 and batting .292, the Yankees defeated the Dodgers in six games, culminating with Reggie Jackson's three home runs in the final game at Yankee Stadium.

Baker's numbers declined in 1978, his batting average falling to .262. In the post-season the Dodgers once again defeated the Phillies to win the National League pennant. Baker hit .467 in four games but drove in only one run. Once again, the Yankees defeated the Dodgers in six games to win the World Series.

Although a players' strike shortened the 1981 season by two months, Baker enjoyed an excellent year. His batting average, .320, again proved to be the third-highest in the National League. For the first time in his career, Baker made the All-Star team, and he also won his first Gold Glove Award for his outstanding fielding. In the World Series the Dodgers avenged their two previous losses by defeating the Yankees in six games. (Baker hit only .167 in the series, collecting four hits and one RBI.)

In 1982 Baker chalked up a solid .300 batting average, 171 hits, 23 home runs, and 88 RBIs, which earned him another spot on the All-Star team. The next year, however, the Dodgers' management wanted to make room in their lineup for their young stars, such as Pedro Guerrero and Candy Maldonado. After Baker had a sub-par season, the Dodgers released him. He spent the next three years playing with, first, the San Francisco Giants and then the Oakland Athletics, who both used him in part-time roles. The Athletics released him after the 1986 season. At 37, with no other offers, Baker retired from baseball. In his years as a player, he missed the 2,000-career-hits mark by only 19 and had the distinction of being one of the few players who never spent any time on the disabled list.

Like many athletes who retire from sports, Baker was unsure about his future. An unexpected development decided his next career move. During an appearance on ABC's *Nightline* in 1987, Dodgers vice president Al Campanis sparked a firestorm when he said, as quoted by Bill Dwyre in the *Los Angeles Times* (April 7, 1987), that African-

Americans "may not have some of the necessities to be a field manager or general manager." Many commentators and civil rights organizations cited Campanis's remarks as proof that racism was still widespread in baseball, 40 years after Jackie Robinson broke the color barrier. The fact that there were no African-American managers or general managers in baseball at the time gave credibility to allegations of racism. In response to those charges, baseball commissioner Peter Ueberroth announced that teams would hire more minorities in executive, management, and coaching positions. In 1988 Baker accepted an offer from the San Francisco Giants to serve as the team's hitting coach.

Baker, who worked for the next four years under the longtime manager Roger Craig, also had ambitions to manage a team. After a fifth-place finish in 1992, the Giants fired Craig and tapped Baker as the new manager. Although pleased with the opportunity, Baker wondered if he had the ability to manage a major-league team. "I wasn't sure I was ready," he told Mark Newman for the *Sporting News* (September 13, 1993). "I had so many things to learn. . . . It wasn't apprehension, it was more of a matter of uncertainty because I'd never been in that situation before." To give him some experience, the Giants had Baker manage the Scottsdale Scorpions in the Arizona Fall League, which had been created by baseball clubs to give their top minor-league prospects, as well as potential coaches and managers, additional playing time in the off-season. Baker found the experience beneficial, telling Newman that he learned how to run a pitching staff.

In his first season as manager, in 1993, Baker turned the Giants around. Although the team was plagued by a series of injuries, Baker guided the Giants to 103 victories, one short of the first-place Atlanta Braves, who were still in the Western Division at the time. Baker immediately became known as a "hands-on" manager who paid close attention to his team in order to spot both strengths and weaknesses. During pregame workouts Baker often talked to players to see how they were doing. "I look in a guy's face and it tells me a lot. Maybe he hasn't slept because he's worrying," he explained to Lowell Cohn for the *San Francisco Chronicle*, as reprinted in the *Chicago Tribune* (May 9, 1993). "I mean, I know I'm the manager and they know I'm the manager, but I want them to understand we're in this together. I just think it's necessary." Some sportswriters also attributed the Giants' resurgence to their powerful lineup, which included Robby Thompson, Matt Williams, Barry Bonds, Will Clark, and Willie McGee, and to a solid pitching staff, which boasted two 20-game winners (Bill Swift and John Burkett) and reliever Rod Beck, who saved 48 games that season. In assessing the team's success, however, Newman wrote, "Baker instilled the confidence he exuded as a clutch player, massaged egos on a team full of veterans and made one right move after another in a season of largely unrecognized adversity." At the end of the season, Baker received the National League Manager of the Year award, which recognizes managers who improve their teams the most.

A players' strike in 1994 cut short what might have been a successful season for Baker and the Giants. When playing stopped, in August, the Giants were locked in a fight with the Dodgers for the National League Western Division title. Although the team had a losing record (55–60), the Giants finished a close second. The strike continued into the next season, resulting in the cancellation of the first 18 games. After the strike ended, in late April 1995, Baker watched as chronic pitching problems doomed the Giants to a last-place finish. The Giants' troubles continued in 1996. This time, poor pitching combined with a weak offense led the Giants to finish in last place again, with 94 losses. Despite widespread speculation in the media that Baker's job was in jeopardy, the Giants granted him a two-year extension in July 1996.

Off-season acquisitions of first baseman J. T. Snow and second baseman Jeff Kent helped the Giants bounce back in 1997. The team won 90 games, finishing in first place in the Western Division, before the Florida Marlins swept them in the first round of the play-offs. After the season Baker won the National League Manager of the Year award for the second time. The Giants also extended Baker's contract through 2000.

Baker's hopes for postseason success for the Giants were frustrated again in 1998. Jeff Kent suffered an injury, which contributed to a slump after the All-Star Game, and the San Diego Padres won the division title. Still, the Giants finished in a tie with the Chicago Cubs for the National League's wild-card berth, which was to be decided with a one-game play-off. Trailing by five runs in the ninth inning of the game, the Giants made a valiant comeback effort. But Barry Bonds, the three-time MVP, at bat with the bases loaded and no one out, managed only a sacrifice fly. The Cubs killed the Giants' rally and won the game, 5–3.

Nonetheless, by 1999 Dusty Baker had earned a reputation as one of baseball's best managers. Sportswriters frequently praised his leadership abilities, citing his skill at motivating players and achieving successes despite managing one of the lowest-paid teams in baseball. In an interview with Dennis Tuttle, a writer for the Sporting News (April 12, 1999), Baker described how he managed the team: "The stars are going to play. That's the same today as it was in my day and the same as it was any day before. But in order to keep people strong and healthy and ready to play in case something happens, role players have to be ready to jump in." Baker added that he is honest when telling his players their respective roles on the team and always keeps his door open, so that his players can discuss any concerns or problems they might have.

Baker and the Giants looked forward to the 1999 season. "The San Francisco Giants have been to the World Series, but the team has never won a world championship," he said to Ebony (July 1998). "I want to be the first man to bring a world title to this city, and I want to do it in [Candlestick Park] before we move to the team's new Pacific Bell Park in 2000." An injury that sidelined Barry Bonds for 10 weeks frustrated Baker's and the Giants' dreams of another trip to the postseason. With Bonds limited to only 102 games, the Giants struggled to a second-place finish behind the Arizona Diamondbacks.

As they did twice before under Baker, the Giants roared back after having a disappointing season. With Bonds and the rest of the team healthy, the Giants dominated the Western Division throughout 2000. Although they finished in first place, with 96 victories, the Giants once again failed to make it beyond the first round of postseason play. After the Giants had won the first game of the play-offs, the New York Mets won the next three games. Several sportswriters (and a few angry fans) asserted that Baker had made several bad judgment calls that together had cost the Giants the series. For example, in Game 2, Baker chose not to use the relief pitcher Robb Nen, who had saved 41 games during the season, and in the eighth inning, the Mets scored two runs against pitcher Felix Rodriguez, going on to win the game 5–4. In Game 3 Baker used many players in an attempt to squeeze out a victory. The game went into extra innings, and in the bottom of the 13th, the Mets' Benny Agbayani clinched his team's victory with a home run off the rookie Aaron Fultz, who was forced to pitch because Baker had already used his other pitchers. In the fifth inning of the final game, which the Giants lost 5–1, Baker did not send in a pinch hitter for pitcher Mark Gardner, who came to bat with the bases loaded and two outs. Gardner popped out to end the inning, costing the Giants a golden opportunity to score. After the game a defiant Baker addressed the criticisms, saying, as quoted by Bruce Jenkins in the San Francisco Chronicle (October 9, 2000), "I'm hearing from people who know less than me about what I've done. Myself? No problem. I'm going to live with me. I'm not gonna let other people control my self-esteem." Jenkins also dismissed the criticisms, writing that Baker "is the same manager and the same man who has brought so much joy to Giants fans" and should remain "in a Giants uniform for many seasons to come." After the season Baker was honored with his third National League Manager of the Year award.

At about this time Baker hinted that he might not return as the Giants' manager in 2001. His contract had expired, and the baseball world speculated that he would manage another team. In October, however, he signed a lucrative, two-year contract with the Giants. Although his exact salary was not disclosed, Henry Schulman and Susan Slusser estimated in the San Francisco Chronicle (October 20, 2000) that Baker was being paid at least $2 million a year.

The Giants struggled throughout the first half of the 2001 season; they were even briefly in last place. Baker's efforts to guide the team to their third first-place finish was overshadowed by Bobby Bonds's quest to break Mark McGwire's single-season home-run record (70), set in 1998. "It's an honor to have been a part of this—something that all the guys will remember, forever and ever," Baker said to Vicki Michaelis for *USA Today* (September 11, 2001), "but the focus still remains on the pennant." In the second half of the season, the Giants rebounded, battling the Dodgers and the Diamondbacks for first place. But the team came up short, finishing two games behind the Diamondbacks, who were powered by two 20-game-winning pitchers, Curt Schilling and Randy Johnson. In a game against the Dodgers on October 6, Bonds hit two home runs to break McGwire's record. The Giants, however, lost that game, 11–10, and were officially eliminated from the play-offs.

Dusty Baker is the co-author (with Jeff Mercer and Marv Bittinger) of *You Can Teach Hitting: A Systematic Approach for Parents, Coaches and Players* (1995). Off the field he devotes his time to promoting several charities, among them the Sacramento Children's Home for Abused Youths. Baker is married and has three children, including one from a previous marriage. He and his family live in Bruno, California. — D.C.

Suggested Reading: *Chicago Tribune* III p13 May 9, 1993; *Dusty Baker.com*; *Ebony* p84+ July 1998, with photos; *New York Times* (on-line) Oct. 7, 2001; *San Francisco Chronicle* E p1 Aug. 11, 2000, G p1 Oct. 9, 2000; *Sporting News* p9 Sep. 13, 1993, with photos, p39 Apr. 12, 1999, with photo; *Sports Illustrated* p76+ Aug. 23, 1999 with photos; *USA Today* C p3 Sep. 11, 2001, with photo

---

Reuters/Fred Prouser/Hulton/Archive

Beckinsale, Kate

July 26, 1973– Actress. Address: c/o P.A. One, Box 21, Honinton, Devon EX14 1YH, England

The British actress Kate Beckinsale has been building her career on the silver screen since 1993, when she appeared in the actor-director Kenneth Branagh's version of *Much Ado About Nothing*. Two years later, at the age of 22, she earned rave reviews for her work in the film *Cold Comfort Farm*, which, as Lynn Hirschberg wrote for *New York Times Magazine* (April 22, 2001), "established her cool, direct and rather brainy style of

acting." In 1996 she played the title role in the British television miniseries *Jane Austen's Emma*. (She also generated a tempest in a teapot in Great Britain by publicly criticizing the American actress Gwyneth Paltrow's markedly different portrayal of the same character in the feature film *Emma*, released several months earlier.) Beckinsale's subsequent film credits include roles in *The Golden Bowl* and, most recently, the big-budget production *Pearl Harbor* (2001), in which she was cast as a nurse in love with two U.S. Army Air Corps pilots. She has also appeared in a handful of plays on the British stage. In an interview with Nancy Mills for the New York *Daily News* (May 20, 2001), she said that "every single article" published about her has mentioned her father, who, in his 20s, became "a huge TV star in England," as she put it to Lynn Hirschberg, and who died at the age of 31. "My father's death—well, his fame and his death—have given me a strong sense of the power of film," she told Hirschberg. "The work, if it has resonance, will outlive me."

Kate Beckinsale was born on July 26, 1973 in London, England, to the British actress Judy Loe and the British actor Richard Beckinsale. From her father's first marriage, she has a half-sister, the actress Samantha Beckinsale. Beginning in 1970 Richard Beckinsale starred in a series of popular British sitcoms—*Lovers*, *Rising Damp*, *Porridge*, and *Bloomers*. He died on March 19, 1979, after suffering a massive heart attack while asleep. Kate was five years old. "Other actors who knew him kept telling me how devastated they were when he died," Beckinsale recalled to Lydia Slater for the London *Daily Telegraph* (November 23, 1996, online). "I was constantly in the position of having to console them for my father's death. It's easy, when you're four feet taller than the person you're talking to, to think they don't really understand what's going on. But I was so devastated, and I knew exactly what had happened. I'm very respectful of small children now." Beckinsale told Lynn Hirschberg, "I learned very early that . . . very healthy people can drop dead in a second. . . . Suddenly, everything was over, but then again it wasn't. My father has been dead for 22 years, and he's still on TV all the time. I'm so used to seeing him. Whenever there's a really significant moment in my life, he's on the TV. . . . At first, it was hard to watch him, but now I see it differently. Now it almost feels like he's watching me."

Four years after Richard Beckinsale's death, Kate's mother became romantically involved with the director Roy Battersby, who has a daughter and four sons. "They all came to stay for long weekends and holidays; they were around a fair bit," Beckinsale recalled to Dina Rabinovitch for Interview (July 1998). "At first I didn't like [the] boys: They seemed like these terrible foul-mouthed creatures. I was very pious and good at the time." Beckinsale was leery of being part of a "blended" family, as she told Lydia Slater. "Step-families are odd things. Everything I'd ever read about them as a child was negative. Stepfathers are supposed to poison you and beat you. I thought I was going to be separating peas and beans on a stone floor at night. . . . I was convinced I was going to be relegated, that we would sell the house where I'd always lived and it would all be awful." She added, "And of course, none of it happened. Roy is a wise and understanding man. He made it much easier for me, because he wasn't trying to be a replacement for my father." Meanwhile, she had begun to develop an interest in acting; as she told Sean M. Smith for Premiere (June 1998), "Growing up, I was always putting on shows and wanting to be the center of attention, and then changing my mind at the last minute and hating it."

While attending the Godolphin and Latymer School, a day school for girls in West London, Beckinsale twice won the prestigious W. H. Smith Young Writers' Competition, once for short stories she had written and once for poetry. For five years during her teens, she battled anorexia; at 15 she weighed only 70 pounds. "I always felt that anorexia was the form of breakdown most readily available to adolescent girls," she told Dina Rabinovitch. "I had five years of intense Freudian analysis, which I don't think a lot of girls my age do. . . . My family didn't respond to my anorexia as a physical illness, which was terribly important." Thanks to psychotherapy, she began to deal with her unresolved grief and anger over her father's death and other anxieties that had contributed to her illness; indeed, she told Lydia Slater, "Anorexia was the best thing that ever happened to me. It opened a channel. I wouldn't be an actress if I hadn't had it." She also told Slater that during her treatment she finally realized that she "had to choose between being a person or a professional anorexic. You can't commit to anything else when your mind is exhausted and homed in on one thing."

Her anorexia, which left her with permanently impaired vision, was under control by the time Beckinsale entered Oxford University's New College, where she studied the languages and literatures of France and Russia. She viewed college as an opportunity to explore the liberal arts; she was unsure about pursuing an acting career, even after winning a small part in a British television movie, One Against the Wind, in 1991, and a larger part in another TV movie, Rachel's Dream, the following year. Her next acting job was her first big-screen role: she portrayed Hero in the actor-director Kenneth Branagh's adaptation of Shakespeare's Much Ado About Nothing (1993), which co-stars Branagh, Emma Thompson, Robert Sean Leonard, Keanu Reeves, Denzel Washington, and Michael Keaton. Beckinsale, whose scenes were shot during her summer holiday from school, described the experience to Lynn Hirschberg as "a full-out tortured time. When I was cast, I didn't know who Keanu Reeves was, and he was my love interest in the film. He turned out to be lovely, but I was just a little pile of angst." Beckinsale had few speaking lines in the movie, and her performance made little impression on critics. Additionally, she was the only main character not billed on the movie poster. Nevertheless, she felt rewarded, as she recalled to Louis B. Hobson for the Calgary Sun (May 25, 1998, as quoted on Canoe.ca), not least because of what she learned from Emma Thompson. "I think every young actress should do her first movie with Emma," Beckinsale told Hobson. "She really brings you down to earth. She doesn't tolerate any superficiality. She is also wonderful with the crew. They all love her. It's humbling to see someone who is a true star be so gracious."

While continuing her undergraduate studies, Beckinsale performed in the little-noticed films Uncovered (1994), Prince of Jutland (1994), Marie-Louise ou la permission (1995), and Haunted (1995). She dropped out of college in 1995 to play the lead character, Flora Poste, in Cold Comfort Farm (1995), directed by John Schlesinger. (The screenplay was written by Malcolm Bradbury, who adapted it from Stella Gibbons's same-named, classic satirical novel, written in 1932 and perenially popular in Great Britain.) Beckinsale told Louis B. Hobson that she "desperately wanted" the role of Flora, an urbane young woman who, after becoming orphaned, goes to live with her unkempt, eccentric country cousins, the Starkadders, and sets about reforming them. After her audition, though, Schlesinger thought the actress was "too young," as she told Hobson. "I was 21, which was the right age, but he thought I looked 16. I wrote him a letter telling him why I had to play the part." "Impressed with my spirit and determination," as she recalled to Hobson, Schlesinger gave her a second audition and was won over. According to Janet Maslin, in a review of Cold Comfort Farm for the New York Times (May 10, 1996), Beckinsale portrayed Flora "with the perfect snippy aplomb." In the National Review (June 17, 1996), John Simon wrote, "The fetching Kate Beckinsale in the role of Flora Poste has an imposing brow, a meltingly compelling gaze, and plenty of poise," and Terrence Rafferty, writing for the *New Yorker* (May 13, 1996), called Beckinsale's performance "charming and canny." Made for British TV, the movie, whose cast included Ian McKellen, Eileen Atkins, and Stephen Fry, got a mostly warm critical reception in the U.S., but it was shown primarily in art houses and thus had only a limited audience.

Beckinsale next appeared in *Jane Austen's Emma*, a made-for-television miniseries that aired on British TV in November 1996 and on the American cable station A&E in February 1997. She hesitated before accepting the role, because, as she told Lydia Slater, "I thought, oh God, not another Jane Austen costume drama. But Emma herself is such a nasty piece of work she seems marvelous, completely modern." She added, "The characters I like tend to be flawed, but I try to show their sympathetic side, too. Everyone kept telling me Emma was just an awful nightmare, but I'd hate to see her played as completely unlikeable. She thinks she's happy, but she isn't, and she behaves as she does out of desperation." *Jane Austen's Emma* was broadcast in the U.S. half a year after the debut of the feature film *Emma*, starring Gwyneth Paltrow in the title role, which inevitably led to comparisons of both the films themselves and the performances of Beckinsale and Paltrow. Caryn James, in the *New York Times* (February 15, 1997), expressed the view that the big-screen *Emma* "was all about brightness and pretty gardens. It was a slick commercial Emma, whose appeal depended on Ms. Paltrow's graceful looks; not a bad idea, but not nearly what Austen had in mind. . . . Ms. Beckinsale's Emma is plainer looking than Ms. Paltrow's, and altogether more believable and funnier." In an interview with Sarah Lyall for the *New York Times* (February 16, 1997), Beckinsale herself described Paltrow's portrayal of Emma as "a bit silly." "I really don't believe that there's only one interpretation of anything," she explained, "but I personally wouldn't have chosen to do it like that. I wouldn't want to waste a good character."

The next three feature films in which Beckinsale starred—*Shooting Fish* (1997), *The Last Days of Disco* (1998), and *Brokedown Palace* (1999)—had varying degrees of critical and commercial success. *Shooting Fish*, a farce directed and co-written by Stefan Schwartz, co-stars Stuart Townsend and Dan Futterman as young con men and Beckinsale as a smart medical student whom they hire as their secretary and who becomes their accomplice. In Great Britain, *Shooting Fish* was the third-highest-grossing film of 1997. For Whit Stillman's generally well-reviewed independent film *The Last Days of Disco*, which is set in the early 1980s, Beckinsale adopted an American accent to play Charlotte, a sharp-tongued, catty young woman who works in publishing and, accompanied by her former college roommate (played by Chloë Sevigny), spends her nights dancing in posh New York clubs. "I

thought [Charlotte] was pretty odious and pretty good fun, and it was enjoyable to play her," Beckinsale told Dina Rabinovitch. "I think if you choose to play a part you must acknowledge some hideous part of yourself that is vaguely similar. I don't think that I am like Charlotte but I wouldn't have been able to play her if I didn't understand her a bit. It's one of the risks of being an actor: You have to face the fact that you've got nasty pieces of work inside you." Beckinsale starred opposite Claire Danes in the largely ignored *Brokedown Palace*, about two American high-school graduates who are imprisoned in Thailand on charges of drug possession.

In 2001 Beckinsale appeared in *The Golden Bowl*, produced by Ismail Merchant and directed by James Ivory from Ruth Prawer Jhabvala's adaptation of Henry James's last novel. Set in the early years of the 20th century, the story focuses on the complex relationships among an American millionaire, Adam Verver (Nick Nolte); his daughter, Maggie (Beckinsale); Amerigo (Jeremy Northam), an impoverished Italian nobleman who marries Maggie for her money; and Maggie's best friend, Charlotte Stant (Uma Thurman), who had had an affair with the prince before his marriage and resumes it after she marries Adam Verver. Some months before Beckinsale began work on *The Golden Bowl*, she gave birth to her daughter, Lily. "I was carrying 20 pounds extra weight" (gained during her pregnancy), she told Nancy Mills, "so it was interesting not to be the sexy, beautiful lead. People say Maggie is the boring and mousy one, but actually it was a brilliant role, and emotionally I was totally overwrought because I'd just had a baby."

After filming *The Golden Bowl*, Beckinsale accepted the role of Evelyn in *Pearl Harbor*. Produced at a cost of $140 million and directed by Michael Bay, whose credits include *The Rock* (1996) and *Armageddon* (1998), the film depicts a love triangle involving a nurse (Beckinsale) and two Army Air Corps pilots who are best friends, played by Ben Affleck and Josh Hartnett. The story is set against the Japanese air attack on the American naval base at Pearl Harbor, on the Hawaiian island of Oahu, on December 7, 1941—the event that triggered the entry of the United States into World War II. "The script for *Pearl Harbor* made me cry," Beckinsale told Lynn Hirschberg. "I've been offered big, stupid Hollywood movies before, and it's easy to say no. . . . I thought, in all sincerity, I would perform in this if it was being staged at a small theater in Wales. I had no idea what a 'Michael Bay movie' was. It was the script that convinced me." "My rule for a script is, Would I be just as happy doing it in the Chiswick Town Hall?" she explained to Sarah Lyall, referring to a section of London. "But there's so much stuff around that I really don't want to do: lots of incredibly obscure period things and things where girls have to get their clothes off. Also, if it's badly written—it doesn't matter what it is—I'd be too embarrassed to say the lines. I think that's why doing a literature degree slightly stumps you as an actress. You can't say bad lines with a straight face." Reviewers disagreed with Beckinsale's high opinion of the screenplay; most described it as awash in corny dialogue. While agreeing that the depiction of the bombing of Pearl Harbor was spectacular, critics condemned the love story as trite and complained about the many glaring historical errors in the film. Nevertheless, in the month after its release, in May, the film grossed over $160 million at the box office.

In October 2001 Beckinsale starred opposite John Cusack in the romantic comedy *Serendipity*, which was generally judged to be contrived but sweet and well acted. She has occasionally performed in plays staged in Great Britain; her credits include roles in Anton Chekhov's drama *The Seagull*, with the Thelma Holts Theatre Company, in Chester, England, in 1995, and in works by two young British playwrights, both of which were mounted in London in 1996: *Sweetheart*, by Nick Grosso, and *Clocks and Whistles*, by Samuel Adamson.

Beckinsale's "clear, pale skin, slight physique and feline self-possession gave her a distinct Audrey Hepburn air," Sarah Lyall wrote after interviewing her in 1997. Lyall also wrote that she is "not known for mincing words, or for compromising." The actress lives in London with her daughter and the child's father—her longtime boyfriend, the Welsh actor Michael Sheen, whom she met when they co-starred in *The Seagull*. — K.S.

Suggested Reading: *Interview* p102+ June 1998, with photos, p70+ June 2001, with photo; (London) *Daily Telegraph* (on-line) Nov. 23, 1996; *New York Times* II p35+ Feb. 16, 1997; *New York Times Magazine* p68 Apr. 22, 2001, with photo; *Newsweek* p48 May 14, 2001, with photo; *People* p71+ June 4, 2001; *Premiere* p84+ June 1998, with photos

Selected Films: *Much Ado About Nothing*, 1993; *Cold Comfort Farm*, 1995; *Shooting Fish*, 1998; *The Last Days of Disco*, 1998; *Brokedown Palace*, 1999; *The Golden Bowl*, 2001; *Pearl Harbor*, 2001; *Serendipity*, 2001

Selected Television Miniseries: *Jane Austen's Emma*, 1997

Selected Plays: *The Seagull*; *Clocks and Whistles*

Bennett, Lerone

Oct. 17, 1928– Writer; editor; historian; poet.
Address: Johnson Publishing Co., P.O. Box 538, Chicago, IL 60690-9813

As an African-American growing up in Mississippi during the 1930s and 1940s, the journalist and historian Lerone Bennett Jr. dealt with racism and violence nearly every day. One evening in 1941, when the 13-year-old Bennett was at a dance, a group of white policemen came in, looking for a suspect among the gathering of African-Americans. The officers lined all the men against the walls of the dance hall for interrogation. As Bennett recalled to Ken Ringle for the *Washington Post* (August 27, 1993), "As the sheriff started around the hall questioning people and searching them, I noticed he would periodically just haul off and slam someone across the face with his fist or his pistol for no reason at all. And I watched as he came around and figured he was hitting about every fourth or fifth person. So I tried to weasel my way so I wouldn't be in the wrong spot. That was how you survived. That was Mississippi."

Although Bennett did his best to be silent and inconspicuous that night, he has followed a very different course since he began his writing and editing career. As a longtime editor for *Ebony*, he has helped its readership grow from about 125,000 to more than nine million per issue. In his historical works, Bennett has described the hardships of African-Americans, highlighted their achieve-

Courtesy of Lerone Bennett Jr.

ments, and offered new interpretations of history—such as those in his groundbreaking book *Before the Mayflower* (1962) and his recent, controversial study of Abraham Lincoln, *Forced into Glory: Abraham Lincoln's White Dream* (2000). Without mincing words or glossing over hard truths about the United States, Bennett has become recognized as a leading expert on African-American history. As Ken Ringle wrote, "If Bennett didn't create the booming field in black history . . . he's at least helped drag it out of the classroom and into the public arena, revitalizing in the process the timeless debate over who and what we are as a nation."

Lerone Bennett Jr. was born in Clarksdale, Mississippi, on October 17, 1928 to Lerone Bennett Sr. and Alma Reed Bennett. From an early age he was taught to value education and reading. His grandmother—whom he described to Ringle as "the greatest person I've ever known"—had 13 children and no way to educate them, since there were no schools for black children in the countryside surrounding Jackson, Mississippi, where she lived. Prevailing against the indifference of her husband and the discouragement of many others, she took her children to Jackson so that they could get an education. "She raised all of those children so that everyone who wanted to go to college went to college," Bennett told Ringle. As a boy Bennett himself was an avid reader and student, and he soon took an interest in history. "I got this mad idea," he said to Ringle, "that if I could just find out why Mississippi was the way it was . . . why racism existed, I would first of all be in a position to understand it, and secondly be in a position to maybe do something about it. This had nothing to do with academics. To me it was a question of survival: a matter of life and death."

Bennett had always wanted to be a lawyer, but after hanging around the offices of two African-American newspapers in Jackson, he became involved in journalism. According to Ken Ringle, he wrote his first editorial at the age of 11. (Ringle did not report whether it was published.) After graduating from Lenier High School, he enrolled at Morehouse College, in Atlanta, Georgia, where he earned an A.B. degree in 1949. Afterward, he went to work as a reporter for the African-American–owned *Atlanta Daily World*, a newspaper that covered issues related to segregation, education, and African-American business. He became city editor of the paper in 1952; he left the following year, to accept an associate editor position at *Jet* magazine. In 1954 Bennett took a job as associate editor for *Ebony*, a magazine of African-American culture for which he would work in a series of positions. *Ebony* was, and is, one of the most prominent publications for African-Americans. Launched in 1945, it was meant to document the successes of blacks at a time when those achievements often went unnoticed. As the founding publisher, John H. Johnson, wrote in his 1989 autobiography, *Succeeding Against the Odds* (which Bennett co-authored), "We wanted to see Dr. Charles Drew and Ralph Bunche and Jackie Robinson and the other men and women who were building the campfires of tomorrow. . . . We intended to highlight Black breakthroughs and pockets of progress. But we didn't intend to ignore difficulties and harsh realities."

In 1958 Bennett was promoted to the position of senior editor at *Ebony*. Four years later he published *Before the Mayflower*, which grew out of a series of articles he had written for the magazine. *Before the Mayflower* is an extensive history of African-American people, documenting periods from the distant past in Africa up to the time of the civil rights leader Martin Luther King Jr. The book's title refers to the fact that the first Africans to come to America were brought on a Dutch slave ship bound for Jamestown, Virginia, in 1619, before the Pilgrims arrived in what was to become Massachusetts aboard the *Mayflower*, in 1620. In the first chapter, "The African Past," Bennett revisited the great empires of Africa's Nile Valley and the western Sudan and showed that the ancestors of American slaves lived in a society in which scholarship was respected and university life was relatively common. "Africa, long considered the 'Dark Continent,'" Bennett wrote, "is now regarded as the place where man first received light. Ancient Africans, long considered primitive and ignorant, are now revealed as creative contributors to Egyptian civilization and builders of powerful states in the Sudan." In the succeeding chapters Bennett followed the history of Africans in America. He pointed out the irony in the fact that they fought in the Revolutionary War in the name of a Declaration of Independence that failed to acknowledge their rights. When African-Americans were enslaved, Bennett stated, they did not submit meekly to this treatment; beginning in the 18th century, there were numerous slave revolts in various areas of the country. In "The Generation of Crisis," Bennett wrote of Frederick Douglass and the many other people who contributed to the abolitionist movement before the Civil War. He described the contributions of African-Americans to the Civil War effort as well as their activities during Reconstruction, the short-lived era of material and spiritual prosperity that blacks enjoyed after the war ended. The concluding chapters of *Before the Mayflower* detail the struggles of W.E.B. DuBois, Marcus Garvey, and Martin Luther King Jr. for black liberation. As John Henrik Clarke wrote in *Freedom Ways* (Fall 1965), "Lerone Bennett proves, in the concluding chapters of his book, that the great human drama now being called 'The Black Revolution in the U.S.A.' has long historical roots and it cannot be fully understood until it is seen in this context."

Although *Before the Mayflower* was not immediately recognized as one of the great books of African-American history (it would later sell well over a million copies), it received favorable reviews at the time of its publication. In *Teachers College Record* (November 1963), R. N. Current wrote, "Viewed as history, the book has the limitations that necessarily pertain to any partisan account of an ethnic or racial group. Within these limitations, the author has done a remarkable job." For *American History Review* (July 1963), Benjamin Quarles wrote, "Whether or not one is familiar with the book's content, he may well be moved by the unusual ability to evoke the tragedy and the glory of the Negro's role in the American past."

Bennett's next book was *The Negro Mood* (1964), a collection of five essays analyzing aspects of the civil rights movement, then at its peak. Bennett wrote in the preface, "In five essays organized around the general theme, The Negro Mood, I have attempted to dig beneath the surface and expose the psychic mechanisms of the Black Fury that is rolling across the land. . . . The Negro rebellion is, in fact, four different rebellions: a rebellion against the conservative within and the conservative without; a rebellion on the streets and a rebellion in the thoroughfares of the mind."

In *Freedom Ways* John Henrik Clarke praised the volume for what he felt was an insightful take on familiar themes: "In essence, the essays in the book *The Negro Mood* are about the changing power relations between blacks and whites," he wrote. "If this were Lerone Bennett's only book, his status as a social historian would still be secure." Saunders Redding, however, felt that the book did not stand out from the many works then being published about the civil rights movement. In *Saturday Review* (January 16, 1965), he called *The Negro Mood* "high-flown and polyphonic, with insufficient regard for logic and precision of expression."

Bennett, while at Morehouse College, had been one year behind Martin Luther King Jr. He had also participated in the 1963 March on Washington, in which King delivered his famous "I Have a Dream" speech. He was, therefore, as qualified as any historian to write a biography of the great civil rights leader. *What Manner of Man: A Biography of Martin Luther King Jr.*, published in 1964, the year King won the Nobel Peace Prize, offered the most in-depth study of King up to that time. A writer for *Library Journal* (July 1965) thought that the book read more like a tribute than a biography. "It is almost embarrassing in its awe and overwhelming praise," the reviewer wrote. Paul Schlueter, however, reviewing the book for *Christian Century* (September 22, 1965), believed that Bennett had written an even-handed treatment of King. "Affectionate . . . but unsparingly critical when necessary," Schlueter wrote, "*What Manner of Man* is far more than a puff piece hurriedly thrown together to capitalize on recent civil rights events. . . . It is by all odds one of the most stirring and courageously Christian biographies ever written about a religious leader." Bennett was given the Patron Saints Award by the Society of Midland Authors for *What Manner of Man*.

Bennett continued to illuminate the history of African-American protest in his next book, *Confrontation: Black and White* (1965), which documents protests in the 17th century and works its way into modern African-American rebellion. Most critics considered the book a valuable historical work. In 1967 Bennett revisited a theme that he had touched on in *Before the Mayflower*: that of the momentary period of relative African-American equality immediately following the Civil War.

Black Power U.S.A.: The Human Side of Reconstruction, 1867–1877 focused on the years when African-American men were finally able to hold office in the South. During that period, every southern state elected African-Americans to its legislature; 20 southern blacks served in the U.S. House of Representatives, and two were elected as U.S. senators from Mississippi. As Bennett wrote in the preface to the book, "An understanding of the triumphs and failures of the Reconstruction is indispensable for an understanding of the triumphs and failures of the Second Reconstruction we are now undergoing."

In 1968 Bennett became a visiting professor of history at Northwestern University, in Chicago. That year he also published *Pioneers in Protest*, a book of biographies of African-American abolitionists. He left Northwestern in 1969, the year he became a senior fellow at the Institute of the Black World, in Atlanta. In 1972 his book *Challenge of Blackness* appeared. Three years later his companion volume to *Before the Mayflower*, titled *The Shaping of Black America*, examined the history of Africans in the United States, with an emphasis on the origins of slavery. In that book he argued that racism was consciously introduced into the American colonies by whites as a way of exerting control. In *Best Seller* (April 1975), Norman Lederer called this a "shaky concept," and a reviewer for *Choice* (July/August 1975) wrote, "In presenting racism as a consciously contrived scheme by sinister (and unnamed) manipulators of what he calls 'the system,' [Bennett] has overlooked the individual dimension and sheer caprice inherent in American racism." A. C. Gulliver, however, thought that Bennett's argument was well-supported. In the *Christian Science Monitor* (May 1, 1975), he wrote, "Bennett treads old ground but with new emphasis. . . . For the knowledgeable, the uninformed, or the merely curious, [this] is a valuable and very readable [book]."

Bennett received a Literature Award from the American Academy of Arts and Letters in 1978, the year before his work *Wade in Water: Great Moments in Black History* was published. Speaking about his book as it relates to African-American youths, Bennett told Ringle, "I think they're down in a hole and want desperately for you to give them some magic answer that will get them out. And of course there is no magic answer. I tell them life is a constant struggle, and even if you do everything right there's no certainty of success. I tell them their only sure hope is excellence. Without excellence this society will eat them alive." Accordingly, in *Wade in Water* Bennett provided stories that demonstrate the excellence achieved by various African-Americans throughout history. Written in a narrative style, with ample attention paid to time and setting, the book includes such chapters as "Nat Turner's Bloody Sermon," "The Private War of Harriet Tubman," "Prelude to Protest," and "The Day They Marched."

In 1981 Bennett was given a Lifetime Achievement Award from the National Association of Black Journalists, and in the following year he received a Candace Award from the National Association of 100 Black Women. Meanwhile, he continued his work for *Ebony*, where in 1987 he was promoted from senior to executive editor, a position he still holds. In 1996 he was honored with a Salute to Greatness Award from the Martin Luther King Jr. Center for Nonviolent Social Change. A Trumpet Award from Turner Broadcasting System followed in 1998, and a Candle in the Dark Award was given to him by Morehouse College in 1999.

The year 2000 saw the publication of one of Bennett's most controversial books, a study of the 16th U.S. president titled *Forced into Glory: Abraham Lincoln's White Dream*. In 1968 Bennett had written an article for *Ebony*, "Was Abe Lincoln a White Supremacist?," in which he had concluded that Lincoln was in fact a bigot who actively campaigned against freedom and opportunity for African-Americans. Most Lincoln scholars at the time discounted the article as being marred by poor scholarship. Bennett therefore spent years augmenting his research before publishing his 650-page book, in which he did not stray from his original conclusion. "If Lincoln had had his way," he argued, "Oprah Winfrey, Martin Luther King Jr., Jesse Jackson Sr., Lena Horne, Muhammad Ali, Hank Aaron, Maya Angelou, Malcolm X, Rosa Parks . . . and even Clarence Thomas would have been born in slavery." As Bennett told Lia Merriweather for *Detours* (February 12, 1999, on-line), "Abraham Lincoln was a racist, believed black people were inferior, opposed citizenship for black people, wanted to deport black people, and never in his whole life had a rational idea about the race problem in America." In *Forced into Glory* Bennett noted that Lincoln was fond of racist jokes and of referring to African-Americans as "niggers." As an Illinois legislator, Lincoln opposed abolitionists, supported fugitive slave laws, and endorsed state laws barring African-Americans from voting, serving on juries, holding office, or intermarrying with whites. In addition, Bennett wrote, the Emancipation Proclamation, issued by Lincoln on January 1, 1863 (after the start of the Civil War, in 1861) to free slaves in the Confederate states actually accomplished little toward that end and, in fact, represented Lincoln's attempt to reverse the Second Confiscation Act, which freed the slaves of owners who supported the Confederacy. (The Emancipation Proclamation did not outlaw slavery in certain Union-controlled areas of the Confederacy or in border states, whereas the Confiscation Act could potentially free slaves owned by any Confederate loyalists.) Furthermore, Bennett asserted, Lincoln's real ambition regarding African-Americans was to deport them from the U.S. and "make America a Great White Place." As for the fact that slaves were in fact freed and given citizenship at the end of the Civil War, in 1865, Bennett maintained that Lincoln was "forced into glory" by radical Republi-

cans such as Thaddeus Stevens and Charles Sumner. Bennett told Robert Stacy McCain for *Insight* (July 3, 2000) that he wrote the book not just to debunk Lincoln as a person but to reveal Lincoln's heroic status in America as—in Bennett's view—an indication of America's unwillingness to come to terms with racism. "The myth," Bennett said, "is an obstacle to understanding. Lincoln is a metaphor for our real determination to evade the race problem in this country."

Critics were divided on the merits of *Forced into Glory*, with one camp maintaining that Bennett had painted an unfair portrait of Lincoln by choosing facts selectively, while the other felt that Bennett had done a service for the United States by dispelling the myth of "Honest Abe." James M. McPherson was one of the former. In the *New York Times Book Review* (August 27, 2000, on-line), he conceded that *Forced into Glory* "must be taken seriously," but also accused Bennett of "distortions of interpretation" and "distortion by omission." For example, McPherson pointed out that the Second Confiscation Act—which Bennett cited as a more important precursor to the Emancipation Proclamation—freed slaves only after it was determined in court, case by case, that their owners were indeed Confederates. Therefore, if abolitionists had continued to depend on the Second Confiscation Act, the process of emancipation would have been so slow as to be virtually nonexistent. Responding to Bennett's claim that the Emancipation Proclamation freed slaves in areas where Lincoln had no power of enforcement (in the Confederate states) and maintained slavery where he did have power (Union-controlled areas of the Confederacy), McPherson wrote, "The Emancipation Proclamation . . . was based on the president's war powers as commander in chief to seize enemy property (i.e. slaves) being used to wage war against the United States. Since Union-controlled exempted areas were not at war with the United States, Lincoln had no constitutional power over slavery in those areas."

By contrast, far from finding fault with Bennett's scholarship, Kam Williams celebrated *Forced into Glory* as a courageous, truthful, and overdue work. In *Black World Today* (May 22, 2000, on-line), he wrote, "*Forced into Glory*, well-written and painstakingly documented, knocks a national icon off his pedestal, yes. But, more significantly, it exposes the duplicitous nature of a national philosophy which has made a habit of extreme dissociation between its words and its deeds." The reaction of Eric Foner, professor of history at Columbia University, in New York City, fell somewhere in between McPherson's and Williams's. In the *Los Angeles Times Book Review* (April 9, 2000), Foner wrote, "Bennett presents compelling evidence of how historians have consistently soft-pedaled Lincoln's racial views. Previous scholars, he rightly points out, downplay or ignore Lincoln's commitment to colonizing blacks outside the country, a position he . . . advocated publicly for almost his entire political career." Nevertheless, Foner argued, "Bennett is not content to show that Lincoln held racist views. Racism, Bennett insists, was Lincoln's most deeply held belief, 'the center and circumference of his being.' The Great Emancipator, he asserts, was, in reality, 'one of the major supporters of slavery in the United States' and 'in and of himself, and in his objective being, an oppressor.' These statements are totally unfounded." In answering the question, "Which was the real Lincoln, the racist or the opponent of slavery?" Foner concluded, "The unavoidable answer is both. . . . If America ever hopes to resolve its racial dilemmas, we need to repudiate the worst of Lincoln, while embracing the best."

In May 2000 Bennett participated in a hearing to address the issue of monetary reparations for descendants of American slaves. The hearing was held by the finance and human relations committees of the Chicago City Council. Bennett emerged during the hearings as an outspoken advocate of reparations. As quoted in *Jet* (May 15, 2000), he said of his ancestors, "They came up from slavery, up from segregation, up from horror. And in the end, by some miracle no historian can explain, they not only survived, but they prevailed, giving this country a new music and new spirit and the take-off capital that made the skyscrapers around us possible. It is that miracle, it is that gift, it is that debt, that we bring before this body today, with the hope that you will join us in ensuring that they did not labor and die in vain." Chicago subsequently joined Detroit, Cleveland, and Dallas in approving a measure aimed at federal hearings on slavery reparations.

Bennett continues to work as executive editor of *Ebony*. His poems, short stories, and articles have appeared in such publications as *Rhetoric and Literature*, *Coming of Age in Philosophy*, and *Myths and Motifs in Literature*. In 1966 Bennett was awarded an honorary doctorate of humane letters degree by Morehouse College. He has been similarly honored by the University of Illinois (1980), Lincoln College (1980), Morgan State University (1981), Vorhees College (1981), Morris Brown College (1986), Rust College (1987), Boston University (1987), Lincoln University (1988), and Winston-Salem State University (1989). His work has been translated into French, German, Japanese, Swedish, Russian, and Arabic. In 1956 Bennett married Gloria Sylvester, with whom he has four children: Joy, Constance, Courtney, and Lerone III. — P.G.H.

Suggested Reading: *Black World Today* (on-line) May 22, 2000; *Detours* (on-line) Feb. 12, 1999; *Freedom Ways* p481+ Fall 1965; *Jet* p4+ May 15, 2000; *Los Angeles Times Book Review* p10 Apr. 9, 2000; *New York Times* (on-line) Aug. 27, 2000; *Washington Post* C p1 Aug. 27, 1993, B p1 Jan. 21, 1995

Selected Books: *Before the Mayflower: A History of the Negro in America, 1619–1962*, 1962; *The Negro Mood*, 1964; *What Manner of Man: A Biography of Martin Luther King Jr.*, 1964; *Confrontation: Black and White*, 1965; *Black Power U.S.A.: The Human Side of Reconstruction, 1867-1877*, 1967; *Pioneers in Protest*, 1968; *Challenge of Blackness*, 1972; *The Shaping of Black America*, 1975; *Wade in Water: Great Moments in Black History*, 1979; *Forced into Glory: Abraham Lincoln's White Dream*, 2000

Courtesy of Seymour Benzer

Benzer, Seymour

Oct. 15, 1921– Geneticist; behavioral scientist.
Address: Biology Dept., M/C 156-29, California Institute of Technology, Pasadena, CA 91125

In his profile of the geneticist and behavioral scientist Seymour Benzer for the *New Yorker* (April 5, 1999), Jonathan Weiner wrote, "Benzer's pioneering work with flies has put him at the center of one of the most controversial issues in science: the extent to which our genes shape who we are and what we do." In conducting his wide-ranging and often pioneering research, Benzer has maintained the work habits he established more than five decades ago. As Jonathan Weiner noted, "He always wore many layers of clothing; he did his best work in the middle of the night; and he amazed [his friends and colleagues] by the things he ate," among them snakes, caterpillars, ducks' feet, and cows' udders. Much of his work has involved fruit flies, known to scientists as *Drosophila melanogaster*, in a laboratory at the California Institute of Technology (Caltech). There, he has often experimented far into the night, attempting to find flies with genes that had altered their tiny owners' sense of time, their ability to mate, or their capacity to remember learned behavior. Modest about his achievements, which include groundbreaking work in physics during the 1940s, gene mapping in the 1950s, and linking behavior to genetics beginning in the 1960s, Benzer has until recently received little notice outside the worlds of biology and genetics. He has been a member of the National Academy of Sciences since 1961 and has won several major international honors, including the Gairdner Award (1964), the Lasker Award (1971), the National Medal of Science (1983), the Thomas Hunt Morgan Medal for his lifetime contribution to genetics (1986), the Wolf Prize for Medicine (1991), and the Crafoord Prize, from the Royal Swedish Academy of Sciences (1993). The Pulitzer Prize–winning journalist Jonathan Weiner profiled Benzer in *Time, Love, Memory*, published in 1999, thus bringing the scientist's discoveries to a larger audience.

The third of the four children of Polish-Jewish immigrants, Seymour Benzer was born on October 15, 1921 in New York City. His parents, Mayer and Eva Benzer, both of whom worked in the garment industry, raised him and his three sisters in the Bensonhurst section of the borough of Brooklyn. As the family's only son, Benzer was favored, and thus was given fewer chores than his sisters; he divided his ample free time between his homemade basement laboratory, where he did chemistry experiments, and playing stickball with neighborhood children. For his bar mitzvah, celebrated when he turned 13, he received a microscope as a present. On the first slide that he made, he placed a sample of his own sperm. Houseflies were another early subject. He graduated from high school at age 15 and then enrolled at Brooklyn College, where he paid his tuition with a New York State Regents Scholarship. Eager to dive into advanced biology, he asked to skip the introductory course, which was more akin to natural history than hard science. His request was denied, and "being a stupid, pigheaded, cocky young guy, I told them the hell with it, and didn't take any biology at all," he told Weiner.

In 1942 Benzer earned a B.A. degree in physics. The same year he married Dorothy Vlosky, nicknamed Dotty, and moved with her to Indiana, where Benzer did graduate work at Purdue University, in West Lafayette. He was awarded a master's degree in physics in 1943 and a Ph.D. in 1947. At Purdue, in the latter years of World War II, Benzer worked in a secret wartime laboratory with scientists attempting to develop germanium semiconductors for use in radar devices. Silicon semiconductors, which were being used at that time, tended to burn out when subjected to high voltages. Benzer discovered a crystal form of germanium that withstood such voltages. He and his supervi-

sor in the lab, Karl Lark-Horovitz, were ultimately awarded six patents for their research discoveries, and the crystal form of germanium was later used at Bell Labs to develop the first transistor.

Benzer's career path changed in 1946, after he read *What Is Life?*, by the Austrian quantum physicist Ernest Schrödinger. The German quantum physicist Max Delbrück had earlier offered ideas regarding the physical makeup of genes, and Schrödinger's book identified this issue as the key question in all of science. Intrigued, Benzer registered for a summer course on bacterial viruses that Delbrück had initiated at Cold Spring Harbor Laboratory, on Long Island, New York. "Within one day," as Benzer told Weiner, he developed a passion for the subject matter and decided to switch his focus to biology. His colleagues at Purdue were dismayed; many of them, as Weiner noted in his article, "were planning to form electronics companies and get rich." "People thought I was nuts," Benzer told Weiner. "Here it was, the semiconductor thing was booming."

Abandoning semiconductors and electronics, Benzer took a leave of absence from Purdue in 1948; the leave stretched into a four-year odyssey into the world of genetics. During that time he worked with four future Nobel laureates in three different laboratories: at Oak Ridge National Laboratory, in Tennessee; at Caltech with Delbrück, who won the Nobel Prize in Physiology or Medicine in 1969; and as a Fulbright scholar at the Pasteur Institute in Paris, where Benzer worked with Jacques Lucien Monod and François Jacob under the direction of André Lwoff, all three of whom shared the 1965 Nobel Prize in Physiology or Medicine. Benzer also spent a summer working with Cornelius van Niel at the Stanford Marine Station, at Pacific Grove, California.

Benzer returned to Purdue in 1953, to teach physics and biophysics as an associate professor. (He was promoted to professor of biology in 1958.) Soon afterward Francis Watson and James Crick published their findings about the double-helix structure of DNA. Benzer had been engaged in his own genetic research, with viruses and bacteria; he was trying to understand the physical structure of their genes and searching for a possible relationship between their genes and those of larger organisms. Benzer's experiments expanded on the work of the geneticist Thomas Hunt Morgan, who had attempted to map the genes of the fruit fly *Drosophila* at Columbia University around the turn of the 20th century. In biology in the 1950s, "what was needed was to connect [Watson and Crick's] studies with the classical maps of the genes started by Morgan," Lewis Wolpert, writing for the *New York Times Book Review* (May 2, 1999), noted in his assessment of *Time, Love, Memory*, which serves as a biography of Benzer as well as an account of his work. Benzer made that connection "brilliantly," Wolpert continued, "focusing in great detail on a single region of virus DNA; he discovered the fine structure of the gene and how it could change by mutations. He discovered mistakes in a gene—deletions and insertions, rather like the typos we all come across."

Benzer spent a decade mapping rII, a chromosomal region of the bacteriophage T4 (a bacteria-infecting virus), doing pioneering work on splitting the gene. To diagram the interior of a gene in minuscule detail, he created a map that stretched across the walls of his laboratory; when he presented it at conferences, its unfurling made a memorable impact on colleagues. Through his experiments with bacteriophage T4, he became the first to show that the internal structure of a gene itself is linear, similar to the arrangements of various genes on a chromosome. Using a mutant strain of bacteriophage T4 that should not have been able to multiply and overtake a strain of the bacteria *E. coli* (as the normal form of T4 could), Benzer then combined the first mutant with strains of T4 that had different genetic mutations. By recombining their genetic structures, the T4 mutants were able to restore their original genetic makeup and reproduce, as evidenced by their destruction of the *E. coli*. Using that system, Benzer was able to detect recombination between two mutations, even if they were only one nucleotide unit away from each other on the DNA of the bacteriophage. That was the key to constructing a fine-structure map of the gene, related to the structure of its DNA. Benzer spent a sabbatical year in 1958–59 at Cambridge University, in England, working with Francis Crick, James Watson, and the geneticist Sydney Brenner.

Despite his research successes, as well as Purdue's willingness to transfer his professorship to the Department of Biology, Benzer felt restless. In the *New Yorker*, Jonathan Weiner described the prevailing attitude of the time: "By the early sixties, molecular biologists had learned so much about the gene that they doubted whether they would ever encounter any further mysteries to equal the ones they had dispelled." Benzer remarked to Weiner, "It was a little bit like the physicists at the end of the nineteenth century saying 'All we have left to do is find one more decimal place.'" While vacationing at Cold Spring Harbor with his family in the early 1960s, however, Benzer was inspired by a new problem, one that would lead him to blaze a trail in a new field: behavioral genetics. Observing his daughters playing on the beach, he found their differences remarkable; his daughter Barbie had always been more energetic than his daughter Martha, while Martha had always been more placid. Benzer had noticed his daughters' distinctive personalities and behavioral characteristics almost from birth and, as Weiner noted, "he didn't think that he and his wife could possibly have made that much difference in the temperaments of the two girls—the difference had to be in the genes." This revelation inspired Benzer to plunge into the "nature versus nurture" debate, which focuses on the influence of environment on personality, on the one hand, and the influence of heredity, on the other. Weiner described Benzer's

motivation: namely, to "try to trace the connections between the gene and the brain, and between brain and behavior." In an effort to understand the physiology of the brain better, he asked his wife to buy from the butcher brains of different species—cow, sheep, goat, chicken, and pig. Working at home in the middle of night, he dissected the brains, examined them, and then cooked and ate them.

In the interest of pursuing his new topic, Benzer went to Caltech in 1965 as a visiting researcher and worked with the psychobiologist Roger W. Sperry, who would later win the Nobel Prize in Physiology or Medicine, in 1981. Benzer's laboratory at Caltech was in the same building where Thomas Hunt Morgan had done his final research; following in Morgan's footsteps, Benzer began to experiment with fruit flies, creating mutant strains and looking for changes in behavior. His first breakthrough was with flies that had maladjusted internal clocks. Ordinary fruit flies hatch at dawn and in the following days maintain a daily routine that always includes becoming active at sunrise, even if they are in a darkened room. In 1968 Benzer and Ronald Konopka, a graduate student, isolated strains of flies whose clocks were broken—some of the flies woke up too early, others "slept in," and still others never went to sleep. Benzer and Konopka linked the various errors in timing to a single gene on the X chromosome and named the gene "period." Benzer and his student Jeff Hall isolated genes that were linked to the fruit flies' courting and mating rituals. One male fly exhibited courting behavior but never mated; Hall named it "celibate." Another male fly began copulation but stopped himself halfway through and rarely produced offspring; he was christened "coitus interruptus." A group of mutant male flies discovered by another researcher were observed exhibiting mating rituals to one another, and the mutant gene responsible was named "fruitless." Other experiments, conducted with Benzer's students Chip Quinn and Duncan Byers, tested the flies' capacity for memory and learning, resulting in the discovery of the mutant "dunce." Throughout the arduous process of working with the insects, Benzer insisted that his research, which many of his students have since continued in their own laboratories at other academic institutions, had relevance to human genetics. "Often the discovery of a gene in the fly has led straight to its discovery in human beings, because key sequences in both genetic codes are very much alike," Weiner wrote in the *New Yorker*. He continued, "Our clocks apparently work so much like fly clocks that, in laboratory tests, some of our protein gears mesh perfectly with the flies' gears, like parts of the same watch—even though human beings and flies have not shared an ancestor since the Cambrian Period, six hundred million years ago."

Named the James G. Boswell Professor of Neuroscience at Caltech in 1975, Benzer took a brief break from his work in 1978, after the death of his wife, Dotty. He thought about dropping his research with flies and moving on to something else. "Well, I'd jumped before," he told Weiner. But late in 1978 he met Carol Miller, a young neuropathologist associated with the medical school at the University of Southern California. Both were driven to unlock the secrets of the brain—he of flies and she of human beings. They traded tools, tips, and case histories before falling in love and marrying, in 1980. At around that time Benzer began working with flies that had inherited the propensity to develop brain defects, naming each mutant after some food that resembled the shape of its lesions.

Benzer's honors include being named a 1998 Ellison Medical Foundation Senior Scholar (which brought him a grant worth almost $1 million). In 2001 he won the National Academy of Sciences Award in the Neurosciences. His work is not without critics, however. According to a rumor, he was once nominated for a "Golden Fleece Award," with which then– senator William Proxmire of Wisconsin identified projects that, as a member of Congress, he considered examples of wasteful or useless government funding. Benzer himself keeps on the lookout for genetic studies that prove to have been based on weak foundations and whose authors later retract their findings; according to Weiner, Benzer "keeps a file of headlines pertaining to genes and behavior, so that if their claims are discredited he can use them in his lectures as cautionary tales."

Benzer and Carol Miller live a quiet life in San Marino, California; they are the parents of one son, Alexander, born in the mid-1980s. Ignored by the recent debate on cloning because of his focus on fruit flies, Benzer has continued with his experiments. In the late 1990s he found himself in the spotlight, after his laboratory published findings of a mutant fly that had outlived its normal 60-day life span by approximately 40 days. The discovery of the fly, named "methuselah" after the biblical figure who lived to the age of 969, "seems a fitting [77th birthday] present for [Benzer], who still works late into the night and loves the smell of fly food," Lewis Wolpert reported. Shortly after the discovery was made public, Weiner asked Benzer if he was planning to travel during his upcoming vacation. "To me, getting back into the lab would be enough of an adventure," Benzer replied. — K.S.

Suggested Reading: *New York Times Book Review* p33 May 2, 1999; *New Yorker* p44+ Apr. 5, 1999, with photo; *U.S. News & World Report* p62 June 28, 1999; *Notable Twentieth-Century Scientists*, 1995; Weiner, Jonathan. *Time, Love, Memory: A Great Biologist and His Quest for the Origins of Behavior*, 1999

Bethune, Gordon M.

Aug. 29, 1941– Chairman and CEO of Continental Airlines. Address: Continental Airlines, 1600 Smith St., Mail Code: HQS EO, Houston, TX 77002

In 1994, when Gordon M. Bethune left Boeing to become the president and chief operating officer (COO) of Continental Airlines, the Houston-based carrier's on-time performance and lost-baggage record were worse than those of any other major airline. Worker morale had reached such dismal levels that some employees, embarrassed to be associated with the company, routinely removed the Continental logo from their uniforms; and that year, according to *Fortune*, the company's losses reached $619 million on revenues of $5.7 billion. These were not recent developments, either: Continental had lost money in 12 of the previous 18 years; had gone through 10 CEOs in 10 years; and had declared bankruptcy twice, in 1983 and 1990. When Bethune stepped in, Continental appeared to be heading for a third—and final—bankruptcy.

Within months of taking the reins at Continental, Bethune—who by then had been named chairman and chief executive officer (CEO)—initiated a complete turnaround. In the first quarter of 1995, the company posted dramatic improvements in on-time performance and baggage handling and even

Continental Airlines

started to turn a profit. Since then Continental has consistently received high marks on the U.S. Department of Transportation's indices of customer satisfaction (which measure on-time performance, baggage handling, denied boardings, and customer complaints) and has proven to be among the most financially successful airlines in the industry. Robert Levering, a managerial consultant and the co-author of *The 100 Best Companies to Work for in America*, told Brian O'Reilly for *Fortune* (December 20, 1999), "I've been doing this for 20 years, and I've never seen a turnaround of the workplace culture as dramatic as this one." *Air Transport World*, a trade publication, named Continental the Airline of the Year for 1996 and 2000; in 1996, 1997, 1999, and 2000, Continental received the *Frequent Flyer*/J. D. Power and Associates Award for best airline on flights of 500 miles or more; and in 1998 and 2001 *Fortune* magazine included the airline on its list of the "100 Best Companies to Work for in America." In 1996 *Business Week* named Bethune one of the top 25 global managers, and in 1999 *Worth* magazine ranked him among the top 50 CEOs in the U.S.

Gordon M. Bethune was born in Austin, Texas, on August 29, 1941. His father flew airplanes that dusted crops with fungicides and insecticides; his mother sold *Americana* encyclopedias. Bethune is said to have been something of a hellion when he was growing up. At 17, after a failed attempt to enlist in the army the year before, he dropped out of high school and joined the navy. The results of a standardized test indicated that he would excel at aircraft maintenance, so the navy began training Bethune as an aircraft mechanic and electrician. "They sent me right back to school," he told O'Reilly. "Just the thing I wasn't looking for: a structured environment." Bethune remained in the navy for 20 years, working with a variety of aircraft maintenance teams. Among his most vivid memories of his time in the service is that of a 90-day stint on KP for threatening to toss a shipmate overboard.

The skill with which Bethune carried out his assignments earned him repeated promotions, and in time he became the youngest chief petty officer in the peacetime navy. As an officer he gained a reputation for establishing rapport with the enlisted men under his command—a managerial style that would later distinguish him at Continental as well. Andrew Jampoler, a former commanding officer of Bethune's, recalled to O'Reilly, "Gordon always knew where the important work was getting done. He spent his life on the flight deck, talking to the men who turned the wrenches. He was superb at motivating people. When it came to getting spare parts for the engines, there was nobody like him. He had a web of relationships throughout the wing that enabled him to get whatever he needed." "In the Navy," Bethune explained to *salesguy.com*, "a mechanic is just a mechanic. We weren't into shining shoes and inspection. You and your boss were measured by how many airplanes you had working every day. And if you don't like your boss, the airplanes didn't get fixed quite as fast, you know? I had some jackass bosses I had to sweat for. We didn't fix every airplane as quick as we could, be-

cause we weren't motivated to. But if we loved the guy, we would kill for him!"

In 1978 Bethune returned to civilian life. The next year he joined Braniff Airways, as supervisor of subcontracted mechanics. In May 1982 Braniff went bankrupt. Soon afterward Bethune accepted an offer to join Western Airlines as vice president of engineering and maintenance. In 1984 he switched to Piedmont Airlines, where he eventually became senior vice president of operations. While working at Piedmont Bethune completed a bachelor's degree in general studies at Abilene Christian University, in Dallas. He left Piedmont in 1987, after the company was bought out by USAir, and began working for the aerospace giant Boeing as vice president of its Renton Division, the subsidiary that oversees the manufacture and engineering of the 737 and 757 aircraft. To polish some of his rough edges, Boeing sent Bethune to an executive training program at Harvard University, in Cambridge, Massachusetts, which he completed in 1992.

In the fall of 1994 Bethune accepted an invitation to join Continental Airlines as president and chief operating officer. When asked by O'Reilly what motivated him to leave Boeing—where he was rumored to have been a candidate for the position of chief executive officer—and join a company on the brink of collapse, Bethune joked, "I was stupid. When they told me I could be co-pilot, they didn't tell me that the engines had died and the tail was falling off." Before long, though, he realized how dire Continental's situation really was. Speaking with Perry Flint for *Air Transport World* (April 1997), he described Continental when he first arrived there as "the most dysfunctional place I've worked in my life." As Bethune saw it, Continental executives were so obsessed with cutting fares that quality and morale suffered. "You can make a pizza so cheap nobody will buy it," he told Adam Bryant for the *New York Times* (November 12, 1996). "Have you ever seen a successful company that doesn't have a good product and where people don't like coming to work every day?"

In late 1994 Bethune and his friend Greg Brennemann, a management consultant who had been working for Continental since 1993, met at Bethune's Houston home to take stock of the situation. "Gordon and I literally sat down at his dining room table over multiple bottles of wine for three nights in a row and wrote down everything we thought was brain-dead about Continental," Brennemann told Ted Oehmke for *Texas Monthly* (June 1998). The two emerged three days later with a four-point plan—the "Go Forward Plan," as they christened it—to set things straight at Continental. (The four points, which have since become mantras at the airline, are "Fly to Win," "Fund the Future," "Make Reliability a Reality," and "Working Together.") At the heart of Bethune and Brennemann's plan was a proposal to distribute to employees about $3 million every month in which on-time performance improved—about half the amount of money that Continental was then losing per month because of delayed flights. They also recommended shutting down Continental Lite, an unsuccessful and costly attempt to duplicate Southwest Airlines' profitable short-haul strategy on the East Coast; strengthening hubs in Houston, Cleveland, and Newark; focusing on luring back the business travelers who had abandoned the airline over the years; and making the improvement of labor relations a top priority. "Our employees were like abused children, and management was the abusive parent," Bethune told Oehmke. "For years they had been beaten, slapped, made to kneel bare-legged on uncooked rice, or whatever."

Thus, Bethune had a clear sense of the changes he wanted to see. But as COO he didn't have the authority to implement his plan in its entirety, especially, as has been reported, because there was friction between Bethune and Robert Ferguson, Continental's CEO. When Ferguson announced his resignation, in late 1994, a month after the meeting between Bethune and Brenneman, Bethune approached Continental's board of directors with the "Go Forward Plan" and declared that if the board named him Ferguson's successor, he would make the airline profitable again. When the board hesitated, Bethune, who had just turned down the job of president and chief operating officer at United Airlines, threatened to leave Continental. "I told them, 'You guys don't want me to run it? Fine. You run it," he recalled to Oehmke. "I told majority shareholder David Bonderman, 'Hey, David, you'd better get up off your ass and come down and run this company.' And he says, 'You know, Gordon, I don't want to do that.'" According to Oehmke, Bethune was named chairman and CEO two hours after delivering his ultimatum.

As one of his first moves, Bethune named Brenneman president and chief operating officer, and the two set to work implementing their proposed changes. They immediately took steps to dismantle Continental Lite and carried out a major purge of upper management. ("Either we tried the prefrontal lobotomy and it didn't work or, quite frankly, they just weren't smart enough to cut it," Brenneman told Oehmke.) Still, Continental was in such miserable shape that for several months after Bethune took charge, the company teetered on the brink of bankruptcy, with several million dollars in unpaid bills. Bethune's history with Boeing proved useful at this juncture: as Continental's creditors grew increasingly restive about the outstanding payments, Bethune eased some of the financial pressure by persuading Ron Woodard, then president of Boeing, to temporarily release some of Continental's deposits on future airplane deliveries. "If we had had to file [for bankruptcy]," Bethune told Oehmke, "we would have had to liquidate. I would have resigned, and Continental would have been history."

Meanwhile, Bethune's efforts to cut down on the number of delayed flights had begun to bear fruit. In February 1995, one month after he promised a $65 bonus to each employee every month that Continental finished among the top five airlines in on-time performance, the company ranked fourth; in March 1995 the company took top ranking in on-time performance for the first time in its history, then repeated that feat in April. Ultimately, Bethune dispensed $65 checks three more times in the course of 1995. Recalling his colleagues' initial skepticism toward his plan, he told John Huey for Fortune (November 13, 2000), "One of my associates said, 'You are not going to get anybody's attention with $65 a month.' I said, 'I bet if Donald Trump spots three $20s and a $5 on the sidewalk, he picks them up!'"

The turnaround at Continental gathered momentum throughout 1995. In July the company announced the largest quarterly profit in its history, and for four consecutive months beginning in August of that year, the airline finished first in the U.S. Department of Transportation's ratings of baggage handling. In December Business Week named Continental the best New York Stock Exchange stock of the year, and the company ended 1995 with its largest annual profit ($224 million) ever. At first Bethune's critics attributed his success to initiatives that had been set in motion before he took charge; skeptics also pointed to a strong economy and, in particular, to a good year throughout the airline industry. But by the end of 1996, after a year in which the airline repeated (and in many ways improved upon) its 1995 performance, Bethune had been widely credited with having put the airline back on its feet.

Business at Continental continued to improve steadily throughout the second half of the 1990s. In 1996 the company reported earnings of $319 million; in 1997 that figure climbed to $383 million, and in 1998 it rose again, to $385 million. As of January 2001 the airline had posted a profit for six straight years. During the same period Continental opened a number of new routes, including flights to Brazil; Ireland; Scotland; Singapore; Tokyo, Japan; Bangkok, Thailand; and Seoul, South Korea. Meanwhile, in early 1998, Northwest Airlines bought a controlling stake in Continental for $519 million. The two airlines agreed to maintain separate managements and identities while combining schedules and frequent-flier programs. While Bethune originally supported the deal, in early 2000 he expressed an interest in buying back the controlling shares from Northwest, against the wishes of that airline's management. In late 2000 an antitrust suit brought by the U.S. Justice Department restricted Northwest's rights over Continental.

When asked about the reasons for his success at Continental, Bethune said to Bryant, "We all [knew] what needed to be done. But the difference between those guys and me is that I got enough people to help me get it done." He elaborated on this managerial approach in his book, From Worst to First: Behind the Scenes of Continental's Remarkable Comeback—A Flight Plan for Success

(1998), co-authored with the journalist Scott Huler; in it he wrote, as cited by *surferess.com*, "Under the old style of management, as symbolized by [the old airline-employee manual], employees were limited on every side. A passenger with an unusual situation was a dangerous character to be avoided, not a challenge to be resolved. No matter what employees did, the manual probably told them that it was wrong. . . . We changed that. We set up a committee to reorganize and rewrite the manual. And we don't call it a manual anymore, we call it guidelines. The new guidelines are supposed to help employees solve problems—give them a sense of where the boundaries are when they run into trouble. But in the general pursuit of their jobs, we want them to use their heads and use their resources. We don't want robots, we want team members."

Known for his plainspoken, even coarse, manner, Bethune regularly spices his conversation with expletives. He is also reported to have a taste for off-color jokes, and he makes no secret of his fondness for driving his Porsche at speeds far in excess of 100 miles per hour. However, because many employees seem to feel that Bethune is genuinely concerned with improving morale, his earthy style is generally perceived as honest and straightforward; indeed, in 1998 employees bought him a Harley-Davidson motorcycle as a token of their appreciation.

Bethune serves on the boards of directors of the Sysco Corp. and Honeywell. He is married and has three children. — P.K.

Suggested Reading: *Fortune* p176+ Dec. 20, 1999, with photos; *New York Times* D p1 Apr. 14, 1995; *Texas Monthly* p58+ June 1998, with photo

Selected Books: *From Worst to First: Behind the Scenes of Continental's Remarkable Comeback—A Flight Plan for Success*, 1998

Courtesy of Mert Atlas and Marcus Piggott

Björk
(Byerk)

Nov. 21, 1965– Singer; songwriter; actress.
Address: c/o Elektra Records, 75 Rockefeller Plaza, New York, NY 10019

"If I have a philosophy," the Icelandic singer, songwriter, and actress Björk told Jeremy Helligar for *People* (September 25, 1995), "it's that I support the beautiful side of anarchy." A former member of the Icelandic pop group the Sugarcubes, Björk has had great success as a solo artist with her albums *Debut*, *Post*, and *Homogenic*. In 2000 she delivered a powerful, award-winning performance as the star of Lars von Trier's unconventional musical drama *Dancer in the Dark*, a film for which she also composed and arranged the score and wrote the lyrics. Her waif-like features, outrageous fashion choices, and blend of cheerful sensuality and innocence have led some journalists to label her eccentric. The "weirdo tag," as she has called it, does not bother her, Björk told Amy Raphael for *Spin* (September 1995); indeed, she finds it flattering, because "it makes me seem more interesting than I am." Although she has often been characterized as otherworldly, the subjects of most of Björk's songs are everyday life and human relationships. "There's a lot of pop music that is escapism, trying to paint this imaginary, beautiful paradise, this place you never go to," she told Bob Kemp for *Time Out New York* (September 18–25, 2000, on-line). "It's very important that pop music take reality and make magic out of it."

Björk Gudmundsdóttir was born on November 21, 1965 in Reykjavík, the capital of Iceland. In an interview with David Ansen for *Newsweek* (September 25, 2000), she described herself as "the most energetic, happy, optimistic sort of person." She has attributed her manic energy in part to Iceland's environment. "We've got this awkward thing, which is twenty-four-hour darkness in the winter, and twenty-four-hour daylight in the summer," she told Jon Savage for *Interview* (June 1995). "There is snow from October or November until mid-March. It means that in the winter you're just inside and you write all the books you were going to write and get everything done on your own, and then in the summer you go absolutely mad. Like bears after hibernating." According to Björk, one advantage of living in Iceland is the availability of both modern amenities and wilderness. Icelanders, she told Greg Tate for *Paper Magazine* (October 2000, on-line), "are still where people in Europe were 300 years ago in our relationship with nature. My family still hunts for half the food we eat."

Björk's mother and father, who had been a couple since both were 14, divorced when Björk was a year old; afterward she and her mother lived in a communal setting with seven adults and a number of children. (Björk has three brothers and three sisters from three sets of parents.) "Can you imagine being brought up by seven grown-ups who all hate work, and all they want to do is play games with you all day long, and tell you four-hour-long stories, and make kites?" Jonathan Van Meter quoted her as saying in *Spin* (December 1997). Björk's mother exposed her to rock and roll, while her grandmother preferred jazz. "Like all children I reacted against my mother's music, so anything to do with improvisation, guitars, psychedelics—I wanted structure," Björk told Greg Tate. "I think emotionally it's very natural to be fluid. You don't know what you're going to feel like in 15 minutes. But that's why I like music to be the opposite, to be something that can bring out emotion because it's very beautifully structured. Otherwise it's a big mess."

For 10 years beginning when she was five, Björk studied classical flute and piano; before long she was regarded as a prodigy. "When I was learning the flute, if they showed me a song I didn't like, I couldn't play it," she told Greg Tate. "I couldn't obey any rules and had to play my own songs, wear my own clothes my own way and was just very stubborn about this idea of identity." By the time she was 11, Björk had released her first album, a collection of Icelandic folksongs. The album sold 5,000 copies—an impressive number in a nation with a population of approximately 265,000. (The comparable figure for the United States, whose population is upwards of 280 million, would be more than five million.) As a teenager Björk sang with a number of punk bands; one of them, Kukl, recorded two albums to which she contributed. The 1982 Icelandic documentary *Rokk í Reykjavík* (Rock in Reykjavik) includes performances in which she participated. At 19, after she discovered that she was pregnant, she and the baby's father, Thor Eldon, married. On June 8, 1986 their son, Sindri, was born. (The couple divorced within a few years.)

In 1987 Björk co-starred in the director Nietzcha Keene's English-language film *The Juniper Tree*, a tale about witchcraft that Keene based on a fairy tale by the Brothers Grimm. That same year she joined Bad Taste, an artists' collective that managed an independent record label and a publishing company. Soon afterward she and Eldon formed the Sugarcubes, along with four others from Bad Taste: Bragi Olaffson, Einar Benediktsson, Margret ("Magga") Ornolfsdottir, and Sigtryggur ("Siggi") Baldursson. The band's first single, "Birthday," received favorable attention from the British press. In 1988 the Sugarcubes signed with Elektra Records and released *Life's Too Good*, the first of their four albums. During the next year or so, they embarked on a world tour with two British bands: the dance-music group New Order and the rock ensemble Public Image Ltd. In 1990 Björk, who, like the other members of the Sugarcubes, was pursuing her own interests at that time, recorded a jazz album entitled *Gling-Gló*. Also that year she worked with Graham Massey, of the trio 808 State, to make the album *Ex:El*. A number of Björk and Massey's collaborations were featured on the Sugarcubes' final recording, a collection of remixes entitled *It's It* (1991). In 1991 Björk moved to London, England, and the following year she left the Sugarcubes.

Björk's first solo album, *Debut* (1993), was produced by the techno artist Nellee Hooper, who had worked earlier with the British groups Soul II Soul and Massive Attack. The album soon became a club favorite; its sales exceeded 2.5 million copies worldwide, and two of its singles, "Human Behaviour" and "Big Time Sensuality," became Top 20 hits. Inspired by both jazz and electronic music, *Debut* features songs that Björk "had written in the evening when my kid was asleep," as she recalled to Jon Savage. Having learned that as a child she had often sung outdoors, Hooper recorded many of the vocals for Björk's next album, *Post* (1995), on a beach in the Bahamas, right outside the studio. *Post* includes the song "Isobel," which combines elements of techno and classical music, and collaborations with the British rap musician Tricky (Adrian Thaws), the hip-hop artist Howie B, and Graham Massey. "I called the album *Post* because a lot of it seemed directed back home to Iceland," Björk told Amy Raphael. "I was telling everyone how it felt moving from a little town to a big cosmopolitan city. How it was exciting and scary at the same time." Björk made a cameo appearance in *Prêt-à-Porter* (*Ready to Wear*, 1994), Robert Altman's spoof of the high-fashion industry.

In 1996 Björk, along with many other well-known musicians, performed in the first Tibetan Freedom Concert, held in San Francisco; organized by the Milarepa Fund, the event raised money in support of the Tibetan people's nonviolent struggle to free their country from Chinese domination. (*Free Tibet*, a video of the concert, was released in 1998.) Björk's next album, *Telegram*, which offers remixes of songs from *Post*, came out in 1996. That was a difficult year for the artist, who suddenly found herself the target of tenacious tabloid journalists. On one occasion, at Bangkok International Airport, in Thailand, a group of paparazzi, frustrated by her refusal to talk to them, attempted to interview her son. Infuriated, Björk attacked one of them—an action that was recorded on videotape. "They were asking [my son] questions against his will," Björk recalled to Greg Tate. "That was one of three times in my life when I've lost control and become physically aggressive. Fortunately, or unfortunately, because there were so many cameras going, it [got] broadcast around the world." Later in 1996 a racist American fan, disturbed to learn of her upcoming wedding to the black British producer and deejay Goldie, sent Björk a letter bomb. Thanks to a video in which the fan recorded himself making the bomb and then committing suicide, the British police intercepted the package before it reached her. (Björk and Goldie later canceled their nuptials.) Reporters soon began camping outside the singer's London home every day.

To escape such invasions of her privacy, Björk spent some time in southern Spain, where she rested, jet skied, and recorded the highly introspective, emotionally raw *Homogenic* (1997), an album that Jonathan Van Meter described as a "minimalist masterpiece." Produced by Björk herself, *Homogenic* includes collaborations with the Icelandic String Octet (identified on various Web sites as Björk's "band") and with Mark Bell, a member of the techno-music group LFO. Björk told Van Meter that *Homogenic* was "the record that's closest to the music I hear in my head." On her tour to promote the album, Björk was accompanied by the octet, Bell, and the sound engineer Allan Pollard, who remixed the artist's music as it was performed, an approach that required her to improvise at times.

"Even though my arrangements are quite experimental, I'm very conservative when it comes to song structure," she told Jonathan Van Meter for *Spin* (December 1997). "So it's this beautiful relationship between complete discipline and complete freedom. . . . Usually I write about one song a month. I never write them down. The chord structure, the bass line, the lyric, the melody, it just goes around in my head when I'm in taxis or whatever. I know what instruments, I know what noises, and I could arrange these things on my own—sometimes I do—but I love working with people so much. They almost operate like my midwife—they get the song out. If I'm lucky, it all comes at once. With lyrics, sometimes it's a very strong feeling, then I've got to work it out, almost like a scientist. . . . First, I only sing noises, then I slowly go into Icelandic and then do hints of English. I always write in Icelandic, and when I translate it to English it adds to the song and then maybe I translate back to Icelandic and then back to English. I actually get quite a lot out of the translation."

In 2000 Björk starred in the Danish director Lars von Trier's film *Dancer in the Dark*. Von Trier hired Björk after seeing her performance in the video for the song "It's Oh So Quiet," directed by Spike Jonze, an elaborately staged production that paid tribute to both Jacques Demy's film *The Umbrellas of Cherbourg* (1964) and the Busby Berkeley musicals of the 1930s and 1940s. *Dancer in the Dark* was the final entry in what von Trier termed his "Gold Heart Trilogy," the other two films in the series being *Breaking the Waves* (1996) and *The Idiots* (1998). "All three films are marked by emo-

tional regression, fear of abandonment and deliberately simplified personal and moral dilemmas," Gavin Smith explained in a profile of the director for *Film Comment* (September/October 2000). "Each one features a pure, childlike, selflessly giving heroine who comes into conflict with the social order: her uncompromising emotional absolutism and freedom from self-consciousness are sufficiently disconcerting to raise questions about her mental state. And at the center of each film is the harrowing spectacle of this childwoman sacrificing herself body and soul for love. . . . In the process she achieves a kind of sanctification and transcendence through martyrdom." Set in Washington State in the 1960s, *Dancer in the Dark* focuses on Selma Yeskova, a Czech immigrant who is losing her sight. Selma works long hours in a factory to pay for an operation for her 12-year-old son, who has inherited her visual disorder. Daydreaming to escape the miseries of her daily existence, she imagines herself as the star of theatrical musicals. An action by one of her neighbors leads to devastating consequences for Selma.

Björk worked for more than a year on the film's score, which she composed, arranged, and recorded with an 80-piece orchestra. After having completed "three albums that were all about me," she found the experience of writing songs from another person's point of view liberating, as she recalled to David Toop for an Elektra Records on-line biography of her. In an interview with Elvis Mitchell for *Esquire* (October 2000), Björk said, "I felt Selma was a very poetic creature. For Lars, being poetic means being intellectual. It means educated—it means snob. For me, it doesn't. You can be working class, you can never have read a book in your whole life. I think you can be dressed in a pink feather boa and still be speaking the truth. I fought quite hard for Selma in the lyrics: *The time it takes a tear to fall a rose to grow a thorn, is the time it will take for you to forgive me.* I would say that's quite naïve, but poetic and passionate and romantic."

The complicated musical numbers in *Dancer in the Dark*, which was shot on digital video, were recorded by 100 cameras in fixed positions. Whenever Selma begins to fantasize, the image brightens, and what she imagines is depicted in kaleidoscopic montages of dancing and singing factory workers that struck Gavin Smith as "hallucinatory swirl[s]." "The idea was to cover the dance in one go, so that the singing could be live, and we would only do the whole thing once, accepting all the mistakes," von Trier told Smith. *(Von Trier's 100 Eyes*, Katia Forbert Petersen's documentary about the making of *Dancer in the Dark*, was produced in 2000.) During the shooting of one sequence, Björk became so incensed about what she regarded as the butchering of her carefully constructed soundtrack that she left the set and did not return for four days. "On my own albums, each song usually has 20 separate music tracks," she told Stephen Garrett for *Time Out New York* (September 21–28, 2000, on-line). "On this movie, it's . . . 110—the 80-piece orchestra, and then each song has 40 tracks of on-location noises. During production, the crew would chop the songs up, because they, say, needed 11 more seconds of the dancers doing swirls. When I had 100 Danish people telling me to stop being so fussy about chopping up music I've spent so many months on, I walked out." Lacking a written agreement regarding her role as composer, she continued to argue about the handling of her songs "all the way to the very last week," as she told Greg Tate.

To play the painfully introverted Selma, Björk immersed herself completely in the character's emotional life. "I gave all and more," she told Glenn Kenny for *Premiere* (October 2000). "My friends came over to visit me on the set and didn't recognize me. They worried about my mental health, because they'd never seen me like that." She told Kenny, "Going through what Selma was going through was very painful. It was painful just to wake up in the morning"; portraying Selma, she said, was like "signing on to war, going to the Vietnam War. I believed I might die."

During filming there were persistent rumors about Björk and von Trier's troubled working relationship. At a press conference held when the film debuted at the Cannes Film Festival, in France, von Trier recalled the shooting as "terrible," as Jonathan Van Meter wrote for *Vogue* (September 2000). "What can I say? Björk is not an actor, which was a surprise to me because she seemed so professional, and she really isn't. I enjoyed working with her, and I will never do it again," he told Van Meter. Björk claimed that reports of her frequent disputes with the director were "blown . . . a little bit out of proportion," as she told Stephen Garrett. "But this *was* painful for me. Lars is very attracted to pain; he says that openly. For him, pain equals truth—and being happy is lying. I don't agree with that. But maybe that's also why I was attracted to working with him in the first place."

Some observers felt that Björk's lack of acting experience was what had enabled her to deliver an unusually believable performance. "She cannot act," Catherine Deneuve, who portrayed Selma's best friend in the film, stated at the Cannes press conference, "she can only *be*, and some of the situations are so hard in the film that she was so much in pain that she could not recover and go on." Much of the film's dialogue was extemporaneous, and the director often placed his handheld camera very close to Björk's face, heightening the intensity already generated by the melodramatic narrative. "The upside was that this is some of the best performance I have ever seen," von Trier told Jonathan Van Meter for *Vogue*. "The downside is that it was so painful for her that I became the bad guy who had to drag her through this every day." *Dancer in the Dark* received the prestigious Palme d'Or at Cannes, and the festival jury named Björk best actress. Björk told Glenn Kenny that when word of her Cannes honor reached her, "I immediately

thought it was for the music. And when they told me it was for the acting, my feeling was, 'I don't want to sound ungrateful, but it's not where my heart is.' My heart definitely belongs to sound." "I've Seen It All," a duet with the Radiohead singer Thom Yorke that was featured on *Selmasongs* (2000), Björk's seven-song soundtrack album for *Dancer in the Dark*, earned Academy Award and Golden Globe nominations for best song. Despite widespread praise for her performance in the film, Björk has declared that she has ended her career as a film actress.

Björk's latest album, *Vespertine*, which was recorded in the U.S., Britain, Spain, Denmark, and Iceland, was released in the fall of 2001. In an interview with Gideon Yago for *Sonicnet.com* (March 5, 2001), Björk said that whereas *Homogenic* was "very emotional and confrontational, both in the melodic sense of the strings and the distorted beats, *Vespertine* is sort of the opposite—very introverted, very quiet and peaceful." It is "very much about inventing your own paradise, but underneath your kitchen table, so it's very secretive," she explained to Yago. "It's sort of about being on your own in your house with your laptop and whispering for a year and just writing a very peaceful song that tiptoes. It's all about reaching those euphoric highs and those ecstacy moments, but with no outside [stimulus]. All it takes is inside you." On Björk's tour in support of the album, she was accompanied by an Inuit choir from Greenland; a 54-piece orchestra; the harpist Zeena Parkins (who at times played an electric instrument of her own invention); and Matmos, an electronica duo from San Francisco.

Performances by Björk are available on several videos, among them *Volumen* (1993), a compilation of music videos for such songs as "Bachelorette," "Venus as a Boy," "Hunter," and "Joga"; *Vessel* (1994), which includes portions of interviews with Björk and a live show in which she sang the tracks from *Debut*; and *Björk: Live at Shepherd's Bush Empire* (1997), which shows her in performance at a theater in London. Her single "All Is Full of Love" came out on both video and DVD in 1999. — C.L.

Suggested Reading: *Esquire* p168+ Oct. 2000, with photo; *Film Comment* p22+ Sep./Oct. 2000, with photos; *Interview* p86+ June 1995, with photos; *New York Times* II p73 Sep. 9, 2001, with photo, E p5 Oct. 8, 2001, with photo; *Premiere* p82+ Oct. 2000, with photos; *Spin* p61+ Sep. 1995, with photo, p92+ Dec. 1997, with photos; *Vogue* p612+ Sep. 2000, with photos

Selected Recordings: with the Sugarcubes—*Life's Too Good*, 1988; *It's It*, 1991; as solo artist—*Debut*, 1993; *Post*, 1995; *Telegram*, 1996; *Homogenic*, 1997; *Selmasongs*, 2000; *Vespertine*, 2001

Selected Films: *Dancer in the Dark*, 2000

Courtesy of David Powers

Blackburn, Elizabeth H.

Nov. 26, 1948– Molecular biologist. Address: Box 0448, UCSF, San Francisco, CA 94143-0448

Elizabeth H. Blackburn's research into the molecular biology of telomeres—the microscopic genetic material located at the ends of chromosomes in cell nuclei—has shed new light on how DNA is transmitted and preserved in cellular division. (DNA, or deoxyribonucleic acid, is the molecular basis of heredity.) Her work is of great interest from a purely scientific point of view, because it contributes to biologists' understanding not only of how cells reproduce but how they age as well. Her discoveries also hold the promise of valuable practical applications, especially in the treatment of cancer.

Telomeres (from the Greek words *telos*, or "end," and *meros*, or "part"—thus, "end parts") are the natural ends of eukaryotic chromosomes. ("Eukaryotic" refers to cells that possess a nucleus. Chromosomes, which are composed of chemical building blocks called nucleotides, are the structures that contain an organism's genetic information; in eukaryotic organisms, chromosomes are found in the cell nucleus and are usually linear or stringlike in shape.) During mitosis, the process of division by which nearly all cells reproduce, chromosomes and the genetic information they contain are copied, thus producing two nuclei and, at the culmination of the process, two cells. For the most part, chromosome duplication is carried out with the help of an enzyme known as DNA polymerase. But DNA polymerase cannot duplicate the last few nucleotides located at chromosome ends; to ensure such duplication, and thereby prevent the progressive deterioration of a chromosome's genetic infor-

mation over several generations, another mechanism is necessary.

Telomeres, which consist of several repeating blocks of a short DNA sequence (specifically, TTAGGG, where T, A, and G represent the chemical bases thymine, adenine, and guanine, respectively), play a crucial role in maintaining the integrity of the genome (that is, the chromosomes) during mitosis. In an interview with the Australian Broadcasting Corporation (on-line), Blackburn, drawing an analogy between shoelaces and chromosomes, likened telomeres to the plastic tips that prevent shoelaces from fraying. Since DNA polymerase can't copy the nucleotides at the chromosome ends, some of a telomere's repeating DNA sequence is snipped off during cell division. In 1985 Blackburn discovered another enzyme, called telomerase, which works to lengthen the shortened chromosomes by attaching newly made copies of the telomere's repeating DNA sequence to the chromosome's end. (Blackburn told the ABC interviewer that she and her colleagues coined the word "telomerase" after getting "a little tired" of repeating the original name they gave the enzyme—"telomere terminal transferase.") A sort of evolutionary stopgap, telomerase makes it possible for cells to divide and reproduce over several generations. "It saves the chromosome's bacon," Blackburn told the ABC interviewer. "It's not elegant or clever. In fact it's kind of clumsy. But it works and has done so for billions of years for every creature, apart from bacteria."

Many researchers, Blackburn among them, believe that there is a connection between the amount of telomerase present in cells and the incidence of cancer and cellular aging. Roughly speaking, scientists suspect that an overabundance of telomerase is responsible for cancer, which is the uncontrolled proliferation of cells, and that a shortage of the enzyme causes cellular senescence, wherein cells die off and are not replaced. The precise nature of the link between such phenomena and the presence of telomerase is imperfectly understood and constitutes the focus of much of Blackburn's current research. Ultimately, such research may contribute to scientists' more complete understanding of cancer and aging and may lead to many practical applications. As Blackburn wrote in a research abstract for the Kirsch Foundation, a philanthropic organization that has provided grants for medical research, "Manipulating telomerase activity has potential therapeutic uses, both in activating the proliferation of normal cells in order to renew aging human tissues, and in treating cancer."

The second of seven children, Elizabeth Helen Blackburn was born on November 26, 1948 in Hobart, on the Australian island of Tasmania. Both of her parents, as well as several relatives, were physicians. Speaking with a correspondent for the American Society for Cell Biology (ASCB) newsletter (December 1997, on-line), Blackburn recalled that Tasmania, which even today remains sparsely populated, "was an idyllic place for growing up. I remember summers staying at the Eastern shore of Tasmania when we would go to a beach, then spurn it as 'too crowded' because we could see some one else on it, and go to a neighboring beach." Blackburn's early contact with the natural world sparked her interest in biology. "I have always been interested in biology and living things," Blackburn told the ASCB interviewer. "My mother tells me I used to horrify her when as a preschooler I would pick up and croon to poisonous jellyfish and stinging ants, telling them how much I liked them. As a teenager I became interested in the underlying basis of biology, which I identified in my mind as biochemistry. I loved the names and structures of amino acids and proteins, and I even had a poster of amino acids up on the wall of my room at home."

When Blackburn was a teenager, her family moved to Melbourne, on the southeastern tip of mainland Australia. After she completed high school, she enrolled at the University of Melbourne, where she chose to major in biochemistry. (Because she did not follow in the footsteps of her parents and other relatives and become a physician, she told the ASCB, she was considered the "black sheep of the family.") As an undergraduate Blackburn attended one of the university's women's colleges, which she has characterized as "very supportive." She received a B.S. degree in biochemistry in 1970, and one year later earned a master's of science degree in the same subject. Recognizing her potential, several of her faculty advisers urged her to pursue doctoral studies abroad; taking their advice, she entered Cambridge University, in England, which attracted her not only because of its strong biochemistry program but also because an aunt and uncle lived nearby.

Blackburn remained at Cambridge until 1975, when she was awarded a Ph.D. in molecular biology. Speaking with the ASCB, she described her experience at Cambridge as "total heaven": for the most part, she was free to pursue her own research interests, and the faculty were helpful and approachable. (Blackburn has recalled having tea with Francis Crick, who, together with James Watson, revolutionized molecular biology in 1953 by describing the helical structure of the DNA molecule.) Her mentor at Cambridge was the biochemist Frederick Sanger, who has won two Nobel Prizes in chemistry—the first, in 1958, for his determination of the molecular structure of insulin, and the second, in 1980, for his discovery (along with the Americans Paul Berg and Walter Gilbert) of the sequence of nucleotides in the DNA of a virus. While at Cambridge Blackburn met her future husband, John Sedat. (Sedat is also a molecular biologist, but the research interests of husband and wife do not significantly overlap.) Blackburn next enrolled at Yale University, in New Haven, Connecticut, where she did postdoctoral research on the repeating DNA sequence encoded in the telomeres of single-celled organisms. (This work eventually led to the discovery of telomerase.) Joe Gall, who collaborated with Blackburn at Yale, described her to ASCB as "completely original. Once she got started, I watched in amazement as she used new techniques she had learned in Sanger's lab."

In 1978 Blackburn and her husband moved to Berkeley, California, where she took a job teaching molecular biology at the University of California at Berkeley. (Sedat joined the faculty of the University of California at San Francisco [UCSF], a campus dedicated solely to graduate and professional study in the health sciences.) Blackburn taught at Berkeley until 1993, when she accepted a position in the Department of Microbiology and Immunology at UCSF. She is currently the chairperson of, as well as a professor in, the department; she also holds the title of professor in the UCSF Department of Biochemistry and Biophysics.

In addition to her research, Blackburn has taken an active role in the broader scientific community. As the president of the American Society for Cell Biology in 1998, she worked to promote strong mentor relationships between young researchers and established scientists and to make the profession of cell biology more accessible to women and minorities. "We don't do research in isolation," she explained to the ASCB. "If people are feeling competitive over funds and they don't feel free to share ideas, that really slows down science." She has also urged the scientific community to be more accepting of those scientists who take breaks from their careers to raise their children. "It doesn't make you a bad scientist if you value family. I'd like to see people being taken seriously as scientists even if some time in their life is spent being an active member of society and of their family. I am for socializing and humanizing the culture and practice of science," Blackburn said.

Blackburn is a foreign associate of the U.S. National Academy of Sciences and a fellow of both the American Academy of Arts and Sciences and the Royal Society of London. For her work on telomeres and the discovery of telomerase, Blackburn received the 1998 Australia Prize (awarded annually by the Australian government for excellence in science and technology in service of humanity), the 1998 Gairdner International Prize (awarded by the Canada-based Gairdner Foundation), and the 1999 Keio Medical Science Prize (awarded by Japan's Keio University Medical Science Fund).

Blackburn and her husband, John Sedat, live in San Francisco. The couple have one son, Ben. In her spare time Blackburn enjoys reading mystery novels, especially those by Amanda Cross. — P.K.

Suggested Reading: Australia Broadcasting Corporation (on-line); Gairdner Foundation Web site; *New Scientist* 2000 (on-line) Apr. 2, 2000, with photo; *Notable Twentieth Century Scientists*, 1995

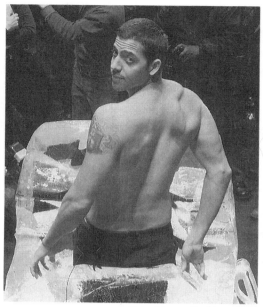

Peter Morgan/Archive Photos

Blaine, David

1973(?)– Illusionist; performance artist. Address: c/o Jason Weinberg & Associates, 122–124 E. 25th St., New York, NY 10010

"Magic is not about having a puzzle to solve. It's about creating a moment of awe and astonishment. And that can be a beautiful thing," the illusionist and performance artist David Blaine told Brett Martin for *Time Out New York* (April 1–8, 1999, on-line). Blaine eschews the flashy costumes and pyrotechnics that are used by stage magicians such as David Copperfield and Lance Burton, preferring instead to perform what is generally called close-up magic; rather than make an entire building "disappear" before a large audience, as Copperfield has famously done in the past, Blaine, who refers to himself as a "mystifier," causes playing cards to appear in unexpected places or bites coins in half and then restores them. While he has been accused by other magicians of performing old tricks that can be learned from a $10 kit from any magic shop, the appeal of his act lies not with the illusions themselves but with the style in which Blaine presents them. He has cultivated a mysterious, vaguely ominous persona, enhanced by the mostly black clothing he wears and by his piercing gaze. ("I started [the gaze] when I was 11 or 12," he told Martin. "My friends would say, 'You're so weird. Why do you look at people like that?' Because it's like I'm looking *into* people.") His image is hipper than that of most other well-known magicians, and Blaine has gained a sizeable following of fans.

In addition to close-up magic, Blaine—a master of publicity—has recently been performing what he calls "feats of endurance," which have no overt element of illusion; in 1999, for example, he was buried alive in a Plexiglas coffin for a week, and in 2000 he was encased in a gigantic block of ice for almost three days. Blaine has had three highly rated ABC television specials, and he recently signed a book deal worth a reported $1 million.

David Blaine has revealed little of his early life, including his actual last name; Blaine was originally his middle name. "I always change stories," he admitted to a reporter for *Papermag* (February 1999, on-line). "It's so boring to hear the same story over and over." He added, "A friend of mine, who is a really good private investigator, tried to track down some info on me. He couldn't find anything—not even a birth certificate." By most accounts he was born in about 1973 in the New York City borough of Brooklyn. His mother, Patrice White, a teacher who was of Russian, Dutch, and Jewish ancestry, and his father, who, according to Blaine, was "Latin, mixed up with Italian," parted ways either before or within two years of his birth.

Blaine traces his interest in card tricks and other kinds of magic to his preschool years. Magic, he explained to David Handelman for *Time* (May 19, 1997), "made people smile. I've always had an ability to communicate with people, and magic was just a device that enhanced that." His mother, whom he described to Ian Parker for *TV Guide* (November 25, 2000) as "my hero," encouraged him in his enthusiasms. "Anything that I did, she believed in, she supported," he said. For example, she raised no objection when, as a child, apparently as a test of endurance, he declined to eat anything for six whole days.

In the early 1980s his mother remarried, and the family moved to Passaic, New Jersey, where Blaine remained until he finished high school. He then moved back to New York City, where he waited on tables and practiced his magic on unsuspecting passersby on the streets. He briefly attended classes at the Neighborhood Playhouse acting studio, "to help with what I do," as he told Cynthia True for *Time Out New York* (May 15–22, 1997, on-line). His mother's death, from cancer, when he was about 19, left him feeling as if he were "in a tornado spinning round and round with nothing to hold on to," as he recalled to Brett Martin. When, during their 1999 conversation, Martin asked him when he had "pulled out of it," he replied, "I *haven't* pulled out of it."

At night Blaine frequented trendy New York City clubs, such as the Tunnel and Bowery Bar, and he often performed his illusions for the other patrons. Before long he attracted the attention of celebrities, among them Robert De Niro, Woody Allen, and Madonna, and he was soon being invited to do magic at their private parties. After sending a short tape of his act to ABC-TV executives, Blaine was signed to do his first televised special, *Street Magic*, which aired in May 1997. With the help of several commercials directed by Spike Lee, one of his fans, *Street Magic* attracted 10.6 million viewers, who were drawn to the subtle but extraordinary effects Blaine achieved. "It's like *Candid Camera* meets magic," Blaine said of the show in an interview for *People* (May 26, 1997). *Street Magic* was taped in various locations across America, including the East Village, in New York City; the Boardwalk, in Atlantic City; and San Francisco's Haight Ashbury district. The unscripted reactions of Blaine's audiences ran from amusement to terror to tears as he appeared to transform cards into other cards, rotate his arm at a physically impossible angle, and levitate. "I'm interested in magic creating an emotional transition," he told Brett Martin. "I like to make a person question what they believe is real." The magic community was unimpressed by Blaine's television premiere, noting that several of his illusions had widely known solutions. For example, when Blaine appeared to levitate a few inches into the air, he was actually performing a move in which one toe, hidden by the pant leg and opposite shoe, stays on the ground to support the magician. It is difficult to perform the trick at exactly the correct angle to convince the audience, and the many times that Blaine failed were edited out of the finished special. Brett Martin reported that *Magic* magazine, the industry's biggest independent periodical, received outraged letters from other illusionists. *Magic*'s tricks editor and columnist Jon Racherbaumer explained the controversy to Brett Martin: "The rank-and-file magicians who watch David's show look at what he's doing and say, 'Hey, I can do that.' What they fail to realize is that (a) obviously they're *not* doing it, and (b) the fact that all performance is really about the audience, not you."

In 1999 Blaine, who had always idolized the great magician and escape artist Harry Houdini, paid homage to his predecessor by spending a week buried six feet underground in a transparent coffin. (Houdini had wanted to be buried alive, but he died, in 1926, before he had completed plans for the stunt.) Blaine was provided with an air supply, three ounces of water a day, and a catheter, to expel urine. He also had some of the comforts of home: maroon pajamas, a white blanket and pillow, and a collection of writing by the French author Voltaire, as Austin Fenner reported for the New York *Daily News* (April 7, 1999). The coffin was placed beneath a giant, clear container of water across from Trump Place, at 68th Street and Riverside Drive, in Manhattan, so that he was on display continuously. "It's not a trick," he explained to Brett Martin. "It's a test of endurance—of what the human body and mind can stand." He insisted to reporters that he was well-prepared for the event, noting that he had undergone a four-day trial run in his home, and that medical personnel were available to him throughout the stunt. Blaine's feat was successful, and he emerged from the coffin a few days before the airing of his second television special, *Magic Man*.

Despite lingering criticism of his burial—he was accused of projecting a hologram into the coffin instead of being there himself, or of having food or extra water buried with him—*Magic Man* drew even more viewers than *Street Magic*. In the broadcast, instead of card tricks like those from his first special, he performed mind benders, such as reviving a dead housefly. In one particularly memorable illusion, as an audience member concentrated on a mental image of a deceased friend, the name of the friend materialized in ash on Blaine's stomach. In another segment he sent a homeless man in New York to buy an instant lottery ticket from a corner store. When the man returned and scratched off the numbers using the "magic coin" Blaine had lent him, he found the ticket to be worth $1,600. Still, Blaine avoids professing a connection with the supernatural. "I'm not a mind reader," he told Ian Parker. "In truth, I'm just an entertainer, just a performer. When you go to see a great movie, or a great play, it affects you and leaves you afterwards inspired. That's what the goal of magic is, to create for someone a moment where they feel inspired or uplifted."

Blaine next endured more than two and a half days of standing upright in a hole carved out of a six-ton block of ice; the event was filmed as part of his third television special, *Frozen in Time*, which aired on November 29, 2000. The location he chose for this feat, Times Square in Manhattan, had great significance for him, as he explained to the *Magic Directory* (December 4, 2000, on-line): "In his 1922 movie, *The Man from Beyond*, there is an image of Houdini frozen in ice, although he never actually tried this challenge. That movie premiered at the Times Square Theater at 42nd and Broadway, so I wanted to be frozen here in Times Square." There were considerable health risks associated with Blaine's stunt—hypothermia, frostbite, blood clots, and dehydration—so he trained in ice-filled bathtubs for a year before the event. On November 27, 2000 he entered the ice, a segment of an Alaskan glacier that had been carved out to allow a two-inch clearance around his body, slathered with insulating gel to maintain his body temperature; he wore only pants, special boots designed to maintain circulation in his feet, a catheter, and wires to monitor his vital signs. While enduring the cold and exhaustion, he was subjected to criticism from skeptics, including Penn Jillette, of the magic/comedy team Penn and Teller, who theorized that Blaine had pumped hot air into the opening to stay warm and increase the space around his body. When he was cut out of the ice 61 hours and 40 minutes later, on November 29, he had set a new world record for ice encasement (the previous record, which was attained by a person lying down, was 57 minutes); he was also dehydrated, in pain from having stood for so long, and delusional. "I thought I had died; I thought that I had woke up and that this was where I was. This was death," he told Ralph R. Ortega for the New York *Daily News* (December 1, 2000). After a brief appearance on the television news show *Good Morning America* following the event, Blaine vanished to recuperate. According to his Web site, in his next stunt Blaine will stand for almost two days, without any safety equipment, atop an 80-foot pole 13 inches in diameter. "If it is windy and I fall—goodbye," he wrote. To complete the feat, he will jump down, his fall cushioned by boxes placed around the base of the pole.

Although Blaine has claimed that maintaining a romantic relationship in the public eye is nearly impossible, he was linked for a while with the pop singer Fiona Apple. He has often been seen socializing with the actor Leonardo DiCaprio and other young stars. Blaine currently lives with the model Josie Moran in Manhattan. He is reportedly devoted to his teenage half-brother. Robert De Niro's production company has purchased the rights to *Trick Monkey*, a screenplay, written by Jim Uhls, that is based on Blaine's life. (Blaine has said that he has no interest in playing himself in the movie.) During breaks in his training regimen for new stunts, he is writing a book, tentatively titled "Mysterious Stranger." "I want the book to have things that can get people hooked on magic," he told Keith Kelley for the *New York Post* (June 21, 2000, on-line), "mathematical puzzles and simple effects that you can flip people out with anytime." Blaine intends to include clues in the book that will lead one lucky reader to a buried treasure chest, filled with $100,000 in gold coins. He is working with Dave Phillips, a cryptographer, to encode the clues. — K.S.

Suggested Reading: *davidblaine.com*; *Entertainment Weekly* p36+ Nov. 24, 2000, with photos; *Papermag* (on-line) Feb. 1999; *Time* p97 May 19, 1997, with photos; *Time Out New York* (on-line) May 15–22, 1997, Apr. 1–8, 1999; *TV Guide* p24+ Nov. 25–Dec. 1, 2000, with photos

Selected Television Specials: *David Blaine: Street Magic*, 1997; *David Blaine: Magic Man*, 1999; *David Blaine: Frozen in Time*, 2000

Ray Stubblebine/Archive Photos

Blakemore, Michael

June 18, 1928– Theater and film director; actor; novelist. Address: 18 Upper Park Rd., London NW3 2UP, England

The theater and film director Michael Blakemore is known for his ability to coax strong performances from actors, most notably in works that require ensemble acting. Blakemore, who has worked in England and the United States as well as in Australia, his native country, spent several years as a stage actor before trying his hand at directing. His directorial credits include the plays *A Day in the Death of Joe Egg*, *The Resistible Rise of Arturo Ui*, *Noises Off*, *City of Angels*, and, in 2000, *Copenhagen* and a revival of *Kiss Me Kate*, for both of which he won Tony Awards. Many journalists have incorrectly referred to Blakemore as an English director, perhaps, it has been suggested, because Australia has been slow to develop a reputation for accomplishments in the arts. "In a sense, you can't win in Australia," he told Mel Gussow for the *New York Times* (August 16, 1995). "If you stay there, then people are inclined to say you're not good enough to make it overseas, and if you leave, they say that you think you're too good for Australia."

Speaking about his role in bringing a playwright's vision to life on the stage, Blakemore told Benedict Nightingale for the *New York Times* (March 12, 1995), "My job is not to give my view of the text, but to realize the text, which is a different thing altogether." While directing has been said to attract personalities that crave power, Blakemore told Michael Behr for the London *Guardian* (December 21, 1970) that he regarded his craft as "essentially an exercise in self-effacement. In other words, I'm always astonished when critics go into great detail about the nature of the direction of a play, or indeed a film, because, in fact, it's really impossible for an outsider to arbitrate. All you can say is that something that is well-directed has about it essentially a sense of government, of rightness."

Michael Howell Blakemore was born in Sydney, Australia, on June 18, 1928 to Conrad Blakemore and Una Mary (Litchfield) Blakemore. "Growing up in Australia, one was very conscious that there was a world elsewhere, and the knowledge intimidated us all every single day," he told Gordon Gow for the London *Guardian* (May 30, 1973). "One felt that life was fairly real in Australia, but it was *really* real in New York and London and Europe." Film rather than theater first attracted Blakemore to drama; the films of the 1940s, he told Matt Wolf for the *New York Times* (May 6, 1990), were a "formative, if disastrous, influence on my life." That is, they were disastrous from the point of view of his father, an eye surgeon who expected his son to become a doctor. "He was scandalized by the thought of his son going anywhere near the theater," Blakemore told Leslie Bennetts for the *New York Times* (December 30, 1985). "But I knew what I wanted to do from a very early age." Nonetheless, Blakemore completed three years of medical school before leaving Sydney, in 1950, to enter the Royal Academy of Dramatic Art, in London, England.

Blakemore described his first several years as an actor to Benedict Nightingale as a "hard slog with no breaks." He landed his earliest roles in 1952, in plays for the Birmingham Repertory Theatre, the Belgrade Theatre in Coventry, and the Royal Theatre of the Bristol Old Vic. In 1957 he toured Eastern Europe with Laurence Olivier in a production of William Shakespeare's *Titus Andronicus*. Blakemore gained his first cinema experience in 1964, as a personal assistant to the director John Boorman, on the set of the rock-and-roll comedy *Catch Us If You Can*. "I was there specifically to coach the [musical group the] Dave Clark Five in the mysteries of acting, but I was on the film for the entire ten weeks," Blakemore recalled to Michael Behr. "It was a marvellous if disturbing way of assimilating the climate of movie-making."

In 1966 Blakemore began to direct for the Glasgow Citizens' Theatre; within two years he had become the organization's co-artistic director. When his good friend Peter Nichols could not find a producer willing to stage his latest play, he turned to Blakemore for help. Blakemore agreed to direct the play—*A Day in the Death of Joe Egg*—guiding it through productions at the Glasgow Citizens' Theatre and London's West End Theatre before making his American directing debut on Broadway with it, in 1968. *A Day in the Death of Joe Egg*, which starred Albert Finney and Zena Walker, focuses on the struggles of a couple whose daughter is profoundly disabled. The comedy in this tragic story arose "from a very frank admission of our indifference to other people's suffering," Blakemore told Michael Behr. "We're really acknowledging the absurdity of ourselves, as well as the absurdity of other people. . . . We take ourselves and our concerns with a desperate seriousness that we don't allow other people." The play introduced both Blakemore and Nichols to an international audience and led to a Tony nomination for the director. (The prize went to Mike Nichols, for his direction of *Plaza Suite*.)

The year 1969 marked the publication of Blakemore's only novel, *Next Season*, a roman à clef based on the 1959 season at Stratford-upon-Avon,

England, during which the Royal Shakespeare Theatre mounted three productions in one summer. Sales of the book were poor, despite favorable reviews, but *Next Season* later became a cult favorite, especially among actors who recognized Blakemore's thinly veiled references to such actors as Laurence Olivier, Charles Laughton, Paul Robeson, Edith Evans, Albert Finney, and Vanessa Redgrave. Barely disguised depictions of the directors Tyrone Guthrie, Peter Hall, and Tony Richardson also appear in the novel, which Blakemore described to Mel Gussow as an insider's account of a "fickle and unfair profession," as he considered it then.

Beginning in 1971 Blakemore directed a series of successful plays at the National Theatre in England. The first was a production of Eugene O'Neill's *Long Day's Journey Into Night*, starring Laurence Olivier. This was followed by the first British production of Ben Hecht and Charles MacArthur's *The Front Page*, a classic comedy, first produced in 1928, that Blakemore described to Nan Robertson as "a diamond-hard farce, without any of the sentimentality that has increasingly crept into American comic writing." Next he directed Shakespeare's *Macbeth* (with Diana Rigg and Anthony Hopkins) and Anton Chekhov's *The Cherry Orchard*. In his interview with Gordon Gow, he noted that comedy can take many forms, and each must be interpreted individually. "Acting can veer into the area of self-congratulation, where the actors tend to smile when the laughs come," he explained. "So I advise players doing *The Front Page* to concentrate on the drama and let the comedy look after itself, whereas in the Chekhov I tell them to seek out the comedy and let the drama look after itself. But it isn't a work that should necessarily inspire gales of laughter, so I haven't tried to impose deliberate comic business—just that tactful detachment. And I don't want it to look like a foreign world, as if these characters and situations could only exist in Russia. I want audiences to recognise that this is exactly how certain people they know might behave."

In 1976 Blakemore resigned his position as an associate director for the National Theatre over differences with its artistic director, Peter Hall. (He later returned to the theatre, at the request of Hall's successor, Richard Eyre; given the chance to direct the play of his choice, he staged Arthur Miller's 1964 drama *After the Fall*.) In 1981 Blakemore directed his first film, an autobiographical tale entitled *A Personal History of the Australian Surf*, which blended newsreels, family photographs, and short narrative scenes centering on the one subject that united him and his father. His second film, *Privates on Parade* (1983), starring John Cleese, is an adaptation for the screen of a play by Peter Nichols that Blakemore had directed for the Royal Shakespeare Company in 1976.

In 1983, on Broadway, Blakemore directed Michael Frayn's satirical *Noises Off*, about a disaster-prone troupe of actors who are rehearsing a fictional, lowbrow British sex farce called *Nothing*

On. The play—particularly the second act, in which the cast acts out parts of *Nothing On* as well as the "backstage" fumbling of the cast and crew—has complicated slapstick bits, performed at fever pitch, that require careful choreographing so as to avoid injury to the actors. "There's an enormous amount of rushing back and forth through slamming doors and up and down steep stairs, and split-second timing involving the hectic passing around of some potentially mutilating props such as an ax and a whisky bottle," Blakemore told Nan Robertson for the *New York Times* (December 16, 1983). "Michael Frayn had meticulously prepared the script, with a double column typed on the pages showing the action going on out front and backstage at the same time." He also told Robertson, "The idea with farce is to convulse the audience with mirth: as benign a form of manipulation as you can imagine. When it works, it generates mass hysteria."

In 1984 in London, and 1986 on Broadway, Blakemore directed another Frayn work, *Benefactors*. Set in the late 1960s, it concerns two English couples (played by Glenn Close, Sam Waterston, Mary Beth Hurt, and Simon Jones) and, as the director described it to Leslie Bennetts, "is primarily about change, the way that the world is constantly in flux, so much so that if we perceived it, it would be impossible to live." Elliptical and fragmented, the script offers few stage directions. "It seemed to me essential that it move like a movie, very quickly," Blakemore told Bennetts. "The tail end of one scene provides an ironic comment on the first line of the next scene. It moves like a film cut." Except for Jones, the actors in the New York production of *Benefactors* were American, which gave Blakemore an opportunity to observe the stylistic differences between British and American actors. "In a lot of English writing, what people say is both what they mean and what they feel, and an English actor is more likely to go to the text as a way of finding out what the text means," Blakemore told Bennetts. "An American actor is more likely to burrow underneath to find something else that will bring the reality of the play to life. Americans tend to invite confrontation, whereas English people tend to evade it, and I think the confrontations, the twists and turns of the plot have a certain vigor here that perhaps they didn't in London. The emotional intensity is greater here." Perhaps as a result, it seemed to Blakemore that American audiences were much better able than their British counterparts to recognize the social issues explored in the piece.

Directing Chekhov's *Uncle Vanya* at the Vaudeville Theatre in London, in 1988, proved to be a challenge for Blakemore, because the play is "so dense, so concise," as he explained to Martin Hoyle for *Plays and Players* (June 1988). "On one page there's so much going on, there's a danger of gliding over without realising the incredible texture" of the work. In an unusual move, Blakemore changed the locale of the well-known play to rural Australia and the time to 1919. "It's a useful device for me since the great problem of Chekhov is the style—remarkably plain and unadorned," he told Hoyle. "In the English translation, with samovars and double-barreled names, it becomes *fabled*—absolutely against the original intention to show ordinary people as they are; particular and eccentric."

Blakemore directed two Broadway hits in 1990: the musical *City of Angels*, a Cy Coleman/Larry Gelbart/David Zippel collaboration mounted at the Virginia Theatre, and Peter Shaffer's play *Lettice and Lovage*, which had enjoyed success in London before its opening at the Ethel Barrymore Theater. *City of Angels* is a fantasy about a struggling screenwriter and his relationship with one of his characters. "I actually loathe musicals usually," Blakemore admitted to Matt Wolf, "and I've never thought of myself as a musical director, but I got the script and was delighted with it. . . . I also wanted to prove that it is possible to spend 4.5 million bucks to get a musical show on and, by planning it carefully and really thinking hard before we go into rehearsal, not to get it on stage by a process of trial and error and bloodshed and hysteria and guys getting sacked and me getting sacked and getting replaced and maybe getting re-engaged again. . . . I think that's all rubbish." *Lettice and Lovage* starred Maggie Smith, as a woman who leads increasingly imaginative guided tours in a singularly boring home owned by Great Britain's Preservation Trust, and Margaret Tyzack, as the Preservation Trust official who fires her; the women's initial dislike for one another evaporates when they realize that they share a passionate disdain for the modern world. Later that year Blakemore was honored with an Outer Critics Circle Award for best director for each of the two productions.

In 1995 Blakemore returned to acting, in *Country Life*, his film adaptation of *Uncle Vanya* (again set in post–World War I rural Australia). He had completed the script in 1983, but it took him until 1995 to secure funding to produce the film. Blakemore took on the part of Alexander Voysey, a theater critic, after Nigel Hawthorne was forced to withdraw from the cast.

On June 4, 2000 Blakemore won Tony Awards for best director in both the musical and drama categories. The former was for a revival of Cole Porter's *Kiss Me Kate*, about a couple whose appearance in a production of Shakespeare's *Taming of the Shrew* is affected by their offstage relationship. The latter Tony was for Michael Frayn's *Copenhagen*, in which Margrethe Bohr, the wife of the Danish physicist Niels Bohr, observes and comments on a 1941 meeting between her husband and the German physicist Werner Heisenberg. "All I can say is 'Thank you America,'" the director stated in one of his acceptance speeches, according to Robin Pogrebin in the *New York Times* (June 5, 2000). "And of course by America I mean New York, and by New York I mean Broadway." *Kiss Me Kate* won a total of five Tonys, the same number that it earned when it premiered, in 1948.

Blakemore moves quickly from one project to the next, seldom taking the time to bask in the glory of his successes. "I get a buzz for about 24 hours after a show is successful, and then I just move on to the next thing," he told Leslie Bennetts. "I think there's a vacuum at the heart of success. It's lovely to be successful, but it doesn't actually mean as much as you thought it was going to." For Blakemore, the preparation process that precedes each production is far more exciting than the actual performance—especially those moments "when you smell that you're on to something, and suddenly you think you might have a present worth delivering," he told Bennetts. "That can be very thrilling."

Blakemore has one son from his first marriage and two daughters from his second, to the set and costume designer Tanya McCallin. (McCallin's many theater and opera credits include her husband's 1988 *Uncle Vanya*.) The couple live in London. Surfing is Blakemore's main recreational activity. — C.L.

Suggested Reading: (London) *Guardian* p8 Dec. 21, 1970, with photo, p12 May 30, 1973, with photo; New York *Daily News* p3 Dec. 11, 1983, with photos; *New York Times* C p3 Dec. 16, 1983, with photo, C p13 Dec. 30, 1985, with photo, II p5+May 6, 1990, with photo, C p11 Aug. 16, 1995, with photo; *Plays & Players* p12 June 1988, with photo

Selected Plays: *A Day in the Death of Joe Egg*, 1967; *The National Health*, 1969; *Long Day's Journey Into Night*, 1971; *The Front Page*, 1972; *Macbeth*, 1972; *The Cherry Orchard*, 1973; *Knuckle*, 1974; *Noises Off*, 1982; *Lettice and Lovage*, 1987; *City of Angels*, 1989; *Copenhagen*, 1999; *Kiss Me Kate*, 1999

Selected Films: *A Personal History of the Australian Surf*, 1981; *Privates On Parade*, 1983; *Country Life*, 1995

Blind Boys of Alabama

Gospel singers

Fountain, Clarence
Nov. 28, 1929–

Scott, George
Mar. 18, 1929–

Carter, Jimmy
Feb. 11, 1932–

Address: c/o Charles Drieve, P.O. Box 975, Jonesboro, GA 30237

The Blind Boys of Alabama have been exciting crowds since the 1930s with the style of gospel singing known as "jubilee." Pioneered by the Golden Gate Quartet in the 1930s, jubilee singing features jazzy harmonies of traditional gospel melodies sung over sparse accompaniment. For most of their history, the Blind Boys, the majority of whom are indeed legally blind, have been led by Clarence Fountain, a man known for possessing a rough and mighty voice that has been called a gospel version of the soul legend James Brown's. "We can sing anything," Fountain told Jason Gross for *Rock's Backpages* (May 2001, on-line). "If you want me to sing you a contemporary gospel tune, we can do that. If you want us to sing a fast jubilee up-tempo song, we can do that. You want us to sing five-part harmony, we can do that. You want us to sing traditional, that's what we're noted for, we can do that." Now one of the few surviving groups from the Depression era, the Blind Boys of Alabama are arguably more popular now than at any other point during their long career. They have been nominated

for three Grammy Awards, and their most recent album, *Spirit of the Century* (2001), combines the group's classic harmonies with the work of contemporary blues musicians and even features versions of material popularized by the likes of the Rolling Stones.

The Blind Boys of Alabama began their career in 1937 as the Happyland Jubilee Singers at the Talladega (Alabama) Institute for the Deaf and Blind. "We were just a bunch of happy guys," Fountain, born in Tyler, Alabama, on November 28, 1929, told *Afgen.com*. The quintet was originally led by Velma B. Traylor and included Fountain; George Scott, born in Notasulga, Alabama, on March 18, 1929 and known for his distinctive style of guitar playing and powerful tenor voice; bass singer Johnny Fields; and J. T. Hutton (the only one with sight). Fountain, who lost his vision after developing pink eye as a child, has a remarkable sense of hearing. "There was a joke going around when I was in Alabama," he told Errol Nazareth for the *Toronto Sun* (December 12, 1997, on-line). "People would say I could hear a rat tiptoeing on a lead carpet in New Orleans!" Inspired by such great gospel groups of the era as the Soul Stirrers, the Happyland Jubilee Singers practiced whenever they had free time at their school—which did not allow gospel singing. Particularly influential to the young singers was the gospel group the Golden Gate Quartet. "Those were the people that we really patterned ourselves after," Fountain informed *Afgen.com*. "They made the current chords and we made 'em too. They didn't sing hard, they just sang jubilee. They sang a lot of music." However, for Fountain the sounds of other musicians were not simply to be copied. "I didn't want to sing like them," he told Jason Gross. "I just wanted to be like ME." Whenever they could, Fountain and his fel-

Longtime members of the Blind Boys of Alabama (left to right):   Courtesy of the Rosebud Agency
Jimmy Carter, Clarence Fountain, George Scott

low jubilee singers would sneak out of the school to play shows for a nearby camp of soldiers. In 1940 the group was augmented by baritone Olice Thomas. In 1945 the Happyland Jubilee Singers decided to drop out of school to tour the country. "We had an advantage over all the rest of the gospel groups," Fountain explained for the official Blind Boys of Alabama Web site, "because you hardly ever see a bunch of blind guys on stage in concert. That was an exciting time."

Tragedy struck the up-and-coming group in 1947 when Traylor, who was fond of handling guns, died as a result of an accidental gunshot. The remaining singers kept performing, however, adding the Reverend Paul Exkano to the group to share lead-vocal duties with Fountain. In 1948 the group made their first records, including "Stand By Me" (later popularized, with different lyrics, by Ben E. King) and "I Can See Everybody's Mother but I Can't See Mine," for the Coleman label. It was around this time that the Happyland Jubilee Singers changed their name to the Blind Boys of Alabama. "We changed our name when the Five Blind Boys of Mississippi came along and were doing really well," Fountain told *Afgen.com*. "The only distinction was that one group was from Mississippi and one was from Alabama. You could go to which one you liked the best. We were tryin' to kill each other for real," he joked. The two groups began an epic rivalry, stealing vocalists from each other and often squaring off in "Battles of the Blind Boys." During such contests, which would often conclude with Fountain performing a duet with his Mississippi counterpart, Archie Brownlee, ambulances were often seen rushing frenzied fans to the hospital. In 1951 Reverend Exkano left the

Blind Boys of Alabama; he was replaced by a former Mississippi Blind Boy, Percell Perkins. Perkins would later leave and have his spot taken first by Joe Watson and, finally, by Jimmy Carter, another ex–Mississippi Blind Boy, who was born in Birmingham, Alabama, on February 11, 1932.

During the 1950s the Blind Boys of Alabama became increasingly popular in the gospel-music world, releasing 11 LPs, but they had limited mainstream success. As the next decade began, a number of gospel singers, among them Sam Cooke, decided to turn to secular music in order to be heard by a wider audience—and to make more money. On several occasions record executives asked Fountain and the Blind Boys to name their price for making the same move. The group turned each offer down. "I wouldn't switch for all the tea in China," Fountain explained to John Kelly for *Muse* (on-line). "Many times I had the opportunity—but I think that's not the thing to do. I wouldn't mix it because you cannot serve two masters at once. You gotta love one and hate the other or vice versa. I love the Lord and my choice was to serve the Lord." Fountain later added, "My thing was that I wouldn't work for a man that wouldn't pay me. And the Devil, he doesn't have anything for me. He might pay me in money, but when you compare that to your soul, that's nothing. So I said I'll work for the Lord because I know I'll get paid. He's a just God and his word is true." As soul music became increasingly popular in the 1960s, gospel performers lost a large segment of their fan base, and the Blind Boys of Alabama played to smaller and smaller crowds. Although the group occasionally experimented with a soul sound, they never lost track of their musical and spiritual priorities. "We only wanted to sing Gospel," Fountain said for *fez-festival.com*. "Sure, we wanted to be popular, but we only wanted to sing Gospel. Our theme is Jesus and that is where we put all our strength and inspiration." In 1969 Fountain decided to leave the group to pursue a solo career. He would return nine years later for *The Soldier Album*.

The Blind Boys of Alabama saw their popularity soar in the 1980s. In 1983 they appeared in the musical *Gospel at Colonus*, the gospel adaptation by Lee Breuer and Bob Telson of the Greek playwright Sophocles' *Oedipus at Colonus*, written in the fifth century B.C. *Gospel at Colonus*, which starred Morgan Freeman, later moved to Broadway, where the Blind Boys performed as members of the cast for 15 weeks. The show went on to win two *Village Voice* Obie Awards for the 1983–84 season, one for best musical. "After *The Gospel at Colonus* we were able to sing to masses of people and travel all over," Fountain told *globalvillageidiot.net*. "We should have done it 20 or 30 years ago, but it just wasn't our time to do it then. Things come when you least expect it—it doesn't come when we want it to come, but in God's own time. I have no complaints about that, you take it as it comes. . . . It broadened the audience, it made us able to sing to more people, which was what I wanted to do all my life, anyway. So we could sing in a way where everybody could come in and listen."

The Blind Boys of Alabama continued to record and tour in the 1990s. In 1994 they received a National Endowment for the Arts National Heritage Fellowship, presented by Hillary Rodham Clinton, who was then the First Lady. In their seventh decade of music making, the group played such events as the Philadelphia Folk Festival, the King Biscuit Blues Festival, and the Beale Street Music Festival. They appeared on the BET cable series *On Jazz* and even showed up on an episode of the popular teen soap opera *Beverly Hills 90210*. In 1995 they became the first group signed to the new House of Blues gospel label, releasing their first live album, *I Brought Him with Me*. Recorded over three nights at the House of Blues in Hollywood, the album received worldwide acclaim; on it, the Blind Boys proved themselves to be quite versatile, tackling a capella harmonies and blues-based songs. Fountain, however, thought the record could have been better. "I tried to get those crazy folk to record it in a church but they wouldn't listen to me," he told Errol Nazareth. "[The House of Blues] was spending the money so what could I say? The atmosphere would've been different."

The Blind Boys followed up that record in 1997 with *Holdin' On*. In 2001 they released *Spirit of the Century*, on which they collaborated with the producer John Chelew and an all-star cast of blues musicians that included the harmonica player Charlie Musselwhite, the bassist Danny Thomson, the guitarist John Hammond, and the drummer Michael Jerome. Put out by the pop star Peter Gabriel's Real World label, the album features blues songs, performed in their original style, that were made into

rock hits by Tom Waits, the Rolling Stones, and others. "We were brought up in school to sing the music that comes before us," Fountain said, as quoted on *globalvillageidiot.net*. "When you can sing to the masses of people, and sing whatever's in your path to sing, if it's in your right way of thinking, and as long as it's in the gospel, then that's good for us." In one of the album's tracks, the Blind Boys sing the lyrics of "Amazing Grace" to the tune of "House of the Rising Sun." The album generally received good reviews, although David Cantwell, writing for *Westword Online* (May 3, 2001), noted that Fountain, "who's used to flying above far sparser accompaniment, feels muted by the lineup's fussy, antiseptic version of the blues. Of course, part of this may be the result of Fountain's own diminished capacities . . . and part because of the more blues-based songs he's singing, which don't demand the ecstatic release that comes with being possessed by the spirit. It's the NPR-ready playing, though, that leaves the album so flat." Still, the critic added that Fountain was "such a great singer that even his whispers sound like those of a sinner on his knees in prayer." "Everybody seems to like it, so what can I say? I can say, the lord is really blessing us in our old age," Fountain told Jason Gross. "He's got a way of doing things that is beyond our understanding. I think it's our time now. I think we reap the benefits with this. It's God's own time—he does things the way he wants it done and can't nobody do nothing about it. You have to stick with him."

The Blind Boys of Alabama continue to maintain a hectic international tour schedule augmented by several younger members. Currently a septet, the group consists of Fountain; Carter; Scott; Caleb Butler, bass; Donald Dilion, rhythm guitar; Ricky McKinnie, drums; and Joey Williams, lead guitar and road manager. "The music's changed through the years," Fountain told *globalvillageidiot.net*. "But we can always go back to our basic thing and come up with some songs that people never heard before, or re-arranged in a new way. We know how to do what needs to be done, in a gospel way. And there's a difference between singing gospel and blues and rock'n'roll, and we've learned to stick to what we know, we've been all over the world singing gospel music, so we've done pretty well." — G.O.

Suggested Reading: *Afgen.com*; *globalvillageidiot.net*; *Muse* (on-line); *Rock's Backpages* (on-line) May 2001; *Toronto Sun* (on-line) Dec. 12, 1997

Selected Recordings: *I Can See Everybody's Mother But I Can't See Mine*, 1948; *Sweet Honey in the Rocks*, 1950; *Living' on Mother's Prayers*, 1950; *Come Over Here the Table Spread*, 1953; *When I Lost My Mother*, 1953; *Stand By Me*, 1954; *Marching to Zion*, 1954; *I'll Never Walk Alone*, 1957; *My Mother's Train*, 1958; *The Original Blind Boys*, 1959; *God Is on the Throne*,

1959; *Fix It Jesus Like You Said You Would*, 1969; *The Soldier Album*, 1978; *I'm a Changed Man*, 1989; *Brand New*, 1990; *I'm Not That Way Anymore*, 1991; *Deep River*, 1992; *I Brought Him With Me*, 1995; *Holden' On*, 1997; *Spirit of the Century*, 2001

Courtesy of the NAACP

Bond, Julian

Jan. 14, 1940– Chairman of the national board of directors of the NAACP; journalist; educator. Address: NAACP, 4805 Mt. Hope Dr., Baltimore, MD 21215

A veteran of the civil rights movement, Julian Bond has been chairman of the national board of directors of the National Association for the Advancement of Colored People (NAACP) since 1998. Active in the student protests to desegregate eating establishments in the South, in the 1950s and 1960s Bond was the communications director for the Student Nonviolent Coordinating Committee (SNCC) and president of the Atlanta chapter of the NAACP before becoming, in 1968, the first African-American ever nominated for vice president. He also served four terms as a member of the Georgia House of Representatives and six terms in the Georgia state Senate. In addition to his duties as NAACP chair, Bond is a columnist, educator, and public speaker; his smooth persona and photogenic looks make him one of the most recognizable figures of the civil rights movement.

Although many battles have been won, civil rights activists continue to engage in the struggle for equal opportunity in the United States. Bond is acutely aware of the class issues underlying discussions of race in America. "We have to acknowledge that, throughout American history, the effort to integrate the poor and underclass—not just blacks—into the mainstream was never more than half-intended," he said in an interview for *New Perspectives Quarterly* (1998). "The structural changes in the capitalist system necessary to eliminate poverty, such as more equitable distribution of wealth and full employment," have never been part of the government's agenda, he continued. "So, the well-meaning attempts to provide more and better schools and better housing, as much as those were unquestionably needed, were doomed to failure as a means of ultimately eliminating poverty." In an interview with Henry Louis Gates that aired on the PBS program *Frontline* on February 10, 1998, Bond was asked whether he thought the goals of the civil rights movement had been accomplished. "We won in the sense that we eliminated legal segregation in America," he responded. "That is no more; that is finished. If you look at the young people I teach and compare them with myself at that age, their lives are so much richer and fuller. Opportunity is so much greater they can do things that I couldn't imagine doing. So in that sense sure, this was an enormous victory. We vanquished in the space of about five years a system that had been in place for almost 100 years. We confused discrimination and racism. We confused the poverty caused by discrimination with poverty caused by larger structural flaws in the economy. . . . So we won, but we haven't won."

The son of Horace Mann Bond and Julia Agnes (Washington) Bond, Horace Julian Bond was born on January 14, 1940 in Nashville, Tennessee, and grew up in Lincoln, Pennsylvania. His father was the president of Lincoln University, the nation's oldest private black college, and as a result Julian had the opportunity to meet such luminaries as the German-born physicist Albert Einstein, the African-American performer and activist Paul Robeson, and the African-American scholar and activist W.E.B. DuBois. Bond attended the George School, a Quaker preparatory institution, where he was the only African-American student. He first felt the effects of racism and prejudice when a dean at the George School insisted that he refrain from wearing his school jacket on a date with a white girl. "He clearly didn't want the school associated with . . . an interracial relationship," Bond told Jacqueline Trescott for the *Washington Post* (May 25, 1979). As a young man Bond was interested in film, but his focus soon turned to writing. His family moved to Atlanta, Georgia, in 1957, when his father became a dean of the School of Education at Atlanta University; that year Bond entered Morehouse College, an historically black school in Atlanta, as an English major. While at Morehouse he took a philosophy course taught by the civil rights leader Martin Luther King Jr. and was one of the founders of the *Pegasus*, the school's literary magazine. Bond also worked as a reporter for the *Atlanta*

Inquirer and co-founded the Committee on Appeal for Human Rights (COAHR), an organization that conducted a series of sit-ins in whites-only establishments that served as a catalyst for the desegregation of lunch counters throughout Atlanta.

In 1960 COAHR merged with the Student Nonviolent Coordinating Committee (SNCC, pronounced "snick"), a protest organization cofounded by individuals including Bond and John Lewis, who became the group's chairman. The following year Bond became SNCC's communications director, responsible for all of the organization's public-relations efforts, including its official newsletter, the *Student Voice*. In 1961 he married Alice Louise Clapton, with whom he would have five children. Around this time Bond decided to leave Morehouse and work full-time for the *Atlanta Inquirer*; later he would become the newspaper's managing editor. Meanwhile, as a member of SNCC, he took part in civil rights efforts and voter-registration drives in Georgia, Alabama, Mississippi, and Arkansas. Bond suffered a concussion as a result of a beating by police on March 7, 1965, when he participated in a demonstration against police brutality in Selma, Alabama; the day of the doomed march across Edmund Pettus Bridge became known as "Bloody Sunday," and television images of the violence perpetrated by the police bolstered public support for the Voting Rights Act, signed into law that year.

Bond told Henry Louis Gates that he and the other members of SNCC came to regard themselves as "the bad boys and girls of the civil rights movements" and found it increasingly difficult to remain nonviolent in the face of brutality and humiliation at the hands of their opponents. "I think the nature of the work we did, the low pay we were getting, the negative experiences we had with government and that sort of orthodox liberalism in the United States just soured us on the chance of any progress being made using techniques that we made or the techniques that King suggested that we made," he told Gates. This change in attitude led some activists to adopt a more militant stance, and soon organizations such as the Black Panthers, which advocated self-defense, began to have greater influence in the movement.

Bond remained with SNCC until November 1965, when legislative redistricting facilitated his election to the Georgia House of Representatives. But his support of a SNCC statement critical of the United States' involvement in the Vietnam War angered his fellow legislators, who prevented Bond from taking his seat for over a year. The voters reelected him in a special election held in February 1966 and again the following November. That same year the Supreme Court ruled that his exclusion was unconstitutional; Bond officially took his seat in 1967. At the 1968 Democratic National Convention, held in Chicago, he led an insurgent delegation known as the Georgia Loyal Democrats in their protest against the exclusion of blacks from the democratic process. Bond took an active role in

the convention, seconding the nomination of Eugene McCarthy for president and in turn being nominated for vice president, making him the first African-American in U.S. history to be nominated for that position. He later withdrew his name from nomination, because at 28 he was seven years shy of the constitutional minimum age for a vice president.

In 1971 Bond returned to Morehouse College to complete his B.A. in English. He also became the first president of the Southern Poverty Law Center, founded that same year by Morris Dees and Joe Levin; he served in that post until 1979, when he became president emeritus (a title he still holds). In 1973 Bond became the president of the Atlanta chapter of the NAACP, the organization founded in 1909 to combat racial injustice, specifically segregation and lynching. His decision to join the NAACP may have surprised some; despite its reputation as a key component of the civil rights struggle, during the 1960s the NAACP and SNCC had taken decidedly different approaches. "The *institution* [NAACP] and its politics just seemed so out of touch to us," Bond recalled to Claudia Dreifus for the *Progressive* (August 1998). "They opposed the sit-ins. They didn't like direct action. They didn't like civil disobedience. They believed in law and litigation. And we were tired of that. We didn't want that. It took too long." Bond's opinion of the organization was not entirely negative: "We respected their grassroots, though," he continued. "In Alabama, Mississippi, and Georgia, it was the NAACP people we were working with. What we didn't respect was the bureaucracy and hierarchy because it was slow and cumbersome and bureaucratic and didn't do anything."

In 1974 Bond was elected to the Georgia state Senate; two years later he was forced to cancel his campaign for the U.S. presidency because he was unable to raise enough money. As a state senator he helped pass into law 60 bills, including one that instituted a pioneering sickle-cell-anemia testing program and one that provided low-interest loans for low-income Georgians buying homes; he also served on the Human Resources, Governmental Operations, and Children and Youth committees and as chairman of the Committee on Consumer Affairs. Bond's political career came to an unceremonious end in 1986, when he was defeated by former city councilman and fellow SNCC alumnus John Lewis in a primary race for the Fifth Congressional District, in Atlanta. Although Bond had the support of such celebrities as Senator Edward M. Kennedy of Massachusettsx, Bill Cosby, the Temptations, and Cicely Tyson, Lewis's reputation for being less militant than his opponent, as well as his aggressive media campaign, led to his victory. The sometimes bitter tone of the race strained Bond's friendship with Lewis; Bond was hurt by rumors that he used drugs, and he felt especially insulted by Lewis's request that he submit to a drug test. Complaints about his history of absenteeism (he had missed a quarter of all roll calls) also hurt his chances at being elected. By the end of the campaign, Bond found himself with a debt of $150,000. Meanwhile, his marriage had begun to dissolve, and in 1987 Alice Bond told Atlanta police that her husband had used cocaine; this information was made public soon after she filed charges of physical attack against Carmen Lopez Butler, alleged to be Bond's lover and drug dealer. Julian Bond denied that he had ever used cocaine, and although his wife later retracted her statements accusing him of drug use and adultery, the couple were divorced soon thereafter. Bond married Pamela Horowitz, a Washington, D.C.–based lawyer, in 1990.

Since 1991 Bond has taught government at American University, in Washington, D.C., where he now holds the title of distinguished professor in residence, and he has taught history at the University of Virginia since 1993. He has been a visiting professor at several schools, among them Drexel University, in Philadelphia, Pennsylvania; Williams College, in Williamstown, Massachusetts; and Harvard University, in Cambridge, Massachusetts. He was elected chairman of the national board of directors of the NAACP in 1998, succeeding Myrlie Evers-Williams, the widow of slain civil rights activist Medgar Evers. As chairman he hoped to improve the organization's use of technology and to find a solution to its financial troubles. "The '90's has seen corporate America withdraw from its social and economic responsibilities of the late '60's and '70's," Bond told Yao Atiim Seidu for the *Atlanta Tribune* (July 1, 1998, online), shortly after accepting the position. "I would like to be a part of refocusing an agenda and a dialogue that makes America work for all of its citizens." He also told Seidu that he hoped to "make the NAACP the organization of record as it relates to all matters concerning race." Bond has launched a campaign to raise $50 million and is responsible for editing *Crisis*, the organization's official publication, founded by W.E.B. DuBois. Since he accepted the position of chairman, the NAACP has focused on issues such as education and the practice of racial profiling by law-enforcement officers.

Bond's poems and articles have appeared in such publications as the *New York Times*, the *Nation*, *Playboy*, *Ramparts*, and the *Atlanta Constitution*. In 1964 Langston Hughes included works by him in the anthology *New Negro Poetry U.S.A.* Bond has also written nonfiction books, among them *Black Candidates—Southern Campaign Experiences* (1968) and *A Time to Speak, A Time to Act: The Movement in Politics* (1972). From 1980 to 1997 he was the host of *America's Black Forum*, a television news program based in Washington, D.C. Bond has appeared in films including *Greased Lightning* (1977), starring Richard Pryor, and also in the 1970s he guest-hosted the popular television comedy program *Saturday Night Live*.

For decades Bond has been a sought-after public speaker. He has received honorary degrees from 15 universities and has served on the boards of directors of many organizations, including the American Civil Liberties Union and the National Federation for Neighborhood Diversity. In 1998 Atlanta mayor Bill Campbell declared July 12 "Julian Bond Day."

Bond told Jack E. White for *Time* (July 27, 1998) that the notion of white supremacy remains one of the key issues facing civil rights organizations such as the NAACP. "It still means so much to those who practice it. It defines who they are. It makes them feel they are better than others. It ensures them positions in employment and college admissions they otherwise might not have. It still puts a lid on the dreams of black people, though to a lesser extent than in the past because of the civil rights movement." Bond does not believe that the struggles facing African-Americans today can be blamed on a lack of black leadership, as many commentators have suggested. "I don't think we have any real leadership problems," he told Hilary L. Hurd for *Emerge* (May 1998). "If I may say so, I think we have a followership problem. It strikes me that one difference between today and 35 years ago is that we had a movement then. We had large numbers of people—north, south, east, west, small towns, big cities—engaged in various civil rights battles. They were marching, they were registering voters. . . . They were engaged. We don't have that same engagement in our communities today. You know, if I had a dollar for every time I've been to some place and somebody said, 'You know, there's a big race problem here. I wish the NAACP would take care of it. I wish Jesse Jackson would come here and take care of it.' Well, the NAACP can't take care of all these things. Jesse Jackson can't take care of all these things. We need to go back to the place where people say, 'Gee, I think I'll take care of it. I think I can do something about it.'" — C.L.

Suggested Reading: *Atlanta Tribune* (on-line) July 1, 1998; *Emerge* p36+ May 1998, with photos; *New Perspectives Quarterly* p31+ 1998; *Progressive* p32+ Aug. 1998, with photos; *Time* p27 July 27, 1998, with photo

Selected Books: *Black Candidates—Southern Campaign Experiences*, 1968; *A Time to Speak, A Time to Act: The Movement in Politics*, 1972

Boyd, John W.

Sep. 4, 1965– President of the National Black Farmers Association. Address: National Black Farmers Association, 7063 Northumberland Hwy., Heathsville, VA 22473

In January 1999 the United States Department of Agriculture (USDA) agreed to pay a total of more than $300 million to black farmers who had sued it for race-based biases in awarding loans and sub-

Courtesy of National Black Farmers Association
John W. Boyd

sidies and to other farmers who could prove that they had been victims of racial discrimination. For many years black and other minority farmers had labeled the department the "last plantation" because of its alleged discriminatory practices. Spearheading the campaign that led to the settlement was John W. Boyd, an African-American farmer who founded the National Black Farmers Association in 1995. By protesting in front of the United Nations headquarters, in New York City, and the White House and by meeting with national leaders, the group succeeded in getting the USDA to reinstate its Office of Civil Rights and draw up recommendations, recently put into action, for helping minority farmers. In 2000, after years of fighting discrimination at the grassroots level, Boyd made an unsuccessful bid to represent the Fifth Congressional District in the U.S. House of Representatives.

Born in New York City on September 4, 1965, John W. Boyd grew up in South Hill, Virginia, on his family's 200-acre farm, which one of his great-grandfathers, a former slave, bought after working as a sharecropper. After reaching adulthood Boyd inherited the farm, where he grew tobacco and raised chickens and cattle. As with thousands of other American farmers, he needed loans from the USDA to remain solvent. In 1992 he received a federal loan of $120,000 to build a new poultry house. After he fell behind in his payments, the USDA rejected his applications for loans to buy chicken seed. "I tried for nine years to get a farm operating loan," David Firestone quoted him as saying in the *New York Times* (January 5, 1999). "Back in 1992, the county supervisor for the department threw my application in the trash. He said they didn't have

any more money. When [an] investigator asked him why he had made only two black farm loans, he said black farmers were lazy." Boyd's financial woes figured significantly in the decision of his wife to leave him. In 1993 he was forced to file for bankruptcy.

Boyd's experiences with USDA representatives convinced him that the agency was discriminating against black farmers. Many other black farmers had been similarly rebuffed in their requests for financial assistance from the department, which was seen as a "lender of last resort," but to which black farmers were often forced to turn, as larger commercial banking institutions usually stayed away from backing them. However, that the USDA would practice discrimination was not hard for blacks to believe; the USDA had been the last government department to integrate and once practiced official segregation in its program delivery. As black farmers were considered to be a higher credit risk, the USDA, according to Boyd, leveled higher interest rates on their loans. Furthermore, Boyd alleged, the USDA would often delay loan approvals for black farmers until late in the crop season, while some of their agents would alter loan applications, to increase the chances that black farmers would be turned down. These and other complaints of more overt instances of racist behavior by the USDA had fallen on deaf ears, especially after the department's Office of Civil Rights was disbanded, in 1983, during the administration of President Ronald Reagan. Thus, black farmers had to seek outside assistance for their complaints against the agency—an expensive course of action that took a great deal of time. Determined to end these perceived injustices, in 1995 Boyd formed the National Black Farmers Association.

One day in December 1996, Boyd found federal officials erecting a sign in his yard in preparation for the auctioning of his farm. "I took a power saw and cut it down," he recalled to Charisse Jones for *USA Today* (January 5, 1999). "It was degrading to me that my great-grandfather, coming out of slavery, was able to raise 12 children, make payments and keep this farm. And here I am . . . generations later, supposed to be a free man, with no access to credit. If I had lost the family farm, I feel I would've failed as a man and a farmer." The USDA granted the call of U.S. secretary of agriculture Dan Glickman for a moratorium on all imminent farm foreclosures, thus making it possible for Boyd and other farmers in similar situations to retain ownership of their land.

The black farmers' group soon began pressuring the Department of Agriculture on what it called discriminatory practices, which, Boyd said, had caused farmers like himself to declare bankruptcy. "It's hard enough to make a living farming without adding discrimination to your problems," Boyd declared, as quoted by Michael Fletcher in the *Washington Post* (on-line). "It's not just one farmer here and another one there; it's happening all over." The pressure put on the USDA by Boyd and his group prompted Dan Glickman to reinstate the Office of Civil Rights in his department; that office soon recommended 92 actions that the USDA could take to help black farmers. In 1997 Boyd and his group met with President Bill Clinton, who pledged $600 million in loans and programs that were partly aimed at black and other minority farmers. Meanwhile, two civil-action lawsuits were filed against the USDA on behalf of large numbers of black farmers. Boyd noted that there had been several discrimination cases filed against the USDA by black farmers since 1968, but not one had been settled. "We want to go back to 1968," Boyd told the *Militant* (January 20, 1997), as quoted in *World History Archives* (on-line). "Everyone with complaints filed with the USDA since then should be compensated, not just those facing foreclosure right now."

In 1998 Boyd asked Glickman to declare a state of emergency to rescue black farmers in the U.S. After waiting in vain for such a declaration as well as for the money the administration had promised, the group protested at the United Nations headquarters; they maintained that, since African-Americans were direct descendants of African slaves who had helped build the United States into an economic force but were never compensated, they deserved assistance. They further maintained that, by refusing them assistance after the abolition of slavery, the government had violated their human rights and forced blacks to continue to exist at the bottom of the American agricultural system. At such protests, Boyd would often bring a mule, named Struggles; once, he even roped Struggles to the gates of the White House. In July 1998 the National Association for the Advancement of Colored People (NAACP) voted to support Boyd's group. Boyd had told the civil rights group, as reported by *USA Today* (July 16, 1998), "I seriously believe that there is a conspiracy to take black farmers' land in this country." Boyd said that through discrimination by the USDA, the number of black farmers and the acreage of farmland they owned had plummeted. According to the U.S. Census Bureau, in 1900 blacks owned 14 percent of American farmland; in 2000 African-Americans owned less than 1 percent. In 1920 there were 925,710 black farmers; in 1992, there were 18,816. The rate of decline among black farmers was five times as great as the rate among white farmers.

In January 1999 the USDA agreed to pay more than $300 million to settle the class-action lawsuits filed against it by black farmers, which meant that on average each farmer who could claim discrimination would receive about $50,000 and have some outstanding loans forgiven by the USDA. Although the department did not admit it had ever discriminated, it did agree that the way in which it had handled bias claims was flawed. While Boyd had originally asked for $3 billion, he and his colleagues still celebrated the agreement. "It's a tremendous victory for black farmers across the nation," David Firestone quoted Boyd as saying. "We

met with the President. We tied a mule to the White House gate. We lobbied Congress. And finally farmers are getting some relief for the way they were treated in the past." In the court case against the USDA, Boyd and his fellow litigants proved that the processing period for loans for blacks was much longer that that for whites, and that a greater portion of their applications had indeed been denied. White farmers, it was shown, would wait an average of 84 days for decisions regarding approval of loans, while blacks would wait an average of about 222 days. Similarly, 84 percent of white farmers were approved for loans, while only 56 percent of blacks got approval. Furthermore, whites received, on average, about three times as much money in USDA subsidy programs. Boyd and his associates were still concerned, however, that many of the officials in the USDA who they claimed were guilty of discrimination still held their jobs and would not be disciplined. "Is this fair? No," Boyd said, as quoted by *U.S. News* (on-line). "But this is a victory bringing the government to its knees."

Despite that victory, the USDA turned down 40 percent of farmers who filed claims to receive settlement money, on the ground that they had not proved that they had been discriminated against. Each farmer who claimed such discrimination had to prove that a white farmer in a similar situation had been approved for loans that he or she had been denied. There had also been delays in payment. Boyd called the number of claims denied "way too many," and also said that the settlement was "too little, too late," as quoted by Danielle Knight of the Inter Press Service (on-line). "It's not enough here for a lifetime of losses, a lifetime of pain and suffering," he said. In December 1999 Boyd and some of his followers protested in front of the Department of Agriculture headquarters, claiming that continued discrimination was leading to continued foreclosure of black-owned farms; the number of such farms had now dropped below 18,000. "No one has been held accountable for their actions," Boyd said, according to a National Black Farmers Association press release (on-line). "None of the decision making officials have been terminated for the act of discrimination. That is totally unacceptable. I will not let this issue go until Agriculture treats all of its customers fairly."

In 2000 Boyd ran successfully in the Virginia caucus (which serves the same purpose as a primary) for the nomination of the Democratic Party to represent Virginia's Fifth District in Congress. He then faced the incumbent, Virgil Goode, an attorney who ran as an independent. On his campaign Web site, Boyd stated, "For too long the working people and voters of the Fifth District have been taken for granted and ignored. This campaign is their cause. We will show that we can 'Do-Something' to improve our schools, we can 'Do-Something' to bring new technologies and jobs to our region, we can 'Do Something' to ensure quality health care and retirement security for our people, and we can 'Do-Something' to cut waste in government and return money to the pockets of the people." On Election Day, despite his spirited campaign, Boyd lost to Goode, 68 percent to 31 percent.

Boyd continues to own his farm in South Hill, Virginia, currently concentrating on raising poultry. "My grandfather always said land knows no color," Boyd told Charisse Jones. "But I didn't have the money to spray my tobacco . . . to buy fuel. The land doesn't discriminate. People do." — G.O.

Suggested Reading: *New York Times* A p1 Jan. 5 1999; *USA Today* A p9 Jan. 5, 1999; *Washington Post* A p1 Dec. 11, 1996

Courtesy of Google
Larry Page (left) and Sergey Brin

Brin, Sergey, and Page, Larry

Brin, Sergey
Aug. 1973– Co-founder of Google Inc.; computer scientist

Page, Larry
Dec. 1972– Co-founder of Google Inc.; computer scientist

Address: Google Inc., 2400 Bayshore Pkwy., Mountain View, CA 94043

The Internet entrepreneurs Sergey Brin and Larry Page, who met as graduate students in 1995, developed the technology behind the popular Internet search engine Google. In 1998 they founded Google Inc., with Page as chief executive officer and Brin

as president. A year later they officially unveiled the company's Web site, *Google.com*. As of mid-2001, with its index of more than 1.6 billion Web pages, *Google.com* ranked as the world's largest search engine. Paralleling the buildup of indexed sites is the increase in the number of Google searches requested by Internet users: in mid-2001, according to Google's home page, Google was processing approximately 100 million queries daily, a figure that represents a growth rate of 20 per cent per month since the inception of the site. The name Google comes from "googol," a mathematical term for the number equal to 10 to the power of 100 (10^{100}), or the numeral 1 followed by 100 zeros (which represents a number greater than the estimated number of atoms in the universe). Brin and Page chose the name to indicate the magnitude of their mission, which is, as Brin told *OLinux* (online), "to organize the world's information, making it universally accessible and useful."

About half of Google users' searches are performed by *Google.com*; the rest are executed by Internet partners who maintain their own Web sites and possess licensing agreements with Google. Brin told Jason Black and Jonathan Hill for *Internet World* (June 1, 2001) that Google has made such arrangements with more than 150 corporate customers in 30 countries, among them Cisco Systems, Yahoo!, NEC, Red Hat, and Netcenter, a property of AOL Time Warner. The company, too, has grown, from a staff of two to more than 200, about half of whom carry out technology-related assignments, to enable the company to retain its position as a leader in its field. The Google search engine is unique in that it locates sites based on pertinence and popularity rather than text wording, which often yields misleading hits. In addition, unlike many other search engines, Google does not produce results linked to advertisers—so-called preferential returns; instead, it has opted for an unbiased, user-focused approach. That strategy has proved to be extremely successful: *Google.com* has earned close to 50 industry awards and accolades, among them three Webby awards, the most coveted prize in the Internet world; *PC World*'s World Class Award for best search engine in 2001; and a 2001 Net Award for best site and best search engine. In addition, it was named a *Forbes* Favorite for being "best of the Web" in 2000 and 2001. Contrary to speculation that the company would go public during the third quarter of fiscal year 2001, Google Inc. has remained privately owned. On August 6, 2001 Larry Page stepped down as the company's CEO; he was succeeded by Eric E. Schmidt, the chairman of the board and former CEO of Novell. Page now serves as president of products, while Brin has assumed the job of president of technology.

Sergey Brin was born in Moscow, in what was then the Soviet Union, in August 1973. He immigrated to the United States with his parents, Michael and Eugenia Brin, when he was six years old. The family settled in College Park, Maryland, where Michael Brin accepted a professorship in mathematics at the University of Maryland. Sergey Brin attended the same university; he graduated with a B.S. degree in 1993, with high honors in mathematics and honors in computer science. He then enrolled at Stanford University, in Stanford, California, where he earned a master of science degree in 1995. He remained at Stanford to work toward a Ph.D. The subject of his research for both his master's and his doctorate was data mining, which, as he explained to Black and Hill, is "the analysis of large amounts of data," by means of which one can "find patterns and trends" and potentially useful relationships among bits of information.

Lawrence Page was born in December 1972 in East Lansing, Michigan, to Carl and Gloria Page. His father was a pioneer in the field of computing and one of the first University of Michigan graduates to earn his doctorate in computers, in the mid-1960s. He later served as a professor of computer science at Michigan State University, in East Lansing. Page's mother, too, taught computer programming at Michigan State. His older brother, Carl Jr., founded eGroups, an Internet company based in San Francisco; in 2000 he sold it to Yahoo! for a reported $450 million in stocks.

As early as 1979 Larry Page had access to a computer in his home. "I turned in the first word-processing assignment in elementary school," he told Andy Henion for the Lansing State Journal (April 29, 2001, on-line). "No one even knew what a dot-matrix printer was." When he was 18 years old, Page built a usable, four-foot-wide inkjet printer out of Lego building blocks. After he graduated from East Lansing High School, Page enrolled at the University of Michigan to pursue a degree in computer engineering. As an undergraduate he received several leadership awards for his efforts toward improving the school's College of Engineering, which was expanding in response to the growth of the World Wide Web. He also served as president of the university's branch of Eta Kappa Nu, the national engineering and computer-engineering honor society. He received a B.S. degree in engineering in 1995, with honors. He then began working toward a graduate degree at Stanford University; his research focused on the Web.

Brin had been working toward his doctorate for about two years when, in 1995, he met Page at Stanford. "When Larry joined [the Stanford Ph.D. program], he started dabbling with the Web and started gathering large amounts of data," Brin told Robert McGarvey for Technology Review (November/December 2000). "That data intrigued me, and I wanted to run various experiments on it." "We didn't even intend to build a search engine originally," Page explained to Olga Kharif for BusinessWeek Online (March 13, 2001). "We were just interested in the Web and interested in data mining. And then we ended up with search technology that we realized was really good. And we built the search engine. Then we told our friends about it

and our professors. Pretty soon, about 10,000 people a day were using it."

The technology Page referred to was a system he and Brin christened PageRank, which consists of a complex network of mathematical algorithms designed to rank Web sites on a scale of importance. Importance is determined by both the number of links between one site and other sites and the importance of the various sites to which it is linked. PageRank demands that higher-ranking sites have external validation. It therefore places Web sites with links to themselves low on its scale of importance—or eliminates them altogether. (Many creators of Web sites copy the site hundreds or thousands of times, to increase its perceived value; their goal is to generate traffic and thus gain maximum advertising revenues.) "There are millions of variables, but we manage to do a lot of math, very fast, and in the end we rank pages in a way that's very close to how you would do it intuitively," Brin explained to McGarvey. "A lot of math" indeed: each PageRank ranking is calculated by means of an equation consisting of 500 million variables and more than two billion terms. More than 6,000 computers are needed to perform the equation.

Brin and Page tried in vain to sell their PageRank technology to such companies as Yahoo! and Altavista. "They realized we had something more advanced," Brin told Black and Hill. "But they were really saying, 'Well, our search is 80 percent as good as the next guy's, so that's good enough.' And they were expanding their chat, their message, and their e-mail. . . . And we're saying, Look, search is important. It's important for people to be able to find information quickly, easily, accurately, and objectively. And we really work hard on that. And that's why Google is better." Certain that a huge business opportunity existed, Brin and Page took steps to set up their own company. Using three credit cards, they bought $15,000 worth of disks, with the capacity to store, in total, a million megabytes of information. Then they formulated a business plan. On the strength of that plan, Andreas "Andy" Bechtolscheim, a co-founder of Sun Microsystems, gave them $100,000 in start-up money. Next, in 1998, they established Google Inc. By September of that year, they had raised almost $1 million in private funding, which carried them through the first 12 months of operation. By the end of that time—during which Google's user base had grown by 20 percent each month—Brin and Page had gotten additional financial support from some of the industry's largest venture capitalists, including a total of $25 million contributed separately by John Doerr, of Kleiner Perkins Caufield & Byers, and Michael Moritz, of Sequoia Capital, each of whom had helped to fund the launches of Apple, Amazon.com, Cisco Systems, Yahoo!, and Netscape. (Doerr and Moritz currently sit on Google's board of directors.) Despite Google's initial success, $25 million was an unusually large investment, in view of Google's modest size and unproven record. News of the infusion of cash raised Brin and Page's profiles considerably, and even led to the coinage of a new term—"to do a google," which means to raise capital while the precise nature of one's business remains unclear. "To google" is another informal term that has come into use; it means to search for information on the Web.

To keep pace with the growth of the Web—which, experts estimate, expands by more than 1.5 million pages every day—Brin and Page have tried to develop new software and expand the number of Google's computers continually. Brin told Jason Black and Jonathan Hill that the company needs to install more than a thousand new computers each month just to keep up with the increasing number of Web pages that require indexing. Brin and Page maintain that Google was the first search engine to index over a billion pages—an assertion with which many industry experts agree. (Inktomi, one of Google's many competitors—and the one from which it seized the much-sought-after Yahoo! account, in June 2000—disputes that claim.) Still, by most estimates, roughly half the Web remains unindexed. The huge amount of work to be tackled does not faze Page or Brin. As Brin told Leslie Walker for the *Washington Post* (October 28, 1999), "We get smarter, not worse, as the Web gets bigger. . . . That's our competitive advantage."

Google's founders have so far turned down all offers from prospective buyers of their company. Page explained to Robert McGarvey, "We're growing at a good rate, we have been successful at attracting good people and we are increasing our traffic tremendously. We believe we are going to dominate the market—and if you believe that, it's hard for anyone to pay you enough to justify selling. Search is the number-one application on the Web. And it's easy for people to try out different search engines so they can compare. They notice differences and they tell their friends. Friends tell friends. And that's how we grow." Because the company has been able to rely on such word-of-mouth publicity, Google has spent relatively little on advertising, compared with other dot-com companies.

If Google Inc. were to go public, Brin and Page would probably become multimillionaires. The company itself, located in the heart of California's Silicon Valley at a location referred to as the Googleplex, provides its employees with luxuries rarely available in the workplace: a full-time masseuse, yoga classes, meals prepared by two gourmet chefs, a pool table, and bedrooms. Twice weekly, workers compete in a hockey match in the company's parking lot. The table in the company's boardroom is reserved for Ping-Pong. In 1998, just months before he would have finished the requirements for his Ph.D. degree, Brin suspended work on his doctorate to work full-time on the expansion of Google Inc. (He has yet to complete the degree.) He and Page are both single and live in California's Silicon Valley. Brin was recently named second on *Women.com*'s "The Internet's Most Eligible Bachelors" list. — J.H.

Suggested Reading: *Brandweek* IQ p10 Nov. 27, 2000, with photo; *BusinessWeek Online* Mar. 13, 2001; *Fortune* p298 Nov. 8, 1999, with photos, p280 Aug. 14, 2000, with photo; *Internet World* p54+ June 1, 2001, with photos; *Lansing State Journal* (on-line) Apr. 29, 2001; (London) *Times* MBA p10 Jan. 26, 2000; *Maclean's* p46+ May 8, 2000; *New Statesman* p129 July 10, 2000; *Online* p41+ May/June 2000; *Technology Review* p108+ Nov./Dec. 2000, with photos; *Time* p66+ Aug. 21, 2000, with photos; *USA Today* B p02 Aug. 7, 2001; *Washington Post* F p20 Feb. 22, 1999, E p1 Oct. 28, 1999, with photo

---

Liba Taylor/Courtesy of International
Planned Parenthood Federation

Brueggemann, Ingar

1940(?)– Director-general of the International Planned Parenthood Federation. Address: International Planned Parenthood Federation, Regent's College, Inner Circle, Regent's Park, London NW1 4NS, England

Ingar Brueggemann has served as the director-general of the International Planned Parenthood Federation (IPPF) since September 1995. The IPPF was founded in 1952 in Bombay, India, by the leaders of national family-planning associations in India, Germany, Hong Kong, the Netherlands, Singapore, Sweden, the United Kingdom, and the United States. Based in London, England, the IPPF currently links national autonomous family-planning associations from more than 180 countries. The organization's mission is to set international standards for the safety of birth-control devices and establish informal rules regarding the provision of contraceptive services. It also tries to rally policy setters, opinion makers, and the media in its member countries to support its core objective: to provide high-quality family-planning services worldwide, as well as services that promote reproductive and sexual health. The IPPF's Web site states: "While governments everywhere have the responsibility of ensuring that health services are available nationwide, IPPF and its members act as the conscience of the family planning movement and as catalysts in tackling issues which government services may be unwilling or unable to deal with, such as the distribution of new methods of contraception, sexuality education, individual counseling, the prevention of unsafe abortion and services for disadvantaged groups and for young people." Under Brueggemann's leadership the IPPF has augmented all of its activities aimed at fostering the well-being of women and children worldwide. It has also worked increasingly to apply reproductive-health and family-planning approaches to tackling the interrelated problems of overpopulation, disease, and famine, particularly in developing countries, where they are most acute. For about two years before she joined the IPPF, Brueggemann worked for the Berlin-based German Foundation for International Development, and for nearly three decades before that, she served as an administrator with the World Health Organization.

Ingar Brueggemann was born in Germany in about 1940. She received her primary-school education in Germany and the United Kingdom, then earned graduate and postgraduate degrees in education and the social sciences from Munster and Marburg Universities, in Germany. In 1966 Brueggemann got a job with the World Health Organization, and during the next quarter-century she became one of the organization's leading social scientists. In 1978, at the WHO/UNICEF (United Nations Children's Fund) conference on primary health care, held in Alma Ata, in what was then the Soviet Union, she served as secretary to one of the principal committees concerned with family planning as a critical element of maternal and child health. In the late 1970s and early 1980s, she held the position of secretary of the Programme Committee of the World Health Assembly; WHO's major policy body, the assembly consists of delegates from each of WHO's member nations. From 1985 to 1988 Brueggemann directed WHO's Programme for External Coordination for Health and Social Development at WHO's headquarters, in Geneva, Switzerland. In that post she strived to coordinate the mobilization of nongovernmental organizations' resources for health-related programs. From 1989 to early 1993, Brueggemann served as director of WHO's office at the headquarters of the United Nations, in New York City. As the official representative of the organization's director-general, she served as an adviser on health-policy issues for various branches of the U.N., including the United Nations Development Programme, the United Nations Population Fund, and UNICEF. Brueggemann left WHO in 1993 to chair the Development Policy Forum of the German Foundation for International Development, a government-funded organization.

In September 1995 Brueggemann was appointed secretary-general of the International Planned Parenthood Federation. (Soon thereafter her title was changed to director-general.) Within a week of taking office, she traveled to Beijing, China, to address the World Conference on Women. Underscoring the vast disparity in living conditions and physical health between women in the developed world and those in Third World nations, Brueggemann issued a call for universal gender equality, access to reproductive-health and family-planning services, and an end to forced servitude and all forms of violence against women. "You just can't speak in the same breath of the situation of the vast majority of women who exist in the underdeveloped countries and of the situation of the minority who live in the industrialized countries," she said in her address at the conference, as quoted on the IPPF's Web site. "They belong to the same planet, but they are worlds apart. In far too many countries women are forced to slave as beasts of burden fetching water and gathering brushwood for fuel, to work endless hours in the fields or to sit for hours on end in hot and crowded market places trying to sell a few wares, to feed hungry husbands and children before they can satisfy their own hungry stomachs, to clean the homesteads and the latrines, and at the end of the day to submit to sexual submission, in too many societies after having had their clitoris mutilated as a child. For them, a satisfying reproductive life is a distant dream. Is it any wonder that health for them is a distant dream too?"

Later in 1995 Brueggemann presided over the IPPF's adoption of its Charter on Sexual and Reproductive Rights. The charter sets forth 12 basic human rights relating to sexual and reproductive freedom: the right to life (which refers specifically to pregnant women whose lives may be endangered by their pregnancies); the right to liberty and security of each individual, including women's right to be protected from genital mutilation and forced pregnancies, abortions, or sterilization; the right to equality and freedom from all forms of discrimination, including equal access to "information, education, and services related to development, and to sexual and reproductive health"; the right to privacy, specifically with regard to birth-control and related information and services; the right to freedom of thought, with no religious restrictions; the right to information and education, specifically regarding "the benefits, risks and effectiveness of all methods of fertility regulation"; the right to choose whether or not to marry; the right to decide whether or when to have children; the right to health care and health protection, including "the right to be free from traditional practices that are harmful to health"; the right to the benefits of scientific progress; the right to freedom of assembly and political participation, specifically regarding groups formed "to promote sexual and reproductive health and rights"; and the right to be free from torture and inhuman or degrading treatment.

In a meeting held in Copenhagen, Denmark, in November 1996, Brueggemann addressed the IPPF's Central Council. As quoted on the IPPF Web site, she said, "If those who pioneered our Federation in Bombay in 1952 could see us today, they would hardly recognize our activities and the way we are conducting them. Things must have appeared much simpler in those days. Too many women were having too many children and fewer infants were dying, and as a result there were too many mouths to feed. Governments started to intervene, often in too impersonal a manner and at the expense of human rights, keeping in mind only demographic factors. Bilateral and multilateral agencies also intervened, with the single goal of keeping down population growth in developing countries, and with little if any understanding of the human and social factors involved. So a group of dedicated individuals decided to look after their own family planning interests, and the initiative gradually snowballed to include family planning associations in every continent."

In March 1997 Brueggemann spoke before the Finnish Parliamentary Group on Population and Development, in Helsinki, placing the subjects of reproductive health and family planning firmly within the greater context of uncontrolled population growth and its environmental consequences. In November of that year, she delivered her second major address to the IPPF's Central Council, this time in Johannesburg, South Africa. With the federation reeling from deep budget cuts—the result of a drop in donations worldwide—Brueggemann painted a picture of a darkening financial future: "The donor world has changed with the times. It is faced with pressing demands to alleviate poverty, to diminish illiteracy, to resolve political and military strife, to protect the environment from further degradation, to overcome developmental stagnation, and to combat new threats to health as well as many old ones that have raised their ugly heads again; and all this following an information revolution that has brought all these problems to their electronic doorstep in what has come to be known as the global village. We have to compete with the demands emanating from all of these catastrophic situations. And we will only be able to do so if we demonstrate that our activities are vital for the future existence of humankind on planet earth," she declared, as quoted on the IPPF Web site.

In a speech given at the World Bank Conference in April 1998, Brueggemann talked about high infant mortality rates and the dangers of childbirth in the developing world. The following month she spoke in Beijing, at a ceremony celebrating the 18th anniversary of the founding of the Chinese Family Planning Association. In June, in the commencement address at the Harvard University School of Public Health, in Cambridge, Massachusetts, she reasserted the IPPF's belief that sexual and reproductive rights are basic human rights, and offered (as quoted on the IPPF Web site) this distillation of the organization's position on abortion: "Among many people, particularly in this country, the very word 'abortion' is taboo. What is the Federation's stance regarding abortion? It plays no planned part of planned parenthood. In no case should abortion be used as a method of family planning. Safe abortion, and I repeat safe, should only be used as a last resort when contraceptive methods have failed. For what is the alternative for so many women? Twenty million women undergo unsafe abortions each year. All over the world unsafe abortions are carried out because safe abortions are not available for women pregnant against their wishes. This applies in particular to teenage girls, large numbers of whom die or are maimed for life every year by unsafe abortions carried out in unhygienic surroundings by unqualified persons. For them, safe abortion carried out as a very last resort as early as possible, and certainly not after the twelfth week of pregnancy, is the only way of ensuring that they remain alive and retain their dignity." Earlier, in April 1998, in a speech given at the World Bank headquarters, in Washington, D.C., on World Health Day, Brueggemann said that an estimated 60,000 to 120,000 women die each year as a result of unsafe abortions.

In May 1999 Brueggemann challenged the Vatican—arguably the most influential opponent of birth control and abortion in the world—by asking for a review of the papal state's observer status in the U.N. and suggesting that the Catholic Church be granted the same nongovernmental status as other major world religions. The attack on church power came in response to Pope John Paul II's earlier condemnation of efforts to provide abortion-inducing pills to Kosovan refugee women who had been raped by Serbian troops in the war-torn former Yugoslavia. The Vatican has consistently opposed the allocation of funds for contraception or abortion, finding justification for its policy in religious orthodoxy. Many family-planning advocates believe that the global problems of overcrowding, disease, and famine could be slowed, particularly in countries with large Catholic populations, if the church were to relax its stance on birth control to some degree. Opponents of the IPPF and its mission also include the Protestant anti-abortion group STOPP International (Stop Planned Parenthood International).

In July 1999 in New York City, Brueggemann was a featured speaker at the second U.N.–sponsored International Conference on Population and Development (the first had taken place in Cairo, Egypt, in 1994). In her speech she referred to the growing political involvement of family-planning associations. "IPPF and family planning associations are in the vanguard of efforts to ensure that the rights, inherent and explicitly stated in the Cairo Programme of Action, are clarified and made a reality," she stated. "Because many existing national policies and laws are, we believe, still contrary to these rights, our Family Planning Associations are working with other human rights partners to encourage and assist governments to introduce the necessary changes." In her conclusion she spoke of the "key role of sexual and reproductive health and rights in promoting equality and development."

Among the IPPF's key initiatives in 2000 was *Sexwise*, a radio program offering sex education, produced in partnership with the British Broadcasting Corporation (BBC) and broadcast in 11 languages to an estimated 60 million listeners in Africa, the Arab world, Latin America, and Asia. The program, which referred listeners to related Internet and printed material, dealt with such topics as foreplay and intimacy, masturbation, homosexuality, unsafe abortion and its consequences, sexual coercion, prostitution, HIV and other sexually transmitted infections, and contraceptive methods. Brueggemann has been instrumental in increasing the IPPF's focus on the AIDS virus. (According to WHO statistics, by 2000 AIDS had claimed 18.8 million lives worldwide, while an additional 34.3 million people had been infected with HIV, 95 percent of them in developing countries.)

Family-planning associations were faced with new challenges in 2001, not only in the developing world but in the United States as well, where President George W. Bush, in one of his first acts after taking office, moved to block federal funding to international family-planning associations that provide or support abortion services. Also in early 2001, congressional Republicans threatened to sharply restrict access to mifepristone, more commonly known as RU-486, a pill that induces abortion if taken within days of conception. RU-486 was widely available in Europe for several years before it was approved by the federal Food and Drug Administration (FDA), in September 2000.

Ingar Brueggemann wears eyeglasses and has a prominent dimple on each of her cheeks. A bio on the IPPF Web site refers to her as Mrs. Brueggemann. — G.K.R.

Suggested Reading: International Planned Parenthood Federation Web site; *New Republic* p6 June 15, 1998; *Unesco Courier* p20 July/Aug. 2000

Burnett, Mark

1960(?)– Television producer. Address: c/o CBS Television Network, 524 W. 57th St., Third Fl., New York, NY 10019-2902

Mark Burnett is the creator and executive producer of the hugely popular television series *Survivor*, which he has described as "*Gilligan's Island* meets *Lord of the Flies* meets *Ten Little Indians* meets *The Real World*." A native of Great Britain who served with the British Army Paratroop Regiment, Burnett parlayed his own enjoyment of the rigors of outdoor adventure into a series of successful "Eco-Challenges," in which teams from around the world competed for cash prizes. A variation on those events—filmed on a Pacific island and involving 16 contestants—became the first televised *Survivor*, which aired in the U.S. in 13 weekly installments beginning in June 2000. Approximately 20 million viewers tuned in each week to watch this "unscripted tropical soap opera," as John Leo dubbed it in *U.S. News & World Report* (June 19, 2000). On *Survivor*, contestants separated into two teams; each week, the losing team was required to vote one of its members off the island—forcing all involved to work together and scheme against one another simultaneously. An estimated 65 million North Americans watched the final episode, in which the $1 million winner of the challenge was revealed. With two additional *Survivor* series to his credit, Burnett has become an influential figure

Courtesy of Eco-Challenge Foundation

in what has been dubbed reality-based television. He has also been credited with helping to open the door to revenue sharing between the networks and producers. "The endgame here, the game we're all in, is selling," Burnett told Bill Carter for the *New York Times Magazine* (January 28, 2001). "Selling productions in stores. I'm a content provider. My show creates an interest, and people will look at it, but the endgame is still going to a store and buying something—a car, deodorant."

Mark Burnett was born in England in about 1960. He grew up in East London, in a house built by the Ford Motor Co., his father's employer. His mother worked in a car-battery factory next to the Ford plant. "I was an only child and never criticized my whole life. Unconditional love. You can't ask for more," he told Bill Carter. At the age of 18, Burnett joined the elite British Army Paratroop Regiment and saw action in such hot spots as Northern Ireland and the Falkland Islands. In one battle, 24 of the 300 soldiers in his regiment were killed. "Real stuff. Horrific," Burnett recalled to Carter. "But on the other hand, in a sick way, exciting." After he completed his active duty, he left the regiment, because merely participating in training exercises did not interest him.

In 1982 Burnett moved to Los Angeles, California. From there he planned to move to Central America, where, he had heard, one could earn money as a "weapons and tactics adviser," as he recalled to Carter. However, when his mother told him that she felt uneasy about his going there, he changed his plans. (He always heeded his mother's advice "unwaveringly" during those years, Carter reported.) Instead, he worked for a while as a live-in nanny and chauffeur in Beverly Hills. His first employers, he told Jan Golab for *Los Angeles* (January 1996), hired him in part because "no one else who applied spoke English as a first language, and I was the only one who'd played semipro soccer." He recalled to Golab, "When I called and told my parents, they couldn't believe I'd suddenly gone from being a soldier in the Falklands to driving a Mercedes-Benz in Beverly Hills." In addition to his work with the family, he coached soccer and basketball and taught swimming.

Burnett's next boss, an insurance mogul, helped him obtain his green card. At that man's suggestion, he enrolled in a management-training program, and after completing the course, he began selling insurance. He left that field after he began reaping large profits at another venture: selling used clothing, which he would purchase for $2 an item, at Venice Beach, in California. Before long he owned five such clothing stands. His success with that enterprise landed him a job as a vice president at an entertainment-industry publishing company, where he learned about marketing, advertising, and corporate budgeting. Fond of implementing new ideas, he marketed a tax-preparation program, an insurance plan to protect taxpayers in the event of an Internal Revenue Service audit, a credit-card-protection service, and a low-interest credit card, which he created with Public Action, a consumer group. He reportedly sold his share of the credit-card business in 1992 for more than $1 million.

Burnett was not happy, though; thanks to the self-help seminars he attended, he realized that he was not quite "self-actualized," as Carter put it.

Then he read an article about an adventure race, a multi-day challenge in which contestants traversed difficult terrain to a final goal. He recognized, as he told Carter, that such an event "would be a great marketing-television kind of thing—people on the edge of death, racing for a prize." Burnett soon entered adventure races himself, and he founded and trained Team American Pride, the first American adventure-race team, with the idea of televising their activities. With a business partner, Brian Terkelsen, a former investment banker and outdoor enthusiast, he arranged to have the Prime Network underwrite the shooting of a documentary on Team American Pride. Burnett, Terkelsen, and the other members of the team participated in two 10-day adventure races, in Madagascar and Oman; kayaking over rough seas, trekking through inhospitable wilderness, and climbing mountains, the adventurers suffered from the constant attacks of biting insects in Madagascar and the lack of sufficient food and clean water in Oman. (In the latter country, according to Burnett, his team got lost in the desert for four days and escaped death from dehydration only by chance: a Bedouin whom they met led them to a pool of stagnant water that contained dead animals.) "An adventure race is a brutal thing," Burnett said, as quoted by Golab, "but that's what it's designed to be. It's designed to take you to your absolute lowest low, so that you learn something about yourself."

Burnett analyzed the races in which he had participated and realized he would have to make some changes. "It wasn't well organized," he explained to Golab. "There were no structured briefings. I knew I'd have to improve on that. Americans expect things to be well organized. The French and other cultures have more of a 'whatever' attitude." Through various contacts he got in touch with the chief programmer for MTV, Doug Herzog. He assured Herzog that he could create and organize a successful event, dubbed "Eco-Challenge," in which—drawn by the chance to earn fame and a $50,000 cash prize—adventure teams from around the world would endure the hardships of trekking through rugged wilderness. Herzog agreed, and after other sponsors joined in, the first Eco-Challenge was organized; the 10-day, televised event took place in southern Utah in 1995, with 50 international teams hiking, horseback riding, swimming, rafting, and mountaineering. Only 21 teams completed the race, which many contestants described as the toughest such competition they had experienced. "I had two goals in mind when I founded Eco-Challenge," Burnett told *Mountainzone.com*. "One was obviously very commercial. It's a for profit business and I hoped to make excellent returns on my investment. Number two, I'd hoped to have a really good time making that money." By his own account, Burnett plotted the details of the race as it progressed. "I never panicked," he told Carter. "What's the point? That'll get you killed in war. It's not that I'm that good. It's a kind of naivete. I didn't realize it should be difficult."

Following the success of the TV special *Eco-Challenge*, which aired on MTV in 1995, ESPN hired Burnett to do a follow-up "mini-challenge" as part of its newly developed *X-Games* series. The second Eco-Challenge was held in Maine. Since then, the competition has become an annual event, held in such places as Patagonia, Australia, Borneo, and Morocco and recorded by large camera crews. In 2000 the race began airing yearly on the USA network. All Eco-Challenge teams are required to carry whatever trash they generate during the contest. Before each challenge, Burnett organizes an environmental service project at the site of the event. In Utah project participants gathered 70 tons of recyclable metals at an illegal dump; in British Columbia, they cleaned trash from a tributary important to spawning salmon; in Australia, they planted more than 1,700 trees along the eroded banks of a river. Several years ago, as a business venture linked with the competitions, Burnett formed his own travel company.

Burnett seized another opportunity in 1996, when he met Charlie Parsons at a party. The creator of the hip British morning TV show *The Big Breakfast*, Parsons told Burnett about his idea for a game show involving castaways on an island, which he had thus far failed to sell. Burnett acquired the American television rights to the concept from Parsons. After four years without success in their attempts to interest an American network in their proposal, they sold *Survivor*, as they called it, to CBS. Burnett acquiesced to CBS's request that he sell the advertising slots for the series himself, under the condition, he told reporters, that he and CBS would split any profits equally, in what would be the first such revenue-sharing agreement for a TV production. CBS has denied Burnett's account of the agreement, insisting instead that the producer received half of the additional ad revenues that accrued when CBS expanded the *Survivor* finale. In response to that denial, Burnett told Carter, "I won't continue calling this one revenue-sharing. But it doesn't matter to me as long as I'm paid well." In what is known as "associative marketing," products of *Survivor*'s eight corporate sponsors appeared prominently during the show.

The first 13 installments of *Survivor*, which aired weekly in the summer of 2000, featured 16 "castaways." Chosen from a pool of 6,000 hopefuls, they came from various walks of life, with professions ranging from former Navy SEAL to truck driver. After being flown to Pulau Tiga, an unpopulated island in Malaysia, they were divided into two teams and then left to find their own food, water, and shelter. Each week, the teams were presented with challenges, such as having to eat insects or stand as long as possible with at least one hand on an "idol"; the losing team had to vote one member off the island. At a certain point, the two teams, or tribes, merged, continuing to vote one person out each week; alliances were formed and then abandoned. The final castaway (chosen from among the remaining four people by the seven members who had last been voted off the island) was Richard Hatch; a corporate trainer from Rhode Island who had played the game both strategically and ruthlessly, Hatch won $1 million in cash.

The popularity of *Survivor* surpassed the predictions of virtually everybody associated with the show. On the heels of its success, CBS broadcast a second installment, *Survivor: The Australian Outback*; that series, set on a 50,000-acre cattle ranch in a remote part of Australia, debuted after the Super Bowl, on January 28, 2001, with a new group of castaways. The next *Survivor* installment, which aired in the fall of 2001, took place in the African nation of Kenya.

In addition to *Survivor* and *Eco-Challenge*, Burnett has two other adventure-based reality programs in the works, for both of which he will be paid 50 percent of advertising revenues. The first, *Combat Missions*, which will premiere on the USA network, will feature teams of past and current Green Berets, former Navy SEALs, and members of other elite forces. Eight teams of four will be dropped from helicopters and will be charged with rescuing hostages, among other tasks. "The show is something I thought about for many years," Burnett told *Daily Variety*, as quoted on *E! Online*. "We are making it so viewers feel like part of it, what's in the minds of the people doing these missions and that they're people with families, brave people who protect us all." Burnett's other upcoming show, tentatively titled "Destination Mir," will air on NBC. Its contestants will participate in a training process for astronauts, though one that is modified for television. Burnett hopes to arrange a trip for the winner on the new International Space Station or on a spaceship that would carry him or her in orbit around Earth. He has also organized a special Eco-Challenge for members of the United States armed forces, which will take place in Alaska in June 2001.

With Martin Dugard, Burnett co-wrote *Survivor: The Ultimate Game* (2000), which is billed as the official companion book to the show. In association with the Los Angeles School District, Burnett has established the Eco-Challenge Youth Foundation, which gives inner-city children a chance to play outdoor sports. In 1996 he established the Eco-Challenge Adventure School in Malibu, California, a joint project with Point Mugu State Park.

Burnett lives with his wife, Dianne, and their two young sons in Malibu. "You know what's great about America?" he said to Carter. "Being working class and not having that classic education in England, you're going to struggle. You know what Americans care about? Results. You do well here, people say, 'Good for you.'" — G.O.

Suggested Reading: *Los Angeles* p56+ Jan. 1996, with photo; *Moutainzone.com*; *New York Times Magazine* p22+ Jan. 28, 2001, with photo; *TV Guide* p28+ Jan. 20–26, 2001, with photo

Courtesy of the White House

Bush, George W.

*July 6, 1946– President of the United States.
Address: The White House, 1600 Pennsylvania
Ave., N.W., Washington, DC 20500*

NOTE: An earlier article about George W. Bush appeared in *Current Biography* in 1997.

In January 2001 George W. Bush became the 43d president of the United States, following the most bitterly contested presidential election in more than a century. He had lost the popular vote but defeated his Democratic opponent, Vice President Al Gore, in the Electoral College—and then only after a 36-day battle over vote recounts in the state of Florida. He faced a Congress almost perfectly divided along party lines and a public just as divided over the legitimacy of his presidency. During the campaign, Bush—the son of a former president— had sought to become known as a new type of Republican, alternately describing himself as a "compassionate conservative" and a "uniter, not a divider," and had touted his ability to bring people together across party lines during his five years as governor of Texas. In the early months of his presidency, this approach proved to be successful with Congress, which passed his trillion-dollar tax cut and has been in deliberations over his proposed public-school reforms and 2002 budget.

Bush ran for president on a primarily domestic agenda: tax cuts, school revitalization, and reforms for Social Security and Medicare. Just seven months and 22 days into his term, that agenda, his presidency, and the country as a whole were forever altered. In the wake of the terrorist attacks on September 11, 2001, which destroyed the World

Trade Center in New York City and severely damaged the Pentagon, just outside Washington, D.C., the president became a source of inspiration to a country in mourning and rallied other nations in the U.S.-led war on international terrorism. On September 20 Bush addressed the country in a joint session of Congress and spoke to a citizenry united by a new sense of patriotism. "Great harm has been done to us. We have suffered great loss. And in our grief and anger we have found our mission and our moment. Freedom and fear are at war. The advance of human freedom—the great achievement of our time and the great hope of every time—now depends on us," he said, as quoted in the *New York Times* (September 21, 2001). "Our nation, this generation, will lift a dark threat of violence from our people and our future. We will rally the world to this cause by our efforts, and by our courage. We will not tire, we will not falter, and we will not fail."

The first child of George Herbert Walker Bush and the former Barbara Pierce, George Walker Bush was born on July 6, 1946 in New Haven, Connecticut, where his father was then completing his undergraduate degree at Yale University. The younger George Bush was born into an illustrious family: his paternal grandfather, Prescott Bush, served as managing partner of the Wall Street firm of Brown Brothers, Harriman and Co. and later became a U.S. senator from Connecticut, while his father distinguished himself as a combat pilot during World War II and as captain of the Yale baseball team.

When the elder George Bush graduated from Yale, he received an offer to work for Brown Brothers but turned it down, deciding instead to take his young family to western Texas, where an oil boom was underway. After working as a salesman for an oil-field supply firm, he co-founded a company in Midland, Texas, that negotiated natural-gas and oil-rights deals with landowners. By this time the family had grown to include a daughter, Pauline Robinson Bush, known as Robin. By the mid-1950s George H. W. Bush had become a millionaire. While they were raised in an upper-class environment, the younger George Bush and his siblings never regarded themselves as wealthy, in part because their parents dismissed any ideas of entitlement their children might have had, believing instead that they needed to earn their own way in life. (Barbara Bush, however, did persuade her husband to set up educational trust funds for the children.) Though his parents were strict, George W. Bush grew up respecting and admiring them, especially his father.

Although he was not born in Texas, George, of all the Bush children, was the one "who would become the truest Texan, who had memories of the oil business, of sleeping in the back seat of the station wagon while his father waited for a well to come in," according to George Lardner Jr. and Lois Romano in the *Washington Post* (July 26, 1999). He attended Sam Houston Elementary School and is remembered as being an active and entertaining child who sought to be the center of attention.

His energy and antics helped to assuage the grief his parents felt after his sister Robin died of leukemia, in October 1953, shortly before her fourth birthday. George provided support for his mother in particular; she often left the younger children in his care. (His brothers, Jeb, Neil, and Marvin, were born in 1953, 1955, and 1956, respectively; his sister Dorothy was born in 1959.) As Lardner and Romano noted, Barbara Bush did not realize how much she was depending on young George until "she heard her son tell a friend that he couldn't come out because he had to play with his mother, who was lonely. 'I was thinking, Well, I'm being there for him,' she recalled. 'But the truth was he was being there for me.'" Robin's death led to the formation of a great bond between mother and son, who also shared outspoken personalities and sharp wits. Though Bush resembles his father physically, his vibrant personality is said to stem from his mother.

In the late 1950s the Bushes moved from Midland to Houston, Texas, where George H. W. Bush's oil company had transferred its headquarters. The younger George Bush, who had just finished seventh grade at San Jacinto Junior High, where he had won his class presidency, quickly made friends at the Kincaid School, a private academy in Houston. There, he became a class officer and joined the school football team. After he had attended private school in Houston for two years, his parents decided that he should begin 10th grade at Phillips Academy, in Andover, Massachusetts, where his father had been educated and had left an indelible mark. (Though Bush's grades were mediocre, he was accepted at the exclusive institution as a "legacy" student.)

At Andover, as the school is commonly known, the 15-year-old Bush felt the full length of his father's shadow. As an Andover student, the elder Bush had famously ignored the counsel of then-Secretary of War Henry L. Stimson, who in his commencement address told students to complete their education before enlisting in the armed forces. Instead, he became the youngest commissioned navy pilot in World War II. Comparisons with his father at such a competitive and elite institution caused the younger Bush a great deal of anxiety. While his father had excelled at academics and baseball, Bush was only an average student and player, though he made the varsity baseball and basketball squads. He ingratiated himself with his classmates, however, with his quick wit and engaging personality. (His caustic remarks earned him the nickname "Lip.")

Again following in his father's footsteps, Bush journeyed to New Haven in the fall of 1964 and enrolled at Yale, but he found the university quite different from the one his father had attended. The college traditions of fraternity parties, football, pep rallies, and secret societies were waning as college students became more politically active, particu-

larly by participating in civil rights rallies and protests against the Vietnam War. For many then coming of age, the 1960s were a confusing time, when societal mores were changing and traditional American values were being questioned. To Bush—who was raised in conservative Texas and grew up worshiping a father who had risked his life in war to defend American ideals—questioning such values was repugnant.

While the war was on the minds of most Yale undergraduates, the members of Bush's fraternity, Delta Kappa Epsilon, were more interested in frat-house activities. Bush was known as a "good-times guy" who liked to drink and play pranks. Still, in meetings of the Skull and Bones—Yale's most elite secret society, to which Bush's father and grandfather had also belonged—Bush and other members talked not only about their love lives and dreams but also about what to do once they had graduated and were facing the draft. Bush's own thoughts on the war were complicated by his father's public support of U.S. policy in Vietnam and recent election to the U.S. House of Representatives. Though he would later question the motives behind U.S. participation in the Vietnam War, Bush "believed that his father's position was correct—we're involved, so we should support the national effort rather than protest it," Robert J. Dieter, Bush's roommate at Yale, told Lois Romano and George Lardner Jr. for the Washington Post (July 27, 1999).

Bush was eager to leave Yale, primarily because of what he considered to be the "intellectual snobbery" of the university's vocal left wing. The school served, however, as an incubator for his own political philosophy. In a Washington Post (July 23, 2000) article, Hanna Rosin noted, "Like many conservatives his age, Bush was in his way consumed by [the 1960s], defining himself and much of his agenda . . . by what he saw then and didn't much like." He later came to articulate what he "didn't much like"—cynicism, intellectual elitism, anti-Americanism, and what he saw as continual self-analysis bordering on navel-gazing. He concluded that the country should replace the ideology of the so-called hippie generation with one of personal responsibility and self-reliance—convictions much more in tune with those of his father's generation than with the beliefs of many in his own. Bush graduated from Yale in 1968 with a bachelor's degree in history.

He then volunteered for the Texas Air National Guard, agreeing to spend two years in flight training and another four in part-time service so that he could become a pilot, like his father. He ultimately became a lieutenant and signed up for a program that rotated National Guard pilots overseas, but the program was later canceled. "Had my unit been called up, I'd have gone . . . to Vietnam," Bush remarked, as quoted in a Washington Post (July 28, 1999) article by George Lardner Jr. and Lois Romano. "I was prepared to go." For some facing the prospect of the draft, the National Guard represented an escape route from Vietnam, and there has been speculation that the elder Bush's status as a congressman helped his son to make the shortlist of applicants. But many of Bush's friends and supporters believe that in choosing the National Guard, he was attempting to find a compromise among his own feelings about the war, his father's position, and the stance of those protesting U.S. involvement in Vietnam. "In a sense he was trying to remain a centrist in a time when there wasn't anything left at the center," Craig Stapleton, Bush's cousin through marriage and a friend for over 25 years, told Lardner and Romano. "He didn't dodge the military. But he didn't volunteer to go to Vietnam and get killed, either."

After completing his active National Guard duty, in 1970, Bush took an apartment in Houston and began looking for work while fulfilling his reserve duty periodically. He secured a job at an agricultural company, but, finding it to be dull, he quit before long. For a time in 1971, he was tempted to join the race for a seat in the state legislature, but he decided against it. In the following year Bush was involved in an episode that would become infamous: after taking his younger brother Marvin out for drinks, he drove back to his parents' house, crashing into neighbors' garbage cans on the way home. When his father confronted him about his behavior, Bush challenged him to a fight. Though the two never came to blows, the incident convinced the elder Bush that his restless son needed direction, and he found the younger George a job as a counselor for inner-city youngsters in Houston's Third Ward. The experience was sobering for Bush, who made a favorable impression on his fellow volunteers, most notably former pro-football great "Big Cat" Ernie Ladd, who told Lardner and Romano, "If he was a stinker, I'd say he was a stinker. But everybody loved him so much. He had a way with people. . . . They didn't want him to leave."

Bush left Houston to enroll at Harvard University's Business School, in Cambridge, Massachusetts, where he hoped to find some direction. He received his M.B.A. degree in 1975 and went straight back to Texas, in search of a field in which he could apply his newly acquired business skills. He started out by freelancing in the oil business as a "landman," one who researches titles to mineral rights so that oil companies can lease those rights. In 1977 he formed his first oil and gas exploration company, Arbusto Energy Inc., but then quickly turned his attention to running for a congressional seat once he heard that Midland's longtime representative, George Mahon, was retiring. After announcing in July 1977 that he would run in the following year's election, Bush quickly gained on Jim Reese, the Republican front-runner. During the campaign Bush traveled the sprawling 19th Congressional District with his new wife, the former Laura Welch, solidifying his support. The primary resulted in a run-off, which Bush won. But he lost the general election to the Democrat, Ken Hance, who called Bush an Ivy League outsider

and accused him of "riding his daddy's coattails." (The elder Bush, who had served as a U.S. congressman and as director of the CIA, among other posts, was gearing up to run for the 1980 Republican nomination for president.)

Bush returned to the oil business just as quickly as he had made up his mind to join the congressional race. Looking for investors for Arbusto, he was aided by his uncle Jonathan Bush and by other family and Ivy League contacts. He quickly found all the funding he needed; in the late 1970s many investors were entering the oil-exploration business because of rising oil prices and the ever-present hope of finding an "elephant," or striking oil. But in the hit-or-miss business of oil exploration, Bush's success rate was no better than average. Of the nearly 100 wells his company had drilled by 1985, only 50 percent ever hit oil or gas. As a result, many of Bush's investors lost money, and the company faltered. The firm had already had a public offering of stock in 1982 and merged with a larger company, Spectrum 7, in 1984, but was still unable to generate a significant profit. (Bush, however, had reaped $362,000 from the sale of the company to Spectrum.) After oil prices collapsed, in 1986, Bush and his partners began to look for another company to take over Spectrum. Thus did the Harken Energy Corp. agree to buy Spectrum and absorb its debts in exchange for shares of stock. According to Lars-Erik Nelson in the *New York Review of Books* (February 24, 2000), Harken wound up "paying Bush $530,000 for stock in a company that was facing foreclosure." (When Bush sold his Harken stock four years later, rumors of insider trading circulated and prompted a probe by the Securities and Exchange Commission. While the commission found that Bush had failed to submit a notice for the sale of the stock, no charges were filed.)

The year 1986 was significant for George W. Bush. First, though he remained a stockholder in Harken and drew a $10,000-a-month salary as a consultant there, his career as a full-time oil executive came to an end. Second, he began immersing himself in politics again, becoming involved in his father's bid for the 1988 Republican presidential nomination. (George H. W. Bush was then serving his second term as vice president of the United States under President Ronald Reagan.) Third, he quit drinking, shortly after his 40th birthday. In the previous year the Reverend Billy Graham, a longtime Bush family friend and spiritual adviser, had talked with Bush at his father's home in Kennebunkport, Maine. After that conversation Bush began to study the Bible regularly and became a much more devout Christian. He also started to think that his drinking—in which he was said to indulge not daily but in binges—was, in his words, "beginning to crowd out my energies and could crowd, eventually, my affections for other people." (It has been speculated in the media that Bush also took illegal drugs, an accusation to which he has never responded directly. During the 2000 presidential campaign, his representatives maintained in various statements that he had not taken any illegal drugs during the previous 25 years.)

Newly sober, Bush moved to Washington, D.C., in 1987 to work at his father's campaign headquarters. Though called "Junior" by other staff members, he quickly earned their respect by becoming, in his words, a "loyalty thermometer," measuring colleagues' commitment to his father and settling disputes among them. He also made sure that all aides and reporters showed his father proper respect and chastised anyone who didn't. He displayed political savvy by keeping his father's campaign "on message," and his manner charmed those around him. He proved to be such a success in helping to win the presidency for his father that many aides began discussing the possibility of his running for governor of Texas in 1990. However, he—as well as his wife and his mother—felt that before he could succeed in politics, he would first have to find success in a field that would put distance between himself and his father in the public mind.

Shortly after his father was sworn in as the 41st president, Bush returned to Texas, uncertain about his future. A former oil partner had called him before the election to find out if he was interested in putting together a group to buy the Texas Rangers, the Major League Baseball team based outside Dallas. After considering the offer, Bush said that he was interested, both because of the opportunity to establish an identity apart from his father's and because of the other people involved in the deal. Those included William O. DeWitt Jr., of the oil-exploration company Spectrum 7, which had merged with Bush's firm, as well as the Rangers' owner, Eddie Chiles, a Bush family friend, who was "in financial trouble and was eager to sell," as Lois Romano and George Lardner Jr. explained in the *Washington Post* (July 31, 1999).

Bush and DeWitt quickly lined up investors, many of them from the East Coast, and bought 86 percent of the team for approximately $75 million. Bush received a 5 percent share of the team, which he bought with the $500,000 he had received as a loan after putting up his Harken stock as collateral. It was agreed from the beginning that Bush, along with the Texas financier Edward "Rusty" Rose II, would run the team, with Rose working behind the scenes and Bush in the more public position of managing partner. Bush relished that position; he went to most of the home games, sitting in the stands with the fans instead of in the owners' box and serving as a virtual head cheerleader for the team. He used his public-relations skills to help sell the public on moving the Rangers from their converted minor-league ballpark to a state-of-the-art, $200 million stadium in Arlington, Texas, bought primarily with taxpayers' money. The Ballpark, as it is known, was a huge success, boosting annual attendance by 50 percent and helping to generate more revenue for the team, so that it could afford top players. That, in turn, helped the performance of the team: the Rangers hadn't won a title since the early 1970s, when the team moved from Washington, D.C., to Texas; in the 1990s they won three division titles in four years.

As the public face of the Rangers' ownership, Bush made a good impression on the team's fans and his employees alike. "You know, this guy fired me," baseball manager Bobby Valentine told Romano and Lardner during the presidential race. "The honest truth is that I would campaign barefoot for him today." Moreover, Bush profited from his baseball experience. In addition to coming out of his father's shadow to a degree, he earned $15 million on his total investment of just over $600,000, plus an additional 10 percent return on his investment when the group sold the team after eight years.

Meanwhile, in 1993, with the new Rangers ballpark scheduled to open the following year, his finances secure, and his public persona more clearly defined, Bush decided to run for governor of Texas in the 1994 election. His opponent would be Ann Richards, who had won the office in 1990. Some observers believed that Bush was running to avenge his father, whom Richards had belittled at the 1988 Democratic National Convention as having been born "with a silver foot in his mouth." Bush, however, dismissed such speculation and focused on running a campaign with a very clearly defined agenda.

When Bill Clinton defeated George H. W. Bush in the 1992 presidential election, Bush had realized that his father's reelection campaign had lacked a coherent message. After he decided to run for the Texas governorship, he was careful to craft a platform with specific proposals, such as decentralizing public education, reforming the state juvenile-justice system, and overhauling welfare. He was also careful not to let himself be goaded into going "off-message" by a ridiculing Richards. (During the campaign she repeatedly referred to Bush as "Shrub" and pointed to his lack of experience in public office.) Richards and her supporters hoped that they could, by discussing Bush's drinking and suggesting that he had had questionable business dealings, cause him to blow up in public—but they were unsuccessful. On Election Day Bush won 53 percent of the popular vote, with many women, Hispanics, and younger voters supporting him. In addition, he became only the second Republican elected to the Texas governorship since Reconstruction.

After taking office, in January 1995, Bush made good on a campaign promise to work well with Democrats, who controlled both houses of the Texas state legislature. At the same time, he was able to push through a significant number of his initiatives, including the restoring of local authority to schools and the raising of education standards; the reduction of the state's welfare rolls by more than 50 percent; and the two largest tax cuts in the history of Texas (totaling over $3 billion). By reaching out to Hispanic and black voters in his state, Bush was able to win reelection in 1998 by a record 69 percent of the popular vote—with 49 percent of Hispanics, 27 percent of blacks, and 66 percent of women supporting him. Many media pundits criticized the governor, however, for not doing more for south Texas, one of the poorest Hispanic regions in the country, even though Bush, according to Lars-Erik Nelson, "stood up to the National Republican Party and refused to go along with a campaign to bar illegal immigrants from the public schools." Bush has also been criticized for Texas's relatively frequent and often seemingly indiscriminate use of the death penalty, which included the execution of mentally retarded prisoners and of women such as Karla Faye Tucker, who had killed two people but embraced Christianity while waiting for her death sentence to be carried out. Critics in the media have also attacked Bush for taking the side of large corporations on environmental-protection issues, most notably in a fight involving the Texas Clean Air Act. In the *New Republic* (August 16, 1999), John B. Judis wrote, "Collectively, Texas's cities suffer from the worst air pollution in the country," and went on to note, "Bush, heeding the wishes of the state's leading industries . . . blocked the correction of a problematic provision in the state's 1971 Clean Air Act that exempts older plants from complying with the law's regulations."

None of these criticisms of Bush's governorship prevented him from becoming, by early 1999, the Republican front-runner for the 2000 presidential election. By June of that year, he had already raised $37 million for his campaign, primarily through longtime friends and associates; he thus won the money race for the Republic nomination before the election season truly got underway. Other early contenders for the nomination, including Elizabeth Dole, Senator Orrin Hatch, and former vice president Dan Quayle, dropped out relatively quickly, unable to compete with Bush's cash juggernaut. By September 1999 the Bush campaign had collected more than $60 million in contributions.

Bush's financing lead did not translate into a lock on the Republican nomination, however. Before the primaries the Bush team sought to make their candidate appear "presidential" by keeping him above the political fray, which had the unwanted effect of making him seem too confident and remote to voters. Bush skipped the debates among the Republican contenders that took place before the New Hampshire primary, and as a result he finished almost 20 percentage points behind Senator John McCain of Arizona in that primary's popular vote. The campaign retooled after that, allowing Bush's natural charm to play on both voters and the reporters following his campaign. He gave nicknames to reporters, called his campaign plane alternately Retooled One and Accessibility Two, and made a continuing effort to transmit his message while looking more at ease on the stump. Time and again he hammered home the themes he had successfully exploited in Texas, such as

school reform and tax cuts, while emphasizing issues of national importance, among them Social Security reform, better Medicare coverage for senior citizens, and increased military spending. He also favored the development of an anti-ballistic missile shield to protect the United States from attack. Overall, he sought to define himself as a new type of Republican, a self-styled "compassionate conservative" who felt that policies should be based on the philosophy of limited government but who also cared about the above-named areas of common concern. The approach paid off: in the Super Tuesday national primary in March 2000, Bush triumphed in California, New York, Ohio, and other large states, as well as in Georgia, Maine, Maryland, and Missouri—effectively ending McCain's bid for the presidency.

Bush coasted into the Republican National Convention in Philadelphia, Pennsylvania, ahead of the presumed Democratic nominee—Vice President Al Gore—in opinion polls, due in part to his selection of Dick Cheney as his running mate. That choice seemed odd to some, since Cheney, who had been the senior Bush's secretary of defense, had also been the man in charge of George W. Bush's search for a vice-presidential running mate. Many others, though, as Howard Fineman pointed out in *Newsweek* (August 7, 2000), saw Cheney as "a bold pick," given Cheney's lack of "pizzazz" and the fact that he hailed from Wyoming, a state with few electoral votes. And as Fineman observed, "Bush knew the biggest fear in the minds of voters: that he might be out of his depth, at least at first, in the Oval Office." By choosing the veteran Cheney, Bush removed a considerable defect in his candidacy—his lack of foreign-policy experience.

During the three televised presidential debates in October 2000, the Democratic nominee took advantage of the lack of specifics in Bush's proposals. Gore, a noted master of minutia in regard to public policy, hammered away at everything from the details of Bush's tax cut to his idea that a percentage of Social Security money should be given to younger workers directly, so that they could invest it as they wished. Bush responded with assertions that his opponent was using "fuzzy math" and that the accuracy of Gore's statements should be questioned, since he had been known to stretch the truth about his own accomplishments in the past. Polls taken shortly after the debates found the candidates in a statistical dead heat, with voters criticizing both Gore's manner, particularly in the first debate, and Bush's seeming lack of knowledge on specific issues.

On November 7, 2000 Americans went to the polls to choose the 43d president of the United States, but they would not find out who that man would be for another 36 days. Around eight in the evening, television networks named Gore as the projected winner in Florida—a state crucial to Bush's gaining the 270 electoral votes needed to win. About two hours later, however, the networks retracted that projection, and shortly thereafter they gave Florida to Bush and proclaimed him to be the next president. Minutes after that announcement, Gore telephoned Bush to concede, only to call him back less than an hour later to retract his concession, since it appeared that more votes were coming in for Gore, putting the outcome of the election in question.

For the next five weeks, Florida was the scene of a flurry of legal actions, beginning with Gore's request to have the ballots recounted manually in four largely Democratic counties: Palm Beach, Dade, Broward, and Volusia. After Bush was declared the unofficial winner in Florida by 327 votes out of six million cast, following a second machine count, his team asked state officials to put a stop to the manual counts. But the Florida Supreme Court allowed the hand counts to continue and gave the counties in question five days to complete them. The Florida secretary of state, Katherine Harris, a Bush supporter, did not extend the deadline for certification to allow all counties to complete their hand recounts. On November 26 Harris certified all votes tallied up to that point, pronouncing Bush the winner in Florida by 537 votes. Gore's team then contested the results of the election in Florida, first in a circuit court and then before the Florida Supreme Court.

At the same time, the U.S. Supreme Court began listening to the Bush team's arguments that Florida's Supreme Court had overstepped its authority by forcing Harris to include the manual recounts in the certified results. The U.S. Supreme Court then sent the case back to the Florida Supreme Court, asking it to clarify its reasoning for including manual recounts in specific counties. Several days later, on December 8, a divided Florida Supreme Court ordered manual recounts in all counties where there were a significant number of "undervotes," or punch-card votes that had not been registered by machine because the cards had not been punched through completely. The next day the U.S. Supreme Court, in a divided ruling, halted the manual recount and authorized a hearing on the matter, set for two days later.

On December 12, 2000, in a highly controversial, five-to-four decision, the U.S. Supreme Court ruled that the Florida Supreme Court had not set sufficiently clear rules for manually counting votes (the state court had said only to count as votes those ballots showing "clear intention"), and that any further delay in the certification of the state's electors would jeopardize their immunity from congressional reexamination after December 12, the date for final certification. Conservatives on the court, in a majority decision, contended that because different methods had been applied to recounts in different counties, the inexact standards prescribed by the Florida Supreme Court for manual recounts violated the guarantee of "equal protection under law" specified in the 14th Amendment to the U.S. Constitution. Shortly after that decision was reached, Gore conceded the election to Bush.

Sworn in on January 20, 2001, Bush came to the presidency with what was perceived as the weakest mandate in more than a century: though he had gained enough electoral votes in Florida to win the presidency, he had lost the popular vote by about a half-million ballots; he faced an evenly divided U.S. Senate and a razor-thin Republican majority in the House of Representatives; and the economy was slowing after a nearly eight-year boom. But, as Jonathan Alter pointed out in Newsweek (December 25, 2000–January 2, 2001), Bush's "strengths match up well with the historical moment: Bush is a conciliator by nature who prides himself on working across the aisle." He immediately set about meeting with congressional leaders, in the hope of finding legislative areas of agreement.

Bush put his Cabinet together quickly by surrounding himself with trusted, longtime advisers: Condoleezza Rice as national security adviser, Colin Powell as secretary of state, and Donald Rumsfeld as secretary of defense, among others. He also set his agenda in motion swiftly, with several executive orders. The first, issued just days after he took office, stopped federal funding of international family-planning groups—a reversal of President Bill Clinton's policy, which had itself overturned President Ronald Reagan's 1984 order to stop funding of abortions overseas. In February Bush signed two executive orders that allowed the government to increase funding of social services provided by religious groups. That act fulfilled a campaign promise that many had questioned on the grounds that it violated the separation of church and state.

Bush's first presidential trip to a foreign country was his visit to Mexico, where he met with the new Mexican president, Vicente Fox Quesada. It had long been a staple of Bush's ideology to promote better trade relations with Mexico, as well as with other nations in the Western Hemisphere. He remarked in a speech given in Miami, Florida, on August 25, 2000, which cited the growing Hispanic population and social influence in the United States, that closer connections to other nations in the Americas are important to U.S. interests: "Those who ignore Latin America do not fully understand America itself. And those who ignore our hemisphere do not fully understand American interests. . . . Our future cannot be separated from the future of Latin America." In April Bush traveled to Quebec City, in Canada, where he and other leaders in the Western Hemisphere signed a commitment to complete negotiations on a Free Trade Zone of the Americas, which would include all of North and South America by 2005. In June Bush made his first presidential trip to Europe, where he met with the leaders of Spain, Sweden, Poland, Slovenia, and Russia to discuss economic ties, environmental issues, and the proposed U.S. missile defense shield.

The first international crisis of the Bush administration occurred in April, when a Chinese fighter jet forced a U.S. surveillance plane flying over international waters to make an emergency landing in China, following a collision between the U.S. plane and a Chinese jet—which resulted in the disappearance and presumed death of the Chinese pilot. The 24-member U.S. crew was held for 11 days, during a time of tense negotiations between the U.S. and Chinese governments. The Chinese government demanded an apology as well as a promise that the United States would stop all surveillance flights near its coasts and would not sell arms to Taiwan, which China considers a renegade Chinese province. The United States expressed regret for the death of the pilot but refused to budge on the issues of surveillance flights and arms sales to Taiwan. The U.S. crew was returned home after the Bush administration signed a document stating that it was "very sorry" for the loss of the pilot. Later in the month, the U.S. sold a number of warships as well as eight diesel submarines to the Taiwanese government. In addition, in television interviews, Bush promised to do "whatever it took" to defend Taiwan against an invasion by forces from mainland China. "Our nation will help Taiwan defend itself," he said in a CNN interview. "At the same time, we support the one-China policy, and we expect the dispute to be resolved peacefully." This statement was considered a bold departure from those of previous administrations, which had kept their positions on the issue purposely vague.

At home, Bush—never considered a firm supporter of environmental conservation—made a number of controversial decisions with regard to environmental regulations. Most notably, he said that the United States would not support the Kyoto Accords of 1997, which called for the reduction of carbon emissions, declaring the accords "unfair to America." He also reversed a campaign promise to have the Environmental Protection Agency (EPA) regulate carbon dioxide as a pollutant, and he has on more than one occasion suggested opening up the Arctic National Wildlife Refuge to oil exploration in order to shore up reserves and keep prices down. Environmentalists were outraged by Bush's proposals, and he has since reversed some of his decisions, including one that would have raised the permissible amount of arsenic in drinking water. He has also pledged to sign a phase-out of a dozen highly toxic chemicals known as POPs (persistent organic pollutants) and has asked Congress to ratify this worldwide treaty.

Overall, Bush's first 100 days in office were smooth and successful. The House and Senate passed his trillion-dollar tax cut; his 2002 federal budget went to conference committee. He has also made what he considered to be "good progress" on his education-reform package, getting such liberal senators as Edward M. Kennedy of Massachusetts to support him on issues including mandatory student testing. Though other, more daunting legislative challenges—such as Social Security and Medicare reform—awaited him, Bush remained optimistic about getting Republicans and Democrats to work together. In his first address to a joint session of Congress, on February 27, 2001, he proclaimed,

"Together, we are changing the tone in our nation's capital. And this spirit of respect and cooperation is vital—because in the end, we will be judged not only by what we say or how we say it, but by what we are able to accomplish."

The president especially needed this spirit of cooperation after the events of September 11, 2001, when a group of 19 terrorists hijacked four commercial airplanes and crashed three of them into the Pentagon and the twin towers of the World Trade Center, killing more than 5,000 people and sending ripples of fear and shock through the nation. (The fourth plane crashed in a rural section of Pennsylvania, reportedly after passengers attempted to regain control of the aircraft.) Bush learned of the attacks while visiting a school in Sarasota, Florida, and quickly issued orders to ground all commercial flights and send fighter jets to protect New York and Washington. Meanwhile, the Secret Service, believing that the White House and Air Force One were targets, moved the president first to Barksdale Air Force Base, near Shreveport, Louisiana, and later to Offutt Air Force Base, outside Omaha, Nebraska, for his protection. Bush quickly tired of bouncing around the country and demanded to return to the U.S. capital. "I don't want some tinhorn terrorist keeping the President of the United States out of Washington. People want to see their President, and they want to see him now," he said, according to the White House adviser Karl Rove, who spoke with Nicholas Lemann for the *New Yorker* (October 1, 2000).

In the week following the attacks, Bush set out to console Americans and prepare them for a long war on international terrorism. After addressing the nation from the Oval Office on the evening of the attacks, he spent the night and the following day in consultation with his national-security team and the leadership of the House and Senate. On September 12 he visited the damaged Pentagon and, for the first time, described the terrorist attacks as constituting an act of war. A day later he spoke to New York governor George Pataki and New York City mayor Rudolph Giuliani and promised them whatever assistance they needed in rebuilding damaged areas of the city and in helping the families of those who perished during the attacks and subsequent rescue attempts. (Bush and Congress have since approved a $40 billion aid package.)

Calling for a "national day of prayer and remembrance," on September 14 Bush attended the Washington National Cathedral with former presidents Gerald Ford, Jimmy Carter, George Bush, and Bill Clinton. Addressing those assembled, he said, as quoted in the *New York Times* (September 16, 2001), "Today we feel what Franklin Roosevelt called 'the warm courage of national unity.' In every generation, the world has produced enemies of human freedom. They have attacked America because we are freedom's home and defender. And the commitment of our fathers is now the calling of our time." That afternoon he arrived in New

York City to tour the World Trade Center site and rally the thousands who had been working around the clock to free the estimated 5,000 people trapped in the rubble. Using a bullhorn to address the cheering crowd, the president proclaimed: "The people who knocked these buildings down will hear all of us soon."

On September 20 Bush appeared before Congress in a nationally televised address to speak about the suspected perpetrators of the attacks and about how the government planned to combat them. He spoke of the international terrorist network Al Qaeda, believed to have been responsible for the earlier bombings of U.S. embassies in Tanzania and Kenya as well as the bombing of the USS *Cole* near a port in Yemen. This group, led and funded by Saudi exile Osama bin Laden, has been aided by the radical Muslim Taliban government in Afghanistan. In his speech, Bush demanded that the Taliban turn over terrorists hiding in their country, dismantle the terrorists' training camps, and free any Americans currently being held. He went on to note: "These terrorists kill not merely to end lives, but to disrupt and end a way of life. With every atrocity, they hope that America grows fearful, retreating from the world and forsaking our friends. They stand against us, because we stand in their way. We are not deceived by their pretenses to piety. We have seen their kind before. They are the heirs of all the murderous ideologies of the 20th century. By sacrificing human life to serve their radical visions, by abandoning every value except the will to power, they follow in the path of fascism, Nazism and totalitarianism. And they will follow that path all the way, to where it ends: in history's unmarked grave of discarded lies. . . . We will direct every resource at our command— every means of diplomacy, every tool of intelligence, every instrument of law enforcement, every financial influence, and every necessary weapon of war—to the disruption and defeat of the global terror network."

In the weeks following that address, Bush directed his administration to conduct the war on terrorism on many fronts: the government has frozen assets of known international terrorists, increased its use of surveillance satellites and intelligence gathering, and begun military intervention in Afghanistan. On October 7, after the Taliban refused to hand over members of the Al Qaeda network, the United States and Great Britain launched air strikes against Taliban and Al Qaeda targets inside Afghanistan. American and British special-forces teams later began working on the ground inside Afghanistan in a further attempt to dismantle terrorist capabilities.

In addition to fighting the war, Bush has had to work to strengthen the U.S. economy, which had been unsteady before the attacks and has suffered greatly since. In addition, he has sought to comfort a nation grown even more fearful since terrorists began sending the lethal spores of anthrax bacteria through the mail to U.S. news agencies and government offices. Though he faces the greatest domestic and international crises since Franklin Roosevelt occupied the White House during the Great Depression and World War II, he remains resolute. "I will not forget this wound to our country and those who inflicted it. I will not yield, I will not rest, I will not relent in waging this struggle for freedom and security for the American people," President Bush promised toward the end of his September 20 address before Congress. "The course of this conflict is not known, yet its outcome is certain. Freedom and fear, justice and cruelty, have always been at war, and we know that God is not neutral between them."

George W. Bush has been married to Laura Bush, a former teacher and librarian, since 1977. They have twin daughters, Barbara and Jenna, born in 1981. The Bushes own a 1,500-acre ranch in Crawford, Texas. — C.M.

Suggested Reading: *New York Post* (on-line) Sep. 21, 2001; *New York Review of Books* p4+ Feb. 24, 2000, p53+ Jan. 11, 2001; *New York Times* A p10 Aug. 17, 1999, A p23 Nov. 30, 1999, p1 Sep. 16, 2001, A p2+ Sep. 17, 2001, A p1+ Sep. 21, 2001, A p1+ Oct. 8, 2001; *New Yorker* p70+ Oct. 1, 2001; *Newsweek* p31+ Feb. 28, 2000, p32+ Aug. 7, 2000, p32+ Dec. 25, 2000–Jan. 1, 2001, p31 Oct. 9, 2001; *People* p56+ Nov. 8, 1993; *Salon.com*; *Time* p40 Aug. 9, 1999, p80 Aug. 16, 1999, p42 Mar. 5, 2001; *Time* (on-line) Nov. 5, 2001; *U.S. News & World Report* p18+ Aug. 9, 1999, p38+ Mar. 19, 2001; *Washington Post* A p1+ July 25, 1999, A p1+ July 26, 1999, A p1+ July 27, 1999, A p1+ July 28, 1999, A p1+ July 29, 1999, A p1+ July 30, 1999, A p1+ July 31, 1999, A p1+ July 23, 2000, A p1+ July 24, 2000, A p1+ July 25, 2000, A p1+ July 26, 2000, A p1+ Apr. 23, 2001

Bush, Laura

Nov. 4, 1946– First Lady of the United States; former teacher and librarian. Address: The White House, 1600 Pennsylvania Ave., N.W., Washington, DC 20050

"Laura is able to live an interesting life that is apart from the political campaign, which I find totally appealing," George W. Bush, then the governor of Texas, commented about his wife to Julia Reed for *Newsweek* (November 22, 1999), early in his successful campaign for the presidency of the United States. "Politics doesn't consume her, and as a result, it doesn't totally consume me." Only the second First Lady of the United States to have earned an advanced degree (the first was Hillary Rodham Clinton), Laura Bush worked as an elementary-school teacher and librarian in Texas for more than a decade before she married, at the age of 32. As the

Rick Wilking/Archive Photos

Laura Bush

First Lady of Texas for five years, beginning in 1995, she worked on several programs aimed at promoting literacy among children and on projects that aided both children who had been abused or neglected and the caseworkers assigned to them. She also helped to raise money for various charities. As the new First Lady of the United States, she plans to continue her focus on education and children.

An only child, Laura Bush was born Laura Welch on November 4, 1946 in Midland, Texas, where her parents—Harold Welch, a successful real-estate developer, and Jenna Welch, who worked as a secretary in her husband's office—raised her. She has said that she felt lonely in her early years and spent a great deal of time reading. Even before she entered elementary school, she knew that she wanted to be a teacher when she became an adult; she liked to line up her dolls and pretend that they were her pupils. Her parents dreamed of sending her to college; as she said during her speech to the 2000 Republican National Convention, as quoted in the *Washington Times* (July 31, 2000), "Neither of my parents graduated from college, but I knew at an early age they had that high hope and high expectation for me. My Dad bought an education policy, and I remember him telling me, 'Don't worry, your college education will be taken care of.'"

Bush attended Southern Methodist University, in Dallas, Texas, where she received a bachelor's degree in education in 1968. After she graduated she worked as a teacher in a series of Texas public elementary schools, the first of them in Dallas. "Many of my second, third and fourth grade students couldn't read," she said in her 2000 Republi-

can National Convention speech, "and frankly, I'm not sure I was very good at teaching them. I tried to make it fun by making the characters in children's books members of our class." In 1974, while teaching in Houston, Bush, who loved reading as much as she loved teaching, earned a master's degree in library science from the University of Texas.

Meanwhile, her friends had tried to set her up with George W. Bush, who lived in her apartment building, but she had repeatedly turned them down. As she told Julie Bonnin for *Austin360.com* (April 18, 1999), "I thought he was someone who was interested in politics and that he would be someone I wouldn't be interested in because I was so uninterested in politics at that time." In 1977, when Welch was working as a librarian at Dawson Elementary School in Austin, Texas, the two were introduced at a barbecue. They arranged a date, during which they played miniature golf; three months later, on November 5, 1977, they married. "I think it was a whirlwind romance because we were in our early thirties," Laura Bush told Skip Hollandsworth for *Texas Monthly* (November 1996). "I'm sure both of us thought, 'Gosh, we may never get married.' And we both really wanted children. Plus, I lived in Austin and he lived in Midland; so if we were going to see each other all the time, we needed to marry." The couple settled in Midland, where in 1975 George W. Bush had established an independent gas and oil exploration company, called Bush Exploration.

Interviewers have often noted the striking differences in the personalities of George W. and Laura Bush. George W. Bush has said that his wife's steadiness has helped calm him down, while Laura Bush told *Good Housekeeping* (on-line) that her husband "adds a lot of excitement" to her life. "I think that's one of the reasons I was attracted to him. He was high-energy and fun and had a great sense of humor. He still makes me laugh a lot. That's very relaxing, I have to say. It's such a great personality trait; it sort of defuses tension."

Before she met George W. Bush, a Republican, Laura Bush was a registered Democrat. Nevertheless, the day after they were married she joined him to launch his campaign for a seat in the United States House of Representatives. During the campaign Laura made a few speeches, but she was not used to appearing before crowds, and by her own account, she felt shy and uncomfortable. George W. Bush lost the election and returned his attention to his business. In 1981 Laura Bush became pregnant. Toward the end of her pregnancy, she suffered complications, and she underwent a cesarian section five weeks before her due date. On November 25, 1981 she gave birth to fraternal twin daughters—Jenna and Barbara, named for their maternal and paternal grandmothers, respectively—and thereafter concentrated on raising her children. In 1984 George W. Bush merged his company with another small firm, Spectrum Corp., and became its president. He profited handsomely when, in 1986, the Harken Energy Corp. bought Spectrum. That same year, after developing a massive hangover after his 40th birthday party, he swore off alcohol—as his wife had been urging him to do for years. "Anyone who stops some habit like that has to do it himself. I did talk to him about it, of course," Laura Bush told Patricia Kilday Hart for *Redbook* (August 1999). "I wanted him to quit drinking—I felt like he was drinking too much."

After the 1988 presidential election, won by her father-in-law, then–Vice President George Bush, George W. and Laura Bush moved to Dallas, where George W. planned to start another business. Instead, along with a group of local investors whom he rounded up, he bought the Texas Rangers baseball team; soon afterward he became the club's managing partner. Laura Bush felt gratified that her husband had found an occupation that he enjoyed so much. For that reason she felt uneasy when he told her that he had decided to run for governor of Texas in 1994. After determining that he truly wanted to be governor and was not mainly interested in adding to the Bush family legacy, she helped him campaign. "We grew close during the baseball games because of the amount of time we spent with each other," George W. Bush told Julie Bonnin. "We could think about things and talk. We grew very close during the [1994] campaign because it was like we were in combat to a certain extent, fellow warriors."

After George W. Bush's victory in the gubernatorial election, Laura thought she might simply try to continue living the life of a homemaker, albeit in the governor's mansion. But she came to hold a different view of what her role as the First Lady of Texas should be; as she told Skip Hollandsworth, "I finally said, 'Well, if I'm going to be a public figure, I might as well do what I've always liked doing,' which meant acting like a librarian and getting people interested in reading." With that in mind, she invited a group of Texas writers to read at an inaugural event. Then she began to travel throughout the state, with the aim of bringing attention to the issue of illiteracy and encouraging the establishment and improvement of reading programs. In 1996 she delivered a short speech on education at the Republican National Convention, in San Diego, California. In 1998 she became involved in an early-childhood development initiative, called the Reach Out and Read program, aimed at helping parents and other caregivers to prepare preschool children for formal instruction in reading. Reach Out and Read included a family literacy project for Texas that was run in collaboration with the Barbara Bush Foundation for Family Literacy, which was founded by Laura Bush's mother-in-law and awards grants nationally.

As the Texas First Lady, Laura Bush also worked with Community Partners to establish Adopt-A-Caseworker programs, which link Child Protective Services caseworkers with community groups that provide the caseworkers with financial and moral support. She also got involved with Rainbow Rooms, which provide caseworkers with clothing, toiletries, toys, and other items needed by children rescued from abusive homes or negligent custodians. In addition, she served on the boards of various institutions, among them the University of Texas Graduate School of Library and Information Science Advisory Council and the Reading Is Fundamental Advisory Council. She also founded the Texas Book Festival, which celebrates state authors and has raised $900,000 for stocking Texas public libraries, and she raised funds for the arts and for programs that promoted breast-cancer awareness.

The comfortable margin with which George W. Bush won reelection as governor of Texas in 1998 led many high-profile Republicans to encourage him to run for the Republican presidential nomination in 2000. Laura Bush, however, had misgivings about his pursuing the presidency. "From [his] '92 campaign, I realized there was an image out there that was not him," she told *Good Housekeeping* (on-line). "That worried me, and it was one reason I think I was reluctant when people started talking about George running for president. We talked about that. Because you don't like to see someone characterized in a way that you know they're not. Of course, in a very partisan political race, your opponents will try and paint a picture of you that's not true. There is labeling and stereotyping. And the way the press reports things, people look one-dimensional, and everyone is really much more complicated than that."

After her husband made up his mind to run, Laura Bush worked vigorously in his behalf, while at the same time keeping a low profile, doing few interviews, and spending time with her daughters. During her 100 days on the campaign trail, she visited many schools, talked about education, and gave speeches. "I always think of myself as basically reserved and shy," she told Julie Bonnin. "I wouldn't have thought of this before I started giving speeches, but reading over the top of a book like I did millions of times as a children's librarian is great practice." Although she found campaigning "exciting," to use her word, the experience was painful at times. In particular, newspapers published a report of an incident that occurred when she was 17: after running a stop sign, she crashed into the car of her boyfriend at the time, injuring him fatally. "It was hard to have that come out," she told Rita Braver for *CBS.com* (on-line). "Although I expected it to come out. . . . It was certainly no secret. All of my friends knew, everyone in Midland knew. But that's hard."

As the nation's First Lady, Laura Bush intends to focus on issues of education and reading. "We certainly need to recruit new teachers," she told an interviewer for *Teachervision.com* (on-line). "Teachers should be paid more. We need to look at school buildings and make sure they're safe, that they are an environment that we would want our children to spend their time in. How do our schools look? Parents can help landscape schools and make sure they look really good for children." In contrast to the controversial and politically active previous First Lady, Hillary Rodham Clinton, Bush has said that she has no interest in advising her husband or pursuing her own political agenda. She even moved her office from the West Wing (where Hillary Clinton had set her up office) to another part of the White House. Although she reportedly disagrees with her husband on such subjects as abortion and the death penalty, she was quoted by John Hanchette for *USA Today* (June 23, 2001, on-line) as saying, "If I differ with my husband, I'm not going to tell you about it." In October 2001 she launched a national drive to end prejudice among schoolchildren.

Laura Bush is known for her calmness, sincerity, and politeness. "I'm not a worrier. I think it's just a temperament. People are born with their temperament, and I have that," she told *Good Housekeeping* (on-line). She quit smoking in 1992. Her hobbies are reading, gardening, and cooking. On several occasions while she was First Lady of Texas, she

went with friends on rafting trips in the Grand Canyon and birdwatching vacations in Belize. She is reputed to be compulsive about the cleanliness of her homes, which include her family's 1,600-acre ranch in Crawford, Texas. According to John F. Dickerson in *Time* (January 1, 2001), she and her husband address each other with the nickname "Bushie." "I would most like to be known as an advocate for children," she told Julie Bonnin. "I would like to help parents be very informed so they can make great decisions for their young children. I think being a parent is the most important job any of us will ever have and our relationships with our families and our children are our most important relationships." — G.O.

Suggested Reading: *Austin* [Texas] *American-Statesman* (on-line) Apr. 18, 1999, with photos; *Good Housekeeping* (on-line); *Newsweek* p42+ Nov. 22, 1999, with photo; *Texas Monthly* p120+ Nov. 1996, with photo

George DeSota/Getty Images

Calderón, Sila M.

(cal-der-OHN, SEE-la)

Sep. 23, 1942– Governor of Puerto Rico. Address: Office of the Governor, La Fortaleza, San Juan, PR 00901

On January 2, 2001 Sila M. Calderón was sworn in as governor of Puerto Rico, becoming the first woman to hold the post since the U.S. Congress, in 1952, granted Puerto Rico the power to elect its

own governor. (Puerto Rico was ceded to the U.S. at the conclusion of the Spanish-American War in 1898. Fifty-four years later its people voted in favor of U.S. Commonwealth status. One of the islands that make up the West Indies, with an overwhelmingly Hispanic population of nearly four million, the Commonwealth of Puerto Rico has a representative in Congress—though that delegate cannot vote, except in committees.) Calderón has been active in Puerto Rican politics since 1973. She became mayor of Puerto Rico's capital, San Juan, in 1996; four years later she represented the Popular Democratic Party (PPD) in a gubernatorial campaign whose platform featured two key points: the maintaining of Puerto Rico's status as a U.S. commonwealth, rather than the pursuit of statehood, and the immediate and unconditional cessation of test bombing by the U.S. Navy on the island of Vieques, located off the coast of Puerto Rico. During the campaign Calderón attacked the administration of the incumbent governor, Pedro Rosselló, for its acquiescence to naval activity as well as its desire to bring about Puerto Rican statehood, which many feared would rob the island of its cultural identity. Many political experts cited Calderón's refusal to budge on the subject of Vieques as a primary reason for her victory over the New Progressive Party (NPP) candidate, Carlos Pesquera, whom she defeated by a margin of 3.2 percent of the popular vote—or a difference of just over 53,000 votes of the almost 1.7 million ballots cast. One of the new governor's first acts was to create a noise-pollution law in direct opposition to the navy's bombing exercises, thus pressuring the U.S. government to evacuate military personnel training in the area. While the U.S. announced that it would withdraw its forces by 2003, the bombing continued, prompting Calderón to file a restraining order against the navy for acting in breach of the noise-pollution law. She spearheaded a referendum in which Vieques residents voted overwhelmingly in favor of the U.S. navy's immediate withdrawal from the island. Although the vote was ruled unconstitutional by a judge in Puerto Rico in October 2001, it fueled Calderón's cause, which drew support from prominent figures on the U.S. mainland, notably Governor George Pataki of New York.

Sila Maria Calderón was born into a wealthy family on September 23, 1942 in San Juan. Her father, César A. Calderón, was an entrepreneur whose business holdings included ice-cream factories and hotels. Her mother, Sila Serra Calderón, was a homemaker. In a New York Times article, cited by the Puerto Rico Herald (January 18, 2001, online), Calderón was quoted as saying of her childhood, "Girls of certain families didn't have to work. My American friends would work as waitresses in the summer and I would go off to Europe with my parents." The article also noted her father's admiration for the PPD and her early exposure to the rich history of her native island.

Calderón chose to attend university on the U.S. mainland, enrolling in 1960 at Manhattanville College, in Purchase, New York, a short distance from New York City. There, she studied political science, receiving her bachelor's degree with honors in 1964; her senior thesis was on Puerto Rico. She then returned to her native island and in 1970 enrolled at the University of Puerto Rico, where she earned her master's degree in public administration in 1972. (In 1989 Calderón was awarded an honorary doctorate in humane letters from Manhattanville and was named the university's most distinguished alumna.)

Calderón got her first job in politics in 1973, having impressed her labor-relations professor, who, upon being appointed Puerto Rico's secretary of labor, named Calderón as his executive assistant. She next served as special assistant for economic development to Governor Rafael Hernández Colón. During this time Calderón also worked in the private sector, as a board member of Citibank Puerto Rico. Meanwhile, her political career continued to gain momentum. In 1985 Calderón became Puerto Rico's first woman to hold the post of chief of staff of the governor's office. Over the next four years, she would become secretary of the governorship, secretary of state, and lieutenant governor. In 1988 Secretary of State Calderón—filling in for an absent Governor Hernández Colón—signed into law a measure that required workers, volunteers, and applicants at child-care centers to obtain certificates showing that they had never been convicted of felonies. In 1989 Calderón left behind a highly successful public-service career to become president of the Commonwealth Investment Co. in San Juan, where she worked until 1995. During this period Calderón also sat on the boards of directors at BanPonce, Banco Popular de Puerto Rico, and Pueblo Internacional Inc., a supermarket corporation.

Until January 1995 Calderón also directed the Cantera Peninsula project, a joint public and private operation devoted to social rehabilitation and economic development of one of the poorest areas of San Juan. This work led to her return to government later in the year, when she won the PPD nomination for mayor of San Juan. During her campaign Calderón echoed her party's opposition to Puerto Rican statehood. The next year, following her victory in the general election, she became the second female mayor in the city's history. (The first was the popular Felisa Rincón de Gautier, who held the post from 1946 to 1968.)

Much of the press coverage of Calderón's four-year tenure as mayor revolved around the Puerto Rican statehood debate between the two major political parties of Puerto Rico. Then-governor Roselló and most others in the NPP were pro-statehood, while Calderón and the PPD, of which she was now president, strongly favored maintaining Puerto Rico's status as a U.S. commonwealth. In 1998 Roselló initiated a referendum on the issue, through which he hoped to prove to the U.S. Congress that Puerto Ricans desired statehood. Calderón, for her part, urged citizens to vote "none of the above" on the December ballot, the other four choices being statehood, either of two forms of independence, and a modification of the island's commonwealth status. On the day of the balloting, 46.5 percent of voters opted for U.S. statehood while 50.2 percent voted "none of the above." The result proved a devastating blow to the already crippled Roselló, whose administration had been steeped in controversy and reports of corruption since the beginning of his second term. Still, the governor refused to acknowledge the results of the referendum as a defeat, instead arguing that votes for "none of the above" amounted to abstentions—and therefore that the majority of voters had chosen statehood. Calderón argued against the governor's position, claiming that the results of the referendum clearly showed Puerto Ricans' desire to continue the island's commonwealth status; under that arrangement, Puerto Ricans have U.S. citizenship, pay no federal taxes, and, while they are permitted to vote in U.S. national primary elections, do not have the right to do so in U.S. general elections. (Puerto Rico receives more than $13 billion in annual aid from the U.S. government.) In the New York Times (December 15, 1998), Mireya Navarro quoted Calderón as saying, "The impression that has been given outside Puerto Rico is that we live in crisis or that we feel like second-class citizens and that is not so." Calderón was also quoted by the New York Times, as reported in the Puerto Rico Herald, as saying, "We are proud of our [U.S.] citizenship and share the same love of democracy and liberty. At the same time we have our own culture we want to protect." She told Martin Kettle for the London Guardian (December 15, 1998), "We have gone to the ballot boxes and said, 'No, this country is ours.' We continue being Puerto Ricans forever. We want to live as Puerto Ricans and die as Puerto Ricans."

With regard to San Juan's economy, Calderón's record as mayor gained her popularity among both local and international business leaders. She explained to *global-review.com*, "My education and training was in political science, but my work experience has been in the private sector and so now when I focus on a problem, I do it from a business angle. . . . [Government] has to dedicate itself to the business of governing and producing results, which is the same for governments as the bottom line is for companies. In many city halls, the focus is on politics; my focus is good government." In 1999, even though San Juan stood directly in the path of Hurricane Lenny, which cost the city $22 million in damage-relief funds, the city treasury ended the year with a $9.8 million surplus.

Calderón won the Puerto Rican governorship on November 7, 2000. On the following January 2, she was officially sworn in as Puerto Rico's first female governor. Complementing her own victory, the PPD also won a majority in the Puerto Rican Congress, allowing the new governor greater leeway in pursuing her agenda. The first move Calderón made was to sign into law the Noise Regulation Act of 2001, which prohibited activities along the shores of Puerto Rico that produced noise of 190 decibels or greater. The law was in direct defiance of navy bombing on Vieques and thus, in essence, outlawed any training exercises, which the navy had been conducting on Vieques for more than 60 years. When the navy failed to stop its exercises, Calderón filed suit in the U.S. District Court for the District of Columbia.

Calderón's continuous pressure on the navy forced the hand of newly elected U.S. president George W. Bush, who soon announced his plans for the navy's gradual withdrawal from Vieques, to be completed by 2003. Calderón remained dissatisfied, citing medical reports that showed the disproportionate number of cancer victims on the island, which she has attributed to navy testing. As of November 2001 neither the navy nor Calderón had backed down on the issue. In honor of her efforts in this area, organizers of New York City's 2001 Puerto Rican Day celebration dedicated the associated parade to Governor Calderón.

Calderón lives in San Juan with her second husband, Adolfo Krans. She has three children (one son and two daughters) and five stepchildren. — J.H.

Suggested Reading: *global-review.com*; *Holland Sentinel* (on-line) Jan. 3, 2001; (London) *Guardian* p12 Dec. 15, 1998; *Miami Herald* (on-line) Jan. 2, 2001; *New York Times* I p16 Sep. 29, 1996, with photos, A p18 Sep. 19, 1997, A p16 Dec. 15, 1998; *Puerto Rico Herald* (on-line) Jan. 18, 2001, with photo; *Politico* (on-line) Feb. 23, 2001, with photo; *PR Newswire* p1 Nov. 7, 2000

Calle, Sophie

1953– Conceptual artist. Address: c/o Donald Young Gallery, 933 W. Washington Blvd., Chicago, IL 60607-2218

In 1980, when Sophie Calle was discovered almost by accident by a French art curator, she was deeply ambivalent about being an artist. Two decades and dozens of exhibitions later—including shows at the Whitechapel Art Gallery and the Tate Gallery in London, the Museum of Modern Art in New York City, and the Musée d'Art et d'Histoire in Geneva, Switzerland—Calle was still maintaining that the aim of her work was to improve and shed light on her life rather than offer self-consciously "artistic" statements. Calle is a practitioner of conceptual art, a loose term that originated in the 1960s to describe art that eschews traditional mediums. Usually, such artists avoid the imitativeness often seen in painting, sculpture, photography, and other conventional forms in favor of a direct expression of concepts. In most of her work, Calle combines text with either photography or an arrangement of objects. Much of it has a distinctly voyeuristic quality, as in *Hôtel*, for which she secretly photographed people's belongings while working as a chambermaid, and *Suite Vénitienne,* for which she followed a man through Venice, pho-

Courtesy of Donald Young Gallery, Chicago

tographing him without his knowledge. Such works, Ginger Danto wrote for *ARTnews* (May 1993), "have been variously called spying, surveillance, voyeurism, even stealing. It's as if Calle's artful interception of others' lives constitutes a form of theft or violation." Often, Calle has also turned her gaze inward, though she frequently blurs the line between autobiography and fiction, tampering with the notions of identity and point of view. She has avoided assigning explicit meanings to her works, preferring to leave that task to her audience. In the *Los Angeles Times* (April 3, 1995), David Pagel characterized the odd crosscurrents that make Calle's work challenging and compelling to many viewers: "The best way to think of Calle's work," he wrote, "is as a cross between Andy Warhol's ironic distance and Oscar Wilde's passionate insistence that artifice is an essential part of reality. Ranking among the most interesting artists today, Calle combines alienation and sincerity in fascinating narrative fragments. Her literary art bends the rules of Conceptualism, dispensing with a search for desire's origins to intensify desire's symptoms."

Sophie Calle was born in France in 1953. Her father was a physician, art collector, and critic who became director of the Carré d'Art, a museum of modern art in Nîmes. When Calle was young her parents separated; she stayed with her mother, who later became a book critic and press attaché. "From an early age," Alan Riding wrote for the *New York Times* (April 28, 1999), "Sophie Calle organized her life around rituals. She gave her goldfish and pet birds elaborate funerals, with music and tiny coffins. She demanded to be awakened with a glass of orange juice when her mother returned home from a party, no matter the hour. In the week before her grandfather's birthday she would mail him countdown letters daily."

After graduating from high school, at the age of 17, Calle traveled in the United States, Mexico, and Asia, financing her trip by working as a barmaid, field hand, and drawing model, among other jobs. In 1978, while staying with a photographer in California, she took a series of photographs of gravestones inscribed with the words "mother," "father," "brother," and "sister," and she developed a passion for photography. After she returned to France, in 1979, she had a reporter take pictures of her while she donned a blond wig and performed a striptease act at a nightclub. As has happened with many of her projects, years passed before *Le Striptease*, as it was called, went on exhibit. "My work is linked to improving my life," Calle told Riding, explaining that "art" is often a secondary purpose of her work. "I organize rituals to satisfy a specific need, to deal with fear of being alone, to get married, whatever. I have organized many that I never expected to exploit. Sometimes I used the material years later. Some I have never gone back to."

For nine days in April 1979, strangers, at her request, slept in Calle's bed while she took pictures of them in slumber—a work she called *Sleepers*. She, too, was photographed while asleep. She also kept a journal of her observations of the sleepers and recorded their answers to various questions. One of the participants showed the work to her husband, Bernard LaMarche Vadel, who, as curator of the Paris Modern Art Museum, was organizing an exhibition of young artists. At Vadel's invitation, Calle entered *Sleepers* in the show. In 1980 Calle began following people around Paris, taking pictures and recording her observations. "When I came back from traveling I felt lost in my own city," Calle told Danto. "I had forgotten everything about Paris. I had no habits. I didn't know anyone. I had no place to go, so I just decided to follow people—anybody. For the pleasure of following them, not because they particularly interested me. I allowed them to determine my route. Eventually, I became attached to these people, so I took a camera. I photographed them without their knowledge, took note of their movements, then finally lost sight of them." One evening, at an art show, Calle met a man whom she had briefly followed earlier that day before losing him in a crowd. He mentioned that he was planning a trip to Venice. Taking their unlikely meeting as a sign, Calle followed him there, without his knowledge. Disguised in a wig, she pursued him through Venice, taking pictures and notes. The work was published in her first book, *Suite Vénitienne* (1983).

Calle was by then well on her way to developing the theme of voyeurism—which served as a point of departure for examining individuals' ways of defining other people. In 1981 she took a job as a chambermaid at a Venice hotel so that she could take pictures of the guests' intimate belongings. The collected photos of those items make up her book *Hôtel* (1984). "Part of our fascination with [*Hôtel*] and *Suite Vénitienne*," Mark Durden wrote for *Art Monthly* (December 1998/January 1999), "is the way in which we are invited to participate with Calle in her voyeurism, we see from her viewpoint, we step into her shoes as it were. The work appeals to the voyeur in us, allows space for our own fantasies about other people's lives." For a 1981 exhibition called *La Filature (The Shadow)*, Calle had her mother hire a detective to follow and photograph Calle herself throughout Paris. *La Filature* marked a new trend in her work, in which she turned her voyeuristic eye on herself to reveal her intimate feelings and secrets. Calle never knew exactly when the detective planned to tail her, and he did not know that Calle knew of him. While he documented her actions, she took photos and noted her impressions. In the *Tech* (March 2, 1990), the Massachusetts Institute of Technology campus newspaper, Paul Groh reported that, as Calle revealed in her notes, she first had her hair specially fixed "to please" the photographer. "She then [took] him for an exhaustive chase through Paris in a type of flirtatious game. She want[ed] to 'show him' the places she love[d], such as the park where she received her first kiss." In the resulting exhibit, in which her photos, notes, and the photographer's pictures were displayed together, "Calle's colorful description of the day is sharply contrasted with the banal photographs and text of the detective," Groh wrote. "For Calle, the day was imbued with meaning; for the detective, the day was merely reporting the facts."

In 1983 Calle found a man's address book on the street, and after making a copy and sending him the original, she interviewed some of his acquaintances to assemble a portrait of him, titling the work *Le Carnet d'Addresses* (*The Address Notebook*). (Some sources give the title as *L'Homme au Carnet*.) Over the course of a month, without disclosing the subject's name, Calle published a written "portrait" in the Paris daily *Libération*. The man retaliated by sending a nude photo of Calle (perhaps shot during one of her stripteases) to the newspaper, which published it as a reply. Years later the man still refused to speak to Calle.

Calle's fame increased throughout the 1980s; during that decade she had solo and group shows in many parts of the world. In 1989 Deborah Irmas's book *Sophie Calle: A Survey* was published. In 1991 Calle introduced *Last Seen*, an exhibit based on the 1990 theft from the Isabella Stewart Gardner Museum, in Boston, of works by Degas, Rembrandt, Vermeer, and other artists. For *Last Seen* Calle interviewed people associated with the museum, asking them to describe the stolen works. In addition to photographs of empty pedestals, bare walls, and labels of the lost works, she displayed the transcripts of these interviews. In 1992 Calle created an exhibit called *Autobiographical Stories*, which consisted of a series of five-foot-high photographs paired with large-format descriptive texts of a purportedly autobiographical nature. For example, a photo of a crumpled wedding dress was accompanied by a text describing a tryst to which Calle had brought a wedding dress. It is unclear whether the stories are true. "What is between truth and fiction is the activity," Calle explained to Danto. "The text and images are the reports of that reality."

In 1993 Calle released her first full-length video, *Double Blind* (called *No Sex Last Night* in the United States), a collaboration with Greg Sheppard, a filmmaker whom she considered her boyfriend when she made it. She and Sheppard planned a trip across the U.S. "at a time when our relations were very tense," as Calle told Danto. "Since we did not speak to one another, the idea was to buy two small cameras and each speak to the camera, which became our partner in dialogue. . . . The idea was to do something together, even if it was creating a conduit for all the hate." They repeatedly videotaped slept-in motel beds, accompanied by Calle's mantra, "No sex last night." Toward the end of their trip, Calle persuaded Sheppard to marry her in Las Vegas; their marriage is still legally intact, though Sheppard and Calle are no longer together. The video she put together was shown at the Whitney Biennale theater and at small art houses in New York, Colorado, Austria, Italy, and elsewhere, and it received many positive reviews. John G. Hanhardt, senior curator of film and media arts

at the Solomon R. Guggenheim Museum, in New York City, called it, according to Danto, "an extraordinary first work in video, demonstrating how one can use the medium to look at oneself through one's relationship to another person." In *Esquire* (February 1993), Michael Hirschorn wrote of *Double Blind*, "As far as drawn-out postmodern conceits go . . . [it is] surprisingly compelling."

In 1994 Calle created an exhibit, called *Calle's Objects*, specifically for the Boymans–van Beuningen Museum, in Rotterdam, the Netherlands. Like many of Calle's other works, it was in part an examination of the way belongings describe their owners and help them describe themselves. On an "Acoustiguide" recording for museum-goers, Calle spoke about various objects of hers that were dispersed throughout the museum. In *Art in America* (January 1995), Tony Godfrey wrote of the exhibit, "What was most fascinating was not, as one would suppose, the way the project reconstructed the museum and Acoustiguide, but how it enlivened one's experience of the place. What anecdotes and fantasies, one wondered, were once attached to those jugs, those buckets, that 1930s bakelite telephone, etc.? The museum became a repository of lost fantasies, desires and remembered lives."

Each year from 1980 to 1993 Calle held birthday parties in which the number of guests corresponded to her age that year. After each gathering she kept her gifts displayed in a glass cabinet; the next year, she replaced the old gifts with the new ones. In 1998 she prepared for the Art Now room at the Tate Gallery, in London, a special exhibition, *The Birthday Ceremony*, which consisted of 14 cases, each filled with one year's birthday presents. Calle included perishable items, such as chocolates, as well as flowers, bottles of champagne, a matador's cape, and a book by the Marquis de Sade, among many other gifts. As Marie Anne Mancio noted in *Make, the magazine of women's art* (September/November 1998), Calle's mother subverted her project by giving her unwieldy presents—a washing machine, for example—thus forcing Calle to place in the case the manufacturer's warranty or other evidence of the gift rather than the gift itself. Once again blurring the line between fact and fiction, Calle admitted that not all the items had been given to her as gifts. "The result is more than an aesthetic collection of covetable objects," Marie Anne Mancio wrote, "it succeeds in provoking questions about the efficacy of gifts as indicators of identity; for instance, does a present tell us more about the donor than the receiver?"

Also in 1998 Calle created an installation called *Double Game*, in collaboration with the novelist Paul Auster. Auster's 1992 novel, *Leviathan*, featured a character named Maria who was based on Calle. Among the projects Maria undertakes in the novel are "The Chromatic Diet," for which, each day for a certain period, she eats foods of a single color, and "Days Under the Sign of B, C & W," in which she structures her days around letters of the alphabet. For "C," for example, Maria spends the day at Montparnesse Cemetery at her future tomb, on which the words "Ciao, Ciao" are inscribed. After reading the novel, Calle asked Auster to create a fictional character whose identity Calle could assume. In response, he offered her a set of guidelines, titled "Personal Instructions for S. C. on How to Improve Life in New York City (Because She Asked)." Among the five pages of instructions was the suggestion that she "cultivate a spot." Calle chose to "improve" a phone booth by cleaning it up and putting in it some flowers, a chair, a notebook and pencils, an ashtray, a magazine, and a sign that read, "Have a Nice Day." Photographs of the booth, along with a written record of people's comments on her additions, were included in Calle's *Double Game* installation, which was exhibited at the Camden Arts Centre, in London, among other places. Calle also included copies of Auster's guidelines and her descriptions of how she had executed the project. Life-size re-creations of previous installations of Calle's that Auster had described in *Leviathan* were presented alongside highlighted text in relevant passages of the book. Calle's book about the installation, also called *Double Game*, was published in 1998. Debora Miller wrote of the book in *Library Journal* (October 1, 2000), "It is both unusual and thrilling to witness an exchange between artists of such high caliber from different fields, and this stimulating duel of wit and inventiveness is loaded with details, keen observations, and fascinating imagery. Beautifully designed, the book is chock-full of photographs, lists, and notes documenting Calle's investigations."

In 1999 Calle was invited to prepare an exhibition for the Freud Museum in London, located at the site of the home and office of Sigmund Freud, the founder of psychoanalysis. "After having a vision of my wedding dress laid across Freud's couch, I immediately accepted," Calle recalled, as quoted on the *Amazon.com* Web site for a book based on the exhibit, *Appointment: Sophie Calle and Sigmund Freud* (2001). In the exhibition in London, Calle interspersed among Freud's belongings her own texts, many of them comical, and objects from her life, including the blond wig she had worn as a stripper. According to Alan Riding, before the opening Calle worried that the show would be considered irreverent, but critics and the public gave it good notices.

Calle lives and works alternately in New York City and outside Paris. — P.G.H.

Suggested Reading: *Art in America* p109 Jan. 1995; *Art Monthly* p29+ Dec. 1998/Jan. 1999; *ARTnews* p100+ May 1993; *Esquire* p19 Feb. 1993; *Interview* p126 Oct. 2001; *Library Journal* p86+ Oct. 1, 2000; *Los Angeles Times* p10 Apr. 3, 1995; *Make, the magazine of women's art* p27 Sep./Nov. 1998, p37+ Mar./May 1999; *New York Times* C p17 Feb. 29, 1993, p1 Apr. 28, 1999; *Village Voice* p62+ Oct. 12, 1993

Selected Books: *Suite Vénitienne*, 1983; *Hôtel*, 1984; *Des Histoires Vraies*, 1994; *Double Game*, 1998; *Souvenirs de Berlin-Est*, 1999; *Absence*, 2000; *Disparitions*, 2000; *Fantômes*, 2000

Canin, Ethan

July 19, 1960– Writer; educator. Address: Graduate Program in Creative Writing, University of Iowa, 102 Dey House, 507 N. Clinton St., Iowa City, IA 52242-1408

The writer Ethan Canin is perhaps best known for *Emperor of the Air* (1988), a collection of nine short stories that reminded many critics and readers of the fiction of John Cheever. Observers noted the maturity of Canin's voice as he wrote about characters ranging from the adolescent son of a grocer to a biology and astronomy teacher in his late 60s. The volume, Canin's first, became a surprise bestseller, unusual enough for a writer's first book but even more rare for a collection of stories; it also earned him the prestigious Houghton Mifflin literary fellowship, which is given periodically to beginning writers of exceptional promise. (Previous recipients include such literary heavyweights as Robert Penn Warren, Elizabeth Bishop, Philip Roth, and Edward Hoagland.) In a review of *Emperor of the Air* for the *Washington Post* (January 20, 1988), Jonathan Yardley wrote, "The phrase 'auspicious debut' has for so long been used so casually and frequently by reviewers that it no longer means anything; this is a pity, for Canin's debut is indeed auspicious." Christopher Lehmann-Haupt also offered critical praise for the book, writing in the *New York Times* (January 25, 1988), "The way these stories transcend the ordinariness of human voices is . . . startling."

At the time of the book's publication, Canin was a 27-year-old, fourth-year medical student at Harvard University. For the next few years, he juggled his medical and literary careers before turning to writing full-time. In addition to *Emperor of the Air*, Canin is the author of *Blue River* (1991), *The Palace Thief* (1994), *For Kings and Planets* (1998), and *Carry Me Across the Water* (2001).

Of Jewish descent, Ethan Canin was born on July 19, 1960 in Ann Arbor, Michigan. His father, Stuart, was a violinist, and his mother, Virginia, a painter. The family moved several times during Canin's youth, following his father's musical pursuits first to Oberlin, Ohio, and then to Philadelphia before settling down in San Francisco, where Canin spent most of his childhood. His writing talents were first noticed while he attended the San

Jane Martin/Courtesy of Random House

Ethan Canin

Francisco University High School; one of his teachers, Danielle Steel, who would go on to win fame as a romance novelist, wrote the following appraisal of Canin's abilities, as quoted by *Publishers Weekly* (December 18, 1987): "Ethan has an extraordinary gift for writing. His work is nothing short of marvelous, crystal clear, perfect in nuance, adept in delivery." Canin received an "A" from Steel for his assignments, a "B+" for effort, and an "A+" for his final project. "I was so flattered," Canin told William Goldstein for the *Publishers Weekly* article, going on to explain his perplexity over Steel's approval of his work. "The stuff is terrible," Canin admitted. "I don't know what the other kids could have been doing to make me get an A."

Upon graduation from high school, Canin dismissed his teacher's suggestion that he follow a career in writing. Instead, he enrolled at Stanford University, in Stanford, California, to pursue a degree in engineering. In an interview for the *Writer* (May 2000), Canin told Lewis Burke Frumkes that his continuing to write was an accident. "I wandered into an English class one day," he recalled, "simply because it was listed on the next page in the course catalogue after engineering. I was looking for another class and ended up taking a creative writing course. . . . I began reading the stories of John Cheever, and that changed my life. Suddenly, I just wanted to be a writer." Like Steel, Canin's Stanford professors enjoyed his writing—enough to send two of his stories, on his behalf, to magazines, where both were accepted. One, called "Abe, Between Rounds," appeared in *Redbook* in August 1981.

After receiving his bachelor's degree, Canin entered the University of Iowa's esteemed Writers' Workshop, an M.F.A. (master of fine arts) program. The workshop was not what he had expected. In an interview with Jane Rosenzweig for the *Atlantic Online* (November 25, 1998), Canin recalled his unhappiness as well as his disillusionment during this two-year period. "I wrote almost nothing when I was in the workshop," Canin told Rosenzweig, "and I learned nothing. I was paralyzed—utterly paralyzed." Some of his memories of the Iowa Writers' Workshop, however, were positive. "At the same time," he continued, "I know I wouldn't have been a writer if I hadn't come to the Iowa workshop. . . . Iowa is sometimes overwhelming, but when you leave you look back on your days here with nostalgia. You have two years to wander around this little Midwestern town with a hundred other impractical romantics, worrying about your next paragraph. Where else are you going to find that life?"

By the time he received his M.F.A. degree, Canin had all but given up on his career as a writer. He began taking undergraduate classes in order to fulfill his requirements for medical school, crediting the novelist John Irving with influencing his decision. He told Frumkes, "John Irving came to give a class. He read one of my stories and didn't like it at all. . . . I wondered, 'What have I done here?' I had a scientific background. I liked people, basically. And in a colossal failure of imagination, I went to medical school." In an interview with Nicholas A. Basbanes for *LitKit* (1998, on-line), Canin explained, "Writing had always been my first love, and the only reason I went into medicine in the first place was because I feared I could never support myself as a writer."

In 1984 Canin entered medical school at Harvard University, in Cambridge, Massachusetts. While there, far from abandoning his writing, he not only continued to produce short stories but had them published in such high-profile magazines as the *Atlantic*, *Esquire*, and *Ploughshares*. His work was also anthologized in the 1985 and 1986 editions of *Best American Short Stories*. During this time the publishing company Houghton Mifflin approached Canin with the idea of bringing out a collection of his work. Canin told Rosenzweig that he wrote most of *Emperor of the Air* during his first year at Harvard, "because I wasn't supposed to be writing. Miraculous trick. The idea of invention when you're in medical school is just beyond the pale." In his review of *Emperor of the Air* for the *New York Times*, Christopher Lehmann-Haupt wrote, "One can't help noting gratefully how much these remarkable stories are preoccupied with matters of ultimate concern—of life and death, of youth and aging, of wealth and poverty and of the heart not only as the seat of human emotions but also as the organ that pumps lifeblood through the system." Jonathan Yardley agreed, writing in the *Washington Post*, "Canin produces . . . evidence of unusual maturity." For *Emperor of the Air,*

Canin won the Heinfield Transatlantic Review Award in 1989, the same year that he was given a National Endowment for the Arts grant.

Following the overwhelmingly positive reception of *Emperor of the Air*, Canin took a year's leave from medical school in order to concentrate on his next writing project. He traveled to Quito, Ecuador, and spent the better part of 1988 producing his first novel, which would be published three years later as *Blue River*. This book focuses on Edward and Lawrence Sellers, two very different brothers who are reunited after 15 years. *Blue River* received decidedly mixed reviews. Many critics, while judging the book to be good for a first novel, expressed their preference for his earlier work. In the *New York Times* (October 10, 1991), Christopher Lehmann-Haupt described *Blue River* as "promising but flawed" and added, "You have a wonderful future as a writer, Ethan Canin, but in *Blue River* you slipped." Jonathan Yardley, in the *Washington Post* (October 23, 1991), reached a similar conclusion: "[*Blue River*] is a narrative long on psychologizing but short on vivid character and incident—by no means a bad book, but well short of what its author is capable."

Canin continued to pursue a career in medicine. He graduated from Harvard Medical School in 1992 and immediately moved back to San Francisco, undertaking a residency at the University of California San Francisco Medical Center. Writing, though, remained very much a part of his life. Over the next three years, he would divide his time among pursuing a medical career, teaching writing at the University of Michigan, the University of Iowa, and San Francisco State University, and completing his third literary offering, *The Palace Thief* (1994), a collection of four novellas and the winner of the 1994 Commonwealth Club Gold Medal for Literature. Most critics agreed that *The Palace Thief* represented Canin's return to form and at least a partial fulfillment of the promise he had shown with *Emperor of the Air*. Dan Cryer wrote for *New York Newsday* (February 21, 1994), "Ethan Canin's achievement is one of both artistry and humanity." Abby Frucht in the *New York Times* (February 20, 1994) also praised *The Palace Thief*, writing, "Mr. Canin watches over his characters in much the same way that if you believe in God, you might imagine Him hovering over humankind—biting His mischievous tongue, stepping aside as we make our most touching, our most devastating mistakes."

As with his earlier works, publicists for this book took advantage of a selling point that went beyond the quality of the writing: the fact that Canin was a young, handsome doctor. He embarked on an extensive promotional tour. Joanne Kaufman, in the *Wall Street Journal* (March 22, 1994), explained why Canin's readings often attracted "many bookish young women," writing, "Mr. Canin is 33 years old and a hunk." While he was uncomfortable with all the attention, Canin found that the experience increased his confidence as a writer. In 1995 he left his post at the hospital and took on writing full-time. "I got halfway through my medical residency," he told John Kenyon for *IowaAlive.com*, "but I realized that if I became a practicing doctor, I wouldn't ever write again." The decision, though, was not an easy one to make. Indeed, the prospect of leaving the medical profession behind "terrified him," Robin Pogrebin reported in the *New York Times* (November 10, 1998). Canin explained to her, "I was leaving the most secure job in the world for the least secure, leaving a job I knew I could do for a job I still to this day have no idea whether I can do."

An opportunity that arose the next year, 1996, helped to calm Canin's fears: he was offered a tenured teaching position at the Iowa Writers' Workshop, from which he had graduated 12 years earlier. In addition to the financial security it provided, the position allowed Canin to maintain the flexible schedule he needed to finish his second novel, *For Kings and Planets* (1998). The story revolves around the characters Orno Tarcher and Marshall Emerson, freshmen at Columbia University in 1974. Orno is a wide-eyed midwesterner who is dazzled by his new friend Marshall, the son of two Columbia professors with connections to the Kennedy family. The book is a study in the attraction of opposites, one that Greg Johnson, in a review for the *Washington Post* (September 12, 1998), called "skillfully evoke[d]." Even more than *Blue River*, however, *For Kings and Planets* inspired a full spectrum of responses from critics. Lehmann-Haupt, writing for the *New York Times* (September 10, 1998), called the new book "shimmering" and concluded, "*For Kings and Planets* leaves you wounded and healed." Three days later, though, Rand Richards Cooper proclaimed in the *New York Times Book Review* (September 13, 1998) that the book was "a greedy monster of a novel that swallows up its creator's virtues and leaves only his weaknesses on display. . . . [Canin] should file *For Kings and Planets* under Lessons Learned and move on."

Canin's most recent book is *Carry Me Across the Water* (2001), a short but complex novel whose main character, August Kleinman, is a 78-year-old widower trying to make sense of his life. A number of critics agreed that the novel was less successful than some of Canin's earlier work. Michiko Kakutani of the *New York Times* (May 4, 2001) wrote, "This novel suffers from a certain lack of passion. It's a highly professional, highly polished performance, but in the end it remains just that: a performance that's conscientious and carefully fashioned, but somehow not deeply heartfelt." Kakutani concluded that the life of the story's hero was "devoid of any real interest." Other reviewers, however, were more generous. Carmela Ciuraru, in the *Wall Street Journal* (May 11, 2001), conceding that Canin had not "entirely sorted out Kleinman's jumble of memories," nonetheless called the book "compelling for its sensitive, elegiac portrayal of aging and grief."

A film version of the title story from *The Palace Thief*, starring Kevin Kline, will be released by Universal Studios in early 2002. Canin will have a cameo role in the movie. He currently resides in Iowa City, Iowa, with his wife, Barbara, and their two children. — J.H.

Suggested Reading: *Los Angeles Times* E p1 May 22, 2001; *New York Times* E p9 Sep. 10, 1998, with photo, VII p12 Sep. 13, 2001; *Publishers Weekly* p19+ Dec. 18, 1987, with photo; *Washington Post* C p2 Jan. 20, 1988; *Writer* p19+ May 2000; *Contemporary Authors* vol. 135, 1992

Selected Books: *Emperor of the Air*, 1988; *Blue River*, 1991; *The Palace Thief*, 1994; *For Kings and Planets*, 1998; *Carry Me Across the Water*, 2001

John Spellman/Retna Ltd.

Capriati, Jennifer
(cap-ree-AH-tee)

Mar. 29, 1976– Tennis player. Address: c/o Saddlebrook Resort, 5700 Saddlebrook Way, Wesley Chapel, FL 33543

Jennifer Capriati's career in tennis has had two distinct phases. The first began three weeks shy of her 14th birthday, when she turned professional and became an overnight sensation in the game. Faring well against experienced players, she won the hearts of spectators with her ponytail and infectious grin. Four months before she turned 15, she was ranked among the top 10 in women's tennis, thus becoming the youngest professional ever to

achieve that level. At 16 she won the gold medal in women's singles tennis at the 1992 Summer Olympic Games. Then, after a dismal performance in the 1993 U.S. Open, when she was 17, she virtually abandoned the game. During the next 14 months, she had highly publicized run-ins with the law and even contemplated suicide. The second phase of Capriati's career began in November 1994, with her initially fitful return to the sport. Her performance improved markedly later in the decade, after she began training with a new coach and undertook a rigorous exercise regime. She again reached the top tier of international tennis in 2001, when she won both the Australian and the French Opens. (She was the first woman to accomplish that feat since Steffi Graf in 1988.) "I'm glad [my troubles] happened when I was younger, because I was still young enough to come back and play tennis," she told Laura Okmin for *CNNSI.com* (February 5, 2001). "That's what I found myself really missing—just being out there, the excitement, competing, being in front of the public, performing." Speaking of her life in tennis, she told Christopher Gerby for *tennis-ontheline.com* (February 1, 2001), "I wouldn't trade it. It is interesting and I've had a lot of opportunities that other people don't get."

Born on March 29, 1976 in New York City, Jennifer Capriati is the older of the two children of Stefano Capriati, an Italian-born actor and stuntman, and his American-born wife, Denise, a flight attendant. After the birth of her brother, Steven, the Capriati family relocated to Florida. Stefano Capriati, a club-level tennis competitor, noticed his daughter's flair for the game when she was three years old, and not long afterward, in 1980, he persuaded Jimmy Evert, a tennis instructor and the father of the 1970s tennis sensation Chris Evert, to take on Jennifer as a pupil. At age seven Jennifer began playing in junior tournaments, where, as her father told Doug Smith for *USA Today* (March 6, 1990), "she lost [in the] first round every week." But she was in love with the game and continued to train with Jimmy Evert, developing powerful ground strokes and a two-handed backhand that became one of her signature moves. At 11 she was unrivaled in her age category and often presented a threat to players five or six years her senior. Competing against teenagers up to age 18, she won the U.S. Clay Court and Hard Court Championships when she was 12. Stefano Capriati petitioned the Women's International Tennis Association (WITA) to allow his daughter to turn professional 18 months before the minimum age of 14, but his request was denied, and Jennifer continued to play on the junior circuit. During the 1989 tennis season, she won the French Open junior title, on clay, becoming, at 13, that event's youngest winner. (Capriati held that distinction until 1993, when the 12-year-old Martina Hingis won the French Open junior title.) Also in 1989 Capriati won the U.S. Open junior title, on a hard court, and reached the quarterfinal of the grass-court Wimbledon junior event in singles; she and her partner, Meredith Mc-Grath, won the junior doubles title at both Wimbledon and the U.S. Open.

Thanks to a change in WITA's rules that allowed girls to become professionals in the month of their 14th birthday, in early March 1990 Capriati turned professional. She had already signed endorsement deals for Prince tennis rackets and Diadora tennis shoes and apparel. Cheered by Chris Evert and advised by her tournament doubles partner, Billie Jean King, Capriati played in her first professional event, the Virginia Slims tournament of Florida, that same month. "I'm really excited," she told Doug Smith. "I know I'm going to a new level. I'm just so psyched. I hope I go out there and do really well." Displaying verve and mental toughness, Capriati played aggressively as she streaked into the finals, before capitulating, 6–4, 7–5, to Gabriela Sabatini, a 1988 U.S. Open finalist and—at age 22—a top contender in women's tennis. In June 1990 Capriati competed in the French Open, the first Grand Slam event of her fledgling professional career. (The other Grand Slam competitions are the Australian Open, the U.S. Open, and the Wimbledon Championships, held in London, England.) Capriati was the youngest competitor ever to reach the semifinals, where she lost to the 16-year-old Monica Seles, 6–2, 6–2. Fighting off five match points in the final game had given her hope of a comeback, she told Thomas Bonk for the *Houston Chronicle* (June 8, 1990): "I thought if I kept fighting, maybe I could win the game and the next one and that game and that game and that game and then get back into the match." Later that summer she made it to the fourth round at Wimbledon, where she was both the youngest seeded player (12th) in Grand Slam history and the youngest to win a match at Wimbledon. Less than six months after beginning her professional career, she had earned almost $190,000 in prize money and had concluded endorsement deals worth more than $2 million. In October of her debut season, she won the Puerto Rico Open, defeating Zina Garrison and thus becoming the fourth-youngest player to win a professional event. At the age of 14 years, 235 days, she garnered a top-10 ranking in women's tennis.

Capriati set another record in 1991, when, as the youngest woman ever to reach the Wimbledon semifinals, she defeated the nine-time Wimbledon champion, Martina Navratilova, in the fourth round. (Navratilova had not suffered a defeat so early in the tournament since 1977.) Capriati defeated Monica Seles in the final of a tournament in San Diego, in July, but then lost to Seles, 6–3, 3–6, 7–6 (7–3), in the semifinal of the U.S. Open later that year, in an epic match in which Capriati again was the youngest female semifinalist ever to compete. After she won the Canadian Open, the U.S. media hailed her as the nation's most promising hopeful in women's tennis.

Capriati's third professional season, 1992, was the first in which she played in every Grand Slam event. She did not make it past the quarterfinals in any of the four events, but with her earnings at Wimbledon, she became the youngest player to reach $1 million in career winnings. (Martina Hingis broke that record later in the 1990s.) One of the highlights of her career came at the 1992 Summer Olympics, in Barcelona, Spain, where she won the gold medal in singles tennis by defeating Steffi Graf, 3–6, 6–3, 6–4.

Capriati's reign as a princess of international tennis began to falter in 1993. For the second year in a row, she failed to advance past the quarterfinals in any of the Grand Slam events. Her relationship with the press became increasingly strained, as she came under fire for her lackluster performances, weight gain, and even flaws in her complexion. As Jody Goldstein wrote for the *Houston Chronicle* (March 21, 1993), "Every pimple or imperfection on the teen-age face was a major catastrophe, thanks to an endorsement contract with Oil of Olay skin products." "Everything felt like a fairy tale in the beginning," Capriati told Goldstein. "Then people came to realize that I really am a real person. Maybe I'm not the perfect thing . . . they thought I was in the beginning." Rumors circulated about Capriati's loss of fitness and her tense relationship with her father, who was also serving as one of her coaches. The nadir of this phase of her career occurred in the first round of the 1993 U.S. Open, held in September, when she was ousted by the Russian qualifier, Leila Meskhi. In an August 31, 1993 interview archived on *FastScripts* (online), Meskhi noted that Capriati had made many mistakes and had soon exhibited signs of serious fatigue. "I started out OK, but at the end of the match I couldn't wait to get off the court," Capriati told a *New York Times* reporter, as quoted in the *Los Angeles Times* (September 26, 1994). "Totally, mentally, I just lost it, and obviously it goes deeper than just one match. I really was not happy with myself, my tennis, my life, my parents, my coaches, my friends. . . . When I looked in my mirror, I actually saw this distorted image: I was so ugly and fat, I just wanted to kill myself, really." Her confidence shattered, Capriati walked away from tennis after the U.S. Open.

Capriati returned to Florida and became a full-time student at Pasco County High School. In December 1993 she was cited for shoplifting an inexpensive ring from a Tampa, Florida, department store; she denied the charge, maintaining that she had inadvertently left the store with the ring after trying it on. Following that incident her parents arranged for her admission to a psychiatric hospital for a two-week evaluation. "She emerged from her involuntary stay bitter and angry," Julie Cart reported in the *Los Angeles Times* (January 19, 1996). Six months later, in May 1994, Capriati was arrested at a motel in Coral Gables, Florida, on charges of possession of marijuana. Her mug shot, disseminated worldwide by the news media, showed her with disheveled clothes, glazed eyes, and a nose ring—seemingly the antithesis of the smiling, perky, pony-tailed teenage tennis phenomenon of a year or two before. Capriati did not serve time in jail for the misdemeanor charge but was ordered to participate in an in-patient drug-rehabilitation program. At that point her corporate sponsors dissolved her contracts. Speaking of the period that followed her arrest and rehabilitation, Capriati told Cindy Shmerler for *Tennis* magazine (May 2000), "The worst part is what I went through afterwards, with all the media attention. Just the total reaction, my reputation going down the drain." Capriati has never offered, even to her parents, a full explanation of her thoughts and actions during this period. She has admitted, however, to caving in to peer pressure and has attributed the poor choices she made to her youthfulness.

Later in 1994 Capriati decided that she wanted to play tennis again, but on her own terms. Tennis, she told the *New York Times* interviewer, "[is] just a game to me now. I don't care about being No. 1, but I'm ready and willing to give it a battle." Reportedly suffering from a groin injury, she delayed her comeback from September to November 1994, when she played at an event in Philadelphia. She lost a three-set match to Anke Huber in the first round; nevertheless, she said after the match, as quoted by Julie Cart, "I learned I really love this game and it doesn't matter to me if I win or lose." After the Philadelphia tournament she disappeared from the tennis scene again. Conflicting reports emerged regarding her physical condition, the identity of her coach, and her plans, if any, to return to professional tennis. Capriati did not play a single professional match in 1995, the year in which her parents divorced.

Rumors that Capriati would receive special dispensation to play on the U.S. Olympic tennis team in July 1996 and defend her gold medal proved unfounded. She returned to competition by participating in a 1996 tournament in Essen, Germany, where she reached the quarterfinals before succumbing to Jana Novotna in three sets. Capriati nosed back into the women's tennis rankings, at 103d, in April 1996 and hovered there, despite first-round losses at both the French Open and the U.S. Open. (She withdrew from Wimbledon because of an injury.) During a tournament in Chicago, she reached her first final in three years, before losing once again to Novotna. Injuries to a hip sidelined Capriati for two of the 1997 Grand Slams, and she lost in the first round of both the Australian Open and U.S. Open. During the 1998 tennis season she did not compete at the first two Grand Slams and fared poorly in the others, losing in the second round of Wimbledon and the first round of the U.S. Open.

Soon afterward Capriati began training with Harold Solomon, whose earlier students included Mary Joe Fernandez, who ranked number four in women's tennis for a total of about three months in 1990 and 1991, and Jim Courier, who ranked number one in men's tennis for a year and a half in 1992–93. Capriati also started working out with a personal trainer; she shed nearly 30 pounds, thereby regaining a sleek, muscular physique. "I was sick of losing," she told Robin Finn for the *New York Times* (September 5, 1999), describing her thoughts at the beginning of her intensified training, "sick of not reaching my full potential that I think I can reach still." Although she was defeated in her first several tournaments of 1999, including a second-round loss at the Australian Open, Capriati won a tune-up event for the French Open, in Strasbourg, as well as one in Quebec City. During the French Open she surged through the first three rounds before falling to Lindsay Davenport in the fourth. After a second-round exit at Wimbledon, she played at the U.S. Open, where she defeated the 1997 French Open champion, Iva Majoli; Seda Noorlander, her nemesis at that year's Wimbledon; and Nathalie Tauziat, the 11th seed. In a fourth-round match that reprised the 1991 semifinal, Capriati faced Seles and lost again, 6–4, 6–3. Perhaps the hardest part of the U.S. Open for Capriati was the post-match interview. She had prepared a statement requesting that the media stop asking questions about her turbulent adolescent years. "I feel like I've started a new chapter in my life, and I need to leave the past behind," the statement read in part, as quoted by Cindy Shmerler. But the press ignored her plea, and Capriati left the interview in tears. She explained to Shmerler, "I know from now on that everything I do won't always be interpreted the way I want it to be."

By the end of 1999, Capriati's world ranking had rebounded to 23. She opened the 2000 Grand Slam season with a semifinal showing at the Australian Open, which she reached by winning matches against Dominique Van Roost, Patty Schnyder, and Ai Sugiyama. In the semifinals she was defeated by Lindsay Davenport, the number-two seed in the tournament, in a 6–2, 7–6 (4) loss. She did not fare as well in the remaining Grand Slams of the year, but she was a finalist at the Bell Challenge, in Quebec City, and the winner of an event in Luxembourg. At the end of 2000, she was ranked 14th, her highest level since 1993. At around that time she ended her professional relationship with Harold Solomon and reinstalled her father as her primary coach. "I have so much confidence in him," Capriati told a reporter for *Real Sports* magazine (2000, on-line). "My dad started me playing tennis. My game is because of what he taught me."

Capriati started the 2001 season with a bang, finally capturing, at age 24 in the Australian Open, her first Grand Slam win. Seeded 12th in the event, she faced Monica Seles for the sixth time in Grand Slam events and emerged victorious from their quarterfinal match, 5–7, 6–4, 6–3. In the semifinals she defeated the defending champion, Lindsay Davenport, 6–3, 6–4, and in the final she eliminated the 1999 Australian Open winner and number-one seed, Martina Hingis, 6–4, 6–3. "Who would've thought that I would have ever made it here after so much has happened?" Capriati exclaimed during the trophy ceremony at center court, as quoted on *CNNSI.com* (January 26, 2001).

"Dreams do come true if you keep believing in yourself. Anything can happen." Continuing her comeback, she reached the finals of tournaments in Oklahoma City and Miami. Her next great triumph was on the clay courts of the French Open; seeded fourth, she beat the 12th-seeded Belgian Kim Clijsters in a marathon match of more than two hours. "I never thought I'd be standing here 11 years later, after playing my first time here when I was 14 years old," she said during the trophy presentation, as quoted on *ESPN.com* (June 9, 2001). "Really, I'm just waiting to wake up from this dream." At Wimbledon, where Capriati was hoping to capture a third Grand Slam win, she was upset in a semifinal by a young Belgian player, Justine Henin, 2–6, 6–4, 6–2. In the final major of the season, the second-seeded Capriati advanced to the semifinals of the U.S. Open, where she was upset by the fourth-seeded Venus Williams, who went on to win the event. Despite the loss, heading into the 2002 season, Capriati remained among the top five players in women's tennis.

Capriati has been romantically linked to the Belgian tennis player Xavier Malisse. She lives in Wesley Chapel, Florida, with her dogs, and enjoys reading, watching movies, skiing, and playing tennis with her brother, Steven, a college player for the University of Arizona. — K.S.

Suggested Reading: *CNNSI.com* Jan. 26, 2001, Feb. 5, 2001; *ESPN.com* June 9, 2001; *New York Times* VIII p1 Sep. 5, 1999, with photo, A1, D7 June 9, 2001, with photo; *People* p54+ Feb. 12, 2001, with photo; *Sports Illustrated* p52+ June 18, 2001, with photo; *Tennis* p89+ Sep. 1997, with photo, p89+ Sep. 1997, with photos, p14+ Sep. 1998, with photo, p10 Nov. 1999, with photo, p106+ May 2000, with photo, p139+ July/Aug. 2001, with photo; *USA Today* C p1 Mar. 6, 1990

Eddie Adams/Outline Press

Castro, Fidel

Aug. 13, 1926– President of Cuba. Address: c/o Cuban Interests Section, Swiss Embassy, 2630 16th St., N.W., Washington, DC 20009

NOTE: Two earlier articles about Fidel Castro appeared in *Current Biography* in 1958 and 1970, respectively.

On January 2, 1959, 33-year-old Fidel Castro accomplished the unthinkable: he led a small band of rebel troops to victory against an army of 30,000 professional soldiers, marching into the Cuban capital of Havana and proclaiming himself leader of a provisional government. It was a victory that the historian Herbert L. Matthews would describe as "a true epic, without parallel in the Western Hemisphere." Although Castro then espoused the idea of a democratic-socialist state, within a few years he had come to embrace Marxism-Leninism. Cuba as rebuilt by Castro became a mass of contradictions: a state that depended on the Soviet Union for aid yet rabidly criticized its benefactor; a nation in which vast improvements were made in healthcare and other areas affecting the working class while human rights were constantly violated. Attempting to promote revolutions in regions throughout the world, Castro has lent troops to dozens of rebel forces, ranging from those in Angola, in Africa, to the Sandinistas in Nicaragua, in Central America. As the 21st century dawned, however, Castro had become an isolated figure. With the Soviet Union undergoing reform in the 1980s before collapsing in the early 1990s, Cuba has been left without its main ally and trade partner. Castro is now the only remaining head of state in the Americas to wear a military uniform as well as the last to decry a free-market economy. While pundits have predicted his downfall dozens of times, he has weathered several internal threats, U.S.-sponsored assassination attempts, economic woes, and the worldwide collapse of communism to enter the new millennium with a seemingly firm grip on power in the last Communist state in the Western world.

Fidel Castro Ruz—whose countrymen generally refer to him by his given name—was born on August 13, 1926 (some sources give the year as 1927) on his family's sugar plantation, near Birán, on the northern coast of Cuba's Oriente Province. His father, Angel Castro y Argiz, who had come as an immigrant laborer from Galicia, Spain, eventually acquired an estate of more than 23,000 acres. (When Castro visited Galicia in 1992, he was quoted in the London *Guardian* [July 29, 1992] as saying, "It doesn't sound too good to say I am the son of a land-owner, so let us rather say I am the grandson of exploited Galician peasants.") After the death of his first wife—who had borne him two children, Lidia and Pedro Emilio—Angel Castro married Lina Ruz González, the family cook in the Castro household, who was also of Galician background. Their children are Angela; Agustina; Ramón (an official in the Cuban agrarian-reform program); Fidel; Raúl (who is vice president of Cuba); Ernma; and Juana (who opposed her brother's policies and defected to the United States in 1964).

As a boy Castro worked in the sugarcane fields on his father's estate. His scantily educated parents apparently had no intention of sending him to school, but Fidel was so determined to obtain an education that at six or seven he talked them into letting him do so. In Santiago de Cuba he attended the Colegio Lasalle and the Colegio Dolores, both Jesuit institutions. After graduating from the latter, in 1942, he entered the Colegio Belén, a Jesuit preparatory school in Havana, where he excelled in Spanish, history, and agricultural studies and was voted the school's best athlete for 1944.

In 1945 Castro enrolled in the Faculty of Law at the University of Havana, where he studied civil law, diplomacy, public administration, and the social sciences and became president of the militant University Students' Federation. In September 1947 he took time out from his studies to participate in an unsuccessful attempt to overthrow the Dominican Republic dictatorship of Generalissimo Rafael Trujillo. In April 1948, as one of the organizers of a student congress at Bogotá, Colombia, Castro took part in the violent uprising known as the Bogotazo. Because of his then-liberal political orientation, he occasionally clashed with Communists in the student movement. Castro recalled in a speech in December 1961 that his ideological development as a Marxist did not fully take form until after he had come into power.

After obtaining his doctoral degree in law from the university, in 1950, Castro established a law practice in Havana with two partners. As a lawyer he championed the poor and disadvantaged. A member of the Partido del Pueblo Cubano—also known as Partido Ortodoxo—which was founded by the liberal reformer Eduardo Chibás, Castro became a candidate for a parliamentary seat representing a Havana constituency in the national election scheduled for June 1952. The elections were canceled, however, when, on March 10, 1952, General Fulgencio Batista overthrew the government of President Carlos Prío Socarrás in a coup d'état and established a military dictatorship. The new government terminated a case against forced labor on the part of enlisted soldiers on the estates of army officers and civil officials, which Castro had brought to the courts.

After the coup Castro submitted a petition to the Court of Constitutional Guarantees, in which he charged that the dictator had violated the Constitution of 1940 through his seizure of power. The court rejected the petition, ruling that "revolution is the fount of law." Having failed to end the dictatorship by legal means, Castro helped to organize a rebel force of young idealists, dedicated to democracy and social justice and to the 1940 Constitution.

On July 26, 1953 a force of some 165 men led by Castro attacked the Moncada Barracks in Santiago de Cuba with the hope of fomenting a popular revolt in Oriente Province. Both that attack and an accompanying raid against the Bayamo garrison ended disastrously for the rebels, half of whom were killed while most of the rest, including Fidel Castro and his brother Raúl, were imprisoned. After conducting his own defense with an impassioned speech ending with the words "La historia me absolverá" ("History will absolve me"), Fidel Castro was sent to the Isle of Pines to serve a 15-year sentence. Commenting on the Moncada attack, Herbert Matthews wrote in his book *Fidel Castro* (1969) that it had "a similar significance for the Cuban Revolution as the fall of the Bastille eventually had for the French Revolution."

Released under a general amnesty on May 15, 1955, Castro tried for a time to conduct his campaign against the Batista regime on a nonviolent level, but the government blocked his access to the mass media. In July he went to Mexico City, where, amid harassment by Mexican authorities, he organized Cuban exiles into what became known as the 26th of July Movement. In Mexico City he met Ernesto "Ché" Guevara, a young Argentine physician, who was to become a key figure in the Cuban revolutionary movement. On December 2, 1956 on the yacht *Granma*, acquired with money contributed by former president Prío Socarrás, Castro landed on the north coast of Oriente Province with a force of 82 men.

The invaders were again badly defeated—with only 12 men, including the Castros and Guevara, remaining of the original force. Nevertheless, that handful of survivors gained a foothold in the Sierra Maestra mountains, where they waged continuous guerrilla warfare against the Batista government with a growing force of volunteers. The timing could not have been better, as revolutionary dissent was rising among certain groups in Cuba, especially among the student population; as a result Batista was forced to close schools and universities for some time. Castro's forces, numbering between 800 and 1,000 men, destroyed sugarcane crops and attacked government troops, with the intent of disturbing the "economy to the extent that the mass of workers will be driven from passivity to active revolt," as reported in the *New Republic* (February 17, 1958). Stating that he was fighting for "political rights, and after that for social rights," as he was quoted as saying in *Time* (April 14, 1958), Castro advanced Socialist, rather than Communist, policies. Indeed, at the time the Cuban Communists were opposed to Castro's revolutionary movement.

Castro proclaimed "total war" against the Batista regime, beginning on April 1, 1958. His guerrilla forces scored victory after victory against the government in the months that followed and inspired a massive civil resistance movement in the cities. By late December Batista had realized his defeat, and on New Year's Day, 1959, he went into exile in the Dominican Republic. On the following day Castro's forces marched triumphantly into Havana, while the city of Santiago fell to the rebels. Castro proclaimed, "Let the thieves of yesterday and today beware! Let them beware! Because the Revolution's laws may reach out to draw in the guilty of every period. Because the Revolution has triumphed and has no obligations to anyone whatsoever. Its only obligation is to the people, to whom it owes its victory."

In the next few days Castro established a provisional government with himself as commander in chief of the armed forces, while Manuel Urrutia Lleo, a liberal judge who had defected from the Batista regime, became president. Heading the new Cabinet, composed largely of middle-class liberals, was Premier José Miró Cardona, a law professor. On January 6, 1959 the two houses of the legislature were dissolved, and all provincial and local officials were removed from office. A day later the United States recognized the Cuban provisional government.

The early days of the revolutionary government were marked by wholesale arrests, trials, and executions of Batista supporters by firing squads. Replying to denunciations of the executions from the U.S. and other countries, Castro reminded his critics of the atrocities committed by the Batista regime and declared that the revolutionary courts would remain in place until "all criminals" were tried. The Cuban Communist Party, outlawed under Batista, was again permitted to operate. On February 16, 1959, following the resignation of Cardona, Castro was sworn in as premier of Cuba, while the post of armed-forces commander went to his brother Raúl. Visiting the U.S. that April, Castro promised that Cuba would adhere to the agreement that permitted the United States to lease the naval base at Guantánamo; that no foreign property would be confiscated; and that his government was aligned with the Western democracies.

An agrarian law adopted in May 1959 established a National Institute of Agrarian Reform, of which Castro became chairman. The law provided for the distribution of land to landless families and for the abolition of tenant farming, while greatly limiting foreign landownership. Consolidating his power, Castro forced President Urrutia to resign on July 17, 1959, after accusing him of sabotaging the revolution. The presidency was then filled by Osvaldo Dorticós, a lawyer, who had been minister of laws of the revolution. By late 1959, however, the real power in Cuba had come to reside with Fidel Castro and his immediate associates.

Meanwhile, relations between Cuba and the United States were deteriorating, largely as a result of the Castro government's expropriation of American-owned properties for what was considered inadequate compensation. Increasing counterrevolutionary activity in Cuba was attributed by Castro to U.S. influence. An agreement between Cuba and the Soviet Union, providing for the purchase of Russian oil by Cuba and of Cuban sugar by the USSR, was signed between the two governments in February 1960. A few months later the United States sharply reduced the quota for sugar imports from Cuba. On his visit to New York City in September 1960 for the 15th session of the United Nations General Assembly, Castro had a friendly meeting with Soviet premier Nikita S. Khrushchev, and in his address to the General Assembly, Castro attacked United States policies toward Cuba. On January 3, 1961, after the Castro government had seized nearly all United States–owned properties and had reached additional agreements with Communist nations, the United States government broke diplomatic relations with Cuba.

On April 17, 1961 a force of some 1,300 Cuban exiles under the unofficial auspices of the United States Central Intelligence Agency launched an invasion attempt at the Bahía de Cochinos (Bay of Pigs), on Cuba's southern coast. After the invaders were defeated and most of them taken prisoner, Castro declared triumphantly that the revolution had "destroyed . . . the army organized during many months by the imperialist Government of the United States." Castro's victory over what he has called the "foreign mercenary invasion forces" enhanced his stature in his own country and at the same time drew him closer to the Communist world. In his May Day 1961 speech, he called Cuba "a Socialist country" and declared that the government would no longer hold elections but would thenceforth depend on the direct support of the people at mass rallies—a system that he apparently did not further explain. "The revolution does not contemplate giving the oppressive classes any chance to return to power," he added. On December 2, 1961 he proclaimed "a Marxist-Leninist program adapted to the precise objective conditions existing in our country." A Marxist political party, the Organizaciónes Revolucionarias Integradas (ORI), with Castro as first secretary, was established on March 23, 1962. It was replaced in 1963 by the Partido Unido de la Revolución Socialista (PURS), which in October 1965 became the Partido Comunista de Cuba. Cuba's industry was nationalized and its agriculture collectivized. While Castro had originally stated that he wanted Cuba to be a nation in which everyone had access to the media, no opposition press or political party was permitted to operate, and public speech was tightly monitored, with dissidents jailed or executed.

Meanwhile, in October 1962 Castro's Cuba became the focal point of an international crisis after U.S. president John F. Kennedy revealed that, according to intelligence reports, the Soviet Union was building bases in Cuba for long-range ballistic missiles. Those weapons, according to Kennedy, constituted "an explicit threat to the peace and security of all the Americas" and threatened to upset the nuclear balance between East and West. On October 23, 1962 Kennedy proclaimed a quarantine on all military equipment going to Cuba and established a blockade that was backed by the Organization of American States. Castro replied that Cuba was amassing weapons for purposes of defense and accused the United States of violating "the sovereign rights of our country and all the peoples." The Cuban missile crisis, as the episode would be known thereafter, subsided a few weeks later, when Khrushchev agreed to the removal of the missiles and Kennedy called for an end to the blockade. Meanwhile, after negotiations between the Castro government and attorney James B. Donovan, representing the Cuban Families Committee, an agreement was reached under which the 1,113 prisoners captured in the Bay of Pigs invasion were to be exchanged for food and medicines valued at $53 million. Castro said of the agreement in January 1963 that for "the first time in history imperialism has paid war indemnification."

After the missile crisis, relations between Cuba and the Soviet Union cooled somewhat. Castro, who was not a party to the negotiations between Kennedy and Khrushchev, criticized the latter for not obtaining greater concessions for Cuba. He declared in January 1963 that the Soviet-American agreement was not binding upon Cuba, and he indicated that he might turn to Communist China for support. Cuba continued, however, to receive substantial Soviet economic and military aid, and on several occasions the Castro regime sided openly with the Soviet Union against the Chinese. On the other hand, Castro took the Soviet Union and other European Communist nations to task in 1967 for establishing ties with oligarchic Latin American regimes and for failing to support revolutionary guerrilla forces in the Western Hemisphere. In February 1968 several pro-Soviet Cubans, including Aníbal Escalante, were imprisoned by the Castro regime as "traitors to the revolution." Castro gave only a lukewarm endorsement to the Soviet invasion of Czechoslovakia in August 1968, declaring that although there was no legal basis for the Soviet action it was necessary to prevent the Czechs from "marching toward a counterrevolutionary situation . . . and into the embrace of imperialism."

In 1968 Castro launched a new revolutionary offensive to step up productivity and extirpate the last vestiges of private enterprise. On January 2, 1969—the 10th anniversary of the Cuban Revolution—Castro called for a "year of decisive effort" to rescue the country's lagging economy. He announced a long-range agricultural development program, while postponing indefinitely the country's previously announced industrial drive. On July 14, 1969 Castro officially launched the 1970 sugar harvest, which, he declared, would continue until the record goal of 10,000,000 tons was reached.

Castro's 1960s reforms were quite effective, as workers and peasants benefitted from improved working conditions, health care, housing, and education and the black and mulatto populations—constituting about 27 percent of the 8,100,000 people who lived in Cuba at that time—were largely integrated into the mainstream. On the other hand, Castro himself admitted that crime, delinquency, illiteracy, and industrial inefficiency continued to plague his country. Vigilante groups known as Committees for the Defense of the Revolution kept a close watch on citizens' activities. The year 1976 saw the first Socialist constitution, which institutionalized the Communist Party of Cuba and installed Castro as first secretary of the party and president of the Council of State.

On the world stage, Castro attempted to promote revolutions throughout Central and South America and Africa. This became another source of tension between the Soviet Union and Cuba, for while the Soviets advocated revolution through the work of Communist organizations, Castro supported guerrilla movements. After Ché Guevara was killed while leading guerrilla forces in Bolivia in October 1967, Castro's support of revolutionary activity in Latin America died down for a while. By the mid-1970s, however, that support had been rekindled. Among other acts, Castro sent troops to Angola in 1974 to support the eventually victorious Marxist rebels, maintaining as many as 57,000 troops in that unstable nation until a peace treaty was signed, in 1988. Castro also sent troops to prop up the Marxist dictatorship in Ethiopia in 1977. In the 1980s he supported the El Salvadoran guerrillas and the Sandinista regime in Nicaragua.

The 1980s saw Cuba and the United States at odds over Cuban emigration. In 1980 some 10,000 disenfranchised Cubans sought asylum in foreign embassies in Havana. When Castro later pulled back the restrictions on emigration, 125,000 Cubans left Cuba for Florida, creating an immigration nightmare for the United States and straining the relationship between the two nations, which only recently had come to agreements on fishing rights and travel rights. Roughly 3,000 of the immigrants were found to have either criminal records or mental problems and were jailed. Castro refused to accept them back into Cuba. Tensions were eased in June 1984, when Democratic presidential candidate Jesse Jackson secured the release of a number of U.S. citizens jailed in Cuba as well as 22 Cuban dissidents. Following this action, the 3,000 unwanted Cuban exiles began to be returned. However, the U.S. government's establishment of the U.S.-based, anti-Castro radio station Radio Martí, run by Cuban exiles, in May 1985 severely damaged any goodwill that had been established in U.S.-Cuban relations. Castro suspended the immigration agreement in 1988, prompting a return of "undesirable" immigrants from Cuba to the U.S.

In 1986, while even the Soviet Union under Mikhail Gorbachev—the general secretary of the USSR's Communist Party—was beginning to initiate economic and social reforms, Castro criticized the steps that had been taken in the past five years toward liberalization of the Cuban economy, such as home ownership and free farmers' markets, or markets not controlled by the government (which earlier he had approved). Denouncing those developments as precursors to corruption, Castro moved toward a hard-line position that would put Cuba in an increasingly isolated position. As the Soviet Union began to face its own economic problems in the late 1980s, aid to its longtime ally was drastically cut, and with the collapse of the Soviet Union, in 1991, trade between Moscow and Havana dropped dramatically as well. Although Castro was quoted in the London *Guardian* (February 22, 1992) as saying that the collapse of the Soviet Union was "far worse for us than the October [missile] crisis," he remained committed to Communist principles. In an interview with Tomás Borge for the *Guardian* (May 30, 1992), Castro quoted from a speech he had made in 1989: "We must be more realistic than ever. But we must speak, we must warn imperialism not to have illusions about our revolution and about the idea that our revolution might not be able to resist if there is a breakdown in the socialist community; because if tomorrow or any other day we wake up to find that there is a great civil conflict in the USSR, or even that the USSR has disintegrated . . . even in those circumstances Cuba and the Cuban revolution would carry on fighting and carry on resisting!"

As a result of the loss of Soviet aid and trade, once amounting to about $5 billion per year, Castro was forced to make some concessions to keep his nation solvent. He thus encouraged Western investment and attempted to revitalize Cuba's tourist industry. Restrictions on overseas travel were lifted as well, prompting many Cubans to move to the United States. One source of difficulty for Castro was an increase in trade restrictions on Cuba, leveled by the United States in 1993 in an attempt to undermine Castro; indeed, some observers predicted that the Cuban leader would be toppled within the year. Yet Castro proved as resilient as ever, promoting the use of bicycles in an attempt to lower the amount of fuel used and sending city workers on 21-day furloughs to grow food in the country. In 1992 the National Assembly voted to reform the 1976 constitution, allowing for limited elections in 1993. However, despite fuel and energy shortages and a sugar harvest only half as large as it should have been, only 10 to 15 percent of Cubans protested the listed candidates by turning in blank ballots in the February 1993 elections, a sign that many Cubans were still behind their leader. In 1994 Castro began to allow for more reforms, such as the legalization of self-employment and free farmers' markets. As a result of the legalization of the free farmers' markets, Castro was able to lower food costs, which had been spiraling out of control in Cuba in recent years.

Despite the reforms the 1990s saw crackdowns on Cuban dissidents, including jailings and executions. In *First Things* (May 1998), the journal of the Institute on Religion and Public Life, its editor-in-chief, Richard John Neuhaus, wrote, "The conservative estimate of the number summarily executed by [Castro's] regime is five thousand. Uncounted thousands more have died in prison or drowned at sea trying to escape Castro's liberation." When asked by Tomás Borge to give his definition of democracy, Castro responded, "Democracy, as Lincoln defined it, is the government of the people, by the people, for the people. . . . And I say that bourgeois capitalist democracy does not entail any of these elements, because I wonder how one can speak of democracy in a country where there is a minority with huge fortunes and others who have nothing. . . . I think that our system is incomparably more democratic than any other, incomparably more democratic than that in the United States." Asked on the U.S. Spanish-language TV network Telemundo about the tightly controlled media system in Cuba, Castro said, as quoted in the *New York Times* (November 19, 1995), "[Political dissidents] have no access, and they will have none, because we are not going to give any opportunities to those who want to destroy the revolution."

Various strategies have produced tentative economic growth and a reduction in Cuba's deficit. The reestablishment of trade with Russia has helped the economy, and Castro has also established a solid trade relationship with Canada, a nation that has sent large shipments of aid and investment capital to Cuba. Yet the embargo enforced by the United States remained in place. To a degree, Castro was able to use the embargo to his advantage, blaming Cuba's economic woes on the United States. Nevertheless, in 1994, more than 20,000 Cubans left their homeland in boats bound for the United States. Intercepted by the U.S. Coast Guard, the refugees were detained at the U.S. naval base at Guantanamo Bay. The situation was eased by an agreement between the two countries that stated that 20,000 Cubans would be allowed into the United States annually, in return for a tightening of emigration restrictions in Cuba. In 1996 tensions once again heightened, when the Cuban military shot down two American planes manned by anti-Castro exiles carrying out relief missions for Cuban refugees. As a result, U.S. president Bill Clinton signed into law a bill that tightened the U.S. embargo of Cuba. While observers again expected a collapse of Castro's regime, the Cuban leader's hold on power seemed as solid as ever in January 1998, when Pope John Paul II visited Cuba. Allowed to speak on human-rights abuses in the island nation, the Pope gave Castro a public-relations boost by condemning the continued American embargo of Cuba. Castro's visit that summer to other nations of the Caribbean proved to be moderately successful in terms of expressions of support for his regime and also demonstrated that he could leave Cuba for long periods of time with no fear of revolt.

U.S.–Cuban relations improved to a degree in 1998. The Pentagon announced that the 50,000 mines placed around the Guantanamo military base in 1961 would be removed, while President Clinton eased the embargo restrictions against Cuba, allowing Cuban citizens to purchase American food and agricultural equipment. The last few years have brought an increasing number of calls to lift the embargo entirely. Critics have pointed out that Cuba no longer poses a threat to national security and have charged that turning a deaf ear to the poor and hungry in the neighboring island is immoral. In October 2000 President Hugo Chavez of Venezuela signed an economic and political agreement with Castro according to which Venezuela promised to supply one-third of Cuba's oil imports at low rates. Venezuela, which has the largest oil reserves of any nation outside the Middle East, also agreed to grant Cuba long-term credits and to accept a barter arrangement for the repayment. The two leaders also spoke about the need for their nations and others in the developing world to remain friendly and form alliances. In December 2000 a visit to Cuba by Russian president Vladimir Putin opened the door to the reestablishment of close economic relations between the two former allies. In March 2001 Castro and the president of South Africa, Thabo Mbeki, signed a cooperation treaty aimed at helping to develop drugs to fight the AIDS virus. Castro announced that Cuba would produce generic versions of such drugs. After meeting with Castro in April 2001, President Jiang Zemin of China agreed to lend Cuba $400 million. The next month Castro set up the Ministry for Auditing and Control, with the goal of ending corruption and black-market activity in Cuba.

Earlier, in November 1999, the United Nations voted 155 to two to condemn the economic embargo waged against Cuba by the United States. That embargo was eased somewhat by the U.S. Congress in 2000, as both the Senate and the House of Representatives voted to allow the sale of food and medicine to Cuba. Castro, however, denounced the changes as insignificant and as nothing more than a public-relations maneuver by the U.S. During an appearance before a House Appropriations subcommittee in April 2001, three months after the inauguration of George W. Bush as president, U.S. secretary of state Colin Powell acknowledged that Castro had "done some good things for his people" and was "no longer the threat he was," but he said that there would be no softening of the sanctions against the island nation while Castro remained in power.

Earlier, in November 1999, Elián González, a five-year-old survivor of a wrecked boat carrying illegal immigrants to the United States, was picked up off the coast of Florida after floating for three days in an inner tube; his mother and stepfather had perished in the disaster. Elián's father, Juan Miguel González, and his grandparents demanded that the boy be returned to Cuba, a call echoed by Castro. Instead, Elián was placed in the care of his paternal great-aunt and great-uncle in Miami, Florida, who immediately began a large-scale campaign to keep the child in the United States, stating that they could offer him a better life in Miami than the one he would resume in Cuba. An emotional and heated political battle soon broke out between Cubans in the island nation and those in the exiled Cuban community, located primarily in Miami. In Havana millions of protestors marched on the United States mission, and Castro roared, as quoted on BBC News (December 6, 1999, on-line), "We are going to move heaven and earth . . . it will be a war, an international battle." U.S. officials announced that courts in Florida would decide the matter. After months of tense legal battles and large-scale protests in both Miami and Cuba, Juan Miguel González arrived in the United States in April 2000. After his Miami relatives repeatedly failed to deliver Elián into the hands of the U.S. Immigration and Naturalization Service (INS), INS agents, authorized by then–attorney general Janet Reno, raided the family's house and brought Elián to his father. Afterward, the Miami relatives attempted through court appeals to keep Elián in the United States, but their efforts were unsuccessful, and the boy and his father returned to Cuba in June 2000. A political goldmine for Castro, the Elián González episode helped cement his hold on power, drawing Cubans together in nationalistic fervor to have the boy returned to their country—and in triumph over the United States.

Still, in October 2001 Castro spoke to around one million people in Havana, condemning terrorism against the United States and elsewhere. He expressed sympathy for the victims of the September 11 attacks in the United States and offered medical assistance.

Known as a powerful speaker and magnetic personality, the six-foot-tall Castro usually dresses in an olive-green guerrilla uniform of the type he has worn since the revolution. His famous beard is now gray. In a rare display of physical weakness, in late June 2001, while giving a nationally televised speech, he had to rest offstage for a while after experiencing a feeling of faintness. While Castro recovered and later finished his speech, the episode renewed speculation about the 74-year-old leader's health and the future of Cuba.

Castro enjoys listening to classical music and reading "every type of literature," praising the works of José Martí, Pablo Neruda, and his long-time friend Gabriel García Márquez. He claims to have read Don Quixote, by the Spanish writer Miguel de Cervantes, about six times. A former athlete, Castro still follows American baseball passionately; according to anecdote, he and his fellow revolutionaries would listen from their hiding place in the Sierra Maestras to New York Yankees baseball games. Although Castro has long been known for smoking cigars, he gave up the habit in 1985. His other interests include scuba diving and underwater fishing. He is a devout Roman Catholic. Castro married Mirta Diaz Balart on October 12, 1948; she divorced him in 1955. Their son, Fidel, attended school in the United States and later studied at the University of Havana. According to Juano Tamayo in the *Miami Herald* (October 8, 2000, online), Castro has five sons by a second wife, Dalia Soto del Valle. He allegedly has an out-of-wedlock daughter, Alina, by Natalia Revuelta. His companion of nearly 30 years is Isabel Coto. Castro's younger brother and fellow revolutionary, Raúl, has held several posts in the Cuban government, currently serving as first vice president and head of the armed forces. Many expect the 70-year-old Raúl to step in as leader should Castro become incapacitated or die.

Castro is notoriously evasive in discussions about himself, often steering conversations back to the Cuban revolution. "Castro does not matter," the Cuban leader said in an interview with Diane Sawyer, as quoted in the *New York Times* (March 7, 1993), "he is ready to give his life for the revolu-

tion." Still ending speeches with the phrase, "Socialism or death! Fatherland or death! We will prevail!," he said of himself a decade ago, as quoted in the *Washington Post* (August 12, 1991), "I am the way I am. I have always been that way. . . . If you act honestly, others will understand that you are honest. If you act courageously, others will understand that you are courageous." He then added, "I believe in the importance of human values." — G.O.

Suggested Reading: *Castro Speech Database* (online); *CNN* (on-line); (London) *Guardian* p7 Feb. 22, 1992, p25 May 30, 1992, with photo, p7 July 29, 1992, with photo, p11 Dec. 21, 1993, with photo; *New York Times* p18 Mar. 7, 1993, E p3 Nov. 19, 1995, with photo; *Observer Review* p18 Aug. 11, 1988; *Time* p26+ Jan. 26, 1998; *Washington Post* C p2 Dec. 15, 1991; *World Monitor* p24+ Mar. 1991, with photos

William Philpott/Archive Photos

Chao, Elaine L.

Mar. 26, 1953– U.S. Secretary of Labor. Address: Office of Public Affairs, U.S. Dept. of Labor, 200 Constitution Ave., N.W., Rm. S-1032, Washington, DC 20210

Elaine L. Chao, the United States' 24th secretary of labor, is the first Asian-American woman to hold a Cabinet position. A native of Taiwan who spoke no English when she arrived in the U.S. at the age of eight, Chao has built a successful career in ad-

ministration. She initiated significant reforms as president of the United Way, the nation's largest charity organization, and developed new programs as director of the Peace Corps. She also held government posts during the presidencies of Ronald Reagan and George Bush. As a member of an ethnic minority in the U.S., Chao has emphasized hard work and self-reliance as the keys to success. "In all my jobs and personal appearances," she told an interviewer for *Jade Magazine* (on-line), "I have never allowed others' perception of me to dominate my goals and my behavior. I have always sought to be recognized for my own achievement and merit. In today's world that's a goal that's becoming increasingly easier to accomplish." As secretary of labor Chao faces an unstable economy and controversy over her opposition to affirmative action. According to her profile on the Department of Labor Web site, she advocates, in her words, "a strong and productive workforce in which everyone can participate . . . where jobs and opportunities are available for those leaving welfare, job training is accessible for those left behind, disability never bars a qualified person from the workplace, and where parents have an easier time balancing the responsibilities of work and home."

Elaine L. Chao was born on March 26, 1953 in Taipei, Taiwan. Her parents, James S. Chao and Ruth M. L. Chao, were both refugees from Communist China who met in Taiwan. "Growing up with their stories gave me a tremendous appreciation for the sacrifice of my parents," Chao told Elizabeth Becker for the *New York Times* (February 26, 2001). "The story of China is one disaster after another." Her parents lived in Taiwan for a number of years and had three daughters, Elaine being the eldest, before James Chao immigrated to the United States. After settling on Long Island, New York, he juggled three jobs and began studying toward a college degree to prepare for his family's move to America. In 1961 Elaine arrived in the United States with her mother and her two younger sisters; three more sisters were later born into the family. On her first day of school in New York, the eight-year-old Chao, as is the custom in Taiwan, bowed respectfully to her teacher—a gesture that was met with laughter from the whole class. "I know what discrimination is," Chao told Becker, apparently referring to that incident. Two years later young Elaine, who under her father's tutelage worked diligently on her English each night at home, was elected class president. James Chao, whose job as an apprentice merchant seaman in Shanghai had enabled him to leave mainland China, established a shipping business, Foremost Maritime Corp., which grew into a successful firm and became well-known in international shipping. "I was very lucky to grow up in a family that believed in hard work and education," Chao told Becker.

In 1971 Chao graduated from high school in Syosset, Long Island, and that summer she held two jobs. "I had to beg my father," she told Caitlin Liu for the *New York Times* (September 8, 1996). "I had to convince him that to be American, I had to get a summer job." To explore the possibility of a career in law, she worked as a librarian's assistant at the Manhattan law firm of Haight, Gardner, Poor & Havens, where she discovered that she liked the advocacy side of that profession. She also worked as an intern at the Rusk Institute of Rehabilitation Medicine at New York University, where she determined that a career in medicine was not for her. "I was like a little sponge," she told Liu, "soaking up all the information and tucking it away for future reference." Chao attended Mount Holyoke College, in South Hadley, Massachusetts, where she received a bachelor's degree in economics in 1975. Four years later she earned an M.B.A. from the Harvard Business School, in Cambridge, Massachusetts. After she completed her master's degree, she found a job as a senior lending officer at Citicorp, in New York City, where she handled the financial affairs of a portfolio of shipping companies. She held that position until 1983, when she was named a White House fellow in the administration of President Ronald Reagan. Highly competitive and prestigious, the White House fellowships program gives people with no prior government experience year-long positions at the White House. During her fellowship Chao met Elizabeth Dole, who was then the secretary of transportation; Dole later became a driving force behind Chao's appointment as deputy transportation secretary in the administration of President George Bush. Following her White House fellowship, Chao worked briefly as an administrator at St. John's University, which has campuses in New York City and on Long Island. In 1984 she was named vice president of syndications at BankAmerica Capital Markets Group in San Francisco, California, where among other projects she arranged a $3 billion loan to the Chevron Corp. that enabled it to purchase Gulf Oil.

In 1986 Chao moved to the nation's capital to take the position of deputy maritime administrator at the United States Department of Transportation, where her responsibilities included overseeing the daily operations of a 1,000-person staff. She also managed a $400 million annual budget, much of which was used to subsidize American shippers and shipbuilders who were having difficulty competing internationally. Two years later she was named chairman of the Federal Maritime Commission, in Washington, D.C., a post never before held by a woman. In 1989 Chao became deputy secretary of the United States Department of Transportation, thus becoming the highest-ranking Asian-American appointee in the executive branch in U.S. history. During her tenure Chao helped the department respond effectively to such catastrophes as the bombing of Pan Am flight 103, a major earthquake in the San Francisco Bay area, Hurricane Hugo, and the Exxon-Valdez oil spill.

In September 1991 Chao left the Department of Transportation to become director of the Peace Corps. Founded by President John F. Kennedy in 1961, the Peace Corps grew to become the world's largest international volunteer organization; in 1992, under Chao, it sent 6,000 volunteers to 91 countries. Chao expanded the organization's reach by establishing the first Peace Corps missions to the Baltic nations and the newly independent states of the former Soviet Union. Rather than teaching English, helping villagers build wells, or doing other types of work that Peace Corps volunteers have traditionally done, the volunteers who served in those countries were charged with training people in the mechanics of entrepreneurship and the running of small businesses, with emphasis on business planning, privatization, management, credit, and banking. "[While] in the past [the Peace Corps] has been known for building irrigation systems," Chao told Amy Kaslow for the *Christian Science Monitor* (May 15, 1992), "today's Peace Corps volunteers will also be known for building financial, legal, and distribution systems." The initiative prompted an unprecedented response from would-be volunteers; according to Kaslow, after the programs in the former Soviet bloc were announced, the Peace Corps received about 900 phone calls a day, quadruple the previous average number, with the majority of callers voicing interest in the new programs. Although the governments of the Baltic and former Soviet states extended a formal invitation to the American volunteers, the initiative drew criticism from some who took issue with what they perceived as the promotion of capitalist doctrines by Americans. Others were concerned that the new programs would divert resources from the Peace Corps missions in Africa and other parts of the developing world.

In 1992 Chao left the Peace Corps to serve as the president of the United Way of America. The country's largest institution of private charitable giving, the United Way serves as an umbrella for 2,100 community-based branches nationwide. "United Way of America is a challenge that I could not decline," Chao was quoted as saying in the *Washington Post* (August 27, 1992). "I did not seek the position, but I am looking forward to it." Under the charity's previous president, William Aramony, United Way's revenues had dropped by 42 percent, due in large measure to controversy brought about by his expensive travel arrangements and financial mismanagement. Aramony had been forced to resign when it was found that millions of dollars had been misappropriated, some of it transferred from United Way to several organizations it controlled and some used to purchase condominiums in New York and Florida. Aramony, who was also criticized for accepting an annual salary of nearly $500,000 and spending United Way funds lavishly while on business trips, was convicted of fraud in 1995 and ordered to pay back to the United Way $2.02 million.

To restore the confidence of donors—as well as that of the local branches, which pay dues that help fund the operating budget of the national organization—Chao took some dramatic steps, which included accepting a salary of $195,000, less than half of what Aramony had earned; cutting the charity's operating budget by 30 percent; and laying off one-third of the staff. Donations climbed about 1 percent a year during her first two years with United Way, and in 1995, they rose by about 3.5 percent, to approximately $3.2 billion, surpassing the amount raised in the year before the scandal was revealed. When she left the United Way, in 1996, saying that she had completed her work there, the National Charities Information Bureau recognized the organization as a leader in nonprofit ethics and accountability. Ironically enough, her leaving caused an ethical controversy. As thanks for her help in reviving the organization, United Way board members planned to give Chao a $292,500 bonus collected from their personal funds. When news of the gift became public, negative press followed, with commentators suggesting that the money should be donated to the charity itself. Editorialists also noted that the sum of money was precisely the amount that Chao would have received had she stayed with United Way another 18 months, leading some to suspect that the money was in fact severance pay. The United Way and its board strongly denied that allegation, contending that the payment was intended to reward Chao, who had declined raises in her salary during her tenure, for her excellent work. As a result of the negative press, Chao refused the money, stating, as quoted in the *Washington Post* (June 18, 1996), "The misinterpretation of this gesture, considering the substantial achievement of the past few years, is unwarranted. Nevertheless, to spare United Way of America, an organization that I love and whose reputation I have worked so hard to restore, any criticism, however unjustified, I have decided to decline this payment."

In 1993 Chao had married Mitch McConnell, a conservative Republican senator from Kentucky who became known for his opposition to campaign-finance reform. Her decision to leave the United Way stemmed in part from her desire to lead a less hectic life and start a family. (She and McConnell have three children from his previous marriage, which ended in divorce.) But Chao was unable to have a child of her own. "Women think they can order their lives in a sequence, but sometimes nature doesn't cooperate," she told Elizabeth Becker. "That was an important lesson for me."

Despite her professed interest in slowing down, Chao engaged in a number of projects after leaving the United Way. She joined her husband's successful campaign for reelection in 1996 and also campaigned for Bob Dole in his failed run for the presidency that year. In addition, she launched a speaking tour through the Program Corporation of America and joined the Heritage Foundation, a Washington-based conservative think tank, as a distinguished fellow. There, she served as an expert on philanthropy, civil society, and the nonprofit sector and as senior editor of *Policy Review*, which is published by the foundation. In 1998 Chao was named chairman of Heritage's Asian Studies Center Advisory Council, which advises the foundation on Asian policy and security issues, according to its Web site. While at Heritage Chao became known for her support of the flat tax, a plan under which all Americans would pay income taxes at the same flat rate. Many in the charity field and on the political left oppose that scheme, which was brought to national attention by the unsuccessful 1996 and 2000 presidential hopeful Steve Forbes, the publisher of *Forbes*, in part because it would eliminate the deduction for charitable giving; if such a plan were implemented, charity officials fear, donations would drop. Chao, however, believes that because the flat tax would leave Americans with more spendable income, its implementation would increase charitable giving. "People don't give primarily because of the tax break they will receive," Chao stated, as quoted in *Heritage Today* (Fall 1999) and published on the Heritage Foundation Web site. "They give first and foremost because they believe in the cause and mission of the organization."

During this period Chao was also invited to serve on an alumni board for Harvard University. The policies of the school's admissions office, she later said, made her realize that affirmative action was hurting Asian-Americans. Harvard officials did not want to exceed their quota in admitting applicants of Asian descent, even though such applicants had the highest test scores and grades. Thus, in effect, Asian-Americans were being held to higher standards for admission than those of other races, a practice Chao believes is patently unfair. As she has said, as quoted in the *New York Times* (January 12, 2001), "I think we should heed to the overall core value of this country that equal opportunity applies for all, and that there should be the same standards for everyone." "I believe most Americans don't care for preferential treatment based on race," she said, as quoted in *Heritage Today* (Fall 1999). "We're a country based on merit, built by immigrants of all ethnic backgrounds who worked hard and took risks. Our society is replete with these wonderfully stirring stories."

In January 2001 President-elect George W. Bush nominated Elaine Chao for the position of secretary of labor. His original choice for the job, Linda Chavez, had withdrawn when it became clear that she had misled the FBI and the Bush transition team by failing to notify them that an illegal immigrant had lived in her house and performed chores. After being confirmed by the Senate with bipartisan support, Chao hired her husband's former chief of staff and press secretary to work in those jobs for her. "My husband has one of the subtlest political minds in the country," she told Elizabeth Becker. "I'm interested in finding the best people, and I can't help it if I'm poaching from his staff." Although initially conciliatory regarding Chao's appointment, members of organized labor and others expressed wariness about her conservative record, which they felt indicated that she would place U.S. business interests ahead of government protections for workers. Early in his tenure President Bush issued four executive orders that in the words of an AFL-CIO spokeswoman are "opposed by organized labor," as reported by Reuters and published on *Yahoo! News* (February 15, 2001, online). The same report stated that Chao had asked the president to delay his action until he could meet with labor leaders, but he declined. Soon afterward, in March 2001, the Senate and the House voted to overturn a Clinton administration ergonomics regulation designed to combat workplace injuries caused by repetitive strain, which affect approximately one million U.S. workers. In a written statement quoted by the Associated Press as published on *Yahoo! News* (March 6, 2001, online), Chao pledged to "pursue a comprehensive approach to ergonomics, which may include new rule-making that addresses the concerns leveled against the current standard." Such concerns include what critics viewed as the vagueness of the Clinton regulation and the large amounts of money that many businesses would have to spend to adhere to it. In light of the recent U.S. economic slowdown, Chao stated, as quoted by Reuters and published on *Yahoo! News* (March 9, 2001, online), that she favored George W. Bush's program of "a quick and substantial tax cut to breathe new life into our hardest-hit manufacturing sectors."

In June 2001 the nation's two largest farmworkers' unions sued the Labor Department for failing to raise the minimum wages of more than 30,000 foreign guest workers. (Federal law requires the department to announce annually the rate that must prevail in each state.) In response to the September 11, 2000 terrorist attacks on New York City and Washington, D.C., the department gave $2.5 million to the State of New York to process the

ensuing increase in unemployment-insurance claims and distributed $25 million to help workers who had lost their jobs as a result of the attacks.

Chao's honors include being named an Eisenhower Association fellow in 1984. In 1986 she received the Goucher Outstanding Young Achiever Award from the National Council on Women, and in 1988 she was included on a list of 10 Outstanding Young Women of America. In 1991 she was named Person of the Year by the New York Foreign Freight Forwarders & Brokers Association for distinguished service in the fields of government, transportation, and banking. In 1994 she earned the Harvard University Graduate School of Business Alumni Achievement Award, the highest honor awarded by the Business School. She has received 11 honorary doctorate degrees from colleges and universities nationwide, and has served on the boards of directors of Dole Foods, the National Association of Securities Dealers, the Millipore Corp., and Northwest Airlines. She is also on the board of the China Foundation. "America is the greatest country on earth," Chao has said, as quoted in *Heritage Today* (Fall 1999). "In everything I've done, I've tried to preserve and protect the basic freedoms that make America a land of opportunity." Discussing her identity as an Asian-American with an interviewer for *Jade Magazine* (on-line), Chao asserted, "Asian Pacific Americans can teach mainstream America a great deal about the strength and benefits of a strong family, high emphasis on quality education, a strong entrepreneurial spirit. There's much we can teach others about the Asian philosophy of taking the long term point of view, doing things in moderation, having patience and proper respect for others. It's this sharing of values that makes our country grow stronger." — G.O.

Suggested Reading: *Chicago Tribune* VI p1+ Jan. 26, 1992; *Christian Science Monitor* p8 May 13, 1992; *Jade Magazine* (on-line); *New York Times* A p18 Aug. 27, 1992, with photo, A p17 Jan. 12, 2001, with photo; *New York Times* (on-line) Feb. 26, 2001, with photo; *Washington Post* A p18 Aug 27, 1992, with photo, D p1 June 18, 1996, with photo

---

Chase, David

Aug. 22, 1945– Television writer; director; producer. Address: c/o Home Box Office Inc., 1100 Sixth Ave., New York, NY 10036

David Chase has written, produced, or directed several of the most highly regarded television series of the past 30 years, including *Almost Grown*, *Northern Exposure*, and *I'll Fly Away*. Most recently Chase created *The Sopranos*, an extremely successful weekly HBO Mob drama starring James

Archive Photos

David Chase

Gandolfini and Edie Falco, which has picked up several awards and won high acclaim for its realism in depicting the lives of a contemporary Mafia family. In its first season the show attracted as many as 10 million viewers a week. Much of that praise is for the show's clever juxtaposition of Mob activity and suburban life. In one such episode, "College," the head of the Mob family, Tony Soprano, drives his teenage daughter to a college for an interview. After dropping her off, he tracks down a mob informant and strangles him to death; then he returns to the school and picks up his daughter. "It's the end of the millennium, and things are weird even for the Mob," Chase was quoted as saying in *TV Guide* (February 6, 1999). "It's what I love about them—these guys are surprisingly bourgeois." *The Sopranos*, which entered its third season in March 2001, has developed a cult following that includes members of the Mafia, whom FBI wiretaps have caught discussing the show.

David Chase was born David DeCesare in Mount Vernon, New York, on August 22, 1945. His father worked in a hardware store. Chase grew up in the New Jersey suburbs of New York City. As a child he was a fan of old gangster movies starring such actors as Edward G. Robinson, who appeared in the classic *Little Caesar* in 1930, and James Cagney, the lead performer in the similarly standard-setting *Public Enemy* (1931). "*Public Enemy* was the movie that started by love affair with the gangster film," he told Bill Carter for the *New York Times* (February 28, 2001). Chase was fascinated by the Mob, becoming excited when his father told him that the fathers of some of the children in his school were involved with Mafia activity. Chase received his B.A. from New York University and his M.A. in

film from Stanford University, in Stanford, California.

Chase co-wrote the low-budget horror film *Grave of the Vampire*, which was released in 1972. The film tells the story of a half-man, half-vampire who is conceived when a vampire rapes a human woman. Despising his vampire side as an adult, he sets out to find and confront his biological father. Chase was also credited with the story for the television film *Scream of the Wolf* (1974), in which a successful big-game hunter comes out of retirement to track down a killer animal. The hunter soon begins to suspect that the wolf in question might be supernatural. Chase also worked as story consultant and story editor for the television series *Kolchak: The Night Stalker*, which aired from 1974 to 1975. The horror/drama show starred Darren McGavin as Carl Kolchak, a Chicago newspaper reporter who, in the course of hunting down mysterious killers each week, found himself investigating paranormal and supernatural activities. Kolchak could never convince his editor (Tony Vincenzo) that what he had experienced was real. Chase also served as a story consultant on the television show *Switch* (1975–78), in which an ex-detective (Eddie Albert) and a man he had sent to prison (Robert Wagner) teamed up to form their own detective agency. From 1976 to 1980 Chase was a co-producer of the successful television crime drama *The Rockford Files*, starring James Garner, which won a 1980 Golden Globe Award for best television drama series.

Chase's screenplay for the 1980 television film *Off the Minnesota Strip* won him an Emmy Award for outstanding writing in a limited series or a special. The film, which Chase also co-produced, tells the story of a Minnesota teenager (played by Mare Winningham) who runs away to New York. Alone and without money, she is sheltered by a pimp and soon begins working as a prostitute. After her parents (Hal Holbrook and Michael Learned) take her home, she is forced to readjust to the midwestern, middle-class lifestyle she once abhorred. In 1985 Chase was one of several directors who worked on the one-season renewal of the television program *Alfred Hitchcock Presents*, which retold some of the episodes from the original show while offering new tales of the bizarre. In 1988 he directed the acclaimed but short-lived CBS drama *Almost Grown*, about Norman and Susie Foley (portrayed by Timothy Daley and Eve Gordon), a couple on the brink of divorce. The show used pop songs to trigger flashbacks to earlier events in the couple's three-decade-long relationship. "Music has always been intrinsic to me with movies. . . . As a writer I've always been inspired by music," Chase said in an interview for HBO (on-line). "I listen to music when I'm trying to think and I just like it." For his next television project, Chase served as an executive producer on the enormously successful television comedy/drama *Northern Exposure*, in which a New York doctor (Rob Morrow) just out of medical school sets up a practice in the tiny, remote

Alaskan village of Cicely, whose residents include a group of eccentrics.

Chase was also involved in the production of another highly praised television series, *I'll Fly Away*, which aired from 1991 to 1993. That show, for which he shared a PGA (Producer's Guild of America) Golden Laurel Award for television producer of the year in 1993, was set in a small southern town in the 1950s and focused on a white lawyer (Sam Waterston) who gets involved in civil rights cases as the civil rights movement begins to gather steam. Meanwhile, the caretaker of his children (Regina Taylor), who is African-American, becomes more aware of her own rights. In 1996 Chase wrote *The Rockford Files: Crime and Punishment*, a television movie in which James Garner reprised his role as Jim Rockford from the original series. For the movie, Chase also served as supervising producer and director. He shared writing credits for the low-budget film *Kounterfeit* (1996), in which an ex-criminal gets involved in a counterfeit money operation. When the counterfeiters are found out, a policeman is killed, and his sister tracks down the men responsible.

Most recently, Chase created the HBO series *The Sopranos*, on which he also serves as executive producer and occasional director. All the major networks passed on *The Sopranos* before HBO picked up the show, which is about the day-to-day life of one Mafia family. "I want to tell the story about the reality of being a mobster—or what I perceive to be the reality of life in organized crime," Chase told Robin Dougherty for *Salon* (June 20, 1999, on-line). "They aren't shooting each other every day. They sit around eating baked ziti and betting and figuring out who owes who money. Occasionally, violence breaks out—more often than it does in the banking world, perhaps." The series gave Chase a chance to write on a subject that had always fascinated him and an opportunity to explore neglected elements of the gangster genre. "Those [old gangster] films were always about a guy and his father," he was quoted as saying in *TV Guide* (February 6, 1999), "and I thought it would be interesting to explore [Tony's] relationship with his mother." The head of the family, Tony Soprano (James Gandolfini), undergoes a midlife crisis; feeling anxious about his Mob life as well as about his relationship with his aging mother, Livia (Nancy Marchand, who died in June 2000), he seeks help from a psychiatrist (Lorraine Bracco). "Actually," Chase told Robin Dougherty, "it's based on my own family dynamic—a guy who is in therapy because his mother is driving him crazy. "Whatever came into my mother's mind, she said it," Chase told Steve Daly for *Entertainment Weekly* (January 7, 2000). "There was no censorship at all. And if you challenged her, she'd say, 'You're not going to change me. *I* know how to talk to people.'" Chase later told Daly that during the Vietnam War his mother told him, "I'd rather see you dead than avoid the draft." In an effort to bring an additional level of realism to the show, he spoke to a former Mafia insider for details on Mob life. "When it comes time to be violent, the show is very violent," Chase told Josh Walk for *Entertainment Weekly* (January 15, 1999, on-line). "The hope is that you don't lose yourself thinking that these people are cuddly teddy bears. You see other parts of them that are very human and full of foibles and even sweetness, but they are very brutal men."

The Sopranos has earned several awards as well as nominations for various honors. Among others, Chase shared a Director's Guild of America Award in 2000 for the show's pilot. He also shared an Emmy the previous year for the writing of the episode "College." The show won a Golden Globe Award in 2000 for best dramatic TV series. In the summer of 2001, it received 22 Emmy nominations, more than any other show on television. It went on to win four Emmys—those for best actor, actress, and writing in a drama series and best makeup in a series. "*The Sopranos* gets everything right, from its uniformly superb cast . . . to its deft deployment of mob lingo . . . to its use of music," Scott Von Doviak declared in a review for *Culturevulture.net* (on-line). Chase has signed with HBO to serve as executive producer through a fifth season of *The Sopranos*. (The fourth season is scheduled to begin in September 2002.) Although in his original conception of the show, *The Sopranos* would air no more than four seasons, those close to Chase have reported that he has become intrigued by new story ideas. "This is beyond my wildest dreams," he told Bill Carter for the *New York Times* (January 11, 2000). "[Before the first season] we'd be out there shooting, myself and the cast, and we'd say to ourselves, Who's going to watch this? We were having a really good time doing it. And I guess it's the Puritan ethic: if you're really enjoying yourself, you're going to be punished." The enormous critical and popular acclaim notwithstanding, Chase, by his own account, worries about making a misstep. "I could sit here and say, listen, I'm an artist, we artists do things for ourselves and pleasing ourselves," he told Carter. "And there's a certain truth to that. I think you have to be somewhat true to your vision. Otherwise you'd go crazy chasing something all the time. But we're social animals. We're like dogs. If the other dogs turn on you, it's going to hurt. You're going to feel bad. You don't want the rest of the pack to turn on you, the pack that first embraced you."

HBO has given Chase the go-ahead to make the film *If I Fell*, a romance that takes place on the fringe of the music business. Chase wrote the screenplay and is slated to direct the movie. Recently, he signed a deal with Columbia Pictures to direct the film *Female Subjects*. — G.O.

Suggested Reading: *Entertainment Weekly* (on-line) Jan. 15, 1999, Jan. 7, 2000, with photos; *New York Times* E p1+ Jan. 11, 2000, with photos, E p1+ Feb. 28, 2001, with photo, C p1+ July 16, 2001, with photo; *Salon* (on-line) Jan. 20, 1999; *TV Guide* p42 Feb. 6, 1999, with photos

Selected Feature Films: as writer—*Scream of the Wolf*, 1974; as co-writer—*Grave of the Vampire*, 1972; *Kounterfeit*, 1996

Selected Television Shows or Films: as story editor and consultant—*Kolchak: The Night Stalker*, 1974–75; as writer and co-producer—*The Rockford Files*, 1976–80; *Off the Minnesota Strip*, 1980; as director—*Almost Grown*, 1988; as co-director—*Alfred Hitchcock Presents*, 1985; as co-executive producer—*Northern Exposure*, 1990–95; as producer—*I'll Fly Away*, 1991–93; *The Rockford Files: Crime and Punishment*, 1996; as writer, executive producer, and co-director—*The Sopranos*, 1999–

Courtesy of Congressman Clyburn's office

Clyburn, James E.

July 21, 1940– U.S. Representative from South Carolina; former chairperson of the Congressional Black Caucus; social activist. Address: U.S. House of Representatives, 319 Cannon House Office Bldg., Washington, DC 20515

In 1993, when U.S. representative James E. Clyburn of South Carolina took office, he became the first African-American member of Congress from that state since the late 1890s. From 1999 to 2001 Clyburn was chairperson of the Congressional Black Caucus, a position currently held by Democratic representative Eddie Bernice Johnson of Texas. He was also active in the civil rights movement and served for 19 years as the South Carolina commissioner for human affairs. Known for his ability to ease tensions between political rivals in order to achieve common goals, Clyburn has credited his father with teaching him that "if you disagree with somebody's ideas and you don't have alternative solutions to offer, then you don't have the right to disagree," as he told Carol B. Barker for the Orangeburg, South Carolina *Times and Democrat* (January 25, 1999). Clyburn described himself to Barker as being "driven to disprove every negative that exists about black people. . . . When I was elected to Congress, I went there to prove that a black person could represent South Carolina in the United States Congress as good, if not better, than any white person, and I'm driven to do that."

James E. Clyburn was born in Sumter, South Carolina, on July 21, 1940. His father was a fundamentalist Christian minister; his mother was a beautician. Clyburn's interest in politics began in childhood: at the age of 12, he was elected president of the local youth branch of the National Association for the Advancement of Colored People (NAACP). He has recalled announcing his political ambition in his mother's beauty shop, only to be warned by one of her customers that he must not mention such matters aloud. "We knew what the rules were," Clyburn explained to Betsy Rothstein for the *Hill* (February 17, 1999). "This lady wasn't throwing water on my dreams. She was just telling me, 'Son, be careful, you can't have those kinds of dreams—you're the wrong color.'" He soon became acquainted with the indignities that blacks had to suffer in the segregated South, particularly during one instance in which he and his father stopped at a local gas station. "I remember my father being chased out of this filling station with some of the most vile language you could hear," Clyburn told Rothstein. "He was asking for directions to a church."

Clyburn carried the memories of such experiences to South Carolina State University, in Orangeburg, and during his junior year he joined the burgeoning civil rights movement. He took part in many sit-ins and demonstrations throughout the state and was arrested on several occasions. He met his future wife, Emily England, outside the Orangeburg County courthouse, where he was one of 400 demonstrators released simultaneously on bail. After graduating from South Carolina State University with a B.S. degree, in 1962, Clyburn worked as a high-school world-history teacher, an employment counselor, and the director of two youth and community development projects in Charleston, South Carolina. (As a congressman he would dismiss as "silly" the efforts of some educators to have so-called black English officially recognized.) In 1971 he joined the staff of Governor John C. West; after dropping out of law school, Clyburn was appointed by West to head the South Carolina Human Affairs Commission. During this time Clyburn also served as president of the National Association of Human Rights Workers (1980–81). He remained with the Human Affairs Commission until 1993.

Redistricting in 1990 resulted in the creation of a black majority in South Carolina's Sixth District. In 1992 Clyburn was elected to the U.S. House of Representatives from that district with 65 percent of the vote, a historic victory that made him the first African-American to represent the state since the 1890s (when his great-uncle George Washington Murray was in office). In the latter half of his first term, Clyburn was president of the House "freshman class." He worked closely with Republicans and business leaders in an attempt to forge bipartisan partnerships; in an effort to stay informed, he regularly hosted town-hall meetings with his constituents. He sat for some years on the Veteran Affairs Committee and the Transportation and Infrastructure Committee, among others, and was also the ranking member of the Veteran Affairs' Oversight and Investigation Committee. During the 106th Congress (1999–2001), Clyburn was appointed to two important groups: the Democratic Steering Committee and the House Appropriations Committee. He was also the Democratic whip for Zone Eight, which has jurisdiction over South Carolina, North Carolina, Georgia, and Tennessee.

Unlike many of his fellow liberals, as a congressman Clyburn has supported the balanced-budget amendment and congressional term limits; at the same time, he has backed the formation of enterprise zones, which give tax breaks to businesses operating in economically depressed locations. He has been an advocate for the owners of small tobacco farms in his constituency, asking his fellow representatives to consider the interests of those farmers in the event of sweeping legislation concerning tobacco. He said, as quoted by *Politics in America 2000*, that while "all of us know there's no future in tobacco," he felt "compelled to advocate fair treatment for . . . the affected families, many of whom have little hope for a decent living otherwise," until "alternative crops are developed." He supported President Bill Clinton's "mend it, don't end it" recommendation regarding affirmative action, voting in 1998 against prohibiting the practice in higher education. He was also an outspoken critic of the welfare-reform legislation passed in 1996. "Welfare reform should not mean help denied," Clyburn declared on the floor of the House, as quoted in *Politics in America 2000*. "I think we can all agree that the welfare system is in need of reform. But the Republicans' idea of welfare reform is to callously toss welfare recipients off the government rolls without much thought to getting or keeping them on payrolls." Clyburn engaged in a successful campaign to name a new courthouse in Columbia, South Carolina, after Matthew Perry, the first black federal judge in the state. (His efforts were opposed by Senator Strom Thurmond, who wanted to see his own name adorn the building.) In late 1998 Clyburn voted against impeaching President Clinton for perjury in connection with Clinton's affair with Monica Lewinsky, a White House intern.

Also in 1998 Clyburn was elected chairperson of the Congressional Black Caucus by a rare unanimous vote. Formed in 1971, the caucus represents the interests of the African-American House Democrats, who currently number 37. Clyburn's approach to the chairmanship was low-key in comparison with that of his immediate predecessor, Congresswoman Maxine Waters of California; more adept at conciliation than Waters, Clyburn frequently called private meetings to discuss concerns with rivals. "I came out of an administrative background," Clyburn told Kevin Merida for *Emerge* (March 1999). "I guess I'm the consummate managerial type. I view myself as being the captain of the football team, not necessarily the quarterback." He realized that there would be no point in trying to imitate Waters's fiery brand of leadership. "We all remember the [1963] March on Washington because of Dr. [Martin Luther] King's speech," Clyburn told Merida. "But Bayard Rustin organized the march, and it would not have been successful without him. We're going to really mess up if we try to play each other's roles. So I am not going to try to be Maxine Waters. I can't live up to that role." As chair of the Congressional Black Caucus, Clyburn focused on issues including environmental racism (for example, the placement of waste-treatment plants in African-American or Hispanic neighborhoods), the reevaluation of methods for conducting the census, and the appointment of black judges to the federal courts. He also worked with J. C. Watts, currently the only Republican African-American in Congress; although the two men have a good relationship, Watts declined an invitation to join the organization. When Clyburn first arrived at the Congressional Black Caucus, he found the atmosphere at the organization to be "caustic," as he told Betsy Rothstein. "It was real, as they say, 'down and dirty.'" But while its members maintained their differences, Clyburn told Rothstein in 1999 that "adjustments have been made and the caucus is a real family—as much of a family as it ever was." During his tenure as chair of the caucus, Clyburn "earned a reputation as a diplomatic yet progressive political leader," as a writer for *Jet* (December 25, 2000–January 1, 2001) phrased it. When his two-year term as chair ended, in early 2001, he was succeeded by Representative Eddie Bernice Johnson of Texas. In 2000 Clyburn won election to a fifth term in Congress, with a resounding 72 percent of the vote.

In the wake of the 2000 presidential election, which George W. Bush won following a 36-day period of vote recounts and legal battles in Florida and charges of voter suppression in that state's minority communities, Clyburn expressed deep skepticism about the Bush presidency. "I'm not interested in whether or not Colin Powell is secretary of state or [Powell's] son is chairman of the Federal Communications Commission or Condoleezza Rice is national security adviser," he told Roxanne Roberts for the *Washington Post* (December 15, 2000), referring to prominent African-Americans in the Bush administration. "What does that do for the constituents I represent who are telling me how much they fear a Bush presidency and what it would mean for public education, for affirmative action, and what it means—right now—for basic voting rights?"

Clyburn, who is a passionate golfer, holds memberships in the NAACP and the Omega Psi Phi fraternity. He is both a Mason and a Shriner and has been awarded honorary doctorates by a dozen academic institutions. He and his wife, Emily, have three daughters—Mignon, Jennifer, and Angela—and two grandchildren. The couple live in Columbia, South Carolina. — C.L.

Suggested Reading: *Congressional Quarterly* p135 Jan. 16, 1993, with photo; *Emerge* p25 Mar. 1999, with photo; *Hill* (on-line) Feb. 17, 1999; (Orangeburg, South Carolina) *Times and Democrat* A p1+ Jan. 25, 1999, with photos; *Politics in America 2000*

Sandra Johnson/Retna Ltd.

Columbus, Chris

Sep. 10, 1958– Film director; screenwriter.
Address: c/o Beth Swafford, Creative Artists
Agency, 9830 Wilshire Blvd., Beverly Hills, CA
90212-1825

Known as the writer and director of some of the most popular motion pictures of the 1980s and 1990s, and also as one of the nicest, most relaxed people in the film industry, Chris Columbus has begun his third decade of filmmaking by directing the movie version of the first book in the extremely

popular *Harry Potter* series. Although frequently lambasted by critics, Columbus's films, often released around Christmas, have captivated audiences around the world and enjoyed enormous success at the box office. Two of his films, *Home Alone* and *Home Alone 2*, are among the 50 top-grossing American movies of all time. Columbus made his reputation by writing and/or directing such family films as *The Goonies* and *Mrs. Doubtfire*; he has recently begun to direct more adult-oriented movies, including *Stepmom* and *Bicentennial Man*.

Christopher Columbus was born on September 10, 1958 in Spangler, Pennsylvania. His father was a coal miner and factory worker who moved his family to Warren, Ohio, not long after his son was born. His mother was also a factory worker. An only child, shy and often alone, Chris would pass the time watching horror movies on television, building models of monsters, and reading comic books, of which he collected around 1,000. As a child he dreamed of drawing for Marvel Comics. Columbus attended co-ed Catholic schools, where he did well in English and in classes that involved drawing and other artistic skills. He did not have an active social life during his high-school years. "Saturday night I was mostly watching *The Carol Burnett Show* with my parents," he told Jim Jerome for *People* (December 14, 1992). "I did have a couple of dates, but they were exercises in nervousness." At 15 he watched Francis Ford Coppola's celebrated gangster saga *The Godfather* and was inspired to make films. He decided that the only ways to escape from the factory town of Warren were "to make movies or become a rock 'n' roll star. But I can't sing, so that was out," he told Terri Minsky for the New York *Daily News* (June 30, 1985). With the 8mm camera his parents bought for him, he and his friends began to make films, many of them comic sketches inspired by *Saturday Night Live*, which had just premiered on NBC. Upon the release of *Jaws* (1975), directed by the 26-year-old Steven Spielberg, Columbus thought, as he recalled to Minsky, "If he can do this when he's 26, so can I."

In his senior year of high school, Columbus was offered a full scholarship to attend nearby Kent State University, but one of his Jesuit teachers suggested that he consider film school. Columbus applied successfully to the Directors Program at the Tisch School of the Arts of New York University (NYU), in New York City. At NYU he found himself at odds with many of the students and members of the faculty, who wanted to create films that communicated their angst. By contrast, Columbus wanted to make movies that would let viewers laugh and enjoy themselves. During his sophomore year he made his first sale to Hollywood: the script of the semiautobiographical "Jocks." While "Jocks" was never made into a movie, its sale seemed to him to be a breakthrough. Later he wrote another partly autobiographical script, for a film entitled *Reckless*, which he also sold—and which represented a bad experience for him. "It was awful," he told Johanna Steinmetz for the *Chicago Tribune* (July 1, 1987). "You know when you're writing that you're forcing it. You're constantly lying to yourself. Then you take the script to Hollywood, and everyone tells you, 'It's great, kid!' Then you leave, and they go off and get someone else to rewrite it." As a junior he wrote "Night Shift," which, like "Jocks," sold but was never produced. In 1980, the year Columbus received a B.F.A. degree in film production, he met Monica Devereux, a choreographer, at a Halloween party. After three dates, Columbus proposed to her, and they were married three years later.

In 1984 *Reckless* was made into a film, Columbus's first, featuring Aidan Quinn as a rebel and former convict who falls for a rich girl, played by Daryl Hannah. Talking with Minsky about the film, which was set in Weirton, West Virginia, and was extensively rewritten by others, Columbus said, "I saw it as a visual 'Born to Run,' but it came out as 'Last Tango in Weirton,' with a sex scene in a boiler room, of all places." Better luck came when Columbus's script for *Gremlins*, which had been rejected repeatedly, was picked up by Steven Spielberg. On hearing that Spielberg would produce the film, Columbus recalled to Minsky, "I thought, I should jump up and down, but I couldn't move. Right then, my life changed." Directed by Joe Dante, *Gremlins* (1984) was a megahit, grossing over $148 million in the U.S. alone. Set in a quintessential American small town, the story begins when a man buys his son a cute little creature, which comes with detailed instructions. The boy fails to follow the instructions, and the town is invaded by the small, strange, and malicious creatures of the title. "I was inspired by mice running around a loft I lived in in New York," Columbus told David Sterrit for the *Christian Science Monitor* (October 23, 1987). "I used to sleep with my arm draped over the side of the bed, and I used to worry that a mouse would come along and take a bite. I realized it's scary to have things running around in the dark, and that's where *Gremlins* came from." For the final version of the movie, Columbus and Spielberg downplayed the script's darker elements—avoiding altogether, for example, the carnivorous inclinations of the Gremlins. With that successful film to his credit, Columbus began working as a writer at Spielberg's Amblin Entertainment. "[Spielberg] was the godfather," he told Jerome. "I was made privy to his filmmaking secrets. If I had a problem, I could run down with three pages of script, and he and I would make changes. You can't beat that." Meanwhile, Columbus set up his own production company, 1492 Productions, and bought a penthouse apartment in New York City.

In 1985 *The Goonies*, written by Columbus, was made into a film by Amblin Entertainment. The film follows a group of delinquent kids who, to save their neighborhood from a land developer, go on a quest for hidden treasure, pursued by a family

of bad guys. The movie was a hit among children and young adults and grossed over $61 million in the U.S. Another Amblin project written by Columbus, *Young Sherlock Holmes*, was released the same year. That film received mixed reviews and failed to find a large audience. Columbus was also behind the concept for *Galaxy High School*, a cartoon that aired briefly on TV in 1986 and concerned an intergalactic high school attended by aliens as well as humans. The following year Columbus made his directorial debut, with the comedy *Adventures in Babysitting*, which starred Elizabeth Shue as a reluctant babysitter who leads the kids in her care through numerous adventures and mishaps after agreeing to pick up a friend stranded at a Chicago bus station. The movie fared well at the box office but received mixed reviews. Rita Kempley noted for the *Washington Post* (July 3, 1987), "[Columbus] doesn't shake the excitement out of this screenplay; he smoothes the climaxes into the transitions as if he were mixing house paint. Nevertheless Columbus . . . is supplying basically benign viewing for kids." "You can't afford to make a *Blue Velvet* right away," Columbus told Johanna Steinmetz, referring to David Lynch's jarring cult film of 1986. "The film has got to be somewhat accessible your first time out, or you might not direct again, and since I want to spend the rest of my life doing this, I want to be careful."

In 1988 Columbus wrote and directed *Heartbreak Hotel*, which perhaps stands as his least successful outing—both critically and commercially—to date. The plot concerns an Ohio teen who kidnaps Elvis Presley after a 1972 concert in order to cheer up his mother, an alcoholic Presley fan who is spending her birthday in the hospital. Despite having been kidnapped, the singer becomes attached to the family and begins helping them out in various ways. "It's bad—awesomely bad, contrived, awkward and filled with unintentional laughs . . . the movie finds so many different approaches to its badness that it becomes endearing," Roger Ebert noted in his review for the *Chicago Sun-Times* (September 30, 1988).

Asked to write the script for the third movie in the *Indiana Jones* series—about the adventurous archaeologist—Columbus was fired by Spielberg after turning in two unsuccessful drafts. It wasn't long, however, before Columbus was back on the "A" list of Hollywood directors. He was signed to direct John Hughes's script for the comedy *Home Alone* (1990), which tells the story of a young boy who is accidentally left behind by his parents during their Christmas vacation in France. In the course of fending off two burglars who have targeted his neighborhood, the boy learns to take care of himself. The film grossed over $285 million in the United States alone, making a star of the child actor Macaulay Culkin in the process; in addition, it was nominated for a Golden Globe Award as best motion picture–comedy/musical. It is currently the 12th highest-grossing film of all time. Critical reaction was mixed at the time of its release, however.

While many found the script to be unrealistic in its depiction of a child left alone, most praised the performance of Culkin, who they felt carried the film. Columbus's next movie was *Only the Lonely* (1991), which he wrote and directed. Basically a remake of the film *Marty* (1955), as virtually every reviewer of the movie pointed out, *Only the Lonely* centers on a 38-year-old Chicago cop, played by John Candy, who lives with his dominating mother. He falls in love with a shy woman he meets at a bar, only to have the romance complicated by his relationship with his mother and the opinions of his friends. "[The story is] based on a combination of people I've known," Columbus told Paul Galloway for the *Chicago Tribune* (May 25, 1990). "It doesn't mean I'm breaking away from anything I've been doing. It's just that now that I'm older, I probably feel more comfortable making movies from this perspective." The film received mediocre reviews, which disappointed Columbus. "It's the best picture I've ever made," he told Jerome. "Thank God there's cable and video, and it can take on a life of its own."

In 1992 Columbus co-wrote the generally well-received animated feature *Little Nemo: Adventures in Slumberland*. More prominently, he directed *Home Alone 2: Lost in New York*. A retread of the earlier film, *Home Alone 2* finds Culkin's character on his own in the Big Apple, where he encounters the same crooks from the first movie. The sequel was almost as great a commercial success as its predecessor (it took in over $175 million in the U.S.) and just as big a critical flop. While many objected to the level of violence in what was billed as a family film, Columbus was unapologetic. "We throw out gags if we feel kids could duplicate them," he told Jim Jerome. "I have to laugh when people question the so-called violence—the same people, myself included, who grew up watching cartoons where Bugs Bunny would blow off Daffy Duck's head with a shotgun, his beak would fall off and he'd put it back on." Columbus followed *Home Alone 2* with another successful comedy, *Mrs. Doubtfire* (1993), which starred Robin Williams as a caring but irresponsible father whose wife, reaching the end of her patience, files for divorce and is given custody of the children. Wanting to see his kids more often than his visitation rights allow, the father disguises himself as an elderly Scottish woman and lands a job as his wife's housekeeper. Although critical of the film in general, many reviewers praised Williams's performance, and the movie won a Golden Globe Award for being the year's best motion picture in the comedy/musical category.

Columbus next co-wrote and directed *Nine Months* (1995), which starred Hugh Grant and Julianne Moore as an unmarried couple who discover that they have conceived a baby. This development frightens Grant's character, who leaves his girlfriend in order to "play the field," but who—after seeing an ultrasound image of the baby—realizes where he belongs. Again, while audiences flocked to the film, critics were not impressed. Peter Stack noted for the *San Francisco Chronicle* (July 12, 1995), "*Nine Months . . .* is good for a few laughs but soon turns tiresome, veering incongruously between slapstick antics and mushy sentimentality." He added, "Columbus takes male pregnancy phobia about as far as he can. And then, in the Columbus fashion, he drives it into the ground."

After producing the Arnold Schwarzenegger comedy *Jingle All the Way* (1996), Columbus directed *Stepmom* (1998), which he also produced. The film starred Susan Sarandon as a divorced mother who has custody of her children. Her ex-husband lives with a woman half his age (Julia Roberts)—who must learn how to be a good mother, once Sarandon's character is diagnosed with cancer. While the actresses were generally given good notices, the film itself did not fare as well among critics. In a scathing review for the *New York Times* (December 24, 1998), Janet Maslin wrote, "Columbus gives the film a lavish look and thick skin about storytelling cliches, directing the most contrived encounters as if they were utterly new." In the *San Francisco Chronicle* (December 25, 1998), Ruth Stein offered a dissenting opinion: "*Stepmom* is a perfect holiday picture. It's uplifting and reaffirming about the virtues of all families including stepfamilies." The film was a big box-office hit. The following year Columbus directed Robin Williams in *Bicentennial Man*, based on an Isaac Asimov short story. Like many of Columbus's other movies, the film performed quite well at the box office, pulling in over $58 million, but received almost universally negative reviews. Roger Ebert noted in his assessment for the *Chicago Sun-Times*, "[It] begins with promise, proceeds in fits and starts, and finally sinks into a cornball drone of greeting-card sentiment."

Columbus executive-produced Henry Selick's surrealistic *Monkeybone* (2001). Partly animated, the movie concerns a cartoonist (Brendan Fraser) who, while in a coma, finds himself in the world he has created. Columbus was signed to direct the movie version of J. K. Rowling's wildly popular young-adult novel *Harry Potter and the Sorcerer's Stone* after Spielberg turned it down. The movie, which stars Daniel Radcliffe as Harry, was scheduled to be released on November 16, 2001. Columbus is also producing and writing the story for *The Fantastic Four*, based on the comic book of the same name; that project, on hold for some time because of its high budget, is currently in the pre-production stage. Its tentative release date, 2003, is also the expected release date of the second film in the Potter series, *Harry Potter and the Chamber of Secrets*, which Columbus also agreed to direct.

Columbus and his wife, Monica, have two daughters and a son. The director owns an apartment in Manhattan and a 19th-century house in San Francisco. Columbus has cast his father-in-law in walk-on rolls in several of his films and has found small roles for other members of his wife's family as well. His favorite films are *City Lights*, *On* the Waterfront, and *The Godfather* and its first sequel. Beyond collecting rock CDs, Columbus has few hobbies. "I have a simple lifestyle," he told Jerome. "I'm not a golfer, I don't play the horses, don't do indoor rock climbing. I try to read a novel a week, I write, take walks in Riverside or Central Park. My friends are still the same gang from NYU days. I really don't do anything else but spend time with Monica and the children. Family has always come first. When everything else is going well in your home life, it's easier to create." When asked by David Sterrit whether he preferred writing or directing, Columbus replied that he would rather direct, adding, "There's nothing that compares with getting a great performance out of an actor—when you're working and working, and finally it clicks, and you've got it!" — G.O.

Suggested Reading: *Chicago Tribune* V p3 July 1, 1987, V p1 May 25, 1990; *Christian Science Monitor* p22 Oct. 23, 1987; (New York) *Daily News* p17 June 30, 1985; *People* p121+ Dec. 14, 1992

Selected Films: as director—*Home Alone*, 1990; *Home Alone 2: Lost in New York*, 1992; *Mrs. Doubtfire*, 1993; *Stepmom*, 1998; *Bicentennial Man*, 1999; as director and writer—*Adventures in Babysitting*, 1987; *Heartbreak Hotel*, 1988; *Only the Lonely*, 1991; *Nine Months*, 1995; as writer—*Reckless*, 1984; *Gremlins*, 1984; *The Goonies*, 1985; *Young Sherlock Holmes*, 1985

Davy/Velente/Prestige/Getty News

Cruz, Penelope

Apr. 28, 1974– Actress. Address: c/o William Morris Agency, 151 El Camino Dr., Beverly Hills, CA 90212

"Screen beauties are hardly a novelty," Matt Wolf wrote for the *New York Times* (November 29, 1998), "but even within the realm of celluloid sirens, the Spanish actress Penelope Cruz elicits unusual adoration from her directors." Indeed, if the directors with whom she has worked are to be believed, Cruz has the potential to join Marlene Dietrich, Ingrid Bergman, and Audrey Hepburn as one of the few foreign-born actresses to become a major Hollywood presence. "Sometimes, some-

body comes along who has such a magic, it doesn't matter if [she has an accent]," Billy Bob Thornton, who directed Cruz in *All the Pretty Horses*, told Sean M. Smith for *Premiere* (March 2001). "She's going to have a very, very long career. She's too strong to hold down." The screenwriter and director Cameron Crowe, who worked with Cruz in *Vanilla Sky*, is similarly effusive. "[Cruz is] the kind of person you see in a movie, and it's like, wow! Yet for someone that beautiful, she doesn't lead with her looks," he told Richard Corliss for *Time* (October 9, 2000). "Her silent moments are as great as when she speaks. Everybody says 'Audrey Hepburn' when they speak about her, and that's one of the big Audrey parts of her: she can turn a little silent moment into a one-act play. She also has this sense of humor that's waiting to pounce. The cool thing is she doesn't play 'girlish' like a lot of American actresses who go through all these light romantic comedies and end up playing cute for years. She never played cute; she played substance and soulfulness—very romantic, but not in a gooey way." While it might be premature to lend such remarks full credence, it seems clear that Cruz—who has appeared alongside many of Hollywood's leading men, including Matt Damon in *All the Pretty Horses*, Nicolas Cage in *Captain Corelli's Mandolin*, Johnny Depp in *Blow*, and Tom Cruise in *Vanilla Sky*—is currently poised to become a household name.

The eldest of the three children of Encarna Cruz, a hairdresser, and Eduardo Cruz, an auto mechanic, Penelope Cruz Sanchez was born in Madrid, Spain, on April 28, 1974. According to Corliss, her given name was inspired by a ballad by the Spanish singer and poet Joan Manual Serrat, who sang: "Penelope, your sad eyes glow at the sound of a distant train." As a young child Cruz spent many hours in her mother's beauty salon. "I grew up observing women," she told Smith. "All these different women, different attitudes, coming there to be pretty. I used to sit there and observe how they related to each other, to my mother. It was very interesting. It was like a good acting school."

Early on, Cruz aspired to become a dancer. When she was four years old, her parents, recognizing that she needed an outlet for her excess energy, signed her up for ballet classes. "I found a way to communicate my feelings without words," Cruz told Smith of those lessons. "It's like I was born with the desire to communicate emotions. When I started to do it in a very intense way, like four hours a day, I was much happier, releasing all that adrenaline. I feel it now sometimes. I have to exercise to transform that energy into another one that doesn't drive me crazy."

After several years of intensive study, Cruz's enthusiasm for dancing began to wane. "It's a very sadistic thing," she told Smith. "You get used to bleeding and smiling at the same time." She began studying acting, too, and by early adolescence, acting had displaced dance as the principal focus of her energies. "I found a lot of magic in [acting], a lot of order to that chaos," she told Smith. "I felt like a child. I was completely in love with it. I still feel like that. You can always keep learning with acting, because the school is life and yourself and your friends and your relationships. I'm fascinated by it! It is infinito!" Cruz acquired a talent agent at 15, and shortly thereafter she appeared in a commercial for Schweppes orange soda.

One year later Cruz made her film debut, with a minor role in *El laberinto griego* (The Greek Labyrinth, 1991), a Spanish thriller written and directed by Rafael Alcázar. In 1992 she appeared in her first prominent role, as Silvia, a teenage seductress who works in an underwear factory, in the director J. J. Bigas Luna's sexual farce *Jamón jamón*. (With English subtitles, the film appeared variously as *Ham Ham* and *Salami Salami*.) Perhaps because of its sexual content, *Jamón jamón* tended to polarize those few American critics and moviegoers who saw it. Rita Kempley, for example, writing for the *Washington Post* (October 23, 1993), dismissed the movie as "a tribute to throbbing Latin manhood, as cretinous and sophomoric as it is pretentiously surreal. . . . Basically, [*Jamón jamón*] is soft pornography with its nose in the air." Roger Ebert, on the other hand, who reviewed the film for the *Chicago Sun-Times* (February 11, 1994), praised *Jamón jamón* for its exuberant nerve. "It is frankly outrageous, it has the courage to offend, it is not afraid of sex, and it goes over the top in almost every scene. It takes a certain kind of moviegoer, I suppose, to enjoy a film like this; of course it's in bad taste, of course it's vulgar, of course it flies in the face of all that is seemly, and, of course, that is the idea." In Spain, where the film was much more widely shown, Cruz's sultry performance quickly catapulted the 17-year-old actress to the unofficial role of national minx—much to her consternation. "There was very strong energy around me," she told Smith, "and I didn't know how to handle it. I had a strong rejection of anything sexual or sensual for a while. I cut my hair very, very short. I didn't do any love scenes, not even kisses, for many years. . . . No one forced me to [make the movie]. I felt very happy doing it. But I also suffered for it."

At about the same time that *Jamón jamón* was released, Cruz was seen in Fernando Trueba's *Belle époque* (1992), a sexual comedy set in an idyllic rural district on the eve of the Spanish Civil War. She played the virginal Luz, the youngest daughter of a benevolent artist and anarchist. In the course of the film, Luz, along with her three sisters, becomes enchanted by Fernando, a handsome deserter who one day shows up at their father's doorstep. When first released in the United States (with English subtitles), *Belle époque* received scant distribution; consequently, it escaped the notice of most American moviegoers. In Spain, however, the film garnered nine Goyas (Spanish Oscars) and thus helped to cement Cruz's fame in her native country. Cruz received a bit of notice elsewhere in Europe and in the United States after *Belle époque* won the 1993 Academy Award for best foreign film.

In the next few years, Cruz appeared regularly in Spanish cinema, averaging three or four films annually, including Fernando Colomo's *Alegre ma non troppo* (1994), Álvaro Fernández Armero's *Todo es mentira* (*Life's a Bitch*, 1994), Alfonso Albacete and Miguel Bardem's *Más que amor, frenesí* (*Not Love, Just Frenzy*, 1996), and Manuel Gómez Pereira's *Amor perjudica seriamente la salud* (*Love Can Seriously Damage Your Health*, 1996). But despite her growing stature in Spain, both Cruz and the films she appeared in during the early to mid-1990s remained largely unknown outside her native country. In 1997 Cruz made a brief appearance (her character gives birth on a bus) in Pedro Almodóvar's *Carne trémula* (*Live Flesh*). Also that year, in Alejandro Amenábar's *Abre los ojos* (*Open Your Eyes*), she played the girlfriend of a Lothario whose handsome features are disfigured in an auto accident, then reconstructed; and in *Niña de tus ojos* (*The Girl of Your Dreams*, 1998), she portrayed a Spanish actress who becomes the reluctant plaything of Joseph Goebbels, Hitler's propaganda minister. For that last role, Cruz won a Goya Award for best actress.

Cruz made her English-language acting debut alongside Woody Harrelson, Billy Crudup, and Patricia Arquette in Stephen Frears's *The Hi-Lo Country* (1998), a Western set in New Mexico in the wake of World War II. Although she was initially apprehensive about acting in a foreign language, Cruz says she found it to be a liberating experience. "It gives you an additional kind of freedom because you don't hear yourself so much," she told Smith. "With that freedom, I can take more risks. There is not so much self-criticism, which can destroy a performance." Cruz's role in *The Hi-Lo Country*, together with her portrayal of a nun who becomes pregnant by a transvestite in Pedro Almodóvar's international hit *Todo sobre mi madre* (*All About My Mother*, 1999), finally brought her to the attention of mainstream English-language moviegoers.

Recently, Cruz has taken major roles in a string of American productions. In Fina Torres's *Woman on Top* (1999), she played Isabella, a heartbroken

Brazilian woman who moves to San Francisco and becomes the talk of the town as the hostess of her own cooking show. While reviewers were generally less than impressed with the movie, most singled out Cruz for praise. "Cruz has everything it takes to be a big star," Bob Graham wrote for the *San Francisco Chronicle* (September 22, 2000), "except maybe, in this case, the right movie." "Torres just doesn't know what to do with Cruz," Stephanie Zacharek wrote for the on-line magazine *Salon.com*. "Cruz is so excruciatingly lovely that her beauty needs to be treated as a great joke, as if she were some extraterrestrial being who has landed here to charm and beguile us. Torres gets the feel exactly right when she shows us a stand of limp tulips on the street that magically spring to attention as Isabella passes by. But aside from that one gently witty moment, *Woman on Top* is just a string of cute gags and pouting on Isabella's part that's supposed to signify soul-searching."

In *All the Pretty Horses* (2000), Billy Bob Thornton's cinematic adaptation of Cormac McCarthy's same-titled National Book Award–winning novel, Cruz played Alejandra, the romantic interest of Matt Damon's character, John Grady Cole. The movie received lukewarm reviews, and most critics judged Cruz to have been overshadowed by Damon. "Poor Ms. Cruz must utter some of the corniest woman-in-love lines this side of *The Bridges of Madison County*," A. O. Scott wrote for the *New York Times* (December 25, 2000), "and, to put it as kindly as possible, she's no Meryl Streep." Still, some reviewers were evidently taken with Cruz's performance. Among them was Edward Guthmann, who declared in the *San Francisco Chronicle* (December 25, 2000), "Best of all are Damon's scenes with Cruz—at a community dance, embracing in a moonlit pond—which are some of the most lusciously romantic in memory."

Blow (2001) represented a departure for Cruz: appearing alongside Johnny Depp, she played a cocaine addict with a sailor's mouth. "No one has ever seen her do that before—just [expletive] yell and scream and go nuts," Ted Demme, who directed *Blow*, told Smith, "which is why I think she wanted to do it." "If you don't get the fuss about Spain's voluptuous Penelope Cruz . . . ," Peter Travers wrote for *Rolling Stone* (on-line), "her take on [the the Depp character's] wife, Mirtha, will turn you around. It's a stormy, smoldering tour de force." Writing for *Salon.com*, Stephanie Zacharek expressed the view that Cruz is "best when she's allowed to run free as a sullen, sulky beauty who snorts coke while pregnant ('I quit smoking!' 'she fires back at George, hilariously, when he reproaches her) and cavalierly mispronounces words (she brands George as a *hype*-ocrite)."

In *Captain Corelli's Mandolin* (2001), set on the Greek island of Cephalonia under the Italian occupation in World War II, Cruz portrayed Pelagia, a local beauty who swoons for Captain Antonio Corelli (Nicolas Cage), an easygoing, opera-loving, mandolin-strumming Italian officer who com-

mands a band of singing soldiers. The movie was adapted from Louis de Bernières's 1994 novel *Corelli's Mandolin*. "Ms. Cruz, apparently optimistic about her corner of Hollywood's gilded cage, once again proves her inability to give a bad performance even under the worst of circumstances," Jessica Winter wrote for the *Village Voice* (August 15, 2001). "Her perfectly modulated emotional range and undaunted conviction while spouting pap is heartening and cumulatively poignant." *Vanilla Sky*, directed by Cameron Crowe and scheduled for release in late 2001, will pair Cruz with Tom Cruise; the film is a remake of *Abre los Ojos*.

When not acting, Cruz says she enjoys spending time with her family, which includes a younger brother, Eduardo, and a younger sister, Mónica. While she was in Greece filming *Captain Corelli's Mandolin*, her mother and brother came to stay with her on location. But having family members with her on the set isn't always possible. "Sometimes I miss them," she told Smith, "but I am used to saying, 'See you later.' In our profession, it's something we have to learn. I spend more than half of the year out of Spain."

Cruz is also active in charitable endeavors, and is reported to have donated her entire paycheck from *The Hi-Lo Country* to the Calcutta-based mission founded by Mother Teresa. — P.K.

Suggested Reading: *New York Times* p30 Nov. 29, 1998; *Premiere* p70+ Mar. 2001, with photos; *Time* p109 Oct. 9, 2000, with photos

Selected Films: *El Laberinto griego*, 1991; *Jamón jamón*, 1992; *Belle époque*, 1992; *Alegre me non troppo*, 1994; *Todo es mentira*, 1994; *Más que amor, frenesí*, 1996; *Amor perjudica seriamente la salud*, 1996; *Carne trémula*, 1997; *Abre los ojos*, 1997; *Niña de tus ojos*, 1998; *The Hi-Lo Country*, 1998; *Todo sobre mi madre*, 1999; *Woman on Top*, 1999; *All the Pretty Horses*, 2000; *Captain Corelli's Mandolin*, 2001; *Blow*, 2001; *Vanilla Sky*, 2001

Cuban, Mark

1958(?)– Businessman. Address: Dallas Mavericks, Reunion Arena, 777 Sports St., Dallas, TX 75207

Mark Cuban has always been a basketball fan. In fact, it was his and his friend Todd Wagner's desire to listen in to their college team's faraway games on the radio that brought him his first billion dollars. Realizing that there would be a market for sports events, speeches, and local radio programming on the Internet, the two formed AudioNet (later renamed Broadcast.com), which provided live broadcasts to millions of listeners nationwide. After selling the company to Yahoo!, Cuban put him-

Jane Hwang/Associated Press

Mark Cuban

self even closer to the sport he loved by purchasing his favorite professional basketball franchise, the Dallas Mavericks. While many scorned the move when it was announced, Cuban has managed to transform the Mavericks from one of the laughing-stocks of the National Basketball Association (NBA) into a play-off contender. In the process he has introduced a new management style to professional sports, one based on the theory that athletes perform best when treated well. Accordingly, Cuban sees to it that his players have what makes them happy, from high-quality towels to personal multimedia systems in their lockers. He also travels with and works out with his team and has befriended the players and support staff. Jerry Reynolds, the director of player personnel for the Sacramento Kings, told Richard Hoffer for *Sports Illustrated* (November 6, 2000), "He's made his team better in every area—talent, operations, it's all stronger. And interest is higher." Cuban, who started his first, successful business—MicroSolutions—when he was barely out of college, told *ABC News* (on-line), "When I got into the PC [personal computer] business [I was told], This is the way it's always done. We'll never need a PC. We'll never need audio or video over the Internet. . . . And you shouldn't get so close to your players. And you shouldn't go out there and travel. Shouldn't, shouldn't, shouldn't—is usually an indication I'm doing things right."

Mark Cuban was born in about 1958 in Pittsburgh, Pennsylvania. His father, the son of Russian-Jewish immigrants, was an auto upholsterer. Cuban has described his boyhood self as a goofy-looking kid with funny teeth and large glasses who dreamed of becoming a professional baseball or

basketball player. As he grew a little older, he turned his eyes to business. At age 12 he started his first enterprise, selling garbage bags door-to-door. "I did pretty well," Cuban told Rebecca Vesely for *Business 2.0* (on-line). "I was certainly the only kid out there selling garbage bags." When he was older, in addition to other ventures, Cuban sold powdered milk door-to-door, and after *Pittsburgh Press* employees went on strike, he and a friend drove to Cleveland, Ohio, to collect the *Plain Dealer* newspaper for resale in Pittsburgh. "It was easy when I realized [selling] wasn't about taking something from somebody, but about helping," Cuban told Hoffer. "If I can help you, you'll buy from me. I've always been the best salesman everywhere I've been. Whatever I was selling, I believed in."

Because it was the least expensive of the top 10 business schools in the country, Cuban chose to attend college at Indiana University. No longer wanting to be, as he told Hoffer, "the short, fat kid who wasn't getting any easy dates," in college Cuban lost weight, joined the rugby team, and ran successfully for freshman dorm president. Since he was too young to drink alcohol, he took the hardest courses first, predicting that when he came of age, he would want to party a great deal. As a freshman he attended graduate-level business classes, but during his sophomore year he had to drop them, after the dean of the business school discovered that Cuban was in effect an MBA student. (Cuban was allowed to keep the course credits he had already completed.) After turning 21 Cuban earned money by promoting parties at the Bloomington National Guard Armory, running an off-campus bar, and giving disco lessons. He also swept floors at a computer store, but found that he enjoyed computers so much that he couldn't resist trying to sell them and work at them—which led to his being fired.

Cuban graduated from Indiana University in 1981 with a B.S. degree in business. He then moved to Dallas, Texas, to sell software. He lived with five other men in a three-room apartment. During that period, without ever having taken a computer class or even owned a computer, he founded MicroSolutions, a computer consulting business. "The goal was to say yes to anything," he told *ABC News.com* (on-line). "I used to stay up all night. 'You want this written in dbase? You want it in BASIC? Sure I can do it.' [But] I'd have no clue." Thanks to his strong work ethic, the company grew and was included on *Inc.* magazine's list of the 500 fastest-growing privately held companies four years in a row. In 1990 Cuban sold MicroSolutions to CompuServe, becoming a millionaire in the process. Almost immediately he formed Radical Computing, a venture-capital and investment firm that specialized in high-technology companies. Over the next few years, Cuban would live in what amounted to semi-retirement, moving to Los Angeles, trading stocks, and taking acting classes.

In 1994 Cuban returned to Dallas. During that year he and a fellow Indiana graduate, the attorney Todd Wagner, discussed their desire to listen to the Indiana Hoosiers basketball games being played hundreds of miles away. Realizing that this could be accomplished over the Internet and that it would also be a good business venture, the two immediately went to work. "The same lightbulb went off for us that did for [the cable TV mogul] Ted Turner when he saw all the satellites going up around the world," Cuban told Vesely. "The Internet just seemed a perfect fit." "We started out in the second bedroom in my house," Cuban recalled during the *ABC News.com* (on-line) chat. "I think to get started we spent 3,000 dollars on a computer, 40 dollars on a radio, and sixty dollars a month for an ISDN line [which uses digital connections to transmit data worldwide], and just worked out of my house for a long time. And after a while, as good things started to happen, Todd and I had friends that started to threaten us if we didn't let them put in money." Cuban and Wagner persuaded a local Dallas radio station to feed its broadcasts over the Internet, and soon the two made similar deals with more stations; local programming, sports games, and speeches became available on-line. Cuban and Wagner called their new, Web-based radio business AudioNet—changing the name to Broadcast.com when they began to move into video broadcasting. As co-founder, Cuban oversaw general operations, including marketing and sales, technology, and strategic partnerships. The company soon became one of the few Internet sites to attract significant advertising while also earning money by setting up on-line video broadcasts for corporations. In 1998 the company went public, enjoying the most successful day in the history of IPOs (initial public offerings) when the stock price rose to $62.75 a share from $18.00. In addition to radio and video streaming, Broadcast.com provided access to NASA transmissions from space, flight-control communications from the Dallas–Fort Worth International Airport, transmissions made via police scanners from major U.S. cities, an audio-book library, and 3,000 musical recordings. By 1999 users could access more than 425 radio, TV, and cable networks. That year the company broadcast a Victoria's Secret runway show, thereby overloading Internet servers when 1.5 million people logged on to watch the event.

In 1999 Yahoo! acquired Broadcast.com for more than $6 billion worth of Yahoo! stock. Cuban, who stayed on as the head of the Broadcast.com division, emerged from the deal with a paper worth of $1.7 billion, while more than 300 of Broadcast.com's 330 employees, who had shares in Broadcast.com stock, became millionaires. "I thought, 'Oh my goodness! This is really happening!,' he told *ABC News.com* during the on-line chat. "It was just as amazing to me as it would be to anybody else. Even though we worked very, very hard, it was somewhat like winning the lottery." With his new riches Cuban made what turned out to be the largest on-line purchase in the short history of the Internet, when he bought a Gulf Stream 5, the fastest corporate jet in the world, for $41 million. He also bought a Dallas mansion (which, as of late 2000, he had yet to furnish).

In 2000 Cuban bought his favorite NBA franchise, the Dallas Mavericks, for $280 million. The deal was scoffed at in many circles, as the Mavericks, considered one of the worst teams in the NBA, had been valued at only $125 million as recently as 1996; the team had not made the play-offs in 10 years and had in its last few seasons compiled win-loss records so bad as to be almost unprecedented. "I'm a huge basketball fan," Cuban said during the *ABC News.com* chat, "and like every other Mavs fan who sat through all the losing years, I would sit there and fume, and say I could do this better. So when I got the chance to, financially, I said why not?" His first major move as owner was to sign the outspoken and flamboyant basketball star Dennis Rodman to a contract—a decision that brought derision from some when it was found that the contract allowed Rodman to show up late for games and skip practice, among other luxuries. Cuban also let Rodman stay in his guesthouse until the NBA found out about the arrangement and ruled it a salary-cap violation. Soon afterward, however, Rodman's defensive game was found to be lacking, and he was let go.

This was only the beginning, as Cuban quickly became the NBA's most notorious owner, creating headlines with every move he made and sitting behind the Mavericks' bench during every game, loudly cheering and complaining about the referees. He put his e-mail address on the Dallas scoreboard and asked fans to give their input; about 400 people a day answered this call, and Cuban began responding to them all personally. Meanwhile, he upgraded his players' luggage and hotel accommodations, sent limos to their houses to pick them up during an ice storm, and bought them each a special side chair for use at games, as well as a personal stereo, flat-screen monitor, DVD player, and Sony PlayStation. He flew with the team from game to game on his Gulf Stream 5 jet, where he could monitor what they were eating. "When you treat your employees well, they don't have any excuses but to work hard," Cuban said for the *ABC News.com* chat. "I want every employee to know that I care about them, that I want them to succeed, and that I'm going to expect 100 percent from them. It doesn't matter if they are a player, a receptionist, or a sales person." Cuban also defied convention by working out with his players and making trades himself, a practice usually reserved for a team's general manager. The responses from NBA owners and coaches and the press were mixed. Some praised Cuban for his hands-on approach to the game, while wondering aloud whether they would soon have to follow his lead in spending large sums to make their players happy. Others, less pleased with a person they saw as an amateur and a show-off, took every opportunity to criticize the new owner.

It did not take long for Cuban to silence many of his critics. After he bought the team, in the middle of the 1999–2000 season, the Mavericks surprised nearly everyone when they missed the play-offs by only a few games and won 16 of their last 21 games of the season to finish with a record of 40–42—after a 10–24 start. In the off-season, Cuban was at the nucleus of the first trade in the history of the NBA to involve four teams. He then went against tradition again, by hiring an extra assistant coach, giving his team a total of four assistant coaches. Ticket sales went up for the 2000–01 season, which the Mavericks finished with a record of 53–29, thereby making the play-offs for the first time since 1990. The team beat Utah in the first round of the play-offs, three games to two, before falling to San Antonio, four games to one. Cuban's passion for the game and his team got him into trouble with NBA officials that season, however. He was fined five times in amounts totaling $395,000, incurring the first four fines by criticizing officials and the fifth by sitting on the baseline of the basketball court, where owners are not allowed. His largest fine—for $250,000—came after he showed replays on the scoreboard related to a disputed call that went against Dallas.

Cuban's ideas regarding basketball extend beyond his own team. He has pitched several ideas to the NBA, such as a system that would "chart the refs," so that coaches could learn about the past tendencies of referees and strategize accordingly; digitized scouting film, so that coaches could have instant computer access to information on prospective players; and introduction of a "clutch average," which would rank players according to how well they performed in certain clutch situations. (The NBA has not thus far shown interest in his ideas.) Cuban is currently planning to build a new sports arena for the Mavericks, which will cost $340 million and will include at each seat such features as instant messaging, video games, and electrical outlets for palm pilots, allowing fans access to real-time statistics.

Cuban, who currently lives in Dallas, also has homes in New York and Los Angeles. He is known for his charisma—and for his extensive knowledge of the technology industry. "I think as bandwidth becomes more available to homes and businesses," he stated on the ABC News.com chat, "that people will travel less for business, work from home more. I think we'll see dramatic improvements in health care, with high speed connections between doctors, hospitals, patients, and the elderly. There will be so many ways that our lives will be impacted, that we will wonder how we ever got along without it." In 1999, in collaboration with Intel, he unveiled "The Black Box," a PC with a 27-megabyte hard drive and DVD-ROM, which can be hooked up to a TV set.

Cuban has insisted that he has not let success inflate his ego. "I think my family and my friends, my girlfriend, keep me very humble," he said on the ABC News.com chat. "And if I was to let any of this go to my head, they would probably give it a good smack. It hasn't helped my basketball game, it hasn't made it any easier to stay in shape. Other than making it easier to buy things, you still have to go through the same trials and tribulations, and that would make anyone humble." — G.O.

Suggested Reading: *ABC News* (on-line); *Broadcasting & Cable* p57 Oct. 18, 1999, with photo; *Business 2.0* (on-line); *New York Times Magazine* p64+ Mar. 5, 2000, with photo; *Sports Illustrated* p80+ Nov 6, 2000, with photos; *Texas Monthly* p122+ Sep. 1999, with photos

---

Courtesy of Coca-Cola Co.

Daft, Douglas N.

1944(?)– Chairman and CEO of Coca-Cola. Address: Coca-Cola Co., One Coca-Cola Pl., Atlanta, GA 30313

On December 5, 1999 M. Douglas Ivester, the chairman and CEO of Coca-Cola Co., announced to the company's board of directors that he planned to retire in the spring of 2000. With the assent of the board, Ivester named as his successor Douglas N. Daft, a native Australian who had spent most of his 30-year career with Coca-Cola in Asia. (Daft was named president and chief operating officer as well.) Ivester's departure was not entirely unexpected—under his two-year tenure, the value of Coca-Cola stock had plunged from $85 to around $47 per share—but his choice of Daft to replace him was "something of a surprise," as Marc Cohen, an analyst for Goldman Sachs, told Stephen Romei for *finance.news.com*, in a statement representative of the conventional wisdom on Wall Street. "I thought others were more favorably situated," Cohen explained. But, apparently unlike several other, more obvious candidates for CEO, Daft reportedly enjoyed the support of the investment guru Warren Buffett, Coca-Cola board member Herbert Allen, and former Coca-Cola president Donald R. Keough, all of whom are powerful behind-the-scenes players at the company. According to several observers, Buffett, Keough, and Allen felt that Daft's experience overseas made him uniquely qualified to lead the soft-drink giant. "Most of [Daft's] experience with the company has been in the Far East," Prudential Securities analyst George Thompson pointed out, as quoted by Greg W. Prince in *Beverage World* (January 15, 2000), "an area which should provide a significant amount of the company's incremental growth over the coming five to 10 years. We view this as an excellent training ground to deal with issues in the rest of the markets around the world."

Coca-Cola came into existence in 1886—about 83 years before Daft joined the company. It was invented by John S. Pemberton, an Atlanta pharmacist, and named by Frank Robinson, Pemberton's bookkeeper, for the two principal ingredients in the syrupy concoction—coca leaves (all traces of cocaine have been removed since 1903) and kola nuts, which contain caffeine. ("Magic . . . [is] . . . not an ingredient in the secret formula," but rather "something that emerges from the imagination of everyone who is touched by Coca-Cola," according to the company's 2000 annual report, as reprinted on the official Coca-Cola Web site.) Marketed as a "brain and nerve tonic," Coke originally sold for five cents a glass at a local pharmacy; in its first year, sales averaged nine drinks per day in all of Atlanta.

In 1891 Asa G. Candler, an Atlanta entrepreneur with a knack for marketing, purchased the full rights to the Coca-Cola recipe for $2,300. Thereafter, the company expanded rapidly. By 1895 the beverage was being sold throughout much of the United States, and by 1898 Coca-Cola had penetrated Canada and Mexico as well. By the time Candler retired, in 1916, the company had developed an extensive bottling network, as well as a distinctively shaped bottle "that anyone would recognize, even if it was felt in the dark," according to the company's Web site. In 1919 Ernest Woodruff, an Atlanta banker, bought the firm for $25 million; that same year Coca-Cola went public. Under Woodruff, Coca-Cola continued to grow, thanks in part to a string of popular, folksy advertising campaigns.

The globalization of the Coca-Cola brand name accelerated during World War II, when numerous bottling facilities were established in Europe and Asia to expedite delivery of the drink to American troops. After the war the company branched out into other beverage sectors, with the introduction of the orange-flavored Fanta, in 1955; the lemon-lime–flavored Sprite, in 1961; and the diet soda Tab (named with the assistance of a computer), in 1963. In 1960 the Coca-Cola Co. acquired the Minute Maid Co., known chiefly as a producer of orange juice. Throughout this period the company continued to promote the Coca-Cola brand name through memorable slogans and jingles. In a high point of the company's advertising efforts, an international group of young people, in an apparently spontaneous act, gathered on a hilltop in Italy in 1971 to sing "I'd like to buy the world a Coke," one of the company's popular advertising jingles.

Currently, the Coca-Cola Co. is a corporate giant that ranks 118th on the Fortune 500 and 328th on the Global 500 lists; it has operations in more than 200 countries and generates annual revenues of over $14 billion. Worldwide, more than one billion servings of Coca-Cola are swallowed daily—close to 2 percent of all the drinks consumed on the planet. (In fact, according to *Internet Doorway* [on-line], if Old Faithful, the famous geyser in Yellowstone National Park, were filled with all the Coke produced to date, it would continue to erupt, about 19 times daily, for more than 1,577 years.) Coca-Cola has become the quintessential icon of American capitalism; in 1988, according to an independent survey, it was the world's most recognizable trademark. Sales of the company's flagship beverage continue to constitute its core business, and such products as Diet Coke, Cherry Coke, Sprite, and Fanta make the company a major presence in other sectors of the nonalcoholic-carbonated-beverage industry. Moreover, through subsidiaries such as Minute Maid and partners such as Nestlé S.A., Coca-Cola markets an array of instant coffees, teas, juices, and herbal beverages—more than 500 "flavor combinations" in all, according to the company's Web site.

In recent years Coca-Cola has experienced a string of setbacks, all of which contributed to the plunge in the value of the company's stock under M. Douglas Ivester. One major reason for some of those reverses was a business strategy, pursued by Ivester and his predecessor, of boosting Coca-Cola's profits at the expense of its bottling network. (The bottling facilities are franchises in which Coca-Cola owns a minority stake and to which it sells cola concentrate. According to Patricia Sellers in *Fortune* [March 6, 2000, on-line], the bottling network "makes the drinks, buys the trucks, delivers the cases, does the local marketing—all with Coke's help.") By charging bottlers in Asia and Latin America high rates for franchise rights, Coca-Cola reaped significant profits in the short-term but left the bottlers unprepared to weather financial troubles. With the advent of the Asian and Russian economic crises of the late 1990s, and similar financial difficulties in Latin America, local bottlers suffered a decline in sales, and passed their losses on to Coca-Cola.

Coca-Cola also suffered a number of public-relations embarrassments under Ivester. In April 1999 eight current and former African-American employees filed a racial-bias suit alleging discrimination in promotions, terminations, and pay. (In the summer of 2000, just as the company announced it had reached a tentative settlement, the lawyers Willie E. Gary and Johnnie Cochran filed a $1.5 billion racial-bias suit on behalf of four new plaintiffs.) In June 1999 France, Belgium, Luxembourg, and the Netherlands banned sales of Coca-Cola after several children drank contaminated Coke and required hospitalization. (The company subsequently ordered a product recall in Belgium at an estimated cost of $34 million.) Coca-Cola also faced criticism in the United States from health activists who objected to the company's practice of making exclusive vending arrangements with cash-strapped school districts. (In at least one instance, Marc Kaufman wrote for the *Washington Post* [March 23, 1999], "the school district . . . urged principals to increase sales of Coke products to keep the profits flowing from vending machine contracts.") Coca-Cola's mounting woes pushed the company's board to pressure Ivester to leave, thus opening the way for Daft to replace him.

Douglas N. Daft was born in Sydney, Australia, in about 1944. He joined Coca-Cola in 1969, as a planning officer in Sydney. Two years later he was transferred to Indonesia, where he handled planning, marketing, and operations. "My job there was simply to sell Coca-Cola, lots of it," he told Joanna Slater for the *Far Eastern Economic Review* (April 20, 2000, on-line). "I worked hard selling Coca-Cola for three years. Then we launched Fanta, . . . and the business just tripled and quadrupled." By the early 1980s Daft had transferred to Malaysia, where he became acquainted with Donald R. Keough. In 1984 he was named president of Coca-Cola's Central Pacific Division, which is in charge of operations in China, Indonesia, Malaysia, Singapore, and Thailand. Four years later he was appointed president of Coca-Cola Japan. "I had to learn how to communicate in Japan," Daft told Slater, "and I don't mean speak Japanese. For example, if I want to have a meeting with the chairman of a company, first of all someone goes and talks through what the meeting will be all about. By the time we get there, both parties know if there are any controversial issues and what the outcome of the meeting will be." In 1991 Daft transferred to the company's Atlanta headquarters to assume the post of president of the Pacific Group, which oversees operations in China, Japan, India and Australia. In October 1999 he was named head of the Middle and Far East and Africa Groups and the Schweppes Beverages Division. On December 5, 1999, the same day that Ivester announced his resignation, Daft was promoted to president and chief operating officer of the Coca-Cola Co., as well as chairman-designate. He was promoted with the backing of Coca-Cola board member Warren Buffett, the chairman and CEO of Berkshire Hathaway Inc., an investment firm that holds about 8 percent of Coca-Cola's capital stock; Herbert Allen, who owns or controls about .5 percent of Coca-Cola stock; and Donald R. Keough, a longtime acquain-

tance of Buffett's, who is an adviser to the Coca-Cola board of directors.

While still chairman-designate Daft began taking steps to decentralize the company. On January 26, 2000 Coca-Cola announced it would eliminate 6,000 jobs worldwide, or about one-fifth of its workforce, as part of a larger plan to transfer more power to local operations. "The world in which we operate has changed dramatically, and we must change to succeed," Daft declared, according to Justin Bachman in an Associated Press (January 26, 2000) report. "We must think local and act local, taking our business to where our business is. This will allow us to sell more products." "Daft spent his career building and running the business in Asia," John Sicher, the editor and publisher of *Beverage Digest*, noted, as quoted by Martha M. Hamilton in the *Washington Post* (January 27, 2000). "He knows what the Coke troops on the ground can do and intends to give them a lot more power." In response to sagging morale in the wake of the layoffs, Daft declared May 8, the day Pemberton created Coca-Cola, a paid holiday for the company's employees.

Daft has been described as "people-oriented" and a "backslapper," in contrast to his predecessor, who was characterized as a "tough, unapproachable taskmaster" and "as driven as they come." He routinely puts in 12-hour workdays and is reported to own more than 500,000 shares of Coke stock, valued at about $32 million in late 2000, as well as $20 million in stock options. — P.K.

Suggested Reading: *Beverage World* p12+ Jan. 15, 2000; *Far Eastern Economic Review* (on-line) Apr. 20, 2000; *Fortune* (on-line) Mar. 6, 2000, Mar. 19, 2001; *Journal of Business Strategy* p14+ Sep./Oct. 2000, with photos; *New York Times* C p2 Dec. 7, 1999, with photo, III p1+ Feb. 6, 2000, with photo; *Wall Street Journal* B p1+ Dec. 7, 1999, with photo

D'Angelo

Feb. 11, 1974– Soul singer; songwriter; instrumentalist. Address: c/o Virgin Records, 90 University Pl., New York, NY 10003-4506

With the release of D'Angelo's debut album, *Brown Sugar*, in 1995, accolades began pouring in from many quarters, proclaiming this singer, songwriter, and multi-instrumentalist the savior of R&B, a musical genre that had been in decline—in the opinion of many—since the 1970s. "Marrying Marvin Gaye's sensual vulnerability with Stevie Wonder's earnestness, . . . Prince's rascally falsetto to Curtis Mayfield's grain and poignancy, D'Angelo brings hope and delight to R&B fans who have been numbed by prefabricated, oversexed and all-too-obvious acts and recordings," the poet, novelist,

Jon Ricard/Retna

D'Angelo

and journalist Rohan B. Preston wrote for the *Chicago Tribune* (October 24, 1995). "And yet he does not so much imitate these masters; they simply inform him as he attempts to take that knowledge to another level." More than two million copies of *Brown Sugar* were sold. D'Angelo's long-awaited sophomore effort, *Voodoo* (2000), featured the smooth vocals—delivered in his famed falsetto—and solid instrumentation that characterized its predecessor, while offering more improvisational nuances. Some critics speculated that *Voodoo*'s more experimental character and lack of hooks might keep the album off the charts, but it has turned out to be at least as commercially successful as *Brown Sugar*. D'Angelo's 2001 Grammy Award, which recognized him as the year's best R&B vocalist, has solidified his position at the forefront of the "new soul" movement that he helped to create.

D'Angelo was born Michael D'Angelo Archer in Richmond, Virginia, on February 11, 1974. His father and one of his grandfathers were preachers, and at an early age he began singing in a church choir. He started learning piano at three. "My oldest brother was playing classical music, and I remember hearing him play 'Flight of the Bumblebee' and Bach, and it made me really want to play," he recalled for *CNN* (June 20, 2000, on-line). "I used to go to the piano after he finished practicing and bang on it." Beginning when he was nine, each Sunday D'Angelo would play the piano and organ at his grandfather's church, and after a while he directed the choir there, too. His musical taste was never restricted to church-related music, however. His mother, Mariann Smith, was a big admirer of Marvin Gaye and other soul musicians, and D'Angelo—who has identified Gaye as one of his major inspirations—would spend hours at the piano picking out tunes by such artists or acts as Donna Summer and Earth, Wind, and Fire. In time he became proficient on drums, bass, and guitar as well as piano.

In his teens D'Angelo added rap to his diverse list of musical influences. "Rakim and KRS-One were my heroes," he told Cheo H. Coker for the *Los Angeles Times* (August 18, 1995). "We used to [have rap competitions] in the bathroom during high school, and I used to call myself Chilly Chill. That stuff is definitely still in me too. All rap is street soul. They just have a different method." At about 16 D'Angelo formed a band called Michael Archer and Precise; in addition to their own material, the group interpreted songs by Al Green and Smokey Robinson, and they won several talent shows. D'Angelo was performing with a rap group called IDU (Intelligent, Deadly but Unique) in 1991 when he signed a publishing deal with EMI, which led to a record contract. Soon after joining EMI's roster, he was invited to compete on Amateur Night at the Apollo Theater, in New York City's Harlem, the venue where such legendary figures as Ella Fitzgerald, Sarah Vaughn, and Pearl Bailey got their first major exposure. He won three separate competitions at the Apollo. With his prize money, he bought musical equipment so that he could do his own recording.

In 1994 D'Angelo's song "U Will Know" was released as a single by the group Black Men United, and it was used as the theme of Doug McHenry's movie *Jason's Lyric*. The next year EMI released *Brown Sugar*. Taking after Prince, another of his favorite musicians, D'Angelo played nearly all the instruments on the album. The songs, most of them lean and stripped down, without complex orchestrations, are dominated by throbbing drum beats and bouncy bass lines and are punctuated by D'Angelo's electric-piano riffs and splashes of guitar. Crooning in his smooth, buttery style, D'Angelo often soared into a falsetto, as in the album's title track, a veiled tribute to marijuana that became a hit single. Most of the songs, however, are about traditional romances, in the style of classic soul music. In "Me and Those Dreamin' Eyes of Mine," for example, D'Angelo sings, as quoted on the *D'Angelo's World* Web site, "Ooh wee baby, you've redefined my vision of love it seems / Your love be da cherry in my chocolate covered dreams / So it seems, my oh my, / Me and those dreaming eyes of mine."

Critical response to the album was overwhelmingly positive. In the London *Guardian* (July 7, 1995), Garry Mulholland wrote of *Brown Sugar*, "The range of talent on display here . . . leaves you breathless to hear what the wonder kid will come up with next. For lovers of true soul music, this is the album we've been waiting for. History and relevance, heartbreak and strutting confidence. *Brown Sugar* is the best soul album since . . . since . . . you know, I really can't remember when." A reviewer for *Rolling Stone* (May 13, 1999) named

Brown Sugar among the best albums of the 1990s and wrote, "After years of imitators, a true son of Stevie Wonder, Marvin Gaye, Sly Stone, Curtis Mayfield, and Prince . . . emerged from an attic in Richmond, Virginia." To many critics D'Angelo embodied a new, more musically interesting alternative to the overtly commercial R&B that ruled the airwaves in the mid-1990s. Coker, for instance, noted, "It's easy to see why critics and fans are beginning to dub him the savior of soul. This entertainer appears to be a figure who can single-handedly bring an integrity and purity back to a genre that has sacrificed true feeling for over-production and cliche." *Brown Sugar*, which went double platinum, earned D'Angelo an American Music Award as favorite new artist, two Soul Train Music Awards, and five Grammy nominations.

The extent of his sudden fame was illustrated during the summer of 1995, when hordes of people gathered outside the site of a D'Angelo concert in New York City, clamoring to get seats to see the new R&B phenomenon. Even such celebrities as the R&B trio TLC, the film director Martin Scorsese, and Prince were turned away. The doorman denied D'Angelo himself entry for more than a half hour, until his identity could be confirmed. Though new-soul releases by Maxwell, Erykah Badu, Lauryn Hill, and Macy Gray came on the heels of *Brown Sugar*—and, by seeming to cast D'Angelo in the role of leader of a new musical trend, might have buoyed his confidence—the expectations stirred by his album had an inhibiting effect on him, resulting in a five-year hiatus before his next recording was released. "I felt pressure," D'Angelo admitted to Kimberly Davis for *Ebony* (April 2000), "but I held on. It was important for me to hold on to what I was believing in, to what I was thinking about. I was just trying to make some good music."

Although he was not recording during those five years, D'Angelo was not inactive. In 1996 a recording of one of his concerts, *Live at the Jazz Café*, was released overseas by EMI U.K. He was a guest on B.B. King's album *Deuces Wild* (1997) and on *The Miseducation of Lauryn Hill* (1998), and he contributed to the soundtrack albums for the films *Scream 2* (1997), *Belly* (1998), and *Down in the Delta* (1998). In February 1997 his son, Michael, was born to his fellow R&B artist Angie Stone, who by the time of the baby's birth was no longer his girlfriend.

At the end of January 2000, D'Angelo released the long-awaited *Voodoo*. Whereas *Brown Sugar* was largely a solo effort, on *Voodoo* D'Angelo collaborated with a half-dozen artists, among them the drummer Ahmir ("?uestlove") Thompson, the trumpeter Roy Hargrove, and the rappers Q-Tip, Method Man, and Redman. "There's strength in numbers, especially with what we're doing," D'Angelo told Davis. "We all share like-minded visions, so it's important for us to network, to get together and to talk and vibe and play together." The album had a looser, more improvisational feel than

Brown Sugar. "A lot of stuff is live and it's the first take," D'Angelo explained, as quoted by Shawn Rhea in the New Orleans *Times-Picayune* (March 10, 2000). "We'd come in and just tape for hours and hours and just play and play, and I would pick the best of the batch and write the song to that jam session. A lot of what you are hearing is just us up in [the studio] jamming." *Voodoo* also offered a larger musical palette than *Brown Sugar*: "Spanish Joint," for example, careens through syncopated Latin rhythms enriched by a jazzy bass line and the trumpet work of Roy Hargrove; "Devil's Pie" eschews prominent vocal melodies for a laid-back, funky groove and low-key singing. In *Voodoo*'s lyrics, D'Angelo dealt not only with the topic of romance but also with faith and fatherhood, the latter of which he experienced anew with the birth in the fall of 1999 of his daughter, Imani, whose mother's identity he has refused to disclose. In "Africa," for instance, as transcribed on the *D'Angelo's World* Web site, he sang, "Ever since the day you came / my whole world began to change / I knew then to dedicate my life, / for your own / everyday I see you grow / and remember what you already know / I receive the love / that radiates from your glow."

The publicity surrounding *Voodoo* was greatly escalated, and almost overshadowed, by the video for the single "Untitled (How Does It Feel)," in which D'Angelo, nude from the waist up and looking muscular and fit, stands against a black background and sings about love. Most critics agreed, however, that *Voodoo* offered a lot more than D'Angelo's highly marketable image. In the *Village Voice* (March 28, 2000), Robert Christgau wrote, "The pecs and pubes of the video are a feint, one of many; although the music can be sexy and lunky and fun and woman-centered, that's just part of the sonic concept. Which is unique." Assessing the album for *Entertainment Weekly* (January 21, 2000), Matt Diehl quipped, "[D'Angelo's] falsetto just may serve as women's answer to Viagra," and then advised, "If you're looking for an antidote to the processed-cheese-disease that's infected today's pop, a little bit o' *Voodoo* is just what the witch doctor ordered." Shawn Rhea, appreciative of *Voodoo*'s eclecticism, wrote, "The singer seems to have channeled the brilliance of his musical forefathers, living and dead, during the crafting of this album. It is a complex, intricate collection of songs that, like voodoo, is simultaneously secular and spiritual, sensual and sacred, earthbound and ethereal." By the middle of 2000, *Voodoo* had sold more than 1.3 million copies and had earned D'Angelo three nominations for the 15th annual Soul Train Music Awards, held in 2001.

The singer maintains residences in New York City and Richmond. His musical mission has changed little in the past decade. "I consider myself very respectful of the masters who came before," he told Davis. "In some ways, I feel a responsibility to continue and take the cue from what they were doing musically and vibe on it. That's what I want to do. But I want to do it for this time and this generation." — P.G.H.

Suggested Reading: *Chicago Tribune* V p5 Oct. 24, 1995; *Ebony* p78+ Apr. 2000; *Entertainment Weekly* p29+ Feb. 4, 2000; *Gentlemen's Quarterly* p92+ Nov. 1995; *Interview* p106+ Feb. 1999; (London) *Guardian* p14 July 7, 1995; *Los Angeles Times* p1+ Aug. 18, 1995; *New York Times* II p28 Apr. 7, 1996, E p25 Feb. 23, 2001; *Rolling Stone* p36+ July 10, 1997; *Time* p85+ July 6, 1998; *USA Today* D p14 Nov. 1, 1995

Selected Recordings: *Brown Sugar*, 1995; *Live at the Jazz Café*, 1996; *Voodoo*, 2000

Enrique Marcarian/Archive Photos

de la Rúa, Fernando

Sep. 15, 1937– President of Argentina. Address: Casa Rosada, Buenos Aires, Argentina

The October 1999 electoral victory of Fernando de la Rúa, the presidential candidate of Argentina's center-left Alianza coalition, ended a decade of rule by the Justicialists, the party of Juan Perón. With a 10-point lead over his chief rival, the Peronist Eduardo Duhalde, de la Rúa dealt the Justicialist Party its worst defeat ever in a presidential election. Yet the result hardly signaled a radical departure from the status quo; in fact, on most substantive policy issues—and especially on economic issues—de la Rúa had not offered any fundamental alternatives to those of Carlos Menem, the outgoing Justicialist president. What he did offer was a different political style, one that promised restraint and openness in a political culture often noted for its extravagant personalism. Voters clearly wanted something new, especially since the country was

mired in its second economic slump of the decade; but with memories of hyperinflation (in the late 1980s) and years of military dictatorship (in the late 1970s and early 1980s) still fresh in the minds of most Argentineans, the impulse for change was tempered by caution. As Roberto Bacman, an Argentinean pollster, told Clifford Krauss for the *New York Times* (October 24, 1999), "Everyone wants change, but moderate change, with more transparency and honesty."

Fernando de la Rúa was born on September 15, 1937 in Córdoba, Argentina's second-largest city. He attended the University of Córdoba, where he studied law, and earned his doctorate with a thesis entitled, in English translation, "Extraordinary Appeal to the Court of Cassation in Argentine Legislation." Shortly after completing his legal studies, at the age of 26, de la Rúa became one of the youngest members of the constitutionally elected Radical Party government of Arturo Illia. De la Rúa served under Illia as an adviser in the Interior Ministry from 1963, the year Illia came to power, until 1966, when the government was toppled by a military coup led by General Juan Carlos Onganía. In April 1973 de la Rúa returned to politics and was elected to represent Buenos Aires, the nation's political and cultural capital, in the Senate, Argentina's upper congressional house. (Prior to 1995 the Senate was composed of two members from each of Argentina's 23 provinces as well as two members from Buenos Aires, which is known as the federal district; since then, each province has been represented by three senators.) Later that year, he became the vice-presidential running mate of the Radical Party candidate Ricardo Balbín. (Balbín lost to Juan Perón, who made a comeback that year after 18 years in exile.) According to the *Economist* (November 21, 1998), de la Rúa served as a congressman for 23 years, until 1996. (Other sources suggest that de la Rúa's congressional career was interrupted after a 1976 military coup.) As a legislator, he was regarded as dedicated but lackluster. He was known chiefly for promoting laws regulating sports and organ transplants, as well as for his support of the rights of indigenous peoples.

The Unión Cívica Radical (Radical Civic Union, or Radical Party), with which de la Rúa has been affiliated since his youth, traces its history to the late 19th century and has traditionally represented the moderate left in Argentine politics. Throughout the most recent period in which the country was ruled by a military junta (1976–83), the Radical Party took the lead in pressing for a return to civilian rule. By 1983 the military regime had been discredited by a faltering economy as well as by its defeat in the 1982 Falklands War (or Malvinas War, as it is known in Argentina, in which that nation attempted to wrest control of the Falkland Islands from Great Britain). Under pressure, the military permitted free elections in October 1983, and the Radical Party scored a decisive victory. Not only did its candidate, Raúl Alfonsín, win the presidency; the party also gained control of the Chamber of

Deputies, Argentina's lower congressional house. While Alfonsín won praise for his prosecution of those responsible for human-rights violations under the junta, the country's mounting economic woes led voters to reject the Radical Party in national elections held on May 14, 1989. (Alfonsín, who was constitutionally ineligible for reelection, did not run.) Rather, the presidency went to Carlos Menem, whose populist campaign promised economic relief while also claiming some of the credit for the restoration of civilian rule. (Menem, who had been jailed for political reasons under the junta, was the first Peronist leader to endorse the Alfonsín government, in 1983.) In 1997 the Radical Party joined with the left-leaning Frepaso, or Front for a Country in Solidarity, a breakaway faction of the Justicialist Party, to form the Alianza coalition.

Earlier, in 1996, de la Rúa had become the first elected mayor of Buenos Aires, a post that had previously been filled by presidential appointment. (The job of administering Buenos Aires, a sprawling city of almost 12 million inhabitants, is one of the most prominent political posts in the country.) As mayor, de la Rúa managed to convert a $600 million budget deficit into a surplus without cutting public services. In fact, he extended the subway, invested in cultural events, opened shelters for battered women and the disabled, and initiated a widely publicized waste-recycling program. He accomplished this in part through sound fiscal policies, but also by cracking down on the corruption and cronyism that had sapped the public coffers for years. His administration charged several former mayors and city officials with accepting bribes from city contractors and canceled a number of irregular rental agreements between the city and allies of former administrations. "The biggest demand of the electorate of my country is for an end to corruption and much greater openness," de la Rúa said in an interview cited by Calvin Sims in the *New York Times* (November 10, 1997). "We will persecute the corrupt until the end."

De la Rúa's emphasis on fighting corruption was politically deft; indeed, it was chiefly his reputation for austerity and honesty that allowed him to defeat Eduardo Duhalde, the Justicialist Party candidate, in the October 1999 presidential elections. Although the country was experiencing acute unemployment, de la Rúa did not fundamentally challenge Menem's economic program (the cornerstone of which was a scheme of the Argentinean currency board—a special monetary authority—that fixed the value of the Argentine peso on par with that of the U.S. dollar). That was because voters tended to blame the disastrous hyperinflation of the late 1980s, which precipitated food riots and plunged millions into poverty, on Radical Party mismanagement; Menem, despite the country's recurrent economic troubles, was widely credited with having ended the crisis. De la Rúa focused instead on corruption, an issue that, according to polls, had remained a top concern of Argentinean voters throughout the 1980s and 1990s. By doing

so, he was able to attack the Peronists without departing from their economic agenda. As Graciela Romer, an Argentinean political consultant, explained to Sims, "In a country like Argentina, which has an expanding economy, large foreign investment and at the same time high unemployment, people start to think that the reason they can't get a job or buy the things they need is because someone in power, in other words government officials, is pocketing the money."

To underscore his anticorruption strategy, de la Rúa ran a number of television advertisements that contrasted his drab political style with Menem's flamboyant antics. De la Rúa began his most celebrated spot by flatly declaring, according to Krauss, "They call me boring." Next, the ad cut to a picture of Menem posing in a Ferrari, followed by a shot of an actor, understood to represent a Justicialist politician, pocketing a bribe. "I'm going to end this party," de la Rúa intoned in a voice-over. "Those who are bored with me are on their way out." While the advertising campaign failed to generate much enthusiasm, it did achieve its intended effect: by election day, polls indicated, most Argentineans regarded de la Rúa as dull but uncorrupt. As Romer told Anthony Faiola for the *Washington Post* (October 25, 1999), "De la Rúa is viewed as an honest man, and that's what Argentines are desperate for."

De la Rúa also benefitted from disarray in the rival Peronist camp, which never managed to mount a unified campaign. Dissension in the Peronist ranks emerged early after Eduardo Duhalde, the governor of Buenos Aires Province, who eventually won the Justicialist Party nomination, opposed Menem's plans to run for a third term. (Menem's serving a third term would have required a constitutional amendment.) The resulting schism was never fully healed, and Menem's eventual endorsement of Duhalde was lukewarm at best. (The day after Duhalde's defeat, "Menem 2003" posters sprang up across Buenos Aires; soon thereafter, Duhalde supporters responded with posters that charged, "Menem did it.")

As expected, de la Rúa won the election by a landslide. With 48.5 percent of the vote, compared with only 37.9 percent for Duhalde, he was able to secure the 10-point lead necessary to avert a runoff. (Argentine law requires a runoff unless a candidate obtains either a 10-point lead or an absolute majority of the vote.) Yet, while de la Rúa declared the final result "a clear mandate," as Clifford Krauss reported in the *New York Times* (October 25, 1999), his Alianza coalition failed to win control of the Senate, which remained in Peronist hands, and came up four seats short of a majority in the Chamber of Deputies. The Peronists also retained 14 of the 24 provincial governorships (two others of which were held by independents), and continued to dominate the Supreme Court. Further undermining de la Rúa's electoral victory was the fact that his Alianza coalition comprised two parties, which he would need to hold together in order to govern effectively.

Thus, in spite of his decided victory at the polls, it was clear from the beginning that political exigencies would vastly curtail de la Rúa's executive powers. In stark contrast to Menem, who had ruled virtually by fiat (Menem's Justicialist Party had commanded a majority in the Senate, the largest minority in the Chamber of Deputies, and a majority of provincial governors, and could count on the sympathy of the judiciary), de la Rúa would be forced to negotiate with his political opponents in order to get anything done. For some commentators, such a shift in the distribution of power appeared to herald a new era in Argentine politics; in the words of Mariano Grondona, a correspondent for the Buenos Aires daily *La Nación*, as quoted in the *World Press Review* (January 2000), "This drastically diminished power will force de la Rúa into a new style of government. For more than 10 years, Menem behaved along the lines of our classical strongmen. . . . de la Rúa, on the other hand, will have to build consensus for each of his initiatives. . . . Menem ruled; de la Rúa will have to persuade. . . . Perhaps a new political culture is coming into being. The essence of government will no longer depend upon one man. From now on, the citizenry will look not to a sole protagonist but an entire political class."

Upon taking office, in December 1999, de la Rúa took a number of measures, as promised, to crack down on political corruption. He established a special anticorruption agency to investigate charges of official misconduct; took steps to disclose government expenditures to the public; and, in a symbolic gesture, put up for sale Menem's presidential jet, *Tango 01*, opting instead to travel by commercial airline. Nonetheless, the indictments of major political figures that many Argentineans had awaited failed to materialize.

In the sphere of foreign affairs, de la Rúa initiated a slight shift to the left. Whereas Menem had cultivated close relationships with the United States (so much so that after his attempt to bring Argentina into NATO in 1999, the local Buenos Aires press derided his "carnal relations" with Washington), de la Rúa adopted a posture similar to that of such traditionally nonaligned Latin American countries as Brazil and Mexico. Shortly after taking office, de la Rúa declared that Argentina would no longer contribute troops to multinational peacekeeping operations. He also publicly advised General Lino Oviedo, a former Uruguayan army chief who sought political asylum in Argentina after accusations that he had plotted the assassination of his country's vice president, to seek a new home elsewhere. At the same time, he reassured President Bill Clinton that Argentina remained committed to its relationship with the United States: "I told President Clinton we would work together for peace and against drug trafficking," he declared at a press conference, as quoted by Krauss.

De la Rúa's greatest challenge lay in tackling the economic recession he had inherited from Menem. The slump, set off by the Asian and Russian financial crises of 1998 and further exacerbated by a January 1999 currency devaluation in neighboring Brazil, had driven unemployment to almost 14 percent by the end of 1999. The national GDP (gross domestic product) had fallen by more than 3 percent that year, and the national poverty rate had reached 29 percent, as compared with 22 percent in neighboring Chile. Income differences between rich and poor were also widening.

While de la Rúa was able to plant much of the blame on Menem, he left many of his predecessor's policies in place. Since many economists predicted that the end of the recession was around the corner, his strategy seemed sensible: as a correspondent for the *Economist* (October 30, 1999) noted shortly after the election, "Mr. de la Rúa's good fortune is to have won just as the recession appears to have reached bottom—enabling him to be fortuitously associated with the rebound." Indeed, optimistic forecasts were made soon after de la Rúa took office, in December 1999. Market analysts, considering the strong economic recovery in Brazil, the recent passage (under Menem) of a "fiscal responsibility law" requiring the government to eliminate the federal deficit by 2003, and de la Rúa's own reputation for fiscal discipline, predicted a modest but significant growth in the GDP of 3 percent for 2000. Standard & Poor, the American credit-rating agency, changed its assessment of the Argentine economy from "negative" to "stable." Finally, the International Monetary Fund offered the Argentine government a contingency credit of $7.4 billion, considerably more than had been expected; this, too, was seen as a vote of confidence in the country's economic prospects.

Nevertheless, Argentina's economic difficulties proved frustratingly intractable in 2000, as the expected recovery failed to occur. Rather, the country hovered in an economic limbo between recession and recovery. Although the economy did grow, growth was sluggish—less than one-half of 1 percent; unemployment edged up to nearly 16 percent, and the government's efforts to reduce the deficit, impeded by the anemic economy, were less successful than had been hoped. For the most part, Argentina's economic difficulties stemmed from causes beyond the government's control, such as low prices for agricultural goods on the international market and the low value of the European euro. Still, independent and government economists alike continued to predict a recovery; as Jose Luis Machinea, de la Rúa's economic minister, told a bankers' association, as quoted by Krauss in the *New York Times* (December 8, 2000), "The Argentine economy is going to grow a lot faster than people expect. An era of prosperity is coming for Argentines."

De la Rúa suffered a major political setback in late 2000 in the wake of a bribery scandal. The scandal, which tied several ministers and a number of senators to an alleged vote-buying scheme, prompted de la Rúa to reshuffle his cabinet; but, because he retained two of the ministers implicated in the scandal, that move only aggravated the situation. In early October four congressmen announced their decision to leave the Alianza coalition, and Carlos Alvarez, de la Rúa's vice president and a key ally in the Alianza coalition, resigned in protest. In an interview with Kevin Gray for the *Houston Chronicle* (October 12, 2000, on-line), Felipe Noguera, a political consultant, characterized the affair as "a crisis of de la Rúa's strategy of fighting corruption and focusing on the way you do things rather than the things you do." By December the president's approval rating had plummeted to a dismal 7 percent. Although de la Rúa was showing signs of a comeback by January, his political allies were understandably concerned about the upcoming midterm congressional elections, scheduled to take place in October 2001.

The Alianza coalition suffered a decisive setback in those elections, and the Justicialist Party gained control of both houses of Congress. Although many saw the results as a plebiscite against de la Rúa's economic policies—Argentina was still mired in recession—a record number of voters expressed dissatisfaction with the entire political system by either leaving blank or intentionally spoiling their ballots. (Argentinean law requires citizens to vote.) After the results of the election had become known, a humbled de la Rúa conceded his party's defeat and acknowledged, according to Hector Tobar in the *Los Angeles Times* (October 15, 2001), that "after this election, I know many things must change. . . . I understand the impatience and the anger of the people. I will not cover my ears." "The de la Rúa administration will be even weaker after the election," the political analyst Rosendo Fraga told Tobar. "As a result, its big political challenge will be to maintain its ability to govern."

When asked by a reporter about hobbies and avocational interests, de la Rúa replied, as quoted by Krauss, "I recognize that I am not No.1 in soccer, chess or golf, but I enjoy them all." On another occasion, de la Rúa, who has written five books on legal procedure, declared, "I'm really a university professor more than a politician," then added, "I do serious things and I do them seriously." De la Rúa is married to Ines Pertine. — P.K.

Suggested Reading: *Economist* p39+ Sep. 4, 1999; *Economist* (on-line) Oct. 30, 1999, with photo; *Houston Chronicle* (on-line) p16 Oct. 12, 2000, with photos; *New York Times* I p3 Oct. 24, 1999, A p1+ Oct. 25, 1999, A p6 Oct. 26, 1999, I p20 Oct. 31, 1999

Deakins, Roger

May 24, 1949– Cinematographer. Address: c/o International Creative Management, 8942 Wilshire Blvd., Beverly Hills, CA 90211

With the more than 40 feature films to his credit—among them *Stormy Monday, Thunderheart, Passion Fish, The Shawshank Redemption, Dead Man Walking, Courage Under Fire, Kundun, The Siege, The Hurricane,* and *Anywhere But Here*—the British-born cinematographer Roger Deakins has created a distinctive, documentary-like visual style, by emphasizing naturalistic light that gives his work an air of realism. Deakins began his career as a camera operator for documentaries, a job in which he learned many of the skills he has employed in his feature films to achieve the naturalism for which his cinematography has become known. He has worked on six films with Joel and Ethan Coen, among them *Fargo,* the black comedy that brought the Coen brothers their first mainstream success and Deakins the second of his four Oscar nominations, and *O Brother, Where Art Thou?*, which traces the odyssey of three fugitives from a Depression-era southern chain gang and earned the cinematographer his most recent Academy Award nomination. "If I bring anything to the Coen Brothers' films, it's my ability to change tack and create a different mood from film to film," he told Ryan

Joel Lipton Photography

Mottesheard for *indiewire.com* (October 30, 2001). Deakins has also served as director of photography for music videos by such artists and acts as Eric Clapton, Marvin Gaye, Madness, Level 42, and

Meat Loaf, and was largely responsible for the look of the jazz icon Herbie Hancock's breakthrough video for "Rock It" (1983). His most recent credits include, in 2001, two feature films—the Coen brothers' *The Man Who Wasn't There* and Ron Howard's *A Beautiful Mind*—and, for HBO, *Dinner with Friends*, directed by Norman Jewison.

Roger Deakins was born on May 24, 1949 in the small coastal town of Torquay, in southeastern England. As a teenager he hoped to become a painter, but the work of such photographers as Walker Evans, Henri Cartier-Bresson, and Sebastiao Salgado inspired him to study still photography in college. "I loved observing life and being able to capture what I saw with my camera," he told Pauline Rogers for her book *Contemporary Cinematographers and Their Art* (1998), as excerpted for *Reelmind.com* (2000, on-line). "It was just what I had been trying to do with paint." Later, in 1972, he entered the National Film School in London. After he graduated he had difficulty finding work. Eventually he was hired to shoot industrial films and rock concerts, and he soon made a name for himself as a cameraperson for documentaries. In his interview with Pauline Rogers, he said, referring to the violence between black guerrillas and white Rhodesian soldiers in the 1970s in what was to become the independent nation of Zimbabwe in 1980, "My first real opportunity came when I was asked to film the war in Rhodesia for the African National Congress. For a few weeks, we clandestinely filmed the effect the white separatist regime was having on the black African population, before we were discovered not to be the tourists we purported to be."

Deakins next worked as part of a crew assigned to document the Whitbread Around the World Yacht Race for Associated Television (now called Central Television), in Great Britain; he got that job by convincing the producers that he was an experienced seaman, although he had been on a yacht only once before. Along with the sound recordist Noel Smart, he spent nine months on the yacht, under less than ideal conditions for their purposes. "Often, the most dramatic times to shoot were also the most dangerous for the boat itself," he recalled to Pauline Rogers. "We were after all members of the ten-man crew. At one point, the rudder broke as we were surfing down-wind in a particularly heavy sea somewhere in the Southern Ocean. Noel and I were part of the watch on deck, so we had to trim the boat and make things safe before we could record anything."

During the first half of the 1970s, Deakins returned to Africa, to document the struggles of two united insurgent groups—the Eritrean Liberation Front and the Eritrean Popular Liberation Forces—in their losing battle to gain independence for the Ethiopian province of Eritrea. For six weeks he and a sound recordist traveled on supply trucks in the troubled province, which lies along the Red Sea. "The great thing about documentaries," he told Pauline Rogers, "is you learn to be conservative

and you learn, almost instinctively, when to shoot and what material is really important to tell a story." Later in the 1970s he was hired as the director of photography for a British television series entitled *Walcott*; shot mostly at night, the show focused on the experiences of a black detective in London's East End.

The British motion-picture writer and director Michael Radford, who had worked with him on documentaries, was impressed with Deakins's approach on *Walcott*, and he hired him to film *Another Time, Another Place* (1983); the cinematographer's debut feature film, it was shot in Scotland. The two next collaborated on an ambitious adaptation of George Orwell's novel *1984*. Told that shooting in black and white, as he would have preferred, would not be wise from a commercial standpoint, Deakins desaturated the negatives to give the film a bleached, desolate look. Produced in only about six months and starring John Hurt and Richard Burton (in his last role before his death), the film was released in 1984 and earned mixed reviews. Deakins and Radford later worked together on a third film, *White Mischief* (1987).

Meanwhile, Deakins had begun to collaborate with other British filmmakers as well. Working with the director Alex Cox, he filmed *Sid and Nancy* (1986), the story of Sid Vicious, the bassist for the British punk-rock group the Sex Pistols, and his relationship with his American girlfriend, Nancy Spungen, whom he was accused of stabbing to death in 1978. (Vicious died of a drug overdose less than four months after the murder.) The film was shot on location in London, Paris, San Francisco, and New York City, in the last of which climactic scenes were filmed at the Chelsea Hotel, where Spungen was killed. Operating a handheld camera, Deakins used fluorescent lighting for many scenes, to give the film the look and feel of a documentary. After shooting *Sid and Nancy*, Deakins left the close-knit and experienced crew with whom he had worked for some time and settled in the United States. He soon gained new colleagues, including Bill O'Leary, who has served as Deakins's gaffer on every one of his American-made films. Two pictures that he filmed for British directors before his move to the U.S. came out in 1988: James Dearden's *Pascali's Island* and Mike Figgis's *Stormy Monday*.

Deakins counts Bob Rafelson's *Mountains of the Moon* (1990) as being among the films in which he takes the most pride. In that movie, Patrick Bergen starred as Sir Richard Francis Burton, the British explorer, writer, and linguist who, with John Hanning Speke, led two expeditions in Africa during the 19th century in a successful quest for the source of the Nile, the world's longest river. Because of the ruggedness of the terrain, Deakins was forced to shoot with far less equipment than normal. One of his favorite sequences shows the explorers' arrival at a lake where they mistakenly believe they have reached their goal. For that scene, Rafelson had in mind seven or eight shots, all of which he hoped to capture near sunset. As Deakins recalled to Pauline Rogers, "I told him that I thought we could do it if we planned our shots carefully and did the whole scene in the last hour of sunlight. It was impossible to fudge that look during the day, as we were in a completely open area of desert and I remember the days being blindingly hot. We laid out and rehearsed about five different dolly shots and other camera angles and were ready to shoot by 2:30 in the afternoon. Holding Bob back from shooting until 4:30 when the light was right was the hardest battle of all!"

Deakins's work for Ethan and Joel Coen's serio-comic *Barton Fink* (1991), about a socially conscious but self-absorbed New York playwright (played by John Torturro) who suffers writer's block in Hollywood, was honored with awards from the Los Angeles and New York film critics' associations and the National Society of Film Critics. Speaking of his working relationship with the Coens, Deakins told Ryan Mottesheard, "I think after doing *Barton Fink*, we just sort of clicked. They felt I understood what they were trying to do. They're so nice to work with and they're so demanding and challenging and I get so much from it. And it's loyalty as well. They're very loyal to me." Two other Coen brothers films on which he collaborated—*Fargo* (1996) and *O Brother, Where Art Thou?* (2000)—earned Academy Award nominations for best cinematography; *Fargo* won an Independent Spirit Award in the same category, from the Independent Feature Project. Deakins also served as the cinematographer for the Coens' films *The Hudsucker Proxy* (1994), *The Big Lebowski* (1998), and, most recently, the black-and-white, noirish *The Man Who Wasn't There* (2001), which co-stars Billy Bob Thornton, Frances McDormand, Jon Polito, James Gandolfini, and Michael Badalucco. In a review of *The Man Who Wasn't There* for the *New York Times* (October 31, 2001), A. O. Scott wrote, "At times the movie seems like a collaboration between [Thornton] and Roger Deakins. . . . Deakins's mastery of the focal and textural possibilities of black-and-white recalls old Hollywood masters like the prolific James Wong Howe and like Gregg Toland, [the latter of whom] shot *Citizen Kane* and *The Best Years of Our Lives*. He is as eclectic as the Coens themselves. In one breathtaking sequence a family reunion in the Northern California countryside transports us from the gloom of film noir into the bleached sunshine of Italian neo-realism. But his camera work is especially tailored to the lines of Mr. Thornton's face and the comb tracks in his silvery hair. The rest of the movie, with its corkscrew plot and whiplash reversals, may fade quickly and pleasantly from memory, but that face remains emphatically there."

Deakins's first Oscar nomination honored his work in *The Shawshank Redemption* (1994), the writer/director Frank Darabont's adaptation of a Stephen King novella; a nomination for an equivalent award for cinematography came from the British Academy of Film & Television Arts as well. Co-starring Tim Robbins and Morgan Freeman, *The Shawshank Redemption* focuses on two inmates who become friends while serving life sentences at a maximum-security facility. Deakins shot the prison scenes on a soundstage and on the grounds of an actual prison. "The hardest lighting challenge was to maintain a consistency of look from set to set and location to location," he told Pauline Rogers. "This is probably the toughest thing on any film. I didn't want the conventional blue, cold light look or harsh backlighting with shafts of fake sunlight piercing heavy smoke. I wanted the kind of light that naturally seeps through small barred windows set in oversized stone walls." For an outdoor scene in which the Freeman character makes an important discovery, Deakins used natural light to illuminate a huge oak tree as the actor walked toward it. The shot required a great deal of preparation, in part because the site was far from a road, making it difficult to position the crane that Deakins wanted to use; the sogginess of the ground posed another challenge. "It looks like a simple shot," Deakins said to Pauline Rogers. "No way!" In addition to an Oscar nomination, *The Shawshank Redemption* earned Deakins an award from the American Society of Cinematographers and a Bronze Frog from Camerimage (the International Film Festival of the Art of Cinematography, held annually in Poland).

As director and co-screenwriter, Tim Robbins worked closely with Deakins to convey a sense of the developing relationship between the two main characters in *Dead Man Walking* (1995). Based on the same-titled 1993 nonfiction book by Helen Prejean, which is subtitled "An Eyewitness Account of the Death Penalty in the United States," the film depicts the bond that Prejean, a nun (portrayed by Susan Sarandon), forges with a violent killer (Sean Penn) on death row. "We had all these conversations [in the script] between Susan and Sean with this wire mesh between them," Deakins told Pauline Rogers. "It tended to be very distracting. . . . Tim wanted this feeling of the barrier between them breaking down as they grew to accept each other for who they were. So we played the first of these scenes with the camera backed up and the mesh in focus. This made Sean hard to see and his character more removed. At one point, we even played a hot light on the wire mesh, as though sunlight were hitting it, obscuring Sean's character completely. Later with longer lenses and slowly tracking the camera close to the wire, we progressively revealed Sean to Susan and to the audience. We even used pieces of larger mesh wire for some close up shots. Still later in the film, the two are separated by a cell block door which in the real building had had a fine wire mesh window for communication. This we changed to plexiglass with holes to speak through. We did this in part to use reflections to heighten the bond which now existed between the characters."

Martin Scorsese solicited Deakins's assistance in re-creating the lost culture of Tibet for *Kundun* (1997), the director's deeply spiritual portrayal of the current Dalai Lama's early life. The cast included many Tibetans, most of whom had never acted before. The documentary-like atmosphere their presence lent to the making of the film pleased Deakins. Presumably, the film could not be shot in Tibet, which is under the control of Communist China. Having failed to get permission from the government of India to shoot the film in that country, Scorsese and Deakins made the movie on the border of the part of the Sahara Desert that lies in Morocco. In an interview with *American Cinematographer* (February 1998, on-line), Deakins expressed amazement at Scorsese's extraordinarily copious preparation before every scene. "If he wanted a particular scene to be a long, moving camera shot on dialogue, he would have that down, maybe along with a couple of close-ups he wanted to use to heighten specific parts of the sequence," he said. "On another scene, he might have things broken down into a much more conventional series of close-ups on dialogue. He did this even before locking down the locations or actually seeing the final sets!"

Scorsese left to the cinematographer many decisions concerning lighting, lenses, and other technical matters. "After seeing the sets and locations, I would take Marty's script notes and transform them into little diagrams showing where the camera would be for each shot, which order to shoot things in, and so on," Deakins told the *American Cinematographer* interviewer. "Overall, I felt as if I had a lot of input; Marty gave me quite a bit of his trust, and I did the best I could to get what he really wanted." Once the crew arrived on location, Deakins arranged as much of the lighting as possible before shooting, to facilitate quick moves from one setup to another. One sequence in the film, in which the Dalai Lama is dreaming, required a zoom lens (a device he has rarely used): a tight close-up of the Dalai Lama's eyes "pulls back and tilts down to reveal him standing amid this array of dead monks in red robes," as Deakins explained for *American Cinematographer.* "The camera then begins rising straight up until he's back in frame at full figure, surrounded by this sea of bodies. There was no way of tracking with the 75' Akela crane we used, so in order to get the size we wanted on the Dalai Lama's face at the beginning, and still have a move with fluid feeling, we used the zoom to widen out at the end of the move. As the camera neared 50' and rising, the perspective shift on the wide end of the lens became very slight; this allowed the effects people at Dream Quest Images to continue the move even further while adding extra bodies to fill the outer edges of the frame." For his cinematography for *Kundun*, Deakins was honored with an Academy Award nomination and awards from the American Society of Cinematographers, the New York Film Critics Circle, the National Society of Film Critics, and the Boston Society of Film Critics.

In 1998 Deakins worked with the director Norman Jewison on *The Hurricane,* the Oscar-nominated film about the boxer Rubin "Hurricane" Carter, who spent 18 years in prison for a murder he did not commit. Once again, Deakins tried to create a visual style for the film that would be "as naturalistic as possible," as he told An Tran for *Cinematography World* (January 11, 2000, on-line). "I saw [the film] as being a document of this man's life. The camera work is low-key and the lighting is unflashy, so it doesn't draw attention to itself. I hate when you have a story that's inherently moving and strong, and you try to beef it up with flashy photography. . . . You should let the story go on its own course and tell itself." Referring to the prison settings of *The Hurricane* as well as those of *The Shawshank Redemption* and *Dead Man Walking,* he told An Tran, "I wanted to really contrast the colors between the world [Carter] lived in before prison and in the prison itself. Freedom was the best part of his life. He was about to be a world champion boxer. Everything was great. I wanted that feeling of color and time, contrasted with the jail interior, though there's much more color in *Hurricane* than there was on the other two films. I didn't feel I was repeating myself in any way, but even if I was, the most important thing is the story; that's always what attracts me. If it's interesting, powerful, and has something to say, then I'll do it."

An article on the Kodak Web site in early 2001 discussed Deakins's use of digital technology to create the sort of "dry, dusty" images that he and Ethan and Joel Coen wanted for *O Brother, Where Art Thou?* (The name of that movie, which premiered at the end of 2000, is the same as that of a film that the hero of the 1941 Preston Surges–directed classic, *Sullivan's Travels,* talks about making.) Working with the film colorist Julius Friede, Deakins selectively eliminated or desaturated various colors. For example, for a scene shot in a forest, "which was actually more of a swamp," as he explained on the Kodak Web site, they made some green leaves "kind of brown." "The audience isn't going to notice that on a conscious level but it suits the look and the mood, and blends with the rest of the scene," he noted.

In the mid-1990s Deakins served for a time as co-faculty chair at the American Film Institute's Center for Advanced Film and Television Study (now known as the AFI Conservatory), located in the hills overlooking Los Angeles. At the 2000 Hawaii International Film Festival, he received the Eastman Kodak Award for excellence in cinematography.

When asked by *Moviemaker* (on-line) to describe what distinguishes a successful director of photography (D.P., in cinema jargon), Deakins replied, "I think, for lack of a better term, it would be a point of view. Everybody sees the world from their own perspective and this uniqueness is what the D.P. brings to the film. . . . It's tough now because so much of the industry is driven by economics, which means you're a hero if you can throw up a few soft lights and knock off a whole bunch of shots. This goes against having an idea and feeling of what is absolutely right for that story you're telling. But, if you choose carefully and find the right director, your way of seeing will leave an impression." — C.L.

Suggested Reading: *American Cinematographer* (on-line) Feb. 1998; *Cinematography World* (on-line) Jan. 11, 2000; *indiewire.com* Oct. 30, 2001; Kodak Web site, 2000; *Reelmind* (on-line) 2000; Rogers, Pauline. *Contemporary Cinematographers on Their Art*, 1998

Selected Films: *1984*, 1984; *Sid & Nancy*, 1986; *Stormy Monday*, 1988; *The Long Walk Home*, 1990; *Barton Fink*, 1991; *Thunderheart*, 1992; *Passion Fish*, 1992; *The Shawshank Redemption*, 1994; *Dead Man Walking*, 1995; *Fargo*, 1996; *Courage Under Fire*, 1996; *Kundun*, 1997; *The Siege*, 1998; *The Big Lebowski*, 1998; *The Hurricane*, 1999; *Anywhere But Here*, 1999; *O Brother, Where Art Thou?*, 2000; *The Man Who Wasn't There*, 2001; *A Beautiful Mind*, 2001; *Dinner with Friends*, 2001

Courtesy of Dan DeCarlo

DeCarlo, Dan

Dec. 12, 1919– Comic-book artist and writer. Address: c/o Bongo Comics Group, 1440 S. Sepulveda Blvd., Los Angeles, CA 90025

Even the most casual comic-book reader has seen the work of Dan DeCarlo. In his four decades with Archie Comics—which publishes the adventures of the never-aging, red-haired teenager Archie Andrews and his pals—DeCarlo refurbished the look of the famous *Archie* series, modernizing it and helping to make it one of the highest-selling comic books in the industry. "Without bragging," DeCarlo told Leslie Eaton for the *New York Times* (February 19, 2001), "I did create a different, new Archie that everyone copied." In addition to his work on the *Archie* books, DeCarlo created *Josie and the Pussycats*, which follows the escapades of a teenage all-girl rock group. That comic book spawned two car-

toon series and a feature film that arrived in theaters in April 2001. "In his own way, he's had a tremendous influence on popular culture," the comics artist Paul Dini said of DeCarlo for the Web site *kclive.com*. "Not every child embraces superhero comics . . . but every kid has read an Archie comic at some point. You could argue that he and [Disney comics artist] Carl Barks are the most widely seen comic artists."

Dan DeCarlo was born on December 12, 1919 in New Rochelle, New York. While growing up in his poor neighborhood, DeCarlo idolized the artist Norman Rockwell and dreamed of becoming an illustrator himself. After graduating from high school, he spent three years at the Art Students League, in New York City. His studies there were apparently cut short when he was drafted into the military, following the Japanese attack on Pearl Harbor—the event that triggered the United States' entrance into World War II. For four and a half years, DeCarlo served with the 8th Air Force as an artist and draftsman, drawing cartoon mascots for the fighter planes, among other duties. Most of his time in the service was spent in Europe; in Belgium, on a blind date, he met Josie Dumont. Smitten with her, but unable to speak French, he communicated his feelings through cartoons drawn on his letters to her. The two were married in 1945, and DeCarlo was discharged from the army a year later.

After returning to the States, DeCarlo struggled to find work as an artist. "Jobs were scarce and apartments were worse," he told Leslie Eaton. Eventually he landed a job with Timely Comics (which eventually became Marvel) for $75 a week. There, he created some of his first cartoon characters, including Millie the Model and Sherry the Showgirl.

In the 1950s, after Timely let its staff go, DeCarlo began freelancing. Following his assignments for D.C. Comics, Ziff Davis, and other companies, he began doing work for Archie Comics, publisher of the popular *Archie* series. Those successful comic books chronicled the misadventures of the amiable teenager and his friends, Jughead, Reggie, and Moose, as well as his girlfriends, the blond, down-to-earth Betty and the rich, snooty, raven-haired Veronica. When DeCarlo started at Archie Comics he was dissatisfied with the limited creativity the artists were allowed. "It was copying Bob Montana, and I didn't like it," he told a writer for the Web site *comicbookresources.com* (May 18, 2000), referring to the series' original artist. "It was too hard, looking up and looking down. So I stopped. A few weeks later, [editor Harry Shorten] called me up and asked me why I'd stopped. 'Is it the money?' And like any good businessman, I said, 'No, I just don't like looking up and looking down.'" DeCarlo went back to freelancing for Archie Comics and was allowed to draw in his own style. He soon began modernizing the look and tone of the comic, and thanks to the revamping, sales began to increase. With such spin-off books as *Betty & Veronica*, DeCarlo and head writer Frank Doyle added to the stories such elements as the love triangle formed by Archie, Betty, and Veronica, which is now a focal point of the books. In 1957 DeCarlo joined Archie Comics full-time, and other artists were ordered to imitate his style, just as they had earlier been told to copy Montana's. "At one point, [the company] even made me produce a seminar, once a week," he told *kclive.com*. "They would videotape me drawing and explaining how I do this, and how I do that."

Wanting to create his own teenage-themed comic book, DeCarlo toyed with several ideas; when his wife came home one day with a bouffant hairdo, he was instantly inspired. "I said, 'That's it!' I fashioned my girl to look like that," he told Ed Matthews for the Web site *slushfactory.com*. DeCarlo named his creation Josie (after his wife) and outfitted her in a slinky cat suit modeled on a costume Josie DeCarlo had worn at a party. He then matched her up with a pair of teenage friends, Pepper and Melody, and in about 1963, *She's Josie* was born. Not long afterward, DeCarlo made the girls musicians, and the comic book became *Josie and the Pussycats*. (At some point during this period, a new character, Valerie, was added.) The *Josie* series was so successful that the characters began making regular appearances in the *Archie* books. Throughout the 1960s *Josie and the Pussycats* as well as *Sabrina, the Teenage Witch* (which DeCarlo co-created) were among the flagship publications of Archie Comics. In 1970 an animated version of the *Josie* series debuted on TV, with a then-unknown Cheryl Ladd providing the singing voice for Melody. An instant hit, the show was followed by *Josie and the Pussycats in Outer Space* in 1972.

Those developments marked the beginning of DeCarlo's troubles with his employers. The first show had been approved, scripted, drawn, and produced without DeCarlo's knowing of its existence. That situation was made possible by the fact that DeCarlo had created the characters, so Archie Comics contended, on a work-for-hire basis—meaning that the characters became the property of the company. DeCarlo has insisted that as Josie's creator, he had the rights to the character. (This scenario is not unique in the comic-book industry; a number of cartoonists have been left without a share of the millions of dollars made through their characters. Prominent among them are the late creators of Superman, Jerry Siegel and Joe Shuster.)

In spite of the fact that the characters he had created were bringing in a fortune he did not share, DeCarlo continued to work for Archie Comics. Meanwhile, *Josie*-themed games, dolls, coffee mugs, and record albums were flying off store shelves. At the same time, *Sabrina, the Teen-Age Witch* was also a moderately successful cartoon series. In 1996 a live-action *Sabrina* came to television and proved to be a ratings smash. A lawsuit over the rights to the Sabrina character is pending.

The final straw came when Archie Comics sold Universal Pictures the rights to turn *Josie and the Pussycats* into a feature film. In March 2000 DeCarlo filed suit against Archie Comics, asking for proper compensation for having created Josie, in light of how successful the character had become. In response to the suit, DeCarlo was fired. He had gone to the Archie Comics office to drop off his work on *Betty & Veronica* and was "trying to sneak out," as he told *kcline.com*, when the publisher, Michael Silberkleit, handed him a letter informing him of the company's decision. Silberkleit released a statement that was quoted in part in Eaton's article: "Since we, at Archie Comics, have always viewed Dan DeCarlo as a member of our 'family,' we were very hurt when he sued us."

In January 2001 DeCarlo's suit was dismissed by Judge Lewis A. Kaplan, who ruled that he had been too late in bringing the matter to the attention of the court. DeCarlo had considered suing Archie Comics back in 1970, when he heard about the creation of a *Josie and the Pussycats* Saturday-morning cartoon. He had contacted a lawyer from the Cartoonists Association, who had told him that, while he could win a lawsuit, the settlement probably wouldn't amount to much—and that he might well be fired during the process. For these reasons, DeCarlo had opted not to sue, a decision that cost him the case three decades later. "I followed the wrong advice, and if I hadn't, I probably would have won this time," he told Robert Wilonsky for the *Cleveland Scene* (February 15, 2001, on-line). "That's the thing that really killed my case. They say I should have acted earlier and why did I wait so long. What I can't understand is there's no statute of limitations on thievery and ownership, is there? Doesn't seem fair." (The film version of *Josie and the Pussycats*, which stars Rachel Leigh Cook and Tara Reid, opened on April 11, 2001 to dismal reviews and ticket sales.)

DeCarlo currently works for Bongo Entertainment, the comic-book company run by Matt Groening, the creator of *The Simpsons*. DeCarlo provides layouts and page designs and occasionally draws characters for the company's various magazines. While he is happy with his present job, he has often expressed dismay at his treatment by Archie Comics. "Sometimes I feel like a loser," he confessed to Wilonsky. "I really do. I hate to say that. It's just *sometimes.* Sometimes I feel good . . . But a lot of nice things didn't happen to me." — J.K.B.

Suggested Reading: *Cleveland Scene* (on-line) Feb. 15, 2001, with photos; *New York Times* B p1+ Feb. 19, 2001, with photos

Selected Comics: *Showgirls*; *Betty and Veronica*; *She's Josie*; *Josie and the Pussycats*; *Sabrina, the Teen-Age Witch*

Armando Gallo/Retna Ltd.

Del Toro, Benicio
(ben-EECE-ee-oh)

Feb. 19, 1967– Actor; producer; director; writer. Address: BDT Mail, P.O. Box 1712, New York, NY 10021

"I knew I had to be someone," Benicio Del Toro told an interviewer for the *Detroit News* (January 25, 2001), speaking about his decision to pursue a career as an actor. "Actually, becoming someone is not the thing. It's to find something I really liked. And I got lucky. I fell in love with what I do, and when you do that, nothing else matters. Rain, shine, you're okay." A native of Puerto Rico, the professionally trained Del Toro made his debut on the silver screen in 1988, in the role of Duke the Dog-Faced Boy, in *Big Top Pee-Wee.* His name recognition increased significantly thanks to his comical depiction of Fred Fenster in *The Usual Suspects* (1995), in which, despite his character's nearly unintelligible speech, he stood out among a cast that included Kevin Spacey, Chazz Palminteri,

and Gabriel Byrne. In Steven Soderbergh's critically acclaimed film *Traffic* (2000), in which the actor spoke mostly in Spanish, Del Toro's depiction of a small-town Mexican policeman eager to do the right thing earned him 10 awards, among them an Oscar and a Golden Globe as best supporting actor. In an interview with Lori Talley for *Back Stage West* (December 28, 2000), the six-foot four-inch Del Toro said, "I think the reason people are reacting so positively to this character and this movie is because I really understood how important it is for the actor to be a storyteller."

"More than any other actor I've ever met, Benicio is not in pursuit of fame or recognition," the screenwriter and director Christopher McQuarrie told Stephanie Stokes for *Zingasia.com* (May 19, 2001, on-line). "I think he's a guy who has a great disdain for popularity. He's very resistant to playing a leading man. He would rather create a character." According to the actor and director Sean Penn, who cast him in his movies *The Indian Runner* and *The Pledge*, Del Toro is "like an acting animal, this guy who comes out of the forest to make movies better," as Stokes quoted him as saying. "He's fearless, and he has a distinctive imagination for character. He's one of the few actors who can make flamboyant choices that never just say, 'Look at me.' He's not showy. If he stands out, it's only because the rest of the people haven't risen as high to the bar."

The younger of the two sons of Gustavo Del Toro and the former Fausta Sanchez, Benicio Del Toro was born in Puerto Rico (in either Santurce, in Old San Juan, or San German, according to various sources) on February 19, 1967. His mother, father, and godmother, as well as a grandfather and an uncle, were lawyers, and his family expected him to follow them in that profession. When he was nine years old, his mother died, a victim of hepatitis; three years later his father relocated the family to rural Pennsylvania, where he evidently became a farmer. The move was difficult for the rebellious, 12-year-old Benicio, and he began getting into scrapes. One incident involved a man who hit him on his head with a baseball bat. (The man was later sent to prison for killing a police officer.) Determined to steer his son onto a straighter path, Del Toro's father, whom Del Toro has described as strict, enrolled him at a boarding school. There, the youth played basketball as a way to fit in. "I really liked to hot-dog," he told Devlin Gordon for *Newsweek* (January 8, 2001). "Behind-the-back stuff, no-look passes." His friends at school nicknamed him Benicio Del Turnover.

After graduating from the boarding school, Del Toro enrolled at the University of California at San Diego, where he planned to major in business. During his freshman year he won a part in a campus theater production. Before his sophomore year he dropped out of college and moved to New York City, to study acting at the Circle in the Square Theatre School. "My family freaked when I told them I wanted to be an actor," Del Toro told one interviewer, as quoted by *Mr. Showbiz* (on-line). "It was like telling them I wanted to be an astronaut. On top of that, it was like saying that in order to be an astronaut, I was going to have to drive a cab in New York for five years." Dismayed members of his family did not speak to him for a while. (His father has since become keenly interested in his achievements and seeks out information about him on the Web.)

After struggling to make it in New York, Del Toro returned to the West Coast, this time to Los Angeles, where he lived with his older brother, Gustavo, who was then studying medicine. His first big break came when he won a scholarship to attend the Stella Adler Academy of Acting. (According to Lori Talley, the scholarship resulted from his performance in a production mounted at a Lafayette Theatre student drama festival, in New York.) The legendary Adler, who was then in her late 80s, demanded much of her students. "Acting, creating, interpreting, means total involvement," she once said, as quoted on the academy's Web site; "the totality of heart, mind, and spirit. Acting is the total development of a human being into the most he or she can be and in as many directions as you can possibly take." Adler "was kinda like [the college basketball coach] Bobby Knight, you know?" Del Toro told Steve Pond for *Premiere* (February 2001). "I'd love to play basketball for Bobby Knight. . . . Everybody's lazy at moments. You need somebody to push you so you can learn to push yourself. Stella was like that. Stella made Bobby Knight look like mashed potatoes."

Del Toro's first professional roles were on television shows, among them *Private Eye*, *O'Hara*, and *Miami Vice*. Like many other Hispanic actors, he was often cast as a gangster or a drug dealer. In his first role in a feature film, as Duke the Dog-Faced Boy in *Big Top Pee-Wee* (1988), he received virtually no notice from critics. The part of a drug lord in the celebrated NBC miniseries *Drug Wars: The Camarena Story* (1990) gave him more screen time than he had had previously, but overall Del Toro felt that his career was stalling before it had really begun. "I wasn't making a living, and I was struggling hard," he told Steve Pond. "I never put a clock on it, but there were moments at night when I'd think, 'Man, I really believe in this, but it's not panning out—what should I do? Maybe I have the wrong approach, maybe I should be a yes-sir kind of guy.'" But he did not give up, and in the next few years Del Toro landed small parts in a half-dozen pictures, among them the small, independent film *The Indian Runner* (1991), Sean Penn's directorial debut; the little-noted *China Moon* (1991); the big-budget spectacle—and box-office bomb—*Christopher Columbus: The Discovery* (1992); the Spanish-language movie *Huevos de oro* (Golden Balls, 1993); Peter Weir's critically admired *Fearless* (1993); and George Huang's *Swimming with Sharks* (1994).

In 1995 Del Toro appeared in Bryan Singer's *The Usual Suspects*, an unusual whodunit about a group of thieves who work with one another after being put together in a lineup. Del Toro portrayed the mumbling thief Fred Fenster, whose "strangled, whispery delivery," as Michael Sragow wrote in a review for *Salon.com* (September 6, 2000), "compels police to tell his character to speak English. (He *is* speaking English.)" Hal Hinson, in his assessment of the film for the *Washington Post* (August 18, 1995), wrote, "The strangest performance is turned in by Benicio Del Toro, who as Fenster speaks in an accent closely resembling that of Vincent Van Gopher in the old 'Deputy Dawg' cartoons; about one out of every three words is intelligible, but he gets a laugh every time he opens his mouth." For his work in *The Usual Suspects*, Del Toro won the 1995 Independent Spirit Award (given by the Independent Film Project/West) for best supporting male actor.

Suddenly a hot actor in the world of independent filmmaking, Del Toro was cast as Benny Dalmau, the best friend of the real-life painter Jean-Michel Basquiat, in *Basquiat* (1996). The film was directed by the painter Julian Schnabel, who, like the title character, achieved enormous professional success in the 1980s. Of Haitian and Puerto Rican descent, Basquiat (played in the film by Jeffrey Wright), in his teens, was a penniless graffiti artist who lived briefly on the streets. At 19 he became an art-world sensation whose paintings sold for as much as $25,000 apiece; in 1988, at 27, he died of a heroin overdose. While not a mainstream success, *Basquiat* earned an enthusiastic response from critics, as did Del Toro's performance. In a representative assessment, Desson Howe, writing for the *Washington Post* (August 16, 1996), described his acting as "marvelous." Del Toro won his second Independent Spirit Award for his work in *Basquiat*.

Del Toro had two additional supporting roles in 1996. In Tony Scott's *The Fan*, he portrayed a baseball player who gets on the wrong side of a murderously obsessed fan (Robert De Niro) who is stalking a star center fielder (Wesley Snipes); in Abel Ferrara's *The Funeral* (1996), he played a mobster in 1930s New York. His performance in the latter impressed Leah Rozen, who, after praising two other members of the cast (Christopher Walken and Annabella Sciorra), wrote for *People* (November 4, 1996), "The real grabber . . . is Benicio Del Toro, . . . who, as a rival gangster, shows sufficient looks and swagger to suggest he just might be Brad Pitt's evil twin."

The actress Alicia Silverstone handpicked Del Toro to star with her in Marco Brambilla's action-comedy *Excess Baggage* (1997), which she also produced. "I went to see *Usual Suspects* and I couldn't concentrate on the film, I was so taken by him," Silverstone told Alison Pollet for *Premiere* (November 1996). "He's wonderful to watch." "Del Toro steals [the movie] with his performance as a car thief who becomes an unwilling kidnapper

. . . ," Roger Ebert wrote for the *Chicago Sun-Times* (on-line), in one of the few even partially positive reviews of *Excess Baggage*. "The movie is often very funny, and a lot of the credit goes to Del Toro, who creates a slow-talking, lumbering character who's quite unlike his image in *Usual Suspects*." For his next film, *Fear and Loathing in Las Vegas* (1998), Del Toro gained 50 pounds to play Oscar Zeta Acosta, nicknamed Dr. Gonzo, a drug-addicted lawyer and traveling companion to Raoul Duke (Johnny Depp), the alter ego of the writer Hunter S. Thompson. (Thompson epitomized what he himself dubbed "gonzo" journalists.) Directed by Terry Gilliam, the film—like the same-named book, which was published in 1971 with the subtitle "A Savage Journey to the Heart of the American Dream"—is a fictionalized account of Thompson's drug-addled journey from Los Angeles to Las Vegas to report on a motorcycle race and a district attorneys' conference about drugs. In interviews Del Toro has complained that he was not pleased with the way the film turned out after editing.

In 2000 Del Toro co-starred as Javier Rodriguez, a Mexican cop, in Steven Soderbergh's *Traffic*, a multilayered, documentary-style film that shows the ways in which the U.S.–Mexican drug trade affects people in many walks of life. Rodriguez "is a good man caught in a bad world where he might not have a choice," Del Toro observed to Lori Talley. "The 'bad guy' is the system and the corruption around the illegal drug trade." He also told her, "My character is responsible for telling the story. [Soderbergh] gave me free rein. I was able to bring this character to life in my own way." Soderbergh, for his part, credited Del Toro with making the story "much more emotional, more interesting and truer to the culture the character sprang from," as he put it to Stephanie Stokes for *ZingAsia.com*. Soderbergh also told Stokes, "He's extremely bright and has lots of ideas, the lion's share of which are really good. We'd meet every few weeks for a few hours, and a lot of it was, 'Wouldn't it be more interesting if . . . ?' He had a huge influence on the story."

Most of Del Toro's dialogue in *Traffic* was in Spanish, which he normally speaks with a Puerto Rican accent. To prepare for the part, which required him to have a Mexican accent, he studied with a language coach. "It wasn't easy for me," he admitted to Talley. "It was serious work. I really had to work hard with the Mexican accent. However, it was a great idea. I think it adds a special dimension to the movie. The audience can't help but feel like they are in the same place as the character—as though they are really looking in at this world." To portray Rodriguez, Del Toro also educated himself about the work of Mexican drug-enforcement officers. Kenneth Turan, the film critic for the *Los Angeles Times* (December 27, 2000, on-line), proclaimed Del Toro's performance to be the finest in the film; the actor, he wrote, has "always been much admired for his subtle power,"

but his "nuanced authority has never been more on view" than it was in *Traffic*. In a review for *Salon.com* (December 27, 2000, on-line), Charles Taylor wrote, "Best of all is Del Toro, with his perpetually sunken eyes. He has the kind of look that directors have heretofore used for crooks and crackpots. The stroke of casting him here is that his weary, unshaven countenance masks a straight-arrow hero, a guy who tries to come on as wised up, but desperately wants to believe that fair play and honor are still possible. . . . He's one of those rare actors who can make moral disillusionment seem attractive." For his performance in *Traffic*, Del Toro won, in addition to the Oscar and Golden Globe Award, best-supporting-actor honors from the Online Film Critics Society, the National Society of Film Critics, and the film critics' associations of New York, Toronto, Las Vegas, and Florida, and two awards from the Screen Actors Guild (for his work individually and as part of an ensemble).

Del Toro's most recent credits include roles in Christopher McQuarrie's *The Way of the Gun* (2000), co-starring Ryan Phillippe, in which he portrayed a kidnapper; Guy Ritchie's *Snatch* (2000), featuring Brad Pitt, in which he played a jewel thief; and Sean Penn's *The Pledge* (2001), with Jack Nicholson, in which he was cast as a mentally disabled American Indian. Del Toro wrote and directed the independent film *Submission*; starring Matthew McConaughey, it was shown at the Venice Film Festival in 1995. He is slated to appear in two films scheduled for release in 2002: *The Hunted* and *The Assumption of the Virgin*. — C.M.

Suggested Reading: *Back Stage West* (on-line), Dec. 28, 2000; Benicio Del Toro Web site; *Entertainment Weekly* (on-line) Sep. 1, 2000; *Los Angeles Daily News Weekend* (on-line) Mar. 9, 2001; *Newsweek* p63 Jan. 8, 2001, with photo; *People* p69+ Apr. 16, 2001, with photo; *Premiere* p95+ Nov. 1996, with photos, p70+ Feb. 2001, with photo; *ZingAsia.com* (on-line) May 19, 2001

Selected Films: *Money for Nothing*, 1993; *Swimming with Sharks*, 1994; *Basquiat*, 1996; *The Fan*, 1996; *The Funeral*, 1996; *Excess Baggage*, 1997; *Fear and Loathing in Los Vegas*, 1998; *Snatch*, 2000; *The Way of the Gun*, 2000; *Traffic*, 2000; *The Pledge*, 2001

Reuters/Steve Marcus/Hulton/Archive
*The members of Destiny's Child (left to right):
Kelly Rowland, Beyoncé Knowles,
and Michelle Williams*

Destiny's Child

R&B group

Knowles, Beyoncé
Sep. 4, 1980–

Rowland, Kelly
Feb. 11, 1981–

Williams, Michelle
July 23, 1980(?)–

*Address: c/o Columbia Records/Sony Music
Entertainment Inc., 550 Madison Ave., New
York, NY 10022-3211*

In 1997, after performing for years without a record
contract, the female R&B vocal group Destiny's
Child signed with Columbia Records and exploded
onto the music scene with their eponymous debut
album. Since then they have sold upwards of
15 million albums and singles worldwide, thereby
earning more than a dozen gold, platinum, and
multiplatinum certifications from the Recording
Industry Association of America. They have also
earned comparisons to such renowned soul groups
as the Supremes and captured two Grammy
Awards and a half-dozen other impressive honors.
Destiny's Child, which began as a trio that performed under a series of other names, is led by Beyoncé Knowles, who "owns one of her generation's
strongest, most distinctively memorable voices,
which by all accounts is saturated in silk, satin and

serious soul," according to a writer for *MusicStarP-
ages* (on-line). The group, managed by Knowles's
father, Mathew Knowles, currently also includes
Michelle Williams and Knowles's cousin Kelly
Rowland. Earlier, for a time, the ensemble was a
foursome, with Knowles, Rowland, LaToya Luckett, and LaTavia Roberson. A disagreement over
Mathew Knowles's management led Luckett and
Roberson to quit; they were replaced in early 2000
by Williams and Farrah Franklin, the latter of
whom was fired after about six months. Despite
such internal disputes and disruptions, Destiny's
Child has released two additional albums—the
highly successful *The Writing's on the Wall* and,
most recently, *Survivor.* "A lot of people don't
have any concept of how many sacrifices we have
to make," Beyoncé Knowles told Christopher John
Farley for the Canadian edition of *Time* (January
15, 2001, on-line). "You have to accept it, because
if you don't, you won't last."

A daughter of Mathew Knowles, who sold medical scanners at the time of her birth, and Tina
Knowles, who owns a Houston, Texas, hair salon,
Beyoncé Knowles was born on September 4, 1980
in Houston, where she grew up. As a child she
showed a strong talent in singing, and in about
1990 two Houston businessmen recruited her,
along with two other Houston natives—LaTavia
Roberson (born on November 1, 1981) and, later,
Kelly Rowland (born on February 11, 1981)—to
form a preteen R&B act, which the men managed.
To hone their skills, the trio began spending their
free time studying videotapes of such legendary
R&B acts as the Supremes and the Jackson 5. After
joining with two other girls, Knowles, Rowland,
and Roberson sang in the Houston area venues under such names as GirlsTyme and Something
Fresh.

In 1992 the group appeared on an installment of
the nationally syndicated television show *Star
Search*, on which contestants performed in a specific category for a cash prize. The girls felt devastated when they lost. "We were kind of nervous
about it," Roberson was quoted as saying on *Music-
StarPages* (on-line), in about 1997. "They made us
. . . do a rap song, although we wanted to sing.
They even made a new hip-hop category for us.
Looking back on it now though, it was a learning
experience we'll never forget." Soon after their appearance on *Star Search*, Mathew Knowles quit his
job and, despite having no experience in the music
industry, took over as the girls' manager. He became Rowland's legal guardian as well, and
brought LaToya Luckett (born on March 11, 1981)
on board. He then arranged a deal with the R&B
songwriter and producer Darryl Simmons and
landed a contract for the quartet, then named the
Dolls, with the record label Elektra. But Simmons
busied himself with several other projects and
spent very little time with the girls. With no
recordings from the Dolls to sell, Elektra dropped
the group. "We felt like our life was over," Beyoncé
Knowles told Rob Brunner for *Entertainment*

Weekly (September 1, 2001). "We thought we would never get signed again."

Encouraged by positive responses to their performances as the openers for such acts as Dr. Hill, Nas EFX, Immature, and SWV, the girls continued to sing publicly in Houston. In 1997 the quartet signed a contract with Columbia Records and changed their name to Destiny's Child. (They had first settled on "Destiny," which Tina Knowles had suggested after seeing the word in the Book of Isaiah of the Old Testament, and then learned that that name was already copyrighted. They added the possessive and the word "Child" after consulting with Mathew Knowles and Columbia.) Destiny's Child's first recording, the song "Killing Time," was used on the soundtrack to the film *Men in Black* (1997). The following year they released their first single, "No, No, No (Part II)," which also features the popular rapper Wyclef Jean. "Boy I know you want me," the words read, "I can see it in your eyes / But you keep on frontin' / Won't you say / What's on your mind / 'Cause each and / Every time you need me / You give me signs / But when I ask you / What's the deal / You hold it all inside / If you wanna be with me / You gotta keep it real / Tell me what's goin' on / Tell me how you feel / 'Cause boy I know you want me / Just as much as I want you / So come and get my love / It's all here for you." The refrain begins, "You'll be sayin' / No, no, no, no / When it's really / Yeah, yeah, yeah, yeah." The song hit number three on the *Billboard* charts. "That was our turning point and we all knew it," Knowles recalled, as quoted on *Music-StarPages* (on-line). "So when it was time to make our album, we never looked back. We were so glad to finally have the opportunity that all of the problems of the past seemed to disappear." Their debut album, *Destiny's Child*, sold over one million copies. The recording failed to impress John Bush, however, who wrote for the *All Music Guide* (on-line), "Much of the album sounds indistinguishable from all the other female groups out there." After touring in the U.S. with Wyclef Jean, the band performed in Europe, supporting such acts as Boyz II Men, K-Ci & Jo Jo, and Uncle Sam. At the fourth annual Soul Train Lady of Soul Awards, held in 1998, Destiny's Child won in three of the nine categories: best R&B or soul single by a group, for "No, No, No"; best R&B or soul album of the year by a group, for *Destiny's Child*; and best new R&B, soul, or rap artist.

Created with the help of several top R&B producers, Destiny's Child's second album, *The Writing's on the Wall* (1999), has sold more than nine million copies. The album contains the Top 10 R&B singles "Bills, Bills, Bills," about a boyfriend who has become a sponger; "Jumpin' Jumpin'," which advises people to have fun in clubs without their current boyfriends or girlfriends; and "Say My Name," in which the singer expresses her suspicion that her man is being unfaithful. It also includes the Top 40 single "Bug-A-Boo," about a boyfriend whose incessant calls to the singer's beeper

and phone have become intolerable, and "So Good," in which the singer declares that, despite predictions of failure from the person or people being addressed, she has made it. Rob Brunner wrote for *Entertainment Weekly* (July 16, 1999) that with *The Writing's on the Wall*, Destiny's Child had "prove[d] themselves to be more capable of confident, inventive R&B than many of their contemporaries. . . . With a snaky lead vocal that slithers around staccato harmony parts, the aptly titled album opener 'So Good' coolly mixes restrained productions and playful melody." Brunner complained, however, that *The Writing's on the Wall* "gets bogged down by too much banal balladry . . . proving Destiny's Child to be capable of sounding exactly like any other group of snooze-inducing slow-jammers." According to Stephen Thomas Erlewine in the *All Music Guide* (on-line), "Even when the album fails to deliver memorable songs, it always sounds alluring, thanks to the perfect combination of vocalists and producers." "When you listen to our album," Kelly Rowland told an interviewer for *Jet* (August 2, 1999), "every woman and every man will love it because it talks about real relationship issues. It deals with the side of love that people tend to run away from, like if a relationship is going to work out or if it isn't. We're really touching bases for real love this time." According to the Sony Web site, *The Writing's on the Wall* ranked in the Top 40 on the *Billboard* album chart in 47 out of 52 weeks in the first year after its release. In early 2000 Destiny's Child were nominated for two Grammy Awards, for best R&B song and R&B vocal performance by a duo or group, and were honored by the NAACP (National Association for the Advancement of Colored People) with an Image Award for *The Writing's on the Wall*. They also performed with the former star of the Supremes, Diana Ross, on the VH1 television special *Divas 2000: A Tribute to Diana Ross*.

But despite their successes, all was not well within the group. In March 2000 Columbia Records announced that both Roberson and Luckett had left Destiny's Child. The split was acrimonious, and Roberson and Luckett later sued the group, stating in their legal papers, as quoted by Christopher John Farley, that Mathew Knowles's "greed, insistence on control, self-dealing and promotion of his daughter's interests at the expense of [Roberson and Luckett] became the dominant forces in Destiny's Child." People associated with Destiny's Child countered by charging that Roberson and Luckett had been lazy and were not contributing much to the group. Both sides agreed, however, that what had triggered the rupture was Roberson and Luckett's contention that Mathew Knowles had not avoided a conflict of interest in managing a group of which his own daughter was a part. The two women wanted to have their own manager. "We had never heard *anything* about them wanting another manager until we got the letters" from Roberson and Luckett's attorney, Beyoncé Knowles told Rob Brunner. "At first we were thinking, 'Well, maybe they *should* get their own manager and we should try to work it out.' But you can't have two managers. It was crazy." The feuding parties settled out of court for an undisclosed sum.

After briefly performing as a duo, Knowles and Rowland decided to replace the two departed members. "Beyoncé and I had a lot of fun and got a great response, stronger than we thought," Rowland told Gary Graff for *CDNow* (August 9, 2000, on-line). "But we decided to get two new girls for the fans. We knew they missed seeing other images in the group; that was part of the Destiny's Child image—four different images." The two new members were Michelle Williams, of Rockford, Illinois (born, according to various sources, on July 23 or December 1, 1980), and Farrah Franklin. Both Williams (a one-time pre-med student at the University of Illinois) and Franklin appeared in the video for the band's single "Say My Name." In July 2000 Destiny's Child announced that Franklin was leaving because she could not handle the heavy workload; she had skipped major promotional appearances and had stormed out of a meeting of the band, they said. Franklin admitted that she had missed group events, but in an interview with Gene Geter for *genegeter.com* (on-line), she contended that she had been ordered to make appearances even when she had felt sick. She faulted the behavior of Mathew Knowles and also of Tina Knowles and Beyoncé Knowles's younger sister, Solange, both of whom are heavily involved in the activities of the group. She found out the group had dropped her, she said, only when she happened to watch MTV News.

Instead of replacing Franklin, Destiny's Child decided to remain a trio. Later in the summer of 2000, after releasing their single "Jumpin' Jumpin'," the group toured the United States with the pop star Christina Aguilera. Rowland broke her foot on stage during the tour but carried on nevertheless, sitting on stage during performances. Destiny's Child's next single, "Independent Women (Part 1)," taken from the soundtrack to the film *Charlie's Angels* (2000), became the group's first number-one hit in England. Indeed, it debuted at the top spot there, making Destiny's Child the first American all-female group to achieve that feat. In mid-2000, at the Soul Train Lady of Soul Awards, Destiny's Child won in the categories of best R&B or soul single for a group, with "Say My Name," and best R&B or soul album of the year, for *The Writing's on the Wall*. At the Billboard Music Awards ceremony, held in December 2000, the trio was named artist of the year—the highest honor; they were also named the year's best duo or group, best hot-100-singles artist, and best hot-100-singles group. In addition, in January 2001 Destiny's Child was recognized as best R&B group at the American Music Awards ceremony and took home the Sammy Davis Jr. Entertainer of the Year Award at the Soul Train Lady of Soul Music Awards. Also in 2001 Destiny's Child received nominations for five Grammy Awards and won two, for best R&B song and best R&B performance by a duo or group, both for "Say My Name." That song also earned the 2001 NAACP Image Award for outstanding duo or group.

In May Destiny's Child released their third album, *Survivor*—the first of their recordings to feature each member of the group in turn singing lead on every song. According to Stephen Thomas Erlewine in the *All Music Guide* (on-line), *Survivor* is "a record that tries to be a bold statement of purpose, but winds up feeling forced and artificial." Kerry Porter, writing for the British periodical *Q* (July 2001), felt that parts of the album were praiseworthy but concluded, "For all the early sassiness, *Survivor* loses its way over a hefty 18 tracks. Clever pruning would have [deleted] the more pedestrian beats and . . . the wince-inducing dalliances with balladry and gospel medley territory."

In addition to *Men in Black* and *Charlie's Angels*, Destiny's Child has contributed songs to the feature films *Why Do Fools Fall in Love?* (1998), *Life* (1999), and *Romeo Must Die* (2000). The three singers are planning to record solo albums, all of which are to be released at the same time. Knowles's album will contain pop and R&B songs, Williams's will focus on gospel, and Rowland's will feature what is known as alternative R&B. Rowland became the first member of the group to go solo, with the song "Angel," recorded for the soundtrack to the big-screen comedy *Down to Earth* (2001), starring Chris Rock. In her first major acting role, Knowles starred in the MTV production *Carmen Brown: A Hip Hopera*, which was based on Georges Bizet's opera *Carmen*. In the *New York Times* (May 8, 2001), Caryn James described the MTV version as "an audacious blend of drama, hip-hop, movie musicals and visual flash, not to mention shrewd marketing and casting." Speaking of her experience in making *Carmen Brown*, Knowles told Jancee Dunn for *Rolling Stone* (May 24, 2001), "Besides Kelly and Michelle, I'm not around people our age for more than forty-five minutes. So I was around people my age for a month and a half, and I made friends. So it was more than a movie for me."

Knowles, Rowland, and Williams are all devout Christians. — G.O.

Suggested Reading: *Ebony* p164+ Sep. 2000; *Entertainment Weekly* p42+ Sep. 1, 2000, with photos; *Jet* p56+ May 14, 2001, with photo; *Newsweek* p54+ May 21, 2001, with photo; *Rolling Stone* p52+ May 24, 2001, with photo; *Seventeen* p152+ Nov. 2000, with photo; *Time* p128 Jan. 15, 2001, with photo; *Time Canada* (on-line) Jan. 15, 2001

Selected Recordings: *Destiny's Child*, 1997; *The Writing's on the Wall*, 1998; *Survivor*, 2001

Selected Films: Beyoncé Knowles—*Carmen Brown: A Hip Hopera*, 2001

Claudia Prieler/Courtesy of Carl Djerassi

Djerassi, Carl
(jer-ASS-ee)

*Oct. 29, 1923– Organic chemist; writer. Address:
Dept. of Chemistry, Stanford University,
Stanford, CA 94305*

In 1999, when the London *Times* compiled its list
of the 30 most important people of the millennium,
many familiar names were included. Isaac Newton, Galileo, William Shakespeare, Ferdinand Ma-
gellan, Mozart, Charles Darwin, Louis Pasteur, and
Albert Einstein all got their due. One name, however, was unfamiliar to many: that of the organic
chemist Carl Djerassi. Known as the father of the
Pill, the first oral contraceptive, Djerassi has been
a controversial figure since his invention took the
world by storm in the 1960s and forever changed
society's view of sex. Djerassi's contributions to
science extend beyond that groundbreaking
achievement. His name is on the patent for the first
antihistamines, and following his work on the Pill,
he was a pioneer in the development of pest-
control substances. Over the last decade Djerassi
has turned to writing fiction. He has published several books of "science-in-fiction," a term he coined
himself; in those works he has explored the fallibil-
ity of scientists and the societal conflicts raised
through their quests for recognition. He is also the
author of two plays as well as books of essays and
volumes of poetry.

Carl Djerassi was born on October 29, 1923 in
Vienna, Austria, the son of Jewish parents—
Samuel and Alice Djerassi—who were both physicians. His rearing was largely nonreligious. He
spent the first years of his childhood in Bulgaria,
his father's native country, returning to Vienna to

start school. Samuel Djerassi specialized in treating venereal disease in the days before the advent
of penicillin; Carl Djerassi's bar mitzvah was post-
poned when a wealthy syphilis patient arrived at
his father's clinic.

It was around this time, when Djerassi was in his
early teens, that he discovered his parents had divorced when he was six. His father had stayed in
Bulgaria, seeing the boy during his visits to Vienna
or when Carl visited him in the summers. "I suppose I was simply too young and generally too happy to wonder that my parents didn't live together,"
Djerassi told Nicholas Wroe for the London *Guardian* (August 26, 2000, on-line). He found out the
truth when his father introduced him to his girlfriend.

In 1938, during the *anschluss*—the incorporating of Austria into Nazi Germany—Djerassi's father
returned to Vienna and remarried his mother in order to take the family out of the country; once they
were safely away from Austria, thanks to Samuel
Djerassi's foreign nationality, the marriage was annulled. Djerassi's mother then traveled to England
to arrange her and her son's entry into the U.S. Carl
Djerassi, meanwhile, remained in Bulgaria, where
he learned English.

Djerassi and his mother arrived, with next to no
money, in the U.S. in 1939. Realizing that an education was of the utmost importance for his future,
the teenage Djerassi wrote a letter to Eleanor
Roosevelt, the wife of President Franklin Delano
Roosevelt, explaining his situation and asking for
financial assistance. Eleanor Roosevelt passed
Djerassi's letter on to the Institute of International
Education. As a result, Djerassi was offered a scholarship to a Presbyterian college in Missouri. He
completed his chemistry degree at Kenyon College,
in Gambier, Ohio, at age 19, then pursued postgraduate studies at the University of Wisconsin.
During that time he married his first wife, Virginia.

Djerassi became a naturalized U.S. citizen in
1945. Shortly thereafter he moved to New Jersey to
work for CIBA, a Swiss pharmaceutical company.
In 1949 he began working for Syntex S.A., in Mexico City, Mexico, where he started out by studying
the uses of cortisone. Soon he was researching the
treatment of certain types of menstrual disorders as
well as cancer. In 1951, by synthesizing different
hormones, Djerassi—along with Min Chuch
Chang, Gregory Pincus, and John Rock—formed
the foundation of what would become known as
the Pill, the first synthetic contraceptive that could
be taken orally. The Pill was made available to the
public in the early 1960s, and, by divorcing sex
and pregnancy, inaugurated a period of great social
change. Because it separated sex from fertilization
far more successfully that had earlier methods of
contraception, it helped to bring about the concept
of "free love," which involved having sex without
fear of impregnation or regard for societal mores.
Free love became an element of the 1960s counterculture, along with drug use and rock music.

Following the advent of the Pill, Djerassi became something of a celebrity. In 1973 he was awarded the National Medal of Science for his work. He remained modest about his discovery, however. "Yes I am proud to be called the father of the Pill," he told Nicholas Wroe. "But identifying scientists is really only a surrogate for identifying the inventions or discoveries. Maybe it is true that Shakespeare's plays would never [have] been written if it wasn't for Shakespeare. But I'm certain that if we didn't do our work then someone else would have come along shortly afterwards and done it."

In 1968 Djerassi founded his own company, Zoecon, which developed new approaches to insect control. As the decade closed he came out openly against the United States' involvement in the Vietnam War. Several years later it was revealed that, because of his involvement in the Democrat George McGovern's 1972 presidential campaign, Djerassi had been placed on the infamous enemies list of Republican president Richard Nixon.

Since the invention of the Pill, Djerassi has spent a great deal of time discussing—and facing controversy over—its possible side effects. The main accusation is that the Pill increases the risk of blood clots in women; some have linked the Pill to an increased risk of cancer and to excessive bleeding during menstruation. Djerassi has dismissed those claims, pointing to studies that place the number of blood clots in users of the Pill at 15 to 25 per 100,000, compared with 60 per 100,000 for pregnant women; he also asserts that links between the Pill and cancer or excessive bleeding during menstruation have never been proven. Djerassi is an outspoken proponent of oral contraceptives' being made available without prescription and is critical of the government's decreased funding for the further development of the Pill.

Today, Djerassi is an accomplished author with several novels, memoirs, and plays to his credit. He writes "science-in-fiction," which he has defined as fictional writing based on science, often discussing the social and personal dilemmas brought about by achievements in that field. He believes that discussions of his fiction can also serve as forums for examining the moral and ethical implications of scientific advances. "The more different ways we have of teaching certain difficult things the better off we are. I think that we as scientists should educate the public about the scientific and technological advances so that society can decide how to best use them. This is my missionary obsession," he told Nicholas Wroe. "Just because you have won a Nobel Prize doesn't mean you're qualified to make these important judgements. Ethics is a social construct and is something that society should establish. But in order to make educated decisions about this you must be aware of it."

In Djerassi's first novel, Cantor's Dilemma (1989), a well-known biologist develops a theory to explain why cells become cancerous; he knows that his theory can win him the Nobel Prize. When he finds out that his lab assistant may have falsified some of the lab results, he attempts to cover up the inconsistencies so that the prize can be his. Djerassi followed up his 1990 nonfiction work Steroids Made It Possible with The Pill, Pygmy Chimps, and Degas' Horse: The Remarkable Autobiography of the Award-Winning Scientist Who Synthesized the Birth Control Pill (1972). Next came his second science-in-fiction book, The Bourbaki Gambit (1994), which involves four scientists who are forced into retirement but decide to continue their research under a collective pseudonym. The group make a significant discovery that threatens to tear them apart. The book Marx, Deceased (1996) is about a novelist, Stephen Marx, who, wondering how he will be remembered, stages his own death. He begins writing under a new name, then becomes romantically involved with a journalist who has uncovered his deed. Meanwhile, his wife, who believes she is a widow, begins a relationship with a critic who is writing an evaluation of Marx's career. The critic harbors a grudge against Marx because the novelist had an extramarital affair with his wife.

In 2001 Djerassi published This Man's Pill— Reflections on the 50th Birthday of the Pill, in which he discussed common criticism of the oral contraceptive—from religious fundamentalists who blame its invention for the general moral decline of mankind, and from feminists who see the Pill as the ultimate manifestation of the patriarchal nature of society, since it was developed to be used exclusively by women. The bulk of the book explores how the Pill affected Djerassi himself, forcing him to explore social ramifications he had not initially considered. ("Until 1969, I would have described myself as a 'hard' scientist, the proudly macho adjective employed by chemists and other physical scientists to distinguish their work from the 'soft,' fuzzy fields such as sociology or even psychology," Djerassi wrote in the book.)

Oxygen (2001) is a play co-written by Djerassi and Roald Hoffmann. Its action alternates between the years 2001 and 1777. In the present day the Nobel Foundation decides to inaugurate a "Retro-Nobel" Award for important discoveries that preceded the creation of the Nobel Prize. One such discovery is that of oxygen, which raises the question of who should be credited. The setting then shifts to 1777, when three men vied for that distinction. The play premiered at the San Diego Repertory Theatre on April 2, 2001.

The subject of Djerassi's play An Immaculate Misconception (1998) is assisted reproductive technologies (ART), the process by which an egg can be successfully fertilized with the injection of a single sperm under a microscope, followed by the insertion of the egg into a woman's uterus. Djerassi told Norman Swan for the Health Report (November 20, 2000, on-line), "Sex of course still continues to be done in the usual way and that's for reasons that we always do: love, lust, pleasure. But reproduction separately, fertilisation, under the microscope, so to speak, . . . this separation of sex and reproduction . . . was not possible before, so therefore implicit in every sexual act was the fact that you might get pregnant, and that of course is you might say the Catholic dictum: you should not have sex for fun, you should have sex with at least the possibility, you can do it for fun but only with all the possibility of reproduction. Well that stopped in a way you could say in 1960, with the introduction of oral contraceptives and IUDs, because these are the two methods of contraception that separated sex from conception." Djerassi believes that the future of birth control lies with ART. He foresees a future in which young men will deposit sperm in banks for later artificial insemination, then undergo vasectomies, making sex and reproduction two entirely separate endeavors. "I'm trying to smuggle important scientific ideas out to the general public. The vast majority of legislators haven't got the foggiest idea about science or technology, and yet many of the decisions they make are based on these things," he told Martha J. Heil for *Discover* (June 2000).

Djerassi has received 18 honorary doctorates in addition to many other honors, including the first Wolf Prize in Chemistry, the first award for the Industrial Application of Science from the National Academy of Sciences, and the American Chemical Society's highest award, the Priestley Medal. He is one of only a few scientists to receive both the National Medal of Science and the National Medal of Technology. He is the author of more than 1,200 scientific publications and seven monographs. An art collector, Djerassi owns one of the most significant collections of works by Paul Klee.

Djerassi divorced his first wife in 1950 and his second wife, Norma, in 1976. He was married again on June 21, 1985; his third wife, Diane Middlebrook, is a writer and professor at Stanford University. Djerassi's daughter, Pamela, was born in 1950; she committed suicide at age 28. Djerassi founded the Djerassi Resident Artists Program (an artists' colony on his California ranch) in her memory in 1979. The program has benefitted more than 1,000 writers, painters, choreographers, and sculptors. He has one son, Dale, from his second marriage. — A.T.

Suggested Reading: *Discover* p24+ June 2000, with photos; *Health Report* (on-line) Nov. 20, 2000; (London) *Guardian* p6+ Aug. 26, 2000, with photos; *She Bang Magazine* (on-line), May 8, 2001; Djerassi, Carl. *The Pill, Pygmy Chimps, and Degas' Horse*, 1992

Selected Books: *Cantor's Dilemma*, 1989; *The Pill, Pygmy Chimps, and Degas' Horse: The Remarkable Autobiography of the Award-Winning Scientist Who Synthesized the Birth Control Pill*, 1992; *From the Lab into the World: A Pill for People, Pets, and Bugs*, 1994; *The Bourbaki Gambit*, 1994; *Marx, Deceased*, 1996; *Menachem's Seed: A Novel*, 1997; *No*, 1998; *This Man's Pill—Reflections on the 50th Birthday of the Pill*, 2001

Selected Plays: *An Immaculate Misconception*, 1998; *Oxygen*, 2001

Djukanovic, Milo

(djoo-KAN-oh-vitch, MEE-loh)

Feb. 15, 1962– President of Montenegro. Address: Predsjednik Republike Crne Gore, Podgorica, Crna Gora

President Milo Djukanovic of the Republic of Montenegro, known to many of his constituents as "Milo the Blade," was for many years something of a political anomaly in what remains of Yugoslavia: a leader who espoused democratic values and declined to exploit ethnic tensions for political gain. Djukanovic's democratic credentials are not entirely beyond dispute; he started his political career as a puppet of Slobodan Milosevic, who, as president first of Serbia and later of Yugoslavia, figured prominently in the Balkan wars of the 1990s. (Accused of war crimes, Milosevic will soon be tried by the International Criminal Tribunal for the Former Yugoslavia.) Moreover, Djukanovic has been involved in numerous shadowy (and perhaps even criminal) business transactions, and, according to Blaine Harden in the *New York Times Magazine*

(April 25, 1999), he is widely believed to have used government funds to line his own pockets. But he has managed to stand up for ethnic tolerance—he has made efforts to promote the civil rights of Muslims and ethnic Albanians, several of whom are included in his cabinet—and has pushed for democratic reform in a trying environment, often at considerable risk to his person and with little direct support from outside Montenegro.

About 650,000 people live in Montenegro, a small, mountainous republic that is bordered by Albania, Serbia, Bosnia and Herzegovina, and the southeastern coast of the Adriatic Sea; it is Serbia's only remaining partner in the Federal Republic of Yugoslavia, a political entity that once consisted of six republics. (The other four were Bosnia, Croatia, Macedonia, and Slovenia.) While Serbians and Montenegrins share both a language (Serbian) and a religion (Orthodox Christianity), the two republics do have distinct histories: unlike Serbia, Montenegro was never entirely conquered by the Ottoman Empire, and at the 1878 Congress of Berlin, it was recognized as an independent state. Then, in 1918, at the end of World War I, Montenegro, together with Croatia and Slovenia, was united with

Reuters/Petar Kujundzic/Hulton/Archive
Milo Djukanovic

Serbia to form the Serb-dominated royalist state that, in 1929, was formally designated Yugoslavia. After World War II Yugoslavia—and with it Montenegro—became a Communist state ruled by Josip Broz Tito (widely known as Marshal Tito), an ethnic Croat who, until his death, in 1980, sought to curb Serbian influence. While Montenegro remained allied with Serbia throughout the 1990s wars (Montenegrin paramilitary units have been linked to war crimes in Bosnia and Croatia), and profited in many ways from an increase in smuggling made possible by the various conflicts, it has become, especially in recent years, both increasingly democratic and increasingly resentful of its larger neighbor. As a Montenegrin political scientist told Masha Gessen for the *New Republic* (June 26, 2000), "Now Yugoslavia is like a bad marriage in which one spouse constantly beats the other. The wife has locked herself in her room, but she hasn't left yet, though she intends to." "It is as if Austria, having united with Germany in the Anschluss of 1938, had opted to reclaim its independence in 1944," Christopher Hitchens wrote for *Vanity Fair* (November 1999).

Montenegro's tangled historical relationship with Serbia is further complicated by the fact that few people, in Montenegro or elsewhere, are able to pinpoint exactly what it is that separates Montenegrins from their Serbian neighbors. According to Gessen, a recent poll indicated that about one-quarter of Montenegrins also consider themselves Serbs; of the majority who consider themselves ethnic Montenegrins, one-third qualify that allegiance by defining themselves as Montenegrins of Serbian provenance. (The converse might be said of many Serbs. The parents of Slobodan Milosevic

are Montenegrin, as is Radovan Karadzic, the Serbian nationalist and indicted war criminal responsible for much of the so-called "ethnic cleansing" in Bosnia-Herzegovina.) Yet, in spite of such difficulties in distinguishing Serbs and Montenegrins, many in Montenegro continue to assert a distinct national identity. This perplexing state of affairs has led one Yugoslavian sociologist, as quoted by Harden, to speak of "a kind of permanent schizophrenia" with regard to ethnic and national identity in Montenegro. Moreover, about 14 percent of Montenegrins are Muslim, and about 8 percent identify themselves as ethnic Albanians. Polls show that slightly more than 50 percent of Montenegrins favor independence from the Federal Republic of Yugoslavia, a cause that Djukanovic has recently embraced.

Milo Djukanovic was born in Niksic, a small city in south-central Montenegro, on February 15, 1962. He was educated in Niksic and Podgorica, the Montenegrin capital, and received a degree in economics in 1986. Earlier, in 1979, Djukanovic, who was politically active from a young age, had joined the League of Communists of Yugoslavia. (Until the collapse of Communist rule, in 1989–90, the league was the only authorized political party in Yugoslavia.) By the time he graduated from college, Djukanovic had become a member of the party's Central Committee, and after the Montenegrin branch of the Communist League rechristened itself the Democratic Party of Socialists of Montenegro (DPSCG), he continued to play an active role in the organization.

Early in his political career, Djukanovic was closely allied with Slobodan Milosevic; indeed, he was originally something of a Milosevic protégé. In 1991, in a gambit to wrest power from old-guard Communists still loyal to Tito's vision of Yugoslavia, Milosevic installed Djukanovic as prime minister of Montenegro. (The prime minister, as the head of government, directs the day-to-day administration of national affairs. The president of Montenegro, as the chief of state, is entrusted with representing the country abroad. He is also empowered to call for parliamentary elections, appoint justices to the Constitutional Court, propose candidates for prime minister to the Parliament, and call for national referenda to alter or amend the constitution. The current president is Filip Vujanovic.) At first regarded as a little more than a Milosevic henchman, during the early and mid-1990s, Djukanovic began to free himself from his mentor's influence. He accomplished this chiefly by establishing an independent source of income. By allowing Italian cigarette smugglers (many of them linked to the Mafia, according to local rumor and the Italian media) to use Montenegro as a base of operations in return for a "transit fee," Djukanovic built an exceedingly lucrative operation that was estimated to have provided the Montenegrin government with about 10 percent of its income. Since Milosevic had little control over the Italian cigarette smugglers, and smuggling provided a source of revenue that was unaffected by the economic sanctions imposed on Yugoslavia by the United States and the European Union in 1991, it provided Djukanovic with a measure of political independence as well. Such questionable business transactions notwithstanding, Djukanovic, in contrast to Milosevic, increasingly espoused democratic reform and ethnic tolerance. (For his part, Milosevic is reported to have resented Montenegro's growing financial autonomy; nonetheless, for years the two leaders did not discuss their differences in public.)

The growing tensions between Djukanovic and Milosevic surfaced in the mid-1990s through Milosevic's wife, Mirjana Markovic, the ultra-left leader of the Yugoslav United Left Party, whom many Montenegrans and Serbs regarded as "a low-wattage Stalinist shrew," according to Harden. (The reference was to Joseph Stalin, the longtime dictator of the Soviet Union.) In her weekly newspaper column, Markovic branded Djukanovic the most notorious smuggler in Yugoslavia—an accusation that many viewed with considerable irony, given that Markovic's only son, Marko, also had a fair claim to that title. Djukanovic retorted that Markovic was, as Harden paraphrased it, "an irrelevant woman whose Chinese-oriented Marxist party . . . was so small that its entire membership could fit on a bus."

The conclusive break between Milosevic and Djukanovic came during the winter of 1996–97, when three months of mass demonstrations, triggered by Milosevic's refusal to recognize the democratic opposition's victory in November municipal elections, severely tested the Serbian leader's political survival skills. Djukanovic took advantage of the political crisis to publicly distance himself from Milosevic. "It would be politically crazy for Milosevic to remain in any political position in the political life of Yugoslavia," Djukanovic declared, as quoted by Jonathan C. Randal in the *Washington Post* (June 14, 1997). On several other occasions he called Milosevic "yesterday's man." Nevertheless, Milosevic proved to be highly resilient; he successfully weathered the unrest of early 1997, and by early summer he had recovered enough of his former clout to sidestep a constitutional ban that had blocked him from serving a third four-year term as president of Serbia, a position he was scheduled to relinquish in December. (Milosevic accomplished this by running, unopposed, for president of Yugoslavia—then chiefly a ceremonial office—and subsequently transferring many of his former powers to his new post.) As Milosevic went about consolidating power in his new office, Djukanovic continued to be a thorn in his side, by opposing efforts to strengthen the federal presidency.

Djukanovic's split with Milosevic precipitated a schism in Djukanovic's political party, the DPSCG, since its president, Momir Bulatovic—who was president of Montenegro then—remained loyal to the Serbian leader. Both Djukanovic and Bulatovic declared their candidacies for the fall 1997 Montenegrin presidential election, and over the summer the two repeatedly clashed as each declared himself the official representative of the DPSCG. Eventually, the courts ruled both eligible to run. During the campaign Bulatovic emphasized his support of Milosevic and accused Djukanovic of preparing to lead Montenegro out of the Yugoslav federation (a charge that Djukanovic at the time denied); for his part, Djukanovic pledged to accelerate economic and democratic reforms and vowed to guarantee the civil rights of the Muslim and ethnic Albanian minorities. In the election, held on October 19, 1997, Djukanovic secured a slim, 5,000-vote margin of victory, and Bulatovic's campaign manager conceded defeat. However, on the day before Djukanovic's inauguration, in January 1998, Bulatovic, along with 10,000 armed protestors, stormed the Presidency Building in Podgorica—an attempt to trigger a violent crackdown by a police force loyal to Djukanovic and thus, according to Harden, give the Yugoslav Army, which had remained loyal to Milosevic, a pretext to intervene and depose Djukanovic. (Previously, Milosevic had employed similar tactics against political rivals to great effect.) After 37 police officers were injured, when one of the protesters lobbed a hand grenade at the building's entrance, Djukanovic's forces responded with tear gas and stun grenades; no one was killed and no arrests were made after the crowd was dispersed. That restraint effectively defused the standoff and denied Milosevic an excuse to move in on Djukanovic.

During his first year as president, Djukanovic continued to walk a political tightrope by pursuing a pro-Western policy while refusing to call for secession from the Yugoslav federation. That became dramatically more difficult in March 1999, when NATO (the North Atlantic Treaty Organization), in response to a Serbian military offensive against the ethnic Albanian population in the province of Kosovo in Serbia, launched a 78-day bombing campaign against the Yugoslav Republic. While most of the NATO bombing was confined to Serbia, Serb military units in Montenegro were targeted as well, which badly undermined Djukanovic's efforts to promote pro-Western policies. Officially, the government declared itself neutral, but the bombing of Montenegro starkly polarized the population into pro-Serbian and pro-Western factions. "It is hard, very hard to speak and work for a democratic and pro-European policy," Djukanovic warned shortly after the start of the bombing campaign, as quoted by Harden in the *New York Times* (April 5, 1999). "NATO bombs have allowed Mr. Milosevic to create a new division in the Yugoslav political scene. Patriots are those who support his policies and anyone who criticizes him is a traitor. In Montenegro, pro-Milosevic forces are becoming much more aggressive." "The bombing has really made a horrible mess for this republic," Milka Tadic, an independent Montenegrin journalist, said, as quoted by Harden. "Djukanovic was put in this horrible political situation of being bombed by his allies. It gave the nationalists and the regular people of this country who are very confused a perfect reason to say that this Government does not want to defend itself from outside attacks."

By late April Djukanovic and Montenegro were in a highly precarious position, and a growing number of voices warned of either an imminent coup or civil war. In addition to grappling with a highly polarized populace and a national economy virtually shut down by the conflict, the Djukanovic government struggled to accommodate thousands of ethnic Albanian refugees who had entered Montenegro from neighboring Kosovo. "The bombs mean that before this story is printed Djukanovic could be put in prison or killed," Blaine Harden wrote for the *New York Times Magazine* (April 25, 1999). In the *New Republic* (May 10, 1999), Anna Husarska wrote, "It feels like The Day Before The Coup in Podgorica," as rival military factions, loyal to Milosevic and Djukanovic, respectively, stepped up their activities in the capital. While repeatedly enjoining NATO to end the bombings, which he branded "irresponsible," Djukanovic continued to denounce Milosevic, whom he called "insane, autistic, and autocratic," according to Harden. Milosevic, in turn, pronounced Djukanovic a "traitor."

From the summer of 1999, when the NATO bombings ended, until Milosevic's electoral defeat in the September 2000 Serbian presidential election and his fall from power the following month, the two Yugoslav republics were poised in a tense standoff: Milosevic made ominous gestures toward the smaller republic, while Djukanovic grew more assertive with regard to Montenegrin independence, progressively loosening his government's ties to Serbia without actually breaking away. In late May and early June 1999, Djukanovic's government first announced it would no longer recognize the military as an organ of the Yugoslav federation, then initiated criminal proceedings against several officers stationed in Montenegro. Later, the Djukanovic government announced its intention to cooperate with the International Criminal Tribunal for the Former Yugoslavia. That meant that should he set foot in Montenegro, Milosevic, who had been indicted by the tribunal, would be subject to arrest and deportation to The Hague, in the Netherlands, the seat of the tribunal—despite the fact that he was still nominally president of Yugoslavia. Djukanovic took a further step toward independence in late 1999, when he announced that Montenegro would adopt the German mark as an alternative currency to the Yugoslav dinar. Throughout this tense period, government officials in Montenegro and abroad, as well as the media, continued to pronounce the small country the likely site of "the next Balkan war."

The September 24, 2000 election of Vojislav Kostunica as president of Yugoslavia, and the ouster of Milosevic in October, led to a nonviolent denouement. While Kostunica, a moderate Serbian nationalist, has stated that he opposes independence for Montenegro (indeed, Djukanovic, to pro-

test Kostunica's pro-Yugoslavia stance, called upon Montenegrins to boycott the September elections), he has said that he is willing to settle the matter democratically. Kostunica told Ljubeta Labovic for the Podgorica weekly *Monitor* (September 1, 2000, on-line) that he favors "a referendum in both states. If a majority is for the common state, then a new constitution; if a majority is against a common state, then two independent states." If Montenegro secedes, Kostunica, as president of the Federal Republic of Yugoslavia, will be out of a job, as the federal republic will cease to exist.

In early 2001 the Djukanovic government continued to press for independence. As Branko Lukovac, the Montenegrin foreign minister, wrote for the *Washington Post* (February 17, 2001), Djukanovic "has committed our country to independence from its federation with Serbia. He has pledged to accomplish this democratically and transparently. And he is committed to working patiently and in good faith with the new democratic leadership in Serbia to seek a mutually acceptable redefinition of our historical relationship. He has opened a broad public dialogue on this issue and is committed to a referendum, which we expect to be held this summer." However, parliamentary elections held in April appeared to have checked the movement toward independence, at least temporarily. With 42 percent of the vote, Djukanovic's secessionist "Victory Belongs to Montenegro" coalition only narrowly defeated the opposition "Together with Yugoslavia" coalition, which emerged from balloting with 40.6 percent of the vote. (Djukanovic had been hoping for two-thirds of the vote so that he could claim a clear mandate for independence.) "This result is a big step backwards for Djukanovic," Darko Brocic, a Belgrade political analyst, said, as quoted by Justin Brown in the *Christian Science Monitor* (April 24, 2001). "He will theoretically be able to hold the referendum, but he will lose a lot of his supporters and may not have enough votes to win." Indeed, on May 24, Djukanovic, while continuing to insist that there existed broad popular support for independence, announced that he was postponing indefinitely a referendum on that issue.

According to the *Wall Street Journal* (April 19, 1999, on-line), his nickname, "Milo the Blade," salutes his intelligence. Djukanovic and his wife, the former Lidija Kuc, have one son, Blazo. — P.K.

Suggested Reading: *New York Times Magazine* p38+ Apr. 25, 1999, with photos; *U.S. News & World Report* p45 Nov. 15, 1999, with photo; *Vanity Fair* p111+ Nov. 1999, with photos

Courtesy of Carolyn Olshaker

Douglas, John E.

June 18, 1945– Criminologist; crime writer; former FBI official. Address: c/o Charles Scribner's Sons, 1230 Ave. of the Americas, New York, NY 10020

Between 1979 and 1982, 22 African-American children were killed in predominantly black neighborhoods in Atlanta, Georgia. Law-enforcement officers guessed that the murders might be hate crimes perpetrated by members of the Ku Klux Klan or the American Nazi Party. The FBI profiler John Douglas had a different theory. Douglas, who later became the head of the FBI's National Center for the Analysis of Violent Crime, thought that the murders could not be attributed to a single person; one of the murderers, he suggested to the police, was probably an African-American man in his mid-20s who was not married, had a peripheral connection to the music business, and was a police buff. The authorities eventually linked two of the murders to Wayne Williams, who fit Douglas's description precisely. Douglas is one of the originators of the technique known as criminal profiling, in which the likely characteristics of the perpetrator of a particular crime—such as the person's age, education, employment, race, height and weight, and behavioral history—are deduced by analyzing the details of the crime. Douglas's profiles have contributed to the arrests and convictions of many murderers, rapists, kidnappers, and other felons. To those unfamiliar with the techniques of profiling, the close similarities between Douglas's description of a possible guilty party and the actual culprit often seem almost miraculous. Thanks to fictionalized portraits of him in books,

on TV shows, and in such movies as *The Silence of the Lambs* (1991), Douglas has gained many admirers. In 1995, after 25 years with the FBI, he retired and, mainly in collaboration with Mark Olshaker, began writing true-crime books based on his own experiences and profiling techniques. His dozen books include the best-seller *Mindhunter* (1995).

John Edward Douglas was born on June 18, 1945 and grew up on Long Island, New York. He graduated from Hempstead High School, where he had demonstrated more interest in sports than in academics. An animal lover who wanted to be a veterinarian, he enrolled at Montana State University in Bozeman, a school noted for its veterinary program. After two years he was forced to leave, because of low grades. Soon afterward he joined the air force; he was stationed at Cannon Air Force Base, near Clovis, New Mexico. Under the G.I. Bill, he attended Eastern New Mexico University in Portales. He was "living in the cellar of a house with no windows," as he recalled to Marjorie Rosen for *Biography* (October 1997), when, by chance, he met an FBI agent at a local health club. Seeing the man's "nice house," "nice wife," "nice car," and generous paycheck, as he recalled to Rosen, gave him the idea that a job with the FBI might provide relief from his unfulfilling circumstances.

For six years after he joined the FBI, in 1970, Douglas worked in Detroit. In 1976 he transferred to the FBI's Behavioral Sciences Unit, as a member of which he studied applied criminal psychology at the FBI Academy. He earned an M.S. degree and a Ph.D., both in psychology, and subsequently taught a course in criminal psychology for police officers throughout the U.S. Having become a specialist, he came to believe that there were serious flaws in the discipline, because so little of the knowledge categorized as criminal psychology had been gleaned from interviews with actual criminals. In their talks with felons, Douglas had discovered, psychologists and law-enforcement officers had seldom asked about motives or posed probing questions about the perpetrators' accounts of their crimes. To acquire more accurate and illuminating information, he interviewed more than 100 murderers, rapists, kidnappers, arsonists, and other criminals. During the course of his research, he spoke with Richard Speck, who murdered eight student nurses in Chicago in 1966; Charles Manson, who is serving a life sentence for the murders of the actress Sharon Tate and four others in 1969; James Earl Ray, who assassinated Martin Luther King Jr. in 1968; Sirhan Sirhan, who killed U.S. senator Robert F. Kennedy, also in 1968; John Wayne Gacy, the killer of 33 young men and boys; David Berkowitz (known as the "Son of Sam"), who murdered six people in New York City in 1976 and 1977; and the serial killer Ted Bundy, who slaughtered at least 36 young women in the 1970s. "I'd let the guy talk," Douglas told Rosen, "let him project the blame onto someone else, even the victims. Then I'd challenge him. I'd say, 'I know your case. I looked at the crime-scene photos. You cannibalized that woman.' What they like is when you tell them about themselves. Then they open up." Through his investigations, Douglas found that the majority of violent criminals were white males of above-average intelligence and that as children most of them had been abused or neglected and had a history of bed-wetting, arson, and cruelty to animals.

The process of profiling involves looking closely at all the details of a crime with the goal of drawing probable inferences about the perpetrator. "To understand the artist, you must look at the art work," David Bowman quoted Douglas as saying in *Salon.com* (July 8, 1999). Although the techniques used in committing crimes vary, every violent criminal, according to Douglas, has a "signature"—something from which he or she derives satisfaction in the course of the crime. Some, for example, need to inflict pain, while others need to hear their victims beg for mercy. Douglas soon began to develop procedures and techniques for identifying signatures and deducing other facts about the culprit. "You examine a crime scene with all its particular attributes in order to develop a general physical and psychological description of the person who committed the crime—a profile," Douglas explained to Paul Reid for the *Houston Chronicle* (October 13, 1996). "Then, in logical terms, you build a set of suspects who fall within the profile. Then, you move logically back to the particular. You try to find the specific criminal within that group." For Douglas, the process of profiling requires both imagination and intuition. "I try to imagine what the victim would have been saying at the time of the attack," he told Amy Wallace for the *Los Angeles Times* (December 8, 1995). "I try to think how [the offender] would have been reacting. I even visualize the expression on his face. . . . I can see the style of hair, maybe the kind of clothing this guy would be wearing."

Partly because of the unorthodox nature of Douglas's techniques, for some time many FBI agents did not accept them. Especially resistant were those who had been strongly influenced by the politically and socially conservative J. Edgar Hoover, who wielded enormous power as head of the FBI from 1924 until his death, in 1972. "It's '77, '78, '80, and I'm doing this stuff," Douglas told Bowman, "but the Hooverites are still around. They want to deal in blacks and whites, and I want to deal in grays." His ideas met with a more favorable reception among members of local and state police forces. But after his profiling techniques led directly to the apprehension of several murderers, his ideas gained greater acceptance within the FBI.

One of his successes was the case of the so-called Trailside Killer, who slaughtered eight women and a man in woodlands surrounding San Francisco Bay between 1979 and 1981; many of the victims had been shot in the head, execution style, while they were kneeling, and also had multiple stab wounds. The police, assuming that the killer had lured many of his victims to the places where they died, believed that he would be an attractive charmer. Douglas, by contrast, surmised that the killer had deep feelings of inadequacy and a speech impediment and, as a child, had wet his bed, set fires, and hurt small animals. He proved to be correct: David J. Carpenter, who in 1984 was sentenced to death for the murders, had a severe stutter and in every other way matched Douglas's profile.

Another case that Douglas helped to solve, in the early 1980s, involved 12 prostitutes and strippers whose bodies were found in remote areas surrounding Anchorage, Alaska. All had died of gunshots from a hunting rifle. Asked by law-enforcement officials for his assessment of various people who were under suspicion, Douglas pointed out a man whom the police considered one of the least likely suspects: Robert Hansen, a small, married man with pockmarked skin and a stutter, who owned a local bakery and hunted game animals. Douglas told the police that, as serial killers often do, Hansen had probably kept "trophies" from his victims. In 1983, on the strength of Douglas's expert opinion, the police obtained a warrant to search Hansen's home—thus setting a legal precedent, according to which a criminal profile could serve as the basis for issuing a search warrant. Again, Douglas's prediction was accurate: as he recalled to Bowman, "In his house they found jewelry belonging to a dozen women he killed, along with a map with X's on it that showed where each woman was buried."

In the early 1980s Pennsylvania police contacted Douglas about a woman whose body had been found at a town dump. She had been sexually assaulted and mutilated, and some of her hair had been cut off. The police told Douglas that they thought the killer was a known robber who had been seen near the site by witnesses. But Douglas thought otherwise. "You're dealing with two people here, not one, and one of them was very close to the victim," he explained, as he recalled to Michael Ryan for the *Houston Chronicle* (July 12, 1992). "You don't have to look beyond the people you've already interviewed. It's probably someone who has been very cooperative." From experience, Douglas had learned that sexual assaulters rarely mutilated their victims, as had happened in this case. Furthermore, the removal of hair—a very personal memento—suggested that at least one of the men had been close to the victim. Further evidence for that theory was the disposal of the body in a public place, where the perpetrators knew that it would probably be found and then properly buried. Armed with this information, the police arrested the woman's boyfriend and his brother. The two confessed to the crime, explaining that the brother had sexually assaulted the woman, and her boyfriend, fearing that someone would find out, had killed her.

As Douglas's methods found acceptance and he grew busier, he started becoming a workaholic. "I had so many cases, I'd go to bed, having read one, and force myself to dream about it," he told Wallace. "I used to come up with ideas in the middle of the night—I'd get up and write [them] down." One day in 1983, while in Seattle, Washington, investigating the so-called Green River murders (named for the waterway where the assumed serial killer of 49 women had left many of their bodies), he began feeling ill. That night he collapsed in his motel room and lost consciousness. Two days later, when colleagues of his found him, his temperature had reached 107 degrees. He was later diagnosed with viral encephalitis, which had been aggravated by stress. "They packed me in ice," he told Bowman. "I was in a coma for a week. I came out of it paralyzed. I had to go through five months of rehabilitation."

On July 10, 1984 the FBI established the National Center for the Analysis of Violent Crime (NCAVC), to provide investigative support for law enforcement personnel on all levels; soon afterward Douglas was named its director. Four years later his first book, *Sexual Homicide: Patterns and Motives*, on which he collaborated with Robert K. Ressler, Ann W. Burgess, and Horace J. Heafner, was published; the information it contains was based on studies conducted by the FBI. Again working with Ressler, Burgess, and Heafner, Douglas wrote *Crime Classification Manual* (1992), a handbook for categorizing criminals and their motives. By 1991 NCAVC was being consulted in connection with more than 1,000 homicides each year, as well as kidnappings, cases of child molestation, terrorism, arson, and bombing, among other crimes, and Douglas's reputation had grown apace.

Publicity about Douglas and his work influenced writers of fiction and scriptwriters working in television and film. In her 1990 crime novel, *Postmortem*, Patricia Cornwell used Douglas as the model for the fictional FBI profiler Benton Wesley, a character who would resurface in several of her subsequent books. Characters based on him have also appeared in the graphic TV series *Profiler*, which debuted in 1996 and features a female crime fighter named Sam Waters (played by Ally Walker), and *Millennium* (1996–99), about a former FBI agent who tracks down messianic murderers. Douglas has lamented inaccuracies in the way profiling is portrayed on such shows. "What they've done is misinterpret my books," he told Bowman. "If I watch *The Profiler*, it drives me crazy when [Walker, as Waters] gets this look on her face, and she has these flashbacks and starts seeing blood and gore." Perhaps partly because of such representations (or misrepresentations), some got the impression that profiling was too unscientific to be reliable. One Pennsylvania defense attorney, for example, according to Amy Wallace, referred to Douglas as "voodoo man." Douglas himself has maintained that profiling is mostly an exercise in logic; nevertheless, on occasion he has alluded to

what seem to be mystical aspects of it. In *Mindhunter: Inside the Elite Serial Crime Unit* (1995), which he co-authored with Mark Olshaker, Douglas wrote, as quoted by Wallace, "I try to . . . put myself mentally and emotionally in the head of the offender. If there is a psychic component to this, I won't run away from it, though I regard it more in the realm of creative thinking."

Some critics of profiling fear that it could lead to false arrests. Roy Black, a Florida lawyer, told Paul Reid, "Profiling is just categorizing. You can see where that can go . . . if statistics show that 80 percent of liquor store holdups are done by black males, then the police are going to start automatically looking for black males instead of at the evidence when a store gets robbed." Moreover, some of Douglas's profiles have contained significant errors. An example is the profile he composed for the FBI of the so-called Unabomber, who succeeded in eluding capture during the 17 years in which, by means of 16 mail bombs, he killed three people and maimed 23 others. Douglas listed the Unabomber's probable characteristics in 1995, after the *New York Times* and the *Washington Post* received a 35,000-word "manifesto" in which the Unabomber condemned what he described as a corrupt technocracy that was destroying the freedom of individuals at the behest of a corporate and governmental cabal. According to Douglas, the Unabomber probably had a wife or girlfriend, drove an old-model car that was in good shape, lived in the San Francisco Bay Area, and would strike again after his manifesto was published in newspapers. But the Unabomber—later identified as Theodore J. Kaczynski—never sent another mail bomb after the manifesto was published, and when he was captured, in 1996, he turned out to be a never-married man who had apparently never formed an intimate relationship with a woman, did not own a car, and lived in a tiny cabin in a Montana forest. In an online interview for *USA Today*, Douglas pointed out that profiling is not infallible and that it is just one of many law-enforcement tools. "I'm the first one to tell anyone who asks for assistance that profiling is not a substitute for a thorough and well-planned investigation," he said.

Douglas's best-selling, semiautobiographical book *Mindhunter: Inside the Elite Serial Crime Unit*, which he wrote with Mark Olshaker, came out in 1995, the year he retired from the FBI. In an assessment of *Mindhunter* for the *New York Times* (November 12, 1995), the horror novelist Dean Koontz wrote, "Douglas sets out to produce a good true-crime book, but because of his insights and the power of his material, he gives us more—he leaves us shaken, gripped by a quiet grief for the innocent victims and anguished by the human condition." Charles P. Thobae, writing for the *Houston Chronicle* (January 7, 1996), found *Mindhunter* to be mostly successful, but he complained that Douglas had revealed "a narcissistic side in his autobiographical narrative. . . . The reader sometimes gets the sense that Douglas is a glib grandstander who considers the notoriety he received from *Silence of the Lambs* to be a fitting climax to his FBI career."

At around this time Douglas and Olshaker formed a company and signed a five-book contract with Simon & Schuster Inc. In 1996 they published *Unabomber: On the Trail of America's Most-Wanted Serial Killer*. This was followed in 1997 by the best-selling *Journey into Darkness: Follow the FBI's Premier Investigative Profiler as He Penetrates the Minds and Motives of the Most Terrifying Serial Killers*. Focusing next on crimes against women, Douglas and Olshaker published *Obsession: The FBI's Legendary Profiler Probes the Psyches of Killers, Rapists, and Stalkers and Their Victims and Tells How to Fight Back* (1998). Their next effort was *Anatomy of Motive: The FBI's Legendary Mindhunter Explores the Key to Understanding and Catching Violent Criminals* (1999), which examined such notorious killers as Lee Harvey Oswald, who assassinated President John F. Kennedy in 1963; Charles Whitman, who shot 13 people from a clock tower at the University of Texas at Austin in 1966; and Timothy McVeigh, who was found guilty of the April 19, 1995 bombing of the Alfred P. Murrah Building, in Oklahoma City, Oklahoma, in which 168 people were killed. In *Biography* (July 1999), Marjorie Rosen wrote that *Anatomy of Motive* was "impeccably researched and brimming with information about killers and their crimes," but warned, "For those who have read the Douglas-Olshaker oeuvre, this book covers some familiar territory." Douglas joined Olshaker to write a crime novel, *Broken Wings* (1999), about an FBI profiler named Jake Donovan who, while investigating the murder of the director of the FBI, is stalked by a right-wing paramilitary organization whose members hold a deep grudge against the bureau. In their most recent collaboration, *Cases That Haunt Us: From Jack the Ripper to JonBenet Ramsey, the FBI's Legendary Mindhunter Sheds New Light on the Mysteries That Won't Go Away*, Douglas and Olshaker show how the use of profiling techniques might have led to convictions in various well-known unsolved murder cases. "In the end," Rodger Lyle Brown suggested in the *New York Times* (December 31, 2000), "it seems [Douglas] is using the profiling angle as a pretext to retell these perennial crime favorites for the true-crime buffs who can't get enough."

Since his retirement from the FBI, Douglas has served as a consultant on criminal cases. In 1997 John and Patricia Ramsey of Boulder, Colorado, hired him to investigate the murder of their six-year-old daughter, JonBenet, a beauty-pageant star, whose body was found in the basement of the family home on the day after Christmas in 1996. The police regarded the girl's parents as major suspects in the case, because they and their son were reportedly the only people in the house with JonBenet on the night that she was killed; there was no sign of forced entry anywhere in the house, and there were no footprints in the snow surrounding the house

after the murder. But after he interviewed the father and mother, Douglas announced that he believed that they were innocent of the crime. His assessment met with much criticism. Gregg McCrary, one of his former FBI colleagues, faulted Douglas for failing to talk to the parents separately, so as to compare their versions of events, and for basing his conclusions on their words rather than their actions. The identity of JonBenet Ramsey's killer remains unknown. In another case, in conjunction with the TV show *America's Most Wanted*, Douglas tried in 1999 to track down Angel Maturino Resendez (also known as Rafael Resendez-Ramirez), the "Texas railroad killer," who was accused of killing nine people near train tracks in Texas, Kentucky, and Illinois. Resendez eluded U.S. law enforcers until he surrendered, in July 1999.

In an on-line interview for *ABCNews.com* (June 22, 1999) and on other occasions, Douglas has said that murderers are "made and not born." He also believes that if potential murderers are not identified and given help by about the time they are in junior high school, there is little hope of rehabilitating them. "I have conducted interviews with serial killers where I've felt that had this person been raised in the right environment, they wouldn't have turned out the way they did," he told *ABCNews.com*. "However, I don't excuse behavior once they have perpetrated a violent crime. I know from my research that they basically have no remorse for what they have done, that they do know right from wrong, and that at the time that they committed the crime they were making choices. My empathy is for the victims of these violent offenders who we seem to forget as years go by. . . . I often feel the perpetrators are not punished strongly enough. I discount the notion of rehabilitation for any of them."

In 1972 Douglas married Pam Modica. The couple divorced during Douglas's hectic years with the FBI and then reunited, after he retired. They have three children: Erika, Lauren, and Jed. — P.G.H.

Suggested Reading: *Biography* p63+ Oct. 1997; *Denver Post* B p1 Jan. 30, 1997, B p3 Jan. 30, 1997; *Houston Chronicle* p8 Apr. 28, 1991, p8 July 12, 1992, p31 Jan. 7, 1996, p1 Oct. 13, 1996; *Los Angeles Times* p1 Dec. 8, 1995; *New York Times Book Review* p54 Nov. 12, 1995; *Salon.com* July 8, 1999

Selected Books: as author—*Guide to Careers in the FBI*, 1998; *John Douglas's Guide to the California Police Officer Exams*, 2000; *John Douglas's Guide to Police Officer Exams*, 2000; as co-author with Robert K. Ressler, Ann W. Burgess, and Horace J. Heafner—*Sexual Homicide: Patterns and Motives*, 1988; *Crime Classification Manual*, 1992; as co-author with Mark Olshaker—*Mindhunter: Inside the Elite Serial Crime Unit*, 1995; *Unabomber: On the Trail of America's Most-Wanted Serial Killer*,

1996; *Journey Into Darkness: Follow the FBI's Premier Investigative Profiler as he Penetrates the Minds and Motives of the Most Terrifying Serial Killers*, 1997; *Obsession: The FBI's Legendary Profiler Probes the Psyches of Killers, Rapists, and Stalkers and Their Victims and Tells How to Fight Back*, 1998; *Anatomy of Motive: The FBI's Legendary Mindhunter Explores the Key to Understanding and Catching Violent Criminals*, 1999; *Broken Wings*, 1999; *Cases That Haunt Us: From Jack the Ripper to JonBenet Ramsey, the FBI's Legendary Mindhunter Shed New Light on the Mysteries That Won't Go Away*, 2000

Henny Garfunkel/Retna Ltd.

Dunst, Kirsten

Apr. 30, 1982– Actress. Address: c/o Iris Burton Agency, 8916 Ashcroft Ave., Los Angeles, CA 90048

At the tender age of 19, the actress Kirsten Dunst has already had a career that would make a 35-year-old jealous. Dunst first caught the public's eye with her portrayal of a young vampire in the film adaptation of Anne Rice's novel *Interview with the Vampire* (1994). Appearing alongside the heart-throbs Tom Cruise and Brad Pitt, the 11-year-old Dunst captivated audiences with her performance and led Brendan Lemon to proclaim in *Interview* (June 2000), "From her first lines as the most appalling specter in Rice's vampire realm . . . Dunst revealed the unmistakable attributes of a great actress—a commanding, unassuagable presence; a face almost obscenely fluent in emotional disclo-

sure; a voice already an instrument, not an appliance." Since her work in that movie, which garnered her a 1995 MTV Movie Award for breakthrough performance in a film as well as a 1995 Golden Globe nomination for best supporting actress, Dunst has appeared in nearly two dozen more films, including *Wag the Dog, Drop Dead Gorgeous, The Virgin Suicides, Get Over It*, and *crazy/beautiful*. Brendan Lemon, in his article about the actress, concluded, "In a time when actors are expected to have the physical perfection and emotional range of fashion models, Dunst does what the greatest performers are revered . . . for: She claws to the rock-bottom of her characters, conveying them so convincingly that even her most disturbing observations keep us watching."

Kirsten Caroline Dunst was born in Point Pleasant, New Jersey, on April 30, 1982. Her German-born father, Klaus, worked as a medical-services executive; her mother, Inez, had owned an art gallery. Klaus Dunst remained in New Jersey after separating from and eventually divorcing his wife, who moved with Kirsten and her younger brother, Christian, to Los Angeles in 1992 for the sake of Kirsten's career in show business. Long before the relocation, Kirsten Dunst had known what she wanted to do with her life. When she was three, her parents, at the urging of admiring strangers, had signed her up with the Ford modeling agency in New York City, which eventually led to acting assignments. By the time Dunst was seven years old, she had appeared in more than 70 television ads. This exposure paved the way for her first appearance on the big screen, in an uncredited role as Woody Allen's daughter in his segment (one of three) in the 1989 film *New York Stories*. From the beginning, Dunst enjoyed the hectic pace of the actor's life. She told Michael Sauter for *Biography* (August 2000), "No one ever had to push me into anything. I loved going on auditions. It was so exciting to me. When I wasn't working, I'd be so upset. I cried when I couldn't go into New York and work." Shortly after her appearance in *New York Stories*, she won a part in the film adaptation of Tom Wolfe's celebrated novel *The Bonfire of the Vanities* (1990), in which she was the daughter of the character played by Tom Hanks.

It was at this point that Dunst moved with her mother and brother to the West Coast, where the young Dunst earned small parts in several more films before being asked to audition for the difficult role of the child vampire, Claudia, in *Interview with the Vampire*. When Dunst read for the part, she surprised one of the film's co-producers, Stephen Woolley, with her maturity and talent. In an interview with Kristine McKenna for the *Los Angeles Times* (November 8, 1994), Woolley explained, "We started looking at 6-year-olds, which is about Claudia's age in the book, but the role is too demanding for a 6-year-old. We needed a child with a mind capable of grasping the fine points of the difficult monologues Claudia has, and Kirsten was the first actress we saw. She gave a wonderful reading but we thought it was too good to be true, so we saw thousands of other girls. In the end we came back to Kirsten—she's quite extraordinary in the part." Tom Cruise, who starred with Dunst in the film, was also impressed with the 11-year-old's talent. "There seems to be the experience of a 35-year-old actress in the body of this little girl," Cruise was quoted as saying in *People* (November 28, 1994). For her work in *Interview with the Vampire*, Dunst won a Young Star Award from the *Hollywood Reporter*.

After turning in a well-received performance in *Little Women* (1994), Dunst starred with Robin Williams in the 1995 fantasy *Jumanji* (based on a children's story by Chris Van Allsburg). She played the orphaned Judy, who, as Dunst explained to Jane Ganahl for the *Chicago Tribune* (December 29, 1995), "can't deal with the fact that her mom and dad are dead. She deals with it through her lies." While the film itself was not showered with praise, Dunst received kudos, particularly for her ability to act alongside absent characters—such as man-eating plants—that were added later through special effects. She explained this process to Louis Parks for the *Houston Chronicle* (December 14, 1995): "You just use your imagination. Just close your eyes and picture it. Then open them and pretend." After her performance in *Jumanji*, the entertainment press pronounced Dunst a member of the latest "Brat Pack," a group of popular young actresses who included Christina Ricci, Gaby Hoffman, and Thora Birch. (All three appeared in the 1995 release *Now and Then*, an opportunity passed up by Dunst, who told Jane Ganahl, "I didn't take it . . . because they wanted me to gain weight and play the chubby girl. And I won't ruin my body for any role.") At about this time, Dunst, now a teenager, was named to *People* magazine's 1995 list of the 50 most beautiful people. Following a few television appearances, including a recurring stint on the series *ER*, Dunst returned to the big screen in 1997, in the political spoof *Wag the Dog*, which starred Dustin Hoffman and Robert De Niro. Although she had a relatively small part in the film, she won favorable notices for her performance as a young actress playing an Albanian orphan in a fake war staged to hoodwink the American public.

After lending her voice to the *Animated Adventures of Tom Sawyer* and winning her second Young Star Award, for her portrayal of Verena in *Strike!*, both in 1998, Dunst landed two lead roles in 1999, in *Drop Dead Gorgeous* and *Dick*. In both of those feature films, she showed audiences the range of her talent by venturing into the world of comedy. *Dick* found the actress playing a 1970s high-school student who, during a class tour of the White House, stumbles upon a scheming President Richard Nixon. Fearing that she has learned too much, Nixon then hires her and her friend, played by Michelle Williams, as his official dog walkers in an attempt to monitor their movements. The two seemingly oblivious girls prove to be Nixon's downfall, as they report his doings to the *Washington Post* reporters Bob Woodward and Carl Bernstein. While the film received only mixed reviews, Dunst and Williams drew in the teenage crowd, further establishing themselves as film stars. In the *Houston Chronicle* (December 16, 1999), Bruce Westbrook wrote, "Dunst and Williams are lovable, clueless and a hoot, piercing a monstrous scandal with adorable naivete." In the "mockumentary" *Drop Dead Gorgeous*, which also starred Kirstie Alley and Denise Richards, Dunst played a beauty-pageant contestant. "Dunst is saddled with a role written in crude, broad strokes . . . ," Peter Travers wrote for *Rolling Stone* (August 19, 1999). "Yet [she] brings warmth and sly humor to the role."

The year 2000 proved to be a significant one for Dunst, both professionally and personally. She turned 18, graduated from high school, and starred in no fewer than four feature films. The first was *The Virgin Suicides*. That movie, which is based on Jeffrey Eugenides's popular novel and represented the directorial debut of the filmmaker Francis Ford Coppola's daughter, Sofia, received a great deal of attention from critics, most of it positive; Dunst also garnered her share of approval for her performance as Lux, one of five sisters who come to tragic ends after suffering under a dictatorial Catholic mother. The role of Lux, dark to be sure, was a departure from Dunst's recent assignments, and she impressed critics with her ability to handle the transition. In a review of the film for the *Boston Globe* (May 5, 2000), Jay Carr wrote, "Kirsten Dunst is the standout. . . . [Her character] seems partly composed of light—an airy, golden apparition, yet heavy with thwartedness until her yearning and rage and confusion boil over."

Dunst next portrayed the cheerleader Torrance Shipman in the popular if not critically acclaimed comedy *Bring It On*. Capping off a successful year, she also starred in *Deeply* and *Lucky Town Blues*. She carried that momentum into the following year with a starring role in the teenage comedy *Get Over It* (2001), opposite the teen idol (and her then-boyfriend) Ben Foster. Critics agreed that the chemistry Foster and Dunst enjoyed off-screen was apparent in the film. Bob Thomas, in the Albany *Times Union* (March 14, 2001), wrote, "Foster carries the load as the frustrated Berke . . . [while] Dunst brings depth to her role as his would-be sweetheart." An article published in the New Orleans *Times-Picayune* (March 16, 2001) described Dunst's performance as "self-possessed" and "scarily professional." Dunst then played the sexually awakened Nicole Oakley in the 2001 release *crazy/beautiful*. Of her decision to take on this "adult" role, Dunst told Jana Meier for the *Houston Chronicle* (July 7, 2001), "I'm just tired of all these stupid girl movies with stupid characters." While the movie tackled mature themes, Dunst agreed to appear in it only on the condition that it contain no nudity. She had earlier passed up the chance to star in the Oscar-winning *American Beauty* (1999), which would have called for her to appear nude opposite the film's star, Kevin Spacey. She told Meier her reasons for avoiding such roles: "I wouldn't want to exploit myself in a certain way because [of my audience] of young girls," she said. "Everybody's growing up so fast, I wouldn't want to rush their process." Most recently, Dunst took on the role of Mary Jane Watson, the love interest of the protagonist's alter-ego, in the director Sam Raimi's *Spider-Man*, due for release in May 2002. She has also started her own production company, Wooden Spoon, with her mother, Inez.

Throughout her childhood Dunst attended school when possible, though most of her education took the form of on-set tutoring. In 2000 she graduated from Notre Dame High School in Los Angeles and even managed to attend her senior prom. Although she has on many occasions expressed her desire to attend college, she has put those plans on hold for the time being to concentrate on her career in acting.

Dunst currently lives in Los Angeles with her mother and brother. — J.H.

Suggested Reading: *Biography* p93+ Aug. 2000, with photos; *Chicago Tribune* pL+ Dec. 29, 1995, with photo; *Houston Chronicle* p9 July 7, 2001, with photos; *Interview* p80+ May 2000, with photos; (London) *Guardian* Friday5 May 19, 2000, with photo; *Los Angeles Times* p1 Nov. 8, 1994, with photos; (New Orleans) *Times-Picayune* (on-line) p5 Mar. 16, 2001, with photo; *People* p137 Nov. 28, 1994, with photos; *Rolling Stone* p44+ July 19, 2001, with photo; *Us* p26+ Aug. 1998, with photos; *US Weekly* (on-line) p36+ July 9, 2001, with photos

Selected Films: *New York Stories*, 1989; *The Bonfire of the Vanities*, 1990; *Interview with the Vampire*, 1994; *Little Women*, 1994; *Jumanji*, 1995; *Mother Night*, 1996; *Wag the Dog*, 1997; *True Heart*, 1997; *The Animated Adventures of Tom Sawyer*, 1998; *Small Soldiers*, 1998; *Strike!*, 1998; *Drop Dead Gorgeous*, 1999; *Dick*, 1999; *The Virgin Suicides*, 2000; *Bring It On*, 2000; *Deeply*, 2000; *Luckytown Blues*, 2000; *The Crow: Salvation*, 2001; *Get Over It*, 2001; *crazy/beautiful*, 2001

Courtesy of Cable Risdon, 1999

Edwards, Bob

May 16, 1947– Host of National Public Radio's Morning Edition; radio journalist. Address: Morning Edition, National Public Radio, 635 Massachusetts Ave., N.W., Washington, DC 20001

"I love radio," the radio news anchor and journalist Bob Edwards told a reporter for *Southern Living* (February 23, 2001, on-line). "It has a magic quality. It's very personal. You think the voice is talking just to you. . . . We have millions of listeners, but I try to talk as if I were having a one-on-one conversation." Since 1979 Edwards has hosted the National Public Radio (NPR) program *Morning Edition*, which, with an estimated six to nine million listeners tuning in nationwide each weekday morning, is currently the most popular program on public radio. Trained in broadcast journalism, Edward worked briefly for a CBS-affiliated radio station before joining the staff of NPR, in 1974. "I think [NPR] sets the standard for broadcasting for radio and television," he told a reporter for *JournalismJobs.com* (October 2000, on-line), which is associated with the *Columbia Journalism Review*. "I think we're doing the right things for the right reasons. We're not doing it to sell products. We're not doing it to be popular. We're doing it because in our judgment these stories are important to do, and at this length and this much depth." In addition to anchoring *Morning Edition*, Edwards conducts brief interviews for the show; his subjects have included politicians, government officials, scientists, business executives, teachers, athletes, artists, writers, musicians, and other people whom he regards as newsworthy—about 800 of them per year. He has become well-known for his deep, calm voice, easygoing manner, and intimate style of interviewing. "I'm still affected by the illusion of radio, the illusion that the person on the radio is talking only to me," Edwards told Steve Weinstein for the *Los Angeles Times* (November 2, 1989). "When you watch television, you're not under any kind of illusion like that . . . you're always part of a huge mass audience. In radio, you don't have that sense of that mass audience. I don't know why. It's magic."

One of the two sons of Joseph Richard Edwards and the former Loretta Bernadine Fuchs, Robert Alan Edwards was born on May 16, 1947 in Louisville, Kentucky. He and his brother grew up in Louisville, where his father worked as an accountant for the city and his mother was a bookkeeper. "I fell in love with the radio when I was three years old. It was my buddy," he told Ken Adelman for the *Washingtonian* (March 2000). The family radio was a large, 1939 Zenith console, and he liked to feel the vibrations of the cloth that covered the radio's speakers; he also enjoyed listening to soap operas (with his grandmother) and other programs. "These voices came out of the box, as well as music and news and drama," he told the *Journalism-Jobs.com* interviewer, to whom he also said, "I wanted to be one of the voices in the box." As a child, he told Art Jester for Knight Ridder Newspapers (November 8, 1999, on-line), "I could tell you all the stations in town, their formats, the names of the disc jockeys and the times they were on the air. And then at night, there were those big, clear-channel stations in far-off exotic places like Cincinnati, Nashville, Chicago, and most of all, New York. I dreamed of going to those places."

After he graduated from St. Xavier High School, a Catholic school, Edwards enrolled at the University of Louisville, where he majored in commerce and supported himself by working as a theater usher, delivery person, and bookkeeper. While at college, he explained in his interview with *JournalismJobs.com*, he "got interested in news because the world was coming apart. The civil rights movement, the antiwar movement, the women's right[s] movement. That focused my radio ambitions toward news." In 1968 he found a position at WHEL, a tiny station in New Albany, Indiana (directly across the Ohio River from Louisville) that operated only in the daytime. "It was like working at a little paper where you learned to set type, sell ads, do obituaries, cover fires," he told *Journalism-Jobs.com*. "That's what working at a small radio station is like. You have to spin records, fix the plumbing, try to sell ads. It's a good place to learn." He added, "The audience is small so you can be bad." Before he graduated from college, he applied for jobs in broadcast journalism with his hometown radio and television stations, but all of them turned him down. "They all told me that Louisville was too big-time for a beginner," he explained to Jester. "I've still got the rejection letters." He earned a B.S. degree in 1969.

At about that time Edwards was drafted into the United States Army and sent to South Korea, where he anchored and produced television and radio broadcasts for the American Forces Korea Network in Seoul. The Vietnam War was raging in 1969, and more than half a million American troops were stationed in Vietnam. "Broadcasting saved my life," Edwards told the interviewer for *Southern Living*. "I mean, just look at me. I'm a big, tall, awkward, clumsy, white target. I would not have lasted 30 seconds on the front line in Vietnam."

After his military service ended, in 1971, Edwards enrolled at American University, in Washington, D.C., where he earned an M.A. degree in communications in 1972. His experience in military broadcasting helped him land a job that same year as a weekend anchor at WTOP-AM, Washington's all-news CBS affiliate. In 1974, four years after its creation, he joined NPR. He served as co-host of *All Things Considered*, alongside Susan Stamberg. "When I came to NPR . . . it was so new and such a small operation," he explained to the *Southern Living* reporter. "I thought it would be just a short-term thing, a stepping stone to one of the bigger networks. But the growth has been great." In 1979 NPR prepared a pilot of an early-bird companion to *All Things Considered*, a news magazine to be called *Morning Edition*, and sent it to every affiliated station. The pilot, hosted by two people, got a thumbs-down response everywhere. "There was just a unanimous feeling that this could not go on the air. It was like a bad local television program in a small market," Edwards recalled to Jacqueline Conciatore and Steve Behrens for *Current* (May 25, 1998), a biweekly magazine about public broadcasting. "In a word," Edwards told Art Jester, "it stunk." Edwards and another NPR anchor were asked to fill in for 30 days, until new hosts could be found. Despite the radical change in his routine—which now required his presence at the station by about 2 a.m.—"I got into it and enjoyed it," as he told Conciatore and Behrens. Within a few months his co-host had quit, and Edwards had become the permanent host of *Morning Edition*.

In the beginning Edwards and the show were on shaky ground. "We were so unprepared," he told Frank Ahrens for the *Washington Post* (May 14, 1999), describing his first broadcast day, November 5, 1979. The day before, followers of Iran's leader, Ayatollah Ruhollah Khomeini, had seized the United States Embassy in Tehran and taken 52 Americans hostage, but, as Edwards recalled, "If you were to look at [NPR's] rundown of that day, you wouldn't even see Iran on it." A major obstacle to wide coverage of national and international events was the paucity of NPR bureaus—at that time there were only three, in New York, Chicago, and Los Angeles, and none overseas, where a lone contact called in reports. (Currently, NPR mainains more than 30 bureaus and offices around the world.) Another problem, at least from Edwards's point of view, was the subject matter of some of the stories prepared for *Morning Edition*. "There would be the occasional brilliant piece of journalism, and in between would be a lot of stuff that you really don't need to get through the day," he told Conciatore and Behrens. "We were big in the folk arts." He recalled to Clea Simon for the *Boston*

Globe (February 11, 1999), "We had an early producer who would do pet care and cooking and gardening. I did my best to sabotage that. Which is not to say I don't enjoy features and talking to musicians. But no gardening." Edwards has remained firm in his commitment to thorough reporting of serious news, which is presented in six-to-10-minute segments. "If we're not going to provide some depth, then I don't think we have a function anymore," he told Clea Simon. "The headlines are what passes for news in commercial radio. Commercial radio has abandoned news. They do a lot of talk, and they may talk about public affairs, but not news."

Segments on *Morning Edition* often include sounds associated with the subject at hand—those of a factory, for example, or a ballpark, a classroom, a playground, or a forest. But, as Edwards pointed out to *JournalismJobs.com*, "there are no pictures to distract. The pictures are created by the listener, with a little help from the broadcaster. The pictures are perfect. If you're showing pictures, different things in that picture can distract from the spoken word." *Morning Edition*'s two-hour weekday broadcast, which, depending on the station, airs again once or twice in succession, also includes special features. (Between some segments there are 23-second anecdotes that are meant to amuse, such as accounts of the bumbling of various would-be thieves.) During the spring of 2001, the special features included the reports "The Changing Face of Adoption"; "Bob Marley Remembered," about the Jamaican reggae icon who died in 1981; "Kismet the Robot," about a device produced at the Artificial Intelligence Lab at the Massachusetts Institute of Technology; "World War II Internment Camp Letters," with readings from letters by youngsters who were among the 120,000 people of Japanese ancestry interned in camps in the U.S. after the Japanese attack on Pearl Harbor; "Mary Sojourner," about a contemporary American writer and environmentalist; and "The Medici Archive Project," which described the efforts of Edward Goldberg in Florence, Italy, to catalog nearly three million letters written during the period (1537–1743) of greatest influence of the Medici family.

Almost every Friday for nearly a dozen years beginning in 1981, Edwards talked with the legendary sports commentator Red Barber, who was 40 years his senior. Barber, who died in 1992, called Edwards "Colonel Bob," a teasing reference to the fact that he had been named an honorary colonel of the Commonwealth of Kentucky. Their four-minute conversations were not limited to the world of sports but encompassed such subjects as racism, the arts, the English language, principles of journalism, family, and cats. Edwards's book *Fridays with Red: A Radio Friendship* (1993) contains biographical information about Barber and excerpts from what Edwards considered their most interesting conversations. In addition, Bill Ott wrote in a review of *Fridays with Red* for *Booklist* (September 15, 1993), "The affection shared between the two men—so apparent on the air, whether Barber was reflecting on the 1947 World Series, discussing his love affair with camellias, or quoting from the Old Testament—comes through every bit as vividly on the printed page. Friendship is a notoriously difficult subject to write about; approached directly, it invariably turns well-meaning prose to mush, but here, sheltered by the all-powerful force field of Red Barber's personality, we slip into friendship sideways. . . . A few chapters into the book, though, we know we're among friends."

Virtually every article about, and every interview with, Edwards has mentioned his unusual schedule. He rises at 1 a.m. and within an hour arrives at the NPR studios in northwest Washington, D.C. There he reads wire services' news reports, records interviews with newsmakers in Europe or Asia, and produces pieces for upcoming broadcasts. Edwards told Conciatore and Behrens that, in a quest for interviews or comments, he has often awakened U.S. politicos, including conservatives who view public broadcasting as too liberal. "We'll get people out of their beds and set them up to talk to me live the next morning. This is Washington. You've seen people shy of being in front of microphones? Or at least on the telephone—at least we'll give them that: they can sit in their jammies and talk to me and then go back to bed. You can get any member of Congress. Boy, they will cancel anything to be able to be on somebody's radio program." He tries to make his interviewees comfortable. "I don't want to intimidate people," he told *Southern Living*. "I'm a relaxed, easygoing guy, and I hope people are relaxed with me. They're more forthcoming if they're comfortable."

The two-hour live broadcast begins at 5 a.m.; it is replayed at 7 a.m. and 9 a.m., with inserted news updates. In the studio Edwards chain-smokes and drinks many cups of coffee. While listening to the two rebroadcasts of the show, he solves crossword puzzles, often doing the *New York Times*, *Washington Post*, and *USA Today* puzzles simultaneously. He leaves the studio at around noon and is in bed soon after 6 p.m.; an electric fan that drowns out household noise helps him fall asleep. Edwards has never gotten entirely used to his work schedule, and he admitted to Conciatore and Behrens that he does not get enough rest, as a result of which he has on occasion suffered physically. "I've come to just really respect sleep," he told the interviewers. "Sleep cures so many things—physically, emotionally, psychologically. Sleep is magnificent."

Edwards's distinctive voice and speech have occasionally drawn criticism. "When I went on *Morning Edition*, the engineers didn't think I could make it because of my voice," he told Art Jester. "They thought in the morning a voice had to be peppy. They thought mine was too laid back." On March 16, 1998, in his short-lived *New York Times* column, the music critic Greil Marcus wrote that Edwards's "soothing, avuncular tone . . . conveys a distinct sense of disengagement with the subjects he is presenting. . . . What comes across is a sense of boredom with the world." Edwards apparently did not feel offended by what Marcus had written; he told Conciatore and Behrens that, with those words, Marcus had "paid me a lot of compliments, although he didn't mean to. I remember [*Morning Edition*'s original producer] Jay Kernis telling me that when I started this program, 'You should sound like you were here yesterday and you're going to be here tomorrow, and no matter what's going to happen, the sun is going to rise tomorrow.' . . . Well, that's exactly what Marcus accused me of doing. Indeed, there's all this bad stuff going around out there. But it isn't the end of the world, the sun will rise tomorrow. That is what a host should do. Without being happy-talk."

Edwards and *Morning Edition* have won a dozen broadcasting prizes. Among them, in addition to the George Foster Peabody Award, are the 1984 Edward R. Murrow Award from the Corporation for Public Broadcasting (a source of funding for NPR); Gabriel Awards, in both 1987 and 1990, from Unda-USA (an arm of Unda-World, the International Catholic Association for Radio and Television); and the Alfred I. duPont–Columbia University Award for excellence in radio journalism, in 1995 (for "The Geographic Century," a co-production of NPR/*National Geographic* that was presented on *Morning Edition*'s series "Radio Expeditions"). "I'm still excited at being at the microphone and talking to listeners," Edwards told *JournalismJobs.com*. "I love that. It's the most basic element of what I do and I still enjoy it very much."

Bob Edwards is tall and lanky, with graying blond hair. He told *JournalismJobs.com* that when listeners meet him, most tell him that he looks nothing like what they imagined. "It's just that people have an image—whatever that image is. I think that [radio broadcasters] should never have our pictures taken. [Listeners] shouldn't know [what we look like.] Let 'em keep the mystery." Edwards has served as a national vice president of AFTRA (the American Federation of Television and Radio Artists) since 1988. He and his wife, Sharon, who met at NPR in the mid-1970s, married in 1979. Their children are Brean Campbell (her son from a previous marriage) and two daughters—Susannah, a college student, and Eleanor, a teenager who is being home-schooled. The couple live in Arlington, Virginia, and, in the same state, own a 19th-century log cabin, which they are restoring. Edwards's leisure activities include genealogical studies, softball, and tennis. — K.S.

Suggested Reading: *Current* May 25, 1998, on-line; *JournalismJobs.com* (on-line) Oct. 2000; *New York Times* C p1 May 14, 1999, with photo; *San Francisco Chronicle* E p1 Oct. 6, 1999; *Southern Living* (on-line) Feb. 23, 2001; *Washingtonian* p31+ Mar. 2000, with photo

Selected Books: *Fridays with Red*, 1993

Courtesy of *Catholic New York*

Egan, Edward M.

*Apr. 2, 1932– Catholic archbishop of New York.
Address: Archdiocese of New York, 1011 First Ave., New York, NY 10022-4134*

Edward M. Egan was appointed by Pope John Paul II to succeed John Cardinal O'Connor as archbishop of New York City, following O'Connor's death in May 2000. Now a cardinal in the Catholic church, Egan is an expert in canonical law; for more than a decade beginning in 1973, he served as a judge of the Sacred Roman Rota, a Vatican court of appeals that deals primarily in marriage law. He also spent 12 years as the bishop of the culturally diverse Bridgeport diocese of Fairfield County, Connecticut. Egan is known for his administrative and fund-raising skills; his staunch conservatism has brought criticism from gay-rights groups and liberal Catholics. He speaks Latin, Italian, French, and Spanish as well as English and is, additionally, a talented classical pianist. Since he was appointed archbishop of New York, he has urged his congregation to fight racism, poverty, euthanasia, and abortion. The Archdiocese of New York was established in 1850 and serves 2.4 million Catholics in 412 parishes in the New York City boroughs of Manhattan, the Bronx, and Richmond (also known as Staten Island) as well as seven other New York State counties: Dutchess, Orange, Putnam, Rockland, Sullivan, Ulster, and Westchester.

Edward M. Egan was born in Oak Park, Illinois, on April 2, 1932, the third of the four children of Thomas Egan, a sales manager, and Genevieve Costello Egan, a homemaker and onetime schoolteacher. Catholicism was an important part of family life in the Egan home. In 1943 Edward and his brother Thomas contracted polio, a disease that had reached epidemic proportions in the nearby city of Chicago, Illinois. Edward Egan spent three weeks in the Cook County Contagious Disease Hospital, followed by six months of recovery at home. Unable to sit up for three months, he received weekly visits from a physiotherapist, who encouraged him to pray before the altar that his family had set up on his dresser. Although Egan had recovered by age 12, he continued to make weekly visits to physiotherapists. The illness caused both brothers to miss two years of school but did not prevent Edward Egan from rising to the top of his class upon his return to St. Giles, a Catholic parochial school in Oak Park. There, Monsignor Lawrence Frawley, recognizing his potential as a student of theology, persuaded him to forfeit a scholarship to Fenwick High, a prestigious private school, in favor of Chicago's Quigley Preparatory Seminary.

Egan had grown up in a home with a grand piano, and by the time he entered Quigley Preparatory Seminary, in 1946, he had become an accomplished classical pianist. He was also a popular student who led his class academically; he was elected student president and edited the student newspaper and yearbook. After he graduated, in 1951, he entered St. Mary of the Lake Seminary in Mundelein, Illinois. The seven-year program combined traditional college courses with four years of theological study. Egan's classes in theology were held at Gregorian University in Rome, Italy, as part of the St. Mary curriculum. He was ordained as a Catholic priest there in 1957 and received a licentiate in sacred theology the following year. He was then appointed ninth curate at Holy Name Cathedral in the Archdiocese of Chicago. Egan spent four nights a week teaching classes for potential converts to Catholicism and served in the mornings as chaplain for patients of Wesley Memorial Hospital. He was soon hired as the secretary to Albert Cardinal Meyer, who abolished racial segregation in all Catholic institutions in Chicago and expanded the diocese to include 30 additional parishes.

In 1960 Egan became the assistant vice rector at Pontifical North American College in Rome, where he taught theology and canonical law. Three years later he graduated summa cum laude with a degree in canonical law from Gregorian University. He returned to the Archdiocese of Chicago in 1966 to serve as secretary to John Cardinal Cody, who supported civil rights and plans to desegregate public schools through the busing of students to schools in distant neighborhoods. "I saw Cardinal Cody take a lot of heat for good causes," Egan once said, as quoted by Mary Ann Poust in *Catholic New York* (June 22, 2000, on-line). "He was admired in the black community, and they were tough years." Following the Second Vatican Council, in 1968, Cardinal Cody appointed Egan to the position of secretary for commissions on Human Relations and Ecumenism. Egan implemented the council's recommendations on the subject of ecumenism—

interdenominational Christian fellowship—by creating a set of guidelines known as "The Interdiocesan Program for Ecumenism," which became the standard for interfaith activities throughout Illinois. He also established ecumenical commissions in a number of parishes and made public appearances before Jewish and Protestant organizations. From 1969 until 1971 he was the co-chancellor for the Archdiocese of Chicago.

From 1973 until 1985 Egan served as a judge for the Sacred Roman Rota, which is one of two courts in the Vatican judiciary system and is the court of appeals for canonical cases involving marriage. His work for the Rota influenced many students of theology, who widely quoted his decisions—rulings that Gregorian University's Father Michael Hilbert described to Brian Caulfield for *Catholic New York* (June 22, 2000, on-line) as "models of logical thinking and good application of the law." In 1983 Egan was one of six canonists chosen to review the final draft of Pope John Paul II's Code of Canon Law, a series of 1,752 new doctrines. Two years later the Pope appointed him vicar for education under Archbishop John O'Connor of New York, a position he held for three years. While in New York Egan supervised the drafting of guidelines for Catholic schools and parish catechetical programs. Sister Joan Curtin, the director of the Catechetical Office, described Egan to Claudia McDonnell for *Catholic New York* (June 22, 2000, on-line) as "a man of deep faith and spirituality and high energy for the sake of the Gospel." Egan publicly opposed sex education, declaring that as far as such matters were concerned, only abstinence should be taught on school grounds. According to Joshua Green in *American Prospect* (July 31, 2000), Egan told City Council members, "Try decency. Try chastity. Try Western civilization."

In November 1988 Egan was appointed bishop of the Bridgeport diocese of Fairfield County, Connecticut. The diocese serves a diverse population of 390,000 (out of a total population of 800,000), and its various churches offer Mass in close to 20 languages. In an effort to meet the needs of 12 parishes that serve Hispanics, Egan set up an exchange program with Colombia aimed at bringing priests with a knowledge of Spanish culture to the diocese. Egan also successfully turned around the diocese's failing school system, closing schools and consolidating the student body, a bold move that forced hundreds of students—many of whom were members of minority groups—into the public-school system. His restructuring left 33 schools supported by 88 parishes and brought stability to a system affected by the departure of large numbers of Catholics from the inner city.

By this time Egan had acquired a reputation as a successful fund-raiser skilled at reaching out to executives at such corporations as General Electric and IBM. Thomas Sweeney, director of development for the diocese, told Mary Ann Poust that Egan was a "good strategist. Once the project is identified, a price tag put on it and it's determined to be a good cause, he's comfortable talking to individuals—or to small groups or even larger groups—asking them to support that good cause. Prominent people connect with him, and he's able to convince them that what he's doing is a good thing, and they can enjoy doing it with him." In 1995 and 1996 a fund-raising campaign known as "Faith in the Future" exceeded its stated goal of $30 million, raising $45 million to pay for the diocese's schools. The 200 staff members of the diocese's Catholic Charities organization operated 31 facilities, including soup kitchens, mental-health clinics, and day-care centers; under Egan's guidance the group's budget doubled, to $9.5 million, making it the largest private social service in Fairfield County.

Egan's tenure in Bridgeport was not without controversy, however. He was one of two bishops in the U.S. who endorsed the Catholic Alliance, a right-wing organization, created by Christian Coalition founder Pat Robertson and its then-executive director, Ralph Reed, that represented an affiliation between conservative Catholics and Evangelical Protestants. Egan later became one of five bishops on the group's all-Catholic advisory board, which had become independent of the Christian Coalition. The Catholic Alliance was opposed by the National Conference of Catholic Bishops, whose opinions on such subjects as welfare reform, health care, and the economy have generally diverged from the positions on these same subjects adopted by evangelicals. Other groups, such as the California Catholic Conference, publicly disassociated themselves from the Catholic Alliance, which soon came to focus exclusively on the issue of abortion. In 1993 Egan successfully campaigned to defeat a proposal to distribute birth-control devices in public schools in Bridgeport, and in 1997 he criticized Father Robert Nugent and Sister Jeannine Gramick of New Ways Ministry for ministering to lesbians and gay men and their families. (According to its Web site, New Ways "provides a gay-positive ministry of advocacy and justice for lesbian and gay Catholics and reconciliation within the larger Christian and civil communities.") Egan tried to stop Nugent from conducting workshops in the Bridgeport area for families with gay members; according to Paul Schindler in Lesbian & Gay New York Online (Issue 133, 2000), "Only when Nugent publicly challenged Egan did the bishop back off his outright ban on the event." (In 1999 the Vatican prohibited both Nugent and Gramick from providing pastoral services for homosexuals.)

Days before he was appointed the new archbishop of New York, Egan became embroiled in a scandal concerning more than two dozen lawsuits filed against the diocese, in which the plaintiffs accused priests of engaging in sexual activities with children placed in their care. (Most of the alleged incidents cited in the lawsuits were said to have occurred before he was appointed bishop of Bridgeport.) Egan reportedly contended that priests are independent contractors and that the church is

therefore not liable for their actions; he also maintained that canonical law should take precedence over civil law in matters between the church and its parishioners. His position prompted the Roman Catholic priest and author Andrew M. Greeley to write a piece for the Daily Southtown (July 9, 2000, on-line), a Chicago newspaper, in which he charged that the diocese's handling of the case under Egan "repeated all the classic mistakes made in dioceses during the 1980s and added some special twists of its own. It has reassigned accused priests, denied the accusations, stonewalled, refused to extend pastoral sympathy to the victims, and threatened to sue the victims for defamation." Greeley commented that Egan's actions reflected "the church's apparent propensity to protect priests from the consequences of their sexual pleasure while at the same time imposing strict rules on the sexual pleasure of others."

When John Cardinal O'Connor died of brain cancer, on May 3, 2000, several names were submitted to Pope John Paul II for consideration as O'Connor's successor, among them Archbishop Justin Rigali of St. Louis, Missouri, Archbishop Edward O'Brien of the military archdiocese, and Bishop Henry Mansell of Buffalo, New York. In the end, however, Egan became the ninth archbishop in the history of the Archdiocese of New York, assuming the post on June 18, 2000. He told Jeffery L. Scheler for U.S. News & World Report (May 22, 2000, on-line) that his first reaction to the news was to say to himself, "Edward, get down on your knees and beg the Lord to give you a hand, and don't get up too quickly."

During his first months as archbishop, Egan consulted with representatives from offices throughout the archdiocese and then initiated various changes. Among them were layoffs at the organization's headquarters and at St. Joseph's Seminary; the closures of three schools; and the eradication of 11 offices. On several occasions he joined Rudolph Giuliani, the mayor of New York City, in denouncing the decision of the Brooklyn Museum of Art to display work that some perceived as sacrilegious. In March 2001 Egan and 44 other archbishops were elevated to the College of Cardinals by Pope John Paul II in a week-long ceremony in Rome that was attended by thousands of Catholics from all over the world. During the ceremony the Pope assigned each new cardinal a church in Rome, making all of them honorary priests of the city's diocese.

Following the September 11, 2001 terrorist attacks that destroyed the World Trade Center, Egan honored the victims and their families in masses held at New York's St. Patrick's Cathedral. "I am sure that we will seek justice in this tragedy as citizens of a nation under God in which hatred and desires for revenge must never have a part," he told attendees of one Mass, as reported by James Barron for the New York Times (September 17, 2001). "I am sure that we'll allow no group or groups in our diverse but united community to be accused or abused because of the outrageous misdeeds of these individuals. I am sure that we will not harbor thoughts of war of any kind without careful, careful consideration of what is right and just before the one God and father of us all."

Egan has been awarded honorary degrees by St. John's University, in New York City, the Thomas More College of Liberal Arts, in Merrimack, New Hampshire, and Western Connecticut State University.— C.L.

Suggested Reading: *American Prospect* p15+ July 31, 2000; Archdiocese of New York Web site; *Catholic New York* (on-line) June 22, 2000, with photos; *New York Times* A p1, B p8 May 12, 2000, with photo, A p1+ June 17, 2001, with photos, A p9 Sep. 17, 2001, with photos; *Newsweek* p63 May 22, 2000, with photo

Brian Dear/Archive Photos

Elliott, Sean

Feb. 2, 1968– Forward for the San Antonio Spurs. Address: San Antonio Spurs, 100 Montana St., San Antonio, TX 78203

Sean Elliott, a talented forward with the San Antonio Spurs basketball team, is known for his grace on the court and his ability to sink long shots. Elliott, who began his professional career on the Spurs' All-Rookie Second Team, is the Spurs' all-time leader in three-point shots made and attempted. After leading the Spurs in their victory against the Portland Trail Blazers for the National Basketball Association (NBA) championship in 1999, he underwent a kidney transplant. When he rejoined

the team, in March 2000, he became the first athlete in history to return to professional sports after recovering from that operation. Elliott's perseverance and skillful playing have inspired both his fans and his teammates. "Every time I see his enthusiasm," Spurs center David Robinson told Thomas Fields-Meyer and Michelle McCalope for *People* (March 27, 2000, on-line), "I realize how fortunate we are to do what we do." Elliott, who was named to the All-Star team in 1993 and 1996, has become a spokesperson for the National Kidney Foundation.

Sean Elliott was born in Tucson, Arizona, on February 2, 1968 to Odiemae Elliott, a nurse, and Robert Elliott, a medical technician. (The couple divorced in 1978.) He has two brothers, Noel and Robert. "When Sean was born, Noel took him on as his," Odiemae Elliott told Carol Lin for *CNN Sports Illustrated* (July 28, 2000, on-line). "He used to fight off anybody else who tried to touch him." Early evidence of Elliott's determination surfaced after he hurt his knee while playing basketball at Tucson's Cholla High School. (The school has since renamed its gymnasium for him.) "The doctor told him, 'No more basketball,'" Noel Elliott told Jackie MacMullan for *Sports Illustrated* (January 31, 2000). "Sean rehabbed, got back out there, hurt his knee again. The doctor told him, 'Forget about basketball.' Sean said, 'I can't.' So the doctor said, 'Well, you better wear a knee brace.' Sean will do whatever it takes." During his senior year of high school, Sean Elliott averaged 33.4 points and 14.1 rebounds per game and was sought after by recruiters from many colleges. He chose to attend the University of Arizona, where he played as a starting forward for four years. He completed his years at Arizona as the leading college scorer of all time: with a final total of 2,555 points, he broke the record previously set by Kareem Abdul-Jabbar (2,325). He was also named national player of the year in five polls during his senior year and received the John Wooden Award for college player of the year.

Elliott was the third athlete chosen by the San Antonio Spurs in the NBA college draft for the 1989–90 season, during which he made the league's All-Rookie Second Team. He and fellow rookies David Robinson and Terry Cummings helped the Spurs win the Midwest Division title, and the team ended the season with a record of 56–26. Elliott's scoring average steadily increased over the course of the next three seasons, and in a demonstration of his unusual endurance, he was the only player on his team to play in all 82 games in both the 1990–91 and 1991–92 seasons. By his fourth year of regular-season play, Elliott was considered one of the NBA's best players, and he was chosen to compete on the Western Conference All-Star Team in 1993.

During the 1993 off-season, the Spurs traded Elliott to the Detroit Pistons in exchange for Dennis Rodman. Elliott found it difficult to thrive in his new environment. "Detroit was known at the time for banging and knocking people around," the former Pistons coach Don Chaney told Mike Wise for the New York Times (June 23, 1999). "And Sean came in basically as a West Coast player, a finesse type guy. So a lot of the players wanted him to become that guy. And that's not who he is." During the 1993–94 season, Elliott suffered from fatigue, injuries, and retention of water in his face and arms. "I'd get my ankles taped before the game, and afterward my ankles were really skinny from where the tape had been, but the rest of my leg was fat and swollen from the water buildup," he told Jackie MacMullan. "They started calling me Peg Leg."

In mid-season the Pistons traded Elliott to the Houston Rockets for Robert Horry and Matt Bullard. Soon afterward a physical examination conducted by a Rockets' doctor revealed abnormally high levels of protein in his urine and an excess of creatinine in his blood—two clear signs that he had kidney disease. "I didn't really believe that this would progress to a life-threatening stage," Elliott told Connie McNamara for Reader's Digest (2000, on-line). "I just figured I'd be able to get through it." The Rockets nullified the trade, depriving the forward of the opportunity to extend his contract for $3 million per season. A few days later doctors announced that Elliott's illness could be treated in six weeks to four months and would not affect his career. Elliott began taking cyclosporin, a medication that decreased the amount of protein in his urine. Houston won the NBA championship that year, and the Pistons finished with a disappointing record of 20–62. Elliott was traded back to the Spurs in the off-season.

The forward made a significant comeback in the 1994–95 season, averaging 18.1 points per game and finishing 18th in points in the league. The Spurs ended the season with the best record of any team in the NBA and advanced to the Western Conference Finals, where they were defeated by the Houston Rockets. Elliott returned to All-Star status the following season, the best of his career up to that time: he achieved two career highs, with 161 three-point shots and an average of 20 points per game. During the 1996–97 season he was plagued by chronic tendinitis in his right quadriceps; undergoing surgery in February 1997, he missed the end of the season. Elliott continued to play even after an orthopedic surgeon recommended that he retire. The following season tendinitis in his left quadriceps forced him to drop out before the end of January, and he underwent another operation. Elliott returned in 1998 as a starter in the first 50 games of the season, averaging 11.2 points per game, the third-best average on his team. In February 1999 he became the team's all-time leader in three-pointers, and on May 4 he scored the 10,000th point of his career, in Portland, Oregon.

The 1998–99 season had been delayed by a strike, so teams played every day to make up for lost time. Elliott experienced serious fatigue, and in March the kidney specialist John Rienick told

him that he required either a kidney transplant or regular hemodialysis treatments. Still apparently unaware—or unwilling to accept—that his kidneys were failing, he elected to finish the season. "My friends and family noticed that I looked ragged every day," he told Connie McNamara. "I was pretty much in a state of denial." During the second game of the Western Conference Finals, Elliott made a seemingly impossible shot over the extended arms of Portland Trail Blazers forward Rasheed Wallace; nearly throwing the ball out of bounds, he sank a three-point shot with less than 10 seconds left in the game. His unforgettable move, which came to be known as the "Memorial Day Miracle," enabled the Spurs to beat Portland 86–85. The team went on to sweep the Trail Blazers, thus earning their first NBA championship. Elliott later learned that during the play-offs his kidneys had been functioning at 10 percent of normal capacity. "The Memorial Day Miracle was nothing compared to what Sean Elliott did during the playoffs," the Spurs' team physician, David Schmidt, told Mike Wise for the New York Times (July 22, 1999). "I talked to a couple of kidney specialists around the country, and for him to play the way he played during the play-offs was the much bigger miracle." Elliott did not tell his teammates about his illness until after the season had ended.

Days after the victory celebration, Elliott was diagnosed with focal segmental glomerular sclerosis, a chronic condition of unknown origin that prevents the kidneys from properly filtering waste materials from the blood. When doctors told him that he had no recourse but to choose between hemodialysis and a transplant, he agreed to the latter. Elliott did not have to add his name to the long list of people awaiting a new kidney, because each of his brothers offered to donate a kidney, and Noel's proved to be a perfect match. (Chances of rejection of a transplanted organ are less than one in 10 when the organ comes from a blood relative.) In July Elliott held a press conference to announce the upcoming operation, which took place the following month at Methodist Specialty and Transplant Hospital in San Antonio, Texas. Sean Elliott had a second round of surgery a few days later, to correct a leak in the connection between the transplanted kidney and his bladder. "That's finally when I broke down and acted like a little baby," he told Jackie MacMullan. "I kept thinking, how in the hell am I going to come back from this?"

Eager to return to the game, Elliot followed his doctors' orders conscientiously and began weight training less than a month after the operation. In October 1999 he began running up and down the stairs in the Alamodome, the Spurs' hometown arena. The next month, in an incident that was not made public at the time, he collapsed and vomited after working out on the Alamodome steps. "For a minute," Elliott told Jackie MacMullan, "I thought I was dying." After being taken to the hospital, he spent half a day hooked up to intravenous fluids. In December Elliott was hospitalized again, this time with pneumonia. "That's when I had serious doubts if I was going to make it back," he told Mark Brown for *WFAA.com* (April 26, 2000). "It took so much out of me. I wasn't able to get out of bed without losing my breath. But the doctors had warned me that this could be one of the complications of being immunosuppressed [a reference to the anti-rejection drugs he was taking]. I had to go back out there and try to get back in shape and that's what I did." The following month Elliott sneaked onto the court to participate with his teammates in one-on-one drills while Spurs coach and general manager Gregg Popovich was working with other players. "One-on-ones are great for getting in shape," Elliott told Jackie MacMullan. "You play defense, and then, a second later, you're on offense. There's no downtime." On his 32d birthday he got permission to resume full-contact practices with the team. During his recuperation Elliott also provided commentary for the Spurs' televised games.

On March 14, 2000, seven months after his kidney-transplant operation, Elliott returned to the court to join the Spurs in a game against the Atlanta Hawks. The event marked the first time a professional athlete had resumed his career following a kidney transplant. He received a standing ovation from a sold-out crowd of 26,708 fans at the Alamodome, and the Hawks' Dikembe Motombo hugged and congratulated him before facing the forward for the opening tip-off. Elliott played for the first five minutes of the game, colliding with Motombo before being replaced by Jerome Kersey. He then played a total of seven more minutes; after missing both a 22-foot jump shot and a layup in the third quarter, he evaded defender Roshown McLeod to make an impressive slam dunk. Although he fell twice during the game, he was not injured. The Spurs went on to defeat the Hawks by a score of 94–79. For the remainder of the season, Elliott averaged 20 minutes per game; he scored a season-high 15 points in 25 minutes in a game against the Utah Jazz on April 14. In the play-offs he averaged 10 points per game. Elliott was present on the court throughout the 2000–01 season—his 12th with the NBA and the final year of his contract with the Spurs—as well as during the Spurs' three play-off rounds. Although he has not officially retired from basketball, Elliott will not be playing during the 2001–02 season; instead, he and Joel Myers will provide the color commentary for the Spurs' televised games.

Thanks to the publicity surrounding his transplant operation and recovery, the six-foot eight-inch, 220-pound Elliott gained "a whole new fan base," as he told Mark Brown. "Pretty much every arena I've been in and everywhere I go I run into someone who has had a transplant or who is going to donate. They ask me all types of questions: What is it going to be like? How am I going to feel? What do I have to worry about?" Among those who have been inspired by Elliott's historic comeback are his fellow team members. "It's great not just for basketball but for a lot of different people who have been

in situations like Sean," Spurs guard Avery Johnson told *CNN Sports Illustrated* (March 15, 2000, on-line). "Just to see how he's going to give a lot of transplant patients hope . . . transcends basketball." According to the former Spurs owner Red McCombs, the impact of Elliott's return to basketball has reached "far beyond sports." As McCombs told *ESPN* (March 14, 2000, on-line), "It is a story of heart. It is a story of the medical greatness that we've got in this country. He will finish out his career as a great player."

During a live chat for *NBA.com* (August 23, 2000), Elliott spoke about the effect of his recovery on his brother Noel. "He knows inside that because of him, I was able to resume my career and my life," Elliott said. "And when you have that kind of power, no one can take that away from you. My brother's been on Cloud 9 ever since I walked out of the hospital. He spent some time with me before and he saw my condition, so when he sees me take the court, he goes absolutely crazy."

Elliott later learned that African-Americans and Native Americans have a higher risk of contracting kidney disease than Caucasians. He also discovered that many people enjoy active lives despite having to undergo regular hemodialysis treatments. (It is possible to receive the treatment at home and while sleeping.) In an effort to educate others about kidney disease, Elliott became a spokesperson for the National Kidney Foundation. In August 2000 he launched a national education campaign sponsored by the American Association of Kidney Patients, the National Kidney Foundation, and the Baxter Healthcare Corp., which specializes in therapies for life-threatening conditions. He also hosted the U.S. Transplant Games, a competition featuring athletes who have received organ transplants, held at Disney's Wide World of Sports Complex, in Orlando, Florida.

Elliott and his wife, Akiko, are separated; together they have one daughter, Jordan. The athlete's recreational interests include working out and playing golf. He also loves to nap. — C.L.

Suggested Reading: *New York Times* D p3 June 23, 1999, with photo, D p4 July 22, 1999, with photo; *Sporting News* p39 Feb. 21, 1994, with photo; *Sports Illustrated* p48+ Jan. 31, 2000, with photos; *Washington Post* D p3 Feb. 10, 1994, with photo

Jeff Christensen/Archive Photos

Eminem

Oct. 17, 1972– Rap artist; songwriter. Address: c/o Interscope Records, 2220 Colorado Ave., Santa Monica, CA 90404

Since the release of his first album, *The Slim Shady LP* (1999), which has sold more than three million copies, the rapper Eminem has emerged as one of the most popular and controversial figures in the pop music world. Also known as Slim Shady and Marshall Mathers III, Eminem seems eager to arouse ire: on "My Name Is," his 1999 hit single, he proclaimed, "God sent me to piss off the world!" In his often autobiographical songs, he has targeted women, homosexuals, the media, and even his mother and his then-wife. His lyrics often evoke vivid and violent imagery and contain many references to drugs. In "I'm Shady," for example, Eminem raps, "Think I've got a generation brainwashed / To pop pills and smoke pot 'til they brains rot / Stop they blood flow until they veins clot / I need a pain shot, and a shot of plain scotch / Purple haze and acid raindrops." Eminem's songs employ a sharp wit, a fertile imagination, and distinctive rhythms; according to many critics, Eminem, a white man who grew up poor and spent his adolescence and teen years in Detroit, offers a new voice to rap. "His rhymes sting like a lungful of crack because they're the rantings of an all-too-real demographic," Pat Blashill wrote for *Details* (May 1999). "He sounds like a working-class invisible man without a job or a hope in the world." Eminem's first album won two Grammy Awards; his second, *The Marshall Mathers LP* (2000), earned three Grammy Awards and sold more than five million copies within the first month after its release—the greatest number ever for a solo artist within that time span.

Eminem was born Marshall Bruce Mathers III on October 17, 1972 in St. Joseph, Missouri. His mother, Debbie Mathers-Briggs, and father, Marshall Mathers II, were in a band called Daddy Warbucks, a small act that, before Eminem's birth, toured clubs and motels in several western states. Eminem never got to know his father; he was raised by his mother, and both he and the media have characterized his early years as difficult and impoverished. As N'Gai Croal put it in *Newsweek* (May 29, 2000), "The rapper's sociopathic facade masks the lingering hurts of his Dickensian childhood." He and his mother rarely stayed in one place for long, living in various locations in Missouri and Michigan. Then, when he was 11, they moved into a housing project in a primarily black section of Detroit. His mother, in an interview with M. L. Elrick for the *Detroit Free Press* (June 30, 2000, on-line), said that between 1978 and 1989 Eminem attended 15 to 20 schools.

Eminem began listening to rap at the age of nine, when his uncle gave him a recording of the soundtrack to the movie *Breakin'*. Rap music offered him solace during his troubled years in Detroit. One of the few white kids in his neighborhood, he was often picked on and sometimes physically attacked. Once, a blow from another student left him in a coma for five days. (Eminem later rhymed about the incident in "Brain Damage," a song from *The Slim Shady LP*.) On another occasion, at 16, as he was walking through the parking lot of a local mall, a car full of black youths pulled up near him, and one of the young men got out of the car, hit him in the face, and then pulled out a gun. Eminem escaped further violence when the gun-waving driver of another car let him into his vehicle. Another source of pain was his father's failure to contact him; the post office returned to him as undeliverable most or all of the letters he wrote to his father.

In 1989, after failing the ninth grade three times, Eminem dropped out of Lincoln High School, in Warren, a suburb of Detroit. Afterward he found work as a cook at a local restaurant called Gilbert's Lodge; he spent much of his leisure time experimenting with different styles of rap and perfecting his skill at inventing lyrics. Sometimes he would sneak into a local high school with a friend to compete in lunchtime rap contests. On Saturdays he performed at open-mike competitions at a Detroit hip-hop store. Because he was white, many patrons would question his ability to rap. "As soon as I grabbed the mike, I'd get booed," Eminem told Anthony Bozza for *Rolling Stone* (April 29, 1999). "Once [expletive] heard me rhyme, though, they'd shut up." In December 1995 he became the father of a daughter, Hailie, whose mother, Kimberly Scott, he had dated sporadically since the late 1980s.

EMINEM

In 1996 Eminem released an album, *Infinite*, on a local label. "*Infinite* was me trying to figure out how I wanted my rap style to be, how I wanted to sound on the mic[rophone] and present myself. It was a growing stage," he explained on his official Web site. The album, which did not exhibit his now-trademark stinging lyrics, sense of humor, or offbeat delivery, attracted little notice. His failure to gain recognition made him bitter. "After that record, every rhyme I wrote got angrier and angrier," Eminem told Bozza. During this time he lived with Kimberly and their daughter in a dangerous neighborhood. One day a stray bullet came through their window, striking a wall. A few weeks before Christmas 1996, Eminem lost his job, leaving him with little money to buy his daughter a gift for her first birthday. His predicament led him to write "Rock Bottom," in which he complained, "Minimum wage got my adrenaline caged / Full of venom and rage / Especially when I'm engaged / And my daughter's down to her last diaper / That's got my ass hyper." (He later included "Rock Bottom" on *The Slim Shady LP*.)

One day during this low period, Eminem invented his alter-ego Slim Shady, who became the persona through which he could rant about his problems, vent his anger, and express his sense of humor. "When I started using the whole Slim Shady name," he explained to N'Gai Croal, "it gave me the chance to take what was wrong with my life and turn it back on [others]."

The day before Eminem was to compete in the 1997 Rap Olympics, an annual competition held in Los Angeles, he and his family were evicted from their apartment; desperate for a place to sleep that night, he broke the lock. The stress of those events notwithstanding, he captured second place at the Rap Olympics. He attracted further notice by performing on a popular San Francisco Bay area rap radio show hosted by Sway and King Tech. While in California he and his manager succeeded in getting a copy of his latest demo, *The Slim Shady EP*, into the hands of executives of the Interscope label.

Before long Eminem came to the attention of the rapper and producer Dr. Dre. "Dre's coworkers told me, when Dre first came to them with me, they were like, 'No white rappers!'" Eminem recalled to Matt Diehl for *Rolling Stone* (February 18, 1999). "And Dre said, 'I don't give a [expletive] if this guy is green or yellow, this is my next project.'" With Dr. Dre's help, Eminem won a contract with Interscope. His first album for the label, *The Slim Shady LP* (1999), which evolved from the *Slim Shady* demo, is filled with dynamic, catchy grooves. In February 1990 "My Name Is," the first single from the record, hit the Top 40 charts. *The Slim Shady LP* went on to sell 480,000 copies in its first two weeks; it soon went triple platinum, with three million copies sold. *The Slim Shady LP* won the 1999 Grammy Award as best rap album, and "My Name Is" earned a 1999 Grammy as best rap solo performance.

Many reviewers of *The Slim Shady LP* agreed that Eminem was a talented lyricist, capable of clever turns of phrase, and a skilled performer. "He does know rhythm," Barry Walters wrote for the *Village Voice* (March 30, 1999), "and he plays with and against his beats nimbly, almost joyfully." Some critics felt that Eminem's angry, scathing lyrics would have grated if they hadn't also frequently been turned against himself. "If he didn't pick on himself so much," Walters wrote, "Eminem's cinematic rage would be oppressive. Instead, it's cartoony and sad, comedic and tragic." Similarly, N'Gai Croal noted, "By flipping the razor-sharp lyrics on himself, Eminem subverts the smirking superiority that plagues mainstream rap, a wily underdog move that lets him get away with more than he could otherwise." In *Billboard* (February 20, 1999), Chuck Taylor wrote, "His ability to poke fun at current trends in our culture will leave both male and female listeners on the edge of their seats waiting to hear what or whom he will pick on next."

Taylor's positive assessment notwithstanding, *Billboard*'s editor in chief, Timothy White, quickly became one of Eminem's most outspoken critics. In a front-page editorial for *Billboard*'s March 6, 1999 issue, he berated the rapper for "exploiting the world's misery" and dwelling on such themes as "drugging, raping, and murdering women." Those angered by Eminem's lyrics included his girlfriend, Kimberly; the couple's relationship had always been stormy, and, as he did with many of his experiences, Eminem referred to their disagreements in his songs. In "'97 Bonnie and Clyde," for example, Eminem raps about taking his daughter to a lake so that she can help him dispose of her mother's body after he kills her. "Here you wanna help Dada tie a rope around this rock? / Then we'll tie it to her footsie, then we'll role her off the dock / Here we go, count of three. One, two, three, whee! / There goes Mama splashing in the water / No more fighting with Dad, no more restraining order."

Eminem's mother, too, publicly expressed anger at him for his references to her in his songs (and his derogatory comments about her in interviews). In "My Name Is," for example, Eminem raps, "Ninety-nine percent of my life I was lied to / I just found out my mom does more dope than I do / I told her I'd grow up to be a famous rapper / Make a record about doin' drugs and name it after her." In September 1999 Debbie Mathers-Briggs filed a $10 million defamation lawsuit against her son. "She asked him to lay off, stop ridiculing her, to stop demeaning her and stop defaming her on numerous occasions," her lawyer, Fred Gibson, told Croal. "This was the last action she had available to make him stop."

Neither the lawsuit nor bad press succeeded in stopping him, however. Eminem's second album, *The Marshall Mathers LP*, was at least as provocative as the first. In "Kill You," over halting beats and sound effects reminiscent of video games,

Eminem raps about his anger toward women. The opening lines attack his mother and seem to defend his father: "When I was just a little baby boy my mamma used to tell me these crazy things / She used to tell me my daddy was an evil man, she used to tell me he hated me / But then I got a little bit older and I realized she was the crazy one / But there was nothing I could try to say or do to change her 'cause that's just the way she was." In "The Way I Am," Eminem vows that he won't be cowed by media criticism. Over a plodding beat and piano loops, he shouts, "All this controversy circles me / It seems like the media immediately points a finger at me / So I point one back at them, but not the index or the pinky."

The Marshall Mathers LP aroused the indignation of the Gay and Lesbian Alliance Against Defamation; in a publicly issued statement excerpted in Rolling Stone (May 31, 2000, on-line), the group charged, "Eminem's lyrics are soaked with violence and full of negative comments about many groups, including lesbians and gay men. While Eminem certainly has the freedom of speech to rap whatever he wants, it is irresponsible for UNI/Interscope Records as a company to produce and promote such defamatory material that encourages violence and hatred." In a conversation with Anthony DeCurtis for Rolling Stone (July 15, 2000, on-line), Eminem claimed that his use of the word "faggot" in his songs was meant to be funny. "The kids listening to my music get the joke," he said. "They can tell when I'm serious and when I'm not." Referring to his "Up in Smoke" tour with Dr. Dre, which extended from mid-June until the beginning of August 2000, he continued, "Nobody wants to talk about the positive [expletive] I'm doing. There's millions of white kids and black kids coming to the tour, throwing their middle fingers up in the air, and all having a common love—and that's hip-hop. Me and Dre are changing the world right now, as we're on this tour. I feel that we are making racism less and less and less. As far as gay people, that's their business. Truthfully, I don't care. It's none of my business."

The Marshall Mathers LP quickly jumped to number one on the charts and sold 1.8 million copies in its first week; in its first month it sold more than five million copies. Once again, many critics praised the musicality of Eminem's work, and some found cause for celebration in his lyrics, but a significant number seemed conflicted about the album. "The Marshall Mathers LP is indefensible and critic-proof," Will Hermes wrote for Entertainment Weekly (June 2, 2000), "hypocritical and heartbreaking, unlistenable and undeniable; it's a disposable shock-rap session, and the first great pop record of the 21st century." In a review for MTV.com (May 12, 2000), Kurt Loder wrote, "'Artful' is unavoidably the right word in regard to this guy. . . . Marshall Mathers has a razor-sharp and ferocious command of language; a level of verbal skill that, in another context, would surely qualify as poetic. . . . On the other hand, might he not

also just be some lucky sociopath, working out his problems on multi-platinum albums? Your call." Some critics felt that Eminem had gone too far with The Marshall Mathers LP, and that his lyrics had deteriorated into simple taunts. "Eminem shadowboxes with nonexistent enemies," Ethan Brown wrote for New York (June 26, 2000), "wasting his narrative skills throwing sucker-punches at vulnerable targets: women, gays, and even his own mother." In Columbia Journalism Review (September/October 2000), Michael Hoyt berated the media for failing to denounce Eminem's hateful lyrics. "Eminem and his ilk have their First Amendment right to spew their poison. The critics have the right, and I would argue the duty, to sound the warning bell when they do."

On June 4, 2000 Eminem got into an argument with Douglas Dali, an associate of the Detroit-based band Insane Clown Posse; according to a police report, Eminem brandished an unloaded pistol at him. (Dali later pressed charges.) Then, in the early hours of June 5, Eminem stormed into a bar where Kimberly Scott Mathers (whom he had married in June 1999) had gone with some friends. There he allegedly pistol-whipped a bouncer who he said had been kissing Kimberly. The latter incident led him to be charged with two felony counts, one for assault and the other for carrying a concealed weapon. On June 7, 2000 Kimberly issued a statement, reprinted in the Detroit Free Press (on-line), which read, in part, "I would . . . like to state that, since my husband has had no problem trying to make me look like an unfaithful wife, that every time I find a picture of him with other women, or read in magazines that he's involved with 'groupies,' I don't go and show up where he is, making a huge scene and getting our faces put all over the TV and papers." One month later, while Eminem was giving a concert nearby, Kimberly attempted suicide, by slashing her wrists in an upstairs bathroom of the couple's home. (Her mother found her before she did any serious damage to herself.) Eminem later filed for divorce.

Meanwhile, Eminem's popularity had swelled. Tickets for the "Up in Smoke" tour had sold well; The Marshall Mathers LP had become a top-seller in Canada as well as the U.S.; his single "The Real Slim Shady" had hit the Top 10; and the video of the single had reached number one on the MTV Top 20 Video Countdown. At the 2001 Grammy Award ceremony, he won awards for best rap album, best solo rap performance (for "The Real Slim Shady"), and best duo or group rap performance (for "Forget About Dre," with Dr. Dre). By embracing and performing a duo with the singer and gay-rights campaigner Elton John at the Grammys, Eminem disarmed some who have criticized him for writing homophobic lyrics.

Ironically, Eminem has complained that his newfound, long-coveted fame has become a new source of hardship for him, in part because numbers of his fans and enemies often gather outside his home, in a Detroit suburb. As he told Brian Mc-

Collum for the *Detroit Free Press* (June 30, 2000, on-line), "Not only did I never think I'd get this big, it's like I'm still refusing to believe it. I don't like having security hold my hand to walk out to my mailbox. There's something inside of me that refuses to believe I can't walk down the street, or be as normal as I want to be." — P.G.H.

Suggested Reading: *Columbia Journalism Review* p67 Sep./Oct. 2000; *Entertainment Weekly* p76+ June 2, 2000, with photo; (London) *Guardian* I p7 Feb. 23, 2001; *MTV.com* May 12, 2000, with photos; *New York* p153 June 26, 2000, with photo; *Newsweek* p63+ May 29, 2000, with photos; *People* p139+ July 24, 2000, with photos; *Rolling Stone* p31+ Feb. 18, 1999, with photos, p42+ Apr. 29, 1999, with photos; (Syracuse, New York) *Post-Standard* A p7 Apr. 7, 2001; *Village Voice* p71+ Mar. 30, 1999, with photo

Selected Recordings: *The Slim Shady LP*, 1999; *The Marshall Mathers LP*, 2000; as contributor— *Dr. Dre 2001*, 2000

Reuters/Sue Ogrocki/Hulton/Archive

Epstein, Samuel S.

Apr. 13, 1926– Pathologist; environmental scientist; physician; educator. Address: School of Public Health, University of Illinois Medical Center, 2121 W. Taylor St., Chicago, IL 60612

"Most scientists try to be impartial," Tony Mazzocchi, a labor-rights activist and former vice president of the Oil, Chemical, and Atomic Workers' Union, told Steve Fiffer for *Chicago* (April 1999).

"But Sam is never equivocal. He hates disease and he hates those who cause disease. He never retreats." Mazzocchi was speaking of Samuel S. Epstein, a pathologist and professor of environmental medicine who is among the world's leading authorities on cancer prevention. He is also a controversial figure, because of his decades-long criticism of cancer-research organizations that he and others have referred to as the "national cancer establishment" (particularly the federal National Cancer Institute and the not-for-profit American Cancer Society). Epstein has long maintained that many types of cancer could be eliminated through the proper regulation or removal of known carcinogens found in food, cosmetics, pesticides, cleaning and other household products, and the environment. He has further charged that the medical profession has failed to act on this knowledge, because at stake are billions of dollars in grant money to researchers and the profits of pharmaceutical companies, all of which depend on emphasizing what he has referred to as "damage control"—the diagnosis, treatment, and cure of cancer rather than its prevention. "We're talking about high crimes and misdemeanors. From the public health standpoint, the cancer establishment's refusal to act on freely available information is tantamount to criminal offenses," he told David Moberg for *Utne Reader* (March/April 1999).

Epstein has written or co-written approximately 280 articles and 13 books, among them *Hazardous Waste in America* (1982), *The Safe Shopper's Bible: A Consumer's Guide to Nontoxic Household Products, Cosmetics, and Food* (1995), and *The Breast Cancer Prevention Program* (1997). The best known of his books is *The Politics of Cancer* (1978); a revised and updated edition, entitled *The Politics of Cancer Revisited*, was published in 1998. Epstein has served as a consultant to U.S. House and Senate committees and appeared before several of them as an expert witness, most notably to call for the banning of pesticides harmful to humans, among them chlordane and DDT; to condemn the use of Agent Orange in Vietnam; and to warn of the dangers of sex hormones injected in cattle raised for human consumption. Those activities provided impetus for the passage of critical environmental legislation, including the Clean Water Act (1972), the Toxic Substances Control Act (1976), the Resource Conservation and Recovery Act (1976), and the Clean Air Act (1990). Epstein told Derrick Jensen for the Chapel Hill, North Carolina *Sun* (March 2000), "We need Nuremberg-type trials to hold industries accountable for these sorts of public health crimes. The tobacco industry would be one example, but there is a wide range of other industries whose executives we need to begin holding accountable. Scientists, too. There are a vast number of indentured scientists in this country willing to jump through any hoop for the sake of profit. In addition, we need to bring to account regulatory officials and members of expert advisory committees—all the people who are supposed to be overseeing public health but are instead facilitating the poisoning of the American people, and, in fact, the people of the world." In 1998 Epstein earned the Right Livelihood Award—widely known as the "alternative Nobel Prize"—for his "exemplary life of scholarship wedded to activism on behalf of humanity," as Fiffer reported, and for his contributions to cancer prevention.

Samuel Stanley Epstein was born in Middlesbrough, a town in Yorkshire, England, on April 13, 1926. His father, Isidore Epstein, was a rabbi; a world-renowned Hebraic and Talmudic scholar, he also earned a doctorate in literature. One of his books, *Faith of Judaism* (1954), is still in print and has been translated into more than 20 languages. Isidore Epstein served as editor of the first English translation of the Babylonian Talmud (the vast compendium of Jewish oral law and rabbinical commentaries on the laws), a work that fills 30 volumes. His father's "fanatic obsession with justice and human rights," Samuel Epstein told Fiffer, was one inspiration for his interest in fighting social injustice and exposing what he described to *Current Biography* as "the profit-driven misuse of science, resulting in avoidable disease and death." Samuel Epstein briefly attended a yeshiva (an Orthodox Jewish school for males). During the 1940s he was a member of an activist youth group affiliated with the Irgun, a Jewish underground military organization whose goal was to end British control of Palestine and establish a Jewish state there. Epstein translated English material into Hebrew for the group during the illegal immigration into Palestine of Jews fleeing the Holocaust.

Epstein considered studying either international law or diplomacy before deciding to focus on the biological sciences. In 1944 he entered Guys Medical School, in London, as a pre-med student. In 1946, as a reward for his outstanding grades on his final examinations, he was granted a one-year leave to continue his studies wherever he wished. He chose the University of London, from which he graduated with a B.S. degree in physiology in 1947. He then went back to Guys, where he earned bachelor of medicine and bachelor of surgery degrees in 1950. Next, he spent a year as a house physician and general practitioner at St. John's Hospital in London before returning to the University of London, where he received a diploma in tropical medicine and hygiene, for which he also studied bacteriology and parasitology (1952); a diploma in pathology (1954); and an M.D. degree (1958), for which he wrote a thesis dealing with experimental pathology. Concurrently, from 1952 to 1955 he served as a specialist in pathology with the Royal Army Medical Corps, an experience that furthered his fascination with the nature of disease. During that time he also worked in a military hospital in West Germany, where he performed autopsies, sometimes on people who had died in car crashes involving Volkswagens. "We saw the same set of injuries, so I got very interested in car design and avoidable accidents," Epstein told Steve Fiffer. In

1953 he earned three military awards, two for his achievements in tropical medicine and one for his accomplishments as a surgeon. From 1955 to 1958 he worked as a lecturer and pathologist at the Institute of Laryngology and Otology at the University of London.

For the next two years, as a British Empire Cancer Campaign research fellow, Epstein worked at the Chester Beatty Cancer Research Institute and the Hospital for Sick Children in London. During that time one of his superiors conducted a study of children with neuroblastoma, a rare cancer that affects the nervous systems of children. The results of the study, he claimed, showed that large doses of vitamin B-12 could cure them. Skeptical about that claim, Epstein repeatedly asked to review his superior's clinical data, but the researcher refused to show him the records of his work. Undeterred, Epstein and another doctor broke into a safe containing the children's medical files. "The claims were bogus," Epstein told Steve Fiffer. "He had taken kids who had had surgery and other therapy and then given them B_{12} and said they were cured because of the vitamins." The head of the hospital confirmed that the elder scientist's claims had been falsified, and after Epstein threatened to alert the public, he agreed to halt the research. Later, to force health organizations and government agencies to take action on what he viewed as public-health crises, Epstein adopted the same strategy, threatening to go public with information that might be damaging to the medical industry.

In 1960 Epstein moved to the United States, where he established the first laboratories in the nation devoted to toxicology and cancer. He took positions with the Children's Cancer Research Foundation (1961–71) and the Harvard University Medical School (1962–71), both in Boston, Massachusetts. (He later became an American citizen.) In 1963 he was named a diplomate in public health and medical laboratory microbiology by the American Board of Microbiology.

A turning point in Epstein's career came three years later, after he informed a top-ranking Food and Drug Administration official of his finding that griseofulvin, an antibiotic used to treat athlete's foot, causes cancer. "He told me, 'It's been approved. You should have told us before it was on the market,'" Epstein recalled to Steve Fiffer. (As he remembered the conversation during his interview with David Moberg, the official exclaimed, "Are you serious? This is on the market. We can't do anything about it.") "That started me on another track," Epstein told Moberg. "If you're going to stay in this field, you've got to shift some attention to politics"—specifically, public policy on cancer. During the next decade he appeared many times before congressional committees and talked with federal-agency and union officials in an effort to end the sale and use of harmful products. His testimony about the dangers of DDT, Aldrin, and other insecticides sprayed on corn, cotton, and other crops contributed to the Environmental Protection

Agency's decision to ban their use. In 1967 Epstein joined the board of directors, and chaired the Boston chapter, of the Committee of Responsibility, a group of doctors and others who brought Vietnamese children badly injured during the Vietnam War to the United States for medical treatment and then took them back to Vietnam. He spent seven months in Vietnam, where he successfully set up the evacuation program despite obstacles emanating from the Vietnamese bureaucracy, the U.S. military, and the American embassy. He later testified on the health hazards of 2,4-D and 2,4,5-T, the herbicides contained in Agent Orange, a defoliant widely used by the U.S. military during the Vietnam conflict. That appearance, along with his 1972 testimony before the Commerce Committee of the U.S. Senate, was instrumental in persuading Congress to ban the military use of Agent Orange in the same year. Earlier, in 1969, he had received the Society of Toxicology's Achievement Award for his efforts to alert the public to the hazards of various poisons. In 1972, in collaboration with Tony Mazzocchi, he organized a strike against Shell Oil to protest occupational hazards in Shell facilities.

From 1971 to 1976 Epstein held three titles at the Case Western Reserve School of Medicine, in Cleveland, Ohio: professor of environmental health and human ecology, professor of pharmacology, and director of environmental health programs. In 1976 he became a professor of occupational and environmental medicine at the Abraham Lincoln School of Medicine and School of Public Health at the University of Illinois, where he conducted research in toxicology and carcinogenesis (the development of cancer). He has been professor emeritus at the university since 1999 and still conducts research there.

In 1977 Epstein won a National Conservation Achievement Award from the National Wildlife Federation. The following year saw the publication of Epstein's book *The Politics of Cancer*, which presents documented evidence that certain U.S. corporations knowingly withheld information about health risks posed by their products. *The Politics of Cancer Revisited*, published two decades after the first edition, contains a new section in which Epstein showed that although $20 billion had been spent on cancer research since 1971, there had been no significant improvement in treatment or survival rates for many types of cancer. The book also describes the deliberate weakening of federal regulatory agencies during the presidential administrations of Ronald Reagan and George Herbert Walker Bush.

Epstein has also written many articles and letters to the editors of newspapers and magazines criticizing the American Cancer Society and the National Cancer Institute, both of which he has accused of having "misled and confused the public and Congress by repeated false claims that we are winning the war on cancer," as Steve Fiffer quoted him as saying. Furthermore, Epstein has charged that those organizations have "myopically fixated

on damage control—diagnosis and treatment—and basic genetic research, with not always benign indifference to cancer prevention." According to Epstein, only 600 of the 80,000 chemicals whose use has been approved by federal agencies are known to be carcinogens—a relatively small number, so that removing them from general use, and thus taking a huge step in cancer prevention, would not be overly disruptive to the economy or people's lives. "The American Cancer Society [ACS] is the world's largest nonreligious charity," he told Derrick Jensen in March 2000. "It takes in more than $600 million a year, ostensibly to fight cancer, and its cash reserves approach a billion dollars. But the vast majority of the ACS's budget goes for salaries, executive benefits, overhead, and other administrative expenses. Less than 16 percent of all the money raised is spent on direct services, such as driving cancer patients home from the hospital after chemo[therapy], or providing pain medication." Epstein has frequently noted that in 1992, in a statement that appeared to support his charges, the *Chronicle of Philanthropy*, a leading charity watchdog, maintained that the ACS was "more interested in accumulating wealth than in saving lives."

Epstein has repeatedly emphasized that spending money on prevention is not in the best interests of the drug companies, which maintain close ties with university and other research organizations; additionally, scientists are not inclined to speak out for fear of losing their grant money. According to Epstein, "The ACS has consistently come out in support of the pesticide industry, has actively campaigned against the Delaney Clause [a federal regulation banning the deliberate addition to food of any substance shown to cause cancer], and has refused to support the Clean Air Act. It's shocking—or it would be, if it weren't so consistent." For example, in an article entitled "The High Stakes of Cancer Prevention," published in 2000 in *Tikkun*, Epstein and Liza Gross wrote that when studies conducted in 1971 proved "that diethylstilbestrol (DES) caused vaginal cancers in teenage daughters of women who had taken the drug during pregnancy, the ACS refused to testify at congressional hearings on whether the FDA should ban the drug's use as an animal-feed additive." In 1977, Epstein and Gross charged, the ACS "called for a congressional moratorium on the [federal Food and Drug Administration's] proposed ban on saccharin, going so far as to advocate its use by nursing mothers and babies in 'moderation' despite clear-cut evidence of its carcinogenicity in rodents and very suggestive evidence of bladder cancer in humans." Offering more evidence for his accusations against the ACS, in "American Cancer Society: The World's Wealthiest 'Nonprofit' Institution," published in 1999 in the *International Journal of Health Services*, Epstein wrote that in 1982 the ACS "adopted a highly restrictive cancer policy that insisted on unequivocal human evidence of carcinogenicity before taking any position on public health hazards. Accordingly, the ACS still trivializes or rejects evidence of carcinogenicity in experimental animals." In the same article he noted that members of the board of trustees of the ACS Foundation have included "corporate executives from the pharmaceutical, investment, banking, and media industries," among them executives of companies that manufacture and sell chemical fertilizers, herbicides, and drugs administered to chemotherapy patients.

Epstein has also taken to task such respected newspapers as the *New York Times* and the *Washington Post* for failing to run articles and letters to the editor that are critical of the drug and chemical companies; he has attributed those omissions to the fact that the newspapers receive enormous amounts of advertising revenues from those companies. "Time and again, we see that government and industry are both willing to sacrifice human lives on the altar of profits, with the mainstream media there to support them all the way," he told Jensen. Directors and senior staff members of the National Cancer Institute and the American Cancer Society have attempted to refute Epstein's findings, by denying his claims that they have neglected prevention and citing falling cancer rates and improved treatment of certain forms of cancer. In his talk with Steve Fiffer, Epstein countered, "The 'reversal' in the overall mortality rates is not only minimal but exaggerated, and more likely due to improved access to health care rather than to advances in treatment and survival and to a reduction in lung cancer deaths from smoking in men." While recognizing that smoking is the leading avoidable cause of cancer, Epstein has demonstrated that smoking accounts for only one quarter of the increase in cancer cases since 1950, and he believes that about one-fifth of these cancers are caused by occupational exposures to carcinogens other than those in tobacco and cigarette smoke. He has also gathered what he regards as irrefutable evidence that the proliferation of cancer since 1950 is linked to inadvertent and avoidable exposure to petrochemical products. "Between 1940 and 1990, the total annual production of synthetic organic chemicals increased from 1 billion to more than 600 billion pounds," he explained to Derrick Jensen. "Over the last few decades, our total environment has become pervasively contaminated with a wide range of toxic and carcinogenic chemicals, some of which are persistent—that is, long-lived. When I say 'total environment,' I mean our air, water, soil, consumer products, food, and workplace. Even our own body fats have become contaminated. This is true from the North Pole to the South, not only for humans but for a wide range of marine life and wildlife, as well."

On February 4, 1992 Epstein made public a statement entitled "Losing the War on Cancer After 20 Years." Endorsed by 65 other experts on public health and cancer prevention, it pointed to a 44 percent increase in cancer cases since 1950 and severely criticized the cancer establishment for indifference to cancer prevention. The statement,

which was timed to coincide with the 20th anniversary of the launch of President Richard Nixon's "war against cancer," inspired Epstein to launch the Cancer Prevention Coalition (CPC), in 1994; the organization, chaired by Epstein, aims to make cancer prevention America's top priority through a campaign of outreach, education, and advocacy, in the hope of reducing cancer rates to pre-1940 levels. The CPC has submitted four separate petitions to the Food and Drug Administration, calling, respectively, for labels on talcum powder to warn women that the application of such powder in the genital area raises the risk of ovarian cancer; a ban on lindane-based shampoos, which are used to treat head lice, mainly in children (lindane is derived from benzene, a known carcinogen); labels on nitrite-preserved hotdogs, to warn of the risk of childhood brain cancer and leukemia; and the mass mailing of a letter that would warn all women with silicone and polyurethane breast implants of the risk of breast cancer. Epstein has published many cancer alerts through the CPC's Web site. "Public release of this information has been widely criticized by many industries and their trade associations," he told Steve Fiffer, but "none have successfully challenged its accuracy." Thomas Mancuso, a research professor emeritus at the University of Pittsburgh Graduate School of Public Health, told Fiffer that although Epstein's views have limited his access to the funding available to other researchers, his work has been impeccable. "He has the science," Mancuso explained. "When you're fighting government or corporations, they get very good scientists to make their cases. He faces the best scientists of their vested interests, so he has to have the corresponding knowledge."

In 1995 Epstein and David Steinman co-wrote *The Safe Shopper's Bible*, a consumer guide to carcinogenic ingredients and contaminants in food, cosmetics, toiletries, and household products; the book also provides information on safe alternatives manufactured by non-mainstream companies. In conjunction with its publication, Epstein held a press conference with the consumer advocate Ralph Nader, at which they presented the "Dirty Dozen," a list of products with carcinogenic or otherwise toxic ingredients. In *The Breast Cancer Prevention Program* (1997), which he co-wrote with Steinman, Epstein argued that, contrary to widespread belief, breast cancer can be prevented, through proper diet, exercise, and the avoidance of the prolonged use of oral contraceptives and exposure to toxins in the home and workplace. Epstein told Derrick Jensen that five independent studies have shown that aspirin is effective in reducing the risk of breast cancer, but since aspirin is not patentable—and thus not especially profitable for drug companies—those companies encourage instead the use of tamoxifen, a chemotherapy drug that, according to Epstein, triples patients' risk of developing uterine cancer and may also lead to liver cancer, liver failure, blood clots, and painful complications for women going through menopause.

Epstein is one of the leading experts on the health risks posed by Monsanto's genetically engineered bovine growth hormone (rBGH), which increases milk production, and on the dangers of sex hormones used to fatten cattle. "In 1989, someone dropped off at my office a batch of documents that had been stolen from the Food and Drug Administration's files on Monsanto," he told Derrick Jensen. "Included was a Monsanto document from 1987 indicating that the company was fully aware of rBGH's danger and was conspiring with the FDA to suppress information critical to veterinary and public health." In 1997 Epstein assisted the European Union (EU) in defending before the World Trade Organization (WTO) the EU's ban on beef derived from cattle injected with either rBGH or sex hormones; the WTO upheld the ban. Although the movement to expose corporate wrongdoing in the food industry has gained momentum much faster in Europe than in the U.S., Epstein is confident that once consumers in the U.S. have been adequately informed of the dangers posed by certain products, they will use their buying power to force the manufacturers to reconsider their choices of ingredients. "I am very optimistic about the American public," he told Steve Fiffer. "I believe that once they really get hold of an issue, they can use the marketplace as an alternative to regulation." More recently Epstein has spoken out against the use of the genetically engineered human growth hormone (HGH) as an anti-aging drug. His book *Got (Genetically Engineered) Milk: The Monsanto rBGH/BST Milk Wars Handbook*, will be published on the Internet in the near future.

Epstein has been a member of several professional societies, among them the American Association of Pathologists and Bacteriologists, the American Association for Cancer Research, the Environmental Mutagen Society, the Society for Occupational and Environmental Health (of which he is president), and the New York Academy of Sciences. His work has earned him more than a dozen awards and honors in addition to the Right Livelihood Award, including the Environmental Justice Award, from the Citizens Clearinghouse for Hazardous Wastes, in 1989; a Lifetime Achievement Award from the National Coalition Against the Misuse of Pesticides, in 1991; and the 1999 Annual Award of the Bioneers, an environmental organization. A recent article in which Epstein criticized the ACS was awarded the 2000 Project Censored Award, which is sometimes referred to as the "alternative Pulitzer Prize" for investigative journalism.

Epstein and his wife, Cathy, live in Chicago, Illinois. He has three children from a previous marriage. — C.L.

Suggested Reading: (Chapel Hill, North Carolina) *Sun* p4+ Mar. 2000, with photos; *Chicago* p76+ Apr. 1999, with photos; *Utne Reader* p22+ Mar./Apr. 1999, with photo

Selected Books: as author or co-author—*The Politics of Cancer*, 1978; *Hazardous Waste in America* (with Carl Pope and Lester O. Brown), 1982; *Cancer in Britain: The Politics of Prevention* (with Lesley Doyal), 1983; *The Safe Shoppers' Bible: A Consumer's Guide to Nontoxic Household Products, Cosmetics, and Food* (with David Steinman), 1995; *The Breast Cancer Prevention Program* (with David Steinman and Suzanne LeVert), 1997; *The Politics of Cancer Revisited*, 1998; as co-editor—*The Mutagenicity of Pesticides: Concepts and Evaluation*, 1971; *Drugs of Abuse: Their Genetic and Other Chronic Nonpsychiatric Hazards*, 1971; *The Legislation of Product Safety: Consumer Health and Product Hazards*, Vol. I, 1974, Vol. II, 1976

Courtesy of Aprille Ericsson-Jackson

Ericsson-Jackson, Aprille J.

Apr. 1, 1963– Aerospace engineer; educator. Address: NASA Goddard Space Flight Center, Guidance, Navigation, and Control Center, Code 572, Greenbelt, MD 20771

Aprille J. Ericsson-Jackson, an aerospace engineer at NASA's Goddard Space Flight Center (GSFC), in Greenbelt, Maryland, has the distinction of being not only the first African-American female to receive a Ph.D. in mechanical engineering from Howard University, in Washington, D.C., but also the first American to receive a doctorate in that field with an aerospace specialization. At GSFC she works to ensure that spacecraft will perform well during NASA missions. Ericsson-Jackson has also worked hard to increase diversity in the sciences, regularly visiting schools as a member of both Women of NASA and GSFC's Speakers Bureau and encouraging young women and minorities to pursue careers in scientific fields. She often tells students, "Shoot for the moon and even if you miss you'll still be among the stars."

Aprille J. Ericsson-Jackson was born on April 1, 1963 in the New York City borough of Brooklyn. Her parents separated when she was eight, and her mother raised Aprille and her two sisters in Brooklyn's Roosevelt housing projects. Ericsson-Jackson discovered her talent for math and science while attending Marine Park Junior High School, where she was the only black student in the Special Progress program, which included instruction in mathematics, earth science, biology, and chemistry. Thanks in part to the encouragement and support of her mother, she achieved outstanding scores on state and city exams and once won second place in her junior high's science fair. She passed the entrance exams for all three of New York City's highly competitive public technical high schools. At the age of 15, she moved to Cambridge, Massachusetts, where she lived with her grandparents while attending the Cambridge School of Weston, a prestigious private college-prep school that gave her a full scholarship three years in succession. She enjoyed sports and proved to have a talent for football, basketball, and softball, playing on student teams.

In the summer after her junior year of high school, Ericsson-Jackson participated in UNITE (now known as Minority Introduction to Engineering, or MITE), a two-week program for African-American students that inspired her to consider a career in aerospace engineering. "Over the course of the program, we were exposed to several engineering disciplines," she told Michael Baine for *Space.com* (September 22, 2000). "One was civil engineering, where we made small bridges that were tested by loading until failure. That was my first attempt at designing anything as a pseudo-engineer. The director of the program was a biomedical engineer, which also interested me, but I decided I did not want to be a medical doctor because of the memorization needed and I did not want to do civil engineering/architecture because buildings and structures did not move." Ericsson-Jackson also visited an air-force base in New Hampshire, where her performance at the controls of a flight simulator indicated a level of ability comparable to that of a pilot. She maintained excellent grades and scored high on her PSATs; she also found the time to volunteer as a physical-education instructor at a number of local elementary schools.

Ericsson-Jackson was accepted as a student at the Massachusetts Institute of Technology (MIT), in Cambridge. During her freshman year she attended an aerospace-engineering seminar in which she learned about "the different disciplines within aerospace," as she told Michael Baine. "It also al-

lowed me to meet various faculty members in the department and exposed me to their research. . . . I kept up my grades and was accepted into the aero/astro program." As an undergraduate at MIT, Ericsson-Jackson worked on several projects related to manned space missions. In 1986 she received a B.S. degree in aeronautical and astronautical engineering from MIT. With the help of a number of grants, she then attended Howard University, as a graduate student in the Large Space Structures Institute. She also delivered technical papers in Germany, Canada, England, and throughout the United States. She earned both a master's degree (1990) and a Ph.D. (1995) in mechanical engineering, making her the first African-American female to receive a doctorate in this discipline from Howard University.

Ericsson-Jackson was hired by the National Aeronautics and Space Administration (NASA) in 1992. She currently works in the Guidance, Navigation and Control Center of NASA's Goddard Space Flight Center, where she concentrates on satellite projects such as the X-Ray Timing Explorer (XTE) and the Tropical Rain Forest Measurement Mission, testing spacecraft designs by conducting simulations of performance. Her most recent work has been on the Microwave Anisotropy Probe (MAP), a satellite designed to seek out clues to the origins of our galaxy, the Milky Way, by measuring the properties of cosmic microwave background radiation found in the sky. MAP launched on June 30, 2001, and, as Charles Bennett, the MAP Science Team's principal investigator, told *Current Biography*, it "is now successfully in its nominal orbit at the second Earth-Sun Lagrange point . . . a million miles from Earth." Bennett added, "All systems are working very well."

In an autobiographical statement Ericsson-Jackson sent to *Current Biography*, she wrote that in the future she hopes to work as "a mission specialist for the astronaut program, [an] Aerospace Engineering professor; and an advisor to the White House through the Office of Science and Technology Policy."

Believing that the Internet is a key component of disseminating information on technical careers to those who need it, Ericsson-Jackson has created an E-mail list through which she provides information to those interested in learning more about educational and employment opportunities in the sciences. "The Internet can also bring new resources to the African-American community," she told *ZD-Net* (on-line). "In Washington, lots of African-American kids use public computers to look for funding for college and to apply online. Who's to say that the corner bookie couldn't have earned an MIT degree if he had been given the opportunity? It costs money to be online, unfortunately, and a lot of people still can't afford the cost of a system that's fast enough, with a printer and everything else you need. And one of the things that's really sad is that teachers and educators lack Internet access, and their schools are missing out. Hopefully all that will change."

Ericsson-Jackson is a recruiter for GSFC; she has applied to NASA's astronaut program, but has thus far been unable to participate due to an asthma condition and surgical repair of both knees. She has taught at Howard University's Department of Mechanical Engineering and is an adjunct professor in the Department of Mechanical Engineering and Mathematics at Bowie State University, in Maryland, where she was hired to improve the engineering curriculum. She created two new courses for freshmen and sophomores at Bowie. Should she fulfill her goal of becoming a professor at Howard University, Ericsson-Jackson hopes to create and chair an aerospace department. She is a member of a number of organizations, including the American Astronautical Society, the American Institute of Aeronautics and Astronautics, the American Society of Mechanical Engineers, the Society of Women Engineers, and Sigma Xi. She also participates in many community-outreach pro-

grams and has visited the White House for meetings on issues related to science, engineering, and technology. In 1997 Ericsson-Jackson received the Women in Science and Engineering (WISE) Award, which recognizes the best female engineer in the federal government. The following year NASA's African-American Awards Committee named her one of GSFC's outstanding African-Americans. She received special recognition at the Black Engineer Awards ceremony sponsored by *U.S. Black Engineer and Information Technology Magazine. iVillage.com* included her on its list of "Women Who'll Rule" in the near future.

Ericsson-Jackson's many hobbies include reading, sports, woodworking, sewing, and baking. She lives in Washington, D.C. — C.L.

Suggested Reading: *NASA Quest* (on-line); *Space.com* (on-line) Sep. 22, 2000

Herman Estevez/Courtesy of St. Martin's Press

Evanovich, Janet

1943(?)– Writer. Address: P.O. Box 5487, Hanover, NH 03755

"When I grow up, I want to be Grandma Mazur," the mystery writer Janet Evanovich told Claire E. White for *Writers Write—The Internet Writing Journal* (January 1999). She was referring to the sharp-witted, spunky grandmother who attends funerals for recreation and has been known to carry a stun gun—one of a host of colorful supporting characters who inhabit the pages of Evanovich's re-

soundingly successful series of mystery novels featuring Stephanie Plum, an untrained bounty hunter who lives and works in Trenton, New Jersey. The series began with *One for the Money,* in 1994, and continued with *Two for the Dough,* in 1995; the most recent, *Seven Up,* arrived in bookstores in mid-2001. Audio versions of books in the Stephanie Plum series have also sold well. A stay-at-home mom when she began writing, Evanovich persevered for some 10 years during which she received nothing but rejection letters for her efforts. In the 14 years since she sold her first manuscript—a romance novel—she has produced several bestsellers and launched a personal Web site that, by her own account, gets a million hits each month. The eighth Plum mystery is scheduled to be published in the summer of 2002.

Janet Evanovich was born in about 1943 and raised in South River, New Jersey. On her Web site she recalled having an active imagination as a youngster. "I read all the Black Stallion books by Walter Farley," she told Claire E. White. "Then I'd run around and pretend I was a horse. I did that for years! The other really dominant literary influences on my life were Little Lulu, Betty and Veronica, and Uncle Scrooge"—all of whom are comic-book characters. When she got a little older, she liked to pretend that she was an opera singer. "My mother would send me to the grocery store down the street, and off I'd go, caterwauling at the top of my lungs," she recalled for her Web site. Evanovich had a close relationship with her aunt Lena, on whom she based Grandma Mazur, one of her fans' favorite characters; Lena was, in her words, "a good egg." "She understood that the realities of daily existence were lost in the murky shadows of my slightly looney imagination," the writer reported on her Web site.

Evanovich attended South River High School, where she was "the school artist . . . a painter," as she recalled during an on-line chat co-hosted by *Talk City* and *Borders.com* (July 22, 1998). After she graduated she entered nearby Douglass College (part of Rutgers, the state university of New Jersey) as a fine-arts major. Between her junior and senior years in college, she married Peter Evanovich, who at that time was earning a Ph.D. degree in mathematics from Rutgers. Within a few years of earning her bachelor's degree, she had become the mother of a son, Peter, and a daughter, Alex, and her husband had begun teaching college mathematics. After her children were both in school, she began writing, either before they came home or after they had gone to bed; she had realized by then, as she told a *Literary Guild*/Yahoo on-line chat (July 5, 2000), that she "wanted a larger audience" than she could get through painting and "liked to entertain." But for 10 years none of her manuscripts was accepted for publication. "I have no idea why I continued to write when I received so much rejection . . . ," she told Claire E. White. "I suppose it was just too important to me to give up. And probably my ornery disposition kept me going." Her husband and, when they got older, her children, too, always supported her, she said during the *Literary Guild*/Yahoo chat.

Finally, in 1987, Evanovich, using the pseudonym Steffie Hall, sold a romance manuscript to an imprint called Second Chance at Love for $2,000. The sale provided inspiration enough for Evanovich to leave the job where she had been working as a temp for a few months and devote herself full-time to writing romance novels. Now aiming to help defray the cost of her children's college educations, she published 12 novels in five or six years, but she grew bored with the format. "I actually was forced out of romance," she told PJ Nunn for the *Charlotte Austin Review* (2000, on-line), a Canadian publication. "I wanted to write bigger books with more action, sort of like the movie *Romancing the Stone*, and I couldn't get any of the romance editors to give me a contract." Writing mysteries, she decided, would be a better pursuit for someone with her personality and aspirations. "I knew I wanted to do good basic entertainment, so that meant I had to keep it short," she explained to Michelle Griffin for the *Age*, an Australian newspaper (March 20, 2000, on-line). "I wanted something people could read in one or two days. I wanted to write in the first person. . . . There are very few places where first person is accepted but crime was one of them." Additionally, Evanovich thought that mystery novels would be a better venue for her styles of humor and dialogue. "I prefer writing action to relationship, because I suck at internal narrative," she admitted in an interview with *Page ONE* that was reprinted on *BookBrowse* (on-line). "I have more freedom of language with mystery. Okay, so I have a trash mouth. I'm from Jersey, what can I say." To perfect her dialogue-writing skills, she took classes in improvisational theater.

Evanovich spent the next two years or so researching her new genre, by reading and watching movies. "I wanted to move into crime fiction, but I really knew very little about law enforcement," she explained in her *Literary Guild* chat. She knew that she did not want to make a private investigator her protagonist, because, she said, she did not think she could compete successfully with Sue Grafton, whose series of mystery novels features a private investigator called Kinsey Milhone. Her creative juices started to flow the day that she saw the 1988 film *Midnight Run* on television; an action comedy directed by Martin Brest, *Midnight Run* stars Robert De Niro as a bounty hunter who stands to gain $100,000 if he can track down a bail-jumping accountant, played by Charles Grodin, and return him to Los Angeles. "I immediately knew this was it," she said during the *Literary Guild* chat, describing her excitement at the idea of inventing a fictional bounty hunter. "And there's the added advantage that bounty hunters don't have to wear cop shoes."

Evanovich made the acquaintance of several bail bondsmen whose names she found in the Yellow Pages, and although none would allow her to tag along when the time came to make an arrest, she succeeded in learning a lot about their routines, modus operandi, and equipment. She later discovered that accuracy was not overly important to her readers; usually, she explained during the *Literary Guild* chat, they are "more interested in my characters than in my crimes." She also spent time with the Trenton police and learned how to handle a gun. In fleshing out her protagonist, she drew from details of her own life—including memories of growing up in the suburbs of New Jersey— as well as her daughter's. "Inevitably," Claire E. White wrote, "fans ask Evanovich if she is really Stephanie. The similarities are there; they are both from New Jersey, they both love Cheetos, have owned a hamster, and have shared 'similar embarrassing experiences,' according to the author." "I wouldn't go so far as to say Stephanie is an autobiographical character, but I will admit to knowing where she lives," Evanovich told White. The writer told Bruce Tierney for *Bookpage* (July 2000, on-line) that television sitcoms suggested a model for the series. "It's like *Seinfeld*," she explained, referring to the long-running comedy series that starred Jerry Seinfeld. "Stephanie is Seinfeld, the central character everybody revolves around."

Stephanie Plum arrived on the mystery scene in *One for the Money*, during the summer of 1994. An out-of-work lingerie buyer, she has been reduced to hocking her furniture to pay her rent. At the behest of her well-meaning but overbearing parents, she agrees to interview for a job at her cousin Vinnie's bail-bond agency. After learning that the clerk position has been filled, she agrees out of desperation to take on the task of finding criminals who have failed to appear for their court dates. Her first assignment is to bring in Joe Morelli, a wily former policeman accused of murdering an unarmed man.

The novice bounty hunter winds up getting the wrong people angry with her, among them the prizefighter and violent offender Benito Ramirez. "Literature this isn't," Dwight Garner wrote for the *Washington Post* (August 28, 1994), "but Evanovich's pluck and good humor win us over. As late-season beach books go, *One for the Money* goes down like a tall, cool drink." Evanovich's debut mystery won the Crime Writers Association's John Creasy Award for best first novel and the Dilys Award from the Independent Mystery Booksellers Association. Almost overnight, Evanovich sold the movie rights to the book to Tri-Star Pictures. (A film version of her book has yet to appear.) With the profits from *One for the Money*, the Evanovich family moved to a house in New Hampshire, where the writer set up her desk near a window with a view of the Connecticut River Valley.

The second in the Stephanie Plum series, *Two for the Dough*, was equally well received. In a review of *Two for the Dough* for *Tangled Web UK*, an on-line site devoted to mystery fiction, Val McDermid described Evanovich as "one of the best of the new breed [of mystery writers]. She writes stylish smartassed prose that keeps the pages turning and the smiles flickering round the corners of your mouth. Her novels may lack the heart of Sue Grafton or the guts of Sara Paretsky, but for sheer readability, it's hard to fault her." *Two for the Dough* won the Crime Writers Association's Last Laugh Award. The next book in the series, *Three to Get Deadly* (1996), was awarded a Crime Writers Association Silver Dagger.

By 1997, the year *Four to Score* was published, Evanovich had settled into a regular routine: 50-hour weeks in front of her computer, interrupted by book tours throughout the United States and other parts of the English-speaking world to promote each new novel. "Being a writer is fun," she told the *Page ONE* interviewer. "Writing a book is hard work." Before going to bed she peruses her Web site for feedback from her fans. Speaking of her book tours, she told Elisabeth Sherwin for the *Davis* [California] *Enterprise* (October 8, 2000, on-line), "I'm a real ham. The hard part for me is coming home from the book tour and not talking about myself for 22 hours a day." While she has enjoyed meeting her fans, Evanovich has complained of feeling pressure to produce a book every year.

The fifth Stephanie Plum mystery, *High Five*, appeared in 1999. "Steph has a spunky, earthy appeal—like a hot dog at the beach with a few grains of sand," Paula Chin noted for *People* (August 23, 1999). The titles of *Hot Six* (2000), which debuted at the top of the *New York Times* and *Wall Street Journal* best-seller lists, and *Seven Up*, published in June 2001, were the winning entries in book-naming contests that Evanovich conducted at her Web site. Her as-yet-unnamed eighth Stephanie Plum novel is scheduled to be published in mid-2002.

Evanovich's entire family has become involved in her career—her husband as the manager of her business (Evanovich Inc.), her son as her financial manager, and her daughter as the creator and administrator of her Web site and occasional companion on book tours. An on-line store at her Web site offers for sale T-shirts that have the words "Plum Crazy, evanovich.com" on the front and a picture of cartoon hamsters representing characters from the Plum series on the back. Also available are key tags, each with a quote from one of her books on one side and a cartoon hamster on the reverse.

Evanovich, who has a contract to write a total of 10 Stephanie Plum novels, hopes to publish a title unrelated to Plum some day. A devotee of writing groups, she is a member of Sisters in Crime (an organization of women mystery writers and writers of both sexes whose protagonists are female) and Romance Writers of America. During annual visits to New Jersey, she tries to pick up new slang to use in her books. The compliments she most appreciates, she told the *Literary Guild*, come from her fans. "I get a lot of letters from women who have lost partners or who are going through hard health times. I get a lot of letters from women who are in chemo. And they tell me that my books make them feel better and I think that's pretty terrific." — K.S.

Suggested Reading: *Age* (on-line) Mar. 20, 2000, with photo; *Bookpage* (on-line) July 2000, with photo; *Davis* [California] *Enterprise* (on-line) Oct. 8, 2000; *Literary Guild Chat Archive* (on-line) July 5, 2000; *Writers Write* (on-line) Jan. 1999, with photo

Selected Books: *One for the Money*, 1994, *Two for the Dough*, 1995, *Three to Get Deadly*, 1996, *Four to Score*, 1997, *High Five*, 1999, *Hot Six*, 2000; *Seven Up*, 2001

Evans, Donald L.

July 1946– U.S. Secretary of Commerce. Address: U.S. Department of Commerce, 1401 Constitution Ave., N.W., Washington, DC 20230

For the past 25 years, George W. Bush's most trusted friend has been Donald L. Evans, a fellow oilman and Republican. Both arrived in Midland, Texas, during the oil boom in 1975 and developed a rapport almost immediately. After helping Bush raise money for his two successful runs for governor of Texas and the first stages of his run for the White House, Evans was named chairman of Bush's 2000 presidential campaign. After winning the election that fall, Bush nominated Evans to serve as secretary of the United States Department of Commerce. Among all of Bush's advisers, none are as close to him as Evans, who some commenta-

Donald L. Evans

tors have said is as dear to Bush as a brother. "All of his advisers are his friends and are loyal to him, and he trusts them. But it's a little different with us," Evans told Frank Bruni for the *New York Times* (April 30, 2000). "It's different when you have a long-term friendship that's stood the test of time." When Bush went to Camp David, Maryland, the presidential rustic retreat, two weekends after the September 11, 2001 attacks on the World Trade Center and the Pentagon, Evans was the only top government official to accompany him.

The second of three children, Donald L. Evans was born in Houston, Texas, in July 1946. His father worked as a manager for the Shell Oil Co. in Houston. Evans attended Memorial High School in Houston, where he excelled in playing golf. In 1965 he entered the University of Texas at Austin. He was a member of the Texas Cowboys, a University of Texas service organization that was involved with leadership development and entertaining at charitable fund-raisers; he received the organization's Bill McGill Award. He was also a member of the Omicron Delta Kappa and Sigma Alpha Epsilon fraternities. Evans received high grades in college and graduated with a B.S. degree in 1969. After a couple of years away from school, Evans returned to the university, to pursue a master's degree in business administration, which he earned in 1973.

In 1975 Evans joined Tom Brown Inc., an oil-exploration and -production company located in Midland, Texas. Although he was hired as an executive, Evans wanted to see the business from the bottom up, so he spent two months working as a roughneck (a slang term for "laborer") on the company's oil rigs before returning to executive work.

By this point Evans had married the former Susan Marinis, who had grown up in Midland. When George W. Bush, who had gone to elementary school with Susan, returned to Midland during the Texas oil boom, he looked her up and met Donald Evans. The two soon became good friends and often played basketball and golf together. Evans also invested in some oil wells owned by Bush's firm.

Some months after the birth of the Evanses' second child, Jennifer, in 1976, the couple learned that the baby was mentally disabled. "It's devastating for someone to tell you that your daughter is retarded," Donald Evans once said, as quoted by Frank Bruni. "But once you get through that, it causes you to really get a deeper understanding of why you're here, what you're doing here. It gave me a chance to get reminded, in a big way, that I'm here to serve others." Bush was a strong source of support during this period, bringing the two men closer together. "It was more than business," Evans told David Firestone for the *New York Times* (July 5, 1999). "We shared a lot of the same values and beliefs. Both of us were out there at the same age, building our families, pursuing the American dream, both of us believing our highest calling in life is to serve other people, getting involved in United Way, our church, immersing ourselves in the community."

In 1978, when Bush ran unsuccessfully for Congress, Evans helped raise money for his campaign. The following year Evans became president of Tom Brown Inc. In 1985 he became CEO of that company. That same year he and a group of friends pressed Bush to get into an adult Bible study group. Evans later gave his friend a guide for reading the entire Bible in daily segments over the course of a year. In 1989 Evans became a member of the advisory council of the College of Business Administration at the University of Texas at Austin. Evans was also involved in community work, serving as a trustee of Memorial Hospital and Medical Center in Midland from 1990 until 1994 and as chairman of the Beefeater Ball of the Midland Cerebral Palsy Center. In 1994 Evans was the leading fund-raiser in George W. Bush's first run for the office of governor of Texas. In addition, Evans was always around to make sure that Bush did not get overtired while campaigning. After Bush's victory, Evans was appointed chairman of the 1995 Texas Inaugural Committee. Bush also appointed him to a six-year term on the board of regents of the University of Texas System. The board named him chairman two years later and reelected him to that position in 1999.

When George W. Bush ran for governor in 1998, Evans was once again his principal fund-raiser. In 1999, when Bush ran for the presidency, Evans was named national finance chairman. By the time the primary season was over, the Bush campaign had raised over $80 million, more than any other candidate had ever collected during the primaries. "This is the easiest fund-raising I've ever done in my life," Evans told David Firestone. "Usually political campaigns are a tough sell, and you always worry that someone's going to ask you for something in return. This time, you call someone and they say, 'Oh, I'm so glad you called me. I was wondering how to make a contribution.'" Evans set up the Bush network of "Pioneers," people committed to raising $100,000 each. In addition, he was responsible for calling upon governors who had endorsed Bush to "push their state check-writing operations into overdrive," as Firestone put it. "Behind every check, there's a willing heart," Evans told Firestone. "To me, it's not a check, it's a person, someone who cares about this great country." During the primaries, Evans was also there to comfort Bush during the tenser moments and relax him with idle conversation. "He knows that I don't particularly care for advice sometimes, just conversation," Bush was quoted as saying by Frank Bruni. "There's that mental down time that candidates need—not to be always on, always answering and figuring out the next step. If he asks me a question, I can tell him I don't want to answer it without hurting his feelings."

After Bush was assured of his party's nomination—following the withdrawal of his rival John McCain, a U.S. senator from Arizona, in March 2000—Evans was named chairman of Bush's presidential campaign. Frank Bruni noted in the *New York Times* (April 29, 2000) that the appointment "suggested the degree to which Mr. Bush wants to keep control over his presidential bid concentrated away from Washington, among the Texans who have already brought him this far." Although Evans had little political experience, Bush trusted him. "He is an experienced chief executive. . . . He has my complete confidence," Bush said, as

quoted in the same article. As chairman of the campaign, Evans helped coordinate the activities of the rest of the Bush team. In December 2000, after Bush was declared president-elect, he nominated Evans for the position of secretary of commerce.

On January 20, 2001, after his confirmation by the U.S. Senate, Evans was sworn in as the 34th secretary of commerce. With a budget of $5.1 billion, the Commerce Department promotes U.S. business development and job creation, international trade, and technology. Among its divisions are the Bureau of Export Administration; the Bureau of the Census; the Minority Business Development Agency; the National Oceanic and Atmospheric Administration; and the Patent and Trademark Office. According to Evans, as quoted on the Department of Commerce Web site, the mission of the department is "to create an environment in which American businesses and American capital can thrive at home and abroad." The same Web site reported that Evans "has set out an aggressive agenda, with a focus on open and fair trade; e-commerce; accurate and timely economic data; sound science; and development of cutting-edge technology."

On March 23, 2001 Evans told a private gathering of Silicon Valley executives that the construction of new nuclear-power plants is the long-term answer to the nation's recent energy woes, an idea still widely rejected for health and environmental reasons. While many on the political left attributed the energy crisis that temporarily gripped California in the winter of 2000–01 to the deregulation of electric companies, Evans supported deregulation and blamed the way that it had been carried out. Although both he and the Bush administration have come under attack for their stands on environmental issues, Evans was quoted by Reuters (April 22, 2001, on-line) as saying, "When people look at [Bush's] record on the environment in the years ahead . . . they will say he is pro-environment." Regarding the Free Trade of the Americas pact, under discussion in Quebec City in April 2001, Evans responded to protestors' claims that the agreement would be harmful to the environment and to labor: "We take the perspective that as you increase prosperity . . . that's good for labor, that's good for the environment," he said, as quoted by Reuters. "But should there be linkage of that to protectionism? No there should not." He later added, "This is going to take some time to work through. . . . I'm not taking a position on trade sanctions or fines or how labor or environment will be or won't be included in the agreement. . . . These are all issues that need to be discussed."

Before he became secretary of commerce, Evans was a major force behind Native Vision, a program that provides services to approximately 10,000 Native American children. He was a member of the Independent Petroleum Association of America, co-chairman of the Midland Wildcat Committee, and a director of the Permian Basin Petroleum Association and the Permian Basin Petroleum Museum. He has also been a member of the Young Presidents' Organization-49ers and the Rocky Mountain Oil and Gas Association. He sat on the board of the Scleroderma Research Foundation of Santa Barbara, California, and was active in the United Way of Midland, the YMCA, and Young Life of Midland. At the First United Methodist Church of Midland, Evans was at various times chairman of the church's finance committee, the administrative board, and the staff/parish relations committee.

Evans currently lives in Washington, D.C. He is said to speak with a Texan drawl and to carry himself in a dignified manner. He and his wife, Susan, have two daughters and a son. — G.O.

Suggested Reading: *Business Week* Apr. 2, 2001, with photo; *Nation* p19+ Jan. 29, 2001; *New York Times* A p7 July 5, 1999, with photo, A p33 Dec. 21, 2000, with photo; *New York Times* (on-line) Apr. 29, 2000, Apr. 30, 2000

Stewart Mark

Farhi, Nicole
(FAHR-ee)

July 25, 1946– Fashion designer. Address: 10 E. 60th St., New York, NY 10022; 16 Fouberts Pl., London W1F 7PJ, England

Prior to 1999, when the French-born fashion designer Nicole Farhi opened her flagship U.S. store in New York City, she enjoyed only a limited reputation in this country. In the United Kingdom, however, which she had called home since she moved there from France in her late 20s, Farhi was already a household name. Often dubbed "the

Donna Karan of London," a reference to one of the most commercially successful female designers in the States, Farhi was known for simple, elegant designs that focused on comfort and wearability rather than attention-grabbing colors and revealing patterns. In the last two years she has taken the U.S. by storm and established herself as an international force in fashion. Farhi's store on Manhattan's East Side now features—in addition to her full line of men's and women's fashions—home furnishings and an ultra-chic restaurant, called Nicole's. In addition to New York and London, Farhi has stores in Manchester, England; Oslo, Norway; and Tokyo, Japan.

Nicole Farhi was born on July 25, 1946 in Nice, France. Her father, Ephraim, a Turkish Jew, had left his homeland in the 1920s and emigrated to southeastern France, where he met and married Nicole Farhi's mother, Corinne Babani, also of Turkish descent. Ephraim "Freddy" Farhi owned and operated a rug dealership until his death, in 1979. When Nicole Farhi turned 18 years old, she moved north, to Paris, to pursue an art education. She soon found that painting and drawing, which brought her much satisfaction, did not provide her with a living wage. As she explained to Andy Beckett for the London *Guardian* (September 27, 1997), "I wanted to do something that would make some money, quickly. I was asked to do some sketches for a fashion magazine, *Depeche Mode*. I did my sketches, and then they said, 'Why don't you design?'" Upon her graduation from art school, Farhi took that advice and began to procure freelance assignments from various clothing makers. Much of her early work was done for the children's-clothing industry. She then created designs for the popular denim company Lee Cooper, which in turn led, in 1973, to a permanent contract with the French company Pierre D'Alby. One licensee of the company's products at the time was Stephen Marks, a British retailer. Before meeting Farhi, Marks had founded his own, small clothing-design and -manufacturing company in his native country and hoped to expand it into a full-time operation. Marks told Louise Chunn for the London *Guardian* (October 5, 1992), "I had another designer working for me at first, but Nicole would come over from Paris and criticise everything we were doing, so I said, you do it then." Farhi took him up on his offer and moved to London. She later became romantically involved with Marks; their daughter, Candice, was born in 1975.

Like her work at Lee Cooper, Farhi's designs at Marks's company, French Connection, demanded an adherence to a fairly rigid style; the clothes were to be mass-produced and therefore had to suit factory criteria for production. This meant that Farhi's designs could not change dramatically from year to year. Still, her design expertise helped to bring about the company's emergence as a world-recognized clothing manufacturer.

Ten years after the birth of their daughter, Farhi and Marks separated. Their professional collaboration, however, continued to flourish. It was Marks who suggested that Farhi develop her own signature line of clothing, which he would back financially. The clothing label Nicole Farhi first appeared in 1989. Meanwhile, Farhi continued to serve as French Connection's head designer until 1991. She described to Chunn the importance of Marks in her life: "I believe that the great chance in my life was meeting Stephen. He has backed me all the way, because he believes in fashion and is not afraid of anything—spending money, opening shops, working hard." Farhi further explained that she and Marks "have always got on" and have maintained good relations since their divorce. Marks continues to run the company he founded, which is now called the French Connection Group PLC and still owns the Nicole Farhi line. "I probably could never have my own business," Farhi told Andy Beckett. "I don't understand finances at all."

In only its second year of operation, the Nicole Farhi line began to garner much critical praise. Farhi was awarded the British Design Council's Award of Design Excellence for her 1991 collection. The following year she was nominated for a Designer of the Year honor at the British Fashion Awards, held in London. While she did not win the award, the nomination greatly enhanced her reputation. Since then Farhi has been recognized seven more times at the British Fashion Awards. She won the Contemporary Collections award for three consecutive years beginning in 1995. In 1993 she opened her first concession in Harvey Nichols, an upscale London retailer. A year later her first private boutiques opened in London and New York. In 2000 she was named Designer of the Year by *FHM*, a British men's magazine.

Meanwhile, in 1992 Farhi received an invitation from the Tony Award–winning British playwright David Hare to attend the London opening of his play *Murmuring Judges*. (Farhi had designed the costumes for the lead actress in the production.) In a conversation with Libby Callaway for the *New York Post* (September 6, 1999, on-line), she said of meeting Hare, "I saw him and my heart went bloop and missed a beat." Shortly thereafter the designer and playwright took up residence together; they were married in 1994. Farhi told Callaway, "There's a big change in my life that corresponds to when I met David. My collections became better, I started using more colors. . . . And if I look at the gross [earnings] of the company, it's improved." Farhi also told Callaway about an unforeseen consequence of her marriage: "I remember giving an interview very soon after getting married, and the journalist said, 'We are very proud that you have crossed over to the intellectual world.' I thought, how strange . . . because I never thought about it that way. But the journalist said [the marriage] gives the fashion world status, that it makes fashion seem like not just a fleeting thing, and makes it sound like something that is serious." Farhi herself had a different view of the matter. In an Associated Press article (April 14, 2000, on-line), Carol Deegan quoted the designer as saying, "I'm just doing clothes, I'm not doing art. I'd do something else if I want to do an art show."

Unlike those of many fashion designers, Farhi's runway shows have tended to be conservative; she has eschewed theatricality, instead choosing to stake her reputation on the clothes themselves. She admitted as much to Louise Chunn: "I realise I'm not so much fun to write about as more extreme designers. But this is what I do. I had no expectations when we started out, so I don't feel disappointed or ignored." In fact, Farhi is dismissive of runway shows in general; she was quoted in an article for *In Style* (January 2000) as saying, "I love doing a [clothing] line but hate presenting [it] on the runway, whittling down six months' work into 20 minutes. You can't do it justice. . . . When your clothes become a welcome part of someone's life, that's real style." Her designs have been worn by such international figures as the British first lady, Cherie Blair, and the actresses Cate Blanchett, Nicole Kidman, and Dame Judi Dench.

Farhi's anti-industry attitude, and her connection with a company that mass-produces clothing, have led many critics to dismiss the designer's styles as being geared toward the tastes of the unsophisticated. (They are not usually geared toward the frugal; the price of a Farhi dress sometimes exceeds $1,000.) Stephen Marks described Farhi's collections to Louise Chunn as "wearable. . . . [They] can easily be worn with items from previous seasons and [the clothes] last well." Marks admitted that any lack of critical acceptance suffered by Farhi is his own doing. "We're just a bit too commercially successful for Nicole to be rated in the way she should be. . . . She's close to being a design genius but the press want their designers to be wacky and not terribly together; they don't want to know how well we're doing. Nicole proves that the press don't know what . . . they're talking about and the public do. They vote with their purses."

When Farhi and Marks decided to expand their operation to include a large retail space in New York, they hired the design firm Michael Gabellini to handle the duties. The New York–based firm, which had designed award-winning boutiques for the fashion gurus Jil Sander and Giorgio Armani, chose an historic building in which to house the new Nicole Farhi. Located at 10 East 60th Street in Manhattan, the 20,000-square-foot structure, built in 1901, had housed the legendary Copacabana nightclub—which, in its heyday in the mid-20th century, regularly hosted such entertainers as Frank Sinatra and Tony Bennett. Like Farhi's collections, the store was designed to be simple yet elegant. Mirroring her flagship store in London, the New York location would also have a restaurant. Speaking of the design, Farhi told Jessie Carry for *FoodandWine.com* (March 2000), "I wanted the store to be friendly and to have very friendly food."

To this end Farhi brought in Annie Wayte, who had been executive chef of her London location, to head the New York restaurant. She also hired the American chef Anna Kovel to serve as Wayte's second-in-command. The New York Nicole Farhi carries home furnishings as well as men's and women's clothing. After the terrorist strikes in the United States on September 11, 2001, the London *Guardian* (September 17, 2001) reported, Farhi canceled the scheduled presentation of her spring/summer 2002 fashion show in London, out of respect for those who had lost their lives as a result of the attacks.

Farhi is still based in London; she lives in Hampstead, a traditionally artistic enclave in the city's north, with her husband, who—since he met

Farhi—has been knighted for his theatrical achievements. When Alan Jackson, writing for the London *Times* (September 19, 1998), asked the designer whether she takes advantage of the title she is now afforded, she answered, "No, I don't. I'm not Lady Hare. I will always be Nicole Farhi." — J.H.

Suggested Reading: Associated Press (on-line) Apr. 14, 2000, with photo; *FoodandWine.com* Mar. 2000; (London) *Guardian* p31 Oct. 5, 1992, with photos, p3 Sep. 27, 1997, p22 July 25, 2000; (London) *Times* p9 Sep. 19, 1998; *New York* (on-line) Sep. 13, 1999; *New York Post* (on-line) Sep. 6, 1999, with photo; *New York Times* F p1 Aug. 19, 1999, with photos, F p12 Nov. 10, 1999, with photo

---

Farrelly, Peter and Bobby

Peter Farrelly
Dec. 17, 1956– Screenwriter; director; producer; novelist

Bobby Farrelly
1958– Screenwriter; director; producer

Address: c/o Bumble Ward, 8383 Wilshire Blvd., Suite 340, Beverly Hills, CA 90211

In the 1990s the films of Peter and Bobby Farrelly spawned the genre of "gross-out" comedy, in which few subjects are taboo; films such as Paul Weitz's *American Pie* (1999) and Todd Phillips's *Road Trip* (2000) have since gone to great lengths to outdo the plethora of memorably outrageous comic episodes that made the Farrelly brothers' *Dumb and Dumber* (1994) and *There's Something About Mary* (1998) popular. Although the Farrelly brothers typically build visual gags around bodily fluids, physical handicaps, and imperiled domestic animals, there is an undercurrent of gentleness and sentimentality in their films. Audiences have connected with their work in part because of its emphasis on characterization and the filmmakers' display of sympathy for the underdog. "The people we laugh at in our movies are those who aren't nice," Bobby Farrelly told *Mr. Showbiz* (on-line). "They're the bad guys. The joke is usually on them. The nice people [also] have things happen to them, but it's just the foibles of being human, like the embarrassment of going through life. It's not anything personal."

Although some reviewers have raised objections to the Farrelly brothers' willingness to push—or cross—boundaries of good taste, the films appear to be critic-proof. "There's two lines," Peter Farrelly explained to Jess Cagle for *CNN.com* (July 27, 1998). "There's a line that the critics will tell you is there. And then there's the real line. And the real line is what we go towards. We never cross that

line. . . . We know when we cross the line. That's when they don't laugh, because the audience won't laugh if it's truly mean-spirited." The often scatological nature of their material harkens back to the vaudeville tradition, in which working-class characters used humor as a means of dealing with the difficulty of everyday life. Jeanine Basinger, the chair of the film-studies program at Wesleyan University, who includes *There's Something About Mary* in her American film comedy class, told John Brodie for *Gentlemen's Quarterly* (June 2000), "[The Farrelly brothers] are to the year 2000 what Preston Sturges was to 1944. They are the freewheeling, antiestablishment voice of comedy. In Sturges's day, a lot of people found him utterly vulgar, and now he seems like the height of sophistication." The Farrellys are so determined to make their audiences laugh that they test-screen each film and have eliminated sequences based on the comments they receive. "Nobody tests movies more than we do," Peter Farrelly told *IGN Movies* (June 22, 2000, on-line). "I don't think there's anyone in the business who does. . . . We get so much feedback from just listening. You know when someone's finding it funny and when they're not. So we show it ten times or so before we even show it to the studio."

Peter and Bobby Farrelly endeavor to make the film set a comfortable environment for actors, hoping that they will thus feel free to experiment. "Our feeling is that the most important thing on a set is that actors have enough confidence to try different things," Peter Farrelly told Anson Lang for *Bold Type* (June 1998, on-line). "If there's stress or tension they won't go out on a limb because they won't want to embarrass themselves if they don't feel completely comfortable. . . . Even the best actors, like Jim Carrey and Bill Murray—these guys will hit it 8 or 9 out of 10 times, they'll be on something incredibly funny, but 1 out of 10, 2 out of 10, they'll fall flat on their faces. That's what makes them great actors . . . they take those chances, they don't play it safe. It doesn't always work, but if

Peter (left) and Bobby Farrelly   Bill Davila/Retna Ltd.

you're on a comfortable set, you don't mind failing, because you know you're among friends." Wild hairdos and tacky clothing feature prominently in the brothers' 1996 film *Kingpin* and *There's Something About Mary*, and the characters engage in physical comedy that some actors might find humiliating. "To me, [the Farrelly brothers'] genius is that they get actors to do things that you never thought you'd do," Ben Stiller, who starred in *There's Something About Mary*, told Kendall Hamilton for *Newsweek* (July 20, 1998). "Not until months later, when you see it up on screen, do you realize what you've done."

The Farrelly brothers labored for nearly a decade before they sold their first script, completing 15 unproduced screenplays and doctoring many more for big studios. They have since become one of the most popular comedy teams in Hollywood and have established a production company, Conundrum Entertainment. Discussing the brothers' partnership, Bobby Farrelly told Jess Cagle, "I think the reason it works first of all is there's a different level of trust. And basically we both share the same vision. It's a warped vision, but we share it. And I think that we're able to protect that vision more, because the people that come at you try to get you to water down what it is that you see." Since they first achieved success, with *Dumb and Dumber*, the Farrelly brothers have found work for their friends, who frequently appear in their films and sometimes direct their screenplays. (They have cast amateurs as actors, but their directors are professionals.) They take pride in being "the anti-Coens," Peter Farrelly told Kendall Hamilton, a reference to the highly regarded filmmakers Joel and Ethan Coen, who are also brothers. "Nobody analyzes our films—and we don't want them to."

Peter John Farrelly was born on December 17, 1956 in Phoenixville, Pennsylvania. Bobby Farrelly was born in Cumberland, Rhode Island, in 1958. They grew up in suburban Cumberland with their father, Robert, a doctor; their mother, Mariann, a nurse; and three sisters. Peter and Bobby Farrelly shared a room, played sports together, and spent time with the same group of friends. When he was a senior in high school, Peter Farrelly had a relationship that would play a large part in his decision to become a writer. "Her name was Cordo," he told Jeff Giles for *Newsweek* (July 3, 2000). "She was on every level a tremendous girl: gorgeous, kind, athletic, cool. And then I broke her heart the next year. . . . I did all the bad things. I was just scared. We didn't talk for a year, and then right when we were thinking about getting back together, she fell out of a car and died. I certainly don't want to use her as some . . . romantic thing that happened to me in my childhood, but she never knew how crazy I was about her, and her death really affected me. . . . When I became a writer, it was really to write something about her."

Peter Farrelly received a B.A. degree in business from Providence College, in Rhode Island, in 1979. After graduation he spent a few years as a salesman for U.S. Lines Inc., a shipping company. When his employment there ended, he suddenly found himself without direction, and he decided to pray for guidance. It soon occurred to him that he should write about his life experiences. Farrelly began filling notebooks with story ideas and succeeded in entering the graduate creative-writing program at the University of Massachusetts. In 1984, after one year there, he transferred to the writing program at Columbia University, in New York City, where he collaborated with Bennett Yellin, a friend whom he had met at the University of Massachusetts. Together they wrote a comedy entitled "Dust to Dust," about a Mafia-run funeral home; although it did not sell, the screenplay caught the attention of the film director David Zucker and the comedian Eddie Murphy. In 1985 Peter Farrelly left the East Coast for Los Angeles, where he worked on scripts for Paramount, Columbia, and Disney. He received an M.F.A. degree from Columbia University, through correspondence courses, in 1987. In the following year he published a novel, *Outside Providence*, about his apparently brief experience at a boarding school.

Bobby Farrelly attended Rensselaer Polytechnic Institute, in Troy, New York, where he played hockey and received a B.S. degree in geological engineering. "I was like a knucklehead, I barely stayed above the grade-point average where they throw you out," he told Mim Udovitch for *Rolling Stone* (July 6–20, 2000). "But all the time I was there, little did I realize, all the parties I went to, I was doing research." Like his brother, Bobby Farrelly went into sales following graduation, and he later invented the Sun Spot, the world's first circular beach towel. "The theory was that, as the sun moves, rather than move your towel—you just move your body," Peter Farrelly explained to Jeff Giles. "But it turns out that people don't mind moving their towel. They like to stretch out now and then." Although they did not live near one another, Peter Farrelly often sought his brother's advice. "For about two years, every time [Yellin and I] wrote a screenplay I'd send it off to my brother because I trusted his instincts with comedy, and story . . . ," Peter Farrelly told Alson Lang. "Finally after a couple of years of this I felt like we were taking advantage of him, because he was doing a lot of the work but he wasn't getting any credit, so we ended up writing a screenplay with him, and it was our best one." That screenplay, for a sequel to *Dragnet*, was never made into a film. The trio worked together until 1992, when Yellin left California.

The Farrelly brothers made money by touching up screenplays written by others; meanwhile, over a 10-year period, they collaborated on 15 ultimately unproduced scripts of their own. They were pleased when a script they had written for the popular television program *Seinfeld* was produced in 1992, but they yearned to make their own films. "Eventually our agent told us, 'Pick out your best script, make up your mind you're going to make this movie no matter what happens, and just tell people it's going to get made,'" Bobby Farrelly told *Mr. Showbiz*. "He convinced us to attach ourselves as directors and make the movie—raise whatever [funding] we needed, and then something might happen." The Farrellys found the break they were looking for when Jim Carrey, the comic actor then best known for his work on the TV show *In Living Color* and the film *Ace Ventura: Pet Detective* (1994), expressed an interest in appearing in the film, which was entitled *Dumb and Dumber*. "That

night we called David Zucker, who we'd written a script for," Peter Farrelly told Jeff Giles, "and we said, 'We're in a nightmare situation. We're beginning a major motion picture, and we don't know what we're doing.' He said, 'Relax. Just be honest with your crew. If you pretend you know what you're doing and you don't, they'll let you drown.' So we worked out a signal with our first assistant director, J. B. Rogers. When I was supposed to yell 'Action,' [Roger would] signal me, and [when the shot was completed] Bobby would yell 'Cut!'"

Peter Farrelly made his directing debut with the film, which stars Carrey and Jeff Daniels as dim-witted roommates who have various misadventures while traveling to Aspen, Colorado. Co-written by the Farrelly brothers and Bennett Yellin, *Dumb and Dumber* earned over $340 million worldwide, making it one of the largest-grossing films for a first-time director in the history of cinema. Peter Farrelly found directing to be "the biggest scam in the world," he told Kendall Hamilton. "I wish everybody could direct one movie because you know what? Everybody could." Peter and Bobby Farrelly then co-directed *Kingpin*, a comedy about a former bowling champion (played by Woody Harrelson) who attempts to recapture his glory by coaching an Amish man (Randy Quaid) with a talent for the game.

The release of *There's Something About Mary*, which the Farrellys co-wrote, co-produced, and co-directed, solidified the brothers' reputation as purveyors of the "gross-out" comedy films that were so vilified by critics—even as audiences flocked to them and other filmmakers struggled to replicate their success. "We never thought this would appeal to everyone," Bobby Farrelly told Jess Cagle. "And, you know, some people just don't get it." *There's Something About Mary* stars Ben Stiller as Ted, an unpopular teenager who is surprised when Mary (Cameron Diaz), one of the most beautiful girls in his class, agrees to accompany him to the prom. But their date is brought to an abrupt halt when Ted catches his genitals in his zipper and is taken from Mary's home by ambulance, as most of the neighbors look on. (Like many scenes in the Farrelly brothers' films, the notorious zipper sequence was based on a real-life occurrence.) Years after losing touch with Mary, Ted finds himself unable to forget her, so he hires a private investigator, Healy (Matt Dillon), to look for her. But Healy himself becomes obsessed with Mary, who is unaware that the two men—among others—are competing for her affections.

The comic set pieces in *There's Something About Mary* involve masturbation, the abuse of domestic animals, and mental retardation. Although many critics focused on the shocking aspects of the film, the Farrelly brothers won over audiences by populating the story with flawed but likable characters. Peter Farrelly told Ian Caddell for *Reelwest.com* that the scene in *Mary* he found "most memorable" is the one in which Healy, reporting back to Ted about Mary, "lies to him, saying 'she's

250 pounds and she's on welfare and she has a bunch of kids and she's in a wheelchair.' . . . And [Ted] says 'I don't care.' That's what makes the movie, because you feel [Ted] deserves her. Anyone can fall in love with Cameron Diaz. So what! Why should you root for that? But when he doesn't care what she looks like years later, that's what makes it work." Some took issue with the film's portrayal of Mary's brother, a mentally disabled man who becomes violent whenever anyone touches his ears. But the Farrelly brothers have insisted that the humor in his scenes grows naturally out of the situations in which the characters find themselves. "It's not malicious in any way," Cameron Diaz told Jess Cagle. "We're not making fun of mentally challenged people. We're making fun of the people who make fun of mentally challenged people."

Peter Farrelly's second novel, the semi-autobiographical *The Comedy Writer*, was published in 1998. The story is narrated by Henry Halloran, a struggling Hollywood screenwriter, who has seen a woman jump off a building to her death and writes about the experience for the *Los Angeles Times Magazine*. Discussing the incident that inspired the novel—Farrelly's unsuccessful attempt to talk a woman out of jumping from a roof—Farrelly told Marcus Dunk for the London *Daily Express* (March 25, 2000, on-line), "In the piece I mentioned that before she killed herself, I asked her to have coffee with me so she could talk about what was bothering her, and after the article came out, I was contacted by about 30 to 40 seriously depressed people who were also suicidal, asking me to have coffee with them. I ended up running all over southern California for about three weeks meeting with people and just listening to them all while I was trying to write comedy. . . . I was really disappointed that I hadn't helped this woman more. I tried, and it could have gone either way, but it didn't go the right way so when these people called I was really open to them. But on the other hand, I changed my phone number, so it wasn't like I wanted to do it for a career. But in any case it gave me the idea for this book." *The Comedy Writer*'s many comic situations are counterbalanced by serious themes, such as the difficulties encountered in relationships.

The following year saw the release of a movie based on Peter Farrelly's first novel, *Outside Providence*. Co-written by the Farrellys and directed by their friend Michael Corrente, the film stars Shawn Hatosy as Timothy Dunphy, a working-class teen whose father (Alec Baldwin) is forced to send him away to a private school when the son gets in trouble with the law. (Corrente had purchased the novel for one dollar in a used-book shop in East Hampton, Long Island, and later bought the movie rights for the same amount. "[Peter Farrelly] wrote about this white trash kid from Pawtucket, and that was me," Corrente told Dana Kennedy for the *New York Times* [August 29, 1999]. "It sounds goofy, but that's what moved me so much about the book. It

was my story.") Although the film was more serious than the brothers' previous work, it was marketed as an outrageous comedy, over Peter Farrelly's objections.

The Farrelly brothers' film *Me, Myself & Irene* (2000) stars Jim Carrey as a mild-mannered man who, after years of putting up with humiliation and abuse from others, develops a split personality. Both his meek self and his new, aggressive side pursue Irene (Renée Zellweger) romantically. *Say It Isn't So* (2001), produced by Peter and Bobby Farrelly and directed by J. B. Rogers, is a comedy about incest and mistaken identity. The brothers' film *Osmosis Jones*, is a partially animated comedy about a battle between a group of germs and the immune system of a man who eats a tainted meatball. The film, directed by the Farrelly brothers and starring Bill Murray and Chris Rock, was released in August 2001. It was followed in November by *Shallow Hal*, about Hal Larson (Jack Black), who, in his quest for physically perfect women, epitomizes shallowness. After an unexpected encounter with the self-help guru Tony Robbins (playing himself), Hal sees women's inner beauty rather than their bodies. He falls in love with Rosemary (Gwyneth Paltrow), a kind, humorous, 300-pound Peace Corps volunteer who, in his eyes, is shapely and beautiful. "This movie is anything but an affront to heavy or unattractive women," Peter Farrelly said, as quoted on *Premiere* (on-line). "Our goal has always been to make a movie that's funny and sweet and ultimately a tearjerker." Some moviegoers, however, complained that the filmmakers had muddled the idea that beauty is in the eye of the beholder and had failed to properly convey the message that character is more important than looks. On the other hand, the film critic A. O. Scott of the *New York Times* (November 9, 2001), observing that *Shallow Hal* is "comparatively restrained when it comes to bodily effluvia and leering dirty jokes," went on to add, "The most shocking thing about it may be its unabashed sincerity. There are enough moments of demented comedy to make you aspirate your popcorn, but by the end you may find yourself, with some amazement, sniffing back tears."

Peter and Bobby Farrelly live in Duxbury, Massachusetts—Peter with his wife, Melinda, and Bobby with his wife, Nancy, and their two children. — C.L.

Suggested Reading: *Gentlemen's Quarterly* p150+ June 2000, with photos; *New York Times* II p9 Aug. 29, 1999, with photos; *Newsweek* p64+ July 20, 1998, with photos, p54+ July 3, 2000, with photos; *Rolling Stone* p94+ July 6–20, 2000, with photos

Selected Films by Bobby Farrelly: as director—*Kingpin*, 1996; as writer and producer—*Outside Providence*, 1999; as writer and producer—*Dumb and Dumber*, 1994; as director and producer—*Osmosis Jones*, 2001 as writer, director, and executive producer—*There's Something About Mary*, 1998; as writer, and director, and producer—*Me, Myself and Irene*, 2000; *Shallow Hal*, 2001

Selected Films by Peter Farrelly: as director—*Kingpin*, 1996; as producer—*Outside Providence*, 1999; as writer and director—*Dumb and Dumber*, 1994; as director and producer—*Osmosis Jones*, 2001; as writer, director, and executive producer—*There's Something About Mary*, 1998; as writer, director, and producer—*Me, Myself & Irene*, 2000; *Shallow Hal*, 2001

Selected Books: by Peter Farrelly—*Outside Providence*, 1988; *The Comedy Writer*, 1998

Michael Nichols © 2001 National Geographic Society

Fay, J. Michael

Sep. 19, 1956– Conservation biologist. Address: Wildlife Conservation Society, 185th St. and Southern Blvd., Bronx, NY 10460

"Almost half of Earth's original forest cover is gone, much of it destroyed within the past three decades," the conservation biologist J. Michael Fay stated in 1997, during testimony before a congressional committee investigating the economic development of Africa's natural resources. "Africa contains one of the three large blocks of the world's tropical forests. Originally Africa had about 6,799 km² [square kilometers]. Today only 2,302 km², or 34 percent, remains. Much of what has been lost has been as a result of the rapid expansion of the logging industry followed by uncontrolled land

use in every country with forest in Africa in the last 30 years. These logging operations are having catastrophic consequences for the ecosystems, the flora and fauna, the economy and the people of these forests." As a scientist employed by the Wildlife Conservation Society (WCS), which is based at the Bronx Zoo, in New York City, Fay has taken a pivotal role in efforts to protect what remains of central Africa's tropical forests. Not only has he worked to establish national parks and preserves, he has also made efforts, in collaboration with magazines such as *National Geographic*, to raise public awareness about the destruction of these unique ecosystems.

J. Michael Fay was born in Plainfield, New Jersey, on September 19, 1956. He grew up in New Jersey and in Pasadena, California. He first traveled to central Africa in the 1980s, to do fieldwork on lowland gorillas in the Central African Republic for his doctoral degree; with the help of a Pygmy tracker and the financial support of the National Geographic Society, Fay spent several weeks following a group of the reclusive primates. He took to this sort of research immediately.

Soon after Fay returned to the United States to write his dissertation, Richard Barnes, a well-known elephant biologist, asked him to conduct a survey of forest elephants under the auspices of the European Community; the work was to be done in a tract of uninhabited land in the northern part of the Republic of Congo, in west-central Africa. (A distinct subspecies of the African elephant, forest elephants are smaller than their savannah relatives and have straighter tusks.) Bounded by swamps to the south and east, hills to the north, and the unnavigable Ndoki River to the west, the region in which Fay worked has long remained virtually inaccessible. It is home to a variety of large mammals, including (in addition to elephants) western lowland gorillas, chimpanzees, leopards, and bongos (a type of forest antelope)—what some conservation biologists term "charismatic megafauna," because of their usefulness in promoting conservation projects. (By contrast, such small creatures as mongooses and shrews seldom generate much human sympathy, even when they or their habitats are endangered. The same holds true for animals not traditionally considered appealing, such as bats or insects.) The forest, which had never been logged, also contained more than 300 bird species and at least 1,000 plant species. Yet, in spite of its remoteness, it was threatened by logging, since many of the surrounding areas had already been depleted of their stock of valuable African mahogany—often with dire consequences for the entire forest ecosystem, as well as for the local peoples who depended upon it for their livelihoods.

In his 1997 congressional testimony on logging, forest ecosystems, and people in northern Congo, Fay gave a detailed account of logging procedures in the region. First, detailed maps are drafted and used to record the locations of individual, commercially valuable trees. Next, a network of logging roads is constructed—an undertaking that is often very damaging to the forest and that is often accompanied by activities that further harm the ecosystem, such as unchecked hunting and slash-and-burn agriculture. Furthermore, because most logging firms rarely hire the local people who had depended on the forest for their livelihoods, indigenous groups like the Pygmies "are marginalized and usually live in extreme poverty," as Fay testified. Ultimately, he concluded, forest ecosystems harvested in such a manner are "damaged beyond repair."

Fay soon became involved in efforts to protect the region in which he had conducted his research. By 1991 he had been named director of a project launched jointly by several international organizations (most prominently the Wildlife Conservation Society) and the Congolese government with the goal of establishing a wilderness preserve. But while the Congolese government expressed interest in cooperating with the WCS and other groups, it was not willing to divert financial resources for conservation projects. As cited in Fay's congressional testimony, transcribed on the Web site of the U.S. House of Representatives, the Congo's minister of agriculture, animal husbandry, water, forests, and fisheries relayed to the U.S. Congress via Fay, "The priority of the Republic of Congo is development for its people. If this necessitates the destruction of the forests of the country, it will be done. Conscious of the need to conserve its forest resources, which are essential for the long term development of the country, the Republic of Congo accepts efforts to conserve and sustainably manage its forests. It is a question of funding and training. If the resources for management do not come from the outside, it is highly unlikely that the Government of Congo will make these resources available."

The government's position notwithstanding, Fay helped secure the necessary funding for the proposed preserve, and in December 1993 a one-million-acre site was officially designated the Nouabalé-Ndoki National Park. Further, Fay helped negotiate a management plan with the Congolese government, indigenous people, and a number of logging companies active in the region, whereby a central section of the park was designated off-limits to all but conservation-related activities, while sustainable logging, subsistence hunting, and tourism were to be permitted in a so-called buffer zone on the periphery of the park. Such buffer zones are intended to be sustainable sources of revenue, thus demonstrating, according to Fay, that wilderness preservation can be combined with, and can even enhance, the long-term economic development of surrounding areas. As Fay pointed out in his congressional testimony, for many years foreign logging companies (most of them based in Europe), rather than local people and the Congolese government, have profited most from the exploitation of central African forest resources; whatever benefits accrue to the Congolese

are meager and short-lived. Fay has expressed the hope that the Nouabalé-Ndoki National Park will serve as a model for preserving other wilderness areas in central Africa.

Throughout the 1990s, in addition to managing the Nouabalé-Ndoki National Park, Fay continued to promote conservation projects in the Congo. After it became evident that large numbers of elephants were being poached for their ivory in spite of the international ban on the ivory trade that went into effect in 1989, Fay took measures to reduce the number of elephants slaughtered for their tusks. Since the actual hunters of the elephants—local villagers—did not profit significantly from the illegal trade (they were paid small sums to provide raw ivory to exporters), Fay approached them with a counterproposal. "We went into every village that was identified as a center of poaching," he told Gloria Chang for the Discovery Channel Canada (May 26, 1997, on-line). "We said 'Listen guys, there's a problem. There's lots of elephants being killed. We know you're killing them so let's try to solve this problem together.' . . . And that's exactly what we did. . . . We just went over to the shooters and said we think we can offer you more than you're getting now." By outbidding the ivory traders, Fay was able to hire a number of former poachers as wardens entrusted with guarding the elephants. The result, Fay told Chang, has been a sharp drop in the number of elephants killed for their ivory.

In his most recent project—a 2,000-kilometer trek through tropical forest from the Central African Republic through northeastern Congo to the coast of Gabon, for the purpose of collecting data about plants and animals—Fay was able to indulge his love of field research while building on his previous work in wilderness preservation. In a playful allusion to a research technique known as a transect survey, which involves traversing the site under study in a straight line and collecting data along the way, Fay dubbed his undertaking the Megatransect. He didn't travel in a straight line, though: rather, his itinerary wound through the forest all the way to the Atlantic coast. Fay has expressed hope that the information he gathered along the way will be used by the governments of the Central African Republic, Congo, and Gabon to protect ecologically valuable lands and to promote sustainable development; as John Hart, a WCS senior scientist, told Richard Stone for *Science* (August 6, 1999), the Megatransect "offers an unprecedented opportunity for an ecological snapshot on a large scale." The expedition, which was sponsored by the National Geographic Society and was featured in *National Geographic*, is also expected to generate public support for the conservation of central Africa's forests. "I want people to feel the magic of walking on an elephant highway through groves of ancient trees," Fay told David Quammen for *National Geographic* (October 2000).

Fay has likened his trek through Africa's equatorial forests to the early-19th-century expedition conducted by Meriwether Lewis and William Clark in the American West, before white people began settling there. "The parallels are overwhelming," he told Stone. Fay went on to explain his sympathy for Lewis, who was killed—by his own hand, most historians believe—three years after completing the expedition. Fay speculated to Stone about the reasons for Lewis's death: "He just couldn't handle the fact that the area west of the Mississippi was going to be completely colonized," he said. "It just drove him crazy, he loved that place so much."

Fay now considers the central African forests his home. "I plan on dying out here," he told David Quammen while on a trek. "I'll never go back to live in the U.S." In one recent instance when he did return—to drum up support for his conservation work and to set up a computer database for keeping track of his research—Fay lived much as he did while exploring the bush. According to Elizabeth Royte in the New Yorker (May 14, 2001), Fay slept on the floor of his hotel room or even on the streets, foraged for food, and often went outside to urinate. (An assistant of Fay's at National Geographic stressed that this arrangement was temporary.) "I'm not trying to make a point by not sleeping in a bed and by not driving a car," Fay told Royte.

"You just don't need all this stuff. I hardly buy food. People are always giving me something—a cookie or a banana in the office. There's food everywhere. You go for cocktails and there are hors d'oeuvres and cheese and crackers. After that, you go out for dinner! Who can eat all this stuff?"

"Behind his wire-rimmed glasses, with their round, smoky lenses, he bears a disquieting resemblance to the young [film director] Roman Polanski," Quammen, who accompanied him during some of his research expeditions, wrote about Fay. "Say something that's doltish or disagreeable, and he'll gaze at you silently the way a heron, hungry or not, gazes at a fish. But on the trail he's good company, a man of humor and generous intellect. He sets a punishing pace, starting at daylight, never stopping to lunch or rest, but when there are field data to record in his yellow notebook, fortunately, he pauses often." — P.K.

Suggested Reading: National Geographic p2+ Oct. 2000, with photos, p2+ Mar. 2001, with photos, p75+ Aug. 2001, with photos; National Geographic Society Web site; New Yorker p50 May 14, 2001; Save the Elephants Web site; Science p825 Aug. 6, 1999; U.S. House of Representatives Web site, Mar. 19, 1997; Wildlife Conservation Society Web site

---

Ferrer, Rafael

Jan. 25, 1933– Painter; sculptor; art educator.
Address: c/o Nancy Hoffman Gallery, 429 W.
Broadway, New York, NY 10012

In his paintings and sculptures, Rafael Ferrer uses bright colors and theatrical references to present humorous and sensual interpretations of everyday life. In developing his technique, the largely self-taught Ferrer, a native of Puerto Rico, was influenced by surrealism and Abstract Expressionism as well as the work of such modernist painters as Henri Matisse and Paul Gauguin. Some of Ferrer's work has also paid homage to the sculptors Alberto Giacometti and David Smith. "It is the brilliant color of Mr. Ferrer's paintings that invariably makes the first impression," Michael Kimmelman wrote for the New York Times (November 6, 1992). "And then it is his technical facility, which allows him to construct sophisticated plays of light and shadow and complex arrangements of forms yet still suggest the plain-spokenness of folk art."

Rafael Ferrer was born in Santurce, Puerto Rico, on January 25, 1933. From the time he was six months old, his family spent part of every year in New York City. From 1948 to 1951 Ferrer attended the Staunton Military Academy, in Staunton, Virginia, where he learned to play drums. As an undergraduate at Syracuse University, in Syra-

Self-portrait by Rafael Ferrer/Courtesy of
Nancy Hoffman Gallery

cuse, New York, he was a member of a popular Latin jazz group made up of musicians from the Crouse College of Fine Arts, which includes the university's School of Music. "Through these friends I began to meet painters and writers—a group of intense young people involved in various aspects of early twentieth century modernism," Ferrer recalled in *Drawing*, the catalogue that accompanied a 1995 exhibit of his drawings at the Nancy Hoffman Gallery, in New York City. "I began to paint on my own and this activity revealed to me something totally new: The intense pleasure of solitary work, and the immense dignity it conferred. Slowly I began to see the counterpoint between painting and drumming. The implacable intensity—indeed the intolerance of the professional musician—had found fertile ground in the internal needs of my psyche."

Ferrer left Syracuse University and later enrolled at the University of Puerto Rico in Mayaquez, where he studied painting. In 1953 he visited Paris with his instructor—and mentor—the Spanish painter Eugenio F. Granell; there he met several surrealist artists and writers, including André Breton, Man Ray, and Wifredo Lam. After earning a bachelor's degree, in 1954, he moved to New York City, where he supported himself as a drummer with jazz bands in Spanish Harlem. Playing this music taught him "to bring out the tropical, primitive, emotional conditions of one's roots into the open, and to rejoice in their messiness and to be . . . proud of their contradictions," as he told Robert Hughes for *Time* (February 28, 1977). For a short time he worked as an assistant stage manager on Broadway, a job he landed with the help of his half-brother, the actor José Ferrer.

After Ferrer returned to Puerto Rico, in 1959, he devoted himself to painting. In 1964 he had his first solo exhibition, at the University of Puerto Rico; during the next two years, his work was also featured in exhibits at local galleries. In 1966 Ferrer moved to Philadelphia, Pennsylvania, with his wife, Irene Alvarez, and their two children. He supported his family by teaching art, first at the Philadelphia College of Art (1967–77) and then at the School of Visual Arts, in Manhattan (1978–80), to which he apparently commuted from Philadelphia. Ferrer's first exhibition in the States took place in 1966, at the Pan-American Union headquarters in Washington, D.C.; it featured lighthearted sculptures fashioned from found objects, among them a typewriter and a barber pole. "I am making machines into humans," he explained to Carolyn Lewis for the *Washington Post* (June 15, 1966). "If my work seems funny, why, a sense of humor is essential in so terrible a world."

In the late 1960s Ferrer engaged in what came to be known as process art, which involves creating temporary installations with ice, leaves, or other ephemeral or degradable materials. He contributed a grease-covered haystack to the Whitney Museum's *Anti-Illusion* show in 1969; *Fuegian House with Harpy Eagle*, a structure made of two dozen 300-pound blocks of ice and a crayon drawing of an eagle, was exhibited at the Whitney Museum's Biennial exhibition in 1973. The art critic Peter Schjeldahl, writing for the *New York Times* (January 25, 1970), expressed the view that Ferrer's process art possessed both "a free-wheeling audacity" and "evidence of taste and resourcefulness to match."

During this period Ferrier spent time in both Puerto Rico and New York, and he found fault with each. "I don't like the messiness of the people [in Puerto Rico]," he told Kay Larson for *New York* (June 20, 1983). "But when I come to the States, I don't like the puritanical attitude. I don't like the restraint of the Americans. I don't like the fact that they're afraid of sex and anything that is too red or bright orange." But the vastness and complexity of the United States fascinated him. "I saw the North American Giant as tired, bleeding from excesses which were never meant to produce pleasures except perhaps those of a puritanical order, foreign and strange," he told Robert Hughes.

Ferrer spent much of the 1970s traveling in Europe, South America, and the United States; he also lived and worked in a house he had bought in Boqueron, Puerto Rico. Using an array of materials, including dried leaves, animal skins, plastic roses, wire, beads, burlap, and neon, he began to examine themes of travel, exploration, and colonization. Among other works, he created a series of uninhabitable tents, which Hughes described as "not so much environments . . . as three-dimensional paintings." Some of the tents have no openings; the openings of others are too small to be entered. "Their subject is landscape: moons and sand, licorice colored skies, cave darkness, vines," Hughes wrote. Ferrer's easel paintings during this period contained expressive figures and images of nightlife, drums, and human sexuality. In 1982 Ferrer married Françoise Stuart Crandall (he and Alvarez had divorced some years before). He began making frequent visits to the Dominican Republic and sometimes summered in Maine. In 1987 he built a house in the Samana Province of the Dominican Republic. Recently, in acts of homage to various artists, among them Alberto Giacometti, Giorgio Morandi, and David Smith, he created a series of paintings that show imagined views of the interiors of their studios.

Ferrer was the subject of a 10-year retrospective at El Museo del Barrio in New York City in 1983. His work is in the permanent collections of various museums, including the Metropolitan Museum of Art, the Whitney Museum, and the Museum of Modern Art, all in New York; the Philadelphia Museum of Art; Chicago's Museum of Contemporary Art; and the Lehmbruck Museum, in Duisburg, Germany, which specializes in modern sculpture. Ferrer is represented by the Nancy Hoffman Gallery, which mounted a career retrospective of his work in 1995. He has received fellowships from the National Endowment for the Arts (in 1972, 1978, and 1989), a Guggenheim Foundation Award (1972), and grants from the Pew Foundation and the Adolph and Esther Gottlieb Foundation. He has been a visiting professor at many universities. For some years he and his wife divided their time between their homes in the Dominican Republic and Philadelphia. Currently, they live in New York. — C.L.

Suggested Reading: *Arts Magazine* p26+ Nov. 1985, p92 Mar. 1990; *New York* p80+ June 20, 1983; *New York Times* II p27 Jan. 25, 1970, with photo; Emanuel, Muriel, ed. *Contemporary Artists*, 1983

Selected Paintings: *La Luna*, 1977; *Sudan*, 1977; *Puerto Rican Sun*, 1983; *Narciso: La Memoria Era Sola La Mitad* (Narcissus: The Memory Was Just the Half of It), 1989; *Abstract*, 1999; *The Mind*, 1999

Courtesy of Timothy Ferris

Ferris, Timothy

Aug. 29, 1944– Journalist; science writer.
Address: Graduate School of Journalism,
University of California, Berkeley, CA 94720; c/o
Owen Laster, William Morris Agency, 1350 Ave.
of the Americas, New York, NY 10019

Although, by his own admission, he took only one science course in college and performed poorly in it, Timothy Ferris has established a reputation as one of the best science writers in the world. Through the force of his curiosity and writerly gifts, he has produced some of the most acclaimed and widely read volumes on astronomy and cosmology in publication. With lucidity and lyricism Ferris has made the mysteries of, and theories about, the universe comprehensible to a generation of readers, through such popular titles as *Coming*

of Age in the Milky Way, The Mind's Sky: Human Intelligence in a Cosmic Context, and *The Whole Shebang: A State-of-the-Universe(s) Report.* "To be a writer is to mandate your own continuing education . . . ," he observed to an interviewer for *Contemporary Authors* (1990). "It's been a matter of brute force, of doggedly insisting on figuring things out and not quitting until I have."

Timothy Ferris was born on August 29, 1944 in Miami, Florida, the son of Thomas A. Ferris, a publicist, and the former Jean Baird, a literary critic. He discovered science before he had even entered grade school. "My initial interest [in astronomy] had to do with the idea that this world had had an origin," Ferris told *Contemporary Authors.* "This was revealed to me by a book that I read when I was about five years old. I was astonished by the idea that the earth under our feet had been put together at some finite point in the past." Ferris's parents fueled his interest further in 1956, when they gave their 12-year-old son a telescope, through which he spied Mars for the first time. But young Tim had no plans to pursue a career in astronomy or any other science. "My father was a writer, and I've always thought of myself as a writer," he told *Contemporary Authors.* "I was 16 when I first attempted to write a book, and I had written a lot of fiction by that time. It really never occurred to me to be a scientist, and I don't think I would have been particularly good at it. It was natural for me to be a writer."

Ferris attended Northwestern University, in Evanston, Illinois, where he earned a bachelor of arts degree in 1966. He next enrolled at law school, but he "disliked" it, as he confessed to the *Contemporary Authors* interviewer, "and simply walked out one day—it was just too nice a day to stay in class—and I never went back." Ferris moved to New York City, where he worked as a reporter, first for the United Press International news service (1967–69) and then for the *New York Post* (1969–71). He left the *Post* for an associate editorship at *Rolling Stone*; in 1973 he was promoted to contributing editor, a title he held until 1980.

Meanwhile, thanks to various writing assignments, Ferris's fascination with science had revived, and he had opportunities to indulge that interest professionally. As a journalist he covered the *Viking* landing on Mars in 1976. The following year he played more of an insider's role in a landmark National Aeronautics and Space Administration (NASA) project: the inauguration of the ongoing Voyager Interstellar Mission (VIM), whose objective, according to VIM's official Web site, is "to extend the NASA exploration of the solar system beyond the neighborhood of the outer planets to the outer limits of the Sun's sphere of influence, and possibly beyond." The primary goal of VIM's two unmanned spacecraft, *Voyager 1* and *Voyager 2*, which were launched a month apart, was to fly close to the planets Jupiter, Saturn, Uranus, and Neptune and transmit pictures of the planets and their moons back to Earth. The spacecraft completed that task by 1990; both continue to fly in opposite directions away from the sun, exploring farther into the outer reaches of our solar system than any other manmade object ever has. Currently, *Voyager 1* is 70 times farther from the sun than is Earth—so far that its radio messages, traveling at the speed of light, take almost 10 hours to arrive at NASA's Earth-based mission-control center. Both craft have enough power left in their nuclear batteries to continue their journeys until the year 2020. Scientists hope that within the next 10 years *Voyager 1* will pass out of our solar system and into interstellar space. Anticipating the possibility that humans or, perhaps, other life forms in outer space will discover the *Voyager* spacecraft in the distant future, VIM commissioned the making of a recording that would contain encoded images and samples of sounds, languages, and music from Earth. A committee headed by the famed astronomer and author Carl Sagan chose the contents of the recording; Timothy Ferris served as producer, which, as he informed *Current Biography*, meant "work[ing] from the start to the finish of the project on virtually all aspects of its content except the pictures—specifically, serving on the committee that chose the music selections, while also helping with the voices and coordinating most other aspects of production."

At about this time Ferris began to gain notice as a serious chronicler of the skies and the study of astronomy. His first book, *The Red Limit: The Search for the Edge of the Universe* (1977), is a narrative history of the scientific developments that formed the basis for Albert Einstein's groundbreaking general theory of relativity, which in turn is the cornerstone of modern astronomy and cosmology. "[The book] sets out the foundations of the modern view over a wide historical range . . . ," the physicist Philip Morrison wrote in his review of *The Red Limit* for *Scientific American* (September 1977). "The intimacy of its reportage and the thoughtful framework in which the author sets the issues mark this book as exceptional, particularly for readers far from the physical sciences." Commenting on the author's narrative style, R. C. Cowen wrote for the *Christian Science Monitor* (May 23, 1977) that Ferris "writes colorfully and gives insight by describing the scientists' own struggles to understand. This is a compelling story in its own right." On the merits of the book (for which Carl Sagan wrote the introduction), Ferris was awarded the American Institute of Physics Prize in 1978.

Galaxies (1980), Ferris's second book, is a photographic survey of the Milky Way and galaxies beyond, with all pictures selected and all text written by Ferris. The volume's lush illustrations and Ferris's typically concise and engaging prose moved T. E. Margrave, in a review for *Library Journal* (November 1, 1980), to label the 182-page work a "tour de force." *Galaxies* was nominated for an American Book Award in 1981. Ferris followed *Galaxies* with a similar effort, *Spaceshots: The Beauty of Nature beyond Earth* (1984). Containing

78 photos of planetary and lunar surfaces, unique galactic features, and such phenomena as solar eclipses, *Spaceshots* is an examination of the aesthetic appeal of the natural world, particularly the heavens. Critics described Ferris's introductory essay to the book, which addresses the notions of nature, beauty, and the evolution of the universe, as "sensitive" and "poetic."

For his next endeavor Ferris turned to a different medium, writing and narrating the television special *The Creation of the Universe*. First aired on PBS in 1985, the special earned Ferris an Emmy nomination and an award from the American Association for the Advancement of Science. He coauthored with Bruce Porter the well-regarded textbook *The Practice of Journalism: A Guide to Reporting and Writing the News* (1988). Also in 1988 Ferris published his fourth book on cosmology, *Coming of Age in the Milky Way*. Similar to *The Red Limit* in that it recounts the stories of key scientists and discoveries that have contributed to humankind's understanding of space and time, *Coming of Age* was lauded by the science writer Marcia Bartusiak in the *New York Times Book Review* (July 17, 1988) as "an exhilarating, wide-ranging journey" that "provides a perspective missing in most popular cosmology books, which lately have tended to highlight speculations of the present without reference to the many yesterdays of astronomy. It is a welcome and refreshing slant." While chiding Ferris for what she felt was a too-hurried treatment of the numerous astonishing developments in astronomy in the 20th century, Bartusiak called him "a master analogist who conveys his insights on the history of cosmology with a lyrical flair." For *Coming of Age* Ferris was nominated for the Pulitzer Prize and was awarded his second American Institute of Physics Prize, both in 1989.

By this point in his career, Ferris was recognized as a top-ranking journalist—as confirmed, for example, by the Guggenheim Fellowship he received for 1986–87—yet some people questioned him as to why he was limiting his focus to science. His response, as he told *Contemporary Authors*, was that "science is the foremost intellectual adventure of our time. It is to our time what painting and sculpture were to the Renaissance; it's what philosophy was in the age of [the 18th-century German philosopher Immanuel] Kant; it's *the* game in town." Furthermore, Ferris asserted to his *Contemporary Authors* interviewer, fewer reportorial beats are more amenable to journalistic inquiry: "I've been treated quite hospitably by the scientists. For one thing, the scientific community is a dream for a reporter to cover, because it is the opposite of secretive; it operates on maximum free exchange of information. . . . Generally in science the assumption is that everyone will try to make as clear to you as possible what they're doing and why. . . . It's the opposite of a military installation. . . . One is less often in the business—as in, say, political reporting—of trying to dig out information that others are trying to keep hidden."

Ferris began the 1990s by co-editing, with Clifton Fadiman, *The World Treasury of Physics, Astronomy, and Mathematics* (1991). In his fifth book-length work of cosmology, *The Mind's Sky: Human Intelligence in a Cosmic Context* (1992), he explored the connections between the inner universe of the human mind and the outer universe of the cosmos, "as seen through the lenses of two innovative fields of scientific research—neuroscience, and the search for extraterrestrial intelligence," as Ferris explained in his introduction. The book is structured as a series of thematically linked essays that Ferris claimed could be read in any order the reader wished. Jim Bencivenga, writing for the *Christian Science Monitor* (February 25, 1992), found that the topics treated in the work's "tidy three sections" resist "linear organization and must be approached more like a picaresque novel, vignette by vignette." Several reviewers, finding fault with the rambling nature of *The Mind's Sky*, used such adjectives as "contrived" and "disjointed" to describe the way the book was arranged. However, few quibbled with the author's writing and research: in the *New York Review of Books* (February 13, 1992), Alan Lightman declared, "Ferris writes with intelligence, imagination, and dramatic flair," while Dava Sobel, in the *New York Times Book Review* (February 9, 1992), termed *The Mind's Sky* "an informed, inspired investigation of the intellect and the infinite . . . anchored in hard science and good sense."

Ferris's book *The Whole Shebang: A State-of-the-Universe(s) Report* (1997) is a return of sorts to what he does best—surveying the scientific landscape for the general reader. The book opens with a review of the major concepts in cosmology, from the Big Bang theory to Einstein's theories of relativity, then presents an overview of current theories and technologies. It also offers Ferris's informed guesses about the astronomic breakthroughs that seem likely in the near future. *The Whole Shebang* was greeted with a warm critical reception. After airing mostly "academic objections," as he called them, James Trefil, in the *Los Angeles Book Review* (May 18, 1997), judged *The Whole Shebang* to be "an enjoyable book that should draw new readers into the current discussions about the origin and evolution of the universe." Ferris's most recent book, *Life Beyond Earth* (2001), is based on a television documentary that he wrote; the film aired on PBS stations in 1999.

Timothy Ferris lives in San Francisco. He spends moonless nights in the Rocky Hill Observatory, which he designed, in Sonoma County, California. A true polymath who has taught five separate disciplines at four universities, including Brooklyn College, in New York City, and the University of Southern California, in Los Angeles, he currently holds the title of professor emeritus at the University of California at Berkeley and is at work on another multimedia project. "I'm writing a book called 'Seeing in the Dark' about stargazing. I'm interested in making a film of that book," he revealed

to an interviewer for *Astronomy* (April 2000). "It will be very different, with both extremes of scales but no middle. You have the vastness of the universe and the interior world of the eye and mind at the other end of the telescope, and nothing inbetween. I've become fascinated by this hourglass-shaped dynamic: the infinite out there and the infinitesimal world within every person. So it's a film about those two universes, but I have to get the book written first." — T.J.F.

Suggested Reading: *AnnOnline* (on-line), 1997; *Astronomy* p52+ Apr. 2000, with photo; Greater Talent Network Web site; Mathematical Sciences Research Institute Web site; *New Yorker* p32+ Feb. 3, 1986; *Contemporary Authors* new revision series Vol. 30, 1990, Vol. 73, 1999

Selected Books: *The Red Limit: The Search for the Edge of the Universe*, 1977; *Galaxies*, 1980; *Spaceshots: The Beauty of Nature beyond Earth*, 1984; *Coming of Age in the Milky Way*, 1988; *The Mind's Sky: Human Intelligence in a Cosmic Context*, 1992; *The Universe and Eye: Making Sense of the New Science*, 1993; *The Whole Shebang: A State-of-the-Universe(s) Report*, 1997; *Life Beyond Earth*, 2001; as co-author—*The Practice of Journalism: A Guide to Reporting and Writing the News* (with Bruce Porter), 1988; as editor—*The Best American Science Writing, 2001*, 2001; as co-editor—*The World Treasury of Physics, Astronomy, and Mathematics* (with Clifton Fadiman), 1991

Selected Sound Recordings: *Great Science Writers of the Decade*, 1995

Selected Video Recordings: *The Creation of the Universe*, 1985; *Life Beyond Earth*, 1999

Foley, Mick

June 7, 1965– Writer; former professional wrestler. Address: c/o Author Mail, 7th Fl., HarperCollins Publishers, 10 E. 53d St., New York, NY 10022; c/o WWF Entertainment, P.O. Box 3857, Stamford, CT 06902

Some people possess athletic ability; some have intellectual gifts. Mick Foley, neither an athlete nor an academic, was bestowed with an inordinately high tolerance for physical pain, which he used to great advantage in his career as a professional wrestler. The six-foot four-inch, 300-pound Foley, known variously as Cactus Jack, Mankind, and Dude Love, participated in matches with tacks scattered on the mat, barbed wire in place of ropes, and explosives at ringside. A mainstay in professional wrestling during its resurgence in the 1990s, Foley—in his various incarnations—won the

Rich Freeda/Courtesy of HarperCollins

Mick Foley

hearts of wrestling fans around the world. When he retired from professional wrestling after 16 years, he became an author, writing two best-selling books about his career as well as two children's books.

Michael Francis Foley was born in Bloomington, Indiana, on June 7, 1965. His family moved to East Setauket, on Long Island, New York, when he was a young boy. His father, John, was an athletic director at a local school; his mother, Beverly, was a gym teacher. Growing up, Foley did not excel at sports. He was, however, a wrestling fan from a young age, and he loved jumping off tall structures, in imitation of one of his heroes, the wrestler Superfly Jimmy Snuka.

Foley was first trained as a wrestler in 1983 by Dominic De Nucci, a former World Wrestling Federation (WWF) athlete who became interested in working with Foley after seeing a film (made by Dan Zucker) of the teenager jumping off a friend's garage onto a stack of boxes and mattresses. The jump was part of a 53-minute "mockumentary," *The Loved One*, in which Foley portrayed Dude Love, a loser turned pro-wrestling superstar who wins the WWF championship belt. (The story told in the homemade film would prove to have strong similarities to Foley's career.) Then a student at the State University of New York (SUNY) at Cortland, Foley drove 400 miles to Freedom, Pennsylvania, each weekend to train at De Nucci's professional wrestling school. During the weekends, to save money, Foley slept in his car, sustaining himself on peanut-butter sandwiches. He made his professional wrestling debut on June 24, 1983, competing under the name Cactus Jack Manson and defeating Kurt Kaufman. Foley worked his way slowly up

the ranks of various independent wrestling federations, often earning as little as $10 for a night's work. He made a name for himself on the circuit by having utter disregard for his body, willingly grappling in thumbtack-covered rings with barbed wire for ropes. (Meanwhile, he earned a degree in communications from SUNY–Cortland in the late 1980s.)

Foley also worked as a "fall" wrestler—one who enters the ring for the purpose of being defeated by bigger-name opponents—at World Wrestling Federation television tapings. In that role he learned the ropes of the WWF while losing to the likes of Bruno Sammartino, Junkyard Dog, Chief Jay Strongbow, and Superfly Jimmy Snuka. Foley sustained his most serious injury of this period on March 16, 1994 in Munich, Germany. In a match against WWF champion Big Van Vader, Foley, wrestling as Cactus Jack, performed his "hangman" routine, which involved putting his neck between the second and third ropes, then intertwining them. "The end result is the illusion of a man being hanged by his neck while his body kicks and writhes in an attempt to get out . . . the man actually is hanging by his neck and the body really does kick and writhe in an attempt to get out," Foley explained in his autobiography *Have a Nice Day! A Tale of Blood and Sweatsocks* (1999). On this particular date, for a prior match on the card, the officials had tightened the ropes. Immediately after beginning his hangman stunt, Foley had to abort to avoid death by strangulation; in the process he tore off two-thirds of his ear. Still, he continued the match for two minutes before being pinned. Foley's career injuries include four front teeth knocked out, five ribs broken, eight concussions, and more than 325 stitches. Photos of a bloodied and battered Foley are commonplace in the annals of professional-wrestling photography and are centerpieces of his two autobiographical books.

Have a Nice Day! A Tale of Blood and Sweatsocks was originally handwritten on 760 pages of notebook paper by Foley, who has claimed to have never owned a computer or typewriter. He wrote the book without a ghostwriter and partially from the perspective of his most popular wrestling persona, Mankind—a deranged fellow who wore a mask, reminiscent of the fictional madman Hannibal Lecter from the movie *Silence of the Lambs*. The book was a surprise success, garnering favorable reviews and reaching the number-one spot on the *New York Times* nonfiction best-seller list. His second book, *Foley Is Good and the Real World Is Faker than Wrestling*, hit bookstores in May 2001 and debuted at number one on the *New York Times* nonfiction best-seller list. "This No. 1 seller thing, it's not too different from winning a championship belt. Once a best-seller, always a best-seller. There aren't too many of us out there," Foley told Adam Platt for the *New Yorker* (December 20, 1999).

One match highlighted in *Have a Nice Day!* was a 1995 clash between Foley and another of his childhood heroes, Terry Funk. The match, for which Foley wrestled as Cactus Jack, was for the championship at an International Wrestling Association Death Match tournament, held in Japan. The ring was rigged with barbed wire and C4 explosives. By its conclusion Foley had suffered a large burn on one arm and cuts that required more than 40 stitches. "I had seven stitches in my hand, fourteen behind the ear, twelve in my head and seven over my eye as well as second degree burns. For that I got three hundred dollars," Foley explained to John Powell for *SLAM! Wrestling* (May 5, 1999). Highlights of the match were featured in *Beyond the Mat* (1999), a controversial documentary about professional wrestling, directed by Barry W. Blaustein. The film begins with the explanation that wrestling is fake, but goes on to emphasize that much of the punishment absorbed by the actors is real. In one of the film's most disconcerting scenes, Foley's wife, Colette, and the couple's two older children, Dewey and Noelle, are shown at ringside, reacting in horror to a particularly savage contest in which Foley participated. "Unfortunately, one of our worst moments has been documented on film," Foley told Brian Masfield for *USA Today* (March 29, 2000). "I stress to my kids that if they're going to wrestle each other, there's no throwing each other on the head. They've been given many lectures on human anatomy and physiology. They know what not to do to each other, and they know what hurts their Dad." The more gruesome images in *Beyond the Mat* notwithstanding, Foley is presented in the film as a sensitive, kind family man. "People feel I have a death wish, or that I'm a masochist, but I feel like if I take my risks now I'll have the ability to retire when I'm 35 or 36 and spend time with my kids. So it's not like I'm going to miss being hit in the head with chairs, it's just something I feel I do very well," Foley said in *Beyond the Mat*.

Also featured in the film is Foley's now-legendary "Hell in a Cell" match, which took place in 1998 in Pittsburgh, Pennsylvania. Foley lost consciousness for two minutes after being thrown off the top of a steel cage from a height of 16 feet by his opponent, the Undertaker, and landing on the Spanish announcer's table. Later, Foley was body-slammed on the top of the steel cage, whose roof collapsed, sending him crashing to the mat. The match was stopped at that point. Foley, who wrestled as Mankind for the match, lost one whole tooth and half of another, which got lodged in his nose. Because of the enormous amount of punishment he absorbed, Foley's performance in that match is regarded as one of the greatest in professional-wrestling history.

"After the Hell in a Cell match [the WWF promoter] Vince McMahon stood right there when they were stitching me up," Foley told Brian Mansfield. "Then he brought me into his office and said, 'I cannot tell you how impressed and thankful I am for what you just did; you've got to promise me you'll never do it again.' He then introduced me to the word 'governor,' which I guess is the apparatus

on a car or bus that stops it from going too fast. So he placed a governor on me." The governor took the form of Mr. Socko, a ragged sock puppet that Foley's Mankind began using as a comic prop. The introduction of the puppet, which shared its name with Mankind's finishing move, was part of a softening of Mankind's image; suddenly the character, whom Foley had created after reading Mary Shelley's novel *Frankenstein*, was a good guy. He changed his ring attire from ripped-up brown and black clothes to a white shirt and dress pants, and even went through a period of wearing a tuxedo. As a result, Mankind became a fan favorite. During that year, 1999, Foley made over $1 million for the first time in his career. His character inspired a comic-book series illustrated and written by Jerry Beck.

During his wrestling career Foley's appeal was based on his taking punishment without regard to winning or losing. Inevitably, his ring antics took a toll on his body. The multiple injuries he suffered have made it difficult for him to walk without pain. "I'd say I was a physical wreck for the last few years of my career," Foley told Dinitia Smith for the *New York Times* (May 22, 2001, on-line). In the same article Foley admitted that he once sat in his kitchen for 20 minutes and stared at his lawn sprinkler before working up the courage to turn it off, because he knew that that simple act would cause him a great deal of pain. Foley retired in 2000, following Wrestlemania XVI, at which he wrestled in a four-way title match against Triple H, the Rock, and Big Show. That match was the first in which Foley wrestled under his own name. Since his retirement Foley has returned to the World Wrestling Federation as a commissioner.

In 2000 Foley published *Mick Foley's Christmas Chaos*, a children's book about a boy who restores the spirit of Christmas to a broken-hearted Santa Claus. Foley wrote the text; the illustrations were provided by wrestling announcer Jerry "the King" Lawler. Foley was inspired to write the book after meeting a young boy who was being treated for severe burns at one of the Shriners Hospitals for Children, where Foley had gone as part of his book-signing tour for *Have a Nice Day!* Foley has donated the proceeds from the book to the hospital. "I dedicated the book to the little guy, and his family is very happy about it," he told *WrestleFanz* (November 20, 2000, on-line). Foley's second children's book, *Mick Foley's Halloween Havoc*, will arrive in bookstores in the fall of 2001.

Foley lives in Smithtown, New York, with his wife, Colette, and their children, Dewey, Noelle, and Mick Jr. In the house is what Foley calls "the Christmas Room," a permanently Santa-themed basement. He listens to Christmas carols year-round and makes pilgrimages with his children to Santa's Village, a Christmas-themed park in New Hampshire's White Mountains. He told Arthur Levine for the *Syracuse American* (November 19, 2000), "I find that it grounds me. It's a chance to escape and become a kid again. I don't want to live

in the big scary world of pro wrestling all the time."
— A.T.

Suggested Reading: *New York Times* (on-line) May 22, 2001; *New Yorker* p34+ Dec. 1999; *SLAM! Wrestling* (on-line) 1999; *Syracuse American* p20 Nov. 19, 2000, with photo; *USA Today* D p1+ Mar. 29, 2000, with photo; Foley, Mick. *Have a Nice Day! A Tale of Blood and Sweatsocks*, 1999, *Foley Is Good and the Real World Is Faker than Wrestling*, 2001

Selected Books: *Have a Nice Day! A Tale of Blood and Sweatsocks*, 1999; *Mick Foley's Christmas Chaos*, 2000; *Foley Is Good and the Real World Is Faker than Wrestling*, 2001; *Mick Foley's Halloween Havoc*, 2001

Selected Films: *Beyond the Mat*, 1999

Selected Television Shows: *Raw Is War*, 1997; *WWF Smackdown*, 1999

Courtesy of Ben Fong-Torres

Fong-Torres, Ben

Jan. 7, 1945– Writer; editor; radio broadcaster. Address: Myplay, inc., 1600 Bridge Pkwy., Redwood City, CA 94065; Rock and Roll Hall of Fame, One Key Plaza, Cleveland, OH 44114

The journalist and radio broadcaster Ben Fong-Torres served as news editor for *Rolling Stone* from 1969 to 1981, years during which the magazine was considered to be the final word on rock and roll and the counterculture. "One might say that the qualities that once made the magazine a cultural touchstone seem to be those of Fong-Torres himself," Carl Rosen wrote for *Billboard* (November 6, 1999), "for you couldn't hope for a more upbeat, sane, and dryly revealing observer of popular music's halcyon era." Fong-Torres has also written for *Esquire, Gentlemen's Quarterly, Parade, Playboy, Sports Illustrated, American Film,* and *Harper's Bazaar;* served as the host of several radio programs; and authored *Hickory Wind: The Life and Times of Gram Parsons* (1991), the memoir *The Rice Room: Growing Up Chinese-American—From Number Two Son to Rock and Roll* (1994), and *The Hits Just Keep on Coming: The History of Top 40 Radio* (1998). He has contributed to and edited a number of anthologies of material previously published in *Rolling Stone,* and his articles and interviews for the magazine were collected in *Not Fade Away: A Backstage Pass to 20 Years of Rock and Roll* (1999), a volume that also includes a selection of his writings for other publications as well as his recollections of the circumstances under which the stories were written. Fong-Torres is currently the editorial director at *Myplay.com,* and he serves as a curator for the Rock and Roll Hall of Fame, in Cleveland, Ohio. He was portrayed by the actor Terry Chen in Cameron Crowe's film *Almost Famous* (2000), which is based loosely on Crowe's days as a teenage reporter for *Rolling Stone.* Fong-Torres was one of the first Asian-American journalists to achieve mainstream success, thus providing the inspiration for a generation of young writers. "I'm the old man of the pack," he told Kimberly Chun for *AsianWeek.com* (October 19, 2000). "I'm the old, old dweeb. It's just a matter of fact that I'm the first one, but I don't know that it means anything. There should have been more. And there are more now."

Ben Fong-Torres was born on January 7, 1945 in Alameda, California, to Richard and Connie Joe Fong-Torres. (The family name was originally Fong; Richard Fong-Torres added the Filipino surname in the 1920s in order to circumvent the Chinese Exclusion Act, a measure implemented to curtail Chinese emigration to the United States.) Along with his two brothers and two sisters, Ben Fong-Torres was raised in the Chinatown section of Oakland, California. He spent much of his youth assisting in the operation of the family's restaurant, called the Silver Dragon. (His sister Shirley Fong-Torres is a well-known San Francisco culinary expert. She is the founder and owner of the Wok Wiz Chinatown Tour and Cooking Center in that city and has written a popular cookbook and a guidebook to San Francisco's Chinatown.)

The Fong-Torres children spoke English with more fluency than their parents but only a limited amount of Chinese. The result was what Fong-Torres described in an article for *Asianconnections.com* as a "lifelong language barrier" between the parents and their offspring, one that led to frequent misunderstandings. To the dismay of their parents, the Fong-Torres children embraced

American pop culture, and Ben became a devoted fan of Elvis Presley, *MAD* magazine, and rock and roll. He was very close to his older brother, Barry. "We were both, in our own ways, rebellious," Ben Fong-Torres wrote for *Asianconnections.com.* "Born into Chinese traditions, into a hard work ethic, we did our duties and earned good grades, but managed to upset our parents with our independence. He dated girls who weren't Chinese, and he studied not law or medicine, but criminology. I told my parents I'd rather be a disc jockey than a dentist."

Fong-Torres was a student at San Francisco State University during the height of the student protest movement, a time when such countercultural events as the Human Be-Ins were in vogue, and FM-radio deejays, who had great freedom in picking their lineups, increased awareness of the variety of rock music being produced. Many rock bands, including Big Brother, the Holding Company, and Great Society, led by Grace Slick, performed on the university's campus. Fong-Torres studied radio, television, and film and served as editor of the student newspaper. After graduating from San Francisco State with a B.A. degree, in 1966, he worked briefly as an announcer and writer for the San Francisco radio station KFOG.

Until that point Fong-Torres had been the "laziest job seeker in the world," as he confessed to Lynne Margolis for *Starpolish.com* (February 25, 2001). His roommates persuaded him to pursue a job at *Rolling Stone*, the counterculture magazine founded by Jann Wenner in 1967. Fong-Torres contacted the magazine the following year with a tip about a film Dick Clark planned to make about the hippie scene in the Haight-Ashbury section of San Francisco; soon afterward, he was hired as a reporter. His first article for *Rolling Stone* appeared in the publication's eighth issue, and he was then assigned to cover an ongoing strike by hippie radio personalities at a local FM radio station. While he became a regular contributor to the magazine, the pay was low, so Fong-Torres took a job as an editor and writer at an employee newspaper of the Pacific Telephone Co. He also volunteered two nights a week as an editor for *East West*, a bilingual newspaper based in Chinatown.

In May 1969 Fong-Torres became *Rolling Stone*'s news editor, a position that made him responsible for the content of the first few pages of the magazine. The editorial offices, which Jann Wenner had obtained rent-free, were located in a loft above a printing plant and next door to a slaughterhouse. Although most of the staff wore long hair and dressed casually, they took their work very seriously. "The informality of the office setup recalled my college paper," Fong-Torres wrote in his introduction to *Not Fade Away*. "Only here, this small group of people were professionals, taking the best of journalistic rules and traditions, yet creating their own unique publication." Being news editor taught him "two things," he wrote. "First, the news was whatever interested us,

whether it came over the phone, by mail, or through an experience the night before at a club, concert, or friend's house. . . . Second, I discovered that titles were meaningless. Whatever we called ourselves, we did a multitude of jobs. We all wrote; we all edited; we all made assignments; we all pitched in with captions, headlines, and story ideas."

During his 12 years at *Rolling Stone*, Fong-Torres wrote more than 400 articles, 37 of which were cover stories. "I was not a rock critic," he explained in the introduction to *Not Fade Away*. "I was trained, at San Francisco State, to be a reporter and editor, and that's what I did at *Rolling Stone*. . . . I did not crit. What I did was meet pop, rock and R&B artists, engage them in conversation, and, through quotes and observations, tell their story." *Rolling Stone* built its reputation on entertainment coverage that did not shy away from exposing artists' flaws and idiosyncracies, however unflattering such exposure may have been. Although Fong-Torres was a fan of many of the musicians and celebrities he wrote about, his admiration for them did not prevent him from exploring both their personal ambitions and insecurities. "I enjoy learning, and telling success stories—even when, and sometimes especially when, success takes the artist on difficult turns," he wrote in *Not Fade Away*. "I like telling what happens when the artist encounters setbacks, misfortune, or outright failure. How he deals with the ups and downs of the high-profile, high-stakes life he's chosen: That's the story I'm looking for."

Fong-Torres conducted interviews with musicians, groups, and other celebrities, including Bob Dylan, the Rolling Stones, Janis Joplin, Paul McCartney, Elton John, Stevie Wonder, the Jackson 5, Linda Ronstadt, Marvin Gaye, Diana Ross, the Grateful Dead, Diane Keaton, and Steve Martin. Fong-Torres also conducted the last interview with Jim Morrison before the Doors' lead singer's death, in Paris in 1971. One of Fong-Torres's favorite pieces was an interview he conducted with Ray Charles, in which the singer for the first time spoke about his heroin use; the article earned Fong-Torres the prestigious Deems Taylor Award for Magazine Writing in 1974.

Fong-Torres's profiles of rock stars often inspired impassioned feedback from readers. "George Harrison once did a tour where he refused to exploit his Beatles past to the dismay of many of the fans who showed up hoping to hear his greatest hits," the writer told Jeremy M. Helfgot for *Tonos.com*. "In the story that I wrote, I thought that I gave him the credit for standing up for his principles, but at the same time I reported the response from critics, promoters, and his own staff people, who all thought that as much as George should be his own man he was still taking money from fans who had a set of expectations of the kind of show they might get. . . . It got tremendous response from people who felt that I was the one criticizing George, even though I was just a messenger. . . .

But George and I had a great interview together backstage, so that was no problem."

From 1970 to 1979 Fong-Torres worked as a weekend deejay at radio station KSAN. During that time he also wrote a syndicated radio special entitled *San Francisco: What a Long, Strange Trip It's Been*, based on interviews conducted for an issue of *Rolling Stone* that commemorated the 10th anniversary of the Summer of Love, a series of musical and cultural events that took place in San Francisco in 1967, at the height of the counterculture's influence. The program received an award for broadcast excellence from *Billboard* magazine. A television interview that Fong-Torres conducted with the comedian Steve Martin for *Evening Magazine* earned him a Northern California Emmy Award in 1977. In 1981 he left *Rolling Stone*, and the following year he traveled to China, where he wrote the script for a television special entitled *Cycling Through China*, which was seen in Asia, Europe, and the United States.

From 1983 to 1992 Fong-Torres worked as a feature writer and radio columnist for the *San Francisco Chronicle*. He left the newspaper to write his memoir, *The Rice Room: Growing Up Chinese-American—From Number Two Son to Rock and Roll*, which sold enough copies to be included on the *San Francisco Chronicle*'s best-seller list. The book tells the story of Fong-Torres's early childhood and the development of his love for rock music. *The Rice Room* also documents efforts on the part of the author and his siblings to assimilate into American culture and includes his account of his brother Barry's shooting death, in 1972. Barry Fong-Torres had been working as a probation officer and counselor to troubled youths in Chinatown, and although his murder remains unsolved, there has been speculation that he was killed by gang members. (Ben Fong-Torres remained silent about his brother's murder until 1984, when he wrote about the killing for the *San Francisco Chronicle*.)

In 1993 Fong-Torres became the managing editor for *Gavin*, a weekly trade magazine of the radio and recording industry. "I'd long admired [*Gavin*'s] late founder, Bill Gavin, for his pioneer work in programming and charting popular music for radio," he wrote in the epilogue to *Not Fade Away*. "He was the unseen, uncredited man behind *Lucky Lager Dance Time*, the show that, in the early fifties, introduced me to rock and roll and R&B as well as pop hits." In addition to his duties as managing editor, Fong-Torres wrote stories about Atlantic Records co-founder Ahmet Ertegun and the singers Pat Boone, Garth Brooks, and Alanis Morrissette. During this time he spent one year as the host of *Fog City Radio*, a two-hour weekly program on KQED, the National Public Radio affiliate in San Francisco. *Fog City Radio* featured performances by, and interviews with, a wide range of accomplished authors, musicians, and broadcasters, such as the country songwriter and actor Kris Kristofferson, the writer Amy Tan, and the comedi-

an and writer Steve Allen. Fong-Torres left *Gavin* in order to write *The Hits Just Keep on Coming*, a history of Top-40 radio in the United States. In 1999 Fong-Torres was hired as editorial director for *Myplay.com*, an Internet music site, and began writing for *Asian Connections.com*. Since 1999 he has written the script for the annual Rock and Roll Hall of Fame induction ceremony, and he recently accepted an invitation to join the museum as a curator.

Fong-Torres's career received widespread attention in 2000, when he was portrayed in the movie *Almost Famous*, directed by Cameron Crowe. In the early 1970s Fong-Torres gave Crowe, then 15 years old, his first assignment for the magazine and served as his assignment editor for the next two years or so. "We had been around for six years and were looking for young energy," Fong-Torres told Susan Wloszczyna for *USA Today* (September 14, 2000, on-line). "A number of artists hated us for giving them negative record reviews. We liked the idea of sending a fresh-faced, buoyant, positive kid out there to get doors open." (In 1979 Jann Wenner landed a three-picture deal with Paramount Pictures. He assigned one screenplay each to Fong-Torres, Crowe, and Hunter S. Thompson, a frequent contributor to the magazine, but only Crowe completed a script; he went on to write or direct a number of popular films, including *Fast Times at Ridgemont High* and *Jerry Maguire*.)

Journalists no longer enjoy the unfettered access to artists that Fong-Torres and his colleagues were afforded in the 1960s and 1970s. "Back then, unlike today, you had real, full, solid access to most of the people you were covering," he told Lynne Margolis. "Especially because you were from *Rolling Stone*; at one time, we were pretty much the only game in town. Today, with all the technology . . . [and] all the mainstream media now covering rock 'n' roll and other pop culture, there is no such thing as exclusivity. *Rolling Stone* is still *Rolling Stone*, so they can still probably get a pretty good lead on being the first to cover a particular act, but back then, we were really all there was. . . . We were the only ones who could give the band a good review and mean something to their career." Today, such career-making power lies largely in the hands of the record companies and artists themselves, who regularly "pick and choose which media they want and which magazines and newspapers and networks and programs they want to appear in, and what billing they get and covers they get," Fong-Torres explained to Margolis.

Although Chinese-American journalists were a rarity in English-language publications when Fong-Torres began his career, he did not feel that his ethnicity affected the way he was perceived in his professional life. "If I could do the job, I had the job," he wrote in the introduction to *Not Fade Away*. "And on the job, meeting with musicians, managers, publicists, concert promoters, and record company executives, I never sensed any surprise on their part as they discovered that the guy from *Rolling Stone* was Chinese. Far more often, I would hear that, from having heard my name on the phone, they expected a Latino ('Torres') or perhaps a Scandinavian ('Von Taurus,' maybe?)."

In 1993 Fong-Torres appeared as a contestant on the game show *Wheel of Fortune*, winning cash and prizes worth close to $100,000. Another notable television appearance took place in 2000, when he performed his impression of Bob Dylan on Dick Clark's TV show *Your Big Break*. On "Rainy Day Bookstores," a track featured on the album *Stranger than Fiction* (1999), Fong-Torres demonstrated his ability to mimic other famous entertainers, such as Elvis Presley. *(Stranger than Fiction* was produced as a benefit for PEN [Playwrights, Editors, Essayists and Novelists] and features songs performed by such writers as Stephen King, Amy Tan, and Norman Mailer.) Fong-Torres has often been called upon as an emcee for public events, and he has sometimes conducted public interviews with celebrities such as Robin Williams.

Fong-Torres lives in San Francisco with his wife, Dianne Sweet, whom he met while studying at San Francisco State University. "I started writing because I was a ham and wanted attention, and

from reading my favorite magazines, *Mad* and *Dig*, it seemed easy," he told *Contemporary Authors* (1980). "Now I write because, although it ain't easy, it's the best work in the world." — C.L.

Suggested Reading: *Asianconnections.com*; *Asianweek.com* Oct. 20–26, 2000, with photo; *USA Today* (on-line) Sep. 14, 2000; *Contemporary Authors* vol. 93–96, 1980; Fong-Torres, Ben. *Not Fade Away: A Backstage Pass to 20 Years of Rock & Roll*, 1999

Selected Books: as writer—*The Motown Album: The Sound of Young America*, 1990; *Hickory Wind: The Life and Times of Gram Parsons*, 1991; *The Rice Room: Growing Up Chinese-American—From Number Two Son to Rock and Roll*, 1994; *The Hits Just Keep On Coming: The History of Top 40 Radio*, 1997; *Not Fade Away: A Backstage Pass to 20 Years of Rock and Roll*, 1999; as editor—*The Rolling Stone Rock 'n' Roll Reader*, 1972; *What's That Sound? The Contemporary Music Scene from the Pages of Rolling Stone*, 1976

Fox Quesada, Vicente

July 2, 1942– President of Mexico. Address: Office of the President, Los Pinos, Puerta 1, Col. San Miguel, Chapultepec 11850, Mexico DF, Mexico

With the July 2, 2000 electoral victory of Vicente Fox Quesada, the presidential candidate of the conservative National Action Party (PAN), the Institutional Revolutionary Party (PRI) lost its grip on the Mexican government for the first time in more than 71 years. Indeed, until that day, the PRI was the longest continuously ruling political party in the world, a pervasive presence in Mexican society that maintained its hold on power by means of a sprawling network of labor unions, business interests, mass organizations, and state enterprises. (Through the years PRI has even been implicated in the killings and "disappearances" of a number of opposition politicians.) Although, when it controlled the government, the PRI always kept up a democratic façade, by holding ritual presidential elections every six years, in the 1980s and 1990s it turned increasingly to vote-buying schemes and even outright fraud to ensure its dominance in the face of the opposition parties' growing momentum. And right up to the eve of the 2000 vote, there was concern outside Mexico as well as within the country that the PRI might attempt to steal the election—a concern that PRI officials did not always try to allay. "In this election, you are going to see the machinery of the PRI, like few parties in the world have," Emilio Gamboa Patron, a PRI

Elizabeth Daliel/AP

campaign manager, declared, as quoted by Julia Preston in the *New York Times* (July 2, 2000) on the eve of the vote. "I'll bet not even the party in China has a machine like the one we have built up over the years."

Fox's presidential victory thus marked the culmination of a long effort on the part of many Mexicans of disparate social and political backgrounds to reform the political system. Although his party, the socially conservative PAN, has often been compared to the Republican Party in the United States, the analogy has flaws, as Andrew Reding pointed out in *World Policy Journal* (Fall 1996). While wealthy Americans represent one of the core constituencies of the GOP, the PAN is predominantly middle class. (The Mexican upper class has traditionally supported the PRI.) In American political terms, Reding suggested, the PAN is best conceived as "a hypothetical GOP limited to the Christian Coalition and Reagan Democrats—highly populist, nationalist, family-oriented, and suspicious of trade deals negotiated by economic elites." Fox has succeeded in retaining the core constituency of the PAN while keeping the party's leadership at arm's length.

The challenge to PRI rule began in earnest during the 1988 presidential campaign; in that election, Cuauhtémoc Cárdenas, the leader of the left-leaning Democratic Revolutionary Party (PRD), nearly defeated the PRI candidate, Carlos Salinos. (To this day, many Mexicans believe that the PRI victory that year was fraudulent.) In the following years opposition candidates from both the left and the right (including Fox) made steady gains, winning seats in the legislature as well as a number of governorships. In 1994 the reform movement acquired a crucial ally in the person of Ernesto Zedillo, a PRI member who captured the presidency that year. Over the strident objections of his party's old guard, Zedillo ushered a series of crucial electoral reforms through Congress; thanks in large part to those reforms, the 2000 elections were among the fairest in modern Mexican history.

Among those who voted for Fox were many who had supported democratic reform in the 1980s and 1990s and who, regardless of whether they felt much enthusiasm for Fox, concluded that almost anything would be preferable to six more years of PRI rule. Coming from all quarters of Mexican society, those voters included workers, the wealthy, members of the military, and even former Communists who felt that ousting the PRI took precedence over ideological differences. Although talks about a possible coalition between the PAN and the PRD broke down in late 1999, Fox succeeded in winning the support of many PRD followers. Moreover, he was able to count on both the political base of the PAN, which consists of young, upwardly mobile professionals (leading one pollster, quoted by Douglas W. Payne in *Dissent* [Fall 2000], to dub the Fox victory a "yuppie revolution"), and conservative Catholics.

The second of nine children, Vicente Fox Quesada was born on July 2, 1942 in Mexico City. His mother, Mercedes Quesada, immigrated to Mexico from Spain as an infant; his father, José Luis Fox, a prosperous landholder, was the son of an immigrant of Irish descent who came to Mexico by way of Cincinnati, Ohio, with the hope of relieving his asthma in a kinder climate. Fox grew up on his father's 1,100-acre ranch in San Francisco del Rin-

cón, in the central Mexican state of Guanajuato. In a campaign autobiography quoted by Sam Dillon in the *New York Times* (July 4, 2000), Fox recalled his exposure to a broad range of Mexican society during his childhood. "Something I'm proud of is that I became good friends with the children of the smallholders and peasants," he wrote. "With them I shared my infancy, my playthings, my house and my food. From that time I began to understand our country's painful inequalities." Repeatedly during his presidential campaign, Fox declared that the fight against poverty and inequality would be his "supreme priority" as Mexico's leader.

The region of central Mexico in which Fox was raised influenced the development of his political beliefs in other ways as well. Traditionally, Guanajuato and its neighboring states have been strongholds of Catholic activism. In 1926 thousands of Mexican peasants and Catholic militants from the region launched an insurgency against the secular (and often anticlerical) republican regime that had come to power in the wake of the 1910 Mexican Revolution. The rebels, commonly known as the Cristeros, fought the government for more than three years before surrendering. Fox has often acknowledged his fascination with the Cristero rebellion: he collects books on the subject, and during his presidential campaign, he often concluded rallies with an old Cristero battle cry: "If I advance, follow me! If I stop, push me! If I retreat, kill me!" Some commentators, comparing the Cristero rebels to the right-wing forces of General Francisco Franco in the civil war in Spain during the 1930s, have suggested that such rhetoric betokens an alarming nostalgia for antidemocratic beliefs; others have pointed out that the militant ecclesiasticism of the 1920s has long since metamorphosed into democratic conservatism.

In 1964 Fox earned a degree in business administration from the Universidad Iberoamericana, a Jesuit institution in Mexico City. His attendance at a domestic university sets him apart from the many others among the country's political elite who have studied at foreign institutions. (Fox's two immediate predecessors in the Mexican presidency, Ernesto Zedillo and Carlos Salinas, hold degrees from Yale and Harvard, respectively.) After his graduation Fox went to work for Coca-Cola de Mexico as a route supervisor. "At the university, they taught me to reflect and to analyze," Fox said in a 1999 interview cited by Dillon. "But working at Coca-Cola was my second university education. I learned that the heart of a business is out in the field, not in the office. I learned strategy, marketing, financial management, optimization of resources. I learned not to accept anything but winning. I learned an iron discipline for getting results." By all accounts a talented manager, Fox quickly rose through the corporate ranks at Coca-Cola de Mexico; in 1975 he was named chief executive. He has recalled that dealing with red tape was his chief nuisance at the company. "What I hated most about those years at Coca-Cola was the time I had to spend dithering with the government," he said in a 2000 interview cited by Dillon. Particularly irritating to him were the meetings at Los Pinos, the Mexican White House, to which the president would summon Fox and other prominent business executives "so we could listen to a lot of foolishness."

In 1979 Coca-Cola invited Fox to direct its Latin American operations, whose main offices were in Miami, Florida, and Atlanta, Georgia. Unwilling to relocate to either of those cities, he left the company and returned to Guanajuato. There, he helped several of his brothers manage Grupo Fox, a family business that consists of a footwear factory and a vegetable farm. As a result of the currency devaluations of the 1980s, the banking crisis of 1994, and, especially, the advent of the North American Free Trade Agreement (NAFTA), which went into effect on January 1, 1994, a sharp divide opened up between small businesses and large corporations in Mexico. While large firms, which often rely on exports and have access to foreign capital, were for the most part insulated from currency fluctuations and have generally benefited from free-trade agreements, small enterprises in Mexico in the last two decades have had to struggle to survive. The Fox brothers weathered the economic turbulence by taking out many loans from Mexican banks and by exporting their footwear and their produce. (Since a portion of Grupo Fox's income was in dollars rather than pesos, Fox and his brothers were able to offset, to a degree, the repeated devaluations of the Mexican currency.) "Every micro, small and medium-sized entrepreneur in this country is a hero for surviving, growing and exporting under these circumstances," Fox told Dillon. "I'm not embarrassed to say the businesses of the Grupo Fox are still highly leveraged, because that's the situation of all Mexican businesses." Later, during his presidential campaign, Fox would claim that his experience at both Coca-Cola and Grupo Fox had given him a unique understanding of business in Mexico.

According to Fox, until the late 1980s his only brush with politics occurred when PRI-organized squatters attempted to seize a part of his farm. "I never, ever, thought I'd be in politics," he explained to Sam Dillon for the New York Times (May 11, 1998). "My father told us that nothing would offend him more, because only thieves and crooks go into politics here." Then, in 1988, the political leader Manuel Clouthier, a friend and fellow businessman who was running for president on the PAN ticket that year, encouraged Fox to join him in his drive to end the PRI's political monopoly. (Clouthier died the next year.) Joining a growing wave of opposition to PRI rule across Mexico, Fox launched a campaign for the local congressional seat and won by a three-to-one margin. Although he ran on the PAN ticket, he established an independent fund-raising organization—the Friends of Fox—to distance himself from the party's leadership.

Almost immediately, Fox got himself noticed. As its first item of business after the elections, the PRI-dominated Chamber of Deputies, the lower house of the Congress, ratified the 1988 presidential victory of Carlos Salinas, the PRI candidate, despite the fact that many Mexicans regarded his win as fraudulent. (With early returns showing a considerable lead for the left-leaning opposition candidate Cuauhtémoc Cárdenas—whose celebrated father, Lazaro Cardenas, was a co-founder of the PRI and served as Mexico's president from 1934 to 1940—the PRI-controlled election board suddenly announced that the computers tabulating the ballots had crashed "due to atmospheric conditions." By the time counting was resumed, Salinas had taken the lead.) After the ratification of the vote, Fox rose to the Chamber of Deputies podium with two charred ballots taped to his head (to represent Salinas's big ears) and imitated the president-elect: "I've felt obligated to ask many of my friends to set aside moral scruples to help me achieve this victory, which I had to do because Mexico isn't ready for democracy . . . ," he said, as reported by Andrew Reding for the World Policy Journal (Fall 1996). "The truth is that the people did not vote for me; my friends had to stuff the ballot boxes."

After serving one two-year term in the Chamber of Deputies, Fox returned to Guanajuato, where he ran for governor in 1991. Although popular among voters, Fox had made powerful enemies by openly challenging Salinas, and as the day of the election approached, the PRI mobilized its extensive resources to punish the upstart candidate. First, Salinas reversed a court decision that had prohibited a second opposition candidate—a carpetbagger, according to Reding—from running and siphoning off some of Fox's support. Then, on election day, more than 500 of the state's 3,850 polling stations counted more votes than there were registered voters. After the balloting, the PRI-controlled electoral commission certified the questionable victory of the PRI candidate. Fox protested the commission's action, and several thousand citizens turned out in the state's major cities to support him. Under pressure, the PRI tacitly conceded it had practiced fraud, then succeeded in installing a more docile member of the PAN (whose name had not been on the ballot) in place of both their original "winner" and Fox.

In 1995 Fox made another bid for the governorship of Guanajuato. The obstacles that had thwarted him in 1991 no longer faced him, because an independent electoral commission had been established and Salinas was in self-imposed exile in Ireland. (Salinas, whose term had expired in 1994, had fled Mexico in March 1995, after his older brother, Raúl Salinas, was arrested for allegedly masterminding the killing of a prominent PRI official. The brother was later found guilty of that murder.) In May 1995 Fox was elected governor of Guanajuato by a landslide, defeating his opponent by a two-to-one margin—the largest ever for an opposition candidate in a Mexican gubernatorial election.

From the time when he first sought the governorship, Fox was open about his presidential ambitions, and as early as 1993 opponents and supporters alike recognized him as a viable presidential candidate. But a provision in the Mexican Constitution, according to which a presidential candidate had to be born in Mexico to "parents who are Mexican by birth," prevented him from running in the 1994 election. Under public pressure to rewrite that and several other articles pertaining to the electoral system, the PRI-dominated legislature amended the Constitution so as to allow a prospective candidate to run if he or she had one parent born in Mexico and had lived in the country for at least 20 years. The legislature also stipulated that the new regulations would not take effect until 2000—a proviso that Fox and his supporters claimed was added expressly to exclude him from the 1994 race. "The only reason it's been extended to 2000 is Vicente Fox, that's clear to everybody," Fox said, as quoted by Anthony DePalma in the *New York Times* (September 4, 1993). PRI officials countered that a law should not be changed to accommodate one person. In any event, with the change in the Constitution, Fox declared his intention to run for president in 2000.

Taking a long windup, Fox inaugurated his campaign in 1997. He spent the next two and a half years barnstorming across Mexico in his trademark cowboy boots and Stetson hat—"As everyone loves to notice," Paul Berman wrote for the *New York Times Magazine* (July 2, 2000), "Vicente Fox, at a rugged 58, is the Marlboro Man"—and even made appearances in the United States. (The 10 million Mexican citizens living north of the border, while currently not permitted to vote for president in absentia, wield considerable influence at home; in fact, Eddie Varon Levy, a Mexican citizen who lives in Los Angeles, won election to Mexico's Chamber of Deputies in July 2000.) In the final weeks of the campaign, Fox ran neck and neck with Francisco Labastida Ochoa, the PRI candidate, and far ahead of Cárdenas, the PRD candidate, and several other hopefuls. About 64 percent of Mexico's nearly 59 million registered voters came to the polls on July 2, 2000; more than 43 percent of them cast their ballots for Fox, giving him the presidency by a margin of more than six percentage points.

After his electoral victory Fox made it clear that fighting corruption in the military, the police, and the government would be one of his top priorities. To that end, he said, he would create a Ministry of Security modeled on the American FBI. He also required his cabinet members to take their oaths of office in public—a first in Mexican politics—and to pledge not to accept any bribes. By late 2001, however, Fox had made little headway in rooting out corruption. A preinauguration promise to establish a "transparency commission" to investigate PRI-era abuses remained unfulfilled, and his appointment, in May, of a military prosecutor as attorney general drew criticism from human-rights

groups. The murder, in October, of Digna Ochoa, one of Mexico's most prominent human-rights lawyers, led many to wonder whether Fox would succeed in cleaning house; some even questioned the president's commitment to doing so. "This is a horrible, tragic blow to human rights protection in Mexico," Curt Goering, the deputy executive director of Amnesty International U.S.A., declared, according to Ginger Thompson in the *New York Times* (October 22, 2001). "The rhetoric of the Fox administration indicated that he was prepared to deal with human rights issues differently than in the past. Well, in the aftermath of an event like this, that rhetoric rings hollow."

A second immediate concern involved negotiating an end to the Zapatista uprising that has been smoldering in the southern state of Chiapas since 1994. In his inaugural address, on December 1, 2000, as reported by James S. Torrens for *America* (January 8–15, 2001), Fox spoke of the debt Mexico owed to "the original peoples of this land who go on suffering intolerable injustice, marginality and inequality. I have been, am and will be committed to a new relationship between indigenous peoples and the Mexican state." Soon after his inauguration Fox moved to satisfy one of the Zapatistas' demands by sending to Congress an Indian rights bill, the so-called San Andrés Accords, that would grant indigenous villages more autonomy. In late April the Mexican Congress overwhelmingly approved an amended version of the legislation—one that indigenous groups had opposed. "If we were to compare this legislation to a tree, it would be more like a bonsai than a great oak," Luis Hernández, a political adviser to the Zapatistas, said, as quoted by Ginger Thompson in the *New York Times* (April 30, 2001). "It is decorative and pretty, but it is not a tree that provides any shade of protection to indigenous communities." Soon thereafter the Zapatistas broke off talks with the Fox government.

Fox has also sought to enlarge Mexico's international stature by taking a more active role on the world stage. In particular, he appears to envision his country as a future advocate for all of Latin America. "Mexico is determined to play an active role in the work that will be required, by its nature and importance, by all the nations of the Americas," he said in a speech before the Organization of American States during a state visit to Washington, D.C., in September 2001, according to Ginger Thompson in the *New York Times* (September 8, 2001). He further questioned the utility of the 1947 Inter-American Reciprocal Assistance Treaty, also known as the Rio Treaty. (In Fox's view, the 54-year-old treaty between the United States and several Latin American countries, designed to prevent the spread of communism, was an obsolete relic of the Cold War.) Later that month Fox challenged (symbolically if not in practice) his country's historically noninterventionist foreign policy by pledging "unconditional support" for the United States in the wake of the terrorist attacks on Washington, D.C., and New York. In October Fox's efforts to boost his country's international standing were further strengthened when Mexico won a two-year seat on the United Nations Security Council.

In relations with Mexico's northern neighbor, Fox has continued to press the United States to make its border more open to Mexican workers, and has expressed a desire to expand NAFTA into a European-style common market. In February 2001, in his first official trip outside the U.S., President George W. Bush traveled to Fox's Guanajuato ranch to discuss the relationship between Mexico and the United States. Although the meeting was overshadowed by American air strikes on Iraq and failed to produce any major shifts in policy, it was widely seen as indicating a change in tone. In March, continuing to address the concerns of Mexicans living in the United States, Fox paid a two-day visit to California, during which he promised to press the Mexican Congress to allow Mexican citizens to vote from abroad. In a September 6, 2001 address before a joint session of the U.S. Congress, Fox urged American lawmakers to grant legal rights to millions of undocumented Mexican immigrants.

In his social views, Fox leans toward religious conservatism. He has expressed opposition to abortion even in cases of rape and has suggested that he disapproves of the secular character of public education. According to Paul Berman, Fox has also labeled homosexual sex "a degenerate act which goes against human nature." Still, he has often shown himself to be more a pragmatist than a conservative ideologue. During his presidential campaign, after it became clear that such positions were probably scaring off voters who would otherwise be attracted to him, Fox issued a statement in which he sought to reassure his critics: "I commit myself to maintain the lay character of the Mexican state and public education," he said, as quoted by Berman. "I commit myself to maintain the liberty, diversity and pluralism of Mexican society and never to use the power of the state to impose lifestyles, religious beliefs or codes of personal behavior. To respect the liberty of creation, of culture and of expression of all the groups who form Mexican society." His words left some people unconvinced; among them was Rosario Robles Berlanga, the popular former mayor of Mexico City, who called him an "authoritarian-in-waiting." Others cautiously accepted his newly avowed moderation. As the Mexican author, editor, and former diplomat Carlos Fuentes wrote for the *Houston Chronicle* (July 6, 2000) shortly after Fox's victory, "I think that all of us Mexicans accept his message of openness and conciliation. I think that we should also remain alert so that feeling the authority of victory, the old moralistic PAN tendencies toward clericalism, homophobia and [misogyny] don't reappear."

Fox's first marriage, to Lillian de la Concha, who was working as an executive secretary at Coca-Cola when they met, ended in divorce. (His wife, he has said, left him for another man.) Fox retained custody of the four children from that marriage. On July 2, 2001 he was married to his official spokesperson, Martha Sahagún. He is the author of a campaign autobiography, *Vicente Fox a Los Pinos* (1999). — P.K.

Suggested Reading:*Economist* p31 July 8, 2000; *New York Times* A p1+ July 4, 2000, with photo; *New York Times Magazine* p34+ July 2, 2000, with photos; *World Policy Journal* p61+ Fall 1996

Selected Books: *Vicente Fox a Los Pinos*, 1999

Courtesy of IAC Group

Francisco, Don

Dec. 28, 1940– Television personality. Address: 9405 N.W. 41st St., Miami, FL 33178

In his almost 40 years on the air, Don Francisco, the gregarious host of the hit Latin American television variety show *Sábado Gigante* ("Giant Saturday"), has presided over hundreds of talent and dance contests, awarded millions of dollars in game-show prizes, and helped launch the careers of scores of buxom spokesmodels (the glamorous-looking women who assist TV hosts). In 1986 Francisco secured a deal with Univision, the world's most-watched Spanish-language television network, and moved the taping of his four-hour TV show from Santiago, in his native Chile, to Miami,

Florida. Enjoyed by a weekly worldwide audience estimated at more than 90 million viewers, *Sábado Gigante* was certified in 1993 by the *Guinness Book of World Records* as the longest-running program in television history.

The heavyset, impeccably tailored Don Francisco, who gave up his trademark cigar some time ago, after becoming gung-ho on maintaining a healthful lifestyle, is also known for his devotion to humanitarian causes. Since 1978 he has staged an annual telethon in Chile to aid handicapped children and raise money for hospital construction in South and Central America. For six years in the 1990s, he served as ambassador to Latin America for UNICEF (the United Nations Children's Fund), working to call attention to the child-labor problem in Latin America and Asia. In 2000 he endowed a scholarship for Hispanic students at Florida International University in Miami and was named to the university's board of directors.

Don Francisco was born Mario Kreutzberger on December 28, 1940 in Talca, Chile. His parents, Erick and Annie, were German Jews who fled the Nazis at the outbreak of World War II. His mother, a classically trained singer whose career was ended by the move to South America, gave Mario singing lessons. Although his peers reportedly mocked his early attempts at classical singing, he enjoyed success during his teens as a theater actor. It was in this context that Kreutzberger coined the persona of Don Francisco, a funny-talking, slightly lecherous emcee who charmed women and enabled men to laugh at their own repressed desires.

In 1959 Kreutzberger's father, a successful tailor, sent him to New York City to study tailoring. Alone in a Manhattan hotel room, he encountered television for the first time. "I turned it on and saw the image, black-and-white, and I thought, 'Incredible,'" he told a *People* magazine interviewer for an article called "The 40 Most Fascinating People on TV" (September 2, 1996, on-line). After his return to Chile, about a year later, he gravitated to the television station on the campus of the Pontificia Universidad Catolica de Chile, in Santiago, where he did odd jobs and observed the goings-on. His break came on August 8, 1962, when Don Francisco went on the air for the first time. Overnight, the weekly broadcast, which at its inception extended for eight hours, became the most popular television show in Chile.

Although the set has been renovated periodically and there is always a demand for new female spokesmodels, *Sábado Gigante*'s basic variety-show format has changed little over the years. Many staff members, including the show's producer, chief editor, and musical director, have worked with Don Francisco for decades. "It was my idea to make the program like soup, to melt everything inside," Don Francisco explained to Jordon Levin for the Danbury, Connecticut, *News-Times* (June 5, 2000, on-line). "There are interviews, humor, games, singers, everything—but all in small tablets. People like change. When I started in TV,

there was no remote control. So the idea was to try and do the remote control in people's minds."

While watching *Sábado Gigante* is tantamount to a shared cultural experience for millions of Latin American families, non-Latino critics have complained about the show's dated look, format, and attitude toward women. "*Sábado Gigante*'s production people seem to have learned their trade by watching *Captain and Tenille*-era variety shows," Henry Goldblatt wrote for *Fortune.com* (August 18, 1997), referring to a bland 1970s song-and-dance cavalcade. "It's like a high school talent show that never ends," Devin D. O'Leary wrote in a review for the *Tucson* [Arizona] *Weekly* (April 16, 1997, on-line), in which he expressed more surprise than criticism. Perhaps because there is nothing else quite like it on the air, *Sábado Gigante* attracts a considerable cult following of non-Spanish speakers.

A typical installment of *Sábado Gigante* includes any or all of the following: comic soap-opera skits, such as the popular and long-running "La Familia Fernandez" and "Hospital Gigante"; a tear-jerking, true-life segment in which people who have not seen each other for a very long time are reunited; a children's pageant in which a new Miss Chiquitita ("Miss Very Small") is crowned; a travel-guide segment; an amateur-talent contest in which losers are hounded offstage by a trumpet-blowing man wearing an executioner's hood; and several game-show segments, which culminate in the predictable finale—the awarding of a new car to a member of the studio audience.

Old-fashioned commercial pitches are also prominent; advertisers are said to love Don Francisco for his willingness to integrate advertising and program content, as talk-show hosts did in decades past. Don Francisco goes a step further, leading his studio audiences in sing-alongs to commercial jingles and appearing with barely dressed women in skits about the products. In addition, political figures ranging from Prime Minister Indira Gandhi of India to Vice President Al Gore have sat for interviews with Don Francisco. A booking on *Sábado Gigante* is de rigueur for Latin American celebrities and musicians making the promotional rounds.

Off-camera, Don Francisco becomes Mario Kreutzberger, described by friends as intelligent, thoughtful, and serious—"someone you don't want to invite to a dinner party because he will bore everyone," as the producer Marcelo Amunategui told *People* jokingly. Kreutzberger lives with his wife of 39 years, Teresa Muchnick, in a well-appointed mansion in the exclusive Miami enclave of Indian Creek Island. The couple have three grown children. Kreutzberger spends about two weeks each month taping *Sábado Gigante* in Miami and the rest of his time taping travel segments for the show, attending to his charity work, and visiting Chile. He has claimed to have taken only one week off from taping in almost four decades, when his mother died, in 1974. A health enthusiast, he begins each day with a rigorous exercise regimen and carefully watches his weight; he also claims to eat eight jalapeno peppers daily. He spends most evenings dining and relaxing with friends.

Among those well qualified to draw the distinction between Mario Kreutzberger and his television alter ego are the attractive Latina spokesmodels who provide "eye candy" for the Don and his viewers of all ages. Former model Maria Torres described the *Gigante* experience to Adolfo Mendez for *Latino.com* (April 19, 2000): "You have to go over your lines and memorize, and then you go out there and deal with Don Francisco harping on you for every little thing you do." Current *Sábado Gigante* spokesmodel Mirabel Rodriguez told Jordon Levin, "Mario Kreutzberger is one person. He's very introverted, observant, always thinking. Once the cameras come on, he's Don Francisco—jokester, womanizer, clown." "With the years you separate your personalities," Kreutzberger told Levin. "I think it's a need you have to be private, to be your own person."

In February 2000 Don Francisco joined with the music-industry executives Larry Rosen and Sergio Rozenblat and the Spanish pop-singing icon Julio Iglesias to create *aplauso.com*. The Web site provides information in Spanish, English, and Portuguese on Latin music and entertainment. — G.K.R.

Suggested Reading: *Advertising Age* S p1+ Sep. 26, 1988; *aplauso.com*; *News-Times* (on-line), June 5, 2000; *People* (on-line), Sep. 2, 1996; *Sábado Gigante* Web site

---

Ed Geller/Retna Ltd.

Fraser, Brendan

Dec. 3, 1968– Actor. Address: c/o William Morris Agency, 151 El Camino Dr., Beverly Hills, CA 90212

Since he made his movie debut, with a single line in the little-noticed *Dogfight*, in 1991, Brendan Fraser has become a Hollywood star. "Blessed with sex appeal and a great sense of comic timing," as a writer for *Entertainment Weekly* (March 2, 2000) put it, and "known for his gentleness, intelligence, and good looks," as Alexander Wohl wrote for *Biography* (August 2000), Fraser has appeared in two dozen films, ranging from such comedies as *George of the Jungle* to the poignant psychological drama *Gods and Monsters*. In many of his films, he has been cast as what Miranda Spencer, writing for *Biography* (June 1999), described as "sweet fish-out-of-water characters." "The careers I admire are built on diversity," Fraser told Alexander Wohl. "Starting off you need to have a calling card that will say 'I can do this and I can do that'—extremes from the sublime to the ridiculous. . . . I'm always looking to make small discoveries and maintain a sense of availability to learn and to be challenged and to find a way to put that into whatever role I'm going to play next. I know that without making diverse choices I probably won't be able to maintain my interest, and once my interest goes away there's no reason in doing it any more."

A citizen of both Canada and the United States, Brendan James Fraser was born on December 3, 1968 in Indianapolis, Indiana, to Peter and Carol Fraser. His father was a Canadian tourism official, and his mother worked in sales. Along with his three older brothers, Brendan grew up in both Europe and North America; the family rarely lived in one place for more than four years, and he became skillful at adapting to new situations. "I remember being the new kid all the time, and that causes a lot of anxiety. But there was a joy in redefining yourself each time," he recalled to Rebecca Ascher-Walsh for *Entertainment Weekly* (October 7, 1994). The Frasers eventually settled in Toronto, Canada, where Fraser attended Upper Canada College, a highly regarded prep school for boys that accommodates both boarders and day students. He often felt alienated at the school. "I was intimidated rooming with the sons of Cabinet members and the Prime Minister," he told a reporter for *Time* (June 22, 1992). "They all wanted to become politicians. I wanted to be an actor."

Fraser studied fine arts, with a physical performance focus, at the Cornish College of the Arts, in Seattle, Washington. After he earned a B.A. degree, in about 1990, he found employment at Seattle's Intiman Theater and the Laughing Horse Summer

Theater, in Ellensburg, Washington; he acted in such plays as *Waiting for Godot*, *Arms and the Man*, and *A Midsummer Night's Dream*. He has cited the actor, pantomimist, and clown Bill Irwin, whom he saw perform in Seattle, as one of his major influences.

In 1991, thanks to his one-line role in Nancy Savoca's *Dogfight*, he met River Phoenix, who starred in the film. Observing Phoenix was life-changing, he told Brendan Lemon for *Interview* (August 1994). "I was working with this guy of 19 who was already doing all this wonderful work. I shook his hand, and he said, 'I'm sorry we didn't get to work together,' and it really inspired me. I remember riding my bike home that night thinking, O.K., this is what I want to do: I want to work for the camera." Passing up a scholarship to attend graduate school at Southern Methodist University, he left Seattle for Hollywood, having been invited for an interview with the casting director Sharon Bialy, who earlier, while scouting in Seattle, had turned him down for the role of a Latino character. Within a short time of his arrival, Fraser had acted in two television movies. He next captured a part in Robert Mandel's *School Ties* (1992), which has been credited with launching his career as well as those of Matt Damon, Ben Affleck, and Chris O'Donnell. In that film, which is about anti-Semitism at an exclusive prep school in the 1950s, he played David Greene, a Jewish star quarterback who keeps his faith hidden from his peers. To create a realistic portrait of Greene, Fraser, who is not Jewish, drew on some of his own distressing boarding-school experiences, which included "being dragged from his bed . . . and thrown in the trunk of a car," according to Alexander Wohl. "I had to do this project because it would help exorcise some of the ghosts that lingered from boarding school . . . ," Fraser told Jamie Diamond for the *New York Times* (June 21, 1992). "Boarding school is creepy and seductive all at the same time. I never felt that I had a grip on it. But this role gave me another crack at it, and I got the opportunity to re-examine my past."

Also in 1992, Fraser was cast in the film *Encino Man*, in the part of Link, a frozen Cro-Magnon man defrosted by two California teenagers. Recalling his audition for the role, he told Susan Spillman for *USA Today* (June 10, 1992), "They turned a camera on me, and I think I wrestled the plants in the office. They wanted to see an actor who was willing to look ridiculous." Although critics panned *Encino Man*, they commented favorably on Fraser's goofy physical presence. During the next five years, Fraser appeared in more than a dozen films, most of which won mixed reviews at best, as did his performances. *Airheads* and *With Honors*, both of which premiered in 1994, are typical of those pictures.

Fraser's big break came in 1997, when he won the lead role in *George of the Jungle*, a live-action remake of a 1967 animated film and a late-1960s television series. He loved the part, finding it phys-

ically challenging, fun, and even meaningful. In an interview for *Mr. Showbiz* (on-line), he compared George, a Tarzan wannabe, to the legendary Greek hero Odysseus: "I think that the quality of the character of Tarzan has to do with its basis in mythology. If you look at the lore, it's essentially *The Odyssey*: a character is transported to a netherworld by some conveyance. . . . He's stranded there, must rise to power. . . . He deposes an evil leader, encounters a woman, loses her by some mistake or abduction, must retrieve her, delving deeper into the jungle or netherworld, and to retrieve her, return home, but not in glory, to encounter his worst foe, which turns out to be, of course, humanity. To overcome that foe is probably the enduring essence of the myth. . . . And then he's rewarded warmly with a jungle wedding." A Disney production directed by Sam Weisman, *George of the Jungle* was a surprise hit that appealed to both adults and children.

Fraser next appeared as Clayton Boone in Bill Condon's *Gods and Monsters* (1998), a fictionalized account of the last months of the British expatriate filmmaker James Whale, who directed the classic 1930s movies *Frankenstein* and *Bride of Frankenstein*. Based on Christopher Bram's novel *Father of Frankenstein* (1995), *Gods and Monsters* follows the physical and psychological disintegration of the homosexual Whale (portrayed by Ian McKellen) and his complex relationship with his new, muscular yardboy, the fictional Boone. *Gods and Monsters* and its stars (who included Lynn Redgrave, cast as Whale's housekeeper) won critical raves; Condon earned an Academy Award for best adapted screenplay. In an interview with Bonnie Siegler for *People* (February 22, 1999, on-line), Fraser said, "I'm so thankful the film is getting such attention because the relationships in the movie are not easy and not really meant to be perfect. . . . It was such a wonderful adventure because we had such a strong sense of purpose."

Fraser starred opposite Alicia Silverstone in Hugh Wilson's *Blast from the Past* (1999), which follows a singularly unworldly 35-year-old after he emerges from the bomb shelter in which he and his parents have lived since his birth. In another 1999 Hugh Wilson picture, *Dudley Do-Right*, Fraser—one of whose great-grandfathers was a member of the Royal Canadian Mounted Police, known as Mounties—played a handsome but dim-witted Mountie named Dudley. "As an old man, I would have regretted not making a mountie movie if I had the chance," the actor told Alexander Wohl. Like *George of the Jungle*, *Dudley Do-Right* is based on a 1960s TV cartoon series, but unlike *George*, it impressed neither moviegoers nor critics.

In Stephen Sommers's tongue-in-cheek action-adventure flick cum horror movie *The Mummy* (1999), Fraser played a 1920s adventurer who unwittingly releases a mummy from entombment, thus enabling it to cause much mischief. The film, a remake of a 1932 Boris Karloff vehicle, got mixed reviews, but it grossed more than $155 million at the box office and helped to boost Fraser's star power. Following the release of *The Mummy*, the actor's asking price per film reportedly doubled. In Harold Ramis's *Bedazzled* (2000), a remake of Stanley Donen's same-titled 1967 film, Fraser took the part of the character originally played by Dudley Moore, that of a nerd who sells his soul to the devil (Peter Cook in the 1967 version, Elizabeth Hurley in 2000) in a desperate attempt to win the affections of one of his co-workers.

In 2001 Fraser starred in *Monkeybone*, a dark, experimental comedy directed by Henry Selick. Using live action, claymation, and computer effects, *Monkeybone* tells the story of a comic-book illustrator (Fraser) who, after a freak accident, finds himself in the purgatory-like "Downtown," where he must fight off Death (played by Whoopi Goldberg). The film's visual effects earned praise, but critics trashed the humor as infantile, the story as amorphous, and the character development as insufficient. In his most recent role, Fraser again played Rick O'Connell, this time in the highly anticipated 2001 film *The Mummy Returns*. Like its predecessor, it received mixed critical ratings but an enthusiastic response from the American movie-going public. The film earned $68.1 million during its first weekend (a record for a non-holiday weekend release) and a total of $202 million over the course of its spring and summer run, placing it 35th (88th when adjusted for inflation) in the list of all-time most profitable movie releases, according to *filmsite.org*.

Fraser's hobbies include photography; he owns a collection of vintage Polaroid cameras. Photos that he took while on the set of *The Mummy* were published in the June 1999 issue of *Premiere*. Fraser has been married since 1998 to the former Afton Smith, a one-time actress, with whom he lives in Los Angeles. — K.S.

Suggested Reading: *Biography* p46+ Aug. 2000, with photos; *Entertainment Weekly* p50+ Oct. 7, 1994, with photos; *Interview* p108+ Aug. 1994, with photos; *New York Times* II p14 June 21, 1992, with photo; *People* (on-line) May 31, 1999; *Premiere* p60+ June 1994, with photos; *Seventeen* p153+ Aug. 1994, with photos; *Vogue* p400+ Sep. 2000, with photo

Selected Films: *Encino Man*, 1992; *School Ties*, 1992; *Airheads*, 1994; *The Scout*, 1994; *With Honors*, 1994; *George of the Jungle*, 1997; *Gods and Monsters*, 1998; *Blast From the Past*, 1999; *The Mummy*, 1999; *Dudley Do-Right*, 1999; *Bedazzled*, 2000; *Monkeybone*, 2001; *The Mummy Returns*, 2001

Friedman, Jane

Sep. 19, 1945– President and chief executive officer of HarperCollins Publishers. Address: HarperCollins Publishers, 10 E. 53d St., New York, NY 10022

Jane Friedman is the president and chief executive officer of HarperCollins, the book-publishing company that ranks second only to Random House in the English-language market. Friedman transformed the once-struggling operation into an industry leader; during fiscal year 2000 HarperCollins reaped revenues of $1 billion and saw an 85 percent increase in profits. Her career began at Random House, where she held many high-ranking positions and became a pioneer in the audio book market as the founder of Random House Audio Publishing. Friedman enjoys the respect and admiration of both her colleagues and her competitors. Jeannie Luciano, the publishing director of W. W. Norton & Co.'s trade division, told *CNN.com*'s *Book News* (November 24, 1999) that Friedman had "turned [HarperCollins] around. I think she was a stabilizing force when she arrived. She's very highly regarded; people like her, feel that she's a real book person. Plus, I think she has terrific marketing instincts." Friedman described herself to *Book News* as "extremely driven. I'm an extremely focused person. I'm obsessed about details. I'm very straightforward, no hidden agen-

George Lange/Courtesy of HarperCollins Publishers

das." As a publicist, Friedman developed the concept of the national book tour; one of the first tours she organized was that of the celebrity chef Julia Child, in the late 1960s. "It was a fabulous experience because we were pathfinders," she told *Book*

News. "It hadn't really been done. . . . I have wonderful memories of Julia Child making mayonnaise in a spinning restaurant over a department store in Minneapolis at 7 o'clock in the morning and having a thousand people show up to the event. It was one of the highlights of my career, and I was about 22 years old." Friedman has since worked with authors including Anne Rice, Tom Peters, Toni Morrison, Michael Crichton, and John Le Carré and has published audio versions of books by Tom Clancy, Nelson DeMille, Sue Grafton, and Patricia Cornwell.

Jane Friedman was born on September 19, 1945 in the New York City borough of Brooklyn. As a young girl growing up on Long Island, New York, she exhibited a passion for books and an interest in the stock market. Friedman's father was a commercial artist, and her mother a model; close to both of her parents, she claims to have acquired a sense of aesthetics from her mother and learned the value of confidence and determination from her father. Friedman graduated from New York University with a B.A. degree in English in 1967. The following year she was hired by Knopf, a subsidiary of Random House, as a Dictaphone typist in the publicity department. From that position she moved quickly up the ranks, becoming first a publicist and then an associate publisher. In 1985 she founded Random House Audio Publishing, a successful audio-book venture and one of the first of its kind. Five years later Friedman became the publisher for Vintage Books, where she supervised the development of the imprint's paperback books. (Vintage Contemporaries editor Gary Fisketjon used the imprint to bring attention to overlooked backlist authors such as Raymond Carver and also to introduce to the public new writers, among them Jay McInerney.) Two years later Friedman was also named executive vice president of Knopf Publishing Group, which comprises Knopf, Vintage, Random House Audio, Pantheon/Schocken, the Everyman's Library, Vintage Español, and Random House Large Print Editions.

In November 1997 Friedman accepted the position of president and CEO of HarperCollins, replacing Anthea Disney, who had been named chairman and CEO of News America Publishing Group. Friedman was also responsible for HarperCollins's publishing operations around the world, in countries including the United Kingdom, Canada, Australia, and New Zealand. In the mid-1990s HarperCollins—a subsidiary of News America, which is a division of Rupert Murdoch's News Corp.—had seen its profits decrease by 80 percent, and the company had cut costs by canceling more than 100 book contracts with mid-list authors, or those whose books usually sell between 20,000 and 30,000 copies. Rupert Murdoch put the company up for sale but could not find a buyer; rumors that Murdoch would sell HarperCollins persisted throughout the remainder of the decade. "I realized what people needed was support," Friedman told *Book News* about her first impression of Harper-

Collins. "I went out to breakfast, lunch and dinner with internal people and external people. Building morale. I spoke to Harper authors who were feeling shaky." Friedman soon found that the pace and atmosphere at HarperCollins was significantly different from the environment she had encountered at her previous place of employment. "I have no idea what my day is going to be like here, although I did know what most of my days would be like at Knopf," she told Gayle Feldman for *Publishers Weekly* (August 24, 1998). "This change is invigorating. There's no chance for me to have a mood; I feel an amazing sense of youth and energy coming from the unknown. But taking this job was like going from having one kid to two—it's more than double the responsibility."

Friedman drastically reduced the number of books published by HarperCollins, to concentrate the company's efforts on promotion; she also employed a sophisticated computer system to monitor sales figures and demographics, so as to determine how many copies of books to send to each store. This policy caused the books' rate of return from booksellers to drop from 40 percent in 1997 to 28 percent the following year. Friedman created two new imprints: HarperPerennial Classics, formed to keep the company's backlist in circulation, and HarperEntertainment, designed to exploit the possibilities in movie and television tie-ins. Her decision to increase the print run of *James Cameron's Titanic*, the companion book to the film starring Leonardo DiCaprio and Kate Winslet, from 20,000 to 400,000 copies paid off; both the book and the film were hugely successful.

HarperCollins published 34 titles that appeared on the *New York Times* best-seller list in 1998, including *I Know This Much Is True*, by Wally Lamb; *Mars and Venus Starting Over*, by John Gray; *Low Country*, by Anne Rivers Siddons; and *A Night Without Armor*, by Jewel Kilcher, as well as paperback editions of *Divine Secrets of the Ya-Ya Sisterhood*, by Rebecca Wells; *The God of Small Things*, by Arundhati Roy; and *The Perfect Storm*, by Sebastian Junger. In 1999 HarperCollins acquired William Morrow and Co. and Avon Books from the Hearst Book Group. "We have created a company that brings together some of the finest authors and imprints in publishing today," Friedman told *Authorlink.com* (September 1999), "a publishing program that combines the energy, quality and heritage of these three companies." The following year the company bought Amistad Press, one of the country's leading publishers of books by African-American authors.

HarperCollins had 57 titles on the *New York Times* best-seller list in 2000, with 14 titles on the list in one week, among them *Moment of Truth*, by Lisa Scottoline; *Daughter of Fortune*, by Isabel Allende; *Have a Nice Day!*, by Mick Foley; and *Dr. Atkins' New Diet Revolution*, by Robert C. Atkins. Among HarperCollins's recent best-sellers are *The Vendetta Defense*, by Lisa Scottoline; *Long Time No See*, by Susan Isaacs; *Body for Life*, by Bill Phillips; and, for younger readers, several books by Lemony Snicket (*The Bad Beginning, The Ersatz Elevator, The Reptile Room, The Vile Village*) and *Where Do Balloons Go?*, by Jamie Lee Curtis. HarperCollins's 2001 titles include *A Cook's Tour: In Search of the Perfect Meal*, by Anthony Bourdain; *Simple and Direct*, by Jacques Barzun; *Ten Stupid Things Couples Do to Mess Up Their Relationships*, by Laura Schlessinger; *The Bulgari Connection*, by Fay Weldon; and, for children, the biography *Langston Hughes*, by Alice Walker.

Friedman's work has often been recognized by her peers in the publishing industry. In November 1998 she was included on *Vanity Fair*'s list of 200 Women Legends, Leaders and Trailblazers; the following year she was the recipient of the LMP (Literary Market Place) Person of the Year Award, and *Ladies' Home Journal* named her one of America's 100 Most Important Women. She was also named one of the 100 Most Influential Women in Business for 2000 by *Crain's New York Business*. Friedman serves on the Advisory Council of New York Is Book Country, an annual outdoor festival. She is also co-chair of the publishing division of the United Jewish Appeal (UJA), as well as vice chair of the UJA's Entertainment, Media and Communications Division. Friedman's other memberships include the American Advisory Committee of the Jerusalem International Book Fair, the board of the Association of American Publishers, the board of Poets & Writers, and the Advisory Committee to the MFA program in creative writing at the New School University (formerly the New School for Social Research), in New York.

Friedman has raised two sons and two stepsons. The latter are the children of her longtime partner, Jeff Stone, an Internet developer and the creator of a series of books, known as *Chic Simple,* that offer advice on such subjects as fashion and interior decorating. — C.L.

Suggested Reading: *Business Week* p74+ June 14, 1999, with photos; *Crain's New York Business* p1+ Nov. 9–15 1998, with photo; *Publishers Weekly* p10 Nov. 3, 1997, with photo, p29+ Aug. 24, 1998, with photos, p34 Apr. 17, 2000

Courtesy of Francis Fukuyama

Fukuyama, Francis

Oct. 27, 1952– Social scientist; writer; educator. Address: George Mason University, 3401 N. Fairfax Dr., Arlington, VA 22201

In 1989 Francis Fukuyama, a little-known social scientist and mid-level government official, published an article announcing that the "end of history" had arrived. Although it appeared in an obscure conservative journal, the *National Interest*, the article received substantial attention in magazines and newspapers in many parts of the world. Fukuyama did not mean that the world was literally coming to an end. Rather, he contended that history, which he defined as not just the recording of past events but as the clash of opposing ideologies, had reached its conclusion, since no other system would ever displace those of liberal democratic governments. While they did not share his viewpoint, legions of academics, journalists, and commentators, and even a number of world leaders, found it necessary to express an opinion about Fukuyama's "end of history" thesis. The year 1992 saw the publication of Fukuyama's book *The End of History and the Last Man*; since then, Fukuyama—the author of several other books, most recently *The Great Disruption: Human Nature and the Reconstitution of Social Order* (1999)—has joined the ranks of those often referred to as "public intellectuals."

Francis Fukuyama was born on October 27, 1952 in Chicago, Illinois. His paternal grandfather immigrated to the United States from Japan in 1905 to avoid being drafted during the Russo-Japanese War. After settling in the "Little Tokyo" section of Los Angeles, California, his grandfather opened a hardware store. In an interview with Benjamin Wattenberg, the host of the PBS series *Think Tank* (October 9, 1999), as posted on the PBS Web site, Fukuyama recalled that his father's family was interned in concentration camps in the United States during World War II. After the war Fukuyama's mother, the former Toshiko Kawata, emigrated from Japan to the United States, where she met his father, Yoshio Fukuyama, who was an ordained minister in the United Church of Christ and taught religious studies at the Chicago Theological Seminary and Penn State University.

Fukuyama lived in Chicago for two years. In 1954 his family moved to New York City. Fukuyama recalled to Current Biography, "I attended a private school that required me, in the sixth grade, to ride the subway one and a half hours each way to get to school. I was very nonathletic and spent my time doing things like attending astronomy classes at the Hayden Planetarium or, when I was a bit older, going to jazz clubs in Greenwich Village." Fukuyama enrolled at Cornell University, in Ithaca, New York, in 1970. There, he took a course with Allan Bloom, who was highly regarded in academic circles for translating the works of such classical thinkers as Plato and Jean-Jacques Rousseau. Bloom and his students, including Fukuyama, spent hours outside class talking about philosophy and classical literature. (In 1987 Bloom would receive national attention for his book The Closing of the American Mind, a blistering indictment of the state of culture and higher education in the United States.) Fukuyama told Current Biography that Bloom, who became his "chief intellectual mentor," encouraged him to study classical Greek in order "to read Plato and Aristotle in the original, as part of my study of political philosophy." Fukuyama received a B.A. degree in classics from Cornell in 1974. That fall, he entered Yale University, in New Haven, Connecticut, to take classes in comparative literature. He studied under Paul de Man, a well-known deconstructionist. "It was kind of an intellectual side journey," Fukuyama recalled to James Atlas for the New York Times Magazine (October 22, 1989).

An earlier occurrence had relegated his study of literature to "side journey" status. As part of his undergraduate education, Fukuyama had spent the first half of 1974 in Paris, France, attending as an observer classes taught by the intellectuals Roland Barthes and Jacques Derrida. "I was turned off by their nihilistic idea of what literature was all about," Fukuyama told James Atlas. "It had nothing to do with the world. I developed such an aversion to that whole over-intellectual approach that I turned to nuclear weapons instead," he continued, explaining his decision to concentrate on political science. In 1975 he went to Cambridge, Massachusetts, to pursue a doctorate in that subject at Harvard University. Fukuyama earned graduate fellowships from Harvard's Center for International Affairs in 1978 and 1979.

During his doctoral studies Fukuyama won several appointments that gave him valuable work experience. In the summer of 1976, he had an internship at the U. S. Arms Control and Disarmament Agency in Washington, D.C. For about a year he worked in Los Angeles as a consultant for Pan Heuristics Services, a consulting group that focuses on national-security issues. In 1979 the Rand Corp., one of the nation's best-known public-policy think tanks, hired him as an associate social scientist at

its office in Santa Monica, California. For Rand, Fukuyama wrote several papers that analyzed the Soviet Union's military and foreign policies toward Iraq, Afghanistan, and Pakistan. For his Ph.D. thesis, Fukuyama explored several threats of military intervention in the Middle East made by the Soviet Union between 1956 and 1973. On the basis of his research, he concluded that the Soviets had been bluffing in every case. He received his doctorate in 1981.

That same year the U. S. Department of State brought Fukuyama aboard as a member of its policy-planning staff. The focus of his work was the Middle East, especially the turmoil in Lebanon and the peace agreements being worked out between Israel and its Arab neighbors. As a member of the U.S. delegation, Fukuyama attended negotiations between Egypt and Israel on Palestinian autonomy. In 1983 he rejoined the Rand Corp. in California as a senior staff member of its political-science department. There, as he explained to Current Biography, he conducted research whose main focus was Soviet foreign and military policy. In 1989 he went back to the State Department as the deputy director of the policy planning staff. His areas of interest were political and military affairs in Europe and issues relating to the Soviet Union.

Earlier, in 1979, Fukuyama had begun publishing articles on a regular basis, contributing to such journals as Current History, Commentary, Middle East Contemporary Survey, Foreign Affairs, Comparative Strategy, and the National Interest. Although he gradually became well known among foreign-policy scholars and government officials, Fukuyama remained largely unknown to both the media and the general public. In 1987 he co-edited a book with Andrzej Korbonski, The Soviet Union and the Third World: The Last Three Decades, to which Fukuyama contributed an article that discussed Soviet policies with regard to Third World nations.

In 1988, while he was still working for the Rand Corp., Fukuyama submitted an article to the National Interest, a journal edited by the neoconservative intellectual Irving Kristol. The article, "The End of History?," was published in the Summer 1989 issue. Fukuyama began the article by suggesting that journalists, political pundits, and even scholars, who were all anticipating the imminent end of the Cold War, were ignoring the wider, historic implications of the unfolding events. "What we may be witnessing is not just the end of the Cold War, or the passing of a particular period of post-war history, but the end of history as such, that is, the end point of mankind's ideological evolution and the universalization of Western liberal democracy as the final form of human government," he wrote. He went on to add, "The state that emerges at the end of history is liberal insofar as it recognizes and protects through a system of law man's universal right to freedom, and democratic insofar as it exists only with the consent of the governed." (The "end of history," he stressed, did not mean the end of violent conflict or of the many problems that plague society, such as poverty, crime, racism, and unemployment.)

To support his thesis, Fukuyama cited the ideas of the German philosopher Georg Wilhelm Friedrich Hegel (1770–1831), who defined history as the attempt to resolve the conflict between opposing "ideological" forces, which include religion, culture, and prevailing moral values. These forces, in turn, are created and driven by "contradictions" within a system. Hegel argued that this conflict would eventually be resolved, leading to the elimination of any contradictions and bringing history to an end. The final result would be a society governed by the principles of reason. In his own time, Hegel believed that history ended in 1806, the year France, under Napoleon Bonaparte, defeated Prussia at the Battle of Jena. Hegel, Fukuyama wrote, believed that Napoleon's victory represented the triumph of "the ideals of the French Revolution, and the imminent universalization of the state incorporating the principles of liberty and equality." Several decades later the German philosopher Karl Marx (1818–83) used Hegel's ideas to delineate the different stages of history, also propelled by contradictions, that he felt were leading toward a definite historical conclusion represented by the triumph of socialism. Fukuyama observed that many intellectuals often ignore Hegel because he is seen as a "precursor" to Marx, whose ideas have been discredited with the decline of communism and the growing acceptance of the free market. Fukuyama maintained, however, that on their own, Hegel's ideas still had merit and could explain the forces driving democratic movements in nearly every part of the world.

In a January 1992 interview with Brian Lamb, the host of the C-SPAN network's program *Booknotes*, as published on the *Booknotes* Web site (January 17, 1992), Fukuyama explained that Hegel's "theory of history" was "based, not on economics, but on what he called the struggle for recognition . . . that we as human beings want to be recognized as human beings with a certain dignity and human freedom." This search for recognition, Fukuyama continued, underlies "the relationship of masters and slaves. It's the path that lies behind, in a certain way, religion and movements like nationalism." Fukuyama believed that this "search for recognition" explained the forces behind contemporary democratic movements. Democratic governments, he noted, recognize the dignity of human beings by giving them individual rights. As a larger consequence, the Hegelian contradictions and clashes of ideology that drive history disappear, leading to history's end and the universal establishment and acceptance of democracy.

Fukuyama concluded his essay by predicting that life in the "posthistorical world" would be a "very sad time" because the "struggle for recognition, the willingness to risk one's life for a purely abstract goal, the worldwide ideological struggle that called forth daring, courage, imagination, and

idealism, will be replaced by economic calculation, the endless solving of technical problems, environmental concerns, and the satisfaction of sophisticated consumer demands." Although he believed that the end of history was inevitable, Fukuyama wondered if "this very prospect of centuries of boredom at the end of history will serve to get history started once again."

Fukuyama predicted that his essay would receive no more attention than his previous publications. The response to it, however, was overwhelming. "The End of History" became one of the most talked-about articles of 1989. Not only was the *National Interest* flooded with letters to the editor, from individuals including Allan Bloom, the historian Gertrude Himmelfarb, and Senator Daniel Patrick Moynihan of New York; many prominent newspapers and journals around the country, such as the *New York Times Magazine*, the *Washington Post*, the *New Republic*, the *National Review*, *Time*, the *Nation*, *Newsweek*, *Harper's Magazine*, *Commentary*, the *American Spectator*, the *Los Angeles Times*, and *Newsday* all devoted substantial attention to Fukuyama's thesis. The essay was also translated into many foreign languages and became the subject of intense discussion in such nations as the United Kingdom, France, Italy, the Netherlands, South Africa, Japan, Brazil, Australia, South Korea, and even the Soviet Union. Soviet president Mikhail Gorbachev and British prime minister Margaret Thatcher also expressed their opinions of the essay. Several months later, in the fall of 1989, when communism began to collapse in Eastern Europe, Fukuyama's essay gained even greater relevance. Fukuyama suddenly found himself thrust into the public spotlight, and his arguments became the subject of intense debate. "Frankly, I wasn't expecting this kind of reaction," he admitted to Bob Sipchen, a reporter for the *Los Angeles Times* (September 21, 1989). "I wanted the thing to be quite speculative and thought provoking. I guess I succeeded beyond my expectations."

Although Fukuyama was praised for writing an intellectually challenging essay that raised important issues, many scholars, historians, journalists, and commentators rejected his thesis. Criticism transcended political and ideological affiliations. One of the gentler criticisms came from Charles Krauthammer, who argued in his syndicated column in the *Houston* [Texas] *Chronicle* (September 18, 1989) that Fukuyama had ignored the role of human nature in driving history. "I would invoke, instead, 3,000 years of history that have amply demonstrated man's potential for evil," Krauthammer wrote. "If evil is inherent in human nature, it will inevitably find its political expression. Hence conflict. Hence history." Other critics suggested that Fukuyama had downplayed potential challenges to democracy from such forces as nationalism, Islamic fundamentalism, and even communism, which still governed as powerful a nation as China and could also make a return in countries plagued by poverty and strife.

Fukuyama told Lamb that many critics had misunderstood his arguments or dismissed them after seeing only the title of his essay. In an article published in the *San Francisco Chronicle* (December 20, 1989), Fukuyama replied to his critics, writing that many of those who disputed his thesis simply did not accept Hegel's definition of history as the clash of opposing ideologies rather than the recording and discussion of past events. "To refute my hypothesis, then, it is not sufficient to suggest that the future holds in store large and momentous events," he argued. "One would have to show that these events were driven by a systematic idea of political and social justice that claimed to supersede liberalism." Fukuyama left the State Department in 1990 to write a book, an expansion of the thesis he had articulated in the *National Interest*. The book, *The End of History and the Last Man* (1992), like the essay that spawned it, sharply divided readers.

Fukuyama remained in the public eye, publishing two more books and many articles for different publications. His book *Trust: The Social Virtues and the Creation of Prosperity* (1995) explored how culture influences a nation's economic well-being. Fukuyama argued that societies with high levels of trust among individuals and clubs and other voluntary groups are far more likely than other societies to facilitate economic growth and prosperity. Trust, he argued, builds "social capital," which encourages cooperation, which in turn facilitates economic growth, making regulations and legal contracts less necessary. To support his thesis he compared such "high-trust" nations as the United States, Germany, and Japan with "low-trust" nations such as France, Italy, and China. The data he cited indicate that high-trust nations are more prosperous overall than low-trust nations. Fukuyama warned, however, that the United States in recent decades had been changing into a low-trust nation.

Fukuyama's next book, *The Great Disruption: Human Nature and the Reconstitution of Social Order* (1999), is his most ambitious to date. In it he asserted that the United States' transformation from an industrial economy to an information-driven one, and the availability of birth control, which separates sex from reproduction, had unleashed many social ills—such as teen pregnancy, drug abuse, the breakdown of the family, illegitimacy, and high crime rates. Nevertheless, he expressed optimism, arguing that these social problems are in decline, and that the damage they have brought to people's lives is being repaired. Based on his readings of both the natural-law teachings of the Greek philosopher Aristotle and the scientific community's increased knowledge of genetics, Fukuyama suggested that human beings possess innate desires to adhere to socially accepted norms and build communities. As they observe how socially irresponsible behavior disrupts society and people's lives, people gradually follow their instincts to accept society's norms in an effort to halt social decay and then heal the damage to society to the point at which social ills are no longer disruptive. Although self-healing eventually restores social order, this process can take decades, or even longer, he wrote. As for the implications of his findings for public policy, Fukuyama, advocating a conservative approach to the problems he mentioned, opposed government solutions. Instead, he favored a "bottom-up" approach, one that would allow local religious communities and private organizations to help guide people to socially responsible behavior.

In 1996 Fukuyama became the Omer L. and Nancy Hirst professor of public policy at George Mason University's School of Public Policy, in Arlington, Virginia. In an article for the *National Interest* (Summer 1999), he reassessed his "end of history" thesis in light of the events that had taken place in the 10 years since he published his original essay. He stood by his claim that no other system would ever pose a significant challenge to liberal democracy. The economic crises that took place in Russia and Asia during the 1990s, he argued, "are in the end correctable by policy and do not constitute systematic challenges to the prevailing liberal world order." He conceded, however, that the argument he had used to support his view that history had come to an end was "fundamentally flawed," acknowledging that he had failed to consider the role of science in human affairs; technological advances such as genetic engineering, he wrote, could radically alter human nature and interaction.

Francis Fukuyama is married to the former Laura Holmgren. The couple have three children: Julia, David, and John. His next book will discuss the political issues behind biotechnology. — D.C.

Suggested Reading: *Booknotes* (on-line) Jan. 17, 1992; Francis Fukuyama Web site; *Houston Chronicle* p12 Sep. 18, 1989; *Los Angeles Times* p1+ Sep. 21, 1989, with photo; *Nation* p302 Sep. 25, 1989; *National Interest* p3+ Summer 1989, p16+ Summer 1999; *New Statesman* p44 Mar. 6, 1992; *New York Review of Books* p7+ Mar. 6, 1992; *New York Times Magazine* p38+ Oct. 22, 1989, with photos; *San Francisco Chronicle* Z p1 Dec. 20, 1989; *Washington Post* C p1+ Mar. 16, 1992, with photos

Selected Books: *The End of History and the Last Man*, 1992; *Trust: The Social Virtues and the Creation of Prosperity*, 1995; *The "Virtual Corporation" and Army Organization* (with Abram Shulsky), 1997; *The Great Disruption: Human Nature and the Reconstitution of Social Order*, 1999; as editor—*The Soviet Union and the Third World* (with Andrzej Korbonski), 1987

Sabina Louise Pierce/AP

Gandy, Kim

*Jan. 25, 1954– President of the National
Organization for Women. Address: NOW, 733
15th St., N.W., Washington, DC 20005-2112*

As president of the National Organization for
Women (NOW), Kim Gandy is responsible for leading the nation's largest and most powerful feminist
organization. Founded in 1966 by 28 women's
rights activists—among them Betty Friedan, the
author of the feminist classic *The Feminine Mystique* (1963)—NOW is charged with "bring[ing]
women into full participation in the mainstream of
American society now, exercising all privileges
and responsibilities thereof in truly equal partnership with men," according to the organization's official Web site. Specifically, NOW aims to protect
abortion rights; revive the Equal Rights Amendment, which has been ratified by 35 states, three
short of the number necessary for its addition to
the Constitution; achieve economic equality between the sexes; support civil rights for racial and
sexual minorities (most of the latter being homosexuals); and end violence against women. In the
short term NOW is expected to pursue that agenda
by fighting President George W. Bush's anticipated
nominations of ideological conservatives to the
federal judiciary, and by putting political pressure
on members of the U.S. Senate to reject such candidates. "They have more to fear from women's votes
than they have to fear from right-wing political and
religious zealots," Gandy recently declared, as
quoted by the *New York Times* (July 2, 2001).

Gandy has been a member of NOW since 1973;
she was named the group's national secretary-
treasurer in 1987 and its executive vice president

in 1991. On July 1, 2001, at a national conference
attended by an estimated 1,000 NOW delegates,
she defeated Toni Van Pelt, the former head of
NOW's Florida chapter, to win election as the organization's president. In an address to the delegates
shortly before the balloting, Gandy stressed her extensive experience as a NOW leader. Patricia Ireland, the outgoing NOW president (who, according
to NOW bylaws, could not run again), had endorsed Gandy. "From an organizational standpoint," Ireland told Katti Gray for *Newsday* (July
26, 2001), "this is not a time to have someone in the
presidency who's going to have a steep learning
curve. Kim, after 14 years, is able to take the baton
from my hand without missing a beat. I don't have
to worry about if she's going to be running fast
enough. She's already hitting her stride."

In her speech to NOW delegates, Gandy called
upon the organization's members to reach out to
politically moderate women, especially those who,
while supporting equal rights for women, may not
identify themselves as feminists. (Toni Van Pelt, a
businesswoman, had called for NOW to embrace a
renewed radicalism.) Gandy also labeled President
Bush "and the right wing that stands behind him"
a "threat to our lives and our rights," as the *Houston Chronicle* (July 1, 2001) quoted her as saying.
Between January 2001, when Bush was inaugurated, and July 2001, NOW membership increased by
about 10 percent.

Kim Allison Gandy was born on January 25,
1954; sources differ as to whether her place of birth
was Shreveport or Bossier City, Louisiana. Her
mother, the former Roma Rae Young, was a homemaker; her father, Alfred, was the vice president of
a local bank. Gandy has recalled that while her parents always encouraged her to pursue her own interests, they tacitly recognized the barriers ambitious women faced at that time. "My parents never
told me there was nothing I couldn't do," she told
Gray. "I've heard that from a lot of strong women,
as though their parents knew they would hit a lot
of obstacles outside the home." Neither her mother
nor her father was especially politically minded,
and Gandy told Gray that the origins of her activism are unclear. "I guess it's hard to find the roots
of that sort of thing. But my dad said to me once
that I would always take up for the underdog. You
know, if someone was picking on someone smaller
than them, I'd go wave my finger in their face. And
I was a skinny kid."

A bright student, Gandy skipped the first and
12th grades. At the age of 16, she enrolled at Louisiana Tech University, in Ruston. She studied mathematics, a subject in which she earned a B.S. degree in 1973. Her growing awareness of discriminatory social attitudes toward women led her, that
same year, to join the local NOW chapter.

In interviews, Gandy has described two experiences that were pivotal in her decision to become
a NOW member. First, while at Louisiana Tech,
she married a graduate student of mathematics.
Several years later the two divorced, in part be-

cause of gender issues. "He came from a traditional family in Cantor, Mississippi," she told Gray. "Left to his own devices, our marriage would not have been much different from our courtship, which was pretty equitable. Once we got married, he said doing the dishes was my job." Second, while applying for a job with the telephone company South Central Bell, where she worked from 1973 to 1977, Gandy discovered that, in Louisiana, marital property laws entitled a husband to dispose of his wife's income as he pleased. (Those laws were annulled by the Louisiana State Legislature in 1980, thanks in part to Gandy's lobbying efforts.) Both experiences led Gandy to think about the ways in which marriage, as a legal institution, is biased against women and sexual minorities. "It has, over long years, disadvantaged women and in many ways continues to," she explained to Gray. "It is, in some ways, unfair. Gay and lesbian couples don't get the same legal benefits from it. For someone like me, who is employed and employable and a lawyer, marriage does not carry many threats. But the average woman often does not know what she is getting into, and what kind of contract the state will make for her."

Gandy's deepening involvement with NOW inspired her to enroll at the Loyola University School of Law, in New Orleans, from which she received a J.D. degree in 1978. After she was admitted to the Louisiana state bar, that same year, she served for one year as a senior assistant district attorney in New Orleans. Thereafter, she became increasingly active in support of women's rights. In 1979 she established a private law practice specializing in such issues as child support, marital property rights, domestic violence, sexual and racial discrimination, and child custody cases in which the mother was lesbian. In one of her most successful cases, Gandy won a $184,000 judgment in a sex-discrimination suit against the United States Air Force. In addition to running her private practice, Gandy served on the New Orleans City Planning Commission; was an officer of several organizations—the Association of Democratic Women, the Lesbian and Gay Political Action Caucus, and the Association of Women Attorneys; served as founding director of New Orleans' Metropolitan Battered Women's Program; founded the Louisiana Women's Lobby Network; and drafted several bills, including the Louisiana Child Support Enforcement Act and the Louisiana Domestic Abuse Assistance Act. In 1982 Gandy was elected to NOW's national board and became regional director of the organization's Mid-South Division; she held the latter position for four years.

When Molly Yard decided to run for the presidency of NOW in 1987 (then–president Eleanor Smeal had announced that she would not seek re-election), she asked Gandy to join her slate by running for the post of national secretary-treasurer. "I was weighing the pros and cons," Gandy told Gray. "My dad said, 'You're going.' I said I wasn't so sure. I didn't know if I wanted to be a little fish in a big pond. He said I'd go to the place where I could fight for the most underdogs at once." Gandy heeded her father's words, and she won the election. (Yard's bid for the NOW presidency was successful as well.) Immersing herself in her new job, Gandy closed her New Orleans law practice and moved to Washington, D.C.

In addition to overseeing the finances of NOW's political action committees during her four years as national secretary-treasurer, Gandy helped draft two pieces of federal legislation: the Civil Rights Act of 1991, which entitles "women to a jury trial and monetary damages in cases of sex discrimination and sexual harassment," as the official NOW Web site explained, and the Freedom of Access to Clinic Entrances Act, popularly known as the "Abortion Clinic Access law," which aims "to permit individuals to have freedom of access to certain medical clinics and facilities" (in particular, abortion clinics), according to the Library of Congress on-line archives. The latter bill was signed into law by President Bill Clinton on May 26, 1994. Throughout this period Gandy remained active in Louisiana politics. In 1991 she took an active role in the campaign to thwart former Ku Klux Klan leader David Duke's bid for the governorship of Louisiana. (Duke was defeated, largely because of a large turnout by African-Americans and other members of minority groups.)

In 1991, the year in which Patricia Ireland began her first term as the NOW president, Gandy was elected NOW's executive vice president. In that role, she was responsible for supervising the organization's administrative staff and overseeing NOW's legislative agenda, the lawsuits it was pursuing, and relations with the federal government. Among NOW's accomplishments during Gandy's tenure was a favorable Supreme Court ruling in *NOW v. Scheidler* (1994); according to the NOW Web site, the Court "affirmed NOW's right to use federal anti-racketeering laws against anti-abortion extremists who organize others to bomb and block clinics and to intimidate patients and health care providers."

According to Gray, Patricia Ireland has characterized Gandy as "a very kind person." "She does not carry a grudge very well," Ireland said. "We have her friends carry them for her—and remind her of the things we should be mad about." Gandy currently makes her home in Washington, D.C., where she lives with her husband, Christopher "Kip" Lornell, an ethnomusicologist and part-time professor of Africana Studies at George Washington University. Gandy and Lornell have two daughters, Elizabeth Cady Lornell and Katherine Eleanor Gandy. Regarding the girls' surnames, Gandy explained to Gray, "It felt right to share. The kids say, 'This is my sister Cady Lornell. This is my sister Katherine Gandy, but we call her Max.' There's nothing abnormal about it to them." — P.K.

Suggested Reading: *New York Times* A p11 July 2, 2001, with photo; *Newsday* B p6+ July 26, 2001, with photos; NOW Web site; *Who's Who of American Women, 2000–2001*

Andrew Redington/Allsport

Garcia, Sergio

Jan. 9, 1980– Golfer. Address: c/o PGA European Tour, Wentworth Dr., Virginia Water, Surrey GU25 4LX, England

The Spanish golfer Sergio Garcia was nicknamed El Niño—the Kid—by the Spanish press "when I was very small," he told Harry Blauvelt for *USA Today* (July 16, 1998). "Now, I have grown up a little. The problem is, when I'm 30 years old, we'll have to come up with another one." Garcia's skills have been admired by professionals and fans the world over, and he has honed his talent with discipline and confidence. "I have always wanted to play," he explained to John Huggan for *Golf World* (April 2, 1999). "I love to practice. I have given a lot of things up, but when you want to do something with your life, that is always the way." As a teenager Garcia accrued stature in the European Amateur circuit, earning opportunities to play as an amateur in the British Open. After emerging as the lowest-scoring (hence the most successful) amateur on the course during the 1999 Masters tournament, he turned pro, and won two Professional Golfers' Association (PGA) events in Europe that year. Bouncing back from a disastrous outing at the 1999 British Open, he finished as the runner-up to Tiger Woods, considered the greatest young player on the PGA tour, at the 1999 PGA Championship

in Medinah, Illinois, losing the tournament by only one stroke. Regarded as one of the sport's newest legends, Garcia plans to work his way to the ranking of number one in the world.

Garcia was born on January 9, 1980 in Castellon, Spain, to a golfing family. His father and swing coach, Victor, signed on as the club professional at the Club de Campo del Mediterraneo in Castellon when it opened, and his mother, Consuelo, ran the pro shop. His older brother, Victor Jr., earned a golf scholarship to study at the University of South Carolina, and his younger sister, Mar, has played on the Spanish girls' circuit. Even before Garcia received his first set of clubs, at age three, he took practice swings around the house with feather dusters and brooms. Beginning at age five, he challenged members at the Club de Campo del Mediterraneo to competitions on the putting green. "I would play them for Cokes or ice creams," he told John Huggan. "Most of the time I would win. I liked to win." He got full-sized clubs at age nine and won his club's championship at 12. By age 13 he was a scratch player—that is, he consistently scored par at every hole—and a year later he had played in his first European PGA event, the Mediterranean Open. To groom him for worldwide success, his parents hired an English tutor and staged mock press conferences, at which he discussed his rounds.

Garcia put himself on the international golfing map at age 15, when he became the youngest person ever to win the European Amateur Championship. The European Amateur crown entitled him to play in the 1996 British Open. His success in the amateur ranks continued; he won the 1997 Catalonia Open, a Spanish PGA event, despite playing as an amateur. Being part of the European circuit put Garcia in contact with the bigwigs of professional golf, including his famous countryman Seve Ballesteros, a three-time British Open winner, who became his professional mentor. "I learned a lot from watching Seve, what a big fighter he is, to never give up. And also some magic shots. . . . He didn't teach me. It's something you can't teach. These shots are something that's inside you, and you have to see them in your imagination. From watching Seve, I am now able to let this magic out," he told E. M. Swift for *Sports Illustrated* (September 27, 1999). Many were surprised by his unusually good short game, his speed, and his driving distance, which regularly topped 300 yards. "I probably hit it so far because of the way I swing," he told Harry Blauvelt. "When I was young, I was so short that I had to swing very fast. Like Indiana Jones snapping a bullwhip." Garcia reached his full height, five feet 10 inches, before his 18th birthday, in 1998. Although he was still playing as an amateur, he made the cut in 12 of the 13 professional events he attempted. "I feel almost like a pro because I've played in so many pro events," he explained to Blauvelt as he was preparing for the opening round of the 1998 British Open. Ubiquitous at marquee events, he attracted the notice of many of the world's best golfers; even after Garcia was cut in the beginning rounds of the 1996 British Open, Tom Lehman, the 1996 British Open winner and the 1996 PGA Tour Player of the Year, invited Garcia to pose with the Claret Jug, the British Open trophy, in anticipation of his future success in that event.

In 1998 Garcia won both the British Boys and British Amateur crowns. He also earned the top spot at the Spanish Amateur and reached the semifinals of the U.S. Amateur. His success at the British Amateur event entitled him to play in the 1999 Masters Championship, held in Augusta, Georgia. He survived the cut and the opening rounds at the Masters and finished play as the lowest-scoring amateur—the first European ever to do so—with a tie for 38th place. Immediately after the 1999 Masters, Garcia turned professional. Within days, his popularity and skill had commanded lucrative contracts with Adidas and Acushnet, makers of Titleist and Cobra golf equipment. The 1999 Spanish Open, held in Barcelona, was the scene of Garcia's first appearance as a pro; he finished 25th.

Garcia's first season as a pro had extreme peaks and valleys. In his U.S. professional debut, the GTE Byron Nelson Classic, he finished in a tie for third. He won the Irish Open, his sixth pro event, in early July 1999, and followed up that triumph with a second-place tie at Loch Lomond, in Scotland. Although confident going into the 1999 British Open, he was pummeled by the course and the winds. He shot an 89 and an 83 in the first two rounds and thus did not progress further. "I couldn't do anything," he confessed to Clifton Brown for the *New York Times* (July 16, 1999). "The wind wasn't as hard in practice. Everything came out the wrong way." Just a month later Garcia was the first-round leader by two strokes at the 1999 PGA Championship, shooting a six-under-par 66 and tying the course record, apparently heeding the wisdom he had shared with Harry Blauvelt the previous year: "I always think under par. You have to believe in yourself." Garcia was happy to quiet the questions about his sub-par performance at the British Open: "I think I proved myself today," he said to Clifton Brown for the *New York Times* (August 13, 1999). "The British Open is done, so I don't want to hear any more questions about that. The difference was that here, I played well, everything went the right way and I made putts." By the fourth round, Garcia and Tiger Woods were locked in battle for the top spot. Even with a spectacular rescue of par on the 16th hole, where he made it to the green from between two tree roots, Garcia was unable to overtake Woods and lost by one stroke. Regardless of his finish, Garcia was thrilled by the experience and his new friendly competition with Woods. "The crowds were amazing," he told Clifton Brown for the *New York Times* (August 16, 1999). "I said when I turned pro that I wanted to be the No. 1 golfer in the world. So I knew I was going to be a rival for Tiger. But I said I always wanted to be a rival being friends, like we did today." Garcia's perfor-

mance at the PGA Championship also qualified him to play on the 1999 European Ryder Cup team, which ultimately lost to the American team. Garcia's final triumph of the 1999 season was his victory at the German Masters in October.

Garcia faltered slightly in the 2000 season. In four of 15 pro events, he finished in the top 10; in two, the Canadian Open and the Buick Classic, he placed third—his best performances for the year. He did, however, beat Tiger Woods in an unofficial, one-on-one, made-for-television event in August 2000. The "Battle at Bighorn" pitted the two friendly adversaries against each other in Palm Desert, California. Garcia has worried, though, about comparisons to Woods: "I just want to be recognized as Sergio Garcia, not the European Tiger Woods," he told *Golf Plus* (May 20, 1999, on-line).

Still exuding youthful confidence, Garcia tried to recapture the magic of his debut season in the 2001 tour. In Europe he won the Trophée Lancôme, beating the defending champion, Retief Goosen, after being down four strokes with only four holes of play remaining. He was cut after the opening rounds of the Masters and the PGA Championship. At the British Open he tied for ninth with a five-under-par outing. Also that year Garcia won his first two United States PGA Tour events: the MasterCard Colonial, in May, and the Buick Classic, in June. As of the end of October 2001, he had finished in the top 10 at seven of the 17 PGA events he had entered that season and had earned more than $2.5 million in prize money. "I do what I love," he told Kevin Cook for *Sports Illustrated* (May 24, 1999). "I play golf, and if I play well, I can make a living. I don't have to be stuck in an office all day, sitting down, so I think I'm a fortunate kid." — K.S.

Suggested Reading: *Golf Magazine* p204+ Apr. 1999, with photos; *New York Times* D p1 Aug. 16, 1999, with photos; *Sports Illustrated* p64+ July 19, 1999, with photo, p32+ Aug. 23, 1999, with photos, p62+ Sep. 27, 1999, with photos; *USA Today* C p3 Apr. 8, 1999, with photo

---

Garrison, Deborah

Feb. 12, 1965– Poet; editor. Address: Alfred A. Knopf, 201 E. 50th St., New York, NY 10022

Poetry collections usually attract few buyers, and of those that have sold well, few have earned critical acclaim in respected periodicals. Among the small number of volumes that fall into the latter category is Deborah Garrison's book, *A Working Girl Can't Win: And Other Poems* (1998), a highly accessible collection that deals with the everyday struggles of a young working woman trying to make sense of her hectic life. Sales figures for the hardcover edition of *A Working Girl Can't Win*

Tony Cenicola/NYT Pictures

Deborah Garrison

have reached 20,000—making it a best-seller among books of poetry, which usually sell around 1,000 copies—and a paperback edition is now available. Garrison wrote the poems in *A Working Girl Can't Win* over a period of 10 years, often after hours at the *New Yorker* magazine, where she worked from 1986 until 2000. Currently, she is the poetry editor at the publishing house Alfred A. Knopf as well as a senior editor at Pantheon Books, a division of Knopf, where she edits fiction and nonfiction.

The second of Joel and Naomi Gottlieb's three daughters, Garrison was born Deborah Gottlieb on February 12, 1965 in Ann Arbor, Michigan. Her father, an anesthesiologist, died of heart failure when she was 14 years old. Her mother, an accountant specializing in nonprofit institutions, was 40 when she was widowed. "She had these three girls to take care of, and her whole life ahead of her, and she went ahead and did it," Garrison told Dana Jennings for the *New York Times* (April 23, 2000). Around the time of her father's death, Deborah began to develop an interest in poetry, and during her teens she began writing poems. She attended Brown University, in Providence, Rhode Island, where she earned a B.A. degree with honors, in 1986, and was elected to Phi Beta Kappa. She later received a master's degree in English from New York University. In her interview with Jennings, she said that she began to get serious about her poetry only after joining the staff of the *New Yorker*, in 1986; she began there as a word processor and worked her way up to editor. "I was inspired to write by the talent at the *New Yorker*. There was a desire to please a literary parent." During her early years at the magazine, she would re-

main after her workday ended, to type and retype her poems on an electric typewriter. After returning to her apartment, in the East Village section of New York City, she would revise them in her head during her frequent bouts of insomnia. "You feel very free to let your mind go in any direction, and you know you have the night," she recalled to Jeanne Tift for the Random House publication *At Random* (February 1998, on-line). "That's really when I've had most of my ideas. I find that distracted, nighttime thinking brings me much closer to the writing self."

At the *New Yorker* Garrison edited the work of such esteemed writers as Martin Amis, Simon Schama, John Irving, and Joan Acocella, an experience that aided her in developing a critical eye and also enabled her to accept criticism about her own work. Her work as an editor did not, however, help her to think of herself as a writer. As she told Tift, "So much of being an editor involves judgment, and when you write, basically you want to let go of all your inhibitions and find some other part of yourself that isn't so controlled. It's hard to do that sometimes after a long day examining other people's sentences. I wish I knew how to press the button and say, 'Okay, now I'm in poetry mode.'" Thus influenced by her editorial mindset, she worked on her poetry only intermittently until 1995, when an editor at Random House suggested that she put together a collection.

Though many of Garrison's poems appeared in *Elle*, the *New York Times*, *Slate*, and even the *New Yorker*, she did not collect them until 1998, the year that Random House published *A Working Girl Can't Win: And Other Poems*. The collection focuses on a young working woman who seeks to balance her professional and private lives, who is devoted to her husband but fantasizes about flirting with other men, and who has a strong sense of herself as a woman but still wonders what her late father would think of her now. In an assessment for *Newsweek* (February 23, 1998), Jeff Giles called *A Working Girl Can't Win* "a wonderful collection, full of candor, bereft of b.s. It will speak both to women and to those hunting for clues to same. . . . Garrison's poems are full of ambivalence—how could any honest poems about love and work not be?—but they don't seem soaked in self-pity. That's partly because the language is so user-friendly, partly because it's full of such unexpected rhymes and sly humor." (One example of such rhymes and humor can be found in the title poem: "Is she Jewish, / self-hating? Past her sell-by date, / or still ovulating?"Another example can be found in "An Idle Thought": "I'm never going to sleep / with Martin Amis / or anyone famous.") Walter Kirn, writing for *Time* (March 30, 1998), reacted similarly, calling Garrison's collection "an airy, appealing first book," and adding, "As Garrison's book proves, not all good poems are hard poems, and sometimes the lines you can hum are also the lines you can't forget." Garrison's positive reviews are best represented by Nicholas Christopher's concluding paragraph in the *New York Times Book Review* (March 8, 1998): "*A Working Girl Can't Win* is an intense, intelligent and wonderfully sly book of poems that should appeal as much to the general reader as to the poetry devotee, a book in which working women and men—overwhelmed, overstimulated, and often overcome by love—ought to find Garrison clearly and generously speaking their language. However emphatically this particular working girl tells us she can't win, she certainly can write."

Other reviewers have not praised the book. Some, like Judy Clarence in *Library Journal* (February 15, 1998), felt that the poems showed that Garrison could turn a phrase but were thin on subject matter. "One only wishes that Garrison would use her vivid skills with the language ('the sun's fuzzy mouth sucking the day back') to explore issues and scenery that more deeply touch the reader's soul . . . ," Clarence wrote. "Garrison entertains but shallowly." In a harsh appraisal for *Parnassus: Poetry in Review* (Volume 24, No. 1, 1999), David Catron speculated that the acclaim lavished by some critics on the book could be attributed to Garrison's acquaintance with people in the literary world. "Like the verdict in the State of California vs. Orenthal James Simpson, [the acclaim] stands as proof that it is sometimes possible to get away with murder if one has the right connections. . . . [This book] is a study in mediocrity. Very few of its 28 poems rise above the level of workshop doggerel. Indeed, many are so poorly conceived and sloppily executed that they fail to reach even that modest altitude." By her own account, Garrison has ignored such criticism, for the most part, and has continued to write poems.

As the poetry editor at Alfred A. Knopf since February 2000, Garrison is concerned that people will assume that the poems she herself has written reflect her poetic taste. "My own poetry is irrelevant to my role as an editor," she told Dana Jennings. "My book would have never been on the Knopf list." She hopes to increase sales of Knopf's poetry books by paying attention to marketing details, ranging from the title of each book to the way the volume is presented to Knopf's sales force. But her most important function at Knopf is editing. "My job is to ask [each writer], 'What are you really trying to say here?'" she told Jennings of the occasional trouble spots in her authors' poetry. "People only respect you for you saying what you think. . . . And poetry has more burden to be clear than any other form."

Deborah Garrison and Matthew C. Garrison, an attorney, have been married since 1986. The couple have two daughters, Daisy and Georgia, and live in Montclair, New Jersey. — C.M.

Suggested Reading: *At Random* (on-line), Feb. 1998; *Cybergrrl* (on-line); *New York Times* I p19 Sep. 4, 1995, E p9 Feb. 26, 1998, I p31 Aug. 15, 1999, XIV p1 Apr. 23, 2000, with photos; *New York Times Book Review* p15 Mar. 8, 1998; *Newsweek* p68 Feb. 23, 1998; *Parnassus: Poetry in Review* p306+ Vol. 24 No. 1 1999; *Time* p68 Mar. 30, 1998, with photo; *Contemporary Authors* vol. 169, 1999

Selected Works: *A Working Girl Can't Win and Other Poems*, 1998

Gary, Willie E.

July 12, 1947– Personal-injury lawyer; philanthropist. Address: Gary, Williams, Parenti, Finney, Lewis, McManus, Watson, & Sperando, 221 E. Osceola St., Stuart, FL 34994

Willie Gary's life story reads like a modern retelling of a Horatio Alger novel. Through hard work and determination, Gary rose from extremely modest beginnings to become one of the most successful malpractice and personal-injury lawyers in the country. During the course of his 27-year career, he has built a reputation in the legal community as a lawyer who rarely loses a case and whose oratory, which draws on the rhetorical traditions of the Baptist church, has been known to reduce juries to tears. As H. T. Smith, a Miami attorney who has worked with Gary, told Charles Whitaker for *Ebony* (October 1987), "Willie Gary doesn't just handle cases, he brings them to life. For him, each case is a living, breathing entity. That's why you can't beat him." One of Gary's rivals told Jonathan Harr for

the *New Yorker* (November 1, 1999), "He acts like he's the most important guy in the world. The thing is he makes everybody else around him feel important, too. That's his genius."

The recipient of a 1995 NAACP Image Award (from the National Association for the Advancement of Colored People), Gary was named Lawyer of the Year in 1996 by *Lawyer Weekly USA* and has received honorary doctorate of law degrees from eight universities. He serves as general counsel to the Reverend Jesse Jackson and as a member of the boards of trustees of several colleges. He is also the chairman of the Gary Foundation, a philanthropic organization that, according to Gary's Web site, strives "to give youth the opportunity to reach their dreams by giving them alternatives to crime and drugs—such as education."

The seventh of the 11 children of Turner and Mary Gary, Willie Gary was born a twin in Eastman, in south-central Georgia, on July 12, 1947. At the time of his birth, his mother suffered medical complications (his twin did not survive); in order to pay the resulting medical bills, his parents were forced to sell the small parcel of land they owned

Courtesy of Willie E. Gary

Willie E. Gary

and farmed outside the town. The family never recovered from this financial blow, a circumstance that, from early on, Gary was determined to redress. "From the time that I was very small, my Dad always said that he knew I would be special because of what happened when I was born," Gary told Whitaker. "That sort of did something for me. It made me want to be somebody to prove that my Dad was right."

From Eastman, the family moved to Pahokee, Florida, where they occupied a three-room wooden shack surrounded by rows of sugarcane and beans. In winter and spring they would work the fields; in late summer they would become migrants, traveling north in their truck to harvest fruit and vegetables in Georgia and the Carolinas. More onerous to him than the hard labor, Gary recalled on his official Web page, were the obstacles that this way of life placed in the way of his education: the migrant children routinely left school at noon to help gather the crops, and sometimes, when the family was on the road, he missed school altogether. "I always wanted to learn," Gary told Kathleen Teltsch for the *New York Times* (February 5, 1992), "and I remember riding in trucks to the fields I would study the words on the billboards. If I didn't understand them, I'd ask the white boss in the field to explain." At a young age he formed an ambition to earn a college degree.

To achieve that goal, Gary took up football in high school, with an eye toward winning an athletic scholarship. But at five feet, seven inches, he was small for the game, and despite his best efforts, the school that he hoped to attend, Bethune-Cookman College, in Daytona Beach, Florida, denied him a place on its team. In desperation, he made his way to Shaw University, an historically black school in Raleigh, North Carolina, whose team, he had heard, might still have openings. Upon his arrival, he learned that the roster was full. He refused to give up, though: instead, he stayed at Shaw, sleeping on a dormitory sofa, living on food supplied from the cafeteria, and making himself useful by cleaning the football team's locker room. When one of Shaw's defensive players was sidelined with an injury, Gary jumped at the offer of a chance to fill in. His determination during the game so impressed coaches and university officials that he was also offered a scholarship. "That day I did more than win a spot on the team," Gary told Teltsch, "I won in life. I was only one step away from having to go back to the orange groves." He served as captain of the football team from 1969 to 1971.

While in college, Gary married Gloria Royal, his childhood sweetheart. When he learned that she was pregnant, he opened a landscaping business to help cover the couple's financial needs. The enterprise prospered, and by the time Gary graduated from Shaw, in 1971, with a bachelor's degree in business administration, he was earning about $25,000 a year. But rather than devote himself exclusively to his thriving business, he decided to pursue a law degree. As he told Whitaker, "I felt that law was the way that I could do the most for my family and my people." In the fall of 1971, he entered North Carolina Central University School of Law, in Durham. Although, as he told Harr, he felt like a "country bumpkin" in law school, he applied himself to his studies with great zeal. In three years he missed only two classes, all the while operating his landscaping business on the side.

In 1974, after earning his law degree, Gary returned to Florida, settling in the town of Stuart. He gained admittance to the state bar and, in 1975, opened his own law concern—thus becoming the first African-American to do so in Martin County, Florida. His firm did well from the beginning, and within a few months, Gary had won his first major civil suit—a $250,000 settlement on behalf of a widow whose husband, a black truck driver named Charlie Hayes, had been killed when he swerved to avoid an elderly white motorist by the name of Ella Dancy. Although the insurance company that represented Mrs. Dancy originally offered Mrs. Hayes $20,000, Gary persuaded an all-white jury to increase that amount tenfold. "I was told that Mrs. Hayes couldn't get a fair trial in this county," he recalled telling the jury in his closing argument, as cited by Harr. "Maybe I'm naïve, but when you raised your hand and swore you'd render a fair verdict, I believed you." On the heels of that victory, Gary negotiated his first million-dollar settlement, in Jacksonville.

Since then, Gary has won more than 100 other lawsuits involving settlements amounting to at least $1 million apiece. Among them are some high-profile, high-stakes personal-injury and malpractice suits, most notably the $500 million judgment in 1995 against the Loewen Group International, a Canada-based funeral-home company—the largest sum ever awarded by an American jury. The case was essentially a contract dispute. Jeremiah O'Keefe, a small-business owner who operated eight funeral parlors and a funeral-insurance firm in Mississippi, charged Loewen with reneging on an agreement to turn over its Mississippi insurance business to him in return for the sale of three funeral homes. Although Gary specializes in personal injury rather than in contract disputes, he was persuaded to take the case after he became convinced that Ray Loewen, then director of the Loewen Group Inc., had intentionally defrauded O'Keefe. During the trial Gary persuaded a jury that Loewen's breach of contract was part of a larger scheme to monopolize the entire U.S. funeral-home market. He asked for $1 billion in compensatory and punitive damages and, as one juror told Harr, came within one vote of getting that amount. The award was later reduced to $175 million, of which Gary's firm reportedly received $69 million for its legal services. (As a rule, his firm claims 40 percent of every award.)

Other lucrative cases that Gary has won include an approximately $40 million settlement with a Florida power company in a multiple-victim electrocution case, a $17 million malpractice suit on behalf of a three-year-old who, as an infant, suffered brain damage caused by improper treatment for meningitis, and a $23 million malpractice settlement resulting from a botched circumcision. In April 2000 Gary filed a $1.9 billion suit against Burger King, alleging that the fast-food giant had defrauded his client, the African-American fast-food entrepreneur LaVan Hawkins. "This is a case about corporate greed and a scheme to use our client as a pawn and it's just not right," Gary declared, as quoted in the *Atlanta Tribune* (on-line). In July 2000 Gary teamed up with the attorney Johnnie L. Cochran Jr. (best known as a member of the team that defended O. J. Simpson at his murder trial) to file a $1.5 billion suit on behalf of four Coca-Cola Co. employees, alleging racial bias on the part of the soft-drink company.

Gary's firm has expanded considerably in the past quarter-century. Gary, Williams, Parenti, Finney, Lewis, McManus, Watson, & Sperando, as it is currently known, has two offices in Florida (in Ft. Pierce and in Stuart) and satellite offices in Texas, Mississippi, and Louisiana; employs a staff of more than 130; retains a corporate jet (christened *Wings of Justice*) for its attorneys and clients; and has "routinely grossed more than $100 million a year" since the mid-1980s, as Gary told Carolyn V. Clarke for *Black Enterprise* (August 1993). Gary lives in a $10 million, 40-room Mediterranean-style villa in Sewall's Point, Florida. Known for his lavish spending, he owns two Bentleys and a Mercedes-Benz, among other cars, and a custom-made watch that cost more than $50,000; according to Harr, "He can match the excess of any corporate mandarin."

At the same time, Gary "realize[s] the importance of giving back" to the community, as he told Ronald Roach for *Black Issues in Higher Education* (March 4, 1999). "I'd still be in the sugar cane fields of Florida if others hadn't given me the opportunity to prove myself." Gary has donated $10 million to his alma mater, Shaw University—thus joining the most charitable individual benefactors of historically black colleges, a group that includes Bill Cosby and Oprah Winfrey—and has also given substantial monetary gifts to several other schools. Through his foundation, which bears his name, he awards college scholarships to needy students. For the past few years, he has organized a golf tournament—the Gary Celebrity Golf Classic, through which he has raised several hundred thousand dollars for scholarships. He has also served on the boards of trustees at Shaw, North Carolina Central University, Bethune-Cookman College, and Edward Waters College. "Gary has a great legal mind," Jesse Jackson told Roach, "but what really impresses me about him is that he hasn't caught amnesia, like a lot of people in his position. He remembers where he came from, and he has reinvested in those roots."

In November 2000 Gary joined a number of prominent class-action and civil rights lawyers, among them Johnnie Cochran and the Harvard law professor Charles J. Ogletree, in preparing a lawsuit seeking reparations for African-Americans who descended from slaves. In a forum on racial reparations sponsored by *Harper's Magazine* (November 2000), Gary explained why he felt that such a suit (which has not yet been filed) is necessary: "After the [Civil War], former slaves were promised forty acres and a mule, and we never got it. . . . I don't think that the fact that it's 135 years later should be a hindrance to people waking up, realizing that it was a grave injustice. And until America accounts for its actions, this friction is always going to be there."

Gary and his wife, Gloria, have four adult children: Kenneth, Sekou, Ali, and Kobie. — P.K.

Suggested Reading: *Black Enterprise* p68+ Aug. 1993, with photos; *Ebony* p127+ Oct. 1987, with photos *Forbes* (on-line) Nov. 11, 1999; *New York Times* B p7 Feb. 5, 1992, with photo; *New Yorker* Nov. 1, 1999

Sergio Perez/Archive Photos

Garzón, Baltasar

1953(?)– Judge. Address: Audiencia Nacional, García Gutiérez 1, 28071 Madrid, Spain

In October 1998 Judge Baltasar Garzón of Spain made international headlines when he issued a warrant for the arrest and extradition to Spain of General Augusto Pinochet, the former Chilean dictator whose military regime was responsible for more than 2,000 assassinations, the unexplained disappearances of more than 1,000 people, and numerous cases of torture in the 1970s and 1980s. In early 2000, after Pinochet had been detained under house arrest for some 18 months, British officials ruled that the elderly general was unfit to stand trial because of his poor health; still, the legal battle that Garzón inaugurated was widely viewed as "a milestone for international human rights law," as the human-rights group Amnesty International declared on March 24, 1999 in an official statement posted on its Web site. "His arrest and the ensuing legal developments have marked the beginning of a new era for human rights." "The entire Pinochet affair, despite the 84-year-old general's escape, represents a huge step towards bringing future Pinochets to justice," an editorialist for the London-based *Economist* (March 4, 2000) wrote shortly after the general was released from British custody.

Pinochet's legal battle began on October 16, 1998, when Garzón, after learning that the former dictator was in London for treatment of a herniated disk in his spine, formally requested his extradition to Madrid, Spain's capital, to stand trial for "crimes against humanity." Because Pinochet had written an amnesty clause for himself and several

of his subordinates into the Chilean constitution before relinquishing power to a civilian regime, in 1990, he was immune from prosecution in his native country. On foreign soil, however, his legal status was less certain. In Spain, a number of laws originally intended to facilitate the prosecution of Basque separatists allow officials, in certain instances, to reach beyond national borders to bring terrorists to trial. These laws, Garzón maintained, provided him with the legal authority to prosecute Pinochet. Moreover, various treaties concluded between Great Britain and Spain require the extradition of individuals wanted for grievous crimes; Garzón also cited such treaties in calling for Pinochet's extradition. While the application of the treaties to Pinochet's particular case was not beyond dispute, British officials determined that there were sufficient legal grounds to serve the warrant for Garzón, and on October 17, 1998 law-enforcement officers from Scotland Yard, as the Criminal Investigation Department of the London Metropolitan Police is informally known, placed the general under arrest.

Complicating Garzón's attempt to prosecute Pinochet was the tangled relationship between international law and various local (usually national) legal institutions and traditions. Although a basis for international human-rights law has existed on paper for many years, in practice many national governments and national legal bodies have been reluctant to cede judicial authority to transnational entities. "We have been trying to create an international human-rights court since the 1950s," Garzón told Laurie Goering for the *Chicago Tribune* (May 14, 2000). "In 1998 a convention was approved, but the U.S., Russia and China have not signed." Consequently, there are few means with which to enforce existing international treaties, and the international arena, in fact if not on the books, has tended to be relatively lawless. As the *Economist* (January 15, 2000) pointed out, "Although a clutch of human-rights treaties passed since the second world war have supposedly outlawed murder, torture and arbitrary arrest by governments, dictators all over the world have continued to employ such methods with impunity, safe in the knowledge that, even if they lost power, they were beyond the reach of the law."

At the heart of the Pinochet case was the precise legal definition of two related concepts: sovereign immunity and jurisdiction. Each is of considerable importance in the enforcement of international law. Roughly speaking, sovereign immunity is the legal assurance that heads of state cannot be tried in foreign courts. In essence the notion of sovereign immunity represents an extension of the principle of national sovereignty (the ideological basis of the independent nation-state) to political leaders. While the idea of sovereign immunity is sanctioned by long-standing legal tradition, it has also served the more pragmatic aim of making international diplomacy possible: like the related concept of diplomatic immunity, sovereign immunity is intended to allow state officials to interact on a transnational level, free from parochial legal harassment and politically motivated prosecution. Strictly interpreted, the principle of sovereign immunity dictates that the president of the United States, for example, cannot be tried in, say, Cuba, even if the Cuban government were to charge him with having committed crimes on Cuban soil. Similarly, Pinochet's allies argued that he could be tried in neither England nor Spain.

There are, however, notable legal precedents in which the principle of sovereign immunity has been interpreted weakly or even abrogated altogether. The most significant of these, and the one that Garzón cited in his attempt to extradite Pinochet, is the Nuremberg Charter, a document drafted by the victorious Allied powers (including Great Britain) at the end of World War II. The Nuremberg Charter provided the legal basis for the prosecution of Nazi war criminals; it is also the legal cornerstone of the international tribunals established in the late 1990s to prosecute war crimes in Yugoslavia and Rwanda. Principle III of the Charter directly contradicts the notion of sovereign immunity; it states, "The fact that a person who committed an act which constitutes a crime under international law acted as Head of State or responsible Government official does not relieve him from responsibility under international law." (Crimes punishable under international law, according to the charter, include "murder, extermination, enslavement, deportation and other inhuman acts done against any civilian population.") The major issue at stake in the Pinochet affair was whether or not former heads of state, as opposed to current heads of state, enjoy sovereign immunity for crimes allegedly committed during their tenures in office. Pinochet's supporters argued that they do; Garzón, in his request for the general's extradition, took the opposite position.

Ultimately, Garzón and his British supporters won this argument: in March 1999 the judicial committee of the House of Lords, Great Britain's highest court, ruled that there was no fundamental legal reason why Pinochet should not be tried in Spain for the human-rights charges brought against him. More precisely, the court ruled that a former head of state accused of violating an international human-rights treaty does not enjoy immunity from prosecution and thus can be tried in the criminal courts of any country that is a signatory to the treaty that he stands accused of violating. Thus, although Pinochet's ill health eventually led to his release, Garzón and his allies had cleared one of the fundamental legal hurdles before the general's extradition and trial. They also set an important legal precedent, among the repercussions of which was the ruling of a Paris court in October 2000 that Libyan leader Colonel Muammar al-Qaddafi could in theory stand trial in France for the shooting down of a French airliner over West Africa in 1989. (Going beyond even the Pinochet precedent, the French court rejected the defense that Qaddafi, as a head of state, enjoyed sovereign immunity.)

The second, related legal issue at stake was that of jurisdiction—specifically, the issue of extraterritorial jurisdiction. In common practice, the authority of a particular court to interpret and apply the law is restricted to certain places, beyond which the court has no power to adjudicate. In particular, the courts of one country usually do not rule on crimes committed abroad. But again, there are exceptions: Britain, for example, claims jurisdiction for crimes committed abroad when the accused is a British citizen; Spain and Germany claim the authority to try cases in which their nationals are the victims of crimes. Many scholars of international law and human-rights groups go even further, arguing that for the most grievous crimes—including genocide, terrorism, and torture—there exists a "universal jurisdiction" that overrides national legal boundaries. By charging Pinochet with "crimes against humanity," then, and not just with the disappearance of Spanish nationals, Garzón was invoking precisely such a notion, and the decision by the House of Lords legal committee that Pinochet could stand trial in Spain was a victory for advocates of universal jurisdiction.

Some critics, however—particularly political conservatives—charged that Garzón's attempt to prosecute Pinochet had been politically motivated. Charles Krauthammer, for example, writing for the *Washington Post* (October 23, 1998), called Pinochet's arrest "a blow for the most ideologically selective justice," and William F. Buckley Jr., who had been a staunch supporter of Pinochet in the 1970s, declared in the *National Review* (December 31, 1998) that "political passion is the prime mover" in the case. As evidence, critics pointed out that the Spanish effort to try Pinochet had long been supported by the Salvador Allende Foundation, named in honor of the democratically elected president whom Pinochet had forcibly deposed; moreover, Joan Garces, the former legal, economic, and political adviser to President Allende, had long represented Pinochet's victims. (On the other hand, the Spanish case was originally filed by Miguel Maravet of the Union of Progressive Prosecutors, an independent Spanish professional association. "The crimes of [Pinochet's] regime," according to the *Economist* [November 28, 1998], "were never in dispute. These have been well documented.") Buckley further suggested that Garzón would not have prosecuted human-rights violations by a leftist ruler: "If Baltasar Garzón protested Fidel Castro's recent appearance in Spain, his cries went unheeded." (In his interview with Goering, Garzón noted, "Spanish law gives immunity to those in power, which means for instance we can't prosecute Fidel Castro.")

In fact, the danger of selectively applying international law was acknowledged across the political spectrum. Marguerite Feitlowitz, for example, writing for *Dissent* (Spring 1999), pointed out, "There is also some legitimate concern that if Spain should prevail in these extradition hearings, it could encourage vendettas against former officials and heads of state. The worry is that the international travel required for government, diplomatic, and financial business will be endangered out of sheer vengeance." Amnesty International, in its March 24, 1999 press release, also stressed the need for a nonpartisan trial: "The law rather than politics should determine whether Pinochet and anyone else accused of similar crimes is in fact guilty or innocent." As might be expected, Garzón and his supporters rejected the charge that they were politically motivated: as the judge stressed in an interview with T. R. Reid for the *Washington Post* (January 16, 2000), "In a nation of laws, the politicians do politics but the law must be left to judges and lawyers. And it is fundamental that the law cannot be bent for political purposes."

The son of an olive farmer, Baltasar Garzón was born in the southern Spanish region of Andalusia in either 1953 (according to Feitlowitz) or 1955 (as Alvaro Tizon reported for the Consortium for Independent Journalism [January 13, 1999, on-line]). As a youth he spent several years in Catholic seminaries in preparation for a career in the clergy. Although he later abandoned that plan in favor of a legal career (reportedly, he was expelled from the seminary for serenading his future wife), colleagues of his have reported that Garzón brings an almost religious zeal to bear on his legal endeavors; indeed, he himself has characterized his dedication to human-rights causes as a "mission." During his school years Garzón displayed a taste for bullfights, rock and roll, and flamenco music.

Garzón worked at a gas station to finance his legal education. After he completed his law degree, he began a steady rise through the ranks of his profession. At the age of 32, he was appointed to the Audiencia Nacional, the highest criminal court in Spain, where he serves as one of six investigating judges. There, Garzón took on a number of high-profile cases in which drug traffickers, Mafia bosses, and international terrorists were prosecuted. At one point he brought charges against and secured the conviction of a number of high-ranking government officials, including a former interior minister, for their ties to government-sponsored death squads that targeted suspected Basque terrorists. The resulting scandal helped bring down the government of the Socialist prime minister Felipe Gonzalez. Garzón has also prosecuted several Basque organizations for promoting terrorism, thus demonstrating, according to his supporters, his impartiality.

By aggressively pursuing such cases, Garzón made a number of enemies. Because he routinely received death threats, a phalanx of bodyguards always accompanied him in public, and he made a practice of switching meeting-places to thwart would-be attackers. Once, he even found a microphone hidden in his bed. In spite of the hostility his work has provoked, Garzón has said that he does not feel intimidated. "I don't have time to be afraid," he told T. R. Reid. "Anyway, it's my choice to do what I do. This is the mission I have chosen."

Garzón's work on high-profile criminal cases won him the admiration of the general public and the Spanish media, who bestowed the sobriquet "Superjudge" upon the young magistrate. While critics have charged Garzón with grandstanding and exceeding his jurisdiction in an effort to attract media attention, his supporters, as quoted by Feitlowitz, have called him "visionary," "courageous," and "the man the whole Establishment wants to kill."

In 1996 Garzón began investigating the disappearance (and presumed murder) of hundreds of Spanish citizens in Argentina under the military dictatorships that ruled the country from 1976 to 1983. The case was originally filed by Carlos Castresana, a Spanish attorney unconnected with the events, and was assigned to Garzón according to the National Court's usual procedure, in which judges get assignments in turns. Although Garzón eventually issued international warrants for the arrest of several former Argentinean military dictators, including General Leopoldo Galtieri, Argentina's leader from December 1981 until July 1982, that action was widely interpreted as a symbolic gesture: such warrants were rarely carried out. However, in late 1997 the former Argentinean military officer Adolfo Scilingo, who had admitted to participating in mass executions whereby political dissidents were drugged, chained, and thrown into the Atlantic Ocean from planes, voluntarily traveled to Spain to testify before Garzón. When Scilingo admitted that he personally had taken part in the executions, Garzón ordered him arrested, and the case received international attention. Later, in early 1998, Garzón caused a diplomatic stir by issuing a subpoena for a visiting Argentinean congressman suspected of involvement in human-rights abuses. In *U.S. News & World Report* (December 7, 1998), Linda Robinson wrote that the official subsequently "barricaded himself in a hotel, called a press conference to denounce the judge, and then fled the country."

While investigating human-rights abuses in Argentina, Garzón began to uncover evidence that linked several of the alleged perpetrators to the Pinochet regime in Chile. In particular, ties between the Argentinean military and the notorious Operation Condor—the code name for a joint effort among the military leaders of Chile, Argentina, Bolivia, Paraguay, and Uruguay to "purify" the southern part of South America of leftists and political dissidents—pointed to Argentina's western neighbor. In sworn testimony, for example, some Argentineans told Garzón that they had been tortured by men with recognizable Chilean accents. Moreover, a declassified FBI cable sent to Washington from Buenos Aires, Argentina, on April 9, 1976, as quoted by Feitlowitz, referred to Chile as the "headquarters" or "center" of Operation Condor. Finally, Feitlowitz reported, Garzón obtained a letter addressed to Pinochet from Manuel Contreras, the head of the Chilean secret police, in which Contreras requested funds for the "neutralization of the principal adversaries of the Junta who live abroad," in Contreras's words.

Such evidence led Garzón to collaborate with another Spanish judge, Manuel Garcia-Castellon, who, like Garzón, was investigating the disappearance of Spanish nationals in Chile. Garcia-Castellon, too, had come across Operation Condor and had uncovered evidence linking the clandestine operation with General Pinochet. He wanted to summon Pinochet for questioning but was prevented from doing so by the amnesty that shielded the general in his native Chile. In 1998, however, when Garcia-Castellon learned that Pinochet was seeking a European clinic to treat his health problems, he persuaded Garzón, whose popularity in Spain gave him more clout, to take the case. Garzón agreed, and shortly thereafter issued the warrant for Pinochet's arrest.

Although Garzón's attempt to prosecute Pinochet received much more press than his investigation of human-rights abuses in Argentina, he continued to work on the latter case while the international spotlight was trained on the onetime Chilean leader. A few hours before he issued the extradition warrant for Pinochet, Garzón froze the bank accounts of 152 Argentine officers implicated in human-rights abuses during the 1970s and 1980s.

In November 1999 Garzón formally requested extradition of 98 Argentineans—including two former presidents, Jorge Videla and Leopoldo Galtieri—accused of involvement in the disappearance of some 600 Spaniards and Argentineans between 1976 and 1983. Carlos Menem, then president of Argentina, immediately attacked Garzón for overstepping the bounds of his jurisdiction; the Argentinean leader further characterized the Spanish judge as a "showgirl" hungry for media attention. Other critics pointed out that, unlike their Chilean counterparts, Argentinean civil courts had already tried some of the military leaders whom Garzón sought to prosecute. Shortly after Pinochet's release, Garzón told Goering, "I will continue with my work on terrorism and corruption, and with the ongoing investigation of 'dirty war' crimes in Chile and Argentina."

The judge and his wife have three children. — P.K.

Suggested Reading: *Chicago Tribune* (on-line) May 14, 2000; *consortiumnews.com* 1999; *Dissent* p33+ Spring 1999; *Economist* (on-line) Nov. 28, 1998; *Washington Post* A p29 Jan. 16, 2000, with photo

---

Gaskin, Ina May

1940– Midwife; writer; president of the Midwives Alliance of North America. Address: Midwives Alliance of North America, 4805 Lawrenceville Hwy., Suite 116-279, Lilburn, GA 30047

During childbirth there is sometimes a condition known as shoulder dystocia, in which, after the baby's head has emerged, its shoulders remain stuck behind the mother's pelvis. When this happens the obstetrician will often place the laboring mother on her hands and knees in order to expand the pelvis and dislodge the infant's shoulders. This procedure is called the Gaskin Maneuver. Before it was publicized, in the *Journal of Reproductive Medicine* in May 1998, the obstetrician frequently resorted to either breaking the infant's collarbone to extract the child or pushing the baby back into the uterus for removal by cesarean section. The Gaskin Maneuver is notable not only for its simplicity and efficiency, but for being the first obstetrical procedure ever named for a midwife—Ina May Gaskin.

Gaskin had first learned about the benefits of the all-fours position while studying with traditional Mayan midwives in Guatemala during the 1970s. In 1976 she published *Spiritual Midwifery*, which is considered a seminal reference book. Often referred to as the "mother of modern midwifery," Gaskin is one of the founding members and the current president of the Midwives Alliance of

Courtesy of Ina May Gaskin

North America (MANA), a professional organization devoted to setting guidelines for training in midwifery and establishing competency and safety standards for those practicing in the field.

Ina May (Middleton) Gaskin was born in Marshalltown, Iowa, in 1940. Her father, a farmer, lost his family farm during the 1930s Depression and became a fire-equipment salesman. Her mother was a home-economics teacher; she taught her daughter to sew her own clothes, which Gaskin still does. A tomboy, Gaskin loved to wrestle with her brother and refused to wear dresses. She was also a voracious reader and a good student, and she planned on a career in engineering. When she graduated from high school, however, in 1958, she couldn't win a scholarship to study what she has called "men's subjects," such as math and science, and turned to English instead. She worked her way through community college for two years before transferring to the University of Iowa, in Iowa City, where she earned a bachelor's degree in 1962. At age 19 Gaskin had gotten married, and when she completed her undergraduate education, she and her husband joined the Peace Corps, the international volunteer organization founded by President John F. Kennedy in 1961. For two years the couple taught English in Malaysia. Upon their return Gaskin enrolled at Northern Illinois University, in De Kalb, and in 1967 she earned a master's degree in English.

While she was a graduate student, Gaskin became pregnant with her first child. As a curious teenager she had read *Childbirth Without Fear*, by Grantly Dick-Read, a British gynecologist who believed that much of the pain of childbirth could be allayed without anesthesia. Although Dick-Read's methods were not in widespread use during her pregnancy, Gaskin hoped for a natural, unmedicated delivery, such as those described in the book. Although she discussed her wishes with her doctor beforehand, her experience was not what she had envisioned. "During birth at the hospital, I was left alone and treated like I had done something nasty," she told Katie Allison Granju for *Salon.com* (June 1, 1999). "Then I was approached by a gang of masked attendants who came in the room and treated me like a ritual victim. They used forceps [to extract the infant], and then I wasn't allowed to see my baby for 18 hours." Soon after the birth, Gaskin, her husband, and their infant daughter, Sydney, left the Midwest for San Francisco, which in the late 1960s was the center of a massive countercultural movement. There, Gaskin regularly attended lectures on a variety of topics, including religion, politics, vegetarianism, and sex, given by a popular teacher named Stephen Gaskin, who later became her second husband.

Stephen Gaskin had amassed a large group of followers, and in 1970 several hundred of them joined him on a five-month-long speaking tour across the U.S. to advance a message of nonviolence. Ina May Gaskin, now pregnant again, was among those traveling in a caravan of colorfully painted buses. One evening a woman in the group went into labor while on one of the buses; she gave birth to a healthy baby boy, with her husband, rather than a doctor, delivering the infant and tying off

the umbilical cord with a clean shoelace. "I didn't do anything but watch in awe," Gaskin told Dorothy Foltz-Gray for the *Iowa Alumni Quarterly* (Winter 1995). "The mother was so happy. She looked very beautiful. . . . And she didn't seem to be in pain. I was high as a kite for days." During the course of the lecture tour, 10 more babies were born, and Gaskin, who showed a natural talent at midwifery, began to assist at the births. One birth was that of her own son; two months premature, he lived only 12 hours. Gaskin has said that his death strengthened her resolve to help other women have satisfying labors and healthy babies. (Sydney died of a brain tumor in 1986; Gaskin currently has three grown children.)

Newspaper stories about the "hippies" giving birth on their buses began to appear in towns where the caravan stopped. A sympathetic obstetrician in Rhode Island who visited the group gave Gaskin and a few of the other women some rudimentary training in midwifery. "He gave a hands-on seminar on how to recognize any complications we were likely to encounter, and what to do if we did, demonstrating how to stimulate a baby to breathe, what to do if the umbilical cord was wrapped tightly around the baby's neck, what to do if the mother hemorrhaged," Gaskin told Granju. "He taught us sterile technique and provided us with some necessary medications and instruments, my first obstetrics textbook and gave us instructions on how to provide good prenatal care."

Stephen Gaskin had seen a parcel of land for sale in Summertown, Tennessee, and soon after the lecture tour ended, he and about 250 followers purchased a 1,750-acre plot and established a vegetarian commune, which they named the Farm. They lived in tents on the land for more than a year, until permanent structures could be built. Gaskin and several other women founded a clinic to which residents of the Farm, who were mostly of childbearing age, as well as women from the surrounding areas came for prenatal care and childbirth. John Williams, a physician who lived about 15 minutes from the commune, agreed to help when there were complications during a delivery. "One thing I always treasure about him is that he never, ever got cross if I called him up in the middle of the night," Gaskin told a reporter for *Newsweek* (December 28, 1992). "Pamela, one of our midwives, called him up once and said, 'There's something blue coming out [of the mother].'" Gaskin continued, "We didn't [know] the medical terminology, not even anatomy. So he got in his pickup, drove on out, and he says, 'Oh, that's her cervix.' He got a sterile glove, pushed it back, and out pops the baby's head, and then we learned, oh, you're supposed to do that."

Determined to share what she had learned, Gaskin wrote *Spiritual Midwifery*. A combination of prenatal advice, first-person birth stories, photographs, and instructions for helping laboring mothers, the book was produced on the Farm's own printing press. (It has since been revised many times and has been published in four languages; the number of copies sold to date has surpassed 500,000.) In it Gaskin maintained that childbirth can and should be a spiritual and empowering experience, and that it should take place without unnecessary medical intervention or trauma. This was dramatically opposed to the accepted wisdom of the day, which held that only trained physicians in fully equipped hospitals should deliver babies. In the year 1900, when it was general practice for women to give birth at home with the help of other women, fewer than 5 percent of births in the U.S. took place in hospitals. By 1939, that figure had risen to 50 percent. By 1970, in part because of pressure from such organized medical groups as the American Medical Association and the American College of Obstetricians and Gynecologists, it was almost unheard-of for a woman to give birth without medical intervention, including anesthesia and fetal monitoring, and almost 100 percent of U.S. births took place in hospitals.

People who came of age during the social upheaval of the 1960s often mistrusted authority figures, including doctors, and in that climate *Spiritual Midwifery* quickly sold 80,000 copies. "Somebody in Crete delivered a baby in a cave using my instructions, and another in a log cabin in Alaska," Gaskin told the *Newsweek* reporter. "It was all word of mouth. Just the constant stream of visitors to the Farm, and some newspaper stories." Gaskin was soon in demand as a speaker, both in midwifery circles and at mainstream medical venues, such as medical schools, despite the fact that she had no formal medical training and—since Tennessee had no legislation regulating midwifery—was unlicensed. She became widely known for her talent at winning the confidence of medical professionals and making them receptive to her point of view. A reporter for the professional publication *Ob. Gyn. News* (April 15, 1979) wrote, for example, "A lay midwife who practices in a spiritual community in rural Tennessee elicited praise and encouragement for her home-birth procedures from some physicians attending the annual conference of the American Society for Psychosomatic Obstetrics and Gynecology." The report continued, "Remarks among some physicians in the audience initially indicated a negative, almost condemning attitude, but reactions changed markedly after they listened to Ms. Gaskin and viewed the tapes [of her working]." Robbie Davis-Floyd, an anthropologist and the author of *Birth as an American Rite of Passage* (1992), described Gaskin to Granju as "warm, funny, good-hearted, brilliant, politically savvy and aware—a postmodern hippie who holds a very strong space for her alternative knowledge system yet moves with fluidity and ease in the professional, political, and medical realms."

In 1982 Gaskin helped found MANA, a group that includes both certified nurse-midwives with formal medical training and lay midwives, also called direct-entry midwives, who have developed their skills through self-study, apprenticeships, or organized midwifery-training programs. MANA is dedicated to providing "the credibility and political strength necessary to promote midwifery as an accepted part of the maternal-child health care system in North America," as an essay on the official MANA Web site stated. In 1987 the group created the North American Registry of Midwives (NARM), an agency dedicated to establishing standardized criteria and administering professional certification for any midwife, whatever course of training she has chosen. Through NARM an applicant demonstrating adequate knowledge, skills, and experience can be designated a certified professional midwife (CPM). Thanks in large part to the group's efforts, direct-entry midwives are now legally recognized in 29 states, can be licensed in 17 states, and can get reimbursed for their services by Medicaid in six states. In early 2001 there were an estimated 4,000 certified nurse-midwives and 6,000 direct-entry midwives practicing in the United States. While that is still far fewer than in other countries, approximately 250,000 women currently use their services every year, many in hospitals, with the approval and backup of physicians.

In May 1998 the *Journal of Reproductive Medicine* published an article in which Gaskin and her co-author, Joseph Bruner, a professor at the Vanderbilt University College of Medicine, in Nashville, Tennessee, detailed her approach to treating shoulder dystocia during labor by positioning the mother on her hands and knees. Although midwifery had been gaining acceptance in the medical community throughout the previous two decades, the publication of Gaskin's findings in a respected journal and the naming of the procedure in her honor were considered watersheds in the profession. The success of Gaskin's approach to childbirth is evident in that fact that while the national rate of cesarean sections is about 25 percent of all births, fewer than 2 percent of deliveries by Farm midwives require surgical intervention.

Gaskin continues to live on the Farm, which at its peak had 1,500 inhabitants; it now has approximately 200. Over the course of her career, she has delivered more than 1,000 babies, and as of this writing, she delivers an average of six monthly. She recently delivered her own granddaughter. Gaskin, whose long, gray braid and warm smile have become her trademarks, remains passionate about the importance of midwifery. "The rate of teen pregnancy in the United States is the highest in the industrialized world," she told Carol Wiley Lorente for *Vegetarian Times* (July 1995). "We have the highest maternal health care costs, yet our infant mortality rate is high, millions of women don't get adequate prenatal care and our rate of breast-feeding is low. Education and care by midwives in the neighborhoods and communities could help avoid these problems." She concluded, "When we as a society begin to value mothers as the givers and supporters of life, then we will see social changes in ways that matter." *Babies, Breast-Feeding, and Bonding*, her second book, was published in 1987. Gaskin has said that her favorite recreational activity is playing with her grand-daughter. — M.R.

Suggested Reading: *Iowa Alumni Quarterly* p34+ Winter 1995, with photos; *Newsweek* p1+ Dec. 28, 1992, with photos; *Salon.com* June 1, 1999, with photo; *Vegetarian Times* p104 July 1995, with photo; Huddle, Norie. *Surviving: The Best Game on Earth*, 1984

Selected Books: *Spiritual Midwifery*, 1976; *Babies, Breast-feeding, and Bonding*, 1987

Courtesy of Lynn Gaubatz

Gaubatz, Lynn
(GOW-bats)

1956– Bassoonist. Address: Levine School of Music, 2801 Upton St. N.W., Washington, DC 20008-3829

The bassoon, the largest of the woodwind instruments and the one with the lowest register, is often called the "clown of the orchestra," and its sound has been likened to that of a baritone with a bad cold. Contributing to the bassoon's buffoonish image is the fact that, ever since the Russian composer Sergei Prokofiev used one to introduce the grumpy grandfather in his symphonic fairy tale *Peter and the Wolf*, the bassoon's deep, sonorous tone has often been coupled with ludicrous and comical characters on film and television soundtracks. In actuality, the bassoon "can sound throaty and not of this world, . . . has a large, full, mellow noise," . . . [and] can be extremely powerful and heavy,"

according to an article written for *ThinkQuest* (on-line), and in recent years there have been hints that it may be coming into its own as a serious solo instrument. "It's long overdue for a boom," the bassoonist Daniel Smith told *Classic CD* magazine (on-line). "It's the next [instrument] that's going to happen." Among the bassoonists to watch, according to various critics, is Lynn Gaubatz, a performer who has drawn the sort of attention usually reserved for violinists, pianists, and cellists. Indeed, much in the manner of the best-known instrumental celebrities, Gaubatz has performed solo recitals in Europe, North and South America, and Africa; has had her performances broadcast on radio stations worldwide, including PBS, Radio Nacional de España, Radio Nacional de Venezuela, and the Voice of America; was the first bassoonist to perform a solo recital at the Kennedy Center, in Washington, D.C.; and, in what may be a sign of crossover appeal beyond the confines of the classical-music world, was named "One of America's 10 Most Outstanding Working Women" by *Glamour* magazine in 1988.

Lynn Gaubatz was born into a Catholic family in 1956 in Dallas, Texas, and raised in the town of Odessa, in western Texas. She took up flute in junior high school along with a friend and played in the school marching band. Soon, rather serendipitously, she switched to the bassoon. What prompted the switch was the music teacher's custom of seating the instrumentalists according to how well they performed on a test—the "chair test," so named because, for example, the violinist who played best would be seated in the "first chair" in the violin section. As Gaubatz told *Current Biography*, "We would have chair tests every week and I would always end up first chair or second chair with my best friend, and I didn't like the competition feeling because I thought it was hurting our friendship. The band needed a bassoonist and an oboist. Somebody raised their hand and said, 'I'll play the oboe'—I didn't know what any of these instruments were—and I said, 'Well, I'll do the other thing.' . . . I fell in love with it immediately. . . . I had a knack for exactly that instrument." Because bassoon teachers were scarce in the Odessa area, Gaubatz often taught herself, learning by trial and error; nevertheless, she advises aspiring musicians to seek out a dedicated teacher to help them avoid bad habits.

While Gaubatz continued to play the bassoon throughout high school, she never considered becoming a professional musician, because, as she told *Current Biography*, "I had never heard of anyone making a living at it, except if you were a band director, and I knew I didn't want to do that." Thus, when she enrolled in Boston University, with the support of a National Merit Scholarship, she chose a double major in music and pre-med. Midway through her undergraduate years, when she realized that she could work as a professional bassoonist, she "just dumped everything else."

GAUBATZ

After earning a bachelor's degree from Boston University, in 1978, Gaubatz studied at the New England Conservatory of Music, in Boston, and the Northwestern University School of Music, in Evanston, Illinois, where she earned a master's degree in 1980. A year later she accepted the post of bassoon professor at the prestigious Mozarteum Conservatory, in Salzburg, Austria, where she taught until 1984. She has continued to collaborate and perform with the Austrian flutist Helmut Zangerle and other musicians she met during her tenure there. After leaving Salzburg Gaubatz performed as a soloist with orchestras under such famous conductors as Leonard Bernstein, Seiji Ozawa, and Sir Georg Solti. Bernstein, who was also a world-renowned composer, declared Gaubatz's playing "inspirational" when he first heard her on the instrument and judged that her potential as a bassoonist was unlimited. For some years, until 1990, she served as the principal bassoonist with the Maryland Symphony Orchestra. Since 1997 she has been a member of the Salzburger Mozart-Solisten, an Austrian chamber-music ensemble.

In the course of building her career, Gaubatz has grappled with a problem that has contributed to bassoonists' widespread lack of recognition: the misperception that there is little first-rate material for soloists to perform. In fact, Gaubatz told Current Biography, there is a wealth of music for the bassoon: in addition to highly regarded bassoon concerti by the 18th-century composers Mozart and Vivaldi, there exist several bassoon sonatas by another 18th-century composer, Georg Philip Telemann, and some classic works by Beethoven. Moreover, 20th-century music is particularly rich in compositions for the bassoon, with important works by Saint-Saëns and Stravinsky, whose perennial concert favorite The Rite of Spring features a solo bassoon in its opening bars.

Gaubatz has further expanded her repertoire by adapting existing works that were composed for other instruments and by collaborating with composers to create new works for the bassoon. When encouraging composers to write material for the bassoon, Gaubatz urges them not to worry about taxing her skills. As she stated in a press release on her Web site, "When composers writing music for me ask what the limitations of the instrument are, I always tell them they should write the music however they feel it should be. It's MY job to figure out how to play it. So far, no one's stumped me yet." Among the works composed especially for her is Wolfgang Pillinger's Kleine Suite von "Kein Platz für Idioten", for which she performed the world premiere. Of the works she has tackled that were not written with the bassoon in mind, some are famously difficult even for their intended instruments. Referring to two piano pieces (by Rimsky-Korsakov and Chopin, respectively) meant to be played at lightning speeds, she wrote for the press release, "I love the audience's reaction when I tear into 'Flight of the Bumblebee,' 'The Minute Waltz,' or some other piece traditionally considered unplayable on the bassoon. I was very proud when composer Russell Woollen told me that my 'Flight of the Bumblebee' sounded downright 'MENACING'!"

In addition, Gaubatz is researching, publishing, and performing works by composers who were persecuted by the Nazis before and during World War II. Some of those musicians lost their lives under the Nazi regime; their works and those of others were labeled entartete Musik—"degenerate music"—and banned. "Tracing the careers of these composers who fled the Nazis, many of whom made their way to England and the US, is fascinating and humbling," Gaubatz said in another press release posted on her Web page. "I hope to keep their music and their legacy alive by not just performing this music, but also by recording it."

Gaubatz is known among her colleagues for her ability to "jump in," or perform with little or no notice, when contacted by an orchestra or music festival suddenly in need of a principal bassoonist. "My friends say this facet of my solo career gives new meaning to the phrase 'Impromptu Musicales', but I have always LOVED performing anywhere, anytime, and it's a great feeling to be able to jump into a crisis and solve it by doing what I love more than anything else—making music," she wrote for her Web page.

Lynn Gaubatz makes her home in Falls Church, Virginia, a suburb of Washington, D.C. She teaches bassoon and chamber music at Mount Vernon College (a division of George Washington University) and the Levine School of Music, both of which are in Washington. In 1999 she performed as a soloist in Trondheim, Norway, at the ceremony in which Antero B. da Silvo, the leader of the East Timor Students' Solidarity Council, earned the international Students' Peace Prize. She has also played at benefit concerts, to raise money for a community music school in Washington, a group supporting nuclear disarmament of the former Soviet Union, and an organization called Musicians Against World Hunger. She is a winner of the National Young Artists Competition, the Lara Hoggard Performance Award for Young Artists, the Aspen Music Festival Wind Competition, the Boston University Concerto-Aria Competition, and the Northwestern University Concerto Competition. Her other honors include a Leonard Bernstein Fellowship to the Tanglewood Music Center, in Lenox, Massachusetts, and the Henry B. Cabot Award for Musicianship, given by the Boston Symphony Orchestra. — P.K.

Suggested Reading: Salzburger Mozart-Solisten Web site; Washington Post V p4, Sep. 18, 1997

Office of the Governor

Gilmore, James S. III

Oct. 6, 1949– Governor of Virginia; chairman of the Republican National Committee. Address: Office of the Governor, State Capitol, Third Fl., Richmond, VA 23219

James S. Gilmore III, the Republican governor of Virginia since January 1998 and the chairman of the Republican National Committee since early 2001, has earned a reputation as a politician more interested in implementing policies than espousing ideologies. Making good on a pledge he made during his gubernatorial campaign, he has reduced taxes in Virginia by approximately $1.5 billion. A hard-liner on issues related to crime, he supports the "three strikes and you're out" policy, which requires life imprisonment after a third conviction for a felony. He is known as a friend of business, particularly of high-tech enterprises such as America Online, which maintains its headquarters in Virginia. Taking action to improve education at all levels, he has reduced tuition at Virginia's public colleges and universities by 20 percent and ensured that all revenue from state lotteries will be spent on public education. Before he was elected governor of the Commonwealth of Virginia (as the state is officially named), he served as Henrico County commonwealth's attorney and Virginia attorney general, among other posts. In 2000 he cochaired the Republican National Convention.

James Stuart Gilmore III was born in Richmond, Virginia, on October 6, 1949. His father, James Stuart Gilmore Jr., was a butcher; his mother, the former Margaret Kandle, was a church secretary. After he graduated from J. R. Tucker High School, Gilmore paid his way through the University of Vir-

ginia at Richmond by working as a grocery-store cashier. After he earned a B.A. in foreign policy, in 1971, he volunteered for the U.S. Army. He graduated with honors from the Army Intelligence School and completed the required course work at the Defense Language Institute in Monterey, California. As a member of the 650th Military Intelligence Group, he was stationed in Mannheim, West Germany. He received a Joint Service Commendation Medal for service connected with NATO (the North Atlantic Treaty Organization).

After his discharge from the army, Gilmore entered the University of Virginia Law School, where he earned a J.D. degree in 1977. He was practicing law when, in 1982, he was elected Henrico County's Republican Party chairman, a position he held until 1986. In 1987 he won election as commonwealth's attorney for the county—a position analogous to that of a district attorney. He was reelected in 1991. Early in his campaign for Virginia attorney general, in 1993, his opponent, William D. Dolan III, questioned the appropriateness of a Gilmore fund-raising letter. According to Donald P. Baker, writing for the *Washington Post* (September 10, 1993), the letter contained the sentence, "Your early contributions to my campaign now, when it is most needed, will not be forgotten when I am attorney general." Dolan's complaint did not significantly affect Gilmore's campaign, and he was elected attorney general by a comfortable margin.

In 1995 Attorney General Gilmore charged a large insurance company, Trigon Blue Cross Blue Shield, with deceptive billing practices, and he threatened to block Trigon's attempt to convert to a for-profit business. Those moves took many by surprise, not only because of Gilmore's self-proclaimed sympathy toward business but also because Trigon had contributed $3,000 to Gilmore's most recent election campaign. Critics said that Gilmore's actions amounted to no more than political posturing, as Trigon had adopted new, acceptable billing practices before Gilmore had won the election. But many observers praised Gilmore for his stance. As attorney general Gilmore increased security in the vicinity of African-American churches after a series of fires, believed to have been set by arsonists, destroyed several houses of worship.

In 1997 Gilmore announced his candidacy for the governorship of Virginia. (Virginia state law prevents incumbent governors from serving successive terms, so the then-governor, George Allen, could not run that year.) Gilmore's platform was similar, in many respects, to Allen's, who gave Gilmore his endorsement. They both supported welfare reform, stricter educational standards, and a tougher stand on parole. In *Policy Review* (September/October 1997), Bernadette Malone wrote, "It has been said Gilmore is to Allen as George Bush was to Ronald Reagan. Gilmore is cautious, more process-oriented than ideological, and on a few issues—like gun rights and abortion—simply more liberal." Like Allen, Gilmore declared his support for parental notification when minors seek abortions. After his election he reversed his stand, on the ground that the Supreme Court had found parental notification unconstitutional in such cases. Later still, he said that he would not support notification requirements even if the Supreme Court had not found them unconstitutional. On taxes Gilmore's position was unequivocal: he supported cutting Virginians' taxes, particularly the unusually high property tax on automobiles, which he pledged to reduce to zero on cars whose book value was $20,000 or less. Like his opponent, the state's Democratic lieutenant governor, Donald S. Beyer, who campaigned under the slogan "Education First!," Gilmore proposed increasing the education budget, though not by as much as Beyer advocated. He promised to spend $240 million on merit-based scholarships and to freeze tuition at public colleges. While Beyer called for raising teachers' salaries, Gilmore suggested only a cost-of-living raise, to leave funds available for hiring additional teachers and thus reducing class sizes. On Election Day Gilmore triumphed, with 56 percent of the vote. He was sworn in as governor on January 17, 1998.

In contrast to George Allen, whose cabinet was heavy with aggressive, highly partisan conservatives, Gilmore surrounded himself mainly with moderates. Immediately setting to work to lower taxes, in his first two years in the governor's office, he pushed successfully for more than a dozen tax cuts. After they are all phased in, the cuts approved by the legislature will total approximately $1.5 billion.

Maintaining his tough stance on crime, in 1998 Gilmore presented a 21-point plan aimed at decreasing gang activity and drug use. Under his leadership Virginia established a statewide version of the Richmond-initiated "Project Exile," which calls for a mandatory five-year sentence for gun-wielding felons. Gilmore's Substance Abuse Reduction Effort (SABRE) strengthened anti–drug-law enforcement as well as drug-treatment and prevention efforts.

In October 1998 Gilmore became involved in the case of Hugh Finn, a one-time news anchorman who had suffered severe brain damage as the result of a car crash in 1995. Comatose for more than three years, he was being cared for in a Virginia nursing home, where he was fed through a tube inserted into his abdomen. His wife, Michele, maintained that he had once told her he would not want to be kept alive in such circumstances, and she sought to have the feeding tube removed. Finn's brothers and parents went to court to prevent Finn's wife and sister from taking Finn off life support, and Gilmore joined their cause. A judge ruled in Michele Finn's favor, and the feeding tube was removed; Hugh Finn died eight days later. After his death Gilmore tried to prevent Michele Finn from being compensated for her court expenses. In an on-line interview posted on *Washingtonpost.com*, Gilmore defended his actions; referring to Finn's parents and brothers, he said, "The family has as-

serted that Hugh Finn was communicating and was not in a persistent vegetative state. As such, I was in court for a total of three and a half days. I didn't think that was too much for Hugh Finn, who had done nothing wrong, when we routinely take years to make these kinds of decisions in death penalty cases. I opposed compensation because law doesn't require the taxpayer to pay unless the action was without foundation."

Early in 1999 Gilmore again became a combatant in a highly publicized quarrel, this time between Virginia and New York over the disposal of garbage. Virginia, which is surpassed only by Pennsylvania in the quantity of out-of-state trash that it imports, had long deposited refuse from New York in its landfills. After rumors circulated that Waste Management Inc., a New York City firm that brought trash to Virginia by barge, planned to increase its shipments, Gilmore succeeded in getting the legislature to ban garbage barges in his state and to restrict the construction of new landfills. A court ruling later overturned the ban, on the grounds that it violated the interstate-commerce clause of the Constitution.

Meanwhile, despite his actions against New York, Gilmore's own environmental record was being subjected to criticism. For example, Kenneth R. Plum, a Democratic member of the Virginia General Assembly, pointed out in a *Washington Post* (September 26, 1999) op-ed piece that in January 1999 Gilmore had helped to kill legislation that would have regulated the disposal of garbage generated within Virginia. While trash exported to Virginia from other states went into lined and regulated landfills, Plum reported, most in-state trash was dumped into unlined, unregulated landfills. Plum also derided Gilmore's decision not to intervene against "Tulloch ditching," the unregulated practice of draining nontidal wetlands, and he urged an investigation into the administration's environmental policies.

On the education front, Gilmore oversaw the institution of the Standards of Learning (SOLs) program, which aims to improve the teaching of such core subjects as math, science, English, and history. He established so-called Best Practice Centers, to provide teachers with various kinds of training and resource materials; helped pass legislation that transfers all revenue raised from the state lottery to public education; and provided $26 million in new funding to two historically African-American colleges, Norfolk State University and Virginia State University in Petersburg.

Acting on his belief in the close links between education and technology, Gilmore took steps to nurture the high-tech industry in Virginia. In an article for *ASEE Prism* (April 1999), a publication of the American Society for Engineering Education, he wrote, "Science and technology will continue to dominate in the next century. . . . All states and their institutions of higher education must prepare themselves to meet the challenges of our growing, technology-driven economy." The governor offered tax breaks to several Internet and high-technology companies, including one of $18 million to America Online, as an inducement to erect a new corporate building in Virginia. (Other high-tech companies based in Virginia include Uunet Technologies, Psinet, Network Solutions, and Capital One.)

The Governor's Commission on Information Technology, which Gilmore created, produced the first comprehensive set of laws governing the Internet within a state. The Internet Policy Act, passed by Virginia's General Assembly in 1999, prohibited unsolicited bulk e-mail; established a Virginia secretary of technology, the first such post in any state; and extended Virginia's Freedom of Information Act to include material posted on the Internet and in e-mail emanating from government offices. In December 1998 Gilmore was named chairman of the Advisory Commission on Electronic Commerce, a federal panel charged with studying Internet tax issues. The commission's report urged Congress to keep e-commerce tax-free.

Gilmore co-chaired the 2000 Republican National Convention, held in Philadelphia, Pennsylvania. He chairs the Congressional Advisory Panel to Assess Domestic Response Capabilities for Terrorism Involving Weapons of Mass Destruction. He also serves as chairman of the Southern States Energy Board, as a member of the Technology Committee of the National Governors' Association, and as vice chairman of the Republican Governors' Association. In December 2000 then–president-elect George W. Bush named Gilmore chairman of the Republican National Committee. The appointment was seen as being partly a reward for Gilmore's aggressive campaigning on Bush's behalf during the presidential race. In announcing his choice, Bush described Gilmore, as quoted in the *New York Times* (December 23, 2000), as a "fellow who knows what it means to set an agenda, build consensus to achieve an agenda and lead." Gilmore's term as governor of Virginia ends in January 2002.

Gilmore is married to the former Roxane Gatling, a professor of classics at Randolph-Macon College. The couple and their two sons, Ashton and Jay, live in Richmond, Virginia. — P.G.H.

Suggested Reading: *Chronicle of Higher Education* A p35 Nov. 14, 1997; *Industry Week* p10+ Mar. 20, 2000; *National Review* p10+ Nov. 10, 1997; *New York Times* pA9 Oct. 10, 1998, B p3 Jan. 13, 1999, C p4 Apr. 26, 1999, A p14 Dec. 23, 2000, A p16 July 20, 2001; *Policy Review* p12+ Oct. 1997, with photos; *Washington Post* D p3 Sep. 10, 1993, with photos, B p1 Aug. 12, 1995, with photo, B p1 Dec. 31, 1997, B p8 Sep. 26, 1999, V p2 May 10, 2000

Goff, M. Lee

Jan. 19, 1944– Forensic entomologist. Address: Dept. of Plant and Environmental Protection Sciences, University of Hawaii at Manoa, Honolulu, HI 96822

"Know maggots, will travel." Those words appear on the business card of M. Lee Goff, a forensic entomologist and professor of entomology at the University of Hawaii at Manoa. In the United States, Goff is one of fewer than 20 specialists in forensic entomology, whose practitioners apply knowledge about the anatomy, physiology, stages of development, and behavior of insects to legal matters—most often, murder investigations. His job entails collecting the insects, insect eggs and larvae, or evidence of the past presence of insects from decomposing corpses and then, in his laboratory, analyzing what he has found. Knowing, for example, the times of year when a particular insect species reproduces, and taking into account such variables as weather and characteristics of the soil, ground cover, or other aspects of the site where a corpse has been found, he has often deduced a victim's time of death with startling accuracy. Based on his conclusions, detectives have issued search warrants and challenged alibis, thereby identifying murderers. "I have entered into an area where insects, crime and our criminal justice system inter-

Courtesy of M. Lee Goff

sect with the very darkest aspect of human nature," he told Jim Borg for *Honolulu* magazine (May 1999). In a lecture that he gave at California State University at Chico, as reported by Roseanne

Langlois for *Inside Chico State* (March 2, 2000), he said, "I may not be able to prevent a murder, but I can keep [the murderer] from doing it again."

For over 15 years Goff has contributed his expertise to criminal investigations as a consultant to the medical examiner of the city and county of Honolulu, Hawaii. He has also worked occasionally on cases from other jurisdictions in Hawaii or other states. Goff has witnessed the transformation of forensic entomology from an obscure pursuit regarded with suspicion among law-enforcement authorities to a discipline that is recognized as rigorously scientific and of proven value. Every year since 1996 (with the exception of 1999), he has taught a week-long course at the Forensic Sciences Research and Training Center of the FBI Academy in Quantico, Virginia, using the decaying corpses of 50-pound pigs for his demonstrations. He wrote about his methods and experiences in *A Fly for the Prosecution: How Insect Evidence Helps Solve Crimes* (2000); intended for a lay audience, it received generally positive reviews, most of which included caveats for squeamish readers. In his assessment of *A Fly for the Prosecution* for the *Sciences* (July/August 2000), Laurence A. Marschall wrote, "The field [of forensic entomology] requires a rare combination of qualities—among them, a deep knowledge of insect life cycles, a knack for deductive reasoning and a strong stomach. Goff has them all."

An only child, Madison Lee Goff—known as Lee—was born on January 19, 1944 in Glendale, California, a suburb of Los Angeles. His parents, Madison and Margaret Goff, who had met while involved in theater, divorced when he was three; afterward Goff was raised primarily by his mother, who worked as a switchboard operator. He attended public elementary schools in Glendale and graduated from Glendale High School. Interested in science since his early years, he had a particular fondness for marine biology, thanks largely to his experiences while scuba diving off the California coast and his fascination with films made by the pioneering oceanographer and marine biologist Jacques-Yves Cousteau. But until college, he told *Current Biography*, "I don't think I had actually viewed it as a real career possibility."

Goff spent a year at Glendale Junior College, where a zoology professor encouraged him to delve further into marine studies. After visiting Hawaii to surf, he relocated to Oahu, Hawaii's most populous island, and enrolled at the University of Hawaii at Manoa. To pay for tuition and living expenses, he performed in small clubs as a singer and guitarist. Finding it necessary to supplement his income, in 1964 he answered a want ad for a part-time marine-biology technician at the Bishop Museum of Natural and Cultural History, in Honolulu. But the ad had been placed in error: the marine-biology job was intended for a volunteer. Goff interviewed instead for a paid position in the museum's entomology division, and, despite his complete lack of experience with insects, he got the job.

That serendipitous occurrence led him to turn his attention from marine biology to entomology. In 1966 Goff earned a B.S. degree in zoology.

Upon his graduation from college, Goff was drafted into the United States Army. He told *Current Biography*, "I wound up in pathology because they didn't seem to know what to do with me once they had me." His undergraduate experience in a zoology lab proved to be useful during his two-year tour of duty, during which he was assigned to work in the morgue of the Fort Ord, California, army hospital. In addition to gaining expertise in human anatomy, he became accustomed to working with corpses and learned to detach himself from the victims. Also while in the army, Goff occasionally tested riot-control gases in Maryland's Edgewood Arsenal.

After his military discharge Goff became a research assistant at the Bishop Museum's Department of Entomology. His research was in acarology, the study of mites and ticks, with a focus on their roles as disease transmitters. In 1971 he worked for six months at Hawaii Volcanoes National Park, as a participant in the International Biological Program (IBP), which was under the combined auspices of the Bishop Museum and the University of Hawaii. He managed the IBP's field station, which was responsible for maintaining weather stations and conducting research on park ecosystems.

In 1971 Goff entered a master's program in biology at California State University at Long Beach. His projects there involved the reclassification of a subgenus of chigger mites that, during the initial part of their life cycle, feed on birds, reptiles, and mammals. He had a particular interest in the subgenus *Leptotrombidium*, which transmits *Rickettsia*, a bacterium that causes typhus fever in Asian and Pacific regions. After he completed his M.S. degree, in 1974, he worked briefly in the parasitology and endocrinology lab of the Kaiser Hospital, in Harbor City, California.

Goff earned a Ph.D. in entomology from the University of Hawaii at Manoa in 1977. He then returned to the Bishop Museum as a full-time acarologist. His first exposure to forensic entomology was another "accident," as he labeled it in a talk with Kojo Nnamdi for a WAMU broadcast of the radio series *Public Interest* (May 18, 2000). It stemmed from his attendance at a meeting of the Entomological Society of America in the mid-1980s. With a museum stipend of only $18 a day to cover his expenses, he could not afford a room at the hotel where the meeting was being held and stayed instead at less expensive lodgings. To avoid having to cross a road during the times when it was dangerously busy or having to take a long, roundabout route to get from his hotel to the meeting site, he would walk there very early in the morning and return late at night. Thus it was that early one morning he attended a talk given by C. Lamar Meek, a Louisiana State University mosquito expert who was also among the handful of entomologists involved with forensics at that time. Meek talked about human decomposition in relation to insects and ended his lecture with a description of a particular murder investigation. His account intrigued Goff, who, unlike many others in the audience, was not fazed by images of pig and human corpses in advanced states of decay. Soon afterward Goff determined that with few exceptions, the entomological literature did not address forensic issues. Eager to forge his own path in the field, he approached Charles Odom, who was then the medical examiner of Honolulu, to offer his expert assistance in criminal investigations. Although Odom had misgivings, he agreed to discuss the proposition with Goff at an eatery. "By the end of the meal," Goff recalled in *A Fly for the Prosecution*, "we had decided that if we could discuss maggots and decomposing bodies while eating curry over rice, we could probably work together."

Goff encountered a few stumbling blocks in his new pursuit. First, there was little opportunity to practice his skills, because the homicide rate in Hawaii was low. Second, bodies decomposed so quickly on Oahu, because of the warmth and wetness, that in many cases there was little or nothing left for him to work with. In addition, as Goff recalled in his book, administrators at the Bishop Museum seemed uncomfortable about the possibility that his involvement in police investigations would attract publicity. In part because of their disapproval, in 1983 he left the museum to join the faculty of the Department of Entomology at the University of Hawaii at Manoa, in Honolulu. He soon discovered some of the benefits of academia, prominent among them the greater ease with which he could secure funding for his research and the willingness of an eager cadre of graduate students to help him with his forensic projects—even though, as he told Laurence A. Marschall, "most people do not share my enthusiasm for maggots."

Goff's primary means of transportation is a motorcycle, so when he sets out for the place where a body has been found, he "tend[s] to travel fairly light," as he told Terry Gross for the National Public Radio series *Fresh Air* (May 17, 2000). His equipment includes a collapsible net; forceps, scalpels, and other tools for scraping and collecting insects, insect eggs, or insect remnants present on the corpse; insect-rearing chambers, in which larvae grow; and, for his own health and safety, gloves and a simple respirator. "When insects go into the body, we look at those with the most advanced development. Then we work backward to determine the time of death," Goff explained in his 2000 lecture at California State University at Chico. The odor of a corpse quickly draws flies, which then lay eggs on the remains. Within a day or so the eggs hatch into larvae—called maggots, in the case of flies—which feed on the flesh. The maggots, in turn, attract predatory insects, such as wasps. Burying beetles and other scavengers join in after that. In Hawaii, Goff told Jim Borg, "there are more than 200 different kinds of insects and other arthropods that may be found associated with a decomposing body." Because there is little variation in the order in which all those species arrive, the presence of particular species on a corpse offers clues about the passage of time since death. Other clues come from the extent of development of larval species, which, depending mostly on weather, proceeds according to a fixed timetable. If decomposition occurs at a time of the year when insects are scarce or not out in the open at all, Goff will not find any entomological evidence.

Most of Goff's work is done not in the field but in his laboratory. His studies of rotting pig carcasses—which, for purposes of his research, are close substitutes for human remains—have proved invaluable in his investigations of decomposing humans. After persuading representatives of the U.S. Department of Agriculture that the pigs did not suffer unduly, he received permission to kill the pigs, and then bury them, in ways that re-create the conditions under which humans are killed and their bodies disposed of. He has left some pig corpses in dense vegetation in very humid areas and others on dry, exposed ground. He has wrapped their bodies tightly in blankets to approximate conditions under which insects find their way to concealed corpses. After killing the pigs, he has used the bodies to replicate the murders of humans by hanging, arson, drowning, or other means. "A corpse is like an island in the sea, different from the surrounding environment," he reported to Burl Burlingame for the *Honolulu Star-Bulletin* (June 9, 2000, on-line). "It is an instant source of nutrients, an expendable resource, and what happens to it affects the site as well." Goff's investigations also indicate the presence of drugs or poisons in a corpse, because such substances affect the development of the insects that feed on its flesh. His large collection of data notwithstanding, Goff told Christopher Kemp for *Salon.com* (December 13, 2000), "I think I've got more questions now than when I started."

A case to which Goff has frequently referred when guest lecturing is that of a young woman whose body was found in a sugarcane field on the Hawaiian island of Kauai, where the climate is hot and wet. "The body was very decomposed and not a lot of physical evidence remained," he recalled to Kemp. There was enough, however, for Goff to estimate that death had occurred 34 to 36 days before his arrival at the site. The police learned about a man who had been with the victim 33 days before. After obtaining a search warrant based solely on Goff's time-of-death estimate, they discovered through the use of luminol (a chemical that attaches to the hemoglobin in blood and makes it glow) that the man had killed the woman in his apartment, dragged her body down the stairs of his building, placed her in the trunk of his car, and left her corpse in the sugarcane field. The man was convicted of her murder. Goff has also helped the police in investigating cases of living victims of elder or child neglect in which improperly treated wounds, such as bedsores, attracted insects.

In addition to his consulting work, Goff teaches courses in entomology at the University of Hawaii and is a popular guest speaker at universities. He is a co-founder of the American Board of Forensic Entomology, whose members he refers to as the "Dirty Dozen." In his week-long seminar for FBI recruits, he stresses the importance of insect evidence and demonstrates ways to collect and analyze it; his daily lectures are followed by practical sessions in which 50-pound pigs serve as the victims. Goff hopes to incorporate DNA technology into his work, to identify larval species without having to rear the larvae to adulthood in his lab. (Many insects look alike when they are in the larval stage.)

Goff remains an avid surfer and uses a Harley-Davidson motorcycle as his primary means of transportation. Drawing from several of his past cases and writing "from the entomological perspective," he is working on a novel about a serial killer. He and his wife, Dianne, have two grown daughters, Dana and Alaina. The couple live in Kaneohe, Hawaii. — K.S.

Suggested Reading: *Honolulu* p22 May 1999, with photo; *Honolulu Star-Bulletin* B p1+ June 9, 2000, with photos; *New York Times Book Review* p20 Sep. 10, 2000; *Salon.com* Dec. 13, 2000

Selected Books: *A Fly for the Prosecution: How Insect Evidence Helps Solve Crimes*, 2000

Steve Granitz/Retna Ltd.

Goldberg, Bill

Dec. 27, 1966– Professional wrestler; animal-rights activist. Address: c/o World Championship Wrestling, Turner Broadcasting System, One CNN Center, Atlanta, GA 30348

Soon after he made his debut appearance with World Championship Wrestling (WCW), in 1997, the professional wrestling superstar Bill Goldberg grew accustomed to having stadium-filling crowds chant his name. The incredible strength of this six-foot four-inch, 285-pound former pro football player, as well as old-fashioned charisma and a devotion to wrestling's theatrics, rapidly made Goldberg a favorite among fans. "Going through a little bit of pain, getting hit with a chair or two and may-

be bleeding a little bit is the least I can do to satisfy my public," he told Danya D'Itria in an interview for *iCAST* (November 13, 2000, on-line). Goldberg amassed an unparalleled winning streak during his first year and became an enormous presence on the WCW tour, winning the world-championship belt in the summer of 1998. One of only a handful of Jewish wrestlers to rise to prominence, he welcomed the obligations that came with his new status as a role model for Jews and non-Jews alike. "It's a big responsibility to take on, but I take on that responsibility with open arms," he assured Blake Eskin for the *Forward* (June 12, 1998, on-line). Goldberg has also used his fame to promote his favorite charitable causes: the Make-A-Wish Foundation, for critically ill children, and the Humane Society of the United States, for which he became a celebrity spokesperson in 1998.

The youngest of four children, William Scott Goldberg was born on December 27, 1966 in Tulsa, Oklahoma. His father, Jed, was an obstetrician and gynecologist, and his mother, Ethel, was a concert violinist. From childhood, he wanted to play football like his older brothers, Michael and Steve. "By the time he could walk," his mother told Bruce Frankel for *People* (December 14, 1998), "he was hiking a football." Early on, Goldberg learned a love of animals from his sister, Barbara, who gave him his first pet; as he told Tracey Middlekauf for *People* (June 29, 2000 on-line), his dog, Rocky, a Rottweiler, was his "best friend" while his parents were divorcing, during his high-school years. He played football for Thomas Edison High School in Tulsa, and during his free time he used his size and bulk as a bouncer at a Tulsa club. He won a football scholarship to the University of Georgia, where he majored in psychology and earned accolades as an outstanding defensive lineman. While in college he also endured what his WCW biography called "by his own admission . . . the worst experience of his life." Experimenting with marijuana the day before a surprise, random drug test, he was suspended and missed playing in the Gator Bowl.

In 1989 Goldberg followed the career path of his brother Steve (who had briefly played for the Oakland Raiders and Minnesota Vikings) and entered the National Football League (NFL) draft. In the 11th round he was selected by the Los Angeles Rams but was cut from the team during preseason training. After being whittled from the Rams in the preseason again the following year, in 1991 he joined the World League of American Football, a new (and short-lived) international league. He spent one season with the Sacramento Surge, which won the 1992 league championship. Goldberg reentered the NFL when he was signed by the Atlanta Falcons, for whom he played nose tackle (some sources say he was a linebacker) in 14 games over the next three seasons. His football career ended in a 1994 preseason game, when abdominal muscles were torn from his pelvis—an injury that was both unusual and excruciating. "I was a piece of junk," he told Bruce Frankel, and he was unable to recover sufficiently to play for the Carolina Panthers, an expansion team that had signed him for the 1995 season.

Retired from football, Goldberg became a personal trainer and spent his days in Atlanta's gyms. During this time he met the wrestler Diamond Dallas Page and went for the first time to a live wrestling event at the invitation of the WCW stars Lex Luger and Sting, who accompanied him there. "I thought, 'This is kind of cool,'" he told Bruce Frankel. So taken with what he saw that he decided to give it a try himself, he endured the rigorous training at the WCW Power Plant, where WCW executives observed his moves and were impressed by his intensity and strength. When he debuted with the WCW, in 1997, wrestling fans immediately saw that Goldberg had no pretenses. "I'm no-frills," he explained to Bruce Frankel. Unlike many other professional-wrestling personalities, he did not apply make-up, don a mask or wig, or wear a fancy costume. Making his entrance amid music and pyrotechnics, Goldberg sported only black bikini briefs, a shaved head, and a menacing scowl. He refused even to take a pseudonym, as most wrestlers do. According to Bruce Frankel, he "briefly considered 'The Warlord' and 'Mossad,' after the Israeli spy agency," but as Goldberg told Blake Eskin, "I didn't think ['The Mossad'] would go over so well."

Goldberg won his first professional match, against Hugh Morrus, late in 1997. He then compiled an unrivaled winning streak, victorious in more than 170 matches through 1998. After he defeated veteran wrestler Raven to become the WCW United States champion in April 1998, he barreled on to defeat Hollywood Hulk Hogan for the WCW world-championship crown in Atlanta on July 6 of that year. Over the course of his long string of victories, Goldberg developed his thunderous taunt: "Who's next?" He also perfected his signature moves, the Spear and the Jackhammer. "My motto is force equals mass times acceleration," he explained to Blake Eskin, describing the Spear—a

dash across the ring toward his adversary, who is often flattened by the attack. Goldberg similarly found the Jackhammer to be an effective way of ending matches. "It's basically holding a guy upside down straight in the air, and, when the time is right, I drop him right on his back and he doesn't get up from that," he told Eskin. Goldberg retained the title of world champion for almost six months, a remarkable accomplishment in an organization that often sees a new champion arise every few weeks. Then, on December 27, 1998, he lost to Kevin Nash in Washington, D.C., as part of Starrcade. The loss ended his unbeaten streak.

Thrown from his top perch, Goldberg continued to appear in WCW matches but also turned his attention to a new sideline: acting. He appeared in *Universal Soldier II: The Return* (1999), with Jean-Claude van Damme, and starred as himself in the David Arquette wrestling comedy *Ready to Rumble* (2000). Acknowledging his lack of acting experience and the fact that the roles he played were not terribly challenging, he announced to Danya D'Itria: "I would definitely aspire to act as a career. But I wouldn't take that responsibility on unless I was totally prepared for it. I've taken one acting class in my life. . . . Going into it half-heartedly and half-prepared would be an injustice to myself." Goldberg also told D'Itria that he would "never" want to become a manager or trainer in professional wrestling, a sentiment that indicated his frustration with the feuds and politicking among wrestlers that are considered part of the entertainment.

The theatrical aspect of wrestling had unintended consequences for Goldberg in late 1999. Although wrestlers are often hurt in scripted matches, he had escaped serious injury in the ring up to that time; but after one show, still in character for his television audience, he almost lost the use of his arm. Confronting some of his opponents in a parking lot, Goldberg smashed a limousine window. That much had been scripted; what was improvised was the use of his bare hand rather than a sledgehammer. The resulting damage required dozens of stitches and took him out of the ring for months.

While Goldberg recuperated from his injury, he devoted himself to personal appearances for the WCW and to activities on behalf of the Humane Society. During the 106th Congress (1999–2001), he appeared twice before congressional committees investigating animal fighting. "I know that when I step into the ring, that's my choice, but these animals, they have no choice," he said, as Michele Orecklin reported for *Time* (February 15, 1999). Staunchly against cockfighting, dogfighting, and rattlesnake roundups, while on Capitol Hill he sought a meeting with Republican representative Steve Largent of Oklahoma to discuss why that state was one of three where cockfighting remained legal. Largent refused to meet with him, leaving Goldberg to muse to Orecklin: "I'm not sure why he wouldn't see me. I would think he'd want me in his corner, but we'll just see who the most popular man from Oklahoma is." What motivated him to defend animals? "To do nothing with [my success] would be worse than not having it," he told Middlekauf. "So I turned my energy into doing as much as I could for the community." An advocate for pet adoption, Goldberg, with his longtime girlfriend, Lisa Shekter, maintains a menagerie near Atlanta that includes dogs, cats, birds, and horses.

Goldberg has also invested a great deal in his relationship with his fans. "I do [what I do] because I walk down the hall and I see a kid's eyes light up, and I see a kid extend his hand or extend a piece of paper and want to shake my hand, want to get an autograph from me. And I know that there's no money in the world that could give that kid that happiness that they derive from getting my autograph or shaking my hand," he explained to Danya D'Itria. Refusing to downplay his Jewish roots, Goldberg contemplated having a Star of David emblazoned on his trunks. "I've never once tried to hide my heritage," he told Rick Reilly for *Sports Illustrated* (June 12, 2000). "I'm proud of being Jewish." In the past, "Jews wrestled only with their identity . . . ," Rabbi Irwin Kula told Dave McKenna for the *New Yorker* (September 7, 1998). "What [Goldberg's success] says is: 'Look at us! . . . We're not weak and wimpy! We're the heavyweight champ!'" While wrestling, Goldberg has never been confronted with anti-Semitism, but he has said that he would not hesitate to go after a heckler spouting epithets during a match. "They pay us a lot to wrestle, but they don't pay us to listen to that," he told Blake Eskin.

Although Goldberg's family members were initially shocked by his decision to be a wrestler, they are now enthusiastic about his participation in the

WCW. "My parents thought I was crazy," he told Frankel. "But now they're proud." "Some people give me an attitude about it," Ethel Goldberg told Rick Reilly. "They say, 'How could you let your son do that? Don't you have to be low class to be a wrestler?' But my son does wonderful things for people with his wrestling. Children's hospitals. Make-A-Wish. The animals." Late in 2000 Goldberg published an autobiography, *I'm Next: The Strange Journey of America's Most Unlikely Superhero*, with the help of his brother Steve.

Though he does not often publicly discuss his plans, Goldberg told Danya D'Itria that for the present he is happy to be part of "the hottest male soap opera out there, and . . . one of the leading characters. And you throw in a little violence, you throw in some theatrics—a lot of theatrics—and you throw in a lot of acrobatics . . . with good story lines and beautiful women and, my God, I mean, it's got a little bit of everything for everybody." — K.S.

Suggested Reading: *Forward* (on-line) June 12, 1998; *People* p121+ Dec. 14, 1998, with photos; *People* (on-line) June 29, 2000; *Sports Illustrated* p106 June 12, 2000; *Time* p89 Feb. 15, 1999, with photo

Selected Books: *I'm Next: The Strange Journey of America's Most Unlikely Superhero* (with Steve Goldberg), 2000

Selected Films: *Universal Soldier II: The Return*, 1999; *Ready to Rumble*, 2000

Golden, Thelma

Sep. 22, 1965– Museum curator. Address: Studio Museum in Harlem, 144 W. 125th St., New York, NY 10027

Thelma Golden "is fast becoming recognized as one of those pivotal centrist figures in African-American life," Greg Tate declared in the *Village Voice* (May 22, 2001). "An art world zephyr who seems to know everyone and be everywhere at the same time, a Black postmodernist with race-woman drive and what used to be called the popular touch," as Tate described her, Golden is the deputy director and chief curator for exhibitions at the Studio Museum in Harlem (SMH). Certain since childhood about her career goals and immersed in the curatorial field since her high-school years, she worked at the SMH before joining the staff of the Whitney Museum of American Art as an assistant curator, in 1988. She thus became, in her early 20s, one of only a handful of African-

Americans to hold a prestigious post at a major U.S. museum. Following a stint at the Jamaica Arts Center for the Performing and Visual Arts, she rejoined the Whitney, where she provoked much indignation among art critics as a co-curator of the museum's 1993 biennial, and where she also generated a great deal of discussion as the curator of the show *Black Male: Representations of Masculinity in Contemporary American Art*, which opened the following year. She left the Whitney in 1998 and in 1999 returned to the SMH to work with her mentor, Lowery Stokes Sims, who had become the museum's director earlier that year. "For the venerable, invaluable but formerly staid Studio Museum," Greg Tate wrote, "she and Sims are performing not just a makeover but a resurrection."

Thelma Golden was born on September 22, 1965 in the New York City borough of Queens, New York, where her father owned an insurance brokerage firm and her mother was a homemaker. She grew up in St. Albans, a section of Queens whose residents are mainly middle- and upper-class

Djamilla Rosa Cochran/Courtesy of Studio Museum in Harlem

Thelma Golden

African-Americans. Golden attended private schools in the New York metropolitan area through high school. Her extracurricular activities included taking dance and piano lessons and attending theatrical events. From an early age Golden knew that she wanted to become a museum curator. She recalled to Diane Haithman for the *Los Angeles Times* (April 23, 1995), "I think I, in going to museums as a young child, really realized that someone did that—I didn't have a name for it, but it was clear that someone put those things up, somewhere. As soon as it became clear to me what that job was, that was the job I wanted." When she was 12 years old, Golden read about Lowery Stokes Sims, who managed the collection of 20th-century art at the Metropolitan Museum of Art (known informally as the Met) in New York and was the first African-American woman to hold such a high position at a major museum. By her senior year in high school, Golden had become a curatorial apprentice to Sims at the Met.

Golden was accepted for admittance by two all-women's colleges: Barnard, an affiliate of Columbia University, in New York City, and Smith, in Northhampton, Massachusetts. She enrolled at the latter, because her parents believed that she would benefit from being away from the city. At Smith, where she majored in both art history and African-American studies, Golden discovered that other black students "didn't bother with visual art," while art-history students and professors "didn't discuss African Americans," as Greg Tate reported. During her summer breaks from college, she continued to intern at the Met. In the summer following her junior year, she also began an internship at the Studio Museum in Harlem. While working at

SMH she formed the view that the museum ignored the opinions and ideas of the artists represented there; she also noted that it failed to present the work of a broad selection of contemporary black artists. (As she told Tate, the SMH "felt like my parents' museum.") Further, it seemed to her that the SMH staff took little interest in the aesthetics of installation. Such impressions led her to conclude that the atmosphere at the museum was unprofessional. Nevertheless, after she graduated from Smith, with a B.A. degree, in 1987, she accepted a full-time job as an associate curator at the SMH.

In 1988 Golden learned of an opening for an assistant curator at the Whitney Museum and successfully applied for the position. Soon, however, she began to experience creative differences with Thomas Newton "Tom" Armstrong, who then directed the Whitney. She also wanted to handle the works of more African-American artists than her job allowed. So, after a year, Golden left the Whitney to serve as the visual-arts director at a facility that promoted the work of black artists: the Jamaica Arts Center for the Performing and Visual Arts, in the Jamaica section of Queens, New York, directed at that time by Kellie Jones.

In 1991 Golden learned that Tom Armstrong was no longer at the Whitney; he had been replaced by David A. Ross, who, while at his previous post, at the Institute of Contemporary Art, in Boston, Massachusetts, had pursued what was considered a more progressive artistic agenda. Golden succeeded in being rehired at the Whitney. In addition to holding the title of associate curator, she was given the job of director of the Whitney Museum of Contemporary Art at Philip Morris, the museum's branch at that company's New York City headquarters. In those capacities Golden organized exhibitions featuring many prominent artists, among them Romare Bearden, Jane Dickson, Jacob Lawrence, Suzanne McClelland, Lorna Simpson, Matthew McCaslin, Glenn Ligon, and the installation group Leone & Macdonald.

In 1993, in collaboration with Elisabeth Sussman, Golden co-curated the Whitney Biennial, a large, influential show that presents highlights of the contemporary American art scene. She was then a 27-year-old with a short résumé; describing to Peter Plagens for Newsweek (May 14, 2001) the task assigned to her, Golden compared it to that of a novice baseball player who comes up to the plate in "the bottom of the ninth, game tied, at Yankee Stadium." The consensus of most of those who reviewed the exhibition was that she and Sussman had struck out. In a representative assessment, Deborah Solomon wrote for the Wall Street Journal (March 5, 1993), "The 1993 Whitney Biennial easily qualifies as the most disturbing museum show in living memory. . . . As if taking its cue from the world of fashion, it has tended to favor the frenetic pursuit of novelty over the sober approach you might expect of a museum." Solomon also complained, "Most of the politics in the '93 Biennial are sexual politics, explored with all the subtlety of a sledgehammer." Alan Rusbridger, in the London Guardian (April 26, 1993), described the show as "the most Politically Correct exhibition of all time." Viewers of the exhibit, on paying the entrance fee, were given buttons that read, "I can't imagine ever wanting to be white." The philosopher and art critic Arthur Danto, writing for the Nation (April 19, 1993), concluded his critique with a reference to the buttons: "I and most of those with whom I have spoken felt as if we had been . . . caught up in a moralizing rampage. I can't imagine ever wanting to have had anything to do with the 1993 Whitney Biennial exhibition."

Golden found herself at the center of controversy again a year later, when the show Black Male: Representations of Masculinity in Contemporary American Art opened at the Whitney and later went on tour in the U.S. The exhibition included photographs, paintings, mixed-media constructions, videos, and films by 29 individuals, among them Robert Mapplethorpe, Adrian Piper, Jean-Michel Basquiat, Renee Cox, and David Hammons, and included depictions of crime, poverty, homelessness, and homosexuality, among other subjects. Many critics dismissed the contents of the show as degrading, demeaning, stereotypical, or even pornographic, but others found much to praise. Among the latter was Linda Nochlin, who wrote for Art in America (March 1995), "Although black masculinity is the unifying theme of the exhibit, its representation is as varied as the imaginations of the artists, who may be black, white, male, female, gay, or straight. The impressions of black manhood that they articulate are variously negative and positive, stereotypical and questioning,

ambiguous and interestingly ambivalent, and realistic and abstract. In general, the show is characterized by sophisticated imagery and visual inventiveness." Also impressed was Christopher Knight, who wrote for the Los Angeles Times (April 27, 1995), "While [Black Male] was assembled to combat and dismantle mass-media stereotypes, it smartly refrains from erecting an equally bogus and restrictive conception of social and cultural role models for black men. One-dimensionality is routine in pop culture, but this show puts its faith squarely in the complex ambiguities of art, where uncertainty is both life-affirming and contrary to the mummification required of a role model."

Golden, meanwhile, remained steadfast in defense of her artistic selections for Black Male. In her interview with Diane Haithman, she said, "This show is not about representation. This is not a documentary survey on black men as they live and breathe today, it is not a catalogue of types. It is about the way in which contemporary artists have looked at black masculinity." She also told Haithman, "The day I decided I didn't want to be a 19th-Century European curator, I knew I would never have the experience of people coming and going 'ooh' and 'aah,' the way they do around the Monets. It just doesn't happen." She also rejected claims that she was, by including "negative" images of black males in the show, encouraging racism. "I'm so finished with that," she told Haithman, "the positive/negative thing? I'm done with that. I can't even go there anymore. . . . It's a simple way to talk about things. But this work is much more complicated than that." In spite of (or, more likely, because of) the furor, the number of visitors to the Whitney increased during the run of Black Male, as Golden noted with satisfaction during an interview with Rhonda Reynolds for Black Enterprise (February 1996). "People were starving to see a show about African-American art, but not necessarily what I was showing—but I never saw more people come into the Museum. They came to see what the controversy was about. Either way I'm just happy they came."

The year 1998 marked the opening of another major show curated by Golden: a major retrospective of the work of the African-American artist Bob Thompson. Thompson (1937–66) was a figurative expressionist painter whose work had received short shrift in the years following his death, "partly because his blend of abstraction and figuration defied easy assimilation by the prevailing narrative of post-war art and partly because the mainstream paid little attention to African-American artists," as Marcia E. Vetrocq wrote in an assessment of the show for Art in America (December 1998). An important member of the Beat Generation, Thompson had associated with many well-known writers, musicians, and artists, among them Allen Ginsberg, Jack Kerouac, and Ornette Coleman. The Whitney retrospective of Thompson's work enjoyed critical success, as did the accompanying 388-page catalogue, Bob Thompson (1998), which

Golden wrote in collaboration with Judith Wilson and Shamim Momim.

Earlier, David A. Ross had announced that Golden would head the curatorial team for the 2000 Whitney Biennial. Then, later in 1998, Ross left the Whitney; he was succeeded by Maxwell L. Anderson, who a month after his appointment made clear his plans to assign Lisa Phillips, the Whitney's contemporary-art curator, the job of assembling the 2000 Biennial, with Golden working under her. (Ultimately, six outsiders curated the exhibition.) Anderson also reorganized the staff, and when Golden learned that she would not be given a specialized area of the museum's collection to oversee, as other curators had, she resigned her position. For the next year she worked as special-projects curator for the huge private art collection of the software mogul Peter Norton, whose interest in the arts and in Golden's professional opinions had often brought him and Golden together. (Norton, who contributed a substantial portion of the funds for the *Black Male* show, resigned from Whitney's board of trustees when Golden left the museum.)

In 1999 the Studio Museum in Harlem announced the appointment of Lowery Stokes Sims as its new director. In an interview with Holland Cotter for the *New York Times* (February 28, 2000), Sims, who in her last position at the Met had curated its modern-art collection, said, "The first thing I wanted to do was hire Thelma." Golden accepted the post of deputy director for exhibitions and public programs at the SMH. (Her title was recently changed to deputy director and chief curator for exhibitions.) High on Sims's agenda—and Golden's—was a reexamination of the SMH's mission to reflect changing attitudes. As Sims explained to Cotter, "The museum was founded when the mainstream wasn't paying attention to African-American art. As an institution, it was a response to that neglect. Then in the 1980s the mainstream woke up and started to take notice." In the 1980s and 1990s, Golden told Greg Tate, "Black artists and those of us presenting them were . . . trying to make work informed by culture, race, gender, ethnicity, nations, and trying to define it in ways that were a very complex combination of content and form. . . . But then that became, thank goodness, the norm, and many Black artists moved to the forefront of our consciousness in terms of contemporary art practice in ways that didn't have to be explained through a Black History Month label. So there was no longer any need to have all those paragraphs before you got to the work on why you were showing the work and what this means and da da da pluralism we are the world hold hands kumbaya." Golden intended to concentrate on filling the SMH with art that spoke for itself. Indeed, as Peter Schjeldahl wrote in the *New Yorker* (June 11, 2001), "'Post-Black' is the term that Golden boldly applies to the sensibility of artists for whom racial identity has become an optional reference."

Golden's first major show after she rejoined the SMH opened in 2001. Called *Freestyle* and co-organized with Christine Y. Kim, it included works in traditional and nontraditional media by 28 African-American artists, most of them thus far unsung. "The best thing about my show is that I have no colon," Golden told Jerry Saltz for the *Village Voice* (May 16–22, 2001, on-line), referring to the absence of that punctuation mark and a subtitle in the exhibition's name. "*Freestyle* . . . stands on its own," Saltz explained. "Like a lightbulb, it needs no explanation: the minute you see it, you know why you needed to see it." Saltz also wrote, "Seeing so much new work by so many young and unknown or emerging artists is thrilling. . . . Although the exhibition is not thematic, many of the issues addressed in *Freestyle* are familiar: social cruelty, the bottomless confusion of the divided self, the crushing weight of being defined from without. Nevertheless, urgency, emergency and bitterness have been replaced by something that could be called radical intelligence. Humor is prevalent, be it twisted or covert; answers are understood as elusive and illusory; the moral failure of America is often at the fore but never moralized about." Peter Plagens was similarly enthusiastic: "There are a few deliberately offhand-looking paintings, some messed-with photography and some MTV-length videos playing in a viewing room in the back of the museum. And nearly every participant holds the de rigueur Master of Fine Arts degree from a big university or topflight art school. . . . But somehow *Freestyle* is different. Its collective passion and grit . . . keeps the show from devolving into the hyperclever anomie that infects almost every other revue of emerging artists these days. *Freestyle* puts the museum on the map not only as a place to see some good contemporary art, but as an institution that might help lead it away from its current fascination with the adolescent side of pop culture." According to Horace Brockington, writing for *New York Arts Magazine* (May 31, 2001, on-line), the exhibition was "certain to move the Studio Museum out of a frozen state towards re-defining itself." In addition to its artistic "resurrection," the SMH is currently undergoing a physical renovation, scheduled for completion in 2003, that will expand its exhibition space by 12,000 square feet. A café and auditorium will be added, along with a new façade.

Thelma Golden has lived in the Park Slope section of Brooklyn since 1990. — J.H.

Suggested Reading: *Black Enterprise* p90+ Feb. 1996, with photo; *Essence* p64 Nov. 1994; *Los Angeles Times* p5 Apr. 23, 1995, with photos, p1 Apr. 27, 1995, with photo; *Nation* p533 Apr. 19, 1993; *New York Times* E p1 Feb. 28, 2000, with photo, B p2 May 1, 2001, with photo, E p36 May 11, 2001, with photo; *New Yorker* p90+ June 11, 2001, with photo; *Newsweek* p60 May 14, 2001; *Village Voice* p49+ May 22, 2001, with photo; *Wall Street Journal* A p7 Mar. 5, 1993

Selected Books: *1993 Biennial Exhibition*, 1993; *Black Male: Representations of Masculinity in Contemporary American Art*, 1994; *Bob Thompson*, 1998

Courtesy of El Cajo Productions

Goldsmith, Jerry

Feb. 10, 1929– Composer for film, television, and concert halls; educator. Address: c/o Savitsky & Co., 1901 Ave. of the Stars, Suite 1450, Los Angeles, CA 90067-6087

One of the most admired and sought-after composers in Hollywood, Jerry Goldsmith has written music for upwards of 250 films and television shows since he began his career in the early 1950s, scoring for CBS. His movie credits include *Lilies of the Field* (1963), *Seven Days in May* (1964), *Von Ryan's Express* (1965), *Planet of the Apes* (1968), *Patton* (1970), *Chinatown* (1974), *Gremlins* (1984), *Basic Instinct* (1992), *L.A. Confidential* (1997), *Mulan* (1998), and, in 1999, *The Mummy*, *The House on Haunted Hill*, and *The 13th Warrior*. Proficient at composing for Westerns, dramas, science-fiction fantasies, period romances, and virtually every other type of film, he has written compositions ranging from Wagnerian-style anthems to Strauss-like waltzes to cool jazz to pieces that reflect the influence of Central American and Arabic music. Well known for his use of unusual "instruments"—stainless-steel mixing bowls, glass "rub rods," bells submerged in water, and a 15-foot-long percussive device called a blaster beam—and for his intentionally discordant music for action and suspense films, Goldsmith has created many scores that are widely considered far superior to the titles for which he wrote them. "Apart from the sheer musical talent he brings to a film, perhaps Goldsmith's most important contribution is his superb dramatic instinct, an unerring sense of where music should—and shouldn't—go in a film. He refuses to settle for a conventional scoring approach and prefers to go against the dramatic grain, to work against the audience's emotional expectations," Gary Crowdus wrote for *Cineaste*, as quoted on the Gr8 Music Store Web site.

The recipient of one Academy Award—for his music for the 1976 horror movie *The Omen*—and 17 additional Oscar nominations, Goldsmith has entered his sixth decade of composing without any sign of slowing down. For the 72-year-old composer, writing for film continues to offer excitement and new opportunities. "A large part of being good is being experienced," he told Gary Dretzka for the *Chicago Tribune* (December 6, 1998), "and I couldn't have 40 years of experience if I was 23, so it's rather exciting. The challenge still is to write a good, original piece of music. There have been some ups and downs, but I'm a very lucky person." For the "Film Music Masters" video series, Fred Karlin directed a documentary about Goldsmith, compiled from old and mid-1990s footage. In a review of the documentary for *Films in Review* (March/April 1996), as quoted on the Gr8 Music Store Web site, Jack Smith wrote, "For Goldsmith, composing for films is clearly an emotional experience, his response to what's on the screen; it's one of the reasons he's endured the ins and outs of Hollywood over the years. What's intellectually or politically fashionable at one time or another is bridged by the universality of emotions displayed by Goldsmith's long roster of [film-music] titles. Emotion is one certain thing that we all can share, anytime, any place, at any point in history. As a composer, Goldsmith instinctively knows this, and that's what keeps him at the forefront of an increasingly fickle industry."

Goldsmith's prodigious output also includes his contata *Christus Apollo*, set to text by the science-fiction writer Ray Bradbury, which premiered in 1969, with the composer conducting the Southern California Chamber Symphony; Music for Orchestra, which was performed for the first time by the St. Louis Symphony in 1971; *Fanfare for Oscar*, which has been used in all Academy Award telecasts since 1998; and *Fireworks—A Celebration of Los Angeles* (1999), which was commissioned by the Los Angeles Philharmonic. Goldsmith has served as a guest conductor with the London Symphony Orchestra, the Royal Philharmonic Orchestra of London, the Royal Scottish National Orchestra, the Budapest Festival Orchestra, and many other ensembles. He has also taught courses in music composition for motion pictures at two universities. He is the honorary president of the Goldsmith Film Music Society, which was founded in Great Britain in 1982 to promote interest in music for cinema, especially Goldsmith's. The society publishes a 60-page journal three times annually and has members in more than 25 countries worldwide. In 1995 *Variety* named Jerry Goldsmith an American Music Legend.

The composer was born Jerrald Goldsmith on February 10, 1929 in Los Angeles, California. His father, Morris Goldsmith, played the violin, and his mother, known as Tessy, played the piano. For as far back as he can remember, Goldsmith has been interested in music; he has been playing the piano since he was six. School, on the other hand, bored him, and when he was nine, his father took him out of school and began hiring private tutors to educate him. Morris Goldsmith strongly encouraged his son to use his musical gifts and engaged some of the best music teachers in the Los Angeles area to train his son five hours a day. As a child and young adult, Goldsmith studied piano with Jakob Gimpel, and later he studied theory and counterpoint with the composer Mario Castelnuovo-Tedesco. He dreamed of becoming a classical composer, but after watching the movie *Spellbound*, with music by the celebrated Hungarian composer Miklós Rózsa, he became bent on writing scores for films. When he was about 18, he attended classes in film composition taught by Rózsa at the University of Southern California (USC). He attended classes at Los Angeles City College as well as USC but did not earn a bachelor's degree.

In 1950 Goldsmith got a job in the music department of CBS as a clerk-typist. Soon afterward he was given the chance to compose for the company. His early assignments included one score a week for the radio programs *Romance* and *CBS Radio Workshop*. With the rise of television in the mid-1950s and the consequent demise of radio dramas, Goldsmith switched to television, scoring for such CBS series as *Gunsmoke*, *Have Gun Will Travel*, *Wagon Train*, and *The Twilight Zone*. In 1952 he made his debut as a composer for the silver screen, with the uncredited score for *Don't Bother to Knock*, starring Marilyn Monroe. His first credited score was for the 1957 Western *Black Patch*.

In 1960 he left CBS to work at Revue Studios, where the legendary film composer Alfred Newman had hired him to score a series of thrillers for television. In 1962 Newman gave Goldsmith the job of writing the score to the film *Lonely Are the Brave*, an unusual, allegorical Western that starred Kirk Douglas. His score for John Huston's *Freud* (1962), in which Montgomery Clift played the pioneering Viennese psychiatrist, earned him his first Academy Award nomination. Thanks to that honor, Goldsmith found himself in high demand; during the next eight years, he produced on average six film scores a year, making that decade his most prolific. He also earned three additional Oscar nominations in the 1960s, for *A Patch of Blue* (1965), starring Elizabeth Hartman as a blind woman and Sidney Poitier as the man who befriends her; *The Sand Pebbles* (1966), set in 1920s China, which features Steve McQueen, Richard Attenborough, and Richard Crenna as crew members of an American navy ship and Candice Bergen as a missionary; and *Planet of the Apes* (1968), for which Goldsmith worked on the music while wearing a monkey mask. Already known for his experimental orchestrations, Goldsmith specified that in some sections of the *Planet of the Apes* score, the horn players blow without mouthpieces and the bass clarinetist finger the notes without blowing, thereby making tapping sounds.

Planet of the Apes marked one of nine collaborations between Goldsmith and the director Franklin J. Schaffner, the first two being projects for the television series *Studio One*, in 1948, and *Playhouse 90*, in 1956. The two next worked together on *Patton*, in which George C. Scott played the brilliant and controversial World War II general George S. Patton Jr. Goldsmith's rousing score for *Patton* brought him great acclaim and another Academy Award nomination. He earned two more Oscar nominations for his scores to the Schaffner films *Papillon* (1973), with Steve McQueen as the title character, an imprisoned petty thief who repeatedly tries to escape, and *The Boys from Brazil* (1978), in which Laurence Olivier played a Nazi hunter who is tracking down the infamous Nazi surgeon and World War II criminal Josef Mengele—who, in a science-fiction twist, has made several clones of the German dictator Adolf Hitler.

Earlier in the 1970s Goldsmith had begun experimenting with the synthesizer, while continuing to write scores for large orchestras. His haunting music for Roman Polanski's brooding film noir *Chinatown* (1974) received an Academy Award nomination for best score, as did his musical accompaniment for *The Wind and the Lion* (1975), John Milius's fictionalized version of an incident in the early 1900s in which a Berber radical kidnapped an American in Morocco. With the menacing music he wrote for the horror picture *The Omen* (1976), Goldsmith won his first—and so far only—Academy Award. His song "Ave Satani" for *Omen* was nominated for best song. In 1979 Goldsmith also wrote the disturbing score to Ridley Scott's film *The Alien*, the cast of which included Sigourney Weaver, John Hurt, and Tom Skerritt. Also that year Goldsmith began his association with the *Star Trek* franchise, scoring *Star Trek: The Motion Picture*, which captured another Oscar nod. Since then he has written the scores for three more *Star Trek* films; his theme for the television show *Star Trek: Voyager* earned him an Emmy in 1995. He is slated to score *Star Trek X*, scheduled to be released in 2002.

In the 1980s, disregarding the growing trend in which film scores are created by stringing together popular songs—a practice that he has lamented—Goldsmith accumulated 41 credits. His score for the ghost story *Poltergeist* (1982), which Steven Spielberg wrote and Tobe Hooper directed, received an Oscar nomination, as did his music for Roger Spottiswoode's *Under Fire* (1983), in which Nick Nolte played an American journalist who gets involved with Sandinista rebels in Nicaragua. Also in 1983 he scored the music for *Twilight Zone: The Movie,* about which he told Richard Harrington for the *Washington Post* (April 12, 1993), "It's the first thing I've written in a long time that I don't mind listening to myself. I usually get bored with [a score] afterwards. . . . It's quite intriguing and one of the best things I've ever done." In the same interview, talking about his way of working, Goldsmith said, "I try to be as subjective as I can with the characters and try to make the music very subjective. I think that I have a great deal of versatility and I think my dramatic sense happens to be quite good, so my approaches are quite unusual. In terms of standard film scoring, I've tried to always find a different way of doing certain things."

In 1986 work that Goldsmith has ranked with his best—music that he wrote for Ridley Scott's sword-and-sorcery fantasy *Legend* (1985)—was rejected in favor of a pop-rock soundtrack fashioned from previously recorded music. The next year he captured another Academy Award nomination, for his score for the basketball film *Hoosiers* (1986), about a 1950s small-town high-school basketball team that wins the Indiana state championship against great odds. Earlier in the 1980s, among other television shows on which he collaborated, Goldsmith wrote music for *Amazing Stories, H.E.L.P,* and the miniseries *Masada,* for which he won his second Emmy Award.

In the 1990s Goldsmith scored nearly 50 films, among them Paul Verhoeven's *Total Recall* (1990), based on a science-fiction story by Philip K. Dick; Verhoeven's controversial *Basic Instinct* (1992), an urban murder mystery that starred Michael Douglas and Sharon Stone; the densely plotted, violent crime drama *L.A. Confidential* (1997), directed by Curtis Hanson; and Disney's animated *Mulan* (1998), based on a 2,000-year-old Chinese legend about a girl who disguises herself as a boy and joins the emperor's army. The latter two scores earned Oscar nominations; the *Mulan* soundtrack sold more than 500,000 copies, making it one of several Goldsmith movie scores to reach gold certification.

Although there are more electronic aids available to the modern-day film composer than existed in past decades, Goldsmith notes that the amount of time between the assignment of a score and the due date has diminished. "If you're lucky, you have five weeks to compose 60 to 70 minutes of music," he told Dretzka. "Thirty years ago, you'd get 10 weeks to produce 40 to 50 minutes of music." By his own account, his favorite score among those he has composed is that for *Islands in the Stream* (1977); the directors he has most enjoyed working with are Schaffner, Steven Spielberg, and Michael Crichton. His collaborations with Crichton include *Coma* (1978), *The Great Train Robbery* (1979), *Runaway* (1984), and *The 13th Warrior* (1999).

In addition to his film work, Goldsmith has been a regent's lecturer in the Department of Music at the University of California at Los Angeles (UCLA). He has performed his film music in concert and has conducted such orchestras as the San Diego Symphony and, in Great Britain, the Royal Philharmonic. The reluctance of many orchestras to perform film music has diminished in recent years. "I've found that orchestras rather enjoy playing music from films, because it's a nice diversion from Beethoven and Mozart," Goldsmith told Gary Dretzka. "It gives them a chance to do a little bit more, especially the brass. They go nuts for it." Goldsmith's music has also inspired three ballets: *Othello* (1971), which he wrote for the National Ballet of Australia and which is now part of that troupe's permanent repertoire; *A Patch of Blue* (1970), which was choreographed for the San Francisco Ballet; and *Capricorn One,* adapted and presented in 1989 by BalletMet in Columbus, Ohio.

Goldsmith is known for his amiability and cooperative spirit, among both directors and musicians in Hollywood orchestras, the latter of whom are notoriously cynical about composers and conductors. "Writing the music is 50 percent of it. If you can't get it performed right, then you're cooked," Goldsmith told Dretzka. "It's the musicians' skill and artistry that makes it all happen." His most recent work includes the score to Paul Verhoeven's *Hollow Man* (2000), a remake of James Whales's 1933 classic *The Invisible Man.* "Growing as a creator—that's what is exciting about what I do," Goldsmith told Harvey Siders for *BMI* (Spring 1975). "It's too easy to become settled in your ways . . . but it's much more exciting to keep inventing new ideas . . . looking for new paths. So with all the complaining [film composers] do, and the lack of time . . . it's still an opportunity to express ourselves that few composers that have preceded this era have ever had."

Goldsmith has earned seven Emmy Awards, for his music for the TV movies *The Red Pony* (1973), *QB VII* (1973), and *Babe* (1975), among other efforts, and seven Golden Globe nominations. With more than 200 recordings to his credit, he has also won seven Grammy Awards. His many other honors include the Max Steiner Award from the National Film Society, in 1982; the first annual Richard Kirk Award, from BMI, in 1987; the Golden Score Award from the American Society of Music Arrangers and Composers, in 1990; and a Career Achievement Award from the Society for the Preservation of Film Music, in 1993. He earned an honorary doctorate of music degree from the Berklee College of Music, in Boston, in 1990. In 1992–93 he taught a graduate course at the University of Southern California School of Music, and he has taught at the UCLA Department of Music since 1998. That year he gave the Academy of Motion Picture Arts and Sciences' Margaret Herrick Library his collected written works, for use by music scholars.

From his first marriage, to the singer Sharon Hennigan Goldsmith, the composer has four children. His eldest daughter—who performed some of the vocals on Goldsmith's score for Blake Edwards's *Wild Rovers* (1971)—and second daughter are teachers. His youngest daughter is in show business. His son from his first marriage, Joel Goldsmith, has composed film and television soundtracks and has sometimes collaborated with him. Jerry Goldsmith and his second wife, the former Carol Sheinkopf, a lyricist, have a son, Aaron. Carol Goldsmith wrote the words to the song "The Piper Dreams" from *The Omen*. The composer and his family live in Beverly Hills, California. — G.O.

Suggested Reading: *All Movie Guide* (on-line); *Cahiers du Cinema* p17 Dec. 1997; *Chicago Tribune* p6 Dec. 6, 1998; *Cineaste* p46+ vol. 21 no. 1, 1995; *Films in Review* p77+ Mar./Apr. 1996; Goldsmith Film Music Society Web site; Hollywood Film Festival Web site; UCLA Department of Music Web site; *Washington Post* pD7 Apr. 12, 1983

Selected Film Scores: *Lilies of the Field*, 1963; *The List of Adrian Messenger*, 1963; *A Patch of Blue*, 1965; *Van Ryan's Express*, 1965; *Our Man Flint*, 1965; *The Blue Max*, 1966; *Sand Pebbles*, 1966; *The Flim-Flam Man*, 1967; *Planet of the Apes*, 1968; *Justine*, 1969; *Patton*, 1970; *Tora! Tora! Tora!*, 1970; *Rio Lobo*, 1970; *Escape from the Planet of the Apes*, 1971; *Wild Rovers*, 1971; *Papillon*, 1973; *One Little Indian*, 1973; *Chinatown*, 1974; *The Wind and the Lion*, 1975; *The Omen*, 1976; *Logan's Run*, 1976; *Islands in the Stream*, 1977; *Coma*, 1978; *Capricorn One*, 1978; *Damien: Omen II*, 1978; *The Boys from Brazil*, 1978; *Alien*, 1979; *The Great Train Robbery*, 1979; *Star Trek: The Motion Picture*, 1979; *The Raggedy Man*, 1981; *Outland*, 1981; *The Secret of NIMH*, 1982; *Poltergeist*, 1982; *First Blood*, 1982; *Inchon*, 1982; *Twilight Zone: The Movie*, 1983; *Psycho II*, 1983; *Under Fire*, 1983; *Gremlins*, 1984; *Rambo: First Blood Part II*, 1985; *Legend*, 1985; *Hoosiers*, 1986; *Innerspace*, 1987; *Lionheart*, 1987; *Extreme Prejudice*, 1987; *The 'burbs*, 1989; *The Russia House*, 1990; *Total Recall*, 1990; *Not Without My Daughter*, 1991; *Sleeping with the Enemy*, 1991; *Basic Instinct*, 1992; *Malice*, 1993; *Six Degrees of Separation*, 1993; *Dennis the Menace*, 1993; *The River Wild*, 1994; *I.Q.*, 1994; *Angie*, 1994; *First Knight*, 1995; *City Hall*, 1996; *Star Trek: First Contact*, 1996; *L.A. Confidential*, 1997; *Air Force One*, 1997; *Mulan*, 1998; *The Mummy*, 1999; *The Haunting*, 1999; *The Hollow Men*, 2000

Selected Radio Scores: *CBS Radio Workshop*; *Escape*; *Suspence*; *Romance*; *Hallmark Hall of Fame*, all in the early 1950s

Selected Television Scores: *Hallmark Television Playhouse*, 1951; *General Electric Theater*, 1953; *Gunsmoke*, 1955; *Playhouse 90*, 1956; *Have Gun Will Travel*, 1957; *Wagon Train*, 1957; *The Twilight Zone*, 1959; *City of Fear*, 1959; *Boris Karloff's Thriller*, 1960; *Ben Casey*, 1961; *Kraft Mystery Theater*, 1961; *Dr. Kildare*, 1961; *Freud*, 1962; *The Man from U.N.C.L.E.*, 1964; *Room 222*,

1969; *The Homecoming: A Christmas Story*, 1971; *The Waltons*, 1972; *The Red Pony*, 1973; *Police Story*, 1973; *QB VII*, 1974; *Babe*, 1975; *Masada*, 1981; *Amazing Stories*, 1985; *Star Trek: The Next Generation*, 1987; *Legend*, 1995; *Reflections on Ice: Michelle Kwan Skates to the Music of Disney's 'Mulan'*, 1998

Selected Orchestral Works: *Christus Apollo*, 1969; *Music for Orchestra*, 1971; *Fanfare for Oscar*, 1998; *Fireworks (A Celebration of Los Angeles)*, 1999

Chemical Heritage Foundation

Good, Mary L.

June 20, 1931– Chemist; educator; business executive; former U.S. undersecretary of commerce. Address: Venture Capital Investors LLC, 400 W. Capitol Ave., Suite 1845, Little Rock, AR 72201-4857

A former undersecretary of the U.S. Department of Commerce, a former senior vice president for technology at AlliedSignal Inc., and the holder of an endowed chair at the University of Arkansas, Mary L. Good has pursued successful careers in three separate fields: government, industry, and academia. Currently, she chairs the board of directors of the American Association for the Advancement of Science and is a managing member of Venture Capital Investors, a group of Arkansas business leaders who support technology-based enterprises. Good has earned many honors, among them the American Chemical Society's Priestly Medal, the highest award bestowed by that organization; the

National Science Foundation's Distinguished Public Service Award; the American Association for the Advancement of Science Award; the Albert Fox Demers Medal from Rensselaer Polytechnic Institute; and the American Institute of Chemists' Gold Medal.

The daughter of John W. Lowe, a school superintendent, and Winnie Mercer Lowe, a schoolteacher, Good was born Mary Lowe in Grapevine, in the Dallas–Fort Worth area of Texas, on June 20, 1931. One of four children, she grew up mainly in Arkansas. After she graduated from high school in Willisville, she enrolled at the Arkansas State Teachers College (now the University of Central Arkansas), in Conway. She has told interviewers that, unlike some of her colleagues, as a child she did not plan to become a scientist. "I never even had a chemistry course until college," she told Carol Kleiman for the *Chicago Tribune* (May 20, 1985). She also noted to Kleiman that her relatively late exposure to the subject "might have been for the better because some high school courses at that time weren't very good." When she entered college, Good intended to major in home economics, in large part because she considered it a useful subject, but she soon abandoned that plan. "In my freshman year," Good told Janice R. Long for *Chemical and Engineering News* (May 13, 1996), "I took my first chemistry course. My teacher was an elderly professor who was absolutely fantastic. He loved his students and he loved his subject. I had a ball. The upshot was that by the second semester I had changed my major to chemistry. I loved working in the lab, particularly wet chemistry, the qualitative analysis lab."

In 1950 the 19-year-old Good earned a bachelor's degree in chemistry. She completed her undergraduate education in just three years by attending classes in the summer as well as during the fall and spring terms. She did so partly, as she explained to Long, because the four siblings in her family were all close in age, and she "needed to get through and out so the younger ones could go to school." Good won a fellowship from the University of Arkansas at Fayetteville to pursue graduate study in inorganic chemistry and radiochemistry. She completed a master's degree at that school in 1953 and earned a doctorate there in 1955. Meanwhile, in May 1952, she had married Billy Jewel Good, who was then a graduate student in physics. The couple have two children: Billy John, now a biologist, and James Patrick, an architect. "Fortunately," Good told Kleiman, "I was never told I couldn't have a career and a family. It was difficult at times, but Bill is very supportive."

Before she completed her graduate education, Good began teaching chemistry at Louisiana State University in Baton Rouge—a job she took in part because her husband wanted to complete his doctorate in physics, and Louisiana State, unlike the University of Arkansas, offered a doctoral program in that field. Her decision to pursue a career in academia was further influenced by the fact that she

was a young mother. "I had a nine-month-old child at the time," she told Long, "and in those days an academic schedule offered more flexibility than an industry job would have." Good was promoted from instructor to assistant professor in 1956. Two years later she transferred to the New Orleans campus of Louisiana State University, where she was named associate professor. By 1963 Good had become a full professor, a position that she held for 17 years. In 1974 she received an endowed chair and was named Boyd Professor of Chemistry. During her academic career Good published nearly 100 research papers and a number of review articles. She also wrote the textbook *Integrated Laboratory Sequence: Volume III—Separations and Analysis* (1970). "What I really enjoyed [was] working with the students," she told Long, "particularly my graduate students. There were close to 20 who worked with me over the years, and I keep in touch with many of them."

In 1980 Good left academia to become the director of research at UOP Inc., a branch of Signal Research Center Inc., an energy and technology conglomerate with annual revenues of $6 billion at that time. "I couldn't turn it down," she told Long of the UOP job offer. "It was so challenging and so interesting, I had to see if I could succeed. . . . At the time, I had pretty much accomplished all I wanted to at the university." Among her accomplishments at UOP, which focused on energy and petroleum research, was the synthesis of a chemical that discouraged barnacles from clinging to painted boats and docks. Good prospered at UOP, and in 1985 she was named president and director of research for Signal Research Center.

Signal underwent extensive restructuring in the wake of the buyouts and acquisitions that swept the chemical industry in the 1980s, and in 1985 it merged with the Allied Corp. to form AlliedSignal Research and Technology Laboratory, a $12 billion-a-year company that produced chemicals, fibers, plastics, and aerospace and automotive parts. In 1986 Good was named president of engineered materials research at AlliedSignal, and in 1988 she became senior vice president for technology, a post she held for five years. The year 1988 also saw the publication of the book *Biotechnology and Materials Science: Chemistry for the Future*, which she edited.

Meanwhile, Good had become increasingly involved with the public sector. In 1980 President Jimmy Carter appointed her to the board of the National Science Foundation (NSF), an independent government agency that makes policy recommendations to Congress and the president. President Ronald Reagan reappointed her to that post in 1986; from 1988 through 1991 she served as chairman of the NSF board. In 1991 President George Bush appointed her to the President's Council of Advisors on Science and Technology.

Good entered public service full-time in 1993, when President Bill Clinton appointed her undersecretary of commerce for technology—the highest-ranking technology post in the Department of Commerce. Good served as undersecretary for four years, during which time she stressed the need for government support of emerging technologies and worked extensively on the administration's Partnership for a New Generation Vehicle, also known as the "Clean Car" initiative. After the Republicans gained control of both houses of Congress in 1994, Good has said, she devoted much of her energy to fighting the efforts of GOP lawmakers to dismantle the Department of Commerce, which to some freshman legislators was a symbol of bloated government. She told Long in 1996 that she and her colleagues were spending "so much time defending what we are doing that it has been very hard to get progressive kinds of things done. We fought to defend the budget positions of these programs. We even fought to defend this office itself." Good explained that in her view, such attacks on the Commerce Department were misguided, because "the federal workforce looks like all the others [in the private sector]. There are a few leadership folks who work very hard, do very good things, are very imaginative and creative, who keep things going. There is a huge group, who—if they have good leadership and are inspired to do things—work very well, put out a solid day's work. And there is

a small fragment who are not very good. I have seen exactly the same in my other two careers." In early 1996 Good served as acting secretary of commerce for nine days, after Ronald H. Brown, who had headed the department since 1993, was killed in a plane crash.

Good stepped down from her government post in 1997 to become Donaghey University Professor at the University of Arkansas at Little Rock. At that time she was also named a managing member of Venture Capital Investors LLC. In early 2000 Good succeeded the renowned biologist and paleontologist Stephen J. Gould as president of the American Association for the Advancement of Science, the world's largest organization of scientists; she currently chairs the association's board of directors.

In her spare time, Good enjoys canoeing and studying Scottish history. After she accepted the job with UOP, her husband took early retirement and devoted himself to painting. In addition to their two sons, the couple have four grandchildren. — P.K.

Suggested Reading: *Chemical and Engineering News* (on-line) May 13, 1996, with photo; *Chicago Tribune* IV p11 May 20, 1995, with photo

---

Googoosh

Feb. 7, 1951(?)– Singer; Iranian pop icon.
Address: c/o Caltex Records, 9045-A Eton Ave.,
Canoga Park, CA 91304; c/o Tarweej-Net Yemen
Business Promotion, P.O. Box 18495, Sana'a,
Yemen

In her heyday, the Iranian singer, actress, and pop icon Googoosh "was Iran's Barbra Streisand, Linda Ronstadt, Cher, Edith Piaf and Madonna rolled into one: not just a magnificent singer but a fashion trailblazer and a symbol of modernity," as Jon Pareles described her for the *New York Times* (August 28, 2000, on-line). Having become a star of Iranian radio at age six and appeared in her first movie at eight, Googoosh won a recording contract as a teenager. She emerged as a hugely popular performer during the late 1960s and 1970s, as she sang of love and romance. While her songs "drew on Western styles, they held onto both the fervor of Persian love poetry and the sliding, quivering, impassioned phrasing of traditional Persian music," according to Pareles. In 1979, at the height of her popularity, her career was effectively ended, after the Ayatollah Ruhollah Khomeini and his Islamic revolutionary followers wrested power from Shah Mohammad Riza Pahlavi. Googoosh, who was visiting the United States when the takeover occurred, made the risky decision to return to Iran and submit to the strict regime rather than spend her life in exile. Forbidden from performing in

public and recording, Googoosh nonetheless retained her cult status, as well as her legions of avid fans throughout Iran and abroad. Although she completely retreated from public life, a small underground industry developed around her music, and copies of her albums remained in demand throughout her time in seclusion. In 2000, after being permitted to leave Iran for the first time in more than two decades, she reentered the spotlight with several concert tours abroad. Her performances were greeted with an emotional frenzy that swept several generations of Iranian exiles on three continents. While sellout crowds attended her concerts throughout the U.S., Canada, Europe, and parts of the Middle East, Iranian consumers looked forward to bootleg copies of *Zoroaster*, the new album she recorded while in Canada. "I didn't have any new songs, any new performances during these 21 years. Three generations are in touch with me and they have a connection with my songs. That makes me surprised," she told Joanne Suh for *CNN Worldbeat* (October 9, 2000, on-line).

Nicknamed Googoosh in childhood, the performer was born Faegheh Atashin on February 7, 1951, according to a profile on the *IranMania* Web site; other sources say she was born in 1950. She spent her first years in a province of northwestern Iran that is now part of Azerbaijan. As a toddler she moved to Tehran, the capital of Iran, with her father, Saaber Atashin; sources are divided as to whether her mother had died or her parents had divorced. Her father, a descendant of Russian immi-

Kevin Frayer/AP

Googoosh

grants, was part of an Azeri performance troupe, and by the age of three Googoosh was taking part in some of their dance routines; at age four she was singing with them. "When I was a little girl, I start[ed] to learn how to perform on stage," she explained to Joanne Suh. Her vocal talent and natural ease as a performer put her in demand. She sang on a radio show for children that was broadcast throughout Iran, and she made her movie debut at age eight, acting in *The Fear of Hope*. At 15 she recorded her first album and became a regular on the cabaret and club circuit. While she was still a teenager, she married Mahmood Ghorbani, a cabaret owner, partly, according to *IranMania*, to remove her business dealings from her father's control; other sources say she married at age 23. She gave birth to a son, Kambiz, soon afterward and continued to record albums and perform live. Kambiz Ghorbani, who has one child, has lived in Toronto and Los Angeles since 1979.

By the 1970s Googoosh had become one of the most popular—if not *the* most popular—singers in Iran, and she attained the status of a pop icon. Iranian women scrambled to keep up with the fashion trends she started. She popularized miniskirts, and when she had her long hair cut to a short bob, the style became—and still is known as—a "Googooshi" cut. Blending traditional themes of love and loneliness with Western jazz riffs or a rock beat, her music appealed to every age group in Iran. Although the lyrics to most of her songs are in Farsi (modern Persian), Iran's official language, she expanded her audience by also singing in Armenian, Turkish, and Arabic.

In the 1970s, after her marriage to Ghorbani ended in divorce, Googoosh acted in several movies, released more albums to astounding success, and had a second, brief marriage. During the 1979 events that resulted in the overthrow of the Shah, Googoosh inadvertently became embroiled in Iranian politics. She was in the United States when the Shah was ousted, and she was forced to choose between returning to Iran, at great personal peril, or staying in exile for the duration of the new regime. Her decision was further complicated when the Ayatollah Ruhollah Khomeini, the new ruler of Iran, ordered all female singers to stop recording and performing, on the grounds that their singing was "decadent" and contrary to Islamic law. All traces of their work—cassettes, records, posters, movies, and memorabilia—were destroyed, and the clerics who ruled the country imposed strict regulations on acceptable entertainment.

Unsure of what to do and facing suspicions that she was an agent in the ousted Shah's secret service—rumors that increased the dangers of returning to Iran—Googoosh remained in Los Angeles until she was too homesick to stay. "I was dying a slow death [in L.A.], so I thought I might as well get done with it," she told Mike Theodoulou for the *Christian Science Monitor* (July 19, 2000, on-line). Her safety was not threatened when she returned, although she was later forced to spend a month in jail; Googoosh has claimed that she cannot remember the exact charges and has insisted that she was not harmed. "My imprisonment was so brief that I am ashamed to talk about it, compared to all those people who have gone to jail in the country. It was a land where so many have been to prison. I wasn't tortured, I was not in any discomfort," she told

Theodoulou. Meanwhile, many other Iranian musicians and artists had left or were leaving the country, feeling that they could not abide by the new restrictions. "I don't think that any artist can face it, if you tell them they can't sing or can't act or can't live with your art for this long—for 20 years you can't work," Googoosh explained to Joanne Suh. Googoosh, however, elected to end her career and live a quiet life in Tehran. She retained only a small circle of friends. In public she even wore a chador, a black garment that covers the entire body and hair of a Muslim woman. "For almost 22 years I stayed in my apartment, sitting on a couch and read[ing] books. I didn't go out much," Googoosh said at a news conference in Toronto, as reported by Farnaz Fassihi for the New Jersey *Star-Ledger* (November 22, 2000, on-line). "Sometimes I went out to buy fruit and shop at the supermarket."

Googoosh's hidden life contributed to her mystique; purported sightings of the star generated the sort of excitement that was associated with alleged Elvis Presley sightings in the U.S. after that singer's death. Despite her lack of new recordings, Googoosh's music stayed at the forefront of Iranian culture and enjoyed a huge following among ordinary citizens on the black market. Iranian expatriates in Los Angeles still produce bootleg copies of her records, which are smuggled into Iran and discreetly sold at kiosks or behind the counters of music stores, where they have been perennial best-sellers. "Googoosh's popularity cuts across the generations," Tom Hundley wrote for the *Chicago Tribune* (July 7, 2000, on-line). "For fans now in their 50s, her songs recall a happier, more carefree time in Iran. For new fans in their teens, her music is a link with social freedoms they have never known." As Farnaz Fassihi wrote, "Taxis blast her music in the traffic-ridden streets of Tehran. Children learn their first dance steps with her songs. A Persian wedding without her voice is unthinkable. Her voice has become the unrivaled voice of Iran."

The road to Googoosh's comeback began in 2000—more than a decade after the death of the Ayatollah Ruhollah Khomeini—when she secured permission to leave Iran, for the purpose of making a movie in Cuba in early 2001 with her husband, the Iranian film director Massoud Kimiai. (The spelling of his given name also appears in various sources as "Masoud" or "Masud," and that of his surname as "Kimia'ie" or "Kimiayee.") According to *googooshmusic.com*, the film will be called "Taskheer Shodehgaan" and is about "a mentally challenged woman who is in love with her scarecrow." Permission was granted by Mohammad Khatami, who was elected president of Iran in 1997, and the minister of culture and Islamic guidance, Ataollah Mohajerani, both of whom lean toward the slow introduction of governmental reforms. The news that Googoosh would be free to leave Iran prompted an offer for a concert tour. (The identity of the promoter has not been made public in easily accessible sources.) "It was a mira-

cle for me because I didn't have any plan to have a concert. I always wanted to have a concert in my country for 70 million people—my people. But I haven't had this chance to have this performance, and so I forgot about performance," Googoosh told Joanne Suh. She recorded a new CD, *Zoroaster*, in Canada before kicking off a North American tour in Toronto. Jon Pareles described one of her concerts, at the Nassau Coliseum, on Long Island, for the *New York Times*: "Onstage, Googoosh had all the trappings of a Western pop diva: giant video screens, scaffolding full of lights and an eight-violin string section along with her pop-rock band. But she was decidedly modest, wearing long dresses and gesturing almost entirely with graceful arms and hands." He added that Googoosh "treats the peaks of her songs like a Persian singer, letting notes slide and cascade as if her melodies were melting in the heat of her emotion." Googoosh was surprised and touched by the devotion of her fans in the sellout crowds; many of them knew all the lyrics to her songs and were moved to tears by the performance, as she herself was at times. "I felt like crying when I see this huge [crowd of] people," she explained to Suh. "When I see people kept loving my songs, my performance, I'm trying to keep this love for them on the stage."

Googoosh's North American tour, which extended through March 2001, was followed by stops in Europe and parts of the Middle East. On March 24 she performed in the sheikdom of Dubai, a member of the United Arab Emirates, before an audience of more than 20,000 people, many of whom had flown from Iran to attend the concert. There is no indication that she will be allowed to perform when, as planned, she returns to Iran. "I don't know what will happen," she told Mike Theodoulou. "But I am hopeful because our revolution is at a stage where democracy is being rehearsed and built. I am very optimistic." — K.S.

Suggested Reading: *Chicago Tribune* (on-line) July 7, 2000; *Christian Science Monitor* (on-line) July 19, 2000, with photo; *CNN Worldbeat* (on-line) Oct. 9, 2000, with photos; *New York Times* IX p3 July 4, 1993, with photo; *Time Europe* (on-line) Aug. 28, 2000, with photo

Selected Albums: *Jadeh*; *Doe Panjereh*; *Mordab*; *Fasle Tazeh*; *Nemeh Gomshodeh Man*; *Harf*; *Ahanghaye Eshghi*; *Zoroaster*

Selected Films: *Panjereh*; *Bita*; *Nazanin*; *Dar Emtedad Shab*

Pat Pollard/Courtesy of R. C. Gorman

Gorman, R. C.

July 26, 1932– Artist. Address: Navajo Gallery, P.O. Box 1756, Taos, NM 87571

The artist R. C. Gorman, whose prolific output of paintings, ceramics, sculpture, serigraphs, and lithographs has earned him the sobriquet "the Picasso of the Southwest," is among the leaders of the so-called modern Indian art movement in the United States. While in the West "modernism" is usually defined as an attempt to break with tradition and thereby find new forms of expression, for Native American artists, as Rennard Strickland wrote for *American Indian Art Magazine* (Spring 1985), modernism is rather an effort to "span the old and the new in a unique way." Gorman's artworks, which often portray scenes from Navajo life and freely incorporate elements of European and Mexican art, blend the traditional and the contemporary. They are also hugely popular, demonstrating, as Strickland put it, that "success is an equal opportunity goddess." In the Navajo Gallery, in Taos, New Mexico, which Gorman has owned since 1968, the artist has exhibited not only his own work but that of dozens of other Native Americans and artists of other ethnicities. His work is in the permanent collection of the Metropolitan Museum of Art, in New York City, which, in 1973, chose him alone among living Native American artists to be represented in its exhibition *Masterworks of the Museum of the American Indian.* Two years later the Museum of the American Indian, in New York City, selected Gorman as the lead-off artist in its 1975 series on contemporary American Indian art.

Gorman's life and art are the subjects of several books, among them *R. C. Gorman, a Portrait* (1983), by Stephen Parks, *R. C. Gorman: The Graphic Works* (1987), by Ben Q. Adams and Richard Newlin, and *R. C. Gorman: A Retrospective* (1990), by Doris Monthan. Gorman himself has produced a four-volume series of cookbooks, called *Nudes & Foods,* featuring his own paintings, and he has self-published books that offer photos of his bronze sculptures and reproductions of his two-dimensional works. When asked how he felt about being compared to Picasso, the fun-loving, down-to-earth artist replied, as reported on the Web site of Sandstone Creations Inc., "I feel good about it! But, maybe it makes Picasso turn in his grave!" When asked how he would like to be remembered, he told the same interviewer, "That I was a hard worker. That I cared about people."

Rudolph Carl Gorman was born on July 26, 1932 in the town of Chinle in the Navajo Indian Reservation in northeastern Arizona, along the border with New Mexico. In interviews he has mentioned having brothers and sisters. Gorman's father, Carl Nelson (C. N.) Gorman, was a painter in his own right; he studied under Norman Rockwell and the Russian-born artist Nicolai Fechin and worked for a while as a commercial artist. In the 1970s C. N. Gorman lectured on Navajo history, culture, and art at the University of California at Davis, where he had helped to establish the Department of Native American Studies. (The C. N. Gorman Museum, which opened in 1973 on the campus of the university and features artists from northern California, was named in his honor.) During World War II C. N. Gorman volunteered to serve with the U.S. Marines in the Pacific theater. As one of 400 Navajo "code talkers," he worked as a radio operator, often on the front lines, using a code based on the complex, unwritten Navajo language; that code, one of the most successful in military history, defied Japanese efforts to crack it, and it enabled the marines to relay orders, coordinate troop movements, and convey military intelligence without fear of detection in every assault they conducted in the Pacific from 1942 to 1945.

Rudy, as R. C. Gorman was known as a child, saw little of his father while he was growing up, because the elder Gorman usually worked far from the reservation during the boy's early years and also because he and his wife separated when Rudy was still very young. In his father's absence, Gorman was raised by his mother, Adella, and members of her family. While Gorman's mother spoke to her son exclusively in English and urged him to adopt American ways, his maternal grandmother imparted to him Navajo traditions and stories. The old tales fired his imagination, and Gorman has credited his grandmother with sparking his ambition to become an artist. "My grandmother introduced me to beauty," he has said, as quoted by Doris Monthan. Gorman's mother recalled to Monthan taking her son to his grandmother's "sheep camp," some miles west of where they lived.

"Rudy always wanted to go herding sheep with his grandmother . . . ," she said. "That was at Waterless Mountain between Black Mesa and Hopi country. We had a lot of rocks there, and when he was out herding sheep, his grandmother told me he would draw on a rock with another rock. I guess those rocks were just like a blackboard to him. His cousins tell me those drawings he did on the rocks are still there." Rudy also drew with sticks in sand and "sculpted" with mud.

In an interview with Susan Lawrence Rich for *Radiance* (on-line), Gorman named Mickey Mouse, the child actress Shirley Temple, and cars as the earliest subjects of his drawings. He soon progressed to drawing images of women. Once, during art class at the Chinle public school, Gorman sketched a picture of a naked woman; the resulting spankings, from both his teacher and his mother, did not discourage him, though, and he never stopped drawing the female figure. In her introduction to *R. C. Gorman: A Retrospective*, Monthan observed, "If . . . [Gorman] has a 'signature work' it is his Navajo women, placidly going about their business of building fires, picking corn, nursing babies, walking across the desert, or, more often, majestically reclining with an enviable serenity. They transmit to the viewer a dignity and timelessness that proclaims: 'We are, we always have been, we always will be.' It is this strength and sense of security which the women in his early life gave to Gorman."

For several years during World War II, Gorman and his family lived in Flagstaff, Arizona. He spent one unhappy year at a Catholic boarding school, at age 12, before entering the Ganado Presbyterian Mission school, another boarding school on the reservation, in 1945. In his youth Gorman was a voracious reader and an excellent student all-around. In Ganado High School he wrote plays that were performed at the student theater and composed songs with the help of a pianist friend. Jenny Louis Lind, an art teacher at the school, introduced him to oil paints. "She encouraged me to do what I felt like doing. . . . She was probably the greatest influence on my life," Gorman recalled to Monthan. During his teens, he told Monthan, "I took it for granted that I was an artist, but it didn't occur to me that I might make a living with my art. So I thought I'd be a dentist or a merchant seaman or an airline pilot." He graduated from high school near the top of his class, in 1950.

In the following year, impelled by a desire to see the world, Gorman enlisted in the navy. Up until then he had never ventured beyond the borders of Arizona and New Mexico or been away from the reservation for any length of time. He told Monthan that he loved the four years he spent in the navy. "It was a tremendous education—so many men from so many backgrounds; yet, I had a real sense of belonging." In the military, surrounded by men away from their wives and girlfriends, Gorman found his skill in depicting the female form to be a valuable asset. Copying from photographs, he would graft drawings of the faces of his buddies' loved ones onto scantily clad, buxom figures. "The men loved it," he told Monthan. "I usually charged the officers seven dollars and the enlisted men, two."

After his discharge from the navy, Gorman returned to Flagstaff and enrolled at Northern Arizona University (then known as Arizona State College), where he studied art and literature. The work of such artists as Rembrandt, Gauguin, Dali, and Van Gogh became important to him, more for their technique and use of color than for their subject matter. "Dali knows just what to do with color," he explained to Monthan, "Rembrandt creates mood, and Van Gogh, there again it's color, but also the wild excitement of rhythm—color chasing color, flying, colliding, exploding. Those are all influences I felt." He was even more profoundly affected by the work of such 20th-century Mexican painters and muralists as Diego Rivera, David Alfaro Siqueiros, and José Clemente Orozco. Although his previous work had drawn upon European, Native American, and mainstream American traditions, Gorman had never felt a deep artistic kinship with any particular painter or school. That changed, however, when he first saw the work of Orozco and Rivera during a trip to Mexico. "I was really turned on," he explained to Monthan. "It's the only place where museums had impressed me—where the painting overwhelmed me. The first time I saw Orozco, I could hardly believe it. It was close to me, close to my people. I confess I have been bored by the paintings of the great classic painters that you see in most museums. But there—Orozco, Rivera, Siqueiros—these were real people painting real people!" After he returned to the U.S., Gorman won a grant from the Navajo Tribal Council to study in Mexico. He chose the graphic-arts program at Mexico City College (now the University of the Americas), where he intensively studied the Mexican modernists and further developed his own style of painting.

In about 1960 Gorman settled in San Francisco and began exhibiting his works in local galleries. Gradually, his works attracted the attention of prominent artists, collectors, and gallery owners. In 1964 Gorman and his father presented a dual show at the Philbrook Museum of Art, in Tulsa, Oklahoma, and they mounted another father-and-son show in 1965, at the Heard Museum, in Phoenix, Arizona. In 1964 John Manchester invited R. C. Gorman to give a solo show at his gallery, in Taos, New Mexico. Gorman's work sold well, and the two became close friends; indeed, Gorman told a 1971 interviewer, as quoted by Monthan, "He has been like a guiding father to me." The next year the Manchester Gallery mounted another Gorman exhibit. In 1966 the artist had two one-man shows in the San Francisco Bay Area, and information about him and his work began appearing in magazine articles focusing on art of the American Southwest. Also in 1966 Gorman co-founded an organization called American Indian Artists; based in San Francisco, it sought to promote the work of representatives of the modern Indian art movement. Toward that end, the group helped to organize shows at various venues. During the 1970s an increasing number of solo shows of Gorman's work were mounted in the American West. In 1975 the Museum of the American Indian in New York City featured his art in a one-man exhibit. By the end of the decade, he was showing his work in Europe and Japan as well as in the U.S.

In 1968 Gorman bought the Manchester Gallery and renamed it the Navajo Gallery; it is the primary distributor of his work. Through its Web site, the gallery currently sells three decades' worth of Gorman posters; lithographs; serigraphs (original silkscreen prints); ceramics—specifically, vases of various sizes, decorated with painted figures; paper sculptures, which resemble friezes; and original oil pastels and acrylics. With few exceptions, the subject of each piece is a woman, a woman with a child, or several women, occasionally placed in a landscape but usually set against a monotonal background. Every figure is drawn from life. "It's necessary for me to work from a live model—the rapport we establish creates a sort of psychic energy," Gorman told an interviewer, as quoted by Monthan. "We may not say much, but there are vibrations and they set the mood for the drawing. If she is down, depressed, it comes through; if she is happy, or relaxed, then that comes through in the drawing."

Critics have often noted that, while his work is rooted in the Navajo experience, it appeals to a diverse audience. One reviewer quoted by Monthan observed, "While Gorman's subject matter is derived from his Navajo heritage, it clearly transcends that. There is universality in his work." While some critics have charged Gorman with excessive commercialism, even his detractors have admitted that his influence on American Indian art has been tremendous. Referring to Fritz Scholder, another major figure in modern Native American art, Rennard Strickland wrote, "It is true that [Gorman and Scholder] are flamboyant and controversial, commercial and popular successes. It is equally true that they are talented and creative, and that without them there might be no significant Indian painting movement at all. . . . It is difficult to imagine modernism in Indian art without Scholder and Gorman."

The Gormans, Portrait of the Navajo Artists aired on National Public Radio in 1983. R. C. Gorman is the subject of the 1987 video film Navajo Artist R. C. Gorman, produced by Harold Joe Waldrum, and two videos produced in 1988 by Jack Peterson: American Indian Artists and Medicine Flower and Lone Wolf & R. C. Gorman. Gorman has earned an honorary degree from Northern Arizona University. The San Francisco city government proclaimed March 19, 1986 "R. C. Gorman Day," and in May of that year, he received the Humanitarian Award in Fine Art from Harvard University. "I'm not politically inclined—toward 'Red Power,'

that sort of thing," Gorman has said, as quoted by Monthan. "I'm Indian, yes, but the only time I realize I am is when I'm told I am. I see myself first of all as an artist. Yet, on the other hand, I'm very proud of the fact that I'm an Indian with a certain amount of ability." Gorman lives in Taos with his cat, Lola, and other pets, among them iguanas, skunks, and pigs. He maintains close ties with his extended family and the local community, and he recently donated a portion of his earnings to a scholarship fund for minority students. He enjoys cooking and eating, which he has said boosts his creativity; swimming in his Olympic-size pool; and maintaining his gold Mercedes.

According to Doris Monthan, the artist is "amusing, unpredictable, and flamboyant," and "is never seen without his headband." Ben Q. Adams, the founder and director of Western Graphics Workshop, which has printed many of Gorman's lithographs, told Monthan, "When R. C. arrives at the workshop . . . the atmosphere is immediately changed, and all the activities of the shop, for the most part, revolve around him. Because of the speed with which he works, he demands constant attention, and new stones and plates are prepared while he works on the key image. He is constantly joking and has many things on his mind. While he is drawing he is often concerned about his Mercedes, whether it needs to be washed or needs some minor repair. He also likes to think about some gourmet food. . . . He likes to dance around the shop to Spanish music, so we have the radio tuned into a Spanish station for him. . . . His energy never stops." — P.K.

Suggested Reading: American Indian Art Magazine p36+ Spring 1985; Radiance: The Magazine for Large Women (on-line); Monthan, Doris. R. C. Gorman: A Retrospective, 1990

Selected Books: R.C. Gorman: The Graphic Works, 1987; The Radiance of My People, 1992; R.C. Gorman's Nudes & Foods, 1994

Gowers, Timothy

Nov. 20, 1963– Mathematician. Address: Cambridge University, Dept. of Pure Mathematics and Mathematical Statistics, Centre for Mathematical Sciences, Wilberforce Road, Cambridge, England CB3 0WB

Timothy Gowers specializes in a branch of mathematics that is concerned with infinite dimensional spaces—a mind-bending idea that, for many people, might evoke thoughts of a Grateful Dead show rather than a complex theoretical construct. Gowers's research has earned him the highest professional honor awarded to mathematicians—the Fields Medal, established by and (against his wish-

Courtesy of Cambridge University

Timothy Gowers

es) named for the Canadian mathematician John Charles Fields (1863–1932), who felt that outstanding mathematical discoveries should be recognized with the equivalent of a Nobel Prize. (A Nobel Prize does not exist for mathematicians.) The Fields Medal is given to four individuals every four years at the International Congress of Mathematicians. Widely publicized by the film *Good Will Hunting*, in which Matt Damon plays a mathematical prodigy, the medal is solid gold, features a profile of the Greek mathematician Archimedes, and bears, in Latin, the inscription "to transcend human limitations and master the universe." At the most recent convention of the International Congress of Mathematicians, which took place in 1998 in Berlin, Germany, Gowers—identified as William Timothy Gowers—was among the four people who received the prestigious award. In selecting him for the honor, the award committee cited his contributions to the field of functional analysis. Gowers's work in this field was singled out for its use of methods derived from combinatorial theory, an entirely separate branch of mathematics. According to the *Notice of the American Mathematical Society* (November 1998), functional analysis and combinatorial theory would appear to have little in common beyond the fact that in both disciplines, problems "are relatively easy to formulate, but extremely difficult to solve." The *Notice* writer went on to observe that "a significant achievement of Gowers has been to combine these [functional analysis and combinatorial theory] fruitfully."

William Timothy Gowers was born on November 20, 1963 in England. He received both his undergraduate and graduate education at Cambridge University, where he was a student of Belá

Bollobás, one of the world's foremost authorities on combinatorial mathematics. After completing his Ph.D. degree, Gowers was briefly a research fellow at Cambridge's Trinity College. (Cambridge is made up of 31 self-governing colleges independent of the university proper, each of which is administered by a master and a number of fellows. Among the famous mathematicians associated with Trinity College are Isaac Newton, Godfrey Harold Hardy, Alfred North Whitehead, and Srinivasa Ramanujan.) In 1991 Gowers joined the faculty of University College London. Four years later he returned to Cambridge, where he was appointed a lecturer at and fellow of Trinity College. Since October 1998 Gowers has held the Rouse Ball Professorship of Mathematics at Cambridge.

Functional analysis focuses on infinite dimensional spaces and the mappings between them. (Mappings are rules that assign entities of one space to entities of another space.) To get a sense of the concept of infinite dimensional space, one might use an analogy with the everyday, three-dimensional world. Roughly speaking, the dimension of any space tells us the number of coordinates needed to specify any given point in that space. To completely determine an address in a two-dimensional city grid, for example, you need to specify only two numbers—the corner of Fifth Avenue and 53d Street, for instance. (In that example, a street in the middle of Manhattan Island is comparable to the x, or horizontal, axis in geometry, and an avenue midway between the east and west sides of Manhattan is comparable to the y, or vertical, axis.) We can extend this concept to a third dimension by specifying height as well: the sixth floor of the building at the corner of Fifth Avenue and 53d Street. (The axis in the third dimension is usually labeled z.) In the case of infinite dimensional space, a listing of the coordinates of a given point would never end. One relatively concrete example of an infinite dimensional space is the set of all real mathematical functions on a given interval of the number line—the collection, say, of all functions that assign a real number to every number between zero and one.

Essentially, functional analysis is an outgrowth of calculus; as one might expect, though, it involves a great deal more than the introductory calculus that first-year college students typically encounter. The latter brand of calculus—single-variable differential and integral calculus—was invented independently by the British mathematician and physicist Isaac Newton (1642–1727) and the German mathematician and philosopher Gottfried Wilhelm Leibniz (1646–1716). Since both of those men achieved their most important results in the mid- to late 17th century, introductory calculus is far from cutting-edge mathematics. Rather, it is the mathematical equivalent of the reflecting telescope and the mercury thermometer. Functional analysis is a more recent development. While it is generally considered to have begun with the work of the French mathematician Jean-Baptiste Fourier

(1768–1830), functional analysis is largely a 20th-century development. To this day, it continues to be a fertile field of mathematical research.

Much of Gowers's work in functional analysis can be viewed as building upon the efforts of the Polish mathematician Stefan Banach (1892–1945). In the 1920s and 1930s, the eccentric Banach, usually working in a café rather than his office at the University of Lvov, filled a notebook with problems in and conjectures about functional analysis. Among his signal innovations was the definition of a particular type of mathematical space—specifically, a complete normed vector space, which can be generalized to describe an infinite number of dimensions. Although this type of space (later christened a Banach space) need not possess infinite dimensions (the humdrum, two-dimensional, so-called Cartesian plane, for example, satisfies Banach's definition), it becomes most interesting to mathematicians when considered in an infinite-dimensional setting. As abstruse and impractical as the notion of an infinite dimensional space may seem, the theory of Banach spaces constitutes, as Allyn Jackson wrote for *Science* (August 28, 1998), "part of the tool kit for many areas of mathematics." Moreover, Banach space theory has found applications in quantum physics, where it forms part of the mathematical apparatus physicists use to describe the subatomic world. Quantum physics, in turn, has laid the groundwork for such practical applications as television and the personal computer.

Until Gowers tackled them, several of the conjectures that Banach set forth in his notebook had proved frustratingly intractable, resisting the efforts of mathematicians to verify or refute them. These conjectures are concerned with the inner structure, or symmetry, of infinite dimensional Banach spaces. Banach himself had predicted that, as Marcus du Sautoy, a colleague of Gowers's at Cambridge, put it in the London *Sunday Times* (August 17, 1998, on-line), "a certain class of objects [Banach spaces] in infinite dimensional space would have a great deal of symmetry." By constructing an unsymmetrical space of infinite dimension that nevertheless satisfied Banach's definition—that was also a Banach space, in other words—Gowers was able to provide a counterexample, thus refuting Banach's conjecture regarding symmetry. In the words of du Sautoy in the *Sunday Times*, "Gowers managed to construct objects that from one angle looked nice and smooth but when moved could never fit back into their original outline." Besides providing proof of the fallacy of Banach's conjecture, Gowers's unsymmetrical construction turned out to have other uses as well: as a counterexample, it could be used to disprove a number of other conjectures in functional analysis, rather like a touchstone, which, in earlier times, was used to test the purity of a piece of gold.

A chief reason for Gowers's success in finding an unsymmetrical Banach space was his familiarity with combinatorial theory, a field of mathematics that, in contrast to functional analysis, is concerned with the arrangement and configuration of the elements of finite rather than infinite sets. In particular, combinatorial theory is the branch of mathematics that addresses problems of existence and construction—the conditions under which an abstract entity may be said to "exist," and how one might go about "producing" that entity.

In addition to doing groundbreaking work at the forefront of mathematical research, Gowers has joined the broader debate on the nature of mathematical thought. He has addressed the philosophical issues involved in the teaching of mathematics and the ways in which mathematical pedagogy might dovetail with artificial-intelligence research. Unlike those mathematicians and mathematics educators who claim that intuition is essential in their discipline and that the intellectual process of discovery is inexplicable—that insight comes first and that logical rigor is secondary (though necessary)—Gowers believes that mathematical thought is wholly susceptible to analysis. Consequently, he does not accept the proposition that mathematical talent constitutes an elusive gift that some have and others don't. "There is a tendency, which I deplore, to think of mathematical research, or indeed problem-solving in general, as a mysterious process relying on an ability that can be drawn out of people but not taught," he wrote for his home page on the World Wide Web. Even the skills necessary to perform such difficult mathematical feats as the discovery of proofs and theorems, Gowers claims, may be imparted. Indeed, he attributes most of the difficulties that students experience to a lack of industry rather than a lack of ability.

Gowers also believes that viewing the essence of mathematics as fundamentally inscrutable has led many of his colleagues to dismiss the possibility that computers will someday come up with mathematical breakthroughs. While he concedes that the effort to teach computers to discover nontrivial theorems is beset with difficulties, he feels it is inexcusable to simply give up the attempt. The arguments of those who maintain that computers will never advance beyond simple number crunching, he has said, "remind me of the arguments of the creationists: 'I concede that a moth might change colour as a result of natural selection, but how could the eye have evolved?'" According to Gowers, even the most profound insights can be deduced from simple steps; in line with that idea, he has posted on his home page a tentative strategy for teaching mathematical ability to computers—or for that matter, to students: "I hope to break problems of the form 'How could a computer discover a proof of this result?' into smaller problems still, and eventually arrive at problems sufficiently small for computer scientists to be able to devise appropriate programs."

To demonstrate how this might be done, Gowers has examined on the Web how one might discover such important mathematical truths as the fundamental theorem of algebra and the fundamental theorem of arithmetic. While these Web pages are geared toward undergraduate math students, they are probably not beyond the grasp of interested laypeople willing to stretch their intellectual muscles. "Imagine that you did not know any advanced mathematics," he wrote at the beginning of the page dedicated to the existence of the square root of two, then added parenthetically: "if you actually don't, then that is fine." — P.K.

Suggested Reading: (London) *Sunday Times* (online), Aug. 17, 1998; *Notices of the American Mathematical Society*, p1359 Nov. 1998; *Science* p1265 Aug. 28, 1998

Courtesy of Darrell Green Youth Life Foundation

Green, Darrell

Feb. 15, 1960– Cornerback for the Washington Redskins. Address: Washington Redskins, 21300 Redskin Park Dr., Ashburn, VA 20147-6100

Darrell Green of the Washington Redskins—at age 41 the oldest cornerback in the history of the National Football League (NFL)—holds his team's record for most seasons played (19), has started more games (251) than any other player in Redskin history, and is the only player to remain from the team's glory days, an 11-year period (1982–92) during which the franchise went to the play-offs nine times and won three Super Bowls. Despite his small frame, Green consistently outplays offensive giants, thanks to his effective strategies and exceptional speed. Green has ranked as the fastest man in the NFL four times, and his time of 6.09 seconds in the 60-yard dash has never been broken on the

football field. Off the field, Green has set up two foundations, based in Washington, D.C., that offer guidance in the areas of education, health, and morality to families and children in need. "He is a leader," Tim Johnson, a former teammate of Green's, told Thomas George for the *New York Times* (May 18, 1997). "He sets a standard above the coach's standard. He goes to the edge. It's all-out. There is a tough, hard, competitive side to Darrell. But there is a real soft side only those the closest to him have seen. He is not afraid to cry over the three things that mean the most to him: his relationship to Jesus Christ, his family and his foundation. He has a heart for things that last."

Once shy around members of the media, Green has grown more outspoken over the years about moral and spiritual issues. He often talks of his love of Christ and his positions against abortion and for premarital celibacy. While some of his teammates have complained that he is self-righteous, most consider him a strong leader on and off the field. "If you ever mapped out something for a young player out of college to follow to be a professional football player and a great person, Darrell would be the example," Bobby Beathard, a former Redskins general manager, told Dennis Tuttle for the *Washingtonian* (November 1998). "It shows you what happens when you live a good life and take care of yourself."

Darrell Green was born on February 15, 1960 in Houston, Texas, the fifth of the seven children of Gloria and Leonard Green. He grew up in a tough, poor section of the city. After his parents separated, when he was 10 (they later divorced), his mother was forced to work at a grocery store during the day, clean offices at night, and sew on the side. "I can remember crying, 'Mama, I'm hungry; Mama, I'm hungry,'" Green recalled to Dennis Tuttle for *Sporting News* (October 27, 1997). "Sometimes we didn't have enough food." At night, Green would sleep in the garage with three of his brothers. Determined to prevent Darrell and his siblings from turning to crime, his mother would call her children in to watch television news stories about robberies and urge them never to steal. When his older brothers and sisters left home, Darrell took on more responsibility. "Darrell would go and wash [his younger siblings'] clothes, and he would make them sit still until he got done," his mother told Dennis Tuttle. "He'd prepare the meals. He'd take care of the younger ones." He would often break up fights in the neighborhood, and according to his younger sister, Deborah, he spent more time talking to adults than to kids his own age.

Following the example of his older brother Lester, Green began playing football on the streets of Houston. "We used to play football from one end of the street in front of my house to the other," he recalled to Thomas George for the *New York Times* (January 23, 1992). "I would run from end to end. I was always the fastest then." Playing for an organized neighborhood football team, Green earned his first MVP (most valuable player) award. He attended Jones High School in Houston, where coaches as well as his peers discouraged him from playing football because of his small size. Following their advice, he joined the track team, whose coach had previously worked in the junior high that Green had attended and had apparently taken a dislike to Green, because the boy had shown no interest in track. In high school, apparently out of ill will, the coach did not allow him to run sprints. "I had no respect in high school," Green told Tom Friend for the *Washington Post* (January 31, 1988). "I ran track in 10th grade, and then I came out for football in 11th grade, and everybody was telling me, 'Hey, get back on the track!' And the downfall of it was I got placed on the junior varsity [football] team in 11th grade, and that didn't sit too well." He made the varsity football squad his senior year, but the coaches apparently thought so little of him that he wasn't even given his own jersey. There was no question, though, that his speed was outstanding: he ran the 100 meters in a world-class 10.08 seconds. "I didn't know what that time meant," Green noted to Richard Justice for the *Washington Post* (August 20, 1990). "I just had never followed the sport enough to know that I'd done something special. People still thought I was a track guy going out for football. I thought I was a football player running a little track on the side. That's the approach I had. I might have been small, but I never minded the contact."

Playing cornerback for the only college to recruit him, Texas Arts & Industries (now known as Texas Agricultural and Mechanics, or Texas A & M), in Kingsville, Green had a tough first semester. He was intensely homesick at first, and a pair of upsetting incidents almost caused him to leave the school for good. On one occasion, a friend he had asked to drive him to Houston left without him and was killed in an accident. Another time, Green's cousin, also a freshman with the football team, stabbed a linebacker who had kept bullying him, puncturing his lung. At the end of the semester, completely fed up with what he had experienced of college life, Green took a bus back to Houston, where he found work driving a furniture truck. Although his former coach at Texas A & I had left that school, he repeatedly called Green, urging him to return to college football, either at Texas A & I or another school. Meanwhile, at home, his mother began taking the family to church more often, instilling in Green the beginnings of an unwavering Christian faith. Although his mother did not want Green to play football, he returned to Texas A & I after a year and a half away. Not long afterward, he was taken to a Bible reading by a track trainer. What he heard at the reading led Green to become "saved" as a born-again Christian.

As a junior at the university, Green racked up 56 tackles and four interceptions in 1982 and was named to the Football Coaches All-American Division II team. He was also named the Lone Star Conference Defensive Player of the Year and made the AP First-team Little All-America. Among other

highlights of his senior year, he returned two punts for touchdowns. In addition to his accomplishments in football, Green excelled at track, running the 100-meter event in 10.08 seconds, second only behind fellow student and future Olympic medalist Carl Lewis. Although skeptics doubted that he could make it in the NFL due to his small size, Green left college and was signed by the Super Bowl champion Washington Redskins in the first round of the 1983 draft, becoming the 28th pick overall. "I came to a team that had just beat Miami in the Super Bowl. So I was scared. Scared of Dave Butz and all of our veterans. Scared to let anyone catch a pass on me. These were professionals I was playing with," Green recalled to Jarret Bell for *USA Today* (August 29, 1997). "I'm thinking, 'How dare this little kid come in here and let someone catch a touchdown.' I was scared of my peers. I had a great respect for them. They were grown men." Soon, however, Green proved his worth to the team. In the 1983 preseason he took a punt return for 61 yards against the Atlanta Falcons. In the season's opening game, which was nationally televised, he caught Dallas Cowboy star Tony Dorsett from behind to prevent a touchdown. By the end of his first year, he was the team's fourth-best tackler, with 109, and his 79 solo stops put him first in that category on a 14–2 team that won the NFC East title. He was runner-up as AP NFL Defensive Rookie for the Year and made the *Football Digest* and AP all-rookie teams. In the postseason he ran back an interception for 72 yards against the L.A. Rams. The Redskins made it to the Super Bowl, where they lost to the L.A. Raiders, 38–9.

During the 1980s the Redskins were one of the dominant teams in the NFL, and Green was considered one of their greatest assets. In 1984 he was elected to a starting spot at the first of the NFL's seven Pro Bowls, after a season in which he had 87 tackles and led his team with 14 deflections and five interceptions. The Redskins were once again NFC East champions that year, with an 11–5 record, but lost in the second round of the postseason to the Chicago Bears, 23–19. In 1986 Green bruised his shoulder 12 weeks into the season, which took him out of the lineup for the first time in his career; still, he led his team with five interceptions. Although the Redskins returned to the postseason that year with a 12–4 record, enough for second place in the NFC East, they lost to the New York Giants in the NFC championships, 17–0.

The year 1987 was an exciting one for Green in several ways. The Redskins were once again NFC East champions with an 11–4 record. Green helped his team reach the NFC Championship game with a 52-yard punt return for a touchdown against the Chicago Bears. In Super Bowl XXII, the Redskins demolished the Denver Broncos, 42–10, making for the first Super Bowl win of Green's career. After that season, Green had a revelation regarding his purpose in life outside football. In his interview with Dennis Tuttle, he recalled leaving a Christmas party for underprivileged children: "It's December and it's cold," he told Tuttle. "[The children] don't have on the right clothes. The adults smell like alcohol. It was devastating. I was driving down the [George Washington] Parkway, and I started crying. I felt like it was God saying, 'Yo, Darrell, the celebrity guy. Yeah that one. YOU! You're not doing anything.' And I wasn't. I was just there. Signing a few autographs and picking up a few kids. Really, nothing. Man, those kids needed help. I just cried." After discussing ideas with his pastor, in 1988 he started the Darrell Green Youth Life Foundation, which would offer financial, educational, and spiritual support to needy families in Washington, D.C.

After leading his team in pass deflections in 1988, Green fractured his wrist in week seven of the 1989 season, which kept him out for the year. Returning for training camp in 1990, Green stunned fans and players alike with his running of the 40-yard dash in 4.1 seconds, two-tenths of a second faster than in his rookie season. The team made the play-offs with a 10–6 record that year, but lost in the second round to San Francisco. The following season, Green was tied for first place on his team with five interceptions and managed a team-best 21 passes defensed. Among numerous other postseason accolades, he was unanimously named an All-Pro. During the previous season, Green had been criticized by some for playing too close to receivers to be challenged by quarterbacks. (If the coverage is too tight, quarterbacks won't throw to the receiver and there won't be a chance for an interception or block.) He played further off in 1991 and was thus better able to intercept passes and break up plays. "Right now, he's at the top of his game," Emmitt Thomas, then the Redskins' secondary coach, told the *Washington Post* (October 3, 1991). "Without a doubt he's the best cornerback in the league." Meanwhile, the Redskins accumulated an extraordinary 14–2 record and were champions of the NFC East. In the NFC championship game against Detroit, Green ran for a 32-yard touchdown interception. In Super Bowl XXVI, he also had an interception, as the Redskins defeated Buffalo, 37–24. That year, Green also competed in the World's Fastest Athlete competition, in which he defeated Olympic gold medalists in the 40-meter dash. Meanwhile, in order to receive his bachelor's degree, Green took courses in English and general studies at Howard University, in Washington, D.C. He later transferred to Saint Paul's College, in Lawrenceville, Virginia, where he earned a B.S. degree in general studies/social sciences in 1998.

Earlier, in 1992, after he had signed a three-year, $4.5 million contract, a broken right forearm sidelined Green for seven weeks while his team managed to compile only a 9–7 record, good for third place in the NFC East. In the second round of the play-offs, the team was defeated by San Francisco, 20–13. For most of the rest of the 1990s, the Redskins stumbled under their new coach, Richie Petibon, whom Green staunchly defended. The low point came in 1994, when the Redskins finished the season with a 3–13 record; in the following years the team slowly improved. Green had set a team record in 1993 by recovering a fumble for a 78-yard touchdown run. He was also the only player in the NFC with two interceptions in a single game, accomplishing the feat twice. Meanwhile, he continued to get high numbers in tackles and consistently led his team with passes defensed.

In the winter of 1993, the Darrell Green Learning Center, an after-school facility, opened in northwest Washington. "This is a no-lose program. We educate on every level," Green said. "We take the kid who's not so academically sharp, we take him by his hand. We take the kids who are super-sharp and take them to a high level of technology, with computers and all in between. We feed, we clothe, we counsel. We have everything that's needed for success, and people need to see that. They need to get involved with that and support it." In addition to his work with children, Green also appeared in a video with Phoenix Suns forward A. C. Green, titled "It Ain't Worth It," which featured sports celebrities championing celibacy and abstinence. "We believe in what we're saying," Green told David Aldridge for the *Washington Post* (December 4, 1993). "We believe in the Bible, not that you pass out condoms, but that you teach righteousness. And righteousness is to abstain. The scripture teaches us that God's word doesn't change. It's the same today as it was yesterday. So we don't bring God's word down to another standard according to convenience."

In 1995 Green was re-signed to a two-year, $4 million contract and, at age 34, had his second-best season—in terms of tackles (81)—in 11 years. Meanwhile, the Redskins managed to improve to a 6–10 record. Green earned a trip to his sixth Pro Bowl the following year, after making 78 tackles, including 52 solo stops and three tackles for loss of yards. He added three interceptions to bring his career total to 43, becoming the all-time Redskins leader in that category. At the end of the year, he received the prestigious True Value Man of the Year Award for his on-the-field excellence and service to the community; Green was presented with a trophy and a $25,000 donation to the Darrell Green Learning Center. He also received the Bart Starr Award, which is selected by NFL players, and the Ken Houston Humanitarian Award for his service to the community. In addition, he was named NFL Man of the Year. "Winning the NFL man of the year was the biggest award I've ever gotten because you work for 15 years in one community," Green told Thomas George for the *New York Times* (May 18, 1997). "In it, as you're living, you're preparing to die just like as a player you play preparing to retire. And what that award did was it validated all of my work. It said: 'Darrell, you've had the right idea.' Not 'You're great,' but 'You've taken the right road.' But that award has no period behind it. There is no stop sign there. I must keep on keeping on." At that point, Green began to be asked how much longer he would play the game. "Man-to-man coverage, that's why I've played so long," Green told Jarrett Bell. "The thrill of the challenge. I need that competition. If it's fourth-and-10 and Michael Irvin or Jerry Rice is on the other side, that feels good. I still have that athletic pride. I want to make all the plays." New York Giants quarterback Dave Brown told Leonard Shapiro for the *Washington Post* (October 20, 1996), "He's in phenomenal shape. For playing as long as he has, you'd think he'd stay away from some of that contact. But he still mixes it up and goes after guys. He's still one of the best cover guys in the league, and his competitiveness has rubbed off on the other guys."

In 1999 the Redskins made their first appearance in the postseason in seven years, but lost to the Tampa Bay Buccaneers in the second round of the play-offs. "When we were losing the last few years, we couldn't run the ball," Green told Liz Clarke for the *Washington Post* (November 10, 1999). "The offensive line was in shambles, and we were trying to get where we wanted to be, and we weren't able to do it. Now, we can run the ball." Green recorded 56 tackles and three interceptions that season, bringing his lifetime total to 50. Although, in early 2000, he turned 40—a previously unheard-of age for a cornerback—Green was as excited as ever about playing. The Redskins signed him to a five-year, $10 million contract with a $2 million signing bonus. That season he was the team leader in games played (269) and interceptions (53). In addition, he became the oldest cornerback ever to start an NFL game. In training camp in 2000, he ran the 40-yard dash at 4.24 seconds, reclaiming the title as his team's fastest man. "It's not normal, what I've just done," Green said at the time, as quoted on *sports.excite.com* (May 31, 2000). "You guys have watched it just like I have. My kids have even seen this. This is incredible. I don't have to do anything else. I've already had an incredible career. It's just a great thrill. It's unprecedented. To have the favor of the team, the favor of the owner, the favor of the community, it's humbling. I am the guy, but believe me I am grateful." The Redskins compiled a win–loss record of 8–8 during that season, while Green made 23 tackles and three interceptions.

The team got off to a dismal start in 2001, winning one game and losing five. Green saw less playing time than in the past, as the Redskins put an extra player in the safety position. Commentators noted that Green was no longer consistently able to stop top receivers. Nevertheless, he succeeded in making 12 tackles. In early September Green announced that he planned to retire at the end of the season.

Green is five feet eight inches tall and weighs 184 pounds. He continues to run the Darrell Green Youth Life Foundation and the Darrell Green Learning Center and is also involved in preaching a message of morality through speaking engagements in the D.C. area. "We want to take the kids to the next level," Green explained to Richard Jus-

tice for the *Washington Post* (September 12, 1996). "We try to take the inner-city kids to the top suburban level. Our main concentration is academics, spiritual and moral training and social support. The school systems are not what they should be. We're trying to lift them up. There are so many broken homes, so we try to add a moral ingredient. Because of the financial struggle, we try to back them up in that area by helping with clothes and shoes. It's not like brain surgery. That's where our priorities are." He hosts an annual golf tournament to benefit Hope Springs Farm, which provides care for orphans and underprivileged children. His wife, Jewell, is the owner of Savvy Interiors. The couple have three children: Jerrell, Joi, and Jared. Green has said that he has never smoked or used drugs or alcohol or lied about an injury. While he is known for his upbeat attitude, he has criticized what he sees as negative changes in the locker room and in society. "When I first came to the Redskins, I had a healthy fear and respect for everyone in the organization around me," Green told Thomas George for the *New York Times* (May 18, 1997). "When a player was having a child, we were there. When there was a birthday, we threw birthday parties. It was family. I see the smelly, rude and crude creeping into pro sports just like it is in society. I see our young society with such a lack of respect. I just don't get a 10-year-old calling me Darrell Green instead of Mr. Green. I don't like the earrings and the tattoos. I don't like the lack of love and understanding. And it's crept right into the locker room and it is not just the players. It's the coaches. It's the owners." Green has said that the two most important people to him are his wife and his pastor, Brett Fuller, who, as he told Thomas George, "roped me around the neck and grabbed me and challenged me on a road where I follow the Lord." He has also said that he is very content with the way his life has gone since he signed with the Redskins. "Look at what's happened to me since I got drafted here," Green told Leonard Shapiro. "I've got my wife I've been married to for 12 years, three great kids, eight years of my Youth Life Foundation, a local church I've been part of for 10 years, tons of friends, three Super Bowl appearances, five Pro Bowls, four NFL fastest man titles, and a few dollars in the bank. That's not too bad, is it?" — G.O.

Suggested Reading: *New York Times* B p18 Jan. 23, 1992, with photo, VIII p8 Mar. 18, 1997; *Sporting News* p12 Oct. 27, 1997; *Washington Post* B p1 Oct. 3, 1991, D p1 Sep. 12, 1996, with photo, D p1 Oct. 20, 1996, with photo, D p1 Nov. 10, 1999; *Washingtonian* p66+ Nov. 1998, with photos

Courtesy of *media.mcdonalds.com*

Greenberg, Jack M.

1942– Chairman and CEO of McDonald's Corp.
Address: McDonald's Corp., 1 McDonald's Plaza,
Oak Brook, IL 60523-1928

"Fast food has proven to be a revolutionary force in American life," Eric Schlosser wrote in his introduction to *Fast Food Nation*, his book-length study of fast food and the values it embodies. "What people eat (or don't eat) has always been determined by a complex interplay of social, economic, and technological forces. . . . A nation's diet can be more revealing than its art or literature. On any given day in the United States about one-quarter of the adult population visits a fast food restaurant. During a relatively brief period of time, the fast food industry has helped to transform not only the American diet, but also our landscape, economy, workforce, and popular culture." The undisputed king of fast-food chains—in the United States and around the world—is McDonald's, whose chairman and CEO is Jack M. Greenberg.

McDonald's was first operated by the brothers Richard and Maurice McDonald in the mid-1940s and later expanded into a nationwide franchise by Ray Kroc. Since its inception McDonald's has built restaurants in 120 nations, among them Argentina, Bahrain, Croatia, Egypt, Israel, Japan, and Russia. It has also revolutionized the restaurant business, in more ways than one. Early on, the McDonald brothers pioneered the use of assembly-line manufacturing techniques that emphasized speed and uniformity in the commercial kitchen; those techniques now constitute the very foundation of the fast-food industry. Later, Kroc developed the marketing strategies that have played an important role

in spreading the brothers' fast-food concept across the United States and beyond. Kroc was among the first to promote the franchise model of business, by means of which a centralized and usually well-known company, under certain contractual obligations, sells the rights to its brand name (and thus presumably its customer base) to local entrepreneurs. Influenced by Walt Disney, McDonald's was also one of the first corporations outside the candy and toy industries to specifically target children—a practice now widespread in many other businesses. By constructing brightly colored playground facilities on restaurant premises, offering promotional toys with meals, advertising its products by means of cartoon characters, building restaurants near schools, and, more recently, arranging to have its food served in some school cafeterias, the restaurant has sought to establish brand loyalty at an early age, as well as to influence parents and other caregivers indirectly. "A child who loves our TV commercials and brings her grandparents to a McDonald's gives us two more customers," Kroc explained, as quoted by Schlosser.

For roughly the first decade of its existence, McDonald's occupied a single facility, in San Bernardino, California. That changed in 1955, the year in which Kroc opened the first McDonald's franchise in Des Plaines, Illinois, a Chicago suburb. By the end of the year, two more McDonald's, both in California, had opened their doors. A persistent, ambitious man, Kroc continued to promote the McDonald's concept zealously, and within a few years, his efforts began to produce results: by 1960 there were about 230 McDonald's restaurants nationwide; 10 years later, thanks in part to the patronage of the baby-boom generation, that figure had mushroomed to 3,000.

Today McDonald's is a global force. By the most recent count, the company runs about 29,000 restaurants in 121 countries and continues to grow. It operates more playgrounds than any other private entity in the United States; is one of the nation's largest distributors of toys; has employed an estimated one out of every eight American workers at one time or another; and is the world's largest owner of commercial real estate. Ranked 138th in the Fortune 500 and 366th in the Global 500, the McDonald's Corp. is among the 30 companies used to compute the Dow Jones Industrial Average.

Perhaps even more significant than McDonald's sheer economic muscle, though, is its symbolic import. McDonald's is the most recognizable brand name in the world, surpassing even Coca-Cola in international visibility; indeed, according to a marketing survey cited by Schlosser, the golden arches are familiar to more people worldwide than the Christian cross. That sort of visibility has not been without its price. McDonald's critics are numerous and vocal; they range from statesmen such as French president Jacques Chirac and former Israeli president Ezer Weizman to activists such as José Bové, the French farmer arrested for leading a group of protestors in ransacking a McDonald's restaurant under construction in Millau, France. Among other things, McDonald's has been vilified as an emblem of American hegemony and environmental devastation; it has also been accused of unfair labor practices and of contributing to cultural homogenization and rising obesity rates. Of course, McDonald's has its defenders as well. The company has been praised for reducing its solid wastes, first by switching from Styrofoam to cardboard sandwich containers, in 1990, then by eliminating sandwich containers altogether and replacing them with paper wrappers. In 2000, according to the McDonald's Web site, the company was named "number one in social responsibility" by *Fortune* magazine. The *New York Times* columnist and globalization advocate Thomas Friedman has further pointed out—half facetiously, perhaps—that thus far, no two countries in which McDonald's operates restaurants have ever gone to war. Most significantly, the company continues to do a brisk business, serving some 45 million people per day—despite its critics.

Presiding over this fast-food empire is Jack Greenberg, a former accountant who was named chief executive officer of the McDonald's Corp. in 1998 and chairman of the board of directors in May 1999. (Greenberg succeeded Michael Quinlan, whose predecessors were Kroc and Fred Turner.) In his short time at the helm, Greenberg has already proven agreeable to the corporation's shareholders. When he took charge, McDonald's was experiencing a slight slump in sales, especially in new restaurants. Now, it appears to have recovered, and many attribute the turnaround to organizational changes made by Greenberg, who has sought to curb domestic expansion and decentralize the company's decision-making processes. In recognition of his achievements, Greenberg was named 1999 Executive of the Year by the editors of *Restaurants and Institutions*.

Jack M. Greenberg was born in 1942 and grew up in Chicago. His entry in *Who's Who in America 2001* lists the name of his mother, Edith Scher, but not that of his father. He attended Chicago's DePaul University School of Commerce, from which he earned a B.Sc. degree in 1964; four years later he received a J.D. degree from DePaul University School of Law. Meanwhile, in 1964 Greenberg had joined Arthur Young & Co., a Chicago accounting firm, where he worked as a tax accountant. Greenberg was made a partner at Arthur Young in 1974; by 1981 he had become director of tax services for the firm's midwestern region, as well as for the company's Chicago office. James Cantalupo, who worked with Greenberg at Arthur Young (and who is currently president of McDonald's International), recalled that "both of us were always very aggressive in terms of our career aspirations," according to Amy Zuber in *Nation's Restaurant News* (January 2000).

Greenberg joined McDonald's in 1982 as executive vice president and chief financial officer. Beginning in 1990, shortly after he was promoted to senior executive vice president, Greenberg spent nearly two years managing in the field, with the goal of getting a better sense of the organization's day-to-day operations. During that time Greenberg carried out his CFO duties "only with external audiences," as he told Scott Hume for *Restaurants and Institutions* (July 1, 1999). "During those 20 months or so our accounting and treasury executives were running my piece of the business. . . . But I would get a call from communications chief Chuck Ebeling who'd say, 'I have so-and-so from the *Wall Street Journal* on the phone.' And I'd say, 'Yeah, but I'm on a roof looking at HVAC [heating, ventilating, and air-conditioning] equipment with an operator. If you give me 5 minutes I'll climb down and call him.' So I did the external stuff and people didn't really know that I was doing full-time operations work." "I was working probably 80 hours a week for almost two years," Greenberg told Patricia Sellers for *Fortune* (June 22, 1998). Upon his return to senior management, Greenberg was promoted to vice chairman. The new position entailed handling real-estate matters, purchasing, franchising, human resources, and communications issues for the firm. "When I came back as vice chairman in charge of those staff functions," he told Hume, "I had a much deeper appreciation of the business."

Greenberg gained national prominence in 1997, when, as the newly appointed chairman of McDonald's USA, he engineered a turnaround of the company's faltering domestic operations. "Part of the problem was maybe being spoiled by our success a little bit," Greenberg told Hume. "We'd done things in a particular way for a long, long time and those approaches weren't working as well. I think we were struggling with why, and it was hard to change. . . . As decision-making got more centralized it slowed down and got more distant from the operators who are running the restaurants. And I think we paid a price for that." One year later Greenberg was named president and chief executive officer of McDonald's Corp.; in May 1999 he was appointed chairman of the board.

As CEO of McDonald's, Greenberg has been swift to respond to the organization's critics, who he believes have often been motivated by frustrations and concerns that have little to do with the fast-food leader. In response to the accusation that McDonald's is a homogenizing force, for example, Greenberg told Moisés Naím for *Foreign Policy* (May/June 2001) that McDonald's is "a decentralized entrepreneurial network of locally owned stores that is very flexible and adapts very well to local conditions." Although only one out of 14 members of the company's board of directors holds a non-American passport (that member is Canadian), "in terms of how the business is run—what makes the difference to our customers and to how we conduct ourselves in these markets—this is all done by local nationals," he told Naím. When asked about the charge that McDonald's is anti-union, Greenberg responded that the restaurant's workers, many of whom are teenagers, value the "temporary and seasonal employment" a McDonald's job offers; consequently, "the employees' need for a union to be treated fairly does not exist. . . . That is not anti-union, it's just there's no need for them. People can interpret it any way they want. We just don't see the need." He further pointed out that McDonald's workers are unionized in countries where union membership is required by law. In his conversation with Naím, Greenberg also defended McDonald's environmental record. "We seek out those who have some interest in a constructive dialogue that can help us. Because we had serious environmental issues and we weren't experts, for example, we joined in a partnership 10 years ago with Environmental Defense [then known as the Environmental Defense Fund]. . . . It has made a difference. If you talk to Environmental Defense, they will tell you that our leadership in this area has made an enormous difference over the last 10 years in terms of how American business behaves."

When asked what he would like to accomplish as CEO of McDonald's, Greenberg told Naím that he hoped he and his colleagues "will leave a legacy of some transformation from a traditional single line of business focused on the one brand in a very narrow way to a business that transforms itself so that the brand stands for a lot more things. . . . Take the largest-selling clothing line for children in the United States. It happens to be called McKids. It happens to be licensed to Wal-Mart, but it's our brand and we get a royalty for it. I think the brand can stand for more things and we can sell more things under the brand if we work at it and we create broader customer expectations." Moreover, Greenberg said that he would like to see McDonald's "in the top tier in social responsibility. . . . We're going to transform this company, keeping what's terrific about it, which is this great brand name and business we've been talking about, but also develop this idea of social leadership, which is important to who we are."

Among his fellow executives, Greenberg is held in esteem for his managerial skills. "I think the key thing is that he is a people person," Herb Blutenthal, a Chicago-based securities analyst, told Amy Zuber. "There are a lot of leaders that can manage people, but he has a unique charismatic flair that really energizes people at the company." Similarly, Jack Staley, who worked with Greenberg at Arthur Young, characterized his former colleague as "an infectious personality. People enjoy being with him. He makes people feel good. It is just part of his persona."

In addition to leading the McDonald's Corp., Greenberg serves on the board of directors of Abbott Laboratories, is a member of the Council of the World Economic Forum and the National Policy Association, and serves on the boards of trustees of DePaul University, the Field Museum, and the Chicago Symphony Orchestra.

Greenberg and his wife, Donna, have three children: David, Ilyse, and Allison. In his free time, he enjoys reading and traveling. — P.K.

Suggested Reading: *Business Week* p166+ Apr.10, 2000; *Forbes* p42+ June 15, 1998, with photo; p218+ Nov. 1, 1999, with photo; *Foreign Policy* p26+ May/June 2001; *Fortune* p34+ June 22, 1998, with photo; *Nation's Restaurant News* p90+ Jan. 2000, with photo; *Restaurants and Institutions* p60+ July 1, 1999, with photos; Schlosser, Eric. *Fast Food Nation: The Dark Side of the All-American Meal*, 2001

David Handschuh/New York *Daily News*

Gruber, Ruth

1911– Journalist; photographer; humanitarian. Address: c/o Three Rivers Press Publicity, Random House, Inc., 299 Park Ave., New York, NY 10171

The journalist and humanitarian Ruth Gruber, whose 90th birthday is in 2001, has spent her career documenting extraordinary events and the experiences of people affected by them. After earning a Ph.D. degree at 20, she slipped inside countries under Communist and fascist regimes to observe the lives of ordinary citizens, a feat made possible in part by the fact that "the men didn't think women were smart or brave," as she told Calvin Reid for *Publishers Weekly* (October 11, 1999). Working closely with U.S. president Franklin D. Roosevelt and Interior Secretary Harold Ickes during World War II, she risked her own safety to escort close to 1,000 refugees to the United States. She covered Israel's War of Independence and the trials of Nazi war criminals, and she counted Eleanor Roosevelt, the widow of the president, and Israeli prime minister Golda Meir among her close friends. Over the past 70 years, Gruber has acted as an eyewitness to history and written 15 books and numerous articles. Her most cherished assignment, accompanying European refugees from Italy to America in 1944, was the subject of her 1983 book *Haven: The Unknown Story of 1,000 World War II Refugees.* The book inspired a television miniseries, *Haven,* which aired in early 2001.

Ruth Gruber was born in 1911 in the borough of Brooklyn, in New York City, where she grew up in a modern Orthodox Jewish home. A genealogy Web site prepared by Stephen Rockower, a maternal relation of Gruber's, notes that she had three brothers; according to Joanne Weintraub, writing for the *Milwaukee Journal Sentinel* (February 5, 2001, on- line), she was the fourth of five children. Her parents, David and Gussie (Rockower) Gruber, who had emigrated from Poland (some sources say Russia), owned and operated a liquor store. Gruber has recalled shedding observant Jewish practice when she was a teenager. "At thirteen I said, 'I don't believe any of this anymore,'" she told Max Alexander for *Reader's Digest* (February 2001). "I rebelled against everything. I wanted to move to Greenwich Village and live among the bohemians." Eager to explore the world, Gruber accelerated her studies. She graduated from high school at 15 and enrolled as a commuter student at New York University, where she studied German and journalism. "I had an African American teacher in first grade and she inspired me to write," Gruber explained during an on-line chat hosted by Kidsnet, an educational resource organization (February 8, 2001). She gained acceptance at the University of Wisconsin at Madison, where she earned a master's degree, writing her thesis on a work by the German poet and philosopher Johann Wolfgang von Goethe. In Madison, according to Joanne Weintraub, she experienced anti-Semitism for the first time, both from a professor of German, who "made pointed remarks about pushy, know-it-all students from New York City, especially the ones who spoke Yiddish," and from a German-born dormitory supervisor, who "made Gruber's life so miserable she had to find a room elsewhere." Gruber next accepted a fellowship at the University of Cologne, in Germany, where she received a Ph.D. in 1932; at 20, she was at the time the youngest person in the world to have earned a doctoral degree. "Going to Germany was my dream," she told Max Alexander. "I was in love with the language." She was entranced by German culture but dismayed by the beginnings of the extreme nationalism and anti-Semitism that accompanied the Nazi dictator Adolf Hitler's rise to power in Germany.

After working for a while as a freelance journalist in New York, Gruber, barely out of her teens, returned to Europe. As a foreign correspondent for the *New York Herald Tribune,* she set about documenting the lives of women who lived under Communist and fascist regimes. In the Soviet Union, then led by the Communist dictator Joseph Stalin, she spent time in Moscow before traveling to the Soviet Arctic in 1935–36, hauling her typewriter onto rickety open-air planes. The first Western journalist permitted to travel in that part of the Soviet Union, she even gained approval to enter the Soviet Gulag, a system of forced-labor camps, mainly in Siberia and the far north of the country, in which living conditions were notoriously harsh. After her time in the Soviet Union, she was allowed to reenter Germany in the late 1930s, even though tensions there were mounting and persecution of Jews and other groups had already begun.

Gruber collected her impressions of the people and landscape of the Soviet Yakutsk region in *I Went to the Soviet Arctic,* which was published in 1939. The book caught the attention of Jane Ickes, who shared it with her husband, Harold Ickes, President Franklin D. Roosevelt's secretary of the interior. Secretary Ickes hired Gruber as his special assistant in 1941 and sent her on a research mission to the Alaska District (Alaska's official designation prior to its gaining statehood, in 1959); part of her job was to scout the area for potential homesteads for returning soldiers. She was a field representative for the Department of the Interior until 1946, when Ickes resigned from his post.

Gruber's favorite assignment under Ickes was one she demanded for herself. In the summer of 1944, she learned that 1,000 European refugees were being granted passage to the United States as "guests" of President Roosevelt; due to strict limits on immigration and the refusal of the U.S. Congress to ease those limits, Roosevelt acted on executive authority to grant the refugees haven in the U.S. only while World War II was still being fought. "The indifference haunts me, it haunts me every day," Gruber said during a press conference concerning the television premiere of *Haven,* as Bernard Weinraub reported in the *New York Times* (February 7, 2001). "They knew what was going on. They knew about the death camps. We could have saved hundreds of thousands. It was overt anti-Semitism, plain and simple." Realizing that the overwhelming percentage of the refugees would be Jewish, Gruber pleaded with Ickes to send her to accompany them, arguing that her Jewishness and her knowledge of Russian, German, Yiddish, Polish, and French would offer them psychological comfort. While Ickes agreed, he and Gruber had to persuade the War Refugee Board and the State Department to allow her to go. The government granted permission, which left Gruber's family as the last remaining obstacle. "My parents were terrified when I left on this trip in the middle of the war," she revealed during the Kidsnet chat. Her mother, Gruber told Patricia O'Haire for the New York *Daily News* (February 4, 2001), "was furious. She was already worried about my brother, who was in the Army, and she came down to Washington and told Mr. Ickes to forbid me to go." To offer her a modicum of protection, the government designated Gruber a "simulated general." "If I was captured, as a civilian I could be executed as a spy, but under the Geneva Convention [an international agreement regarding the treatment of prisoners of war], a general must be taken care of," she explained to O'Haire.

In July 1944 Gruber flew to Naples, Italy, to accompany the refugees aboard the *Henry Gibbins*, an army troop transport ship returning to the U.S. with wounded soldiers. Her charges had already been chosen from among tens of thousands of refugees. The decision making had been a trying process for those involved; Gruber noted for Kidsnet that "the first man sent over to make the selection had a nervous breakdown." He and others had attempted, she explained, "to select people who had escaped from concentration camps . . . [and] to select people who could help run the camp [in which the U.S. government planned to house them]—we had lots of doctors, engineers, cooks." The boat, part of a 29-ship convoy, set sail in late July with 982 refugees aboard (approximately 100 of whom were not Jewish), hailing from 18 countries and ranging in age from an 80-year-old Greek man to a baby born a few days earlier and nicknamed "International Harry" by the soldiers on the *Henry Gibbins*. While the boat sailed through the Mediterranean Sea, German submarines and airplane squadrons presented constant threats, and during the Atlantic crossing, Gruber found herself defending the refugees to some of the wounded soldiers, who were convinced that the transport of Jews to America might provoke a German attack. "Ignoring nonfraternization orders given the GIs, [Gruber] picked out the most professional singers among the refugees and the best-looking girls, and, in the finest Hollywood tradition, put on a show. The GI audience loved it," Tom Tugend wrote for the *Jewish Journal of Greater Los Angeles* (July 28, 2000). Gruber also held daily English classes for the refugees, despite the rough crossing. She described the experience for Kidsnet: "We set up a blackboard and everyone who wanted to learn crowded around and I began by teaching them, 'How do you feel?' 'I feel fine.' Many would get seasick and they would stand over the rail of the ship and say, 'I feel fine.'"

An additional part of Gruber's job was to document the stories of her wards and relay them to Ickes and Roosevelt. Although it pained her to listen to the litany of death, starvation, and torture from which the refugees had escaped, the experience strengthened her attachment to Judaism. "Yes, faith played a role [in this mission]," she told Kidsnet. "I have a theory that even though I was born Jewish there was a moment in my life when I BECAME Jewish. It was on our ship that I realized the truth and beauty of my Jewishness. But I think it happens to people of all faiths."

Upon arrival in the U.S., Gruber, now called "Mother Ruth" by her charges, accompanied the refugees via train to the Fort Ontario army base in Oswego, New York. The refugees, who did not have regular visas, were not allowed to contact relatives or friends who lived in the United States, in part because the U.S. government feared they would find means to immigrate illegally. Fort Ontario had barbed wire and searchlights, much like the camps from which many of the refugees had escaped, but Gruber convinced the refugees that they would be cared for in the camp and were not in danger. Working quickly, she obtained permission for the children to attend Oswego schools. Although visitation outside the base was strictly limited, many residents of Oswego eventually came to the camp and befriended the refugees. Few people outside Oswego and Washington, D.C., even knew the story of the 982 people who were saved, despite a piece that ran in *Life* magazine. "Americans did not really know about it," Gruber told Kidsnet. "It became one of the best kept secrets of World War II." Although the refugees rejoiced when World War II finally ended, they faced a forced return to Europe. (Some of the refugees, particularly those who were not Jews, volunteered to return.) Gruber appealed to President Harry S. Truman to supersede the executive order of his predecessor, President Roosevelt, and allow the "guests" to stay. In January 1946 the residents of Fort Ontario were offered permanent haven. The army base was closed, and the refugees were taken to Canada briefly so that they could enter the United States with proper immigration materials. Gruber had finally accomplished her mission to her satisfaction, and the experience "shaped the rest of my life," as she explained to Nadine Brozan for the *New York Times* (August 4, 1994). "It affected everything I wrote and did. Refugees and survival became my obsession."

Her work with the Oswego refugees at an end, Gruber found a new assignment. Hired by the *New York Post*, she went to Europe and the Middle East in 1946 to follow the activities of the Anglo-American Committee of Inquiry on Palestine, co-created by President Truman and British foreign minister Ernest Bevin, which would make recommendations as to whether or not Britain should allow 100,000 Jewish refugees to enter Palestine, then under British jurisdiction. In words and photographs, Gruber chronicled life amid the often deplorable conditions of the Displaced Persons (DP) camps, where Jews who could not return to their homes stayed after World War II had ended. Despite the unanimous recommendation that the displaced Jews should be permitted to immigrate to Palestine, Bevin refused to let them do so. Writing for the *New York Herald Tribune* in 1947, Gruber followed the activities of the United Nations Special Committee on Palestine on a similar mission. While working on that assignment, she received word that the ship *Exodus 1947* was attempting to break the British blockade of the Palestinian coastline and deliver 4,500 refugees to the port city of Haifa. Gruber rushed to Haifa and watched as British vessels attacked the *Exodus 1947* in a skirmish that left three dead and 200 injured. The damaged ship was turned back to Cyprus and its human cargo eventually shuttled to France and Germany, where the refugees reentered DP camps. Gruber followed the ship, documenting the conditions in Cyprus and the stories of those who were forced to return to Europe. "I must live a story to write it," she explained to Adam Segal for the *Canadian Jewish News* (July 20, 2000, on-line). Despite Gruber's skill at evoking sympathy for the refugees, she was the only journalist the British permitted aboard. "It was the ship that launched the nation [of Israel]," she told Segal about the *Exodus 1947*, whose voyage inspired her to cover future developments on the road to Israeli statehood. Gruber related her experiences in *Destination Palestine: The Story of the Haganah Ship Exodus 1947* (1948) and *Israel without Tears* (1950). Her account of the *Exodus 1947* journey influenced the writer Leon Uris, who dramatized the story in his novel *Exodus* (1959).

In the early 1950s Gruber put her career on hold briefly in order to start a family. She married Philip Michaels, an attorney, in 1951, and had a daughter, Celia, and a son, David. Meanwhile, she maintained her status as a special foreign correspondent for the *New York Herald Tribune*, and soon she resumed writing, covering the trials of Nazi war criminals and the fledgling state of Israel. Her next book, *Israel Today: Land of Many Nations*, appeared in 1958. Gruber contributed regularly to several Jewish and secular magazines, including *Commentary*, *Look*, *Saturday Review*, and *Ms.*; beginning in 1961, she published a column in *Hadassah* magazine, the journal of the Women's Zionist Organization of America. Gruber wrote scripts for NBC's radio program *Eternal Light*, which ran from 1944 to 1981 and offered dramatizations of episodes from the ancient Judaic world.

Throughout the 1960s and 1970s, Gruber traveled widely and produced articles and books on subjects ranging from the life of Felisa Rincon de Gautier, a suffragist who became the mayor of San Juan, Puerto Rico, to the migration of Ethiopian Jews to Israel. Her 1978 book, *Raquela: A Woman of Israel*, a biography of the Israeli nurse and health-care pioneer Raquela Prywes, won the National Jewish Book Award. In the early 1980s she returned to the subject closest to her heart, the story of the 982 refugees she had shepherded to freedom. She was still in touch with many of the people who had called her "Mother Ruth," and she made regular appearances at the group's reunions. "She considers it her role to show up," Ray Harding, who was nine years old when he came to the U.S. aboard the *Henry Gibbins*, told Max Alexander. "We think of Ruth as our den mother." Gruber's account of the group's journey, *Haven: The Unknown Story of 1,000 World War II Refugees*, was published in 1983. As she wrote it, "I felt I was re-living every minute of the experience," she revealed for Kidsnet.

Refusing to slow down as she entered her 80s, Gruber wrote her autobiography, *Ahead of Time: My Early Years as a Foreign Correspondent* (1991).

She also discovered a newfound fascination with her adventures and writings on the part of the public. "There seems to be a renewed interest in World War II and the fate of the survivors by a new generation that knows little about the subjects," she told Tom Tugend. Three of her books—*Haven*, *Raquela*, and *Exodus 1947*—have recently been updated and reissued by Random House to considerable fanfare. *Haven* was made into a CBS miniseries, which starred Natasha Richardson as Ruth Gruber and aired in February 2001. (Gruber and her daughter had cameos in the movie, as refugees hoping to be selected to board the *Henry Gibbins*.) Richardson met with Gruber before accepting the part and described the experience to Patricia O'Haire: "Sitting there was this extraordinary woman who singlehandedly made a great deal of difference in the lives of so many people. I was struck by the fact that there is nothing angry or bitter about her, considering the doors that were closed in her face. . . . It would be tough enough for anyone to do what she did now, let alone a young Jewish woman in the '40s." After deciding to play Gruber, Richardson explained her motivation to Max Alexander: "I felt obligated to make this movie because I was shocked to find out that while hundreds of thousands of German POWs [prisoners of war] were sent to America during the war, the Administration could find room for only a few Jewish refugees."

Living by her maxim to "never, never, never retire," as she told Tom Tugend, Gruber is writing her 16th book, about the most interesting women she has met in her long career. She hopes that there will be a large reunion of the Oswego refugees and their descendants at the opening of the Safe Haven Museum, located at what was Fort Ontario, which is slated for the late summer of 2001. (A small section of the barbed-wire fence from Fort Ontario was given to her by the refugees as a souvenir.) Married and widowed twice, Gruber now lives alone in New York City. She has four biological grandchildren—and many more of a different sort. "From these nearly 1,000 people, I must have 5,000 grandchildren and great-grandchildren now," she explained, as reported by Bernard Weinraub. "But how many more grandchildren could I have if we had saved more?" — K.S.

Suggested Reading: *Biography* p71+ Sep. 2001, with photos; *Hadassah Magazine* (on-line) Feb. 2001, with photo; *Jerusalem Post* (on-line) Sep. 13, 2000, with photo; *Milwaukee Journal Sentinel* (on- line) Feb. 5, 2001, with photos; New York *Daily News* Showtime p13 Feb. 4, 2001, with photo; *New York Times* (on-line) Feb. 7, 2001, with photo; *Publishers Weekly* p22 Oct. 11, 1999; *Reader's Digest* p88+ Feb. 2001, with photos

Selected Books: *I Went to the Soviet Arctic*, 1939; *Ahead of Time: My Early Years as a Foreign Correspondent*, 1991; *Exodus 1947*, 1948 (reissued 1999); *Raquela: A Woman of Israel*, 1978 (reissued 2000); *Haven: The Unknown Story of 1,000 World War II Refugees*, 1983 (reissued 2000)

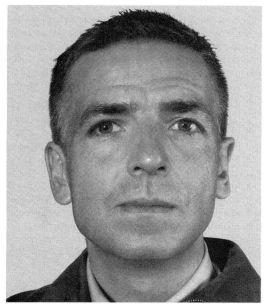

Courtesy of Richard Burbridge

Gursky, Andreas

Jan. 1955– Photographer. Address: c/o Matthew Marks Gallery, 523 W. 24th St., New York, NY 10011

In his enormous color pictures, many of which exceed six feet in both length and width, the German photographer Andreas Gursky presents "a stunning and inventive image" of the world at the turn of the 21st century. That assessment appeared on the Web site of the Museum of Modern Art (MOMA) in New York City, in an introduction to a mid-career retrospective of the 46-year-old Gursky's work mounted by the museum in early 2001. The assessment continued, "His adventurous mixture of contemporary subjects, saturated color, large scale, rich detail, bold abstraction, visual wit, art-world savvy, photographic spontaneity, and flamboyant digital tinkering—all in the service of a polished, signature style—have made his work one of the most distinctive and challenging contributions to contemporary art." According to Calvin Tomkins, who profiled him for the *New Yorker* (January 22, 2001), "Gursky's idea was that in his pictures he would be like 'an extraterrestrial being,' knowing nothing of the world, who looks at contemporary society and tries to figure out what is going on there." His subjects have included apartment buildings, industrial plants, huge retail

markets, the trading floors of international stock exchanges, and sporting events, at sites in Hong Kong, Egypt, Brazil, Japan, Sweden, France, and the United States, among other places, as well as in Germany.

Well-known in his native land since the late 1980s, Gursky has attracted much more widespread notice in recent years, thanks in part to group and solo shows in the U.S. and elsewhere. His work has inspired critics and others to reevaluate photography as an art form. Tomkins, for example, while viewing Gursky's pictures at MOMA, was "suddenly struck," as he wrote, by the realization "that Gursky was laying to rest photography's ancestral inferiority complex with regard to painting." Assessing the MOMA show for the *New York Times* (March 2, 2001), Michael Kimmelman, who described the photos as "eye-poppingly gorgeous," wrote, "Their ambition and fetishized magnificence dispense with the concept that photographs need to tell the truth, . . . as if truth were ever a thing as simple as whatever appeared in a viewfinder. . . . The pictures expose a strangely persistent fallacy: that altered photographs are different from paintings or sculptures or drawings as objects of art. It's an idea that must finally be put to rest in the 21st century. All art involves manipulation, after all—manipulations of color, perspective, scale, whatever, which becomes the measure of its ingenuity and content." Kimmelman also wrote, "The ultimate compliment to any exhibition is to say that the rest of the world looks different after you leave the show. That's certainly the case with Mr. Gursky's midcareer overview."

The only child of Willy Gursky and Rosemarie Gursky, Andreas Gursky was born in January 1955 in Leipzig, in what was then Communist-ruled East Germany. His paternal grandfather and his father were commercial photographers. When he was a few months old, his family, leaving nearly all their possessions behind, slipped across the border to democratic West Germany, to begin their lives anew. In 1957 the family moved from Essen to Düsseldorf, where a major portion of the West German advertising industry was based. In Düsseldorf Rosemarie and Willy Gursky opened what soon became, Tomkins reported, "one of the city's top commercial photo studios."

Although, as Gursky told Tomkins, he "had a very close relationship" with his father and mother and "grew up in this atmosphere of a professional advertising studio," during his youth he believed that he would never follow in his parents' footsteps vocationally. As a child he excelled at sports and particularly enjoyed skiing and tennis; at 16 he became the junior tennis champion of Düsseldorf. In his late teens Gursky began to question the societal and personal values that had enabled his parents to provide him with material comforts. While still in high school, he left home; he lived with classmates until he graduated, in 1975. For reasons of conscience, he refused to enlist in the armed service, as required by law. Instead, in a compromise worked out with the West German military, he worked as a hospital technician for about 18 months.

In 1978, after contemplating a career in social work or psychology, Gursky entered the Folkwang-schule (Folkwang School), an institute of photography in Essen. "I had to do something, and a close friend of mine, who was very interested in photography, persuaded me just to try it with him," he explained to Tomkins. The curriculum emphasized photojournalism; everywhere he went, Gursky brought along two Leica 35-millimeter cameras, each loaded with black-and-white film, and he took pictures on impulse. Among other influences, he studied the work of the renowned French photojournalist Henri Cartier-Bresson. During this period he earned a living as a taxi driver and made his first trip outside Germany: he visited New York City, where he prowled the streets looking for good subjects to photograph. "I was fascinated by the city, but I felt completely lost there," he told Tomkins. Back in Germany, as he approached the completion of his course work at the Folkwangschule, he submitted his portfolio to several magazines in Hamburg, the center of West German magazine publishing, but he received no job offers.

While in New York City Gursky had talked with Thomas Struth, another young German photographer. (Struth has since achieved great success in his field; according to Tomkins, he and Gursky are the "ruling masters" of the "Düsseldorf School" of photography and photo-based art.) Struth suggested that he consider studying photography with Bernd and Hilla Becher at the Staatliche Kunstakademie (State Art Academy), a famous art school in Düsseldorf. Taking Struth's advice, in 1980 Gursky enrolled at the Kunstakademie and a year later began to study with the Bechers, who had set up the academy's photography department. The couple specialized in photos of industrial architecture and were, as Tomkins wrote, "the leading apostles of a rigorous, minimalist approach to photography which was intended, in their minds, at least, to take the medium back to its nineteenth-century roots as impersonal, quasi-scientific documentation." The Bechers instructed their carefully selected students (there were only five when Gursky worked with them) to choose a single subject, such as smokestacks or water towers, and photograph examples of it in similar weather and at the same time of day, using a single-exposure, large-plate camera loaded with black-and-white film and mounted on a tripod. The couple also welcomed their students into their home. "What was important to me about the Bechers was to see how they lived," Gursky explained to Tomkins. "It was so different from my parents, and from advertising. Everything in the house was for photography." Gursky experimented with both inanimate and animate subjects. For a while he concentrated on images of uniformed security guards in lobbies of office buildings; he was amused by the idea that the guards were posted in pairs to keep an eye on each other. Rejecting the Bechers' instruction, he used color film exclusively from that point on.

In what contributed to an informal break with the Bechers, Gursky began to photograph landscapes with a handheld camera. He was particularly drawn to scenes that contained a bit of mystery or drama. His new mentor at the Kunstakademie, Kaspar Koenig, nicknamed Gursky's newest photographs Sonntagsbilder—"Sunday pictures"—because many of them showed people at leisure, swimming, fishing, biking, or otherwise amusing themselves. Gursky shot other subjects as well, planning each photograph precisely, as the Bechers had taught him. In 1987, his last year at the academy, he resumed using a single-exposure camera and a tripod, to gain the high levels of clarity and detail that he sought. He became familiar with the work of others who had adopted similar equipment, among them Michael Schmidt, Robert Adams, Nicholas Nixon, and Jeff Wall. A fellowship bestowed by the school enabled him to concentrate on his own projects and stop the advertising work that he had been doing to support himself. In recognition of his skill and achievements, at the end of Gursky's Kunstakademie career, Bernd Becher gave him the title Meisterschüler—literally, "master student." Soon after his graduation from the Kunstakademie, he had his first solo exhibition, at the Düsseldorf airport.

Since his Sonntagsbilder period, Gursky has chosen as his subjects what Norman Bryson, writing for Art/Text (November 1999/January 2000), labeled "sectors or domains": industry (which Gursky illustrated with, for example, panoramic shots of factory interiors); finance (images of the trading floors of stock exchanges in Chicago and other cities); commerce (with such pictures as 99 Cent [1999], which shows row upon row of shelved products inside a big store); "aesthetics and the museum," in Bryson's words (for example, a photo of three paintings by the 19th-century British artist J. M. W. Turner on exhibit at the Tate Gallery in London); and recreation (a bird's-eye view of the audience at a midnight rave). Some images capture more than one domain. Untitled V (1997), for example, in which scores of athletic shoes in a wide range of colors are neatly aligned on the three tiers of a white, back-lit display case, illustrates commerce and recreation.

Gursky's recent prints are extremely large. Tokyo Stock Exchange (1990), for instance, which shows several hundred black-suited, white-shirted men standing or walking on the exchange's nearly litter-free parquet floor, is six feet two inches by about seven feet one-half inch. The Rhein (1996) measures six feet by a bit over seven feet; it is a horizontal view of a straight section of the Rhine River (as it is spelled in English), in Germany, on an overcast day, without people, boats, or other objects, its grassy banks completely featureless. (Gursky told Peter Plagens for Newsweek [March 19, 2001] that it took three years for him to decide exactly how he wanted to portray the river.) The huge prints are produced in Düsseldorf labs by technicians specially trained by Gursky and others.

Because he uses a camera that records images on individual five-by-seven-inch plates rather than film, Gursky told Plagens, he "cannot react very spontaneously" as a photographer; rather, he explained, "you have to think carefully about what you want. I have a visual idea—that I have been thinking about for a long time—and I prepare for it." Thanks to the latest technologies and his own skill, his panoramas capture both sweeping breadth and exquisite detail. "With Gursky, the details are so rich that the image positively sizzles with information: every grain of sand, every furrow in the carpet, every window in the building . . . ," Bryson wrote. "The implication is that ordinary vision is a weak and unreliable instrument, unable to see the wood for the trees, too caught up in local distractions: the camera, and only the camera, gives access to the totality of the social and of history." In an interview with Veit Görner for *Andreas Gursky: Fotografien 1994–1998*, an exhibition catalog, Gursky said, "You never notice arbitrary details in my work. On a formal level, countless interrelated micro and macrostructures are woven together, determined by an overall organizational principle. . . . A visual structure appears to dominate the real events shown in my pictures. I subjugate the real situation to my artistic concept of the picture." In the 1989 photograph *Niagara Falls*, for example, Gursky angled his lens to capture a tour boat filled with blue-slickered passengers fading into the mist of the pounding falls; lacking context—there is no hint of the commerce on land, for example—the image has an air of drama and mystery.

In 1992 Gursky began to use computers to manipulate his images. For his photo of Nike athletic shoes displayed in a store, for example, he digitally enhanced the shelves and "invented" the reflection below them, as Michael Kimmelman put it. Gursky eliminated a factory complex and its smokestack from his photograph of the Rhine River, and some of his crowd scenes include multiples of portions of the images. For *Shanghai* (2000), which measures approximately 10 feet by six feet nine inches, he combined several photos of the curved, multileveled atrium of a late-20th-century building in China to create what Kimmelman described as a "seamless bending grid." Commenting on that picture, Kimmelman wrote, "What matters is not the process by which it was concocted but the glowing amber color and Minimalist perfection of the result: potent geometry supersedes the ostensible subject of the photograph, which is anonymous modern architecture." By contrast, Norman Bryson found fault with Gursky's approach and results: "The trouble is not that Gursky exaggerates . . . but that he presents his exaggerations with so little pretense of naturalism. In his computer manipulations all the seams show, all of the color retouchings hit you on the head like a hammer. Have you noticed . . . that in Gursky's crowd scenes, ev-

eryone who wears red wears the same red—or blue, or yellow? You would think that in advanced industrial societies, clothes are color-coded." "The twentieth century developed some powerful models for understanding the macro-processes of social life . . . ," Bryson wrote. "Gursky's interest in the photogenic—in how photographs look—threatens this whole social-analytical project by suggesting that the panoramic is, in the end, only a visual stylization." By his own account, however, Gursky seeks more than "visual stylization." When he decided to photograph an example of industry, for example, as he said during his interview with Veit Görner, he "visited over 70 world-famous industrial companies. Most of them had a socio-romantic air I hadn't expected. I was looking for visual proof of what I thought would be antiseptic industrial zones. If these companies had been systematically documented one would have had the feeling one was back in the days of the Industrial Revolution. After this experience I realized that photography is no longer credible, and therefore found it much easier to legitimize digital picture processing."

Gursky has also stepped outside the bounds of traditional photography in that, as he told Calvin Tomkins, he is "working against the medium of photography that asks for a certain moment in time." By enabling him to juxtapose images shot at different times and to otherwise manipulate his pictures, digital technology has made it possible for him to create more-inclusive representations of various domains, with multiple perspectives and an array of details that would probably be absent in works by traditional photojournalists, who generally seek to draw attention to one thing. *Parliament, Bonn* (1998), for instance, portrays not only groups of lawmakers in animated discussions in the brightly lit, colorfully furnished legislative chamber, but also, in the dimly lit upper-level gallery, a hazy view of the visitors, their expressions seemingly indicating either bewilderment or boredom. Gursky's photo of the world-class Sha Tin racetrack, in Hong Kong, which, according to Tomkins, he "shot from the clubhouse roof," shows "the crowd in the infield, the homestretch with its two adjacent tracks (turf and dirt), the tote board, the island of trees in the middle, the backstretch, the high-rise apartment buildings beyond, and the distant mountains—everything but the race itself, which is visible nonetheless (postmodern irony!) on a giant television screen."

In departures from his usual focus, Gursky photographed one of Jackson Pollock's famous "drip" paintings at the Museum of Modern Art in New York City and—in what has been described as a nod to the all-gray works that the German artist Gerhard Richter painted in the 1960s—photographed a portion of a totally gray carpet, in *Untitled I* (1993). Gursky described the latter as "the first picture I made where the narrative aspect was completely lost." But, he added, referring to Richter's work, "That's painting and this is photography, and it's very important that you see this is photography—the texture, the way the light changes."

Gursky, who has traveled widely overseas in his search for subjects, continues to find inspiration in Düsseldorf, where he lives with his wife, Nina, a photographer. With two other artists, he is transforming an unused power station into an enormous studio space in Düsseldorf. The popularity of Gursky's photographs has increased significantly in recent years among art collectors; one of the six prints of *Prada II*, which Tomkins described as "showing three subtly illuminated, empty display shelves on a blank wall," fetched $270,000 at a Christie's auction in November 2000. Prada, a luxury Italian leather-goods and clothing manufacturer, is among several companies that have given Gursky commissions. His early exhibits were small group shows; he has since had major exhibitions in Milwaukee, Wisconsin; Pittsburgh, Pennsylvania; and London. The mid-career retrospective of his work mounted at the Museum of Modern Art in New York City, which extended from March 4 to May 15, 2001, included 40 of his works, dating from 1984 to the present.

From a previous union, Gursky has a young daughter, Cynthia, and son, Victor, who live with their mother. The photographer and his son are fervent soccer fans. A longtime jogger, Gursky ran in the New York City marathon in 2000. "It was one of the greatest experiences of my life," he told Tomkins. He finished the race in four hours, 28 minutes; he plans to run again in 2001 and hopes to finish in less than four hours: "One year older, and half an hour quicker," he quipped. He also enjoys skiing and playing tennis. — K.S.

Suggested Reading: *Art in America* p86+ July 1998; *Art News* p136+ Feb. 2001, with photo; *Artforum International* p104+ Jan. 2001; *Art/Text* p76+ Nov. 1999/Jan. 2000; *British Journal of Photography* p12+ Feb. 3, 1999; *Harper's Bazaar* p230+ Feb. 2001, with photo; Museum of Modern Art Web site; *New York* p119+ Mar. 26, 2001; *New York Times* E p33+ Mar. 2, 2001; *New Yorker* p62+ Jan. 22, 2001, with photo; *Newsweek* p54+ Mar. 19, 2001; *Parkett* p58+ No. 44, 1995; Galassi, Peter. *Andreas Gursky*, 2001

Selected Works: *Niagara Falls*, 1989; *Tokyo Stock Exchange*, 1990; *Salerno*, 1990; *Untitled V*, 1997; *Prada II*, 1997; *Parliament, Bonn*, 1998; *Shanghai*, 2000

Harden, Marcia Gay
(MAR-shuh)

Aug. 14, 1959– Actress. Address: c/o Endeavor Agency, 9701 Wilshire Blvd., 10th Fl., Beverly Hills, CA 90212

"I am the one without an Oscar," the actress Marcia Gay Harden once joked to David Richards for the *New York Times* (November 4, 1992), speaking of her role in the movie *Used People*, alongside such prize–winning luminaries as Shirley MacLaine, Marcello Mastroianni, Kathy Bates, and Jessica Tandy. Harden can no longer claim that distinction: in March 2001 the 41-year-old veteran of the stage and screen won the Academy Award for best supporting actress, for her portrayal of the artist Lee Krasner, the wife of the painter Jackson Pollock, in the biographical film *Pollock*. To many Hollywood observers, Harden's win came as a surprise; the Las Vegas oddsmakers declared her a 12-to-one long shot for best supporting actress, and the media predicted that 21-year-old newcomer Kate Hudson would take home the prize, for her role in *Almost Famous*, a much more commercially successful movie than *Pollock*. In the view of those who have followed Harden's career, however, her Oscar was well deserved. Rather than a fairy-tale rise to sudden fame (as experienced by, for example, Hilary Swank, who won an Oscar for her first big role), Harden has had a long and circuitous career. She has created a number of highly

Bill Davila/Retna Ltd.

original and critically acclaimed roles—in the film *Miller's Crossing* (1990), the Tony Award–winning play *Angels in America* (1992), and the television movie *Sinatra* (1993)—but somehow, until she won the Oscar, she had remained just below the radar of Hollywood fame. Ignoring the advice of a casting director who told her to soften her "nostril-flaring look" if she wanted to make it as a movie star, Harden has steadfastly charted her own course. With dark hazel eyes, bold eyebrows, full lips, and a curvaceous figure, she is a throwback to the 1940s movie queen—a stand-out in a crowd of actresses defined largely by their cuteness and disappearing waistlines. Throughout her career Harden has been buoyed by her own ambitions and deep-rooted confidence. "I always wanted to be in movies, I'm embarrassed to say," she told David Richards. "Yes, I set my cap on a high star, I did. . . . Obviously, I wouldn't be an actress if I didn't think I had a gift."

Marcia Gay Harden was born on August 14, 1959 in Tokyo, Japan (some sources say La Jolla, California). The daughter of a U.S. Navy captain and a former actress on the New York stage, Harden grew up in Japan, Greece, Italy, Germany, and Texas, following the path of her father's military career. "When I was a kid, I changed my identity all the time . . . ," Harden told Richards. "Every couple of years, we would move, which allowed you to get rid of your bad reputation and acquire a new one." Harden also remembers putting on shows with her three sisters and one brother on her family's back porch in Japan, and viewing ancient tragedies performed in millennia-old amphitheaters in Greece. While living in Munich, Germany, Harden took acting classes and began to consider an acting career seriously. After her first commercial part, as a drunk in a military propaganda movie, Harden enrolled in the University of Texas theater program.

After she graduated from college, in 1980, Harden moved to Washington, D.C., where a small but nurturing theater community thrived. There, Harden won two Helen Hayes acting awards and gained attention for a series of bold and confident portrayals, including one as the girl in *Equus*, Peter Shaffer's brutal play about adolescence and sexual obsession, and another as a wheelchair-bound woman in *And They Dance Real Slow in Jackson*. To prepare for the latter role, Harden spent several weeks traveling around Washington in a wheelchair and leg braces. "The first day we went to the Washington Monument," she recalled to Megan Rosenfeld for the *Washington Post* (April 1, 1983). "The guard was very helpful and put me at the head of the line for the elevator. . . . I noticed that mothers would always shoo their children away from me. And people always look to see if you're pretty. Somehow if you're pretty it's a greater tragedy. And if they think you have a boyfriend they seem relieved." Harden worked as a waitress and hostess to support herself during those years, struggling with her impatience to make it in a bigger way. "I get depressed and anxious. I want things while I'm young," she confessed then to Rosenfeld. "Probably I'm not ready for it now, and I won't see that for a few years. But I think I'm ready for a lot. Now."

In 1991 Harden moved to New York City and, in pursuit of a master's degree in fine arts, enrolled at New York University's Tisch School of the Arts. There, while performing in an unseemly role—as a character called Lucy the Fat Pig, a part that called for her to snort and otherwise degrade herself in front of the male lead—Harden was "discovered" by Donna Isaacson, a casting director who was in the audience. "Now here is someone with nerve," Isaacson thought, as she recalled to Margy Rochlin for the *New York Times* (March 4, 2001). "She just went with it. There was no holding back." By so doing, Harden beat out better-known actresses, including Julia Roberts and Demi Moore, for the female lead in Ethan and Joel Coen's *Miller's Crossing*. The Coen brothers had already established a reputation for mining unknown female acting talent; they had cast the relatively unknown Frances McDormand in *Blood Simple* (1984) and Holly Hunter in *Raising Arizona* (1987)—breakthrough movies for those women. In *Miller's Crossing*, an atmospheric period gangster film, Harden played Verna, a tough-talking, gun-toting, poker-faced gangster's moll, and she was lauded for what was repeatedly described as her "silken" performance. The movie was not widely seen, however, and afterward Harden returned to auditioning and doing catering and other odd jobs. "Everyone thinks offers are always pouring in," she told Rochlin. "Offers have never poured in. Never. I was auditioning a lot, but I didn't get the jobs. I had to pay off my school loans, you know?"

Harden appeared in a range of pictures in the 1990s, among them the independent films *Crush* (1992) and *The Spitfire Grill* (1996), such mainstream flops as *Desperate Measures* (1998) and *Meet Joe Black* (1998), and more successful ventures, including the comic *First Wives Club* (1996) and Disney's remake of *Flubber* (1997). "I'm a high-class migrant worker," she told Darrel L. Hope for *Venice* magazine (January 2001, on-line). "I go from job to job and sometimes I'm an artist in that job and sometimes I'm not." Though many critics panned her movies, Harden herself was consistently well reviewed, and words such as "underused" began to appear often in reference to her.

Out of her many roles in the 1990s, critics singled out for special praise Harden's gutsy performance as the 1940s film star Ava Gardner in the CBS television miniseries *Sinatra* (1992). Gardner was Sinatra's second wife, touted by MGM studio as "The World's Most Exciting Animal" and known both for her earthy magnetism and tempestuous behavior, both on and off the set. Harden was loath to take on the role of this Hollywood legend. "I couldn't exactly see myself playing the most beautiful woman in the world," she told Richards. To prepare, she watched Gardner's films and read her autobiography and Kitty Kelley's biography of Frank Sinatra, which describes incidents from his tumultuous marriage to Gardner (including a night that the couple spent shooting out the streetlights of Palm Springs). With the help of several coats of make-up and "fabulous costumes," Harden was eventually able to find Gardner's essence—"that raw, gutsy power she had," as she described it to Richards.

After playing Ava Gardner, Harden transformed herself into Marilyn Monroe, Jacqueline Kennedy Onassis, Audrey Hepburn, Anne Bancroft, and Barbra Streisand—all in the 1992 film *Used People*, in which she played a troubled woman who escapes reality by impersonating famous stars. From the pillbox-and-veil glamour of the widowed Onassis to Bancroft's seductive Mrs. Robinson from *The Graduate*, Harden reinvented herself again and again, a feat that, she recalled to Lois Romano for the *Washington Post* (December 23, 1992), was fun but also challenging. By this point in her career, Harden had embraced her image as a chameleon. "I like it when casting people say, 'Bring Marcia in. She's not totally right, but she can transform,'" she told Jesse Kornbluth for *Vanity Fair* (January 1993). "The only problem with this disappearing thing is that you never leave yourself behind. I never quite convince myself."

Harden is also remembered for her starring role on Broadway in the Tony Award–winning play *Angels in America*, by Tony Kushner. In Parts I and II of this fantastic epic about the American landscape of the 1980s, Harden portrayed Harper, the young, Valium-addicted wife of a gay Mormon lawyer. Some of the most lyrical episodes in the play depict Harper's hallucinations of a frozen Antarctic landscape, where she overcomes her fears and finds happiness with an Eskimo ice-fisherman. Harden was nominated for a Tony Award for her role in *Part I: Millennium Approaches* and won a Theater World Award for her role in *Part II: Perestroika*.

Harden met the actor Ed Harris while playing opposite him in Sam Shepard's *Simpatico* at the New York Shakespeare Festival in 1994. During the run she experienced Harris's legendary intensity and impulsiveness up close. "If Ed feels something coming on, he just does it," Harden told Rochlin. "There was this one point in the play where my character wags her finger in his face. Once, Ed just lunged forward and bit it." The invitation to join the cast of *Pollock*, a biographical film about the life of the American painter Jackson Pollock that Harris had been developing for years, came from Harris himself. "I knew that when Ed said, 'Do you want to be a part of this project?' it wasn't a cruise ship invitation. I knew it was more like getting into a boat, with him handing me a paddle," she told Bob Thompson for the *Toronto Sun* (September 9, 2000, on-line).

Harris directed and produced the film and also starred as Pollock, a pioneer of abstract-expressionist painting who rose to fame in the 1940s and fell into depression and alcoholism in the 1950s. Harden played Lee Krasner, Pollock's long-suffering and similarly volatile wife. Krasner, who as a painter was an important figure in her own right, single-mindedly promoted her hus-band's career and cared for the brilliant, obsessive, tormented Pollock. "She mothered him, nurtured him, bossed him, nagged him, pushed him, and enabled him," Harden told Darrel L. Hope. In order to get inside her character's skin, Harden took painting lessons (which she hated), read everything she could about Krasner, who died in 1984, and mastered her subject's Brooklyn accent; she even rolled around in one of Krasner's old beds. "It was a transformational type of role where I got to look different, sound different, and behave differently and exist in another skin," Harden told Hope. "I love that." Just as the historical Krasner had been as strong-willed as Pollock, Harden matched Harris's intensity on screen. In December 2000 she won the New York Film Critics Circle Award for her portrayal of Krasner.

Harden was alone in a hotel room when she learned about her Academy Award nomination as best supporting actress; lacking anyone she knew to celebrate with, she hugged the room-service waitress. In interviews before the Academy Awards ceremony, Harden said that win or lose, she planned to continue pursuing her love affair with acting. "Just the other day I went out on an audition and I connected to the character and I moved somebody. A woman in the room felt something," she told Hope. "I don't even care if I get the role because it reminded me that I'm an actor, that's why I'm doing this, to move somebody, to make people connect on some level what this crazy life experience is about and for myself to learn what it's about."

Harden's other film role in 2000 was in Clint Eastwood's *Space Cowboys*. In 2001 or 2002 she will appear in the films *Just Like Mona*, about a troubled relationship between a teenage boy and his mother, and *Gaudí Afternoon*, a thriller set in Barcelona, in which Harden plays an American woman who must team up with her husband's mistress to solve a mystery.

Harden appeared as the black-attired, morbid Masha in a star-filled production of Chekhov's *The Seagull* that was presented in New York City's Central Park in the summer of 2001. Currently, she is playing a college professor in the CBS television series *The Education of Max Bickford*, which premiered in September 2001.

In July 1996 Harden married Thaddaeus Scheel, a documentary filmmaker. The couple live in Venice, California, with their young daughter, Eulala Grace. — M.A.H.

Suggested Reading: *Entertainment Weekly* p40 Apr. 6, 2001, with photo; *New York Times* C p1 Nov. 4, 1992, with photos, p20 Mar. 4, 2001, with photos; *Toronto Sun* (on-line) Mar. 10, 2001; *Vanity Fair* p94 Jan. 1993, with photo; *Venice* (on-line) Jan. 2001; *Washington Post* B p7 Apr. 1, 1983, with photo, C p3 Dec. 23, 1992, B p1 Dec. 25, 1992, with photo

Selected Films: *Miller's Crossing*, 1990; *Crush*, 1992; *Used People*, 1992; *The Spitfire Grill*, 1996; *Meet Joe Black*, 1998; *Space Cowboys*, 2000; *Pollack*, 2000

Selected Plays—*Angels in America*, 1993; *Simpatico*, 1994

Selected Television Shows—*The Education of Max Bickford*, 2001–

Hulleah Tsinhnahjinnie

Harjo, Joy

May 9, 1951– Poet; screenwriter; musician; educator. Address: c/o W. W. Norton & Co., 500 Fifth Ave., New York, NY 10110

The work of the award-winning poet Joy Harjo reflects her strong feelings of connectedness to her Native American heritage and to the landscape of the American Southwest. Often autobiographical, Harjo's poems are rooted in memory as well as in myth, history, and the environment. "I feel strongly that I have a responsibility to all the sources that I am: to all past and future ancestors, to my home country, to all places that I touch down on and that are myself, to all voices, all women, all of my tribe, all people, all earth, and beyond that to all beginnings and endings," the poet told *Contemporary Authors* (2000). "In a strange kind of sense [writing] frees me to believe in myself, to be able to speak, to have voice, because I have to; it is my survival." Harjo has written six volumes of poetry; the first, *The Last Song*, was published in 1975, the most recent, *A Map to the Next World: Poems and Tales*, came out in 2000. Her most highly celebrated book is *In Mad Love and War* (1990), which won the William Carlos Williams Award of the Poetry Society of America, among other honors. Harjo has taught creative writing and poetry at a half-dozen universities. She also plays alto saxophone; her readings of her poems to the accompaniment of the band Joy Harjo and Poetic Justice have been recorded on three CDs.

"I don't believe I would be alive today if it hadn't been for writing," Harjo told Laura Coltelli for *Winged Words: American Indian Writers Speak* (1990), as excerpted in *Contemporary Literary Criticism* (1994). "There were times when I was conscious of holding onto a pen and letting the words flow, painful and from the gut, to keep from letting go of it all. Now, this was when I was much younger, and full of self-hatred. Writing helped me give voice to turn around a terrible silence that was killing me. And on a larger level, if we, as Indian people, Indian women, keep silent, then we will disappear, at least in this level of reality. As Audre Lorde says [in her 1996 book, *Sister Outsider: Essays and Speeches*] . . . , 'Your silence will not protect you,' which has been a quietly unanimous decision it seems, this last century with Indian people."

A registered member of the Muscogee Nation (also known as the Creek or Muskoke tribe), Joy Harjo was born on May 9, 1951 in Tulsa, Oklahoma. Her father, Allen W. Foster, was Muscogee; her mother, Wynema (Baker) Foster, was part French and part Cherokee. Native Americans of mixed heritage as well as white families lived in the neighborhood where Harjo was raised, on the north side of Tulsa. Harjo's Muscogee grandmother, Naomi Harjo, and great-aunt Lois Harjo Ball were both painters who earned bachelor of fine arts degrees in the early 1900s; her great-aunt became young Joy's mentor. "From the time I was very small you could always find me drawing, whether it was in the dirt or on paper. That was the one thing that made me happy," Harjo told Marilyn Kallett for the *Kenyon Review* (Summer 1993). As a teenager Harjo studied painting and theater at the Institute of American Indian Arts, an innovative program in Santa Fe, New Mexico. After she graduated, in 1967, she joined a Native American dance troupe and took a number of odd jobs.

Harjo spent one semester as a pre-med student at the University of New Mexico before switching her major to painting. She also took courses in the language of the Navajo Nation. After attending readings by Galway Kinnell, Simon Ortiz, Leslie Marman Silko, and other poets, she gave up painting and began writing poetry. "I found that language, through poetry, was taking on more magical qualities than my painting," Harjo explained to Laura Coltelli. "I could say more when I wrote. Soon it wasn't a choice. Poetry-speaking 'called me' in a sense. And I couldn't say no." Ortiz's performance in particular showed her that "the voice of a poet can be a natural speaking voice, and poetry can include the experience of a person of the Southwest like me," as she explained for the *Heath Anthology of American Literature Newsletter* (Fall 1991, on-line). In 1976 she earned a B.A. degree from the University of New Mexico.

Harjo then entered the prestigious Iowa Writers' Workshop, at the University of Iowa, where she took classes with Leslie Silko. At that time Harjo was a single mother raising two children (a son, Phil, and a daughter, Rainy Dawn). When she first arrived at the university, she told Marilyn Kallett, she felt as if she had "walked into a strange land in which I had to learn another language. This comes from being of native background, from the West, but it also comes from being a woman in that institution. I heard the Director say once to a group of possible funders—I was one of the people they chose to perform for them in the workshop—he told them that the place was actually geared for male writers, which is honest; it was true, but I was shocked. I remember [the novelist] Jayne Anne Phillips and I looking at each other, like 'Can you believe this? Then why are we sitting here?'" Harjo received a master's degree in fine arts from the university in 1978. She told Kallett that although she "learned a lot about technique" at the Iowa Writers' Workshop, she was disappointed to find "the art of poetry had broken down into sterile exercises. And yet, I know I admire some of the work of those people who taught me. But the system had separated itself from the community, from myth, from humanhood."

Earlier, in 1978, Harjo had begun teaching at the Institute of American Indian Arts, where she remained until 1979. Her first full-length volume of poetry, *What Moon Drove Me to This?*, was released the following year; included in the text were nine connected poems originally published in 1975 as a 15-page chapbook entitled *The Last Song*. From 1980 to 1983 Harjo served as a writer and consultant for two private organizations—the Native American Public Broadcasting Consortium and the National Indian Youth Council—and a federal agency, the National Endowment for the Arts (NEA). Harjo's experience with the NEA was at times both "comical" and "bizarre," as she explained to Laura Coltelli. "When I was on the National Endowment for the Arts literature panel I was often the spokesperson-representative for Indian people, black people, all minority people, including women's, lesbian, and gay groups. It was rather ridiculous and angering at the same time, for we were all considered outside the mainstream of American literature. And it's not true, for often we are closer to the center."

Repetition of phrases marked some of the poems in Harjo's second book, *She Had Some Horses* (1983). For example, in a poem about the rape of a child, the line "She thought she woke up" serves as a refrain. Some of Harjo's early poems, such as "Kansas City" and "Heartbeat," feature Noni Daylight, a character Harjo created as a means of telling the stories of women. Noni Daylight began "as a

name I gave a real-life woman I couldn't name in a poem," Harjo explained to Laura Coltelli. "Then she evolved into her own person, took on her own life. And then she left my poems and went into a poem by Barney Bush, a Shawnee poet, and I never saw her again. She never came back!" The image of the moon also recurred in Harjo's early work, as a symbol both of the past and of female energy. Often labeled a feminist writer, Harjo has not hesitated to acknowledge that her poetry is "woman-identified," as she described it to Coltelli. "One of the funniest questions I have been asked as a visitor to an Indian-culture class in a university is, by a male student, 'Where are the men in your poems?' He was offended because he didn't see himself, not in the form that he looked for. I truly feel there is a new language coming about—look at the work of Meridel Le Sueur, Sharon Doubiago, Linda Hogan, Alice Walker—it's coming from the women."

As Harjo explained to Laura Coltelli, her poems "begin with the seed of an emotion, a place, and then move from there." She told Coltelli that she has come to view each poem as the culmination of "an often long journey that can begin years earlier, say with the blur of the memory of the sun on someone's cheek, a certain smell, an ache." The resulting poem is "sifted through a point, a lake in my heart through which language must come." Harjo's work is informed by her belief that art emerges from a place "beyond us . . . from that source of utter creation, the Creator, or God," as she told *Contemporary Authors*. "We are technicians here on Earth, but also co-creators. . . . Ultimately humans have a small hand in it. We serve it. We have to put ourselves in the way of it, and get out of the way ourselves." Harjo's approach does not involve "taking established forms and developing them," as she explained to *Contemporary Authors*. "I admire a finely constructed sonnet but I do not wish to work in that Euro-classical form. I honor that direction, but I am working to find my own place. . . . I am influenced by Muscogean forms, European and African forms, as well as others that have influenced me [such as] Navajo. . . . [The Navajo language] influenced me deeply because intimate to the language were the shapes of the landscape, the history. I became aware of layers of meaning marked by sandhills, by the gestures of the earth." Harjo was also inspired by the civil rights movement and the activities of the American Indian Movement, an organization responsible for sparking "an intertribal awareness in [the U.S.]," as she told Paul Seesequasis for the magazine *Aboriginal Voices* (1995, on-line). "I started writing out of that need for that river of concern. Up to that point a lot of us felt shame for what we were. That movement helped galvanize us and open us up like nothing else."

Harjo collaborated with the astronomer and photographer Stephen Strom on *Secrets from the Corner of the World* (1989), a book of 60 prose poems set in the Southwest, each of which was accompanied by one of Strom's photographs. From 1985 until 1988 she was an assistant professor at the University of Colorado at Boulder, during which time she began playing the saxophone. She spent the following two years as an associate professor at the University of Arizona at Tucson before becoming a tenured professor at the University of New Mexico at Albuquerque, where she taught from 1991 to 1997. She took a leave of absence from academia to concentrate on her work with Poetic Justice.

Poetic Justice evolved out of a collaboration between Harjo and the drummer Susan M. Williams in 1992. In addition to Williams and Harjo, who provides vocals and plays the saxophone, for a while the band featured the guitarist William Bluehouse Johnson, the bassist John L. Williams, the guitarist Richard Carbajal, and Frank Poocha, a percussionist who also performs tribal songs. The band has made three recordings: *Furious Light* (1986), *The Woman Who Fell from the Sky* (1994), and *Letter from the End of the Twentieth Century* (1997); a fourth, tentatively titled "Crossing the Border," is in the works. Following the release of *Letter from the End of the Twentieth Century*, Poetic Justice received an award for Outstanding Musical Achievement from First Americans in the Arts (1998); the recording was also nominated for awards in eight categories at the 1998 National Native Music Awards. The band's music incorporates elements of rock, jazz, reggae, and tribal music. Recently Harjo has been traveling with a rotating group of musicians known as Joy Harjo and Her Poetic Justice Band.

African-American music in particular has "been critical to my development as a writer and musician," Harjo told *Contemporary Authors*. "There is history and a relationship between Africans and Muscogean peoples begun in the southeastern U.S. We've influenced each other, yet this influence is rarely talked about. I can hear the African influence in our stomp dance music, and can hear Muscogean influence in jazz, the blues, and rock. . . . The first poetry I heard and recognized as pure poetry was the improvised line of a trumpet player on a jazz tune on the radio when I was four years old. . . . I've been trying to get it right ever since."

The year 1990 marked the appearance of Harjo's fourth volume of poetry, *In Mad Love and War*, a very personal take on such subjects as politics, heritage, and the healing power of poetry. It contains pieces dedicated to the Native American activists Jacqueline Peters and Anna Mae Pictou Aquash, the jazz saxophonist Charlie Parker, and the pop singer Nat King Cole. *In Mad Love and War* received several awards in 1991, among them the Josephine Miles Award for excellence in literature, the William Carlos Williams Award, and the American Book Award, as well as prizes from the Poetry Society of America and the Before Columbus Foundation. Later, in 1995, the book also received the Delmore Schwartz Memorial Award and the Mountains and Plains Booksellers' Award.

In a review for *Prairie Schooner* (Summer 1992), Kathleen West wrote, "*In Mad Love and War* has the power and beauty of prophecy and all the hope of love poised at its passionate beginning. It allows us to enter the place 'we haven't imagined' and allows us to imagine what we will do when we are there."

The title of Harjo's next volume of poetry, *The Woman Who Fell from the Sky* (1994), refers to an Iroquois creation myth. The book, which contains a number of prose poems, was sold along with a cassette featuring Harjo's poetry and the music of Poetic Justice; it received an Oklahoma Book Arts Award in 1994. In 1997 Harjo and Gloria Bird co-edited *Reinventing the Enemy's Language: North American Native Women's Writing*, a social and political call to arms that includes work by approximately 80 women, among them the writers Louise Erdrich and Mary Brave Bird and various activists, including Wilma Mankiller, Beatrice Medicine, and Winona LaDuke. The year 2000 saw the release of Harjo's fifth full-length collection of poetry, *A Map to the Next World: Poems and Tales*, as well as a children's book, *The Good Luck Cat*, about a girl's friendship with her pet cat, Woogie. "A Love Supreme," a collection of the author's essays, and a volume of new and selected poems by Harjo are scheduled to be published in the near future.

In 1982 Harjo completed a nondegree program at the Anthropology Film Center in Santa Fe, New Mexico. She has since written a number of screenplays, including "When We Used to Be Humans" (which has never been published) and *Origin of Apache Crown Dance* (1985). From 1987 to 1990 Harjo was a member of the board of directors of the Native American Public Broadcasting Consortium. She also completed a songwriting workshop at the Berklee College of Music, in Boston, Massachusetts, in 1998. Harjo provided narration for a series on Native Americans that aired on Turner Network Television and the Emmy Award–winning 1995 *National Geographic Explorer* segment on the Navajo "code-talkers" who, using the Navajo language during World War II, helped to encode military messages that eluded Japanese cryptographers.

Harjo, who currently lives in Honolulu, Hawaii, is a member of the advisory boards of the New Mexico and the national chapters of the writers' organization PEN, and she has served on the editorial boards of such publications as *Contact II*, *Tyuonyi*, and the *High Plains Literary Review*. Her many honors include the Academy of American Poetry Award (1976); a Lifetime Achievement Award from the Native Writers' Circle of the Americas (1995); the New Mexico Governor's Award for Excellence in the Arts (1997); the Lila Wallace–Reader's Digest Award (1998); and a Distinguished Achievement Award from the Western Literature Association (2000). She has received poetry fellowships from the National Endowment for the Arts (1978) and the Wittner Byner Poetry Foundation (1994). In 1998 she received an honorary doctorate from St. Mary-in-the-Woods College, Indiana, and was appointed to the National Council on the Arts by then–president Bill Clinton.

"Today, just about everything inspires me to continue writing," Harjo told an interviewer in connection with the 1998 edition of the *Heath Anthology of American Literature* (one of the many anthologies that include her poetry), as cited on the Georgetown University Web site. "My granddaughter inspires me to think about the future. I have intense dreams and visions that inspire me. And I have an amazement for survival that keeps me writing." — C.L.

Suggested Reading: *American Indian Quarterly* p13+ Summer/Fall 1999; *MELUS* [The Society for the Study of the Multi-Ethnic Literature of the United States] p5+ Spring 1989/1990; *New York Times* C p11 Apr. 21, 1997, with photos;

Progressive p22+ Mar. 1992; *Contemporary Authors* new rev. ser. vol. 91, 2000; *Contemporary Literary Criticism* vol. 83, 1994; Pearlman, Mickey. *Listen to Their Voices: Twenty Interviews with Women Who Write*, 1993

Selected Books: *The Last Song*, 1975; *What Moon Drove Me to This?*, 1980; *She Had Some Horses*, 1983; *Secrets from the Center of the World*, 1989; *In Mad Love and War*, 1990; *The Woman Who Fell from the Sky*, 1994; *The Good Luck Cat*, 2000; *A Map to the Next World: Poems and Tales*, 2000

Selected Recordings: with Poetic Justice— *Furious Light*, 1986; *The Woman Who Fell from the Sky*, 1994; *Letter from the End of the Twentieth Century*, 1997

Jonathan Daniel/Allsport

Harrison, Marvin

Aug. 25, 1972– Wide receiver for the Indianapolis Colts. Address: Indianapolis Colts, P.O. Box 535000, Indianapolis, IN 46253

Since he entered the National Football League (NFL), in 1996, as a member of the Indianapolis Colts, Marvin Harrison has quietly worked his way into the elite ranks of NFL wide receivers. With the exception of 1998, when he was injured, Harrison has led the Colts in receptions every year since he joined the team. In 1999 he led all NFL receivers, with 115 catches for 1,663 yards. At six feet and approximately 180 pounds, Harrison is relatively

small for a wide receiver; he makes up for his size with speed, precise pass patterns, the ability to hold onto the ball, and a good understanding of the game. "I think his mind goes faster than his feet— and his feet are pretty fast," the Colts' wide-receivers coach, Jay Norvell, told David Hughes for the Terre-Haute, Indiana *Tribune-Star* (September 1999, on-line). Along with quarterback Payton Manning (with whom Harrison has cultivated a close friendship) and running back Edgerrin James, Harrison is a member of the Colts' "Big Three," the triumvirate that has transformed the team from one of the worst in the NFL to one of the best.

Marvin Harrison was born on August 25, 1972 and raised in Philadelphia, Pennsylvania. When he was two years old, his father died of a genetic disease, and his mother, Linda, started working two jobs to support the family. She was rather strict, instilling a sense of discipline in Harrison that served him well throughout his school years and is viewed as a great asset by his coaches and other staff of the Indianapolis Colts. "You'd like to put him on a commercial for young players, and say, 'If you want to become a great player, do what Marvin Harrison has done—work every day, including the off-season, and make yourself into a superstar," the Colts' president, Bill Polian, told Paul Attner for *Sporting News* (December 13, 1999).

Harrison attended Roman Catholic High School, in Philadelphia, where he excelled at both basketball and football. As a running back and wide receiver, he won three Maxwell Awards, given each year to Philadelphia's top high-school football player. Having earned a football scholarship, Harrison entered Syracuse University, in Syracuse, New York, in 1991. He lettered in his first year with the school football team, the Orangemen, and became a starting wide receiver in his sophomore year. By the time he finished his senior year, he had broken the school record for total receiving yards—2,718. His 20 touchdowns placed him second on Syracuse University's all-time list, and his total of 135 receptions was the second-best in team history. He was also voted to the All-Big East team. Harrison's farewell game as a Syracuse student was in the Gator Bowl, held in Jacksonville, Florida, in which he made a remarkable seven catches for 173 yards and two touchdowns as his team beat the Clemson Tigers, 41–0.

Though his college performance was impressive, his quiet demeanor both on and off the field kept Harrison from becoming a high-profile player. He was picked 19th overall by the Indianapolis Colts in the 1996 pro draft—a respectable but not exceptional number; three other receivers were drafted before him. He signed a five-year contract worth $5.8 million—a rather modest sum for an up-and-coming football star. At that time the Colts were a mediocre team at best, and Harrison was seen as a ray of hope for them.

Harrison worked hard in the 1996 preseason. He proceeded to lead the team in receptions that year, with 64 catches for 836 yards and eight touchdowns. On December 15, in a game against the Kansas City Chiefs, he caught six passes for 103 yards and three touchdowns, and the Colts won, 24–19. For that achievement, Harrison was named the American Football Conference (AFC) Offensive Player of the Week. "Marvin has all the things you like," the Colts' coach Lindy Infante said to Mike Chappel for the *Buffalo News* (October 6, 1996). "He has all the physical tools, and he's a bright guy who picks up the game plans each and every week. He doesn't play like a rookie. He has a sense for coverages, for finding the soft spot, of when to cut and how to get around people, and those skills will only get better."

In addition to his achievements on the field, Harrison impressed his fellow players with his capacious appetite. Sausages, french fries, ice cream sundaes—when he wasn't playing, he always seemed to be eating. Every week he would order a box of 30 Tastykakes—his favorite snack—to keep in his locker. "He's a freak of nature," the Colts' defensive tackle Tony McCoy told Attner. "I have never seen anyone eat what he eats and keep a chiseled body. His metabolism must be going 100 miles per hour. I gain five pounds just looking at one of those Tastykakes." McCoy, who was Harrison's hotel roommate for road games, later roomed with someone else to avoid the constant temptation to snack.

In 1997 Harrison again led the Colts in receptions, with 73 catches for 866 yards and six touchdowns. As a team, though, the Colts were the worst in the league, with three wins and 13 losses. Things did not improve for them the following year; they posted the same miserable record of 3–13. Harrison played well for the first 12 games of the 1998 season: he had 59 catches for 776 yards and seven touchdowns. A dislocated shoulder forced him out of the lineup for the remainder of the season.

By the spring of 1999, Harrison had fully recovered from his injury, and he opted to attend a 10-week spring training camp to work with the Colts' young, talented quarterback, Payton Manning. He and Manning perfected their timing on various pass routes, usually working on just one route per day until they could execute it flawlessly. Often, when the other players stopped to rest, Manning and Harrison continued to practice. "Marvin and I have a bond, a feel that's hard to describe," Manning told Peter King for *Sports Illustrated* (October 4, 1999). "We go to dinner. We hang around. We spend extra time on the practice field. . . . Even when a play breaks down, we each know what the other's doing."

The dynamic between Manning and Harrison was an essential part of the Colts' transformative, 1999 season, in which they won their division and went 13–3 after having finished in last place the previous two seasons. Going into the third week of the 1999 season, the Colts had one win and one loss and faced a crucial game against the San Diego Chargers and its formidable defense. To the surprise of many, Manning and Harrison picked the defense apart. Harrison hauled in 13 passes for 196 yards and a touchdown (the most catches ever for a Colts wide receiver) as his team sealed a comeback victory, 27–19. Against the Dallas Cowboys on October 31, Harrison blazed by the league's premier defensive back, Deion Sanders, for a touchdown, and the Colts beat the Cowboys, 34–24. "People need to start talking about Marvin Harrison," Sanders later said to Attner. "He's a bad boy. He's not getting all the credit because he's not a flamboyant receiver. He's like a blue-collar worker. He goes out and gets his job done and takes it to the house."

Harrison continued to excel as the year went on. He finished the season with 115 catches for 1,663 yards and 12 touchdowns and was voted to the Pro-Bowl. His receiving record of 1,663 yards was the best in the league that year and the fifth best of all time. He also became the 26th player in the history of pro football to catch 100 or more passes in a season. Toward the end of the year, defenses started to pay special attention to Harrison, by double-teaming him. For that reason he did not score a touchdown in the final seven games of the season; one of them was a play-off game that the Colts lost to the Tennessee Titans. The fact that two of the Colts' other receivers, E. G. Green and Jerome Pathon, were playing while injured added to Harrison's difficulties, because it allowed teams to focus on him to the exclusion of the other receivers. "That comes with the territory," Harrison told Larry Schoolnick for the *Syracuse Herald Journal* (August 30, 2000). "There have been receivers who have been marked men for 10 years or more, guys like Michael Irvin and Jerry Rice, and they kept doing the job. We have an offensive scheme to put me into different situations that will get me the ball."

After the 1999 season Harrison signed a four-year contract with the Colts that was worth approximately $25 million. In 2000 he continued to perform in stellar fashion, leading the team in catches (102) and becoming the fifth receiver in league history to accumulate 100 receptions in two successive seasons. His 14 touchdowns tied a 1959 team record, held by Raymond Berry; he also tied the Colts record set by Berry for touchdown receptions in the most games. The Colts appeared unlikely to make the play-offs when, with three games left in the season, they had compiled a lackluster 7–6 record. But thanks in part to strong performances by Harrison, the team posted victories in their last three games and won a wildcard spot in the play-offs. On December 30, 2000 the Colts lost in overtime to the Miami Dolphins, by a score of 23–17, after squandering several opportunities for a victo-ry. In the first six games of the 2001 season, during which the Colts went 3–3, Harrison led the team with 38 receptions for 545 yards and seven touchdowns.

Harrison, who is not married, lives in Philadelphia during most of the off-season. — P.G.H.

Suggested Reading: (Albany) *Times Union* pC3 Oct. 19, 1995; *Boston Globe* p45 Apr. 19, 1996, with photo; *Buffalo News* C p7 Oct. 6, 1996, with photo; *New York Times* p1+ Oct. 8, 1994, D p7 Nov. 15, 1999; *Sporting News* p18 Dec. 23, 1996, p18+ Dec. 13, 1999, with photo; *Sports Illustrated* p106+ Oct. 4, 1999; *Syracuse Herald Journal* F p5 Aug. 30, 2000; (Terre-Haute, Indiana) *Tribune-Star* (on-line) Sep. 1999, with photo

---

Courtesy of UC Berkeley Office of Public Affairs

Hass, Robert

Mar. 1, 1941– Poet; literary critic; college teacher. Address: 576 Santa Barbara Rd., Berkeley, CA 97407

In his poetry, Robert Hass offers candid depictions of human relationships and presents views of the natural world that reflect the tradition of West Coast nature writers. Hass served as the poet laureate of the United States from 1995 to 1997; a professor of English at the University of California at Berkeley, he has translated works by the 17th-century Japanese poet Bashō Matsuo and helped to translate those by the Nobel Prize–winning Polish expatriate Czeslaw Milosz (although, by his own admission, he knows little Japanese or Polish). Hass's preferred forms include iambic pentameter, haiku, and the prose poem, and he has often employed the long line associated with the poetry of Walt Whitman and Allen Ginsberg. Hass told Yvonne French for the *LC Information Bulletin* (October 30, 1995), published by the Library of Congress, that a longer line provides him with "more breath. . . . It's also a matter of growing up, an accumulation of karma, the stuff that can't be fixed. It's deeply mysterious." In a review of Hass's book *Human Wishes* for the *New York Times Book Review* (November 12, 1989), quoted in part in *Contemporary Literary Criticism* (1996), the poet Carolyn Kizer wrote, "Robert Hass is so intelligent that to read his poetry or prose, or to hear him speak, gives one an almost visceral pleasure. . . . Mr. Hass is a poet of domestic passion—for children, friends, the household, the neighborhood, for women as lovers, women as friends. His publisher speaks of his work as poems of loss, of mutilation. Rather, he is a poet of abundance, a romantic of the breakfast table, of a companionable walk in his California hills."

Although it is perpetually fashionable in intellectual circles to bemoan the death of literature, Hass has maintained that American poetry is enjoying a period of "tremendous vitality," as he put it to Yvonne French. "Three books of poetry are published a day; there are 400 poetry journals on the Internet. . . . Whole areas—Native American, Chinese, Asian, African American, Latino—that have been mute, who have gotten their world spoken for them by others, are writing. . . . A lot of poetry is being recited in bookstores and coffeehouses. Every time the politics get really bad, the poetry gets really good. I think it has to do with the demoralization of what people perceive as the shrinking of the American economy. . . . One economic trend everyone agrees to in the country is the consolidation of wealth and the increase of poverty. The arts get active when reality needs re-aligning." During his tenure as poet laureate, Hass adopted the mantra "Imagination makes communities," encouraging people from all walks of life to try writing poetry. "We are symbol-making beings," he explained to Susan Adams for *Forbes* (May 17, 1999). "Everyone tastes that in some part of their being and wants to say in their own terms what it means to be alive. Poetry is the most common way, because the material of poetry is the stream of language that is constantly going on in our heads. It's very low tech. Anyone can do it."

Robert Hass was born on March 1, 1941 in San Francisco to Fred Hass, a businessman, and Helen (Dahling) Hass. He grew up in the Marin County suburb of San Rafael, California, where he attended private Catholic school. As children, Hass and his brother stayed up late at night reading works by Robert Lowell and Rudyard Kipling. Eventually he became familiar with the poetry of Beat writers as well as members of the San Francisco Renaissance; his greatest poetic influences were Gary Snyder and Kenneth Rexroth. (He has also named William Wordsworth and Ezra Pound as influential in his development as a poet.) In 1962 Hass married Earlene Leif, with whom he had three children: Leif, Kristin, and Luke. He received a B.A. degree from St. Mary's College of California, in Moraga, in 1963, and M.A. and Ph.D. degrees from Stanford University, also in California, in 1965 and 1971, respectively. From 1967 to 1971 he was an assistant professor at the State University of New York at Buffalo; he also taught English at St. Mary's from 1971 to 1974 and 1975 to 1989.

Hass's first book, *Field Guide*, which drew upon the poet's knowledge of the California landscape, was awarded the Yale Series Younger Poets Award when it was published, in 1973. In the *Southwest Review*, as quoted in *Contemporary Authors* (1999), Michael Walters wrote that the book served as "a means of naming things, of establishing an identity through one's surroundings, of translating the natural world into one's private history. This is a lot to accomplish, yet Robert Hass manages it with clarity and compassion." The poet Stanley Kunitz, who selected the book for the Yale award, wrote in his foreword to *Field Guide*, "Reading a poem by Robert Hass is like stepping into the ocean when the temperature of the water is not much different from that of the air. You scarcely know, until you feel the undertow tug at you, that you have entered into another element. Suddenly the deep is there, teeming with life."

Hass's second book of poetry, *Praise*, was published in 1979. Referring to the title, he told Grace Cavalieri for *American Poetry Review* (March/April 1997), "I think that to praise or dispraise, to enchant or disenchant, both of which functions art has, you have to include a lot of one if you're going to do the other. I think poetry that says *yes* has to swallow great goblets of darkness; and poetry that says *no* has to say no in the face of

the fact that there must be reasons why the poet has chosen to live in order to say it." In the Hollins University literary journal *Hollins Critic* (February 1980), Robert Miklitsch, a professor of cultural and literary theory, wrote, as quoted in *Contemporary Authors* (1999), that the publication of *Praise* marked "the emergence of a major American poet."

Hass's next book, a work of nonfiction called *Twentieth Century Pleasures* (1984), contains critical essays on subjects including Robert Lowell, James Wright, Czeslaw Milosz, and Rainer Maria Rilke. His third book of poetry, *Human Wishes*, was not published until 1989. Hass has always taken a leisurely approach to publishing his work; he told David Streitfeld for the *Washington Post* (May 8, 1995), "I never wanted to have, like John Updike said about T.S. Eliot, a 'reluctant oeuvre,' but I do seem to be slow. I tend to write a lot and throw away a lot." Also in 1989 Hass began teaching English at the University of California at Berkeley.

One of the poetic forms for which Hass has felt an affinity is haiku. In 1994 he translated and edited *The Essential Haiku: Versions of Bashō, Buson, & Issa* (the last two names are those of the 18th-century Japanese poet Buson Yosa and the 18th–19th-century Japanese poet Issa Kobayashi). Although he has occasionally written what he calls "Metro Haikus" while riding the subway, Hass usually relies on the discovery of what he refers to as "found haiku," or overheard dialogue that happens to conform to haiku structure. "Two guys in $500 overcoats get on at the Farragut North Station," he recalled to Francis X. Clines for the *New York Times* (December 9, 1996). "And one says to the other, 'Well, if he had been focused, he wouldn't even have considered it.' Seventeen syllables!" From haiku Hass learned a precise attention to detail, something that many commentators on his work have noted. "There's a tremendous tendency, especially in our hurried-up society, to abstract, to not see, not notice," Hass told Kurt Shillinger for the *Christian Science Monitor* (October 12, 1995). "I was attracted to Japanese poetry because it was the poetry of ordinary attention. And it was hugely arresting. . . . For me, the way to anchor and clarify is with a poem—my so-called Zen-clear way of noting detail."

Hass has worked closely with Czeslaw Milosz, assisting him in translating from Polish into English works including *Provinces* (1993), *Facing the River: New Poems* (1995), and Milosz's collected poems. (The men are neighbors and share a publisher.) Milosz first translates a poem into rough English, and then he and Hass work together to shape the piece into what both regard as satisfactory poetry. "Translation is really a problem-solving task," Hass explained to *American Poet* (Spring 1996), in an interview reprinted on the Academy of American Poets Web site. "Every once in a while you see the original and something comes into your head that is also a formal solution to the problem of getting it into lively English, and you feel like you've written a poem. But that's pretty rare."

In 1995, when James H. Billington, the librarian of Congress, chose Hass to succeed Rita Dove as the nation's poet laureate, Hass became the first West Coast native to hold that post. Hass welcomed the opportunity to act as an ambassador for American poetry. "If nobody stood up and said that the life of the imagination in this country matters, it would be a shame," Yvonne French quoted him as saying. "What we lobby for is the mind and the heart. They're not at all in danger in this country, but I think the country is in danger in relation to them." The poet laureate has few official responsibilities—it is assumed that the person will continue to concentrate on his or her regular work—but like Dove, who maintained an exhausting schedule of radio and television appearances, Hass used his position to advocate for poetry and literacy. "I thought it would be an interesting thing to do to go where poets don't go," he told Francis X. Clines. Hass visited business and service organizations such as the Rotary Club, some of which present a different guest speaker each week. He spoke to the businesspeople about "public literacy and the condition of public education, support for the schools, and for the arts in schools," as he told American Poet. "There's massive middle-class flight from public schools, education is desperately underfunded, the rate of literacy is rapidly declining. I think it's useful to have somebody who's not running for office going around and saying, 'This is a catastrophe. If you want schools, and if you want an educated public, you have to pay for it.'"

As poet laureate Hass also wrote a weekly newspaper column, for which he selected a poem and introduced it; the column appeared in the Washington Post and was syndicated in 25 other newspapers around the country. These poems were later compiled in Poet's Choice: Poems for Everyday Life (1998). Another project organized by the poet was "Watershed," a six-day conference sponsored by the Orion Society (an environmental-education organization) and the Library of Congress as well as Hass, which aimed to introduce nature writing to inner-city children. Hass believes that the work of poets can have a concrete effect on the life of the nation. "There are instances: Thoreau read Wordsworth, Muir read Thoreau, [President Theodore] Roosevelt read Muir, and you got national parks," he told Sarah Pollock for Mother Jones (March 1997). "It took a century for this to happen, for artistic values to percolate down to where honoring the relation of people's imagination to the land, or beauty, or to wild things, was issued in legislation."

Hass's most recent book of poetry, Sun Under Wood: New Poems, was published in 1996. Like much of his work, the poems include personal material, such as the breakup of his marriage and his mother's alcoholism. "As an artist, you have the job of working out whatever is given to you to work out," he told Sarah Pollock. "In Sun Under Wood, I found myself realizing that I had to write the poems of middle age, which were to me poems of

what's irreparable in the world, the ways you've [expletive] up in your own life, things you can't change. Yet compared to the scale of injustice in the world, how do I write about this? At some level, you have to be able to say, 'This is my task.' It's in small, local ways that you keep yourself alive and refresh ideas that are always going into dead abstraction." In an assessment of the book for American Poetry Review (May/June 2000), Christopher Buckley wrote that Hass "mitigates the weight" of his confessional tales with an "equally intense view of and attention to the natural world, his willingness to see himself as part of it, existing at that level—a nod to eastern thought."

Hass has earned many awards and honors. In 1978 he was the poet-in-residence at the Frost Place, a Franconia, New Hampshire, farm named for the poet Robert Frost. Praise captured the William Carlos Williams Award; Twentieth Century Pleasures received the National Book Critics Circle Award for Criticism, and Sun Under Wood: New Poems received the same award in the poetry category. Hass has held a Danforth Fellowship (1963–67), a Guggenheim Fellowship (1980), and a MacArthur grant—the so-called "genius" award (1984–89). In 1986 he received the PEN award for translation, and in 1997 he was named Educator of the Year by the North American Association on Environmental Education. Hass has served as a visiting lecturer at the University of Virginia (1974), Goddard College, in Plainfield, Vermont (1976), and Columbia University, in New York City (1982).

Hass has been married since 1995 to Brenda Hillman, a poet who teaches at St. Mary's College; the couple live in Berkeley, California. In addition to his three children from his first marriage, he has one stepchild. — C.L.

Suggested Reading: American Poetry Review p41+ Mar./Apr. 1997, with photos; Christian Science Monitor p1+ Oct. 11, 1995, with photos; Mother Jones p18+ Mar. 1997, with photo; New York Times C p11+ May 8, 1995, with photo, A p1 Dec. 9, 1996, with photo; Publishers Weekly p51+ Oct. 28, 1996, with photo; Sierra p48+ Nov./Dec. 2000, with photo; Contemporary Authors vol. 71, 1999; Contemporary Literary Criticism Yearbook, 1996

Selected Books: as author—Field Guide, 1973; Praise, 1979; Twentieth Century Pleasures: Prose on Poetry, 1984; Human Wishes, 1989; Sun Under Wood: New Poems, 1996; as translator and editor—The Essential Haiku: Versions of Bashō, Buson, & Issa (1994); as co-translator (with Czeslaw Milosz)—Provinces, 1993, Facing the River: New Poems 1995, A Treatise on Poetry, 2001; as editor—Tomas Transtomer, 1987; Rock and Hawk: A Selection of Shorter Poems [by Robinson Jeffers], 1987; as co-editor—Into the Garden: A Wedding Anthology: Poetry & Prose on Love and Marriage (with Stephen Mitchell), 1993; The Best American Poetry 2001 (with David Lehman)

Hendrickson's most important discovery came in 1990, when she found what turned out to be the largest, most complete, and best-preserved skeleton of a *Tyrannosaurus rex* ever unearthed. The 42-foot fossil was named Sue, after Hendrickson, and installed at the Field Museum in Chicago, following a dispute over ownership. In the 1980s in South America, hundreds of miles from the ocean, Hendrickson uncovered a "graveyard" full of ancient whale bones. In 1998–99, with the marine archaeologist Franck Goddio, she dove to recover the ships of Napoleon's that were sunk by the British admiral Horatio Nelson in the Battle of the Nile in 1798. "I just want to feel that discovery moment again," she told Joseph B. Verrengia, explaining the globe-trotting lifestyle she has pursued since the age of 17. "I'm lucky," she told Bruce Frankel for *People* (July 24, 2000). "I think about what I want to do and I do it. Almost no one has that freedom."

The second of three children, Sue Hendrickson was born on December 2, 1949 in Munster, Indiana, a southern suburb of Chicago just across the Indiana-Illinois border. Her mother, Mary, was a teacher (according to some sources, she was a real-estate agent); her father, Lee, worked as a railroad purchasing agent. As a child, she was a voracious reader and a good student with an active inner life. "I was really shy and always walked with my head down, but my curiosity was strong," she told Ritu Upadhyay for *Time for Kids* (March 2, 2001). "I'd go up and down the alley and poke the wire trash burner behind our house, looking for treasures," she recalled to Bruce Frankel. Eventually losing interest in school and growing restless in suburbia, Hendrickson dropped out of high school and left home at age 17. "People make such a big deal about the dropout thing," she said to Joseph B. Verrengia, sharing her frustration over the frequent discussions about her credentials. "I've got a good, logical mind, and I teach myself."

After several years of traveling cross-country and working odd jobs, many in marinas or within sight of the ocean, she landed in Florida, where she lived on a sailboat and made a living restoring boats. A few years later she easily passed the exam for her GED (general equivalency diploma). Interested in sea life, she considered pursuing a degree in marine biology at the University of Washington before concluding that she would feel restricted by academia. (According to several sources, Mary Hendrickson continued to save money for her daughter's college tuition until Sue turned 30.) Hendrickson spent a year in California, working on boats. After being adrift again, she went to the Florida Keys, where she supported herself by diving to capture lobsters, salvage materials from shipwrecks or airplane crashes, or catch tropical fish for collectors. Whenever she failed to recognize a fish she had netted, she took it to Miami for identification; occasionally, the fish turned out to be of a species never seen before.

George Papadakis/Courtesy of the Field Museum

Hendrickson, Sue

Dec. 2, 1949– Marine archaeologist; paleontologist. Address: c/o Scholastic Inc., 555 Broadway, New York, NY 10012-3999

"Never find anything good," the marine archaeologist and amateur paleontologist Sue Hendrickson cautioned Joseph B. Verrengia of the Associated Press, in an article printed in the *Columbia (Missouri) Daily Tribune* (May 14, 2000). "Everyone will want it." A reclusive explorer, Sue Hendrickson has spent her adult life finding and sometimes selling fossils and archaeological artifacts that are among the world's most interesting and revealing. Bored and frustrated by formal schooling, she taught herself about many aspects of paleontology, the study of fossils, and archaeology, the study of cultural remains; she became involved in land-excavation projects before exploring the sea, where she has uncovered scores of shipwrecks, sometimes finding the fossilized remains of the people aboard as well as their possessions. While some scientists have complained that selling artifacts debases the fields of paleontology and archaeology, others—among them academics, collectors, and museum officials—acknowledge that Hendrickson's uncanny knack for discovering artifacts in the murky depths of the sea or under layers of earth is invaluable. "Money has never been the motivation," Hendrickson told Will Hoover for the *Honolulu Advertiser* (September 21, 2000). "I spent years with next to no money at all. I lived on derelict boats most of the time. I've lost more on fossils that I've ever made. It didn't matter because I was doing what I wanted."

During this period Hendrickson began to work on marine archaeology projects, diving to recover wrecked ships and the treasures aboard. "I'm like a kid who didn't grow up," she admitted to Rachel Louise Snyder for *Salon.com* (September 10, 1999). "I do all the things you wanted to do when you were young—digging for dinosaurs and diving for shipwrecks." One diving project took her to the Dominican Republic. She returned there often in the mid-1970s, and once, while hiking in the hills and forests, she discovered the country's amber mines, touring some of them with a group of miners. (In a process requiring millions of years, what is known as amber was formed by resin that oozed from now-extinct species of coniferous trees, trapping insects, seeds, and other objects that came into contact with it. The resin hardened, preserving its captives as fossils.) Performing research on her own, Hendrickson became a self-taught authority on amber and forged a career as a professional collector. She has found some of what have become the best-known samples of amber in the world, discovering three of the six known butterfly remains that were preserved in their original state more than 20 million years ago. She has relinquished pieces to museums—sometimes at a steep discount, sometimes at no charge—as well as to individuals. "I could be better at business," she told Snyder, "but I choose not to be."

The amber-suspended insects that had captivated Hendrickson led her in the early 1980s to explore other fossils. After studying on her own, she became a field paleontologist, raising money for her personal expeditions by diving for lobsters. In 1985 she met the paleontologist Peter Larson, who ran the Black Hills Institute of Geological Research, a South Dakota–based outfit that excavated, catalogued, and mounted fossils for display. Together, Hendrickson and Larson, who were romantically involved for a time, embarked on a series of excavations that culminated in one of the world's most impressive finds. In August 1990 they were working on unearthing a triceratops in South Dakota's badlands when Hendrickson, nosing around with her dog, Gypsy, on a ridge, spotted large vertebra fragments. "I felt drawn to that formation for two weeks," she told Joseph B. Verrengia, adding, "I can't explain it." Each bone had a honeycombed texture, indicating the skeleton of a large carnivore. Larson confirmed that the bones were, in fact, those of a *Tyrannosaurus rex*, and their team began digging frantically. "When I first realized that the few bones emerging from the hillside were *T. rex*, I didn't believe it," Hendrickson told an interviewer for *CNN.com* (May 17, 2000). "I [had] found maybe two carnivorous dinosaur bones before." Spending over two weeks performing arduous work and precise excavation in the baking August sun, the team unearthed a beautifully preserved, nearly whole *Tyrannosaurus rex* skeleton that measured 42 feet in length. The more than 200 bones recovered include the skull, which is five feet long and contains 58 teeth, including

one that, at 12 inches, is the longest *Tyrannosaurus rex* tooth ever found; a *Tyrannosaurus rex* foreleg (only one other has ever been unearthed); and a wishbone (known formally as a furcula). The wishbone is the first ever found among tyrannosaur remains and, according to some scientists, amounts to evidence that birds and dinosaurs have a common ancestor. The skeleton is regarded as the best specimen of its kind in the world. Although its sex is not known, it was named Sue, to honor Hendrickson.

A four-way dispute over ownership of the bones soon ensued, involving the United States government, which claimed that it had a right to the find under the Federal Antiquities Act of 1906; Maurice Williams, on whose property Sue was found, but who had already accepted a $5,000 payment from Larson; the Cheyenne River Sioux, who claimed ownership with the argument that Williams's ranch was part of their tribal lands; and Larson's Black Hills Institute, which had found and excavated the skeleton. To the horror of Hendrickson, who feared that the bones would begin to disintegrate, the *Tyrannosaurus rex* skeleton was seized by the federal government in 1992 and put into storage until the case could be resolved. "It was like taking the Mona Lisa and throwing it in the gutter," she told Bruce Frankel.

Uncomfortable with the media attention surrounding her and Sue, Hendrickson decided to return to her underwater pursuits. She has excavated sites off the coasts of Egypt, the Philippines, the Dominican Republic, Cuba, and Florida. She was part of a diving team that worked to raise the Egyptian queen Cleopatra's palace and parts of the city of Alexandria, Egypt, that sank into the Mediterranean Sea after an earthquake in the fifth century. Hendrickson was a member of another diving team that discovered and excavated the wreck of the *San Diego*, a Spanish galleon that went down in the year 1600 off the coast of the Philippines. Hendrickson has referred to the wreckage of the *San Diego*, where 28,000 artifacts and the remains of 100 crew members were found, as the "Sue of Shipwrecks." "Every day we came up with something amazing," she told Joseph B. Verrengia. The artifacts include a collection of porcelain pieces from China's Ming Dynasty (1368–1644). Some of Hendrickson's expeditions with Franck Goddio were captured in documentary films made for *National Geographic* and the Discovery Channel.

While Hendrickson was occupied with diving, in 1996 a United States District Court awarded ownership of the *Tyrannosaurus rex* bones to Maurice Williams. The following year the skeleton was auctioned at Sotheby's, and a consortium comprising the McDonald's Corp., Disney, and the Field Museum, in Chicago, purchased Sue for $8.36 million, the largest amount ever paid for a fossil. The skeleton would now have a home as part of the Field Museum's collection. Around the time that the restored fossil was unveiled, in May 2000, Hendrickson emerged as a minor celebrity, particularly among young dinosaur aficionados who had followed the restoration of the skeleton and the mounting of the exhibit in Chicago. "Normally, I'm a private person," she explained to Will Hoover during an interview for the *Advertiser* (July 9, 2000). "In the cosmic [scheme] of things, I guess I was supposed to find Sue and give up part of my life doing what I don't want to do to help 'her' inspire kids to learn. I'll do this to a minor degree. I can't do a whole lot. I'm not equipped for it." Although Hendrickson has said that she does not want to write a full-length volume about her experiences, explaining that writing takes too much time, she authored a short book for children, *Hunt for the Past: My Life as an Explorer (A Dinosaur Named Sue)*, published in 2001 by Scholastic Books. She has also turned down offers to have others write books or screenplays about her life. "I don't want to be packaged," she told Rachel Louise Snyder. "I really don't feel I'm that important. Maybe it's because I'm a paleontologist, but we're really nothing. We're not even a second in the universe. Why write a book about me?"

In the late 1990s, after living without a permanent address for more than 30 years, during which she shuttled her belongings from one project site to another, Hendrickson, who is single, built a home in the Bay Islands of Honduras. She is loath to slow down, although her new house and her age interfere somewhat with her world-traveling lifestyle. She successfully fought cervical cancer in 1990 but continues to suffer from a lymph infection that she picked up in the waters off the coast of Egypt. "Getting older is upsetting," she told Rachel Louise Snyder. "The body giving out, all the repairs you have to do." She added, "Now that I have the house, I don't want to leave it when I'm there, and that's scary. That shows me that I'm not just getting older, but that my priorities are changing. I'm satisfied with sitting still, which I never thought I would be." Hendrickson helped, in terms of both finance and physical labor, to rebuild parts of Honduras that were ruined after Hurricane Mitch swept through in the fall of 1998. In May 2000, at the age of 50, she donned a graduation cap and gown for the first time to receive an honorary doctorate of humane letters from the University of Illinois at Chicago. "It's just a total honor," she told David Heinzmann for the *Chicago Tribune* (May 8, 2000). "It's a formal recognition of what I've done." — K.S.

Suggested Reading: *Biography* p70+ Nov. 2000, with photos; Field Museum Web site; *Honolulu Advertiser* (on-line) July 9, 2000, with photo, Sep. 21, 2000, with photo; *New York Times Magazine* p15 May 28, 2000; *People* p129+ July 24, 2000, with photo; *Salon.com* Sep. 10, 1999

Selected Books: *Hunt for the Past: My Life as an Explorer (A Dinosaur Named Sue)*, 2001

Hill, Faith

Sep. 21, 1967– Singer; songwriter. Address: c/o Warner Bros. Records, 3300 Warner Blvd., Burbank, CA 91505; c/o Faith's Friends, P.O. Box 24266, Nashville, TN 37202

"Sometimes I catch myself and realize just how incredible it is to be living out my childhood dream," the singer/songwriter Faith Hill told Sara Switzer for *Glamour* (January 2000). "It brings me to tears." Although she has been a powerful presence in the country scene since the appearance of her debut album, *Take Me As I Am* (1993), Hill did not achieve stardom until the release of her 1998 quadruple-platinum album, *Faith*, which features the crossover hit "This Kiss." With her most recent album, *Breathe* (1999), and the accompanying same-named hit single, Hill became a bona-fide superstar, selling out arenas around the world and representing Cover Girl makeup in several television commercials and print ads. "Everything is going great," Hill remarked on the Warner Bros. Web site in mid-2000. "Each day I try to get as much out of life as I can—to keep it real, sincere and very honest. Hopefully, people can get that from my music. And if I'm lucky, one day there will be a little spot carved away somewhere that says I made a contribution."

Victor Malafronte/Archive Photos

Hill was born Audrey Faith Perry on September 21, 1967 in Jackson, Mississippi, and raised in the nearby town of Star. She was adopted as an infant by Pat Perry, a factory worker, and his wife, Edna, a bank employee. Unlike her adoptive parents, who showed little inclination for music, Hill was passionate about it from an early age. "My mom will tell you I was born singing, but the truth is I started when I was three years old," she told Sara Switzer. She was that age when she made her public debut, performing at her local church. "I held the hymnal upside down and sang as loud as I could, pretending I could read the words out of the book." When she was 10 Hill sang at a women's luncheon. At 13 she began teaching herself guitar; soon she was singing and accompanying herself on the instrument at venues in her area. She enjoyed performing at black Baptist churches, where she was well received and felt overwhelmed by the energy all around her. "People were on their feet the entire time at those churches," Hill told a reporter for *Country Music World* (on-line). "Even my black friends would joke me and say, 'Girl, you've got a black soul. You should've been born black.' I couldn't understand how some people could calmly clap and just mouth those words, because I was filled with that passion." Hill also sang at such events as rodeos and county fairs. "When I was about 16, I sang at the Raleigh, Mississippi Tobacco Spit," she told Peter Castro for *People* (September 11, 1995). "They would have the competition before the entertainment, so they would set these spittoons at the end of the stage and the men and women, some with teeth, some without, would stand way back to see who could spit farthest into the spittoons. It was so gross. They had to clean the stage off with a towel before we played."

After briefly attending Hinds Junior College, in Raymond, Mississippi, Hill left for Nashville to pursue a career in music. To support herself she toiled at a series of unmemorable jobs, including one at the country singer Reba McEntire's management company. "[Hill] was a very outstanding young lady because she was so bubbly and full of life," McEntire told Jeremy Helligar for *People* (July 12, 1999). "That's the way it was, even in the fan-club days, when she was back there stuffing envelopes." Hill next landed a job at the publishing company owned by the country singer Gary Morris. "I was thinking, 'Lord, have I got myself stuck! Maybe I'm going to have to be a secretary for the rest of my life! If I tell 'em I'm a singer I may lose my job,'" she recalled to Jack Hurst for the *Chicago Tribune* (December 12, 1993). While in Nashville Hill met the publishing executive and aspiring songwriter Dan Hill, and the two soon married. Shortly after the wedding, as Hill has told it, David Chase, a staff songwriter at Gary Morris's company, heard her singing along with the radio one day. Impressed with her raw ability, he helped her put together a demo tape and began shopping it around to record executives. Eventually the tape came to the attention of the singer Gary Burr, who hired Hill as a backup singer. One evening during a Burr performance, Hill's singing attracted the attention

of a representative from Warner Bros. Records, who promptly signed her to a deal.

In 1993, having begun to think about having children, Hill began investigating her medical history and, consequently, sought to learn more about her birth parents. "My parents never hid the fact that I was adopted," she told Switzer. "They offered to help me find my biological parents—but I never had the desire until I was an adult." Hill eventually made contact with her biological mother and brother; her biological father, she discovered, had died some years earlier in an automobile accident. "The first time I met my biological mother, I just stared at her," she told Helligar. "I'd never seen anybody who looked anything like me. It was the awe of seeing someone that you actually came from. It fills something." Hill developed a close relationship with her biological mother, but she considers the Perrys her real parents.

Not long after she connected with her mother, Hill's marriage dissolved. "No beating or cheating occurred," she told Mary Kaye Schilling. "I just felt captured." To combat the pain of her divorce, Hill concentrated on writing songs for and recording her first album, *Take Me As I Am*. The disk spawned the hit single "Wild One," which spent four weeks at the number-one spot on the country charts, thus making Hill the first female country artist since 1964 with a song at the top for so long. A second single from *Take Me As I Am*, a cover of Janis Joplin's "Piece of My Heart," also reached number one. "I'd never heard her version until I finished mine," she told a reporter for *Headliner* (Spring 1994), for an article that also appeared on *Country Music World* (on-line). "That's something that just happened. People would ask me what songs I was putting in the record and I'd say, 'I'm doing this old Janis Joplin thing "Piece of My Heart,"' and they'd go, 'You're doing what?' Everybody said, 'Whatever you do, don't listen to it until you finish your version,' which turned out to be a great idea, because it would've been a completely different record. I couldn't have done it." *Take Me As I Am* eventually went double platinum (meaning that it sold two million copies), a rare feat for a debut artist. In 1994 the Academy of Country Music named Hill favorite new female artist, and she earned a *Billboard* award for top female country artist. In addition, she was nominated for a Horizon Award from the Country Music Association and an American Music Award for favorite new artist.

To promote her album Hill launched an extensive world tour alongside such artists as Reba McEntire, Brooks & Dunn, Alan Jackson, and George Strait. Soon after the tour ended, she recorded her second album, *It Matters to Me* (1995). Another smash hit for Hill, it sold more than three million copies and generated the number-one hit single of the same name. After the album's release Hill went on tour with the country singer Tim McGraw (son of the former baseball player Tug McGraw). The pair fell in love; they married on October 6, 1996. In that same year Hill, in collaboration with Time Warner and Warner Bros. Records, founded the Faith Hill Family Literacy Project, which aims to educate people about illiteracy in the U.S. and encourage them to support literacy programs. The inspiration for Hill's involvement in the project was the situation of her father, who was forced to drop out of school at a young age and whose reading ability never progressed beyond the fourth-grade level. "He's done really well," she told Joanna Powell for *Good Housekeeping* (May 1999). "But there's a whole other world out there in reading. I didn't understand how important it was until I became an adult and realized how much he missed out on."

Also in 1996 Hill contributed to two albums for children, *The Best of Country Sings the Best of Disney* and *For Our Children Too*, and recorded a duet with McGraw, "It's Your Love," which spent six weeks at the number-one position on the country charts. At around the time her first child was born, in May 1997, she decided to take time off from recording and touring. "My career had been really busy," she told Chet Flippo for *Billboard* (April 4, 1998). "There were so many things going on that I just wasn't feeling . . . *creative* anymore. I felt like I was in a place in my life where I wasn't saying what I wanted to say musically. I felt real stagnant. I wasn't putting on record what I really wanted to put on. I just needed some inspiration. I needed to live a little bit, get off the road." After an extended break, during which she became pregnant with her second child, Hill returned to recording; she released her third album, *Faith*, in April 1998, a few months before the baby's birth. A more pop-oriented album than her previous efforts, *Faith* includes the single "This Kiss," which helped Hill cross the barrier between country and Top 40 pop stations. "This Kiss" went on to become her first platinum single; the album itself sold more than four million copies and significantly raised Hill's profile. She contributed to the soundtracks to the films *The Prince of Egypt* (1998) and *Message in a Bottle* (1999), and in 1999 she shared the stage with Cher, Tina Turner, and Whitney Houston at VH-1's *Divas Live* concert.

In November 1999 Hill released her fourth album, *Breathe*. Her most successful recording to date, it debuted on the *Billboard* charts at number one; the title track, too, became a hit. Some country enthusiasts, however, chastised Hill for apparently eschewing her down-home roots in favor of a more mainstream sound in *Breathe*. "There seems to be a real aggressive attack right now to preserve the traditions," she told Chris Willman for *Entertainment Weekly* (December 10, 1999). "And I can only do what's real to me. I would never be able to do a record like Loretta Lynn. I did lots of her songs growing up, and Tammy [Wynette], oh Lord, I did *everything* of hers. But I couldn't go out and make a pop record if I tried. And I couldn't go out and make a traditional country record, either, because I'm inspired by too many things—deep gospel,

R&B, soul. There's gonna be those who won't like the new album because they're fans from my first couple of records. But [*Breathe*] is nothing that isn't *me*."

In February 2001 Hill won three Grammy Awards—for best female country vocal performace, best country collaboration with vocals, and best country album. That spring *Breathe* was certified at sales of more than six million copies. In May Hill won the Academy of Country Music award for top female vocalist of the year. That same month her new single, "There You'll Be," was released in conjunction with the film *Pearl Harbor*. The single was a Top-10 staple on MTV throughout the summer. On September 21, 2001 Hill, along with many other performers, participated in the telethon held to raise money for victims of the September 11, 2001 terrorist attacks on the United States. Soon afterward, *There You'll Be: The Best of Faith Hill* was released to international markets. Hill was nominated for female vocalist of the year by the Country Music Association in 2001. Her husband, Tim McGraw, was named entertainer of the year at that year's awards ceremony.

Hill and McGraw are the parents of two daughters, Gracie and Maggie, and are expecting a third child in early 2002. Currently, they spend most of their time traveling, performing, and recording. A devoted mother, Hill has resolved that the family can be apart for no more than three days at a stretch. "When my kids grow up, I want them to know who the hell I am," she told Switzer. "I want them to be able to say, 'My mother taught me how to read, how to appreciate life and how to apply makeup.'" She told Powell, "I've always wanted a family as much as I've wanted my career. I won't lie: it is a lot of work, and I'm tired. Having two little girls so close in age is almost like having twins. But we learned how to pack and get around and do what we have to do. It's amazing what you can wake up every morning and accomplish as long as you're happy." — J.K.B.

Suggested Reading: *Billboard* p20+ Apr. 4, 1998, with photo; *Chicago Tribune* XIII p20+ Dec. 12, 1993, with photos; *Entertainment Weekly* p57+ Dec. 10, 1999, with photos; *Glamour* p56+ Jan. 2000, with photos; *Good Housekeeping* p28+ May, 1999, with photos; *McCall's* p20+ Nov. 2000, with photo; *People* p95+ July 12, 1999, with photos, p86+ Aug. 21, 2000, with photo; *Redbook* p118+ June 2000, with photos

Selected Albums: *Take Me As I Am*, 1993; *It Matters to Me*, 1995; *Faith*, 1998; *Breathe*, 1999; *There You'll Be: The Best of Faith Hill*, 2001

Courtesy of CNN

Hinojosa, Maria
(hin-uh-HOH-suh)

July 2, 1961– Broadcast journalist; radio producer; writer; artist. Address: CNN, 5 Penn Plaza, 20th Fl., New York, NY 10001-1810

The award-winning broadcast journalist Maria Hinojosa has appeared regularly on television and radio programs for nearly two decades. Hinojosa has served as the urban-affairs correspondent for CNN since 1997 and has hosted *Latino USA* on National Public Radio (NPR) since 1993. She also contributes to the NPR shows *All Things Considered* and *Morning Edition*. She has written two books: *Crews: Gang Members Talk with Maria Hinojosa* (1995) and *Raising Raul: Adventures Raising Myself and My Son* (1999). Displaying her fervent pride in her cultural heritage, Hinojosa's work also reflects her belief that a journalist is obligated to provide a forum for people whose stories are often neglected or ignored by the mainstream media. "Growing up as a Mexican immigrant in Chicago, I always had the experience of being the 'other,'" she told *Something About the Author* (1997). "I was the other among my mostly white friends in the states but I was also the other when I would go back to Mexico and my young cousins would tease me about being an 'Americana.' Feeling as an outsider helped me identify with others who might be seen in the same way. Feeling that my 'voice' was never really important, I saw myself in others who were voiceless as well. In my work as a journalist and as an author I hope to give that voice back to the voiceless. All of society's voices and perspectives are legitimate and important. We might not like what we hear but we have a responsibility to listen."

Maria Hinojosa was born in Mexico City, Mexico, on July 2, 1961 to Raul Hinojosa, a physician, and Berta (Ojeda) Hinojosa, a social worker. She was raised in the Hyde Park section of Chicago. In spite of their decision to live in the United States, Hinojosa's family retained a strong sense of cultural identity and visited Mexico once every year. In 1979 Hinojosa enrolled at Barnard College, in New York City, majoring in Latin American studies, women's studies, and political economy. While at Barnard, a women's college that is affiliated with Columbia University, she gained her first experience in radio, as host and producer for Columbia University Radio's *Nueva cancion y demas*; she later became a program director for the station. Hinojosa graduated from Barnard College with a B.A. degree, magna cum laude, in 1984. The following year she began working for National Public Radio as a general-assignment correspondent. In 1987 Hinojosa produced the CBS Radio programs *Where We Stand*, with Walter Cronkite; *Newsbreak*; and the *Osgood File*, in which Charles Osgood offered commentary on events of the day; from 1988 to 1989 she was a producer and researcher for the TV show *CBS This Morning*. In 1991 she became the first Latin American woman to host a live New York television talk show in prime time, when WNYC-TV hired her for *New York Hotline*; WNYC Radio had previously employed her as a general-assignment correspondent. Hinojosa has been a host and guest of WNET's television program *Informed Sources* since 1992 and an anchor for NPR's *Latino USA* and WNBC-TV's *Visiones* since 1993. In 1995 she joined the staff of CNN; in May 1997 she became the first CNN correspondent to be assigned to cover urban affairs exclusively.

Her first book, *Crews: Gang Members Talk with Maria Hinojosa*, was based on interviews (originally broadcast on NPR) the journalist conducted with gang members in the New York City borough of Queens after Brian Watkins, a young tourist from Utah, was stabbed to death on a city subway platform in 1990. Hinojosa focused on a gang associated with the stabbing; her interviews led her to conclude that the young men in the group had been desensitized by the violence they had witnessed on television and in the movies. The book includes nearly unedited transcripts of her conversations as well as a glossary that "translates" her subjects' street vernacular. Hinojosa told Cynthia Hanson for the *Chicago Tribune* (March 28, 1993) that the kids she spoke to had become "disengaged from society" and had come to enjoy the adrenaline rush they experienced from attacking strangers. The original report angered some listeners, who felt that in presenting the gang members' opinions, the program appeared to be condoning their behavior. "A lot of people said, 'Why would you put these kids on the air?,' but I felt that whether we like it or not, we have to hear this stuff," Hinojosa told Hanson. She came to believe that the interviews had served as a form of "audio therapy" for the kids, some of whom began "to rethink who they are and why they do what they do," she told Hanson. "I'm not saying that a couple of interviews are going to change a child's life. I have no illusions that this is a simple thing to go through." *Crews: Gang Members Talk with Maria Hinojosa* is illustrated with photos by German Pérez, an artist from the Dominican Republic, whom Hinojosa married in 1991.

Hinojosa is a member of the National Association of Hispanic Journalists, the National Alliance of Third World Journalists, and the Newswomen's Club of New York. She lectures frequently at colleges and universities and has earned many honors for her accomplishments in journalism and broadcasting. In 1991 her radio report "Crews" was named Top Story of the Year by the National Association of Hispanic Journalists; also that year, her coverage of the South African leader Nelson Mandela for WNYC radio earned her an Associated Press Award. Hinojosa received the National Association of Hispanic Journalists Radio Award in 1993; also that year she was presented with the Deadline Award from the New York Society of Professional Journalists for her NPR report entitled "Kids and Guns." In 1995 *Hispanic Business* magazine included her in its list of the 100 most influential Hispanic Americans; she also received a Robert F. Kennedy Award for the NPR program "Manhood Behind Bars," which focused on the increasing numbers of young men who make the transition into adulthood while incarcerated. In 1999 *Working Mother* magazine named Hinojosa one of the 25 Most Influential Working Mothers. That year she also received from the National Council of La Raza

the Ruben Salazar Award, which was named for a journalist who was killed by a tear-gas canister while covering a Chicano protest rally in East Los Angeles in 1970.

Hinojosa and her husband live in New York City with their son, Raul Ariel, born in 1996, and daughter, Maria Yurema, born in 1998. After the birth of her second child, she took a six-month leave of absence from work. In her 1999 memoir, *Raising Raul: Adventures Raising Myself and My Son*, she described her difficulty in getting pregnant and her experiences as a first-time mother who wrestled with the demands of family and career and sometimes found herself torn between her strong ties to both Mexico and the United States. She and her husband have collaborated on the construction of a series of altars, some of which have been exhibited at the Bronx Museum of the Arts, in the New York City borough of the Bronx, the Cooper-Hewitt National Design Museum (a division of the Smithsonian Institution), also in New York, and the Mexican Fine Arts Center Museum, in Chicago, Illinois. Hinojosa enjoys reading, writing, dancing, hiking, and yoga. — C.L.

Suggested Reading: *Contemporary Authors*, vol. 152, 1997; *Something About the Author*, vol. 88, 1997; Telgen, Diane, and Jim Kamp. *Notable Hispanic American Women*, 1993; *Who's Who in America, 2001*

Selected Books: *Crews: Gang Members Talk with Maria Hinojosa*, 1995; *Raising Raul: Adventures Raising Myself and My Son*, 1999

Hoffman, Philip Seymour

July 23, 1967– Actor. Address: c/o Paradigm Talent Agency, 10100 Santa Monica Blvd. #2500, Los Angeles, CA 90067-4003

An actor of unusual range and versatility, Philip Seymour Hoffman is known chiefly for his portrayal of characters who make audiences wince in embarrassment. "His presence was bracing, in the manner of a pine tree, or a pile of garbage," Claire Dederer wrote for *Salon.com* of Hoffman's roles in such movies as *Boogie Nights* and *Happiness*. "Like any really fine character actor, Hoffman gives off a strong whiff of reality. Hollywood's idea of a loser is Ethan Hawke with chin whiskers. But Hoffman's not a rebel loser, he's a loser loser, the guy at the next table who keeps trying to tell you about his operation. . . . Hoffman isn't someone we want to be. He's someone we want to be better than. Here is an actor whose entire oeuvre can be described in one sentence: 'At least I'm not *that* guy.'"

But Hoffman is neither bent on personifying indignity for its own sake nor eager to goad his audience into gloating over the lost souls whom he portrays. Although his characters are frequently unattractive and painfully awkward and behave in a way that can best be described as mortifying, Hoffman works to endow them with a tinge of pathos as well. "Actors are responsible to the people we play," he told Michael Krantz for *Time* (November 22, 1999). "I don't label or judge. I just play them as honestly and expressively and creatively as I can, in the hope that people who would ordinarily turn their heads in disgust instead think, 'What I thought I'd feel about that guy, I don't totally feel right now.'" The result, more often than not, is ambivalence among moviegoers, who often can't decide whether to cringe or to sympathize. Discussing his work in *Happiness* (1998), for example, in which he played a lonely, sweaty, and sexually frustrated young office worker who rants obscenely (and anonymously) to his attractive neighbor over the phone but is paralyzed with anxiety in her presence, Hoffman told Jill Bernstein for *Premiere* (February 1999), "People were like, 'You're a

Jill Connelly/Archive Photos

Philip Seymour Hoffman

freak—you're good and all, but you played the sicko.' And I'm like, 'Oh, thank you, I guess. Leave me alone.' People have a hard time saying, 'I identified with that.' I mean, nobody is that person, but come on, you don't identify with being so enamored of somebody that you can't get up the nerve to say anything to them?"

Hoffman's willingness to invest himself in unglamorous roles has earned him a reputation as one of the most capable character actors around. Among his admirers is Joel Schumacher, who directed him in *Flawless* and has described him as "quite possibly the best character actor of his generation," as Louis B. Hobson quoted him as saying in the *Calgary Sun* (November 19, 1999). Schumacher added that while Hoffman "will never make $25 million a picture" because he "doesn't have the pretty, pouty, little-boy look that makes young men overnight sex symbols . . . he will work forever and will probably do the most fascinating roles." Hoffman has received several professional honors: the National Board of Review named him best supporting actor for his work in Paul Thomas Anderson's *Magnolia* and Anthony Minghella's *The Talented Mr. Ripley*; the Independent Feature Project nominated him for an IFP/West Spirit Award for his role in *Happiness;* and the Screen Actors Guild nominated him for an award for his work in *Flawless.*

The third of four children, Philip Seymour Hoffman was born in Fairport, New York, a suburb of Rochester, on July 23, 1967. After Hoffman's parents were divorced, when he was nine, his mother raised the children by herself. A civil-rights and women's-rights activist who returned to law school at the age of 37, his mother was "a staunch

feminist . . . ," as Hoffman told Patrick Giles for *Interview* (February 1999). "I grew up with very strong feminist messages. As a result, I battled her in my teenage years because my image of being a man was a deformed one."

Hoffman first took an interest in acting at 15, when a classmate whom he liked told him she was trying out for a part in a school production of Arthur Miller's *The Crucible*. He tagged along, and soon abandoned baseball and wrestling in favor of acting. He took part in several high-school productions and took a summer course at New York City's Circle Repertory Company, then went on to study at New York University's Tisch School of Drama. After he graduated from NYU, in about 1989, Hoffman, like many other aspiring actors, took odd jobs while looking for roles. He made his film debut in the obscure *Triple Bogey on a Par 5 Hole* (1991), written and directed by Amos Poe. After appearing in a few independent films, he landed a minor role alongside Al Pacino and Chris O'Donnell in *Scent of a Woman* (1992). Over the next few years, Hoffman kept afloat with small roles in such films as *My New Gun* (1992), *When a Man Loves a Woman* (1994), and *Nobody's Fool* (1994). His first real breakthrough came several years later, when he nabbed the sizable role of Dusty, a socially maladjusted tornado tracker, in Jan de Bont's *Twister* (1996).

In Paul Thomas Anderson's *Boogie Nights* (1997), set in Southern California in the late 1970s, Hoffman played Scotty, a gay sound technician hopelessly in love with Dirk Diggler (Mark Wahlberg), a rising porn star. Although his was a minor role, Hoffman earned much praise in connection with a scene in which Scotty impulsively plants a sloppy kiss on Diggler at a New Year's Eve party and is immediately rebuffed. "[Hoffman] initially turns away from Wahlberg," Jose Arroyo wrote for *Sight & Sound* (December 2000), "then meets his eye, raises his hand in a pacifying gesture, and says, 'I want to know if you like me.' Later he begs. When he says, 'Can I kiss you?' his mouth remains open, the tone of his voice lowered, as if it's too much to ask and he knows it but still can't help himself. The scene ends in the car he's bought to please Dirk and when he bursts into a tearful chant of 'I'm a [expletive] idiot' it's like an aria that reprises the previous scale of emotions. For the audience it functions as a catharsis of knowledge and understanding." "It might not have been much different from any other unrequited love scene," Dederer wrote, "but something about the way Hoffman's red pleather jacket stretched taut over his gut utterly undid me. . . . He's been creeping me out ever since."

One year later Hoffman took a leading role in an independent film, Todd Solondz's *Happiness* (1998), a black comedy set in suburban New Jersey. While some critics lauded the film for exposing the moral bankruptcy and hypocrisy below the respectable surface of middle-class life, others contended that subverting middle-class mores had become something of a cliché: "Aren't the American suburbs a fairly easy target by now? . . . ," David Denby asked rhetorically in *New York* (October 19, 1998). "It's more than a little naïve, I think, to be shocked that people are out for themselves, that family relations can cover self-seeking and competitiveness." Yet Denby and other critics who expressed mixed feelings about *Happiness* were impressed by Hoffman, who, according to Denby, "does wonders with his sagging belly, his fumbled glasses, his pained smile." Also in 1998 Hoffman appeared in Brad Anderson's *Next Stop, Wonderland*, as an obnoxious Communist proselytizer, and in Joel and Ethan Coen's *The Big Lebowski*, as an officious personal assistant to the millionaire Jeff Lebowski. He further expanded his range with roles in Tom Shadyac's *Patch Adams* (1998) and Paul Thomas Anderson's *Magnolia* (1999), in which he was cast as a hospice nurse.

Hoffman won further acclaim for his work in *Flawless* (1999), in which he played Rusty, a transsexual who gives voice lessons to his neighbor, a homophobic former security guard who has suffered a stroke (Robert De Niro). "The role of Rusty is a cliché," Jose Arroyo wrote, "the sad queen who puts up with abuse under the guise of love while masking her vulnerability with sarcasm and cynicism. But Philip Seymour Hoffman's playing is not—he achieves flamboyance through economy of gesture, vibrancy through stillness and an almost unprecedented degree of expressivity through his voice. . . . The scenes have few values he fails to extract. For instance near the beginning, when Rusty is performing her act in front of some greatly appreciative straight boys, she tells them: 'Guys like you beat my ass once I leave the club. I want you to bend over and kiss my ass. Think of me as a present and it's Christmas.' Hoffman's reading of the first part conveys both accusation and weariness. He speeds up the rhythm and tone to turn the second part into commanding flirtation and then, with a tilt of the head, a lift of the hand and a few sways of the body, nails the laugh of the final part while not sacrificing his character's desire for symbolic revenge." Similarly, Jamie Malanowski, writing for the *New York Times* (November 21, 1999), praised a scene in which the crossdressing Rusty "shrinks into invisibility when he puts on a shirt and tie to attend his mother's funeral. Scenes like [this] are priceless, lingering in the mind long after the rest of the movie has left it, speaking to us about how people resist easy categories and snap assessments." "I'm pretty much a guy guy," Hoffman told Jill Bernstein when asked about how he prepared for the role. "I had to decide what it was about this person that I could identify with, and I came to this little piece of truth about myself: I have known what it's like to want to be someone else. There was a time in my life—and even now—that I assumed somebody else is better than me, sexier than me, more intelligent than me. That's what this guy is about."

In *The Talented Mr. Ripley* (1999), Hoffman provoked ambivalence in moviegoers once again, with his portrayal of Freddie Miles, a sneering preppie expatriate living in Italy who scents out the murderous duplicity of Tom Ripley, played by Matt Damon. Despite an abundance of disagreeable qualities, the Freddie character was surprisingly compelling. Janet Maslin, writing for the *New York Times* (December 24, 1999), called Hoffman's performance "scene-stealingly wonderful." "Best of all is the unstoppable Philip Seymour Hoffman," Kenneth Turan wrote in a review of *Ripley* for the *Los Angeles Times* (December 24, 1999). "His role as the thuggish, arrogant, red-convertible-driving Freddie . . . is pitch perfect." In an interview with Jamie Malanowski, Hoffman explained Freddie's appeal: "He's honest and boisterous, but he comes across as not that great a guy. And that's why I like him, because he's right, he's right, he is right, he's on it, but he's the only one who's on it. And because of that, he's perceived as a jerk, and gets killed. So it's like, 'Who does the audience have sympathy with?'"

In 2000 Hoffman appeared in *Almost Famous*, as the rock critic Lester Bangs, and in David Mamet's *State and Main* (2000), as Joseph Turner White, a touchy, self-promoting writer. Reviewing his work in *State and Main* for the *New Republic* (January 29, 2001), Stanley Kauffmann described Hoffman as "a true talent" who "exhibits another facet of his gifts as the screenwriter in the film, a playwright of individuality learning how to adjust to expediency." In an assessment of *State and Main* for *Salon.com*, Charles Taylor wrote, "Hoffman, who continues to amaze through his sheer range, is as endearingly bewildered here as he was endearingly bearish playing Lester Bangs in *Almost Famous*."

In addition to his film work, Hoffman has appeared in Off-Broadway productions, among them *Defying Gravity* and *Food and Shelter*, by Jane Anderson; *The Skriker*, by Caryl Churchill; *True West*, by Sam Shepard; and Shakespeare's *The Merchant of Venice*. In 1999 he made his directorial debut, with an Off-Broadway production of Stephen Adly-Guirgiss's *In Arabia, We'd All Be Kings*.

"On my down time I do a lot of nothing," Hoffman told Pamela Harland for *Independent Film Magazine* (January 14, 2000), as quoted by ptanderson.com (a Web site devoted to the life and work of Paul Thomas Anderson). "I just kinda read, run and hang out with friends because I haven't had a lot of [free time] lately. I just try to do a lot of nothing. Go to some sports. I like to play tennis. I travel a lot with my work now so if you are travelling all the time you don't want to travel you want to stay home. And when you stay home you really don't want to do too much because you've been going out and getting up early and staying out late all the time. So you just do very little." Hoffman lives in New York City's West Village.— P.K.

Suggested Reading: *New York* p 71+ Oct. 19, 1998, with photo; *Premiere* p88+ Oct. 1999, with photo; *Salon.com* Nov. 22, 1999, with photo; *Sight & Sound* p16+ Dec. 2000, with photos; *Time* p100 Nov. 22, 1999, with photo

Selected Films: *Triple Bogey on a Five Par Hole*, 1991; *My New Gun*, 1992; *Leap of Faith*, 1992; *Scent of a Woman*, 1992; *Joey Breaker*, 1993; *Money for Nothing*, 1993; *My Boyfriend's Back*, 1993; *When a Man Loves a Woman*, 1994; *The Getaway*, 1994; *Nobody's Fool*, 1994; *The Yearling*, 1994; *Twister*, 1996; *Hard Eight*, 1996;

Boogie Nights, 1997; *Patch Adams*, 1998; *Happiness*, 1998; *Montana*, 1998; *Next Stop Wonderland*, 1998; *The Big Lebowski*, 1998; *Flawless*, 1999; *Magnolia*, 1999; *The Talented Mr. Ripley*, 1999; *Almost Famous*, 2000; *State and Main*, 2000

Selected Plays: *Food and Shelter*; *The Merchant of Venice*, 1994; *The Skriker*, 1996; *Defying Gravity*, 1997; *Shopping and [Expletive]ing*, 1998; *True West*, 2000; *In Arabia, We'd All Be Kings*, 2000

Jeff Mitchell/Reuters/Hulton/Archive

Hughes, Karen

Dec. 27, 1956– White House counselor to the President. Address: The White House, 1600 Pennsylvania Ave., N.W., Washington, DC 20500

Karen Hughes, the White House counselor to the president, is, by most accounts, the most powerful woman ever to occupy a staff position at the nation's presidential quarters. As counselor, Hughes manages a staff of 43 White House employees, overseeing the communications, speechwriting, and media offices. She also maintains responsibility for the overall crafting, polishing, and presentation of the president's message. During the 2000 presidential election campaign of George W. Bush, Hughes, serving as communications manager, was one corner of the "Iron Triangle," the collective name given by reporters to the Republican nominee's three right-hand people (the other two being

Karl Rove and Joe Allbaugh). Standing nearly six feet tall, Hughes is an imposing figure who often brandishes her powerful voice in defense of the president during press conferences. As Michele Cottle explained in the *New Republic* (November 29, 1999), Hughes "has a Texas-size voice—a booming foghorn that can easily slice through the nattering of a room of journalists and frequently does, when [she] decides to cut short a 'press availability' that's getting out of hand." *CNN* reporter Charles Zewe told Cottle that Hughes "is someone not diminutive in any sense of the word." By other accounts, Hughes is a kind of presidential mother hen, keeping the chief executive safe from political harm. She has also been referred to as the alter ego of the president, whom she served as director of communications when he was governor of Texas. Hughes's greatest strength, experts have agreed, is her ability to shape the president's thoughts into clear, cogent messages.

Hughes was born Karen Parfitt on December 27, 1956 in Paris, France, where her father, Harold R. Parfitt, was a major general in the U.S. Army Corps of Engineers. Throughout Hughes's childhood the family—which included her younger sister, Beverly—moved often, living by turns in Pennsylvania, Missouri, Florida, Kentucky, Canada, and, in the late 1960s, Panama, where Major General Parfitt served as the last governor of the Canal Zone. In 1969 the Parfitt family landed in Dallas, Texas, and when Hughes's father was again reassigned, this time to Virginia, she stayed behind with a neighbor to complete her final year of high school. In the fall of 1974, she enrolled at Southern Methodist University (SMU), in Dallas. There, she took a journalism course taught by Bob Mann, who later worked as press secretary to Democratic senator Edward M. Kennedy of Massachusetts, and also studied under Lee Elsesser, then news director at the NBC-affiliate KXAS-TV, in neighboring Fort Worth. Finding that she much preferred broadcast news to print journalism, Hughes approached Elsesser about a possible internship at KXAS. He agreed, and in the summer of 1976 she began working as an unpaid assistant at the station. Hughes quickly noticed that the news department was having difficulty compiling enough material for the weekend editions of its broadcasts. She therefore began suggesting stories that she herself could cover. Hughes told Paul Burka for *Texas Monthly* (September 1999) that when she returned to school that fall, "everybody wanted me to stay on so that they wouldn't have to work weekends." Hughes graduated summa cum laude from SMU in 1977 with a B.A. in English and journalism. Elsesser immediately offered her a position as night and weekend reporter at KXAS. For the next seven years Hughes covered a wide variety of stories for the station, ranging from murders to hurricanes to school-board and city-council meetings.

In 1980 she was assigned to cover the presidential campaign of George W. Bush's father, George Herbert Walker Bush; she instantly became enamored of the world of politics. She was introduced to Jerry Hughes, a divorced Dallas lawyer, in 1981, and two years later the couple were married. At this point Karen Hughes began questioning her career choice. As she explained to Dan Balz for the *Washington Post* (July 23, 1999, on-line), "I had gotten married and I had a new stepdaughter. I remember when I was doing the wedding invitations, I got called and sent to a hurricane. I was driving toward the coast and everybody else was driving the other way. I remember thinking, 'Why am I doing this?'" In 1984 she received a call from a friend working in the Dallas office of then–U.S. senator John Tower, who asked Hughes if she would consider leaving television for politics. She immediately went to work as the Texas press coordinator for the reelection campaign of President Ronald Reagan (whose vice president was the elder George Bush), leaving behind the world of journalism.

Having successfully played her part in Reagan's reelection, Hughes continued her political efforts, performing public-relations services for various candidates around Dallas. One of these candidates was Fred Meyer, a Dallas businessman, who ran successfully for the Texas Republican Party chairmanship in 1991. Meyer's victory helped to raise Hughes's profile even more, not just in the world of public relations but in the Republican Party as well. In 1992, as a result, Hughes was asked to move to Austin to become executive director of the Texas GOP. At the time the Republican Party there had only two members who held statewide office; Meyer believed that the party's future in Texas depended on defeating the Democratic incumbent governor, Ann Richards, and getting a Republican into office. The responsibility for making that happen was placed in Hughes's hands. In 1994 she joined George W. Bush's gubernatorial campaign as director of communications. It was an opportune time for Bush and Hughes: apparently disaffected with the Democratic Party, on Election Day voters increased the number of Republicans in the U.S. House of Representatives by 52 and the number in the Senate by 11, thus giving the GOP control of both houses of Congress for the first time in more

than four decades, and they boosted the number of Republican governors by 11. One of those newly elected governors was Bush. From the beginning of their association, it was clear that Bush and Hughes were a good match, both professionally and personally. Hughes told Dan Balz, "When you're together for long days in very high-stress situations, you either end up not liking each other or liking each other a lot, and we ended up liking each other a lot." Hughes remained in Governor Bush's service as director of communications after his election.

As early as 1998, when Hughes helped to bring about a second term for her boss, speculation arose concerning the Texas governor's future in politics—specifically, his potential entrance into the 2000 presidential race. When Bush announced his plans to pursue the U.S. presidency, it was only after securing the support of his director of communications. As Paul Burka reported, Bush told Hughes, "If you have any doubts about this, we need to talk about it right now, because I'm not doing this unless you're coming with me." Dan Balz also discussed the close relationship between Bush and Hughes: "Bush advisors say that, on a personal basis, Hughes is probably the closest to the governor . . . and they say Bush always seems more confident and relaxed when she is around." Throughout the campaign, which was characterized by Michelle Cottle as "one of the most tightly managed . . . in political memory, thanks in large part to the fiercely protective Hughes," Bush's speeches and the time he spent with the media were kept to a minimum; the soon-to-be president was able to avoid questions on controversial subjects to a great extent, as Hughes often intervened in situations that might have tainted her boss's image. Her loyalty to the president is both famous and without parallel. Margaret D. Tutwiler, a senior White House adviser who also served under Reagan and the elder Bush, was quoted by Geraldine Baum and Elizabeth Mehren in the *Los Angeles Times* (April 1, 2001, on-line) as saying, "Karen has no agenda separate from George Bush's success, and that is rare in any staff in the capital, especially inside a White House." Baum and Mehren further pointed out, "That unbending loyalty and single-mindedness have carried Hughes throughout her career."

Hughes has always taken great pride in her role as Bush's confidant and in her ability to sum up his views with all-encompassing catch phrases. Upon hearing Bush describe himself at a press conference as "a conservative with a heart," Hughes came up with the term "compassionate conservative," which Bush has used to characterize himself ever since. After witnessing him interact with children during a campaign visit to a juvenile detention center, she recommended the slogan "Leave no child behind." (Years earlier, those words had been registered as the motto of the Washington-based Children's Defense Fund.) "The objective [of the Bush team] is to have every word that comes out of the campaign—every speech, every press release, every media response—sound like George W. Bush, or at least like Karen Hughes sounding like George W. Bush," in Paul Burka's words. It was no surprise, then, that Hughes took on the task of ghostwriting Bush's autobiography, *A Charge to Keep* (1999). Bush and Hughes have maintained their interconnectedness in the White House. As quoted by Kenneth T. Walsh in *U.S. News & World Report* (April 30, 2001), Republican senator Kay Bailey Hutchison of Texas said, "The White House would never make a strategic decision without Karen in the room." Jeanne Cummings and Jim Vandehei, writing for the *Wall Street Journal* (February 26, 2001), quoted the Texas-based media adviser Mark McKinnon as saying that Hughes "is the president's compass. She advises on everything."

On September 11, 2001, following a series of horrific terrorist attacks on Washington, D.C., and New York City, the U.S. government implemented an emergency response plan in order to prevent further assaults on key buildings and individuals—including the White House and President Bush. Around the country, government offices closed down, tenants in various areas were evacuated, and federal and local police established security perimeters around landmark buildings. As Secret Service agents whisked the president away to secure locations, first in Louisiana and then in Nebraska, the nation's only official source of information was Karen Hughes. By mid-afternoon, as quoted by Todd S. Purdum and Robin Toner in the *New York Times* (September 12, 2001), Hughes had addressed the American public and assured them that their "federal government continues to function effectively," explaining that Bush and other senior members of the government were out of harm's way but still in constant communication with one another. Hughes worked closely with the president onboard Air Force One as he returned that evening to the White House; she listened as he conveyed the outline of the speech he would deliver to the American people in response to the day's grim developments.

Throughout her career Hughes has maintained her close relationship with her family. She took her son, Robert (born in 1987), out of school in 1999 so that he could join her on the campaign trail, where she tutored him. Both her son and her husband, Jerry, have relocated to the nation's capital with her; Robert now attends St. Alban's School, a private institution in Washington. Hughes has also added to her schedule what she calls a "midweek moment": she leaves work early every Wednesday to spend time with her son. She explained to CNN White House correspondent Kelly Wallace (on-line), "I was looking for a way in the middle of the week that I could say [to Robert], you are my priority, you are important and if it means having to walk away from my job once in awhile, I'm ready to do that." Hughes's husband, for his part, has taken time away from practicing law to help care for their teenage son. Hughes's commitment to family stems in large part from her own childhood and greatly

informs her political beliefs. As Paul Burka wrote, "[Hughes's] conservatism comes from her upbringing in a military family and is rooted in God, family, and country rather than economic dogma or social zeal." Burka also quoted the White House counselor as saying that she feels "free to disagree" with the president in private, though the two "have no external disagreements." As for Bush's opinion of his right-hand woman, he told Dan Balz, "People have either got good instincts and good antennae or they don't. Karen has got good instincts. . . . Her voice is one of reason and honesty." As quoted by Kenneth T. Walsh, the president used the following word to describe Hughes: "Indispensable." — J.H.

Suggested Reading: *Los Angeles Times* A p1 Apr. 1, 2001, with photos; *New Republic* p20+ Nov. 29, 1999, with photo; *New York Times* A p27 Nov. 11, 1999, A p1 Nov. 22, 1999; *Texas Monthly* p127+ Sep. 1999, with photos; *U.S. News & World Report* p25 Apr. 30, 2001, with photo; *Wall Street Journal* A p24 Feb. 26, 2001; *Washington Post* (on-line) July 20, 1999, with photo

---

Jackson, Thomas Penfield

Jan. 10, 1937– U.S. District Court Judge for the District of Columbia. Address: U.S. District Court, U.S. Courthouse #2429, Washington, DC 20001

Thomas Penfield Jackson has been a judge for the United States District Court of the District of Columbia since 1982, when he was appointed to the bench by President Ronald Reagan. Among the high-profile cases over which he has presided is the antitrust suit brought against Microsoft, in which he found that the software giant had in fact created a monopoly and ruled that the company be split. (While agreeing that Microsoft was a monopoly, a United States Court of Appeals later nullified that ruling and removed Jackson from the case.) The judge has also been involved in other prominent court decisions, such as the trial of former Washington, D.C., mayor Marion Barry on drug-possession and other charges in 1990.

Thomas Penfield Jackson was born in Washington, D.C., on January 10, 1937. After attending various public schools in Montgomery County, Maryland, he received a music scholarship to St. Alban's School in the District of Columbia, where he was a member of the Washington Cathedral Choir of Men and Boys. He later transferred to Bethesda–Chevy Chase High School, where he played football and edited the school newspaper. After graduating, with an A.B. degree, from Dartmouth College, in Hanover, New Hampshire, in 1958, he joined the U.S. Navy. For the next three years, Jack-

Larry Downing/Archive Photos
Thomas Penfield Jackson

son served as a line officer, a qualified command duty officer, and an officer of the deck aboard the *Chas. S. Sperry*, a navy destroyer in the U.S. Atlantic and Mediterranean fleets. In 1959 he attended the U.S. Naval School of Military Justice, which qualified him to serve as a ship's prosecutor. When his naval service was completed, Jackson attended Harvard Law School, in Cambridge, Massachusetts, where he received a bachelor of laws degree in 1964.

Over the course of the next 18 years, Jackson practiced law, first as an associate and then as a partner at Jackson & Campbell, P.C., where he specialized in general civil litigation. He was admitted to practice in the District of Columbia and Maryland, as well as in their federal courts, in 1965 and 1966, respectively, and in 1970 he was admitted to practice before the U.S. Supreme Court. From 1969 until 1975 he served as a member of the Vestry at All Saints Episcopal Church in Chevy Chase, Maryland. He worked for the reelection campaign of President Richard M. Nixon in 1972. Jackson was serving as the president of the Bar Association for the District of Columbia when, in 1982, he was appointed to the U.S. District Court by President Ronald Reagan; he would remain president of the association until 1983.

One of the most publicized cases of Jackson's judicial career was the 1990 trial of Washington, D.C., mayor Marion Barry, an African-American, who was found guilty of cocaine possession, one of 14 charges against him. (The jury was unable to reach verdicts regarding the other 13, with the exception of one, of which Barry was acquitted.) In October, during his campaign for a seat on the City Council (his mayoralty had ended in 1990), Barry

was sentenced to serve six months in prison without the possibility of parole and to pay a fine of $5,000; he was also required to pay for the cost of his imprisonment and to undergo random urinalysis for one year. According to Michael York and Tracy Thompson in the *Washington Post* (October 27, 1990, on-line), during the sentencing Jackson characterized the former mayor as a "compulsive user of cocaine" who had "given aid, comfort, and encouragement to the drug culture at large, and contributed to the anguish that illegal drugs have inflicted on this city." York and Thompson also reported that the judge showed some sympathy for Barry, referring to him as "deserving of as much compassion as anyone so afflicted" with addiction.

Jackson was later criticized by ethicists as well as members of the legal profession for remarks he made about the case at Harvard University in the fall of 1990. Unaware that two reporters were present, he told the students that there had been overwhelming evidence against Barry, and that he had reason to believe that four of the jurors had been partial to the former mayor. Although the case had already been decided when he made his remarks, some saw Jackson's actions as a serious breach of the unwritten rule against commenting publicly on cases over which one has presided. His indiscretion also did little to discredit the claim made by Barry and others that the former mayor—who, as a result of a "sting" operation, had been caught on videotape smoking crack cocaine—was a victim of a racist justice system. "Looked at in the context of . . . the story the defendant wanted to tell the public, [the Jackson controversy] plays right into [Barry's] hands," the New York University Law School ethics expert Stephen Gillers told Saundra Torry for the *Washington Post* (September 30, 1991). Some saw the comparatively light penalty ($100,000 and community service) that Jackson gave in 1987 to former Reagan aide Michael Deaver for committing perjury as a further indication of the judge's racial bias. Barry and his attorneys succeeded on appeal in having Barry's sentence discounted, on the grounds that Jackson had "not precisely state[d] his reasons for the sentence he imposed," as the *Washington Post* (September 26, 1991) reported. Barry's lawyers also tried to have Jackson disqualified from the former mayor's resentencing, but an appeals court panel ruled two to one that the judge's remarks did not warrant his removal from the case. In September 1991 Jackson again sentenced Barry to serve six months in prison and pay a $5,000 fine. (Barry was reelected mayor of the District of Columbia in 1994.)

The most recent of Jackson's high-profile cases was the highly publicized antitrust case filed by the U.S. Department of Justice's Antitrust Division against the software giant Microsoft in 1997, a case comparable in magnitude to the 1911 decision regarding Standard Oil and the decades-long legal wrangling involving AT&T. Microsoft was accused of violating a 1994 consent agreement with the Department of Justice (in which it had agreed to deal more fairly with competitors) by forcing computer manufacturers to include the browser Microsoft Internet Explorer with the installment of Windows 95 software, a process referred to by the court as "bundling." Jackson said that he would hear the case in as timely a fashion as possible, originally promising to conclude the proceedings in six weeks. (An earlier antitrust case against IBM had been drawn out for more than a decade, until President Reagan ordered it abandoned, in 1982.) In an effort to speed up the process, Jackson ordered both sides to take written depositions from their witnesses and limited the number of witnesses each side could call to 12. In 1997 the Department of Justice asked Jackson for an immediate injunction against the company, while Microsoft implored him to dismiss the case altogether. Jackson granted the injunction in December; when the court reconvened, in May 1998, Windows 98 (the latest version of Microsoft's software at that point) was also made part of the case.

Many commentators contended that Jackson appeared to support the government's point of view from the beginning. He frequently rolled his eyes, scowled, and otherwise expressed frustration with attempts made by Microsoft's lawyers to deemphasize the company's strategy of intimidation. Many journalists noted that the judge's body language often made it appear that he was bored, and more than one journalist reported witnessing Jackson yawning or dozing. One of the most damaging pieces of evidence presented by the government was the videotaped deposition of Microsoft founder and CEO Bill Gates, in which the software magnate appeared nervous and evasive; Jackson was reported to have found some of what Gates said so outrageous that he laughed aloud in the courtroom as the tape was being shown.

The Department of Justice lawyer David Boies was relentless in uncovering the inconsistencies between the public statements of the company's top executives and their E-mail messages, many of which were enlarged and projected on a screen in the courtroom. In late January 1999 Boies referred to an E-mail message in which Microsoft's third-highest-ranking executive, Paul Maritz, stated that the company intended to "cut off Netscape's air supply." Maritz refused to concede that the company considered Netscape to be a threat. Throughout the first phase of the trial, Microsoft's lawyers attempted to downplay the significance of the E-mails, referring to their content as mere "snippets" of information.

The government also produced evidence that Microsoft had persuaded Apple to use Microsoft Internet Explorer rather than Netscape's browser, a product some felt to be superior. Executives from Microsoft's competitors, such as Intel and Apple, testified to being bullied by Microsoft executives to do so. The Department of Justice also claimed that in June 1995 Microsoft had tried to both absorb the Netscape browser into its own product and limit Netscape's access to the browser market. Witnesses

such as Microsoft executive Daniel Rosen refused to answer questions in a straightforward manner, a strategy that angered the judge and made the company look as if it had something to hide. One day at the end of March, Jackson called a 10-minute recess after he raised his voice with Microsoft executive Robert Muglia, who had repeatedly attempted to reinterpret statements made in E-mails that clearly demonstrated Gates's desire to destroy the Java program, developed by Sun Microsystems, another of Microsoft's competitors.

Also at the end of March, Jackson called a two-month recess, during which he presided over a trial involving drug trafficking and murder. When the Microsoft trial resumed, on June 1, 1999, the lawyers were permitted to conduct their initial questioning of witnesses in court. Arguing against the notion that Microsoft had all but completely dominated the software market, the company's lawyers produced an AOL-Netscape document showing that 24 percent of Netscape's browsers were preinstalled, a practice that closed a portion of the browser market to Microsoft. Jackson soon became impatient with Microsoft lawyer John Warden's questioning of AOL's David Colburn, who Warden hoped would verify the importance of Netscape's browser to the AOL-Netscape merger; journalists once again reported that the judge seemed to have already drawn his conclusions regarding the case. The trial came to an end after 76 days of testimony. Although highly publicized, the case did not hurt Microsoft's business—the company's stock value had doubled since the commencement of the trial, and its profits increased by 125 percent. Microsoft also released more than one new version of Windows while waiting for the outcome of the antitrust proceedings.

The judge's decision was scheduled to be released in three parts—findings of fact, conclusions of law, and announcement of the penalty. In November 1999 Jackson released his findings of fact, a 207-page document that stated that Microsoft was indeed a monopoly and that its rivals posed no threat to its dominance. He concluded that the company was so powerful that it could charge whatever it wanted for its operating systems without losing business to its competitors. "Most harmful of all," Jackson wrote in a portion of the findings excerpted by Patrick Thibodeau and Kim S. Nash for *Computerworld* (November 8, 1999), "is the message that Microsoft's actions have conveyed to every enterprise with the potential to innovate in the computer industry. Through its conduct toward Netscape, IBM, Compaq, Intel, and others, Microsoft has demonstrated that it will use its prodigious market power and immense profits to harm any firm that insists on pursuing initiatives that could intensify competition against one of Microsoft's core products." Jackson also concluded that Microsoft had inhibited progress by making computers more expensive and more difficult to use, and that furthermore, its practice of bundling slowed down computer systems and made them more prone to crash. The statement appeared to agree with almost all of the government's findings. Joel Klein, the head of the antitrust division of the Department of Justice, praised the document, telling reporters that the judge's findings had proven "once again that in America, no person and no company is above the law," according to Adam Cohen in *Time* (November 15, 1999). The findings of fact also opened the door for other companies to file lawsuits against Microsoft.

In November Jackson appointed Richard A. Posner, chief judge of the Seventh U.S. District Court of Appeals, in Chicago, to serve as a mediator in the Microsoft case, in the hope that an out-of-court settlement might be reached. Posner assured the Department of Justice that it was not likely that Microsoft could be split; the government agreed to drop the charges on the condition that Microsoft agree to certain terms, such as fair-pricing measures and the creation of an independent committee to monitor all new features to be integrated into Windows software. But Microsoft was reluctant to accept the government's suggestion that they make a group outside the company privy to its decision-making process. When the talks seemed to be slowing down, Jackson threatened to release his conclusions of law before a compromise could be achieved, a development not likely to favor Microsoft; as a result, negotiations were stepped up, but no agreement was reached. In April 2000 Jackson delivered the conclusions of law, which stated that Microsoft had in fact violated antitrust laws. A hearing date was set for May. Soon after the conclusions were published, it was announced that the Department of Justice would recommend that the company be split. Microsoft's stock value fell immediately.

The Department of Justice proposed dividing Microsoft into two companies, one for its Windows operating system and another for its applications software. Gates was vehemently opposed to the recommendation, declaring that the breakup of the company would be "punitive beyond reason," according to Dori Jones Yang in *U.S. News & World Report* (May 8, 2000). Gates warned that the breakup would have an adverse affect on the economy. (Executives from Standard Oil and AT&T had made similar claims when their respective companies were found guilty of antitrust violations, but in neither case had the prediction come to pass.) When Jackson added his support to the breakup plan, Microsoft promised to appeal. Jackson told Greg Stohr for the *Seattle Times* (September 29, 2000) that the breakup was "a last resort" that had resulted from Microsoft's "intransigence," openly admitting that his decision would be vulnerable on appeal. Once again, the judge was criticized for talking to the media while the final outcome of a case was pending, and Microsoft filed legal briefs that charged Jackson with exhibiting a bias against the company. "By repeatedly commenting on the merits of the case in the press," the brief, which was excerpted by D. Ian Hopper for the *Detroit*

News (November 28, 2000, on-line), stated, "the district judge has cast himself in the public's eye as a participant in the controversy, thereby compromising the appearance of impartiality, if not demonstrating actual bias against Microsoft."

Jackson put the final implementation of his judgment on hold while Microsoft took its case to the Supreme Court. When the Supreme Court voted not to hear the case, Microsoft filed a brief with the U.S. Court of Appeals, which in the past had made judgments favorable to the company.

Jackson said that Microsoft's arrogance and dishonesty led to its apparent defeat in the case. Candor on the part of the company's executives would have "dispelled, to a large extent, any inference of malevolent motive," he told Ken Auletta for the *New Yorker* (January 15, 2001). "It would have disclosed that they were genuinely concerned that there might have been some merit to the allegations of improper conduct on their part. . . . In one sense, you have to give Microsoft credit for consistency. It has maintained, and continues to maintain, that it has done nothing amiss." Jackson told Auletta that he believes that Gates "has a Napoleonic concept of himself and his company, an arrogance that derives from power and unalloyed success, with no leavening hard experience, no reverses."

In June 2001 the United States Court of Appeals for the District of Columbia Circuit reversed Jackson's decision to split Microsoft into two companies. The court also found that by discussing the case with journalists before its outcome had been determined, Jackson had committed ethical violations that were "deliberate, repeated, egregious, and flagrant," according to an excerpt of the decision in an article by John Schwartz for the *New York Times* (June 29, 2001). "Public confidence in the integrity and impartiality of the judiciary is seriously jeopardized when judges secretly share their thoughts about the merits of pending cases with the press." Although Jackson was removed from the case, the court upheld his earlier finding that Microsoft constituted a monopoly. In August the case was sent back to the U.S. District Court in Washington, D.C.; late the following month District Court Judge Colleen Kollar-Kotelly ordered the Justice Department and Microsoft to engage in talks and to reach a settlement by October 12. In November Microsoft and the Justice Department announced that they had done so; that settlement, they said, would safeguard computer manufacturers' freedom to choose which software packages to bundle with Microsoft's operating systems and would restrict Microsoft's ability to stifle its competition. The settlement also called for the creation of a "technical committee," to be composed of three experts who were to work in Microsoft's offices and have full access to the company's records. Some commentators have argued that the agreement does not provide the government with ways to enforce its provisions, except through continued courtroom procedures. Lawrence Lessig, for example, reporting for the *New York Times* (November 9, 2001), wrote, "The decree . . . does nothing to establish a more efficient or direct way to hold Microsoft to its promises. It instead relies upon the company's good faith in living up to the letter and the spirit of the agreement—and of the law." Nine states, among them California and Massachusetts, have refused to accept the settlement; a hearing on the matter, to be held in the U.S. District Court presided over by Judge Kollar-Kotelly, is set for March 4, 2002.

Judge Jackson often walks the 21 blocks from his home in Washington, D.C., to the courthouse, on Pennsylvania Avenue. At the beginning of the Microsoft trial, it was widely reported that he seldom used his computer and never communicated via E-mail; by the time the proceedings had concluded, however, he had become well-versed in a number of technical areas. Jackson owns a vacation home in southern Maryland, where he enjoys sailing a boat he christened *Nisi Prius*, which is Latin for "unless before" and has come to mean "trial court." — C.L.

Suggested Reading: *Computerworld* p1+ Nov. 8, 1999; *Fortune* p168+ Mar. 1, 1999, with photos; *New Republic* p14+ July 23, 2001; *New York Times* C p1+ June 29, 2001, with photo; *New Yorker* p40+ Jan. 15, 2001; *Newsweek* p52+ Nov. 8, 1999, with photos; *Time* Nov. 15, 1999; *Washington Post* p5 Sep. 30, 1991, with photo; *Washingtonian* p37+ Apr. 1999

Tami Chappell/Archive Photos

Jakes, T.D.

June 9, 1957– Clergyman; writer; gospel artist.
Address: T.D. Jakes Ministries, P.O. Box 5390, 6777 W. Kiest Blvd., Dallas, TX 75236

"I've been called the shepherd of the shattered," the Pentecostal pastor T.D. Jakes told Pam Lambert and Michelle McCalope for *People* (November 9, 1998). "I think that's a fairly adept description." Jakes is the founder of the Potter's House, a high-tech place of worship in south Dallas, one of the most economically depressed areas in Texas. He is a charismatic speaker whose sermons most commonly address economic empowerment and, in a spiritual sense, reconciliation and healing. His 8,200-seat church, one of the first buildings of its kind, features a state-of-the-art sound system as well as laptop terminals that allow congregants to download, from their pews, notes from sermons they are hearing and other information. In the last five years, the multiracial, nondenominational ministry has grown to include more than 26,000 members. In addition to being a minister, Jakes is a Grammy-nominated gospel artist and the author of more than 20 books, several of which have reached the Christian best-sellers list. His unorthodox weaving of the tenets of pop psychology, capitalism, and Pentecostalism have made him both one of the most popular and one of the most controversial figures in contemporary Christianity. The growth of his congregation has broken records, and his books and recordings have enjoyed a significant following that is not limited to Christian audiences. Jakes is also the host of *The Potter's House* (originally titled *Get Ready with T.D. Jakes*), a television program broadcast in the U.S. four times a week, on the Trinity Broadcasting Network and Black Entertainment Television, as well as in countries including Uganda, South Africa, and England.

"Ministry is completely different in the African-American community," Jakes told Lauren F. Winner for *Christianity Today* (February 7, 2000). "The church is everything. We've never had a president, we've only had preachers. . . . Many of us have not had fathers, so he's the daddy we didn't have. We take pride in him in a way white folks don't understand." "When T.D. Jakes opens his mouth, what comes out is liquid fire," the television and radio evangelist Reverend John Hagee told Pam Lambert and Michelle McCalope. "It impacts your life with a message that doesn't stop when you walk out of there." Jakes's ability to connect with those seeking spiritual guidance has led some to regard him as a possible candidate to succeed the Reverend Billy Graham as the nation's most prominent and influential spiritual figure. "People are really hungry and they want a movement of God and that's happening," Potter's House member

Summer Barton told Christy Lemire for the *Abilene Reporter-News* (April 13, 1998, on-line). "It's not the same old boring service Sunday after Sunday. It's got life to it. People get tired of church and they want something that's going to keep them here."

Jakes has been criticized by some who are put off by his conspicuous affluence; the pastor, who wears expensive tailor-made clothes, owns a Mercedes Benz and a $1.7 million home in Dallas. He has been associated with celebrities including Deion Sanders, Emmett Smith, and Omar Stourtmire of the Dallas Cowboys football team, all three of whom he baptized; Jakes performed the wedding ceremony when Sanders married the model and actress Pilar Biggers. Eugene Rivers, a preacher and activist from Dorchester, Massachusetts, told Lauren F. Winner that he believes that Jakes is doing the African-American community a disservice by "promoting black middle-class consumerism. He is not offering black Christians a developed sense of biblical justice, like we got from Martin Luther King. The prophetic dimension of biblical faith is absent from Jakes's teaching." Jakes makes no apologies for his lavish lifestyle, claiming that he represents for his congregation the success that a person can achieve through hard work and a spiritual life. "To say to me that because I'm a Christian, or because I'm a minister or because I'm black . . . that I'm excluded from everything everybody else has an opportunity to have insofar as the legal pursuit of health and wealth and life is discrimination," he told Bill Broadway for the *Washington Post* (July 26, 1997). "When we get through worshipping and shouting and clapping and singing, we need jobs," Jakes told Pam Lambert and Michelle McCalope. "I'm not here for me, because I got mine. But I can't go to bed until they have theirs." He told Lauren F. Winner that he must "talk about economic empowerment because it is a reality for my people. Pastor Joe Success at First Suburban Christian Church does not need to preach that message." Jakes believes that young African-Americans, some of whom may be tempted to resort to illegal means to escape the difficulty of living in poor neighborhoods, can look to him as an example of someone who achieved prosperity without breaking the law. "One of the reasons they do not go straight is they believe if they go straight, they have got to go to work at Wendy's or Burger King," Jakes told Broadway. "Once they see a black man who is successful, who has written several books and been celebrated [across] the country and overseas, and he's not selling drugs but he's driving the same kind of car the pimp or drug dealer is, and he's not illegal and he's not immoral, it encourages young men. . . . They say, 'Hey, if God can do it for him, he can do it for me, too.'"

Other critics, such as the Christian broadcaster Hank Hanegraaff, have suggested that Jakes is a cult leader, pointing to his friendly relationships with such religious fundamentalists as the Promise Keepers, Jim Bakker, and Robert Liardon, a televangelist whose bizarre claims include ac-

counts of his one-on-one meeting with Jesus and his visit to a heavenly warehouse filled with lost body parts. Jakes is also a bishop responsible for more than 200 churches of the Higher Ground Always Abounding Assemblies, an organization that has aroused suspicions among Christians because of its adherence to Oneness Pentecostalism—a movement that disputes the traditional Christian concept of a Holy Trinity consisting of the Father, Son, and Holy Spirit. Oneness Pentecostalists believe that Jesus Christ alone is God, and for that reason they invoke the name of Jesus rather than all three members of the Trinity when performing the rite of baptism. Christians such as the African-American broadcaster Jerry Buckner have denounced Jakes as a heretic, and others have accused him of subscribing to modalism, an ancient belief that views the Father, Son, and Holy Spirit of the Trinity as different "modes" of God rather than three separate beings. "I believe in one God," Jakes told *Maranatha Christian Journal* (February 22, 2000, on-line). "I believe in the Father, the Son, and the Holy Spirit. I believe that these are distinct and separate in their function. Their distinctives are so separate that each has individual attributes, yet they are one. I do not believe in three Gods. . . . I look forward to the day when Christians do not judge one another by our diverse associations, nor the nuances of semantics, but by our love and the sweet fruit of Christ in our lives."

Thomas Dexter Jakes was born on June 9, 1957 in South Charleston, West Virginia. As a boy he often roamed the hills of his close-knit neighborhood, preaching to an imaginary congregation; his religious fervor earned him the nickname "Bible Boy." His mother, Odith, was a home-economics teacher who taught her three children to cook, sew, and do other household chores. His father, Ernest, an entrepreneur who created a successful janitorial service, developed a kidney disease when his son was 10 and was frequently hospitalized. Jakes inherited his father's business acumen, earning money by delivering newspapers and by selling Avon products and vegetables from the family garden. At the age of 15, he graduated from Center Business College (apparently not a college that conferred bachelor's degrees). Jakes attended religious services beginning at an early age, eventually becoming the musical director at his local Baptist church. He began preaching part-time while also taking psychology courses at West Virginia State College.

In 1980 Jakes established the Greater Emanuel Temple of Faith in Montgomery, West Virginia, a storefront church with an initial membership of 10 that expanded quickly. The following year he married Serita Ann Jamison and took a job with Union Carbide to support his family. Jakes faced a number of obstacles in 1982, when the chemical plant shut down and his father died. His father's long illness and death "had everything to do with who I am today," Jakes told Christy Lemire. "My ability to understand hurting people has to do with being raised in a hospital and talking with kids who were dying around me." As the Greater Emanuel Temple of Faith's congregation expanded, he began preaching full-time and hosted a local radio program called *The Master's Plan*. As the church grew, its headquarters moved first to Smithers, West Virginia, and then to South Charleston; 40 percent of the Greater Emanuel Temple's members were white, an uncommonly high number for a church run by an African-American pastor.

Jakes's television program, *Get Ready with T.D. Jakes*, began airing in 1993. The show was a vehicle for promoting T.D. Jakes Ministries, a not-for-profit organization, founded in 1994, that is responsible for producing his annual conferences. Some of his conferences, which include "Soul Survivors," "When Shepherds Bleed," and "Manpower," have attracted audiences as large as 52,000. A radio version of *Get Ready with T.D. Jakes* was nationally syndicated in 1995. Jakes received his bachelor's, master's, and doctoral degrees from Friends International Christian University, a correspondence school in Merced, California. As he explained to Bill Broadway, the institution "affords ministers an opportunity to pursue their education while they are ministering or pastoring. It's for guys like me who have already gone on [with their careers] and are halfway up the hill. They take credits you have accrued from school and experience and round out with courses until you are eligible for a diploma."

In 1996 Jakes was followed by 50 families when he relocated his ministry from West Virginia to a 28-acre compound in the Oak Cliff section of Dallas that had previously been owned by M. V. Grant, a televangelist imprisoned for tax evasion. The Potter's House is the largest church in Texas; it set records by acquiring 7,000 members in its first year, expanding to 17,000 by the second year, and reaching 21,000 by the third. The church's name comes from the biblical story of Jeremiah, a prophet whose observations of a potter's wheel brought him to the realization that damaged vessels can be made beautiful again. The ministry's dedication to improving the lives of those who live in the neglected south Dallas area is evidenced by its sponsorship of 48 outreach programs, including Raven's Refuge, a ministry for the homeless; Operation Rehab, which ministers to prostitutes; a GED literacy program; and the Transformation Treatment Program, which offers support and rehabilitation to those addicted to drugs and alcohol. When completed, the City of Refuge, launched in 1998, will offer rehabilitation, education, cultural events, and training services in an atmosphere not unlike that of a college campus; it will also house a preschool, a private school serving students from kindergarten through 12th grade, a youth ministry, a performing-arts center, and group homes for both pregnant teenagers and the elderly. The Potter's House has donated satellite dishes to more than 260 prisons in 29 states, so that Jakes's message can be heard by prisoners who seek spiritual guidance. "Most of our Bible was written in prison, by in-

mates," Jakes wrote on his official Web site. "Some of the greatest men that God ever used were incarcerated. In fact Jesus himself was incarcerated, locked up and executed. Jeremiah, Joseph, Peter, and the Apostle Paul were incarcerated. Many of the great people of faith, received their faith in prison—and were able to make a significant contribution to the world."

Jakes's three Sunday church services, described by Christy Lemire as "Andrew Lloyd Webber meets James Brown," are sometimes attended by more than 15,000 people. "He's the perfect preacher for today's society," the *Dallas Morning News* reporter Deborah Kovach Caldwell told Lauren F. Winner. "He taps into the recovery movement, he's appealing to a multiracial audience, and he's a Pentecostal pastor who preaches with intensity." Jakes first delivered his best-known sermon in 1992; titled "Woman Thou Art Loosed!," and based on the book of Genesis, it was aimed at uplifting women who had been abused or otherwise disrespected. He soon turned the sermon into a musical, which would play to packed houses across the nation, and in 1994 a small Christian press, Destiny Image, published a book based on the sermon that went on to sell 1.25 million copies. The success of that volume led to a two-book deal with G.P. Putnam & Sons, which published Jakes's best-selling *The Lady, the Lover, and Her Lord* (1998) and *Maximize the Moment: God's Action Plan for Your Life* (1999). Jakes sang on the recording *Woman Thou Art Loosed! Songs of Healing and Restoration*, which features music from the stage production and earned Jakes a Grammy nomination in 1998. Many women have responded positively to the pastor's willingness to deal in his sermons with such difficult issues as sexual abuse and domestic violence. Describing the impact of the musical, J. Lee Grady, editor of *Charisma* magazine, told David Van Biema for *Time* (December 11, 2000), "It wasn't just 'Read the Bible verse and talk about it.' . . . It was a married black man speaking from a shepherd's heart to wounded women, and they lined up by the thousands."

Jakes's other books include *Can You Stand to Be Blessed?* (1994), *Naked and Not Ashamed* (1995), *Loose That Man and Let Him Go!*, and *The Great Investment: Faith, Family, and Finance* (2000). The year 1997 saw the publication of *Lay Aside the Weight*, an inspirational book based on Jakes's own struggle to lose 100 pounds. Jakes has also released a number of albums, including *Sacred Love Songs* (1999) and *T.D. Jakes Live from the Potter's House with the Potter's House Mass Choir* (1999). In 2001 he released *The Storm Is Over*, on the new label Dexterity Sounds, in partnership with EMIK Gospel. The album hit number one on *Billboard*'s gospel chart in early April, selling close to 30,000 copies by the end of its second week. Jakes Ministries also offers a large selection of videotapes and audiotapes. In May 2001 Mahogany Cards, a division of Hallmark that caters to African-Americans, introduced a line of greeting cards known as

"Loose Your Spirit: Messages of Faith and Inspiration," based on Jakes's writings and sermons. T. D. Jakes's company, Touchdown Concepts, which produces what Jakes has labeled "empowerment entertainment," plans to mount a new play in 2001; in addition, in conjunction with Matt Crouch's firm Gener8xion Entertainment, it is working on a film version of *Woman, Thou Art Loosed.*

"I'm definitely a you-can-do-it person," Jakes told Christy Lemire. "I believe you can do anything. I have an urgency about life that's abnormal. I seize life like a person coming out of drowning seizes air." Those who know Jakes well continually praise his work and express thanks for the positive effect he has had on their lives. Paul Gage, who owns Gage Group Ministries, a consulting and fund-raising firm for religious organizations in the Dallas area, described Jakes to Lemire as "a man of integrity. He is anointed. He is a man of God here to proclaim the good news. Everything about this guy T.D. Jakes seems to be a little magical. It's his personality, his ability to communicate. He is spiritually gifted and equipped beyond the average person, I think." Jakes told Jadell Forman for *Texas Monthly* (September 1998) that his ministry had developed as "a result of loving God, loving people, and having experienced the love of God healing the broken issues of my life. I have an almost compulsive need to bring people into the presence that helped me to survive."

Jakes has been the recipient of several awards and honors. In 1996 *Gospel Today* magazine presented him with the Gospel Heritage Award for Ministry; the following year he was given the key to the city of Dallas, in acknowledgment of the community service provided by Raven's Refuge. In 1997 Jakes was named one of the Ten Most Influential Christian Leaders of the year by *Home Life* magazine, and the recording *Woman Thou Art Loosed! Songs of Healing and Restoration* was awarded the Gospel Music Association's Dove Seal; the following year the same recording was nominated for both a Dove Award and a Grammy Award. Jakes lives in south Dallas with his wife, Serita, who oversees the women's ministry at the Potter's House, and their five children. — C.L.

Suggested Reading: *Christianity Today* p52+ Feb. 7, 2000, with photos; *People* p121+ Nov. 9, 1998, with photos; *Texas Monthly* p120+ Sep. 1998, with photos; *Washington Post* B p7 July 26, 1997

Selected Books: *Woman Thou Art Loosed!*, 1994; *Can You Stand to be Blessed?*, 1995; *Naked and Not Ashamed*, 1995; *Loose That Man and Let Him Go!*, 1996; *Lay Aside the Weight*, 1997; *When Shepherds Bleed*, 1997; *The Lady, Her Lover, and Her Lord*, 1998; *Maximize the Moment: God's Action Plan for Your Life*, 1999; *The Great Investment: Faith, Family, and Finance*, 2000

Selected Recordings: *Woman Thou Art Loosed! Songs of Healing and Restoration*, 1997; *Sacred Love Songs*, 1999; *T.D. Jakes Live from the Potter's House with the Potter's House Mass Choir*, 1999; *Get Ready: the Best of T.D. Jakes*, 2000

Jeffords, James

May 11, 1934– U.S. Senator from Vermont.
Address: 728 Hart Senate Office Bldg.,
Washington, DC 20510-4503

On May 24, 2001 United States senator James Jeffords of Vermont announced his defection from the Republican Party and declared himself an Independent. This move, which by most accounts took his colleagues by surprise, upended the results of the 2000 elections, in which the GOP had secured a one-seat majority in the Senate that depended on the tie-breaking votes of the incoming Republican vice president, Richard B. Cheney. Jeffords's defection, and his subsequent announcement that he would vote largely along Democratic Party lines, shifted control of the Senate back to the Democrats. Jeffords stated in his public announcement, as quoted on his Senate Web site, that he had taken the controversial action "in order to best represent my state of Vermont, my own conscience, and the principles I have stood for my whole life." He further explained, "Increasingly, I find myself in dis-

agreement with my party. I understand that many people are more conservative than I am, and they form the Republican Party. Given the changing nature of the national party, it has become a struggle for our leaders to deal with me, and for me to deal with them." Political observers offered more specific reasons for Jeffords's decision. Gloria Borger, in *U.S. News & World Report* (June 4, 2001), placed responsibility with the presidential administration of George W. Bush, citing its disregard of Jeffords's political importance. The White House, Borger continued, had made a conscious and malicious effort to make Jeffords's political life "unbearable" in response to his tie-breaking vote in opposition to the president's $1.6 trillion tax cut. (Jeffords's last vote as a Republican was for a modified, $1.2 trillion tax cut, which passed both the House and the Senate and was signed into law soon thereafter.) Kenneth Walsh, Terence Samuel, and Angie Cannon, writing for *U.S. News & World Report* (June 4, 2001), also cited the Bush administration's mistreatment of Jeffords as a key reason for his defection. The article went on to note, however, that senior White House officials offered an alternative

Courtesy of Senator Jeffords's Office

James Jeffords

explanation, suggesting that Jeffords "simply got a better deal from the Democrats, that his talk of principle was cover for the real reasons: power and influence." Shortly after Jeffords's announcement on May 24, *Time.com* named him "Person of the Week" for "demonstrating to the White House and the U.S. Senate that revolutionaries often come in surprising packages."

James Merrill Jeffords was born on May 11, 1934 in Rutland, Vermont. He is the son of the late Marion H. Jeffords and the late Olin M. Jeffords, a chief justice of the Vermont Supreme Court. Jeffords attended public schools in the Rutland area through high school, then earned a B.S. degree from Yale University, in New Haven, Connecticut, in 1956. That year he enlisted in the U.S. Navy; he served three years of active duty. (He retired from the U.S. Naval Reserve as a captain in 1990.) After his active stint in the navy, Jeffords enrolled at Harvard Law School, in Cambridge, Massachusetts, from which he received a degree in 1962. He practiced law in Rutland for the next five years before winning his first public post, as Vermont state senator for Rutland County, a position he held from 1967 to 1968. The following year he ran for—and won—his first statewide office, becoming Vermont's attorney general and serving from 1969 to 1973. Jeffords was also a delegate to Vermont state Republican conventions in 1964, 1968, and 1972. In the last-named year he was the Republican gubernatorial nominee, but he was defeated in the general election by the Democratic candidate, Thomas Salmon. In 1975 Jeffords set his sights on Washington. He was elected as Vermont's lone member of the U.S. House of Representatives and served in the 94th Congress as well as the six succeeding Congresses (January 3, 1975–January 3, 1988).

As a U.S. representative, Jeffords displayed his state's unique brand of conservatism, one with strong links to the past. As he explained when he announced that he was becoming an Independent, "The party I grew up in was the party of Ernest Gibson, Ralph Flanders, and Bob Stafford. These names may not mean much today outside of Vermont. But each served Vermont as a Republican Senator in the 20th century. I became a Republican not because I was born into the party but because of the kind of fundamental principles that these and many other Republicans stood for: Moderation, tolerance, and fiscal responsibility. Their party, our party, was the party of [Abraham] Lincoln." During his 13-year tenure in the House of Representatives, Jeffords became the ranking Republican member of the House Education and Labor Committee and also served on the House Agriculture Committee. He co-founded the Congressional Arts Caucus and was one of six founders of the Congressional Solar Coalition. From 1978 to 1979 he served as chairman of the House Environmental Study Conference; he was also an adviser to the 1978 Law of the Sea Conference. Jeffords's moderate approach to conservatism was in evidence many times during his career in the House, where he often voted outside party lines. In 1981, for example, Jeffords was the only Republican to vote against President Ronald Reagan's tax bill, arguing that it would lead to an increased national deficit—a prediction that was borne out. He also opposed aid to the anti-Sandinista rebels in Nicaragua in 1986 and came out on several occasions against limits on abortion.

In 1988 the incumbent U.S. senator from Vermont, Republican Robert Stafford, decided to retire after 18 years of service. Jeffords was immediately touted as heir apparent for the position. He ran and won, easily defeating Democrat William Gray, with 67.9 percent of the vote. In the Senate Jeffords continued to vote outside the Republican box, often championing those issues usually reserved for Democrats and opposing causes embraced by Republicans. In early 1991, with the approach of the deadline imposed by President George H. W. Bush for Iraq's withdrawal of its troops from Kuwait, Jeffords showed reluctance to vote in favor of the president's plan to use force against Iraq. "I'm torn on the resolution," he told Elaine Sciolino for the *New York Times* (January 11, 1991), citing more than 700 phone calls and letters he had received from his constituents, 90 percent of which urged the senator to "oppose any move that would involve the United States in a war." (Members of the House and Senate—including Jeffords—voted 302–230 in favor of military action.) In 1993, with a new, Democratic president, Bill Clinton, in office, Jeffords again broke ranks with his Republican colleagues, becoming the first GOP member of Congress to announce his support of the Clinton administration's health-care plan; the vast majority of his colleagues in both the House and the Senate rejected the measure. As reported in the *Rut-*

land Herald (October 16, 2000, on-line) by Frederick Bever, however, Jeffords has on occasion been more conventional in his conservatism, particularly when it comes to supporting business interests. As Bever explained, in 1997 Jeffords sponsored a bill that paved the way for direct talks between employees and managers, which unions feared would make it possible for employers to avoid collective bargaining. Bever also cited Jeffords's vote to limit the liability of makers of products that harm consumers, as well as his 1999 tie-breaking vote against legislation that would have strengthened the U.S. Department of Agriculture's ability to enforce new meat and poultry inspection standards. Nonetheless, throughout the 1990s, Jeffords was a key ally of the Clinton administration. Bever wrote that Clinton even referred to Jeffords once as his "favorite Republican."

Party lines aside, Jeffords has managed to base his political career on several fundamental issues, which have put him in alliance with most of his constituency. Jessica Reaves for *Time.com* (May 24, 2001) wrote that in Vermont, "conservatives talk about the individual's ascendancy over the government, whereas in Washington you're more likely to hear them talk about the government's moral agenda." Demonstrating that viewpoint, while still a member of the House of Representatives, Jeffords began his effort to amend the Social Security Act to expand health-care coverage to eligible recipients of Supplemental Security Income and Social Security Disability Insurance who return to work. In 1999, long after Jeffords's election to the Senate, the bill was passed as the Work Incentives Improvement Act. As quoted on the National Multiple Sclerosis Society's (NMSS) Web site, Jeffords explained, "My reason for sponsoring this particular piece of legislation is quite simple. The Work Incentives Improvement Act of 1999 addresses a fundamental flaw in the current law. Today, individuals with disabilities are forced to make a choice—an absurd choice. They must choose between working and receiving health care. . . . This is not right." In 1999 the NMSS honored Jeffords as Senator of the Year. Jeffords has consistently supported women's right to abortion, mirroring his constituents' view of the individual's primacy over a perceived national morality. Frederick Bever reported, "Most years, Jeffords gets a 100 percent score from pro-choice organizations (and a 'zero' from the Right-to-Life Committee)." In 1997 the Republican-controlled U.S. House of Representatives approved an Interior Department spending bill that included a provision to abolish the National Endowment for the Arts (NEA), an organization designed to promote and fund the work of artists. Jeffords, who then headed the Senate committee that oversaw the NEA, led a bipartisan challenge to the House's decision and even countered with a proposed increase for the NEA's future budget. Two years later, instead of being eradicated, as House Republicans had proposed, the NEA was awarded an extra $4 million

for the 2000 fiscal year, bringing its total budget to $103 million. Other measures supported by Jeffords are increased spending for AIDS research and financing for special education. He has also gained a reputation as a staunch defender of homosexual rights. In 1999 Jeffords sponsored a bill for the Employment Non-Discrimination Act, which—if passed—will further protect gays and lesbians in the workplace.

Perhaps the most controversial of Jeffords's votes in the Senate came in 1999, during the impeachment trial of President Bill Clinton. On January 7 of that year, the House of Representatives presented the Senate with two articles of impeachment against the president, charging him with lying under oath before a federal grand jury and with committing obstruction of justice, both in connection with Monica Lewinsky—the White House intern with whom the president later admitted to engaging in sexual relations. Jeffords made it very clear from the beginning that he would vote against both articles, again representing the majority opinion of people in his home state, where Clinton enjoyed a soaring approval rating despite the scandal. Jeffords was later joined by several moderate Republican senators, including Arlen Specter of Pennsylvania and John Chafee of Rhode Island (the latter of whom died later that year). The Senate needed at least 67 votes, or the support of two-thirds of its 100 members, in order to secure the impeachment of the president. That support did not materialize, largely because of dissenting Republicans such as Jeffords, who was one of only five Senate Republicans to vote against the obstruction charge and one of 10 to vote against the perjury charge.

With regard to Jeffords's recent decision to become an Independent, many political experts have attributed a large part of his dismay with the GOP, and with the Bush administration in particular, to information published in an article by Melanie Fonder for the *Hill* (May 9, 2001, on-line). The article began, "The Bush administration, angry at Sen. Jim Jeffords . . . , is considering backing a Wisconsin Democrat's [Herb Kohl] proposal to end a program that sets dairy prices in New England." The program, called the Northeast Interstate Dairy Compact, allows six New England states, including Vermont, to set their own milk prices. The compact had long been known as one of Jeffords's top priorities, and, in fact, its loss would almost guarantee his defeat in the next election. The White House, in response to the article, denied any intention of tampering with the compact. Nonetheless, 15 days later Jeffords announced his defection from the Republican Party. Jonah Goldberg, writing for the *National Review* (June 25, 2001), offered this summary of events: "There have been many explanations for the defection of Sen. James Jeffords from the GOP: He is a man of principle. He is a lefty. He cares about education. He is just a weasel. But as the debates raged, an odd consensus emerged on one point: The Northeast Dairy Compact is a Third

Rail of American politics, and even Sir Thomas More would swear the Oath of Supremacy if the sanctity of this obscure price-fixing milk cartel were in jeopardy." (The reference was to the high-ranking Roman Catholic official in 16th-century England who was beheaded for refusing to acknowledge King Henry VIII as head of the Church of England and accept the nullification of the pope's authority in England.)

Jeffords is currently a member of four Senate committees: the Finance Committee, the Special Committee on Aging, the Environment and Public Works Committee, and the Veterans' Affairs Committee. Jeffords is the nation's only Independent senator and one of only three Independent members of Congress, the others being Representative Bernard Sanders, also of Vermont, and Representative Virgil Goode of Virginia. While he spends most of his time in Washington, Jeffords maintains a residence in Shrewsbury, Vermont, with his wife, the former Elizabeth Daley. They have two grown children, Leonard and Laura. *My Declaration of Independence*, in which Jeffords wrote about his departure from the Republican Party, was published in late 2001. — J.H.

Suggested Reading: *Hill* (on-line) May 9, 2001; *National Review* p27+ June 25, 2001, with photo; *New York Times* A p9 Jan. 11, 1991, with photo, A p23 Sep. 30, 1993, with photo, A p15 July 16, 1997, A p23 Feb. 12, 1999, C p2 Mar. 18, 1999; *Rutland Herald* (on-line) Oct. 16, 2000; *U.S. News & World Report* p16+ June 4, 2001, p29 June 4, 2001; *Washington Post* C p5 Sep. 16, 1999; Jeffords, James. *My Declaration of Independence*, 2001

Courtesy of U.S. House of Representatives

Johnson, Eddie Bernice

Dec. 3, 1935– U.S. Representative from Texas.
Address: 1511 Longworth House Office Bldg.,
Washington, DC 20510

In November 2000 Eddie Bernice Johnson, a Democrat, was elected to a fifth term as the representative of Texas's 30th Congressional District, an urban area that includes many of Dallas's African-American neighborhoods as well as parts of the city's downtown. Earlier, as a Texas state legislator in the early 1990s, Johnson had helped to redraw the boundaries of the 30th Congressional District. In 1996 the U.S. Supreme Court ruled that the re-districting was unconstitutional, because it had been done along racial lines; the district was again redrawn, and many of Johnson's supporters feared for her political future. But their worries proved to be unfounded: in the 1998 congressional elections, she won 72 percent of the vote; in 2000 no Republican challenged her, and she received 92 percent of the ballots cast. Johnson began her professional life as a psychiatric nurse; for some years she ran her own consulting company, which focused on commercial enterprises. In her more than eight years in Congress, she has compiled a mostly liberal voting record, though she is mindful of business interests in Dallas. A strong ally of President Bill Clinton, she called upon the black community to support Clinton during his impeachment trial in 1998, because "he's been the best president on our issues," as the *Almanac of American Politics, 2000* quoted her as saying. In addition to serving as a Democratic deputy whip, Johnson is the ranking Democrat on the Subcommittee on Basic Research of the House Committee on Science and serves on the House Committee on Transportation and Infrastructure. Currently, she also chairs the Congressional Black Caucus.

The daughter of Lee Edward Johnson and Lillie Mae Johnson, Eddie Bernice Johnson was born on December 3, 1935 in Waco, Texas. Beyond those bare facts, readily available sources contain little information about her early life. In 1955 she earned a nursing diploma from St. Mary's College in Notre Dame, Indiana. After her graduation she returned to Dallas, where, from 1956 to 1972, she was the chief psychiatric nurse at the Dallas Veterans Administration Hospital. During that time, in 1967, she earned a B.S. degree in nursing from Texas Christian University, in Fort Worth.

Johnson began her career in public service in 1972, when she ran successfully for a seat in the Texas House of Representatives. She thus became the first African-American woman to represent

Dallas in the Texas state legislature. Johnson was reelected to the Texas House in 1974 and 1976. During her second term she was appointed chair of the House Labor Committee—another first in Texas history, as never before had a woman chaired a major state House committee. In 1976, while serving in the legislature, Johnson earned a master's degree in public administration from Southern Methodist University, in Dallas.

Johnson resigned her seat in the House in 1977, during her third term, after President Jimmy Carter appointed her a regional director of the U.S. Department of Health, Education, and Welfare. (In 1979 the Department of Education Organization Act provided for a separate Cabinet-level Department of Education, and the next year the Department of Health, Education, and Welfare was renamed the Department of Health and Human Services.) From 1979 through 1981 Johnson worked for the department in Washington, D.C., as executive assistant to the administrator for primary-health-care policy.

For seven years after she returned to Dallas in 1981 (the year a new administration, headed by President Ronald Reagan, came into power), Johnson served as vice president of the Visiting Nurse Association of Dallas. She also founded Eddie Bernice Johnson and Associates, a consulting firm that helped businesses expand or relocate to the Dallas–Fort Worth area. In 1986 she won election to the Texas State Senate in the 23rd Senatorial District, in the Dallas area. While serving in the state Senate, Johnson continued to operate her business; in 1988 she expanded it to include Metroplex News, an airport-concessions management firm.

As chairwoman of the Texas Senate Subcommittee on Congressional Districts, Johnson took a pivotal role in redrafting the state's congressional districts to reflect population changes revealed by the 1990 census. Texas had grown considerably during the 1980s and was entitled to three new congressional districts. In an attempt to comply with the Voting Rights Act of 1965 and to insure minority representation in Congress, the redistricting plan Johnson helped to create included a new district in Dallas County (District 30) in which African-Americans were in the majority; a new district near Houston (District 29), the majority of whose residents were Hispanic; and a redrawn District 18, also near Houston, in which blacks constituted the majority. All three districts were tortuous geographic constructs, and all were overwhelmingly Democratic. Although Republicans—and even Democrats from adjoining districts who were disturbed that portions of their established constituencies had been siphoned away—objected to the plan, the new district maps were approved by the U.S. Department of Justice in 1991 and used in the 1992 congressional elections. That same year Johnson made her first run for Congress in the 30th District; she won both the primary (with almost 92 percent of the Democratic vote) and the general election (with nearly 72 percent of the ballots cast).

During her first term Johnson served on the House Science, Space, and Technology Committee (now known as the Committee on Science) as well as on the Committee on Public Works and Transportation (now called the Committee on Transportation and Infrastructure); she was also elected Congressional Black Caucus whip. A loyal Democrat and a strong supporter of President Bill Clinton, Johnson voted along party lines 94 percent of the time during her first two years in office. She regularly endorsed gun control and abortion rights, and among her colleagues she was regarded as a social liberal on most issues. On economic issues Johnson was closer to the center; she was hesitant to back the North America Free Trade Agreement (NAFTA), but she voted for the pact after the Clinton administration assured her that NAFTA "would not cause my district to lose additional jobs," as she recalled, according to CNN (on-line).

Meanwhile, opponents of the Texas redistricting plan had begun to challenge the new districts in court. In early 1994 the Texas Coalition for a Color Blind Texas, a group of Republicans from Houston and Dallas, filed a lawsuit charging that the districts—including the 30th—had been racially gerrymandered, in violation of the Fourteenth Amendment to the Constitution. In a preliminary hearing a panel of judges ruled that the 30th District could stand but nevertheless remarked that it "received well-deserved ridicule as the most gerrymandered district in the United States." On appeal, however, a three-judge panel of the U.S. District Court ruled in August 1994 in favor of the plaintiffs; the panel allowed the 1994 elections to proceed as planned, but ordered the state legislature to draft a new plan in 1995. In 1994 Johnson ran unopposed in the primary, then secured over 72 percent of the vote in the general election.

Soon afterward the state of Texas appealed the district court's 1994 decision. On June 13, 1996, in *Bush v. Vera* (named for then–Texas governor George W. Bush and one of the respondents), the U.S. Supreme Court upheld the district court's ruling that Texas's 18th, 29th, and 30th Congressional Districts constituted racial gerrymanders and violated the Equal Protection Clause of the Fourteenth Amendment. (Section 1 of the amendment provides that no state shall "deny to any person within its jurisdiction the equal protection of the laws.") The Supreme Court's decision was grounded in various earlier decisions, notably *Shaw v. Reno* (1993) and *Miller v. Johnson* (1995). In *Shaw v. Reno* the Court ruled that people of any race are entitled to challenge districting plans on grounds of racial discrimination; specifically, a redistricting map violates the Equal Protection Clause if it is "so extremely irregular on its face that it rationally can be viewed only as an effort to segregate the races for purposes of voting, without regard for traditional districting principles." In some respects that statement contradicts the Voting Rights Act of 1965, which strove to guarantee equal electoral opportunity for racial minorities by requiring the government to consider issues of race in drawing district boundaries, among other practices. As a result of the Court's ruling in *Shaw v. Reno*, governmental bodies were required to strike a balance between the demands of the Voting Rights Act, on the one hand, and those of *Shaw*, on the other.

In *Miller v. Johnson* the Court clarified its position on the competing demands of *Shaw* and the Voting Rights Act. To challenge a district on Equal Protection grounds, Justice Anthony M. Kennedy wrote in the Court's opinion, a plaintiff "must prove that the legislature subordinated traditional race-neutral districting principles, including but not limited to compactness, contiguity, respect for political subdivisions or communities defined by actual shared interests, to racial considerations. Where these or other race-neutral considerations are the basis for redistricting legislation, and are not subordinated to race, a state can 'defeat a claim that a district has been gerrymandered on racial lines.'" In *Bush v. Vera* Johnson and her fellow appellants did not deny that they had subordinated such race-neutral considerations as compactness and contiguity in deference to the aim of creating a majority African-American district, in compliance with the Voting Rights Act. However, they argued that they had given other race-neutral considerations—especially the attempt to unite communities of interest and to protect political incumbencies—as much weight as the desire to create a "majority minority district." "Our plan was incumbency protection, pretty much," Johnson told Kenneth J. Cooper and Kevin Merida for the *Washington Post* (January 28, 1994).

The Court rejected such claims, holding that race had been the paramount consideration in the creation of District 30. "The record contains no basis for displacing the District Court's conclusion that race predominated over [other] factors . . .," Justice Sandra Day O'Connor wrote in an opinion in which she was joined by Justice Kennedy and Chief Justice William H. Rehnquist. "The evidence amply supports the District Court's conclusions that racially motivated gerrymandering had a qualitatively greater influence on the drawing of district lines than politically motivated gerrymandering, . . . and that political gerrymandering was accomplished in large part by the use of race as a proxy for political characteristics." In a dissenting opinion in which he was joined by Justices Ruth Bader Ginsburg and Stephen G. Breyer, Justice John Paul Stevens wrote, "I would find these districts constitutional, for each considers race only to the extent necessary to comply with the State's responsibilities under the Voting Rights Act while achieving other race neutral political and geographical requirements. The plurality's finding to the contrary unnecessarily restricts the ability of States to conform their behavior to the Voting Rights Act while simultaneously complying with other race neutral goals."

In August 1996 a panel of federal judges drafted a revised district map for the 1996 congressional elections. The panel annulled the results of the spring 1996 primaries and provided instead for open primaries on November 5; runoffs would be held in those districts where no single candidate won a majority of the votes. In the open primary held in the redrawn 30th District, in which 45 percent of the population were African-Americans, Johnson won 55 percent of the ballots cast in a seven-way race and was thus reelected without a runoff. In the general election held two years later, she secured 72 percent of the vote.

In recent years Johnson has sponsored legislation to bridge the so-called digital divide, which refers to the differences in opportunities available to people who have access to the latest computer, telephone, and Internet technology (and the training that enables them to make optimum use of it) and those who lack such access. She was a strong supporter of the 1998 Next Generation Internet Research Act, which provided funding for research on networking technologies. She also promoted initiatives to boost students' science and math skills and to encourage them to pursue technical careers. A vigorous proponent of permanent normal trade relations (PNTR) with China, Johnson argued, as posted on her official Web site, that "granting PNTR to China is not a vote against unions and labor. In fact, America's leadership in global trade is the only way we can protect our workers. . . . The labor movement must prepare for the new global economy and help us create high-tech, high wage jobs that will lift the standard of living for all of America's workers." Johnson has also worked to end racial profiling.

In December 2000 Johnson was elected chair of the Congressional Black Caucus (CBC), an alliance that currently numbers 37 Democratic African-American representatives. Johnson beat her closest rival for the post, Representative Bennie Thompson of Mississippi, by one vote. As chair of the CBC, Johnson has promised to press for election reform, which she has called the organization's number-one legislative priority. "We need to examine what happened in Election 2000, and why it happened . . . ," Johnson declared, as cited by *Jet* (March 19, 2001). (She was referring to the finding by the National Association for the Advancement of Colored People that numerous African-American voters had reported intimidation by election officials, inaccurate voter registration lists, subjective, vague, or nonexistent ballot-counting standards, and flawed ballot designs in the 2000 general elections.) "Make no mistake about it," Johnson added, "the CBC intends to keep this issue in the forefront. It is the duty of this Congress to assure that the faults in our national election system are corrected before the 2002 elections." She also vowed to press for expanded minority access to capital, improved early health care, and closer American relations with Africa.

Johnson's honors include the Heroes Award, given by the Texas State Conference of NAACP Branches "to an individual who illustrates a lifetime commitment of advancing civil rights," and the President's Award, given by the National Conference of Black Mayors in 2001. The congresswoman married in 1956 and divorced in 1970. She has one son, Kirk, and three grandsons. — P.K.

Suggested Reading: *Jet* p4+ Dec. 25, 2000–Jan. 1, 2001; *New York Times* I p6 Jun. 15, 1996, I p1+ Nov. 23, 1996; *Almanac of American Politics, 2000*; Foerstel, Karen. *Biographical Dictionary of Congressional Women*, 1999; Gill, LaVerne McCain. *African American Women in Congress: Forming and Transforming History*, 1997; U.S. House of Representatives Web site

Tami Chappell/Archive Photos

Jones, Chipper

Apr. 24, 1972– Baseball player with the Atlanta Braves. Address: Atlanta Braves. P.O. Box 4064, Atlanta, GA 30302-4064

As a boy, the Atlanta Braves baseball player Chipper Jones modeled himself after the legendary New York Yankees switch-hitter Mickey Mantle. Mantle represented diligence, enthusiasm for the game, and quiet confidence, and the young Jones tried to embrace the same values. As a professional, Jones has always practiced and played hard and has proven himself to be a dedicated member of his team. He even emulates the old-timers by pulling up his pant legs to expose his stirrup socks. "In many ways, Jones does seem a figure out of another

sports era, a genuine throwback to the days when athletes played hard all the time and wouldn't think about dissing a teammate or a manager . . . ," Harry Stein wrote for *Sport* (July 1998). "In an era when players with outrageous salaries never seem to run out of things to gripe about, Chipper has a genuine appreciation for the life he's getting to live." After seven full seasons of stellar performance and a contract that has made him one of the highest-paid players in baseball, the third baseman remains passionately devoted to the game. Eager to serve as a role model, he has set up a foundation, named for himself, that aims to improve the lives of young people.

The only child of Larry Wayne Jones Sr. and his wife, Lynn, Larry Wayne Jones Jr. was born in De Land, Florida, on April 24, 1972 and grew up in the smaller town of Pierson, Florida. As a young man his father had been drafted as a shortstop by the Chicago Cubs baseball team; choosing to build a career in education rather than baseball, he worked as a secondary-school algebra teacher and baseball coach. Larry Jr. was still a little boy when his father began teaching him the fundamentals of baseball; father and son practiced in the backyard with a tennis ball and a section of PVC pipe. Jones looked and acted so much like his father that everyone described him as "a chip off the old block"—thus his nickname, Chipper. "Chipper and his father are absolute clones," Jones's mother, a professional horsewoman, told Michael Bamberger for *Sports Illustrated* (September 16, 1996). "They stand the same way, they walk the same, they field the same. Watching Chipper play shortstop in high school was like watching Larry play shortstop in college. They are both competitive—to a fault. When Chipper comes home and wants his father to throw him a little batting practice, the next thing you know, Larry's trying to strike him out and Chipper's trying to hit home runs. But that's what makes them so good at what they do."

By the time he was in junior high school, Jones had already become a local phenomenon in baseball. When he entered the eighth grade, at Taylor Junior-Senior High School, his father temporarily resigned from coaching there, because he knew that his son was qualified to replace a senior student as a team starter, and he wanted to avoid accusations of favoritism. As Jones Sr. knew would happen, Chipper got the starting position at shortstop in eighth grade, without his father's intervention. When Jones entered his sophomore year in high school, his father transferred him to a private boarding school, the Bolles School, in Jacksonville, Florida—several hours' drive north of Pierson—because he believed that, in light of Chipper's importance to the school as an athlete, teachers at Taylor were lowering their academic standards for Chipper. Pierson's residents regretted losing Chipper, whom professional baseball scouts, sometimes as many as 40 to 50 at a time, were already coming to see on a regular basis. The town has since named both a street and a ballpark for him.

Jones found Bolles "extremely tough at first," as he recalled on his Web site, *chipperjones.com* (May 15, 2000). But, he wrote, "it turned out to be the best thing that my parents ever did for me. It forced me to grow up, to overcome my fears and insecurities, to be challenged academically, and to play sports in a place where I wasn't already guaranteed a spot because of my past performance. It made [me] prove myself all over again, which was something I needed at the time."

At Bolles, Jones played basketball and football as well as baseball. He led the school baseball team to three straight Class AA baseball championship games, and each year he helped his team eliminate Taylor from the play-offs. At the end of his senior year, in 1990, the Atlanta Braves picked him first in the draft. The relatively modest contract—for $350,000—was negotiated without agents in his parents' living room. "I don't play for money. I play for the love of the game," Jones declared to Ben Kaplan for *Sports Illustrated for Kids* (June 1997). Within a couple of weeks, he was playing for the Braves' Single-A minor-league team.

Jones progressed quickly in the minor leagues. In his first season he achieved a batting average of .326, with 15 home runs and 98 runs batted in (RBIs). In 1993 he was named the Braves AAA minor-league Player of the Year and played eight games with the Braves' major-league club. In 1994 the Braves deemed him ready for the major leagues. Because the team already had an excellent shortstop and third baseman, the Braves opted to start Jones in left field. Jones missed his first year, though, because of a preseason base-running accident in which he tore the anterior cruciate ligament in his left knee. As it happened, much of the 1994 season was lost anyway, because of a baseball strike that began in August and was not settled until April 1995. Jones, who earned nothing during the strike, found himself in a difficult financial position: he had gotten married in 1991, and he and his wife, the former Karin Fulford, were worried that they would not be able to keep up their mortgage payments. To avoid having to sell their home, Jones's wife took a job as a substitute teacher to supplement their income while Jones nursed himself back to health.

When Jones returned to work, in 1995, he was in good shape. He had added some muscle to his six-foot four-inch frame and now weighed 210 pounds. The Braves made him a third baseman, and he immediately attracted notice around the league. Less than midway through the season, Tim Kurkjian wrote for *Sports Illustrated* (June 5, 1995), "If you watch Braves third baseman Chipper Jones play nine innings and then talk to him for 10 minutes, you can't help thinking, This guy *can't* be a rookie. He doesn't play like a rookie, nor does he act, think, or talk like one. In a year in which the rookie crop is not bountiful, it's clear that the 23-year-old Jones, who has been Atlanta's best all-around player so far this season, is going to be a star."

Jones finished the season with a batting average of .265, with 23 home runs and 86 RBIs. In the play-offs, in which the Braves faced the Colorado Rockies, he improved on his regular-season performance. In the first game he saved a run with an impressive defensive play and then hit two home runs, including a game winner in the ninth inning, which enabled the Braves to top the Rockies by a score of 5–4. In the second game Jones began a ninth-inning rally with a double that helped his team achieve a 7–4 win. In the fourth game, with the Braves down 3–0 in the third inning, Jones hit a double to score two runs and then reached home plate after a teammate hit a home run. The Braves won, 10–4, thus eliminating the Rockies. Jones finished the next round, against the Cincinnati Reds, with a .389 batting average and four RBIs. The Braves went on to win the 1995 World Series, by beating the Cleveland Indians in six games. The *Sporting News* named Jones Rookie of the Year, and he signed a four-year, $8.25 million contract with the Braves. In 1996 Jones became a full-fledged star. His batting average that season was .309, he had 30 home runs and 110 RBIs, and he was selected to play in the All-Star Game. The Braves once again made it to the World Series, this time losing the world championship to the New York Yankees in six games.

Meanwhile, Jones was becoming an integral part of the team not only on but also off the playing field. His teammates knew they could count on him to keep track of vital game statistics, because his memory for such things was almost photographic. Also, he proved he had a sense of humor when, before the team was to board a plane one day, a teammate stole his clothes from his locker and replaced them with a clownish outfit of striped pants, plaid jacket, big white shoes, and a big, loud tie. Jones wore the clothing on the flight, much to the delight of his teammates.

In 1997 the Braves racked up 101 wins, more than any other team that season. As he had the previous year, Jones broke the 100-RBI mark, with 111, while batting .295 and swatting 21 home runs. He hit three grand slams (home runs with three runners on base) in the space of only 13 games, setting a National League record for hitting three grand slams in the fewest number of games. Jones was again selected to play in the All-Star Game. That year the Braves lost to the Florida Marlins in the National League Championship Series, partly because of Jones, who cost his team potential runs by making several uncharacteristic base-running errors. Jones was quick to own up to his flawed play. "No excuses," he said to Harry Stein for *Sport* (July 1998). "Those were stupid mistakes—they shouldn't have happened. They won't again." He also told Stein, "I'm not by any means the best player in the game. I've just gotta keep working 'til I get there." Errors on the playing field apparently did not undermine Jones's confidence. In his 1995 interview with Tim Kurkjian, he had acknowledged having what he termed a "necessary arrogance." "I feel I do all things well," he had said, "and I'm intense about it." In 1998, continuing to play with great intensity, he attained a batting average of .313, with 34 home runs and 107 RBIs, and he again made the All-Star team. The Braves won their division, compiling 106 victories, and then lost the National Championship Series, this time to the San Diego Padres in six games.

In October 1998 Jones publicly admitted to having a child out of wedlock with a waitress from Hooters named Jennifer Rutledge. "I went public partly because my wife pressured me to do it," he told Tom Verducci for *Sports Illustrated* (October 4, 1999). "But that was like a weight lifting off my shoulders. I had been living a hypocritical life. I wasn't as quick to look people in the eye, and I didn't want to do that anymore. That was the only good thing that came out of it. I cleared my conscience. I'm paying for my mistakes. I am greatly sorry for them. But I feel it's time to close the door." Bill Zack, the author of *Chipper Jones* (1999), a book for juvenile readers, quoted him on *Bravos Web* (1999, on-line) as saying, "I want to be a better role model. . . . I've gone out to schools and I've been on TV and I've said all the right things and it appears like I've done all the right things . . . kind of saying one thing out of one side of my mouth and behind closed doors doing totally the opposite. It's time I started practicing what I'm preaching." In 1999 Jones and his wife divorced.

As late as May 17 that year, Jones's batting average was only .259, which inspired fears that his personal troubles and fallout from the scandal surrounding his infidelity might hurt Jones's ability to play ball. But he pulled out of his slump—in spectacular fashion. Earlier, in the off-season, the Braves' new batting coach, Don Baylor, had pushed Jones to be more aggressive at the plate and to try for more home runs. Baylor's encouragement paid off: showing that he could hit with power from both sides of home plate, Jones finished the season with 45 home runs. Toward the end of the season, as the Braves were fighting the New York Mets for first place in the National League East, Jones almost single-handedly put the Mets out of the running. In a three-game series, he hit four home runs as the Braves swept the Mets and assured themselves another first-place finish in their division. (Jones had made a habit of excelling at crucial moments. Tom Verducci, reporting in October 1999, characterized him as the best National League hitter in the late innings of close games: at that time he was averaging an impressive .415 in the seventh inning or later, when his team was either tied, ahead by a run, or in position to score the tying run.)

Jones's 1999 season batting average was .319, with 110 RBIs. He was named to the Associated Press All-Star Team and became the first major leaguer ever to hit at least .300 with at least 40 doubles, 40 home runs, 100 walks, and 20 stolen bases. Those statistics were enough to earn him the 1999 National League Most Valuable Player honor. Jones was well aware that his late-season dominance over the Mets was an important factor in his getting the award and gaining renown around the league. "Any time I read a story about the MVP they would point directly to that series," he told Jack O'Connell for the *Sporting News* (November 17, 1999, on-line). "The Mets were only a game behind us when they came in. We knew every game was important, and they were trying to knock us off. Fortunately, I was seeing the ball very well at that time. Those four home runs were huge. I'd like to think my name was already on the map before that, but that kind of jump-started everything."

At that time Jones's salary was significantly lower than those of most of the other top players in the game. After the 1999 season Jones felt that he deserved higher pay, and he threatened to leave the Braves if they didn't offer him a new contract. "I've been a bargain the last couple of years," he told Jon Heyman for the *Sporting News* (March 26, 2000, on-line). "I'm not going to do that anymore. When my day comes, I'm going to take advantage of it. If the Braves are not ready to recognize everything I tried to do for this organization . . . there will be no hard feelings. Just as long as there are no hard feelings if I play somewhere else."

Going into the 2000 season, the Braves gave Jones a six-year, $90 million contract. Some commentators wondered whether the added pressure of being among the highest-paid players in baseball would hurt Jones. Defensively, he did struggle somewhat, committing 25 errors, the most since his rookie year. His batting average with runners in scoring position (.260) was also lower than usual. Nevertheless, he still had an excellent season, with a batting average of .311, 111 RBIs, and 36 home runs. Moreover, he became only the second third baseman in history to hit at least 100 RBIs five seasons in a row. (The first was the Hall of Famer Pie Traynor, in the five years beginning in 1927.) The Braves once again won their division in 2000, then lost to the St. Louis Cardinals in the first round of the play-offs.

The 2001 season was perhaps Jones's finest to date. He batted .330, with 38 home runs and an on-base percentage (OBP) of .427. For the seventh time in his career, he made it to the play-offs with the Braves. The team lost their chance to play in the World Series, though, falling to the Arizona Diamondbacks in six games.

Not long ago Jones set up the Chipper Jones Family Foundation, which works with such organizations as the Cystic Fibrosis Foundation and Boys & Girls Clubs of America with the goal of helping young people. The proceeds from the sales of autographed items offered on his Web site (baseballs, priced at $69 apiece; jerseys, for $279; and bats, for $99) support the activities of the foundation. At present, Jones has agreements with 10 corporate sponsors, among them Mizuno, which manufactures sporting goods; WSB Radio, which broadcasts Braves' games; and Sony PlayStation.

From his liaison with Jennifer Rutledge, Jones has one son, Matthew. In March 2000 he married Sharon Logonov. His recreational activities are hunting and fishing. — P.G.H.

Suggested Reading: *Atlanta Journal-Constitution* E p1 Sep. 17, 2000; Chipper Jones Web site; *Sport* p47+ July 1998, with photos; *Sporting News* (on-line) Nov. 17, 1999, Mar. 26, 2000; *Sports Illustrated* p78+ June 5, 1995, with photos, p26+ Oct. 16, 1995, with photo, p60+ Sep. 16, 1996, with photos, p44+ Oct. 4, 1999; *Sports Illustrated for Kids* p36+ June 1997; *St. Louis Post-Dispatch* D p10 Oct. 21, 2001

Renders/Isopress/Getty Images

Kabila, Joseph

1972(?)– President of the Democratic Republic of the Congo. Address: c/o Permanent Mission to the United Nations, Democratic Republic of the Congo, 866 United Nations Plaza, Suite 511, New York, NY 10017

Joseph Kabila is the president of the Democratic Republic of the Congo (DRC), a position he assumed following the assassination of his father, Laurent Désiré Kabila, in January 2001. The Congo—known variously over the years as the Belgian Congo, the Republic of Congo, and Zaire—has been at war for the last three years, as rebel soldiers from Rwanda, Uganda, and Burundi have fought to take control of the country and thus gain possession of its vast supply of natural resources, which include rich soil, copper, uranium, diamonds, gold, and timber. Zimbabwe, Angola, and Namibia have pro-

vided military support to the struggling nation; Western countries, including the United States, France, and Belgium, also have interests in the region. At the height of the war, rebel forces controlled close to 60 percent of the country. After taking office Kabila met with several world leaders and promised to work to end the conflict in his country. A substantial number of foreign troops have left the Congo since February 2001, following the United Nations Security Council's approval of a plan that both facilitated the withdrawal of those combatants and placed U.N. peacekeepers in the Congo. But some groups remain, among them the Rwanda-based rebels known as the RCD (Congolese Rally for Democracy). Peace negotiations continue, but Kabila has made it clear that no peaceful solution is possible until all the invading troops depart. According to estimates of the New York–based International Rescue Committee, 2.5 million people have died since the war began, many from such causes as preventable diseases and malnutrition.

The third-largest country on the African continent, after Algeria and the Sudan, the Congo is one-quarter the area of the United States and is home to 50 million people from more than 200 ethnic groups. In 1885 King Leopold II of Belgium laid claim to the nation, setting off an extended period of European colonization of Africa; it is estimated that as many as 10 million Congolese died at the hands of the invading Belgian forces. Many Congolese were enslaved well into the 20th century. In 1960 the Congo won its independence from Belgium; Laurent Kabila was a member of a group of rebels who supported Patrice Lumumba, the first prime minister of the Republic of Congo, late in 1960. Mobutu Sese Seko led a coup against Lumumba; five years later, after having ceded power to President Joseph Kasavubu, Mobutu staged a second coup and went on to rule the country for more than three decades. Mobutu's dictatorship was tolerated by the leaders of Western nations in large part because he was anti-Communist.

Meanwhile, in 1967 Laurent Kabila founded the People's Revolutionary Party, which successfully established farming collectives, health-care facilities, and schools and conducted trade in gold, ivory, and diamonds, yet failed for many years in its efforts to remove Mobutu from power. Then, in 1997, Kabila led the Alliance of Democratic Forces for the Liberation of the Congo in a successful campaign to overthrow Mobutu. Kabila declared himself head of state and renamed the region the Democratic Republic of the Congo. Although he promised reform, Kabila soon proved himself to be a corrupt dictator who violated human rights and restricted the press. "During his nearly four years in power, former President Kabila regularly and ruthlessly violated the human rights of the Congolese people, killing, torturing, imprisoning, and causing the 'disappearance' of any who he thought threatened him or his regime," the group Human Rights Watch reported on its Web site in January

2001. "Among those who suffered most were political opponents, leaders of civil society, human rights activists, and journalists." Kabila was generally regarded as an impediment to the peace process, looking the other way as Rwandan and Ugandan allies raped and killed civilians and refusing to allow U.N. troops to intervene. He also supported and armed the Interahamwe militiamen and the Burundian Hutu, who committed genocide in Rwanda in 1994. Uganda and Rwanda, former allies of Laurent Kabila, turned on the leader in 1998, initiating a conflict that drew the nation into civil war.

The newly appointed Congolese president, Joseph Kabila, hopes to revive the Lusaka Accords, a peace agreement that was signed in 1999 by most of the countries involved in the conflict—and that has since been ignored. As he took office, some questioned Kabila's ability to rule the country while surrounded by his father's close-knit circle of advisers, a concern he soon eliminated by dismissing the entire cabinet. In his late 20s or early 30s (his exact date of birth is unknown), Kabila has little political experience, although he served in his father's army as both chief of staff and a major-general. "He never sought power, it just happened," Ernest Neville, Kabila's spiritual adviser, told Sudarsan Raghavan for the Knight Ridder News Service (January 26, 2001). Some Congolese regard the new president, who spent much of his life outside the region, as a foreigner; other commentators have noted that Kabila's inability to speak French, the official language of his nation, may diminish his effectiveness as a leader. "I would like to see the Congo united," Kabila told IRIN (March 30, 2001, on-line). "I would like to see it invaded no more. For the moment, that is my objective. We have lost nearly two million Congolese in this war. One cannot accept such things anymore. The international community must insist on the withdrawal of all these foreign military forces."

Joseph Kabila was born in approximately 1972. (Some sources state that the year may be as early as 1969.) The eldest of 10 children, he is reported to have grown up either in eastern Congo, where his father founded a Marxist/Pan-Africanist political party, or in Tanzania, where his father worked as a diamond and ivory trafficker. Kabila was educated in Tanzania, Kenya, and Uganda, where he learned both English and Swahili. He received military training in Uganda and Rwanda. In 1996 Kabila joined his father in the struggle against Mobutu Sese Seko. After the takeover of the capital city of Kinshasa, in May 1997, Laurent Kabila sent Joseph to China, where the son underwent six months of additional military training. Not long after Joseph's return, Laurent Kabila fired the army's chief of staff, Celestin Kifwa, and replaced him with his son. In August 1998 Joseph Kabila was promoted to the position of major-general of the armed forces.

Laurent Kabila was assassinated by a member of his security force, later identified as Rashidi Kasereka, on January 16, 2001; Kasereka was killed by Kabila's guards as he attempted to flee the scene of the murder. (The assassin's motives are not known.) On the day that his father was interred, Joseph Kabila, assuming the duties—though not the official post—of the presidency, met with the leaders of Zimbabwe, Angola, and Namibia. A week later he embarked on a diplomatic mission aimed at garnering support for a peaceful resolution to the war. He convened with President Thabo Mbeki of South Africa and President Jacques Chirac of France before traveling to the United States, where he spoke before the United Nations and held separate meetings with President George W. Bush, Secretary of State Colin Powell, and Rwandan president Paul Kagame. Kabila also met with James Wolfensohn, president of the World Bank, and representatives of the International Monetary Fund (IMF). He was officially sworn in as president 10 days after his father's assassination; the postponement of the inauguration allowed the Parliament to approve the appointment. (Nobody else vied for the post; the delay stemmed from the absence of established rules for a transfer of power.) "I swear my fidelity to the country," Kabila stated, according to CNN.com (January 26, 2001), "and I will respect the constitutionality of the republic, to guarantee its independence and to unite the Congolese people and to unite the entire country and defend its borders." The new president also promised to hold free elections, open up the diamond market (which had been monopolized by International Diamond Industries, an Israeli company), and welcome international peacekeeping forces.

One of Kabila's first directives was to pay soldiers and civil servants, who had not been compensated for their services for several months. Perhaps in part because he dismissed the members of his father's cabinet in early April and has allowed peacekeeping forces to enter the country, Kabila has gained the support of the international community as well as many Congolese citizens. The new president's commitment to peace efforts, in sharp contrast to his father's many attempts to stall such proceedings, has surprised diplomats. Kabila hopes to renegotiate the Lusaka Accords and lead his nation to a peaceful resolution of the ongoing conflict. "The most important thing I can do for my country is to see an end to this war," he told Ray Suarez for Online NewsHour (February 1, 2001). Kabila has said that he is ready to face the challenges awaiting him and believes that "the future is bright for the Congo," if, as he told Suarez, "the Congolese people will take this opportunity, sit down, talk to each other. But, of course, the occupation must end in order for the Congolese people to do that—in perfect harmony with each other, not being forced by any foreign power, be it Uganda or Rwanda." Although some troops have begun to withdraw from the region, inspiring hope that a peaceful solution to the conflict may be possible,

Kabila's continued military support of the Interahamwe militia and the Burundian Hutu has stalled negotiations with Rwanda, whose leaders have vowed to take revenge on all those responsible for the genocide that took place in that country in 1994. — C.L.

Suggested Reading: *Economist* p43 Mar. 17, 2001, with photo; *New York Times Upfront* p14+ Mar. 5, 2001; *Newsweek* p42+ Jan. 29, 2001, with photo; *U.S. News & World Report* Jan. 29, 2001, p24, with photo

Ruphin Coudyzer/Courtesy of the Market Theatre

Kani, John

1943(?)– Actor; director; playwright. Address: c/o Market Theatre, P.O. Box 8656, Johannesburg 2000, South Africa

Although, by the mid-1970s, when he was about 30, the black South African actor John Kani had become an international success, in his home country he could not legally claim to be an actor; after winning a Tony Award for his Broadway performance in *Sizwe Bansi Is Dead*, Kani returned to South Africa only to be arrested and placed in solitary confinement for performing in that very play. The bitter ironies of Kani's life are rooted in apartheid—a word meaning "apartness" in the Afrikaans language—a legal system that, through a series of laws passed in South Africa in the 1950s, institutionalized the racial segregation of the nonwhite majority and the white minority. Under apartheid, all South Africans were categorized by race—"Bantu," or black; "Coloured," or mixed

race; and "white"—and forced to live and work in separate areas, with more than 80 percent of the land set aside for the less than 15 percent of the population that was white. In the early 1990s the government of President F. W. de Klerk, facing unrest at home and censure abroad, began to dismantle apartheid; in 1994 a coalition government with a black majority was elected under a new constitution.

John Kani's experiences as a black man living under apartheid cannot be separated from his life in the theater. Born at a time in South Africa when, as he put it to C. Gerald Fraser in the *New York Times* (April 1, 1975), "not even your father [knew] what [was] going to happen in your life," Kani defied the odds and became an international acting sensation, playing to both black and white audiences in South Africa and spreading awareness of apartheid through his extended touring productions in the United States and Europe. Kani has spoken of his involvement in theater as both protest and sustenance, a sentiment echoed by the playwright, director, and actor Athol Fugard, Kani's longtime collaborator. "Our common denominator is our anger and our outrage," Fugard told Henry Kamm for the *New York Times* (October 28, 1976). "But anger and outrage are not the basis of our work. Our basis is a celebration, a celebration of the fact that life is worth living and has to be lived."

John Kani was born in about 1943 in the black township of New Brighton, South Africa, near the industrial city of Port Elizabeth. His father was a policeman who struggled to raise 10 children (some sources say 11). Growing up, Kani had hoped to become a lawyer, but an event in 1962 changed the course of his life. While he was at home one day, security police came to his home to look for his older brother, a university student, who was not there. Charged with joining the Youth Brigade of the outlawed African National Congress, his brother spent the next five years in jail, at the Robben Island Prison for political prisoners; Kani never saw him in all that time. The Kani family used up their savings on lawyers to lobby for his freedom, and John Kani went to work on an assembly line at a Ford factory instead of going to college. He toiled on the assembly line for six years. During that period, in 1965, he joined a local theater company, the Serpent Players, out of boredom and frustration. "There are more than a million people living in the township of New Brighton, and there are no restaurants, no clubs, no places to enjoy yourself, one cinema," Kani explained to Kamm in 1976. "You go to work at eight and when you come back you can either sit there and eat and then drink or go to bed with your wife and make another baby. I heard about the Serpent Players, so I went there to see if I could do something with the late parts of the evening."

The Serpent Players was founded in 1956 as an amateur company and turned professional in 1961. In 1965 the company invited Athol Fugard, a white

South African, to join them. Fugard was already well known; his 1961 drama, *Blood Knot*, about two brothers—one who looks black and one who could pass for white—had been banned in South Africa but had won international fame. The collaboration between Fugard and the black Players actors was not only unusual; it was also, technically, illegal. Since government officials did not accept "artist" as an employment category for blacks, Fugard had to employ Kani and another principal actor, Winston Ntshona (one of Kani's childhood friends), as a chauffeur and gardener, respectively—though he had neither car nor garden—so that they would be permitted to travel to his home for rehearsals without fear of arrest. The Players sidestepped rules prohibiting blacks from performing for white audiences by giving shows in private clubs; when performances were held in black townships, Fugard was not allowed to attend. Occasionally, the Players openly defied apartheid laws by using racially mixed casts or performing to mixed audiences in public theaters in Johannesburg and Cape Town.

In spite of these difficult circumstances, the company sustained a high level of artistry, performing classics by Sophocles, Euripides, and Shakespeare and 20th-century works by Jean Genet, Bertolt Brecht, and the Nigerian writer Wole Soyinka, among others. In the early 1970s Fugard and some of the actors, including Kani, began experimenting with what they called "playmaking," in which they developed narratives and improvisational scenes based on their personal experiences under apartheid. Like many theater artists of the 1960s and 1970s, they were inspired by the example of the Polish theater director Jerzy Grotowski, who preached that the essence of theater consists of one performer and one person watching. In Grotowski's vision, costumes, elaborate sets, and other theater staples are secondary to the relationship between actor and audience. This notion of a stripped-down theater worked well in apartheid-era South Africa, because such productions were inexpensive, easy to move from location to location, and based as much on actors and improvisations as on scripts, making them elusive targets for censors. Three plays—collectively called the "statement plays," because of their political content—emerged from the playmaking process: *Statements After an Arrest Under the Immorality Act* (1972); *Sizwe Bansi Is Dead* (1972); and *The Island* (1973). These plays, which had no music or dancing and relied on mime, improvisation, and small casts, were radically different from most popular South African theatrical works.

Sizwe Bansi Is Dead evolved through discussions among Kani, Winston Ntshona, and Fugard, all of whom are credited as its authors. Kani's character, Styles, a township resident, opens the play with a virtuoso, partially improvised monologue that, in various performances, extended from 20 minutes to a record 90 minutes. After years of working as a toadying Ford factory worker, Styles has opened a small photography studio that he calls "a strong room of dreams" for his people. During his monologue Styles speaks directly to the audience, interweaving comments about topical events and the production's locality into the story of his life. At one point he invites an audience member to come on stage and take a closer look at his photographs. For *Livemag.com* (June 1998), Nina Shengold recalled her experience as a high-school senior attending a Broadway production of *Sizwe* and being chosen by Kani to come on stage: "I took hold of Kani's hand, clambered over the footlights and floated across the stage in a humming fog of excitement. I don't remember any of the photographs he showed me, but I'll never forget Kani's face, the burn of his eyes and the sweat on his skin as he begged me to look." In a play in which the characters repeatedly cry, "I am a man!," Styles's photographs are the only evidence of his black customers' essential humanity; as Shengold quotes him as saying, "We own nothing but ourselves. This world, and its laws, allow us nothing except ourselves."

Eventually, the character Sizwe Bansi (played by Ntshona) appears; Sizwe is a rural naïf who has traded identities with a corpse in his desperation to get a work-permit stamp in his passbook. (Under apartheid, all blacks had to carry a passbook, an internal passport that contained the bearer's photograph, an identification number, and more than 90 pages of official stamps, signatures, and data about the person's tribe, home, place of work, marital status, and travel restrictions imposed of the person. Failure to keep a passbook up to date and in good order was a criminal offense.) Sizwe's predicament satirizes the dreary reality of apartheid life—the need for black people to navigate arcane bureaucracies in order to live and work—but it also serves as a heartfelt protest against a system in which a black person's humanity is reduced to his or her passbook number. Kani described the play, which was banned in South Africa in 1976, to C. Gerald Fraser as being about "surviving under pressure," adding that it had to be "as humorous as possible. It has to go with the wind and wave like a reed . . . and hit the master as he turns his face or is rolling on the floor laughing." There were tense moments during some of the public performances for all-black audiences. Kani described to Leo Seligsohn for *New York Newsday* (April 6, 1975) times when audience members became enraged after recognizing in the play elements of their own lives. "Everyone in the audience has a passbook and some know their passbooks are not in order," Kani told Seligsohn. "They become angry. Sometimes they run up to the stage and talk to us. Others in the audience yell, 'Sit down. Sit down.' It can get out of hand."

Kani next collaborated with Ntshona and Fugard on an even more politically provocative project—a play about Robben Island, the notorious prison where many of South Africa's black political prisoners were housed and where Kani's brother spent five years. At the time it was dangerous even to utter the name of the prison, since discussion of the South African penal system was forbidden. To evoke the notion of this "sacred space," as Fugard labeled it in an interview with Peter Rosenwald for the London *Guardian* (January 8, 1974), the playwright spread a large blanket in the grass outside his home. Without telling Kani and Ntshona what he was thinking, he asked them to explore the blanket's parameters, to walk around its edges and then stand in the center. He then repeatedly halved the blanket and asked the actors to repeat their actions, until finally there was room only for the two actors to stand on the folded cloth. According to Rosenwald, Fugard then asked the actors, "What do you think it means?" Their answer was that the blanket represented a cell, and without further conversation the three men understood where the acting exercise would lead. As Kani put it to Rosenwald, he and Ntshona knew that Fugard hoped "to take the island and say something about it. We joined our hands, closed the garage door and after two weeks, fourteen days, we were on stage in Cape Town."

After two experimental performances of the play, which came to be called *The Island*, Kani, Ntshona, and Fugard were invited to the Royal Court Theatre, in London, to continue its development. From there, *The Island* traveled throughout the English-speaking world, and its text was translated into 30 languages. It thus became a lightning rod in the gathering storm of opposition to apartheid. The characters portrayed by Kani and Ntshona are political prisoners and cell mates. On a bare stage, they mime their daily tasks of hard labor with exacting precision—digging, filling imaginary wheelbarrows, pushing them, emptying them, filling them again. When they speak, it is in the familiar, intimate dialogue of men bound together not only by fate but by the four walls of a cell that, according to Richard L. Coe in the *Washington Post* (July 18, 1975), "seemed to get smaller by the minute"—an echo of Fugard's "disappearing-blanket" exercise. Like *Sizwe Bansi Is Dead*, *The Island* mixes humor and pathos. Kani and Ntshona's characters prepare to perform an entertainment for their fellow prisoners, a scene from Sophocles' *Antigone*, and they indulge in slapstick comedy—Ntshona's character dons a woman's wig and bra to play Antigone, while Kani's, as King Creon, preens and poses. But when the two prisoners begin to play out the scene of Antigone's defiance against Creon's unbending authority, the mood suddenly becomes serious. According to Coe, "laughter and kidding are gone," and the relevance to contemporary South Africa of the ancient theme of civil disobedience becomes apparent.

Kani and Ntshona toured with *Sizwe Bansi Is Dead* and *The Island* throughout Great Britain, the United States, and Australia for three years, and everywhere their performances were greeted with ecstatic reviews. Coe noted the actors' intensity: "There is to their every exchange vivid immediacy,

in eyes, voice, and movement. Simple gestures are so direct and fearless that they make their own comments on the text." Others noted the powerful rapport between Kani and Ntshona. After their 1975 Broadway performances, the actors received the first-ever joint Tony Award for best actor (Kani for *Sizwe*, Ntshona for *The Island*). In interviews, Kani and Ntshona frequently spoke about the period they spent abroad as a myth-shattering time, during which they discovered similarities between their own experiences and the experiences of blacks outside South Africa. "It's obvious that things are bad for blacks living in this country," Kani told Joel Dreyfuss for the *Washington Post* (July 11, 1975), referring to the United States. "They are the 90 per cent who are unemployed. They are the 90 per cent standing in the streets with faces that I have seen at home."

As they had while on tour, the actors experienced both elation and disillusionment after they returned to South Africa, in 1976. Kani marveled to Peter Rosenwald, "One of the leading Afrikaans pro-government newspapers, *Die Burger*, headlined an article about our success in Britain: 'Two Fantastic South African Actors?' We have every reason to laugh with pride because that newspaper called us 'South Africans' not 'natives' or 'Bantus.' Not only do our black brothers and sisters share our success but our entire beautiful country shares it." On the wings of their international success, Kani and Ntshona toured South Africa with *Sizwe Bansi Is Dead* and *The Island* in repertory for 10 months, performing mostly for private audiences. Only a few weeks after their return, following a performance of *Sizwe*, Kani and Ntshona were arrested by local officials in Transkei (a black township that had recently been declared independent from South Africa). Accused of insulting Transkei authorities and inciting violence, each actor was placed in solitary confinement, which prompted outrage and protests in the New York and London theater communities. After two weeks both men were released without explanation. Kani was typically philosophical about his poor treatment in his native country. "Abroad we are always being asked, 'Are you bitter?'" Kani told Henry Kamm. "A stupid question. Of course we are. But I am not going to run around and knock my head against the white establishment. I'd only break it, and I need my head. My brains are in it." Kani's resolve was tested in 1985, when his brother Xolile was killed by police. He had been attending a funeral for an 11-year-old boy—who had also been slain by the police—and, as often happened, the funeral had turned into a demonstration, during which Xolile was gunned down. After his brother's death, Kani confessed to William Claiborne for the *Washington Post* (October 8, 1987), he had been filled with thoughts of revenge and had considered leaving the country. "I thought, 'What the hell am I doing in this country?'" he told Claiborne. "'I'm a Tony Award winner. I can get work anywhere in the world. Why am I hanging around here?'" Kani decided to stay and give vent to his anger in South Africa, rather than leave for the United States or Britain.

In the late 1970s Kani became an associate director of the Market Theatre, a 520-seat house that was founded by Barney Simon in 1976 on the site of an old Johannesburg produce market. The theater became a focal point of public protests against apartheid. While books and movies were extensively censored, the theater's activities were mostly ignored, a circumstance that Kani has attributed to its capacity for disguise. "I know that art can wear these beautiful clothes and it is difficult even for a fascist regime to stop you," he told Dreyfuss. During Kani's tenure as associate director, the Market Theatre produced many Shakespearean comedies and tragedies (which, thanks to costumes or acting styles, contained satirical barbs aimed at South Africa), as well as home-grown plays that followed the example of Sizwe and The Island, such as Mbongeni Ngema and Percy Mtwa's Woza Albert! and Ngema's Sarafina! "In the 1980s, if one wanted to know what if felt like to be alive in public in South Africa, one went to the Market Theatre," Robert Greig, a drama critic for South Africa's Weekly Mail and Guardian, declared in the New York Times (February 27, 1994). In 1990 Kani and Simon founded the Market Theatre Laboratory, which works to develop local talent through a drama school, community-outreach programs, and showcase performances.

During the 1980s Kani appeared in two roles that caused a stir in South Africa. In 1981 he played Vladimir to Ntshona's Estragon in Samuel Beckett's Waiting for Godot; the young boy was played by a black actor, and Lucky and Pozzo, the deranged master-and-servant duo, were played by white actors. Kani told John Engstrom for the London Observer (February 15, 1981) that he and Ntshona had always wanted to appear in the play, not for any political reason, but because it is so much fun for actors. According to Engstrom, the play caused a furor when it opened in Cape Town; audiences and critics argued over whether or not it was appropriate for a multiracial cast to perform a traditionally "white" play.

In 1987 Kani became the first black actor in South Africa to play the role of Othello, Shakespeare's tragic Moor. Othello's relevance to contemporary South Africa must have been resoundingly obvious to the white audiences who filled the Market Theatre each night, just as it was to Kani. "Sometimes I think, 'Please, please, can't we change it, just for tonight?'" he told William Claiborne. "Can't we have Iago saying, 'I'm sorry. I made a mistake.'? But it doesn't happen in the play, and it doesn't happen in South Africa. In Othello, the tragedy is inevitable. In South Africa, the tragedy is not inevitable, but the way it's going now, it's going to blow." Only two years had passed since the South African government had scrapped the Immorality Act, which forbade interracial marriage. It had also been two years since

Kani had played Jean, the ambitious servant who seduces his white mistress, in August Strindberg's drama Miss Julie. Kani recalled to Claiborne that when, on opening night, he placed his hand on the thigh of the white actress playing Miss Julie, half the audience walked out, and he needed a security detail in order to leave the theater safely. Kani's appearance as Othello two years later, opposite a blond and blue-eyed Desdemona, occasioned no such public protests, though it received enormous media attention as a milestone in modern South African history. The production marked the first time Kani performed Shakespeare, and he worked hard to master Shakespeare's English; as a student at a Bantu school, he had read Macbeth and Julius Caesar in Bantu, the tribal language of the Xhosa people.

In addition to his work in theater, Kani has had a thriving career as a film actor. His cinematic credits include Master Harold and the Boys (a 1986 film that is based on the same-named Fugard play, in which Kani appeared), Saturday Night at the Palace (1987), A Dry White Season (1989), Sarafina! (1992), and a dozen others. In 1995 Kani and Ntshona revived their roles in The Island for a special performance at the Market Theatre. Many former political prisoners were in attendance, including Nelson Mandela, who became South Africa's first post-apartheid president after enduring 18 years as a prisoner at Robben Island (and eight more years elsewhere). "With every sentence uttered on stage there was a huge sigh from the audience. When we sang, they sang with us. It was incredible," Kani told Justice Malala for the London Sunday Times (February 6, 2000). The production then toured internationally.

John Kani's role in creating the new South Africa has been recognized in many ways: he has been awarded two honorary doctorates; he was elected chairman of the National Arts Council of South Africa, in 1997; and in January 2000 he was honored with an award from the Hiroshima Foundation for Peace and Culture, for his work in helping to forge a desegregated theater.

Kani has rarely talked about his personal life in interviews. As of 1975 he was married and had three children. — M.A.H.

Suggested Reading: (London) Guardian p10 Jan. 8, 1974, with photo; (London) Observer p35 Feb. 15, 1981, with photo; New York Newsday II p3+ Apr. 6, 1975, with photo; New York Times p29 Apr. 1, 1975, with photo, p5 Oct. 28, 1976, p33 July 11, 1977, with photo; Washington Post B p9+ July 11, 1975, with photos, B p9 July 18, 1975, with photo, D p4 Sep. 16, 1987

Selected Theater Work: as co-creator and actor—Statements After an Arrest Under the Immorality Act, 1972; Sizwe Bansi Is Dead, 1972–1976; The Island, 1973–1976, 1995; as actor—Waiting for Godot, 1981; Miss Julie, 1985; Othello, 1987

Selected Films—*Master Harold and the Boys*, 1986; *Saturday Night at the Palace*, 1987; *A Dry White Season*, 1989; *Sarafina!*, 1992

Courtesy of Karen Karbo

Karbo, Karen

1956– Writer. Address: c/o Bloomsbury Publishing, 175 Fifth Ave., Suite 300, New York, NY 10010

Karen Karbo, who originally set out to write screenplays with tragic themes, has instead made her reputation with novels that strike sharp blows at reviewers' funny bones. In *Trespassers Welcome Here* (1989), the story of a group of Russian expatriates in Los Angeles, she captured the foibles and accents of a community desperate to adapt to American mores. *The Diamond Lane* (1991) contrasts documentary filmmaking with Hollywood crassness, and *Motherhood Made a Man Out of Me* (2000) turns a jaundiced eye on the world of motherhood. Her most recent work is the nonfiction volume *Generation Ex: Tales from the Second Wives Club* (2001). In an interview for the *New York Times Book Review* (May 19, 1991), Karbo told Laurel Graeber that she "never tries consciously to be funny," invoking the comic actor Charlie Chaplin's maxim that humor must "come from how you look at life." Her own belief is that life is "hopelessly tragic and hilarious."

Karen Karbo was born in 1956 in Detroit, Michigan, to Joan and Richard Karbo. She was educated at the University of Southern California in Los Angeles, receiving a B.A. in 1977 and an M.A. in 1980. For a screenwriting class, as Laurel Graeber report-

ed, Karbo wrote a script "about a crippled pianist who falls in love with a religious guitar player in the Paris Metro." She told Graeber, "I thought it was *Imitation of Life*," referring to the 1959 film melodrama. "But my instructor said, 'This is the funniest thing I've ever read.' It struck me then that maybe I wasn't aimed for high drama." While writing screenplays in Los Angeles, Karbo supported herself as a dog groomer and a Hollywood agent's assistant, among other jobs. But she found no buyers for her screenplays. "It's depressing . . . when you try to sell your soul and nobody wants it," she told Graeber. So she decided to try her hand at fiction.

Karbo's first book was *Trespassers Welcome Here*. In that novel Karbo explored the lives of four Russian women who have emigrated to Los Angeles and work in the Slavic languages department of a university. Bella Bogoga is obsessed with shopping; Valeria Chalisian teaches "Russian with an Emphasis in Sports Vocabulary," or "Russian for jocks," as it is known on campus; Tanya Zlopak, an actress, is desperate for a Hollywood film role; and Marina McIntyre, who works as a KGB agent, is married to an unsuspecting American. All four women, each in her own way, pursue the American dream.

"Karbo is a very funny writer," Elin Schoen Brockman wrote for the *New York Times Book Review* (May 21, 1989), in an assessment of *Trespassers Welcome Here*. "And what is amazing about her humor is not merely its abundance but its range—from near slapstick to a wry wit, evident even in the wonderfully ironic title . . . and also its depth. For shining through the shenanigans of the various characters are poignant revelations not only about strangers in a strange land, but about their American friends, lovers and nemeses, and about Soviet-American relations at their most intimate and basic."

Like *Trespassers Welcome Here*, *The Diamond Lane* is set in Los Angeles. Karbo told Graeber for the *New York Times Book Review* interview that she conceived of *The Diamond Lane* as a twist on the book *You'll Never Eat Lunch in This Town Again*, a nonfiction Hollywood exposé by Julia Phillips. "I think of it as 'You'll Never Eat Lunch in This Town in the First Place,'" she said. "And the characters are people who would love to have lunch." The adventures of two sisters form the core of the book. One sister, Mouse, has been in Africa with her boyfriend, making a documentary film about tribal marriage customs; the other, Mimi, who is divorced and works as an assistant to a Hollywood film producer, is romantically involved with a married man—who, like her, dreams of success as a screenwriter. "Karbo has done her job brilliantly," Robert Ward wrote of *The Diamond Lane* for the *New York Times Book Review* (May 19, 1991). "Not only is the plot ingenious, but the writing remains deft all the way through. . . . Karbo is smart enough and good enough to know when to slow down and reveal the little terrors that people feel in Tinseltown, but she is also clever and sophisticated enough to know that the Hollywood experience is essentially a comic one. And it remains so even as Mouse and Mimi and their boyfriends stagger toward an unforgettable (and darkly funny) wedding." "Part of what Karbo is satirizing in this novel, in an often very wicked fashion," Judith Freeman commented in the *Los Angeles Times* (June 21, 1991), "is the way the ordinary rituals and activities in life—love, work, marriage—get twisted into the most bizarre shapes when money and Hollywood values enter the picture." Karbo, Freeman continued, "understands the banalities and excesses, the contradictions and absurdities of living in a place where knowing not to put glitter in your stucco is construed as good taste. . . . Karbo sustains her tale by contrasting misery and humor, real filmmaking (real documentary) and the crass commercial product, poor humble Africa and fat, gluttonous America."

Karbo was a contributor to the 1995 volume *Home: American Writers Remember Rooms of Their Own*. Her piece evoked her mother, for whom "the dining room is a vortex of impeccable etiquette and laborious buffets," as Bernard Cooper noted in the *Los Angeles Times* (December 24, 1995). He found Karbo's second-person narrative "hilarious, but never at the expense of the conservative mother who values self-control above other virtues. That Karbo can sustain this tone without one note of condescension is no small feat, and it is a tone that becomes all the more chilling as a tumor slowly destroys her mother's capacity for self-control."

For the 1997 nonfiction book *Big Girl in the Middle*, Karbo served as co-writer with Gabrielle Reece, a tall former professional model who had abandoned that career to join Team Nike in the Bud Light Professional Beach Volleyball Tour in 1991. Reece's story centered on her team's unsuccessful 1996 season, one in which, as the *Publishers Weekly* (May 26, 1997) reviewer wrote, "Captain Reece maintained her perspective and her resolve to keep plugging away. This account should give a boost to the morale of female athletes."

In the 2000 novel *Motherhood Made a Man Out of Me*, Karbo took on the pitfalls of pregnancy and new motherhood. The protagonist, Brooke, has a baby daughter, Stella, whose arrival has effectively ended Brooke's career as a film producer. Brooke's husband, Lyle, is an aspiring artist who repairs photocopiers for a living, spends a great deal of time playing computer games, and generally proves to be less than ideal as a father. Brooke's best friend is the pregnant Mary Rose, who "functions largely as a straight woman for the narrator," David Kipen observed in the *San Francisco Chronicle* (July 5, 2000), "smiling along as Brooke confides yet more witty observations, e.g., 'She didn't see me. No one does of course. Being the mother of a beautiful baby is the next best thing to being in the Witness Relocation Program.'. . . Karbo plainly has a lot to say—much of it amusing—about both

pregnancy and new motherhood. By synchronizing Mary Rose's pregnancy with Brooke's first nine months as a mom, Karbo covers both topics in half the time."

While Ann Hodgman, writing in the *New York Times Book Review* (June 18, 2000), found *Motherhood Made a Man Out of Me* to be "peevishly hilarious," she tempered her praise with mild criticism: "What [Brooke] might as well be saying is: 'I'm trying to tell a whole big story but the baby keeps getting in the way'. . . . Throughout the novel, characters are thrown at us and we're just expected to keep track of them somehow. . . . The city where this is all taking place is never mentioned by name. It must be Portland, Ore., because it's always rainy and people are always watching Trail Blazers games. . . . In the same way, segments of plot bob up without warning from under a thick layer of domestic detail. (The details are very funny; there are just so many of them!) . . . But that's because this book is really about having babies, and it's the plot that keeps getting in the way." Hodgman concluded, however, that "*Motherhood Made a Man Out of Me* should be clutched to the 'corn-silo-sized' breasts of every new mother."

Karbo's *Generation Ex: Tales from the Second Wives Club* was published in the spring of 2001. That nonfiction book examines, from the points of view of five women who meet to trade stories, the complications that result from having "exes" in one's life: an ex-husband, a husband's ex-wife, and the children of the various unions. The *Library Journal* (March 1, 2001) reviewer, who considered *Generation Ex* a self-help book, noted that Karbo had hit "all the major minefields." The *Publishers Weekly* (March 5, 2001) critic termed the exspousal encounter a "hilarious" mix of "screwball comedy, tragic drama, feel-good fantasy and stalker flicks." Laura Jamison, writing in the *New York Times Book Review* (April 8, 2001), also found *Generation Ex* "wildly funny," and she praised Karbo's use of "solid statistics."

Karen Karbo lives in Portland, Oregon, with her husband, a filmmaker. Her previous marriage ended in divorce. She is a contributing writer for *Sports for Women*, and her articles have appeared in other publications, including the *New York Times Book Review*. — S.Y.

Suggested Reading: *Los Angeles Times* p5 June 21, 1991, p1 Dec. 24, 1995; *New York Times Book Review* p11 May 21, 1989, p9 May 19, 1991, p27 June 18, 2000; *New York Times Book Review* (on-line) Apr. 8, 2001; *New Yorker* p95+ Sep. 16, 1991; *Quill & Quire* p29 May 1991; *San Francisco Chronicle* D p1 July 5, 2000; *Virginia Quarterly Review* V p20 Winter 1998; *Voice Literary Supplement* p13 May 9, 1989

Selected Works: fiction—*Trespassers Welcome Here*, 1989; *The Diamond Lane*, 1991; *Motherhood Made a Man Out of Me*, 2000; nonfiction—*Big Girl in the Middle* (with

Gabrielle Reece), 1997; *Generation Ex: Tales from the Second Wives Club*, 2001

Associated Press

Katsav, Moshe
(KAT-sev, MOH-sheh)

1945– President of Israel. Address: c/o Israeli Embassy to the United States, 3514 International Dr., Washington, DC 20008

When, on July 31, 2000, the members of the Knesset, Israel's Parliament, elected Moshe Katsav to be the country's eighth president, he became only the second Sephardic Jew to hold the position. (Yitzhak Navon, the fifth president, was a native-born Israeli of Sephardic descent.) Sephardic Jews, who came to Israel from predominately Muslim countries in the Middle East and North Africa (or who descended from such settlers), comprise 40 percent of the nation's population; they are often referred to as the "second Israel," because they are typically less educated and prosperous than Israel's Ashkenazi Jews, who are of European descent. Katsav's opponent in the election was Shimon Peres; an Ashkenazi Jew who had been educated at Harvard University and New York University, had twice served as Israel's prime minister, and had won the 1994 Nobel Prize, Peres was widely perceived as one of the nation's elder statesmen and was expected to win the election easily. His surprising defeat was seen as a victory for Israel's Sephardic underdogs, who had long felt disenfranchised from the political process. An editorial in the *Jerusalem Post* (August 1, 2000, on-line) stated, "[Katsav] does not arrive at the presidency with as

exalted a resume as some of its previous occupants or the man he defeated. But he has the potential not only to achieve but to raise the stature of the high office he has been chosen to hold." Although the presidency is largely a ceremonial post in Israel—actual power resides with the prime minister and the Knesset—Katsav's election was regarded by some political observers as a sign that at least some power was passing from the hands of the educated Ashkenazi elite. Katsav's victory was also interpreted as a rebuke to Prime Minister Ehud Barak, who had backed Peres.

Moshe Katsav was born in 1945 in Yazd, a small town in Iran. His family members were among the tens of thousands of Sephardic Jews who emigrated to Israel from Middle Eastern nations during the 1950s. The Katsavs arrived in Israel in 1951 and settled in an immigrant tent camp on the northern tip of the Negev Desert. Within a year the camp had developed into a small settlement of shoddy apartment complexes and had been given the name Kiryat Malachi, which translates to "Town of Angels." (Los Angeles Jews had donated much of the money for its development.) Kiryat Malachi soon became, in effect, a ghetto, made up of poor, uneducated Jewish immigrants from Ethiopia, the Soviet Union, Morocco, and Iran. Thanks in large part to the presence of a polyglot population in Kiryat Malachi, Katsav became fluent in Hebrew, English, and Arabic as well as Farsi (modern Persian), the official language of Iran. His parents eventually had a total of eight children; his father supported the family by working in a twine factory.

Katsav graduated from the Ben-Shemen Agricultural School. He then performed his mandatory service in the Israeli Defense Forces (IDF), as a corporal in the communications corps. After he left the military, in 1966, he worked as a reporter for the *Yediot Aharonot*, a daily newspaper. A short time later he began his undergraduate studies at the Hebrew University of Jerusalem, becoming one of Kiryat Malachi's first residents to attend college. (Currently, only a fifth of the settlement's high-school graduates continue their education—a percentage that is far below the Israeli average.) While at the university Katsav became active in politics, serving as chairman of the Gahal Party's branch on campus. The Gahal Party was a predecessor of the Likud-Liberalim Leumi (Unity-National Liberals), commonly known as Likud, a right-wing political bloc established to challenge Israel's Labour Party.

In 1969, while still a student, Katsav was elected mayor of Kiryat Malachi. At 24 years of age, he was then the youngest mayor in the country. For reasons not explained in readily available sources, he served in that post for only one year. He graduated from Hebrew University in 1972, receiving a B.A. in economics and history. Actively pursuing a career in politics, he was elected to a full term as mayor of Kiryat Malachi in 1974 and held the post until 1981. He won a seat in the Knesset in 1977, as a member of the Likud Party. Starting in that year until 1981, he served on the Knesset committee on interior affairs and the environment and the committee on education and culture. He also served as chairman of the Knesset members' lobby for development towns, and he fought for more government services for Kiryat Malachi and other impoverished communities.

Throughout the 1980s Katsav climbed the Likud hierarchy. In 1981 Prime Minister Menachem Begin appointed him to the post of deputy minister of housing and construction. Three years later Prime Minister Yitzhak Shamir, who succeeded Begin, named Katsav minister of labor and social affairs, making him the youngest minister in the Cabinet at the time. In 1988 Shamir appointed Katsav minister of transportation, and in that capacity he received considerable favorable attention in the Israeli press. A series of strikes by railroad workers in the following year inconvenienced tens of thousands of passengers and delayed transportation of important cargo, such as grain and minerals. Katsav settled the dispute by negotiating a 20 percent pay increase for the workers. He also unveiled an ambitious plan that year to improve Israel's roads, where poor conditions were contributing to many car accidents. In 1991 Katsav negotiated an agreement with the Soviet Union that established the first direct air flights between that region and Israel.

In the 1992 election—amid growing discontent among several groups, including the unemployed, the new Russian immigrants, and disenfranchised Sephardim—the Labour Party, headed by Yitzhak Rabin, ousted Shamir's government. After his defeat Shamir announced his retirement, and the Likud Party scrambled to find a new leader. Katsav announced his candidacy; he told Michal Yudelman for the *Jerusalem Post* (August 14, 1992) that he had the ability to "get the Likud Party out of its deep crisis, rehabilitate it and lead it to victory in the next Knesset elections." On March 25, 1993, however, Likud voters elected Benjamin Netanyahu, a former ambassador from Israel to the United Nations, to head the party. Despite his defeat Katsav remained a member of the Likud Party's leadership, becoming its faction chairman—the equivalent of a legislative whip—in the Knesset. He also became head of the Israel-China Parliamentary Friendship League. In 1995 he visited China as part of the first delegation to do so since diplomatic relations had been established between the two countries, in 1992.

Katsav joined Netanyahu in opposing the Oslo Accords, the peace agreements between Rabin's government and the Palestine Liberation Organization (PLO), which had been negotiated in 1993. Like Netanyahu, Katsav believed that the agreements endangered the security of Israel, and over the next several years a number of terrorist attacks on Jewish Israelis by Arabs helped fuel public support for their position. On November 4, 1995 Prime Minister Rabin was assassinated by a Jewish extremist who opposed the peace process. During a memorial held for Rabin in the Knesset, Katsav

said, as reported by Liat Collins in the *Jerusalem Post* (November 13, 1995), "It is a human, national, state and personal pain. There's not one of us who didn't learn to respect Rabin despite differences of opinion."

In the May 26, 1996 election, Israeli voters narrowly returned the Likud Party to power, with Benjamin Netanyahu as prime minister. Katsav became deputy prime minister and minister of tourism. (Tourism has always been one of Israel's most important industries, with more than two million tourists typically visiting the country each year.) Netanyahu, who had pledged never to support the Oslo Accords, moderated his position once he took power. In January 1997 he negotiated an agreement with Yasir Arafat, the chairman of the Palestinian Authority, that called for the withdrawal of Israeli troops from the West Bank city of Hebron as well as a select number of other territories. Katsav, who had also been appointed minister of Israeli-Arab affairs by Netanyahu, surprised many political observers when he exhibited similar moderation. He backed Netanyahu's new agreement and also took several steps to improve relations between Arabs and Jews in Israel. For example, on October 30, 1997 he visited the village of Kafr Kasim to apologize for the 1956 killing of 49 Arab civilians there by the Israeli police. (Each year a memorial service is held for the victims, and while Israeli government officials were always invited to attend, Katsav was the first to accept the invitation.) "I came here to identify with the victims, show them honor, say the victims were innocent, express our sorrow, and say that the victims deserve our apology," he declared, according to Herb Keinon in the *Jerusalem Post* (October 30, 1997). A few months later Katsav expressed moral outrage about the discovery, by means of a poll, that almost half of Israeli high-school students believed that the civil rights of Israeli Arabs should be restricted. "I'm angered and deeply concerned by this kind of attitude," he told Michael Yudelman for the *Jerusalem Post* (January 20, 1998). "Israel's Arabs are equal citizens, although I know a minister's statement is not enough to solve the problem. It must be tackled from the root, by the educational system and society."

By 1999 Netanyahu's government had become crippled by a weak economy, scandal, and stalled peace talks. The One Israel Party (a coalition that included the Labour Party), headed by Ehud Barak, a former general in the IDF, won a landslide victory in that year's election. Netanyahu stepped down as head of the Likud Party and was replaced by Ariel Sharon, a former defense minister, while Katsav continued to serve in the Knesset, as a member of the opposition.

In July 2000 Ezer Weizman, who was then president, resigned after being investigated for bribery and fraud. Likud Party members tapped Moshe Katsav as their candidate for the presidency, while the One Israel Party chose Shimon Peres. The press made much of the seeming disparities between the candidates. Peres had enjoyed a long, distinguished career in Israeli politics and was internationally recognized. By contrast, Katsav, a right-wing legislator from a small town and three-time Cabinet minister, was barely known outside Israel. Katsav campaigned energetically and, as a religiously observant Jew, appealed for support from legislators who represented the religious parties in the Knesset, among them Shas, an ultra-Orthodox faction vehemently opposed to the secularism of many Israeli politicians. On July 31 Katsav defeated Peres, 63–57. Residents of Kiryat Malachi poured into the streets of their town to celebrate his victory. According to various observers, the Knesset's choice of Katsav sent a message to Barak, who, in the opinion of many legislators, had made too many concessions to Yasir Arafat during peace negotiations and had failed to adequately address Israel's social problems. Support for Barak had begun to erode during his first year in office, and a criminal investigation for alleged campaign-finance violations had been initiated. On the same day as the 2000 presidential election, Barak's government barely survived two no-confidence votes in the Knesset. Katsav's somewhat hawkish views were considered by many to be a welcome antidote to those of Barak and Peres, who were thought to be committed to peace at any price. (A large-scale uprising, which started in 1987, was being waged by Palestinians living in the territories that Israel had won during various military conflicts. Like many members of the Likud Party, Katsav strongly supported rigorous military suppression of the uprising, also known as the *intifada*, and opposed any territorial concessions to the Arabs.)

As Israel's eighth president Katsav vowed to represent all sectors of Israeli society during his five-year term. "I want Israeli Arabs to see me as their president, all Jews to see me as their representative; whether they are haredi [ultra-Orthodox], religious or secular, Sephardi or Ashkenazi," he declared during his victory speech, as quoted by Nina Gilbert and Gil Hoffman in the *Jerusalem Post* (August 1, 2000, on-line). Katsav also pledged to avoid partisan disputes and to work to unify the country. "I cannot erase my political views, and I cannot cancel my beliefs," he told Sam Kiley for the London *Times* (August 1, 2000), "but . . . I am locking up my political views for my term as President." In February 2001 Ariel Sharon was elected president, easily defeating Barak. The following June Katsav visited the United States to urge President George W. Bush to pressure Arafat and the Palestinian Authority into accepting a cease-fire in the interests of preserving the peace process, which was being undermined by Palestinian terrorist attacks.

Katsav has been married to his wife, Gila, for more than 30 years. They have five children. — D.C.

Suggested Reading: American Jewish Congress Web site; *Jerusalem Post* (on-line) p3 Nov. 13, 1995, p1 Oct. 30, 1997, p4 Jan. 20, 1998, p1 Aug. 1, 2000; *Jewish Telegraphic Agency* (on-line) July 31, 2000; (London) *Times* (on-line) Aug. 1, 2000; *Los Angeles Times* I p1 Aug. 3, 2000, A p3 May 29, 2001; *Washington Post* A p17 Aug. 1, 2000

Kcho

(KAH-cho)

1970– Sculptor. Address: c/o Barbara Gladstone Gallery, 515 W. 24th St., New York, NY 10011-1104; c/o Regen Projects, 629 N. Almont Dr., Los Angeles, CA 90069

The Cuban sculptor Kcho, who grew up on a small island, has poured his fascination with the sea—and all it represents—into his art. His sculpted boats, rafts, and docks evoke a world defined by the sea and colored by Cuba's recent history of political isolation and ceaseless emigration. Kcho often uses found materials—bottles, driftwood, fishing nets, and other debris washed up onto shore—to make his sculptures and elaborate installations. Since 1991 his work has been exhibited in more than 50 shows and international competitions, and some of his pieces have been acquired for the permanent collections of several major museums. At just over 30 years of age, Kcho is already internationally known in his field.

Kcho was born in 1970 in the town of Nueva Gerona, on Isla de la Juventud, a small island that is a four-hour boat ride from the southern coast of Cuba. "Where I grew up," he explained to Rosa Lowinger in an interview for *Art News Online* (June 2000), "all the limits were liquid." Kcho's father had long wanted to name a son "Cacho," which means "chunk" or "piece," thus signifying that the boy would be a "chip off the old block." His mother objected to giving that name to her newborn, so the infant was named Alexis Leyva Machado. The nickname "Cacho" stuck, though, and during high school the teenager changed the spelling to "Kcho." Kcho's father was a carpenter; he taught his son how to use hand tools and build things. His mother, who was artistic, helped make elaborate decorations for the island's annual carnival.

While Kcho was in elementary school, a teacher noticed his skill at drawing and encouraged him to seek training in art. At 14 he was accepted into the prestigious Escuela Nacional de Artes Plásticas, a fine-arts school in Havana. After briefly studying painting, he switched to sculpture, because, as he told Rosa Lowinger, "painting seemed too methodical, too much about process, and there's an element of deceit in it." He has credited his painter's eye with enabling him to see that, in his words, "trash also has color."

Kcho

Kcho graduated from the fine-arts school in 1990. After failing to gain admittance to the Instituto Superior de Arte, a university-level fine-arts school, he embarked independently on a career as an artist. Within a year a solo exhibition of his work, titled *Paisaje popular cubano* (Cuban Folk Landscape), opened at a Havana gallery, the Centro de Arte 23 y 12. The show included *La peor de las trampas* (The Worst of Traps), a ladder with machete-blade rungs and sides that culminated in fake palm fronds, and the austere piece *Como el garabato se parece a Cuba* (How the Hook Resembles Cuba), a sculpture made from a grass-cutting tool that is long and curved, like the island. Kcho's work was also included in groups shows in Havana and Caracas, Venezuela.

Despite these successes, the 1990s were an inauspicious time for Kcho's debut in Cuba. After the dissolution of the Soviet Union, in 1991, and the fall of Communist regimes in Eastern Europe, the Communist-ruled Cuba lost its major foreign markets and subsidies, and its economy suffered a severe decline. Declaring a "Special Period in Times of Peace," President Fidel Castro instituted strict food rationing and other austerity measures. Like most other Cubans, artists had to make do with less. The members of one artists' collective, for example, as Nina King reported in an article on the Cuban art scene for the *Washington Post Magazine* (April 13, 1997), shared paint and made their own brushes. The climate of scarcity may have prompted Kcho to rely more heavily on found objects. During those lean years many Cubans took to the seas in homemade rafts and rickety boats, hoping to reach Florida and make better lives for themselves. Concurrently, Kcho began to construct boat

frames out of bent wood; for one piece he created a flotilla of toy boats surrounded by pieces of inner tubes near a debris-strewn beach. To Manuel E. González, a Cuban exile who directs the Chase Manhattan Bank's art program in New York, Kcho represented the "quintessential Cuban artist of the 'Special Period,'" as he put it to Lowinger.

The situation in Cuba notwithstanding, during the 1990s other countries grew more hospitable to Cuban artists. In 1991 the U.S. Treasury Department lifted a ban on the import and resale of some forms of Cuban art, by reclassifying paintings and drawings as "informational materials" and thus making them exempt from the trade embargo that has existed on most Cuban goods since 1960, shortly after Castro came to power. President Bill Clinton's "people-to-people" program made it easier for U.S. artists, journalists, and scholars to travel to Cuba; reciprocally, the Castro government made it easier for Cuban artists to travel abroad and sell their works. Kcho became one of the most visible and successful Cuban artists to emerge during this period. In 1992 he left his native land for the first time, and over the next few years, works by him were included in shows in Brazil, Germany, Switzerland, South Africa, and the United States. In 1995 he won the grand prize—$50,000—at South Korea's Biennale, an international art competition, for his work *Para Olvidar* (To Forget), an installation in which a rowboat rested on a pile of empty and half-empty beer bottles, the whole seeming to allude to the Cuban people's sufferings and desire for escape.

Kcho's first U.S. exhibition was mounted at the Barbara Gladstone Gallery, in New York City, in 1996. The show included the piece *Columnar In-*

finida (Infinite Column), a tower of oil drums, bottles, oars, surfboards, and boats. The title refers to the famous "Endless Column" series of one of the earliest modern sculptors, Constantin Brancusi (1876–1957); made of stacked symmetrical forms, Brancusi's "Endless Column" pieces sometimes reached as high as 100 feet. In the New York Times (April 5, 1996), Michael Kimmelman described Kcho's "Infinite Column" series as "dreamy, ad hoc, slightly surreal concoctions that could just keep going up and up."

While many creators of large art installations draw plans, choose materials, and then hire engineers to build their works, Kcho prefers a totally hands-on approach. For an installation in Ghent, Belgium, in 2000, he endured freezing rain and stood in mud and hip-high water for three days in order to "make the drawing in the river" rather than sketch it on paper, as he put it to Lowinger. The resulting installation was a 66-foot-long dock winding down to the water from a medieval castle on the river bank. Kcho's sculptures retain a handmade quality, reflected, for example, in the metal C-clamps that join bentwood pieces and in the ad-hoc appearance of the pieces that incorporate found materials. Kcho has traced some works to chance phrases that strike him as good titles for sculptures-to-be. "I was in a bar last night, having a beer with one of my assistants," he told Lowinger. "A small thing suddenly became something: don't hammer two nails in one line. I was explaining it to him and, at the same time, I knew the expression would be the starting point for a new work. Sometimes it takes me a year or more to do something with them, but my process always begins with the title."

Kcho also uses pencil and paper to work out his ideas. "In a white sheet of paper all you need is light and shadow," he has said, as quoted on the Barbara Gladstone Gallery Web site. "The drawing is the essential vessel of the idea, a poetic vessel." While thinking about his column sculpture (Columnar Infinida), Kcho created drawings 10 feet high, with sheets of paper placed one on top of another, to create a sense of height and volume. These and other drawings, of boats, oars, and lonely piers, appeared in the Barbara Gladstone Gallery in September 2000.

Given Cuba's isolation and uniqueness, it is perhaps not surprising that critics' interpretations of Kcho's artworks take into account his country's politics and recent history. The sea-themed sculptures have also been viewed as the natural expression of someone who was raised on a relatively remote island. The boat sculptures evoke in addition the notion of life as a passage, an idea that can be traced at least as far back as ancient Greek mythology, which held that at death, people's souls ferry across the river Styx to the realm of the dead. "A boat is an ancient human invention," Kcho explained to Susan A. Davis for the New York Times (March 17, 1996). "I don't think there is another mode of human transport that says more about peo-

ple. You go to a lake and see a canoe, then you go to Miami and see boats that look like fairy castles." Nina King regarded Kcho's raft and boat sculptures as allusions to Afro-Cuban history, which began with slaves' forced journeys by ship from Africa to the New World.

Others have spoken of the elegant, slightly surreal physicality of Kcho's sculptures—a characteristic noted, for example, in connection with the ironically titled Lo mas mejor del verano (The Best of Summer), which was shown at a 1994 exhibition in Madrid, Spain. For this installation Kcho hung from a ceiling grid several cheap Cuban rafts ("the kind people fish from or use to escape," he explained to Davis). He also hung various objects that he had found in Spain: fishing nets, bits of wood and baskets, kayaks and oars, an empty water bottle, and old sneakers, all of which were reflected in the gallery's highly polished, black stone floor. "The first thing you noticed was the reflection of the rafts hanging from the ceiling, all going in the same direction," the exhibition's organizer, Dan Cameron, told Davis, "and it dawns on you: I've drowned." Rosa Lowinger had a remarkably similar reaction: "One had the impression of being submerged in water, witnessing a shipwreck from below," she recalled. Kcho created Lo mas mejor del verano in March 1994, four months before food shortages and riots prompted a mass exodus of Cubans, who rafted from the island across the Straits of Florida. "When that happened, I got a little scared because my design became very real," he told Davis. "In everything that comes from Cuba there is a brush stroke of politics." Although—unlike Soviet artists, whose government forced them to adhere to the officially propagated "socialist realism"—Cuban artists have never had to conform to a state-sanctioned style, degrees of censorship and self-censorship clearly exist to this day. Cuban artists rarely make Castro himself the subject of their work, for example; according to Lowinger, "The artists of Kcho's generation tend to cloak their messages in poetry and symbolism."

In recent years Kcho has been personally affected by the continuing thorniness of U.S–Cuba relations. His first New York show was picketed by angry Cuban-Americans, many of whom believed that any support for Cuban artists tacitly lends legitimacy—and hard currency—to the Castro regime. In 1997 Kcho was scheduled to create an exhibit at a Los Angeles gallery, but at the last moment he was denied a visa by the United States—a fairly common occurrence that Cubans refer to as la trauma de la visa. At Kcho's request the gallery's curator exhibited copies of correspondence in which he and Kcho discussed this problem; the gallery also posted the rejection notice from the U.S. State Department. For a 2000 show in Madrid, Kcho created a series of drawings of docks that, when closely examined, spelled out "Elián," a reference to Elián González, the five-year-old survivor of a wrecked boat that had been carrying illegal immigrants from Cuba to the United States in November 1999. Elián's fate launched a political war between anti-Castro Cuban-Americans, who believed the boy should have been allowed to stay in the U.S., and the Clinton administration, which eventually returned him to Cuba and his father. Kcho's work has many such sly political references and allusions, but he has also emphasized its universal themes (loss, impermanence, dreams) that are beyond the realm of politics. "Cuba is not Fidel alone. . . . Cuba is also its artists," he told Lowinger. One sculpture that clearly expresses this sentiment is *Obras Escogidas* (Selected Works). Created in 1997 and installed at the Walker Art Center, in Minneapolis, Minnesota, it consists of a boat made of wooden racks that are filled with Spanish, English, and French texts—Marxist tracts, Western classics, and school textbooks, all of which represent the varied literature that Kcho read as a child. Visitors to the gallery were encouraged to get into the boat and read.

According to Lowinger, Kcho is "as thick and solid as a football linebacker," with a booming voice, "enormous smile, and seemingly boundless energy." He lives in Havana, where he recently began to create mobiles, inspired by his visit to the studio outside Paris where the late American sculptor Alexander Calder worked. —M.A.H.

Suggested Reading: *Art News Online* June 2000; *New York Times* (on-line) Mar. 17, 1996, Apr. 5, 1996; *Washington Post Magazine* W p18 Apr. 13, 1997

Selected Works: *Como el garabato se parece a Cuba* (How the Hook Resembles Cuba), 1991; *La peor de las trampas* (The Worst of Traps), 1991; *Columnar Infinida* (Infinite Column), 1994; *Lo mas mejor del verano* (The Best of Summer); *Para Olvidar* (To Forget), 1995; *Obras Escogidas* (Selected Works), 1997

Courtesy of Southwest Airlines

Kelleher, Herb

Mar. 12, 1931– President and CEO of Southwest Airlines. Address: Southwest Airlines Co., P.O. Box 36611, Dallas, TX 75235-1611

Herb Kelleher is no fan of what he described, in an interview with Donna Rosato for *USA Today* (February 23, 1998), as "the old hierarchical theory of management which says you have to show you're in charge by walking around acting like a brick all day." Instead, the president and CEO of Southwest Airlines cultivates an unorthodox management

style, which has won him the admiration of customers and employees alike. Kelleher has been known to perform rap songs that poke fun at himself, to don a white sequined Elvis Presley costume for a magazine cover, and to appear at company gatherings in drag. Once, when asked to speak before a professional aviation society about his accomplishments, he joked, as cited by Kenneth Labich for *Fortune* (May 2, 1994), "I'm very good at projectile vomiting"—then added, after the laughter had subsided, "I've never had a really *serious* venereal disease." On another occasion, Kelleher even proposed to settle a dispute over a rival's alleged appropriation of a Southwest advertising slogan not by the usual legal avenues, but rather by means of a CEO-to-CEO arm-wrestling match.

There is a method to Kelleher's madness, for beneath the antic disposition there lies an astute businessman. "He is very flamboyant," Seth Schofield of USAir Group Inc. told Richard Weintraub for the *Washington Post* (September 12, 1993), "but probably one of the most disciplined business executives you can meet." A workaholic who routinely devotes 14 hours a day, seven days a week to running Southwest, Kelleher has said that he takes his job, if not himself, seriously. His dedication has paid off. Under Kelleher's charge, Southwest has grown from a small, intrastate airline to the fifth-largest carrier in the U.S. It is the most consistently profitable carrier in the business, having operated in the black for 26 straight years since 1973—a U.S. industry record. Numerous times, the U.S. Department of Transportation has bestowed upon Southwest its "triple crown" award, which recognizes best on-time performance, best baggage handling, and fewest customer complaints, and in a 1993 report cited by Labich, the department called Southwest the "principal driving force for changes occurring in the airline industry." For these and other achievements, Kelleher was named Chief Executive of the Year in 1999 by *Chief Executive Magazine* and was the only airline executive chosen to sit on President Bill Clinton's commission on air travel. As Larry Bossidy, the CEO for Allied Signal, summed up in presenting Kelleher with the CEO of the Year award, "Herb is an unconventional innovator, masterful in breaking all the molds to combine fun, fierce competitiveness, genius, and Elvis impersonations into unique and effective business operations."

The fourth child of a Campbell's Soup Co. general manager and a homemaker, Herbert David Kelleher was born in Camden, New Jersey, on March 12, 1931. He remembers his childhood as being happy until his father died of a heart attack when Herb was 12; shortly thereafter, his older brother was killed in World War II. These losses forced Kelleher to grow up quickly, but they also strengthened his relationship with his mother. "My mother and I were alone," he told a reporter for *People* (May 2, 1994). "We became very close. We'd sit up until 4 a.m. talking about business, politics, everything."

Growing up in Haddon Heights, a Philadelphia suburb near Camden, Kelleher spent several summers working on the factory floor of a Campbell's facility, an experience that he has credited with teaching him a great deal about running a business: "It was like getting a Ph.D. in industrial management—squared," he told Labich of his summer job. After graduating from Haddon Heights High School, Kelleher matriculated at Wesleyan University, in Middletown, Connecticut, where he studied philosophy and literature. He originally aspired to a career in journalism, but switched to law after the legal scholar and Wesleyan trustee Arthur T. Vanderbilt took him under his wing. After earning a B.A. degree, cum laude, Kelleher enrolled at the New York University Law School, from which he graduated in 1956.

After leaving law school Kelleher clerked for a New Jersey Supreme Court justice for two years before taking a job with Lum, Biunno, and Tompkins, a Newark, New Jersey, law firm. He stayed in New Jersey for several years, then relocated to Texas and joined the San Antonio–based firm Matthews, Nowlin, Macfarlane & Barrett. In "A Culture of Commitment," a chapter he contributed to the business anthology *Leader to Leader* (1999), Kelleher explained how an experience at the San Antonio firm informed his later, idiosyncratic management style: "Wanting to learn from the best, I went to see two of the most renowned litigators in San Antonio try cases. One sat there and never objected to anything, but was very gentle with witnesses and established a rapport with the jury. The other was an aggressive, thundering hell-raiser. And both seemed to win every case. That's when I realized there are many different paths, not one right path. That's true of leadership as well."

In 1966 Rollin King, a Texas businessman who planned to start a low-fare, no-frills airline serving Dallas, Houston, and San Antonio, hired Kelleher as an outside counsel. (Although King first approached Kelleher in the latter's San Antonio office, Kelleher told Labich, "I often tell people the whole thing took place in a bar because so many of the good things in life do happen there.") The fledgling airline encountered stiff opposition from the very beginning: lawyers representing the rival carriers Texas International, Braniff, and Continental argued in court that Texas could not support another airline and tried to persuade government authorities not to issue Southwest an operating license. Kelleher, representing Southwest pro bono, fought the case all the way to the U.S. Supreme Court, ultimately winning. In 1971 Southwest Airlines received permission to operate, and four years later the company went public.

In 1978 Kelleher was named chairman of Southwest Airlines (he assumed the titles of president and CEO in 1981) by the board of directors, after Lamar Muse, Kelleher's predecessor at the company's helm, stepped down. Although he had extensive knowledge of the company's legal affairs, Kelleher was short on management experience. "I was apprehensive, just as I expect everyone was," Kelleher told Charles A. Jaffe for *Nation's Business* (October 1991). "So I got everybody together for a meeting. And the first thing I told them was not to worry because I had the most important executive ability down cold. . . . I've always been able to make erroneous decisions very quickly."

Despite his initial trepidation, the board's choice of Kelleher for the top post turned out to be well-founded. After emerging from a series of fare wars in the wake of airline deregulation, in 1978, Southwest began to grow steadily, and it has continued to do so, more or less unabated, to this day. First, the airline expanded beyond the borders of Texas into New Mexico, Louisiana, and Oklahoma. Then, after establishing a solid base in these neighboring states, Southwest branched out to Chicago and Phoenix—cities strategically important for the California and Midwest markets, respectively—as well. More recently, the airline has established footholds on both coasts and has even initiated transcontinental flights. Throughout its rapid expansion, Southwest has remained a profitable venture despite hard times in the airline industry. (Between 1978 and 1991 high fuel costs and deregulation forced 169 airlines to fold or merge with competitors.)

In "A Culture of Commitment," Kelleher offered a simple formula for Southwest's success: "What's the secret to building a great organization? How do you sustain consistent growth, profits, and service in an industry that can literally change overnight? . . . I can answer basically in two words: *be yourself*. That is both a simple and a profoundly difficult goal. It means spending less time benchmarking best practices and more time building an organization in which personality counts as much as quality and reliability. It also means cultivating an ability to embrace paradox. Southwest Airlines has a reputation as the wild and crazy guy of commercial aviation. Yet in many ways we are the most conservative company in our industry."

In the view of many industry analysts, Southwest has indeed managed to set itself apart from the crowd, in terms of both its market niche and less tangible factors, such as company culture and public image. A Harvard Business School case study cited by Labich, for example, determined that Southwest had succeeded in "differentiating itself through its focus on service, operations, cost control, marketing, its people, and its corporate culture." While Southwest is frequently emulated, few rivals have managed to duplicate its achievements.

In contrast to those of most domestic carriers, Southwest's business strategy does not focus primarily on luring frequent fliers away from other airlines. Instead, Southwest attempts to tap the large pool of Americans who fly infrequently, if at all. "Our main competition is the automobile," Kelleher told Richard Woodbury for *Time* (January 25, 1993). "We're taking people away from Toyota and Ford." Consequently, Southwest tends to offer fares priced well below the industry average. When the now-defunct Braniff was charging $62 for a one-way flight between Dallas and Houston, for instance, Southwest was asking a mere $15. Such low prices usually lead to an increase in passenger volume, which is how the airline has managed to come out ahead. In 1993, for example, Southwest began flying between Louisville, Kentucky, and Chicago. Before Southwest entered the market, in 1992, that route had an average weekly traffic of about 8,000 passengers. Within one year, the figure had jumped to 26,000.

Southwest's high-volume strategy works because the airline operates differently from most other domestic carriers. In airline jargon, Southwest is a "short-haul, point-to-point carrier," which means that the airline chiefly makes short, nonstop flights and does not have a recognizable hub. "While a hub-and-spoke system is an efficient way to fill a plane," Kelleher told Charles A. Jaffe, "it isn't so good at using a plane." Instead, the airline favors satellite airports, which tend to be less congested than other facilities, and uses only one type of aircraft, the 737, which results in fewer logistical difficulties for maintenance and flight crews. Moreover, Southwest does not assign seats, serves no in-flight food except for peanuts and crackers, has no first-class section, and requires passengers to re-check their baggage when making connections—even connections on Southwest. In return for such small inconveniences, Southwest has managed to cut its average turnaround time— the time required to unload, refuel, and reboard a plane at the gate—to about 20 minutes, as compared with an industry average of 45 minutes. That means that Southwest requires a proportionally smaller fleet than its competitors, which in turn translates into lower fares.

Southwest has further distinguished itself through its history of unusually good labor relations. The company has experienced only one strike in its 30-year history, a six-day walkout staged by machinists in the mid-1980s, and has never laid off any workers. Southwest's compensation and benefits programs are among the most generous in the industry, and it was the first airline to inaugurate an employee profit-sharing plan. Further, the company has the lowest annual employee turnover in the industry, and those jobs that become available are highly coveted: in 1990, for example, Southwest was swamped with 62,000 applications for 1,400 openings.

Kelleher attributes the company's high morale to a hands-off management style. In "A Culture of Commitment," he wrote, "A financial analyst once asked me if I was afraid of losing control of our organization. I told him I've never had control and I never wanted it. If you create an environment where the people truly participate, you don't need control. They know what needs to be done, and they do it." By most accounts, that approach has won Kelleher the respect of Southwest employees. Michael E. Levine, the executive vice president for marketing at Northwest Airlines, remarked, as quoted by Labich, "Herb is really an extremely gifted labor-relations talent, especially when you consider he has somehow managed to get union people to identify personally with this company."

That identification is most visible in the zany antics of Southwest employees. Flight attendants have been known to break into song aboard planes, for instance, or to surprise boarding passengers by popping out of overhead bins. The company's original uniform included red hot-pants, and Southwest is especially famous for its off-beat in-flight announcements. (Past favorites include the following: "Good morning, ladies and gentlemen. Those of you who wish to smoke will please file out to our lounge on the wing, where you can enjoy our feature film, *Gone With the Wind*." "Please pass all plastic cups to the center aisle so we can wash them out and use them for the next group of passengers.") While such behavior seems to bear Kelleher's stamp, Southwest employees disagree as to whether the CEO's personality has significantly influenced the company's culture. Some say it has, while others maintain that the airline was unconventional from the beginning.

Herb Kelleher was described by Amy Engeler for *Business Month* (August 1990) as "tall and wiry, with a touch of Gene Wilder mania in his bulging blue eyes." Kenneth Labich characterized Kelleher as "the sort of fellow who can barely contain his excess energy." A chain-smoker who consumes five packs of cigarettes per day ("I am determined to keep on doing it, and I don't much care what society thinks about it," he told Labich), Kelleher is also conspicuously fond of Wild Turkey bourbon. ("I met the president of the company that makes the stuff down in Louisville not long ago," he quipped to Labich, "and I told him that he may be just a man to most people—but to me he is a god.") He reportedly sleeps a mere four hours per night and reads two to three books per week. He also enjoys hunting and fishing, and frequently visits Conquistadores del Cielo, a rural Wyoming ranch popular among airline executives. (One associate of Kelleher's told Labich that at the ranch, "there is an unwritten rule that, if you don't want to stay up all night drinking and talking, then you stay the hell away from Herb.") Kelleher is married to the former Joan Negley, the daughter of a prominent San Antonio rancher, and has four children. — P.K.

Suggested Reading: *Fortune* p45+ May 2, 1994, with photos; *New York Times Magazine* p36+ Nov. 9, 1997, with photos; *Time* p55 Jan. 25, 1993, with photo; *USA Today* B p5 Feb. 23, 1998, with photos

---

Kentridge, William

1955– Visual artist; filmmaker; theater director. Address: c/o Marian Goodman Gallery, 24 W. 57th St., New York, NY 10019; c/o Goodman Gallery, P.O. Box 411137, Craighall 2024, South Africa

"All of my work is about Johannesburg in one form or another . . . ," the artist William Kentridge told interviewers for *onepeople.com* (February 1998, on-line), referring to the South African city in which he has lived nearly all his life. "Thematically I suppose I work with what's in the air, which is to say a mixture of personal questions and the broader social questions. Questions this year, questions last year, responsibility, retribution, recrimination, before issues of what histories are hidden in the landscape. Often they're fairly broad questions but generally they arrive through quite a personal or particular starting point." Kentridge has been described as "the first globally acclaimed South African artist of the post-apartheid period," which began with the dismantling, in 1991–92, of the system of institutionalized, government-enforced racial discrimination that had prevailed in South Africa for more than 40 years. He began to make a name for himself in his native land in the 1970s, as a founder of, and actor, designer, and director with, the Junction Avenue Theatre Company—a "theater of resistance" troupe, as Barbara Pollack labeled it in the *Village Voice* (May 30–June 5, 2001). The mission of the company was to reveal the cruelties of apartheid and thereby hasten its end. More recently, he has collaborated on productions mounted by South Africa's renowned Handspring Puppet Company, with which he has worked as a set designer, writer, director, and puppeteer.

Trained in theater and mime as well as fine art, Kentridge also served as an art director in the film and television industries before the mid-1980s, when he began to devote much of his efforts to the work for which he has become best known outside South Africa: a series of animated films that "tell a story" by showing continuously changing charcoal drawings of his own creation. While the films' protagonists are two white, Jewish, middle-aged South African men, the series illuminates questions of guilt and responsibility and other issues that affect all South Africans and, indeed, people and nations everywhere. "In searing images," the art critic Grace Glueck wrote for the *New York Times* (June 8, 2001), "[Kentridge] addresses not only the land itself and its racial problems but also the general human condition, expressed in the longings and frustrations of bourgeois lives played out in the country's deeply dysfunctional setting." Also for the *New York Times* (June 17, 2001), Hilarie M. Sheets wrote, "His art is often viewed through the prism of politics. And yet he roots his work in the local and the specific: for him it's a way of getting at universal truth rather than simply illustrating the recent history of his country."

The highly prolific Kentridge, whose oeuvre also includes etchings, lithographs, and videos, has won all of South Africa's major art prizes and several American awards. His animated film *Stereoscope* (1999) won the Carnegie International Prize, from the Carnegie Museum of Art, in Pittsburgh, Pennsylvania; the previous year he was shortlisted for the even more prestigious Hugo Boss Prize, from the Solomon R. Guggenheim Museum, in New York City, an honor that, according to the Guggenheim's Web site, is given "in recognition of an artist whose career exemplifies a significant new development in contemporary art, one with international cultural reverberations." His work has been exhibited in solo and group shows at galleries and museums in Germany, France, England, Belgium, Sweden, and other European countries as well as South Africa; Cuba, Turkey, Japan, New Zealand, and Australia; and various sites in the United States, among them the Guggenheim Museum, the Museum of Modern Art, and the New Museum for Contemporary Art, in New York City, and the Hirshhorn Museum and Sculpture Garden, a division of the Smithsonian Institution, in Washington, D.C.

The eldest of the two sons and two daughters of Sydney Kentridge and Felicia Geffen, William Kentridge was born into a Jewish family in Johannesburg in 1955. His grandparents came to South Africa a century ago; on one side of his family, they emigrated from Lithuania, and on the other, from Germany. Three of the four were lawyers, as are his father and mother. Felicia Geffen founded the Legal Resources Centre, South Africa's first nonprofit legal-aid provider. Sydney Kentridge, who was knighted in 1999 by Queen Elizabeth II of England for his achievements as a human-rights attorney, was a major figure in the struggle to end apartheid.

William Kentridge with one of his drawings

Peter Rimell/Courtesy of
the Museum of Contemporary Art, Chicago

Among other anti-apartheid efforts, he served as counsel to community members and the Roman Catholic bishop of Johannesburg, Ambrose Reeves, during an inquiry into events on March 21, 1960—"Black Monday"—at the South African township of Sharpeville, where police opened fire on an unarmed crowd of black Africans, killing 69. He represented the family of the black South African Steve Biko, a founder of the Black Consciousness Movement, in an inquiry after Biko died, at age 30, while in police custody in 1977. He also represented Nelson Mandela when South Africa tried Mandela for treason in 1956.

Although William Kentridge was raised in a relatively affluent, safe home, he became well aware early on of the abominable conditions in which most black South Africans lived and the many ways in which apartheid precluded the possibility of better lives for them. In a talk with Phylicia Oppelt for the London *Sunday Times* (October 17, 1999, on-line), he recalled wandering into his father's study one day when he was six years old and seeing photos of some of the victims of the Sharpeville massacre. "If one talks about monumental shocks when one realises that the world is constructed in different ways to the safe, intimate world of a protected childhood, that would certainly be an instance," he told Oppelt. During his childhood he also learned about the pogroms and other acts of discrimination against Jews in pre–World War II Russia and the near-destruction of the European Jewish community by the Nazis during that war.

"My mother would say I started drawing seriously at three, but I drifted into it," Kentridge told Phylicia Oppelt. At the King Edward VII School, a high school for white boys in Johannesburg, he told Oppelt, he "did part-time fine art studies," but not with the goal of making art his career. As a teenager he served on the Johannesburg junior council, whose members represent several dozen of the city's schools; when he was 17 years old, his fellow councilors elected him Johannesburg's junior mayor. (Many South African cities have similar student bodies and junior mayors.) "I was a very arrogant and self-certain 17-year-old," Kentridge told Oppelt. "That was on one level, and, on another, I was a bumbling insecure adolescent. I have a difficult relationship with my past. I feel sorry for him."

In the same interview Kentridge said that he knew he did not want to study law—"I thought I would never know whether I was a good lawyer or simply my father's son"—and that his parents never pressured him to follow in their footsteps. At the University of the Witwatersrand, in Johannesburg, which he entered in 1973, he majored in politics and African studies. In 1975, while an undergraduate, he worked with Malcolm Purkey and other student opponents of apartheid to found the Junction Avenue Theatre Company (JATCO). For years afterward he served as an actor, writer, director, and set designer for numerous productions of the innovative group, which performed in Johannesburg and the neighboring black township of Soweto until 1991. With Purkey (now a well-known theater director) and Steven Sack, he wrote the play *The Fantastical History of a Useless Man* (1976), which examines the causes of the black South African student rebellions of 1976.

After he earned a B.A. degree, that same year, Kentridge studied fine art for two years at the Johannesburg Art Foundation. His teachers included the painter Bill Ainslie, whom Barbara Pollack described as "influential . . . in South African circles." From 1978 to 1980 Kentridge taught etching at the Johannesburg Art Foundation. Midway through that period a solo show of his drawings and prints was mounted at the Market Gallery, in Johannesburg. In 1981 his work was featured in two one-man shows—one, called *Domestic Scenes*, at the Market Gallery, and another at the Association of Arts, in Cape Town, South Africa. He won first prize in a national graphics competition in Bellville, Cape Province, that year. Also in 1981 Kentridge moved to Paris, where he studied mime and theater at l'École Jacques Lecoq, named for the master French pantomimist and drama teacher who founded the school and taught there. A physical trainer, expert in movement, and one-time athlete, Lecoq stressed the importance of process rather than results and encouraged his students to venture into the unknown rather than simply to polish their performances. "I learnt more about painting and drawing from Jacques Lecoq, who taught me theater, than I did from art teachers," Kentridge told *onepeople.com*. In 1982, after completing the Lecoq course, Kentridge returned to Johannesburg. For the next three years or so, he had jobs as an art director, both for feature films and television series, and worked on his own projects as well. *Howl at the Moon*, a 40-minute fictional video that he co-directed in 1981, won the Red Ribbon Award at the 1982 American Film Festival. His 30-minute fictional film *Salestalk* (1984) earned the Blue Ribbon Award at the 1985 American Film Festival. In 1984 he was a co-winner of the Olive Schreiner Award (named for a South African writer and feminist) for JATCO's production of the play *Randlords and Rotgut*, by Ari Sitas. Later, in 1988, he helped to found the progressive South Africa–based, cooperative production company Free Filmmakers.

In 1989 Kentridge made the seven-minute-long *Johannesburg, 2nd Greatest City After Paris*, the first in his ongoing series of animated films. (The lengths of others in the series range from three minutes to nine; all use sound as well as images.) To make his animated films, Kentridge uses a technique that captures "the process of a drawing coming into being," as he put it in his interview with Hilarie M. Sheets. A highly skilled draftsman, he first makes a charcoal drawing and mounts it on a wall. Operating a type of camera in which film can be advanced one frame at a time and that is used to make traditional animated films, he then photographs the drawing. Next, he changes the drawing slightly, by adding something or erasing something that he then redraws. In a single day he may alter the drawing 60 to 100 times, photographing each revision; after a week, he typically will have produced about 40 seconds' worth of film. The "story" in each film is told through several dozen evolving drawings, in which a chain of often bizarre events occurs in a succession of settings ranging from the mundane to the surrealistic. Most of the final drawings in each sequence are preserved; in shows,

some of these works are exhibited along with the motion pictures in which they appear. "[Kentridge] says it's in the physical act of walking between the drawing on the wall and the camera that he finds a sense of what can happen next in his stories," Sheets reported, adding, "The fact that charcoal leaves a trace when rubbed out gives Mr. Kentridge's sequences an imprint of time." In addition to *Johannesburg, 2nd Greatest City After Paris*, the series includes, among other films, *Monument* (1990); *Mine* (1991); *Sobriety, Obesity and Growing Old* (1991); *Felix in Exile* (1994); *History of the Main Complaint* (1996); *Ubu Tells the Truth* (1997); *Weighing . . . and Wanting* (1998); *Stereoscope* (1999); and *Medicine Chest* (2000). In *Medicine Chest*, which was made specifically for the first U.S. retrospective of Kentridge's work, held at the New Museum of Contemporary Art in mid-2001, the film is projected onto the interior of an actual medicine chest. In a review of the retrospective for *artmagazine.co.uk* that also offers an illuminating discussion of Kentridge's approach to his art, Eric Gelber wrote of *Medicine Chest*, "The normal contents of a medicine chest appear intermittently throughout the film, along with barren fields with solitary figures walking through them, [and] a flittering black colored bird. The film has the feel of a daydream, a stream of consciousness. . . . There are no dramatic resolutions to the tenuous 'plots,' but there is continuity through movement and culminating moments."

In *Johannesburg, 2nd Greatest City After Paris*, Kentridge introduced his two principal characters—Soho Eckstein and Felix Teitlebaum—who have also appeared in his later animated films. Both are portly, middle-aged Jewish men who resemble their creator physically to some degree—"mainly because [Kentridge] needs someone close at hand to use as a model," as the artist explained, as paraphrased by Sheets. Invariably dressed in a dark, pin-striped suit—even when, as in *History of the Main Complaint* (1996), he is lying in a hospital bed—Soho is a ruthless yet pitiful businessman (according to different sources he is an industrialist, a real-estate promoter, or a factory or mine owner). Kentridge has depicted Soho as a high-living capitalist whose obsessive concern with reaping the highest possible profits is beginning to share space in his brain with feelings of guilt and remorse, stemming from his belated but painful realization of his role, and those of other whites, in the maintenance of apartheid. (Soho's brain is depicted in some of Kentridge's films.) The sensitive Felix, by contrast, is a more sympathetic figure; a melancholy artist, he is always naked—"I couldn't think of an outfit for him," Grace Glueck quoted Kentridge as saying—and he exudes acute anxiety as he, too, struggles with his memories and his attempts to come to grips with the past and the present. Both he and Soho, Hilarie Sheets wrote, "putter about their daily activities under the weight of remembering and forgetting." "The films can be understood as a sort of diary or daily newspaper of one's self . . . ," Kentridge told Sheets. "It's a real mixture of the political and the social and the personal. Insofar as the films track anything, they try to approximate that process."

The animated films *Felix in Exile* and *History of the Main Complaint* (the latter of which Kentridge made during the period when South Africa's Truth and Reconciliation Commission held public hearings into the human-rights abuses that had taken place under apartheid) were shown at Documenta X, an international exhibition for contemporary art, held in Kassel, Germany, in 1997. Many people who attended Documenta X were unfamiliar with Kentridge's work, and both films attracted an enormous amount of attention. Thanks to the resulting discussions about them, the artist's profile quickly rose in the international art world. "During the 1980's there was the cultural boycott of South Africa, which meant that work got seen very little outside," Kentridge told Hilarie Sheets. "There was never an expectation that it was going to be seen in a large way. In retrospect that was a blessing. It meant I didn't have to try to catch up or surpass what was being done in America. So when there was an interest in these films, I knew what I was doing."

That interest has angered some people. In an article from *Art Monthly* (June 1999) excerpted on the Web, for example, the British artist Eddie Chambers complained that, while only five million of South Africa's 38 million people are white, "no black South African artist has any sort of profile that comes even close to that of Kentridge. The same must be said of South Africa's so-called 'coloured' artists [among the three million South Africans classified as coloured]. . . . In other words, the 29 million [black] majority, along with South Africa's 'coloured' and Indian populations have found themselves being represented, in the art galleries of the world, by a small impregnable clique of white, primarily male South African artists, of which William Kentridge is the prime example." According to Phylicia Oppelt, Kentridge believes that his rise to international prominence is, as Oppelt put it, "the luck of the post-apartheid draw," and can be attributed in part to the name recognition he gained through the earlier shows of his work outside South Africa.

Kentridge has dismissed the criticism that, through his art, he has used the horrors of apartheid to benefit himself. "To try and get a coherent view of South Africa by simply looking at my films or art you would get a completely mixed-up view of the society, because that's not what I'm trying to do," he declared to Oppelt. "I'm not interested in 'Apartheid for Beginners.'" He has also rejected as "ridiculous" the view, expressed by a critic quoted by Oppelt, that, because of the way he has presented Eckstein and Teitlebaum, his animated films "smell just like anti-Semitism."

During the past decade Kentridge has collaborated with the Johannesburg-based Handspring Puppet Company on a half-dozen productions, among them *Woyzeck on the Highveld* (1992), based on the famous 19th-century drama *Woyzeck*, by Georg Buchner; *Faustus in Africa!* (1995), an adaptation of Goethe's tragedy *Faust*; and *Ubu and the Truth Commission* (1997) and *Ubu Tells the Truth* (1997), which are based on Alfred Jarry's absurdist trilogy of the 1890s, the most famous of which is *Ubu Roi*. Using actors, puppets, animation, and music, the works interpret classic European theatrical works from the perspective of contemporary South Africa. Several of the productions have won the Vita Award in South Africa. According to the Web site of the Henson International Festival of Puppet Theatre, one critic described *Woyzeck on the Highvelt* as "a fantastic, stylistic work that simply shatters all standards."

Kentridge told Phylicia Oppelt, "For a Jewish person there is a strong Calvinist work ethic in me. There's never been a sense of dropping out or simply doing nothing. I think there was also a sense of responsibility there, that the least you could do as a privileged white South African was to work hard." In 1997 teachers and students from the Film & Television and Multimedia School at CityVarsity, a Cape Town institution, made the CD-ROM *William Kentridge*, about the artist and his work. A book, also called *William Kentridge*, was published in 2001 in conjunction with the U.S. retrospective of his work. The book was co-authored by the artist, the American museum curators Neal Benezra, Staci Boris, Dan Cameron, and Lynne Cooke, and Ari Sitas, a professor of social studies at the University of Natal, in Durban, South Africa.

Kentridge is married to Anne Stanwix, a physician. The couple live in Johannesburg with their two daughters, Alice and Isabella, and their son, Samuel, who were born in 1984, 1988, and 1992, respectively. — M.H.

Suggested Reading: *artmagazine.co.uk*; Goodman Gallery Web site; (London) *Sunday Times* (on-line) Oct. 17, 1999; *New York Times* E p27+ June 8, 2001, with photos; *New York Times* (on-line) June 17, 2001, with photos; *onepeople.com* Feb. 1998; *Village Voice* p44+ June 5, 2001, with photos; *Washington Post* p53+ Mar. 9, 2001, with photos; Kentridge, William, and others. *William Kentridge*, 2001

Selected Films: *Johannesburg, 2nd Greatest City After Paris*, 1989; *Monument*, 1990; *Mine*,1991; *Sobriety, Obesity and Growing Old*, 1991; *Felix in Exile*, 1994; *History of the Main Complaint*, 1996; *Weighing . . . and Wanting*, 1998; *Stereoscope*, 1999; *Medicine Chest*, 2000

Martyn Goodacre/Retna Ltd.

Kid Rock

Jan. 17, 1971– Rap artist; rock musician; songwriter; founder of Top Dog Records. Address: c/o Atlantic Records, 1290 Ave. of the Americas, New York, NY 10104

"Persistence pays," the rap artist and rock musician Kid Rock told Dimitri Ehrlich for *Interview* (July 1999). "I always believed in myself. I could look in the mirror . . . and ask, 'Are you as good as everybody else?' and I could honestly say, 'No, you're better.' I didn't want to go out and change anything. I just wanted to make the music that was part of my background, which was rock and blues and hip-hop." In 1998, nearly a decade after he first entered the music business, Kid Rock achieved enormous success with *Devil Without a Cause*, an album that sold more than 10 million copies and earned the artist a Grammy nomination. Soon after its release Kid Rock began recording songs that were used on the soundtracks to movies, among them *Any Given Sunday, Mission: Impossible 2, Road Trip, Shanghai Noon, Strangeland,* and *South Park: Bigger, Longer, Uncut.* His exposure increased when a line from one of his earlier recordings, "Ain't no party like a Detroit party / 'Cause a Detroit party don't stop," was adopted by the Detroit Red Wings hockey team as its anthem. Kid Rock records and tours with the Twisted Brown Trucker Band, which includes Jimmie Bones on keyboard and vocals, Kenny Olson on lead guitar, Stefanie Ulinberg on drums and vocals, Uncle Kracker (whose real name is Matt Shaker) on turntables and vocals, and Jason Krause on guitar. (Another band member, the diminutive, foul-mouthed vocalist Joe C, born Joe Calleja, died in

2000.) Kid Rock's music blends elements of southern rock, rap, metal, country, and funk; his performances are high-energy spectacles featuring fireworks, dancers, and the large inflatable middle finger that he uses to sum up the attitude he exhibits on stage. Presenting an image that is equal parts pimp and "trailer trash," Kid Rock keeps his hair long and often wears a derby and a sleeveless T-shirt under a white fur coat. "When hip-hop came in, so many white kids wanted to be a part of that culture, start[ed] wearing their hats sideways, using a little Ebonics," he told Lorraine Ali for *Newsweek* (June 5, 2000). "I thought it's cool to like hip-hop, but it's also cool to be white. You should be proud of what you are. But it's important not to confuse white trash with racism. . . . Let's just say I don't have the most positive stuff in my music and I'm not about politics, so I'm changing things in another way."

Like the rap artist and songwriter Eminem, Kid Rock has been lambasted by critics for the sexist and homophobic aspects of his lyrics; also like Eminem, whom he has described as "a good friend" of his, he has rejected such charges. "Yeah, I use the word 'fag,'" he told Thor Christensen for the *Dallas Morning News* (February 9, 2001), in an article reprinted on *GuideLive* (on-line). "And no, I don't hate gay people. . . . Some of my best friends are gay . . . and they don't get offended when I use the word 'fag' around them. They laugh. I don't hate anybody in this world. But I talk the way I talk and the way I was raised." Echoing many other rap artists, Kid Rock has insisted that his lavish use of profanity and street slang merely reflects his background. "I'm from Detroit," he explained to Max Sidman for *thesynthesis.com.* "I go into McDonald's and I'm used to having someone wavin' a gun in my face. Not to mention that this is the way I talk to all my friends. I'm not gonna switch it up on my record."

A proud single father and the founder of the label Top Dog Records, Kid Rock has cautioned observers not to draw conclusions about his behavior in private life from his brash stage persona. "Not only am I a hard worker, but I'm probably the nicest guy you ever met," he told Jon Wiederhorn for *Dr. Drew.com* (2000). "One thing I've learned is that people are usually the opposite of their image. I mean, I am all that when I'm up on stage, and if someone disrespects me, I'll be the first to lash out at them. But I'm not into being a bad person. Offstage I'm really a nice, genuine, normal person. I like Big Macs and Budweiser."

The third of four siblings, Kid Rock was born Robert James Ritchie on January 17, 1971 in Romeo, Michigan, a suburb of Detroit. As a child he heard a lot of rock and roll at home, and he developed an interest in hip-hop as well as rock early on. "I grew up with a corn field in my backyard, had horses when I was young, spent my early years mowin' lawn and haulin' brush," Ritchie told Max Sidman. "I saw someone scratchin' records on TV one day, and I immediately ruined my mom's stereo. . . . I cut out a piece of felt, threw it on the turntable, and used the volume knob to scratch all the Beatles records." At his parents' request, he would often lip synch Bob Seger and Jim Croce songs at family backyard parties. During the summer following his 14th birthday, Ritchie was kicked out of his house. While boarding with friends in the nearby Mount Clemens housing project, he worked at a car wash and "walked around drinking forties, . . . eating pork rinds, hanging out at the barbershop, riding the bus to Detroit to get records, [and] hanging out with the guys selling drugs on the street," as he recalled to Chris Heath for *Rolling Stone* (June 22, 2000). Ritchie returned home when school started, but the following summer he left again—this time by choice— and briefly sold drugs himself. He continued to immerse himself in hip-hop culture, deejaying at parties, entering talent contests, and appearing with a dextrous break-dance crew known as the Furious Funkers. The dancers were sponsored by a local Burger King restaurant, and Ritchie began to rap introductions for them during their in-store performances. "They'd move the salad bar out of the way," he told Heath, "and we'd get down." Ritchie's deejay skills earned him his stage name: as he explained to Dimitri Ehrlich, attendees at the break-dance shows sometimes exclaimed, "Look at that white kid rock."

In 1988 Kid Rock made his first demos; on the strength of those recordings, he soon landed both an opening spot on a tour with the rap duo Boogie Down Productions and a contract with Jive Records. Kid Rock's debut album, *Grits Sandwiches for Breakfast*, produced by Too $hort and D-Nice, was released in 1990. Soon afterward WSUC, the radio station of the State University of New York at Cortland, was fined $23,750 by the Federal Communications Commission (FCC) for broadcasting the album's opening single, a song about cunnilingus entitled "Yo-Da-Lin in the Valley." (The fine was later rescinded.) A short time later Kid Rock went on a 20-city tour with Ice Cube and Too $hort. "He had a way about himself so that it didn't really matter [that he was white]," the rap artist Yo Yo, also a tour participant, told Sacha Jenkins for *Spin* (October 1999). "He had a good flow. There wasn't too many white boys doing it then, and Cube and them all embraced him. He blended right in."

After Jive Records dropped him, Kid Rock moved to New York City, where he began to experiment with a fusion of rap and metal, a style that would increase in popularity as the 1990s progressed. He made two recordings for the independent label Continuum: *The Polyfuze Method* (1993), the name of which came from a Hair Club for Men commercial, and an EP, *Fire It Up* (1996). In 1996 Kid Rock returned to Detroit, where, using his earnings from sales of the Continuum recordings (many copies of which he had sold out of his basement), he founded Top Dog Records, built his own recording studio, and bought a house. Also that year he released *Early Mornin' Stoned Pimp*,

to which the Black Crowes keyboardist Eddie Harsch and the soul singer Thornetta Davis contributed.

At around this time Kid Rock signed a contract with Atlantic Records. "I won't sit here and lie to you like every other group; I went with Atlantic because they kicked out the cash," he told Max Sidman. "But still, I told them flat out that I really liked them, and they were the first ones at the table. They broke it down for me, everything I wanted. And sometimes, you just gotta take a chance with somebody. You never know what you're going to get dealing with a major, but the guys who signed me were totally straightforward: 'We'll sell some records now, and a few years down the road we might kick you off the label.' I said, 'Fine. That's all I want to hear.'" After receiving a check for his advance from Atlantic Records, Kid Rock celebrated at a local bar. "I gave the bartender five hundred dollars and told everyone that drinks were on me," he told David Jenison for *Woodstock.com* (1999). "I was completely jacked up within twenty minutes. Later that night, some kid—I guess I was with his girlfriend or something—body slams me right off my chair. My buddy sees me go down, so he cracks a bottle over the guy's head. A big brawl breaks out, and the bouncers think I started it. . . . The cops came and hauled us down to county [jail], but we're still all jacked up. We partied in lock-up and had a blast tormenting the cops." Although not yet a star, while in jail he wrote the lyrics to "Only God Knows Why," a ballad about the downside of fame.

At many of his shows, Kid Rock noticed a concertgoer standing on a stool in the front row, singing the lyrics to his songs. The fan was the three-foot nine-inch Joe Calleja, known as Joe C. "It bummed me out because I thought he was some little kid, and his parents were taking him to all my shows and buying him my records," Kid Rock told David Jenison. "I'm not the king of morals or anything, but I thought that was a little twisted. Finally, after one of the shows, Joe C comes up and asks me if I wanted to smoke a joint. That was the final straw. I asked him to take me to his dad, and he got pissed. He started yelling, 'I'm grown! I'm grown!' When I realized he was just a midget, I said, 'Bring your short ass backstage.'" Joe C's stunted growth was a result of his long-term treatment with prednisone, one of the medications he took to combat the effects of celiac disease, which he had had since birth. After he and Kid Rock became acquainted, Joe C appeared on stage with the band, and soon afterward Kid Rock offered him a permanent position and taught him how to rhyme.

Devil Without a Cause (1998) brought Kid Rock instant fame. Thanks to the frequent airing of the song "Bawitdaba" on radio and MTV's enthusiastic support of the "Bawitdaba" video, the album soon went multi-platinum; it eventually sold more than 10 million copies. To promote the recording, Kid Rock toured with the popular rap-metal group Limp Bizkit and made a memorable appearance at

Woodstock '99, held in Rome, New York, to mark the 30th anniversary of the original, three-day Woodstock music festival. He was also nominated for a Grammy Award as best new artist (the prize went to Christina Aguilera). In September 1999, accompanied by Run DMC and Aerosmith, he performed at the MTV Music Awards ceremony; his medley included "Bawitdaba," Run-DMC's classic song "King of Rock," and "Walk This Way," a prototypical rock and rap hybrid that Aerosmith and Run DMC had recorded together in 1986.

Kid Rock's next album, *The History of Rock* (2000), is a compilation of songs from his second and third albums, newly recorded versions of old songs, and a few new singles. The album went double platinum within two months of its release and was supported by Kid Rock's tour with the bands Fuel and Buckcherry. After the death of Joe C, shortly after his 26th birthday, the concert included a tribute to him: as an electronic sample of his vocal contribution to the song "Devil Without a Cause" played, a huge picture of the deceased rapper was lowered from the rafters. "We didn't want to make it sad and do the tribute during 'Only God Knows Why,' because he wouldn't want that," Kid Rock told Thor Christensen. "He'd be like 'Hey everybody! Let's light one up and rock out!' He'd want the party to continue."

In his conversation with Dimitri Ehrlich, Kid Rock expressed the view that music that combines rock and hip-hop (such as the work of the Beastie Boys, Rage Against the Machine, and Korn) has become popular because it represents "rebellion: Loud kick drums and loud guitars. That's what it was in the '70s—how loud could you get your guitars. Then in the late '80s, it was how much bass could you put in your trunk to piss people off? We just put it all together." Kid Rock told Ehrlich that his own music is influenced by "MTV and the radio, Lynyrd Skynyrd, Run-DMC, Eric B, and the best of everything that ever was." By his own account, the musician with whom he feels the deepest affinity is the country-and-western icon Hank Williams. "He's the only person who's had a lifestyle remotely similar to mine," Kid Rock told Sacha Jenkins. "I've read two books in my whole life: *The Girl Who Owned [a] City*, in the eighth grade, and Hank Williams' autobiography, *Your Cheatin' Heart*. There's just something about the things he went through, and the songs he wrote are heartfelt and true."

His popularity has earned Kid Rock endorsement contracts with Borsalino, the manufacturer of many of his trademark hats, and other companies. He has also received substantial corporate gifts, such as $40,000 worth of clothes from Versace, as a result of which he no longer has to buy the clothes he wears on stage. "I get big boxes of Hanes T-shirts free, and I throw them away after I wear them once," he told Devin Friedman for *Gentlemen's Quarterly* (September 2000). "I've got thirty pairs of white Adidas shelltoes that I get free, along with the Pumas. . . . I get five to ten cases of beer

delivered to my house from Anheuser-Busch every month because I'm on their VIP program. . . . I go into Gucci and they give me a discount just for selling a bunch of records. I'm like, 'Sweet.'"

Kid Rock made his acting debut in the film *Joe Dirt* (2001), directed by Dennie Gordon and starring David Spade. He is featured in *All Access* (2001), an IMAX film that also includes performances by Carlos Santana, Sting, Al Green, Sheryl Crow, Moby, Mary J. Blige, and George Clinton, as well as backstage footage. Kid Rock was among the artists who accompanied the legendary soul singer Aretha Franklin at Radio City Music Hall, in New York City, for the 2001 presentation *Live: The One and Only Aretha Franklin*, broadcast on the series *VH1 Divas*. He is currently working on a new album for the Atlantic label and projects for Top Dog Records, including an album by the Dallas-based country singer David Allan Coe. In 2000 Top Dog released *Double Wide*, the debut album of the rap singer Uncle Kracker, Kid Rock's deejay and the co-writer of much of *Devil Without a Cause*. "I've had Top Dog for 10 years now, and I finally have the business side of it worked out to where I can give people I believe in a fair shot," Kid Rock told Jon Wiederhorn. "I'm not into just finding an act, I also [enjoy] shaping that act musically, socially, and in every way. I want to utilize everything I've learned to help them, and hopefully I can [work with] some good songwriters and really talented people. My focus is gonna be talent, not gimmicks."

Kid Rock has custody of his oldest son, Junior, whose parents' rocky, interracial marriage was chronicled in Kid Rock's "Black Chick, White Guy," a song from *Early Mornin' Stoned Pimp* that was re-recorded for *Devil Without a Cause*. The musician has tried to strike a balance between his career and his responsibilities at home. "I live 40 miles outside Michigan in the middle of the woods, and I get home as much as possible," he told Jon Wiederhorn in 2000. "I think I'm doing a very good job being there for my son, who I raise by myself. It's very tempting to go out and play 60 shows this summer and make $20 million, but instead I'm only gonna play for three weeks because I want to spend time with him. There are just some things that are more important than money and music." In a statement made after the death of Joe C, excerpted by Gary Graff for *Wall of Sound* (November 17, 2000, on-line) and reprinted on *ABC-NEWS.com*, Kid Rock said, "Family and friends are everything; without them, all of the fame and fortune means nothing." — C.L.

Suggested Reading: *Gentlemen's Quarterly* p326+ Sep. 2000, with photos; *Interview* p104+ July 1999, with photos; *Newsweek* p70 June 5, 2000; *Rolling Stone* p58+ June 22, 2000, with photos; *Spin* p91+ Oct. 1999, with photos, p74+ Feb. 2001, with photos; *Village Voice* (on-line), July 5–11, 2000

Selected Recordings: *Grits Sandwiches for Breakfast*, 1990; *The Polyfuze Method*, 1993; *Early Mornin' Stoned Pimp*, 1996; *Fire It Up*, 1996; *Devil Without a Cause*, 1998; *The History of Rock*, 2000

Ruth Fremson/AP

Konaré, Alpha Oumar

Feb. 2, 1946– President of Mali. Address: c/o Embassy of Mali, 1900 L St., N.W., Washington, DC 20036

Alpha Oumar Konaré, the popularly elected president of Mali, is often hailed as a model African democrat. Despite having faced a number of formidable obstacles to the pursuit of democratic reform—including widespread poverty, armed insurrection in the north, and a dearth of nonauthoritarian regimes in the region—Konaré, in nine years of office, has in the estimation of most observers managed to stick to his avowed democratic principles. That is not to say there have not been problems. Irregularities in the 1997 national elections elicited criticism from human-rights groups, and many in the opposition claim that Konaré's democratic flourishes are chiefly aimed at impressing the outsiders who provide foreign aid. Still, no one has denied that Konaré has taken important steps to insure freedom of the press and to get ordinary people involved in politics. In fact, Freedom House, the New York–based human-rights organization, has designated Mali a "free" country every year since 1992.

Moreover, because it is one of the world's poorest countries, Mali's relative success in guaranteeing civil and political rights has served as a counterexample to the theory, frequently advanced in the late 1990s, that democracy can flourish only in countries with strong economies and substantial numbers of middle-class citizens. "Democracy has given us social dialogue as a method of government," Konaré told Howard W. French for the *New York Times* (October 16, 1996). "The more people participate, the more importance they attach to the work of building our nation. With participation and transparency we have managed to limit the ethnic tensions that tear at so many African countries and avoid the waste that has ruined so many others."

Mali is a landlocked country spanning an arid, sparsely populated stretch of the Sahara Desert (in the north) and the subtropical upper basin of the Niger River (in the south); it is about the size of Texas and California combined. This geographic division has a corresponding ethnic one: the predominantly Muslim population, which numbers about 11 million, includes a variety of sub-Saharan ethnic groups in the south, as well as traditionally nomadic peoples related to the North African Berbers in the north. Although Mali was ruled for many centuries by a series of prosperous sub-Saharan empires that included parts of Senegal, Burkina Faso, Guinea, and Niger (the last empire was effectively destroyed by a Moroccan army in 1591), today it is strikingly poor. Life expectancy at birth is 50 years, literacy rates hover at about 30 percent, and recurring droughts have brought devastation to the country's primarily agricultural economy.

The recent history of Mali, like that of many other African countries, is interwoven with the history and legacy of European colonialism. From 1898, when the French first gained control of the region, through January 1959, when Mali united with neighboring Senegal to form the semi-independent Mali Federation, the country was known as the French Soudan. Konaré was born under French rule on February 2, 1946 in Kayes, a small city in western Mali on the Senegal River. His father was a schoolteacher who also served as mayor of Kayes.

French rule was characterized by a highly centralized administration run by a governor-general situated in Dakar, Senegal. For the most part, the French disregarded local social and political institutions, at least until the passage of the *loi cadre*, or enabling law, in 1956. (The *loi cadre*, which essentially reestablished local autonomy in internal affairs, was a response to growing nationalist sentiment throughout West Africa in the post–World War II period.) Less than two years after it was founded, on June 20, 1960, the Mali Federation achieved complete independence within the French Community (an association of self-governing former French colonies that pursued a common agenda in matters such as defense policy, economic policy, and foreign affairs). As a political entity, however, the Mali Federation would prove to be short-lived: it collapsed in August 1960, after the secession of Senegal. One month later, on September 22, 1960, Mali proclaimed itself an independent republic.

Mali's first president was Modibo Keita, the leader of the Sudanese Union, the country's foremost nationalist organization under French rule. Soon after Keita took the reins of power, Mali's government evolved into a single-party dictatorship aligned with the Soviet bloc. Keita reigned for eight years before being deposed in 1968, in a bloodless military coup staged by a Sudanese Union faction that opposed the president's increasing reliance on French administrative assistance. Konaré, who opposed the coup, has said he first became involved in national politics at this time. (He was then studying history and geography at the École Normale Supérieure in Bamako, the Malian capital.)

Although the leaders of the 1968 coup had pledged a swift restoration of civil and political rights, such changes were not forthcoming. Rather, infighting among military leaders led to the eventual consolidation of political power in the hands of Lieutenant Moussa Traoré, one of the coup leaders. In 1974 the political organization with which Traoré was associated drafted a new constitution that provided for some limited democratic reforms; however, a series of coup attempts and a severe drought in the north delayed implementation of the new constitution until 1979. That year Traoré, the candidate of the country's sole political party, was elected to a five-year term (later extended to six years) as president and prime minister. In 1985 Traoré was reelected—again as the sole candidate.

Meanwhile, Konaré, who had completed his schooling at the École Normale Supérieure in 1969, taught history and geography for two years in Markala and Badalabougou, cities in the Niger Basin. In 1974 he was named head of research at Mali's Institute of Human Science, and in 1975 he completed a doctorate in history and archeology at the University of Warsaw, in Poland. Three years later, in May 1978, Konaré was named minister of youth, sports, arts, and culture. In 1980 he resigned from government and began working with the underground democracy movement. Throughout that decade he became increasingly outspoken in his criticism of Traoré. He founded two publications—the cultural quarterly *Jamana* and the newspaper *Les Echos*—that raised the bar for independent journalism in the country in terms of outspokenness, and in 1986 he took part in founding the National Popular Democratic Front, a prodemocracy organization.

Traoré held onto power until early 1991, when growing nationwide austerity, coupled with mounting demands for multiparty democracy, led to widespread rioting in the streets of Bamako. Military leaders took advantage of the unrest in the capital to launch another coup. At the head of the army group that seized control of the government was Lieutenant Colonel Amadou Tourmani Touré—coincidentally, a former student of Konaré's. Much as his predecessor had done, Touré announced his intention to reinstitute civilian government once the national emergency had been remedied. Unlike his predecessor, though, he actually followed through on that promise. "I made a coup," Touré told Johanna McGeary and Marguerite Michaels for *Time* (March 30, 1998), "but sometimes you have to give a quick kick to democracy. I watched other officers my age in other countries take over. These men came in to save their countries, then stayed 20 years. But when a country is well managed, the constitution is respected, no captain can come out of his barracks. The vaccination against a coup is good government." In the summer of 1991, Touré convened a national conference in which 1,000 delegates from 42 parties drafted a new constitution based on the principles of multiparty democracy. On January 12, 1992 the constitution was approved in a national referendum that saw low voter turnout. In succeeding weeks the Alliance for Democracy in Mali, or Adema, the party that Konaré had helped found the previous summer and which he fronted, won majorities in both municipal and legislative elections. In the April presidential elections, Konaré attained a solid victory, thus becoming Mali's first democratically elected president. He was inaugurated on June 8.

Upon taking office, Konaré was immediately tested by a growing insurrection among ethnic Tuaregs in the north. (The Tuaregs, a traditionally nomadic North African people, had been severely impoverished by lengthy droughts in the 1970s and 1980s. They also charged the national government, which was dominated by sub-Saharan ethnic groups, with suppressing their language and culture.) The conflict between insurgent Tuaregs and the Malian army reached a peak in 1994; in the following year Konaré's government reached an accord with the rebels—the so-called Timbuktu peace agreement. To celebrate the accord, in March 1996 the inhabitants of Timbuktu, in Mali, burned some 3,000 guns in a bonfire, christened "the flame of peace," at the edge of the Sahara. Thus far, the truce has held. As part of the agreement, some 2,500 former rebels were given jobs in the army and civil service; another 9,500 received demobilization credits or loans to start small businesses. According to Sophie Boukhari in the *Unesco Courier* (January 2000), "only about 10 percent of the former rebels subsequently deserted the army or abandoned their new civilian jobs and the rate of their absorption into the private sector is reckoned to be 70 per cent. . . . The legendary lords of the desert feel uncomfortable in their new situation but they are resigned to working at a regular job."

The presidential and parliamentary elections of 1997, the first since 1992, were plagued by numerous irregularities and sporadic outbreaks of violence. The first round of parliamentary elections, in April, were marred by a shortage of voting slips; although a team of international observers concluded that balloting had been "secret and unrestricted," as quoted by an Amnesty International report (on-line), Mali's Constitutional Court annulled the elections. A number of opposition groups held demonstrations in protest, and many boycotted the presidential elections in May, with the result that Konaré received 95.9 percent of the vote. Protests in June against Konaré's investiture for a second term and unrest in July and August related to rescheduled parliamentary elections degenerated into violence that left two people dead. Government security forces arrested dozens of protesters, some of whom later alleged that they had been intimidated and, in some cases, tortured while in police custody—charges that drew the censure of several international human-rights groups. For his part, Konaré attributed the problems to the country's authoritarian legacy and the youthfulness of Malian democracy. "Since the last election, we have faced some difficulties," he later admitted to Nora Boustany for the *Washington Post* (November 28, 1997). "The difficulties are a fact of life. Democracy is fragile." Nevertheless, he added, "the place for the opposition is not in jail." Although the government established a commission of inquiry in late 1999 to investigate the allegations of intimidation and torture, a lack of funding has prevented the commission from carrying out its work.

During his tenure as president, Konaré has made freedom of the press a high priority, with the result that there are currently more than 40 independent newspapers in the country, published in French and Arabic as well as in a number of local languages. Independent radio stations, of which there are about 40, also play an important role in the national discourse, given the high rates of illiteracy in Mali. Perhaps Konaré's most innovative act has been the institution of an open, national public forum, held for several days in Bamako each December, in which ordinary citizens are given the chance to address the prime minister and members of the national cabinet on national television with their complaints and concerns. Although the forum, which is based on local, precolonial traditions, has been labeled by some in the opposition as a public-relations stunt, many observers believe it has done much to further the cause of democracy in Mali. "This may have all started to please the outside world," Tore Rose, a representative of the U.N. Development Program stationed in Mali, said, as quoted by Howard W. French, "but the important thing is that people have come to believe in their right to criticize and question their leaders, and that is a very powerful agent for change."

Konaré has repeatedly stated that he plans to return to an academic career once his second term of office expires in 2002, despite calls from some of his supporters to alter Mali's constitution to allow a third term. (The 1992 constitution limits the president to two five-year terms.) "I do not underesti-

mate the difficulties, but I do not accept excuses that say Africa should not make an effort to be pluralist . . . ," Konaré told Howard W. French for the *New York Times* (September 7, 1997). "I am certain that pluralism will survive Konaré."

Konaré is married and has four children. — P.K.

Suggested Reading: Amnesty International Web site; *Christian Science Monitor* p4 Feb.13, 1992, with photo; *Economist*, p39 July 26, 1997, p40+ July 10, 1999; *New York Times* I p3 Sep. 7, 1997, with photo; *Time* p34+ Mar. 30, 1998, with photos; *Unesco Courier* p26+ Jan. 2000; *Washington Post* p27 Mar. 24, 1996, p41 Nov. 28, 1997; *Political Handbook of the World, 1998*

Ivan Milutinovic/Archive Photos

Kostunica, Vojislav

(kawsh-TOO-neet-sah, VOY-slahv)

Mar. 24, 1944– President of the Federal Republic of Yugoslavia. Address: c/o Embassy of the Former S. F. Republic of Yugoslavia, 2410 California St. N.W., Washington, DC 20008

In the summer of 2000, the makeshift Democratic Opposition of Serbia, a diverse coalition of 18 opposition parties, asked Vojislav Kostunica to serve as its presidential candidate in national elections scheduled to take place in Yugoslavia on September 24. (Present-day Yugoslavia is made up of two states: Serbia, whose capital is Belgrade, and Montenegro, whose capital is Podgorica.) Kostunica, a 56-year-old constitutional scholar, hesitated to accept the invitation. Referring later to his indecision, he said, as quoted by Steven Erlanger in the

New York Times (October 9, 2000), "It was a joke that among the undecided voters in Belgrade was Kostunica." But Kostunica was also the only opposition leader with a realistic chance of defeating Slobodan Milosevic, Yugoslavia's then–president, who bears a heavy responsibility for the so-called ethnic cleansing campaign carried out in Bosnia-Herzegovina, a former republic of Yugoslavia. Other opposition politicians, notably Zoran Djindjic, the leader of the Democratic Party, and the maverick Vuk Draskovic, the head of the Serbian Renewal Movement, were better known, both at home and abroad. But Djindjic and Draskovic had made grave political miscalculations during NATO's bombing of Yugoslavia in 1999—Djindjic, by spending most of the war in the seaside resorts of Montenegro, and Draskovic, by serving in Milosevic's wartime cabinet; consequently, neither man was a viable candidate. That left Kostunica, the leader of the Democratic Party of Serbia, who, unlike Djindjic and Draskovic, had never compromised his anti-Milosevic stance. (In fact, Kostunica's first meeting with Milosevic took place on the evening of October 6, 2000, just after the Serbian leader decided to concede defeat in the elections.) While Kostunica has said that initially he felt pessimistic about his chances of unseating Milosevic, he ultimately concluded that he could not escape making a run for the presidency. "The choice [of Kostunica] was perfect . . . ," Timothy Garton Ash wrote for the *New York Review of Books* (November 16, 2000). "He had a unique combination of four qualities, being anticommunist, nationalist, uncorrupted, and dull."

Dullness in particular had become a political virtue in a region that had been the target of the 78-day NATO bombing campaign in the spring and early summer of 1999 and that, over the preceding 10 years, had been entangled in four bloody wars—in Slovenia, Croatia, and Bosnia-Herzegovina, all former constituent republics of Yugoslavia, and Kosovo, a section of Serbia. As one independent Yugoslav journalist told Ash, "You know, I want a boring president. And I want to live in a boring country." Kostunica appeared to fit the bill: he was known for his gray rumpled suits, his beat-up Yugo, and his modest Belgrade apartment. Most importantly, he was known for his muted and reserved political style, a sharp contrast to the frequent histrionics of the Milosevic regime. "I am an ordinary, average man," Kostunica declared in a September 20 campaign speech (the text of which was posted on-line, in translation, at *antiwar.com* in 2000). "It has never occurred to me to see myself as some historic greatness." Many in Yugoslavia went to the polls hoping above all for a return to normalcy. As Dragan Velikic wrote for the *Frankfurter Allgemeine Zeitung* (or *FAZ*, October 12, 2000, on-line), as translated by Patrick Kelly for *Current Biography*, "Kostunica's promise to the citizens of Serbia is that he will fight for an ordinary, unremarkable everyday life rather than for myths and territories. This represents a fundamen-

tal change in the political life of the country." Kostunica also said in his September 20 speech, "I only know that what you want, and what I want, of course, is to live in an ordinary, average European country."

Kostunica's candidacy caught many by surprise, including, it seems, Milosevic. As Velikic pointed out, "The Serbian dictator never imagined that a pro-Western opposition would settle on a candidate who had a reputation for being both conservative and uncompromising." Given Kostunica's low-key image, his indisputable Serbian nationalism, and his apparent incorruptibility, the state propaganda machine found it difficult to blacken his name effectively. Still, it tried. Besides spouting vague claims of moral degeneracy, the pro-Milosevic press impugned Kostunica's masculinity by pointing out that while he owns a number of cats, he has never fathered any children. It further alleged that he was a compulsive philanderer with a preference for women under 25. By the end of the campaign, Milosevic apparatchiks were reduced to hurling rotten vegetables at Kostunica. Nevertheless, Kostunica remained strong in opinion surveys. As he and his supporters toured the country in three dilapidated buses, many of those opposed to the Milosevic regime took up caustic rallying chants, such as "Save Serbia and kill yourself, Slobodan" and "Save us from this madhouse, Kostunica."

As most onlookers had expected, Kostunica came out ahead of Milosevic in the September 24 election. His undisputed lead did not, however, assure him the presidency. Since 1989, when he was elected president of Serbia (he won the presidency of Yugoslavia in 1997), Milosevic had become adept at massaging election results in such a way as to ensure his victory while nevertheless retaining the legitimizing trappings of democracy. As Timothy Garton Ash noted, Milosevic "was not a totalitarian dictator. Instead, his regime was a strange mixture of democracy and dictatorship: a 'demokratura.'" On September 26 the State Election Commission, a group stocked with Milosevic supporters, announced that Kostunica had won 48.22 percent of the vote, not 55 percent, as his supporters claimed, while Milosevic had captured 40.23 percent. Because its regulations required that the winning presidential candidate receive over 50 percent of the vote, the commission scheduled a run-off election for October 8. Kostunica and his supporters refused to accept that decision, claiming they had won an outright victory. "We are talking about political fraud and blatant stealing of votes," Kostunica declared, as quoted by a correspondent for CBS Worldwide (on-line). "This is an offer which must be rejected."

In the following days Kostunica supporters began to gather in Belgrade, the capital of Yugoslavia, and to stage mass demonstrations as well as a general strike. By October 5 the ranks of protesters had swelled to several hundred thousand. For the most part, the protests were peaceful. The only patently revolutionary moment came on October 5, when demonstrators in Belgrade stormed and set fire to the federal Parliament building (a symbol of the Milosevic regime) while the police—who had previously been loyal to Milosevic—stood by. At about the same time, in another part of the capital, anti-Milosevic protesters seized control of the state television station, thus depriving Milosevic of his primary means of disseminating propaganda. That evening Kostunica appeared before the Parliament. "Good evening, liberated Serbia," he told the gathered crowds. "Serbia has hit the road of democracy and where there is democracy there is no place for Slobodan Milosevic." The next day Milosevic appeared on national television and officially conceded the presidency to Kostunica, and on October 7 Kostunica was sworn in as president of the Federal Republic of Yugoslavia. It was a surprisingly nonviolent denouement to a tense stand-off with an historically violent regime. "I don't like the word revolution," Kostunica had declared on October 3, as quoted by Steven Erlanger in the *New York Times* (October 3, 2000), "but what is happening in Serbia today is a revolution—a peaceful, nonviolent, clever, civilized, democratic revolution. People are ready to start building a new country."

The son of a respected judge who served on the Serbian Supreme Court, Vojislav Kostunica was born on March 24, 1944 in Belgrade. According to Christiane Srna, a correspondent for the *FAZ* (October 10, 2000), the Frankfurt, Germany–based Serbo-Croatian daily *Vesti* has reported that Kostunica was born at home; Belgrade, which was occupied by the German army during World War II, was being bombed, so his mother was unable to reach a hospital. Kostunica studied law at Belgrade University Law School, from which he graduated in 1966; he earned a master's degree from the law school in 1970 with a thesis titled "The Political Theory and Practice of the Constitutional Judiciary in Yugoslavia." That same year he was named assistant at the Faculty of Law at Belgrade University, where he worked as a lecturer for four years. In 1974 he lost his job, after criticizing as unfair to Serbs the changes that Josip Broz Tito made to the Constitution that year. (Marshal Tito, the Communist leader of Yugoslavia from 1945 until his death, in 1980, was an ethnic Croat.) Also in 1974 Kostunica earned a doctorate from Belgrade University Law School, with a thesis titled "Institutionalized Opposition in Capitalist Political Systems," which dealt with the role of the opposition in a multiparty system. Beginning in 1974 he was employed by the Institute for Social Sciences; he remained there until 1981, when he was appointed senior scientific associate at the Institute for Philosophy and Social Theory. During this period Kostunica authored or co-authored several books, one of which (*Pluralism or Monism of Parties*) charged that the purportedly multiparty system under Tito was a farce. In 1989 Kostunica founded the Democratic Party, which was rechristened the Democratic Party of

Serbia in 1992, after Yugoslavia, which had been made up of six republics, broke apart. (Two of those republics, Slovenia and Croatia, declared independence in 1991; two more, Macedonia and Bosnia-Herzegovina, followed suit in early 1992; soon afterward, Serbia and Montenegro declared themselves the Federal Republic of Yugoslavia.)

After becoming president of Yugoslavia, Kostunica faced a number of challenges. First, there was the question of what to do with Milosevic. Symbolically, that question was intimately connected with the larger question of how the country was to come to terms with its recent, violent past. In some quarters there was desire for revenge, which led to speculation that Milosevic might end up like the Romanian dictator Nicolae Ceausescu, who was executed by his countrymen after he was toppled from power. Others felt that the ex-president should stand trial in The Hague, in the Netherlands, where the International War Crimes Tribunal was convened. Finally, there were those who preferred to forget the recent past and therefore take no steps to punish Milosevic. Before and during his campaign, Kostunica had often declared that Milosevic ought not to be delivered to the war-crimes tribunal, but the international pressure—especially from the United States—to do so was considerable. Toward the beginning of November 2000, Kostunica softened his position somewhat; rather than stating that he would not hand over the ex-president to the tribunal, he said that the issue simply was not on his mind: "Today I am thinking more about the problems of electric power than The Hague tribunal," he said, as quoted by Michael Dobbs in the *Washington Post* (November 3, 2000).

When, on April 1, 2001, Milosevic finally was arrested—by local police, on domestic charges of corruption and abuse of power—Kostunica staunchly opposed the transfer of the former president to The Hague to stand trial for war crimes. "It should never happen," he told reporters, according to Steven Erlanger in the *New York Times* (April 3, 2001). "I think that it's possible to do everything so that it should never happen." Kostunica felt that the International War Crimes Tribunal "practices selective justice, which is not justice at all," as Erlanger reported in the *New York Times* (April 4, 2001). Kostunica agreed with proponents of extradition that Milosevic's arrest marked a turning point in Serbia's return to normalcy. "Its meaning is to make public all the violations of the law and rights committed by the old regime led by Milosevic, so people can have a complete, clear picture. There will be no hide-and-seek—everything will come out. If we speak of the need for social catharsis, then the most important is this one." Yet Kostunica favored trying Milosevic before a domestic court. What his country needed, he said, "is something that from the beginning of the American republic is called self-rule and self-government. How can our people and courts become competent to deal with questions like war crimes unless you're given a chance?" (On June 28,

2001, Yugoslav authorities delivered Milosevic to tribunal officials. While Kostunica had opposed the move, Zoran Djindjic, who in December 2000 was elected to the powerful post of prime minister of Serbia, supported the extradition.)

The task of balancing the conflicting demands for vengeance, justice, and forgetting was further complicated by the fact that the old regime continued to retain many vestiges of power, despite the ouster of Milosevic. In particular, the government of Serbia, Yugoslavia's larger republic, was dominated by Milosevic supporters, including Mirko Marjanovic, the Serbian prime minister, and Milan Milutinovic, the Serbian president. There were also questions regarding the loyalties of the police and military, despite the fact that both had accepted the defeat of Milosevic in early October. As Marko Nikovic, a former Belgrade police chief, told a correspondent for the *Economist* (October 19, 2000), "Negotiations between the democratic alliance and the police will have to start soon, or the police will start co-operating with the old authorities." In contrast to several of his coalition partners, Kostunica favored a cautious approach toward restructuring the army and police. Finally, prior to parliamentary elections scheduled for December 23, Kostunica presided over a transitional government in which several ministries were divided among members of Kostunica's Democratic Opposition of Serbia, the Serbian Socialist Party (which Milosevic founded), and Vuk Draskovic's Serbian Renewal Movement. (Kostunica's coalition secured an overwhelming majority of parliamentary seats in the December elections.)

Kostunica also faced the difficult task of determining the roles of Kosovo and Montenegro in the Yugoslav Republic. Kosovo, while still nominally a Yugoslav province (Serbia comprises three provinces: Serbia proper, Vojvodina in the north, and Kosovo in the south), is eager to break away from Belgrade. Thus far, Kostunica has staunchly opposed its independence, arguing that its autonomy would put the rights of ethnic Serbs in Kosovo at risk. As for the status of Montenegro (in which secessionist rumblings have also been heard lately), Kostunica told Ljubeta Labovic for the Podgorica, Montenegro weekly *Monitor* (September 1, 2000) that he favored "a referendum in both states. If a majority is for the common state, then a new constitution; if a majority is against a common state, then two independent states." The government of Montenegro, fearing that Kostunica would try to reassert Belgrade's control over the republic, boycotted the September election, and less than 30 percent of eligible Montenegrins came to the polls.

Finally, there was the problem of holding the democratic movement together. Even as an opposition movement, the 18-party coalition that backed Kostunica had been notoriously fractious, a weakness that Milosevic had often exploited to his own advantage. Vuk Draskovic, for example, the head of the Serbian Renewal Movement, refused to join the coalition, insisting instead on campaigning independently before the September elections. Moreover, the opposition had virtually no practical governing experience. In August 2001 Kostunica's Democratic Party of Serbia announced its intention to pull out of the Democratic Opposition of Serbia (DPS) coalition, ostensibly in protest over the government's handling of organized crime; by early September, however, the DPS had worked out its differences with coalition partners.

Perhaps the greatest unknown with regard to Kostunica was the precise meaning of his avowed Serbian nationalism. In the wake of his electoral victory, Kostunica was for the most part characterized in the Western media as a "moderate Serbian nationalist." Many of those who emphasized the "moderate" nature of his nationalism also pointed to his strong democratic credentials: he styled himself a Western liberal democrat who, while a sharp critic of U.S. foreign policy (in particular, the American-led NATO campaign of 1999), was nevertheless sympathetic with Western Europe. He was a longtime advocate of multiparty democracy, as demonstrated by his early writings: in 1981 he had translated into Serbo-Croatian the Federalist Papers (written in 1787 and 1788 by Alexander Hamilton and James Madison, with the help of John Jay), and he has also written extensively on the 17th-century British philosopher John Locke and the 18th-century French statesman and political scientist Alexis de Tocqueville, seminal figures in the history of Western (especially American) democratic thought. And finally, he had long played an active role in the Serbian pro-democracy movement. "If I remember correctly," Velikic wrote for the *FAZ*, "the core of the democratic opposition in Serbia was born in his apartment."

For those who emphasized Kostunica's democratic virtues, his nationalism could be regarded as a benign epiphenomenon. Kostunica himself encouraged this interpretation in several interviews with the Western media. For example, as the new president told Jovana Gec for *Der Spiegel* (on-line), as translated by Patrick Kelly for *Current Biography*, "To be a nationalist does not mean to be against other nations. To be a Serb does not mean to be anti-American." Such moderate nationalism also came to the fore before and during the presidential campaign. In an April 14, 2000 speech recorded on bbnet.org, for instance, Kostunica spoke of the need for solidarity among Serbs and then added, "It is also very important that we make our fellow citizens of other ethnicities experience Serbia as their own." Kostunica has often complained that the Serbs have been demonized by the Western media, and has accused the West of indifference with regard to Serbs' human rights. In 1995, for example, when a Croatian military offensive crushed Serb separatists in Krajina (a region of Croatia that had a large population of ethnic Serbs) and sent more than 150,000 Serb refugees streaming into Serbia and Serb-held territories in Bosnia, Kostunica passionately denounced U.S. support for Croatia. He has also accused NATO of ignoring the plight of Serbs in Kosovo.

At the same time, some observers found Kostunica's nationalism anything but harmless. "The limitations of Kostunica and his revolution are disturbing," Leon Wieseltier wrote for the *New Republic* (October 23, 2000), where he is literary editor. "He is an unembarrassed Serbian nationalist, who does not see or does not wish to see that the tribal sentiment of his people, their 'national question,' has been not the solution but the problem." In particular, Kostunica's opposition to the International War Crimes Tribunal in The Hague elicited sharp criticism. Some critics also pointed out that while Kostunica condemned the policy of ethnic cleansing during the 1991–95 war in Bosnia, he had supported the Bosnian Serb leader Radovan Karadzic, who was later charged with genocide by the tribunal for his role in the July 1995 killings of more than 6,000 Bosnian Muslims (Bosniaks) in Srebrenica. Moreover, during a 1998 visit to Kosovo, at a time when the Yugoslav army was driving hundreds of thousands of ethnic Albanians out of their homes, Kostunica was photographed brandishing an automatic rifle, an image that upset many Kosovo Albanians. As Wieseltier further wrote, "It has often been remarked that Milosevic's regime was communism surviving in the form of nationalism; but it is important to observe that in Serbia anti-communism, too, takes the form of nationalism. For this reason, [Kostunica's victory] has been only partially an uprising of conscience."

Kostunica lives with his wife, Zorica, who holds a doctorate in law, in the same modest apartment in Belgrade which they resided before his election. He owns several cats, although the frequently cited figure of 17 may very well be an exaggeration. The couple have no children. — P.K.

Suggested Reading: *New Republic* (on-line) Oct. 23, 2000; *New York Review of Books*, p8+ Nov. 16, 2000, with photo; *New York Times* A p1+ Sep. 4, 2000, with photo, A p1 Oct. 8, 2000, with photos, A p6 Oct. 9, 2000, with photo; *Newsweek* p49 Sep. 25, 2000, with photo; *Time Europe* (on-line) Oct. 9, 2000

Reuters/Enny Nuraheni/Hulton/Archive

Krugman, Paul

Feb. 28, 1953– Economist; writer; journalist; educator. Address: c/o New York Times, 229 W. 43d St., New York, NY 10036

Paul Krugman, according to Brad DeLong, a professor of economics at the University of California at Berkeley, is "the best claimant to the mantle of John Maynard Keynes," one of the most influential economists of the first half of the 20th century.

Krugman, DeLong wrote on his own Web site, in a review of one of Krugman's books, is "an extremely knowledgeable professional economist, an excellent writer, and an incisive critic of what international economic policymakers are doing wrong." A professor of international trade and international economics, Krugman has taught at Yale University, the Massachusetts Institute of Technology, Stanford University, and Princeton (where he is currently on the faculty). He has earned the John Bates Clark Medal, one of the most prestigious honors in his field, and many of his colleagues expect him to win a Nobel Prize some day. He is the author of 18 books on international trade and international finance, some of them highly technical and others accessible to the educated layperson. Especially since the mid-1990s, Krugman has tried to make economic policy intelligible to a more general audience; toward that end, he has written columns for *Fortune*, the on-line magazine *Slate*, and, most recently, the *New York Times*.

An only child, Paul R. Krugman was born on February 28, 1953 and grew up mostly on Long Island, New York. His mother told Sylvia Nasar for the *New York Times* (October 27, 1991) that her son took to history at an early age and enjoyed playing with toy soldiers: "Paul staged the battle of Gettysburg and then he loved to lecture us about it." In "Incidents from My Career," a 1995 essay posted on his Princeton University Web site, Krugman wrote that he grew up "in a safe middle-class suburb" and received "an ordinary education" at "one of the many John F. Kennedy High Schools" in the New York area. In addition to his love of history, Krugman developed a fondness for science fiction. "Science fiction novels . . . may have been what made me go into economics," he wrote in the

1995 essay. "Those who read the stuff may be aware of the classic Foundation trilogy by Isaac Asimov. It is one of the few science fiction series that deals with social scientists—the 'psychohistorians,' who use their understanding of the mathematics of society to save civilization as the Galactic Empire collapses. I loved Foundation, and in my early teens my secret fantasy was to become a psychohistorian. Unfortunately, there's no such thing (yet). I was and am fascinated by history, but the craft of history is far better at the what and the when than the why, and I eventually wanted more. As for social sciences other than economics, I am interested in their subjects but cannot get excited about their methods—the power of economic models to show how plausible assumptions yield surprising conclusions, to distill clear insights from seemingly murky issues, has no counterpart yet in political science or sociology. Someday there will exist a unified social science of the kind that Asimov imagined, but for the time being economics is as close to psychohistory as you can get."

After he graduated from high school, Krugman enrolled at Yale University, in New Haven, Connecticut. He majored in economics but continued to pursue his interest in history (most of his electives were in the latter subject). In 1973 William Nordhaus, a visiting economist from the Massachusetts Institute of Technology (MIT), in Cambridge, recruited Krugman to serve as his research assistant. Krugman became Nordhaus's protégé, and after he earned a bachelor's degree from Yale, in 1974, he began graduate study at MIT. During the summer of 1976, he experienced policymaking first-hand: along with a small group of fellow graduate students, he worked for and advised the central bank of Portugal. He completed his Ph.D. in 1977.

In the fall of that year, Krugman began teaching at Yale. The university also expected him to produce articles based on original research, but, as he recalled in his essay, he felt "somewhat directionless. I was not sure what to work on; I was not even sure whether I really liked research." Then, after several months on the job, he paid a visit to Rudi Dornbusch, his doctoral-thesis adviser, to discuss potential research subjects. "I . . . prepared a list of possible ideas, including as an afterthought the idea of a monopolistically competitive trade model. When he flagged the idea as interesting, I went home to work on it the next day—and knew within a few hours that I had the key to my whole career in hand. I distinctly remember staying up all night in excitement, feeling that I had just seen a vision on the road to Damascus." (His metaphorical remark refers to the biblical passage in which St. Paul experienced an epiphany while journeying to Damascus and embraced Christianity.) Krugman's insight was that economies of scale—the relative savings that result when an industry or enterprise becomes bigger—could motivate specialization by national economies and international trade among them even in the absence of comparative advan-

tage. (The concept of comparative advantage is usually attributed to the British economist David Ricardo, who, in the early 19th century, demonstrated that two countries will benefit from reciprocal trade if each country specializes in manufacturing a product that it is either "most best" or "least worse" at producing. Traditionally, international-trade theory relies heavily on this idea.) Krugman has admitted that his insight was not novel—critics of traditional economic models had often made similar points. But by lending those ideas more powerful and more elegant expression in a series of papers published in professional journals, Krugman won a wider audience for them. Together with those of several of his contemporaries, his postulates became known as the "new trade theory" and provided a rationale for limited forms of protectionism in international trade.

In 1980 Krugman left Yale to teach at MIT. In 1982 he took a leave of absence from academia to work in the administration of President Ronald Reagan as the Council of Economic Advisors' chief staffer for international economics. Krugman has acknowledged that it was "strange" for him to be a part of the Reagan White House ("I was then and still am an unabashed defender of the welfare state, which I regard as the most decent social arrangement yet devised," he noted in his essay), but the deep national recession of 1982 year led him, along with other government officials, to set aside his political differences with the administration, at least in the short term. Krugman wrote most of the 1983 *Economic Report of the President* before leaving his post by the end of the year. "Washington was first thrilling, then disillusioning," Krugman wrote in "Incidents from My Career." "It is the capital of the world, and for a young person it is wonderful to think that you can really have an effect on decisions of global importance. . . . Some people get addicted to that thrill, and will do anything to stay near the center. After a little while, however, I began to notice how policy decisions are really made. The fact is that most senior officials have no idea what they are talking about: discussion at high-level meetings is startlingly primitive. . . . Furthermore, many powerful people prefer to take advice from those who make them feel comfortable rather than from those who will force them to think hard. That is, those who really manage to influence policy are usually the best courtiers, not the best analysts. I like to think that I am a good analyst, but I am certainly a very bad courtier. And so I was not tempted to stay on in Washington."

After his return to MIT, in 1983, Krugman collaborated with the Israeli economist Elhanan Helpman of Tel-Aviv University to write *Market Structure and Foreign Trade: Increasing Returns, Imperfect Competition, and the International Economy* (1985), a "magnum opus," as Krugman called it, which synthesized the new trade theory to which Helpman as well as Krugman had made important contributions. "The book is worthy reading, not only for international economists analyzing foreign markets, but also for those with a more general background," Donna Hill wrote for *Business Economics*, as quoted in *Contemporary Authors* (1999). Krugman himself, in his essay, said of the book, "Not only did it synthesize the field, but by offering a single, comprehensive reference it was a great advertising device."

In the fall of 1988, the *Washington Post* contracted Krugman to write a book about the U.S. economy; it was to be one of a series of "briefing books" for nonspecialists on economic and policy issues, ranging from environmental policy to national defense. Krugman's contribution, *The Age of Diminished Expectations: U.S. Economic Policy in the 1990s*, which he has characterized as "a primer on the U.S. economy" as well as "a kind of stealth textbook on economic theory . . . with sophisticated models hidden under the seemingly plain prose," was published in 1990. While Krugman noted in the preface that the book was "an attempt to describe the way things are, and why" rather than "a political tract or a call to arms," he repeatedly emphasized in the text that fundamental economic problems—in particular, declining productivity and growing inequality in the distribution of income—were not being addressed by the country's political leadership. *The Age of Diminished Expectations* was generally praised for its lucidity and readability; in the *New York Times Book Review* (October 28, 1990), for example, Peter Passell wrote, "[Krugman] is the rare professional economist who knows how to explain the essence of policy issues to a non-professional audience, and he manages it without a hint of condescension. *The Age of Diminished Expectations* is a remarkable achievement: a painless, quick read that tells you much of what there is to know about the great economic issues of the day." Other reviewers found fault with Krugman's pessimism or his restraint; one of them, assessing the book for the *Economist* (September 29, 1990), wrote, "On trade, most notably, but on other issues, too, Mr. Krugman takes his self-consciously low-key approach—his mission is not to excite—too far. . . . Because of this attitude of detachment, *The Age of Diminished Expectations* pales beside Milton Friedman's *Free to Choose*—or even, if that is an unfair comparison, beside *Hard Heads, Soft Hearts*, by Alan Blinder of Princeton University, an author whose political sentiments are closer to Mr. Krugman's. . . . Both these books conveyed a sense of purpose that Mr. Krugman's does not. In return for his marvelous clarity, most readers will happily put up with his somewhat diminished vision of what economics is for. But if, as he grows older, Mr. Krugman also grows angrier, it will be no bad thing."

The Age of Diminished Expectations, which sold moderately well for a book on economics, indirectly led to Krugman's sudden (if short-lived) prominence during the 1992 presidential campaign. In a chapter devoted to the increase in income inequality, Krugman had pointed out that the disparity between rich and poor had mushroomed during the Reagan presidency: "The real income before taxes of the average family in the top 10 percent of the population rose by 21 percent from 1979 to 1987, while that of the bottom 10 percent *fell* by 12 percent." Some two years later, after further reflection on the subject of income inequality, Krugman realized that the trend described in *The Age of Diminished Expectations* had become even more pronounced at the extreme ends of the scale: about 70 percent of the increase in average family income from 1977 to 1989 had gone to the wealthiest 1 percent of families. When he cited that figure in congressional testimony in early 1992, the Clinton campaign seized upon it and used it to impugn the domestic records of the Reagan and Bush administrations. For several months during that time, Krugman waged "a propaganda war," as he characterized it, with the *Wall Street Journal*'s editorial-page writers, who disputed his interpretation of the data. (The *Journal* argued that widening income disparity was a statistical chimera.) "I think I won that war," Krugman later wrote. "In the end, the point was that inequality had indeed increased sharply, and efforts to deny that eventually looked silly."

In the summer of 1992, before the actual election but after he had published an op-ed piece endorsing Bill Clinton's economic plan, Krugman was widely touted in the press as a candidate for chairman of the Council of Economic Advisors. Krugman had indeed been in touch with several Clinton advisers and took part in a campaign meeting with the future president in late summer. But according to Krugman, he soon realized that "the Clinton Administration was going to systematically prefer policy entrepreneurs to real experts." He especially took issue with what he would later brand the "foolish analogy between international trade and corporate competition," which he claimed amounted to economic sophistry. "It is simply not the case that the world's leading nations are in any important degree in competition with each other," he later told Steven Pearlstein for the *Washington Post* (April 3, 1994), "or that their major economic problems can be attributed to failures to compete on world markets." Perhaps because of his outspokenness, Krugman was not offered a job in the Clinton administration.

Krugman expanded his criticisms of policymakers on both sides of the political spectrum in *Peddling Prosperity* (1994), in which he argued that the economic visions of both Reagan and Clinton were little more than snake oil. "The way that a small group of 'supply-siders,' preaching a doctrine that even conservative economists regarded as nonsense, came to dominate American economic policy is one of the wonders of our age," he wrote in his preface to the book. "The story of the 'strategic traders,' who are in effect the liberal counterparts of the supply-siders, is still unfolding." While some questioned Krugman's motives for writing *Peddling Prosperity*—it was suggested that he felt bitter about being passed over for a post in the Clinton administration—the book was generally praised as a primer on recent U.S. economic history and a study of the way in which economic ideas are mangled by demands for political expediency. "Krugman extracts larger lessons about the tension between academically correct and politically useful ideas," Sylvia Nasar wrote for the *New York Times Book Review* (March 13, 1994), "about why the market for economic miracle cures has boomed in the past two decades and, most important, about the real limits of economic knowledge." In defense of the Clinton administration, Larry Summers, then deputy secretary of the Treasury Department, told Pearlstein, "The basic idea of people who worry about competitiveness is that if American firms produce better products and have more markets in which to sell them, America will be better off. That is consistent with almost every economic theory. What Paul has done is elevate scholarly quibbles to high disagreements."

In *Pop Internationalism* (1996), a collection of previously published essays, Krugman continued to take aim at what he termed the administration's "ersatz economics," particularly its vision of international trade as a "win–lose" contest among nations. "You could think of Krugman as a sort of highbrow version of James (The Amazing) Randi, the magician who goes around telling the real story of how rivals bend spoons," Michael Hirsch wrote for *Newsweek* (March 4, 1996). In *The Accidental Theorist: And Other Dispatches from the Dismal Science* (1998), Krugman disputed the economic views of, among others, former secretary of labor Robert B. Reich, French president Jacques Chirac, then–House Speaker Newt Gingrich, the financier George Soros, the political journalist William Greider, and the editors of the *Wall Street Journal*. According to Krugman, such politicians and journalists overstate the contribution of globalization to regional economic instability, unemployment, and declining wages. As he wrote in an op-ed piece for the *New York Times* (February 13, 1997), "Reports of the death of national autonomy are greatly exaggerated. . . . None of the important constraints on American economic and social policy come from abroad. We have the resources to take far better care of our poor and unlucky than we do; if our policies have become increasingly mean-spirited, that is a political choice, not something imposed on us by anonymous forces. We cannot evade responsibility for our actions by claiming that global markets made us do it."

In *The Return of Depression Economics* (1999), Krugman analyzed the prolonged economic stagnation of Japan during the 1990s, as well as the crises in Mexico in 1995, East Asia in 1997, and Brazil in 1998–99, and concluded that insufficient demand, rather than inflation, was the greatest danger to the world economy. In order to stimulate investment, he advised, governments should deliberately engineer moderate inflation, thus encouraging people not to hoard cash. "It is a pity that this excellent book did not come out sooner," an *Econ-*omist (July 17, 1999) reviewer declared. "With the world economy now seemingly on the mend and financial markets buoyant again, Paul Krugman's account of the recent global financial turmoil has lost some of its immediacy. . . . But this expanded essay is still essential reading. . . . *The Return of Depression Economics* is a lucid and punchy analysis of the dangers posed by global financial markets and a wake-up call for complacent or economically ignorant policymakers."

Recently, Krugman has taken a prominent place in the public eye as a regular op-ed columnist for the *New York Times*. In essays that appear twice weekly, Krugman has repeatedly accused the administration of President George W. Bush of "misrepresenting the actual content of its own economic plan," as he put it in his March 29, 2001 column. Specifically, Krugman charged Bush with pitching his tax cut "as a short-run stimulus to spending—as the answer to an economic slowdown that Mr. Bush has done his best to play up," when in fact it was "the creation of someone who believes in the trickle-down theory: make the rich richer, and a rising tide will lift all boats." According to Krugman, the tax cut is an impractical antidote for a slowdown, because "when governments try to fight garden-variety recessions by cutting taxes or increasing spending they almost always get it wrong. By the time Congress has finished negotiating who gets what, and puts the new law into effect, the recession is usually past—and the fiscal stimulus arrives just when it is least needed. Fiscal pump-priming has its place; it's appropriate in the face of deep and persistent slumps. But otherwise we should make budgets for the long run, and let the Fed deal with short-run problems by adjusting interest rates."

"Perhaps in the end the question one should ask of any scholar is what purpose he feels his work serves," Krugman wrote in "Incidents from My Career." "I could claim great nobility of character and tell you that I work for the good of humanity. Or I could try to shock you and tell you that all I care about are the financial and professional rewards. Neither would be entirely false. I am, indeed, a bit of a romantic who believes, rather in the face of the evidence, that good ideas eventually prevail and make everyone's life better. I am also not an ascetic: I will not sneer at a nice honorarium or a free trip to a pleasant location. But the honest truth is that what drives me as an economist is that economics is *fun*. I think I understand why so many people think that economics is a boring subject, but they are wrong. On the contrary, there is hardly anything I know that is as exciting as finding that the great events that move history, the forces that determine the destiny of empires and the fate of kings, can sometimes be explained, predicted, or even controlled by a few symbols on a printed page. We all want power, we all want success, but the ultimate reward is the simple joy of understanding."

Krugman is married to Robin Wells, a member of Princeton's research staff in economics. The couple are co-writing a textbook about principles of economics. — P.K.

Suggested Reading: *Economist* p99 Sep. 29, 1990; *Economist* (on-line) July 17, 1999; *New York Times* F p10 Oct. 27, 1991, with photos, D p1 May 11, 1992, with photos; *New York Times Book Review* p26 Oct. 28, 1990, p24 Mar. 13, 1994, p11+ Mar. 24, 1996; Princeton University Web site; *Washington Post* H p1 Apr. 3, 1994, with photos

Selected Books: *Exchange Rate Instability*, 1989; *The Age of Diminished Expectations: U.S. Economic Policy in the 1990s*, 1990; *Rethinking International Trade*, 1990; *Geography and Trade*, 1991; *Has the Adjustment Process Worked?*, 1991; *Currencies and Crises*, 1992; *What Do We Need to Know about the International Monetary System*, 1993; *Peddling Prosperity: Economic Sense and Nonsense in the Age of Diminished Expectations*, 1994; *Development, Geography, and Economic Theory*, 1995; *The Self-Organizing Economy*, 1995; *Pop Internationalism*, 1996; *The Accidental Theorist: And Other Dispatches from the Dismal Science*, 1998; with Elhanan Helpman—*Market Structure and Foreign Trade: Increasing Returns, Imperfect Competition, and the International Economy*, 1985; *Trade Policy and Market Structure*, 1989

Dan Chung/Archive Photos

Lara, Brian

May 2, 1969– Professional cricket player. Address: c/o West Indies Cricket Board of Control, P.O. Box 616 W, Factory Rd., Woods Centre, St. John's, Antigua

In the West Indies, cricket is much more than a game. Barbados, Jamaica, Guyana, Martinique, and Trinidad and Tobago, along with the 18 other nations identified collectively as the West Indies, share many features of culture and geography, but they are politically separate. Cricket is one of the few institutions that bind these countries together: with the exception of the University of the West Indies, the West Indies cricket team is, as Trevor

Chesterfield wrote for *CricInfo* (January 20, 1999, on-line), "about the only unifying force in the former British colonies of the Caribbean." Thanks to the prominence of the sport in this part of the world, star West Indian cricket players are often treated like folk heroes. Among them is the Trinidadian cricketer Brian Lara, who has reigned as the king of West Indian cricket for the past decade. As an athlete who, as Larry Rohter put it in the *New York Times* (January 6, 1996), "plays with a distinctly West Indian flair and creativity," Lara has endeared himself to fans "who share his upbringing and his aspirations and take delight every time their team trounces their former British rulers." Lara is also one of the best batsmen ever to play the game. He holds two world records for most points scored in a game. (The records are for two different variants of the game: the more prestigious first-class cricket, played over a number of days, a variation of which—test cricket—is played between teams of different nations; and one-day cricket, which is played at both domestic and international levels.) And, in a game in which, according to *cricket.org*, "a batting average [of runs per out] above 30 is very good, 40 excellent, and 50 is legendary," as of September 2000 Lara boasted a career average of 49.67 runs per out in test-cricket matches.

While its beginnings are obscure, cricket has been played in England in one form or another since the late Middle Ages. The earliest known record of the game—an illustration of a man demonstrating a stroke to a young boy—is in an illuminated decree issued by Pope Gregory IX that dates from the first half of the 13th century. For a long time cricket lacked standardized, hard-and-fast rules and thus tended to be played differently from place to place; indeed, hockey, golf, and American baseball are all believed to have evolved from variants of cricket. The rules of cricket as it is now played were codified in the 18th century, when the game experienced a surge in popularity. With the expansion of the British Empire in that century and the next, cricket (along with other aspects of British culture) spread to many countries around the world; it is most popular among the Commonwealth nations. (In recent years the game has also gained favor in countries with no historical ties to the British Empire, such as Italy and Germany.) The International Cricket Council's full members, whose teams routinely compete in test matches, are Australia, India, Pakistan, South Africa, New Zealand, Sri Lanka, Zimbabwe, and the West Indies. Lara has played on the West Indian team in international matches since 1991.

Although the rules of cricket are exceedingly complex (many outsiders regard the game as completely inscrutable), those familiar with baseball often find that, without too much trouble, they can discern roughly what is happening during a game. While baseball and cricket differ greatly in particulars, in essence they are similar: in each sport, two teams take turns batting, in an attempt to score runs, and fielding, in an attempt to end the opposing team's turn at bat, and the team with the most runs wins. A game of cricket usually consists of one or two innings; the number depends upon the version of cricket being played. (In cricket, the word "innings" is used for both the singular and the plural.) Because batsmen do not retire from the field upon scoring, as baseball players do after scoring a run, cricket can make considerable demands on a player's endurance. That is particularly true of high-scoring batsmen, such as Lara, who play until they are stopped, or got "out," by the opposing team. Lara achieved one of his record scores after more than 12 hours of play in a game that lasted three days.

The youngest of 11 children, Brian Charles Lara was born into a Catholic West Indian family on May 2, 1969 in Santa Cruz, Trinidad (just north of Port-of-Spain, the capital city). He first encountered cricket at the age of six, when an older sister gave him a cricket bat. Soon afterward his father and sister enrolled him in what, in an interview with Mark Browning for the *Cricketer* (on-line), he referred to as "the local Harvard coaching clinic," and he became hooked on the sport. "Every Sunday during the season, I went there to learn the game," he told Browning. When he was 14 he left home to live with Joey Carew, a family friend as well as a former batsman for the West Indian cricket team, in order to devote himself more fully to developing his cricket skills. After graduating from secondary school, he entered Fatima College, in Port-of-Spain, where he played on the school cricket team, eventually breaking the youth batting record for the West Indies.

In 1991 Lara graduated to the regional senior team, with which he made his international debut, in a game against Pakistan. Only two years later, in a match against Australia, Lara scored 277 points, the fourth-highest point total in the history of Caribbean cricket, and earned the nickname "Prince of Port of Spain." He was hailed as the next star of West Indian cricket, and many observers declared that he had the potential to become one of the game's all-time greats.

Demonstrating the wisdom of that belief, Lara broke two world batting records in a span of two months in 1994. In April of that year, playing against England for the West Indian team, he set the record for the all-time highest score—375—in a test innings, a feat that the *Washington Post* (April 19, 1994) likened to breaking Wilt Chamberlain's National Basketball Association single-game record of 100 points, which has stood for almost four decades. In June 1994, playing against Durham for the Warwickshire, England, team, Lara shattered the record for a first-class innings with 501 points. (By comparison, a score of 50 is considered good for a batsman, and a score of 100, also known as a "century," excellent.) Upon his return to Port-of-Spain, Lara was greeted by Patrick Manning, the prime minister of Trinidad and Tobago, who declared the next day a "Day of Achievement" in Lara's honor. Some in the British press objected to the philistinism implicit in emphasizing mere scores—as Frank Keating pointed out in the London *Spectator* (August 20, 1994), the British author George Orwell once wrote, "In the eyes of any true cricket-lover, it is possible for an innings of 10 runs to be 'better' (i.e. more elegant) than an innings of a hundred runs." Still, Lara's performance in both games was generally regarded as outstanding.

In the wake of his world records, Lara was swamped with media attention, and he received from Mercury Asset Management, the United Kingdom's largest fund manager, a corporate sponsorship worth about £100,000—the most lucrative sponsorship ever for a cricketer. For the most part, the press responded positively to the announcement of the deal, but before long sportswriters joined players in complaining that success had gone to Lara's head; an incident in which he used a cell phone on the playing field proved especially controversial. Unaccustomed to such disapproval, Lara began to perform irregularly and to quarrel with managers and officials. On several occasions he was fined for being disputatious or for arriving late to a match. In 1995 the historically strong West Indian team suffered a humiliating defeat in a match with an inexperienced Kenyan squad in the Cricket World Cup. "In America," Lara later told a correspondent for the *Electronic Telegraph* (on-line), "you'd hire a publicist and a PR person, but this is cricket and I couldn't pay for all those things, so it was something of an experience and I regret it now. It's tough on that cloud up there, and you need some sort of guidance because you can be really naive. You can be used and abused pretty easily."

Later in 1995 Lara became embroiled in another controversy, when he withdrew from his team to protest the policies of the West Indian Board of Control, the organization that regulates and supervises cricket in the West Indies. In the view of Lara and his supporters, the board treated local players unfairly and often with high-handed paternalism—behavior that struck Lara as an unwelcome vestige of British colonial rule. In addition, Lara reportedly felt that the West Indian team included players who had been chosen not for their athletic ability but because they were favorites of the management. Speaking of his protests, he told Rohter, "This is not only about my cause. We need to insure [that] the real meaning of West Indies cricket keeps going. It's not just a matter of guys going out there to play cricket, it's an upliftment for our people of the Caribbean, and I hope that this matter can bring everything out to be dealt with on a proper basis." Michael Holding, a Jamaican cricket official quoted by Rohter, responded to Lara's charges by claiming that the cricketer was a confused young man who needed "someone to sit down with him until he can realize what life is all about." The feud was resolved after a new coach was hired, in the spring of 1996, and Lara resumed playing.

Shortly after his return Lara was made captain of the West Indian team, a post to which he had aspired for several years. His captaincy proved disappointing, however, for himself as well as his fans. Although he led his team to several important victories, the West Indian team's invincibility, and its domination of international cricket, vanished.

Particularly embarrassing for Lara was a 0–5 defeat in a 1998 series with South Africa, the worst loss in the history of the West Indian team. In early 2000, after another loss, this time to New Zealand in late 1999, Lara resigned as captain, noting in his letter of resignation, as quoted by Rick Eyre for *cricket.org*, the "moderate success and devastating failures that have engulfed West Indian cricket."

In the second half of the 1990s, meanwhile, Lara had continued to perform well as a batsman. In a 1999 match against Australia, he scored his third career "double century," garnering a total of 212 points. That same year he became the fourth West Indian and 17th player in the history of cricket to score more than 6,000 runs in international one-day play. In recognition of both achievements, he was named the International Cricketer of the Year. Moreover, according to a computerized survey of cricket statistics completed in 1999, Lara was the best batsman of the 1990s. Throughout that decade, when not playing test cricket for the West Indian team, Lara was associated with the first-class Warwickshire team. — P.K.

Suggested Reading: *New York Times* B p10 Apr. 19, 1994, A p2 Jan. 6, 1996, with photo; *Sports Illustrated* p60 May 2, 1994, with photo

Lewis, David Levering

May 25, 1936– Historian; biographer; educator. Address: Rutgers University, History Dept., Van Dyck Hall, New Brunswick, NJ 08903

David Levering Lewis is a biographer, historian, and professor at the New Brunswick campus of Rutgers, the state university of New Jersey. One of the country's most highly respected historians, he is recognized for his thoughtful and detailed portrayals of influential African-American intellectuals and social activists. His books include *Martin Luther King: A Critical Biography* (1971), *Prisoners of Honor: The Dreyfus Affair* (1973), *When Harlem Was in Vogue: The Politics of the Arts in the Twenties and Thirties* (1981), and a two-volume biography of the African-American civil rights activist, scholar, writer, and educator W.E.B. Du Bois, each volume of which earned Lewis the Pulitzer Prize for biography, in 1994 and 2001, respectively. In 1999 Lewis was one of 32 recipients of the MacArthur Fellowship, also known as the "genius grant."

David Levering Lewis was born on May 25, 1936 in Little Rock, Arkansas. His mother, Urnestine Bell Lewis, was educated at Atlanta University, and his father, John H. Lewis, graduated from Yale University. When David was seven John Lewis was fired from his job as a high-school principal; his dismissal stemmed directly from his testimony in a successful discrimination lawsuit, in which

Courtesy of Rutgers University

Thurgood Marshall (who later, in 1967, became the first African-American Supreme Court justice) represented the National Association for the Advancement of Colored People (NAACP). The family left Little Rock and moved to Wilberforce, Ohio, where

John Lewis became the dean of the divinity school of Wilberforce University.

About two years later Lewis's father attended a national meeting of Sigma Pi Phi, the oldest African-American academic fraternity. W.E.B. Du Bois, who, like John Lewis, was a member of Sigma Pi Phi, had been invited to deliver a speech at the meeting, and young David, who was present, was introduced to him. When Du Bois, who was then in his 70s, asked the boy what he wanted to do with his life, he was too awestruck to respond. As an adult, Lewis could not recall the subject of Du Bois's speech, but through research he discovered its contents: Du Bois had rejected his well-known concept of the "Talented Tenth," his term for the elite segment of the African-American community, who he had believed was capable of changing— and should have tried to change—the status of black people in America. "Here we were with college presidents and the most successful black brain surgeons and engineers, the whole *crème de la crème* of black America, and Du Bois spoke to them for about an hour and a half about how corrupt they were," Lewis told Mary Ann French for the *Washington Post* (December 13, 1993). "He told them that their jobs, their privilege brought with it obligation to bring the rest behind, that when he had conceived the notion of the Talented Tenth, it was as a leadership class, and what was happening to these guys was that they were conspicuously consuming . . . and that therefore he had decided that the concept wasn't working, and we should now do something in a socialist sense—which is just incredible, to be talking to African American professionals about socialism!"

In 1950 John Lewis was named president of Morris Brown College, one of five schools that make up Atlanta University, and the family moved to Atlanta, Georgia, where he and his wife had grown up. David Lewis finished high school at the age of 14; the following year he entered Fisk University (Du Bois's alma mater), a traditionally African-American college in Nashville, Tennessee. After receiving a B.A. degree in history and philosophy from Fisk, in 1956, Lewis spent one semester at the University of Michigan Law School. He then enrolled at Columbia University, in New York City, where he earned an M.A. degree in history, in 1959. He paid for his tuition at Columbia by caring for an elderly husband and wife, both of whom suffered from cerebral palsy.

In 1962 Lewis, who is fluent in French, completed his Ph.D. in modern European and French history at the London School of Economics and Political Science, in England. In the same week that he received his doctorate, he was drafted into the U.S. Army. He served in Landstuhl, Germany, as a psychiatric technician in the army medical corps, until 1963. Thanks to a job offer from the University of Ghana, in Africa, he got an early release from the armed services. He lectured on British and European history at that university, in the city of Legon, in 1963–64. Lewis then taught modern French history at Howard University, in Washington, D.C. (1964–65), the University of Notre Dame, in Notre Dame, Indiana (1965–66), and Morgan State College, in Baltimore, Maryland (1966–70). He next spent four years as an associate professor at Federal City College, now the University of the District of Columbia. He won research grants from the American Philosophical Society in 1967 and the Social Science Research Council in 1971.

In 1971 Penguin published Lewis's first book, *Martin Luther King: A Critical Biography*, which he had begun working on while the civil rights leader was alive. It appeared about three years after King's assassination, making it one of the first books to be published about the slain activist. The book sold well. Lewis's publisher was surprised when Lewis announced that the topic of his next book would be the notorious Dreyfus Affair: the case of Alfred Dreyfus, a French Jewish army officer who in 1894 was court-martialed for selling military secrets to the German government and received a life sentence of solitary confinement. It was later learned that much of the evidence against him had been forged; nevertheless, at a second court-martial, in 1899, he was again found guilty. Dreyfus later received a pardon from the French president, and in 1906 he was exonerated by a civilian court. "It was the beginning, of course, of modern anti-semitism," Lewis told Mary Ann French. "Nobody could make out why a black professor would write about this topic. The reviews reflect it. Quite odd. They kept looking for some angle." A paperback edition of *Prisoners of Honor: The Dreyfus Affair* came out in 1994.

Lewis left the University of the District of Columbia in 1981 to join the faculty of the University of California at San Diego, as a professor of history. That year saw the publication of his third book, *When Harlem Was in Vogue: The Politics of the Arts in the Twenties and Thirties*. He had briefly considered writing a book about the period in American history between the two world wars, but decided instead to try to counter the prevailing academic approach to the African-American experience, which, he felt, dwelled on the horrors of slavery and shortchanged the work of black activists and thinkers. *When Harlem Was in Vogue* concentrated on the efforts of a small group of elite African-Americans to garner white support for art created by blacks during the Harlem Renaissance, a period during which black culture flourished and whites became both patrons of and artistic collaborators in African-American art.

In 1985 Lewis accepted the position of Martin Luther King Jr. professor of history at Rutgers University at New Brunswick, New Jersey. (He has held the prestigious title "university professor" since 1994.) He has taught courses in African-American history, the civil rights movement, the literature of racism, and global imperialism. During his second year at Rutgers, Lewis received a Guggenheim Foundation fellowship. Along with David C. Driskell and Deborah Willis Ryan, he contributed essays to *Harlem Renaissance: Art of Black America* (1987).

Lewis's next book, *The Race to Fashoda: European Colonialism and African Resistance in the Scramble for Africa* (1988), chronicles the invasion and colonization of Africa in the 19th century by Great Britain, Germany, France, Italy, Belgium, Portugal, and the Boers, who were of Dutch and French Huguenot descent. The idea for the book came to Lewis in Paris in the early 1970s, when he was gathering material for *Prisoners of Honor*. In his quest for documentation for *The Race to Fashoda*, he did extensive research in France, England, Belgium, Turkey, Egypt, Djibouti, Sudan, and Ethiopia. Determined to find out more about the black African point of view, he combed archives in the Sudan and Ethiopia that had seldom been explored. During the course of his research, he "found the normal amounts of suspicion," Lewis told Anne Zusy for the *New York Times Book Review* (February 28, 1988). "The more explaining you have to do about the curious enterprise you're doing, that it's not political and you just want access to documents and don't have an ax to grind, the more likely you are to hear, 'Oh this is really interesting.'" In *The Race to Fashoda*, Lewis established that African blacks had repeatedly attempted to defend their lands against European invaders. "African resistance was broader, deeper, and more concerted and more effective than the intruders themselves usually recognized, or than most of the later accounts reveal," he told Walter Goodman for the *New York Times* (February 3, 1988). Lewis also demonstrated the ways in which the foreigners' actions led to outbreaks of disease, famine, cannibalism, and lawlessness. The book's centerpiece was his description of the battle between French and British forces for Fashoda, a fortress in the Sudan, which followed years of territorial disputes in Africa between Great Britain and France. William Boyd described the book for the *New York Times Book Review* (February 28, 1988) as "elegantly written and thoroughly researched."

W.E.B. Du Bois's personal papers were made available to the public at about the time that Lewis began work on his biography of Du Bois; thus, by an accident of timing, he was the first scholar to have access to much of the material that he used for the book. The first African-American to receive a Ph.D. from Harvard, Du Bois (1868–1963), who pronounced his surname "Du Boyce," was a writer, intellectual, educator, and influential civil rights activist. He co-founded the National Association for the Advancement of Colored People (NAACP) and served as an editor of the organization's magazine, the *Crisis*, from 1910 until 1934. He was at the forefront of Pan-Africanism, a movement that encouraged all people of African descent to work together to combat the effects of European imperialism everywhere in the world. Lewis told Mary Ann French that his eight years of research into Du Bois's life and work required him to look through "110,000 items in [Du Bois's] correspondence

alone; some 100 related manuscript collections; 20,000 pages of Freedom of Information [documents]; . . . 200 or so oral histories; . . . [and, in a reference to Africa,] a continent of secondary reading material." He also traveled "7,000 crisscross miles in the former Soviet Union" and made "patient, sweltering quests for documents in West Africa." Lewis told French that, before starting his work, he had expected Du Bois "to be elitist, highly principled, dazzlingly brilliant, capable of manipulation of the English language like few writers have been, paradoxical and infuriating and supremely admirable and a little hypocritical. And I think all of those things have panned out."

Taking an unorthodox approach to exploring Du Bois's inner life, the biographer persuaded a psychologist to "treat" Du Bois, as impersonated by Lewis, during a series of therapy sessions. These sessions led him to believe that Du Bois—who claimed that his first sexual experience was his rape by an older woman—suffered from a castration complex (the fear of emasculation, a concept introduced to the public in the writings of Sigmund Freud). Lewis subsequently learned a great deal about his subject's complicated and often harsh attitude toward women. "When I began writing, I was less sensitive than I am now to women's issues," he told French. "As a matter of fact, when I wrote one of the chapters in which I try to deal with his relations with his wife, the woman who was the associate editor said, 'You're sounding very smug and unfeeling here, David.' . . . So I began to get it right in that I saw the penalty of being in his life as a woman was a large one . . . even though he was one of the great feminists [and] what he writes about women on the page is exhilarating."

The 735-page *W.E.B. Du Bois: Biography of a Race, 1868–1919* (1994), a comprehensive account of Du Bois's academic accomplishments and the development of his political consciousness, details how race, sex, class, and locale shaped both his personality and his prolific writings. Although he was a world-class scholar, he frequently had to grapple with institutional racism. His many books and articles restored feelings of dignity among members of the African-American community and paved the way for later developments in sociology and political action. In a passage from Lewis's book that Gloria Waite quoted in the *Christian Science Monitor* (December 6, 1993), Lewis wrote that Du Bois was "the paramount custodian of the intellect that so many impoverished, deprived, intimidated, and desperately-striving African-Americans had either never developed or found it imperative to conceal." The biography also examined the philosophical differences between Du Bois and the educator and reformer Booker T. Washington, who believed that if African-Americans worked hard and accumulated wealth, whites would accept them and award them equal citizenship. Du Bois regarded Washington's approach to winning equality as too passive. In a review for *New York Newsday*

(November 21, 1993), Wilson J. Moses, a professor of American history, wrote that although *W.E.B. Du Bois* is "meticulous and scholarly, the work is nonetheless readable and free of academic jargon and pedantic obfuscation." Moses also proclaimed that "on the evidence of this volume alone, Lewis' work will surely remain the standard against which all future efforts must be judged." *W.E.B. Du Bois: Biography of a Race, 1868–1919* was a finalist for a National Book Award in fiction, and it won nine major awards, among them the Pulitzer Prize for biography; the Bancroft Prize, from Columbia University; the Francis Parkman Prize, from the Society of American Historians; and the Ralph Waldo Emerson Prize, from the Phi Beta Kappa Society.

Before the publication of the second volume of his Du Bois biography, Lewis edited two books. The first, *The Portable Harlem Renaissance Reader* (1994), is a compilation of autobiographical writings, essays, critical pieces, political manifestos, poetry, and fiction that traces the Harlem Renaissance from its origins—Lewis has named 1917 as the year it began—to the peak of its renown, in 1935. Lewis divided the Harlem Renaissance into three periods. In the first, white artists exerted a great deal of influence; in the second, the Talented Tenth played a large role; during the last, most celebrated period, the writers themselves were the focus of attention. The book includes essays by Du Bois, Richard Wright (the author of the highly acclaimed novel *Native Son*), the actor, singer, and social activist Paul Robeson, and Marcus Garvey, the influential black nationalist who led a "back to Africa" movement from about 1916 to 1925; poetry by Sterling Brown, Countee Cullen, and Langston Hughes; and fiction by Jean Toomer, Jessie Fauset, and Nella Larsen. Lewis also edited *W.E.B. Du Bois: A Reader* (1995), which offers selections from Du Bois's many books and articles in a single volume intended to be accessible to the general public.

The Life of W.E.B. Du Bois: The Fight for Equality and the American Century, 1919–1963 (2000) picks up Du Bois's life soon after the Harlem Renaissance began, then details his battles with Marcus Garvey, the Pan-African conferences Du Bois organized, his break with the NAACP, and his embrace of Marxism, which led him to doubt the possibility of integration. Lewis described Du Bois's support of both the Japanese government and Germany's national socialism (Nazi) movement, led by Adolf Hitler—a curious development in light of his opposition to anti-Semitism in his writings. Lewis has noted that following his 1936 visit to Germany, Du Bois expressed his dismay at that country's treatment of Jews, comparing the horror of their situation to both the Spanish Inquisition and the African slave trade. Du Bois traveled through Eastern Europe and what was then the Soviet Union, where he was praised for his opposition to America's foreign and domestic policies. In 1960 Du Bois left for Ghana, where he spent the rest of his life in

self-exile. That same year he joined the Communist Party—"in order to, I think it's fair to say, . . . Homerically thumb his nose at what he saw as the increasing rigidification of politics in America, the triumph of the Cold War, as he saw it, the division of the world into two armed camps," as Lewis told Brian Lamb for *Booknotes* on January 24, 1994, as transcribed for the *Booknotes* Web Site. Du Bois died on the night before the historic 1963 March on Washington, during which the Reverend Martin Luther King Jr., one of the many civil rights activists who had been influenced by Du Bois, gave his landmark "I Have a Dream" speech. In a review for the *Village Voice Literary Supplement* (October/November 2000, on-line) of the second volume of Lewis's Du Bois biography, the novelist and essayist Ishmael Reed wrote, "*The Life of W.E.B. Du Bois* succeeds, not only because of its meticulous scholarship, but because, unlike the average American history book, it places African Americans at the center of important events of the 20th century and not outside them. This impressive work also reminds us that at one time in this country, opinion wasn't just a plaything, something that could be packaged as entertainment by showbiz 'Public Intellectuals.' Du Bois paid dearly for his defiance. Like Paul Robeson, he sacrificed wealth for his anticapitalist positions and would probably be outraged that his name and concepts are being merchandised by an alliance of megacapitalists like Microsoft, AT&T, and Time Warner." The second volume of Lewis's biography of Du Bois, like the first, won a Pulitzer Prize.

Lewis and his second wife, Ruth Ann Stewart, have been married since 1994. Stewart is a research professor at Rutgers University's Center for Urban Policy Research and the Edward J. Bloustein School of Planning and Public Policy. Her written works include the book *Portia: the Biography of Portia Washington Pittman, the Daughter of Booker T. Washington* (1977). Lewis and Stewart live in New York City with Stewart's daughter, Allegra. Lewis has two sons, Eric and Jason, and a daughter, Allison, from his first marriage, to Sharon Siskind, which ended in divorce in 1988. — C.L.

Suggested Reading: *Booknotes* (on-line); *Christian Science Monitor* p15 Dec. 6, 1995, with photo; *New York Newsday* p43+ Nov. 21, 1993, with photo; *New York Times* C p21 Feb. 3, 1988, with photo; *New York Times Book Review* p11+ Feb. 28, 1988; *Village Voice Literary Supplement* (on-line) Oct./Nov. 2000; *Washington Post* B p1+ Dec. 13, 1993, with photos

Selected Books: as author—*Martin Luther King: A Cultural Biography*, 1971; *Prisoners of Honor: The Dreyfus Affair*, 1973; *When Harlem Was in Vogue: the Politics of the Arts in the Twenties and Thirties*, 1981; *W.E.B. Du Bois: Biography of a Race, 1868–1919*, 1994; *The Life of W.E.B. Du Bois: The Fight for Equality and the American*

Century, 1919–1963, 2000; as editor—*The Portable Harlem Renaissance Reader*, 1994; *W.E.B. Du Bois: A Reader*, 1995

Rose Prouser/Archive Photos

Li, Jet

Apr. 26, 1963– Actor; martial artist. Address: c/o Steven Chasman, 1411 Fifth St., Suite 405, Santa Monica, CA 90401

The actor and martial artist Jet Li is a legend in his native China, where he won six national martial-arts championships (in both youth and adult competitions) and was one of the leading figures in the Hong Kong kung-fu movie boom of the 1980s and 1990s. Known for his speed and dexterity, the five-foot six-inch actor is also one of the most successful stars to cross over from Asian to American cinema. His debut in an American-made movie came in 1998, when he played a villain and martial-arts expert in *Lethal Weapon 4*. Li's appearance in the film coincided with a surge in both the popularity of Hong Kong kung-fu movies in the U.S. and their influence on big-budget American action films. Thanks to his physical prowess, Li helped shift the emphasis from computerized visual and aural wizardry to the skills of actors. "At a time when special effects are so commonplace that they're no longer special, Jet Li is a one-man *Matrix*," N'Gai Croal and Ana Figueroa wrote for *Newsweek* (March 27, 2000), referring to a 1999 futuristic action movie that was laden with computer-generated effects. In *Time* (April 3, 2000), Richard Corliss wrote of Li, "His martial poses have classic beauty and power. His spin-kicks flout all laws of physics; there's

nothing like Jet Li in a foot fight." Li's second American film was the popular *Romeo Must Die* (2000); it was followed by *Kiss of the Dragon* (2001). In 2001 he starred in *The One*, about a man from a parallel universe.

Jet Li was named Li Lian Jie when he was born, in Beijing, China, on April 26, 1963. His father, an engineer, died when Li was two; afterward his mother struggled to support her three sons and two daughters by selling bus tickets. Li was the youngest of the children, and his mother was extremely protective of him. "Because I was the smallest," Li wrote for his official Web site, "my mother never allowed me to go swimming or ride the bicycle. Any risky activity—any kind of physical exercise that was even slightly dangerous—was off-limits. So while kids my age were out playing in the street, this docile little boy stayed inside." Always an obedient child, Li never even considered challenging his mother's, or any adult's, wishes. When he entered school, at the age of eight, he quickly became a favorite of his teachers, and he excelled at school both because of their favorable treatment and his own desire to please. "Maybe it's because I don't have a father," Li said to Kyle Smith for *People* (April 17, 2000). "I need to become special. Because I don't want my mom to feel sad."

By order of the government, Li and other school-children were sent during the summer of 1971 to the Beijing Sports and Exercise School, where youngsters were randomly assigned to train in different sports. Li was placed in classes in *wushu*, a general term for Chinese martial arts. Wushu involves learning a variety of challenging "forms"—rehearsed progressions of punching, kicking, and other moves; each level must be mastered before the student can progress to higher ones. Advanced students also learn to manipulate the "eighteen arms," traditional Chinese weapons: saber, spear, sword, halberd, axe, battle axe, hook, fork, whip, mace, hammer, talon, trident-halberd, cudgel, long-handled spear, short cudgel, stick, and meteor hammer. At the end of Li's first summer at the school, instructors selected for further training the best 20 or so of the approximately 1,000 students who had studied wushu there. Li was among them, and from that point on, every day after his regular school lessons were over, he and the others practiced wushu outdoors—even during the cold Beijing winters, when punches and kicks stung all the more.

When Li was nine he participated in the first Chinese national wushu competition held since the Cultural Revolution of the 1960s. There were no official placings or standardized routines; rather, a single award for excellence was issued, and Li earned it. Thereafter, Li's academic schooling was reduced to half-days; later, his academic subjects were dispensed with altogether, so that he could concentrate on perfecting his wushu skills and go on to represent China in exhibitions and competitions. After performing in the opening ceremonies for an international table-tennis championship in

1972, Li was invited, along with his wushu teammates, to meet with Zhou Enlai, who was then the Chinese premier.

As he continued to excel in wushu, Li's training became increasingly rigorous, usually lasting eight hours a day. Because of power shortages, electricity was routinely cut off at scheduled times in different parts of China. Li's school had no power on Friday nights, and students were accustomed to having a break then. One Friday evening Li's coach, an extremely strict instructor, awakened the members of the team and ushered them into the gym, where he forced them to practice; with the light of a flashlight, he tried to catch them in errors. This session terrified Li and his teammates. "What if the coach suddenly shone the light on you just as you happened to be taking a little 'break'? The punishment would be unimaginable," Li recalled on his Web site. "We were experiencing true fear. In the pitch black gym, where absolutely nobody could see how hard we were working . . . I trained as I had never trained before." At one point Li stumbled and felt a sharp pain in his ankle, but he was too scared to tell his coach. Two days later a visiting coach came to watch the athletes and, noticing Li's swollen ankle, discovered that the boy had been practicing with a broken ankle.

In 1974 Li was among 30 wushu students chosen nationwide to represent China in a goodwill tour of the United States. Li's training intensified, and six months of exhaustive lessons in Western social etiquette were added to his regimen. Li told Corliss that he was warned by his elders that he and others might be monitored by U.S. officials, so one morning after his arrival in the U.S., he tried an experiment in his hotel room. "I spoke to the flowers in Chinese: 'I like chocolate ice cream.' I said to the mirror, 'I like banana.' When I [returned] to the hotel, I opened the door, and everything I'd mentioned was on the table as if I'd ordered it. 'It's true,' I thought. 'They are listening.'" The U.S. tour ended with a wushu exhibition on the White House lawn before President Richard M. Nixon and Secretary of State Henry Kissinger, among others. Afterward, Li got a chance to meet Nixon, while members of the media looked on. "I remember he say, 'When you grow up, do you want to become a bodyguard?'" Li recalled to Kyle Smith. "I said, 'No, I don't want to protect one person. I want to protect billions of Chinese people.' The Chinese papers loved that. And Henry Kissinger says, 'Little boy, when you grow up, you should become a diplomat instead of a bodyguard.'"

Later in 1974 Li won the Chinese National Youth Sports Competition in wushu, where he had faced athletes as old as 18. In 1975, because of his previous year's win, the 12-year-old Li was eligible to compete with people over 18 in the Third National Games in China, which included contests in various sports. Not long before the competition, Li cut himself badly with a sword during a tournament. "Of course, the entire audience was roaring

'waaaah' in horror, pointing and screaming," Li related on his Web site. "I kept going—punching, rolling, leaping. I didn't feel any pain, just heat. Stuff was dripping. That's all I knew. I just assumed that I was sweating more heavily than usual. At a certain point, as I whipped my face around, I did notice, 'Hey! Here's some blood.' But I did not stop doing my form." Li wore heavy bandages on his head until moments before the start of the Third National Games, thus making his eventual win of the Chinese Men's All-Around National Championship all the more impressive.

In 1976 Li and his wushu team went on a tour of cities in Europe, Asia, Africa, and the Middle East. The following year he won his second Chinese Men's All-Around National Championship and again toured the world. On a flight to Zaire, Li suddenly noticed that the plane had been circling over the airport for quite some time and that the stewardesses looked worried. After a while, the passengers were informed that the landing gear would not descend, and a stewardess distributed stationery so that all those aboard could write their wills. Li's writing skills were rusty from lack of use, and he feared that he would not be able to complete this "assignment" satisfactorily. "I started to feel extremely anxious—not because I was being told to write my will, but because I was staring at a blank sheet of paper," he recalled on his Web site. "It was like being given a pop quiz! I had no idea what to write. I have no clear recollection of how people around me were reacting to the crisis—I just remember panicking: 'I would so much rather be practicing a form or doing drills right now. Anything but writing!'" As it turned out, the landing gear functioned after all, and he was spared from having to write his will. Between 1977 and 1979 Li won three consecutive Chinese Men's All-Around National Wushu championships.

For some time representatives of the Chinese film industry, including the movie producer Fung Chi, had been eyeing Li for roles in kung-fu movies, but Li was small for his age, and they decided that they would wait until he matured physically before casting him. He accepted his first role in 1980, appearing in Shaolin Temple (1982) as a young hero who goes to a traditional Shaolin temple in hopes of recruiting some monks to help him avenge his father's death. (The title refers to China's best-known martial art, Shaolin quan, named for the Shaolin Monastery, which was founded more than 1,500 years ago and became famous for its monks' skill in the martial arts.) During the time that the movie circulated throughout mainland China and Hong Kong, Li's real name was mistakenly presented as Jet Li, apparently in the credits; when he learned the English meaning of "jet," he decided to keep the name. Though he earned only $700 for his work in the movie, Li became a star. After its release he received more than 100,000 fan letters, some of them apparently written in blood.

In 1984 *Shaolin Temple: Kids from Shaolin* (also known as *Shaolin Boys* and *Shaolin Kids*) came to theaters. In that movie two families end their ongoing feud in order to unite against a common enemy. Li made his directing debut in 1986, with a film whose Chinese title was translated (and misspelled) as *Born to Defence* (it is also known as *Born to Defend*); Li also starred in it, as a World War II soldier who, upon his return to China, finds his hometown overrun by thuggish U.S. Navy men and then proceeds to eject them. The year 1986 also saw the release of *Shaolin Temple 3: Martial Arts of Shaolin* (also called *Arahan* and *North and South Shaolin*). Made with a larger budget than the previous films in which he had starred, the picture features Li as Zhi Ming, a northern Shaolin monk who sneaks away from his temple to avenge the deaths of his parents at the hand of a despotic lord named He Suo. In a review that disparaged the plot, Mick LaSalle reported in the *San Francisco Chronicle* (July 18, 1997) that Li's "technical mastery is astonishing."

In 1988 Li starred in *Dragon Fight* (or *Dragon Kickboxer*) and *Dragons of the Orient*. His fame in China skyrocketed two years later, thanks to his leading role in the director Hark Tsui's *Once Upon a Time in China*. Li's character, Wong Fey Hong, is a legendary Chinese hero who has often been depicted in Chinese films. The manager of a wushu school, Wong comes to the aid of his community when it is overrun by drug dealers and American sailors who seek to sell Chinese women into prostitution. One of the side plots involves Wong's romantic interest in a woman who is in danger of succumbing to American cultural influences (which are portrayed as pernicious). In the *Austin Chronicle* (on-line), a reviewer wrote of the film, "Jet Li's brilliantly choreographed fight scenes are an adrenaline-fueled rush, whether it's in a warehouse with too many bamboo ladders lying around, or out in the open with nothing but an umbrella as a weapon." According to Chris Hicks in the *Deseret News* (December 11, 1992, on-line), before the distribution of *Once Upon a Time in China* in the U.S., one reel of the original film was removed so as to shorten the film to two hours; as a result, most American critics found the plot hard to follow.

Once Upon a Time in China generated three sequels. In the first, which reached theaters in 1991, Li once again played Wong Fey Hong. Wong travels to Canton, China, with his lover, called Aunt Yee (though she is not related to Wong), who has just returned from the West. There they encounter the White Lotus Sect, an anti-Western gang led by a man named Kung, who can magically repel bullets. Eventually it becomes clear that the emperor opposes Kung, who must then face the wrath of Wong. In the *New York Times* (September 1, 1993), Stephen Holden wrote of the movie, "From its opening scene of a White Lotus rite in which Kung walks on hot coals and repels cannonballs, the movie is a splendid if frankly fake-looking spectacle," and then added, "Underneath the fun, the

film considers the age-old Chinese debate over Westernization versus traditionalism."

In 1992 Li starred in *The Master*, *Once Upon a Time in China 3*, and *Swordsman II*. That year his manager was murdered, allegedly by one of the criminal gangs that had begun seeking to cash in on Hong Kong cinema when it surged in popularity during the 1980s. In 1993 Li starred in five more kung-fu movies, among them the two-part *The Legend of Fong Sai Yuk* and *The Tai Chi Master*. A documentary about Li, variously called *Shaolin Kung Fu* and *Li Lian Jie's Shaolin Kung Fu*, was released in 1994; it shows Li executing amazing kung-fu moves and offers some biographical information about him. In that same year he starred in *The Bodyguard from Beijing*, *The New Legend of Shaolin*, and *Fist of Legend*. In the last-named film, he played a martial-arts student who returns home after a period of study in Japan to find that his master has been killed. He puts his fighting skills to work in the name of vengeance. "As martial arts heroes go," Mick LaSalle wrote for the *San Francisco Chronicle* (May 28, 1996), "Jet Li in *The Fist of Legend* is something of an ear, nose and throat man. His meticulous hand-work leaves opponents choking and blinking. At one point in this film he puts his fingers in a fellow's mouth and rearranges his jaw, giving him a serious case of TMJ [temporomandibular joint disease]."

The year 1995 saw two more Li movies, *My Father Is a Hero* and *High Risk*, the latter of which spoofs the popular kung-fu movie star Jackie Chan. Li was cast as the stunt double for Frankie, the "Jackie" character in *High Risk*. The double has plenty of work, because Frankie's claim that he does all of his own stunts is highly exaggerated; most of the time, rather than work, he carouses with young women on the set. When Frankie finds himself among a group held hostage in a hotel, he discovers the extent of his dependence on his double's talents. The movie aroused controversy in China and Hong Kong, where Chan's stature is great.

In *Dr. Wai and "The Scripture without Words"* (1996), Li played a successful author of adventure stories who, while suffering a crippling writer's block, imagines himself as his fictional hero. In 1997 he starred in *Once Upon a Time in China and America*, the final installment in his popular series. In that film, which was shot in Texas, Li, as Wong, travels to the American West of yesteryear, where he finds that both cowboys and Indians are experts in wushu. By this time Li was being courted by such American filmmakers as Oliver Stone, Francis Ford Coppola, and Quentin Tarantino. He accepted an offer from the director Richard Donner and the producer Joel Silver to play the villain in *Lethal Weapon 4* (1998). To help choreograph the fight scenes, Li brought to the U.S. several people he had worked with in Hong Kong, including Corey Yuen Kwai, whose credits with Li include *The Legend of Fong Sai Yuk*. In *Lethal Weapon 4* Li portrayed a Chinatown gangster who, as a member of the Asian Triad crime syndicate, is smuggling Chinese citizens into the U.S. and selling them into indentured servitude; he is also planning to sneak into the country some of the syndicate's imprisoned leaders. It's up to the buddy police officers Martin Riggs and Roger Murtaugh (played by Mel Gibson and Danny Glover, respectively) to stop the bad guys. While reviews of the movie were mixed, most critics had kind words for Li. In the *Denver Post* (July 10, 1998), for example, Steven Rosen wrote that the movie "at times falters amid too much comedy and family pathos. What saves it is a mesmerizing, terrifying villain, Chinese martial-arts star Jet Li. . . . His presence gives *Lethal Weapon*'s best, most brutally sensational confrontations a Hong Kong action-movie flavor."

Li next turned down a role in the Oscar-winning foreign-language film *Crouching Tiger, Hidden Dragon* (2000), which became a surprise hit, to star in *Romeo Must Die* (2000), an action movie loosely based on Shakespeare's *Romeo and Juliet*. In an attempt to cash in on the perceived popularity of kung-fu movies among African-American audiences, its scriptwriters made the warring families two California mob clans, one of Asian and the other of African-American descent. Li's character, Han, is an ex-cop who has taken the rap for his criminal father and brother and is serving a prison sentence in Hong Kong. Upon hearing of his brother's murder in Oakland, he promptly escapes from prison amid a storm of martial-arts pyrotechnics and flies to California, where he falls in love with Trish (played by the now-deceased R&B singer Aaliyah), the daughter of the rival, African-American crime boss. This budding romance fuels the violence stirred by Han's brother's death, as a series of mutual misunderstandings provokes a rash of killings among the families. In a couple of scenes, the camera zooms onto Han's victims to show X-ray images of their cracked bones—shots that Li suggested. In another scene in which the director followed a suggestion from Li, Han, unwilling to hit a woman, seizes Trish by the wrists and ankles and, using her hands and feet as clubs, delivers a barrage of blows to her female attacker. Commenting on the scene to Richard Corliss for *Time* (April 3, 2000), Aaliyah said, "I rehearsed for that scene . . . for a month, but Jet and I didn't hook up until the day we shot. That's how dope [good] he is; he doesn't even have to rehearse. He just comes to the set and fights." Though poorly received by critics, *Romeo Must Die* did well at the box office; released in mid-week, it earned $18 million by the end of its first weekend.

In his next film, *Kiss of the Dragon* (2001), which he co-wrote, Li starred as Liu, a Chinese government agent sent to Paris to arrest a Chinese drug lord operating there. Also working on the case is a corrupt French police detective named Richard, who kills France's drug czar and pinning the crime on Liu. On the run in an unfamiliar country, Liu meets Jessica (Bridget Fonda), a prostitute who is afraid to stop working for Richard for fear that he will retaliate by harming her daughter. Jessica has a videotape of Richard murdering the drug czar, but Liu can't turn the tape over to the proper authorities until he removes the daughter from Richard's clutches. Critics generally found the film to be deficient in its plotting but rich in riveting action sequences. While Elvis Mitchell, for example, complained in the *New York Times* (July 6, 2001) that "the filmmakers have lowered the bar in storytelling terms," he maintained that Li's "action sequences are like an oil fire, spilling from one room into the next and lighting the interiors with heat and wreckage. Mr. Li and his fisticuffs choreographer, Corey Yuen, have set a new standard for action here."

Li has been cast as the character Kato (originally played by Bruce Lee) in an upcoming film version of *The Green Hornet*, for which he will reportedly earn more than $5 million plus 5 percent of the film's gross profits. Joel Silver plans to produce a film in which Li will star as the reincarnated first king of China.

In 1987 Li married the actress Qiuyan Huang, with whom he had two daughters; the couple divorced in 1990. He married the actress Nina Li Chi on September 19, 1999 (traditionally, nines signify longevity in Chinese culture). Their daughter, Jane, was born on April 19, 2000. — P.G.H.

Suggested Reading: *Boston Globe* C p1 July 11, 1998; *Denver Post* E p1 July 10, 1998; *New York Times* C p13 Sep. 1, 1993, B p15 May 15, 1999, E p13 July 6, 2001; *Newsweek* p74 Mar. 27, 2000; *People* p29 Aug. 3, 1998, p133 Nov. 16, 1998, p103+ Apr. 17, 2000; *San Francisco Chronicle* D p1 May 28, 1996; *Time* p80 Apr. 3, 2000; *Village Voice* p64 Aug. 13, 1996, p74 July 22, 1997; *Washington Post* p41 Mar. 24, 2000

Selected Films: *Shaolin Temple*, 1982; *Shaolin Temple 2: Kids from Shaolin*, 1984; *Born to Defence*, 1986; *Martial Arts of Shaolin*, 1986; *Dragon Fight*, 1988; *Dragons of the Orient*, 1988; *Once Upon a Time in China*, 1990; *Once Upon a Time in China 2*, 1991; *Once Upon a Time in China 3*, 1992; *The Master*, 1992; *Swordsman II*, 1992; *The Legend of Fong Sai Yuk*, 1993; *The Legend of Fong Sai Yuk II*, 1993; *The Last Hero in China*, 1993; *The Kung Fu Cult Master*, 1993; *The Thai Chi Master*, 1993; *Li Lian Jie's Shaolin Kung Fu*, 1994; *The New Legend of Shaolin*, 1994; *The Bodyguard from Beijing*, 1994; *Fist of Legend*, 1994; *My Father Is a Hero*, 1995; *High Risk*, 1995; *Black Mask*, 1996; *Once Upon a Time in China and America*, 1997; *Lethal Weapon 4*, 1998; *Hitman*, 1998; *Romeo Must Die*, 2000; *Kiss of the Dragon*, 2001; *The One*, 2001

John Spellman/Retna Ltd.

Lindo, Delroy

Nov. 18, 1952– Actor. Address: c/o William Morris Agency, 151 El Camino Dr., Beverly Hills, CA 90212-2775

In the estimation of both colleagues and critics, Delroy Lindo is one of the more versatile actors currently working in film and television. Among the starring roles he has taken in the last five years are those of a loving father, an angel, an incestuous itinerant worker, a civic-minded drug dealer, the explorer Matthew Henson, and Justice Clarence Thomas of the United States Supreme Court. Lindo, who first attracted attention in Spike Lee's film *Malcolm X*—he turned in an award-winning performance as the numbers runner West Indian Archie—has earned plaudits for fleshing out supporting roles as well, in such films as *Get Shorty* and *The Cider House Rules*. Some of the films in which he has appeared have not fared well among reviewers, but even the most withering critical assessments have often contained words of praise for his characterizations. Lindo has also acted extensively in the theater, in works by Shakespeare, Lorraine Hansberry, and August Wilson. While he has not yet achieved celebrity status, "his star has slowly been on the rise" since the mid-1990s, in the words of a writer for the CheckOut Entertainment Network (on-line). Six and a half years ago, when he was 41 years old, Lindo said to Martha Southgate for *Premiere* (June 1994), "Who's to say, if I were a white actor doing the same work, that my career wouldn't have a whole different kind of momentum now? I don't want to beat a dead horse, but it's not a level playing field." Two years later he said, in an interview with Lucas Hilderbrand for *A&E*

Cinemascape (November 7–13, 1996, on-line), "If I look just generally at the film industry and the kinds of parts that are available, then yes, there are of course limitations on the opportunities that would come my way. But I choose not to do that because that's kind of self-defeating. We all understand where we are and the institution of Hollywood that we're dealing with. We understand the structures and limitations. What I prefer to do is look personally at the opportunities that have come my way. When I do that, I'm proud of the fact that I've gotten to do a range of things."

The son of Jamaican immigrants, Delroy Lindo was born in London, England, on November 18, 1952, and grew up in a borough of the city called Lewisham. His first taste of acting came when he was about five, when he played one of the three wise men in a school Nativity play. That role, Lindo recalled to Helen Dudar for the *New York Times* (May 8, 1994), entailed marching down an aisle in kingly regalia and singing the Christmas song "We Three Kings of Orient Are." Lindo remembers how pleased he felt when people in the audience complimented him for saying his lines correctly and enunciating the words clearly. After that, according to Dudar, he "never imagined another working life" other than one connected with acting.

When Lindo was 15 he and his mother moved to Toronto, Canada. There, inspired in part by PBS productions of Shakespeare's *The Taming of the Shrew* and Edmond Rostand's *Cyrano de Bergerac*, he got acting jobs in local theaters. In the late 1970s he won a partial scholarship to study acting at the American Conservatory Theater, in San Francisco. Among his classmates at the school was Denzel Washington. (The school's alumni also include Danny Glover, Annette Bening, and Winona Ryder.)

Lindo landed his first film role—that of an army sergeant in *More American Graffiti* (1979), the sequel to *American Graffiti*—shortly after his graduation. The bulk of his early work, though, was in theater rather than in motion pictures. (A decade would pass before he was cast in another movie.) Most of his stage roles, in turn, were in regional theater, but Lindo found occasional jobs in New York City as well. His Broadway debut came in 1982, in Athol Fugard's *Master Harold . . . and the Boys*, in which the actor served as an understudy to both Danny Glover and James Earl Jones, each of whom played one of the "boys"—waiters in a South African tearoom. When the production toured nationally, Lindo filled the role that Glover had played. He later portrayed the character Walter Lee in several independent productions of Lorraine Hansberry's *A Raisin in the Sun*. When Beth Coleman interviewed him for the *Village Voice* (May 24, 1994), Lindo "visibly wince[d]" at the memory of his first attempt at that role, in 1983, but expressed satisfaction about his second effort, at the Kennedy Center, in Washington, D.C., a few years later. To prepare for the role in the latter staging—which earned him a nomination for the Helen

Hayes Award—he told Coleman, "one thing I did was go to Chicago and literally walk the streets where Lorraine [had] lived. I'm not saying going to Chicago guarantees brilliant work, but as many contacts as I can make to create the authenticity of a character, I will." Lindo later earned an NAACP Image Award for best actor for his work in a Los Angeles production of *Raisin in the Sun*.

Lindo's theater breakthrough came with his portrayal of Herald Loomis in a 1988 Broadway production of August Wilson's *Joe Turner's Come and Gone*. The drama, set in the early 20th century, recounts the efforts of a haunted, brooding man to locate his vanished wife, who left him after a white man forced him into illegal servitude. "Few who saw that production are likely to have forgotten the first-act climax," Helen Dudar wrote, referring to the scene in which Loomis experiences a visionary seizure. Lloyd Richards, who directed the play, told Dudar, "I loved [Lindo] for the unstinting, unfettered investment of self" that he brought to his character. Richards added, "You don't have to build a fire under Delroy. The fire is going all the time." Lindo's performance earned him a Drama Desk Award nomination (presented by a panel of journalists, critics, and writers who cover New York theater) and a Tony Award nomination.

Such critical and professional recognition did not trigger a flood of attractive job offers for Lindo. Indeed, the next role that came his way was little more than a walk-on appearance in a revival of Tennessee Williams's *Orpheus Descending*. "I was speechless," Lindo told Helen Dudar, recalling his reaction to the offer. "I couldn't believe they were serious." During the next few years, his roles included that of Scott Joplin in a 1993 Playwrights Horizon production of Eric Overmyer's fantastical, poorly received musical biography *The Heliotrope Bouquet by Scott Joplin & Louis Chauvan*. He also captured minor roles in a few films, among them *Mountains of the Moon* (1990), about the discovery of the source of the Nile River by the British explorers Sir Richard Burton and John Hanning Speke; the action-comedy *The Hard Way* (1991), which starred Michael J. Fox and James Woods; and the coming-of-age drama *Bright Angel* (1991), written by Richard Ford and directed by Michael Fields. Speaking of the disappointments that followed *Joe Turner's Come and Gone*, Lindo told Dudar, "If I could have one thing in my relationship to this work, I'd pray to have a healthy perspective. You know, if you get into the woe-is-me bag, it's not very usable. What can you do with it?"

Eventually, Lindo's performance in the Wilson play paid off, because the screenwriter and director Spike Lee remembered it when he was casting for his film *Malcolm X* (1992). In Lee's retelling of the slain black leader's life (adapted from *The Autobiography of Malcolm X*, written in collaboration with Alex Haley), Lindo played West Indian Archie, a Harlem numbers boss. A smooth, self-confident hustler when he first encounters Malcolm X (played by Denzel Washington), West Indi-

an Archie reappears years later as a penniless, broken old man. The role was small but demanding, since Lindo had only a few scenes in which to sketch the evolution of his character. He pulled it off, transforming West Indian Archie into one of the picture's more memorable figures. In *By Any Means Necessary* (1992), his book on the making of *Malcolm X*, Spike Lee wrote, as quoted by Dudar, that Lindo's performance "really rocked the set from roof to floor." The actor won an NAACP Image Award for his work in the film.

Lee picked Lindo for the role of Woody Carmichael in his next directorial project, the semiautobiographical *Crooklyn* (1994). Set in Brooklyn in the early 1970s and co-written by Lee, his brother Cinqué, and his sister, Joie, *Crooklyn* focuses on the middle-class Carmichael family: the father, Woody, an unemployed jazz pianist; the mother—and main breadwinner and disciplinarian—Carolyn (played by Alfre Woodard), a schoolteacher; and the couple's four sons and one daughter (Zelda Harris). Lindo jumped at the chance to portray the dreamy Woody, a loving if somewhat truant husband and father. As he told Beth Coleman, "It warmed my heart to have Spike cast me. It's especially gratifying as Woody came right on the heels of Archie. A lot of people would just see a gangster type. What Spike saw, I hope, was a good actor." In her *Premiere* article, Martha Southgate reported that working with the five youngsters who played the Carmichael children proved to be the "hardest challenge [Lindo had] faced as an actor." "I cannot stress enough how fearful it made me," he admitted to Southgate. "Children are so brutally honest. They cut right to the core of things." Another difficulty for Lindo stemmed from the plotline's underpinnings in Lee family history. "I was very aware that I was creating a character on top of certain autobiographical realities," he explained to Southgate. "There were things I did not want to delve into [with the Lees] because they might be too private."

After *Crooklyn* Lindo appeared in a series of mainstream Hollywood productions, often in the company of some of the industry's biggest stars. Perhaps because of his ability, in the words of a writer for Fametracker.com, to embody "charming menace better than any other actor working today," he was cast as a bad guy in several of them. Those screen thugs include Bo Catlett, a star-struck Las Vegas drug dealer, in Barry Sonnenfeld's *Get Shorty* (1995)—a satire of the film industry, based on an Elmore Leonard novel, that co-starred John Travolta, Gene Hackman, Danny de Vito, and Rene Russo. Another is the underworld figure Red, in Steven Baigelman's *Feeling Minnesota* (1996), which features Keanu Reeves, Cameron Diaz, Vincent D'Onofrio, and Dan Aykroyd. In Spike Lee's *Clockers* (1995), an adaptation of a novel by Richard Price about people caught up in street-level drug trading in a black inner city, Lindo portrayed Rodney Little. A morally complex figure, Rodney is a drug dealer who exploits local kids yet gives them the paternal attention they crave and can't get elsewhere; he is also a notary public and small-business owner who wants to provide a good role model for the young drug sellers. In a conversation with a reporter for the *Albany Times Union* (September 13, 1995, on-line), Lindo said, "I met the man Richard Price based Rodney on, so I had a blueprint." He compared Rodney to Charles Dickens's character Fagin, in *Oliver Twist*, who trains young boys to be criminals. "One of the things that makes Fagin enduring as a literary character is that he has human elements that make him compelling and alluring," Lindo said. "As an actor, your job is not to pass judgment, but to dimensionalize. Rodney is a father figure to these kids. . . . I have to maintain a facade, a hardness. But at the same time, it's paternal hardness. As an actor, I'm looking for ways in which I can do that in a human way. It ends up being seductive." In *The Cider House Rules* (1999), which John Irving adapted from his same-titled novel, Lindo depicted Mr. Rose, the likable leader of an itinerant group of apple pickers, who impregnates his own daughter. According to the film critic Roger Ebert, writing for the *Chicago Sun-Times* (on-line), Lindo succeeded in bringing to life a man who "is guilty of incest and yet—somehow, murkily—[is] not entirely a monster."

Lindo has also been cast as characters who are on the side of law and justice. In John Woo's 1996 action thriller *Broken Arrow*, starring John Travolta and Christian Slater, he portrayed Colonel Max Wilkins, an air-force officer intent on stopping a maniac's plot to detonate a stolen nuclear missile in the southwestern U.S.; that supporting role failed to earn even a mention in most reviews. The actor initiated talks with FBI agents to prepare for his role as the FBI agent Lonnie Hawkins in Ron Howard's *Ransom* (1996), a violent thriller about a kidnapping in which he appeared opposite Mel Gibson and Rene Russo. "What I was specifically concerned about was the reality of being a black agent," he told Lucas Hilderbrand. More recently, Lindo has brought a measure of dignity to a variety of oddball roles in several uncelebrated movies. They include Danny Boyle's romantic comedy *A Life Less Ordinary* (1997), in which he played an angel with a mean streak alongside Holly Hunter, Cameron Diaz, and Ewan MacGregor. His depiction of a modern-day Capulet in Andrzej Bartkowiak's *Romeo Must Die* (2000), a Hong Kong version of Shakespeare's *Romeo and Juliet*, eluded the general censure directed at the film. In an otherwise scathing review, for example, Roger Ebert, writing for the *Chicago Sun-Times* (on-line), noted, "Lindo projects competence, calm and strength in every scene." In 2000 Lindo appeared alongside Nicolas Cage, Angelina Jolie, and Robert Duvall as a police detective in Jerry Bruckheimer's *Gone in 60 Seconds*. In the following year he played a criminal mastermind in David Mamet's *Heist*, which also starred Gene Hackman and Danny DeVito.

The variety of characters he has played on the silver screen notwithstanding, Lindo's most nuanced roles have come in movies made for cable-television networks. The first of those projects was *Soul of the Game* (1996), an HBO docudrama directed by Kevin Rodney Sullivan, which focuses on three stars of baseball's Negro League—Satchel Paige (played by Lindo), Jackie Robinson (Blair Underwood), and Josh Gibson (Mykelti Williamson)—during the summer of 1945, when Robinson became the first African-American player to be signed to a major-league team. In the 1997 HBO drama *First-Time Felon*, which recounted the transformation of Greg Yance from one-time gangster to dedicated youth counselor, Lindo appeared as a prison officer. For the 1998 TNT production *Glory & Honor*, he portrayed Matthew Henson, the African-American who accompanied Commander Robert E. Peary on his historic 1909 expedition to the North Pole (as well as on Peary's eight previous, unsuccessful polar treks) but who received none of the acclaim heaped on the other man.

Lindo portrayed Clarence Thomas in the 1999 Showtime movie *Strange Justice*, based on Jane Mayer and Jill Abramson's 1994 book about the Supreme Court justice, whose nomination hearings before the Senate Judiciary Committee were rocked by allegations of sexual harassment made by Anita Hill, a former colleague of Thomas's. "This plot certainly challenged me from a creative standpoint," Lindo told Denolyn Carroll for *American Visions* (August 1999). "It made me ask: How do I make a character whom many people hold strong opinions about compelling? How do I keep him dramatically interesting?" Seeking answers to those questions, Lindo visited Thomas's hometown, Pinpoint, Georgia, and talked to people who had known him. "I spoke to one gentleman who was raised with Judge Thomas and who told me that even as a child Clarence was different, he always had his head in a book, he was always very disciplined, didn't play much with other kids," Lindo recalled to Bernard Weinraub for the *New York Times* (August 22, 1999). "This suggested a person who saw himself, even as a kid, different from other kids, who saw himself not bound up by the environment in which he grew up. That suggested to me an interesting element to his psychological makeup. I decided to develop that." He further explained to Weinraub how he had approached the role of Thomas, whose "politics are not my politics," and about whom he had already formed a strong, apparently negative opinion. "Anita Hill didn't want these hearings public and neither did Clarence Thomas," he said. "They were both forced into it. And basically he was forced into defending himself with every bone and fiber in his body. Here was a man like a cornered animal. It got to a point where I understood why he conducted himself the way he did. I don't think he had any choice."

Lindo told Denolyn Carroll that the speed with which cable projects are completed is sometimes disproportionate to "the complex themes that the films are tackling"; he would have liked time to explore in greater depth, for example, the relationship between Matthew Henson and the Inuit woman who bore him a son. But he praised the cable studios for attempting difficult, important themes. Moreover, as he told Carroll, he found the cable roles personally rewarding: "The films I have done on cable have all focused on subject matter that I am very interested in, socially, politically and historically."

Recently, Lindo produced and directed two documentary projects of his own—an interview with Spike Lee that aired on the Independent Film Channel/Bravo network on June 28, 1999 and an interview with the screenwriter and director Charles Burnett that was shown on the Showtime cable network in February and April 2000. In the case of Lee, the film provided Lindo with the chance to publicly show his gratitude to the director who had played such an important role in his film career. That documentary was faulted by some for eschewing potentially controversial matters; on the other hand, it was praised for showing a side of the feisty director that is seldom revealed in the media. "Famous for never letting down his guard with the press, [Lee] never even gets a chance to put it up with Lindo," Chris Vognar wrote for the *Dallas Morning News* (on-line).

Lindo's wife, Neshormeh, is an artist who at one time served as the educational-programs manager for the Schomburg Center for Research in Black Culture, in Harlem. The couple, who have no children, currently live in California. — P.K.

Suggested Reading: *American Visions* p42+ Aug. 1999, with photos*; Dallas Morning News* (on-line); *New York Times* II p19 May 8, 1994, with photo; *Village Voice* p16 May 24, 1994, with photo

Selected Films: *More American Graffitti*, 1979; *The Blood of Heroes*, 1988; *Mountains of the Moon*, 1990; *The Hard Way*, 1991; *Bright Angel*, 1991; *Malcolm X*, 1992; *Mr. Jones*, 1993; *Bound by Honor*, 1993; *Crooklyn*, 1994; *Get Shorty*, 1995; *Clockers*, 1995; *The Winner*, 1996; *Ransom*, 1996; *Feeling Minnesota*, 1996; *Broken Arrow*, 1996; *A Life Less Ordinary*, 1997; *The Devil's Advocate*, 1997; *Glory & Honor*, 1998; *The Cider House Rules*, 1999; *Gone in 60 Seconds*, 2000; *Delroy Lindo on Spike Lee*, 2000; *Gone in 60 Seconds*, 2001; *Heist*, 2001

Selected Plays: *Master Harold and the Boys*, 1982; *A Raisin in the Sun*, various years; *Joe Turner's Come and Gone*, 1988

Lupica, Mike
(LOO-pik-uh)

May 11, 1952– Sportswriter; novelist. Address: c/o G. P. Putnam's Sons, 375 Hudson St., New York, NY 10014

One of the most well-known and outspoken people in his field, Mike Lupica has been working as a sportswriter and commentator, primarily in New York City, since he was a teenager. During the 15 years that he reported on sports for the New York *Daily News*, he also wrote for such magazines as *World Tennis, Tennis, Sport, Playboy*, and *New York*, and he produced a column for the monthly *Esquire* for 10 years. He has participated regularly on ESPN's Sunday morning TV show *The Sports Reporters*. His writings include several sports-related nonfiction books and five novels, three of which are narrated by a TV reporter. Lupica's dedication to, expertise in, and passion for sports have earned him unusual license to express his opinions freely—and sometimes cantankerously, as his nickname, "The Lip," suggests. "I've been writing . . . for more than 20 years," he told Adam Boyle for the *Independent* (on-line); "it's very liberating, I absolutely don't care what people think." Underpinning Lupica's frequent tirades is a simple love for the games he grew up playing and watching as

Virginia Sherwood, ABC/Courtesy of Mike Lupica

a kid. "I look to sports to celebrate the great moment, the great drama, the great play," he explained to Boyle. "Go back and read every column

I wrote. . . . I'm celebrating the great New York moment in sports."

The son of Benedict and Lee Lupica, Michael Thomas Lupica was born on May 11, 1952 in Oneida, a town in west-central New York State. His father was an avid sports fan, and he would often leave notes for his son in the morning before going to work, to let the boy know what had happened in sports the night before. Young Mike also kept track of his favorite teams by reading articles by such sportswriters as Dan Jenkins, Pete Hamill, and, particularly, Jimmy Breslin, whom he has credited with influencing his choice of career.

Soon after Lupica enrolled at Boston College, in Massachusetts, he got involved in journalism. "I was writing for three school papers and working nights at the *Boston Globe,*" he recalled to Boyle. "So I had clearly decided that this was what I want to do." As an undergraduate Lupica also served as a columnist for the *Boston Phoenix* (1971–75) and for *Boston* magazine and the *Washington Star* (1974–75). In 1975, within a year of his graduation from Boston College, the *New York Post* hired him as a sportswriter. He remained with that newspaper for a year before becoming a columnist for *New York News,* remaining there until 1981. Concurrently, in 1980 he joined the New York *Daily News,* where he worked until 1994, while engaging in many other journalistic and literary pursuits. He was a sports broadcaster for *CBS Morning News* from 1982 to 1984 and for ESPN from 1982 to 1983. For a short time he tried his hand as a radio sports broadcaster, for WNBC, but he disliked the job and soon quit. "The function talk radio really seems to fulfill," he told Boyle, "is it's a place for people to bitch and people will listen to them. It's anger 24 hours a day."

Having made a name for himself in New York, Lupica won the contract to co-author a memoir by the star Yankee slugger Reggie Jackson. *Reggie: The Autobiography,* published in 1984, earned critical praise and became a best-seller. Lawrence S. Ritter, who assessed it for the *New York Times Book Review* (August 19, 1984), reported that the narcissism that permeated the text did not keep him from enjoying the book. "[*Reggie: The Autobiography*] is arrogant, boastful and egotistical," he wrote; "it never allows modesty to get in the way of a good story. . . . Despite all the hype and braggadocio, something genuine keeps popping up. . . . [It] turns out to be one of the better sports autobiographies of the 1980's."

Lupica's first work of fiction, *Dead Air,* came out in 1986. Its hero is Peter Finley, a New York City television reporter, whose adventures provided fodder for two later Lupica novels, *Extra Credits* (1988) and *Limited Partner* (1990). In *Dead Air* Peggy Lynn Brady, a beautiful talk-show host, vanishes, and her husband asks Finley to investigate her disappearance. Peggy, Finley, and many of the other characters work for the Global Broadcasting Co., which is being taken over by a Christian network. A host of dead bodies turn up before Finley discov-

ers why Peggy disappeared. The book received mixed reviews. "Perhaps the book's unrelieved patter and gimmickiness are meant to suggest television's manic self-promotion," Arthur Krystal suggested in the *New York Times* (May 25, 1986, on-line). Krystal also wrote, "For sheer concentration of hyperbole ('there was a hole in the overcoat you could fit all of Mickey's Mouseketeers through'), metaphor ('the mugginess had taken its big hand off the city's throat') and simile ('nibbling on her right ear like it was the smoked salmon appetizer'), no one beats Mike Lupica's . . . Peter Finley."

Extra Credits finds Finley looking into the suicide of a young woman after her girlfriend indicates to him that there may be more to her death than meets the eye. Soon Finley and his wife are set upon by a mysterious attacker who presumably wants Finley to back off the case, but the reporter perseveres. The pseudonymous Newgate Callendar wrote of *Extra Credits* in the *New York Times* (July 31, 1988, on-line), "The plotting is taut, coherent and believable. The writing is sophisticated, the dialogue bright. *Extra Credits* will keep you in the hammock when you should be doing more important things." In its sequel, *Limited Partner,* Finley investigates the deaths of one of his friends, a former New York City bar owner, and the friend's wife, both of whom have apparently died of drug overdoses—the wife on the day after her husband's funeral. The confessions and advice of a cocaine-sniffing New York Mets pitcher help Finley learn the truth about their deaths. Michael Lichtenstein, writing for the *New York Times* (October 14, 1990, on-line), found fault with Lupica's wise-cracking narrator: "Unfortunately, Mr. Lupica's Borscht-Belt one-liners mar *Limited Partner,* and his incessant name-dropping detracts from what might otherwise have been a pretty fair whodunit."

In collaboration with Bill Parcells, who was then the head coach of the New York Giants, Lupica wrote *Parcells: Autobiography of the Biggest Giant of Them All* (1987). In 1988, in addition to *Extra Credits,* Lupica published two books of nonfiction. *Wait Till Next Year: The Story of a Season When What Should've Happened Didn't and What Could've Gone Wrong Did* offers a recap of the tribulations New York baseball, football, and basketball teams endured during the 1987 season. Co-written with the novelist and screenwriter William Goldman, it combined Lupica's somewhat detached reportorial style with Goldman's more gushing prose. Morey Berger, writing for *Library Journal* (December 1988), called it "bittersweet reading for Big Apple fans" and "lots of fun for outsiders, too." Lupica's second 1988 book of nonfiction, *Shooting from the Lip: Essays, Columns, Quips, and Gripes in the Grand Tradition of Dyspeptic Sports Writing,* contains an assortment of Lupica's newspaper and magazine articles. Diane Cole, reviewing the collection for the *New York Times* (May 29, 1988, on-line), wrote that "Lupica's wit can be devastating" and described his columns as "tasty appetizers that leave one hungry for more, a desire satisfied by the handful of lengthier magazine pieces included here."

In 1994, after 15 years, Lupica left the *Daily News* to join the staff of a competing paper, *Newsday*, which is based on Long Island, New York. In 1995 he wrote his fourth novel, *Jump*, a mystery about a basketball star accused of rape. Meanwhile, his reputation for outspokenness had continued to grow. For some time he had been issuing yearly "awards" to sports figures and others whom he deemed worthy of special criticism. For instance, in *Esquire* (June 1995), Lupica gave a "Deion" award (named for the glamorous football and baseball star Deion Sanders, whose utterances Lupica had often criticized) to then–Speaker of the House Newt Gingrich: "His solution to the baseball strike," Lupica wrote, referring to the 234-day players' strike of 1994–95, "was for everybody to get together, pop up some corn, and watch [the baseball movie] *Field of Dreams*. It's a little-known fact, but Newtie also watched a movie before he came up with his Contract with America: *The Sting*. Take the Deion, Mr. Speaker. And, by the way, nice haircut."

In 1996 Lupica channeled his ire into *Mad As Hell: How Sports Got Away from the Fans—and How We Get It Back*. Lupica explained to Boyle that part of the problem with sports was the players themselves: "Somehow we've created this monster," he said, "these kids, from the time they're 13 or 14, from the time they're bigger, stronger, faster than the next kid. Nobody ever says no to them. People just tell them what they want to hear." But Lupica's criticism of sports extended beyond the athletes. A reviewer for *Coach and Athletic Director* (December 1996) wrote of *Mad As Hell*, "[Lupica] comes out slugging, taking on all corporate schemers, frauds, and hypocrites—naming names, places, motives, and laying out the case histories of the bad guys who are defaming his true love." The reviewer concluded, however, that the book would do nothing to "stop evolution, the relentless course of our sports world." Wes Lukowsky, writing in *Booklist* (October 15, 1996), was among other reviewers who agreed that Lupica's outrage was honest but that his analysis of sports was shortsighted and marred by incomplete reporting. "Lupica's mad, all right, but he's not really telling us anything new," Lukowsky wrote. "His solution—call the companies whose products the bad boys sell and tell them you're mad—seems a bit naive. Still, most fans share Lupica's righteous indignation and will enjoy sputtering angrily as they read."

In 1998 Lupica co-wrote *The Fred Book*, the autobiography of the businessman Fred Imus, who is a regular guest on his brother Don's popular talk-radio show. Following the 1998 baseball season, Lupica published *Summer of '98: When Homers Flew, Records Fell, and Baseball Reclaimed America* (1999), in which he reflected on a triumphant New York Yankees team and on the home-run duel between Mark McGwire and Sammy Sosa, as well as on the way sports, and baseball in particular, had brought him closer to his father and his three sons, Christopher, Alex, and Zach. Critics felt that Lupica was at his best writing about what he loves best. "Baseball is a densely woven tapestry of past, present, and future, never more so than when records are falling," George Robinson noted for the *New York Times Book Review* (May 30, 1999). "A few lucky people, writers mostly, get to turn it over and follow strands to show us how the picture is created. This is what Mike Lupica does brilliantly in *Summer of '98*." Brian Koonz, writing for the *News-Times* (April 28, 1999, on-line), gave Lupica perhaps the ultimate compliment for a sportswriter: "Lupica writes every word the way [Joe] DiMaggio played every inning."

In 2000 Lupica penned his fifth novel, *Bump and Run*. It focuses on Jack Malloy, who works in a Las Vegas casino, where he arranges and covers up the illicit activities of the establishment's wealthy clientele. When Jack's extravagantly rich father dies and unexpectedly bequeaths the New York Hawks, a fictional football team, to his son, Jack discovers that the National Football League (NFL) engages in all sorts of nefarious operations. Against the wishes of his siblings, the Hawks' coach, the press, and other team owners, Jack puts the skills he used in Las Vegas to work in an attempt to lead his team to the Super Bowl. Lupica explained in an interview with Michael Hiestand for *USA Today* (November 7, 2000) that the contents of the book aroused the suspicions of his wife, Taylor, whom he married in 1986. "I kept telling her it's a novel," Lupica said. "That doesn't mean you have to have lived that stuff!" Critics were impressed by Lupica's apparent knowledge of football's economics and behind-the-scenes controversies. "This book doesn't make us believe the NFL needs cleaning up; it confirms our belief that the NFL is a hell of a party," Michael Harris wrote for the *Los Angeles Times* (November 28, 2000). "If only we could be invited too." In *Publishers Weekly* (October 9, 2000), Sybil Steinberg wrote, "The brutal revelations about what goes on behind the game are hilarious but slightly disturbing, for the reader senses that beneath the satire and broadly drawn characters there is something more than a thin layer of truth, that somehow there is no hyperbole here."

Lupica's 2001 novel, *Full Court Press*, is about a female basketball player, Delilah "Dee" Gerard, who becomes the first woman to play in the National Basketball Association (NBA). Recruited by the fictional New York Knights, she is used as a marketing tool by the team's owner and ignored by her teammates. Her on-court performances are at first sub-par. Adding to her difficulties, a vindictive sportswriter dredges up scandals from her past. Eventually she hits her stride and leads the Knights into the play-offs past the New York Knicks, but her experience in the NBA is so disillusioning that she is unsure whether to sign the long-term contract offered her at the end of the season. "As always, Lupica . . . entertains with his lively pacing, screwball characters and insider's knowledge of professional basketball," Jeff Zaleski wrote in an assessment of *Full Court Press* for *Publishers Weekly* (September 24, 2001). "Sports fans will likely lap it up, though even they may pine for more suspense and wince at the overabundance of locker-room humor. They also may wish that Lupica . . . would use his considerable expertise to take a harder, or at least a more effectively placed, swing at the business of professional sports."

Lupica lives with his wife and children in New Canaan, Connecticut. As a freelancer, he continues to contribute to the *Daily News* and the *Los Angeles Times*, among other publications. — P.G.H.

Suggested Reading: *Coach and Athletic Director* p83 Dec. 1996; *Esquire* p52+ June 1995; *Independent* (on-line); *Los Angeles Times* E p1 Nov. 28, 2000; *New York Times* (on-line) May 29, 1988, Feb. 4, 1989, Oct. 14, 1990; *New York Times Book Review* p16 May 30, 1999; *News-Times* (on-line) Apr. 28, 1999; *USA Today* C p3 Nov. 7, 2000; *Washington Post* C p3 Mar. 3, 1994

Selected Books: nonfiction—*Reggie: The Autobiography*, 1984; *Parcells: Autobiography of the Biggest Giant of Them All*, 1987; *Shooting From the Lip: Essays, Columns, Quips, and Gripes in the Grand Tradition of Dyspeptic Sports Writing*, 1988; *Wait Till Next Year: The Story of the Season When What Should've Happened Didn't and What Could've Gone Wrong Did*, 1988; *Mad as Hell: How Sports Got Away From the Fans—and How We Get it Back*, 1996; *Fred Book*, 1998; *Summer of '98: When Homers Flew, Records Fell, and Baseball Reclaimed America*, 1999; novels—*Dead Air*, 1986; *Extra Credits*, 1988; *Limited Partner*, 1990; *Jump*, 1995; *Bump and Run*, 2000; *Full Court Press*, 2001

Charles Hopkinson/Camera Press/Retna Ltd.

Lynne, Shelby

Oct. 22, 1968– Singer; songwriter. Address: c/o Island/Def Jam Music Group, 825 Eighth Ave., New York, NY 10019-7416

Singer and songwriter Shelby Lynne's sixth album—*I Am Shelby Lynne* (2000)—was greeted by listeners and critics as a declaration of independence. Its bluesy, soulful music seemed to Michael Gallucci, writing for the *Illinois Entertainer* (October 2000), to be "the work of an artist breaking free of her past and starting all over again"; Chris Willman declared in *Entertainment Weekly* (February 11, 2000) that it had "the liberating feeling of a debut." Containing songs written over a period of years and recorded in sessions in the singer's kitchen, *I Am Shelby Lynne* struck many listeners as intimate and heartfelt, much like an overheard conversation between close friends. Lynne has claimed that she made the album mainly for herself; as she told an interviewer for *Entertainment Weekly* (July 23, 2000, on-line), "I didn't make it to get on the radio. I didn't make it to get great reviews. I just wanted to make a record I could be proud of, because at one point in my career I was wondering if I could do that." The album made Lynne an international star and garnered her a Grammy Award for best new artist—a sign that, after more than a decade of making music, she had indeed broken free of the "country" label and gained popular recognition for her powerful voice and achingly beautiful music.

As many have observed, Lynne's life is the stuff of countless country-music songs. Born Shelby Lynne Moorer on October 22, 1968 in Quantico, Virginia, Lynne was raised in and around Mobile, Alabama. Music was prominent in her home: her father, a vocational-school teacher and onetime officer in the U.S. Marines, played guitar and aspired to be a bandleader, and her mother, a legal secretary, taught her and her sister, Allison, who is four years younger than Shelby, to sing in harmony around the kitchen table. Occasionally, Lynne accompanied her parents to nightclubs in Mobile, where she and her mother performed at the open microphone. By the age of eight, Lynne had decided, with her parents' blessings, to become a country-music star. In an inteview with James McNair for *Top Magazine* (September 1999), she recalled listening to old Ella Fitzgerald recordings with her grandmother when she was a child and occasionally singing along. She was also strongly influenced by recordings made by Billie Holiday, Nina Simone, and Betty Carter, some of the best vocal stylists of the 20th century.

Lynne's childhood was marked by her father's drinking and increasingly violent behavior. One night when she was 17, her father fatally shot her mother and then himself. Lynne has described this horrific event as the "accident" that permanently altered her life—and her voice. "Four years ago, I didn't sing the way I sing now," she told Jack Hurst for the *Chicago Tribune* (December 3, 1989). "I think a lot of anger, a lot of bitterness, comes out in a good song. I can feel it." The media have often dwelled on the pain and tragedy in Lynne's life, but she herself has made a point of giving credit to her parents for her success. "Look, their thing just went to the inevitable, because, well, love can do terrible things to you," she told Brantley Bardin in an interview for *Details* (March 2000). "But however [messed] up they were—and they were, but who isn't?—I've wanted so many times to say, like in a song, how great and cool and perfect I felt they were."

After the tragedy, Lynne told Hurst, she became a "bum": "I wouldn't work, wouldn't go to school, wouldn't do anything—except sit around home all day and write songs and watch TV and sing." Eventually, at her grandmother's prompting, she auditioned for a job as a performer at the Opryland USA theme park, in Nashville, Tennessee. Although she was not hired—probably because her dancing did not measure up to her singing—a local songwriter in the audience was impressed by her performance and persuaded her to record a demo tape of his songs. A Nashville songwriter who heard the tape helped her to win a spot on the cable-television show *Nashville Now*. After her appearance Lynne received contract offers from four record companies—she signed with Epic—and the opportunity to record a single, "If I Could Bottle This Up," with the country legend George Jones. Jack Hurst explained Lynne's sudden entry into "Music City" by emphasizing the unique quality of her voice, which he described as "a mirror of her feelings." "Slow or fast, soft or hard, each song is burned with the fire of an emotion whose purity is of a degree rarely brought to music," he wrote.

Lynne released her debut album, *Sunrise*, on the Epic label in 1989. Laden with anguish over her parents' deaths and the breakup of her brief marriage (she was married by age 18 and divorced soon afterward), *Sunrise* included a rendition of the Floyd Tillman classic "Love You So Much It Hurts." The album's failure to yield a hit single led her promoters to surmise that the music was too "down" for radio play, so they sent her back to the studio to make a more upbeat recording. The result, *Tough All Over* (1990), and its successor, *Soft Talk* (1991), were mainstream country albums that brought Lynne recognition in the country-music world: in 1991 she was proclaimed best new female artist by the Academy of Country Music and given the Country Music Association's Horizon Award for rising new talent; she also won the support of such veterans of the genre as Reba McEntire (who, in an interview, called her the best new female singer), Kenny Rogers, and Randy Travis (she toured with both men). Yet her three albums with the Epic label failed to earn her a popular audience, beyond country's traditional fan base, as her record company had hoped. Moreover, Lynne began to feel boxed-in by Nashville's music scene. Refusing to be coached for interviews or to dress in flashy, sequined costumes, she soon earned a reputation as a troublemaker. But such criticism swayed neither Lynne nor her manager. "We just said: 'What you see is what you get,'" the singer told David Zimmerman during an interview for *USA Today* (February 20, 1990). "If you're ever lucky enough to get signed by a record label, they like you because you're different and when they get you they want to make you look like everybody else." Meanwhile, Lynne's sister, Allison Moorer, had moved to Nashville, with the goal of launching her own musical career, and she occasionally joined Lynne on the road to sing backup. "She makes sure I eat and dress right. She sews, she cooks, she cleans," Lynne told Zimmerman. (A singer and songwriter, Moorer has released two albums since 1998.)

Determined to have more control over her music, Lynne sought a smaller record company after her contract with Epic came to an end. She released her next two albums, *Temptation* (1993) and *Restless* (1995), on two different independent labels. Both were eclectic works that drew from many musical traditions, including jazz, swing, blues, and big band. On the concert tour to promote *Temptation*, which she performed with an 18-piece band known as the Swing Kings, Lynne took on the roles of torch-song singer and jazz diva. "It's so big—and so loud—that [audiences] can't help but sit there and really listen," she told Jack Hurst for the *Chicago Tribune* (December 17, 1993), speaking of the sound she and the band produced. A *Billboard* critic, quoted by Hurst, reported that "the people in the front rows had their hair blown back" and added, "Lynne is probably the only singer in Nashville who can hold her own against a band of this intensity."

Lynne wrote about half the songs on *Restless*, which had a more honky-tonk edge than its predecessor. It contains her song "Slow Me Down," a tribute to the southern way of life. "Being a Southern girl, I like talking about the South and its beauty," Lynne told Robert Loy for *Country Standard Time* (on-line). "The bottom line is I wanted to write a song about true Southern elegance." Also during 1995 Lynne performed the song "If I Never Knew You" with Hal Ketchum for the soundtrack of the Disney animated film *Pocahontas*.

In 1998 Lynne moved back to Alabama, to ponder her next move amid familiar surroundings. A big fan of Sheryl Crow's hit album *Tuesday Night Music Club* (1993), she decided to seek out its legendary producer, Bill Bottrell, who had also worked with Madonna and Michael Jackson. The semiretired Bottrell was lured back to work by Lynne's demo tape, and she, in turn, moved to California to work with him. The two spent a year, mostly in the singer's kitchen, making and recording music—a liberating experience for Lynne. "It's difficult expressing yourself in Nashville," she confessed to Michael Gallucci. "I never really concentrated on songwriting until this record. I really knew that I had something to say, and I said, 'What the hell, I really don't have anything to lose, I'm going to make a record that I like.'" "This is not a reinvention. This is an *acceptance* of who I am," she told Willman. Titled *I Am Shelby Lynne* (2000), the album consists of 10 distinctive tracks, some drawing from soul and R&B, others sounding lush and symphonic, and still others gravitating toward country rock and pop. Many of the songs seem to be expressions of a tortured soul; the single "Life Is Bad," for example, contains the lyric, "I'm looking up for the next thing that brings me down." When Brantley Bardin made a comment to her about her music's overwhelming pessimism, Lynne responded, "Actually, I'm working on that—but hey, show me somethin' good."

Most critics raved about *I Am Shelby Lynne*, and even those who found the music too eclectic or overproduced acknowledged the album as a whole to be a bold and promising departure. In February 2001, after a decade of making and performing music, Lynne won the Grammy Award for best new artist, beating out younger artists on the music scene. "It was weird enough to get the nomination," she told Chuck Crisafulli in an interview after the ceremony, as transcribed for the Grammy Awards Web site. "I never expected to win. It's just wonderful."

Lynne currently lives in Palm Springs, California, where she enjoys the desert, nearly ever-present sunshine, and long drives in her classic, 1968 Cadillac Coupe de Ville, whose radio has "still got that turnin' knob that I love," as she told Bardin. Just over five feet tall, she is reputed to be a tough, no-nonsense woman—"She would never suffer somebody telling her to be nice and sweet and behave," her producer, Bill Bottrell, told Chris Willman. She relishes what she has described as the "old school concept" of putting on a good show when she performs. Lynne's latest album, *Love, Shelby*, was scheduled to be released in mid-November 2001. — M.A.H.

Suggested Reading: *Chicago Tribune* XIII p18+ Dec. 3, 1989, with photo, III p5 Dec. 27, 1993, with photo; *CNN.com* Apr. 18, 2000; *Country Standard Time* (on-line); *Details* p118 Mar. 2000, with photo; *Entertainment Weekly* p47 Feb. 11, 2000, with photo; *Entertainment Weekly* (on-line) July 23, 2000; *Illinois Entertainer* Oct. 2000, on-line; *USA Today* D p1+ Feb. 28, 1990, with photo

Selected Recordings: *Sunrise*, 1989; *Tough All Over*, 1990; *Soft Talk*, 1991; *Temptation*, 1993; *Restless*, 1995; *I Am Shelby Lynne*, 2000; *Love, Shelby*, 2001

Steve Jennings/Retna ltd.

Mahal, Taj

May 17, 1942– Blues musician. Address: c/o Bill Graham Management, P.O. Box 429094, San Francisco, CA 94142

Over the course of his career, Taj Mahal has brought blues music to new generations of listeners. His unique sound, which fuses blues with other musical styles that have African roots, has influenced such diverse artists as the traditional-blues musician Rory Block and the modern rockers Eagle-Eye Cherry and Michelle Shocked. On his nearly 40 albums, Mahal has recorded everything from reggae-influenced blues to Malian fusion. He has won two Grammy Awards and earned four additional Grammy nominations. "My passion is to keep the [blues] tradition alive," Mahal wrote for his official Web site, "both for people of my generation who lived through it and, of course, for the kids who really can learn from it."

The eldest of nine children, Taj Mahal was born Henry St. Clair Fredericks on May 17, 1942 in New York City. His father, a native of the West Indies, was a pianist and jazz arranger who wrote charts for such luminaries as the clarinetist Benny Goodman and the singer Ella Fitzgerald. In order to make ends meet for his large family, he also worked as a molder for Fisk Tires. Mahal's mother, the former Mildred Shields, was a schoolteacher and gospel singer from South Carolina. Mahal's parents and grandparents were followers of Marcus Garvey, the charismatic leader of the Universal Negro Improvement Association, an influential black nationalist organization. The Frederickses moved to Springfield, Massachusetts, six months after Mahal's birth. Jazz was played constantly in their home, except on Sundays, when Mahal's mother would allow only gospel recordings. When Mahal was 12 he saw his father get run over and killed by a tractor in the family's backyard. (His mother later remarried.) "My father's death has been a painful thing, and still is to an extent," Mahal told Stephen Foehr, who collaborated with Mahal on the book *Taj Mahal: Autobiography of a Bluesman* (2001). "I may have resolved it, but I still have trouble." Mahal later added, "My father's death made me realize that I had to be doing the work that I needed to be doing. It made me more serious about doing my stuff, not being frivolous. Instead of lounging around, waiting for stuff to happen, I got busy. I started working as soon as I could, because that was the responsibility of the eldest."As a teenager Mahal worked long hours on tobacco and dairy farms.

Meanwhile, not long after his father's death, Mahal had discovered Mississippi Delta blues through new neighbors who had arrived from the South. Mahal taught himself to play guitar and bass and began to listen to records by such blues greats as Jimmy Reed, Howlin' Wolf, and Big Mama Thornton, as well as to recordings by the rock and roll musicians Chuck Berry and Bo Diddley. He was fascinated by his discovery that much of this music derived largely from traditional African forms.

Mahal attended the University of Massachusetts in Boston, where he studied animal husbandry, veterinary science, and agronomy. As an undergraduate he formed his first group, an R&B band called Taj Mahal and the Elektras. ("Taj Mahal," meaning "Crown Palace," is the name of a 17th-century mausoleum built by an Islamic Indian emperor to honor his second wife. Located in Agra, India, it is considered one of the most exquisite monuments in the world.) The group played at various Boston coffeehouses and college mixers. During this period Mahal became a fan of the electric-blues pioneer T-Bone Walker. He admired Walker's music because, while it contained progressive elements, it also remained true to its African roots. Mahal began to study the history of the blues and related black folk music from West Africa and the Caribbean, as well as zydeco, rock, and jazz. He learned to play many instruments, becoming proficient on the piano, banjo, mandolin, dulcimer, harmonica, and various flutes. At the same time he continued performing on the Boston folk circuit. In 1964 Mahal received a bachelor's degree in agricul-

ture from the University of Massachusetts. He then drove to Los Angeles, California, with Jesse Lee Kincaid, a fellow musician. There, Mahal and Kincaid joined with the guitarist Ry Cooder and the drummer Ed Cassidy to form a blues group called the Rising Sons. The band released only one single before breaking up. In 1992 Columbia Records released the album *The Rising Sons Featuring Taj Mahal and Ry Cooder*, which contained material recorded almost three decades earlier.

Mahal made his eponymous debut album, released in 1968 on the Columbia record label, with Ry Cooder and Bill Boatman on guitar. The record, which includes one original song composed by Mahal, is regarded by many music historians as an essential work of modern blues. Calling it a "startling statement in its time," Bruce Eder, in the *All Music Guide* (on-line), noted, "[Mahal] approached the music with a startling mix of authenticity and youthful enthusiasm. The whole record is a strange and compelling amalgam of stylistic and technical achievements—filled with blues influences of the 1930s and 1940s, but also making use of stereo sound separation and the best recording technology." Some critics, however, felt that the album was nothing more than a slick, commercial take on blues music. (In the liner notes for the album, Mahal wrote, "I could play . . . just exactly like Robert Johnson [a seminal blues musician], but what would be the point of that? This is 1968, not 1926.")

At the end of 1968, Mahal released *The Natch'l Blues*. A more diverse collection of music than his debut, the record encompassed modern soul and also drew from several different blues styles; it featured four original compositions and a rendition of "Corinna," which became a staple of Mahal's live performances. "Not content to mime or reproduce the blues note for note, Taj Mahal announced his intention to leave the path entirely, and then to return, bringing what he'd found," Eric Waggoner wrote of *The Natch'l Blues* for the *Pheonix New Times Online* (October 5, 2000).

Mahal's third recording, *Giant Step* (1969), was a double album, with two sides of solo acoustic blues and two sides featuring a full electric band. Referring to criticism that he had strayed from pure blues, Mahal told Bruce R. Miller for the *Sioux City Journal* (July 5, 1996, on-line),"There were enough songs on my first three albums to be hits. But because of who I am, where I am, where I came from and the angle I was playing, the industry was unfriendly to what I was playing."

In the early 1970s Mahal began to incorporate more black folk traditions into his blues records. *Happy to Be Just Like I Am* (1971) added Caribbean rhythms to acoustic blues, while *Recycling the Blues & Other Related Stuff* (1972) included some gospel-tinged music by the Pointer Sisters. In 1974 he released *Mo' Roots*, which emphasized a reggae sound. At the same time he recorded straightforward blues albums, such as *Ooh So Good 'N' Blues* (1973). *The Real Thing* (1972), a live recording, showcased many of Mahal's explorations. "*The Real Thing* was no mere blues album," Eric Waggoner wrote. "It carried the entire history of African-American music spilling out of both hands, in a joyful mess. If that mess was sometimes diffuse . . . his sheer happiness at being able to build a solid evening's set out of 300 years of musical history was (and remains) an infectious thing to hear." Mahal's albums *Music Keeps Me Together* (1974), *Satisfied 'N Tickled Too* (1976), and *Music Fuh Ya' (Music Para Tu)* (1977) also offered fusions of musical styles.

During the 1980s roots music of all kinds diminished in popularity, and Mahal's career suffered. Unable to generate interest from record companies, Mahal moved to Kauai, Hawaii, where he fished and occasionally recorded children's albums. One of those was *Shake Sugaree* (1988), which, as Thom Owens wrote for the *All Music Guide* (on-line), "leads kids through a musical journey, taking them through the Caribbean, Africa, and the Deep South, telling stories and singing songs all the while. . . . Every song and story is not only entertaining, but educational as well."

Mahal's career began to revive in 1991, when he composed blues music for the highly praised Broadway production of *Mule Bone*, an unfinished 1930 play by Langston Hughes and Zora Neale Hurston that had never been performed. The soundtrack album earned Mahal a Grammy nomination. In the next few years, he made up for his 1980s recording drought by releasing several lauded albums. *Taj Blues* (1992) combined blues with several of the roots-music styles that Mahal had long explored, while *Dancing the Blues* (1993) continued in a more traditional vein. "This is a gloriously contemporary sounding romp through a whole series of songs crying out for revival," Robin Deneslow wrote of the latter record for the London *Guardian* (April 15, 1994). "Taj Mahal treats them with respect and verve." In 1996 Mahal released *Phantom Blues*, featuring guest appearances by the popular musicians Bonnie Raitt and Eric Clapton. In *Phantom Blues* Mahal presented, in their original style, old blues songs that had been remade into pop and R&B hits. "For the most part," he wrote on his official Web site, "this album was designed to go down some familiar trails, but to look for new things. I am committed to retaining the shape and form of these great songs, while putting my own spin on them."

With *Se%7Enor Blues* (1997)—"one of Taj Mahal's best latter-day albums," according to Thom Owens in the *All Music Guide* (on-line)—the artist captured his first Grammy Award, for best contemporary blues album. "Stylistically, it's similar to most of his albums," Owens noted in his review, "but he's rarely been as effortlessly fun and infectious as he is here." Mahal next returned to children's music, with *Shakin' a Tailfeather* (1996). Ross Boissoneau, writing for the *All Music Guide* (on-line), was not impressed by the recording's "overabundance of sincerity." "There's just a

bit too much trying to get across a message and too little just having fun. That's a serious problem for a disc aimed at kids." In 1998 Mahal, while still living in Hawaii, released *Sacred Island*, a collection of Hawaiian music and Hawaiian-flavored blues that he recorded with the Hula Blues Band, which he had formed in 1981. (The band performed once on the National Public Radio series *The Prairie Home Companion* and has been featured on various blues-themed cruises.) Perhaps Mahal's most unusual recent project was *Kulanjan* (1999), on which he collaborated with Toumani Diabate, a Malian musician who plays the kora, a 21-stringed instrument similar to a lute. "Natural, unpretentious, and occasionally sensual, *Kulanjan* is classy world music without the stuffy undertones," Michael Gallucci wrote for the *All Music Guide* (on-line). Taj Mahal's album *Shoutin' in Key: Taj Mahal & the Phantom Blues Band Live* (2000) won the artist his second Grammy Award for best contemporary blues album.

Mahal is known not only for his instrumental prowess and versatile voice but also for his engaging stage presence. In concert he always wears a hat, a brightly colored shirt, and dark glasses. He has composed music for several films, including *Sounder* (1973), *Sounder II* (1976), and *Zebrahead* (1992), as well as television shows. He has also made cameo appearances in a dozen movies, among them the *Sounder* films, *Once Upon a Time . . . When We were Colored* (1996), *Outside Ozona* (1998), and *Songcatcher* (2000). Recently he teamed up with the on-line music site *MusicBlitz* to launch a series of interactive Internet workshops that describe the origins of Chicago, West Texas, and Delta blues. "The fact is that the blues has always been part of modern technology even when Robert Johnson was recording 60 years ago," Mahal was quoted as saying on *Tokyo Classified* (on-line). "And if you don't take the time to put music into some framework, if it doesn't have some hard currency that will pass from one generation to the next . . . from one technology to the next, well, the next generation won't get it."

In a review of *Taj Mahal: Autobiography of a Bluesman* for *Amazon.com*, Richard P. Haight, who identified himself as the book's copy editor, wrote, "Taj Mahal's international concert schedule and complex family relations made him an elusive, sometimes reluctant, contributor to the [book]. Foehr was forced to tell the story as much by contacting Taj's myriad kin, fellow musicians, friends, and others as by getting Taj to tell it in his own words. The result is a rich, multifaceted combination of autobiography and biography that provides a classic example of the genre as well as a fascinating portrait of its subject, the world of the blues, Taj's family and friends, and a history of the blues in the last 40 or 50 years." — G.O.

Suggested Reading: *All Music Guide* (on-line); *New Statesman* p39+ July 24, 1998; *Phoenix New Times Online* Oct. 5, 2000; *Sioux City Journal* (on-line) July 5, 1996; *Taj-mo-roots.com*; Mahal, Taj, and Foehr, Stephen. *Taj Mahal: Autobiography of a Bluesman*, 2001

Selected Recordings: *Taj Mahal*, 1968; *The Natch'l Blues*, 1968; *Giant Steps*, 1969; *Happy to Be Just Like I Am*, 1971; *Recycling the Blues & Other Related Stuff*, 1972; *The Real Thing*, 1972; *Sounder*, 1973; *Ooh So Good 'N' Blues*, 1973; *Mo' Roots*, 1974; *Music Keeps Me Together*, 1975; *Satisfied 'N Tickled Too*, 1976; *Music Fuh Ya' (Music Para Tu)*, 1977; *Brothers*, 1977; *Evolution (The Most Recent)*, 1978; *Taj*, 1987; *Shake Sugaree*, 1988; *Like Never Before*, 1991; *Mule Bone*, 1991; *Taj's Blues*, 1992; *World Music*, 1993; *Dancing the Blues*, 1994; *Phantom Blues*, 1996; *Señor Blues*, 1997; *Sacred Island*, 1998; *Kulanjan*, 1999; *Shoutin' in Key: Taj Mahal & the Phantom Blues Band Live*, 2000

Courtesy of Maki and Associates, Tokyo

Maki, Fumihiko

Sep. 6, 1928– Architect. Address: Maki and Associates, 5-16-23 Higashi-Gotanda Shinagawa-ku, Tokyo 141, Japan

The celebrated modernist architect Fumihiko Maki is known for designs that avoid the clichés of Western and Eastern styles of architecture while integrating the best elements of both. Writing for *Time* (May 3, 1993) the week that Maki was named the winner of the 1993 Pritzker Architecture Prize, Kurt Andersen described the Japanese-born architect as "that rare designer whose buildings are decorous but also fetchingly strange, a little dream-

like." According to Andersen, "Maki's buildings are extraordinary not just because they are intriguingly conceived but also because they are so meticulously made." His architecture, which is devoted to public spaces rather than private dwellings, "reflects a deep commitment to the vitality of community life," and his "structures often blur clear distinctions between the building's interior and the world outside its walls," as Simi Hoque wrote for a Web site maintained by the Department of Architecture of the University of California at Berkeley. The many projects that he has designed as the principal partner of Maki and Associates include, in the United States, the Mark C. Steinberg Hall of Art and Archaeology, on the campus of Washington University, in St. Louis, Missouri, and the Yerba Buena Gardens Visual Arts Center, at the Moscone Convention Center, in San Francisco, California. In Japan his works include dormitories and other buildings on the Kumagaya campus of Rissho University, northwest of Tokyo; the aquarium at Okinawa Memorial Park; the Hillside Terrace housing complex, in Tokyo; the Danish Embassy in Tokyo; the Fujisawa Municipal Gym; the Museum of Modern Art in Kyoto; the Iwasaki Art Museum, in Kagoshima; the Nippon Cultural Center, in Chiba; the Wacoal Spiral and Tepia buildings, in Tokyo; and the Tokyo Metropolitan Gymnasium. In an article about him for *Contemporary Architecture* (1994), the Chinese architect Ching-Yu Chang wrote, "With all his keen interest in theory and technology, Maki is a populist and his buildings display a warmth and sense of excitement and surprise that is rarely found in contemporary architecture."

Maki is a co-founder of the Metabolism Movement in architecture; its name, inspired by that of the biological process, reflects the belief of the Metabolists (as its practitioners are called) that large-scale urban projects, like cities themselves, can change in response to cultural and other societal advances, in large part through the advent of new technologies. In 1964 Maki coined the term "megastructure," to refer to a single complex that incorporates living space, stores, and elements of transportation. The Metabolists have brought dynamic changes to Japan. "Space that reflects the will of a city or society cannot be exhausted," Maki told Bonnie Churchill for the *Christian Science Monitor* (April 26, 1993). "I believe that spaces with strength and nobility can transcend function and survive on an existential level." He has also said, as quoted on the Pritzker Prize Web site, "The problem of modernity is not creating forms, but rather, creating an overall image of life, not necessarily dominated by the concept of modernity." In the view of Heather Willson Cass, writing for *Architecture* (June 1993), Maki's "concern for the physical, social, and cultural context of buildings . . . has distinguished his work from that of other Modernists of his generation." Maki has taught architecture at Harvard University and the University of Tokyo, and he has served as a visiting professor at several other schools.

Fumihiko Maki was born in Tokyo, Japan, on September 6, 1928. His childhood visits to buildings in Japan that had been designed by the American architects Frank Lloyd Wright and Antonin Raymond left a lasting impression on him. In 1952 Maki graduated from the University of Tokyo with a bachelor's degree in architecture. He did his postgraduate work in the United States. In 1953 he received a master's degree in architecture from the Cranbook Academy of Art, in Bloomfield Hills, Michigan, where he was exposed to the work of Eliel Saarinen, who designed the school's buildings and much of its curriculum. The next year Maki completed a second master's degree, at Harvard University's Graduate School of Design, in Cambridge, Massachusetts, where he studied with José Luis Sert. He apprenticed with two prestigious firms: Skidmore Owings & Merrill, in New York City (1954–55), and then Sert Jackson & Associates, in Cambridge (1955–58). From 1956 to 1958 Maki served as an associate professor at Washington University, the site of his first commission in the U.S., the Mark C. Steinberg Hall of Art and Archeology, which was completed in 1960. (His first building project—Toyoda Memorial Hall, at Nagoya University, in Japan—was completed in the same year.) A grant from the Chicago-based Graham Foundation for Advanced Studies in the Fine Arts enabled him to spend two years (1958–60) traveling in Japan, Southeast Asia, India, the Middle East, and parts of Europe. In 1961 Maki joined the faculty of Harvard University's Graduate School of Design, where he taught until 1965 as an associate professor.

Meanwhile, in 1964, Maki had established his own architectural firm, Maki and Associates, in Tokyo. Early on, he resolved that at any one time, his staff would number no more than 35. "I was never attracted to the idea of a large organization," he has explained, as quoted on the Pritzker Architecture Prize Web site. "On the other hand, a small organization may tend to develop a very narrow viewpoint. My ideal is a group structure that allows people with diverse imaginations, that often contradict and are in conflict with one another, to work in a condition of flux, but that also permits the making of decisions that are as calculated and objectively weighed as necessary for the creation of something as concrete as architecture." For some projects Maki and Associates has collaborated with larger firms.

In 1968 Maki became a professor of architecture at the University of Tokyo, where he taught for the next 21 years. In 1969 Maki and Associates completed the first stage of the Hillside Terrace apartment complex, a multiphase project on which Maki worked until 1992, when Phase VI was finished. Intended for multiple uses, the complex developed along with his ideas for it. The earlier sections of the exterior resemble concrete cubes, while intricate arrangements of ceramic tile cover more-recent additions. The unusual flexibility of Japanese workers aided the construction process.

"At construction sites in Japan, workers are always willing to cooperate with architects so that we can do something almost unthinkable in the U.S.—modify our designs in the process of building," Maki told Kurt Andersen, S. Chang, and Yukinori Ishikawa for *Time* (September 21, 1987).

The Fujisawa Gymnasium, completed in 1984, consists of three buildings covering close to 500,000 square feet. The gymnasium proper, which seats 2,000, is notable for its sloping ceiling, which peaks at 262 feet six inches. The structure consists of two connected buildings covered in curved sheets of stainless steel that are reminiscent of 16th-century Japanese armor. "One of architecture's functions," Maki told Kurt Andersen for *Time* (May 3, 1993), "is to waken subconscious memories of shapes." In designing the gymnasium, he was inspired to use "increasingly complex forms," as he told Bonnie Churchill. "Many people say it looks like a frog, or a beetle, or a spaceship. I just wanted to make a very dynamic building. I wanted to make rich interior spaces. . . . The building has become complex enough to yield all kinds of images according to the people who look at it." By his own account, the project led Maki into increasingly complex forms and thus marked a turning point in his career.

In 1993 Maki completed the Yerba Buena Gardens Visual Arts Center at San Francisco's Moscone Convention Center. (The center was one element of a large-scale redevelopment of the downtown section of San Francisco that also included projects by Mario Botta, James Polshek, and I. M. Pei.) The structure, which stands on an L-shaped lot, was designed to provide affordable and flexible exhibition sites. It was also equipped with special glass that allows a generous amount of light to enter the space but filters out ultraviolet rays, which can damage works of art. The architect Bill Lacy, the executive director of the Pritzker Architecture Prize committee, told Bonnie Churchill that Maki "uses light in a masterful way, making it a tangible part of every design as are the walls and the roof. In each building, he searches for a way to make transparency, translucency, and opacity exist in total harmony. He uses detail to give his structure rhythm and scale."

In 1993 Maki was named the winner of the Pritzker Architecture Prize; established by the Hyatt Foundation in 1979, the bronze medal and $100,000 award recognize lifetime achievement. Maki was the second Japanese architect to win the prize, which, in the world of architecture, is equivalent in prestige to a Nobel Prize; the first was Kenzo Tange. (A third, Tadao Ando, won the prize in 1995.) Among Maki's many other honors are the Japan Institute of Architects Award (1963), the Reynolds Memorial Award (1987), the Wolf Prize for Art (which he earned along with Giancarlo de Carlo, in 1988), the Chicago Prize (1988), the Thomas Jefferson Memorial Medal of Architecture (1990), and a gold medal from the Paris-based Union Internationales des Architectes (1993). He and his wife,

Misao, who married in 1960, have two daughters.
— C.L.

Suggested Reading: *Architectural Record* p72+
Mar. 1994, with photos; *Architecture* p21 June
1993, with photos; *Christian Science Monitor*
p14 Apr. 26, 1993; *Time* p68+ Sep. 21, 1987,
with photos, p65 May 3, 1993, with photos;
Casper, Dale E. *Fumihiko Maki, Master Architect*,
1988; Emanuel, Muriel, ed. *Contemporary
Architects*, 1994; *International Who's Who,
1996–97*; Maki, Fumihiko, Botond Bognar, and
Alex Krieger. *Fumihiko Maki: Buildings and
Projects*, 1997

Selected Works: Toyoda Memorial Hall, Nagoya,
Japan, 1960; Mark C. Steinberg Hall of Art and
Archaeology, St. Louis, Missouri, 1960; Hillside
Terrace Apartment Complex, Shibuya-ku, Tokyo,
1969-1991; Fujisawa Auditorium, Japan, 1984;
Nippon Convention Center, Tokyo, 1989; Tokyo
Metropolitan Gymnasium, Tokyo, 1990; Yerba
Buena Gardens Visual Arts Center, San
Francisco, California, 1993

Courtesy of U.S. House of Representatives

Maloney, Carolyn B.

*Feb. 19, 1948– U.S. Representative from New
York. Address: 2430 Rayburn House Office Bldg.,
Washington, DC 20515; 1651 Third Ave., Suite
311, New York, NY 10128*

Carolyn B. Maloney, a Democrat from New York
City, won her seat in the House of Representatives
in 1992 by a very narrow margin against a longtime
Republican incumbent. Her popularity among her
constituents has increased with each successive
election, and she has made a name for herself as a
determined, hard-working crusader for women,
children, and families. Maloney began her political
career as a member of the New York City Council,
where her intensity and scrappiness earned her a
reputation as a "pit bull," according to an anonymous colleague of hers, as quoted on the *Freedom
Channel* Web site. The Paid Parental Leave for Federal Employees Act and the Right to Breastfeed
Act, both approved by the 106th Congress, thanks
in large measure to Maloney's efforts, illustrate her
consistent concern for the welfare of women and
children. Maloney has also worked for campaign-
finance reform, greater government efficiency, increased foreign aid, and stronger environmental
protection.

The daughter of R. G. and Christine (Clegg)
Bosher, Maloney was born Carolyn Bosher on February 19, 1948 in Greensboro, North Carolina. She
graduated from Greensboro College, in 1968, with
the intention of pursuing a law degree. In 1970, after a year at the University of North Carolina
School of Law, in Chapel Hill, she visited New
York City, and her plans changed. "I went up to see
a friend and never left," Maloney told Michael
Janofsky for the *New York Times* (December 26,
1992). "I just fell in love with the place. My father
was furious." Not long after her arrival, she married Clifton Maloney, an investment banker, and
found work in New York City as a public-school
teacher. She quickly moved into administrative
positions with the New York State Board of Education, where her work included training people for
jobs in welfare services. Beginning in 1977 she
worked as an aide in the New York State Assembly,
and later, in the state Senate. In 1982 she ran for the
New York City Council against incumbent Robert
Rodriguez and defeated him by a two-to-one margin. As a councilor she represented primarily East
Harlem, 80 percent of whose residents were members of minority groups.

In 1986 Maloney founded a council subcommittee on city contracts, which computerized the system for keeping track of the approximately
$7 billion per year the city was spending on out-
side help. She also was the chief architect of the
New York City Campaign Finance Act, which
helped to shrink the monetary advantage that in-
cumbents held over political challengers. At about
this time Maloney became a mother for the second
time, thus becoming the first city councilor to give
birth while in office. As a councilor, Maloney focused much of her efforts on women's and children's issues. Among other measures, she proposed legislation to make day care more affordable
and helped create early-childhood development
programs as a member of a joint mayoral-council
commission.

In 1992 Maloney ran for a seat in Congress, to
represent New York State's 14th District, which included most of the Upper East Side of New York

City and portions of the Lower East Side and Upper West Side. In the Democratic primary she triumphed over three other candidates. Her opponent in the general election was the 14-year incumbent Bill Green, a fiscally conservative and socially liberal Republican who was favored to win. But Maloney benefitted from the recent redistricting, which had expanded the constituency to include Astoria, a neighborhood in the borough of Queens, and the Greenpoint section of Brooklyn, both of which had a relatively high proportion of minority populations, who traditionally voted Democratic. On Election Day Maloney triumphed, by fewer than 5,000 votes. She has won each succeeding election by wide margins: 64 to 35 percent in 1994; 72 to 24 percent in 1996; 77 to 23 percent in 1998; and 74 to 23 percent in 2000.

Soon after her swearing-in in 1993, Maloney stirred a controversy within the Democratic Party by refusing to back President Bill Clinton's budget package, despite threats from high-ranking House Democrats that she had no hope of a successful congressional career if she withheld her support. "I did not run for Congress to succumb to threats," Maloney declared, as quoted in the *New York Times* (May 29, 1993). "During the campaign," she went on to say, "I promised along with President Clinton to cut two dollars for every new dollar raised. Then he revised his proposal to one to one. And what we voted on last night was a reversal, two to one." Then, in August, she voted to approve the final, altered version of the plan, claiming, as the *New York Times* (August 4, 1993) reported, that "it basically equalizes the ratio of spending cuts and revenue increases."

Maloney's first House appointments, to the Committee on Government Operations and the Banking, Finance, and Urban Affairs Committee, gave her an opportunity to draw on her experiences in setting fiscal policy as a city councilor. In 1993, once again going against the political grain, she voted against the North American Free Trade Agreement (NAFTA). In 1995 she and Republican Stephen Horn of California successfully sponsored a bill that required government agencies whose debtors still owed money to them to turn the debts over to the Treasury Department for collection. She worked to keep banks from controlling other businesses and leveled allegations against the Federal Reserve Board for subsidizing its check-clearing services in order to compete with private businesses. An avid opponent of wasteful government spending, Maloney won a protracted battle to dissolve the Civilian Marksmanship Program, which for years had provided millions of dollars' worth of free ammunition to civilians. She is also a member of the Joint Economic Committee.

As a congresswoman Maloney has continued to serve as a spokesperson for women and families. On April 21, 1993, at a hearing of the House Subcommittee on Human Resources of the Committee on Ways and Means, she vigorously supported President Clinton's proposal for new funding for child-welfare services. She helped enact various bills that aimed to help women and families, including the Child Support Enforcement Improvements Act of 1996, which gave child-support enforcement agencies more access to the financial information of noncustodial parents and encouraged states to enforce child-support laws. Maloney helped pass the Breast Cancer Early Detection Act of 1997, which provided increased coverage from Social Security for annual mammographies for women 65 and older. The Right to Breastfeed Act of 1999, another of Maloney's bills, protected the right of women to breast-feed on federal property. The Federal Employees Paid Parental Leave Act of 2000, which Maloney and three other representatives introduced, provided six weeks' paid parental leave to federal employees with new babies. Maloney has also introduced several women- and family-related bills that Congress has not yet passed. Among them are the Child Care Tax Credit bill, which would provide tax credits to all companies that give child-care assistance to their employees. Another, the Kiddie Mac bill, aims to facilitate the financing of child-care and child-development facilities; a field hearing for that measure was held on October 8, 1999.

Along with Democratic representative John Dingell of Michigan and others, Maloney introduced the Independent Commission on Campaign Finance Reform Act of 1997, which set up a committee to make recommendations on campaign-finance reforms. This act became an addendum to the 1998 Shays-Meehan campaign-finance bill (proposed by Christopher Shays, a Connecticut Republican, and Martin D. Meehan, a Massachusetts Democrat), which Maloney supported. Maloney helped push through the Federal Election Commission Appropriations Amendment, which passed on July 16, 1998; the amendment increased by $2.8 million the allocation of funds for the Federal Election Commission (FEC), which investigates election-law violations. At about this time Maloney helped to block Republican attempts to oust the FEC general counsel, Lawrence Noble. She contended, along with other Democrats, that Republicans wanted Noble removed because of his investigations into Republican fund-raising.

Maloney's congressional work has also encompassed environmental protection. In 1993 she sponsored a bill for the Northern Rockies Ecosystem Protection Act (NREPA), a proposal to classify 16 million acres in five states as protected wilderness. Opposing lawmakers embarrassed her on the floor of the House when they asked her to define "ecosystem" and to name the head of the Forest Service, the agency that would oversee the new wilderness area—queries that she was unable to answer correctly. Undeterred, she reintroduced the bill in 1998 and again in 1999; the legislation, which stirred further debates in the House, has yet to become law. Maloney also led the successful attempt, via an amendment to a House appropriations bill for the Interior Department that passed on

June 14, 2000, to collect from oil and gas companies billions of dollars in royalties (connected with their sale of raw materials taken from federal land) owed to the federal government.

Since she entered Congress, Maloney has voiced strong opinions on several issues of international import. In 1993 she opposed the Arab boycott of Israel and helped pass the Arab Boycott Arms Sales Prohibition Act, which banned arms sales to any country participating in the boycott. On June 20, 1996 she co-hosted a so-called congressional colloquy on human-rights abuses in Peru, focusing on that nation's imprisonment in 1996 of the American Lori Berenson for alleged revolutionary activities. Maloney's War Crimes Disclosure Act facilitated access to information about individuals who participated in Nazi war crimes in World War II; it was signed into law in altered form on October 19, 1996. A similar piece of legislation, the Nazi War Crimes Disclosure Act, became law on October 8, 1998. In a nod to her Greek-American constituency in Astoria, she helped found the Congressional Caucus on Hellenic Issues. In 1999 her legislation to restore voluntary U.S. contributions to the United Nations Population Fund was incorporated into the Foreign Operations Appropriations bill. On April 7, 2000 she made a passionate speech before President Clinton and others at the World Health Day meeting, urging an increase in foreign-aid spending. During the speech she said, as quoted on the international news Web site *Planetwire*, "As a nation, we offer the young people of the poorest regions of the world a glimpse of the American dream, but all too often, what they get is the nightmare of early teen pregnancy, the nightmare of infant and maternal death."

As the ranking Democrat on the House Subcommittee on the Census, Maloney came under fire from Republicans who decried certain questions on the 2000 census form as a violation of privacy and advised their constituents not to answer them. Republicans also leveled allegations of improprieties against the Census Bureau. According to the Public Broadcasting Service (PBS) Web site (March 30, 2000), Maloney said of the issue, "If you're encouraging, as some members are, their residents and their communities not to fill out the form, they're only hurting their localities because the census shows us where we need schools, where we need senior programs, and it's incredibly important." In June 2000 Maloney voted to defeat an amendment that would have downsized the Census Bureau. In 2001 the administration of President George W. Bush decided to base its political redistricting on "raw" national census figures rather than on figures statistically adjusted to correct likely underestimates of the total U.S. minority population. Maloney criticized the decision and said, as quoted in the *Houston Chronicle* (March 7, 2001, on-line), "There is still a differential undercount. It will result in blacks, Hispanics, Asian Pacific Islanders, American Indians and children being missed in legislative districts above the nation-

al average, and it will result in affluent people being counted twice, leading to an unfair distribution of federal funds."

Maloney's awards include the Military Order of the Purple Heart for Meritorious and Conspicuous Service for veterans, the Ellis Island Medal of Honor, the Hadassah Myrtle Wreath Award, the Global Peace Award from the organization Peace Action, and the Queens Women's Political Caucus's Queens Women of Distinction Award. Her children are Christine Paul Maloney (whose middle name honors Alice Paul, an American feminist and suffragette who began fighting for the Equal Rights Amendment to the Constitution in 1923) and Virginia. — P.G.H.

Suggested Reading: *Barron's* p37 Feb. 23, 1998; *New York Times* p25 Dec. 26, 1992, A p15 Aug. 4, 1993, B p9 Mar. 28, 1995; *Almanac of American Politics, 2000*; Foerstel, Karen, ed. *Biographical Dictionary of Congressional Women*, 1999; *Politics in America*, 1994

Courtesy of SimonSays.com

Marcinko, Richard

(mar-SINK-oh)

Nov. 21, 1940– Writer; motivational speaker; CEO of Richard Marcinko Inc.; former military officer. Address: SOS Temps, 801 N. Pitt St., Suite 418, Alexandria, VA 22314

In the shadowy world of special warfare, there is little Richard Marcinko hasn't seen or done. Throughout a career in the U.S. Navy spanning more than 30 years, Marcinko flouted protocol and upended tradition, earning the nickname "Rogue Warrior." An unconventional thinker who uses his wits and his fists equally well, Marcinko founded SEAL (SEa Air and Land) Team Six, an elite counterterrorist naval unit. Since he retired from the navy, in 1989, Marcinko has applied his talents to the corporate world, heading up two successful businesses: Richard Marcinko Inc., a motivational and team-building company, and SOS Temps, a corporate-security firm. In addition, he is a successful author. The first of his best-selling *Rogue Warrior* books is a memoir chronicling his exploits as a navy SEAL; the others are novels based on his SEAL experiences. He has also written a series of nonfiction books on how to apply SEAL training to the corporate world.

Richard Marcinko was born on November 21, 1940 in the mining town of Lansford, Pennsylvania. "I was born on Thanksgiving Day, and the world's been thankful ever since," he joked to *Current Biography*. His father, George L. Marcinko, worked in the coal mines, while his mother, the former Emilie T. Pavlik, was a homemaker. "I was always independent," he wrote in his autobiography, *Rogue Warrior* (1992), co-written by John Weisman. "I had my own paper route by the age of five. At seven, I was taking off for a day at a time, running through the mile long Lehigh Railroad tunnel to swim in that Hauto reservoir." Growing up in the pro-military afterglow of World War II, he was drawn to the armed forces, Marcinko recalled to *Current Biography*. "I grew up when the towns had victory parades and banners on the homes that said 'Welcome Home Johnny,' and all that," he said. "So going to war was still a good thing. And because of that, there's a certain amount of patriotism that comes naturally when you grow up that way."

In 1952, after the Lansford mines closed, the Marcinko family moved to New Brunswick, New Jersey. There, Marcinko worked a series of odd jobs while attending St. Ladislaus Hungarian Catholic School. In 1958 he dropped out of high school and joined the navy. Most of Marcinko's relatives had served in the military, and Marcinko felt compelled to follow in their footsteps, albeit in his own way. "None of my relatives had gone into the navy," he told *Current Biography*. "And I didn't want to repeat what the others had done."

Arriving at boot camp in Great Lakes, Illinois, Marcinko quickly adjusted to military life. "Talk about gung ho—I even spit-shined the *soles* of my boots," he wrote in *Rogue Warrior*. After completing his basic training, Marcinko was sent to Quonset Point, Rhode Island, where he helped teach survival techniques to naval aviators. While there, he saw the 1951 film *The Frogmen*, starring Richard Widmark, which depicted the heroic deeds of the Underwater Demolition Team (UDT) in the Pacific during World War II. Marcinko was inspired by the film, feeling that service in the UDT was exactly what he was looking for. "That [movie] kind of stoked my interest in being in the navy and still be-

ing proactive and action-oriented," he explained to *Current Biography*. He applied to the UDT program but was deferred, the reason being that he had not yet completed his rudimentary naval training. Eventually, after a dust-up with a senior officer in Naples, Italy, Marcinko was sent to UDT in the hope that the rigorous training would make him less aggressive.

Marcinko sailed through UDT training in Little Creek, Virginia, as well as the strenuous 10-week course in St. Thomas, in the West Indies, in which he learned the skills needed to become a frogman. He was accepted at the Officers Candidate School, graduating in 1965 as an ensign. Assigned to the destroyer *Joseph K. Taussig*, Marcinko soon realized that he had an affinity for leading men. "Somewhat to my surprise I discovered that leading is not easy," he wrote in *Rogue Warrior*. "It takes the same sort of confidence you need to jump out of a plane to order a man to do something that may prove fatal to him—and have him carry out the order instantaneously and without question." In spite of his satisfaction with his position, he yearned to join the SEAL teams, reputedly the toughest and most aggressive units in the armed forces. (According to Marcinko, the widely held assumption that the Green Berets outshine them in toughness and aggressiveness is incorrect. While the Green Berets' training is arduous, he told *Current Biography*, that of the SEALs is even more difficult, and for that reason there are fewer SEALs than Green Berets. Moreover, he said, Green Berets are often parachuted into war zones, whereas SEALs must reach their targets unassisted and while carrying their own gear.) Trained to handle any adverse situations, SEALs are generally selected for the most dangerous covert missions. Marcinko was drawn to the training-intensive life of the SEAL teams, as well as the chance to study unconventional warfare. "You're going to do the most you can with the least available," he said to *Current Biography* of the teams. "You're there to live off the land, and live off your enemy, and pick off things. And when you start doing that, you start to study your enemy and do things that are not taught in our formal schools."

By May 1966 Marcinko had pulled enough strings to get himself assigned to SEAL Team Two. He began his tour of duty in the Vietnam War the following September. In Vietnam Marcinko learned many warfare tactics that he would later apply to his military career. The Vietcong, or North Vietnamese guerrillas against whom he was fighting, "taught me more about war than anybody," he told *Current Biography*. "They were obviously dedicated, they'd been doing it for 20 years. They worked in cells, small teams and could move in a hurry." As he spent more time in Vietnam, he and his teammates began to adapt to the style of fighting used by the Vietcong. "By the early spring of 1967 we were carrying one canteen instead of the regulation two, substituting bullets and grenades for the water weight," he wrote in *Rogue Warrior*.

"We modified our field gear, leaving packs behind in favor of load-bearing vests, into which we punched holes so the pockets would drain both mud and water immediately. We took no changes of clothing or ponchos. We slept in the open, camouflaging ourselves with whatever we had around us. Like the [Vietcong], we became guerrillas—living off the land instead of acting like invaders." For his efforts in Vietnam, Marcinko was awarded a Silver Star, four Bronze Stars, and two navy Commendation Medals.

After returning from Vietnam, in 1968, Marcinko was assigned as special operations adviser for the navy's Amphibious Training Command. Based on his performance there, he was accepted into a navy collegiate program in Monterey, California, where he received a B.A. degree in international affairs. In 1972 he was promoted to lieutenant commander. Not long afterward he was selected as the chief naval attaché in Cambodia. Following eight months of intelligence training, including language and spy skills, Marcinko was sent to Phnom Penh, Cambodia, where he helped that nation's army battle the Communist Khmer Rouge and created a Cambodian marine force, the first of its kind.

In October 1974, after his return from Cambodia, Marcinko was given command of SEAL Team Two. As commander, he led his team on many covert missions, most of them of such a secret nature that he cannot discuss them even now. In addition, he received an education in navy protocol, in the process discovering a lot he didn't like. As he recalled in Rogue Warrior, "Our missions were designed by idiots in Washington . . . who had no idea about the capabilities of SEALs, or the limitations of such elements as terrain, weather, or what the nineteenth-century strategist and philosopher Von Clausewitz referred to as 'friction'—the fog of battle that is a fancy way of restating Murphy's Law: 'What can go wrong will go wrong.'" After leaving SEAL Team Two, in 1976, Marcinko attended Auburn University in Montgomery, Alabama, where he received a master's degree in political science. He then went to Washington, D.C., to take a job in intelligence at the Pentagon.

In November 1979 Iranian terrorists took control of the U.S. Embassy in Tehran, holding all of the American diplomats hostage. After the 1980 operation to rescue them resulted in a collision on the ground between a rescue helicopter and a refueling aircraft, Marcinko began to formulate what he described to Current Biography as "the thesis of my military career." "When the raid failed in Iran, they said, 'We want a full-time counterterrorist force,'" he explained. Marcinko envisioned a fully functional SEAL unit designed exclusively to counteract terrorist activity. Made up of 75 enlisted men and 15 officers, SEAL Team Six (so named to make the enemy believe there were five other platoons of a similar nature) was an unconventional unit from the start. Instead of culling members from the well-groomed ranks of Naval Academy graduates, Marcinko sought out "dirtbags," as he described them

in Rogue Warrior. "Dirtbags with union skills—truck drivers, crane operators, bricklayers, longshoremen. But I wasn't looking for just any dirtbags. I wanted motivated dirtbags . . . the guys who try harder. I went through each candidate's . . . records to see where they ranked in their classes. Whereas the number one man may have breezed through, the guy who was seventy-seventh probably had a bitch of a time in the water, didn't like crawling through mud, and hated demolition—but he never quit."

Over the next three years, Marcinko and his team underwent some of the most rigorous and extensive training in naval history and embarked on several clandestine missions. In 1984, after he had left SEAL Team Six, he was tapped to create a special unit with the job of testing the security of naval bases. Dubbed Red Cell, Marcinko's unit was composed of several members of SEAL Team Six, as well as other highly trained individuals from the world of special warfare. Red Cell's mission was to infiltrate naval bases by any means possible and shine a light on the vulnerabilities of security procedures. "I'd learned in Vietnam that the back door was the best way to hit Charlie," he wrote in Rogue Warrior; "now I'd get to be Charlie and hit the Navy through its own back door." In the ensuing months Red Cell set about assaulting various naval bases around the country. Their activities included a successful—though fake—demolition of Air Force One, which was stationed at Point Mugu Naval Air Station, in Santa Barbara, California. The naval commanders were shocked to learn the extent of their facilities' vulnerability. Even more surprising was the fact that Marcinko's unit accomplished their mission using the most brazen of tactics, such as replacing padlocks with their own store-bought ones or walking onto a base wearing a stolen commander's uniform. "The things that we did in Red Cell were not 007," he explained to Current Biography, referring to the fictional master spy James Bond. "At the most sophisticated level, we broke into places the way a second-story burglar would do, that's all."

In April 1986 Marcinko was dismissed from command of Red Cell, pending an inquiry by the Naval Investigative Service. Based on testimony from John Mason, a former SEAL Team Six member who was on probation for falsifying travel vouchers, the navy compiled enough evidence against Marcinko to convict him for conspiracy. Specifically, the government charged that Marcinko had received a kickback of $100,000 for specialized grenades bought by the military from a company of which he was a silent partner. The investigation dragged on for four years and resulted in Marcinko's being sentenced to 21 months in a federal prison. While there, he penned Rogue Warrior as a way to help defray his legal costs. Co-authored with John Weisman, the book was a best-seller. In response to the overwhelming demand for more books from Marcinko, he wrote Rogue Warrior II: Red Cell (1994), a fictionalized adventure based on his experiences testing naval security. That book was also a hit, and Marcinko began writing at the rate of about a book a year, penning *Green Team* (1995), *Task Force Blue* (1996), *SEAL Force Alpha* (1998), and *Echo Platoon* (2000). In addition, he has published a series of nonfiction books, including *Leadership Secrets of the Rogue Warrior* (1996), *Rogue Warrior's Strategy for Success* (1997), and *The Real Team* (1999).

Currently, most of Marcinko's energy is devoted to his company Richard Marcinko Inc. (RMI). A motivational team-building company, RMI works with corporate clients, mapping strategies and creating more-effective methods for running a business. "The [program] reflects the commonality between combat and whatever the industry is doing, and the need to know the enemy, called the competition," Marcinko told *Current Biography*. In addition to the seminars, RMI hosts "boot camps," in which businesspeople are thrust into intensive, three-day training sessions and taught to think creatively and work together. "I figure out a way to psychologically strip them down and [get them to] hate me so they can form up and screw with me a little bit," he told *Current Biography*. "And then we analyze where we are, and show how it applies to their industry." He also runs SOS Temps, a security firm that has attracted a number of high-profile clients overseas.

Richard Marcinko lives in Alexandria, Virginia, in a house he calls "Rogue Manor." He is married to Nancy Alexander, a contracts manager. The couple have five children, two from Marcinko's previous marriage, to Kathy Black, which ended in 1985. He and his wife recently adopted a baby girl. Marcinko moonlights in Hollywood, helping film directors portray SEALs accurately in movies; he was a consultant on *The Rock* (1996) and *G.I. Jane* (1997). More recently, he joined the crew of Ron Howard's *The Grinch* (2000), using SEAL tactics for coping with torture to help Jim Carrey (who played the title character) deal with the excruciatingly painful contact lenses his role required. Marcinko's latest work of fiction, *Detachment Bravo*, was published in 2001. His 13th book is scheduled to appear in the fall of 2002. Marcinko is developing a movie version of *Rogue Warrior* with the producer Jerry Bruckheimer and is at work on a CD-ROM game.

In the wake of the September 11, 2001 terrorist attacks on New York City and Washington, D.C., Marcinko has been interviewed more than100 times for television and radio. The attacks and the U.S.'s ensuing war against the Taliban in Afghanistan prompted Marcinko to create a radio program, *America on Watch with Richard Marcinko*. The three-hour weekly show, which premiered on the Talk Radio Network on November 3, 2001, features such guests as Tom Ridge, the director of the federal Office of Homeland Security, and offers discussions of current world events and ways in which the U.S. can protect itself against potential terrorist activity. Marcinko has been negotiating with the action-film producer Jerry Bruckheimer to bring a *Rogue Warrior* movie to the big screen. "I'm very fortunate and very lucky that I go through life still being me," he told *Current Biography*. "Retiring didn't necessarily change me, and I'm able to work in the civilian arena without changing my tactics, only modifying it so it's better understood." — J.K.B.

Suggested Reading: *People* p155+ May 4, 1992, with photos; *Publishers Weekly* p51 Apr. 8, 1996; Marcinko, Richard, and John Weisman. *Rogue Warrior*, 1992

Selected Books: *Rogue Warrior* (with John Weisman), 1992; *Rogue Warrior II: Red Cell*, 1994; *Rogue Warrior: Green Team*, 1995; *Rogue Warrior: Task Force Blue*, 1996; *Leadership Secrets of the Rogue Warrior*, 1996; *Rogue Warrior: Designation Gold*, 1997; *The Rogue Warrior's Strategy for Success*, 1997; *Rogue Warrior: Seal Force Alpha*, 1998; *Rogue Warrior: Option Delta*, 1999; *The Real Team*, 1999; *Rogue Warrior: Echo Platoon*, 2000; *Rogue Warrior: Detachment Bravo*, 2001

Martin, Mark

Jan. 9, 1959– Race-car driver. Address: c/o Roush Sports Group, 235-10 Rolling Hills Rd., Mooresville, NC 28117

Blink, as the saying goes, and you might miss him. Averaging speeds of 150 to 160 miles per hour, race-car driver Mark Martin tears up the track, the number "6" painted on the side of his Ford Taurus becoming just a blur. Martin is one of the "perennial frontrunners, the drivers who simply refuse to lose," according to Juliet Macur in *TV Guide* (February 13, 1999). He has been at the pinnacle of the National Association of Stock Car Racing (NASCAR) circuit for a decade, logging more than 150,000 miles and winning millions of dollars in prize money. By the end of the 1999 season, Martin had finished nine times among the five highest scorers in the NASCAR Winston Cup Series. Macur attributed Martin's success to his "uncanny ability to focus," and Martin himself has admitted to being intensely competitive, barely savoring one win before thinking ahead to the next race. His determination and competitiveness have made him popular with the growing number of stock-car racing fans, who have in the past decade made NASCAR racing—which grew out of a culture of moonshine runs on dirt roads in souped-up cars—a $2 billion-a-year industry and the second-highest-rated sport on television, behind pro football.

Mark Martin was born on January 9, 1959 in Batesville, Arkansas. He inherited his love of speed from his father, who "always drove really

David Taylor/Allsport

Mark Martin

fast," as he told a reporter for the *That's Racin'* Web site (June 9, 1999). "I idolized and adored my father . . . ," he said. "He was enthusiastic about speed and controlling speed. I became enthusiastic, too." According to Martin, his father helped him get started in motor sports. By the age of 15, Martin was racing stock cars on the local Arkansas dirt tracks. He won a race in only his third start, and in the same year went on to win an Arkansas state junior championship. "When I started out I just wanted to race. Then, when I found out I could win, then I just wanted to win," Martin told the *That's Racin'* interviewer. "One of the greatest days of my [life] was the day I realized as a young man that I was going to be able to make a living racing cars, instead of working a job and racing cars on the weekend." During the next few years, Martin climbed the tiers of the sport, moving up to higher divisions and beginning to compete on asphalt tracks. In 1977 he began racing in the series organized by the American Speed Association (ASA), becoming Rookie of the Year that first season and winning the championship in each of the next three years.

In 1981 Martin made five appearances in the more prestigious NASCAR Winston Cup Races, and in the following year he drove his first full season, with a family-sponsored team. Although he had eight top-10 finishes that year, he never received payment. Short of funds, he was forced to auction off some of his racing equipment. Martin was able to return to the ASA series for the years 1984–86, pairing for the first time with crew chief Jimmy Fennig, who would later join Martin on a NASCAR team. In 1986 Martin won his fourth ASA Championship.

In 1987 Martin decided to take one more shot at the big leagues—NASCAR racing. He drove a full season in the NASCAR Busch Grand National Series for a car owner named Bruce Lawmaster. Winning a high-profile race at Dover Downs brought him to the attention of Jack Roush, an automobile engineer and racing fan, who was looking to put together a team for the 1988 NASCAR Winston Cup Series. "When I encountered Mark, he was hanging on by his fingernails just to stay in a ride in [the] Winston Cup," Roush told Mike Shropshire for *Sport* (July 1999). Roush appreciated Martin's commitment and his love of cars. "Mark was a hardware guy who was much more interested in how many cars we were going to build, what they were going to be like . . . than he was in how much money he was going to make," Roush recalled. Roush asked Martin to be his driver, and since then the two men have made a winning team, earning 31 Winston Cup victories for the Roush Valvoline team and finishing second in the points standings three times—in 1990, 1994, and 1998.

In 1989 Martin won his first Winston Cup race at the AC Delco 500, in Rockingham, North Carolina, and was duly named National Motorsports Press Association's Driver of the Year. In 1990 he finished second in the overall Winston Cup season, only 26 points—out of thousands—behind Dale Earnhardt. (The Winston Cup series is made up of many different races, and over the course of a season participants accumulate points for wins and pole positions. The Cup is awarded to the racer who has racked up the most points by the end of the full year's schedule of events.) Meanwhile, Martin kept up a part-time schedule in another NASCAR series, the Busch Grand National, in which he has amassed 40 career victories, more than any other driver in the series' history. Martin also won the International Race of Champions (IROC) series four times, in 1994, 1996, 1997, and 1998. For the IROC series, 12 of the world's best drivers compete against one another over four races. The drivers race in the same kind of car, in an attempt to level the playing field in terms of technology and to shift the focus of the race onto the skills of the drivers.

The Winston Cup title has become Martin's holy grail, if only because he has come so close so many times. "He's like Susan Lucci at the Daytime Emmy Awards. Pete Sampras at the French Open. The Utah Jazz in the NBA playoffs," Darrell Fry quipped in the *St. Petersburg Times* (April 12, 2000, on-line), alluding to the fact that the Cup seems inexplicably to elude Martin. A perennial front-runner, in a class with Jeff Gordon, Rusty Wallace, and Dale Jarrett, Martin has finished among the top five in points nine times in the past decade. "Fact is, Mark Martin's too good a driver not to have a Winston Cup title mounted to his hood yet," Shropshire wrote. In 1998 Martin logged his best racing year yet, earning $4.3 million and scoring more overall points in any one season than any driver since Cale Yarborough, in 1977. And yet, to the consternation of his many fans, Martin finished second in the Winston Cup that year, losing to Jeff Gordon.

Gordon and Martin are a study in contrasts. Competition pits Gordon's DuPont Chevy against Martin's Ford; Gordon's youth and boyish good looks against Martin's weather-beaten early middle age; Gordon's seemingly effortless success against Martin's years of struggle and scrappy determination. In 1995, at age 25, Jeff Gordon won the Winston Cup after only two years on the circuit, becoming the youngest racer ever to win the series. He won again in 1997 and in 1998. "Because Gordon bypassed a full apprenticeship at the dirt track minor leagues, in the minds of the stock car traditionalists his act still goes over like Frankie Avalon at a Tennessee turkey shoot," Shropshire wrote. By comparison, Martin is regarded by many as an unflagging fighter. "We didn't have the fastest car," Martin said after winning an upset victory in the Goody's 500, in April 2000, as quoted by Darrell Fry in the *St. Petersburg Times* (April 12, 2000, online), "but I ran like a dog." Fry agreed with that assessment, noting, "Everything Mark Martin has achieved in 18 years of running Winston Cup has come from being on his hands and knees."

After finishing second in a race in August 1998, Martin learned that his father, stepmother, and 11-year-old half-sister had been killed when their private plane crashed in Nevada. Though devastated by this loss, Martin continued to race impressively that year. In 1999 he was involved in a nasty car wreck in a Daytona race, further exacerbating his chronic back pain. Martin suffered from a condition called spondylolisthesis, in which a broken bone in his back causes pressure on the nerves there. In November 1999 Martin underwent lumbar fusion surgery, and after a few months of rehabilitation, he was back in action, his pain alleviated though not completely gone. "Even though he feels pain emotionally and physically, Mark is able to block it out when he needs to. That's what makes him so special," Roush Racing teammate Jeff Burton told Macur.

Martin has credited much of his success to his car and his crew of mechanics. In racing, just as driver competes against driver, pit crew races against pit crew, aiming for the speediest refueling stops, fastest tire changes (as many as 14 per race), and best on-the-fly adjustments and repairs. The cohesion of the team is crucial to success in the grueling Winston Cup schedule, which is made up of several races a month, 10 months a year. "I think the whole Valvoline team looks toward me for emotional leadership," Martin was quoted as saying on the Roush Racing Web site. "You can make a difference in the way your guys feel. They're burned out and they're tired and they have to re-energize every week. . . . I try to set a good example, but, honestly, [crew chief] Jimmy Fennig is the true leader of these guys. He's really the hero when it comes to leadership and keeping a good even-keel."

Martin has been driving a Ford Taurus since 1998. When he won the Las Vegas 400 that year, he became the first driver to win a Winston Cup race with that make of car. Jack Roush, the owner of Martin's team, worked as a Ford engineer in the 1960s—the era of the "muscle car"—and has a reputation for building winning engines. (In addition to owning five Winston Cup racing teams, Roush runs Roush Industries, which has done engineering and prototype services for every major American car company.) In an interview for *That's Racin'*, Martin described the many factors that contribute to winning a race, including a car's gas mileage, horsepower, and aerodynamics, a track's surface and number of turns, and of course luck. "It's my belief that sometimes there are full moons and sometimes there isn't," he said. Roush's engineers improve the stock cars by building lighter chassis (or supporting frames), improving aerodynamics through wind-tunnel research, and increasing fuel efficiency. "We're building stronger chassis that weigh less and engines that put out more horsepower and use less gas," Martin told the *That's Racin'* reporter. "That's why we break the track records almost every year. Cars will continue to go faster and faster and faster until they do something to hold us back."

Martin works on his own body as well. At only five feet six inches and 150 pounds, he is small for his sport; additional weight must be added to his car to reach the minimum 3,400 pounds. Martin maintains a strict racing diet of tuna, wheat bread, water, and pretzels, and is an avid weightlifter, with only 7 percent body fat. He believes this regimen gives him the strength and stamina needed for everyday acts of racing—such as gripping the wheel and dealing with adrenaline surges—and also for keeping his body pliant, making it more likely that he will walk away from an accident.

Martin lives in Daytona Beach, Florida, with his wife, Arlene, and their five children. He has said that because of all the hours he spends driving and fulfilling promotional obligations, he doesn't have as much time with his family as he would like. He has been able to pass on his love of racing to his only son; in May 2000 eight-year-old Matt won his first race in the junior Honda division, and his dad was there to watch. "It was fun because I wasn't his coach, or his crew chief, I was just his Dad," Martin told David Poole for the *Charlotte Observer* (May 12, 2000, on-line).

Martin was presented with the Hometown Hero and Professional Driver of the Year honors at the 2000 Florida Sports Awards. The Hometown Hero award, honoring athletes who help children in their communities, was given in recognition of Martin's work for the Big Brothers Big Sisters of America organization, for which he raised money and helped to lead a recruitment campaign for new mentors in 1999. For the first time in his career, Martin is now racing exclusively in the Winston Cup Series, still hoping for the elusive title. — M.A.H.

Suggested Reading: *St. Petersburg Times* (on-line) Apr. 12, 2000; *Sport* p74+ July 1999, with photos; *That's Racin'* (on-line) June 9, 1999; *TV Guide* p2+ Feb. 13, 1999, with photos

Steve Babineau/Allsport

Martinez, Pedro

Oct. 25, 1971– Baseball player. Address: Boston Red Sox, Fenway Park, 4 Yawkey Way, Boston, MA 02215

At five feet 11 inches and 170 pounds, the Boston Red Sox pitcher Pedro Martinez doesn't look intimidating. Nevertheless, in his 10 seasons in the major leagues, he has become one of the most feared pitchers in baseball. Martinez has been among the league leaders in strikeouts in the past few seasons and has won the Cy Young Award three times. According to the "Profile and Scouting Report" posted on the ESPN Web site (October 2, 1999), "Martinez has the best stuff in baseball. His stuff includes a 92–98 MPH fastball that sometimes seems as if it's skidding across ice. He throws his changeup with perfect arm speed and at a range of angles, so no hitter knows it's coming . . . He also throws his curveball from several different arm angles."

Pedro Martinez was born on October 25, 1971 in Manoguayabo, a small town in the Dominican Republic. His parents worked as civil servants and often had to struggle to support him and his five siblings. "I realize now how much they had to do without," Martinez told Mark Starr for *Newsweek* (April 6, 1998). "Everything was for us. Go to school, learn values, learn how to be a man and be

responsible. I never want to let them down." Like many Dominicans, Martinez loved American baseball. He grew up idolizing the Dominican-born Juan Marichal, an outstanding pitcher with the San Francisco Giants who was elected to the National Baseball Hall of Fame in 1983. Martinez developed his pitching skills by playing with his older brother, Ramon, who made his major-league debut as a pitcher with the Los Angeles Dodgers in 1988.

According to Starr, Ramon told the team's scouts about Pedro. As a result, in 1989 Pedro Martinez gained admission to the Dodger Academy in Santo Domingo. In an interview with Steve Marantz for the *Sporting News* (July 18, 1994), Martinez recalled that while at the academy, he would run to keep in shape. But one of the coaches wanted him to gain weight and threatened to fine him $500 if he was caught running. "But I know I have to keep in shape for pitching," Martinez said. "They let me run sprints and five laps. I wasn't completely comfortable with that. So I pay the security guard at night to let me run."

After two years at the Dodger Academy, Martinez came to the United States to join the Dodgers' organization in the minor leagues. He immediately showed promise: in the 1991 season he advanced to all three minor-league levels (Class A, Double A, and Triple A), and he achieved a combined win–loss record of 18–8. He also recorded 189 strikeouts in 177 innings while giving up 126 hits, and attained an earned-run average (ERA) of 2.28. That year the *Sporting News* named him Minor League Player of the Year. In 1992 Martinez made his major-league debut with the Dodgers, playing alongside his brother, Ramon, who was already an established star. Pedro played in only two games and was credited with one loss. In 1993 the Dodgers used him as a middle reliever. That year his win–loss record was 10–5, and his ERA 2.61. He also became one of the few pitchers with more strikeouts (119) than innings pitched (107).

On November 19, 1993 the Dodgers traded Martinez to the Montreal Expos for second baseman Delino DeShields. The Expos used Martinez as a starting pitcher. In the strike-shortened 1994 season, he won 11 games in 23 starts, and his ERA increased to 3.42. Eleven of his pitches hit batters, a number greater than that of any other National League pitcher in 1994. Indeed, early in that season he had developed a reputation as a "head-hunter"—a pitcher who deliberately tries to hit opposing batters. According to Tim Crothers in *Sports Illustrated* (May 26, 1997), Martinez's close pitches in the first two months of the season led to "three bench-clearing brawls and 12 player ejections." Martinez strongly denied allegations that he was deliberately trying to hit batters. "There's no rule in baseball that says you are not allowed to pitch on the inside corner or close to batters. You don't hit someone on purpose, which I'm not trying to do," he insisted to Marantz. "I'm a power pitcher. I'm supposed to go in and get people out. If I keep throwing over the middle and away, they hit it." Martinez also attributed the wildness of his pitches to his inexperience in the major leagues.

In 1995 Martinez posted 14 wins, but lost a career-high 10 games. His ERA was 3.51, and he recorded 174 strikeouts; again, his pitches hit 11 batsmen. On June 3, 1995, in the top of the 10th inning in a contest with the San Diego Padres, he missed his chance for what up to then had been a perfect game, by surrendering a double to Bip Roberts. Martinez was credited with the win when the Expos scored a run in the bottom of the 10th inning.

Martinez displayed better control in the 1996 season, in which he won 13 games and lost 10. He struck out 222 batters and hit only three. One of the three was Gregg Jeffries of the Philadelphia Phillies, whom he hit during a game on September 24, 1996. Later, when Martinez came up to bat, the Phillies' pitcher Mike Williams retaliated by trying to hit him twice. In response, Martinez charged the mound, an infraction that led to his suspension for eight games.

Martinez enjoyed a successful season in 1997. He won 17 games while losing only eight. His ERA decreased to a career low—and 1997 National League low—of 1.90. He also struck out 305 batters in 241 innings. In *Sports Illustrated* (April 20, 1998), Gerry Callahan noted that Martinez was the first pitcher since the Washington Senators' Walter Johnson, in 1912, to record more than 300 strikeouts and an ERA lower than 2.00 in the same season. On July 13, 1997 Martinez pitched a shut-out against the Cincinnati Reds while giving up only one hit. His performance during the season earned him the National League Cy Young Award. (Later, in January 1998, during a banquet in Boston, Martinez presented his Cy Young Award to Juan Marichal. According to Callahan, Martinez believed that Marichal should have won the coveted award during his career. While the two were flying back together to the Dominican Republic, Marichal returned the award to Martinez.) With Martinez now considered a hot commodity, the Montreal Expos' management believed that they would not be able to afford to retain him after his contract expired, at the end of the 1998 season. Taking action before he could sign a more lucrative contract with another team, on November 18, 1997 the Expos traded Martinez to the Boston Red Sox for the pitchers Carl Pavano and Tony Armas Jr. The Red Sox, apparently eager to keep Martinez, signed him to a six-year, $75 million contract, making him one of the highest-paid players in baseball. A few months later he attended the reopening of a church in his hometown that had been destroyed by fire and that had been rebuilt with money that he had donated. The ceremony "was better than the Cy Young, better than the new contract," Martinez told Callahan. "The people mobbed me and hugged me. The priest blessed me. Everyone had tears in their eyes. It was unbelievable."

Martinez got a warm reception from Boston fans during the 1998 season. Whenever he pitched at Fenway Park, people in the stands cheered him enthusiastically. "It makes me feel good to play for people who eat, drink, and sleep baseball," Martinez told Starr. His record in 1998 was 19-7, with a 2.89 ERA and 251 strikeouts. In the postseason Martinez won the first game of the American League divisional play-offs against the Cleveland Indians, striking out eight batters in seven innings. The Red Sox then lost the next three games, and thus the series, to the Indians. Despite Martinez's formidable statistics, Roger Clemens of the Toronto Blue Jays won the Cy Young Award, having posted slightly better numbers in the categories of wins, strikeouts, and ERA.

Pedro Martinez was pleased when, in 1999, the Red Sox acquired his brother, Ramon, in a trade. The two had not played together since 1993, when both were with the Dodgers. Pedro Martinez posted phenomenal numbers in 1999, leading the American League in wins (23), ERA (2.07), and strikeouts (313). Martinez also won his second Cy Young Award. During the All-Star Game, he struck out five batters and was named the game's Most Valuable Player (MVP). On September 10, 1999 he pitched his best game of the season, striking out a career-high 17 batters during a contest with the New York Yankees. In the postseason the Red Sox faced the Indians once again in divisional play-offs. Martinez started the first game, against the Indians, but he was forced to leave in the fifth inning after he strained his back. The Red Sox lost, 3–2. After losing the second game, the Red Sox made a dramatic comeback, winning the next two games. In the fourth inning of Game 5, after the Indians had pounded the Red Sox pitchers Bret Saberhagen and Derek Lowe for eight runs, the Red Sox brought in Martinez. As the Red Sox's batters chipped away at the Indians' lead, Martinez pitched six scoreless innings and struck out eight batters. The Red Sox came from behind to win the game, 12–8, and the series. In an interview with *Sports Illustrated* (October 12, 1999, on-line), Red Sox pitching coach Jim Kerrigan described Martinez's pitching during the game as "one of the most heroic, gutsy performances I've ever seen." In the American League Championship Series, the Red Sox faced their arch-rivals, the New York Yankees. Once again, the Red Sox's hopes of winning their first World Series since 1918 were dashed when the Yankees defeated them, four games to one. In his only appearance, Martinez won Game 3, pitching seven scoreless innings and striking out 12 batters.

An incident that occurred on April 30, 2000 marred an otherwise successful season for Martinez. In the bottom of the seventh inning of the game that Martinez was pitching that day, a ball pitched by the Cleveland Indians' Charles Nagy hit the Red Sox batter Jose Offerman. Players from both benches immediately ran onto the field, but the umpires prevented a fight. The umpire Tim

Tschida warned both teams that pitchers would be ejected immediately if there was any further trouble. He followed through on that threat the next inning, after Martinez hit the batter Roberto Alomar with a ball. The league then suspended Martinez for five games. As for his statistics during the 2000 season, his wins for the year dropped to 18, but he reached a career-low 1.74 ERA and struck out 284 batters in 217 innings. For the third time in his career, Martinez won the Cy Young Award. The Red Sox, however, failed to make it to the postseason.

The Red Sox's acquisition of the outfielder and power hitter Manny Ramirez in December 2000 led several sportswriters—and the team's legion of devoted but chronically heartbroken fans—to entertain the notion that in 2001 Boston might win its first World Series since 1918. But troubles soon arose. Injuries sidelined Martinez and the star shortstop Nomar Garciaparra for most of the season. The Red Sox placed Martinez on the disabled list in late June, after he tore a rotator cuff muscle in one of his shoulders. Although he was expected to return to the starting rotation in a few weeks, the injury turned out to be more serious than had originally been thought; it kept him off the pitcher's mound for two months. Despite the absence of Martinez and Garciaparra and injuries to other players, for some time the Red Sox managed to keep pace with the first-place Yankees. When Martinez started pitching again, in late August, he felt some discomfort in his shoulder. The Red Sox team physician attributed it to lingering inflammation—a diagnosis with which Martinez disagreed. He sought a second opinion from Lewis Yocum, the team physician for the Anaheim Angels, who announced that Martinez had a minor tear in his shoulder muscle. That finding led to a much-publicized dispute between Martinez and the Red Sox management. Dan Duquette, the team's general manager, declared publicly that Martinez was perfectly healthy and should continue pitching, because "we are paying him a lot of money," as Bob Hohler quoted him as saying in the Boston Globe (September 5, 2001). Outraged by Duquette's comments, Martinez told Hohler, "What I don't appreciate is Duquette saying I'm healthy because, dammit, it's not true. I'm doing the best I can to help the team. I don't need to be pushed." In mid-September the Red Sox placed him back on the disabled list, and his season came to an end. In 18 starts Martinez had finished 7–3 with a 2.39 ERA. The Red Sox ended the season 13.5 games behind the Yankees.

Although Martinez is one of the best pitchers in baseball today, he remains modest and friendly. According to Callahan, he never refuses requests for interviews or autographs. In a conversation with Charles Pierce for Esquire (June 1998), he declared, "What do I mean when I say I pitch from my heart? It means something inside me—a feeling I get. It's in my blood, my body. It's not the money. The money, it never steps inside the white lines. It's my pride, my name. My family's name. My rep-

utation. That's worth more than the $75 million they're paying me." — D.C.

Suggested Reading: *baseball-reference.com*; *Boston Globe* C p1+ Sep. 5, 2001, with photo; Boston Red Sox Web site; *Esquire* p48+ June 1998; *Newsweek* p57 Apr. 6, 1998; *Sporting News* p12+ July 18, 1994; *Sports Illustrated* p38+ Apr. 20, 1998

Courtesy of Teledesic LLC

McCaw, Craig

Aug. 11, 1949– Businessman. Address: Teledesic Corp., 2300 Carton Pt., Kirkland, WA 98033-2127

The telecommunications mogul Craig McCaw is not only one of the major innovators of the cellular-phone industry: he is among the current leaders of what has come to be known as the Information Age, quietly launching a project aimed at connecting people from around the world through services unimaginable only a decade ago. His plan is for a global satellite system that would make it possible for communities without telephone connections to have Internet access, E-mail, and cellular services. Such a system, McCaw feels, would help to end what he perceives as one of the negative aspects of the Industrial Age—the marginalization of Third World societies. "We recognize that we can do something really good and, by the way, not have it viewed as some charitable project that will require someone to pour in huge amounts of money," he told Peter Elstrom for *Business Week* (September 28, 1998, on-line). "It's absolutely the right thing for the world and a good thing for us." Now a multibillionaire, thanks to the sale of his pioneering national cellular service to AT&T in 1994, McCaw has increased his fortune still further through his holdings in the various communications companies he has formed.

Craig Oliver McCaw was born on August 11, 1949 in Centralia, Washington, the second of the four sons of J. Elroy and Marion McCaw. Elroy McCaw, a pioneer in radio and television, had established an empire of media holdings. Among many other acts for which he was famous, he purchased the radio station WINS in New York City and turned it into the first rock and roll station in the United States. Craig McCaw grew up in the posh Highlands district of Seattle, Washington, in the Boeing mansion (an official historical landmark), which his parents owned. As a boy, McCaw had difficulty with his studies and was soon diagnosed as dyslexic. "Growing up, I had trouble fitting in," McCaw was quoted as saying by Brian E. Taptich in the *Alarm Clock* (on-line). "As a dyslexic, I don't think like other people, so I didn't fit very well in a clique." "Dyslexia forced me to be quite conceptual, because I'm not very good at details," he said at his 1997 induction into the Academy of Achievement, as quoted by Taptich. "And because I'm not good at details, I tend to be rather spatial in my thinking—oriented to things in general terms, rather than the specific. That allows you to step back and take in the big picture. I feel blessed about that."

At the age of 16, McCaw held his first job, selling subscriptions for his father's Seattle-based cable company during the summer in return for his first flying lessons, which his parents paid for. Known as a serious and focused teenager, McCaw attended Stanford University, in Palo Alto, California, where he tried—but failed—to take over the vending-machine business that serviced the school. His attempt to operate a small aircraft firm also failed.

In 1969 Elroy McCaw died of a stroke, at the age of 57, while Craig was home from college on a break. That blow was followed by another: the family's discovery that the McCaw media empire had amassed staggering debt. After the Internal Revenue Service and other creditors completed their dealings with the McCaw estate, the family was left with one cable-television company, Twin Cities Cablevision, and a life-insurance payment of $2 million, a small sum in comparison with the family's onetime fortune. After his father's death Craig McCaw took a year off from college to help his mother handle both financial burdens and emotional problems. He then returned to Stanford, where, with his mother's guidance, he ran Twin Cities—left in a trust to him and his brothers—from his dorm room. McCaw took a lesson from the debt his father had accumulated. "I'm picky about the people I do business with," he told Quentin Hardy for *Forbes* (June 12, 2000). "[My father] wasn't picky. I learned to be fastidious about accounting, to be careful about the ethical nature of people. And to keep things simple, to focus on quality."

In 1973 McCaw received a B.A. degree in history from Stanford and set out to restore his family's fortune. Under his leadership Twin City Cablevision began buying remote cable operations, and by cutting costs, raising rates, and expanding and improving service, the company started turning a profit. During this period McCaw began his well-known practice of securing large loans based on even larger expected profits. With their cable business worth $3 million in annual revenue, he and his brothers took out a $10 million loan at 22 percent interest to purchase new cable properties. In 1980 they sold half of their company to Affiliated Publications Inc. for $12 million in order to fund new ventures. Among those was McCaw Cellular Communications, a cellular-phone service company. Although the cellular-phone market was quite small in the early 1980s, McCaw was optimistic. "It seemed to me that if it could be done right and in a big way, cellular phones would be worth a fortune," he told Anthony Ramirez for the *New York Times* (November 15, 1992).

After losing bids to become a carrier for specific cellular territories, McCaw began aggressively purchasing cellular services. Over the course of the decade, both the cable and cellular businesses boomed. By 1988 McCaw Cellular Communications was operating in 127 U.S. cities and had a potential base of 48 million customers; meanwhile, as of 1987, the cable company begun by McCaw's father ranked as the 20th largest in the world. But both businesses needed large infusions of capital to continue to prosper, as there were no more cheap cable systems to be acquired. Deciding to focus on cellular phones, McCaw sold the cable company to the Washington Redskins' owner, Jack Kent Cooke, in 1987 for $755 million. Meanwhile, he continued to purchase cellular companies. In 1990 he obtained 52 percent of Lin Broadcasting, one of the largest cellular companies in the United States and one with access to the profitable New York City market. That year McCaw Cellular reported $1.4 million in revenue with over two million subscribers.

In 1991 Craig McCaw announced that McCaw Cellular had combined its properties in the four largest cellular regions of the country; this was the first move toward a national network, which would be marketed under the name Cellular One. Optimism was tempered, however, by the fact that in the process of acquiring its vast number of cellular properties, McCaw Cellular had racked up $5 billion in debt. To keep the company solvent, McCaw had already sold 22 percent of it to British Telecom. With investors made nervous by the enormous risk he had taken, and with the recession of the early 1990s cutting into revenue growth, McCaw Cellular's stock price dropped by around two-thirds. The company's financial situation was helped slightly by AT&T, which in 1992 bought one-third of McCaw Cellular for $3.8 billion. McCaw, who was the chairman of his company, then decided—against his own instincts: he had faith in his firm and still wanted to lead it—to sell the company to AT&T in 1994 for $11.5 billion, at the time the largest telecommunications merger ever. In order to concentrate on other projects, he declined to join the AT&T board of directors. (His brothers had owned stock in McCaw Cellular but had not held jobs within the company.)

With that sale completed, McCaw formed a holding company, Eagle River, to manage the McCaw family's money. In 1995 he started focusing his attention on another small holding company, Fiberlink, which had been part of McCaw Cellular and was retained by McCaw after the AT&T deal. Renaming the company Nextlink, McCaw turned it into a local phone-service supplier before expanding it into a major broadband provider, which currently serves as a prominent supplier of Internet services. "It's the best thing I have ever done," McCaw told Quentin Hardy. Nextlink, which serves mainly large businesses, saw its market value soar from $1 billion to $10 billion in less than three years, as it became known for quality customer assistance and low prices. In 1998 McCaw, through his Internext company, agreed to pay Level 3 Communications $700 million in exchange for 25 percent of the $10 billion global fiber network the company was building. Level 3 now runs a 16,000-mile fiber-optic network that is able to handle more than 300 million voice conversations at once and is used by Nextlink.

At around the same time as the Level 3 deal, McCaw also formed Nextband Communications LLC, which planned to offer high-speed Internet connections over radio waves to offices that could not be reached in a cost-effective fashion by current satellite or fiber connections. In addition, he made a deal with Nextel, previously a series of radio networks used by taxi dispatchers and those in similar jobs. In return for 26 percent of the company's stock, McCaw agreed to put $1.1 billion into the company over a six-year period. After the deal was completed, McCaw was able to persuade the hardware manufacturer Motorola to improve the sound quality of the company's service. He hired Dan Akerson to run Nextel; Akerson reduced the number of pricing plans and refocused the service for workers who wanted cellular phones that could double as walkie-talkies. By 2000 Nextel had grown from 340,000 customers to 5.6 million.

By far the most elaborate of McCaw's plans to date involves Teledesic, the telecommunications company he formed in 1990. In 1994 McCaw and his friend Bill Gates, the founder and CEO of Microsoft, announced that they had each put up $5 million for Teledesic to launch a satellite network that would provide Internet, cellular-phone, and E-mail service throughout the world with the use of low-flying satellites. At the same time the two businessmen announced that the network would be in place by 2001 and would generate over a half-billion dollars in revenue in its first year of service alone. After five years, they predicted, that number would jump to $6.5 billion. While many

saw the idea as little more than a pipe dream—and a highly expensive one at that—McCaw continued to seek investors, and by the start of 2001 he had raised over $1.5 billion of the estimated $9 billion it would take to launch the system. According to current estimates, the company will launch 288 communications satellites, which will be stationed 800 miles above the earth's surface. Each satellite will cover a specific area of the planet and be able to transmit large amounts of data to any destination in the world. Although Iridium LLC and ICO Global Communications, the network's already-existing competitors (both plan to launch communications satellites), filed for bankruptcy in August 1999, McCaw has remained positive about the future of such projects; in November 1999 he invested $500 million in ICO. "It is our hope that by working with ICO's team and international partners we can bring the company back to good health and make a contribution to global communications, particularly in the developing world," McCaw was quoted a saying by *Internetwire* (November 11, 1999, on-line). "We recognise that this is a big job and that there's a lot of work ahead of us. Our investment in ICO marks the first step in our strategy to widen the technological tools at our disposal and serve a broader group of customers."

McCaw hopes that the satellite project will help to revitalize the economies of Third World nations and, in doing so, help preserve indigenous cultures. According to the company's vision, an antenna dish only a few feet in diameter could provide any town or individual with telephone service, E-mail capability, and the ability to hold video conferences via the Internet. Since about half of the world's people live in countries with less than one telephone line per 100 inhabitants, the implications of McCaw's plan are mind-boggling. "Take a poor village in Guatemala," McCaw explained to an interviewer for *Fortune*, as quoted by Brian Taptich. "They have electricity; they have television; they see our riches and they want them. But where they are, they cannot have them. They don't have communications, and they don't have the tools to make money. Yet they have crops or they weave blankets, things that could be quite valuable if there were not so many middlemen. Indigenous societies would be able to survive, rather than disintegrate as young men and women leave to seek work in the city."

McCaw's net worth is estimated at roughly $1 billion. As the telecommunications market experienced a severe downturn in 2001, McCaw sold many of the possessions he had accumulated during the 1990s, including three houses, three jets, a private island, and his 300-foot yacht. Meanwhile, stock prices of Nextel and XO Communications (the name of the company formed by the merger in 2000 of Nextlink and Concentric Networks) fell to all-time lows. In 2000 McCaw formed the One World Challenge syndicate, a team that includes designers and sailors, to compete for the America's Cup in New Zealand in 2002–03. He was married to his college sweetheart, Wendy Petrack, for 21 years; the couple divorced in 1997. In February 1998 McCaw married Susan Rasinski, a former San Francisco investment banker, with whom he has two children. He is known for being shy and reclusive and also for being eccentric by the standards of the business world. He often talks about the risks of technology as well as the benefits, or discusses how best to strike a balance between work and the rest of life. Sometimes, feeling bored by the confines of the office, he works instead on one of his yachts or at home; on occasion he has started water-gun fights with his colleagues. He once suggested to government regulators that they reserve the radio spectrum for telepathic communication. He has been known to hold his hands up in his office to feel the auras of the people around him.

A major donator to charity, McCaw gave $1 million in 1997 to the Seattle public schools, the largest such gift in the history of Washington State. In 1998 he sponsored the release of the killer whale Keiko (featured in the movie *Free Willy*) from captivity at Sea World. Before Keiko was released, McCaw was allowed to swim briefly with the animal, an experience that he later called "the greatest . . . of my life," as quoted by Brian Taptich. Also in 1998 he tried to stop a whale hunt by the Makah, an American Indian tribe whose reservation is in Washington State, and he donated $15 million to the charity run by the former South African president Nelson Mandela. McCaw lives in Washington with his family. "I'd just as soon be retired," he told Peter Elstrom, "but that doesn't seem to happen. We just keep having these ideas." — G.O.

Suggested Reading: *Alarm Clock* (on-line); *Business Week* (on-line) Sep. 28, 1998; *Forbes* p. 72+ June 12, 2000, with photos; *New York Times* III p5 Nov. 15, 1992, with photo, III p1+ June 4, 2000, with photo, C p1+ Sep. 28, 2001, with photo

Fred Ernst/Reuters/Hulton/Archive

McDonald, Gabrielle Kirk

Apr. 12, 1942– Judge. Address: Women's Division, National Bar Association, 1225 11th St., N.W., Washington, DC 20001

As a judge of the International Criminal Tribunal for the Former Yugoslavia (ICTY), Gabrielle Kirk McDonald presided over the first international war-crimes proceedings since those held at Nuremberg, Germany, at the end of World War II. In 1996 she led a three-judge panel in an historic trial that convicted Dusan Tadic, a Bosnian prison guard, of rape, torture, and murder. Four years later she took the helm of the Women's International War Crimes Tribunal on Japan's Military Sexual Slavery. From the beginning of her career, when she upheld civil-rights laws in the South as an attorney for the National Association for the Advancement of Colored People (NAACP), to her work on the ICTY and the tribunal for the Japanese military, McDonald has gained the respect and support of her colleagues. On April 5, 1999 then–secretary of state Madeleine Albright, at a dinner hosted by the American Bar Association, said of McDonald, "I am profoundly in her debt; as are we all, as well as the people of the Balkans, and people everywhere who love truth and seek to do right." McDonald is currently special counsel to the chairman of Freeport-McMoRan Copper & Gold Inc., a position in which she advises the firm on human-rights issues.

The daughter of a railroad worker, Gabrielle Kirk McDonald was born on April 12, 1942 in St. Paul, Minnesota. Her parents divorced when she was young, and she and her sibling moved to New York City with their mother, Frances, a light-skinned woman whose mother was Swedish and whose father was a black American. In New York McDonald was exposed to racial prejudice for the first time. A landlord, on discovering that Frances's children were black, tried unsuccessfully to force the family out of their residence, and workers in the local beauty parlor objected to working with McDonald's hair—but were forced to do so when her mother held her ground. Racial attitudes also led to McDonald's getting into fistfights, which she "did not like and did not win," as Kitty Felde put it in an on-line profile of the judge. Inspired by her mother's example, however, she was determined to fight racism in her own way, "using her brains instead of her fists," as Felde phrased it.

McDonald studied at Boston University and Hunter College, in Manhattan, but did not earn an undergraduate degree from either school. She nonetheless enrolled at Howard University Law School, in Washington, D.C., in 1966, graduating first in her class. From 1969 to 1979 she was a founding partner—along with her then-husband, Mark McDonald—in the Houston, Texas, law firm of McDonald & McDonald, where she specialized in plaintiffs' discrimination cases. As Kitty Felde reported, the firm's most significant win was a settlement for $1.2 million in back wages for 400 workers at the Lone Star Steel Co. McDonald also joined a group of young lawyers at the NAACP Legal Defense and Education Fund, helping to win the first major legal victory against employment discrimination under the 1964 Civil Rights Act. That 1967 case involved a suit against the Philip Morris Co., which had been accused of hiring black workers only for ill-paying, tedious, dead-end jobs, such as preparing tobacco leaves for processing. McDonald believes that her experiences during this period contributed greatly to her ability to oversee the International Criminal Tribunal for the Former Yugoslavia. "I learned a lot from the civil rights movement. There we were dealing with a minority and with confrontation. And at that time we got new laws and we had to use them to enable people to live and work together," she told Marlise Simons for the *New York Times* (January 13, 1999).

In 1979 McDonald was appointed a federal district court judge by President Jimmy Carter, making her the first African-American on the Texas federal bench and the third female African-American federal judge in the nation. One of her highest-profile cases involved harassment of immigrant Vietnamese shrimp fishermen by the Ku Klux Klan. During the trial McDonald and her family received death threats and were sent one-way tickets to Africa; the Grand Dragon of the local Ku Klux Klan told the judge that she should be removed from his case because he could not get a fair trial from "a Negress." "Of course he got nowhere," McDonald told Marlise Simons. "I said that if race was an issue, then being white was an issue too. I may be a Negress, but I'm a Negress with a black robe and the gavel and the law." McDonald closed down the Klan's paramilitary camps and ordered the group to cease its harassment of the fishermen.

McDonald left the federal court in 1988 to teach law at St. Mary's University Law School, in San Antonio, Texas, and Texas Southern University, in Houston. She returned to the bench in 1993, when the U.S. Department of State recommended her for a spot on the judicial panel for the Yugoslavia tribunal, which then numbered 11 judges. The tribunal was created to try those charged with war crimes during and after the breakup of the former Yugoslavia. Yugoslavia had been comprised of six constituent republics, born in the aftermath of World War II; one of them, Bosnia and Herzegovi-

na, gained independent statehood in 1992. Following this development the Bosnian Serbs carried out a campaign that came to be known as "ethnic cleansing" against the Bosnian Muslims, who outnumbered the Bosnian Serbs but were poorly armed. Elected to the tribunal by the U.N. General Assembly with the largest number of votes of those chosen, McDonald was selected to preside over the tribunal's first trial, the first in half a century in which a person was tried by an international court. The defendant was Dusan Tadic, a Bosnian Serb karate teacher who stood accused of killing two Muslim policemen and beating, raping, and torturing prisoners at local prison camps. On May 7, 1997 McDonald and two of her judicial colleagues, Judge Ninian Stephen from Australia and Judge Lal Vohrah from Malaysia, found Tadic guilty of 11 counts of crimes against humanity. Sentencing Tadic to 20 years in prison, McDonald told him in a voice that betrayed emotion, as quoted in Kitty Felde's on-line profile, "You must bear responsibility for your criminal conduct. To condone your actions even when committed in this context . . . is to give effect to a base view of morality and invite anarchy."

During the time that McDonald served on the tribunal for the former Yugoslavia, more than 90 people were indicted for genocide, war crimes, or crimes against humanity. Deflecting criticism that those tried at the time did not include some of the war's most prominent villains, she told Marlise Simons, "I've never heard a witness say, 'That person is not important enough.' I've never heard a victim say, 'I want someone with a higher rank.' Every individual wants justice in their own case." Discussing the approach taken by the tribunal, McDonald explained to Kitty Felde for the *Los Angeles Times* (February 7, 1999, on-line), "The theory is, and I believe in it, that you focus on personal accountability, individual accountability. Again, borrowing from the Nuremberg concept, that in order to avoid group stigmatization, you look at individuals and try individuals." She lamented the fact that the United States was one of the seven nations to oppose the treaty that would have created a permanent International Criminal Court (ICC), telling Kitty Felde, "It's important for the United States to be a part of the world community. The United States is the superpower, and its absence is sad to me." In 1997 she was elected president of the ICTY, succeeding Judge Antonio Cassese of Italy. Her appointment as president meant that each of the tribunal's three main sections was headed by a woman; Louise Arbour, from Canada, served as chief prosecutor, and Dorothee de Sampayo, of Holland, was the registrar and chief administrative officer. During this time McDonald oversaw the appeals chamber for the International Criminal Tribunal of Rwanda. McDonald's six-year term on the Yugoslavia tribunal ended in November 1999.

While she remained a proponent of the international court, she was critical of many aspects of it, specifically its lack of a police force. "The ICC Statute has established rigorous requirements for the Court's judges, including standards of expertise in criminal and international law, as well as judicial experience," McDonald said, addressing the Preparatory Commission for the International Criminal Court on July 30, 1999, as quoted on the United Nations Web site. "You can, therefore, assume that the Court will have experienced and capable judges who will have the skills to address developments as they occur or evolve. My advice is: trust them, don't tie their hands. The judges are responsible for conducting the trials and the appeals that will be the work of the court, and it is the judges who will control the proceedings. For the judges to effectively manage and direct the proceedings, the rules must be sufficiently flexible to allow them to exercise discretion when necessary. They must allow the judges to address evolving situations and respond to issues that could not be anticipated during the drafting process."

During December 7–12, 2000 McDonald headed the Women's International War Crimes Tribunal on Japan's Military Sexual Slavery, established to seek redress against the Japanese government for acts of sexual violence committed against "comfort women" during the Asia-Pacific War and not prosecuted by the International Military Tribunal for the Far East. The aim of McDonald and her fellow judges was to make advances toward the recognition of gender-based violence committed against women in times of armed conflict. The judges declared that the Japanese government owed apologies and reparations for these crimes.

McDonald is a member of the board of directors of Freeport-McMoRan Copper & Gold Inc., which mines copper in Indonesia and Indonesian territories and smelts and refines the metal in Spain. As special counsel to the chairman, she guided Freeport-McMoRan's adoption of policies that are sensitive to the social and economic needs and human rights of the people living in its areas of operation. With her encouragement, in December 2000 the corporation endorsed the joint U.S. State Department–British Foreign Office Voluntary Principles on Human Rights and Security, which "guide companies in maintaining the safety and security of their operations within an operating framework that ensures respect for human rights and fundamental freedoms" and call for continuing evaluation of those activities, according to a statement issued that month by the Bureau of Democracy, Human Rights, and Labor of the U.S. State Department. According to an on-line bio of McDonald on the Web site of Freeport-McMoRan (which is known as FCX on the stock exchange), McDonald is currently practicing "corporate responsibility law" in New York.

Kitty Felde described McDonald in the Los Angeles Times article as "a tall, elegant woman who laughs easily and often and seems to mother everyone in her circle." In 2001 McDonald was honored by the American Bar Association Commission on Women in the Profession with its Margret Brent

Women Lawyers of Achievement Award. She is the founder of the Women's Division of the National Bar Association. McDonald has two grown children, Michael and Stacy, who are both lawyers. — A.T.

Suggested Reading: New York Times p4+ Jan. 13, 1999, with photos, p7+ Nov. 9, 1999, with photos; Time (on-line) July 28, 1997; Washington Post p26+ Nov. 9, 1999, with photos

---

McGruder, Aaron

1974(?)– Cartoonist; creator of the comid strip The Boondocks. Address: c/o Universal Press Syndicate, 919 N. Michigan Ave., Chicago, IL 60611-1681

As the creator of *The Boondocks*, an edgy, nationally syndicated comic strip influenced by hip-hop culture, Aaron McGruder has managed to inject new life into the funny pages. At first, the reaction among readers unaccustomed to seeing racial politics portrayed in the timeless and often childlike world of the comic strip was something close to shock: according to Christina Denardo in the *ASNE Reporter* (April 2, 2001), the *Los Angeles Times* was swamped with complaints after it first ran *The Boondocks*, and a poll conducted by the *Pittsburgh Post-Gazette* a year after it started running the strip revealed that 70 percent of that paper's readers favored giving *The Boondocks* the axe. Nevertheless, as readers grew accustomed to McGruder's work, most began to warm to the strip: today *The Boondocks* boasts a loyal and diverse following (especially among younger readers), and there is even talk of a one-hour animated TV show. "It's very exciting to see a strip of that quality artistically with writing that strong from someone so young," Lucy Shelton Caldwell, the curator of the Ohio State Cartoon Research Library, said, as quoted by David Astor in *Editor & Publisher* (April 17, 1999). "What these characters signify," John Simpkins wrote for the *New York Times Magazine* (June 24, 2001), "has proved to be equally enlightening and uncomfortable for black and white people alike."

The Boondocks focuses on the daily lives of Huey Freeman, named after Huey Newton of the Black Panthers, and his little brother, Riley, two African-American kids transplanted from their inner-city Chicago neighborhood to a tony, largely white suburb—the "boondocks" of the strip's title. Huey, as his name suggests, is a budding radical; Riley is a "gangsta" wannabe. Supporting characters include Jazmine, a biracial girl; Caesar, a friend from Brooklyn; and Hiro, a Japanese hip-hop fan.

Like Huey and Riley, McGruder, born Aaron Vincent McGruder in about 1974, moved from Chicago to a predominately white suburb—in McGruder's case, to Columbia, Maryland, where

Aaron McGruder

Courtesy of Aaron McGruder

his parents (Bill, a communications specialist, and Elaine, a homemaker) still live. As McGruder is quick to admit, *The Boondocks* draws extensively on his own childhood experiences. "A lot of me comes out in the strip," he told *People* magazine (July 26, 1999). "There are themes of interracial and intraracial alienation, and on top of that some childhood silliness." McGruder has said that the intimidation he experienced as one of the few blacks in his suburban neighborhood was acute. "When you grow up black in the suburbs," the cartoonist told David Astor, "everybody's very kind about their racism, but you know it's there."

As a child, McGruder was an avid comic-book fan as well as a devotee of the *Star Wars* film trilogy. As for newspaper comic strips, he was particularly inspired, he has said, by Berke Breathed's *Bloom County*, Bill Watterson's *Calvin and Hobbes*, and Charles Schulz's *Peanuts*. "*Calvin and Hobbes* is just the best comic strip ever," McGruder told Tom Scocca and Vincent Williams in an interview for the *Baltimore Citypaper* (February 9, 2000, on-line). "And *Peanuts*—*Peanuts* transcends the form. My first exposure, as a small child, to comics was through the *Peanuts* cartoons." (Speaking with Astor, McGruder said he was especially impressed by the "depth of emotion" of Schulz's characters.) Later, McGruder discovered *manga*, a form of Japanese comics that is generally more elaborate and more varied than American comics, and *anime*, the animated series based on them. As numerous readers have pointed out, the illustrative style of *The Boondocks* is greatly indebted to Japanese *manga*.

McGruder attended the University of Maryland, where he majored in Afro-American studies and graduated in 1997, having written a thesis on black

cartoonists. According to the Web site of the African American Literature Book Club (AALBC), the strip was born when McGruder, "dissatisfied with both college and the comic book world," began "playing with the idea of creating a 'black' comic strip—inspired by his love of hip hop and saturated with political and racial satire." *The Boondocks* first appeared in February 1996 on a Web site; within a few months, it had migrated to the *Diamondback*, the University of Maryland's student-run daily paper. After a run of several months in the *Diamondback*, *The Boondocks* also made a brief appearance in the *Source*, a hip-hop magazine. (It was eventually discontinued there because of "legal and contractual disagreements," according to the *Boondocks* Web site.) In 1998 McGruder offered to sell his strip to a number of national syndicates. Several turned it down before Universal Press Syndicate offered McGruder a five-year contract, in December 1998. "The editors were blown away by the artwork," Kathie Kerr, director of communications for Universal Press Syndicate, recalled, as quoted by F. Romall Smalls in *Black Enterprise* (July 2000). "It brought a sense of diversity to the comic pages, and its consistent humor appeals to a younger audience that newspapers want."

The Boondocks entered syndication on April 19, 1999, appearing in about 160 newspapers nationwide—a number that surpasses the first-run figures of such well-known comic strips as *Doonesbury* and *Calvin and Hobbes*. "The reality is that the first two or three months, I was like, 'This [expletive] ain't gonna last. Let me go kamikaze hard and just say a whole bunch of stuff I've been meaning to say before I get canceled,'" McGruder told Jon Caramanica for *Vibe* (July

2001). "Then I *didn't* get canceled." A number of early installments, however, did elicit angry letters from upset readers—among them, blacks who charged the cartoonist with perpetuating negative stereotypes, whites who felt that he was bashing them, and multiracial advocates who accused him of intolerance toward interracial marriage and mixed-race people. In response, McGruder said that his critics suffered from "irony deficiency." "The focus of the strip is race," he told N'Gai Croal for *Newsweek* (July 5, 1999), "just like the focus of *Dilbert* is cubicles." Although two papers canceled the strip, and a number of others, including the *Atlanta Journal-Constitution*, transferred it to the editorial pages, the extra publicity ultimately served to boost the distribution of *The Boondocks*: within six months, the strip was running in about 200 newspapers. Today, that figure stands at about 250.

Recently, McGruder has been focusing more on the commercial possibilities of *The Boondocks*. He has published two anthologies of his strip, *The Boondocks: Because I Know You Don't Read the Newspaper* (2000) and *Fresh for '01 . . . You Suckas* (2001); he is planning an animated *Boondocks* TV series; and according to the AALBC Web site, T-shirts and posters are also in the works. "The *Boondocks* has had a very strong start in a very shaky business," McGruder told Smalls. "It is time to take it to the next level. If you are pursuing art, you have to be prepared to handle it like a business, a commodity. You have to be able to sell it." McGruder recently moved to Los Angeles in order to better promote the strip.

McGruder has continued to court controversy in recent months as well—though not always intentionally, he has said. One strip, which featured Riley hitting a white girl with a toy light saber, drew irate comparisons to the school shootings in Littleton, Colorado. "There's a double standard," McGruder told Margot Hornblower for *Time* (July 5, 1999). "Calvin, in Calvin and Hobbes, abuses a little girl, shoots guns, orders explosives and imagines blowing up his elementary school. Calvin does things I could never do with a black character because people are scared of black males." Another strip, scheduled for publication soon after the September 11, 2001 terrorist attacks on New York City and Washington, D.C., had Huey calling an FBI terrorist tip line to report Ronald Reagan for abetting extremists in Afghanistan. (In a later strip Huey pointed out that, under the Reagan administration, the CIA had trained Osama bin Laden to fight Soviet forces in Afghanistan.) A number of papers refused to print the strip, and over the next three weeks, the New York–based *Daily News* ran *The Boondocks* only once. McGruder, however, stood by his work, insisting that political views were not out of place in the funny pages. "There was plenty to talk about without making light of the situation, and there was real opportunity to make legitimate criticisms of the government and media," McGruder told Jayson Blair for the *New York Times* (October 22, 2001). "I struggled with it, and

I really thought I was going to get canceled from the *Daily News*. But this is one of those critical moments in history, and I did not want to look back and regret not having said something."

In spite of his strong convictions, McGruder seems weary of all the quarreling his strip has stirred up, and he has acknowledged that controversy, while occasionally an effective tool for gaining publicity or making a point, ultimately isn't at the heart of his work as a cartoonist. "Sometimes, the strip isn't going to be about anything controversial, and it's not because The Man is stopping me," McGruder told Caramanica. "The important things are to tell good stories, develop interesting characters, and, of course, you better be funny." — P.K.

Suggested Reading: *Editor & Publisher* p53 Apr. 17, 1999, with photo, p47+ Oct.9, 1999, with photo; *New York Times Magazine* p42 June 24, 2001, with photo; *Newsweek* p59 July 5, 1999, with photo; *People* p131 Dec. 31, 1999, with photo; *Time* p78 July 5, 1999, with photos; *Vibe* p64 July 2001, with photo

Selected Books: *The Boondocks: Because I Know You Don't Read the Newspaper*, 2000; *Fresh for '01 . . . You Suckas*, 2001

McLean, Jackie

May 17, 1932– Jazz saxophonist; educator.
Address: Hartt School, University of Hartford, 200 Bloomfield Ave., West Hartford, CT 06117

Commenting on the jazz saxophonist Jackie McLean's performance at a 1995 concert in New York City, Peter Watrous wrote for the *New York Times* (June 10, 1995), "He can generate an almost unheard-of intensity. Mr. McLean plays with his intonation, making pitches sometimes sound sharp and acid and at other times true. He likes to use jagged lines and hard rhythms. His tone is hard as well, and when he got going on his improvisations his work took on the feeling of an event." McLean has been known for his biting tone, emotional intensity, and crisp rhythmic attack since he came onto the bebop scene, in the 1950s. As that decade progressed he became one of the most recognized practitioners of the fiery, impassioned "hard-bop" style of jazz. Always eager to remain relevant and absorb new influences, McLean incorporated elements of avant-garde jazz into his repertoire in the 1960s, an experimental leaning that became as much a part of his playing in subsequent years as his blues and bebop roots. McLean has also worked as a music educator for more than three decades and has recently released several well-regarded recordings on the Blue Note label, on which he enjoyed much success in the 1960s.

Toshiba-EMI/Courtesy of Blue Note Records

Jackie McLean

John Lenwood McLean was born in New York City on May 17, 1932. From the time he was very young, he was surrounded by music. His father, John McLean, was a jazz guitarist; his mother played piano in church; his godfather, Norman Cobbs, was a saxophonist; and his stepfather owned a record store, where McLean worked and listened to records to his heart's content. The Sugar Hill section of New York City's Harlem, where McLean grew up, was the stomping ground of such jazz luminaries as Duke Ellington, Nat "King" Cole, Benny Carter, Thelonious Monk, Sonny Rollins, and Bud Powell, the last three of whom McLean befriended. From the time he was five years old, McLean often sat in the orchestra pit where Norman Cobbs played saxophone in the band at the famous Abyssinian Baptist Church. Cobbs gave McLean his first saxophone, a soprano sax, when he was 14. When he was a year older, his mother bought him an alto sax, even though McLean, at the time, preferred the deeper tones of the tenor sax, particularly as played by Lester Young. "When I heard Lester Young, that really had an impression on me," McLean told John Diliberto for an article posted on the National Public Radio Web site's "Jazz Profiles." "It seemed as though his instrument was speaking to me personally."

At 15 McLean met jazz pianist Bud Powell, an experience McLean called "a turning point in my life" in an interview with Fred Jung for *Jazz Weekly* (on-line). McLean went to Powell's house nearly every day for one-on-one instruction from the bebop legend. The first musician who made McLean fall in love with his own instrument, however, was alto saxophonist and bebop pioneer Charlie "Bird"

Parker. "When I first heard Bird, that was it," McLean told Jung. "I knew that that was the way I wanted the alto to sound. . . . Everybody that heard Bird was drawn like a magnet to his musical concept. He was truly the greatest musician of his time. He was certainly one of the greatest musicians ever produced on this planet, up at a level of creativity of anybody you can name, even Europe or Africa or China or India or anywhere, just remarkable." Soon McLean started sneaking out of his neighborhood in the evenings to go down to 52d Street in the New York City borough of Manhattan, where Parker often played. Most of the time McLean had just enough time to see Parker walk into the club before having to head home to make his 10 o'clock curfew.

Eventually McLean met Parker, who encouraged his playing and, later, even asked McLean to substitute for him at gigs when Parker was otherwise engaged. McLean's first important gig was with Bud Powell at New York City's Birdland. In 1951 he made his recording debut, with the trumpeter Miles Davis, on *Dig!*, which is considered by some to be the first hard-bop record. (Bebop is characterized by rapid tempos and harmonic complexity; hard bop, which grew out of bebop, is often more percussion-oriented, among other differences.) McLean then had a year of formal music training at North Carolina A & T University, in Greensboro. His gigs in the mid-1950s included work with Paul Bley (1954) and George Wallington's quintet (1955). In 1956 he played and recorded with the bassist and composer Charles Mingus, an experience that McLean found difficult but ultimately rewarding. McLean, at that time, wore his Parker influence on his sleeve, and Mingus discouraged him, sometimes rather harshly, from mimicking his idol. As McLean told Jung, Mingus would say to him, "'Get a style of your own, man. There's a sound and a real style inside of Jackie McLean. Why the hell do you keep on playing Bird's stuff. You can't play anything that he played better than he played it. . . .' He woke me up." From 1956 to 1958 McLean further enhanced his reputation by playing with the drummer Art Blakey's Jazz Messengers.

Meanwhile, McLean's first recording as a leader, entitled *The Jackie McLean Quintet*, was released by the Ad Lib label in 1955. Beginning in 1956, with *Lights Out!*, McLean made a series of records with the Original Jazz label. On *Lights Out!* McLean collaborated with trumpeter Donald Byrd, pianist Elmo Hope, bassist Doug Watkins, and drummer Art Taylor. McLean's Parker influence is still very evident here, even as McLean and his band adhere to the hard-bop style that began to come into its own after Parker's death, in 1955. A reviewer for *The Penguin Guide to Jazz on CD* (1998) wrote of the recording, "*Lights Out* has a directness and simplicity of diction that are not so evident elsewhere [on the Original Jazz recordings]; where McLean does attempt something more adventurous . . . he does so with taste and precision."

In 1959, on the respected Blue Note label, McLean recorded *Jackie's Bag*, the first of 21 classic albums he would record with the label over an eight-year period. On albums such as *Jackie's Bag*, *Vertigo* (1959), *New Soil* (1959), and *Bluesnik* (1961), McLean is still working within the hard-bop framework and incorporating his solid feel for the blues into his improvisations. One can also hear McLean straining to expand into new directions on these albums, however. In *The Penguin Guide to Jazz on CD*, one reviewer wrote that "Minor Apprehension," which was written by McLean and appeared on *New Soil*, has "elements of freedom which are slightly startling for the period and wholly untypical of McLean's previous work." Jackie King, in an article on *All About Jazz* (November 2000, on-line) about *New Soil*, noted that McLean's "tasty solos and great technique give way to one of the best, most self-assured, definitive improvisations you'll ever hear." King called the album "a perfect definition of jazz at its best. Still contemporary, still fresh, and still jazz."

McLean became involved in theater for the first time in 1959, playing the role of the saxophonist in the avant-garde Living Theater production of *The Connection*. He toured with the Living Theater in the U.S. and Europe and later appeared in the film version of the play. "I fell in love with theater then and there," McLean told Mike Zwerin for *Culturekiosque* (September 24, 1998, on-line). "Even my saxophone playing became a lot more theatrical after that." In the 1960s McLean began to depart from the hard-bop style that had brought him so much acclaim in the previous decade. Avant-garde jazz had started to take shape in the late 1950s,

thanks to the efforts of musicians such as the saxophonist Ornette Coleman, who eschewed strict chord progressions in his playing and based his improvisations on a wider variety of factors. Unlike many of the musicians reared on bebop, McLean was receptive to avant-garde jazz, incorporating it into his style. His flexibility helped keep him relevant in the jazz world, according to some commentators. "McLean stepped from under the wings of Charlie Parker," Eric Person wrote for *Down Beat* (October 1993), "not by discarding the bop or blues language, but by augmenting it with the freer expression of the avant garde." On albums such as *Let Freedom Ring* (1962), McLean showed himself capable of incorporating wide intervallic leaps (sudden jumps from the low to the high registers or vice versa) and fully exploring the four-octave range of the alto sax. A reviewer for *The Penguin Guide to Jazz on CD* wrote of *Let Freedom Ring*, "McLean shrugged off the last fetter of bop harmony and pushed through to a more ruggedly individual post-bop that in important regards anticipated the avant-garde of the later 1960s. McLean's phenomenally beautiful tone rings out."

In 1967 McLean collaborated with Ornette Coleman on the album *New and Old Gospel*. For that recording Coleman played trumpet, with which he was comparatively unfamiliar—a move that drew an unfavorable response from many critics of the time. In *Stereo Review* (March 1997), however, Francis Davis asserted that the album contained some of McLean's finest playing. "Never counted among McLean's classic Blue Note albums of the Sixties," Davis wrote, "*New and Old Gospel* deserves a more charitable hearing than it received in its own day—and not just for presenting Coleman in a more or less conventional setting. It offers some of the most riveting McLean available on disc." McLean's last Blue Note album of that period was *Demon's Dance* (1967).

In the mid-1960s McLean had begun working with community groups and college students. Later in the decade he taught music at the University of Buffalo and also became affiliated with the New York State Department of Corrections, where he helped counsel users of narcotics. McLean himself had struggled with a drug habit since the 1950s. "When I was strung out on dope," he explained to Zwerin, "my horn was in the pawn shop most of the time and I was a most confused and troublesome young man. I was constantly on the street, in jail, or in a hospital kicking a habit." The New York City police eventually seized McLean's cabaret card, thus preventing him from playing in clubs, so that when Charles Mingus hired him to play in his band, McLean had to do so under an assumed name. In 1968 he began commuting from New York to Connecticut to teach a saxophone course and serve as a drug counselor at the Hartt School of Music of the University of Hartford. He relocated to Hartford in 1970 and eventually formed the African-American Music Department and a jazz degree program at the school. In 1971 McLean, along with his wife, Dolly, and three other artists, formed the Artists Collective, a community project that today offers music instruction and dance, drama, and visual-arts programs. In an interview with Fred Jung for *All About Jazz* (1998, on-line), McLean explained his involvement in music education: "It is my most important mission besides playing it," he said. "I play it and I study it and I am always working at it, but I have a hunger to go into an environment where young people are and teach about this music."

In the 1970s, while continuing to teach at the Hartt School, where he would become chair of the jazz department, McLean recorded consistently, primarily with the Steeple Chase and Inner City labels. In 1973 he made two albums, *The Meeting* and *The Source*, with the acclaimed saxophonist Dexter Gordon; the two were joined by pianist Kenny Drew, bassist Niels Pedersen, and drummer Alex Riel. A reviewer for *The Penguin Guide to Jazz on CD* called the albums a "'double' of genuine quality" and wrote, "McLean is usually quicker to the punch, but Gordon spins out his ideas (particularly on the standards) with confidence and some in reserve." In 1974 McLean released his first collaboration with his son, René, an album entitled *New York Calling*. Critics generally found the album to be lackluster. It wasn't until *Dynasty*, cut in 1988, that McLean and René, who plays the saxophone and flute, showed their collaborative potential. René wrote some of the songs for the album, bringing in African and Asian musical influences, "to which McLean responds very positively," a reviewer for *The Penguin Guide to Jazz on CD* wrote, "confirming how much on the outside of conventional bop language he always was. The unmistakable tone is still very much intact."

In the 1980s and early 1990s, McLean released few new albums and played few live gigs, concentrating instead on his teaching at the Hartt School. For a time he was unable to interest a major record label in recording his music. Then, in 1993, the Mosaic label issued a four-CD boxed set of McLean's music, *The Complete Blue Note 1964–66*, that featured re-releases of tunes from those years plus some mid-1960s tracks that had not been available until the 1970s. "Clearly it wasn't for lack of inspiration that much of this music languished in the vaults for years," Mike Joyce wrote for the *Washington Post* (December 22, 1993). "After all, not only is McLean in top form much of the time, playing with great rhythmic intensity and commanding a searing tone, but he's surrounded by musicians who frequently play at a similarly challenging level." In 1996 McLean signed with Capitol, a larger recording label, to release *Hat Trick*. The album, which also features Junko Onishi on piano, Nat Reeves on bass, and Lewis Nash on drums, presents fresh approaches to fairly well-known songs, such as "Bag's Groove," "A Cottage for Sale," and "Solar." A reviewer for *The Penguin Guide to Jazz on CD* found that Onishi's unique style worked well with McLean's phrasing: "On-

ishi invests familiar themes . . . with a faintly alienating strangeness, a matter of unexpected extra notes rather than anything identifiably 'wrong.' The effect is almost like having a second, distantly recorded horn player in the ensembles, chiming echoes of a brass line that isn't actually there. . . . Odd, but very effective."

In 1997 McLean signed a contract with Blue Note to release a series of new albums, the first of which was *Fire and Love* (1997). In 2000 he released *Nature Boy*, which consisted of ballads on which McLean plays in a relatively subdued style. "Now that he has resolved to relax, at least on *Nature Boy*," Don Williamson wrote for *52nd Street* (2000, on-line), "the bitter and hard edge to the McLean aggressiveness has faded. We hear instead the deliberate and ruminative means by which he builds a solo through logic and clarity."

In 2001 McLean, along with the pianists John Lewis (who died later that year) and Randy Weston, was awarded a National Endowment for the Arts Jazz Masters Fellowship, a prize worth $10,000. Nearing the age of 70, McLean has become a living jazz icon, yet rather than rest on his reputation, he remains determined not only to keep playing but to expand in new musical directions as well. "I can't just be content to play what I played in the '50s or what I played in the '60s—and I do play some of that," he told Ira Gitler for *Down Beat* (March 1996). "But I'm looking to the future all the time and find what I can play that will be different and still keep the tradition of the music there." — P.G.H.

Suggested Reading: *Culturekiosque* (on-line) Sep. 24, 1998; *Down Beat* p56 Oct. 1993, p32+ Mar. 1996, p18+ May 2001, with photo; *Jazz Weekly* (on-line); *New York Times* I p15 June 10, 1995, II p27+ Feb. 6, 2000; Cook, Richard, and Brian Morton, eds. *The Penguin Guide to Jazz on CD*, 1998

Selected Recordings: as leader—*The Jackie McLean Quintet*, 1955; *Lights Out!*, 1956; *4, 5 and 6*, 1956; *Jackie's Bag*, 1959; *New Soil*, 1959; *Bluesnik*, 1961; *Let Freedom Ring*, 1962; *Destination Out*, 1963; *Action*, 1964; *Jacknife*, 1966; *New and Old Gospel*, 1967; *Live at Montmartre*, 1972; *New York Calling*, 1974; *New Wine, Old Bottles*, 1978; *Dynasty*, 1988; *Rites of Passage*, 1991; *The Complete Blue Note 1964-66*, 1993; *Hat Trick*, 1996; *Fire and Love*, 1997; *Nature Boy*, 2000; with Art Blakey—*Jazz Messenger*, 1956; *Hard Bop*, 1956; *Once Upon a Groove*, 1957; with Miles Davis—*Dig*, 1951; *Diggin'*, 1951; *Young Man with a Horn*, 1952; *Odyssey*, 1955; with Charles Mingus—*Pithecanthropus Erectus*, 1956; *Blues and Roots*, 1959

Also frustrating for Menken is the implication that his music is just for children. "I'm often very surprised to find my animated soundtracks in the children's bin," he told Berger. "It drives me crazy. These are musicals. They're written as musicals." At the premiere for the animated film *Pocahontas*, he told Neil Strauss for the *New York Times* (June 15, 1995), "I get upset when someone comes up to me and goes: 'Alan Menken, it's nice to meet you. My three-year-old just loves your songs.'" He has learned, however, to take such insensitivity in stride, telling Strauss, "I'm now able to translate that in my brain into, 'I love your songs.'"

A middle child, Alan Menken was born on July 22, 1949 in New Rochelle, New York, to Norman Menken, a dentist, and Sheila Menken, a semiprofessional actress. His father would frequently gather the family, which included Menken's two sisters, around the piano to sing show tunes by George Gershwin or Rodgers and Hammerstein. Menken attended public schools in New Rochelle, which was known for the high quality of its school system's music-education division. He also studied piano at home, with a series of private teachers. "I showed an interest in piano at a very young age," Menken recalled to Pamela Sommers. "But I hated to practice, so when my parents left the room I'd make up my own version of the piece. That's how I started composing." One of his piano teachers encouraged him to submit his compositions to the New York State Young Composers program. By the age of 10, he was receiving citations from the program for some of the pieces. In junior high school he also began studying violin and guitar; later, he served for a time as the concertmaster of the New Rochelle High School orchestra. His mother set up a theater in the family's basement for Menken and collaborated with him on a musical adaptation of "A Bintel Brief" (Yiddish for "a packet of letters")—a newspaper column, published in the United States in the Yiddish-language paper *The Forward* during the early part of the 20th century, that contained letters written by Jewish immigrants. The musical was successfully staged at a local synagogue. "I always knew he had to make it in music," Menken's mother told Joseph Berger. "You couldn't imagine how far he would go, but it was in his soul."

Despite his musical talent, Menken envisioned becoming a dentist, as his grandfather and an uncle as well as his father had done. He enrolled at New York University as a pre-med major but hated the course of study. Often he found himself cutting classes to play the guitar or tinker around on a campus piano, so he switched his major to music. After earning a bachelor's degree, in 1971, Menken began to support himself by playing the piano for ballet classes: he met his wife, Janis, then a professional dancer, at one such class, and the pair married in 1972. He also began performing his own songs in area nightclubs, hoping to become a singer/songwriter like Billy Joel or James Taylor. One tune from that period, "Pink Fish," concerned a Texan's first taste of bagels and lox.

Reed Saxon/AP

Menken, Alan

July 22, 1949– Composer. Address: c/o Walt Disney Co., 1450 Broadway, 2d Fl., New York, NY 10018-2201

"The people at Disney consider what I write to be Disney music," the composer Alan Menken told Pamela Sommers for the *Washington Post* (November 25, 1992). "But it's my music." Menken, best known for his award-winning scores to *Beauty and the Beast* (1991) and *Aladdin* (1992), among other Disney animated films, has had a long and varied musical career—a fact that is often overshadowed by his association with Walt Disney Productions. Before composing the infectious pop tunes for his first Disney film, *The Little Mermaid* (1989), Menken wrote jingles, performed his own songs in nightclubs, served as an accompanist in dance classes, and composed the scores for several live theatrical productions, most notably the 1982 stage version of *Little Shop of Horrors*. But thanks to the success of *The Little Mermaid*, which was credited with reviving the genre of feature-length animated musicals and won two Academy Awards, Menken became inextricably linked in the public's mind with Disney. "I love being associated with Disney," he told Joseph Berger for the *New York Times* (July 13, 1997). "At the same time, one of my ambitions over the course of the next 10 years is to have my name, my stylistic profile, my catalogue of songs, come under the umbrella of Alan Menken." He also said to Berger, "The frustration is at moments where I really put my career on the line and my heart and soul into it and see someone slap the word Disney before what I've done and cheapen it with the implication [that] this is just marketing and commercialism."

At his parents' behest Menken attended a workshop at Broadcast Music Inc. (BMI), a music licensing agency; earlier attendees of the workshop, which was run by Lehman Engel, a Broadway conductor and innovative teacher, included several lyricists, librettists, and composers who had later achieved success in their fields. Engel had his students invent songs for existing stage characters, such as Blanche DuBois from Tennessee Williams's *Streetcar Named Desire*. "I realized I really like the challenge of writing for characters, adapting stories, being able to write an entire song score," Menken said to Sommers. "I discovered I had a gift for writing accessible theatrical material that also had some kind of contemporary thing to it." At BMI Menken met Michael Bennett and Steve Brown, with whom he collaborated on a series of mainly unsuccessful projects, among them *Battle of the Giants*, a campy Flash Gordon parody; a musical based on a Jules Feiffer novel; and "Atina, Evil Queen of the Galaxy," a star vehicle for the 300-pound drag queen Divine, which never got past the workshop stage. "I was always the married straight guy among all these wild gay men doing exciting, cutting-edge work," Menken told Sommers, noting with sadness that many of that group had since died of AIDS. During this period, writing commercial jingles provided the greatest portion of Menken's steady income.

Through a mutual friend at BMI, Menken met Howard Ashman, a lyricist from Baltimore, with whom he would form a longstanding partnership. Menken has often referred to their relationship as being similar to a marriage. "I can't say that it was a once-in-a-lifetime collaboration, because I have a long lifetime to go," he told Stephen Holden for the *New York Times* (March 15, 1992), the year after Ashman's death from AIDS. "But I've never been in a room with a mind like that. I've never been in a room with someone who took my music and possessed it as his own the way Howard did." The pair first collaborated in 1979, on a stage adaptation of the Kurt Vonnegut novel *God Bless You, Mr. Rosewater*. Although their musical was not commercially successful, they teamed up again in 1982, to bring to the stage a musical version of *Little Shop of Horrors*, a cult film by the B-movie director Roger Corman. Ashman had long dreamed of turning the movie—which concerns the adventures of Audrey, a man-eating plant, and Seymour, the plant-store clerk who tends her—into a live musical. The resulting show ran for almost six years Off-Broadway and became a cult hit. During that time Hollywood producers voiced an interest in making a film of Menken and Ashman's musical. "Howard's and my introduction to Hollywood was just another adventure," Menken told Pamela Sommers. "At one point, Martin Scorsese wanted to direct. Tom Cruise wanted to play Seymour. The budget kept rising. It was out of our hands." Eventually a production team that included David Geffen was assembled, and filming began. Menken and Ashman wrote a few new songs for the movie,

which starred Rick Moranis, so that the score would be eligible for an Academy Award. (According to Academy rules, a minimum number of the songs from a film score must have been written expressly for the cinema.) "Mean Green Mother from Outer Space" won an Oscar nomination for best original song, becoming the first highly risqué song to be so honored.

On the advice of David Geffen, Jeffrey Katzenberg, the chairman of Walt Disney Studios, hired Menken and Ashman to write the score for *The Little Mermaid*, which Disney was adapting from the same-titled fairy tale by Hans Christian Andersen. (Katzenberg was eager to steer the studio back to the type of full-length animated features, such as *Snow White* and *Cinderella*, that had been so popular in previous decades.) Menken and Ashman, having wearied of the difficulties involved in mounting live productions in New York City, readily agreed to work on the project. "I went back and looked at a lot of different animation and it all touched me," Menken told Neil Strauss, recalling his preparation for the film. "It's so magical, and I really wanted to give *The Little Mermaid* that timeless feel so it would just take you out of this world." Disney animators created an undersea world populated not only with mermaids but with choruses of other singing and dancing marine life as well. It was Ashman's idea to make Sebastian the Crab, one of the movie's most endearing characters, Jamaican, so that Menken could compose several catchy, calypso-style numbers. Ashman also wrote a plaintive ballad, "Part of Your World," for the title character to sing. (Each subsequent Disney feature, including those produced after Ashman's death, has included at least one such ballad.) Incredibly successful at the box office, *The Little Mermaid* won two Academy Awards, for best original song and best original score.

A few days after the Oscar ceremony, Ashman revealed to Menken that he was seriously ill. He was determined to keep working, however, so the pair hurried to finish the score for their next Disney movie, an adaptation of the classic French fairy tale *Beauty and the Beast*. After Ashman's sight failed, Disney hired a reader for him, and the company delivered a speaker phone to his home so that he could work from his bed. Despite his deteriorating condition, he and Menken finished that score and even started one for their third Disney collaboration, *Aladdin*. In March 1991 Ashman died, at age 40. Dedicated to "our friend Howard, who gave a mermaid her voice and a beast his soul," *Beauty and the Beast* premiered eight months later. It eventually grossed $146 million in the United states alone; the soundtrack sold more than three million copies, and the title track, sung over the end credits by the pop stars Celine Dion and Peabo Bryson, became a hit single. Three songs from the film—"Beauty and the Beast," "Belle," and "Be Our Guest"—were nominated for an Academy Award as best original song; the title song won, and the score earned an Oscar as best original score. "The intensity of a life close to the end really came through those songs," Menken told Joseph Berger. "It's tragic what didn't get written. We had a great career ahead of us, and when [Ashman] died I really did feel that my career was going to die with his passing."

Menken went on to complete the score for *Aladdin* (1992) with Tim Rice, a former partner of the British composer Andrew Lloyd Webber. The music for *Aladdin*, a blend of 1940s-style jazz and Arabic music, won an Academy Award for original score, and the ballad "A Whole New World" was named best original song. A second song, "Friend Like Me," which was sung by Robin Williams as the genie, was also nominated in that category. Burying himself in work to cope with his grief over Ashman's death, Menken completed other projects in 1992, among them the soundtrack for a television movie about the life of Abraham Lincoln; a song for the film *Home Alone 2*; and the score for Disney's first live-action musical in more than two decades, *Newsies*, which failed at the box office. Also that year he returned to his theatrical roots, composing the score for an Off-Broadway play called *Weird Romance*, in collaboration with the lyricist David Spencer. That production fared poorly commercially, unlike his next foray into live theater, *Beauty and the Beast*, which was a resounding success. The lavish version of *Beauty and the Beast* that opened on Broadway in 1994 became a long-running hit in New York City and eventually toured all over the world. Menken credited much of the musical's success to Ashman, who had conceived the Busby Berkeley–style sequence in which household objects sing—an audience favorite in both the animated and live versions. The stage version also contained some new songs written by Menken and Rice.

During the next three years, working with various lyricists, Menken wrote the scores for three other Disney animated features—*Pocahontas* (1995), *The Hunchback of Notre Dame* (1996), and *Hercules* (1997). Each grossed well over $100 million, and *Pocahontas* earned Menken two additional Academy Awards. The films' soundtrack albums sold several million copies among them, and many of their songs aired frequently on the radio after their release. Menken's most recent Disney project was the 1997 oratorio *King David*, which was written to celebrate the 3,000th anniversary of the city of Jerusalem, Israel. Written in collaboration with Tim Rice, it was staged at the New Victory Theater (which Disney had purchased and renovated that year), on New York City's famed 42nd Street.

Some critics have charged that Menken's compositions pander shamelessly to pop sensibility. "His work has always struck me as an exploitation of the musically naive mind," the veteran radio announcer/disc jockey Jonathan Schwartz told Berger. But more often, journalists writing about the tunes use such adjectives as "catchy," "infectious," and "appealing." Menken has explained in many interviews that while he borrows from an array of musical idioms, what he composes has his personal stamp. But the reason for the popularity of his work, he believes, has little to do with his style. "I have a great trust in the power of music and song," he told David Patrick Stearns for *USA Today* (December 27, 1994). "I think that [trust] somehow translates to an audience and allows them the space to enjoy it."

Menken, who has won a New York Drama Critics Award, a Drama Desk Award, and the Outer Critics Circle Award, received the 1983 BMI Career Achievement Award for his contributions to musical theater. Said to be quiet and unpretentious, he lives with his wife, Janis, and daughters, Anna and Nora, in a stone cottage in Westchester County, New York. In 1998 he gave New York University $250,000 to endow a scholarship program for students majoring in music composition. The Alan Menken Scholarship is being awarded yearly to a junior in the Department of Music and Performing Arts in the School of Education. — M.R.

Suggested Reading: (New York) *Daily News* p33+ Dec. 6, 1989, with photos; *New York Times* 2 p17+ Mar. 15, 1992, with photos, C p16 June 15, 1995, with photo, II p30 July 13, 1997, with photos; *People* p 73+ Dec. 16, 1991, with photos; *USA Today* D p5 Dec. 27, 1994, with photo; *Washington Post* E p1 Nov. 25, 1992, with photo

Selected Scores: *Little Shop of Horrors*, 1982; *The Little Mermaid*, 1989; *Beauty and the Beast*, 1991; *Lincoln*, 1992; *Newsies*, 1992; *Aladdin*, 1992; *Life With Mikey*, 1993; *The Music Behind the Magic*, 1994; *Pocahontas*, 1995; *The Hunchback of Notre Dame*, 1996

Middelhoff, Thomas

1953– Chairman and CEO of Bertelsmann AG. Address: Bertelsmann AG, Carl-Bertelsmann-Str. 270, D-33311 Munich, Germany; Bertelsmann, 1540 Broadway, 24th Fl., New York, NY 10036

Thomas Middelhoff is the chairman and chief executive officer of Bertelsmann AG, the third-most-powerful media conglomerate in the world, after Time Warner and the Walt Disney Co. ("AG" is an acronym for a German term that means "corporation.") Based in Gütersloh, Germany, Bertelsmann has holdings in the publishing, television, radio, and Internet markets, including BMG Entertainment, the book publishing giants Random House and Bantam Doubleday Dell, RCA and Arista Records, and magazines such as *Family Circle*, *YM*, and *McCall's*. The company also has several online entertainment retail services, including *Barnesandnoble.com*, Bertelsmann Online (*BOL.com*), and CDNow. Worth $15 billion, Bertelsmann AG

Courtesy of Bertelsmann

Thomas Middelhoff

owns, in total, 600 media enterprises in more than 50 countries. "We are not a German company," Middelhoff told Doreen Carvajal for the *New York Times* (October 19, 1998). "We are a real global company." Other successful holdings include CLT-UFA, Europe's leading television and radio company, and Pixelpark, a German software design company. Bertelsmann's projected revenues for 2001 are expected to total $20 billion. Unlike many top multimedia companies, however, Bertelsmann AG does not trade publicly, a strategy that some economists suggest has diminished its stock value. "Bertelsmann is a sleeping giant that's now going to emerge," Steve Case, the CEO of the Internet company America Online (AOL), told Marc Gunther for *Fortune* (November 23, 1998.) "And Thomas will become one of the best-known and most-respected media executives in the world."

Originally a publishing concern, the Bertelsmann company was founded in 1835 by Carl Bertelsmann; its first best-seller was a collection of Christian hymns entitled *Theolemi*. Bertelsmann later expanded its offerings to include works by the 19th-century British poet Lord Byron and the Brothers Grimm (Jacob and Wilhelm), 19th-century writers of fairy tales. In an editorial that appeared in the *Nation* (December 28, 1998), Hersch Fischler and John S. Friedman reported that during the 1930s and 1940s, Bertelsmann, as printer, was the largest supplier of propaganda material to the government of the German dictator Adolf Hitler. Fischler and Friedman also claimed that Heinrich Mohn, the company's CEO during this period, was a member of the SS, an elite arm of the Nazi police. According to the authors, Bertelsmann had previously attempted to cover up its relation-

ship to the Nazis by claiming that the company was shut down during the war for refusing to support Hitler's campaign. (After Fischler and Friedman's article appeared, Middelhoff removed the corporate history from Bertelsmann's Web site and appointed a committee of scholars to investigate the charges. In January 2000 the commission found that, contrary to Bertelsmann's public statements, the company had indeed supported Hitler and had provided the Nazis with propaganda materials. A short time later Bertelsmann announced its decision to donate money to a German compensation fund for those forced into slave labor by the Nazis. In the fall of 2000, Random House, which is owned by Bertelsmann, pledged $1 million to the Holocaust Survivors' Memoirs Project.) Bertelsmann's printing plant was destroyed during World War II; it was later rebuilt by Reinhard Mohn, the great-grandson of the company's founder. Mohn decentralized Bertelsmann's holdings and built the corporation into one of the leading media entities in the world. Middelhoff told Marc Gunther that Mohn was "the most important entrepreneur Germany has ever had, not just because of his economic success but because he created a sense of entrepreneurial culture combined with a sense of social responsibility. Efficiency and humanity are not contradictions at Bertelsmann."

Thomas Middelhoff was born in Düsseldorf, Germany, in 1953; sources have listed his date of birth variously as May 11 and November 5. Middelhoff received a master's degree in business administration from the University of Münster in 1979; he also served as a research assistant at the university's Institute of Marketing from 1980 to 1983. Middelhoff worked in his family's textile plant before joining Bertelsmann as a management assistant in 1986; that same year he earned a Ph.D. in new media from the University of Saarbrucken. Two years later he took over as the managing director of Mohndruck, the company's printing plant in Gütersloh. In 1994 he became the head of corporate development as well as the coordinator for Bertelsmann's multimedia business.

Middelhoff established his reputation as a talented businessman in 1995, when, as a young member of Bertelsmann's executive board, he persuaded the company to purchase 5 percent of AOL, then a relatively unknown Internet service. "Thomas had the insight, before pretty much any other media executive, that this was going to be an important market, and he personally dived into it," Steve Case told Marc Gunther. The previous year Middelhoff had launched AOL Europe, a joint venture with Case that soon became a market leader on the continent. He told Polly Sprenger for the *Standard* (April 24, 2000, on-line) that when AOL Europe was first announced, "almost everybody joked about Bertelsmann, about why we bloody Germans decided to partner with AOL when Compuserve was bigger. They said, these crazy Germans, . . . they don't have any idea what's really going on." AOL went on to become one of the top

Internet companies while the influence of its competitors Compuserve and Prodigy diminished considerably. "If AOL were a flop, I would not be here," Middelhoff told Gunther. "I'm absolutely convinced of that."

Middelhoff moved to New York City in 1997 in an effort to both improve his English and learn as much as possible about American publishing. He arranged meetings with many of the top players in the business world, including Michael Eisner of Disney, Gerald Levin of Time Warner, and the media mogul Rupert Murdoch. Within a year, Bertelsmann AG had acquired Random House, one of the world's most successful and respected publishing companies. Bertelsmann AG has since become one of the largest booksellers on the planet; its various companies combined sell close to one million books every day. Besides Random House and Bantam Doubleday Dell, the company has a 50 percent stake in *Barnesandnoble.com* and also owns Bertelsmann Online, an Internet bookseller that has made it possible for readers to have access to books in many different languages.

The rise of publishing conglomerates has dismayed some observers, among them André Schiffrin, the founder of the New Press. Schiffrin wrote for the *Nation* (July 5, 1999), "In a few years, these conglomerates have managed two seemingly contradictory achievements. They have lost unprecedented amounts of money, and they have eliminated from their lists many of the serious and lasting books on which publishing traditionally relied. Of course, the few remaining independent presses and many of the university presses are doing their best to publish the books that have disappeared from the conglomerate lists. But as the investment of the major publishing houses, which control 80 percent of sales, continues to shift to more commercial fields, the choice of ideas presented to American readers will continue to dwindle." In the case of Bertelsmann, some have criticized not only the choices of books to be cut but the works that have been green-lighted. Recently Bertelsmann published *The Fame of a Dead Man's Deeds: An Up-Close Portrait of White Nationalist William Pierce* on *MightyWords.com*, a Web site it co-owns with Barnes and Noble; some critics have accused the author of the book, Robert S. Griffin, of promoting the ideas of Pierce, who wrote the notorious racist novel *The Turner Diaries.*

In November 1998 Middelhoff became Bertelsmann's CEO, succeeding Mark Wossner, who led the company through 15 years of expansion. That month Bertelsmann AG acquired 82 percent of Springer-Verlag G.m.b.H., Germany's largest publisher of science and technical books, for $597 million. In 1999 AOL proposed a merger, but Bertelsmann's shareholders expressed a desire to remain independent. On other fronts, Middelhoff instructed all employees to do business in English rather than German; he also bought personal computers for all of the company's 74,000 workers.

Recently, the Bertelsmann-owned BMG Entertainment joined several companies in pursuing legal action against Napster, the popular Web site that allowed music fans to download songs by their favorite groups for free, thus cutting into the profits of companies connected to the music business. Bertelsmann AG eventually bought a portion of Napster and agreed to drop its portion of the lawsuit. In return Napster agreed to begin charging its subscribers; part of those fees will now be paid to BMG as royalties. In a keynote speech at Germany's music-industry trade fair Popkomm, excerpted by Wolfgang Spahr for *Billboard* (September 2, 2000), Middelhoff stated, "For all the reservations we have, Napster is cool, a fantastic music brand with the following characteristics: high-quality . . . music; easy to use; global selection for all labels' repertoire; prompt service; and free choice. I ask you: which one of you—and I expressly include Bertelsmann here—is able to offer music fans a comparable service?"

In January 2000 Middelhoff resigned from AOL's board of directors, following that company's merger with Time Warner, one of Bertelsmann's top competitors. In March 2000 Bertelsmann sold its 50 percent share of AOL Europe to America Online Inc. for $8.5 million. That month Bertelsmann Online expanded into the Asian market, a move calculated to increase competition with AOL. In a separate deal, AOL agreed to buy out Bertelsmann's interest in AOL Australia. In February 2001 Bertelsmann took over the RTL group, Europe's largest television broadcaster, for $9 billion, a stock transaction that elevated its interests in the company from 37 to 67 percent. The following month Middelhoff resigned from the board of Vivendi Universal, a competitor with whom Bertelsmann hoped to forge closer business relations.

In April 2001 the Jewish organization UJA-Federation of New York honored Middelhoff at a benefit dinner, at which the Nobel Peace Prize–winning writer Elie Wiesel delivered the keynote address. While the UJA's choice of honoree outraged some Holocaust survivors, Wiesel, who is the honorary chairman of the Holocaust Survivors' Memoirs Project, felt that Middelhoff had earned his trust. Referring to Random House's million-dollar donation to the project, he explained to Tamar Lewin for the *New York Times* (April 30, 2001), "While it was in the end Random House that gave the money . . . , the agreement was with Bertelsmann, and it was Middelhoff who made the commitment. He also called me, and seemed really very upset when the stories of Bertelsmann's past came out. We discussed it at length, and my advice was to come clean, to let everything be open. And I believe he has done that."

Middelhoff serves as a chair of the business steering committee of Global Business Dialogue on Electronic Commerce, made up of executives from multimedia conglomerates who would like to change international Internet policies. In a letter to the organization excerpted by Elizabeth Manus for the *New York Observer* (November 17, 2000, on-line), Middelhoff wrote: "Conflicting policies, rules, overregulation and regional patchwork regulations are obstacles to all companies engaged in electronic commerce on a global scale." Middelhoff has also worked to reduce the sometimes prohibitively high prices some European users must pay for access to Internet services.

Middelhoff is married and has five children. — C.L.

Suggested Reading: *Billboard* p101+ Sep. 2, 2000, with photo; *Fortune* p176+ Nov. 23, 1998, with photos; *New York Times* p1 Oct. 19, 1998, W p1 Feb. 6, 2001, with photo, B p3+ Apr. 30, 2001, with photo; *New York Times Magazine* p72+ June 10, 2001, with photos

Courtesy of the governor's office

Minner, Ruth Ann

Jan. 17, 1935– Governor of Delaware. Address: Legislative Hall, Dover, DE 19901

On November 7, 2000 Delaware, nicknamed the "small wonder" because of its area (48 of the other 49 states are larger) and population (only five states have fewer residents), elected a woman governor for the first time in its history. The winner of that election, Ruth Ann Minner, is one of only 19 women in U.S. history to serve as a governor of any state. (Three of those women succeeded their husbands, who died in office, and four succeeded male governors who left office early.) Minner, universally known as "Ruth Ann," made her way up the

ranks of the Delaware state government after overcoming severe hardships early in life and as a young adult. Her first-hand knowledge of adversity has motivated her to try to change Delaware for the better and has accounted for much of her appeal to ordinary voters. "She's a well-respected woman," Taube Carpenter, a resident of southern Delaware, told the Associated Press in 2000. "She knows what it's like to live paycheck to paycheck, and has had to earn a paycheck, her own paycheck, to feed three kids." In 1974 Minner won a seat in the Delaware House of Representatives, becoming the first woman to represent her district. She served in the Delaware Senate, too, before being elected to her first term as lieutenant governor, in 1992. On Election Day 2000 about 50 percent of Delaware's registered voters went to the polls, and of those, 59 percent cast their ballots for Minner.

A daughter of Samuel and Mary Ann Coverdale, Minner was born Ruth Ann Coverdale on January 17, 1935 in Milford, Delaware. Her parents were sharecroppers, and when she was 16 she dropped out of high school to work on the farm, as her three older sisters and older brother had done. At 17 she married Frank Ingram, with whom she had three sons: Frank Jr., Wayne, and Gary. The Ingrams started a small business (various sources describe it as a pesticide company or an asphalt-paving enterprise) while maintaining a modest farm for the family's use. In 1967 Frank Ingram suddenly died. Beginning on the day of his funeral, the local bank began scrutinizing the expenses of his wife, because, as Minner explained to an Associated Press reporter, as quoted on *blackstocks.com* (June 16, 2000), "I was a widow without visible means of support." According to Delaware bank policies, a woman was not eligible to sign a promissory note for a loan; a man's signature was required for all such transactions. "I couldn't get a credit card. I couldn't get money," she told the reporter. "How was I to survive with three children?" To support her young family, Minner immediately went back to school, at the same time continuing to maintain the family's farm. She completed her high-school education with a general equivalency diploma and then took college classes at Delaware Technical and Community College; concurrently, she worked in a library and as a federal agriculture worker in Delaware and Maryland.

In 1969 Ruth Ann Ingram married Roger Minner. The couple started a car-towing and -wrecking business, and her financial situation became more secure. Spurred in part by her desire to help people beset by hardships, as she had been, she did volunteer work for Delaware's Democratic Party. In the early 1970s she got a job as a clerk in the state House of Representatives. After the 1972 election of Sherman W. Tribbitt, a Democrat, as governor, she became a receptionist in his office.

During this period Minner began thinking of seeking elective office herself. "I never had an intention of getting deeply involved in politics," she told Francis X. Clines for the *New York Times* (January 4, 2001). "But it finally got down to proving some things to myself." In 1974 she ran successfully for a seat in the Delaware House of Representatives from the 33d District, which covers parts of Sussex and Kent counties. (The Delaware House has 41 members; each is elected to a two-year term.) Her priorities included trying to change the laws that prevented women from securing their own bank loans and credit cards. "From the time I was a child, my mother taught me you should help someone else if they had a problem," Minner told Alexandra Marks for the *Christian Science Monitor* (October 17, 2000). "I realized that someone had to take the initiative to make it easier for other women." Restrictions on credit extensions to women were repealed during her time in the House of Representatives. She was reelected in 1976, 1978, and 1980 and served for a while as House majority whip.

In 1982 Minner won election to the Delaware state Senate from the 18th District. (That arm of the Delaware legislature has 21 members, each of whom is elected to a four-year term.) She has said that of all her accomplishments during the 10 years that she served in the Senate, she felt most proud of her role in the passage of the Delaware Land and Water Conservation Act, which, to date, has funded the preservation of 30,000 acres as wilderness. For her work as the chair of the Natural Resources and Environmental Control Committee, Minner was honored by several state environmental groups, among them the Delaware Wildlife Federation and the Delaware Sierra Club. As a state senator she also served on the Public Safety Committee and the Education Committee.

In 1992 Minner was elected lieutenant governor of Delaware. She worked with the new governor, Thomas R. Carper, to build the Delaware economy. Their efforts included promoting agriculture, an important element in Delaware's economy, by offering tax breaks and other financial incentives to farmers who might otherwise have been tempted to sell their land to real-estate developers. Minner also headed the Commission on Government Reorganization and Effectiveness; informally known as the Minner Commission, it "was responsible for recommendations that saved the state impressive amounts of money," as Ralph Moyed reported in the *News Journal* (January 11, 2001, on-line), a Delaware newspaper. Both Minner and Carper were reelected in 1996.

In 2000 Carper made a bid for a seat in the United States Senate, and Minner announced her candidacy for the governorship. Delaware does not have its own television stations, so her many appearances at rallies and speeches at small venues carried more weight than they might have in other states. "You have to meet everyone," Matthew Heckles, Minner's campaign field director, told Yvonne Thomas for the *Review* (November 10, 2000, on-line), the campus newspaper of the University of Delaware. "The amount of people who know her is important, and part of the reason she's so popular." Minner's Republican opponent was John Burris, a businessman from southern Delaware who had previously run for state office. The central issues in the campaign concerned education, health care, the state's growth and development, the environment, and public safety. On Election Day, November 7, 2000, Minner defeated Burris by winning 59.2 percent of the 319,920 votes cast. "There is evidence that many nominally Republican women voted for her," Ralph Moyed reported.

The day after the election, Minner described her victory to Patrick Jackson for the *News Journal* (November 8, 2000, on-line) as a vote of confidence that reflected Delawareans' positive feelings about the changes implemented during Governor Carper's administration. "This election says that after eight years we're in great shape, but we can do better," Minner said. She also attributed her success to her record of public service and her understanding of the particular needs of Delawareans. On January 3, 2001, the day she took the oath of office as governor, she told Francis X. Clines, "I never dreamed I would come this far. . . . I love this work. These days are not to be squandered."

After winning the election, Minner pleased her constituents by drawing on a pool of talented Delawareans to fill cabinet posts, instead of hiring from out of state as her predecessors had done. Her 2001 legislative agenda, released in March 2001, focuses on improving education through funding primary-school reading specialists and after-school academic programs; securing better health care by means of a patients' bill of rights; protecting the environment and the well-being of Delaware residents by requiring that businesses reveal to the public information about environmental hazards and contaminants; improving the state's foster-care system; and guarding residents' safety through stricter drunk-driving and gun-permit legislation.

Minner has cited the late Israeli prime minister Golda Meir, whose career in public service spanned 50 years, as one of her heroes and role models. The governor's second husband, Roger, died of cancer in 1991, but she maintains the business they started together. Her three sons are married, and she has at least a half-dozen grandchildren. As a legislator, Minner won several awards from environmental groups; she has also been recognized as an outstanding small-business owner and honored as the Delaware Mother of the Year and Woman of the Year. She was elected to the Delaware Women's Hall of Fame in 1995. — K.S.

Suggested Reading: *Christian Science Monitor* (on-line), Oct. 17, 2000, with photo; (Delaware) *News Journal* (on-line) Nov. 8, 2000; *Nando Times* (on-line) Nov. 8, 2000; *New York Times* (on-line), Jan. 4, 2001, with photo; *People* p113+ Mar. 5, 2001, with photo; *Philadelphia Inquirer* (on-line) Dec. 12, 2000

Ho/Archive Photos

Miyazaki, Hayao

Jan. 5, 1941– Animated-film director. Address: Studio Ghibli, 1-4-25, Kajino-cho, Koganei-shi 184, Japan

One of the most successful filmmakers in Japan, Hayao Miyazaki is among the few animators the public can identify by name. In such animated motion pictures as *Nausicaä*, *My Neighbor Totoro*, and *Princess Mononoke*—the largest-grossing domestic film in Japanese history—he has vivified his personal vision in stories about the interplay between humans and nature and the marvelousness of existence. Many of those stories feature strong female protagonists. The popularity of Miyazaki's films is especially impressive in light of the fact that they eschew both the catchy song-and-dance routines that have driven the success of recent Disney films and the sex and violence that have made Japanese animation popular worldwide. Instead, Miyazaki relies on plot, character, and breathtaking animation—most notably, for aerial sequences and landscapes—to reawaken what Helen McCarthy, the author of *Hayao Miyazaki: Master of Japanese Animation* (1999), called a "sense of wonder that lies dormant in all of us from childhood to life's end."

Miyazaki can accurately be called an animation auteur, because he is involved in so many aspects of the making of his films. Unlike most of the directors in his specialty, he personally checks—and until recently, redrew—the key animation in his films. His organizational abilities are also extraordinary. With his longtime collaborator, Isao Takahata, Miyazaki set up a sophisticated studio—Studio Ghibli (pronounced "ji-bu-ri")—to attract

the best talent in Japan. The facility's large inhouse staff and production capabilities have given Miyazaki a level of control that is unusual in the world of animation and have helped him create backgrounds and animation whose quality is recognized as rivaling—or in the opinion of some, surpassing—that of Disney. Such directors as Akira Kurosawa (*Rashomon*, *Seven Samurai*), John Lasseter (*Toy Story*), and Gary Trousdale and Kirk Wise (*Beauty and the Beast*) have paid homage to his films. "In my movies for children," Miyazaki told Mark Schilling for *Japan Quarterly* (January–March 1997), "I want to express, before anything else, the idea that the world is a profound, multifarious, and beautiful place. I want to tell them that they are fortunate to have been born into this world." He has also said that after people watch his films, he wants them to think, "I wish things were like this."

The second of four sons, Hayao Miyazaki was born on January 5, 1941 on the outskirts of Tokyo. His uncle headed Miyazaki Airplane, which made parts for Zero fighter planes; Miyazaki's father, Katsuji, was a director of the company. Miyazaki often felt guilt over his family's involvement in World War II and the privileges they enjoyed during the war—plentiful food and access to a car, for example—when so many other Japanese were suffering from shortages of necessities. He was deeply troubled by an incident that occurred when members of his family fled the firebombing of Utsunomiya (about 60 miles north of Tokyo) in a company truck: despite the pleas of a woman on foot, the truck did not stop for her or anyone else. Miyazaki has acknowledged that his memory of the event may not be reliable and that he realizes that there were good reasons for not stopping the truck; nevertheless, he has expressed the wish that he or his brother had told his parents to let the woman ride with them. (In many of his films, he has depicted younger characters endangering themselves to help others.)

In 1947, the year Miyazaki started school, his mother was hospitalized with spinal tuberculosis; she remained bedridden until 1955. (His fear that his mother would die resurfaced as a theme of his film *My Neighbor Totoro*.) While growing up Miyazaki envisioned a career as either an animator or a *manga* (Japanese comic-book) artist. Fond of drawing tanks, planes, and ships, he tried creating his own manga but destroyed his work after realizing how similar it was to that of Osamu Tezuka, a revered manga artist. In his last year of high school, Miyazaki saw Taiji Yabushita's *Legend of the White Serpent*, the first Japanese color animated film. Moved to tears by the movie, he decided to pursue animation. "Looking back at it now, it's just a sappy love story," he told Lewis Beale for the New York *Daily News* (October 24, 1999, on-line), "but it's the mystery of animation that unfolded itself to me. I really do locate the genesis of my becoming an animator in that moment."

Miyazaki attended Gakushuin University, in Tokyo, and studied political science and economics. As an undergraduate he joined a children's-literature group and read a wide variety of children's books. After he earned a degree, in 1963, he got a job at Toei-Cine, the largest animation studio in Asia. He started out as an in-betweener on the animated film *Wan Wan Chushingura* (*Watchdog Woof-Woof*, 1963), the TV series *Okami Shonen Ken* (*Wolf Boy Ken*, 1963), and the short film *Gulliver no Uchu Ryoko* (*Gulliver's Space Travels*, 1964). (Movement in animated films is broken down into segments, the most important of which—the first and last scenes—are drawn by key animators. In-betweeners are responsible for the smooth transition between these scenes.) The work was not very creative, but, inspired in part by *The Snow Queen* (1957), by the Russian animator Lev Atamanov, a film whose quality he hoped one day to match in his own work, he persevered. Miyazaki was soon promoted to key animation for the TV series *Shonen Ninja Kaze no Fujimaru* (*Wind Ninja Boy Fujimaru*, 1964), *Hustle Punch* (1965), and *Rainbow Sentai Robin* (*Rainbow Warrior Robin*, 1966). His Marxist leanings led him to become heavily involved with the animators' labor union, and by 1964 he had become the union's chief secretary. At around this time he married Akemi Ota, a Toei animator; his wife abandoned her career several years after the birth of their second son.

While working on *Wolf Boy Ken*, Miyazaki had met the show's director, Isao Takahata. The two worked together again on *Taiyo no Oji Hols no Daiboken* (*The Great Adventure of Hols, Prince of the Sun*, also known as *Little Norse Prince Valiant*), the first film that Takahata directed. Work on the motion picture started in 1965, during a labor crisis at Toei. Reflecting the idealism of some of the Toei animators, the film was made democratically—anybody could contribute ideas during development and storyboard meetings. Miyazaki's many suggestions impressed his colleagues. The film, which promotes the idea of unity among people, took three years to complete; although it was critically praised, its run in theaters was brief and it fared poorly financially. Takahata never directed a movie for Toei again.

Miyazaki continued to work as a key animator at Toei, on such films as *Nagagutsu o Haita Neko* (*Puss in Boots*, 1969), *Soratobu Yureisen* (*The Flying Ghost Ship*, 1969); *Dobutsu Takarajima* (*Animal Treasure Island*, 1971), and *Ali Baba to Yonjuppiki no Tozoku* (*Ali Baba and the 40 Thieves*, 1971). He also began drawing manga. Beginning in 1969, for about half a year, he produced the manga *Sabaku no Tami* (*People of the Desert*, 1969) for a weekly children's paper, using the pen name Saburo Akitsu.

In 1971 Miyazaki, Takahata, and another colleague, Youchi Otabe, left Toei for A-Pro. At that studio Miyazaki co-directed, with Takahata, several episodes of the television series *Rupan Sansei* (*Lupin III*), based on the manga by the artist Monkey Punch about Lupin, a lovable thief. Miyazaki also came up with the concept for the short film *Panda Kopanda* (*Panda & Child*, 1972), about a girl who has two panda companions. (The earlier arrival in Japan of two pandas from China had set off a panda craze.) Miyazaki wrote the screenplay, handled the design, and drew the layouts and key animation for the project and its sequel, *Panda Kopanda Amefuri Circus no Maki* (*Panda & Child: Rainy Day Circus*, 1973), both of which Takahata directed. Miyazaki has identified these as the first films he made for children, not for himself.

In 1973 Miyazaki, Takahata, and Otabe moved to Zuiyo Pictures, now known as Nippon Animation. They worked on the TV series *Alps no Shojo Heidi* (*Alpine Girl Heidi*, 1974), based on a novel by Johanna Spyri. Takahata directed and Miyazaki designed the scenes and layouts, while Otabe directed the animation and character design. The popular series launched the World Masterpiece Theater television series, devoted to showing classics of children's literature. The trio worked on several other projects for that series, including *Haha o Tazunete Sanzen-Ri* (*Three Thousand Miles in Search of Mother*, 1976), *Araiguma Rascal* (*Rascal the Raccoon*, 1977) and *Akage no An* (*Anne of Green Gables*, 1979).

By the late 1970s Miyazaki had begun to establish himself as a director. *Mirai Shonen Conan* (*Future Boy Conan*, 1978) is the first television series he directed by himself. Based on Alexander Key's novel *The Incredible Tide*, the 26-episode series takes place in 2008, after war has devastated Earth. Miyazaki next directed his first feature film, *Lupin III: Cagliostro no Shiro* (*Lupin III: Castle of Cagliostro*, 1979), in which the thief and his cohorts struggle to free a princess from the clutches of an evil count. One scene, a showdown in a clocktower, inspired footage produced for Disney's *The Great Mouse Detective* (1986). While the Disney film used computer graphics to animate the clocktower battle, the *Lupin III* sequence was drawn entirely by hand.

Miyazaki worked on a variety of projects before he got a chance to direct another feature film. Under the pseudonym Teruki Tsutomu, he directed two episodes of the second *Lupin III* TV series for Telecom. He also directed the first six episodes of *Meitantei Holmes* (*Great Detective Holmes*, also known as *Sherlock Hound*) for the Italian TV channel RAI; the series, in which all the characters are dogs, aired in Japan in 1984. In 1982, because he could not find work as an animator, Miyazaki started the manga *Kaze no Tani no Nausicaä* (*Nausicaä of the Valley of the Winds*) for the magazine *Animage*; he completed it 12 years later, after 59 episodes. The idea for the story came to Miyazaki after he learned that fish—in an example of the amazing ability of living organisms to adapt to extreme conditions—were thriving in Japan's Minamata Bay, where heavy mercury pollution had made the marine life poisonous to humans. (Before the mercury contamination had been discovered, many babies whose mothers had eaten the fish had been born with horrendous defects.)

During the *Nausicaä* manga's first year, the publisher of *Animage*, Tokuma Publishing, approached Miyazaki with an offer to turn the manga into a film. Production started in 1982, the year in which Miyazaki's mother died. (In both the manga and the film, the mother of the heroine also dies.) Produced by Takahata, *Nausicaä* was made in nine months, for about $1 million. Its plot roughly corresponds to that of the first fifth of the manga, though there are significant deviations. In the film, a toxic jungle called the Sea of Corruption has sprung up as a result of a devastating war known as the Seven Days of Fire. Teeming with unusual and frightening creatures who thrive in the polluted environment, the sea emits beautiful spores that are fatal to humans when inhaled. The few human survivors of the war live at the borders of the jungle, where they are slowly dying out. Nausicaä, the princess of the Valley of the Winds, has the rare ability to get along with the jungle creatures. She struggles to dissuade neighboring kingdoms from unleashing a terrible weapon that would eradicate them. (In 1986 an edited version of *Nausicaä*, titled *Warriors of the Wind*, was released in the U.S. The alterations horrified Miyazaki and Takahata, who have since stressed that in any future foreign distribution deal, no cuts can be made to their films.)

Nausicaä (1984), which earned about $6.5 million and won praise from the World Wildlife Fund, marked a turning point in Miyazaki's career. Thanks to its success, Miyazaki and Takahata opened their own office, Nibariki, which means "two-horse power." They then persuaded Tokuma to back the formation of Studio Ghibli; its name is that of a World War II–era Italian scouting plane and also refers to a hot Saharan wind. Miyazaki and Takahata intended the studio, which opened in 1985, to blow a fresh wind through Japanese animation. The studio was to be devoted to theatrical films, which entailed big risks; many animation studios worked in television to support their theatrical releases.

Ghibli's first offering was *Tenku no Shiro Laputa* (*Laputa, Castle in the Sky*, 1986), directed by Miyazaki and produced by Takahata. As with all his films, Miyazaki worked extremely hard on it. He traveled to Wales to research details for the background illustrations, to give the film an early-19th-century feel. In addition to drawing the storyboards and cleaning up the animation, he wrote lyrics to the song that ended the film. The film's title refers to a floating island that figures in Jonathan Swift's 18th-century satire *Gulliver's Travels*. In Miyazaki's story, the key to finding the castle is Sheeta, a girl who owns a mysterious pendant that has been passed down to her. Chased by sky pirates and military men who believe that the castle threatens civilization, she meets Pazu, an orphan child whose father died while looking for the castle. Together they find the floating island and discover both its beauty and its danger.

Nausicaä and *Laputa* are full of action. For his next directorial effort, *Tonari no Totoro* (*My Neighbor Totoro*, 1988), Miyazaki wanted to create a slower-paced film about two girls' summer in the country. Nervous about how it would be received, Tokuma agreed to make the film on the condition that it be released in conjunction with Takahata's upcoming *Hotaru no Haka* (*Grave of the Fireflies*), a dark tale about the effect of World War II on two Japanese children.

A year in the making, *My Neighbor Totoro* is set in Tokorozawa (where Miyazaki currently lives) in the 1950s. It portrays two young sisters, Mei and Satsuki, who have moved with their father to the countryside to be closer to the hospital where their mother is a patient. Mei and Satsuki encounter forest spirits that only children can see. Among them is Totoro, a huge fuzzy creature with a grin like that of the Cheshire cat (from Lewis Carroll's fantasy *Alice in Wonderland*) and a secret home in a gigantic camphor tree. Incorporating several other nods to Carroll as well, the film evokes both the fears and wonders that children experience unbeknownst to their parents. Miyazaki wrote the lyrics to the film's end song.

Although Akira Kurosawa asserted that *Totoro* was one of the few Japanese titles on his list of 100 favorite films, the initial response to *Totoro* among most critics and audiences was tepid. But within two years or so, Totoro dolls were being merchandised, and they became a phenomenon. Merchandising has since given the studio some financial stability; nevertheless, Miyazaki recoils at the thought of erasers and pencils bearing the images of characters from his films. Reflecting the studio's debt to the furry creature, Totoro has become the official logo of Ghibli.

In a conversation with Steve Fritz for *Another Universe* (September 29, 1999, on-line), Miyazaki said he had received a letter from a friend of his saying that his little boy loved *Totoro*. "He's watched it over and over and over and over again . . . over 50 times now," the friend wrote. "I sent him a letter back immediately, saying he was making a terrible mistake . . . ," Miyazaki told Fritz. "Owning a little puppy will teach you a lot more about life than watching Totoro one hundred times." "I think animation is robbing children of the precious time they should be spending getting to know reality themselves," he declared to Fritz.

Miyazaki's next work, *Majo no Takkyubin* (*Kiki's Delivery Service*, 1989), was based on a book by Eiko Kadono. A coming-of-age tale, the film depicts the 13-year-old witch Kiki's struggles to make a living and win friends in her adopted city and thereby become a full-fledged witch. Though she achieves financial independence by starting a high-flying delivery service, the pressure of running the business and the stress from her painful awareness of her differences from other children cause her to lose her ability to fly. More than two-and-a-half million moviegoers went to see *Kiki's Delivery Service*, making it Studio Ghibli's first box-office hit.

Until the release of *Kiki*, Ghibli had hired only temporary help and paid them on a piecework system. As a result, the workers earned only about half of what other animators did, because they devoted so much more time to each image. On the heels of *Kiki*'s success, Miyazaki and Takahata decided to hire permanent workers on salary; doing so, they hoped, would be fairer to the employees, attract the most talented artists, and allow for in-house training and development of staff. When they implemented their plan, in 1990, Ghibli's production costs doubled overnight. At around this time the partners began planning the construction of a new, three-story studio in Koganei City, a Tokyo suburb, for which Miyazaki drew the blueprints.

Ghibli moved into the new studio shortly after release of *Kurenai no Buta* (*Porco Rosso*, 1992). A nostalgic depiction of pilots in the Adriatic Sea region between World Wars I and II, *Porco Rosso* was envisioned as a short in-flight movie for Japan Airlines, but it soon became a full-length project. *Porco Rosso*'s central character is an expert flyer who has the head of a pig—an artistic device that was meant to represent his withdrawal from humanity. While living alone on a beautiful island while fascism overtakes Italy, he meets a young female engineer who helps restore his spirits. *Porco Rosso*, which earned $23.5 million, was the highest-grossing film in Japan that year.

In 1994, the year in which his father died, Miyazaki finished the *Nausicaä* manga. The manga was much different from the movie, which he thought was too simplistic. In the manga's finale Nausicaä learns the ultimate secret of the forest. With the power of a highly destructive ally at her disposal, she is forced to choose between two competing visions of how the world should be organized, one of which recalls a variety of utopian schemes, including Marxism. Miyazaki has said that the writing of the manga caused him to rethink and finally repudiate his Marxist beliefs. Initially, he had questioned whether he was being elitist in depicting Nausicaä as a princess; in time he decided that there was something more basic than class involved in determining one's outlook on life.

Miyazaki has often assisted with other Ghibli releases. He produced Takahata's documentary on the Yanakawa Canal, *Yanakawa Horiwari Monogatari* (1987), and his animated film *Omohide Poro Poro* (*Only Yesterday*, 1991). Miyazaki helped plan the script for *Pompoko* (1994), also directed by Takahata, and he provided the screenplay and storyboards for—and produced—*Mimi o Sumaseba* (*Whisper of the Heart*, 1995), directed by Yoshifumi Kondo. For the last-named film, which was the highest-earning domestic release of 1995, he directed a brief but fantastic aerial sequence. He also directed a pair of commercials for Nihon TV and *On Your Mark*, a music video for the rock group Chage and Aska. In 1996 Ghibli struck a deal with Disney for the distribution of eight Ghibli films.

Miyazaki has continued to create manga, including *Shuna no Ryoko* (*The Journey of Shuna*, 1983), about a prince who steals seeds of the Golden Wheat from the gods to feed his people. *Zasso Note* (*Daydream Data Notes*, 1984–) is a series of short manga, usually war stories, published in *Model Graphix* magazine. More recently, Miyazaki published *Doromamire no Tora* (*Tigers in the Mire*, 1998–99), about Otto Carius, a German tank commander who, with just two tanks, held off a Russian advance in Estonia during World World II. (All the characters in *Doromamire* appear as pigs.)

Miyazaki's latest film, *Mononoke Hime* (*Princess Mononoke*, 1997), was the highest-grossing motion picture in Japanese history until *Titanic*. The work, which marks the first time Miyazaki used computers in the animation process, cost about $20 million to make and grossed over $150 million, beating *E.T. The Extra-Terrestrial* for the box-office record in Japan. Drawing on diverse sources, *Mononoke* takes place in the Muromachi period (1392–1573), when lush, primeval forests still existed in Japan, according to Miyazaki. Not wanting to create a story about samurais and geishas, Miyazaki chose as his central character Ashitaka, a member of a secret northern tribe. Cursed by a demonic animal god and exiled from his village, Ashitaka undertakes a quest to understand why the animal god has succumbed to hatred. His journey leads him to Tataraba, a village of ironworkers who, in striving to survive, degrade the nearby forest, which is protected by large animal gods and a human, San, who was abandoned as a child and has been raised by the wolf god. As the conflict between the humans and the protectors of the forest escalate, Ashitaka struggles to achieve peace between the warring parties. "*Mononoke* is about hatred and whether or not it can be overcome," Miyazaki told Steve Fritz for *Another Universe* (September 29, 1999, on-line). In a statement that accompanied the release of the film, he wrote: "We are not trying to solve global problems with this film. There can be no happy ending to the war between the rampaging forest gods and humanity. But even in the midst of hatred and slaughter, there is still much to live for. Wonderful encounters and beautiful things still exist." In 1999 *Princess Mononoke* became the first Ghibli film to have a theatrical release nationwide in the U.S.

As with his previous films, Miyazaki was involved in nearly every aspect of making the film. Exhausted by the amount of effort he was putting into his films, and concerned about his worsening eyesight and the declining strength of his drawing arm, he announced in 1998 that he would be scaling back his involvement with Ghibli. He actually quit the studio early that year and retired to "Pig House," a space next to the studio that is used for training animation directors. However, he ended up returning to Ghibli a year later. Although he no longer has hands-on involvement with the animation, he has continued to direct. Currently, Miyazaki is making short films for the Studio Ghibli

Museum, in Tokyo; the museum, which he helped design, opened in October 2001. He is also directing a film about a 10-year-old girl who undertakes a journey to the world of spirits to rescue her parents, who have been transformed into pigs.

Speaking about making animated films aimed at children, Miyazaki told Elisabeth Vincentelli for the *Village Voice* (October 27–November 2, 1999), "If a child is raised in a village of only 100, then they can see that they have a value of one one-hundredth of this village. But when you get to a figure of 100 million, what's one one-hundredth million? How do these children find value for their own existence? I felt that I needed to speak to them, and address that concern as an adult." He also told Vincentelli, "Childhood should be what it is for itself, and not some preparation surrendered to a future adulthood. . . . All children are tragic because they're born with infinite possibilities, and really the process of childhood is about cutting off many of those possibilities. So I aim all my films at these tragic children." In a conversation with Lewis Beale for the New York *Daily News* (October 24, 1999, on-line), he said that he and Takahata had "managed to cultivate an audience that is a natural mixture of adults and children. There are many people in Japan who believe that in order to keep children from getting bored you have to sing, dance and jump and run around. We have spent 30 years proving them wrong." — W.G.

Suggested Reading: *AnimeFantastique* p24+ Fall 1999, with photos; *Another Universe* (on-line) Sep. 29, 1999; *Film Comment* p62+ Nov.–Dec. 1998; *Japan Quarterly* p30+ Jan.–Mar. 1997, with photo; *San Francisco Chronicle* Oct. 31, 1999, with photos; *Village Voice* Oct. 27–Nov. 2, 1999, with photo; McCarthy, Helen. *Hayao Miyazaki: Master of Japanese Animation*, 1999

Selected Films: as director—*Lupin III: Cagliostro no Shiro* (*Lupin III: Castle of Cagliostro*), 1979; *Kaze no Tani no Nausicaä* (*Nausicaä of the Valley of the Wind*), 1984; *Tenku no Shiro Laputa* (*Laputa, Castle in the Sky*), 1986; *Tonari No Totoro* (*My Neighbor Totoro*), 1988; *Majo no Takkyubin* (*Kiki's Delivery Service*), 1989; *Kurenai no Buta* (*Porco Rosso*), 1992; *Mononoke Hime* (*Princess Mononoke*), 1997; as animator and/or scene designer and/or layout artist: *Wan Wan Chushingura* (*Watchdog Woof-Woof*) 1963; *Gulliver no Uchu Ryoko* (*Gulliver's Space Travels*), 1964 *Taiyo no Oji Hols no Daiboken* (*The Great Adventure of Hols, Prince of the Sun*, also known as *Little Norse Prince Valiant*), 1968; *Dobutsu Takarajima* (*Animal Treasure Island*), 1971; *Panda Kopanda* (*Panda & Child*), 1972; *Panda Kopanda Amefuri Circus no Maki* (*Panda & Child: Rainy Day Circus*), 1973; as producer— *Omohide Poro Poro* (*Only Yesterday*, 1991); *Mimi o Sumaseba* (*Whisper of the Heart*), 1995

Selected Television Shows: as director—*Lupin III*, 1971; *Mirai Shonen Conan* (*Future Boy Conan*), 1978; *Meitantei Holmes* (*Great Detective Holmes*), 1981; as animator and/or scene designer and/or layout artist: *Okami Shonen Ken* (*Wolf Boy Ken*, 1963; *Shonen Ninja Kaze no Fujimaru* (*Wind Ninja Boy Fujimaru*), 1964; *Hustle Punch*, 1965; *Rainbow Sentai Robin* (*Rainbow Warrior Robin*), 1966; *Alps no Shojo Heidi* (*Alpine Girl Heidi*), 1974; *Haha o Tazunete Sanzen-Ri* (*Three Thousand Miles in Search of Mother*), 1976; *Araiguma Rascal* (*Rascal the Raccoon*), 1977; *Akage no An* (*Anne of Green Gables*), 1979; as producer—*Yanakawa Horiwari Monogatari* (*The Story of Yanakawa Canal*, 1987)

Selected Manga: *Sabaku no Tami* (*People of the Desert*), 1969; *Kaze no Tani no Nausicaä*, 1982– 1994; *Shuna no Ryoko* (*The Journey of Shuna*), 1983; *Zasso Note* (*Daydream Data Notes*), 1984–; *Doromamire no Tora* (*Tiger in the Mire*), 1998

Sonja Pacho/Retna Ltd.

Moby

Sep. 11, 1965– Deejay; singer; songwriter.
Address: c/o MCT, 333 W. 52nd St., #1003, New York, NY 10019; c/o V2 Records, 14 E. Fourth St., New York, NY 10012

"What I strive for is honesty and sincerity," the deejay, songwriter, and singer Moby told Andrew Essex for *Interview* (March 1996), "which means recognizing that I'm a really flawed creature. If people want to judge me, all I can hope for is,

'Well, he's not perfect, but at least he's sincere.'" A deejay in the contemporary sense, Moby does not just spin disks—rather, he adds new material to remixes of existing songs to create original works, which he performs live. His stage performances distinguish him from other deejays in part because of his unpredictable behavior: at some concerts he has removed his clothing or smashed his keyboards, for example. Moby is both a pioneer in the techno-dance movement in music and its most public representative. His song "Thousand," which races along at a tempo of 1,015 beats per minute, was named in the *Guinness Book of World Records* as the fastest single ever recorded. Other Moby recordings, among them "Go," "Next Is the E," and "Drop a Beat," exerted considerable influence on the worldwide rave movement. But Moby, a professed Christian, avoids the heavy drug use practiced by many rave enthusiasts, and he neither smokes cigarettes nor eats meat. He has been a member of various bands, including the Vatican Commandos, Flipper, and the Ultra Vivid Scene, and has recorded under the pseudonyms Voodoo Child, UHF, and Barracuda.

"I want hit singles," Moby told Lorraine Ali for *Rolling Stone* (May 4, 1995). "I want people to know who I am, to be on MTV. Techno is faceless because most of the artists are afraid to put themselves forward. Most of them are terrified, so they sort of made a virtue of insecurity. They are afraid to perform, afraid of what their friends will think. So they make themselves personalityless. There's a lot of timid white guys out there."

Moby believes that resistance to techno among some listeners stems from apathy and ignorance. "Techno is about newness," he explained to Pat Blashill for *Details* (April 1995). "And what people demand of culture right now is a reaffirmation of the aesthetics and mores of what they were brought up with, because we live in a world we perceive to be unstable. We look for stability in the past, in rock 'n' roll that either sounds old or is old, and in movies that are based on TV shows. And I think that people who hate techno are homophobic. Techno and disco culture is generally seen as the province of Latin, black, and gay culture. Disco was the manifestation of all these feminine, gender-weird territories, and I think most white men are really threatened by techno because of these residual things." Moby, for whom dance is of great importance, also told Blashill, "What's spiritual for me is interacting with people. Just looking at how intensely complicated the fabric of existence is, I think that indicates the majesty of God."

Moby, as his parents called him, was born Richard Melville Hall on September 11, 1965 in New York City. He has never determined if it is true, as his parents contended, that he is a great-great-grandnephew of the celebrated 19th-century American writer Herman Melville, the author of *Moby-Dick*. He told Andrew Essex that he is proud of his nickname, because "*Moby Dick* represents the chaotic forces of nature versus the nineteenth-

century rational mind"; nonetheless, he has never read the book. "I've tried reading *Moby Dick* about three times," he admitted to an interviewer for *People* (November 1, 1993), "but the long passages where he gets bogged down describing whales just lose me."

Moby's father was a teaching assistant in the chemistry department at Columbia University, and at some point his mother became a medical aide. When Moby was two years old, his parents divorced; soon afterward his father was killed, when he lost control of his car while drunk and drove it into a brick wall. Moby and his mother moved in with his maternal grandparents in Darien, Connecticut, so that his mother could complete her undergraduate studies. When he was 10 he began listening to the music of Led Zeppelin and taking lessons in classical guitar. His introduction to disco, which occurred at a school dance when he was about 12, marked a turning point in his life. "Without thinking about it, I just shed all my Caucasian inhibitions and danced like crazy," he recalled to Chris Norris for *New York* (March 27, 1995). "I was possessed." A few years later, after he and his mother had moved to Stratford, Connecticut, Moby discovered the punk-rock music of such bands as the Clash, Gang of Four, and the Sex Pistols. Although, as he told Charles Aaron for *Spin* (June 2000), he and his mother were struggling to survive with the aid of public assistance and food stamps, his interest in the politics of punk-rock music "made our little disenfranchisement seem romantic." During Moby's teenage years his mother bought a house in Darien with money inherited from his grandfather. Becoming increasingly bored with suburban life, the 16-year-old Moby and some of his friends formed a straight-edge punk-rock group called the Vatican Commandos. (The term "straight-edge" refers to the members' abstention from cigarettes, drugs, and, in some cases, sex.) The group released an EP entitled *Hit Squad for God*. "We were anti-church, anti-suburbs, anti-long hair, anti-whatever," Moby told Charles Aaron.

Moby soon became convinced that punk orthodoxy could be as stuffy and restraining as he considered organized Christianity to be. "When you find yourself staring at some band in an indie-rock club with 50 other white kids holding Rolling Rocks [a brand of beer], and nobody's moving, you realize your worldview is pretty limited," he told Aaron. While studying philosophy as an undergraduate at the University of Connecticut, Moby read the Gospel according to Matthew and, inspired by the life and words of Christ, he decided to try to be less promiscuous and to stop drinking and using drugs. "I'm not really a cultural Christian, but I love Christ," he told Lorraine Ali. "I try to live up to his teachings but fail all the time. It's this yardstick that I hold up to my life that I can never, ever live up to. It's more interesting than frustrating. . . . I'm too attached to other things: the world, money in the bank, sex, being aggressive." Moby's religious leanings did not engender an affinity with the Christian right. "My goal is to get people to reevaluate Christ separate from Christianity," he told Chris Norris. "Most of the time, when you say 'Christ,' people envision Pat Robertson or Jerry Falwell or the ineffective little man who stood at the front of church every Sunday for an hour and a half and bored you to death. But Christ was this communistic, anarchistic, homeless, weird guy, who was also God and also really understood how people should be."

After dropping out of both the University of Connecticut and, later, the State University of New York at Purchase, which he attended from 1986 to 1988, Moby moved to the East Village section of New York City. There, he set up a studio in an apartment he shared with his best friend, the painter Damian Loeb, and Adrian Bartos (now a New York radio personality known as Stretch Armstrong). He began sending tapes containing mixes of different songs to clubs and radio stations. He landed a job at Manhattan's Club Mars, where he had the opportunity to serve as a deejay at performances of such hip-hop legends as Big Daddy Kane and Run-DMC. Moby found dance culture "atmospheric and sexy and religious" and was fascinated by "how foreign and interesting and wonderful it was," as he told Charles Aaron. "New York was dirty and dangerous, and sexual politics were weird, but at these clubs, Latinos, blacks, whites, men and women were celebrating!"

For his early singles, Moby used various pseudonyms, including Barracuda and Voodoo Child. He had his first hit in England in 1991, with "Go," a song that used Angelo Badalamenti's theme for David Lynch's television series Twin Peaks as its foundation. Soon afterward he began receiving requests for remixes from such artists and acts as Michael Jackson, the B-52s, Brian Eno, and Depeche Mode. "Back then, I didn't even know how to remix," Moby told Andrew Essex. "But suddenly, people were offering me more money to do just one record than I'd made the whole previous year." His success in England also led to a five-album deal with Elektra Records.

During this period Moby received invitations from around the world to serve as a deejay. He became enormously popular in spite of his public decision not to partake in the drug culture that had become synonymous with the all-night parties known as raves. Indeed, as the once loving and supportive culture of raves became a profitable commodity and, as it seemed to him, less aesthetically pure, he lost interest in it. "What disillusioned me about the punk scene is what disillusioned me about the house-music scene and, later on, about the rave scene," he told Charles Aaron. "It was always the tastemakers championing musical virtues I didn't care about. Hardcore punk decided to champion obscurity and aggression. With house music, you'd go to these industry events in '90-'91, and it was so bloodless and *professional*. Techno lost its celebratory quality." Moby's will-

ingness to critique the techno community, coupled with his success, led to a backlash among techno-music fans. "Within that core techno community, I'm a pariah," he told Neil Strauss for Rolling Stone (November 17, 1994). "But I've done a lot to encourage that, too, because I don't like that sort of really conservative, cliquey mind-set. I've turned on my heroes in the past, so it makes sense that people will turn on me. I'd be disappointed if they didn't—to an extent."

Moby has often used his position as a public figure to promote such causes as vegetarianism and environmentalism. The liner notes for his album Everything Is Wrong (1995), an eclectic and challenging mix of hardcore (an aggressive punk subgenre that was especially popular in New York City), blues, disco, and gospel, included two essays and a list of 67 statistics. "Getting people to think is a huge reason why I make records," Moby told Greg Kot for the Chicago Tribune (June 2, 1995). "If it's just a way to make money and gratify your ego, it's such a waste. But if some kid in Ohio starts thinking about vegetarianism or animal rights or the implication of being a member of this industrial society because of something he hears or reads on a record, that's a good tradeoff."

Everything Is Wrong reflected Moby's diminishing interest in the techno movement, which he had been instrumental in popularizing. "Techno has become a little too sophisticated," he told Greg Kot. "What I loved about the dance music was the dancing. But now it seems there are so many other elements that are involved that have nothing to do with the music. You've now got a lot of anal-retentive white guys who are afraid to get sweaty and dance. So they make music that's not particularly challenging: this boring, ambient, esoteric stuff that you can play in your living room but that has no emotion to it."

Moby followed Everything Is Wrong with remixes for Metallica and the Smashing Pumpkins; he also opened for the Red Hot Chili Peppers and Soundgarden and was featured on the Lollapalooza tour. In 1997 he shocked the music industry and alienated many techno fans with Animal Rights, a guitar-laden rock album. "I couldn't help but notice that while dance music had become pretty conservative and dull, the world of rock music had become, for me, pretty exciting," Moby told Larry Flick for Billboard (February 1, 1997). Animal Rights was not well received. "People's response to Animal Rights was just reactionary," Moby told MTV (on-line). "People heard aggression and fast songs using guitars and they immediately dismissed it." (A year later, however, the Chemical Brothers' and Prodigy's guitar-heavy electronic-music albums earned praise as groundbreakers.)

Moby claimed to be surprised that people had reacted so negatively to Animal Rights. "Musicians are not supposed to be corporate friendly people that make predictable, easily palatable records," he told MTV (on-line). "My heroes throughout the world of popular music—from John Coltrane to Billie Holiday to George Gershwin to Miles Davis, Ian Curtis, Bryan Ferry, Bob Dylan, Neil Young— these artists have at times had a lot of commercial success. But at other times they were quite self-involved and idiosyncratic. That's just what we're supposed to do." Like many other artists, Moby has maintained that his primary intention is to please himself. "I just make stuff that makes me happy or makes me cry because life is so messy in the nicest way," he told Lorraine Ali.

The year 1997 also saw the release of Moby's *I Like to Score*, a compilation of music from his movie soundtracks, including a version of the James Bond theme that became a Top 10 hit in the United Kingdom. Soon afterward he decided to leave Elektra Records, having concluded that its executives' financial concerns superseded their interest in producing good music. "In my meetings with some of the people at the company, they talked about market share with this note of terror in their voice," Moby told Robert Hilburn for the *Los Angeles Times* (August 10, 1999). "They were all real nice people and music lovers, but the fear of the CEO had been put in them." Before long Moby signed with V2 Records, an independent label established by Richard Branson, the founder of Virgin Records.

Moby's first release for V2 was *Play* (1999), an album that featured three distinct types of songs. The first incorporated music from *Sounds of the South*, an Atlantic Records boxed set of Library of Congress field recordings made by the music historian Alan Lomax, as well as vocals from an old Columbia Records gospel compilation. "My main interest in these old vocals was more my emotional response to them as opposed to where they came from," Moby told Jocelyn Clarke for *Muse* (2000, on-line). "They appealed to me on a very subjective level. . . . I wasn't trying to be sensitive to the original material. I was trying in a very naive way to make music that I loved. I started out with the vocals in their most unadulterated and unprocessed state, and they worked really well in that capacity and so that's how I used them." Because the field recordings had been recorded a capella, it was not difficult for Moby to incorporate them into his songs. A second group of songs on *Play* features Moby's vocals; the remainder of the album consists of instrumentals.

Play was a huge success, thanks in part to the popularity of the singles "Natural Blues" (which spawned a music video, directed by the photographer David LaChapelle, that stars Fairuza Balk and Christina Ricci) and "Bodyrock," a track reminiscent of old-school hip-hop that borrowed elements of the music of Boogie Down Productions. "I hope I have made an album that can improve the quality of people's lives for a brief little time, and I know that sounds really arrogant," he told Charles Aaron. "But you know, I *am* from the suburbs."

Moby received Grammy Award nominations in two categories for his work on *Play*: best rock instrumental performance (for "Bodyrock") and best

alternative music performance. *Play* spent 78 weeks on *Billboard*'s Top 200 charts; in May 2000 the album was certified platinum by the Recording Industry Association of America, and some months later it was certified double platinum. It has also reached gold or platinum status in more than half a dozen other countries. Moby and *Play* appeared on many music critics' "best of year" lists, in *Spin*, *Rolling Stone*, and the *Village Voice*, among other publications. Also in 2000 the musician completed a long tour and composed the opening theme for John Waters's film *Cecil B. De-Mented*. In addition, Moby earned another Grammy nomination, for best dance recording, for "Natural Blues." He also had his first Top-10 single, "South Side"; along with the No Doubt singer Gwen Stefani, he performed a version of that song that differed from the one on *Play*. In 2001 Moby appeared on PBS's weekly series *Sessions at West 54th* and in the IMAX feature *All Access*, which also offered performances by George Clinton, Carlos Santana, B.B. King, Kid Rock, and Macy Gray. Also that year he organized and headlined Area: One, a summer festival that included such diverse acts as Outkast, Nelly Furtado, Incubus, and the Roots.

Moby is reportedly not troubled by the paradox inherent in his existence as an underground artist with mainstream aspirations. "I spent years immersing myself in esoteric culture—going to avant-garde jazz performances and reading esoteric books and seeing weird self-indulgent movies— and at some point I just had to admit to myself, for the most part, self-indulgent state-subsidized esoteric culture leaves me cold," he told Ted Oehmke for the *New York Times Magazine* (July 4, 1999). "I find myself responding more to . . . stuff that's a little more talked about and a little more utilitarian. When I was 16 years old, I tried to be a good punk rocker, and I listened to punk rock. But I had to admit that I loved classical music, and I loved pop music, and I loved disco. . . . If people actually knew the depths of my love for . . . crummy pop songs, they'd be ashamed on my behalf."

Moby derives inspiration from the passion and determination of such figures as the 19th-century Dutch artist Vincent van Gogh and Mohandas K. Gandhi, who led India to independence in 1947. "I look through history, and my favorite people tend to be unbalanced," he told Lorraine Ali. "They weren't complacent but instead driven by something. Complacent people tend not to accomplish very much. They might have happy lives, and if I could live a day in their shoes, I might feel very jealous of them. . . . That's also why I think I don't want to marry or have children. I want to be emotionally an adolescent until I die. I want to hear a Smiths song at 50 and still be able to cry."

By his own account, Moby has embraced the commercialism of the music industry because he wants his music to reach as many people as possible. "I'm very proud of the music I make," he told *MTV News* (May 31, 2000, on-line). "The reason I want to sell records is that I like the music that I make, and I love the fact that some people might find a place for my records in their home. I like the idea that I can make music to be the soundtrack to people's lives."

An article about Moby's Manhattan apartment appeared in *Gentlemen's Quarterly* in September 2000. — C.L.

Suggested Reading: *Billboard* p9+ Feb. 1, 1997, with photo; *Details* p185+ Apr. 1995, with photos; *Interview* p93+ Mar. 1996, with photos; *Los Angeles Times* D p1+Aug. 10, 1999, with photo; *New York* p48+ Mar. 27, 1995, with photo; *New York Times Magazine* p10 July 4, 1999, with photo; *Rolling Stone* p102+ Nov. 17, 1994, with photo, p58+May 4, 1995, with photos; *Spin* p96+ June 2000, with photos

Selected Recordings: *Moby*, 1992; *Ambient*, 1993; *Everything Is Wrong*, 1995; *Animal Rights*, 1996; *I Like to Score*, 1997; *Play*, 1999

Courtesy of Friends of Morella

Morella, Constance A.

Feb. 12, 1931– United States Representative from Maryland. Address: 2228 Rayburn House Office Bldg., Washington, DC 20515

"I happen to be in love with my district," Constance A. "Connie" Morella, a United States representative from Maryland, enthused to Charles Babington of the *Washington Post* (October 22, 1992). The residents of Maryland's Eighth District, a well-to-do swath of Montgomery County that borders

Washington, D.C., seem to feel the same way about Morella, having returned her to Congress every two years since she was originally elected, in 1986. While over 60 percent of Morella's constituents are registered Democrats, she is a Republican—one whose longevity and popularity in her district apparently transcend partisanship. Her reputation has been that of an independent thinker who is willing to vote against the Republican Party line on such inflammatory issues as abortion and gun control in order to best meet the needs of the people she serves. Representative Henry Hyde, a starkly conservative House member from Illinois, explained Morella's delicate position to Leslie Maitland for the *New York Times* (April 18, 1990): "Why is she a Republican and not a Democrat? That's a good question. But we're delighted, ecstatic almost, to have her in the party. We'd like her to vote with us more often. But to get elected she must reflect her district, and she votes like her predecessors. We also need all the Republicans we can get."

The daughter of Italian immigrants, Morella was born Constance Albanese on February 12, 1931. Her father worked as a cabinetmaker. She grew up in Somerville, Massachusetts, a blue-collar Boston suburb, and attended public schools, later graduating from Boston University with an A.B. degree in English. In 1954 she and her husband, Anthony, also raised in Somerville, moved to the Washington, D.C., area. Morella taught high school in Montgomery County, Maryland, before earning an M.A. degree in English literature from American University, in Washington. Beginning in 1970 she taught English at Montgomery College.

Morella subscribed to Democratic views as a young adult but changed party affiliation in 1962, when she discovered the "progressive Republicanism" of such politicians as John Lindsay, Nelson Rockefeller, and Jacob Javits, who, as she explained to Maitland, believed in "civil rights, individual liberty, and governmental interference only when it cannot be done on an individual level, and then local government can do it best." Her first political experience came in the early 1970s, when she was part of a local commission for women; she worked to ensure that a woman could apply for credit without the signature of her spouse. In 1974 Morella ran for the Maryland General Assembly, but lost. Four years later, however, she won a seat as a delegate in the General Assembly, to which she was reelected in 1982. During 1980 she campaigned as a Republican for the U.S. congressional seat for her home district, the Eighth, but she was defeated in the primary. In 1986 Michael Barnes, a Democrat, vacated that seat; Morella ran for the spot, opposed by state senator Stewart Bainum Jr., and after lagging behind in preelection polling, she won by 6,000 votes. "It was just plain hard work, and the result was stunning," she told R. H. Melton for the *Washington Post* (November 6, 1986).

Morella's first impression of her Eighth District voters has continued to influence her campaigns. "[The 1986] election shows that Montgomery

County voters are very independent," she explained to Melton. "It proves that party label is nothing that's going to keep people from voting for a person." Accordingly, Morella's party affiliation has been all but removed from the literature of her subsequent campaigns. Morella's tenure has been similar to that of a local politician; her district, a short car or subway ride from the U.S. Capitol, has enjoyed day-to-day attention from her that would be impossible if her constituents were farther away. As Babington noted, "Three things are certain in Montgomery County: death, taxes and Connie Morella showing up for every small-town parade and public forum, shaking every hand in sight before she departs." Her constituents appreciate her concern for local issues, and the mutual goodwill even led her to quash rumors that she would run for the Senate in 1994. "I know my county, and I like it," she told Kent Jenkins Jr. for the *Washington Post* (February 1, 1993). "In a statewide race, I don't think I'd be able to do the personal things that I can do so well here." That personal touch has won over thousands of otherwise hard-core Democratic voters and has managed to keep Morella afloat in every race since 1986, no matter how well financed her opponent has been.

After her original swearing-in, in 1987, Morella quickly blazed her own trail. By June of that year, she had come out against aid to the Nicaraguan rebels, voted to override presidential vetoes on clean water and highway-construction bills, and even stood with Democrats to pass a fattened budget that raised taxes. "[The $1 trillion budget] was not an easy vote, but it's one I felt was best for my constituency," she told Eric Pianin for the *Washington Post* (June 28, 1987). Her constituents indeed benefitted: the many federal workers living in her district received a pay raise for fiscal year 1988, and senior citizens' health benefits and cost-of-living adjustments were protected. Although some congressional Republicans were frustrated by her lack of enthusiasm for President Ronald Reagan's policies, most understood her unusual status as a liberal Republican in a Democratic district who, with one rash or upsetting move, could be toppled in the next election. Morella, for her part, was frustrated by the increasing conservatism of her party: "It would have been easier for me to run as a Democrat," she admitted to Maitland. "But you defeat the purpose if you leave the party instead of trying to broaden the base."

One area that Morella has consistently attempted to defend is women's issues: funding for cancer and HIV/AIDS research; affordable child care; women and children's health care; pregnancy prevention among teenagers; and programs to combat domestic violence. She is particularly well known in Congress for her work on the last-named issue, having sponsored the Violence Against Women Act of 1994, which provided a large federal grant to finance counseling, shelters for battered women, telephone hot lines, and other services. In 2000 she sponsored the Violence Against Women Act reau-

thorization to renew the grant and expand the legislation. Her 1996 congressional resolution, aimed at preventing children from being placed in the custody of anyone who had abused his or her spouse, was mentioned in a 1999 television movie, *Shameful Secrets*, in a scene involving a congressional hearing. Morella has often broken ranks with the Republican Party to support abortion and reproductive rights. In early 1989 she joined a group of Republican congresswomen who wrote to the newly inaugurated President George Bush in support of abortion rights. (She told Maitland, "I'm sure the President [Bush] scratches his head sometimes when he looks at my voting record.") Morella's stance, which includes support of even controversial "partial-birth" abortions, has continually made her the darling of both abortion-rights groups and her more liberal constituents. In 1992 she went to the Republican National Convention hoping to persuade the party leadership to remove its antiabortion plank from the presidential platform. "I would like to move the party closer to the center," she explained to Jenkins. In May 1996 she debated then-congressman Tim Hutchinson of Arkansas, a Republican opponent of abortion rights, on the PBS program *NewsHour*, saying, as quoted on-line by *PBS.org* (May 2, 1996), "I think [the abortion plank of the GOP platform] will cost some votes [for GOP presidential candidate Bob Dole] because Americans are middle-of-the-road, and they feel that abortion is personal and should be private, and it has to do with one's personal beliefs, and it doesn't belong on the agenda for politicians."

As a representative with a significant percentage of constituents who work in the fields of science and technology, Morella is a member of the Subcommittee on the Environment, Technology, and Standards of the House Committee on Science. In 1997–98, during the 105th Congress, she pushed successfully for passage of a bill to review and eliminate the roadblocks preventing women, minorities, and the disabled from advancing in scientific professions. Morella also sponsored, in 1999, the Technology Transfer Commercialization Act, allowing technology created in national laboratories to be sold and marketed in the private sector. One of Morella's most important contributions in the area of technology was her role as co-chair of the House Year 2000 Task Force. As early as the 1996 House session, Morella realized that both the government and private industry were far behind in Y2K computer and technology readiness, and she foresaw the chaos that could occur if the problem went uncorrected. For championing this cause, she was honored in 2000 during Federal Computer Week.

Unlike many of her Republican peers, Morella has won the support of both the Sierra Club and the League of Conservation Voters, which placed her on its Environmental Honor Roll for her support of measures to preserve endangered species and American forests. Closer to home, Morella has called for continued federal support of Glen Echo

Park, a popular, historic amusement park and community center located in her district. Glen Echo has been managed by the National Park Service since 1971, but until fiscal year 2000 the federal government had seemed uncertain as to who could best manage the park and its programs. In an online *Washington Post* interview moderated by Bob Levey (April 7, 1998), Morella commented, "Glen Echo Park is a federal treasure and it should be preserved. . . . I am part of this [preservation] committee and hope that we will forge a public-private partnership." Morella has attempted to steer the Congress toward fiscal responsibility, for example by proposing reform of the Internal Revenue Service and an end to the "marriage penalty" tax, and she has usually supported Republican foreign-policy positions; on domestic social issues, however, she has shown liberal leanings. She sponsored the Hate Crimes Prevention Act of 1999, which expanded the role of federal agents in hate-crime investigation and prosecution, and supported federal funding of the arts. An advocate of gun safety, she participated in the Million Mom March, a mass demonstration held in Washington, D.C., on May 14, 2000 to call for sensible gun laws. Earlier, in an act of solidarity with President Bill Clinton, who shared their views, in March 2000 she and other members of the House had visited the White House to call for swift action on gun-safety initiatives. "There is no reason that we should have child-proof cigarette lighters and child-proof medicine bottles, but handguns aren't required to have trigger locks," read a press release from the congresswoman's office, dated March 15, 2000.

Although Morella supported the conservative Newt Gingrich in his successful 1994 bid for the position of Speaker of the House, vast divisions between her and her party followed. Morella's biggest break with the GOP came late in 1998, when she was one of only four congressional Republicans to vote against the impeachment of President Clinton, who was charged with perjury and obstruction of justice in connection with the Monica Lewinsky sex scandal. In the weeks preceding the impeachment vote, she fielded thousands of calls from constituents at her office and at home (her phone number is listed), as well as from the pro- and anti-impeachment factions in Washington. She had supported the motion to censure Clinton, "to find some way to come to a decision where the President would receive more than just an indelible scar in history," she told Harry Jaffe and Chuck Conconi for *Washingtonian* (February 1999). But when the motion to censure was rejected, she was faced with the vote on impeachment itself. Her decision, delayed until the day before the vote, was based on her historical research, which revealed that "impeachment was not meant to be punitive. It is for removal. . . . What he did does not really imperil the county," she explained to Jaffe and Conconi. Despite what she called her "velvet glove approach"—an outwardly gentle manner that reportedly inspires affection even in people who oppose her opinions—Morella's vote in the impeachment hearings only deepened the divide between her and some of her fellow Republicans. "Morella has little clout within the party," Jaffe and Conconi wrote. "And she is virtually a pariah within the Maryland Republican Party. . . . The harshest consequences of Morella's vote may be that any hopes she had of running statewide as a Republican might be dead, especially for the US Senate. Her problems have to do with getting nominated, not getting elected." Such speculation does not seem to bother her, though; throughout the seven terms she has thus far served in the House, her mantra might have been the statement she made to Maitland in 1990: "People didn't send me here to be a robot." In 2000 Morella retained her House seat in a race against a self-financed Democrat, Terry Lierman, who ran on the platform of decreasing the Republican representation in Congress. In March 2001 she became the chair of the House Subcommittee on the District of Columbia, an arm of the House Committee on Government Reform.

Morella and her husband raised nine children—three of their own and six of her late sister's—and have more than a dozen grandchildren. While some might expect Morella—who is 70—to retire soon, she has different ideas. As she told Levey, "My role model is Sen. [Strom] Thurmond," who continues to serve in the Senate at close to 99 years of age. "Enough said." — K.S.

Suggested Reading: *New York Times* A p16 Apr. 18, 1990, with photo; *Washington Post* B p1+ Aug. 9, 1992, with photo, B p1+ Mar. 13, 1995, with photos, D p9 Oct. 9, 1993, p57 Nov. 6, 1986, with photo; *Washingtonian* p34+ Feb 1999, with photos

---

Morris, Errol

Feb. 5, 1948– Filmmaker. Address: Fourth Floor Productions, 678 Massachusetts Ave. #503, Cambridge, MA 02139

The words "eccentric," "peculiar," "odd," "quirky," and "idiosyncratic" are often used to describe the filmmaker Errol Morris, whom one journalist described as being in "a perpetual state of having too many ideas." Among other proposals, Morris has pitched ideas for films about spontaneous combustion, the fate of Albert Einstein's brain (which was stolen from an autopsy room), and a giant, 28-pound chicken. His six feature-length films are similarly offbeat. In the first, *Gates of Heaven*, he explored the pet-cemetery business; in his most recent, *Mr. Death*, he profiled a self-styled expert in execution technology who is also a prominent Holocaust denier. Between those projects, Morris created vivid cinematic portraits of the residents of a Florida swamp town, the participants in a Kaf-

Errol Morris

Courtesy of Magic Lantern, Inc.

kaesque court trial, the brilliant physicist Stephen Hawking, a lion tamer, a topiary gardener, a mole-rat specialist, and a scientist whose specialty is robotics. "I've always thought of my portraits as my own version of the Museum of Natural History, these very odd dioramas where you're trying to create some foreign exotic environment and place it on display," he told Philip Gourevitch for the *New York Times Magazine* (August 9, 1992).

Morris's "nonfiction features"—he dislikes the word "documentary," because he thinks his films do more than faithfully and uncreatively record the truth—are not freak shows. From his hundreds of hours of interviews, he culls statements about issues and ideas that he hopes have wide significance. One of his favorite themes is the way humans connect their private "mental landscapes" to the outside world. "I think all my films have been . . . solipsistic films, on one level," he told David Sterritt for the *Christian Science Monitor* (August 26, 1988). "They're films about people lost in strange, private worlds of self-delusion and fantasy. . . . They're about characters who are suspicious and desperate about what's 'out there' in the world."

Part of Morris's success as a filmmaker stems from his ability to coax his subjects to reveal these interior worlds, sometimes with unexpected outcomes. In *The Thin Blue Line*, for instance, one subject virtually admitted that she had perjured herself in court; her disclosure later helped free an innocent man. The extraordinary revelations Morris has captured on film led the movie critic Roger Ebert to declare him "America's most intriguing documentarian"—albeit one whom Academy Award voters have regularly snubbed. In her *New*

York Times (Sep. 30 1997), review of his1997 film, *Fast, Cheap, and Out of Control*, Janet Maslin described Morris as "a one-of-a-kind filmmaker capable of melding science, philosophy, poetry and sheer whimsy into an elaborate meditation on life's mysteries." "I like the idea of making films about ostensibly nothing," Morris told Mark Singer, who profiled him for the for the *New Yorker* (February 6, 1989). "That's what all my movies are about. That and the idea that we're in a position of certainty, truth, [and] infallible knowledge, when actually we're just a bunch of apes running around."

Speaking of his childhood with Susan Stark for the *Detroit News* (October 18, 1997, on-line), Morris said, "I think you can't . . . articulate this kind of thing when you are very young, but I think I always wanted to be an artist, to deal with ideas"; he then added, "I've always said that the interest isn't film making—it's ideas." A son of Abner Morris and Cinnabelle (Burzinski) Morris, the filmmaker was born on February 5, 1948 in the suburban town of Hewlett, on Long Island, New York, and raised there. His father, a doctor, died of a heart attack when Morris was two. His mother, a graduate of the world-famous Juilliard School, in New York City, supported Errol and his brother, Noel, by teaching music in a public school. An asthmatic, precocious child, Morris learned chess in third grade and gave lectures on astronomy to his fifth-grade classmates. He loved stamps, maps, trilobites, and Frank Baum's fantasy stories about Oz. He was also fascinated by murderers. "It's an obsession I've had since I was a little boy," he told Martha Sherrill Dailey for the *Washington Post* (September 2, 1988). "I grew up in the '50s, when executions were a reality." Preoccupied with death, he concluded in his teen years that "there was no point in going on, but then I realized that life is just an endless series of embarrassments and I'd hate to miss out on all that," as he told Mark Singer.

Morris studied cello at Putney, a Vermont prep school known for its music program; he was also tutored by the renowned music teacher Nadia Boulanger in Fontainebleau, France. (In addition, according to Susan Stark, he was a student at the Juilliard School at some point.) He attended the University of Wisconsin, from which he graduated with a degree in history in 1969. After completing his studies he took up rock climbing, reportedly becoming the first person to wear a white shirt and necktie while scaling the northwest face of Half Dome, in Yosemite National Park, California. For a while he supported himself by working as a cable-television salesmen in Wisconsin and ghost-writing term papers in Massachusetts. Then he entered the graduate program in the history of science at Princeton University, in New Jersey. Because he did not have a background in science, he found his course work rough going, and his unconventional ideas often led to conflicts with his adviser. Once, after he turned in a 30-page double-spaced paper, his adviser wrote a 30-page, single-spaced paper criticizing it.

In search of more congenial academic pastures, Morris went to the University of California at Berkeley to study philosophy. On campus he found a second home at the Pacific Film Archive, one of the few places in the East Bay that regularly screens obscure films. For almost a year he watched several movies a day there. Tom Luddy, who directed the archive at the time, told Mark Singer, "There were a bunch of regulars and a bunch of eccentric regulars, and Errol was one of the eccentrics. . . . What made him eccentric? Well, for one thing, he dressed strangely. Remember, this is Berkeley in the early seventies. And Errol was wearing dark suits with pants that were too short, white dress shirts, and heavy shoes. He looked like a New York person gone to seed. Then, I let him use our library for research, and he was always getting into little frictions with the staff. He felt he could both use the Archive and put it down. He would leave messes. He never bothered to reshelve books. I found myself defending him, which was often difficult, because he would attack me for the programming. He was a film-noir nut. He claimed we weren't showing the *real* film noir. So I challenged him to write the program notes. Then, there was his habit of sneaking into the films and denying that he was sneaking in. I told him if he was sneaking in he should at least admit he was doing it."

An avid reader of such tabloids as the *National Enquirer* and the *Weekly World News*, Morris developed an unusual thesis proposal dealing with movie monsters, the insanity plea, and social scientists' inability to explain criminal behavior. For research on his thesis, Morris attended the trials of serial killers in Santa Cruz, California, then known as the mass-murder capital of the United States. He also made several visits, in 1975 and 1976, to Central State Hospital, in Waupun, Wisconsin, where he conducted interviews with Edward Gein, a taxidermist, serial killer, cannibal, and grave robber whose history was the basis for the films *Psycho* and *Texas Chainsaw Massacre*. Soon afterward Morris moved to Wisconsin, so that he could interview other local murderers. He remained in Wisconsin for nearly a year.

Through Tom Luddy, Morris befriended the eccentric German filmmaker Werner Herzog. Werner shared Morris's interest in Ed Gein, and they developed a theory that Gein had dug underground tunnels to his mother's coffin; they even considered digging into the grave by moonlight to confirm the theory. Herzog later hired Morris as a consultant on the film *Stroszek* (1977), an experience that taught Morris more about the art of filmmaking. With the cash he earned from his consulting stint, Morris traveled to Vernon, Florida, a town known as "Nub City" because an unusual number of its residents had reportedly hacked off their arms and legs to collect insurance payments. Morris wanted to develop a fictional movie based on Vernon, but he got sidetracked when he noticed an article in the *San Francisco Chronicle* about the pet-cemetery busi-

ness. Intrigued, he traveled to California and began filming extensive interviews with Floyd McClure, whose pet-cemetery business had failed, and the Harbert family, who ran the successful Bubbling Well Pet Memorial Park.

In the process of shooting the film, in the spring and summer of 1977, Morris fired three cinematographers (one of whom he had to wrestle for the camera at one point) after conflicts involving his atypical ideas about documentary filmmaking. Rather than try to achieve a "documentary look," with jiggly, handheld-camera shots and natural lighting, Morris had all his subjects sit the same distance from the camera, used artificial lighting, and, relying on a technique he had developed while interviewing mass murderers, interrupted his subjects as seldom as possible. "It's not like *60 Minutes* with a Mike Wallace type trying to wear someone down, impeaching what they say and trying to uncover a lie or a contradiction—the investigative journalist style," he explained to D. C. Denison for a *Boston Globe* (February 12, 1989) article reprinted on Morris's official Web site. "In *60 Minutes* the journalist is the star. In my style of interviewing the camera is the star. . . . Some of the most surprising new facts came from people talking without interruption." Of greatest importance, Morris learned, was keeping the subjects talking and looking as if he was listening, even if he wasn't. "Actually, listening to what people are saying, to me, interferes with looking as if you were listening to what people are saying," he told Mark Singer.

Gates of Heaven (1978), as Morris called his pet-cemetery picture, was made for $120,000, most of which came from his family and a wealthy classmate of his. "You can approach this film in a dozen different ways," Roger Ebert told Scott Pelley, who interviewed him for the *60 Minutes* spin-off *60 Minutes II*. "It just doesn't have a bottom. You can't get to the bottom of it. And you can't decide, no matter how often you see it, if it's a comedy or a tragedy." Ebert praised the movie as one of the 10 best of all time, but it did not receive much publicity when it was screened, except for a brief flurry of stories reporting that Herzog had eaten his shoe when the work was shown in Berkeley. (According to those reports, Herzog had vowed that if Morris ever made a film, he would consume his own footwear; the event was documented by Les Blank in the short 1979 film *Werner Herzog Eats His Shoe*.)

In 1979 Morris returned to Vernon to finish his "Nub City" film. After experiencing both creative and practical difficulties in completing the project (one of the "nubbies" even threatened him with bodily harm), Morris switched his focus to other Vernon residents. On the surface, the film records their thoughts on such topics as worm farming, turkey hunting, cosmology, and the word "therefore"; on a deeper level, the film illuminates their thoughts on life, death, love, and religion. The resulting work, *Vernon, Florida*, was shown at the New York Film Festival in 1981, but it was never nationally distributed and earned little attention, except when it was aired on television, in 1982. Some critics complained that Morris's film presented its subjects as backwater yokels, but Morris disagreed; as he later told Martha Sherrill Dailey, "I don't see myself as apart from any of my characters. I feel very much in the same boat with many of them. Because the movies are funny doesn't mean I am making fun of them."

After completing *Vernon, Florida*, Morris struggled financially. He was offered various Hollywood projects—a film about John and Jim Pardue, a pair of bank-robbing brothers who had killed their father, grandmother, and two accomplices; a work about an Elvis Presley impersonator; and a script based on a short story by Stephen King—but each of them fell through. During this period Morris's brother died of a heart attack. In 1984 Morris married Julia Sheehan, an art historian he had met in Wisconsin in the 1970s. Harassed daily by bill collectors, Morris supported his wife and their son, Hamilton, by working as a freelance private detective for an agency that investigated cases involving securities and commodities. He found that being a good detective was not much different from being a good interviewer, in that for both, he had to induce people to open up to him. "Errol has an incredible ability to get people to talk," Jim Mintz, who had hired Morris to work for the agency, told Philip Gourevitch. "His ability not to fill a silence is unique."

For his next film, which he tentatively titled "Dr. Death, A Series of Seven Stories About Self-Deception or Concepts of Violence in Criminality," Morris wanted to profile James Grigson, a Texas psychiatrist dubbed the "Killer Shrink" and the "Hanging Psychiatrist." At that time in Texas, the death penalty could be imposed only if the prosecution demonstrated that the guilty person would most likely commit a violent crime again. Grigson became known for supplying prosecutors with his "expert" judgment on criminal propensity. In the course of interviewing Grigson and several convicts who had been condemned to death in part because of his testimony, Morris was seized with an idea for a different film, one revolving around a prisoner named Randall Adams. In 1977 Adams had been convicted for murdering Dallas police officer Robert Wood during a routine traffic stop the previous year; his death sentence had been commuted to life in prison because of a technicality. Adams claimed that he had been framed by a man named David Harris, who on the day of the murder had picked up the hitchhiking Adams; the two had spent some time drinking and carousing. A minor at the time of the killing, Harris had been the police's first suspect because he had bragged to friends that he had killed a cop. After his arrest Harris claimed that Adams had shot the officer, and Adams was tried for the murder. In the courtroom Adams maintained that he had left Harris several hours before the murder, but three surprise witnesses placed Adams at the scene of the crime, and their combined testimony led to his conviction.

While investigating Adams's story, Morris obtained files on the Adams prosecution from Henry Wade, the district attorney of Dallas County, who had assigned the case to his assistant Douglas Mulder. In the files, which Wade had refused to release to Adams's attorney, Morris found evidence that the testimony of the prosecution's eyewitnesses was untrue. Morris tracked down the witnesses and filmed them giving accounts that contradicted what they had said in court. One of them even admitted in a rambling monologue that she had failed to pick out Adams in a lineup and that a policeman had told her whom to finger. Morris also located Harris, who soon afterward was convicted of murder in a different case. In a dramatic tape-recorded interview from death row, he admitted to Morris that Adams had not committed the crime.

Morris's film of his investigation, *The Thin Blue Line* (1988), was released just as Adams was launching another appeal. Veering from straightforward documentary, the film included stylish re-enactments, short sequences from noir films, and a score by Philip Glass. "The underlying theme is that human credulity is virtually unlimited," Morris told Bruce Tomaso for the *Chicago Tribune* (August 9, 1989), reflecting on the blatant lies used to convict Adams. "Our desire to believe anything we want to believe is a lot stronger than our desire to seek the truth." Billed as "the first murder mystery that actually solves a murder," *The Thin Blue Line* was the first Morris film to be distributed widely. The film won best-documentary honors from the New York Film Critics Circle and the National Society of Film Critics; to the surprise of many critics, it was not nominated for an Oscar. The work led to a MacArthur Fellowship for Morris, in 1989, and a Guggenheim Fellowship, in 1990.

In 1989, largely because of the evidence that Morris had unearthed and passed along to Adams's attorney, Adams's conviction was overturned. Adams later sued Morris because he felt that he was entitled to a share of Morris's profits from the film. Actually, Morris had earned very little money—the film had cost about $1 million and grossed about $1.5 million. The suit was settled out of court. Morris kept in touch with Harris (who, as of 1999, was still on death row) but not Adams. "I'm very proud of what I did in that case, regardless of whether [Adams] appreciated it or not," he said in a 1999 on-line interview for the publishing house Bedford/St. Martin's. The success of *The Thin Blue Line* led to more Hollywood offers, though as before, some of the projects ended badly for Morris. For example, he was hired by the actor Robert Redford to direct *The Dark Wind* (1991), a film based on a Tony Hillerman mystery novel, but he was fired before editing began. Morris later told Gourevitch, "Mine is a circuitous path. I can't see myself as a Hollywood insider, although I definitely want the Hollywood career." (Since 1989 he has worked on commercials to supplement his income.) Morris's next film project came when Steven Spielberg picked him to direct an adaptation of the best-selling nonfiction book *A Brief History of Time*, by the physicist Stephen Hawking, who has been totally paralyzed and unable to speak for many years, as a result of amyotrophic lateral sclerosis, a neuromuscular disorder better known as Lou Gehrig's disease. (Hawking writes and "speaks" with the help of a specialized computer and voice synthesizer.) Although the movie *A Brief History of Time* (1992) treats such exotic ideas as the reversibility of time and the physics of black holes, it is not primarily a science lesson. Morris told Keith Phipps for the *Onion* (on-line) that it is "about Stephen Hawking's dream about his science, the story of his own biography—but not biography on a kind of factual level, but biography as dreamscape. Of how he himself views his own work, about his own personal or emotional connection to the universe. Which is what I felt about the book, too. I looked at the book as a romance novel." The film won Morris the 1992 Grand Jury Prize for documentary filmmaking and the Documentary Filmmakers Trophy from the Sundance Festival.

For the next several years, Morris pitched various ideas with little success. He also invented the Interrotron, a device based on TelePrompTer technology. (TelePrompTers are transparent screens on which text is projected; the machine enables a person to read text without looking away from his or her audience.) According to the Web site of New York City's Museum of Modern Art, the name "Interrotron" was coined by Morris's wife, to take into account the "mixture of interview, interrogation, and terror" that it represented. Previously, Morris had placed his head next to the camera while talking to his subjects, so that they would look into the camera, but on film their gaze was slightly off center. With the Interrotron, an image of Morris is projected on a glass plate positioned right over the camera lens; another plate projects an image of the subject to Morris. What results, Morris believes, is "true" first-person filmmaking. "Not that you always have to be looking into somebody's eyes," he told Shawn Rosenheim for the *New York Times* (October 30, 1994). "But if there *is* eye contact, every look takes on a completely different significance. The inclination of the head suddenly takes on enormous dramatic power." Though the device may seem awkward and artificial, Morris believes that talking to the filmmaker's image may be less intimidating than directing one's speech to the person's face. As a production designer who worked with Morris noted, talking to the Interrotron is like talking to a television, an object with which most Americans are comfortable.

For *Fast, Cheap, and Out of Control* (1997), which was financed by American Playhouse and the British television station Channel 4, Morris interviewed a lion tamer who had elaborate theories about lion psychology; an expert on a species of rodent, known as the naked mole-rat, who sees parallels between human behavior and that of the mole-rat, which lives in colonies governed by a rigid caste system; a Massachusetts Institute of Technology scientist who works in the field of robotics and believes that automatons will dominate future societies; and a gardener who has spent decades trimming trees and shrubs into elaborate shapes. One of the themes that unites the monologues is the subjects' search for control over life. *Fast, Cheap, and Out of Control* earned best-documentary film honors from the National Board of Review and the National Society of Film Critics, among other groups, and it won the Independent Spirit Award (bestowed by the Independent Feature Project, an organization that serves independent filmmakers).

In his latest film, *Mr. Death: The Rise and Fall of Fred Leuchter Jr.* (1999), Morris focused on a self-described "Florence Nightingale of prisons" whose professional activities included repairing electric chairs and advising prison wardens on ways to make executions more humane; one of his ideas was to allow the condemned person to sit up and watch TV as the lethal injection was being administered. Leuchter's unusual expertise led to a meeting with Ernst Zundel, the publisher of *The Hitler We Loved and Why* and the Holocaust-denial tract *Did Six Million Really Die?* Brought to trial in the 1980s in Canada, where it is illegal to publish false historical accounts that incite racial animosity, Zundel enlisted Leuchter to help him disprove the reality of the Holocaust. Leuchter subsequently spent his honeymoon in Auschwitz (where many Jews had been gassed to death by the Nazis and up to 1,500,000 people are believed to have died) to examine the site and surreptitiously collect samples of the brick from the gas-chamber areas. Summarizing his findings in the infamous *Leuchter Report*, which has been distributed over the Internet and has been cited by numerous Holocaust deniers, Leuchter claimed that there was no residue of lethal gas on the bricks and that the facilities could not have been used as gas chambers because the gas would have leaked and killed the Nazi guards.

Morris became aware of Leuchter through a newspaper article, and he began to think about making a film about the Holocaust from an innovative angle. "Spielberg [in his film *Schindler's List*] has the interesting thesis that anybody can be a hero, whereas I have the far more interesting thesis that anybody can think he's a hero," Morris told Mark Singer. Because of the controversial subject matter, Morris's footage sat on a shelf for several years before the Independent Film Channel agreed to finance the movie. In the course of *Mr. Death*, Leuchter's study of the bricks and his findings are repudiated; but rather than trying to prove that the Holocaust occurred, the film examines why the Holocaust happened. The answer, Morris suggests, lies in the pattern of self-deception of someone like Leuchter, whose actions on behalf of Zundel led to the loss of his consulting business and the collapse of his marriage. Morris doesn't consider Leuchter anti-Semitic. "What happens if you really need to be loved and the only people who will love you are Nazis?" Morris asked Singer rhetorically. He also said, "People do not do evil knowingly. Evil is always construed as some form of doing good. . . . I hope this movie becomes more effective if Fred emerges as more a person like you and me." In 1999 the Durham, North Carolina–based Double Take Documentary Film Festival honored Morris with its Career Award for that year.

In the 1990s several studios considered financing television series proposed by Morris (among them "Oddballs, One-Shots and Curiosities" and "Interrotron Stories"). In March 2000 his first TV series, *First Person*, began broadcasting on the Bravo cable channel. *First Person* consists of half-hour interviews with unusual people. "Stairway to Heaven," for instance (made originally as a half-hour documentary in 1998), profiles Temple Grandin, an autistic professor of animal science and one of the world's foremost designers of humane slaughterhouses, whose intense empathy for cattle informs her career. For some of his *First Person* interviews, Morris has experimented with a new device that employs 20 cameras. Since August 2001 *First Person* has aired on the Independent Film Channel.

In his conversation with Susan Stark, Morris talked about a filmscript that he has worked on for years but for which he had yet to find financial backing. Its plot, based on a true story, concerns the alleged murder of an 87-year-old woman in Michigan and the subsequent trial of the accused killer, who, in what Morris declared was "a miscarriage of justice," was found guilty and sentenced to castration. "Everything you would expect in a Scott Turow mystery is present in this story," he told Stark, referring to the author of such best-selling novels as *Presumed Innocent*. "What was remarkable about the trial itself was that in every single aspect it resembled a murder trial. Except the accused was a dog."

By no means wealthy from his films, Morris lives comfortably in Cambridge, Massachusetts. "To me what makes the world tolerable is that it's insane—that's what keeps me going," he told J. Hoberman for *Interview* (November 1997). The filmmaker is the subject of Kevin Macdonald's 48-minute documentary *A Brief History of Errol Morris*. In his leisure time he plays piano and cello. — W.G.

Suggested Reading: *American Film* p33+ Jan./Feb. 1988, with photos; *Detroit News* (on-line) Oct. 18, 1997; Errol Morris Web site; *Interview* p52+ Nov. 1997, with photo; *New York Times* II p34 Oct. 30, 1994, with photo; *New York Times Magazine* p18+ Aug. 9, 1992, with photo; *New Yorker* p38+ Feb. 6, 1989, p33+ Feb. 1, 1999; *News Observer* (on-line) Apr. 4, 1999, with photo; *Premiere* p21 May 1990, with photo; *Washington Journalism Review* p18+ Apr. 1989, with photos; *Washington Post* D p1+ Sep. 2, 1988, with photo

Selected Films: *Gates of Heaven*, 1978; *Vernon, Florida*, 1982; *The Thin Blue Line*, 1988; *A Brief History of Time*, 1992; *Fast, Cheap and Out of Control*, 1997; *Mr. Death: The Rise and Fall of Fred Leuchter Jr.*, 1999

Selected Television Shows: *First Person*, 2000–

Mosley, Sugar Shane

Sep. 7, 1971– Boxer. Address: c/o Jack Mosley, 722 Val Vista St., Pomona, CA 91768-1653; c/o Bull Pitt Boxing Club, 2715 W. Foothill Blvd., Suite 10, Rialto, CA 92376

The World Boxing Council (WBC) welterweight champion, Sugar Shane Mosley, has traveled a slow road to the top of the boxing world. For years, even though he won all of his fights, most of them by knockout, he was unable to attain the level of fame or the hefty paychecks usually enjoyed by the best in the sport, due to the fact that he was not controversial and lacked a powerful promoter. Eventually, however, his prowess in the ring spoke for itself. As his string of victories grew, resulting in an International Boxing Federation (IBF) lightweight title in 1997, commentators began to take notice of Mosley's blazing hand speed, his power, his mastery of the lost art of the body punch—and his wholesome personality. In the *New York Times* (September 22, 1998), Timothy W. Smith called Mosley the "best pound-for-pound fighter no one has heard of" and observed that his good nature made him the "antithesis of everything that is wrong with boxing." After Mosley, still unbeaten, was named Fighter of the Year by the Boxing Writers Association of America in 1998, he suddenly became seen as the torchbearer for a new breed of boxer. "Where are the tattooed orphans, the repeat offenders, the surly nose-bone-into-your-brain stars we've grown used to?" Richard Hoffer asked in *Sports Illustrated* (April 26, 1999). "Is it truly possible that the sport has been taken over by a bunch of kids with milk mustaches, guys who a year ago were playing trumpet in the school band? In other words, does the changing face of boxing now belong to Sugar Shane Mosley?" The boxer, who moved up to the welterweight division in 1999, is undefeated in 38 bouts, and his 35 knockouts give him the highest knockout ratio of any active title holder.

Shane Mosley was born in the Los Angeles area on September 7, 1971 to Jack and Clemmie Mosley. His upbringing did not conform to the popular im-

Courtesy of Chomie Enterprise

Sugar Shane Mosley

age of a boxer's life. He did not turn to the sport as a way out of poverty or a life of crime; rather, he came from a stable, nurturing, middle-class family. When he was still a baby, his family, which included his two older sisters, relocated to the comparatively quiet town of Pomona, California. His father, who had been an amateur boxer, commuted 100 miles a day to work as a material manager for the University of Southern California Medical Center. His mother also commuted to work; her job was in the accounting department of General Dynamics.

Mosley was such an active child that his nursery-school teacher allowed him to bring his Big Wheel tricycle to school, so that he could ride it while the other children took naps. At the age of eight, he started going to the boxing gym with his father, who acted as his trainer—a role he continues to fill. In his teens he joined the U.S. amateur boxing team, and in 1990, according to Hoffer, Mosley's coach said of him, "He's probably above and beyond any [amateur] in the world at his weight class."

Mosley's amateur boxing career was thriving when, in 1992, he lost a match against Vernon Forrest by a controversial decision, thus failing to qualify for the U.S. Olympic boxing team. Making the Olympic team had been crucial to the careers of many successful boxers, including Mosley's idol, Sugar Ray Leonard (who probably, along with the great boxer Sugar Ray Robinson, inspired Mosley's nickname, although readily available sources do not confirm this). Despite the setback, Mosley continued to box well, and by the time he became a pro, in 1993, his amateur record was an impressive 250–10, and he had racked up three national titles. Nevertheless, without the publicity sur-

rounding an Olympic appearance, Mosley could not attract a prominent promoter. Instead, he found Patrick Ortiz, who was new to boxing and did not have the connections to line up bouts with major contenders. Mosley remained strictly a West Coast phenomenon and needed his parents' help to stay afloat financially. "I was worth millions, or so I thought," Mosley told Hoffer, "but I was living in my parents' garage, making $1,500 or $2,000 a fight."

Furthermore, Mosley was clearly not encountering the level of opposition he was capable of facing. Of the seven matches he fought in his first year as a pro, he won all by knockout. The first fight of his pro career that did not end in a knockout was his 1994 match against Oscar Lopez, which he won by decision. Mosley won his other eight fights of 1994 by either knockout or technical knockout (TKO), which occurs when the referee stops the fight to prevent serious injury to one of the boxers. "I was fighting fights that were less challenging than my sparring sessions," Mosley told Timothy W. Smith for the *New York Times* (May 7, 1998).

Several years into his pro career, Mosley started to pursue contracts with other promoters. As a result of legal battles with Patrick Ortiz, Mosley was prohibited from fighting for 10 months while he waited for his contract with Ortiz to expire. Then, in 1996, Mosley signed a contract with promoter Cedric Kushner, who quickly accelerated the pace of the fighter's career. "You could say that he's been under-promoted," Kushner told Hoffer, "but you would be tragically understating the case."

On August 2, 1997 Mosley fought for the International Boxing Federation lightweight belt, against South Africa's Phillip Holiday. Stepping into the ring, Mosley—who was 23–0 with 22 knockouts—looked as if he had blown his chance for the title: a large dose of creatine, a legal muscle builder, taken the day before, had given him a case of diarrhea that left him dehydrated and significantly lighter. Nevertheless, while not as strong as usual, Mosley was in good enough shape to beat Holiday in a decision that gave him the IBF lightweight title.

Mosley proceeded to defend his belt with authority. In his first title defense, in 1997, he knocked out Manuel Gomez in the 11th round. His five title defenses in 1998 all ended in knockouts by Mosley. He was so formidable that he seemed in more danger of injuring his hands by hitting his opponents than of being hurt by their punches. Speaking of his victory over James Leija on November 14, 1998, Mosley said to Timothy W. Smith for the *New York Times* (November 16, 1998), "In the fifth round I noticed that my left hand was hurting, so I quit throwing the jab so much and started working the body. In the sixth round my right hand started to hurt. But I kept working the body. I think that's what did it for me." The referee stopped the fight in the ninth round in order to protect Leija from serious injury, thus giving Mosley a TKO. (According to Hoffer, Leija's trainer then pleaded with HBO network officials to give his fighter another chance, this time "against somebody human.")

Mosley was named Fighter of the Year by the Boxing Writers Association of America in 1998, and his father was named Trainer of the Year. As 1999 wore on, Mosley had trouble keeping below the 135-pound limit for the lightweight division, so he decided to move up two weight classes to the welterweight division, where he felt he could fight more comfortably. The move was also calculated to put him in the same weight class as the renowned Oscar De La Hoya, whose fame and earnings greatly overshadowed Mosley's at the time and whom Mosley felt he had a chance to beat.

Mosley's first fight as a welterweight took place in California on September 25, 1999 against Wilfredo Rivera, a tough boxer who had 30 wins and who owed his three losses to the two best boxers in the division: De La Hoya (who accounted for one loss) and Felix Trinidad. Commentators voiced concern over Mosley's decision not only to advance two weight classes—a rare event—but also to fight, his first time out, one of the best in his new weight class. Mosley came into the ring brimming with energy, throwing a barrage of punches. After nine rounds the bout seemed about even. At the start of the 10th and final round, Mosley advanced to the center of the ring looking determined, knowing that he needed a knockout to assure a victory. Then, with 22 seconds left in the bout, Mosley hit Rivera with a left-right combination that sent him reeling to the canvas. Rivera didn't get up, and Mosley came away with an impressive victory. Mosley, for the second year in a row, was named Fighter of the Year by the Boxing Writers Association of America, the first fighter ever to win the honor in two consecutive years.

On January 22, 2000, in commanding fashion, Mosley won his second fight as a welterweight by knocking out Willy Wise in the third round. Afterward he secured a fight with Oscar De La Hoya. The match was billed as "Destiny," because the two fighters had grown up near each other in Southern California and had faced each other as young amateurs—a fight Mosley had won. In 1992, the year Mosley failed to qualify for the Olympics, the photogenic De La Hoya had gone on to win the United States' only gold medal in boxing and, along with it, a new nickname, the "Golden Boy." Indeed, De La Hoya seemed to be made of gold: while Mosley was earning less than $1 million per fight, De La Hoya was routinely getting about $15 million. De La Hoya's career earnings exceeded Mosley's by approximately $100 million. In 1999, when Mosley jumped weight classes, De La Hoya's promoter, Bob Arum, had scoffed at the idea of a Mosley–De La Hoya bout. "It's a ridiculous fight . . . ," he told Timothy W. Smith for the New York Times (May 13, 1999). "I don't believe a fight with Oscar is competitive in any way." A year's time had found the two fighters more closely matched in the estimations of fans and commentators, though De La Hoya was still favored to win.

The fight was held in Los Angeles on June 17, 2000. Mosley moved backward almost from the beginning of the bout, fending off his larger opponent with flurries of quick punches. De La Hoya landed few punches in the early rounds, and it seemed that Mosley had the edge. Then, in the middle rounds, Mosley's energy appeared to flag, and De La Hoya started to land his jab with regularity. In the eighth round Mosley switched to a southpaw (left-handed) stance, which helped to keep De La Hoya's jab at bay. By the start of the 12th and final round, the fight was still close: one judge had De La Hoya ahead by three points, while the other two judged Mosley to be ahead. Summoning impressive energy at the climax of a fight that had already been rigorous, the two fighters let their punches fly freely. While both landed hard blows, Mosley's speed helped him to land a few more than his opponent, including a solid right to De La Hoya's head as the bell rang. Two of the three judges awarded the fight to Mosley, thus giving him a win by split decision and making him the new World Boxing Council welterweight champion. "It was a close fight," Mosley told Ron Borges for the Boston Globe (June 18, 2000). "We went toe-to-toe for 12 rounds. We went soul-searching in that last round. We showed we're both great warriors. Oscar is a great champion. I was just the better man tonight." Ring magazine subsequently pronounced Mosley the best fighter, pound-for-pound, in the world.

After beating De La Hoya, Mosley found himself grappling with an unexpected but familiar hindrance: alone at the top of his weight division, he was unable to arrange big-time fights. On November 4, 2000 he made his first welterweight title defense, against Antonio Diaz, whose record was 33–2 and who hadn't lost since 1996. Mosley dominated the fight, landing 144 punches to Diaz's 71. He won every round and knocked Diaz down once in the second round and twice in the sixth before the referee stopped the bout. Next, he dispatched Shannan Taylor in five rounds on March 10, 2001, and Adrian Stone in three on April 24. About an hour after flooring Stone, Mosley publicly offered De La Hoya a rematch, but the "Golden Boy" demurred. Instead, Mosley watched while De La Hoya and other desirable opponents, such as Felix Trinidad, took on other boxers in multimillion-dollar events. Mosley plans to move up to 154 pounds and fight Winky Wright for the junior-middleweight title on January 26, 2002. "Shane's the best out there right now and I can see why nobody wants to fight him," the former heavyweight champion George Foreman said, as quoted in the London Guardian (July 23, 2001). "If I was Trinidad, I'd just keep going up in weight and make sure to stay out of Mosley's way." — P.G.H.

Suggested Reading: Boston Globe D p1 June 18, 2000; (London) Guardian p25 July 23, 2001; Los Angeles Times p3 Sep. 26, 1999, D p5 Oct. 6, 2001, D p7, Oct. 13, 2001; Los Angeles Times (on-line) Mar. 21, 2000, D p1 Nov. 5, 2000; New

York Times C p8 May 7, 1998, D p12 Sep. 22, 1998, D p2 Nov. 16, 1998, p8 May 13, 1999; *Sports Illustrated* p54+ Apr. 26, 1999, with photos, p54+ June 26, 2000

Zahid Hussein/Archive Photos

Musharraf, Pervez

Aug. 1, 1943– Leader of Pakistan. Address: Chief Executive's Secretariat, Islamabad, Pakistan

In a sudden move in October 1999, General Pervez Musharraf, then the chairman of Pakistan's Joint Chiefs of Staff Committee, was sacked by Prime Minister Nawaz Sharif while returning to his home country from Sri Lanka by air. His plane, almost out of fuel, was forbidden to land at its original destination and was instead directed to another airport, hundreds of kilometers away. Within minutes, however, Musharraf's supporters in the army had staged a spur-of-the-moment coup, and the plane was allowed to land. Musharraf then declared himself the new leader of Pakistan, and Sharif was put under house arrest. In a nation that has seen army takeovers before, the news was hardly alarming, and indeed many Pakistanis, angered over their nation's poor economy and widespread corruption, welcomed the change in leadership. Since then, Musharraf has suspended the constitution of Pakistan and held a firm grip on the country's reins, promising to reform the nation's political system and improve its economy before making way for new national elections. While some continue to view his promises with great skepticism, those close to the general maintain that he has no interest in serving as military dictator and that his tenure as leader will ultimately give rise to a much healthier nation. Meanwhile, as he maintains a hard line with neighboring India in discussions over the disputed state of Kashmir, Musharraf has kept alive the hope for a lasting peace between the two nations.

The second of three boys, Pervez Musharraf was born on August 1, 1943 in Delhi, India, four years before the nation won its independence from Great Britain. (Some sources spell his first name "Pervaiz" or "Parvez.") His father was a career diplomat; his mother, who had earned a master's degree in English literature from Indraprastha College, was a homemaker before becoming a secretary for the International Labour Organization. After the creation of Pakistan—formerly a Muslim region of India—as an independent, predominantly Muslim state, in 1947, Pervez's family moved to Karachi, in the new country, where they lived for a few years. (India remained mostly Hindu.) Although they were not a rich family, they were comfortable. Musharraf's younger brother, Naved, later told Shanthi Shankarakumar for Rediff on the Net (on-line), "We are nominal Muslims in that we don't go to the mosque very often and neither do we pray five times a day. I don't know how to read the Quran and neither do my brothers. . . . We are all very secular." In 1950 Musharraf's father was stationed in Ankara, Turkey, and the family moved there with him. Musharraf and his brothers were tutored at home and learned to speak and read Turkish and English fluently. Meanwhile, Musharraf was becoming quite popular with other children. "Even as a child," Naved Musharraf told Shankarakumar, "he was outgoing and extroverted, with a large circle of friends. Friends were attracted to him because he was such fun." Returning with his family to Pakistan after six years in Turkey, Musharraf attended Saint Patrick's High School, a convent school in Karachi. After graduating, he completed his intermediate education (which follows secondary school and precedes undergraduate studies) at Forman Christian College in Lahore, Pakistan. His mother stressed the importance of education and expected her children to do their best at their studies. Pervez Musharraf's brother Javed was known as the smartest of the three boys; Pervez, who excelled at sports, was not very accomplished academically, except in mathematics. Cricket soon became his favorite sport, and he also became very interested in bodybuilding. "He wanted to impress everybody," his brother Naved told Shankarakumar.

In 1961 Musharraf entered the Pakistan Military Academy. Three years later he was commissioned to an elite artillery regiment. In 1965 he saw combat for the first time, as a young officer in the second of the three India-Pakistan wars, the first two of which centered on the disputed region of Kashmir, which both India and Pakistan claim to own. He was later awarded a medal of distinction for gallantry. "If anybody says he's not scared he's telling a lie," Musharraf said during an on-line chat with

Owen Bennett-Jones for BBC News. "I've been through two wars and I've faced bullets, I've seen people dying, if anybody says that he's not scared he's lying. There's a very thin line between bravery and cowardice actually. A brave man is a person who's certainly scared but he controls his emotions and stands—he's a brave man. Another man who is again scared, doesn't control his emotions and gives in and runs away—so there's a very thin line. So I would call myself pretty brave, I am scared certainly but I am a believer in destiny—in my own destiny and therefore that gives me more courage." Musharraf soon volunteered for, and served seven years in, the Special Service Group "Commandos," as Musharraf's Web site bio refers to them. During the 1971 war with India, he served as company commander in a commando battalion. Musharraf rose quickly through the military ranks, even though—unlike most Pakistani army officers—he is not Punjabi; promoted to the rank of brigadier general, he commanded an infantry brigade as well as an armored artillery division.

Among other activities, in the 1980s Musharraf trained mercenaries, who were recruited by various Islamic extremist groups, to fight the Soviet troops in Afghanistan. At camps set up on the Afghan-Pakistani border, religious instruction and military training were given to Afghan refugees, Islamic guerrillas, and Muslim volunteers from other countries. Over the next decade Musharraf held various positions in the military, including deputy military secretary at the military's Secretary Branch and member of the Directing Staff, at both the Command and Staff College, Quetta, and the National Defense College.

On January 15, 1991 Musharraf was promoted to the rank of major general and given the command of an infantry division. Nearly five years later he took command of the distinguished strike corps as a lieutenant general. On October 7, 1998 he was promoted to the rank of general and also appointed chief of army staff, following the departure of General Jehangir Karamant, who had advocated a larger role for the army in the country's decision making. Although Pakistani prime minister Nawaz Sharif had hoped that Musharraf would be more malleable than his predecessor, such was not the case. Musharraf was named chairman of the Joint Chiefs of Staff Committee the following spring; he and Sharif soon found themselves at odds regarding army-government relations as well as the subject of Kashmir. The breaking point between Musharraf and Sharif came during the Kargil invasion in June and July 1999, when Pakistani troops entered Indian-administered territory in Kashmir. Musharraf was one of the main strategists for this operation, which was later called to a halt by Sharif, following pressure from Western nations including the United States. Musharraf expressed anger over what he perceived as weakness on Sharif's part. Lieutenant-General Ziauddin Khawaja then released tapes of conversations between Musharraf and Lieutenant-General Khalid Aziz, ex-

posing the nature of the army's involvement in Kargil to the Pakistani public, which had been made to believe that only Islamic militants had crossed the Kargil border; the release of the tapes angered the military and intensified Pakistani citizens' perception of the army as a rogue element.

It was around this time that protests against Sharif began to erupt, as many Pakistanis blamed the prime minister for mishandling the government and the economy. Pakistan owed the World Bank $1.17 billion in loans, and many Pakistanis were fed up with rising prices and constant corruption. Sharif sent his brother and Khawaja to Washington, D.C., to seek a statement in support of the government, and the U.S. issued a warning to political and military elements in Pakistan wishing to stage a coup. This move angered the army even more, and at a corps commanders' meeting in September, the top army officers vowed to resist any move to oust Musharraf. The decision was later leaked to Sharif, and on October 12, 1999, while Musharraf was returning by airplane from the 50th anniversary celebrations of the Sri Lankan army, he was ousted by Sharif and replaced by Khawaja. "Nobody can sack me," Musharraf reportedly responded, as quoted in the *Week* (October 24, 1999, online), a British news magazine. Within half an hour, at Musharraf's headquarters, an emergency meeting resulted in a plan for a coup. Soon the army had taken over the PTV (Pakistani television) center in Islamabad, just before Musharraf's firing was to be announced. Meanwhile, Musharraf's plane, carrying 200 other passengers as well, was refused permission to land at Karachi. The control tower first told the pilot to fly to India, then to fly to an airport in Nawabshah, 200 kilometers northeast. The army later stated that at the time there was only six or seven minutes' worth of fuel in the plane. The army soon took over the airport in Karachi and allowed the plane to land; they also seized key institutions across the country. When the plane landed Musharraf declared himself chief executive of Pakistan and placed Sharif under house arrest. Sharif would later be charged with corruption, terrorism, and hijacking, and after a protracted court case, he was sentenced to life in prison. The relatively peaceful coup had taken a total of 17 hours to execute.

On October 15 Musharraf officially installed himself as Pakistan's ruler, suspended the constitution, and declared a state of emergency. He also suspended the National Assembly and all provincial assemblies and dismissed local governors. While refusing to set a time line for the restoration of democracy, he stated that he was going to help Pakistan rebuild itself. In a televised address to the nation on October 17, he stated, as quoted by the BBC (on-line), "Fifty-two years ago, [Pakistan] started with a beacon of hope and today that beacon is no more and we stand in darkness. There is despondency and hopelessness surrounding us, with no light visible anywhere around. The slidedown has been gradual but has rapidly accelerated in the last many years. Today, we have reached a stage where our economy has crumbled, our credibility is lost, state institutions lie demolished. Provincial disharmony has caused cracks in the federation, and people who were once brothers are now at each other's throat. In sum, we have lost our honour, our dignity, our respect in the community of nations." He stated that by suspending the constitution, he was establishing not martial law but only temporary restrictions to facilitate the return of true democracy. In one of his first acts, he made it law that by November 16, 1999, defaulters on bank loans were to pay part of what they owed and submit a timetable for paying the balance—or face arrest. As a gesture of goodwill toward India, he pulled Pakistani troops back from the Kashmir border. (Indian leaders made it clear that the gesture did not mean much to them.) Soon Musharraf appointed three retired military officers and a judge to govern the country's provinces. After 13 days in power, Musharraf left for a tour of the Middle East in order to consolidate support for his new regime. On October 25 he appointed members of a National Security Council to administer the government's affairs.

The coup met with disapproval and criticism in the West and resulted in the suspension of Pakistan by the British Commonwealth of Nations, in light of the many unknowns regarding Musharraf's leadership. Since then, Musharraf has faced a mixed reception on the international stage, with the West taking him to task on several issues without condemning him entirely. Although then–U.S. president Bill Clinton eventually made a brief visit to Pakistan after the coup, the U.S. made it clear that the trip did not amount to an endorsement of the regime. Clinton pressed Musharraf on several points but was unable to change the viewpoint of the general, who later stated that the United States and Pakistan had failed to see eye-to-eye on a number of topics—such as Kashmir, Pakistan's nuclear program, and the nation's relationship with the fundamentalist Taliban leaders in Afghanistan. "I'm bothered about the American relationship with Pakistan," Musharraf was quoted as saying by the BBC (on-line), "and we are bothered about the substance of that relationship."

Former prime minister Sharif's party, the Pakistan Muslim League (PML), announced that it would fight the suspension of the constitution in the courts. The Supreme Court eventually ruled that the coup was legal but set a three-year limit for army control of the government. The Grand Democratic Alliance (GDA), a loose opposition coalition led by the Pakistan People's Party, was highly critical of the ruling and questioned the impartiality of the judges. "Why is a three-year period required to restore this fundamental right?" GDA leader Nawabzada Nasrullah Khan said, as quoted by the BBC (on-line). "If it is to improve the economy and complete accountability then the best choice is always a political government elected through the free will of the people." On November 30, 1999

Musharraf's government announced the establishment of 100 special courts to try people accused of corruption or of defaulting on loans. While many began to wonder if the general was going to keep his promises of bringing democracy back to Pakistan, on December 4, 1999 he promised local democracy within a year, and later that month he outlined his government's plans to revive the country's ailing economy. The measures include introducing a sales tax, encouraging oil and gas exploration, and promoting small businesses. Musharraf also pledged to reduce interest rates and cut Pakistan's heavy debt burden.

In January 2000, in a controversial move, Musharraf required all Pakistani judges to state their allegiance to the new military regime or be fired—a policy attacked by the West and by opposition parties in Pakistan. In March of that year, after a series of apparently antigovernment bombings and assassinations and amid fears about violence during a planned visit to Pakistan by President Clinton, Musharraf's government banned outdoor rallies, a decision that Pakistani opposition groups attacked as a movement away from democracy. Musharraf's government defended itself by stating that it could not risk public aggression and violence at a time when it needed to focus on rebuilding the nation. Later that month Musharraf announced that the first local elections would take place between December 2000 and May 2001, with general elections to follow. The voting age was also lowered, from 21 to 18. On April 21, 2000 Musharraf promised that he would end human-rights abuses in Pakistan. He went on to say that laws allowing so-called honor killings, or the murders of women on flimsy charges to satisfy male pride, had to end, as did child labor. He later backed away from his decision to change the country's severe laws against religious blasphemy, after encountering opposition to his plan among some Islamic groups. On August 15, 2000 Musharraf reshuffled the National Security Council, this time including ministers among the members. (He has also recently revived the religious provisions in Pakistan's suspended constitution.)

By this point, cracks in Musharraf's support base were becoming visible. Pakistanis had seen few changes in their living conditions; the economy and employment remained stagnant, and prices had not fallen since the end of Sharif's tenure. In addition, shopkeepers across Pakistan became incensed when Musharraf announced that, with less than 1 percent of the Pakistani population paying income taxes, he was going to make such payments mandatory for more people. Earlier the International Monetary Fund (IMF) had refused to give economic credit to Pakistan unless the nation committed itself to enacting stabilizing economic reforms, such as raising tax revenue. For a couple of weeks, shopkeepers nationwide protested the new tax measures, with some arrested for refusing to take part in a tax survey. Outbreaks of violence related to the protests were reported;

police used tear gas in order to quell dissenters. By July 2001 changes in various policies had led to the beginning of an economic recovery. In recognition of the government's attempts to end corruption and raise the standard of living for the millions living in poverty, the World Bank announced that it planned to give Pakistan millions of dollars in loans over the next year.

Tension over Kashmir has continued since Musharraf established himself as leader of Pakistan. On August 2, 2000, after a couple of border clashes earlier in his rule, widespread violence in the portion of Kashmir under Indian control left 90 people dead. Although India blamed Islamic rebels for the killings, and Pakistan for funding them—a charge made repeatedly over the years—Musharraf stated that he had nothing to do with the attacks. Later that year Musharraf expressed approval when one of the Islamic groups fighting in Kashmir pledged a cease-fire and opened talks with the Indian government. The talks fell through, however, when India refused to let the Pakistani government itself participate in negotiations, which prompted criticism from Musharraf. Later, India, too, declared a cease-fire, and Pakistan withdrew some front-line troops, while declaring that Pakistan would practice restraint on the line dividing Pakistani-controlled and Indian-controlled Kashmir. Kashmiri Islamic separatists continued their attacks, however, and India returned to its policy against negotiating with them, despite Pakistan's insistence that such negotiations take place. In the *New York Times* (October 9, 2001), Musharraf was quoted as saying that the hostility in Kashmir "cannot be identified as terrorism. There is a freedom struggle going on in Kashmir."

Following a catastrophic earthquake in the Indian state of Gujarat in January 2001, Pakistan temporarily set aside its differences with its nuclear rival and offered relief aid for the victims. In an historic move, Musharraf telephoned the Indian prime minister, Atal Behari Vajpayee, to offer his condolences. (It was the first time the two men had spoken since before Musharraf came to power.) In May 2001 India ended its six-month cease-fire in Kashmir; at the same time the Indian government invited Musharraf for face-to-face talks. The Pakistani leader, who had been calling for direct talks between the two nations for months, accepted the invitation despite the flare-up of violence in Kashmir. "I would give credit to Prime Minister Vajpayee for his statesmanship, and his vision and his courage and boldness towards accepting a reality and starting to address an issue which has bedeviled relations between our two countries," he said, as quoted by *BBC News* (May 28, 2001, on-line). The three-day summit, held in July 2001, failed to produce any agreement other than one specifying that the heads of India and Pakistan would meet annually and that the countries' foreign ministers would hold talks twice yearly. Vajpayee later blasted Musharraf for the lack of substantive results at the summit and called the general "clueless" on issues of history and diplomacy. On October 1, 2001 a suicide bomber killed 38 people in the state assembly building in Srinagar, the capital of Indian-administered Kashmir. The bombing came three weeks after the terrorist attacks on New York City and Washington, D.C., and at a time when the United States was recruiting both India and Pakistan for help in its war against terrorism. India accused Pakistan of aiding the Islamic separatists responsible for the October 1 attack, and on October 15, after a 10-month lull in hostilities, India shelled 11 Pakistani military posts in Kashmir.

Earlier, on August 6, 2000, almost all of the opposition parties in Pakistan came together to demand a fresh timetable for new elections. They also passed a declaration criticizing the new regime's economic policies and anticorruption measures. Soon afterward Musharraf announced his devolution plan for the country, which would transfer a great deal of power to hundreds of elected town and district committees. One-third of the seats in the committees would be reserved for women. Elections would be held on a nonparty basis, which would help to avoid corruption, according to Musharraf. Although the opposition attacked the plan, calling it unfeasible, the first phase of the local elections, which took place in December 2000, went smoothly. Citizens in 18 districts voted for local officials, but the low voter turnout disappointed the government. The second phase took place in March 2001. In the aftermath of the March elections, Pakistani authorities arrested several leading opposition leaders and hundreds of activists prior to and during pro-democracy rallies. In a move that angered many in the Pakistani opposition, Musharraf consolidated power in June 2001 by naming himself president of Pakistan while remaining head of the army. Days earlier the then-president, Rafiq Tarar, was removed from office while Musharraf formally dissolved the nation's Parliament and the legislatures in the four provinces of the country. Both the British Commonwealth and the United States expressed concern about Musharraf's actions. The third and final phase of the elections took place in August 2001. Musharraf stated recently that there will be no general elections until October 2002.

In addition to trying to calm those anxious for a return to democracy, Musharraf has had to face a rise in Islamic fundamentalism in Pakistan and the in-fighting between shia and sunni Muslims. In June 2001 Musharraf denounced hardline Islamists for disrupting the Pakistani government and for projecting a false image abroad of Pakistan as a nation that supports terrorism. He later banned two militant groups. In August 2001 police in the Pakistani province of Punjab and in Karachi made large-scale arrests of radical Islamic groups.

The issue of internal stability in Pakistan was greatly magnified after the terrorist attacks on the United States on September 11, 2001 by Islamic militants thought to be backed by Saudi-born Osama bin Laden, a guest of the ruling Taliban in Afghanistan, Pakistan's western neighbor. As the chief supporter of the hardline Islamic regime in Afghanistan, Musharraf was placed in an awkward position when the United States asked him to back its military activity against Afghanistan by providing intelligence, airspace, and logistical support. If he agreed to the American proposal, he risked destabilizing his own country, where there was much support for the Taliban and distrust of the United States. However, if he refused to assist the United States, he could find himself cut off entirely from Western aid and facing the increased influence of India in the international arena. As the United States had demanded that Afghanistan turn over bin Laden or face military strikes, Musharraf made several efforts to defuse the situation by sending diplomatic missions to Afghanistan to persuade the Taliban to turn over their guest. Those efforts were unsuccessful, however; on October 7 the U.S. began its military campaign against the Taliban.

Days later, when Musharraf agreed to work with the United States, irate Islamic fundamentalists began increasingly violent protests across the country, demonstrating their support of bin Laden and opposition to the United States. The protests embarrassed the Pakistani government as they suggested to other nations that Pakistan was a haven for Islamic extremism. In a televised speech defending his decision to support the United States, Musharraf noted that the U.S. was waging a war not against the people of Afghanistan or Islam but against terrorism. He also stated his belief that India, which had already agreed to help the United States, wanted Pakistan to be declared a terrorist state and hoped to see an anti-Pakistani government installed in Afghanistan. "It is not the question of weakness of faith or cowardice," Musharraf was quoted as saying by BBC News (September 19, 2001, on-line). "I am ready to sacrifice my life for Pakistan. I have fought two wars and faced many dangers and, praise be to God, never showed cowardice. However, we do not want to invite trouble for nothing. The future of 140 million people cannot be jeopardized. Even Islamic law provides that if we are faced with two difficulties and we have to select one of them, it is always better to choose the lesser trouble." While he noted that many in his nation had sympathies with Afghanistan, he stated that his government could exert more influence over the situation by helping the international community. Nonetheless, Pakistani militant activity rose following the address.

The benefits to Pakistan of allying itself with the United States soon became evident, however, as the United States government moved toward ending sanctions imposed against the nation and India following nuclear tests in 1998. Among other damages to Pakistan, the sanctions had blocked loans and debt relief for the nation while encumbering plans for a poverty-reduction program. The lifting of sanctions against Pakistan also allowed the World Bank to increase its aid to the nation, while in late October U.S. president George W. Bush signed legislation to end all sanctions against Pakistan and resume all economic and military aid within two years. Bush also promised a package of $500 million in economic aid. When the United States began its air strikes against Afghanistan, Musharraf declared his support for them and his hope that they would be brief. A shake-up in the top levels of the Pakistani army was seen by observers as a means by which Musharraf would rid himself of any high-ranking army figures who might have Taliban sympathies. Musharraf continued to retain diplomatic relations with the Taliban even after all of the regime's other allies ended relations with that government. As a result, the Taliban embassy in Islamabad, Pakistan, became the only place during the war on Afghanistan where the Taliban were able to communicate with the outside world. As the air strikes continued into late October, thousands of demonstrators took to the streets; Musharraf, though, came out in full support of a lengthy campaign in Afghanistan. The nation later announced it would deport any Afghan refugees involved in the increasingly violent demonstrations in support of the Taliban. On October 27, tens of thousands demonstrated in Karachi, Pakistan, in support of bin Laden and the Taliban, in the largest protest in the country since the bombings of Afghanistan had begun. Meanwhile, thousands of armed Pakistani tribesmen massed at the Afghani border to volunteer to fight for Taliban.

Turning his attention to the future of Afghanistan, Musharraf was adamant that no new government could be imposed on the people of that nation from outside, and that any new government should represent all ethnic groups present in the nation. He also warned the Northern Alliance, the armed forces of the previous government in Afghanistan, from taking advantage of the situation and trying to seize power for themselves. Observers noted the likelihood of Musharraf's withdrawing his support of the operation against the Taliban if the Northern Alliance succeeded in replacing the Taliban in Kabul. Musharraf and many others in Pakistan worry that an ethnically non-Pashtun government such as the Northern Alliance would ignite Pashtun nationalism in Pakistan.

Musharraf spends a great deal of his free time playing squash, badminton, and golf; he also enjoys water sports, such as canoeing and sailing. An avid reader, especially of military history, he is also known as a lover of good food, old Hindi film songs, movies, and the ghazals of Mehdi Hasan and Noor Jehan. He married his wife, Sehba, on December 28, 1968. The couple have one son and one daughter, both married. Their son lives and works in the U.S.; their daughter, who studied architecture, now helps her husband run an advertising agency. She has one daughter, Musharraf's only grandchild. Musharraf's brother Naved told Shanthi Shankarakumar that Pervez Musharraf "is a very caring family man, but at the same time, he is very authoritarian and was quite rigorous in training his son. He made sure the boy took part in sports. Pervez laid emphasis on sports, and not so much on studies."

Although Musharraf has said that he is trying to be tolerant in his rule of Pakistan, he insists that he will not put up with blockage of his reform process. "Quite clearly, what Pakistan has experienced in recent years has been merely a label of democracy, not the essence of it," he stated in a televised speech in March 2000, as quoted by the BBC (on-line). "Our people were never emancipated from the yoke of despotism. I shall not allow the people to be taken back to the era of sham democra-

cy." Musharraf has targeted population growth as one of the greatest threats to Pakistan's future and has also established a national commission to protect women's rights. He has said that while he does not want to use nuclear weapons against India, he would consider that option should his own nation's safety be put at risk.— G.O.

Suggested Reading: BBC (on-line); *New Statesman* Oct. 18, 1999; *New York Times* A p12 Oct. 13, 1999, with photo, A p12 Oct. 26, 1999, with photo, A p7 Oct. 9, 2001; *Time* p64+ Oct. 22, 2001; *Week* Oct. 24, 1999

Courtesy of Ford Motor Co.

Nasser, Jacques

Dec. 12, 1947– Former CEO of Ford Motor Co. Address: c/o Ford Motor Co., American Rd., Dearborn, MI 48121

"There's no bad business, only bad strategies," Jacques Nasser told Mukul Pandya for the Wharton Business School's *Leadership Digest* (October 1999, on-line), during his tenure as the chief executive officer of the Ford Motor Co. "You've got to be driven by a goal beyond monetary value. It has to be in your heart, not just an intellectual stimulus. Every single moment for me is a hair-tingling moment." Nasser, a citizen of Australia, served as Ford's CEO from January 1999 to October 2001. He began working for the company in 1968 as a student intern; during the next three decades, he worked for Ford in nearly a dozen countries in various capacities, among them president of Ford

Australia and chairman of Ford Europe. "I've faced a military junta in Argentina and a financial meltdown in the Philippines," he told Suzy Wetlaufer for the *Harvard Business Review* (March/April 1999). "I've faced hyperinflation, closed markets, open markets, Japanese competition—you name it. I've probably packed 100 years of experience into those 30 years." In a conversation with William J. Holstein for *U.S. News & World Report* (January 19, 1998), he said, "I look at things like an outsider because I've been so many places. I think of myself as an insider-outsider."

By his own account, Nasser's mission was to move Ford from second place in earnings among the world's car manufacturers, behind General Motors, to the top spot. Toward that end he pushed strenuously to improve Ford's financial condition and waged an aggressive campaign to induce people to buy Ford's cars, trucks, and sport-utility vehicles (SUVs). During that period Ford was still trying to recover from the scandal that erupted in 2000, involving claims that the Bridgestone/Firestone tires installed on Ford Explorers had caused dozens of fatal accidents. "I am an agent of change. I don't believe in stagnation," Nasser told David C. Smith and Greg Gardner for *Ward's Auto World* (February 1997). "I've entered assignments that have placed me in an environment where action was needed. I could either sit back and just let things roll along and we would have been in a worse predicament. I'd rather face issues up-front. There's no point in offering false hope." On October 30, 2001, after almost three years in the top spot, Nasser was ousted by the Ford Motor Co. (According to some sources, he resigned.) His departure followed recurring clashes with the company's chairman, William Clay Ford Jr., the great-grandson of founder Henry Ford.

Jacques Albert Nasser was born on December 12, 1947 in Amyoun, Lebanon, a mountain village 60 miles north of Beirut. His father, a native of Lebanon, had pursued small-business opportunities in the Caribbean, North America, and France during the Great Depression of the 1930s before returning to Lebanon during World War II. In 1951 the Nasser family, which by then included Jacques's brother, Jaime, moved to Australia, in the hope of finding better economic prospects. They settled in Northcote, a Melbourne suburb. "I didn't look Australian, and when I went to school I was different than the kids in my class," Nasser recalled to Mukul Pandya. "I spoke Arabic, not English. My lunch was tabouli and flat bread, and kids would laugh at me. But I stayed with my food. The lesson I learned was, it's OK to be different. Be yourself. Be your own brand. Stand up for what you believe in."

In school Nasser did particularly well in math and science. Displaying an early entrepreneurial streak, he became part-owner of a discothèque and a bicycle-repair business. As a teenager he developed a passion for cars; according to Marjorie Sorge in *Automotive Industries* (February 1999, online), "He bought used cars at auctions, fixed them up and sold them for a profit." He also applied his tinkering skills to a 1948 Singer automobile, which he purchased with a friend in the late 1960s. After he graduated from high school, he enrolled at the Royal Melbourne Institute of Technology as a part-time student and majored in international business; he earned a diploma in 1972. Earlier, in 1968, he had become a student intern at Ford Australia and had stayed on as a financial analyst, despite his father's questioning his decision to become part of a huge corporation rather than be his own boss.

In 1973 Nasser spent a few months at Ford's Dearborn, Michigan, Truck Operations division. His fondness for opera and jewel-toned suits "didn't fit in with Ford culture," as he told William J. Holstein. "I stuck out like a sore thumb for a while." In 1973 Nasser returned to Australia to become a manager at Ford Australia. By 1975 he had been assigned to Ford's International Automotive Operations. There, he was involved in many aspects of the business, ranging from plant operations to design of new products. He also formed joint ventures with other companies, such as Autolatina, a collaboration between Volkswagen and Ford that served Latin American nations and lasted from 1987 to 1995. During his 15-year tenure with International Automotive Operations, he worked in the Philippines, Thailand, Japan, South Africa, Venezuela, Mexico, Brazil, and Argentina. Fluent in English and Arabic, he learned Spanish and Portuguese during that period. (He also has a rudimentary knowledge of French.)

In 1985 Nasser became the head of operations at a Ford plant in Pacheco, Argentina. A few years before, Argentina's government had moved from military to civilian control and from dictatorship to democracy. Inflation was raging out of control, and when Nasser distributed bonus checks to his managers, they immediately left his office to cash their checks rather than sit and chat with him, knowing that the value of the checks might evaporate momentarily. "The lesson I learned from that was you've got to be quick and nimble," he told Marjorie Sorge. "You have to look at all the opportunities

and strike while you can." Later that year a group of militants, apparently angry about the institution of democratic reforms, held Nasser hostage at the Pacheco plant for three days. He should have felt scared, Nasser told Sorge, but he "really didn't perceive any danger at the time. I just felt they were trying to make a political point." After his release Nasser collapsed from exhaustion.

In 1990 Nasser took the reins as president of Ford Australia. When he had last worked in Australia, Ford had been making a profit, but now the firm was losing revenue and market share. Within three years of Nasser's arrival, Ford Australia's financial health had returned, thanks in part to his willingness to cut the workforce and his success at persuading parts suppliers to agree to higher standards of quality. In 1993 Nasser was promoted again, this time becoming the chairman of the struggling Ford Europe and a vice president of the parent company. In Europe he earned the nickname "Jac the Knife" after he shrank the payroll and closed plants that he deemed insufficiently productive. Acknowledging that many Ford employees feared him, he defended his methods, telling *Newsweek* (November 23, 1998) interviewers, "I do have a strong desire to strengthen this company. The alternative is mediocrity. . . . What would you choose?" In part because of the worldwide financial recession, he achieved only limited success in reversing Ford Europe's downward trajectory. Among the brights spots during his leadership of the division was the introduction of the Ka, a tiny, sporty, three-door model that moved from the drawing board to showrooms in 24 months, instead of the usual 36 months. (Later, Sue Zesiger reported for *Fortune* [June 22, 1998], 24 months became "Nasser's timeline for every new project.") The Ka was not marketed in the United States (it did not meet U.S. safety requirements), but it sold well in Europe, Australia, and South America.

In 1994 Nasser was named Ford's vice president of product development, with responsibility for merging the European and North American car and truck operations. Two years later he was elevated to president of automotive operations—a job, based in Dearborn, that required extensive traveling. He placed high on his list of priorities the weaving of Ford's many divisions into a cohesive global enterprise. "Ford's fiefdoms don't always war with one another, although that can happen, but they don't exactly care about the domain that contains them all," he explained to Suzy Wetlaufer. In an effort to promote feelings of unity, he rearranged Ford's headquarters in Dearborn, putting product designers and creative teams a floor or two below the executive offices; according to Sue Zesiger, he has made it a practice to visit the design studios regularly.

Focusing on global competition during his time as president of automotive operations, Nasser oversaw the acquisition of major stakes in Jaguar and Aston Martin and the increase of its controlling interest in Mazda from a quarter to a third. The company also bought Land Rover from BMW and considered (but rejected) the idea of purchasing the Korean car companies Kia and Daewoo.

On January 1, 1999 Ford's CEO, Alex Trotman, retired, and Nasser was named his successor. As CEO Nasser applied the same business strategies that had served him well in the past. He closed a plant in Lorain, Ohio, and dropped workers elsewhere as well; he eliminated models that did not generate what he viewed as a big-enough profit, among them the Thunderbird, the Aerostar, and the Aspire; and he streamlined factory processes—for example, by using interchangeable platforms for trucks and SUVs. Placing Lincoln and Mercury in Ford's "Premiere Automotive Group," he gave those divisions the go-ahead to begin operating in California. He installed luminaries from outside Ford in executive positions instead of promoting from within. Motivated in part by his memories of discrimination as a child, he also made a major push to increase the racial diversification of the Ford workforce. In 1999 Ford began building a factory in Russia.

In the summer of 2000, news reports began linking the Ford Explorer, an SUV, to fatal rollover accidents in which the treads of its tires (made by the Japanese firm Bridgestone/Firestone) had separated. It was soon revealed that similar accidents had been reported in Venezuela and Saudi Arabia. Amid a growing public outcry about the companies' failure to act earlier, Ford and Bridgestone/Firestone jointly issued a recall of two types of Explorer tires. At Nasser's insistence, the target date proposed by Bridgestone/Firestone for completion of the recall—the spring of 2001—was moved up to November 2000. In full-page ads signed by Nasser and in television spots in which he appeared, as well as on the company's Web site and at its retail outlets, Ford informed customers about the progress of the recall. In addition, Nasser closed three Explorer assembly plants for two weeks so that the recalled tires could be replaced with 70,000 tires already in stock; the temporary shutdown cost Ford $100 million.

Still, Ford was criticized for moving too slowly and not investigating claims until forced to do so. In September 2000 Nasser and the CEO of Bridgestone/Firestone, Masatoshi Ono, testified before the House Commerce Committee regarding the defective tires (linked to some 100 deaths and many more injuries) and the recall. Nasser let much of the blame for the safety problems fell on Ono and the tire company, but he seemed genuinely distressed that Ford products and engineering were implicated in scandal. "We don't want to let anyone down," he told Sue Zeiger for Fortune (September 18, 2000), admitting there had been a "break in trust" between Ford and consumers. "And when something unintended like this happens, it really doesn't matter whose fault it is. We feel morally and emotionally connected to the people who buy our vehicles. If I could find a magic wand that would give me $6\frac{1}{2}$ million 15-inch tires

that I could personally hand carry to every customer, I'd do it." Congressional and other investigators learned that the tires, made to meet Ford's specific design standards, did not have a good safety rating when Explorers were driven at high speeds, especially for prolonged periods and in hot weather. Ford has announced that starting in 2002, purchasers of Explorers will have a choice of Goodyear or Michelin tires.

In the 2001 model year, Ford introduced the Focus; a compact car designed to replace the Escort, it debuted to great acclaim around the world. Intent on forging a "lifelong commitment" to Ford customers, Nasser made plans to bring back the Thunderbird, this time as a luxury two-seater. Earlier, during a May 1999 press conference at Ford's headquarters, he promised that new, environmentally friendly technology was being applied to Ford SUVs, trucks, and vans, so that the emissions from those types of vehicles would eventually meet the emission standards for cars. "It's the right thing to do," he said, as reported by Keith Bradsher for the New York Times (May 18, 1999).

In the belief that every Ford employee has the potential to come up with ideas for improving the company, Nasser ordered executives and managers to participate in seminars in which they were asked to solve difficult problems by teamwork. Almost one-third of Ford's 330,000 employees worldwide received weekly "Let's Chat" bulletins—friendly E-mails from Nasser with news about the company, including new strategies; many responded to him personally, and Nasser—who made sure that every E-mail is answered—engaged in many cyberspace conversations with employees near and far. "You can't say 'I'm going to open up the dialogue,' and then not really open it up," he told Suzy Wetlaufer. "You have to be genuine in what you are doing. I mean, when you get stopped at the newsstand on a Saturday morning and a factory worker comes up to you and says 'I was thinking about that comment you made in your speech the other week,' you can't just say, 'Well, sorry, it's my free time right now. Just send me a note next week.' When you open up change—when you bring its case to your people—you have to stay front and center for their questions." Convinced that the Internet will change the automotive industry, Nasser instituted a program whereby free home computers and very low-cost Internet access were to be provided to all of Ford's salaried employees—about 100,000 people. The program "has sent a very clear message internally about the importance of e-commerce and new technology," he told Laura Washington for Money (June 1, 2000, on-line). "We saw this as a way of improving our skill levels, making us more literate in what we think is probably the most revolutionary technology around." Nasser anticipated that information fed to Ford from customers using the Internet would enable Ford to build vehicles to order, with delivery in five to 10 days. "We have many combinations today because no one is truly certain about what consumers really want," he told Marjorie Sorge for *Automotive Industries* (November 1999).

In July 2001, after urging Nasser without success to appoint a chief operating officer, William Clay Ford Jr. created for himself what was called "an office of the chairman and chief executive." By doing so, he forced Nasser to attend meetings with him regularly and thus share decision making, with the result that he curbed Nasser's power. In the following months, with declining sales and market share, falling profits, and a shaky American economy, rumors began to emerge regarding the security of Nasser's position. Although the company took various cost-saving measures, such as cutting production and decreasing the white-collar workforce by 5,000 employees, Ford's credit rating dropped. In late October 2001 Nasser was relieved of his duties. He was replaced by William Clay Ford Jr.; the head of Ford's North American operations, Nicholas Scheele, was named president and chief operating officer.

Known for his unusual energy and enthusiasm, Nasser is said to sleep no more than five hours a night. He owns several Jaguars. A collector of Swiss watches, he wears a timepiece that displays three time zones at once. "I can be impatient," he confessed to Sue Zesiger in 1998. "And probably unrelenting and intense. I have high personal standards, and I set the same standards for my team."

Nasser and his wife, Jennifer, an Australian-born teacher, separated in 2000; they have since reconciled. The couple have three daughters and a son. — K.S.

Suggested Reading: *Fortune* p79+ June 22, 1998, with photo; *Harvard Business Review* p76+ Mar./Apr. 1999; *New York Times* A p16 May 18, 1999, C p1+ Oct. 16, 2001, with photo; *New York Times* (on-line) Feb. 6, 2001; *U.S. News & World Report* p51+ Jan. 19, 1998, with photo; *Ward's Auto World* p27+ Feb. 1997, with photo

---

Nixon, Agnes

Dec. 10, 1927– Television writer. Address: All My Children, *320 W. 66th St., New York, NY 10023*

Over the course of a career spanning five decades, Agnes Nixon has written some of television's most enduring daytime dramas, including *As the World Turns, The Guiding Light,* and two shows she created—the groundbreaking *One Life to Live* and her personal favorite, *All My Children.* Nixon, who

still writes the latter two shows, was inducted into the Television Hall of Fame in 1993. The actress Susan Lucci, who plays the lovable villainess Erica Kane on *All My Children,* said on the installment of Lifetime Television's *Intimate Portrait* focusing on Nixon, "Agnes is a legend. Agnes is an icon."

Nixon was born Agnes Eckhardt on December 10, 1927 in Chicago, Illinois, the only child of Harry Eckhardt, the owner of the Perfection Burial Garment Company, and Agnes Dalton Eckhardt. Only three months after her birth, Nixon's parents divorced; Harry Eckhardt remained in Chicago, while Aggie (as the baby was called) and her mother returned to her mother's hometown of Nashville, Tennessee. There, they lived with Grandmother Dalton, a prim, severe Irish Catholic who spoke in antiquated threats. "She had a silver-headed cane and she'd stomp it on the floor. . . . She'd say, 'I'll rue ye 'til the day I die!'" Nixon recalled, laughing, during her interview for *Intimate Portrait.* Although several of Grandmother Dalton's 12 grown children still lived at home, Nixon was the only youngster in the house. The Great Depression was pinching purses—Nixon has recalled her refusal to throw rice at an aunt's wedding, wanting instead to make soup with it—and her mother and favorite aunt, Emma, worked as bookkeepers to help support the family.

Nixon reveled in the romantic tales of her Irish ancestors told by Aunt Emma, and she eventually began to make up her own serials, using cartoons she cut from various periodicals. She had an extensive filing system for her paper characters, dividing them by gender, age, and physical position (standing, sitting, walking, etc.), and she involved them in complicated plots. At the Catholic school she attended, St. Cecelia's Academy, the nuns discovered Nixon's imagination and creative-writing skills; at their urging, she wrote plays and staged them in the school auditorium. Nixon felt isolated in the real world, however, in part because she was the only child of divorce at her convent school. "I had a lonely life," she revealed on *Intimate Portrait*. "I had no father . . . I think I had an abandonment complex."

Despite her father's virtual disappearance from her life up to that point, Harry Eckhardt offered to pay for Nixon's college education, which her mother was unable to afford. She accepted his tuition payments, even as his hard-to-please nature and fickle affections made her college years—at Northwestern University, in Evanston, Illinois—tense, and heightened the bad blood between her parents. "I remember saying to myself: Just study him, don't break down, don't commit suicide, just try to take a lesson from him and make sure that no child of yours ever feels as you feel about him," she said on *Intimate Portrait*. At school, Nixon studied drama; intimidated by the acting skills of her classmates, who included the future stars Cloris Leachman and Charlton Heston, she focused on dramatic writing. After graduation she wanted to pursue a career in writing, but her father wanted her to join his burial-garment business as a secretary. He even arranged a meeting between his daughter and Irna Phillips, who in 1930 had created the first radio soap opera; the purpose of the meeting, as Harry Eckhardt saw it, was to persuade Nixon to abandon writing. But after a nerve-racking interview that included a dramatic reading of Nixon's sample half-hour script, Phillips hired her on the spot to write for the serial *Woman in White*, one of four soaps with which Phillips was involved at that time. Thrilled to be saved from working with her father, Nixon became a fast, diligent, and effective writer determined to earn her $100-a-week salary, a princely sum in 1947. "I remember how people talk," she said on *Intimate Portrait*, discussing the ease with which she writes dialogue. "I hear it in my head." While writing for the radio, Nixon never missed a deadline, which made her a valuable asset for Phillips and served Nixon well throughout her own career. "I guess I have some talent, and that's God-given. I don't take credit for that. Only thing I take credit for is the seat of the pants to the seat of the chair," she said as part of an ABC/Disney panel at the premiere of the cable channel SoapNet, as reported by Catherine Seipp in *Media Week* (January 31, 2000).

In 1950 television opened new doors for the soap-opera genre. Irna Phillips relocated to California and asked Nixon, her protégée, to follow suit. Nixon, however, wanted to write for television in New York City, where live prime-time broadcasts were produced at the time. Although she had never even visited New York, she moved there, and within a month she had sold a script for $750. She found more work writing dramas for *Studio One*, *Cameo Theater*, *Somerset Maugham Theater*, and *Philco Playhouse*; she earned enough to finance a European vacation. But loneliness still haunted her, as she revealed to Kristin McMurran for *People* (October 5, 1981): "I would stand in the backyard of my basement apartment and listen to the lilt of laughter and the tinkle of glasses behind the fence. It seemed like the whole glamorous world was on the other side and I was the child whose face was pressed against the candy store window." Then, on a blind date in 1950, she met Bob Nixon, who worked for the Chrysler car company. The two married in the spring of 1951.

Recently married, newly pregnant, and having just relocated to Philadelphia, Nixon immediately tested the condition on which she had accepted Bob Nixon's marriage proposal: that she would be able to continue her writing career. She began writing for the TV serial *Search for Tomorrow*; she worked at home while caring for her young children, mailing her scripts to New York. Irna Phillips soon called to ask her to write for the television version of her wildly popular radio soap opera *The Guiding Light*, and Nixon immediately accepted. With the unwavering support of her husband, she was able to meet both the demands of her family—which had grown to include a son and three daughters by the late 1950s—and the unending deadlines of a serial drama, a balancing act that involved having a Dictaphone with her at the hospital during labor. Phillips and Nixon co-created *As the World Turns* in 1957; Nixon was soon the head writer for both *As the World Turns* and *The Guiding Light*. Hers was a position with considerable power, which she used to bring groundbreaking stories to daytime audiences. In 1962 she wrote a story line for *The Guiding Light* in which one of the female characters discovers that she has uterine cancer and ultimately undergoes a hysterectomy to save her life. Both the CBS network and Procter & Gamble, the sponsor of the show, balked at this plot development, but Nixon insisted on seeing it through. The two sides eventually hammered out a solution that was agreeable to all concerned: Nixon would be allowed to go ahead with the plot, provided the words "cancer," "uterus," and "hysterectomy" did not appear in the script. "It was not to try to break barriers or anything like that, but . . . I thought this is insane—to say that entertainment and public service can never be in the same story," she said on *Intimate Portrait*.

Nixon was invited to become the head writer of the struggling soap opera *Another World* in 1965; under her stewardship, the show became the second-most-popular daytime serial on the air. But Nixon had hoped to create a show of her own, and ABC offered her the chance in 1967. *One Life to Live*, which began broadcasting in July 1968, was immediately recognized for its showcase of timely topics: the Vietnam War, interracial romance, and class distinctions. One of the show's first story lines involved a young white woman, Carla, who falls in love with a black doctor. When they kissed, the country went wild; a television station in Texas immediately canceled the show. But in a surprise twist, it was revealed that Carla was actually a black woman, passing as white to help her acting career. (Ellen Holly, the actress who portrayed Carla, was black.) The socially relevant content of *One Life to Live* attracted a new, younger audience that included college students. Richard Stengel speculated in *Time* (August 15, 1983) that "future sociologists may watch reruns of Nixon's soaps the way students today read Dickens." Nixon had also defended her soaps and their content in letters to the editor of the *New York Times*.

After the runaway success of *One Life to Live*, ABC asked Nixon to create another serial, and she responded with the series *All My Children*, which premiered on January 5, 1970. *All My Children*, which began as a script written during a family vacation, became known as Nixon's favorite among the shows she wrote for and featured characters whose lives were the most like her own. "One of the reasons that Erica [Kane, portrayed since the first episode by Susan Lucci] is my favorite character is because she, too, suffers from an abandonment complex, having been a child of divorce," Nixon explained to Alan Ebert for *Good Housekeeping* (November 1995). Through *All My Children* Nixon injected humor into the soap-opera genre while continuing to use the medium as a canvas for current social issues: premarital sex, drug abuse, domestic violence, and, later, homosexuality and AIDS. The actor Laurence Fishburne, for whom Nixon created a teenage character on *One Life to Live* after being impressed by his performance in a television movie, believes that Nixon's work is representative of television as an instructional tool. He elaborated on *Intimate Portrait*: "I think she's really a bright, shining example of how we can use the medium of television to . . . inform, entertain, and educate ourselves." Nixon herself has always seen her work in that light. "I'm a writer, but I'm also a teacher," she told Richard Stengel. As she did with Fishburne, Nixon has often created roles on her shows for actors and actresses whose work she admires; Tom Berenger and Tommy Lee Jones were two of her other beneficiaries. Already-established celebrities who are also soap fans occasionally have cameo appearances; Carol Burnett and Rosie O'Donnell have even had recurring roles on *All My Children*.

Nixon's responsibility in shaping daytime television became a family affair. In the 1970s, after Bob Nixon left Chrysler, he and Agnes Nixon established Creative Horizons, a production company. Agnes Nixon's duties as producer and head writer became as demanding as her writing, and the effect was all-consuming, as she explained to Kristin McMurran: "We have no summer reruns, like nighttime. We're under pressure to produce 260 hourlong segments a year." But, she has maintained, that is part of the charm of soap operas. Their appeal is in being "the form of entertainment closest to real life," she told *Broadcasting & Cable* (May 31, 1999). "Every day is a new episode . . . it's never repeated." She explained on *Intimate Portrait* that Irna Phillips "taught me how to milk the es-

sence of drama out of the minutiae of everyday life. And that's what we live! We don't live just the high points and the low points. We live minute by minute." While writing her show, Nixon has always tried to maintain the perspective of her viewers, and so she rarely appears on the set. "It's hard for me to see the stars in hair rollers going through rehearsals," she revealed to Kristin McMurran. "I don't want the edge taken off."

In the 1980s Nixon co-created the soap opera *Loving*, which, unlike most of her series, was a half-hour show. She also wrote a three-part television miniseries, *The Manions of America*, which told the story of a 19th-century Irish family, much like Nixon's mother's family, who eventually make their way to prosperity in the United States. Although the story was panned as being "too epic for its own good" by the *Christian Science Monitor* (September 25, 1981) and as "lacking substance" by the *New York Times* (September 27, 1981), the performances of the stars, particularly Kate Mulgrew and Pierce Brosnan, won praise from critics.

Nixon continues to write for her ABC creations, *One Life to Live* and *All My Children*, while tucked away in her third-floor garret in Pine Cottage, a pre-Revolutionary house located in the Philadelphia suburbs and purchased by the Nixons in the 1950s. She has won accolades, Emmys, and millions of fans around the world. Going by the titles of head writer for *All My Children* and daytime story consultant for ABC, she maintains a deep attachment to her characters and still sees her shows as outlets for her creativity and energy. After the death of her husband from cancer, in 1996, she began writing again as soon as she could manage it. Now a grandmother of more than half a dozen, Nixon has no plans to stop writing. "Every day is a new episode and there are no reruns," she told Gwen Kinkead for *Savvy Woman* (April 1989). "And we make 'em laugh, we make 'em cry, and we make 'em wait."
— K.S.

Suggested Reading: *Broadcasting & Cable* p28 May 31, 1999; *Good Housekeeping* p28+ Nov. 1995, with photo; *People* p71+ Oct. 5, 1981, with photos; *Savvy Woman* p58+ Apr. 1989, with photo; *Time* p69 Aug. 15, 1983, with photo

Selected Television Shows: as creator and writer—*One Life to Live*; *All My Children*; as co-creator and writer—*As the World Turns*, 1956; *Loving*; as writer—*Another World*; *Guiding Light*; *Search for Tomorrow*; miniseries—*The Manions of America*, 1981

Selected Radio Shows: *The Guiding Light*; *Woman in White*

Larry Downing/Archive Photos

Norton, Gale A.

*1954– U.S. Secretary of the Interior. Address:
U.S. Department of the Interior, 1849 C St., N.W.,
Washington, DC 20240*

"I've been involved in environmental issues for over 20 years. Over that time I've developed a point of view and a vision about the environment. If I had to boil it down to just one phrase, it might be this: We Americans can conserve our environment—and benefit from it, too. We can preserve America's wild places while protecting jobs and doing our part to help preserve America's prosperity." These words were spoken by Gale A. Norton, a Republican and the new United States secretary of the interior, during her February 15, 2001 introductory meeting with her staff, as quoted on the Department of the Interior's Web site. To her supporters, Norton's view represents a fine compromise between conservationists and industrialists. For while Norton, a former attorney general of Colorado and the first female secretary of the interior, is in favor of opening federal lands to oil and mineral drilling, she has stated that such actions must be done responsibly and with a focus on retaining treasured land. Additionally, many representatives of U.S. industry agree with Norton's libertarian notion that corporations should be self-regulating with regard to environmental policy, and that even the smallest governmental interference with their property rights for the sake of enforcing federal environmental rules should require compensation. Such views, however, anger and worry many Democrats, who believe that Norton's policies will ultimately harm the environment and destroy the land her department was designed to protect.

Gale A. Norton was born in 1954 in Wichita, Kansas. Her family moved to Colorado when she was a child, and she grew up near the Rocky Mountains. "From the time I was a young child growing up in Colorado, I've loved the Rocky Mountains," she was quoted as saying by Mike Soraghan for the *Denver Post* (December 30, 2000, on-line). "A place to hike with my dog, watch an elk in a grove of aspen trees, or contemplate eternity gazing at jagged mountain peaks." She attended the University of Denver, in Colorado, from which she graduated magna cum laude with a bachelor's degree in 1975 and earned a law degree, with honors, in 1978. It was there that she became a libertarian, one who believes that government involvement in the affairs of a nation's citizens and companies should be extremely limited. In 1979 Norton became a senior attorney for the Mountain States Legal Foundation, a conservative think tank with a pro-development outlook, where James G. Watt, a future secretary of the interior, then worked. Moving to Washington, D.C., to work with the foundation, she switched her party affiliation to the Republican Party, which she later described as a move on her part toward "practical politics." She held her position at Mountain States until 1983, when she became a National Fellow at Stanford University's Hoover Institution, where she conducted research on new and resourceful ways to control air pollution. From 1984 to 1985 she served as United States assistant to the deputy secretary of agriculture.

From 1985 to 1987 Norton served as associate solicitor of the U.S. Department of the Interior. In that position she worked closely with the National Park Service and the Fish and Wildlife Service on legal issues regarding endangered species and public lands. Among other efforts, she advocated legislation that would have opened Alaska's Arctic National Wildlife Refuge to oil drilling as well as measures that would have required the government to pay corporations and landowners not to wipe out critical wildlife on their land. After leaving that post, Norton became senior counsel at Brownstein, Hyatt & Farber P.C., a predominantly Democratic firm.

In 1991 Norton won election as attorney general of Colorado, defeating the incumbent. In her new position she dealt with cases involving hospital ownership, gasoline prices, and antitrust enforcement. Praised by conservatives for advocating a reduction in the role of the federal government in setting standards for the environment and health, Norton also worked successfully with Democrats on some issues. In a decision applauded by both her supporters and her critics, she won a major court case whose outcome pressured the federal government to clean up hazardous waste at Rocky Flats and the Rocky Mountain Arsenal. She won kudos from members of both parties for her role as a negotiator of the $206 billion settlement reached in 1997, after the tobacco industry was sued for health damages on behalf of citizens across the nation. In the settlement, the largest in history, Norton successfully represented Colorado and 45 other states. More controversially, she advocated Colorado's "self-audit" law, which allows companies to conduct voluntary audits to ascertain whether they are in compliance with environmental requirements. She also received criticism from both the left and moderate Republicans for her support of Colorado's Amendment 2, which would be ruled unconstitutional by the United States Supreme Court in 1996. The amendment would have nullified state and local laws that prohibited discrimination based on sexual orientation and rescinded existing gay-rights ordinances in Aspen, Boulder, and Denver. At the time Norton stated that while she believed in equal rights for all, she also felt that in order to qualify for constitutional protection, a group had to have a history of being discriminated against, had to be incapable of changing its status, and had to be politically powerless. Noting that in her mind homosexuals did not meet those criteria, she determined that they were not eligible for protection under the Constitution. In 1996 she ran for the Republican Senate nomination from Colorado but was defeated in the primaries. That year she also spoke out in favor of a policy that would forbid Colorado's 28 public colleges from providing race-based scholarships, as she believed the practice to be unconstitutional. She ended her term as attorney general in 1999.

Upon George W. Bush's election as the 43d president of the United States, in 2000, he nominated Gale Norton as secretary of the interior, a choice that surprised many. As quoted by Mike Soraghan, Bush noted that he had chosen Norton for many reasons, among them her reputation "for building consensus on divisive issues." In a speech at the press conference at which Bush announced her nomination, Norton said, as quoted by ABC-News.com (on-line), "An entire one-third of our land is owned by the federal government. Together with the other departments that own that land, the Department of the Interior faces the challenge of seeing that our land is used in an environmentally responsible way." While her nomination prompted praise from industry leaders, environmentalists were outraged and expressed fears about her belief in opening federal land for mining and oil drilling; they also cited her past lobbying for a lead-paint manufacturer, and her desire to let corporations police themselves in matters relating to the environment, as causes for alarm. In addition, she was criticized for a speech she made in 1989, in which she stated that the government should compensate property owners when their property values were decreased as a result of environmental regulations. Despite the intense lobbying by environmental groups and other liberal organizations that opposed her confirmation, the Senate Energy and National Resources Committee approved her nomination by a vote of 18–2, and Norton was confirmed by the Senate by a vote of 75–24. Sworn in on January 30, 2001, she became the first woman to head the Department of the Interior.

In her first month in office, Norton backed Bush's highly controversial attempt to open up 1.5 million acres of the Arctic National Wildlife Refuge to oil drilling. She has stated that it is possible to drill there without damaging the land. "There are techniques that are being talked about that are very high-tech kinds of approaches—things like putting in ice roads and only doing any kind of activity during the dead of winter," she said during a question-and-answer session with the Department of the Interior's Washington, D.C., staff. "So that they might drag their equipment over these roads, but when spring comes, they entirely melt away. And the tundra is left fairly undisturbed, looking at what they call diagonal drilling or drilling so that you can have one well that can access five miles of underground. So we need to do things to ensure that the caribou habitat and the other habitat is undisturbed as much as possible because those are very important resources for us." Her position was attacked by Democrats and conservationists who suspected that even with such planning, oil drilling in the refuge would harm the environment and the indigenous people of the area.

Norton surprised many when she decided not to attempt to overturn former president Bill Clinton's last-minute designation of millions of acres of federal land as national monuments. She did say, however, that there would be attempts to adjust the boundaries of the monuments as well as to alter the rules for commercial activities within them. "I certainly disapprove of the process by which those monuments were generally created . . . but I have not yet heard any calls to repeal any of the monument designations," she told the Washington Post, as quoted by Reuters (February 21, 2001, on-line). On the issue of global warming, Norton has taken a moderately conservative stance. "It does seem, based on my evaluation," she was quoted as saying on the Web page of the Embassy of the United States in Stockholm, Sweden, "which is not a scientific one, that there is beginning to be more of a consensus that global warming is occurring. There is still disagreement as to the causes and the long-term future. And obviously, there is disagreement about what ought to be done in that regard. I will certainly rely on scientific information as it becomes available and evaluate the information as it is presented to me." While she has discussed changing a 1997 U.S. Forest Service decision that banned drilling in areas of the Lewis and Clark National Forest, in Montana, she has said that she is not opposed to the current moratoriums on new offshore drilling in California and Florida.

Norton played a major role in creating the Bush administration's energy plan, which emphasized domestic production of oil and gas and played down environmental concerns. "We have to find a way to pursue the resources that we need and, at the same time, to protect the environment," Norton told Douglas Jehl for the New York Times (May 25, 2001). Norton and the administration later retreated from some of their energy goals and scaled back plans to allow oil companies to drill in about six million acres in the Gulf of Mexico. Under the new plan only 1.5 million acres would be opened to drilling. However, that decision, too, was criticized by environmentalists; even some Republicans accused the administration of caving in to pressure from oil and gas interests. New mining regulations announced by the Department of the Interior in October 2001 changed or deleted some of the provisions of the Clinton administration. One provision that was removed had given the interior secretary the power to prohibit new mining sites on federal land where, it was determined, mining operations would cause long-term harm to communities and the environment. Not surprisingly, the deletion dismayed environmentalists but pleased the mining industry. Norton also said she would ask Congress to overhaul mining laws that dated back to 1872. At around the same time, the department reversed the Clinton administration's ruling that mining near Native American traditional and religious sites was illegal.

In October 2001 the Interior Department went to court as a result of a suit filed by Native American activists in 1996. The suit involved a trust fund established by the federal government in 1887 as a repository for royalties from certain activities conducted by non-Indians on Native American lands. The plaintiffs argued that for many years, up to and including the first months of the Bush administration, the Interior Department had mismanaged at least $10 billion of the royalties that had accrued from the grazing of cattle, logging, mining, and oil drilling, and that therefore the department should be divested of control of the fund. In 1998 a U.S. district judge had decided against appointing an outside receiver to remedy the situation and had allowed the Interior Department to retain control of the fund, though with court supervision. Since then two court-appointed watchdogs have noted the continued failure of the department to manage the fund correctly.

Norton currently lives in the Washington, D.C., area with her husband, John Hughes. The two are known as passionate hikers and lovers of the outdoors. The National Federalist Society once honored Norton as Young Lawyer of the Year, and she received the highest honor of the Colorado Women's Bar Association: the Mary Lathrop Trailblazer Award. She has headed the Coalition of Republican Environmental Advocates, which "emphasizes free-market solutions over environmental regulation," and opposes government intervention in environmental protection. As attorney general of Colorado, she also served as chair of the Environment Committee for the National Association of Attorneys General. She served, as an appointee of former president George Bush, on the Western Water Policy Commission and has also served as Environment Committee chair for the Republican National Lawyers Association and general counsel of the Colorado Civil Justice League. Envisioning her

new role as secretary of the interior, Norton told the Associated Press (February 13, 2001), "The Department of the Interior is often viewed as remote and distant, making decisions that deeply affect people's lives without really understanding the consequences. I would like to be remembered as a secretary who really brought people together and changed our decision-making focus to one that requires Washington to listen to people throughout the country." — G.O.

Suggested Reading: *ABCNews.com*; *Denver Post* (on-line) Dec. 30, 2000, Jan. 31, 2001; *New York Times* A p1+ Dec. 30, 2000, with photo, A p14 May 25, 2001, with photo; *U.S. News & World Report* p14+ Jan. 29, 2001, with photo

---

Courtesy of U.S. Treasury Department

O'Neill, Paul H.

Dec. 4, 1935– U.S. Secretary of the Treasury. Address: Office of the Secretary, Dept. of the Treasury, 1500 Pennsylvania Ave., N.W., Washington, DC 20220

"I'm not going to make a huge case that [a tax cut] is the investment we need to make sure we don't go into a recession," Paul H. O'Neill, the 72d secretary of the treasury and former chairman of the aluminum company Alcoa, remarked during his comparatively little-publicized confirmation testimony before the U.S. Senate, as quoted by Frank Pelligrini in *Time* (January 18, 2001, on-line). "But if we are going to do it anyway," he added, "the sooner the better." Since his new job requires him to play an important role in designing and implementing

Republican president George W. Bush's $1.35 trillion tax cut, O'Neill's comment—with its implied lack of enthusiasm for the plan—raised the eyebrows of Republicans and Democrats alike. "Something doesn't add up about the new Treasury Secretary nominated by George W. Bush," a perplexed William Greider wrote for the *Nation* (January 29, 2001, on-line). As Greider pointed out, some labor leaders, a group that has not traditionally had kind words for those in O'Neill's post, have waxed enthusiastic over O'Neill—who, unlike previous treasury secretaries, has a background in manufacturing and government rather than in banking and finance. For example, George Becker, the president of United Steelworkers of America (a union that represents 22,000 Alcoa workers), told Greider, "I'm not an economist . . . but Paul is a person working people and labor people can talk to. He is an industrialist who believes in the United States and has maintained a strong industrial base in the United States. I think this is far better than having another bond trader in that job." Meanwhile, laissez-faire conservatives have criticized O'Neill for having publicly questioned the wisdom of Bush's tax cut. The fact that O'Neill is not a supply-sider, or one who favors tax cuts, "is less important than his subversion of the president-elect's agenda," John J. Miller and Ramesh Ponnuru wrote for the *National Review* (January 18, 2001, on-line). "Bush has made the argument that tax cuts are an insurance policy against recession for over a year now. He needs spokesmen who will make that case in order to win over a skeptical Washington. One might have thought he would pick a Treasury secretary who would be such a spokesman."

O'Neill's record suggests that he is a pragmatically inclined, moderate Republican with a strong independent streak. He supported the deficit-reducing tax increase put in place by Bush's father, former president George Herbert Walker Bush, and later, in 1992, endorsed the incoming Democratic president Bill Clinton's proposed tax on gas. While hardly an environmentalist (an Alcoa smelter outside Austin, Texas, is one of that state's biggest polluters), O'Neill took part in a number of discussions on global warming sponsored by the Clinton administration. On the other hand, O'Neill staunchly opposed Clinton's 1993–94 health-care initiative and, on one occasion, came close to saying that the corporate tax ought to be abolished altogether. (In an interview with the *Financial Times* [May 21, 2001, on-line], O'Neill called for the elimination of taxes on corporations in favor of taxes aimed directly at individuals, who, he noted, already pay them in the form of taxes charged for products. Such a plan would dispense with the "administrative cost of running the tax process," in his view.) "The escalating codes of tax administration that are driven by an even-more complex tax code add nothing [to] the . . . value of our products . . . ," he said during a 1990 speech at Indiana University, as quoted by Larry Kudlow in the *National Review* (December 20, 2000, on-line). "Here

is an area where the federal government could make a difference. . . . The ultimate reduction would come from simply eliminating the corporate tax. No tax. No tax departments." Such talk notwithstanding, O'Neill declared at his confirmation hearing that his days as "a free-ranging, self-admitted maverick" are over.

If O'Neill's lukewarm endorsement of the Bush tax cut makes him seem an odd choice for the post, it should be remembered that he is a familiar face to many in the current Bush administration. O'Neill worked with then–White House chief of staff Dick Cheney (now Bush's vice president) under President Gerald R. Ford; he was considered as a possible secretary of defense by George H. W. Bush. He is also close to Federal Reserve chairman Alan Greenspan, whom he met in the 1970s, during the Ford administration (and who, like O'Neill, later served on the Alcoa board of directors). "In Paul O'Neill, the president-elect has attracted an exceptional and talented person," Greenspan said, as quoted by Joseph Kahn and Floyd Norris for the *New York Times* (December 21, 2000) shortly after O'Neill's nomination was announced. O'Neill in turn made sure to underscore his ties to Greenspan, who is credited by some with having engineered the economic growth of the 1990s. "I've made it a business to come by [the Fed] on a fairly regular basis and tell him what I thought he was doing wrong," he said in a press conference cited by Gosselin. Because relations between Greenspan and the Bush clan have been strained in the past (some supporters of the elder Bush felt that Greenspan hurt their candidate in the 1992 presidential election by not moving quickly enough to reduce unemployment), O'Neill's ties to the Fed chairman are valuable to George W. Bush.

The son of John Paul and Gaynald Elsie O'Neill, Paul Henry O'Neill was born in St. Louis, Missouri, on December 4, 1935. Because his was a military family, during his childhood O'Neill lived in many different parts of the United States, an experience he has credited with teaching him negotiating skills that would later prove valuable in government and business. "Part of growing up in a military family," O'Neill told a reporter for MSNBC (on-line), "is going different places all the time and being forced to deal with people who never saw you before and didn't have the experience of growing up with you. And that's pretty good training for going into a place where the natural reaction to outsiders is rejection." O'Neill received a B.A. degree in economics from Fresno State College, in California, in 1960, and an M.P.A. (master of public administration) from Indiana University six years later.

O'Neill began his career in government in 1961, as a computer-systems analyst for the Department of Veterans Affairs, where he remained through 1966. In 1967 he took a job as budget examiner in what was then called the Bureau of the Budget, in Washington, D.C., in the administration of President Lyndon B. Johnson; two years later he was named chief of human resources for the Office of Management and Budget (OMB). O'Neill stayed at the budget office throughout the presidential administrations of Richard Nixon and Gerald R. Ford, eventually becoming deputy director. "As a career employee, Paul rose to the No. 2 position at OMB strictly on merit," Ford told Michael Schroeder for *Business Week* (June 27, 1988). "I can say without reservations that he is the most knowledgeable, objective adviser on the budget I ever had." At this time O'Neill also met Dick Cheney and Alan Greenspan, who were also employed in the Ford administration.

At OMB, O'Neill's federalist views led him to strike a middle path between conservatives, who wanted to slash many government programs, and liberals, who wanted to use government resources to promote social initiatives. As Suzanne Woolsey, who worked with O'Neill at the Office of Management and Budget, told Joseph Kahn and Floyd Norris, O'Neill "virtually invented" block grants, whereby the federal government provides matching funds for local programs. (In theory, block grants allow the federal government to support local initiatives without taking control of them.)

In 1977, when Jimmy Carter succeeded Ford as president, O'Neill left government to become vice president of International Paper, the New York–based company that is the world's largest paper and packaging manufacturer. (International Paper is also one of the 30 companies that compose the Dow Jones Industrial Average.) O'Neill served as vice president until 1985, when he was promoted to president.

In April 1987 O'Neill was named chairman of Alcoa, an aluminum manufacturer, by the company's board of directors. Although Alcoa's previous chairman, Charles W. Parry, claimed at the time that his retirement was voluntary (he cited growing medical concerns), Michael Schroeder noted in *Business Week* that the change in leadership was in fact a "boardroom coup." At issue was Parry's controversial vision for redefining Alcoa as a diversified company with operations in aerospace, packaging, and new-materials research, as opposed to the single-interest aluminum producer it had been since 1888. (Parry planned to realize this vision chiefly through acquisitions; in 1985 he forecast that within 10 years, Alcoa would derive over 50 percent of its revenue from businesses unrelated to aluminum.) While Parry's proposed changes made sense to some at Alcoa, which was then faltering because of a worldwide slump in the aluminum market, traditionalists on the board of directors, who preferred to stick with aluminum, quietly began searching for a new chairman. After a plan to recruit the CEO of Cummins Engine Co., the nation's leading manufacturer of diesel engines, fell through, the board (which at the time included Alan Greenspan) turned to one of their own and chose O'Neill, who quickly reversed the course set by Parry. "If we're going to be successful, it will be premised on our ability to be first in the aluminum business," O'Neill told Schroeder.

Under O'Neill, Alcoa recovered from its slump to become, by 1999, the best-performing stock in the Dow Jones Industrial Average. Like Parry, O'Neill pursued a policy of acquisition, but the businesses acquired by Alcoa under O'Neill were almost exclusively aluminum companies. As a result, the aluminum industry in the United States is now highly monopolized. In fact, according to George David Smith, an economic historian at New York University whom Gosselin quoted, "it's probably the purest monopoly in American history."

In 1993 O'Neill demonstrated his willingness to accept some government involvement in business when, working with the Clinton administration, he brokered a deal to persuade the former Soviet republics, then flooding the world market with cheap aluminum, to reduce production in return for loans. He also proved adept at negotiating the divide between government and industry. "It's typical that the industry people come in foaming at the mouth about the need for [private trade] sanctions [against the Russian government]," W. Bowman Cutter, a Clinton administration official, told Kahn and Norris. "Paul was totally balanced. He saw both sides and worked for a principled solution that made sense for everybody."

O'Neill was confirmed by the Senate and sworn in as the 72d secretary of the treasury on January 20, 2001. During his first months in office, he continued to defy expectations. At the first Bush Cabinet meeting, O'Neill angered some administration officials by distributing copies of a 1999 speech in which he had compared the possible consequences of global warming to a nuclear holocaust. Soon afterward he made a casual remark to a German newspaper that, because it was widely interpreted as signaling a change in fiscal policy, roiled foreign-exchange markets. Disparaging remarks that he made about former president Ronald Reagan's economic policies were used by Senate Democratic leader Tom Daschle to attack President Bush's proposed tax cuts. And O'Neill caused the Bush administration some embarrassment by initially refusing to divest himself of more than $90 million worth of Alcoa stock, despite the suggestion from some quarters that not doing so represented a conflict of interest. (O'Neill eventually declared that he would divest his shares slowly, over several months.)

By late 2001 O'Neill appeared to have been reined in somewhat by a Bush administration uncomfortable with his idiosyncratic style. That was particularly evident after the September 11, 2001 terrorist attacks on New York City and Washington, D.C.: while the White House entrusted O'Neill with tracking down the financial assets of Osama bin Laden and the Al Qaeda network, the secretary was conspicuously absent from high-level meetings that focused on working out a national economic-stimulus package and a bailout plan for the airline industry. Moreover, O'Neill's efforts to mitigate fears of a national recession by means of rosy pronouncements on the state of the economy were widely derided in the media as unrealistic, glib, or even disingenuous. "He's the only cabinet member who hasn't really stepped into the national dialogue in a persuasive way," an anonymous "influential Republican" told Joseph Kahn for the *New York Times* (October 2, 2001). "At the White House, disappointment is widespread." In response to such criticism, O'Neill has emphasized that President Bush needed and appreciated independent thinkers. "I've been disappointed that there doesn't seem to be a larger clientele, including in the media, for people who tell the truth," he said during an interview cited by Kahn. "When I do something and it's off the beaten path, people say, 'Oh, my God, this is not the way we play the game.'" He told Kahn, "If I thought I was reducing the president's effectiveness I would leave tomorrow."

Paul O'Neill and his wife, Nancy, have four children—three daughters and one son—and 12 grandchildren. In his spare time O'Neill enjoys watercolor painting. — P.K.

Suggested Reading: *Business Week* p58+ Jun. 27, 1988, with photos; *Los Angeles Times* (on-line) Dec. 21, 2000, with photo; *New York Times* C p1 Oct 2, 2001, with photo, C p1 Oct. 2, 2001, with photo; *New York Times* (on-line) Dec. 21, 2000, with photo; *Time* (on-line) Feb. 27, 2001, with photo

---

Courtesy of Sandra Sunrising Osawa

Osawa, Sandra Sunrising

1941– Filmmaker; poet. Address: Upstream Productions, 6850 35th Ave. NE, #11, Seattle, WA 98115

Sandra Sunrising Osawa has been an independent film and video producer longer than any other Native American in the United States. She has produced more than 40 videos, among them her own documentaries, which touch on current Native American issues. With the airing of her informational series on American Indians on NBC in 1975, she became the first independent Native American producer working in commercial television. In an effort to combat widely held stereotypes about American Indians, Osawa has mostly focused on present-day Native Americans rather than on Native American myths and historical events. "The situation for Native Americans is a bit complicated because we're always painted as people in the past," she told Chon Noriega during a roundtable discussion for the *Viewing Race Project* Web site. "That's something that we struggle with daily; you get the feeling that you're not really an Indian unless you have feathers." Several of her films document Native Americans' attempts to get the United States government to uphold treaties it signed with various Native American nations. Unlike Hollywood films, which Osawa believes neglect many aspects of Native American life, her documentaries tell multiple stories within one overarching narrative. "I don't like to tell a story with just one dimension," she told Noriega, "because certainly with Indian stories, there's never just one dimension. I try to capture multiple facets, such as history, religion, culture, politics and the law, so that you get a complete story. This comes from a resistance to seeing Native Americans portrayed as one-dimensional people."

A member of the Makah Indian Nation, which has lived in coastal areas of the Pacific Northwest for thousands of years, Osawa was born Sandra Johnson in Washington State in 1941. "Sunrising" comes from her mother's Indian name, which, in English translation, was "Cooking Up at the Sunrise," as Osawa told *Current Biography*. According to the Makah Nation Web site, in the Makah language the tribe's name is "Kwih-dich-chuh-ahtx," which means "people who live by the rocks and seagulls"; "Makah," the name by which neighboring tribes called it, means "generous with food." Osawa's father was a commercial fisherman and athlete. A shy child, Sandra was the only person of color in her school in the early grades.

After she reached maturity, Osawa worked for her tribe, serving as its first community-action director. In the mid-1960s she led the Makah War on Poverty program and launched Washington State's first Indian Head Start program. "There was never anything to do on the reservation," she recalled in an interview with Victor Payan, reprinted on the

San Diego Latino Film Festival Web site. "I tried to have a movie night, but it was difficult with no films about us and particularly nothing about Northwest tribes. That always stuck in my mind." She was also influential in developing, for Makah children from grades one through 12, cultural-studies programs that kept alive the language and songs of the Makah while bringing Makah elders into the local schools. In addition, she helped Native American tribes of the American Northwest fight for fishing rights long promised but never delivered by treaties with the United States. The conflict was also a personal one for Osawa, whose grandfather's three sealing schooners had been confiscated by the U.S. government without compensation after seal hunting was banned.

During the fishing-rights protests, Osawa saw first-hand the way biases in the media regarding Native Americans skewed news coverage of Native American concerns. "The media decided how they wanted to cover our story and we pretty much had to go along with it, even though we were desperately trying to bring out the issue of treaty rights," Osawa was quoted as saying in a press release reprinted on the Web site of the PBS documentary series P.O.V. (the acronym for "point of view"). "Day after day, night after night, we would see the protests being presented as Indians on the warpath and no substance at all. I recall feeling very powerless because we weren't able to really access the media very well."

Osawa received a B.A. degree from Lewis and Clark College, in Portland, Oregon. In the late 1960s or early 1970s, she taught at the Clyde Warrior Institute for Native American Studies in Los Angeles. She later enrolled in the graduate program in film at the University of California at Los Angeles (UCLA), having heard that the university wanted to increase the number of minority students in its film school. The idea of gaining a wider audience for Native American stories that were important to all tribes and nations had been developing in Osawa's mind since her days of social activism, and she felt that cinema would be an excellent vehicle through which to reach that goal. At UCLA she met her future husband, Yasu Osawa, a Japanese cameraman, and the two began working together. Sandra Osawa's first film, made at UCLA, was the one-minute Curios. "I decided to try the most difficult thing, a short piece, and was really elated with it," she told Payan. "We shot inside a museum at people coming through looking at Native American curios. Mummies were still being displayed. We shot that and edited the whole thing. . . . It showed how white people really see us, in terms of looking at us behind glass cases."

After one semester Sandra dropped out of UCLA, as did Yasu, because of deficiencies in the program, such as inaccessibility of film equipment. "It would have been nice to have the degree," she told Payan, "but I was impatient at the process of sitting there talking about theory. I wanted to jump in and do something!" She and Yasu soon found

work at the Los Angeles Indian Center, where they published a magazine called Talking Leaf. Yasu designed and provided photographs for the magazine, while Sandra wrote investigative, political articles and poetry that called for social and political reform. In 1975 she produced a 10-part series on Native Americans for NBC, for which the network honored her with an Outstanding Producer Award. The first film for commercial television to be produced, researched, written, and acted by Native Americans, it was later purchased by the Bureau of Indian Affairs (BIA) for use in the BIA school system (one of only two school systems operated by the federal government; the other, operated by the Department of Defense, provides classes for the children of military personnel living on or near military bases). The series covers such topics as Native American religion, family, art, and politics. Despite the 6:00 a.m. time slot to which NBC relegated the series, the films received a great deal of positive feedback from Native Americans as well as non-Indians. At around the same time, Sandra Osawa also wrote the script for When the Geese Fly Low, a PBS documentary on the Northern Cheyenne Indians and their long trek northward. (Displaced from their traditional homes in Montana and North Dakota, the Cheyennes were sent to live in so-called Indian Territory, in Oklahoma, where they suffered from the humidity, scarcity of food and other resources, and outbreaks of disease. In 1879 they journeyed north; attacked by American troops along the way, the survivors reached Montana, where a new reservation was eventually set aside for them.) After the NBC series, Sandra Osawa waited 13 years to direct another film for broadcast television.

Meanwhile, Osawa and her husband, concerned that the Los Angeles smog might harm their health and that of their two young children, had moved to Seattle. There, they found that getting funding for new projects was much harder than in Los Angeles. "How did we know at the time that dropping out of film school would matter when we moved to Seattle," Sandra Osawa told Laura Nielsen Denke for Online (July/August 1998). "People like credentials. How would we know that opportunities were much more restricted in Seattle." Eventually, the Osawas got jobs directing such shorts as Hamatsa Dance, a re-creation of authentic Native American dancing filmed for the Pacific Science Center, in Seattle. In 1981 they co-founded Upstream Productions, a Seattle-based production company.

After years of working on other people's projects and pitching ideas to various organizations and donors, the Osawas, via Upstream Productions, received funding from the Paul Robeson Foundation to produce the half-hour documentary In the Heart of Big Mountain, which aired on the Learning Channel in 1988 as part of The Spirit of Place series. Nominated for the National Cable Television Association's 1989 CableACE Award, the film showed the harrowing effects of a recent mass relocation on one Navajo family.

Next, Sandra Osawa produced the one-hour film *The Eighth Fire* (1992), which aired on NBC and depicted three separate battles over Native American treaty rights that were in progress at the time. That film, directed by Yasu Osawa, was commissioned by the National Council of Churches, which had been forced to cut the funds for the project after the Osawas began filming. Undaunted, the Osawas finished the film without any more financial remuneration, after getting permission to retain ownership of segments not included in the final version of the film. Along with additional filming, those outtakes were featured in Sandra Osawa's 1995 film, *Lighting the 7th Fire*, which premiered on *P.O.V.* It was the first Native American–produced portion of the series. *Lighting the 7th Fire* focuses on the Chippewa Indians of northern Wisconsin, who, in 1983, won a court decision that allowed them to fish outside the boundaries of their reservation, on land ceded earlier to the Indians in treaties. The Indians had been promised such rights for over a century by unfulfilled treaties with the United States government. Fearful that Chippewa spearfishing could extinguish the walleye fish population, non-Indians in the area harassed Chippewa by shooting at them or stoning them. The film took its name from part of a Chippewa prophecy about seven fires, each of which represents a different aspect of life. The sixth fire represents a period of loss, while the seventh fire represents a period when lost traditions are renewed. The Chippewa believe that the seventh fire may signal the restoration of fishing rights. "There are times in our history, just as there were in the civil rights movement, when you can see the tide start to turn," Osawa was quoted as saying in the *P.O.V.* Web site press release. "This story in Northern Wisconsin right now is one of those times. You can see the tide beginning to turn." Later in the same press release, she was quoted as saying, "I wanted to focus more on experiences and give voice to Native American viewpoints because most Americans don't know what it is like to be Indian in 20th century America. This is also what I call my honor song video or my way of honoring people who make a stand, who try to make a stand and who try to make a difference. *Lighting the 7th Fire* is a pat on the back to some of the many people of all races who stand up to right a wrong and thereby inspire us all."

Also in 1995 Sandra Osawa directed the six-minute, black-and-white video *Goin' Back*, which used early 1970s footage that, according to a Web site of the National Museum of the American Indian (a division of the Smithsonian Institution), was "prepared as a tribute to Floyd Westerman's 'Goin' Back' song and as a memorial tribute to Emette Sarracino [a member of the Laguna Pueblo tribe]." In explaining what motivated her to make *Goin' Back*, Osawa said, as quoted on that Web site, "When I went to graduate school at UCLA . . . the whole idea about being in Los Angeles and being Indian was really interesting, because it's the city with the largest urban Indian population in the country. And what struck me was that there was always this talk about 'urban Indians' and 'reservation Indians' and yet in a sense what I found was that the spirit was really the same, no matter where you lived. Especially if you lived in L.A., there was even more of an intensity to go back and maintain your presence, or your roots or to visit, and there was always this continual back-and-forth. Some friends of mine, myself included, would always go back home. So when I heard Floyd Westerman's song about going back, going home, it really triggered the whole image for me in terms of what I saw taking place with the two worlds. People living in the urban world, but really reconnecting strongly with the reservation world. And this whole connection seemed to be perfectly blended in his song."

Sandra Osawa's documentary *Pepper's Pow Wow*, about Jim Pepper, a Native American saxophonist and clarinetist who blended experimental jazz with music of his Native American heritage, premiered in 1996. The film had taken years to finish, due to Osawa's difficulty in getting funding for the project, which she has blamed on potential donors' lack of knowledge about people of significance to Native American communities. To compound her troubles, in 1992, before the film was completed, Pepper died. "Making [this film] . . . was important because it presents a profile of a contemporary Native American man in a nontraditional role," Osawa told Chon Noriega. "Jim Pepper was . . . an innovator of the world music concept as we know it. So the work can be used to change the frozen images of the past and to try to get a different perspective on the present and the future." *Pepper's Pow Wow* was screened at the 1996 Sundance Film Festival and at the 1996 Taos Talking Picture Film Festival in Taos, New Mexico, at the latter of which Osawa was named the "Native American Filmmaker of the Year"; the film won several other awards as well.

Also in 1996 Sandra Osawa directed and produced *Usual and Unaccustomed Places*, which profiles several Northwest Indians and their struggle to secure their tribes' treaty rights. In undertaking that project, Osawa had competed for a commission from the state government, which was encouraging the making of a film about the state's native peoples, in connection with Washington's Centennial Celebration. When the commission was awarded to a non-Indian producer, Osawa and her husband protested, complaining that Washington's Native Americans had thus been prevented from telling their own story and, moreover, that the supposedly strict guidelines for the granting of the commission had not been followed. The *New York Times* ran the story, and after reading the article, an owner of a television station in California gave the Osawas some of the money they needed to start shooting the film. The first part of *Usual and Unaccustomed Places* premiered at the 1997 Sundance Film Festival. Sandra Osawa's most recent film is *On and Off the Res with Charlie Hill* (1999), which premiered at the 2000 Taos Talking Picture Film Festival. The documentary is a profile of the Native American comedian Charlie Hill, whose performances on national television have helped dispel popular misconceptions about native culture.

"[My films] are very spiritual in their basic construction and in their basic message . . . ," Sandra Osawa told Victor Payan. "Whether the [film] is political, which many are, it's still rooted in a strong spiritual feeling. That's probably a departure from how a non-native would produce the same subject area. I doubt it would have that element of spirituality. That's what sets my work apart, and hopefully makes it stronger." Osawa has taught script writing at Evergreen State College, in Olympia, Washington, and video production at Seattle Community College, and has written several dramatic scripts of her own. She was inducted into the Writers Guild in the 1970s, after selling her feature-length script "Upstream at Medicine Creek" to a television station.

Five poems by Sandra Osawa were published in *Dancing on the Rim of the World: An Anthology of Contemporary Northwest Native American Writing* (1990), which contains a smattering of prose amidst many poems. "I was influenced by the poetry of writers with spare and clear imagery," Osawa, who has been writing poetry since fourth grade, told Payan. "I wanted to find images that were somewhat, I want to say simple, but simple could be misunderstood. In terms of being like poetry, the more you refine it, the less words you have to use. I'm driven by poetry with strong, specific imagery. That really reaches people. It's a discipline that guides me to reduce and clear out the clutter. It's hard in documentaries because they are driven by words. So we try finding ways to make words come out as strong as they possibly can." Osawa also contributed two essays to the book *First Fish, First People* (1998), edited by Judith Roche and Meg McHutchinson, an anthology of articles by Native American and Japanese writers that deal with the role of the Pacific wild salmon in traditional cultures and issues connected with the species' conservation.

In the mid-1990s Osawa served as a United Nations Environment Programme fellow at the Center for Media, Culture, and History at New York University. She has identified as the two most rewarding moments of her life her receipt of the NBC award and the airing of *Lighting the 7th Fire* on PBS. She and her husband still own and manage Upstream Productions. Yasu has served as the editor, videographer, still cameraman, and graphic artist for five Upstream documentaries made for national television and for more than 50 made for museums and other nonbroadcast uses. The Osawas are currently engaged in research for a documentary on the Native American ballerina Maria Tallchief, who was a soloist with the New York City Ballet and later became the director of the Chicago Ballet. — G.O.

Suggested Reading: *American Indian Quarterly* p104+ Winter/Spring 1998; *Online* p6+ July/Aug. 1998, with photos; *P.O.V.* (on-line); *Viewing Race* (on-line)

Selected Films: *Native American Series*, 1975; *In the Heart of Big Mountain*, 1988; *The Eighth Fire*, 1992; *Lighting the 7th Fire*, 1995; *Goin' Back*, 1995; *Pepper's Pow Wow*, 1996; *On and Off the Res with Charlie Hill*, 2000

Retna Ltd.

Osbourne, Sharon

1956(?)– Rock manager and promoter. Address: c/o Susan Blond Inc., 14542 Ventura Blvd., Suite 210, Sherman Oaks, CA 91403

Sharon Osbourne, the manager and wife of the heavy-metal doyen Ozzy Osbourne, has been called the most powerful woman in rock. As the chief organizer and promoter of the traveling all-day metal festival Ozzfest, Sharon Osbourne has helped to demonstrate that the genre of heavy metal, once written off as an obsolete relic of the 1970s and 1980s, is still a force to be reckoned with in the world of popular music. The festival, which has grossed over $60 million and played to almost two million fans, has injected new life into the metal scene by pairing established acts such as Ozzy with relatively unknown groups. Of course, it is Ozzy Osbourne who receives top billing and is most readily associated with the festival; but, as Aidin Vaziri wrote for the *San Francisco Chronicle* (August 20, 2000, on-line), "Sharon . . . is clearly the brains behind the operation."

In an interview with Steve Hochman for the *Los Angeles Times* (June 18, 2000, on-line), Osbourne said that she attributes her success, in part, "to being a woman in a man's world." Indeed, the music industry and especially the heavy-metal scene have tended to be overwhelmingly male-dominated. As Osbourne told Nancy Miller for *Entertainment Weekly* (September 1, 2000), "If you're a woman and you say no in business, they call you a bitch. If you say yes, you get [expletive] on by everybody." When she encounters that attitude, Osbourne continued, "I just do what I want and don't give a [expletive] what anybody else thinks." As a result, Osbourne has acquired a reputation for colorful behavior that, in its own way, rivals her husband's notorious onstage antics. (Ozzy is reputed, among other things, to have decapitated a live bat with his teeth during a concert.) Once, according to Pat Blashill for *Spin* (August 2000, on-line), Osbourne trashed the office of a merchandising firm that had crossed her; on another occasion, she told Hochman, she kicked the groin of a promoter who had cheated her on a concert payment. The acclaimed director and filmmaker Penelope Spheeris, whose 1988 documentary, *The Decline of Western Civilization II: The Metal Years*, features a segment on Ozzy, told Blashill, "I've experienced the love of Sharon Osbourne and the wrath of Sharon Osbourne, and they're both very intense. The bottom line is, she'll do anything to protect Ozzy, her children, her dogs, and her empire. And if anyone does anything to encroach upon that, they're . . . dead. She will win."

Osbourne was born Sharon Arden in about 1956 in Brixton, a working-class section of London. Her father, Don, managed the pop group Electric Light Orchestra and was the president of Jet Records. Although he achieved success in the music industry, Don Arden had a prodigal streak that resulted in rapidly seesawing economic fortunes for his family. "Growing up, it was a platinum spoon in my mouth one day, a plastic one the next," Sharon Osbourne recalled to Pat Blashill. Consequently, in spite of her modest roots, Sharon Osbourne spent a portion of her youth in Mayfair, an aristocratic London neighborhood.

It was through her father's management agency that Sharon Osbourne met her future husband. Among the groups that Don Arden managed in the 1970s was Black Sabbath, the legendary proto-metal band that featured John "Ozzy" Osbourne on lead vocals. One day, while Sharon was working as a receptionist for her father's management agency, she met the singer, who stumbled into the office in a drug-induced stupor. "Ozzy walked into my father's office without shoes, with a water faucet dangling from his neck, and sat on the floor. I was terrified," Sharon Osbourne recalled to Montgomery Brower for *People* (July 10, 1989). In 1979, after he was ejected from Black Sabbath because of excessive drinking, Ozzy retreated into a Los Angeles hotel room, where, for a time, he subsisted on alcohol and pizza. Sharon Arden helped him get

back on his feet, by persuading him to embark on a solo career. In the process, she got to know and like the singer.

As Sharon grew closer to Ozzy, her father became increasingly estranged from the couple, apparently because he felt that his daughter was attempting to steal his most lucrative client. The situation reached a climax when, during her first pregnancy, as Sharon told Blashill, her father loosed his Doberman on her. The resulting wounds required 80 stitches, and she subsequently suffered a miscarriage. After she recovered, Sharon broke with her family altogether. "I left my father in such a way, what with taking Ozzy and all, that I was terrified of him," she told Blashill. She said to Brower, "It's absolutely disgusting what happened because it didn't matter that he was my father. It was money that tore us apart." Yet, while she and her father have hardly spoken in the last 20 years, Sharon has credited him with having provided her with invaluable business lessons. As she told Blashill, "I learned from all his [mistakes], and from how he destroyed everything he had. At one time he was a very powerful man, and I watched it all fall away. I learned everything from him. But I don't threaten people. I say what I have to say and it's over. If there is someone I don't want to deal with, I just say, '[Expletive] off. Die. I want you out of my life.'"

On July 4, 1982 Sharon and Ozzy married. By then, thanks in no small part to Sharon's management, Ozzy's solo career had taken off. Speaking with Steve Hochman for the *Los Angeles Times* (June 18, 2000, on-line), Ozzy explained his debt to Sharon: "One day I said to her, 'What right do you have to tell me what to do? You can't sing a [expletive] note.' She said, 'Maybe I can't sing, but you can't read a [expletive] contract.' Oh, right." Ozzy's first solo album, *Blizzard of Ozz* (1981), went platinum; its sequel, *Diary of a Madman* (1981), did even better, registering double-platinum sales.

In spite of those commercial successes, both Sharon and Ozzy were struggling with alcohol addiction. As Sharon recalled to Hochman, "We'd both drink until we blacked out and wake up the next morning with black eyes and bruises—he'd hit me, I'd hit him. And then one morning," she continued, "I woke up and said, 'One of us has to be together enough to deal with the business.' So I quit drinking that day." While Ozzy spent the rest of the 1980s in and out of rehabilitation clinics (succeeding nevertheless in making several platinum-selling albums), Sharon built her reputation as a tough yet personable manager.

By the early 1990s Ozzy had cleaned up his act and stopped drinking, and the Osbournes' married life had begun to approach relative normalcy. However, the singer's career had stalled once again. The 1992 edition of the *Rolling Stone Album Guide*, for example, in a representative review quoted by Hochman, judged that Ozzy's 1991 album *No More Tears* "briefly postpones the inevitable conclusion of Ozzy's saga—extinction." But within a few years, Ozzy's career began to exhibit new signs of life, once again as a result of Sharon Osbourne's persistent efforts. In 1995 Sharon offered her husband's musical services to the promoters of the alternative-rock festival Lollapalooza. But she was turned away, because, she has claimed, the tour's organizers felt that the aging metal stalwart Ozzy had lost his cool cachet. Angry but undiscouraged, she resolved to start an independent festival. Shortly thereafter she persuaded 16 heavy-metal bands to enter the Ozzy fold and sign up for concerts in Los Angeles and Phoenix. Both shows sold out, and Ozzfest was born. While Lollapalooza ended with the 1997 festival, in both 1998 and 1999 Ozzfest grossed, on average, according to Tim Henderson in *Billboard* (June 5, 1999), more per show than did any other U.S. summer concert event. The fifth Ozzfest, in 2000, included, in addition to Ozzy Osbourne, such bands as Pantera, Godsmack, Incubus, Methods of Mayhem, Static-X, Disturbed, Taproot, and Kittie, the only all-female group to perform at that festival.

When Henderson asked Sharon Osbourne to account for the success of Ozzfest, she responded, "I have to be truthful with you. I don't know. It's about giving kids value for money and what they want for the genre of music. The only thing I can put it to is that we don't try and outsmart ourselves. We don't try to bring in 40 singing monks, and we don't try and bring in Tony Bennett. We just do what we do. A lot of times when people get successful, they try and get too smart and they try and put stuff on that impresses themselves and people of their age group. We're talking about the suits that run these things, and they go home and say, 'We've got this and it's so cool,' yet it doesn't work with the kids on the street."

Recently, two bands whom Sharon Osbourne once managed have filed lawsuits against her. In February 2000 Smashing Pumpkins, whose frontman is Billy Corgan, sued her for allegedly misappropriating $150,000 and for allegedly terminating the group's contract without notice. (The previous month Osbourne had split publicly with the band, issuing a press release that immediately became famous among fans. "It was with great pride and enthusiasm that I took on management of the Pumpkins," she announced in the release, as quoted by Blashill, "but unfortunately, I must resign today due to medical reasons—Billy Corgan was making me sick!!!") Responding to news of the Pumpkins' suit, she said in another press release, "It is unfortunate that Mr. Corgan has turned a routine accounting matter into a lawsuit designed to attack my honesty and credibility. Obviously this is just a sad attempt to keep me in his life a little longer because he misses me so much." Less than a month later, two former members of Ozzy Osbourne's band filed a $20 million suit against Sharon Osbourne and her husband, alleging that they had not been properly credited for songwriting contributions.

Sharon and Ozzy Osbourne live with their three children, Aimee, Jack, and Kelly, in Beverly Hills, California. The couple also own five small dogs: Maggie, LuLu, New Baby, Minnie, and Tedd. — P.K.

Suggested Reading: *Billboard* p29 June 5, 1999, with photos; *Entertainment Weekly* p24+ Sep. 1, 2000, with photos; *Los Angeles Times* (on-line) June 18, 2000; *San Francisco Chronicle* (on-line) Aug. 20, 2000; *Spin* (on-line)

Courtesy of U.S. Department of Education

Paige, Roderick R.

June 17, 1933– U.S. Secretary of Education. Address: U.S. Department of Education, 400 Maryland Ave., S.W., Washington, DC 20202-0498

President George W. Bush's plan for education reform, announced during his 2000 campaign and published on the Web site *georgewbush.com*, incorporates major planks of the Republican education platform of recent years, among them increased reliance on standardized testing to gauge student progress and make funding decisions; "parental choice" measures that allow parents to remove children from failing schools and place them in charter or private schools, with tuition paid through government-issued vouchers; and increased school-security measures. Bush's choice for secretary of education, Roderick R. Paige, the Republican former superintendent of the Houston Independent School District, successfully implemented similar reforms in Houston, Texas, in the latter half of the 1990s. Education professionals throughout the country, irrespective of party affiliation, greeted Bush's appointment of this tough former football coach with the undisguised hope that he would be able to reshape the American public-education system, which has fallen into disrepair as the result of decades of fiscal neglect at the federal, state, and local levels.

Roderick Raynor Paige was born on June 17, 1933 in Monticello, Mississippi. His father was a school principal, and his mother was a librarian. As a young man he split politically with his family, registering as a Republican, because, as he told Peter Slevin for the *Washington Post* (December 30, 2000), he perceived Mississippi Republicans, at that time, as being less overtly racist than their Democratic counterparts.

Earlier, Paige had become a quarterback on the football team at Jackson State University, in Jackson, Mississippi, where he earned a degree in physical education in 1955. He spent the next eight years as the head football coach at Utica Junior College, in Utica, Mississippi, before holding the same position at Jackson State in the mid-1960s. He earned a doctorate in physical education from Indiana University, in Bloomington, Indiana, in 1969, writing his dissertation on the reaction times of football offensive linemen.

Paige worked for a year in Ohio, as an assistant football coach at the University of Cincinnati, then became head coach at Texas Southern University, a predominantly African-American institution in Houston, starting in 1971. With a wife and son to support, Paige wanted more stability than coaching had to offer, and he became a tenured faculty member. An excellent organizer, with an exceptional ability to motivate those working under him, Paige became dean of Texas Southern's College of Education, a post that he held for 10 years beginning in 1979.

In 1989 Paige was elected to the board of education of the Houston Independent School District (HISD), the largest public-school district in Texas and the seventh largest in the United States overall. Shortly after arriving on the board, he co-authored a mission statement, "A Declaration of Beliefs and Visions," that advocated fundamental, districtwide reform through decentralization of the school system, a renewed focus on instruction, increased accountability on the part of teachers and administrators, and the development of a core curriculum.

Paige was named to the position of superintendent of schools for HISD in 1994. "I didn't apply for that," he told the audience assembled for a January 11, 2000 forum, "A Successful Initiative for Educating At-Risk Students," held at the Center for Civic Innovation in New York City (a transcript of which appeared on the Web site of the Manhattan Institute). "I didn't come through the traditional superintendent's pipeline. All of a sudden somebody gave me the key to the superintendent's office. I thought about it for a minute, and then committed myself to one of the most awesome responsibilities that I've ever even considered."

After facing down early opposition from the overwhelmingly Democratic teachers' union—and from some Hispanic groups, who felt that a person from their community should have been chosen to run the schools (about one-third of the district's students identify themselves as Hispanic)—Paige began attacking the myriad problems that were plaguing the district. "We realized that never before in public education had we been asked to do so much," he told the forum audience. "Never before had we been faced with such a diverse population of young people overwhelmed by poverty and social decay, and the lack of familiarity with the English language. We had drugs in our middle schools, crack babies: all of these issues that you know so much about. . . . We identified some of the things that we would like to prioritize early on, and one of the things we knew is that . . . you have to have an environment that is safe and conducive to teaching and learning." Paige upgraded security, shaping the HISD police department into the largest school-system police force in the country and the fifth-largest law-enforcement agency in all of Texas. (About 8 percent of public-school districts nationwide have their own police departments, Paige reported in an article on school safety, "Safety Above All Else," published in the *Houston Law Review* [Spring 2000].)

A Texas law passed in response to the shootings that occurred in 1999 at Columbine High School, in Littleton, Colorado, required that any student caught carrying a weapon or making a violent threat be expelled or sent to a disciplinary "alternative" school. After first attempting to set up and run its own alternative schools—an effort Paige later characterized as a costly failure—HISD subcontracted the job of educating disruptive pupils to a private company, Community Education Partners. Even before extra security measures, such as random metal-detector searches, were added in the wake of the Columbine attack, the incidence of students' bringing firearms to HISD schools decreased by 75 percent over the five-year span from 1994 through 1998.

The two main criticisms lodged against Paige during his career with HISD—complaints that resurfaced following his nomination as education secretary by President-elect Bush on December 29, 2000—involved Paige's support of a limited school-voucher scheme and what some saw as his overreliance on standardized-test scores as a determining factor in school-funding decisions. Critics of standardized testing in the district charged that students who did poorly on the Texas Assessment of Academic Skills were quietly discouraged from staying in school by teachers and administrators whose salary bonuses and other financial incentives were tied to high scores. During the forum "A Successful Initiative for Educating At-Risk Students," Paige defended standardized testing and gave a different explanation for an increased dropout rate: insufficiently stringent promotion standards at lower grade levels, which had caused students to advance to high school even when they lacked the basic skills necessary to succeed there. Once the disparity between standards in the lower and upper grades was corrected, Paige said, the number of dropouts would go down.

Criticism of Paige's nomination from within the education community was led by Linda McNeil, a professor of education at Rice University, in Houston, who had studied the Houston public schools in depth for several years. McNeil argued that Paige's emphasis on boosting standardized-test scores resulted in teachers teaching "to the test," at the expense of providing students with a meaningful curriculum. However, because Paige's efforts at improving the woefully drug- and crime-ridden HISD were widely viewed as successful and as a model for improving other urban school districts around the country, few heeded McNeil's rallying cry against the superintendent. Characteristically, Paige kept his stolid demeanor, preferring to allow the statistics to speak for themselves: 73 percent of students in the district passed the Texas Assessment of Academic Skills test in 2000, nearly double the 1995 figure (37 percent).

Paige's most controversial position has been his ongoing support of private-school vouchers. The vouchers, which theoretically would allow students in failing public schools to transfer to private schools—with the public-school district paying all or most of the tuition costs—have been a source of heated debate ever since they were first introduced into the national discussion of education several years ago. While they form a central part of President Bush's plan for education reform, vouchers have traditionally been viewed by Democrats as harmful to the education infrastructure, since they take funds earmarked for public schools and transfer them into private hands, leaving the public-school districts poorer than they were in the first place. The public schools suffer even further, opponents of the vouchers maintain, because the best and brightest students are encouraged to attend private schools, leaving behind the students who are most at risk.

But in a time in which Republicans and Democrats are thought to be ideologically closer than ever before, increasing numbers of Democrats are supporting vouchers as a short-term solution to the education crisis. Nevertheless, some prominent Democrats, among them Senator Edward M. Kennedy of Massachusetts, have warned that a legislative stalemate could result if Bush and Paige are intent on pushing the vouchers issue. Indicating that he would continue to support vouchers as education secretary, Paige wrote, in a November 2000 column for *Education Week* (quoted in an article by Jacques Steinberg in the December 30, 2000 edition of the *New York Times*), "We believe that public funds should go to students, not institutions, and there may be a time when vouchers will be part of the mix."

Paige led Houston in the establishment of charter schools—start-up schools that are organized by groups of parents, administrators, and teachers and funded with money marked for state public education. The charter schools provide a free alternative for a small but growing percentage of mostly low-income and minority students who were formerly enrolled in HISD schools. According to the Bush plan, whose announced aim is to "stop funding failure," a charter school would be allowed to drive a failing, traditional public school out of business, just as a successful retail business triumphs over its less-savvy competitors. Opponents of this approach point out that in the case of education, the quality of children's lives—not just dollars—are at stake.

By the time he was tapped by Bush to be the next education secretary, Paige's get-tough attitude and record of positive changes in the school system had made believers of many who had opposed him at the start of his term as superintendent. "[Paige has] demonstrated he is committed to quality public education and quality urban education," the president of the National Education Association, Bob Chase, said, as quoted by Joetta L. Sack and Darcia Harris Bowman on the Children First America Web site. "If there's any concern, it's his support for some forms of vouchers . . . but he was as the top of the list of people being considered as far as we're concerned." Chase's sentiments were echoed by education professionals across the land. Sack and Bowman quoted Michael D. Casserly, the executive director of the Council of the Great City Schools (an organization of large urban districts), as saying, "President-elect Bush made a wise decision. [Paige] has always been somebody who not only knows the intricacies of how schools work, but is singular in his focus—to improve schools, particularly urban schools."

Paige was confirmed as education secretary by the U.S. Senate on January 20, 2001. Some commentators have argued that, because education is such an important issue for President Bush, Paige has so far been given little latitude to affect policy without close guidance from the White House. By his own admission, Paige has at times felt virtually abandoned in his new job in the nation's capital. "I was here a long time by myself," he told Diana Jean Schemo for the *New York Times* (August 5, 2001). "I'm walking around in this building. I could throw a brick from one end to the other of the corridor and wouldn't hit a soul." Jack Jennings, the director of the Center on Education Policy, a Washington, D.C.–based organization that describes itself as an "advocate for public education and for more effective public schools," told Schemo that he ranked Paige "I, for irrelevant." Furthermore, the federal government contributes only about 7 percent of funding for public-school districts nationally, so questions remain as to how much Bush and Paige can actually accomplish in the field of reforming education, beyond setting an example and guidelines for America's students and educators to follow. (In the past, public schools have suffered largely as a result of low property taxes imposed at the state or local level, a jurisdiction over which Paige has little control.)

Paige, who seres as an usher in his Baptist church in Houston, is known for always wearing alligator, lizard, or snakeskin cowboy boots. He divorced some years ago; for the past decade the Houston entrepreneur Betty Davis-Lewis has been his close companion. Paige has residences in Houston and Washington, D.C. — G.K.R.

Suggested Reading: *Education Week* (on-line) Feb. 14, 2001, with photo; *Los Angeles Times* (on-line) Dec. 30, 2000; *New York Times* A p16 Aug. 5, 2001, with photo; *New York Times* Dec. 30, 2000 (on-line), with photo; *Texas Monthly* p149+ Sep. 2000; *Washington Post* (on-line) Dec. 30, 2000, with photo

Reuters/Michael Mulvey/Hulton/Archive

Palmeiro, Rafael

Sep. 24, 1964– First baseman for the Texas Rangers. Address: Texas Rangers, 1000 Ballpark Way, #400, Arlington, TX 76011

Many experts agree that the Texas Rangers first baseman Rafael Palmeiro is headed for the Major League Baseball Hall of Fame. On September 23, 1999, one day before his 35th birthday, Palmeiro hit his 400th career home run, becoming only the 32d player in major-league history to reach that milestone. He has accomplished that feat with relative modesty, shying away from publicity. That is perhaps one reason why Palmeiro, in a sport filled

with gold-chain flamboyance, has yet to receive the widespread recognition many feel he deserves. Not that he is bothered by this lack of attention: in an Associated Press article (on-line), Palmeiro explained, "I stay out of trouble and don't create any controversy about anything, and I shouldn't. My job is to play baseball." In the 1990s Palmeiro, in addition to his second-ranked 1,719 hits, ranked seventh in home runs, with 353, and fifth in runs batted in (RBIs), with 1,099, right behind such superstars as Mark McGwire, Barry Bonds, and Ken Griffey Jr. In the past seven years alone, only McGwire, Sammy Sosa, and Barry Bonds have hit more homers than Palmeiro's 292, and only Sosa has topped Palmeiro's 868 RBIs. In this same period Palmeiro has hit at least 38 home runs and driven in at least 100 runs each year. Only one other player—Babe Ruth—has hit at least 38 home runs in seven consecutive seasons. And Palmeiro's career is far from over: in 1999 he signed a five-year, $45 million contract with the Rangers.

Rafael Corrales Palmeiro was born on September 24, 1964 in Havana, Cuba. In 1971 he, his parents, and two of his three brothers fled his island homeland, which by then had been ruled by the dictator Fidel Castro for two decades, and settled in Miami, Florida, where Palmeiro remained through high school. His oldest brother, Jose Jr., was forced to stay in Cuba because he was 17 years old at the time of the family's departure and was therefore due to serve in the army. It was not until 1995, in large part because of negotiations between Cuban officials and the Baltimore Orioles' owner, Peter Angelos (on whose team Rafael Palmeiro played at the time), that Jose Jr. was allowed to leave Cuba and reunite with his family. In an interview with Mark Maske for the *Washington Post* (May 7, 1997), Rafael Palmeiro described the reunion. "It was hard," he explained. "It was almost like meeting a stranger. I know he's my brother, but I didn't really know him. I was meeting his family for the first time. When they got here, it was more emotional for my parents." All of Palmeiro's three brothers now live in Miami.

Very early in his life, Palmeiro was taught to play baseball. Referring to the hours of drills he and his brothers endured on the baseball fields of Miami, he told Mark D. Williams for *Baseball Digest* (May 2000, on-line) that his father was "a taskmaster." Palmeiro later attended Jackson High School in Miami, from which he graduated in 1982, after being named Most Valuable Player of the Jackson baseball team. In June of that year, he was selected by the New York Mets in the eighth round of the free-agent draft. But he chose not to sign a contract, instead opting to enroll at Mississippi State University, in Starkville. There, he joined future major leaguers Will Clark and Bobby Thigpen on the university baseball squad. Palmeiro's best year as a college player was in 1984. He finished second among undergraduates in the nation in home runs (29) and third in RBIs (94). With a .415 batting average that year, Palmeiro became the first Triple Crown winner (first in home runs, RBIs, and batting average) in Southeast Conference history. While playing for Mississippi State, Palmeiro was named three times to the All-America baseball team. In the June 3, 1985 free-agent draft, the Chicago Cubs chose Palmeiro as their first-round draft pick and 22d pick overall. This time around, Palmeiro decided to go professional.

After immediate success at the minor-league level, where he was named Eastern League Most Valuable Player for 1986, Palmeiro made his major-league debut with the Cubs, on September 8, 1986. In his 22 games that year, he enjoyed minimal success, batting a mediocre .247 with only three home runs. The next year Palmeiro divided his time between the Cubs and its minor-league farm team in Iowa. He knocked 14 homers in 221 at-bats for the Cubs.

Nineteen-eighty-eight was Palmeiro's first full year in the major leagues. He played in 152 of the Cubs' 162 games, batting an impressive .307, leading National League rookies for the year and placing second overall. His high average, however, came at the expense of his home-run production. Scouts quickly dismissed Palmeiro as merely an opposite-field singles hitter, a far cry from the formidable power hitter the Cubs thought they had drafted. After the 1988 season Palmeiro was traded to the Texas Rangers.

In the following two seasons for Texas, Palmeiro missed only 14 of the team's 324 games. Despite his consistency, he still lacked power at the plate, hitting 22 home runs in 1,057 at-bats. While his batting average rose to .319 for the 1990 season, Palmeiro felt he could do better. He believed that in addition to a high average, he could produce the big hits his team wanted. He told Maske, "Coming up on a veteran team [the Cubs], I saw myself hitting for a high average. I was battling the batting title, and I got away from my approach. I got away from driving the ball. . . . When I got to Texas, I almost had to learn how to do it all over again, learn how to pull the ball and drive the ball again. . . . [Now] I think I can do both."

In 1991 Palmeiro's prediction came true. He emerged as one of the premier hitters of the game, in terms of both power and batting average. In 159 games Palmeiro hit 26 long balls while raising his average yet again, to a soaring .322. He also collected more than 200 hits for the season and scored 115 runs. He proved himself a vital ingredient to the Rangers' success, especially in 1993—the year he hit 37 home runs (then a career high) while preserving a .295 batting average, driving in 105 runs, and leading the American League with 124 runs. On top of his stellar performance at the plate, Palmeiro also demonstrated speed that season, stealing a career-high 22 bases.

With his five-year contract with the Rangers running out at the end of the 1993 season, Palmeiro felt that he was in a position to negotiate a long stay in Texas, where he and his wife had recently purchased a plot of land. On November 22, however, he received a call from the Rangers' president, Tom Schieffer, who told him that the team had decided to sign his former Mississippi State teammate Will Clark to a five-year, $30 million contract. Since Clark—like Palmeiro—played first base, Palmeiro knew that his time in Texas had come to an abrupt end. "I couldn't believe it," he recalled in an interview with Phil Rogers for *Inside Sports* (May 1994). "For two minutes I couldn't say anything." In his conversation with Rogers, he went on to call the Rangers organization "low-class," Schieffer "a backstabbing liar," and even Clark "a mediocre player" and "a low life." Palmeiro accounted for his uncharacteristic outburst by explaining that he had met with Clark only a week earlier, during an alumni game at Mississippi State, where the two had shared their concerns over their respective teams' inabilities to reach contract agreements. (Clark's contract with the San Francisco Giants had also just expired.) Palmeiro had also told Clark about his love of Texas and his half-finished dream home. "The Rangers' whole intent was to sign Will Clark," he told Rogers in retrospect, "not me. I know that. They had all the opportunity in the world to sign me. . . . They just never showed any interest in doing it." When Palmeiro put himself on the market, the Baltimore Orioles were quick to respond: only two weeks later he signed a five-year, $30.35 million contract with the team.

In his first season with the Orioles, Palmeiro lived up to the team's expectations. Three-quarters of the way through the 1994 season, he already had 23 home runs and 76 RBIs and was batting .319. But after the Orioles had played 111 games, the Players' Union announced a strike, and the season was cut short. The next year Palmeiro picked up right where he had left off, turning in 39 home runs and 104 RBIs while maintaining a .310 average. In 1996 he hit another 39 home runs in the regular season, which, along with his 142 RBIs, helped his team make it to postseason play. They would go on to lose to the New York Yankees in the second round of the play-offs, but not before Palmeiro had picked up three more home runs.

Despite two more very successful seasons with the Orioles, Palmeiro was faced with contract arbitration again at the end of 1998, a year in which he had blasted 43 home runs. Both sides of the bargaining table expressed a desire to keep Palmeiro in Baltimore. But as Josh Barr reported in the *Washington Post* (September 23, 1998), the Orioles' owner, Peter Angelos, "said he [would] not break the bank to re-sign" Palmeiro. The team then offered him $21 million over a three-year period, which he and his agent, Jim Bronner, immediately rejected, calling it "an insult." Palmeiro was concerned less about the amount of money than about the length of the contract. Fast approaching 2,000 hits and 400 home runs, he wanted to secure the time he needed to reach those milestones. He also had his eye on the more elusive goals of 3,000 hits and 500 home runs, which he believed he could achieve. During his five-year tenure with Baltimore, his wife, Lynne, and their two sons had maintained residence at their now-completed Texas home, with the hope that he would one day return to play for the Rangers. On the morning of December 1, 1998, Palmeiro telephoned the Rangers' general manager, Doug Melvin, informing him of his desire to return to Texas and asking Melvin to make him an offer—even though the Orioles had just proposed giving him $50 million over a five-year period, meeting his original terms. A few hours later Palmeiro signed a five-year, $45 million contract with the Texas Rangers. (Will Clark, who—because of a nagging back injury—had not measured up to expectations during his time in Texas, was released to make room for Palmeiro.)

In 1999, his first year back with the Rangers, Palmeiro had a banner year, reaching career-best numbers for home runs (47), RBIs (148), and batting average (.324). He also won his third straight Gold Glove award for fielding and was named both the Texas Rangers' Player of the Year and the 1999 *Sporting News* Player of the Year. In the 2000 season Palmeiro became the first Ranger ever to reach the 100 mark in runs (102), walks (103), and RBIs (120) in the same season. He missed repeating that feat in 2001 by only two runs. His record for that season also includes 101 walks, 123 RBIs, and 47 more homers. Palmeiro now occupies 27th place among the all-time career home-run leaders.

Palmeiro is active in several charitable causes. He joined Hal Price Books and Decker Foods to host the "Raffy Readers" summer reading program in 1999 and has worked extensively with the Coors Brewing Company in its "21 Means 21" campaign, a program designed to increase awareness of underage drinking in Hispanic markets. He is also a spokesman for the Juvenile Diabetes Foundation's "Walk to Cure" program, to which he makes a $100 contribution for each of his home runs. Palmeiro lives in Colleyville, Texas, just outside Arlington, with his wife and their two sons, Patrick Ryne and Preston Connor. — J.H.

Suggested Reading: *Baseball Digest* (on-line) May 2000; *Inside Sports* p24+ May 1994, with photos; *New York Times* D p1 Dec. 2, 1998, with photo, D p3 Oct. 5, 1999; *Sports Illustrated* p46+ July 19, 1999, with photo; *Washington Post* C p5 May 7, 1997, with photo, D p1 July 19, 1997, D p1 May 24, 1998, with photo, C p1 Sep. 23, 1998, with photo, D p1 May 15, 1999, with photo

Petersen, Wolfgang

Mar. 14, 1941– Film director; producer. Address: c/o Creative Artists Agency, 9830 Wilshire Blvd., Beverly Hills, CA 90212-1804

The German filmmaker Wolfgang Petersen is known for well-crafted action thrillers such as *Air Force One* (1997) and *The Perfect Storm* (2000). He began his career with films for German television and made his Hollywood debut with *Shattered* in 1991. Working closely with researchers and special-effects technicians, Petersen uses technology to expand the possibilities of the film-going experience. The success of pictures such as *Das Boot* (The Boat, 1981) owes as much to this attention to detail as to suspenseful narratives and masterful editing. Petersen has also explored the fantasy/science-fiction genre in such films as *The Neverending Story* (1984) and *Enemy Mine* (1985), and produced films, among them *Red Corner* (1997), *Bicentennial Man,* (1999) and *Instinct* (1999).

Wolfgang Petersen was born in Emden, Germany, on March 14, 1941. Exhibiting an interest in film at an early age, he made his first movies—imitations of American Westerns—when he was 12. Growing up in the harbor towns of Emden and Hamburg, Petersen spent a lot of his time around boats and the men who worked on them. "The sea was magical to me," he told Kathleen Sharp for *Salon* (July 14, 2000, on-line). "As a 13-year-old, it was a place where my imagination and fantasies

Darren McCollester/Newsmakers

were transported to infinity. Also, when I was 6 or 7 years old . . . something very powerful happened. . . . It was shortly after the war in Germany and we were very, very hungry people. All of a sudden, I remember that out of the mist came these huge ships streaming into the harbor. Again and again. They were mostly American ships, and we were looking up at these ships. Sailors onboard were throwing to us kids below all kinds of goodies, like food and chewing gum. We scurried around like little rats to grab the food. And that added to my idea of wonder coming out of the sea, that the ocean carries us to places far off, like spaceships do."

In 1960 Petersen became an assistant director at the Ernst Deutsch Theater, in Hamburg; he directed his first play there the following year. He then studied acting in Hamburg and Berlin before earning an apprenticeship with Berlin Film and Television. Eventually Petersen directed a number of programs for German television, among them *Tatort* (Crime Scene), an award-winning crime series that featured one of the earliest performances of the actress Nastassja Kinski. In 1973 Petersen's first feature film, *Einer von uns beiden* (One or the Other of Us), was released; the story of a blackmailer who discovers a professor's plagiarism, it went on to earn him the German National Film Prize for best new director. In 1977 he made *Die Konsequenz* (The Consequence), considered to be a sensitive portrayal of male homosexuality. *Schwarz und Weiss wie Taghe and Naechte* (Black and White Like Day and Night, 1978), a fictional film about chess, received the best-director award at the Paris Film Festival.

In 1978 Petersen bought the rights to Richard Neely's novel *Plastic Nightmare*, which was a bestseller in Germany. When he attended the Cannes Film Festival in the hopes of acquiring additional funding for the project, Bavaria Studios invited him to direct another film: *Das Boot*, a harrowing antiwar tale that focuses on a crew of German soldiers aboard a submarine during World War II. With the help of two consultants, a pair of U-boats were painstakingly reconstructed for use in the film. As co-writer and director, Petersen hoped to capture "the smell of reality, the blood, the sweat and the tears, the claustrophobia—so we wanted to make sure every bolt and every screw in the boat was real," as he told Richard von Busack for *MetroActive Movies* (April 3, 1997, on-line). "Our designers were obsessed with reality. I cannot imagine that almost 50 people spent months in one of these cigars without killing each other. That was our task and the challenge—me and my cinematographer, Jüst Vacano—we'd either kill each other or make a great movie." About 250 crew members worked for two years to re-create the experience of submarine warfare, utilizing two full-scale submarines, three replicas, and a 16-foot-high machine that simulated turbulence aboard the ship. "Steadicam existed in 1981, but the cameras were too cumbersome for this small space," Petersen told von Busack. "We never could have gotten it through the hatches. Vacano had an Arriflex, and he added a gyroscope to it to make the camera more stable. He was covered with padding like an ice-hockey player, which was good because he was always running into things. Sometimes it took 16 takes to get the right shot." Originally intended as a six-hour miniseries (it aired on German television in that form), *Das Boot* was released in a 140-minute version in 1981, to international acclaim; the film was nominated for six Academy Awards and came to be considered one of the greatest war films ever produced.

Petersen's next project was *The Neverending Story*, a children's fantasy based on a book by Michael Ende, which had become popular around the world and was translated into 27 languages. Although Ende was displeased with the changes Petersen made in the story, the film was successful enough to spawn two sequels, which were directed by others. Petersen next directed *Enemy Mine* (1985), a science-fiction story that starred Dennis Quaid and Louis Gossett Jr. as a human and an alien, respectively, who are loyal to opposing military forces and learn to set aside their differences after their spacecraft crash-land on a distant planet following a space battle.

For the first film that he directed in the U.S., Petersen returned to Richard Neely's *Plastic Nightmare*, which he retitled *Shattered* (1991). Created as an homage to Alfred Hitchcock, the film starred Tom Berenger as a man suffering from amnesia; Berenger's co-stars included Greta Scacchi as the protagonist's wife and Bob Hoskins as a pet-shop owner and private investigator. Warned of the difficulties that sometimes arose for directors working within the Hollywood studio system, Petersen co-wrote (with Andrew Birkin) and co-produced the film and acquired much of his funding from German investors. "I wanted very much to be in a situation similar to the situation European directors like to be in and are used to being in, with a lot of creative control and control over production, which as you know, is not always the case for directors in Hollywood," Petersen told Paul Chutkow for the *New York Times* (October 6, 1991). "I can really say this is my picture, the way I wanted it to be made."

While *Shattered* was not a financial success, Petersen's next film, *In the Line of Fire* (1993), proved to be popular with audiences, grossing over $100 million. *In the Line of Fire* starred Clint Eastwood as a Secret Service agent haunted by the assassination of President John F. Kennedy, an event he believes he could have prevented. John Malkovich starred as the agent's nemesis, a former CIA assassin who plans to kill the current president. In Petersen's *Outbreak* (1995), Dustin Hoffman and Rene Russo played a divorced couple who reunite to stop the spread of a deadly virus in a small town. The film was based on Richard Preston's popular book *The Hot Zone* (1994), which told the true story of a last-minute effort to prevent a possible outbreak of the Ebola virus at a Virginia laboratory. *Outbreak* also featured Morgan Freeman, Donald Sutherland, Kevin Spacey, and Cuba Gooding Jr. In the Petersen-directed *Air Force One* (1997), Harrison Ford portrayed the president of the United States, who must fend for himself when

Russian terrorists take over his airplane. The cast also included Glenn Close as the vice president and Gary Oldman as the leader of the terrorist group. The researcher Brian McNulty worked with members of the Secret Service and the military in order to lend the film's technical details the verisimilitude that Petersen typically seeks.

The year 1997 also saw the re-release of *Das Boot*, in a restored version that added more than an hour of footage to the film's original running time. In addition, the film was reedited, the soundtrack was remastered, and the subtitles were replaced. "From the very beginning, I tried to recreate the authentic feeling of being in the boat with these men, to really bring across the essence of the claustrophobia and tension," Petersen said in an interview for the Web site maintained by Sony Pictures Entertainment. "With the help of today's technology, we can simulate the ambiance of being in a submarine to a much greater degree. In particular, advances in digital sound technology make an enormous amount of difference. These guys on the submarine had nothing but their ears—they had no windows, no way out. It was extremely important to demonstrate the way in which they relied almost exclusively on sound as their cues for danger. Thus, the more realistic the sound effects, the more audiences will feel what the men felt in the boat." For the Sony Pictures Entertainment Web site, Ortwin Freyermuth, the producer of the restored version, commented on the film's significance: "*Das Boot* was really the first war movie ever to depict German soldiers in World War II as the 17-18 year old kids they were, young men who were totally misled and abused. This is a side of the German war experience that was never seen in a motion picture before *Das Boot*."

Petersen's most recent offering, *The Perfect Storm* (2000), starring George Clooney and Mark Wahlberg, was based on Sebastian Junger's best-selling nonfiction account of the tragic journey of the crew aboard the *Andrea Gail*, which set sail from Gloucester, Massachusetts, in 1991. "I like stories that take place in confined spaces," the director explained to Dayna D'Itria for *iCAST* (November 22, 2000, on-line), when asked about his decision to make a second film about a sea vessel. "You can really go into the characters and see how they react when there is no way to open the door. . . . I also like the element of water, because I think water is the most beautiful, almost mesmerizing element—and it's the most dangerous. I think it's a frightening element. I remember what an incredibly exhilarating feeling it is to ride one side of these huge waves in a fishing boat, and crash down on the other side again. It's like being on drugs, it's just amazing, beautiful. And we show that a little bit with George and Mark when they ride the waves, they're having the time of their lives there. The thing about it is, you very quickly cross a line there. It can go very quickly from something very, very exhilarating and beautiful into pure terror. The power is enormous." Many mem-

bers of the cast and crew established relationships with the family members and friends of the people portrayed in the film, eventually winning their trust and support for the project. In order to create the long storm sequence, Warner Bros. built a tank 95 feet in both width and length and 22 feet deep. Together with the special-effects experts at Industrial Light and Magic, the filmmakers employed blue-screen photography, computer-generated waves, and painted backdrops depicting different weather conditions to create the illusion of a devastating storm. While *Das Boot* had been considered ahead of its time, in terms of its sound editing, cinematography, and realism, technological advances now allowed Petersen to go even further. "I learned on *Das Boot* that it's very important to never connect the cameras to the boat itself," he told Ron Magid for *American Cinematographer* (July 2000). "The cameras have to be independent of the boat to really get the feeling of the movement in the water. We therefore had two, three or four huge crane arms with cameras extending from the edge of the tank, which gave us a third axis of movement. Having the cameras totally away from the boat enhanced the movement of the boat and helped a lot later on to create the illusion that the boat was moving through the waves." The opening scenes, shot in Gloucester, were preceded by images of an actual hurricane—Floyd, as it was named—an unexpected event that produced large waves. *The Perfect Storm* proved to be another success for the director, grossing more than $180 million at the box office.

Petersen and his wife, Maria, live in Los Angeles. — C.L.

Suggested Reading: *American Cinematographer* p50+ July 2000, with photos; *New York Times* II p21+ Oct. 6, 1991, with photos, E p1+ Mar. 30, 2001, with photos; *Salon* (on-line) July 14, 2000

Selected Films: as director—*Einer von uns beiden (One or the Other of Us)*, 1973; *Die Konsequenz* (The Consequence), 1977; *Schwarz und Weiss wie Taghe and Naechte* (Black and White Like Day and Night), 1978; *Das Boot* (The Boat), 1981; *The Neverending Story*, 1984; *Enemy Mine*, 1985; *Shattered*, 1991; as producer and director—*Outbreak*, 1995; *Air Force One*, 1997; *The Perfect Storm*, 2000; as executive producer and director—*In the Line of Fire*, 1993; as producer—*Bicentennial Man*, 1999; as executive producer—*Instinct*, 1999

Deborah Feingold/Archive Photos

Phillips, Sam

Jan. 5, 1923– Record producer; businessman.
Address: Sam Phillips Recording Service, 639
Madison Ave., Memphis, TN 38103-3307

"Sam Phillips is not just one of the most important producers in rock history," Richie Unterberger wrote for the *All-Music Guide* (on-line). "There's a good argument to be made that he is one of the most important figures in 20th-century American culture." In 1951 Phillips produced what has been called the first rock and roll song, Jackie Brenston's "Rocket 88." He also cut early records by such legends as B.B. King and Howlin' Wolf as well as other blues artists, retaining in those recordings a raw energy that no other producer at the time succeeded in capturing on vinyl. "If you had to do something too many times," Phillips has said, "it could really get to where it didn't have the spontaneity. And anything that didn't sound spontaneous really was no good." Later in the 1950s, at his now-legendary Sun Records studio, he recorded the first Elvis Presley singles and produced the work of such rock and roll luminaries as Jerry Lee Lewis and Roy Orbison. In addition, Sun produced several records by some of the best blues and country musicians of the day. After Phillips sold Sun, in the late 1960s, he built a successful career in real estate and as an investor in radio stations. The Sam Phillips Recording Service still operates in Memphis, Tennessee.

Sam Phillips was born into a poor family on January 5, 1923 in Florence, Alabama. As a youngster he worked in the fields alongside African-Americans and became familiar with spirituals and the blues. "Growing up, I loved black people,"

Phillips told Norm Shaw for *BlueSpeak* (June 1996, on-line). "I could listen to them sing forever. I heard a lot of words I could equate with. Sure I was young, but the bigger I got, the more I understood that I had been hearing this stuff all my life." He learned to play many instruments (most likely at school), ranging from the drums to the sousaphone, and with his unusual energy and determination, he dominated his high-school band. He also organized a smaller band, from members of the marching band, to play for the high school, and while serving as president of the 11th grade, he formed a choir. Outside school, by his own account, he learned a great deal about life from an elderly man known as Uncle Silas, who had been blinded by syphilis. The disdain that his close contact with African-Americans provoked in many of his white peers still angered him decades later. "Let me tell you, you cannot express to people how much the black man has meant to our culture," he told Shaw. "People just do not know the integrity of the people. I know what I have learned from black people. I have learned, man, that everyone is the same."

Phillips quit school after the 11th grade and found work as a radio announcer and engineer. His first disc-jockey position was in Muscle Shoals, Alabama. In 1945, now married and a father, Phillips moved his family to Memphis, where he had landed a job as a disc jockey at radio station WREC. In addition to working there, in January 1950 Phillips opened his own studio, the Memphis Recording Studio—the first such facility in that city. He started to record blues artists and, to make ends meet, also recorded at private functions. "My conviction was the world was missing not having heard what I heard as a child," he told Bill Ellis for the Scripps Howard News Service, as reported in the *Naples* [Florida] *Daily News* (January 21, 2000, on-line). "And nobody was crazy enough to do what I did then with no money, just hard work. I was already working myself to death at the radio station and recording weddings and funerals and anything else. I don't feel I made any sacrifice. The only thing that frightened me was that I wanted to make sure that my children—Knox and Jerry, [wife] Becky and my momma didn't suffer from my malfeasance of thinking."

During this period Phillips recorded pieces by B.B. King and Howlin' Wolf (Chester Burnett) and also produced Jackie Brenston's "Rocket 88," which several rock scholars have labeled the first rock and roll record ever cut. "A lot of artists had been kicked around. I hate to say this, but some of the independent labels, they just didn't do black folks right . . . ," he told Bill Ellis. "I'm not saying I'm an angel or anything. But there's nobody in this world that knew more about what they were feeling than me, because I had come through the Depression. I happen to have white skin and that made it better for me. And yet it was so damn bad. I couldn't believe that life could be this bad. And then I'd look around and see my black brothers and know they got what was left of the hog [while] we got the best part of the hog. And so I was equipped." Even on those early records, Phillips's production had a distinct style. He made the sounds of instruments more prominent on recordings than was common at the time and would even record fuzzy guitars. As a result, the blues songs he recorded were rawer, more energetic, and closer to the sound of live music than those produced elsewhere. After producing the disks, Phillips would license the masters to such labels as Chess and RPM. Toward the end of 1950, Phillips started his own record label with his friend Dewey Phillips (no relation), a disc jockey. Called Phillips, the label folded after only one release, "Gotta Let You Go," by the bluesman Joe Hill Louis.

During the 1950s Phillips, who had been sleeping less than five hours a night while trying to work multiple jobs, endured two nervous breakdowns and underwent electric shock therapy. In addition, his failure to pay his income taxes on time led to difficulties with the Internal Revenue Service; reportedly, an agent who saw how ravaged he looked took pity on him and gave him more time to wipe out his debt to the IRS.

In 1951 Phillips quit his job as a disc jockey at WREC. At about the same time, frustrated by the repeated arguments over talent acquisition that he had had with executives at various record labels, he decided to try his hand again at launching a label of his own. In 1952 he started Sun Records, with the motto, "We record anything—anywhere—anytime." Unlike any other label then in business, Sun Records was staffed entirely by women. The label began working with local blues artists, mostly musicians who had never before had a chance to record. "Knowing how poor [the musicians] were and how poor I was, nobody did more in my opinion to help people in a certain way than I did, many ways psychologically, to make them feel they had achieved something in life," Phillips told Jackson Baker for the *Memphis Flyer* (June 8, 2000, online). "One thing I never did. I never slighted one person who came in there for an audition. Not one damn penny did they pay me before we signed a contract and had sessions." In 1953 Sun had its first national hit—"Bear Cat," by Rufus Thomas. (Sun would later lose a lawsuit that was filed to protest the record's similarity to another song.) Over the next couple of years, Sun produced high-quality electric blues records, some of which became successful singles, by such bluesmen as James Cotton, Little Milton, and Junior Parker. The label also produced white country musicians, among them Douglas Poindexter.

In 1954 Phillips met Elvis Presley, then a shy teenager, who, according to various sources, was interested in either recording songs for his mother or making a vanity record for himself. Phillips arranged for Presley to cut a disk on July 5, 1954, with backing musicians who he thought would interact well with the young singer/guitarist. The session wasn't going particularly well until, during

a break, Presley and the other musicians started jamming with Presley on the blues song "That's Alright, Mama." Excited by what he heard, Phillips told the musicians to keep working on that track. Presley ultimately recorded five singles for Sun in the blues and country veins. "I was trying to find a white person . . . who could sing with the same feeling [as a black person] but *not* try to copy these people," Phillips told Jackson Baker. "*That* would have been a joke. I honestly believe had we not done what we did with Elvis, or with somebody, and got that feel over and broke down a little bit of the wall or if somebody else hadn't done the same type of thing, I honestly feel that we would have still had segregation in music." In 1955 Presley recorded his first hit for Sun, "Baby Let's Play House," which reached number 10 on *Billboard*'s country chart.

Toward the end of that year, in a well-known and—in retrospect—shortsighted business move, Phillips sold the contract of the still little-known Presley to RCA for $35,000 ($40,000, according to some sources), so as to keep his label afloat and sign new artists. "I sold Elvis for a reason and that was a legitimate deal," Phillips told Bill Ellis. "And that was done to help take [off] some of the burden put on my many years as an independent. [RCA] gave what then was an awful lot of money." Right after Phillips sold Presley's contract, Sun had its biggest hit up to that date, with Carl Perkins's "Blue Suede Shoes."

Throughout the rest of the 1950s, Phillips continued to record a roster of future rock greats. His decision to switch Sun's focus from blues to rock and roll drew some criticism, from, for example, the former Sun artist Rufus Thomas. Among others whom Sun recorded in the late 1950s were Jerry Lee Lewis, Roy Orbison, Johnny Cash, and Sonny Burgess. Toward the end of the decade, Phillips delegated more responsibility to other Sun producers so that he could spend more time on the business side of the label. Meanwhile, rock and roll was beginning to fade as a style, and Sun was unable to adapt to new forms of rock. Cash, Orbison, and Perkins left Sun for other labels (and future success); Jerry Lee Lewis stayed put, but his career ran into trouble due to scandal. Nevertheless, the label still had some life left in it. The country singer Charlie Rich recorded some minor hits for Sun in the late 1950s and early 1960s; he left the label in 1964. In addition, Carl Mann made the singles charts with "Mona Lisa." Sun continued to release records in the 1960s, but more and more infrequently; by the middle of the decade, the label's operations were beginning to wind down. Phillips wasn't hurting, however, because he had begun investing in radio stations, real estate, and the Holiday Inn hotel chain. In 1969 he sold the entire Sun catalogue to Shelby Singleton. During its 16-year run, Sun had released 226 singles.

The red-bearded Phillips is said to look about 30 years younger than he is. He is known as being down to earth, direct, and proud of his accomplishments but not arrogant. "God didn't make us perfect or He wouldn't have messed around with Adam and Eve and the apple," Phillips told Jackson Baker. "I am honest, and some things turn on the fact of what you believe honesty to be." His children now run the family studio—the Sam Phillips Recording Service—and a music-publishing company in Nashville. A resident of Memphis, which he loves with a "religious fervor," in his words, Phillips currently spends most of his time working with the radio stations he owns in Alabama. "I'll never retire," he told an Associated Press reporter, as quoted in the *Jefferson City* [Missouri] *News Tribune* (July 13, 2000, on-line). "I'm just using up somebody else's oxygen if I retire." In 1986 he was inducted into the Rock 'n' Roll Hall of Fame. In 1997 the University of Mississippi gave

him the title of honorary professor of southern studies. "I'm happy we were able to contribute, at least in my opinion, to what music has done, and is continuing to do, as one of the greatest ambassadors we have, both for nations around the world and racial desegregation," Phillips told Gary Graff for *Elvis World News* (June 17, 2000, on-line). "We now get to hear R&B and don't worry whether it's white or black. I feel like we made a hell of a contribution." — G.O.

Suggested Reading: *All Music Guide* (on-line); *Bluespeak* (on-line); *Naples* [Florida] *Daily News* (on-line) Jan. 21, 2000; *Newsweek* p54+ Aug. 18, 1997; *Rolling Stone* p53+ Feb. 13, 1986, with photos

---

Courtesy of Pritzker Architecture Prize

Piano, Renzo

Sep. 14, 1937– Architect. Address: Renzo Piano Building Workshop, Via Rubens 29, 16158 Genoa, Italy

Architecture is a meeting of art and engineering, beauty and technology, form and function. On a practical level, architecture offers humanity places to live, work, and congregate, and on an aesthetic plane, it helps to give a face to a cityscape, character to a skyline, and personality to a residential neighborhood. Despite all the creativity inherent in architecture, however, one of the field's most lauded living practitioners, the Italian architect Renzo Piano, has resisted the label "artist," preferring

to recognize the building process in its entirety, from concept to construction. "I came to architecture from building, because my father was a builder, everybody was—and is—a builder in my family," Piano told Christopher Andreae for the *Christian Science Monitor* (May 11, 1989). "So I like the concept that architecture is not something that you [just] draw on paper. It's something you draw, you think, and you build."

Piano first gained international attention when he collaborated with the British architect Richard Rogers on the futuristic Georges Pompidou Center in Paris, which was completed in 1977. Since then, he has solidified his reputation as one of the most versatile and inventive architects in the world. His projects have ranged in size and scope from the subtle design of the Menil Collection Art Museum in Houston, Texas, to the imposing grandeur of Kansai International Airport, the world's largest air terminal, in Osaka Bay, Japan. For these and other, equally impressive examples of his work, the Hyatt Foundation awarded Piano the 1998 Pritzker Architecture Prize, the discipline's highest honor. Despite Piano's opposition to being called an artist, the Pritzker jury, in its description of his work, referred to him as exactly that. "Renzo Piano's architecture reflects that rare melding of art, architecture, and engineering in a truly remarkable synthesis, making his intellectual curiosity and problem-solving techniques as broad and far ranging as those earlier masters of his native land, Leonardo da Vinci and Michelangelo," the citation read. "While his work embraces the most current technology of this era, his roots are clearly in the classic Italian philosophy and tradition."

Renzo Piano was born on September 14, 1937 in Genoa, Italy. His father, grandfather, and uncles, as well as one of his brothers, were all building contractors, and it is this legacy that has kept Piano's view of architecture grounded in craftsmanship. "Today, you may still be a 'craftsman' using a computer and test models and scientific instruments

. . . ," he told Christopher Andreae, "and the reason I am making a lot of polemic about this is because usually the architect is accepted as exactly the opposite: as a kind of specialist, an intellectual man." For a profile of him in the *New Yorker* (August 22 & 29, 1994), Piano told Calvin Tomkins that from the age of eight, he "would play around building sites. I was very happy and proud to go with my father to the sites, and it always seemed miraculous to me that what was sand and bricks would one day become a building." Even as a child, Piano was fascinated by the strong but lightweight structures that abound in nature, marveling at such intricate and well-balanced creations as spiderwebs and beehives and wanting to design equally impressive structures himself. He soon grew to admire the work of Filippo Brunelleschi, the 15th-century Italian artist whose mechanically sound designs led to the construction of the Duomo, in Florence.

At the age of 17, having decided that he wanted to study to be an architect, Piano broached the subject with his father, who quickly questioned his intentions. "He looked at me, and he said, 'Why? Why do you want to be an architect? You can be a *builder*,'" Piano recalled to Calvin Tomkins. "That was something I never forgot." Though this conversation did little to steer Piano away from his dream, it would later play into the naming of his architectural firm, the Renzo Piano Building Workshop. "You asked me why I call this place 'workshop,'" Piano said to Tomkins. "I think one reason is that I still feel a little like a traitor. Here we make things, make physical elements, test them, work with them. Keeping the action together with the conception is maybe a way to feel less guilty."

Piano's older brother, Ermano, a builder who constructed a number of his younger brother's designs before his death, in 1991, was instrumental in persuading their father to let Renzo pursue architecture. Previously a lackluster student, Piano began his architectural training in Florence, where he received excellent grades. He then transferred to the Milan Polytechnic Architecture School, from which he graduated in 1964. Newly married, Piano divided his time between Genoa, where he used his father's construction facilities to build—among other things—a plywood sailing sloop, and Milan, where he had been working part-time under the guidance of the architect and furniture designer Franco Albini. Piano has credited Albini with providing him with the bulk of his training. "He was a great architect in Milan—he made nice things—maybe not so famous but great," Piano told the *Architectural Record* (May 1998). "And when I was in school, I wasn't really in school because I was working with Franco Albini and going to school maybe twice a week."

As an adult, Piano retained the affinity for strong but lightweight materials and structures that he had had as a boy. The first notable occasion on which he put that preference into practice came in 1969, when he was commissioned to design the Italian Industry Pavilion to be installed at the 1970 Expo in Osaka, Japan. His design of a lightweight tent structure, supported by cables, was widely noticed in the architectural community. Later that year Piano was introduced to Richard Rogers, who had admired his pavilion. The two men shared an interest in the writings of futurist-cum-philosopher Buckminster Fuller, and their friendship and partnership soon flourished. The pair struggled through the usual paucity of work available to young architects until 1971, when, partly on a whim, they decided to enter the competition for the largest and perhaps most significant architectural commission in 25 years: the Georges Pompidou Center modern-art museum, in Paris.

At the beginning, Piano and Rogers's bid for the Pompidou Center project seemed bound for failure. They worked on their plans right up to the deadline, delivering them to the post office moments before it closed, on the date by which the shipment had to be postmarked to be eligible. According to British postal regulations, their packing tube was too long, so Piano and Rogers had to rush to trim their prints so that they would fit into a smaller tube. The two men shipped the package in time, only to have it returned a few days later because of insufficient postage. Although Rogers was able to persuade the postal clerk on duty to reship the package with the original date stamped on it, the partners were convinced by now that their efforts had been in vain. But out of 681 entries, Piano and Rogers's design, with its distinctive, wide-open spaces and public areas, got the nod.

The resulting Pompidou Center, also referred to as Beaubourg, after the neighborhood it occupies, remains the focus of heated debate. At the beginning, with its inside-out design, exoskeletal structure, and colorfully painted, exposed plumbing and air ducts, the museum scandalized purists in much the same way that the modernist works it houses succeeded in doing decades earlier. Despite the argument over the building's design that has continued among the art world's elite for the past two decades, Beaubourg has become an urban center for the masses, and for many years it attracted greater crowds than the famous Louvre, also in Paris. "We wanted to create a place of curiosity and exploration," Piano told Daniel S. Levy for *Time* (May 4, 1998). By rejecting the traditional, somber, austere setting for institutionalized art and replacing it with an invitingly whimsical structure, Piano and Rogers created a venue for congregation. Unfortunately, the unanticipatedly large number of visitors exacted its toll on the structure, and Piano was commissioned in 1995 to renovate the building, a job that involved minor expansion and space reorganization. The project began in the fall of 1997 and was completed in January 2000. One new space, a 15,000-square-foot gallery, housed a major retrospective of Piano's work in early 2000. The exhibit, which included dozens of models, videos, drawings, and photographs, was arranged "not chronologically but rather around three broad themes: invention, urbanism and sensitivity," as Alan Riding reported in the *New York Times* (March 5, 2000). Later that year the show traveled to the Neue Nationalgalerie in Berlin, Germany.

The Pompidou Center project also took its toll on Piano and Rogers. Exhausted by the work it had entailed, the pair ended their partnership upon the center's completion (though they remain good friends), and each was relatively unproductive over the next few years. Also, Piano's marriage became strained during his time in Paris, resulting in a separation in 1984 and a divorce in 1989.

Meanwhile, in 1981 Piano was invited by the Houston, Texas, socialite Dominique de Menil to her home to discuss plans to construct a museum that would house the impressive art collection she and her husband, John, had amassed. In the early 1970s the de Menils had selected the famed architect Louis Kahn to design a building for their artworks, but the deaths of John de Menil and Kahn, both in 1973, ended those plans. Impressed by the care with which Piano listened to her ideas, which had developed over the decade that had passed since she and her husband had first conceived the project, Dominique de Menil employed Piano for the project.

She had two requirements: that the museum appear small and unimposing on the outside, yet be as spacious as possible on the inside; and that natural light be used to illuminate the exhibited works, so visitors could see those works in the changing daylight, as she had in her home. After making extensive studies of the area's light conditions and examinations of the surrounding neighborhood, which contained small houses, Piano designed a building that looks from the road like a two-story structure but encompasses more than 100,000 square feet of exhibition space. For the ceiling he used what he has described as "leaves"—thin, wave-shaped slabs of reinforced cement that overlap slightly on a steel lattice and support a skylight roof. The leaves provide natural ventilation and allow in sunlight, while diffusing it so as not to damage the exhibited art works. Many consider the Menil Collection Art Museum, completed in 1986, to be Piano's masterpiece. Five years after it was built, Piano was asked to return to the Menil Collection to make an addition, the Cy Twombly Gallery. In a discussion about the museum and his other work, Piano told Alan Riding, "I think style is a very dangerous concept. It's a narcissistic attitude. Why should you worry about style? Worry about coherence. That is a better idea. Style is like a rubber stamp, a designer label; it becomes quite commercial. . . . Style becomes a limitation, a sort of golden cage, in which you worry about being recognized. What I like about the Menil Collection is that the building is a portrait of the client, not of the architect."

Though the brashness of the Beaubourg appears to stand in stark contrast to the subdued contemplativeness of the Menil Collection, Piano has pointed out that the two museums share more than

meets the eye. "We had to destroy a myth in Paris, an exaggerated emphasis on ritual, by creating a place open to all comers," he told Franck Renevier for the London *Guardian* (September 26, 1982). "In Houston the wide-open spaces and immense distances of Texas and a total absence of a structured cultural focus turned the problem inside out. There we had to protect a cultural value, remove it from the urban magma, incite contemplation. Still, what Beaubourg and Houston share is the fact of having abolished the religious, solemn side of museum-going and conventional museum formulas."

Closely linked to Piano's family heritage and his fascination with nature's lightweight materials is his holistic approach to architecture. Piano has altered the direction of architecture by eschewing trends and reigning artistic theories and instead considering buildings' designs in relation to the environments in which they will be placed and in relation to the people or objects the buildings are intended to house. "You have to think about the position of the sun—at four o'clock on a winter afternoon, where is the sun? You think about the wind; sometimes instead of making piazzas you end up making wind tunnels," he explained to Calvin Tomkins. "Gradually, you move into more precise areas, having to do with color, vibration, resonance—and only then do you start to work with architecture." While some might consider such external variables to be restrictive, Piano sees them as liberating. In the same way that some poets use the constraints of meter and rhyme to stimulate creativity, Piano considers a project's parameters as opportunities to make his structures seamlessly become part of the landscapes they occupy.

An example of the merging of these principles in one work is the Piano-designed Kansai International Airport Terminal, opened in 1994. Piano and his associates won the bid in an invitation-only competition among 15 architects, among them such prominent figures as I. M. Pei, Norman Foster, and Jean Nouvel. Constructed on a man-made island in Osaka Bay, Japan, the two-kilometer-long terminal gives the appearance of a huge airplane or glider; the main building is ventilated by natural air flow. In addition, Piano's plans called for a large number of trees to be planted on the landfill around the exterior of the terminal. Piano overlooked one detail, however: the trees might have attracted birds, which would have interfered with, and probably seriously damaged, aircraft. So, "we had to get scientists to find trees that would not attract birds," Piano told Tomkins.

One of Piano's most unusual buildings is the Jean-Marie Tjibaou Cultural Center, in Nouméa, on New Caledonia, a group of Pacific islands under French control. The center (named for a New Caledonian political leader who was assassinated in 1989) offers permanent and changing exhibits of works created by the Kanak, an indigenous people of Oceania, and other peoples native to the South Pacific. Built between 1991 and 1998, the center consists of 10 semicircular wooden structures of different sizes that stand on a peninsula. The design of the buildings' outer shells (which are made of iroko, a wood that requires little maintenance) echoes that of traditional Kanak huts. "These constructions are an expression of the harmonious relationship with the environment that is typical of Kanak culture," Piano explained, as quoted on *geocities.com*'s "Big Buildings" Web site. Each of the buildings makes use of a so-called passive ventilation system; special skylights open when there are light breezes and close when the air currents become stronger. In *Architecture* (October 1998, online), the California-based architect L. R. Findley wrote, "The mysterious forms of [the center] . . . are at once unexpected and beautiful. Rising from tropical vegetation to brush the sky, the center's swelling wooden shapes seem simultaneously alien and indigenous, as impressive as the landscape that surrounds them. . . . In cultural terms, . . . this is a subtle and generous work, a model of diplomacy, and a compelling contribution to . . . [the] Kanak people."

For the 20th anniversary of the Pritzker Prize, on June 17, 1998, the Hyatt Foundation was invited by President Bill Clinton and his wife, Hillary Rodham Clinton, to present its award to Piano at the White House. Because of their interest in building development, the Pritzker family, heads of the Hyatt hotel chain, chose in the late 1970s to honor excellence in architecture. Piano became the 21st recipient of the Pritzker Prize, often referred to as the "Nobel of architecture," which carried with it a bronze medallion and $100,000. Capping a decade of his dominance in his field, the Pritzker award followed a number of other prestigious honors for Piano, including a gold medal in 1989 from the Royal Institute of British Architects, the American Academy of Arts and Letters' 1994 Arnold W. Brunner Memorial Prize in architecture, and a 1995 Praemium Imperiale award for lifetime achievement in the arts.

Piano's workshop is currently concentrating on approximately 20 major projects in Europe and the United States, including the rehabilitation of the Fiat Lingotto factories in Torino, Italy, the Harvard University renovation and expansion project in Cambridge, Massachusetts, and the new, 40-story headquarters for the *New York Times* in Manhattan. In a long, illuminating article for that newspaper (October 22, 2000), Herbert Muschamp described the process by which Piano's design was chosen for the *Times* skyscraper in a competition that drew proposals from the British architect Norman Foster and the New Haven, Connecticut–based architect Cesar Pelli. (David Childs of Skidmore Owings & Merrill and Frank Gehry removed their design from consideration a few weeks before the winner was announced.) After noting the "relational values from which architecture is made: of outside to inside; top to bottom; structure to expression; content to form," Muschamp wrote, "Piano's design embodies those relational values, and more, in radiant form."

Piano, who has handled some of the largest architectural projects of the last three decades, is now in charge of his largest yet: the reconstruction of 185 acres owned by DaimlerChrysler in Berlin's Potsdamer Platz. The cultural center of Germany— some would say of all Europe—during the 1920s and 1930s, Potsdamer Platz was leveled by bombing during World War II. During the Cold War the Platz was not rebuilt, because it straddled the border dividing Communist East Germany and democratic West Germany. To get designs for the site, in 1992 Daimler-Benz, as it was then known, organized a competition in which 14 firms participated. The Renzo Piano Building Workshop, in collaboration with the German architect Christoph Kohlbecker, won first prize. Piano has admitted that the enterprise is daunting. "Cities are beautiful because they are created slowly," he said, according to the profile of him posted on the Pritzker Prize Web site. "It takes 500 years to create a city, and we have been asked to reconstruct a large chunk of Berlin in just five years."

Renzo Piano divides his time between his homes and offices in Genoa and Paris. He married his second wife, Milly, in September 1992. Piano's passion away from work is sailing. His avocation has mingled with his vocation on several occasions; he has designed and built four boats for himself, and he made a foray into professional marine architecture by designing the British luxury ship *Crown Princess* in 1990.

In his 2000 interview with Alan Riding, Piano said, "If you are a bad writer, no one reads your book. If you're a bad musician, no one listens to your music. But if you're a bad architect, you impose something on a city forever. I believe architecture can transform life, it is a utopia, it can bring lightness and beauty and poetry. But the architect has a great responsibility. Aesthetics and ethics are very much connected, but I didn't understand that when I was 30 or when I was 40 or when I was 50." "You know," he added, "my feeling is that you should live as an architect only after you are 50 because for the first 50 years you just learn. I am not joking. You learn and you make so many mistakes. Then, when you reach 50, maybe you can work properly for 50 years. And after that maybe you have another 50 years to teach other people." — T.J.F.

Suggested Reading: *Architectural Record* p75 May 1998, with photo; *Architecture* p39 May 1998, with photo; *Christian Science Monitor* p14 May 11, 1989, with photo; *House Beautiful* p42 Aug. 1998, with photo; *New York Times* II p33+ June 14, 1987, C p16 Jan. 15, 1993, II p48 Mar. 5, 2000, with photos; II p1+ Oct. 22, 2000, with photos; *New Yorker* p52+ Aug. 22 & 29, 1994; *Online NewsHour* June 19, 1998

Selected Works: B&B Italia Offices, Como, Italy, 1971–73; Centre Georges Pompidou, Paris, France, 1971–77; UNESCO Urban Reconstruction

Workshop, Otranto, Italy, 1979; Mobile Construction Unit, Dakar, Senegal, 1978; Menil Collection Art Center, Houston, Texas, 1982–87; IBM Traveling Pavilion, 1984–86; Genoa Subway Stations, Italy, 1983; Institute for Research into Light Metals, Novara, Italy, 1985–87; Columbus International Exposition, Genoa, Italy, 1988–92; San Nicola stadium, Bari, Italy, 1987–90; Rue de Meaux Housing, Paris, France, 1987–91; Kansai International Airport Terminal, Osaka, Japan, 1990–94; Ushibuka Bridge, Kumamoto, Japan, 1989–96; Renzo Piano Building Workshop, Genoa, Italy, 1989–91; Jean-Marie Tjibaou Cultural Center, Nouméa, New Caledonia, 1993–98; Banca Populare di Lodi and Auditorium, Milan, Italy, 1993–2001; reconstruction of a section of Potsdamer Platz, Berlin, Germany, 1996–2000; National Center for science and Technology, Amsterdam, Netherlands, 1994–97; Atelier Brancusi, Paris, France, 1993–97; Beyeler Foundation Museum, Basel, Switzerland, 1994–97; Mercedes-Benz Design Centre, Stuttgart, Germany, 1994–98; KPN Telecom Office Tower, Rotterdam, Netherlands, 1997–2000; Maison Hermès, Tokyo, Japan, 1998–2001

Steve Granitz/Retna Ltd.

Pierce, David Hyde

Apr. 3, 1959– Actor. Address: c/o Silver, Massetti & Szatmony, 8730 W. Sunset Blvd. #440, Los Angeles, CA 90069-2277

Although the highly acclaimed and immensely popular NBC sitcom *Frasier* is named for the character played by Kelsey Grammer—Frasier Crane, a Seattle on-air psychiatrist—the actor David Hyde Pierce has often stolen the show, with his hilarious depiction of Frasier's brother, the stuck-up but lovable Niles. Indeed, since *Frasier* debuted, in 1993, Niles Crane has become one of the favorite characters of the American TV audience. "Because Niles and Frasier are such odd characters—so effete and overcultured and unaware—it makes it easier for people to identify with them," Pierce told Kinney Littlefield for the *Orange County* [New Jersey] *Register* (April 24, 1997, on-line). "You can recognize those traits in yourself and still say, 'At least I'm not as bad as they are.'" A master of deadpan delivery, Pierce has won three Emmy Awards and an American Comedy Award, among other honors, for his skill in bringing Niles to life. The actor began his career in theater, with parts on Broadway, Off-Broadway, and elsewhere. He has appeared in supporting roles in such motion pictures as *Nixon* and *Isn't She Great* and has lent his voice to several animated films, among them *A Bug's Life* and *The Tangerine Bear*.

David Hyde Pierce was born on April 3, 1959 in Saratoga Springs, New York, the youngest of four children—two boys and two girls. His father was an insurance agent, and his mother was a homemaker. Pierce has loved acting since his childhood; as a boy he would practice "death scenes" by repeatedly throwing himself down the stairs in his home. "My parents were so patient, God bless 'em," he told Littlefield. "They'd hear a 'thumpa thumpa thumpa' and know it was just me falling down the stairs." He began perfecting his comedic style early on. "I can vividly recall telling a joke in, like, second grade," he told Alan Carter for *Entertainment Weekly* (November 12, 1993), "and realizing it was funnier if I didn't laugh. I've been deadpan ever since." Pierce also wrote short plays as vehicles for himself and his classmates. "They were always plays where I got to die," he told Luaine Lee for a Scripps Howard News Service article reprinted on *SouthCoast Today* (on-line). "I might do 'Julius Caesar,' where they could stab me to death. There's a Jimmy Stewart movie called *The FBI Story* which I had seen with all these scenes of gangsters getting shot. So I wrote up a play where you could see all these things and I played John Dillinger because I thought that was the coolest death scene, getting shot amidst all these garbage cans." Pierce also studied piano, and his theatrical bent notwithstanding, he dreamed of a career as a concert pianist. When he told his parents he wanted to be a musician, as he recalled to Lee, "they sat me down in the living room and opened the encyclopedia to Albert Schweitzer. They pointed out to me that Albert Schweitzer was a musician, but he was also a world-renowned scientist and did all these other things. And we don't want to narrow our focus too soon, do we?"

At his graduation from Saratoga High School, in 1977, Pierce received the Yaddo Medal for best dramatic-arts student. That fall he entered Yale University, in New Haven, Connecticut, where he soon switched his major from music to English and theater arts. "It became clear to me that not only didn't I have what it takes talentwise to be a concert pianist, but also part of that talent is the interest," he told Lee. "I didn't want to sit for 12 hours in a practice room and didn't want to take all the music history classes that you had to take. There was a lot of other stuff I would rather be doing." In addition, he has said, he had realized that what he loved most about piano was "the performing aspect . . . , not specifically the playing-the-piano part," as he put it to Luaine Lee. After he earned a bachelor's degree from Yale, in 1981, he moved to New York City and enrolled in acting classes. To pay his bills, he worked as a security guard, a church organist, and a tie salesman at Bloomingdale's department store.

Pierce made his Broadway debut in 1982, in the small role of a waiter in Christopher Durang's farce *Beyond Therapy*. The next year he moved to Minneapolis, Minnesota, where he became an ensemble player at the prestigious Guthrie Theater. After he returned to New York City, in 1986, he portrayed Laertes in a New York Shakespeare Festival production of *Hamlet* that starred Kevin Kline. Pierce made his television debut as O'Neill in an episode of *Spenser for Hire* in 1987 and his film debut with a walk-on part as a bartender in James Bridges's *Bright Lights, Big City* (1988). His cinematic career continued with small roles in three other 1988 films—*Rocket Gibraltar*, *Crossing Delancey*, and *The Appointments of Dennis Jennings*. He then joined a touring production of Anton Chekhov's play *The Cherry Orchard*, which traveled in the Soviet Union and Japan in 1988 and 1989. He next appeared as a gay pediatrician in the 1989 Broadway run of Wendy Wasserstein's Pulitzer Prize–winning play *The Heidi Chronicles*. "After that show," he told Steve Pond for the *New York Times* (November 7, 1993), "I thought, 'It can't get any better than this.' It was highly unlikely that I would ever get a better part. So I could stay there and hope to some day do as well again, or I could strike out on something different."

With that thought in mind, Pierce moved to Los Angeles, to audition for various television and film roles. During the next few years, he had bit parts in the films *Vampire's Kiss* (1989), *Civil War Diary* (1990), *Little Man Tate* (1991), and *The Fisher King* (1991). In 1992 he was cast as Theodore Van Horne in the Norman Lear–produced *The Powers That Be*, a television sitcom about a dysfunctional political family that is headed by a bumbling senator. Pierce played the senator's suicidal son-in-law, a congressman who is in love with the senator's clumsy maid. Despite good reviews, the show lasted less than one season. The following year Pierce

appeared in a small role in the film *Addams Family Values* and won a larger part, that of Dennis Reed (the brother of the female lead, played by Meg Ryan), in the hit romantic movie *Sleepless in Seattle*.

Pierce landed his role on *Frasier* almost by chance. A spin-off of the successful and long-running sitcom *Cheers*, *Frasier* focuses on the cultured and intellectual psychiatrist Frasier Crane, played by Kelsey Grammer. When the producers of the series came across Pierce's head shot, they were struck by his physical resemblance to Grammer; after meeting with Pierce, they decided to cast him as Frasier's brother, a role created for him. (Before the character was added to the script, Frasier had had no siblings.) "My chemistry with Kelsey is very hard to define," Pierce told Littlefield. "It's certainly not anything conscious. I think of it almost as acrobats. We know we can try anything, and the other one will be right there for us." Niles, as portrayed by Pierce, comes across as more sympathetic than one might expect of someone who is awkward, pompous, snooty, and out of touch with common people. "I look for ways to make him as close to an actual human being as possible," Pierce told Bret Watson for *Entertainment Weekly* (November 3, 1995). "Because he's in some ways extreme and that's what makes him funny." Niles, a psychiatrist like his brother, is unhappily married to a woman named Maris, who has never appeared on screen. He soon fell for Daphne Moon (played by Jane Leeves), the British live-in physical therapist who ministers to the Crane brothers' injured father. For several seasons Niles's feelings for Daphne went unspoken while he suffered the torments of his marriage and endured the pain of hearing about Moon's love affairs. In *Frasier*'s 2000–01 season—the series' eighth—Niles and Daphne became romantically involved, much to the delight of many longtime fans of the show.

In addition to working on *Frasier*, Pierce acted in Mike Nichols's horror film *Wolf* (1994), which starred Jack Nicholson. He was cast as John Dean, the White House counsel during the presidency of Richard Nixon, in Oliver Stone's *Nixon* (1995). Pierce also supplied the voices of Daedalus, in Disney's animated television series *Hercules* (1998), and Slim the Walkingstick, in John Lasseter's animated movie *A Bug's Life* (1998), for which Disney and Pixar Animation Studios collaborated. Speaking of the latter film, Pierce said, as quoted on *Just Go* (on-line), "I see so much of myself in what they've animated. That was what really blew me away. When you're doing an animated film, you trust that the illustrators and animators will do you justice, because you have no control over it. A lot of what I do comes with facial expressions and the difference between what I'm saying and how I look when I'm saying it. This was beyond my wildest expectations. It was me and better than me and more than me, because it had more hands than I do." In 1999 Pierce portrayed a deaf pianist in Robert Townsend's television "mockumentary" *Jack-*

ie's Back and narrated Jeff Abugov's nature-documentary spoof The Mating Habits of the Earthbound Human.

The following year Pierce played Professor Neumann in David Wain's comedy Wet Hot American Summer and co-starred with Bette Midler and Nathan Lane in Andrew Bergman's Isn't She Great, a biopic about the novelist Jacqueline Susann, whose book Valley of the Dolls has been credited with ushering in a new era of commercialism in publishing. In Isn't She Great, which received mostly negative reviews, Pierce played Susann's prissy editor. Among those who praised Pierce's work in the film was Stephanie Zacharek, who noted for Salon (January 28, 2000, on-line) that he was "the kind of actor who can infuse any stuffed-shirt character with effortless charm, which is exactly what he does here." Pierce provided the voice of Bird in the animated film The Tangerine Bear (2000). He had a small part in the crime-comedy Chain of Fools (2000), played a larger role as Henry in Wet Hot American Summer (2001), and was heard as the voice of Drixorial in the animated film Osmosis Jones (2001). "For voice-over," Pierce told Littlefield, "you have to energize your voice more. But I still value subtlety and throwaway delivery. That's the kind of humor I like to do—not hitting anything too hard, letting people be surprised by the laugh rather than pointing the way to it."

Pierce is known as engaging, nervous, and self-effacing. He lives in West Hollywood with his two Wheaton terriers, Emma and Mabel; according to Mr. Showbiz (2000, on-line), his partner is Brian Hargrove, the producer of the sitcom Caroline in the City. His charitable work involves supporting AIDS research, Habitat for Humanity, and research aimed at finding a cure for Alzheimer's disease. (One of his grandfathers and, he suspects, his father were afflicted with Alzheimer's.) His mother and father both died within the last five years. "There's a sense," he told Lee, "when your parents are gone, that really you're it. You're on your own two feet. It's not your life for them or even with them. It is your life informed by all the things they've given to you and hopefully still observed somewhere by them. But you're on your own in a good sense and maybe, in some ways, a stronger sense." Pierce has strived to keep his private life away from the glare of the media, and unlike most Hollywood actors, he does not have a personal publicist. "I don't go unrecognized, but I can go undisturbed," he has said. He told Lee, "Things that go along with Frasier that are different from what I had with other shows—the fame and financial security and stuff like that—I'm very pleased I have them, but they've never been and still aren't that interesting to me. The people I work with have always been the most important thing to me. That's the way I've been the luckiest."

Pierce's honors include the Q Award, given by Viewers for Quality Television, for best supporting actor in a quality series, which he has won five times. He won Emmy Awards in the category "out-standing supporting actor in a comedy series" for his work in Frasier during the 1994–95, 1997–98, and 1998–99 television seasons. In 1995 the Screen Actors Guild named him outstanding male actor in a comedy series; in 1997 he earned an American Comedy Award for funniest supporting male performer in a television series as well as a CableACE Award as best guest actor in a dramatic special or series for his appearance in an episode of The Outer Limits. The following year he received the Television Critics Award for outstanding individual achievement in comedy. He has occasionally returned to the stage for one-off performances, usually in Los Angeles. — G.O.

Suggested Reading: Mr. Showbiz (on-line); New York Times II p37 Nov. 7, 1993, with photo; People p252 Nov. 17, 1997, with photo; SouthCoast Today (on-line); TV Guide p24+ Sep. 7–13, 1996, with photos, p16+ Feb. 21–27, 1998, with photos

Selected Movies: Sleepless in Seattle, 1993; Wolf, 1994; Nixon, 1995; A Bug's Life, 1998; Isn't She Great, 2000; Osmosis Jones (2001); Wet Hot American Summer, 2001

Selected Television Shows: The Powers That Be, 1992; Frasier, 1993–

Selected Theatrical Productions: Beyond Therapy, 1982; Hamlet, 1986; The Cherry Orchard, 1988; The Heidi Chronicles, 1989

Pincay, Laffit

(PINK-eye, LA-feet)

Dec. 29, 1946– Jockey. Address: c/o Jockey's Guild, 250 W. Main St., #1820, Lexington, KY 40507

"I have a great wish to be the best," the Panamanian jockey Laffit Pincay told Whitney Tower for Sports Illustrated (December 6, 1971) early in his career. Ranked at that time among the world's foremost jockeys, Pincay was inducted into the Thoroughbred Racing Association's Hall of Fame four years later, when he was 29. He has since become renowned as one of the top jockeys in horse-racing history. On December 10, 1999 he chalked up his 8,834th professional victory, thus surpassing the record held by another jockey great—Bill Shoemaker—for most career wins. Less than a year later, on October 28, 2000, Pincay became the first jockey ever to reach the 9,000 mark in victories. In the course of his 35-year career, Pincay has earned five Eclipse Awards for Champion Jockey (from the Thoroughbred Racing Association)—in 1971, 1973, 1974, 1979, and 1985—and has led the U.S. in total annual prize earnings seven times. He has

Ken Levine/Allsport USA

Laffit Pincay

won the Belmont Stakes three times—in 1982, riding Conquistador Cielo; in 1983, with Caveat; and in 1984, aboard Swale. He won the Kentucky Derby once, in 1984, again with Swale. "I just love riding horses," Pincay told Cindy Pearson for *About.com* in 1999, "and that's all I want to do for as long as I can."

The second of four children, Laffit Alejandro Pincay was born on December 29, 1946 in Panama City, Panama. His parents divorced when he was very young, and his father, a jockey and later a trainer of horses, settled in Caracas, Venezuela. "As a kid I hardly ever saw him . . . ," Pincay told Tower in 1971. "I know he came to New York on at least one occasion—to ride Primordial II and win the Display Handicap at Aqueduct [a New York City racetrack] in 1964. I used to meet him once in a while, but seldom now."

As a boy Pincay aspired to become a baseball player, but his small stature (he stands five feet, one inch) led him to choose horse racing instead. At 15 he got a job cleaning the stalls at Panama City's local racetrack. "I would work at the track from six in the morning until 11:30 [a.m.]," Pincay recalled to Tower. "Then I would go to school from two until six or seven at night. It was a year before I could exercise horses, and still another year before I started breezing [leading horses at a leisurely pace around the track] and working them out of the gate. During this time I was being helped tremendously by an old man, a former rider with a great deal of courage named Bolivar Moreno. He had started a school to teach boys like me to become jockeys. Before my time, such [Panamanian] riders as Manuel Ycaza, Braulio Baeza and Heliodoro Gustines mostly taught themselves through experi-

ence on the track—or they were helped by the trainers and the families they worked for. But by the time Jorge Velasquez [born in Panama one day before Pincay] and I came along, Moreno had his school set up. . . . [Moreno] would put a barrel down for us to sit on and use some cord to make stirrups and reins." Pincay came to read about and admire such famous jockeys as Shoemaker, Johnny Longden, John Rotz, Ron Turcotte, Baeza, and Ycaza. "It seemed impossible that I would ever come to the United States," Pincay told Tower. "I never thought I could make it; it was so difficult."

After he started riding, Pincay rapidly emerged as one of Panama's top jockeys, winning more than 400 races in two years. He soon caught the eye of Fred J. Hooper, a famous owner, breeder, and trainer who owned a stable at Arlington Park, in Chicago; Hooper had helped both Velasquez and Baeza launch successful careers in the United States. Hooper signed Pincay to a $500-per-month racing contract and invited him to Arlington Park, where the jockey won his first race. He continued to perform well during the rest of the season. "Out of the first 11 mounts I think I won eight races," he told Tower, "and even though I came late to Chicago I finished as the third leading rider. Then we went to Hawthorne Park [near Chicago] and I was leading rider. Then on to New York, where I believe I finished third." "If you get the opportunity you've got to take it when you can," Pincay later reflected, speaking about his decision to leave his native land. "We Panamanians come [to the United States] with more experience under tougher conditions. At home we start working with broken-down horses. Another thing, the 2-year-olds in Panama are not broken as carefully as they are [in the United States] so it is a lot more dangerous. You've got to be better."

In the following years Pincay proved that his strong debut was anything but a fluke. He rose to the front ranks among jockeys at Hollywood Park, in Los Angeles, and at Aqueduct Race Track, and set the record for the most wins (148) in a Hollywood Park season—a record that still stands. In 1971 Pincay led the U.S. in races won, and he regularly brought in more prize money than any other jockey. (Then, as now, jockeys typically earned 10 percent of the winner's share of the purse.) As early as 1971, Pincay was hailed by Bill Shoemaker, the world's foremost jockey at the time, as horse racing's next top rider. "Laffit is the next champion, whether he beats my lifetime record [of most career wins] or not," Shoemaker told Tower in 1971. "He's the finest rider to come along since I've been in a position to judge."

In the 1980s Pincay continued to win races at a steady pace. He nearly retired from racing in 1985, after his wife, Linda, whom he had married in 1967, committed suicide. "It was very, very tough" for him after her death, Pincay told Nick Charles for *cnn.com* (December 10, 1999). "It was very hard for me because you know I never expected it. You feel very guilty. You blame yourself for a lot of things. You blame yourself because you didn't see it coming. What could you, what could I have done better?" Despite his grief, he returned to racing, to which he remains committed. By 1990 he had brought in more than $150 million in prize money for his horses' owners.

Over the course of his career, Pincay has suffered many injuries. He has broken his collarbone 11 times, his ribs 10 times, and both his thumbs; fractured his spine twice; and punctured a lung twice. Yet he regards his spartan diet, not the constant physical risk to which he is exposed, as the most trying aspect of his profession. Like virtually all jockeys, he keeps a vigilant eye on his weight in order to maintain a competitive edge. Over the years he has tried many special diets; once, because of the effects of malnutrition, he collapsed in the jockeys' room at a racetrack. "I wasn't born to be small," he told Ed McNamara for *espn.com*. "I'm built to be 135 to 150 lbs." (He currently weighs about 115 pounds.) To keep his weight low, Pincay subsists on 850 calories per day (the average American consumes 2,000 calories daily) and devotes several hours each day to stretching and working out on a treadmill. According to his acquaintances he sometimes restricts himself to a single peanut during transcontinental flights—one half at takeoff, the other half upon landing—and regularly scrapes the salt off crackers before eating them. As a result, he "has been able to keep his body in tremendous physical condition over the years," the jockey Chris McCarron told Nick Charles in 1999. "And he's always been a diminutive guy as far as height and everything goes. But when you look at his muscle development . . . it's very, very impressive. I would match him with any athlete in the world." By his own account, Pincay looks forward to relaxing his diet someday. As his older son told Charles, "The first thing he's looking forward to [in his] retirement isn't the fact that he'll be avoiding danger everyday, and not involved with all the accidents that can happen in his sport, but the fact that he can eat like a normal human being."

At present, however, Pincay does not have specific retirement plans. "There's no question in my mind that I could ride for another five years," he told Bill Finley for the *New York Times* (June 10, 2001). "The question is whether I want to do that or not. I'll see how I'm doing and how I feel. A lot will depend on whether I can keep getting on good horses. I'm not going to set any schedule or make any commitments. I'll go year by year and see what happens."

In 1992 Pincay remarried. He and his second wife, Jeanine, have a seven-year-old son, Jean-Laffit. His children from his previous marriage are Laffit III, a New York sportscaster, and Lisa. — P.K.

Suggested Reading: *cnn.com* Dec. 10, 1999, with photos; *espn.com* Apr. 25, 2001; *People* p109+ May 13, 1985, with photo; *Sports Illustrated* p76+ Dec. 6, 1971, with photo

Courtesy of Popeil Inventions Inc.

Popeil, Ron
(poh-PEEL)

May 3, 1935– Inventor; businessman. Address: Ronco Inventions LLC, 21344 Superior St., Chatsworth, CA 91311

Ron Popeil may not be a household name, but the gadgets and appliances that he has invented and then pitched on late-night television include some of the most recognizable artifacts of American consumer culture. Among the familiar and best-selling products in Popeil's portfolio are the smokeless ashtray; Mr. Microphone; the Record Vacuum; the Inside-the-Shell Egg Scrambler; the Ronco 5-Tray Electric Food Dehydrator (a device for producing beef jerky, banana chips, soup mix, and even potpourri at home); GLH ("great looking hair") Formula Number 9 Hair System (a water-soluble, nontoxic spray-on toupee); the Popeil Automatic Pasta and Sausage Maker; and, most recently, the Ronco Showtime Rotisserie & BBQ. Not every Popeil invention has been a success. Bombs include a home handwriting-analysis kit, a do-it-yourself subliminal-message tape, the Hold-Up adhesive sponge board, and a device called the Inside the Outside Window Washer. But in more than 35 years as a supersalesperson, Popeil has seen more hits than misses.

In fact, Popeil has moved such vast quantities of merchandise over the years—over $1 billion worth—and has had such an impact on late-night television and home-shopping programming that he has been dubbed by some the "Einstein of infomercials." (Other sobriquets include the "King of Hair," the "King of Pasta," the "King of Dehydration," and the "Man Who Conquered the American

Kitchen.") Popeil has accomplished all this by bringing the tactics of the county-fair salesman to television. As Malcolm Gladwell pointed out in the *New Yorker* (October 30, 2000), "Ron Popeil didn't use a single focus group. He had no market researchers, R. & D. teams, public-relations advisers, Madison Avenue advertising companies, or business consultants. He did . . . what all the experts said couldn't be done in the modern economy. He dreamed up something new in his kitchen and went out and pitched it himself." "What Henry Ford was to industrial strength and genius, Ron Popeil is to the next generation of American ingenuity," Robert Thompson, an associate professor of television at Syracuse University, has said, as quoted by Ted Anthony for the Associated Press (April 13, 1997, on-line). "He's figured out the very complex negotiations that go on between what American culture produces and how we consume it. People 100 years from now are going to be writing dissertations on him." With the *USA Today* television columnist Jefferson Graham, Popeil wrote *The Salesman of the Century: Inventing, Marketing, and Selling on TV: How I Did It and How You Can Too!* (1995), which is both an autobiography and an instruction manual for would-be entrepreneurs.

The second son of Samuel and Julia Popeil, Ronald M. Popeil was born in the New York City borough of the Bronx on May 3, 1935. His extended family included a number of pitchmen who made their livings by working boardwalks and state fairs; one of them later invented the Ginsu knife. "My cousins could sell you an empty box," Popeil told Gladwell. His father, an inventor and salesman, created such labor-saving kitchen appliances as the Chop-O-Matic and the Veg-O-Matic (a more advanced version of the Chop-O-Matic), as well as the Pocket Fisherman, a collapsible rod and reel. When he was four years old, Popeil's parents divorced, and he was sent to live with his paternal grandparents. Thereafter, he saw his father and mother infrequently. He would spend hours in his grandmother's kitchen, watching her cook, but, as he told Tom Gliatto and John Hannah for *People* (May 3, 1993), "Home life was not there." "My grandfather used to tie me down in bed—my hands, my wrists, and my feet," Popeil told Gladwell. "Why? Because I had a habit of turning over on my stomach and bumping my head either up and down or side to side. Why? How? I don't know the answers. But I was spread-eagle, on my back, and if I was able to twist over and do it my grandfather would wake up at night and come in and beat the hell out of me. I never liked him. I never knew my mother or her parents or any of that family. That's it. Not an awful lot to remember. Obviously, other things took place. But they have been erased."

At 16 Popeil moved to Chicago, where his father, by now a factory owner, manufactured Chop-O-Matics and, in time, Veg-O-Matics. Shortly thereafter Popeil began hawking his father's mer-chandise at the city's Maxwell Street flea market. "The first time I went there," Popeil wrote in his autobiography, as cited by *ideafinder.com*, "the proverbial light bulb went on over my head. I saw all those people selling product, pocketing money, making sales, and my mind went racing. I can do what they're doing, I thought. But I can do it better than they can. So I gathered up some kitchen products from my father's factory—he sold them to me at wholesale, so he made a full profit—and went down on a Sunday to give it a try. I pushed. I yelled. I hawked. And it worked. I was stuffing money into my pockets, more money than I had ever seen in my life. I didn't have to be poor the rest of my life. Through sales I could escape from poverty and the miserable existence I had with my grandparents. I had lived for 16 years in homes without love, and now I had finally found a form of affection, and a human connection, through sales."

Popeil soon persuaded the manager of the flagship Woolworth's store in downtown Chicago to provide him with demonstration space in return for a cut of his revenue. Within a few weeks the young pitchman was earning more money than the store's manager. "He was mesmerizing," Mel Korey, a college friend and former business partner of Popeil's, told Gladwell. "There were secretaries who would take their lunch break at Woolworth's to watch him because he was so good-looking. He would just go into the turn, and people would just come running." ("The turn" is the moment when a pitchman stops performing and starts asking for money.) By his own account, Popeil was earning $1,000 per week at a time when salaries averaged $500 per month. He bought himself a Rolex watch and regularly dined at Chicago's fanciest restaurants.

In 1955, after only a year at the University of Illinois, Popeil dropped out of school to devote himself full-time to pitching merchandise. For several years he worked under his father; their relationship, he told Patrick McGeehan for the *New York Times* (December 11, 1994), was "all business." In 1964 he founded Ronco—later rechristened Ronco Teleproducts, Inc.—with Mel Korey and, for $500, shot a two-minute television spot for the recently developed Veg-O-Matic. Because of the Veg-O-Matic's efficiency, a pitchman demonstrating the appliance needed large quantities of produce on hand—an expensive proposition. Television enabled Popeil to reach a mass audience with a single performance, without spending much money for props. The commercial, broadcast on a number of local stations around the country, was a huge success, and consumers all over the U.S. bought up Veg-O-Matics in droves. At about the same time, Popeil began advertising an invention of his own: the Ronco Spray Gun, a garden-hose nozzle that contained a chamber in the handle for pellets of soap, fertilizer, insecticide, or whatever other water-soluble substance one wanted to project copiously and conveniently. It, too, sold well. In 1964

Ronco pulled in $200,000 in sales; by 1968 the company's revenues had mushroomed to $8.8 million. In 1969 Ronco went public, on the American Stock Exchange.

Throughout the 1970s and early 1980s, the company continued to expand. Popeil became a regular on late-night television, and gadgets such as the smokeless ashtray and Mr. Microphone, while often mocked by comedians and others, became part of American popular culture. By the mid-1980s at least one art gallery had dedicated a show to the "cultural iconography" of Popeil's wares; Dan Aykroyd had parodied Popeil on *Saturday Night Live*; Weird Al Yankovic had written a song about him; and tags such as "It slices! It dices!" (which Popeil had used to pitch the Veg-O-Matic), "But wait! There's more!," and "Isn't that amazing?" had become indelibly linked with Popeil and his products. The additional publicity boosted sales further, driving Popeil's personal net worth into the millions.

Ronco fell briefly on hard times in 1984, when one of its creditors, strapped for cash in the wake of the 1982–83 national recession, forced a liquidation of the company's assets. Ronco's trademarks and inventory were put up for auction, but buyers were scarce; moreover, none of those few prospective buyers proved willing to put up the sums the banks sought. Popeil, however, had retained his large personal fortune, and when the banks approached him, he agreed to buy the rights to Ronco's products for around $2 million. But the whole ordeal had soured him on running a business, and after reconstituting Ronco, he went into semiretirement. While he continued to fiddle with prototypes for new appliances, he left the company's day-to-day operations to others.

Meanwhile, in 1984 the Federal Communications Commission had relaxed limits on the length of television advertisements, thus making possible the half-hour infomercial. By 1991 Popeil was back on the airwaves, pitching his Ronco Food Dehydrator and doing a brisk business. The new format gave him a chance to shine by interacting with an audience, as he had in his youth, and it also allowed him to linger on details of his appliances. Here is Popeil, as cited by Gladwell, pitching his rotisserie oven: "All I'm going to do here is slide it through like this. It goes in very easily. I'll match it up over here. What I'd like to do is take some herbs and spices here. All I'll do is slide it back. Raise up my glass door here. I'll turn it to a little over an hour. . . . Just set it and forget it." While his performances look effortless, Popeil pointed out that a successful infomercial requires considerable skill, since a good pitchman must be equal parts businessman and entertainer. As he explained to David Strick for the *New York Times* (September 3, 1995), "Pick a product, any product on your desk. Introduce the product. Tell all the problems relating to the product. Tell how the product solves all those problems. Tell the customer where he or she can buy it and how much it

costs. Do this in one minute. Try it. You know what it sounds like? It comes out like this: Brrrrrrrrrr." "Ron literally invented the business of direct response TV sales," Steve Bryant, a host on the Philadelphia-based QVC Network (the home-shopping channel), said in an interview with McGeehan. "Ron paints in very definable brushstrokes, and every doubt in the customer's mind is wiped away."

While his latest appliance, the Ronco Showtime Rotisserie & BBQ, is racking up record sales, Popeil has continued to experiment with new ideas. "I have enough money today," he told Anthony, "but I can't stop. If there's a need for these things, I can't help myself." According to Gladwell, Popeil is currently at work on several new products, including a countertop meat-smoker and an automatic bread-and-batter machine (for fish sticks, fried shrimp, and mozzarella sticks).

Popeil and his fourth wife, Robin, a former Frederick's of Hollywood model, currently make their home in Beverley Hills, California. The couple have an infant daughter, Contessa. Popeil also has two daughters, Kathryn and Shannon, from his first marriage, and one daughter, Lauren, from his third. In *The Salesman of the Century*, he discussed the failure of his first three marriages. Popeil enjoys boating, fishing, and spending time in his kitchen, cooking and tinkering with prototypes for new gadgets. — P.K.

Suggested Reading: *New York Times* F p12 Dec. 11, 1994; *New Yorker* p64+ Oct. 30, 2000, with photo; *People* p154+ May 3, 1993, with photos

Selected Books: *The Salesman of the Century* (1995)

Powell, Colin L.

(KOH-lin)

Apr. 5, 1937– U.S. Secretary of State. Address: U.S. Department of State, Washington, DC 20520

United States secretary of state Colin L. Powell has proven to be one of the most perennially popular figures on the American political landscape. Ever since the 64-year-old retired army general rose to national prominence as chairman of the Joint Chiefs of Staff during the Persian Gulf War, in 1991, when he helped to guide the U.S. military to victory over Iraqi forces, he has been compared favorably to such men as Dwight D. Eisenhower and Ulysses S. Grant—generals who successfully entered politics after overseeing military triumphs. Indeed, for a time in the mid-1990s, there was intense speculation as to whether Powell would, like those men, seek the presidency. (He announced in the fall of 1995 that he would not.)

Charles Hopkinson/Retna Ltd.

Colin L. Powell

When news broke in December 2000 that Powell was to serve as secretary of state under the incoming president, George W. Bush—and would thus assume the most powerful office ever held by an African-American in the United States—some likened the general to George C. Marshall, who, as secretary of state after World War II, presided over the reconstruction of a war-torn Europe. It was unlikely that anyone could live up to such inflated expectations, and indeed, several months into the Bush presidency, Powell's star appeared to have dimmed somewhat. His political centrism seemed to be out of step with the conservatism prevailing in the administration, with the result that Powell often appeared to be working with his hands tied. Although Powell told Johanna McGeary for *Time* (September 10, 2001), "I'm not frustrated. There are problems to be solved. And my job is to help the President find the right answer to the problems he faces," close friends reportedly told journalists that the general was dissatisfied with his role in the administration.

Powell's role took on new importance in the wake of the terrorist attacks on the U.S. on September 11, 2001. Immediately after the attacks Powell, like President Bush, struck a bellicose note in his official remarks. Referring to Al Qaeda, the terrorist network of the Saudi Arabian–born Osama bin Laden—who was believed to have masterminded the deadly assaults and to be hiding in Afghanistan—he said, "We will go after that group, that network, and those who have harbored, supported and aided that network, to rip the network up." "When we're through with that network," he added, as quoted by R.W. Apple in the *New York Times* (September 14, 2001), "we will continue

with a global assault against terrorism in general." But behind the scenes Powell was thought to be urging restraint—much as he had done 10 years earlier, during the Persian Gulf War.

In his official capacity as secretary of state, Powell was charged with building diplomatic support in the Arab world for the American-led "war on terrorism." In the weeks following the September 11 attacks, that effort appeared to comprise two elements: first, Powell (as well as President Bush) manifestly tried to win the support of moderate Arabs by suggesting that the United States supported the creation of a Palestinian state. (Bin Laden and others have justified the terrorists' actions in part on what they view as the ill treatment of the Palestinians by the United States and Israel.) Second, the secretary sought to strengthen American ties to Pakistan, which supported U.S. military action in neighboring Afghanistan in the wake of the attacks, by ensuring Pakistani president Pervez Musharraf that the United States remained committed to promoting Pakistan's interests in the long term—even if American relations with India, Pakistan's longstanding adversary, would suffer as a result. "I made the point to [President Musharraf] that this isn't just a temporary spike in the relationship," Powell said at a news conference, as quoted by Reuters (October 16, 2001). "We believe as a result of the actions taken by Pakistan over the last five weeks we truly are at the beginning of a strengthened relationship, a relationship that will grow and thrive."

Colin Luther Powell was born in the Harlem section of New York City on April 5, 1937 to Luther Powell, a shipping clerk in Manhattan's garment district, and Maud Ariel (McKoy) Powell, who worked as a seamstress there. His parents, who had emigrated from Jamaica more than 20 years earlier, impressed upon Colin and his older sister, Marilyn, the importance of education and personal achievement and fully expected their children "to do something with [their] lives."

In about 1940 the family, which Powell recalls as having been "strong and close," moved to the Hunts Point area of the South Bronx, where Powell graduated from Morris High School in 1954. At the City College of New York, he majored in geology and got his first taste of military life as a cadet in the Reserve Officers' Training Corps (ROTC). "The discipline, the structure, the camaraderie, the sense of belonging were what I craved," he wrote in his autobiography, *My American Journey* (1995), as quoted by *ABCNews.com*. Former classmates remember that he displayed rare leadership ability on campus, motivating many other students to succeed. He was appointed commander of the Pershing Rifles, the ROTC precision drill team, and graduated at the top of the college's ROTC class of 1958 with the rank of cadet colonel, the highest rank in the corps.

On graduation, Powell was commissioned a second lieutenant in the United States Army. His first field assignment involved leading a platoon in Germany charged with stopping any westward advance of the Soviet army. A few years later, in 1962, Powell was one of more than 16,000 military advisers sent to South Vietnam by President John F. Kennedy. While marching through a rice paddy one day in 1963—he was assigned to a South Vietnamese infantry battalion patrolling the border with Laos—Powell stepped into a Punji-stick trap, impaling his foot on one of the sharpened stakes concealed just below the water's surface. After that injury, he was given a Purple Heart, and in that same year he was awarded the Bronze Star. In 1968–69, during the height of the U.S. war in Vietnam, Powell returned there for a second tour of duty with the United States Army infantry as a battalion executive officer and division operations officer. He was injured a second time in a helicopter crash landing, during which his rescuing of troops from the burning helicopter earned him a Soldiers Medal. Altogether he won 11 medals, including the Legion of Merit in 1972.

By his own admission, Powell's experiences in Vietnam had a profound effect on his later views regarding the appropriate use of American military force. "Many of my generation of Vietnam-era officers," he later wrote in his autobiography, as quoted by Lawrence F. Kaplan in the *New Republic* (January 1, 2001), "vowed that when our turn came to call the shots, we would not quietly acquiesce in halfhearted warfare for half-baked reasons that the American people could not understand."

On his return to the United States, Powell enrolled in the graduate school of George Washington University, in Washington, D.C., where he obtained a master's degree in business administration in 1971. The next year Powell, by then a major, took his first political position—that of White House fellow, a coveted internship in which middle managers are groomed for larger responsibilities. (Other alumni of the program include former San Antonio mayor and U.S. Housing and Urban Development secretary Henry Cisneros, former national security adviser Robert McFarlane, and CNN chairman and CEO Tom Johnson.) Guided by the insight that "budgets are to organizations what blood is to the circulatory system," as he later wrote in his autobiography, Powell obtained a position in the Office of Management and Budget (OMB), an agency that "had its hand on every department's jugular." For one year he served as assistant to the deputy director of the OMB, Frank C. Carlucci, an appointment that proved to be a career turning point: both Carlucci and Caspar W. Weinberger, then director of the OMB, were so impressed with his competence and quiet efficiency in the administration of President Richard Nixon that each in turn later lured him from a military command to serve as his deputy in Ronald Reagan's presidential administration.

In succeeding years Powell moved back and forth between military command posts and administrative assignments in the national-security establishment. In 1973 he was assigned as a battalion

commander in Korea; the next year he was rotated home to a staff job at the Pentagon. In 1975 Powell, who was by then a colonel, enrolled at the National War College. After completing seven of the nine scheduled months of study, he was given the command of the Second Brigade of the 101st Airborne Division at Fort Campbell, Kentucky. Despite having missed the last two months of the course, he graduated with distinction in 1976. During President Jimmy Carter's administration, Powell served as senior military assistant to the deputy defense secretary and, briefly in 1979, as executive assistant to Secretary of Energy Charles W. Duncan Jr. By that time Powell had been promoted to major general. For the first several months of the Reagan administration, he provided transitional support in the Defense Department under Carlucci, who had just become deputy secretary of defense under Weinberger. In the spring of 1981, Powell began two years as assistant commander of the Fourth Infantry Division at Fort Carson, Colorado.

In July 1983, while serving as deputy commander at Fort Leavenworth, Kansas, General Powell was summoned back to Washington at the request of Defense Secretary Weinberger. As Weinberger's senior military assistant for the next three years, Powell acquired a reputation as the ideal number-two man, carefully screening both information and visitors to ensure a free flow of ideas without burdening his boss with minor details. He also played a major role in organizing U.S. military operations, such as the invasion of Grenada and the bombing of Libya.

During Powell's stint as Weinberger's assistant, the Reagan administration—and in particular, the National Security Council under Robert McFarlane and John M. Poindexter—became involved in an illegal, covert operation to secure the release of American hostages in Lebanon and to raise funds for the Nicaraguan rebel forces, the Contras, by selling arms to Iran. The Iran-Contra affair, as the scandal later became known, led to the appointment of a special prosecutor, Lawrence E. Walsh. Walsh eventually charged Secretary Weinberger with withholding information from Congress about aid to the Contras; however, on December 24, 1992, a few days before the trial was scheduled to begin, an outgoing President George Herbert Walker Bush pardoned the former secretary of defense.

While the pardon put an abrupt end to the proceedings against Weinberger, the investigation, as detailed in a voluminous report by Walsh, also raised questions about Powell's role in the affair. Although Powell was never implicated in any wrongdoing, there was speculation that he may have suppressed information in an effort to cover for his boss. In a 1987 sworn deposition quoted by David Corn for *Salon.com* (March 20, 2000), Powell told investigators looking for documentary evidence that "the secretary, to my knowledge, did not keep a diary." But in a sworn affidavit submitted to Walsh in 1992, Powell recalled that "during the period I worked with Secretary Weinberger

. . . I observed on his desk a small pad of white paper, approximately 5" by 7". He would jot down on this pad in abbreviated form various calls and events during the day. I viewed it as his personal diary." (In 1992, the charge against Weinberger was withholding information; the diary had turned up in 1991.)

In his final report, as quoted by Corn, Walsh wrote that Powell's 1987 deposition statement "hardly constituted full disclosure," that it had been "designed to protect Weinberger," and that it was "at least misleading." However, he also noted that "it would have been difficult to prove that [Powell's 1987] deposition testimony was intentionally false." In a 1992 letter to the court overseeing Walsh, Powell accused the special prosecutor of attempting "to impugn my honor," as quoted by Corn. He further explained that "I was asked by congressional staff in 1987 whether Mr. Weinberger kept any records at all of his daily activities. I replied truthfully that he took notes, but did not have a diary—a permanent record summarizing important events. My 1992 affidavit, on the other hand, focused in depth on the notes I said he took and my understanding that the notes were personal. . . . I described his notes [in 1992] as a diary to convey the idea that they were private and personal, as opposed to an official record."

Meanwhile, in June 1986 Powell had eagerly accepted another infantry command, this time as commanding general of the Fifth Corps, a force of 72,000 troops stationed in Frankfurt, Germany. Along with the assignment went a temporary promotion to lieutenant general. Just six months later, however, he received a call from his former superior, Frank Carlucci, who had just been named to succeed Admiral Poindexter as national security adviser. Carlucci asked Powell several times to join him as his deputy in the White House, but each time Powell declined, explaining that too much of his career had already been diverted to policy positions and that he enjoyed his new military duties. Only after President Reagan himself called to repeat Carlucci's request did the general reluctantly agree to return to Washington in January 1987, explaining: "I'm a serviceman, a soldier, and it looked like my service might be of greater use here."

At Carlucci's urging, Powell reorganized the president's national security staff along the lines recommended by the Tower Commission, which President Reagan had created to investigate the Iran-Contra scandal. Eschewing Poindexter's proclivity for secrecy and compartmentalized relationships, Powell created clear lines of authority and broadened the dialogue to include all interested parties. "I am a great believer that the interagency process works best," Powell told Don Oberdorfer for the Washington Post (March 23, 1987), "when everybody has a chance to say his piece and get his positions out on the table . . . [so] that when we forward the final decision package to the president or present it to him orally, everybody

who played knows he has been properly represented and had his day in court."

On November 5, 1987 President Reagan named Carlucci to succeed Weinberger as secretary of defense and promoted Powell to national security adviser. As head of the National Security Council, Powell took a prominent role in the Reagan administration's unsuccessful efforts—made despite the steady trickle of new information regarding the Iran-Contra scandal—to win congressional support for $36 million in military aid for the Contras. He also played an important part in coordinating the December 1987 summit meeting between President Reagan and Soviet leader Mikhail S. Gorbachev, which resulted in the signing of the intermediate-range nuclear forces (INF) treaty. (As a result of that treaty, the Soviet Union for the first time agreed to mutual on-site inspection as a means of enforcing an arms-control agreement.) Powell opposed heavy spending on the Strategic Defense Initiative, or "Star Wars," program.

At the end of Reagan's second term, in January 1989, Powell briefly returned to the field as commander in chief of the Forces Command, headquartered at Fort McPherson, Georgia. In September 1989, however, he returned to Washington after President George H. W. Bush named him chairman of the Joint Chiefs of Staff. At 52, Powell was the youngest man—as well as the first African-American—to occupy the American military's top post.

In the months leading up to the 1991 Persian Gulf War, Powell's concern for the safety of his subordinates (and perhaps, to a lesser extent, his distrust of civilian authorities) led him to advocate nonintervention, and—after that was rejected as an option—military restraint. Between the Iraqi invasion of Kuwait, on August 2, 1990, and the beginning of the allied military strike, the following January (after Iraq's leader, Saddam Hussein, had ignored the U.S.–imposed deadline for withdrawing his troops), Powell argued that economic sanctions and diplomacy ought to be given more time to work. According to some reports, he even favored abandoning Kuwait and drawing the proverbial line in the sand at the Saudi Arabian border. Further, Powell is reported to have expressed concerns that war with Iraq might trigger an anti-Western backlash among Arab states, or that it might devolve into a prolonged war of attrition. His views brought him into conflict with other administration officials, especially then–secretary of defense Richard R. Cheney, who argued for a swift, large-scale military strike. At one point, as John Barry and Evan Thomas related in Newsweek (March 5, 2001), Cheney grew so exasperated with Powell's unwillingness to cooperate that he drew the general aside. "Colin, you're talking policy and that's not your job," the secretary reportedly said. "I want you to give me military advice. Stop talking policy."

The decision to conduct a large-scale military operation carried the day, and on January 17, 1991, the United States led Operation Desert Storm, the allied attack against Iraq. That same evening, Powell appeared on national television and announced the American strategy for fighting the Iraqi army: "First we're going to cut it off, and then we're going to kill it." Despite that blustery declaration, Powell continued behind the scenes to advocate restraint. Only two days after American troops began the brief, successful ground invasion of Kuwait and Iraq, Powell urged President Bush to declare a ceasefire—against the wishes of military leaders including General H. Norman Schwarzkopf, the commander in chief of the United States Central Command, who wanted more time to pursue Hussein's elite Republican Guard units and to advance toward Baghdad, the Iraqi capital. On this point, Powell prevailed—with deleterious results, according to some of his critics, since shortly after the ceasefire Republican Guard units helped secure Hussein's hold on power by brutally suppressing civilian uprisings that had been encouraged by the United States. In an article published in *Foreign Affairs* (Winter 1992/1993) two years after the war, however, Powell defended his position. "Even if Hussein had waited for us to enter Baghdad," he wrote, "and even if we had been able to capture him, what purpose would it have served? And would serving that purpose have been worth the many more casualties that would have occurred? Would it have been worth the inevitable follow-up: major occupation forces in Iraq for years to come and a very expensive and complex American proconsulship in Baghdad? Fortunately for America, reasonable people at the time thought not. They still do."

Meanwhile, as allied warplanes trapped and destroyed retreating Iraqi forces on the highway joining Kuwait City and Baghdad, Powell expressed concern that the resulting carnage would tarnish the military's reputation. "We don't want to be seen as killing for the sake of killing," Powell advised Bush, as quoted by Barry and Thomas. (While some human-rights groups have said the attack on the so-called "highway of death" constituted a war crime in violation of a Geneva Convention ban on attacking defenseless soldiers, the Pentagon stated that the retreating Iraqis were planning to regroup and attack.)

In 1992 and 1993 Powell once again demonstrated his reluctance to commit armed forces abroad by opposing U.S. intervention in Bosnia, a region then suffering a brutal war and an "ethnic cleansing" campaign carried out by nationalist extremists in the wake of the disintegration of Yugoslavia. In fact, Powell opposed intervention so strongly that he was against even airdrops of food, fearing that such action would inevitably lead to deeper involvement in a protracted conflict. When confronted by Madeleine Albright, then ambassador to the United Nations (and later secretary of state), Powell responded that American troops were "not toy soldiers to be moved around on some sort of global game board," as quoted by Barry and Thomas. "In 1991, I was asked why the U.S. could not assume a 'limited' role in Bosnia," he later wrote in his autobiography. "I had been engaged in limited military involvements before, in Vietnam for starters. I said, 'As soon as they tell me it's limited, it means they do not care whether you achieve a result or not. As soon as they tell me "surgical," I head for the bunker.' I criticized the pseudo-policy of establishing a U.S. 'presence' without a defined mission in trouble spots. This approach had cost the lives of 241 Marines in Lebanon."

Powell notably abandoned his opposition to military intervention in late 1992 and early 1993, when he endorsed the deployment of U.S. troops to Somalia. (The East African country was then suffering a famine caused largely by an ongoing civil war.) Some suggested that Powell may have been moved to reevaluate his noninterventionist views by political pressure at home, or by humanitarian motives. Others, however, have alleged that the general changed his mind in an attempt to preempt orders from a newly inaugurated President Bill Clinton to send troops to Bosnia. (According to this argument, Powell felt that it would be less risky to send troops to Somalia and that the president would be disinclined to intervene in two simultaneous conflicts.) By the time 18 American special-operations soldiers (and more than 500 Somalis) were killed in the Battle of Mogadishu, in October 1993, Powell was no longer chairman of the Joint Chiefs, and thus largely managed to escape blame for that debacle. Still, several members of the Clinton administration—including the president himself—have bitterly suggested that Powell did in fact bear some of the responsibility. (According to Powell's critics, the general had helped escalate the conflict by urging American forces to arrest Somali general Mohammed Farrah Aidid but had refused to authorize the military backup necessary for such an operation.)

Powell articulated his views on the appropriate use of American military force—informally referred to as the "Powell doctrine"—in an article published in the winter 1992–93 issue of *Foreign Affairs*. Simply expressed, the Powell doctrine states that the U.S. should intervene militarily only as a last resort; that when it does intervene, it must have clearly defined political and military goals; and that in such cases, "decisive means and results are always to be preferred, even if they are not always possible." (Also in the article, Powell wrote that the U.S. and its allies had used "overwhelming force quickly and decisively" in the Gulf War; many in the media seized on the words "overwhelming force" to sum up the general's military philosophy.) Before going to war, Powell wrote, policymakers must be able to answer a series of questions: "Is the political objective we seek to achieve important, clearly defined and understood? Have all other nonviolent policy means failed? Will military force achieve the objective? At what cost? Have the gains and risks been analyzed? How might the situation that we seek to alter, once it is altered by force, develop further and what might be the consequences?" While Powell's article offered a fairly elaborate underpinning for his foreign-policy views, many observed that the general had strayed from that scheme in the past, most noticeably in his support for military involvement in Somalia. Powell, for his part, had stressed in the *Foreign Policy* article that his views were intended as a set of rough guidelines rather than as a statement of official policy. "There is . . . no fixed set of rules for the use of military force," he wrote. "To set one up is dangerous."

In spite of Powell's behind-the-scenes opposition to the Gulf War, his public role as chairman of the Joint Chiefs brought him widespread popularity in the wake of the conclusive American victory. As a result, both the Democratic and Republican parties began courting him soon after he retired from the military, on September 30, 1993. Nevertheless, Powell declined to publicly affiliate himself with either party; he chose rather to spend the next two years writing *My American Journey*, his autobiography, which was published in September 1995.

The appearance of *My American Journey* brought to a feverish pitch the speculation that Powell was considering a run for the presidency. Although it was unclear whether he would run as a Democrat, a Republican, or an Independent—if indeed he chose to run at all—the retired general's charisma and strong independent streak appealed to a wide range of centrist voters. While Powell's more liberal social views appealed to many Democrats, moderate Republicans found his emphasis on limited government, fiscal responsibility, and individual responsibility attractive. At the height of his popularity, in late 1995, national polls showed Powell beating both President Clinton and Senator Bob Dole of Kansas, the respective front-runners (and later nominees) of the Democratic and Republican parties, in one-on-one races in 1996. The polls further indicated that if Powell were to run as an Independent in a three-way race against both Dole and Clinton, he would have tied the president with slightly more than one-third of the vote. (Dole would have finished third.)

On November 8, 1995 Powell put an end to speculation by announcing that he would not run for president. He also declared that he would join the Republican Party. (Up to this point Powell, who had served in both Democratic and Republican administrations, had been tight-lipped about his party affiliation.) To enter the race, he said at a press conference, as quoted by Martin Fletcher in the London *Times* (November 9, 1995), would require "a passion to run the race and win the quest; the kind of passion and commitment that I felt every day of my 35 years as a soldier; the kind of passion I do not yet have for political life. For me to pretend otherwise would not be honest to myself or to other people, and because such a life requires a calling

that I do not yet hear, I cannot go forward. I will not be a candidate for president or any other elective office in 1996." Powell further explained that a presidential race would have required too many sacrifices from his family. "General Colin Powell ran his presidential campaign exactly as he would have liked to run the Gulf war," David Frum wrote for *Commentary* (January 1996), "a massive build-up of force culminating in a strategic withdrawal."

After retreating from the presidential race, Powell took advantage of his high profile to promote "America's Promise—the Alliance for Youth," a national campaign to promote volunteerism and to address such problems as violence, drugs, and pregnancy among children and adolescents. According to the organization's official Web site, America's Promise seeks to fulfill its goals by providing the nation's youth with five promises: an ongoing relationship with caring adults; safe places, with structured activities, to go to during nonschool hours; a "healthy start and future," including adequate health care and health education; marketable skills developed through internships, apprenticeships, and a sound education; and opportunities to "give back" through community service. "If we can give kids these basics," Powell told Laura B. Randolph for *Ebony* (July 1999), "we can transform them from potential delinquents and dependents into good citizens. It can't happen overnight, but if we keep at it, it can happen child by child, street by street, neighborhood by neighborhood, city by city." Much of Powell's work for America's Promise involved traveling the country to lecture and solicit contributions from various civic and commercial organizations.

Although he had never ceased to be a media presence—even in semiretirement—Powell reappeared on the national political stage in July 2000, when he spoke at the Republican National Convention in Philadelphia. In his address, Powell once again displayed an independent streak, voicing support for some aspects of the Republican Party platform while criticizing others. He recommended, for example, that policymakers "experiment prudently with school voucher programs to see if they help." (He was referring to a system by which parents could apply toward private school the funds allotted for their children's public-school education.) He defended the education record of the 2000 Republican presidential nominee, George W. Bush, pointing out that as governor of Texas, Bush had "ended social promotions. He increased state funding for education by eight billion dollars. He put new textbooks in every school. He strengthened standardized testing in all Texas public schools, he insisted on teacher competency, and he expanded the charter school movement." At the same time, Powell went on to voice sharp criticism of those in the Republican Party who "miss no opportunity to roundly and loudly condemn affirmative action that helped a few thousand black kids get an education," but who fail to speak out "over affirmative action for lobbyists who load our tax codes with preferences for special interests." He further warned that "the issue of race still casts a shadow over our society, despite the impressive progress we have made over the last 40 years to overcome the legacy of our troubled past." In a post-convention interview with Margaret Carlson for *Time* (August 14, 2000), Powell explained that he had viewed the address as a "great opportunity to talk to millions, to tell Republicans the problem is us, not the kids. I wanted to shake up the way they see things." Powell stumped for Bush in the final days of the 2000 presidential campaign.

On December 16, 2000 Bush, then president-elect, named Powell as his secretary of state, praising the retired general as "an American hero, an American example and a great American story," according to Alison Mitchell, writing for the *New York Times* (December 17, 2000). For his part, Powell sought to reassure those who feared an isolationist foreign policy from the new administration; he also expressed his support for Bush's proposed missile-defense shield. Although some voices questioned the applicability of the Powell doctrine to the post–Cold War world, the choice of Powell was generally applauded in the press—though perhaps more as a conciliatory gesture after a fiercely contended election than because of the retired general's diplomatic credentials. (Bush's opponent in the general election, Vice President Al Gore, had won the popular vote; Bush had triumphed in the Electoral College following highly controversial vote recounts in Florida.) Powell was confirmed by the Senate and sworn in on January 20, 2001 as the 65th U.S. secretary of state.

Although many expected Powell to dominate the Bush administration, given his charisma, celebrity, and global stature, the secretary of state seemed a curiously marginalized figure during his first months in office. Powell did register a number of successes: his handling of the diplomatic standoff with China, after a Chinese fighter jet forced a U.S. surveillance plane to make an emergency landing in Chinese territory following a midair collision, received kudos, as did his success at raising morale among State Department staffers. But his setbacks were prominent, too, suggesting a lack of influence in the administration. His plan to reinvigorate porous U.N. sanctions against Iraq by making them "smarter" foundered due to lack of Russian support, and he was publicly humiliated by the Bush administration on at least two occasions: first, one day after he announced the administration's intention to resume Clinton-era negotiations of a missile-proliferation arrangement with North Korea, the White House, angry at South Korea's lack of support for a missile-defense shield, forced him to retract his position. Later, Bush's rejection of the Kyoto Treaty caught Powell, then on a diplomatic mission to promote missile defense in Europe, by surprise. (Powell was delegated to defend the rejection of the treaty, a move that rankled many Europeans.) "That's one where, you know, I would have done it differently," Powell told Johanna McGeary for *Time* (September 10, 2001).

According to McGeary, the primary source of Powell's early frustrations was a "fault line" between his attitudes and those of the rest of the administration. "Powell is a multilateralist; other Bush advisers are unilateralists. He's internationalist; they're America first. If you wanted to put a label on Powell's foreign outlook, you could call it 'compassionate conservatism'; the others share the second notion but not the first. He is often seen as the Administration's force of moderation, charged with checking its more extreme enthusiasms."

It was initially unclear whether Powell would take a more prominent role in the administration following the September 11, 2001 terrorist attacks on New York City and Washington, D.C., since the Bush administration, in an effort to present a unified front, was tight-lipped about the specific recommendations of—and differences of opinion between—individual Cabinet members and senior advisers. Nevertheless, in the weeks before the American-led military strike against Afghanistan, which began on October 7, 2001, Powell appeared to be urging the administration to exercise restraint. "Well, let's not assume there will be a large-scale war," he said at a press conference, as quoted by William Kristol for the *Washington Post* (September 25, 2001). "I don't know that we should even consider a large-scale war of the conventional sort." While some at the Department of Defense—most notably Deputy Defense Secretary Paul Wolfowitz—pressed for military action against Iraq (and even Lebanon) in addition to Afghanistan, Powell reportedly wanted to limit U.S. military involvement to Afghanistan alone. He further stressed the importance of coalition building in the Arab world in order to shore up support for the American campaign.

During a September 23 appearance on *Meet the Press*, the secretary was questioned about the applicability of the Powell doctrine to the crisis—specifically, about what was thought to be the doctrine's call for "overwhelming force," in light of President Bush's much-repeated point that the American campaign would proceed in a new and unconventional manner. "I've never talked about overwhelming force," Powell responded, as quoted by the *Washington Post* (October 7, 2001). "I've always talked about decisive force, meaning you go to the point of decision and that's where you apply decisive force. In the Persian Gulf War 10 years ago, you had an army sitting out there, easily identifiable, there it was waiting to be attacked, and we applied decisive force against the Iraqi army. It's different this time, and we shouldn't see this in the same context as if there is a large enemy out there that we plan to attack in conventional ways. If the president decides that this is what we should do and have to do, I can assure you that our military will have plans that will go against their weaknesses and not get trapped in ways that previous armies have gotten trapped in Afghanistan."

Powell is married to the former Alma Vivian Johnson. The couple have two daughters, Linda and Annmarie; a son, Michael, who currently serves as chairman of the Federal Communications Commission, a position to which he was appointed by the Bush administration in early 2001; and two grandchildren. In his free time Powell enjoys playing racquetball and restoring old Volvos. — P.K.

Suggested Reading: *Foreign Affairs* p32+ Winter 1992–93, p102+ Nov./Dec. 1995; (London) *Times* p1 Nov 9, 1995; *Nation* (on-line) May 2, 2001; *New Republic* p17+ Jan. 1, 2001; *New Republic* (on-line) Apr. 17, 1995; *New York Times* A p1 Dec 17, 2000; *Newsweek* p38+ Dec 25, 2001, with photos, p34+ Mar 5, 2001, with photos; *Political Science Quarterly* p625+ Winter 1995–96; *Time* p88+ Mar. 13, 1995, with photos, p24+ Sep. 10, 2001, with photo; *Vital Speeches of the Day* p651+ Aug. 15, 2000; *Washington Post* A p21 Apr. 17, 2001; Powell, Colin L. *My American Journey*, 1995

Radiohead

Musical group

Greenwood, Colin
Jan. 26, 1969–

Greenwood, Jonny
Nov. 5, 1971–

O'Brien, Ed
Apr. 15, 1969–

Selway, Phil
May 23, 1967–

Yorke, Thom
Oct. 7, 1968–

Address: WASTE, P.O. Box 322, Oxford OX4 1EY, England

Pigeonholed at first with the "alternative" rock bands that debuted in the wake of Nirvana's success in the early 1990s, the British group Radiohead has continued to explore new musical idioms and to bring experimental ideas and structures into the mainstream, thereby inviting comparisons to performers ranging from Pink Floyd to the Beatles. Radiohead's music—described as ethereal, dense, mournful, and majestic—features the tenor voice of its lead singer and lyricist, Thom Yorke, whose sound is among the most distinctive in rock music today. Yorke founded Radiohead in collaboration with the bassist Colin Greenwood in about 1988; shortly afterward, the group expanded to include the guitarist Ed O'Brien, the drummer Phil Selway, and the guitarist Jonny Greenwood. While the guitars that dominated their early work are still occasionally prominent, their increasing use of synthesizers and sophisticated production technology has pushed the boundaries between electronic music and rock.

Radiohead's first hit single, the so-called loser anthem "Creep," was released in 1992. *OK Computer* (1997), the band's third album, is widely considered Radiohead's masterpiece; several magazines have hailed it as one of the greatest, if not *the* greatest, rock album ever recorded. The group's members—five natives of Great Britain—have downplayed their experimental edge; as Thom Yorke told a writer for *Entertainment Weekly* (October 24, 1997), "We write pop songs. As time has gone on, we've gotten more into pushing our material as far as it can go. But there was no intention of it being 'art.' It's a reflection of all the disparate things we were listening to when we recorded it." Radiohead's influences range from the jazz bassist and composer Charles Mingus to the jazz harpist and pianist Alice Coltrane to the electronic artist Richard D. James, known as Aphex Twin, to the rock icon David Bowie. Radiohead's lyrics, many of which criticize aspects of contemporary life, contain much ingenious wordplay. Speaking about *OK Computer*, Yorke told the writer for *Entertainment Weekly*, "If it's about anything, it's just dealing with noise and fear, and trying to find something beautiful in it"—a statement that might serve as a summing-up of the band's philosophy.

The members of Radiohead were all born within four and a half years of one another in England (with the exception of Yorke, who was born in Scotland and spent his early years there). The oldest of the five is Phil Selway, whose date of birth is May 23, 1967; the youngest is Jonny Greenwood (November 5, 1971). In between are Thom Yorke (October 7, 1968), Colin Greenwood (January 26, 1969), and Ed O'Brien (April 15, 1969). All of them attended the Abingdon School, a private boys' boarding and day school near Oxford. Colin Greenwood and Yorke became friends there when they discovered that they shared a liking for both cross-dressing and the post-punk bands Joy Division and Magazine. They decided to form a band themselves. Their first recruit was Ed O'Brien, whom they approached because he seemed "cool," as one of them put it, and reminded them of the British rock icon Morrissey, the vocalist of the band the Smiths. Christening themselves On a Friday, the trio played a few gigs in 1988, accompanied by a drum machine. After the machine broke down, they sought out Phil Selway, who was playing with another band but agreed to join them. Before long Greenwood's younger brother, Jonny, asked to become a member of their group. Although they considered him too young and inexperienced, they occasionally allowed him to perform with them, on harmonica.

The members of Radiohead (left to right): Thom Yorke, Phil Selway, Ed O'Brien, Jonny Greenwood, and Colin Greenwood

Rankin/Dazed & Confused/Retna

Each member of the band attended a different college. Yorke studied fine art and literature at the University of Exeter; O'Brien majored in politics at the University of Manchester; Colin Greenwood and Selway both studied English, the former at Cambridge University and the latter at the University of Liverpool; and Jonny Greenwood dropped out of college after three months. When the young men returned home on school holidays, they practiced and performed together. After the last of the four older musicians graduated from college, they re-formed the group, in Oxford, with Jonny Greenwood as a full member on guitar. Inspired by the title of a song on the 1986 Talking Heads album *True Stories*, they changed their name to Radiohead. After their first official gig, in 1991, they received more than 20 contract offers from record companies. They still had not made a deal when, in early May 1992, they released the EP *Drill* and opened shows for such established rock acts as PJ Harvey, Tears for Fears, and James. Soon afterward they signed to the EMI/Capitol record label and, in September 1992, released their first single, "Creep." The alienation and romantic frustration expressed in the song—its lyrics proclaim, "I'm a creep / I'm a weirdo / What the hell am I doing here? / I don't belong here"—were to take their place among the group's major themes. "Self-loathing is something we can all relate to," Ed O'Brien explained, as quoted by David Sprague in *Billboard* (May 15, 1993). The single became a minor hit in England. It was followed by the singles "Anyone Can Play Guitar" and "Pop Is Dead."

In February 1993 Radiohead released their first album, *Pablo Honey*, which consisted primarily of mid-tempo, plaintive songs with a heavy focus on guitars. For the most part both the British and American music press ignored the recording. Although noting that it offered "clever lyrics and good hooks," Mario Mundoz wrote for the *Los Angeles Times* (June 27, 1993) that the album did not "really deliver anything you haven't heard before, steering too close to Smiths-like melodies and trying ever so hard to be depressed in the way the Cure popularized." Despite the lack of attention, Radiohead continued to work hard, embarking that summer on a tour of Europe, during which they opened for other acts. The band's fortunes suddenly changed when American MTV and alternative-radio stations started playing "Creep" heavily, apparently having recognized that the song's self-deprecatory lyrics and sharp guitar bursts fit comfortably with the grunge-rock scene that was so prominent at that time. The band soon supported Belly and Tears for Fears on a U.S. tour, during which they found that most concertgoers were interested only in "Creep." Thanks to its success in the U.S., "Creep" was re-released in England at the end of 1993, and this time it made the Top 10, while *Pablo Honey* sold enough copies to earn a gold certification. Radiohead spent the summer of 1994 performing dates around the world. During the year that followed their return to England, the group released *Iron Lung*, a series of EPs, which featured a continuation of the *Pablo Honey* sound with an increased emphasis on low-key acoustic numbers.

Eager to change the media perception that they were a one-hit wonder, Radiohead entered the studio with the producer John Leckie to record their sophomore album. The first results were heard in February 1995, when the single "High and Dry," a soaring acoustic ballad and their most sophisticated record until then, was released. In *The Bends*, which was released the following month, the group added a stronger dose of synthesizers and offered more dynamics than on their debut album. The lyrics, again mostly self-deprecatory, this time tackled the themes of isolation and loneliness as they applied to society in general, rather than just the singer; most critics found them to be of a higher quality than the group's earlier efforts. "Fake Plastic Trees," a mostly acoustic song about lonely people in an age defined by marketing, was released as a single in May 1995 and quickly became a fan favorite.

The Bends received strong reviews from some members of the press, who compared Radiohead favorably to such rock legends as U2 and complimented the band for writing songs that were more mature than their earlier work. "What makes *The Bends* so remarkable is that it marries such ambitious, and often challenging, instrumental soundscapes to songs that are at their cores hauntingly melodic and accessible," Stephen Thomas Erlewine wrote for the *All Music Guide* (on-line). Other critics were less friendly. "The sonics are frequently more compelling than the songs they embellish," Mark Jenkins complained in the *Washington Post* (April 7, 1995). American radio and MTV ignored the singles from *The Bends*, which were very different from "Creep," and record sales were low. Similarly, in Britain, during a summer in which the airwaves were dominated by anthemic Britpop by the likes of Blur, Oasis, and Pulp, Radiohead's somber musings were not popular.

Meanwhile, the band continued to perform live, supporting R.E.M. on their *Monster* tour. The third single of *The Bends*, "Just," was released in August 1995, and thanks to its louder guitars and stark, haunting video, Radiohead began to be noticed again. In 1996 rock radio and MTV began to play "Fake Plastic Trees" in heavy rotation, and *The Bends* returned to the British Top 10 and went gold in America.

During the first half of 1996, the band toured to promote *The Bends*. Then they began work on their third album. Released in July 1997 and titled *OK Computer*, the album found Radiohead moving in distinctly new directions, combining progressive-rock experimentation with punk fury. For some tracks the band abandoned conventional song structures and used various synthesizers and production effects, taking their cue from such diverse sources as the film music of Ennio Morricone, *Bitches Brew*–era Miles Davis, and 1970s German psychedelia. Yorke's lyrics, which in some songs were much more abstract than before, did not dwell on his personal life. "I came to the realization I was being selfish in the past," he was quoted as saying on *MTV* (on-line), "and that was a good thing. It happened after *The Bends*. A drunk bloke comes up in the bar or a girl comes up in the street and says, 'Thank you, that record helped me through a difficult time.' And you stop being the selfish wanker you've always been. . . . I think there was a genuine point where it really was important for me to say things on a personal level to get these things sorted out for myself. But once it was out, it was done. With this album, I am moving on."

Containing multiple sections and ambitious lyrics, "Paranoid Android," the first single from *OK Computer*, was compared to Queen's multi-part operatic single "Bohemian Rhapsody." "Please could you stop the noise," Yorke sang, "I'm trying to get some rest / From all the unborn chicken voices in my head." The surreal animated video of "Paranoid Android" attracted a lot of attention as well. The singles "Karma Police" and "No Surprises" received heavy airplay in both England and the United States. *OK Computer* was acclaimed in the press, with several magazines naming it "album of the year." Noting for *All Music Guide* (on-line) that it had "establishe[d] Radiohead as one of the most inventive and rewarding guitar-rock bands of the '90s," Stephen Thomas Erlewine declared that *OK Computer* was "a thoroughly astonishing demonstration of musical virtuosity, and becomes even [more] impressive with repeated listens, which reveal subtleties like electronica rhythms, eerie keyboards, odd time signatures, and complex syncopations." Apparently surprised by all the praise, Radiohead's members insisted that they didn't think the record worthy of the hype. Yorke told Aidin Vaziri for *Guitar Player* (October 1997), for example, "We got bored with being just a rock band, and we started considering what else was going on around us. Rock wasn't speaking to us. There was no intention to be difficult. Every record we make is, to some extent, the band absorbing stuff we've fallen in love with and then attempting to pay homage to it—and failing." The EP *Airbag/How Am I Driving* (1998), released while the band was touring, featured all the bonus tracks on the singles from *OK Computer*.

Radiohead returned to the studio in 1999 to record their highly anticipated fourth album. Difficulties soon arose, however, because Yorke suffered a bout of writer's block and then, having become fascinated by such experimental electronica acts as Aphex Twin and Autechre (Sean Booth and Rob Brown), would often bring only programmed drum machines or other electronic sound equipment to the studio. "It was about generating bits of work that may be incomplete and may not be going anywhere," Yorke told Danny Eccleston for *Q* (October 1999). "And by the time you finish it, it may be unrecognizable. But it might be far better than what you started with. That's what I hoped we were trying to do—regardless of where the music was coming from, and regardless of which members of the band were involved." His colleagues struggled with Yorke's new vision. "If you're going to make a different-sounding record," O'Brien told Eccleston, "you have to change the methodology. And it's scary—everyone feels insecure. I'm a guitarist and suddenly it's like, well, there are no guitars on this track, or no drums. [We] had to get our heads round that. It was a test of the band, I think."

Despite such stumbling blocks, Radiohead continued recording, and in 2000 its new tracks began to be heavily circulated over the Internet, on Napster and other servers. Although arguments about choices of songs for the new album almost caused the musicians to split up, they launched a tour of Europe and Great Britain over the summer, during which they introduced many of their new songs. *Kid A*, released in October 2000, surprised many listeners by its reliance on a minimalist electronic sound and the near absence of conventional songs. In one song, "The National Anthem," the group incorporated avant-garde, Mingus-style horns. In others, Jonny Greenwood experimented with little-known instruments, using the Ondes Martenot, an electronic instrument that consists of a keyboard, a ribbon, and a ring and is best known for its use in the work of the 20th-century French composer Olivier Messiaen and in the theme of the television series *Star Trek*. Its unusualness notwithstanding, *Kid A* debuted on the American and British album charts at number one, thus becoming the first British album to hit the number-one spot in the U.S. since 1997.

Although critical reaction to *Kid A* was more reserved than it had been for *OK Computer*, most reviewers seemed to like it. In *Entertainment Weekly* (October 6, 2000), David Browne wrote, "Songs float by on the faintest of heartbeat pulses, intergalactic noises streaking like comets across the melodies. Ecclesiastical keyboards gently nudge the songs along." Browne concluded that despite its weaknesses, "it is a genuinely challenging work in a generally unchallenging time." In *All Music Guide* (on-line), Stephen Thomas Erlewine judged *Kid A* to be "a record that's intentionally difficult to grasp, which makes it seem deeper on first listen than it actually is. . . . The music is never seductive—it's self-consciously alienating, and while that can be intriguing at first, there's not enough underneath the surface to make Radiohead's relentless experimentation satisfying. Still, an experiment that yields mixed results still yields results, and there are some moments here that positively shimmer with genius." "With us, it's never going to be a case of 'let's tear up the blueprint and start from scratch,'" Jonny Greenwood told Simon Reynolds for the *Wire* (July 2001). "When the *Kid A* reviews came out accusing us of being wilfully difficult, I was like, 'If that was true, we'd have done a much better job of it.' It's not that challenging—everything's still four minutes long, it's melodic." The band's decision not to release any singles from *Kid A* or to make videos related to it prompted some in the press to accuse Radiohead's members of pomposity. In response, O'Brien explained to Oldham, "There weren't any singles of *Kid A* because there weren't any singles on the record as far as we're concerned. We didn't do videos because there weren't any singles. There's no great mystique to it."

In June 2001 Radiohead released their fifth album, *Amnesiac*, culled from the same recording sessions that generated *Kid A*. Although expected to be a return to the more conventional sound of *The Bends*, the record turned out to be even more dense and experimental than *Kid A*. Nevertheless, it topped the charts in the United Kingdom, while hitting the number-two position in the United States. As with *Kid A*, the album drew heavily from minimalist electronica, with lyrics heavy with paranoid phrases that were reminiscent of nursery rhymes. "You can see the shared genes: the jazz spasms and electronic pulsings, the chill blood, and most of all, the chronic hypersensitivity to the world outside," Victoria Segal noted in her favorable review for *NME* (on-line). "It feels like a record that would blister if you touched it, allergic to modern life, shut away in a protective tent. It reports on half-remembered contact and conflict, blurred images seen through milky plastic." "The human touch and its visceral impact are no longer central to the music," Jon Parales wrote in his critique of the album for *Rolling Stone* (June 21, 2001, on-line). "The songs on *Amnesiac* are barely populated vistas, subdued and ambient but not at all soothing. Electric guitars are scarce, and never heroic. Instead, there are semiautomatic rhythm loops, indecipherable background voices, pockets of static, and writhing string arrangements with electronic penumbrae. And when the band does write a melody with a grand arc, the arrangements leave Yorke sounding not triumphant but stranded." Stephen Thomas Earlewine, in the *All Music Guide* (on-line), wrote, "*Amnesiac* plays like a streamlined version of *Kid A*, complete with blatant electronica moves and production that sacrifices songs for atmosphere." Showing no signs of slowing down, Radiohead revealed in August 2001 that they were already working on a new album, to be released sometime in 2002.

Because of the somber take on modern life in their music, many listeners have assumed that the members of Radiohead are cynical and depressed, but the men have insisted that that is not the case. Many of their lyrics, they have maintained, are based on one incident and do not reflect an overarching view of life. The performers are often described as low-key and polite; Yorke, however, who told Jon Wiederhorn for *Rolling Stone* (September 7, 1995) that he has "always been melodramatic about everything," is known for his emotional outbursts. "The only time I feel comfortable is when I'm in front of a mike," Yorke confessed to Wiederhorn. "I'm obsessed with the idea that I'm completely losing touch with who I am, and I've come to the conclusion that there isn't anything to Thom Yorke other than the guy that makes those painful songs." — G.O.

Suggested Reading: *Addicted to Noise* (on-line); *All Music Guide* (on-line); *Entertainment Weekly* p32+ Oct. 24, 1997; *Guitar Player* p27+ Oct. 1997, with photo; *New Music Express* (on-line)

Dec. 23, 2000; *Q* (on-line) Oct. 2000; *Rolling Stone* p19+ Sep.7, 1995, with photos

Selected Recordings: *Pablo Honey*, 1993; *The Bends*, 1995; *OK Computer*, 1997; *Kid A*, 2000; *Amnesiac*, 2001

STR/Archive Photos

Ralston, Joseph W.

Nov. 4, 1943– Commander in Chief, U.S. European Command; Supreme Allied Commander, Europe. Address: CMR 450, Box 7500, APO AE09705

On May 2, 2000 General Joseph W. Ralston succeeded General Wesley Clark as Supreme Allied Commander, Europe (SACEUR, in military parlance), more commonly known as the commander of the North Atlantic Treaty Organization (NATO). A career U.S. Air Force officer and four-star general who served as an F-105 fighter pilot in Vietnam, Ralston is the second member of the air force to lead NATO in the organization's 51-year history. (The first, Lauris Norstad, was appointed by President Dwight D. Eisenhower and served from 1956 to 1962.) Among his colleagues, Richard J. Newman wrote for *U.S. News & World Report* (June 16, 1997), Ralston is viewed as "a bright, proficient insider who moves smoothly in political circles. But he is also known as a status-quo, business-as-usual commander who has avoided grappling with critical issues the military faces—particularly whether a dramatic rethinking of force structure and strategy is needed to free up an extra $15 billion a year to upgrade planes, ships and other weapons."

Ralston became NATO's leader at a critical juncture in the organization's history. Throughout most of the Cold War, NATO had been the United States' and its allies' answer to the Warsaw Pact, a military alliance of the Soviet Union and Communist nations in Eastern Europe. With the political transformation of the Communist bloc in the late 1980s and the dissolution of the Warsaw Pact in July 1991, NATO began to reevaluate its role in both European and world affairs. In the absence of a common threat, NATO increasingly saw itself, in the words of a fact sheet posted on the NATO Web site on September 12, 2000, as "a catalyst for extending stability and security throughout Europe." In the 1990s the alliance sought to strengthen its relations with Russia and especially the Eastern European countries. NATO first offered the former Soviet satellites limited participation in the alliance, and eventually, in early 1999, accepted three former Communist bloc countries—Hungary, Poland, and the Czech Republic—as full members. A few weeks after that, NATO launched its first military action since its formation, in 1949: a campaign of air strikes against the Federal Republic of Yugoslavia. None of NATO's members had been attacked by Yugoslavia, nor were any national interests at stake; rather, NATO justified the operation as an effort to advance humanitarian goals by protecting ethnic Albanians from violence at the hands of the Serbian military in the Kosovo region of Serbia.

In the sphere of international relations, the notion of disinterested humanitarian intervention is widely regarded as problematic: as an editorial writer for the *Economist* (November 4, 1999) noted, in the Kosovo campaign "the West tore up the code of international conduct which forbids interference in the internal affairs of nation-states, and which has prevailed since the Treaty of Westphalia in 1648 [which brought an end to the Thirty Years War, in Europe]." Indeed, part of the reason why Russia and China objected so vociferously to NATO's action in Kosovo is that the two countries are wary of any precedent that could lead to an infringement of their own national sovereignty.

Ralston himself has suggested that, in the future, NATO will continue to develop and strengthen the internationalist role it took in Kosovo, and in particular, that it will become more closely involved in international politics. In a policy forum billed as "Aerospace Power and the Use of Force," as cited by *PR Newswire* (September 15, 1999, on-line), Ralston stated, "In Kosovo, I believe air power created the conditions for a diplomatic solution. That's how it's supposed to work." He added that the U.S. military will be used increasingly as a "tool in the diplomat's portfolio." Ralston has also suggested that beyond serving as a political instrument, NATO itself will assume certain diplomatic responsibilities. Upon taking command of the military alliance, Ralston announced that one of his top priorities would be enhancing NATO's relations with Russia. "Perhaps we have a window of opportunity now with [Russian] President [Vladimir] Putin taking over," he stated, as quoted by Linda D. Kozaryn in an on-line publication of the American Forces Press Service. "I look forward to meeting with my Russian military counterparts and seeing what we can do to build a better foundation for our relations."

Joseph W. Ralston was born in Hopkinsville, Kentucky, on November 4, 1943. During his grade-school years, his family moved to Norwood, Ohio, near Cincinnati. In high school Ralston took part in a variety of athletic activities, among them basket-ball, track, and cross-country running, and served as vice president of the local chapter of the National Honor Society. When he graduated, in 1961, his excellent scholastic record earned him a scholar-ship to nearby Miami University, in Oxford, Ohio. There, he joined the Air Force ROTC (Reserve Offi-cers' Training Corps).

Ralston's military career is somewhat unusual because, unlike many officers of comparable rank, he attended a civilian institution rather than a mili-tary academy. After he received a B.A. degree in chemistry, in 1965, he began training as a pilot at Laughlin Air Force Base, in Texas. He completed basic pilot training in 1966. Next, he transferred to Nellis Air Force Base, in Nevada, to begin combat crew training. One year later, during the Vietnam conflict, Ralston was stationed at the Kadena Air Base, in Japan, as a member of the 67th Tactical Fighter Squadron (later, the 12th Tactical Fighter Squadron). As an F-105 fighter pilot, he logged more than 2,500 flying hours, including 147 com-bat missions over Laos and North Vietnam.

After completing his active military service, Ral-ston returned to Nellis Air Force Base to work as an instructor pilot. Thereafter, he steadily rose through the air-force ranks, eventually becoming deputy chief of staff for plans and operations at U.S. Air Force Headquarters, in Washington, D.C., in 1994, and then commander, Headquarters Air Combat Command, in 1995. Along the way, he completed a master of arts degree in personnel management at Central Michigan University and studied at both the National War College, in Lang-ley, Virginia, and the John F. Kennedy School of Government at Harvard University, in Cambridge, Massachusetts.

In November 1995 Ralston was officially select-ed by the Department of Defense to succeed Admi-ral William A. Owens as the vice chairman of the Joint Chiefs of Staff, the second-highest-ranking position in the American military. According to Eric Schmitt in the New York Times (November 17, 1995), as vice chairman, Ralston was "expected to advance Admiral Owens's efforts to lead a broad technological revolution to equip and restructure the post-cold-war military to fight the nation's wars. This includes enhancing the military's com-bat surveillance and communications equipment, and making greater use of commercial technolo-gy." In March 1996, after his appointment was ap-proved by both President Bill Clinton and the U.S. Senate, Ralston began serving his two-year term as vice chairman.

For a while it was assumed that Ralston would eventually succeed General John Shalikashvili as chairman of the Joint Chiefs of Staff. In June 1997, however, after admitting to an adulterous affair with a CIA intelligence analyst in the 1980s, Ral-ston bowed to public pressure and reluctantly withdrew his name for consideration for the post—despite the continued support of Secretary of De-fense William S. Cohen. Explaining his decision in an official press release posted on the U.S. Depart-ment of Defense Web site on June 9, 1997, Ralston stated, "This is solely my decision, and I make it with a sense of regret. The regret is not for me per-sonally. . . . My regret is that the public discus-sion surrounding my potential nomination blurred the facts and gave the appearance of a double stan-dard regarding military justice." Specifically, Ral-ston was referring to the case of Lieutenant Kelly Flinn, the air force's first (and, at the time, only) fe-male B-52 bomber pilot. Shortly before news of Ralston's affair became public, Flinn had been forced to leave the military without an honorable discharge after admitting to adultery with the hus-band of an enlisted woman. (In fact, she narrowly escaped a court martial.) Since Flinn and her sup-porters had argued that military authorities were enforcing a double standard, and that a male officer would not have been forced to step down, Ral-ston's situation was popularly viewed as a test case for gender equity. Still, Ralston was never obliged to resign his commission. According to his sup-porters, that was because the general had never lied about his affair to his superiors, as Flinn had, and because Ralston had conducted his affair with a civilian and thus had never jeopardized military order. "The Army doesn't worry about adultery for the sake of adultery," Kenneth Bacon, a Pentagon spokesman, declared, as quoted by CNN (June 5, 1997, on-line). "The Army worries about adultery that could effect the chain of discipline." Accord-ing to Flinn, as quoted by the Economist, "What re-ally matters in these cases is not what really hap-pened but your gender, your rank and who you know."

In the wake of the scandal, it appeared that Ral-ston's prospects for further advancement had been irrevocably damaged. In addition to the loss of his chance to become chairman of the Joint Chiefs of Staff, his two-year appointment to the position of vice chairman was scheduled to expire in the spring of 1998. Thereafter, Ralston would be re-quired by law to either find a new military job within 60 days or retire. By early 1998, however, the commotion about Ralston's long-ago affair had subsided, and in January of that year, President Clinton quietly nominated the general for a second term. Ralston easily won the approval of the Senate Armed Services Committee; the only reference to the events of the previous June came when Senator John W. Warner, a Virginia Republican, praised Ralston for his dignified response to the controver-sy. "Given the unusual circumstances of what hap-pened," Warner said, as quoted by Eric Schmitt in the *New York Times* (February 5, 1998), "you and your wife and family handled that period in a commendable and professional manner." Even those senators who had previously expressed doubts about Ralston were apparently sufficiently impressed with his professional competence to renew his appointment.

Ralston's star got another boost when, in July 1999, Cohen chose him to replace Wesley Clark, an army general, as the military head of NATO. In nominating Ralston for the post, Cohen, as quoted by Elizabeth Becker for the *New York Times* (July 29, 1999), spoke highly of Ralston's "diplomatic skills, his war capabilities and his war record." There were also hints that Clark had rubbed the White House the wrong way during the Kosovo conflict. (An unidentified NATO official, for example, told John Barry and Christopher Dickey for *Newsweek* [August 9, 1999] that Clark "does get in people's knickers to some extent.") While the Clinton administration had strongly opposed the deployment of ground troops in Yugoslavia, for fear that heavy American casualties would result, Clark had insisted that the U.S. Army ought to be involved. Clark was eventually overruled, and the role of NATO in the Balkans was restricted to a 78-day bombing campaign. In announcing that Ralston would be replacing Clark, administration officials downplayed such disagreements between the White House and Clark. National security adviser Samuel R. Berger, for example, in a press conference covered by Elizabeth Becker for the *New York Times* (July 29, 1999), said that "General Clark is a superb commander. The President has the highest degree of confidence in him." But Clark was also asked to retire several months earlier than expected, and some speculated that the administration favored Ralston as more cooperative and less headstrong.

Moreover, the fact that Ralston serves in the air force is also telling. In Kosovo, according to some military analysts, NATO demonstrated that a conflict could be successfully waged with air power alone. According to Richard Hallion, an air-force historian who spoke with Harry Levins for the *St. Louis Post-Dispatch* (August 7, 1999), this success led some to conclude that "the primary means of resolving crises is through the use of air power." That view pleases civilian officials, because air strikes generally result in fewer American casualties than infantry campaigns. The choice of a general in the air force as the head of NATO may mean, as Levins wrote, that political leaders hope the alliance "can win its wars without surface forces." A senior NATO official, as quoted by *Newsweek* (August 9, 1999), agreed that Ralston's appointment heralds a shift toward a preference for air power over ground troops by NATO, but he questioned the wisdom of that approach: "What does this say about the U.S. military's commitment? Commitment to what? To keeping the Army healthy and out of combat?"

NATO launched its third Balkans mission since 1995 on August 22, 2001, when Ralston approved the deployment of alliance troops to Macedonia in an effort to buttress a cease-fire agreement between ethnic Albanian rebels and the Slav-dominated government. (Because NATO officials were wary of becoming entangled in an open-ended mission, the force was charged with a very specific assignment: it was only to collect the rebels' weapons, as stipulated in the cease-fire agreement.)

After the September 11, 2001 terrorist attacks on Washington, D.C., and New York City, NATO, for the first time in its history, invoked Article 5 of the North Atlantic Treaty, which states that an attack on one member of the alliance is an attack on all. While that move set the stage for NATO participation in any subsequent military action—participation that Ralston would oversee—the U.S. Department of Defense told alliance defense ministers in late September that it would not request NATO involvement.

Among his military honors, Ralston has been awarded a Defense Distinguished Service Medal, a Distinguished Service Medal, a Legion of Merit, a Distinguished Flying Cross, and a Meritorious Service Medal. He is married to the former Diane Dougherty, his second wife, and has four children: Christopher, Paige, David, and Sarah. — P.K.

Suggested Reading: *Economist* p7 June 14, 1997, with photo; *Newsweek* p40+ Aug. 9, 1999, with photos; *St. Louis Post-Dispatch* p20 Aug. 7, 1999; *U.S. News & World Report* p34 June 16, 1997, with photo

---

Rania

Aug. 31, 1970– Queen of Jordan. Address: Royal Palace, Amman, Jordan; Jordan River Designs/Jordan River Foundation, P.O. Box 2943, Amman 11191, Jordan

"I am an Arab through and through, but I am also one who speaks the international language," Queen Rania of Jordan said to Daniel Klaidman for *Newsweek International* (June 12, 2000, on-line), almost 15 months after she was crowned by her husband, King Abdullah II. The world's youngest queen, Rania has brought a touch of sophistication to the Jordanian royal family while strengthening its connection to that nation's public: unlike her husband, whose mother is British, and the previous reigning queen, Noor, a native-born American, Rania is a Palestinian who has spent her entire life in the Middle East. She has accompanied her husband on trips overseas, and she is determinedly pushing for reform on domestic issues, ranging from the educational system to prevention of child abuse; at times she has even gone head-to-head with some of Jordan's more conservative voices.

Rania

Courtesy of Jordan Information Bureau

"It's a difficult task because there is really no limitation to your responsibility as a [queen]," Rania told Joseph P. Kahn for the *Boston Globe* (October 26, 1999). When Kahn asked the queen if her prominent role in her husband's court was evidence of her intention to radically change the mores of Jordanians, she replied: "I'm not looking for revolution. It's a matter of taking the best from the past and looking towards the future."

The queen was born Rania Yassin on August 31, 1970 in Kuwait to Faisal Yassin (or Yasin, according to some sources), a pediatrician, and Ilham Yassin. Her father and mother moved to Kuwait in the 1960s, and they raised their three children in a comfortable middle-class environment there. After Rania completed high school, she enrolled at the American University in Cairo, Egypt, where she earned a bachelor's degree in business administration in 1991. That year the Yassin family left Kuwait and settled in Jordan, for reasons connected with the Persian Gulf War, which was triggered when Iraq invaded Kuwait in late 1990, an action that the Palestine Liberation Organization (PLO) supported. After graduating from college, Rania joined her family in Jordan and got a job in banking and then in the marketing department of Apple Computer in Amman, the nation's capital. Early in 1993 Rania was introduced to then–Prince Abdullah at a dinner party given by one of his sisters. Both have recalled that occasion as love at first sight. "We managed to keep it quiet for a while," Rania told Kahn; but Abdullah's life in the public eye made total privacy impossible. The two were soon engaged. King Hussein, Abdullah's father, presided at their royal wedding, on June 10, 1993.

When she married Abdullah, Rania became a princess. She took her new status seriously; in an interview for *Ammar.com* in 1998, she said, "I personally do not think that getting married to a prince and having the title of 'princess' bestowed on me overnight makes me deserving of it. It is something I feel I should earn by contributing positively to society." In 1995 Rania founded the Jordan River Foundation, a private, nonprofit organization whose goal is to encourage income-generating and creative projects designed to help women and children in need. She began by aiding furniture makers and other artisans. As of late 2000 more than 3,500 people were employed in enterprises funded at least in part by the Jordan River Foundation. Rania has also endorsed "micro-enterprise" projects, as such small-scale enterprises are known, initiated by the U.S. Agency for International Development. "Economic participation is a main route through which women can improve their situation and that of their families. As women's levels of income increase, so does the standard of living for the rest of the family," she explained in June 1999 in an address to the International Women's Business Conference, an event that she co-chaired with then–First Lady Hillary Rodham Clinton. Rania has also taken a special interest in health initiatives. She heads the Jordan Blood Society and the Jordan Society for Organ Donation and is a patron of and spokesperson for the International Osteoporosis Foundation, whose main offices are in France and Switzerland.

Rania's life took a dramatic turn in January 1999, when King Hussein, who had been battling cancer, suddenly withdrew the designation of crown prince from his brother Hassan and conferred it on Abdullah, his eldest son. When King Hussein died, on February 7, 1999, Abdullah became the new ruler of Jordan. On March 21, 1999, at the end of the official mourning period for Hussein, Abdullah gave his wife the title of queen. This action led to widespread speculation about possible changes in Rania's relationship with Queen Noor, King Hussein's widow and a stepmother of Abdullah. "People are going to look for negatives. The idea of two queens is intriguing, but we have a very good relationship," Rania told Jeffrey Goldberg for the *New York Times Magazine* (February 6, 2000). For her part, Queen Noor told Goldberg, "I see us all being in transition. Abdullah and Rania and the new people coming in need to make an independent way for themselves."

Since she became queen, Rania has redoubled her efforts on behalf of the people of Jordan, where the birth rate is high (about 26 births per 1,000 people in the year 2000, which is about 18 percent greater than the estimated global rate and nearly twice the rate in the U.S.); unemployment is estimated at between 15 and 25 percent, and poverty is widespread. "I am . . . representing Jordanians and have to constantly be in touch with the people. This is something I intend to do forever," she told an interviewer for Reuters, as reported in the

Shanghai Star (April 14, 2000, on-line) and other newspapers. "The fact that we have a young population means that we have to try to live up to their hopes and aspirations."

Rania has brought new issues to the fore—prominent among them the existence of child abuse among Jordanians. "When I got interested in child abuse four or five years ago, it was a subject that wasn't discussed in Jordan," the queen told Kahn. "There wasn't even any terminology for child abuse at the time. Now people are aware that it's a problem that exists in every community in the world, that it needs to be brought out in the open. We are opening the first center in the [Arab] Middle East to deal with this issue, and we hope it will be a model replicated in other countries." That facility, the Dar al-Aman (Home of Safety), opened in August 2000. Rania has also spoken out against "honor killings"—the murder by male family members of women who are believed to have engaged in premarital or extramarital sex. The Jordanian Parliament has twice rejected legislation that would classify honor killings as homicides. Early in 2000, according to Daniel Klaidman, "Rania gave her blessing to a protest march on the Parliament building over the issue."

While some Jordanians have criticized Rania's unusually active role in Jordanian domestic affairs, the queen has maintained that what she is doing conforms to ideas she and the king share with regard to modern marriage and a modern monarchy. "It's really a partnership. . . . My role is to be supportive as much as I can and contribute as much as I can," she told the Reuters reporter. Fluent in both English and Arabic, she speaks in the former when

talking to Westerners about the empowerment of Jordanian women and in the latter when talking to local groups about the importance of education and technology in Jordanian schools.

King Abdullah and Queen Rania are the parents of three children: a son, Prince Hussein, and two daughters, Princess Iman and Princess Salma, who were born in 1994, 1996, and 2000, respectively. "The fact that we took over this position at a young age means our children are also young," Rania observed to Kahn. "It's a very sensitive and crucial time in their lives." During their leisure time, the royal family have been known to stop in at one of Amman's Internet cafés or at an American hamburger joint with friends. "I think every professional couple faces the same challenge, balancing work life and family life," Rania told Kahn. "In our case, maybe it's a little more exaggerated at times, but we do try to create that balance." Being a mother, Rania believes, has enabled her to empathize with the feelings of women everywhere. "I think we share the same concerns all over the world," she explained to Kahn. "I worry about my children just like every other mother worries about her children. About keeping them close, about keeping contact with them. Going out of our way to make time for them. For me, it's an investment in the future." — K.S.

Suggested Reading: *Boston Globe* E p1 Oct. 26, 1999; *CNN.com* (on-line) Aug. 20, 2000; *Newsweek International* (on-line) June 12, 2000, with photo; *People* (on-line) Apr. 28, 2000, with photo; *Time* (on-line) Feb. 14, 2000

Reeves, Dan

Jan. 19, 1944– Head coach of the Atlanta Falcons. Address: Atlanta Falcons, 4400 Falcon Pkwy., Flowery Branch, GA 30542

Dan Reeves, the head coach of the Atlanta Falcons, is known for his fierce competitiveness and his impressive career totals—171 wins, 140 losses, and one tie in regular games by the end of the 2000 season—which place him among the top coaches of all time in the National Football League (NFL). "Of course everyone in the NFL wants to win," the Hall of Famer and longtime Dallas Cowboys coach Tom Landry, Reeves's mentor and one of his former bosses, told Mike Freeman for the *New York Times* (August 30, 1993), "but what distinguishes the good coaches from the great ones like Dan is never being satisfied to win 12 games, or 13 games [in the 16-game regular season]. The great ones want to win all the games, everything. Some people become satisfied with a little success. Not Dan." A former member of the Dallas Cowboys, Reeves has been involved with the NFL since 1965. In 1981,

after serving as player-coach, assistant coach, and then offensive coordinator for Dallas, Reeves was hired as head coach of the Denver Broncos, thus becoming, at 37, the youngest person ever to hold that position in professional football. Reeves spent 12 years with the Broncos, helping them to earn three American Football Conference (AFC) titles and three unsuccessful trips to the Super Bowl. A four-year stint as head coach of the New York Giants ended in 1997, when he returned to his native Georgia to coach the Atlanta Falcons. Changing their losing ways, the Falcons made it to the Super Bowl during Reeves's second year as their coach and only six weeks after he had undergone emergency quadruple-bypass surgery. "I often wonder what heaven is going to be like," Reeves, who has yet to win a Super Bowl contest, told David Hutchinson for *Inside Sports* (January 1989). "I really do. It's said that life is going to be so much better in heaven. But if that's the truth, is anybody going to suffer a loss in heaven? How are you going to be competitive? I really wonder about that. I enjoy competition. Certainly it's much more fun to win. But I don't know how I could exist without competition. I enjoy it that much."

Dan Reeves

Jed Jacobsohn/Allsport

Daniel Edward Reeves was born on January 19, 1944 in Rome, Georgia. His father, Charles Edward "Edd" Reeves, and his mother, Ann Reeves, raised him and his three siblings on a 275-acre farm just outside Americus, Georgia, where they grew cotton, corn, and peanuts and raised hogs and cows. Having to help with the farm work instilled in him a sense of duty early on; as he told Gerald Eskenazi for the *New York Times* (January 19, 1987), "You learn to get up early, do the work, be part of the family, know your responsibility." Even while suffering a childhood bout with rheumatic fever and a kidney disorder, he remained an active helper. "I can remember sitting back and shelling peas and butter beans and other chores like that because I couldn't physically do other things," he told Samantha Stevenson for the *New York Times* (February 7, 1993). By the time he entered second grade, he had regained good health. In elementary school and junior high, he and his friends often played pickup games of football. Reeves was a three-sport athlete at Americus High School. A standout quarterback on the football team, he contributed to an upset victory of the reigning state champions during his senior year. He was also a guard on the school's championship basketball team and the starting left fielder when Americus High School won the state baseball championship.

After he graduated from high school, Reeves enrolled at the University of South Carolina. In his three seasons as a quarterback with the Gamecocks, he grew close to the team's coach, Marvin Bass, and, despite injuries to his knees, set 10 school records. His exceptional performance notwithstanding, he felt disheartened by the team's poor showing. "When I went to college, I lost," he

told Mike Freeman. "The best record we had was [four wins, five losses, and one tie]. I knew I didn't want to lose anymore." In 1965 Reeves left college to sign with the Dallas Cowboys as a free agent. "I liked him, he was this tough son-of-a-gun," Landry, who recruited him, told Freeman. "But at first I couldn't find a place for him. But he was so tough and competitive that he made me find a place for him." That place was in the offensive line, where Reeves had the role of all-purpose back. After the 1970 season he was named a player-coach, serving as a liaison between his teammates and Landry. During his first tour as a player-coach, the Cowboys faced the Miami Dolphins in Super Bowl VI and won by a score of 24–3. In 1972 his assignment changed from backfield coach to backup quarterback after the number-one quarterback, Roger Staubach, was injured. After the 1972 season Reeves retired from play; he became a full-time assistant coach in 1973.

By this time Reeves, who had married in 1964, had become the father of three children. Less-than-ideal relationships with Cowboys players and growing concerns about his parental responsibilities led Reeves to quit football after the 1973 season. He took a job in real estate (some sources say construction) but became extremely unhappy. In 1974 he rejoined Landry's staff as an assistant coach, and three years later he rose to the position of offensive coordinator. On January 15, 1978, in Super Bowl XII, the Cowboys triumphed over the Denver Broncos, 20–3. Reeves's negotiations the next year for a coaching job with the New York Giants fell apart over his demands for strict control over decisions. In 1981 he accepted the head coaching job with the Denver Broncos. "I thought I'd fit in here and then I found out that [Denverites] hated people from Dallas," he told Gerald Eskenazi. "I had this Super Bowl ring I used to wear from when Dallas beat Denver, and one night in a restaurant a woman said to me, 'You've got a lot of nerve wearing that in this town.'"

During his first season with the Broncos, Reeves led the team to a 10–6 record. In the 1982 season, which was shortened by a players' strike, the Broncos ended with two wins and seven losses. The following year Reeves and the Broncos began a five-season winning streak; they made four trips to the play-offs, and in 1984 Reeves was named the AFC Coach of the Year. In both 1987 and 1988, the Broncos won the AFC crown but lost in the Super Bowl, in contests with the New York Giants and then the Washington Redskins. The team was demoralized by the losses, and Reeves, too, felt upset; as he explained to David Hutchinson, "From my standpoint it's not so much personal disappointment as the fact that so many people you know feel badly because you didn't get the job done, and you're the one who's responsible. You feel like you've let down so many people. . . . I'm sure that deep down inside, everybody still feels that hurt and wants a chance for redemption. But as I told them in training camp, if we look that far ahead we'll never get there. Our immediate goal is to try to win our division. To do that, we have to focus in on one game at a time." The Broncos won the 1989 AFC title, and Reeves earned the 1989 AFC Coach of the Year honor. Then, at Super Bowl XXIV, held on January 28, 1990, the team lost to the San Francisco 49ers, 55–10. Speaking of Denver's third Super Bowl loss in four years, Reeves told Samantha Stevenson, "The most disappointing thing is that we never played to our capabilities, which is the No. 1 thing a coach has to worry about."

Reeves's volatile relationships with his offensive coordinator, Mike Shanahan, and Denver's star quarterback, John Elway, provided the local media with much fodder before, during, and after each season. In 1990 Reeves fired Shanahan for insubordination. He and Elway clashed over personnel decisions, play-calling, and general strategy. "The one thing Elway and Reeves have in common is a near-pathological need to win," Bob Kravitz wrote for *Inside Sports* (October 1992). "It's the reason they butt heads, and it's the reason they have so much success." The Broncos bounced back from their 5–11 1990 season to reach the play-offs in 1991, with a 12–4 regular-season record. They won the divisional play-off, in a game against Houston, 26–24 and then lost the AFC championship to Buffalo, 10–7.

By the end of the 1992 season, his 12th with the Broncos, Reeves had guided the team to 117 wins, 79 losses, and one tie—an outstanding achievement. Nevertheless, Pat Bowlen, the Broncos' owner, citing his desire for greater control over personnel, refused to renew Reeves's contract. Suddenly stripped of his job and fearing that he might never coach again, Reeves became despondent. "It was like a death in the family," his wife told Frank Litsky for the *New York Times* (January 27, 1993). His spirits lifted when, a month after his dismissal, Reeves signed a five-year contract to coach the New York Giants.

In his first season with the Giants, Reeves released the popular linebacker Pepper Johnson, who had openly disagreed with him during training camp, and picked the aging quarterback Phil Simms to be the Giants' starter, releasing quarterback Jeff Hostetler to the Oakland Raiders. Reeves insisted on discipline and hard work, which had reportedly been lacking under the Giants' previous coach, Ray Handley. "You can't have a successful team unless you have rules and regulations, so that everyone is on the same page," he told Samantha Stevenson. He said to Leonard Shapiro for the *Washington Post* (September 1, 1993), "I am demanding. I think you win by working hard, and that's all I ever ask of my players." The Giants responded to Reeves's approach, compiling an 11–5 regular-season record and going 1–1 in the play-offs; the Associated Press honored Reeves as Coach of the Year. The honeymoon did not last, however; the Giants' performance declined, and the relationship between Reeves and the team's general manager, George Young, grew strained. Reeves and the

management quibbled over personnel decisions, including the rating of quarterback Dave Brown. Early in 1997, after three disappointing seasons, Reeves was fired, one year before his contract was to expire.

Soon after his dismissal the Atlanta Falcons, who had had only two winning seasons since their NFC West title in 1980, persuaded Reeves to return to his home state by promising him free rein over all personnel matters. In the 1997 season the Falcons posted a 7–9 record, a marked improvement on the previous year's 3–13. The team ended the 1998 regular season on December 27 with 14 wins and two losses. Earlier, on December 13, during a contest against the New Orleans Saints, Reeves had experienced chest pains; the following day he underwent quadruple-bypass surgery. (In 1990 and 1991 he had undergone cardiac angioplasty, a procedure that clears blocked coronary arteries.) Within a month of the surgery, he returned to work, coaching his team through the play-offs; Atlanta beat San Francisco, 20–18, in the NFC divisional play-offs and then Minnesota, 30–27, in overtime in the NFC championship game. "That's old school [professionalism]," the Falcons' kick returner and wide receiver Tim Dwight told Austin Murphy for *Sports Illustrated* (February 1, 1999). "There's not much we wouldn't do for this guy." In Super Bowl XXXIII, the Falcons faced the Denver Broncos, coached by Mike Shanahan and still headlined by quarterback John Elway. Although the Falcons lost, 34–19, Reeves picked up coaching awards from the Associated Press and the *Sporting News*. The Falcons had losing records in 1999 (5–11), in part because of preseason injuries, and 2000 (4–12). By the end of October 2001, with more than half of the season remaining, the Falcons had compiled a 3–3 record.

Since his heart surgery Reeves has visited medical centers throughout the United States to promote public awareness about heart disease and to advocate the adoption of a low-fat, low-cholesterol diet, daily workouts, and other lifestyle changes, using himself as an example. "Crossing the Goal Line: Dan Reeves' Playbook for Surviving Heart Disease," a booklet that he co-wrote, is distributed by the pharmaceutical firm Merck & Co. "It's important in recovery to set goals," he told Thomas George for the *New York Times* (June 7, 1999). "The message is that when you suffer heart disease your life is not over."

Reeves lives in Atlanta with his wife, Pam, his high-school sweetheart. They have two daughters, Laura and Dana; a son, Lee; and four grandchildren. The coach's autobiography, *Reeves*, which he wrote with the assistance of the sportswriter Dick Connor, was published in 1988. — K.S.

Suggested Reading: *Chicago Tribune* IV p1 Jan. 29, 1988, with photo; *Inside Sports* p20+ Jan. 1989, with photos; *New York Times* B p7 Jan. 27, 1993, with photos, VIII p 9 Feb. 7, 1993, with photos, C p1 Aug. 30, 1993, with photos; *Sports*

Illustrated p44+ Feb. 1, 1999, with photo;
Washington Post B p5 Sep. 1, 1993; Reeves, Dan.
Reeves: An Autobiography (with Dick Connor),
1988

Courtesy of Arista Records

Reid, L. A.

*1956– President of Arista Records; songwriter;
record producer. Address: Arista Records, 6 W.
57th St., New York, NY 10019*

Although Antonio "L. A." Reid was for several
years a drummer with the successful R&B group
the Deele, it is in his behind-the-scenes work in the
world of music that he has been most influential.
In the mid-to-late 1980s, working with Deele band-
mate Kenny "Babyface" Edmonds, Reid wrote and
produced songs for some of the most important
R&B artists of the time. In the process, he won three
Grammy Awards for writing and production, and
had 33 of the songs that he co-wrote and/or co-
produced hit number one on the American singles
charts. In 1989 he and Babyface established their
own record label, LaFace, which would go on to
record some of the most successful and important
R&B acts of the 1990s, including TLC, Usher, and
Toni Braxton. Recently named the president of
Arista Records, Reid is now the head of one of the
largest pop labels in the United States, one that
boasts contracts with Santana, Aretha Franklin,
Carly Simon, and Whitney Houston, among other
musicians and groups. "In my career I've always
kind of been the guy behind the guy," Reid remarked to Larry Nager for the *Cincinnati Enquirer*
(October 17, 1999, on-line). "Even when it was the

Deele and it was in Cincinnati, Ohio, I was the guy
behind those other guys. I wasn't the lead guy. I
was at times maybe the spokesperson, because I
was the leader of the band. But I wasn't the visual
guy, I wasn't the lead singer, I wasn't out front. But
I was kind of married to the business and the creative aspect together. It was never purely creative,
it was always kind of both. And so as I've grown,
I've found that my love, my passion and my talent
is really to make others happen and not necessarily
promoting me."

One of the four children of Emma Reid, the songwriter, musician, producer, and executive was
born Antonio Reid in 1956 in Cincinnati, Ohio. He
was raised in the Cincinnati suburbs of Mount Auburn and Madisonville. "We moved around a lot,"
he told Nager. "I want to say we come from the
ghetto, but the truth is that I don't recall being that
poor. I don't have a rags-to-riches story. My mother
always worked, so I always had clothes and shoes.
When I started getting into music, my mother supported me and was helping me buy instruments."
Reid became entranced by such artists as Led Zeppelin, Jimi Hendrix, Sly Stone, Stevie Wonder, and
Miles Davis, and saved whatever money he could
to buy 45s. He especially loved James Brown. "I
used to have a karate class in Evanston," he told
Nager. "And when I would wait for the bus, I
would go stand in front of the [old King Records
building] and just stare at it. James Brown was
there, and I was drawn to him and the music he
created." Reid attended Hughes High School; by
the time he graduated, in 1974, he was playing
drums in several musical groups. Dave Parker, a
baseball player who was then with the Pittsburgh
Pirates, paid the expenses for one of the groups to
record some of their material. One of the songs was
played on the Pittsburgh radio station WCIN, while
another was later used on a compilation record issued by another Pittsburgh station, WEBN.

Reid later formed a group called Essence, which
played mostly original material. After several personnel changes, they renamed themselves the Deele but continued to play slick R&B and funk. "We
called the group the Deele, because it implied that
we were gonna get a record deal," he told Nager.
One of the new members of the Deele was Kenny
"Babyface" Edmonds. Reid and Edmonds soon became fast friends and successful musical collaborators. "We just really liked each other," Reid recalled to Nager. "Our musical ideas kind of worked
together real well. [Babyface] was a very melodic
guy, and I was a very rhythmic guy. We liked each
other's company, we admired each other's taste,
whether it be in music or in things other than music. We forged an amazing relationship that lasted
many years." In 1983 the group was signed by Solar, the label of the famed R&B group Midnight
Star. The Deele's first single, "Body Talk," released
that year, was featured on an episode of the hit television show *Miami Vice*. Although it hit only number 77 on the pop chart, it reached number three on
the R&B chart. The group followed that song up

with two more charting singles, "Just My Luck" and "Surrender." In 1984 the Deele released their debut album, *Street Beat*, which managed to crack the Top 100 on the national album chart. "Though the record . . . is pleasant, synthesized soul and lite funk, it doesn't show many signs of innovation, and only the hit singles demonstrate much song-craft," Leo Stanley noted for the *All Music Guide* (on-line). During the recording of the album, Reid learned a great deal from Reggie Calloway, the Midnight Star trumpeter and producer, who pro-duced *Street Beat*. "This guy probably doesn't even know how much impact he's had on my life," Reid told Nager. "Reggie kind of taught me the impor-tance of making sure that every song you record is the absolute best song that you can find and has the absolute best performance by the artist. It was that basic training. I like to think of it as boot camp that really sort of paved the way for what we do now at LaFace, and so many of the other artists and labels that I associate with. But it all came from there."

Material Thangz (1985), the Deele's second al-bum, was not as successful as their debut, with only the title cut making its way to the singles chart. Meanwhile, however, Reid and Babyface were becoming known as one of the hottest song-writing/production teams in the R&B world. Reid moved to Los Angeles, where, with Babyface, he produced and wrote for other artists on the Solar label; those performers included Shalimar, the Whispers, and Pebbles. The last-named artist, whose real name is Perri McKissack, married Reid. During the second half of the 1980s, Reid and Babyface produced and/or wrote songs for some of the most popular artists of the time, among them Bobby Brown, Sheena Easton, Karyn White, Paula Abdul, the Jacksons, Whitney Houston, Boyz II Men, and Bell Biv Devoe. The final Deele album featuring Reid and Babyface, *Eyes of a Stranger* (1987), contained two hit singles, "Two Occa-sions" and "Shoot 'em Up Movies," and became a certified gold release.

Despite their success, Reid and Babyface felt that they were missing out on financial rewards. "At that point I decided I wanted some ownership in the game," Reid told Nager. "We were having a lot of success, making a lot of records, selling a lot of records, not making a lot of money. We wanted equity participation and you can't have equity par-ticipation if you're work-for-hire. And as produc-ers we were work-for-hire. So I figured it out. I want a label." In 1989 Reid and Babyface formed LaFace Records, a five-year, $20 million joint ven-ture with Arista Records, which agreed to distrib-ute their products. (The name "LaFace" combined parts of Reid's and Edmonds's stage names.) While Babyface continued writing, producing, and per-forming, Reid mostly stayed behind the scenes. "I've kind of retired from the studio," Reid told Nager. "[Babyface has] obviously kept it up and done an amazing job at it. We still talk every day and have co-ownership of our label. But for the most part, he pursues his career, and I retired to the boring job of being a record company executive."

Reid immediately began looking for artists to sign to the label. In 1991, in one of his first major successes, he signed the all-female R&B group TLC, which was managed by Pebbles. The group had three consecutive Top 10 hits the following year, and their debut album was also quite success-ful. Reid also brought the R&B singer Toni Braxton to the label. Her first album, released in 1993, sold more than seven million copies and earned her Grammy Awards in the categories of best new artist and best female R&B artist. "I look for stars, y'know? More than I look for people who sing or for people who play, I look for people who I think are stars," Reid told Nager. "People who have the ability to make you love them, and to make people around the world love them. And that becomes the most important thing to me. There are great singers all over the world. In any Baptist church in Ameri-ca you can find the greatest singers in the world. But it doesn't always translate to superstardom. I don't know what it is. It's something that I feel when I meet an artist, when I watch an artist. What-ever it is, let's put it this way, TLC has it, Madonna has it, Toni Braxton has it, Usher has it, Puff Daddy has it."

In September 1993 Reid and Edmonds split as a production team. "There were a lot reasons," Reid told Sonia Murray for the *Atlanta Journal-Constitution* (July 2, 2000, on-line). "No. 1 was, I think I used to [upset him] because I would sit in the studio and be on the telephone. . . . No. 2: I started to have a true love of the business and working with other artists. No. 3: In some respects, Kenny might have felt like Kenny needed to grow as a writer and producer and he needed to do it by himself. . . . And I supported that." Reid faced tension in other areas, personal as well as profes-sional, over the next couple of years. In 1995 he and Perri McKissack divorced, and in 1997 Toni Braxton sued LaFace, holding the company re-sponsible for the conditions that led her to file for bankruptcy. Reid responded to the latter develop-ment philosophically, telling Sonia Murray, "It's just a fact of life, at a certain point all labels have legal issues. I think the fact that LaFace was such a proud company, and is such a proud company, that there simply were people around that really wanted to [hurt] this company. And as artists be-come successful, they become prone to listening to people."

In spite of such troubles, LaFace continued to be successful, grossing around $100 million annually. Among the other popular acts signed by Reid were the southern rap groups Outkast and the Goodie Mob and the soul crooner Usher. TLC's *CrazySexy-Cool* (1994) sold more than 13 million copies, mak-ing those artists the best-selling female group in the country. The record was later named the best-selling hip-hop album of the 20th century by the Recording Industry Association of America. In 1995 LaFace announced that it had renewed its agreement with Arista and its parent company, BMG, which invested an estimated $100 million in the label over five years. "We are doing exactly what the major labels do, just on a smaller scale," Reid told Rhonda Reynolds and Ann Brown for *Black Enterprise* (December 1994). "The difference is we understand black artists. We understand how to market them better than anybody." In 1997 LaFace released the soundtrack to the film *Soul Food*; Edmonds produced both the soundtrack and the film, which earned $11.4 million in its first weekend in theaters.

In 2000 Reid married Erica Holton, an Atlanta schoolteacher, in a ceremony on the Isle of Capri, off the coast of Italy. Soon afterward he was named president of Arista. Although the choice of Reid was not controversial, the move itself caused a stir, since it meant that Arista's founder, Clive Davis, was being forced to step down after 25 years at the helm of the label. As a result of the decision, some executives and performers left Arista, explaining that they wanted to work only with Davis; many others, inside and outside the recording industry, were excited to see an African-American chosen to head a major label. Despite the popularity of many African-American recording artists, few blacks held positions of power within the field. Reid was invigorated by the leap from running a small label to being the head of a major record company that was home to superstars. "I really need the challenge," he told Sonia Murray. "I love music first and foremost. And I haven't been able to work in all genres of music. . . . I've been sort of pigeon-holed into the box of doing R&B and obviously some rap music. Although it's music that's crossed over . . . I have to tell you, I'm a little bored. I love working with the artists that I've worked with. I don't like the idea of having a small company, though. Because in a small company, I'm far too dependent on a couple of people, a couple of artists." Regarding his plans for Arista, Reid told the same interviewer that while he wanted to maintain the company's strengths—R&B and pop—he was also interested in opening up new markets. "In recent years, Arista has had marginal success in rock music. That's an area that's really going to require a lot of time and attention. . . . Also, I think when you look at the Latin population in the country and the fact that Arista basically has one artist—which would be Carlos Santana—who makes music that is appealing to that population of people, I think that there's obviously some room for growth there." After Reid was named president of Arista, the company acquired LaFace. In 2001 Reid amazed observers when he signed Whitney Houston to a $100 million multi-album deal. During that year rumors abounded that Reid was under heavy pressure to increase sales.

Reid has three children: Aaron, Ashley, and Antonio Jr. He lives and works in Atlanta and also has an office in New York City. He is a partner in Justin's, an Atlanta restaurant, along with the rapper and producer Sean "Puffy" Combs. Reid helped Combs's Bad Boy Records in its distribution deal with Arista. "All the success and all, I certainly don't take it lightly and I count my blessings," Reid told Nager. "But now, I'm more concerned with having peace and just happiness in life. I'm not trying to say that I haven't been happy and I haven't been peaceful but it just hasn't been at the forefront of my desire, and now it is. Simple as it may sound, I just want peace and love." — G.O.

Suggested Reading: *All Music Guide* (on-line); *Atlanta-Journal Constitution* (on-line) July 2, 2000; *Black Enterprise* p94+ Dec. 2000; *Cincinnati Enquirer* (on-line) Oct. 17, 1999; *Fortune* p40 Apr. 2, 2001, with photo; *Jet* p46+ May 22, 2000, with photo; *New York* p34+ Jan. 29, 2001

Selected Recordings: with the Deele—*Street Beat*, 1984; *Material Thangz*, 1985; *Eyes of a Stranger*, 1987

Armando Gallo/Retna ltd.

Reitman, Ivan

Oct. 27, 1946– Film director; producer. Address: 1482 E. Valley Rd., Suite 477, Montecito, CA 93108

Since he produced the low-budget sleeper hit *Animal House*, in 1978, Ivan Reitman has earned a reputation as one of the most consistently successful directors and producers of comedy in Hollywood. His hits, which include *Stripes*, *Ghostbusters*, *Twins*, and *Dave*, have grossed over $2 billion since 1973. Such mainstream success has led many to question the artistic merit of Reitman's work: the producer Julia Philips, for example, described

Reitman in her 1990 memoir, *You'll Never Eat Lunch in This Town Again*, as quoted by Michael Walker in the *Chicago Tribune* (November 27, 1994), as "a businessman not an artist." While Reitman has not denied that he has a knack for marketing, he has pointed out that his films are more than just mindless entertainment. "I think I am a businessman," he told Walker, "in terms of how I'm not a fool with regards to how the business works. But the films I've made are pretty complicated and have worked for a number of creative reasons." Increasingly (and especially since the release of the 1993 political satire *Dave*), critics have agreed with him. "Whether about summer camp, college, the military or white-collar life," Randall Rothenberg wrote in a representative judgment for the *New York Times* (May 2, 1993), "Mr. Reitman's movies are sweetly cynical comedies about regimented institutions, and they celebrate the kind of wanton rebelliousness that appeals to young people."

The son of Clara and Leslie Reitman, Ivan Reitman was born on October 27, 1946 in Komarmo, Czechoslovakia, a river-port town in what is now southwestern Slovakia. Both of his parents, who were Jewish natives of Czechoslovakia, escaped Nazi persecution during the 1940s; his father fought in the underground resistance during World War II, while his mother survived imprisonment in the Nazi concentration camp in Auschwitz, Poland. When Reitman was four his family fled Czechoslovakia, which by then had become a Soviet-style Communist state, by hiding underneath the floorboards of a tugboat headed up the Danube River for Vienna, Austria. To keep him quiet, his parents fed him tranquilizers. "For a while," Reitman told Brian D. Johnson for *Maclean's* (June 9, 1986), "they were concerned they might have killed me. When they finally lit a candle, I was lying there with my eyes wide open—but out cold." "You have to know one thing," Reitman's father told Joy Horowitz for the *New York Times Magazine* (June 15, 1986). "We were five days in that boat. It was very hard on him. This affects a child. Maybe what he missed as a very young child, this is what he wanted to recapture in high school and college—the crazy stuff." Several months after arriving safely in Austria, the family emigrated to Toronto, Canada, where Reitman's father established a successful dry-cleaning business.

Reitman remained in the Toronto area through his college years, attending McMaster University, in Hamilton, a nearby steel town. In the late 1960s McMaster was an especially fertile seedbed for sketch comedy; as Len Blum, a college friend of Reitman's, recalled to Rothenberg, "It was a very unusual community. . . . There was a competition for attention that was measured in laughter." Reitman, who majored in music, was active in the campus drama society and film club. One summer, with nothing else to do, he persuaded a music-industry executive to sponsor a summer course at the National Film Board of Canada, in Montreal. (The National Film Board of Canada is a public agency that, according to its Web site, "produces and distributes films and other audiovisual works which reflect Canada to Canadians and the rest of the world.") For the class, Reitman made his first movie, a four-and-a-half-minute short entitled *Guitar Thing*. Upon returning to McMaster in the fall, he obtained funding from the student council for a second film, *Orientation*, a 20-minute documentary about the first week of school. Thanks in part to his astute promotional skills, *Orientation* was eventually shown in theaters across Canada.

In 1969, after he graduated with a bachelor's of music from McMaster, Reitman produced his first full-length feature, a risqué art film titled *Columbus of Sex*. Based on the Victorian-era memoir *My Secret Life*, which chronicled the "amatory career" of the anonymous London author, the film received "widespread critical acclaim" from Canada's arts community, as Juliet Ward reported for the *International Movie Database* (on-line). (When Reitman spoke with Brian D. Johnson, however, he called *Columbus of Sex* "a terrible movie.") The picture upset Canada's custodians of public morals; in 1970 Reitman was convicted of violating Canada's decency laws and fined $300.

Reitman turned next to horror, a genre traditionally popular among young filmmakers trying to break into the business. In 1973 he directed the low-budget comedy-horror spoof *Cannibal Girls*. The movie, which was shot without a script, starred Andrea Martin and Eugene Levy (both of whom later achieved fame for their work on *SCTV*, the Canadian version of *Saturday Night Live*). Reitman traveled to Cannes, France, with his future wife, Genevieve, to promote the film. "We put salacious posters all over the main drag to lure buyers into the theaters," he recalled to Johnson. Although *Cannibal Girls* eventually became a cult favorite, it did less well than Reitman had hoped. That frustration, plus the considerable debt that he had amassed in making the film, dampened his enthusiasm for directing, with the result that he decided to devote himself exclusively to producing.

As a producer, Reitman teamed up with the cult director David Cronenberg to put together a number of tongue-in-cheek horror movies—works that Reitman, speaking with Joy Horowitz, characterized as "genre exploitation" films. Among the titles he produced during this period were *Shivers* (1975, released in the United States as *They Came from Within*), *Death Weekend* (1977, also known as *The House by the Lake*), and *Rabid* (1977). Reitman also made brief excursions into stage and television; he produced *Spellbound*, which evolved into Doug Henning's *The Magic Show*, on Broadway, and *Greed*, a made-for-television parody of *The Price Is Right* that featured Dan Aykroyd as off-stage announcer. In 1975 Reitman, who had become a fan of the American satirical magazine *National Lampoon*, produced an Off-Broadway version of the *National Lampoon Show*, which had previously been a touring production. Among the show's cast members were John Belushi, Bill Murray, and Harold Ramis, all of whom Reitman would later work with.

Reitman's next big film project, *National Lampoon's Animal House* (1978), hit pay dirt, breaking the record for the top-grossing comedy film up to that time. (*Ghostbusters*, another Reitman film, broke that record in 1984; it was superseded on the U.S. charts by either *Forrest Gump* or *Home Alone*, depending on one's definition of comedy.) The story of the Delta House fraternity and its fight for the right to party, *Animal House* was hailed by some as a brilliant exercise in grotesque comedy and damned by others as tasteless and disgusting. Critical opinions aside, the movie had a powerful impact on Hollywood filmmaking: it spawned a host of imitators and is generally held to have touched off the long wave of campus comedies that swept theaters in the 1980s. In addition to increasing John Belushi's prominence, the success of *Animal House* led Reitman to reconsider his decision to stop directing; as he told Rothenberg, "It killed me I didn't get to direct it."

In the next few years, Reitman directed two films of his own, both of them starring Bill Murray: *Meatballs* (1979) and *Stripes* (1981). *Meatballs*, a spoof about a camp counselor who becomes a mentor to a troubled camper, became the sleeper hit of the summer by introducing a sentimental streak into an *Animal House*–like burlesque. Although shot on a meager budget—$1.5 million—the film eventually brought in $43 million. *Stripes*, like Reitman's previous movies, made liberal use of slapstick and farce, but it leveled its sights at a new target: the U.S. Army. Although the picture did not please critics—Pauline Kael, for example, writing for the *New Yorker* (July 13, 1981), called it "a flimsy, thrown-together service comedy"—Reitman has said that he eventually shrugged off the bad press. As he told Joshua Klein for the *Onion* (online), "I remember *Time* or *Newsweek* giving it one of those one-paragraph condescending encapsulations, and I sort of quickly learned not to deal with that. Not even to read, just to deal with the movies and try to do the best I could." *Stripes* was a hit at the box office, grossing $85.3 million.

Ghostbusters (1984), also directed by Reitman, continued to mine the vein of youthful comedy that had brought him his previous successes, and it marked his return to the horror spoof as well. Written by Dan Aykroyd and Harold Ramis, both of whom also starred in the film alongside Bill Murray, *Ghostbusters* follows the escapades of a group of paranormal psychologists who earn a living as supernatural exterminators, ridding New York of unwanted ghosts and specters. It soon transpires that the denizens of the beyond, led by the Babylonian demon Gozer, are gathering for an apocalyptic assault on the city, which Murray and his associates—in their typically farcical manner—try to thwart. "We are taking a mundane attitude towards the supernatural," Ramis wrote in the production notes. "We're simply janitors cleaning up someone else's mess with a little bit of high tech-

nology." *Ghostbusters* attracted large audiences in spite of mixed reviews and confirmed Reitman's reputation in Hollywood as a man with a golden touch.

For his next film, the romantic comedy *Legal Eagles* (1986), Reitman attempted to break away from his "schlockmeister" image, by teaming up with the dignified Robert Redford. (For his part, Redford opted to work with Reitman in a bid to loosen up his image.) Although the film generated a stir in the media and ultimately grossed about $50 million, it was only a moderate success, given that it cost $35 million to shoot. Accounting for its problems, Reitman told Rothenberg, "The plot didn't make much sense. I can't even tell you the plot because I don't quite understand it."

In *Twins* (1988) Reitman overhauled Arnold Schwarzenegger's screen image by casting him as the long-lost twin brother of the character played by the diminutive Danny DeVito. The movie proved that Schwarzenegger, then known chiefly for playing hypermasculine action types, could perform effectively in comedy, too. Indeed, the makeover was so successful that Reitman made two more comedies with Schwarzenegger: *Kindergarten Cop* (1990), about a tough policeman who goes undercover as a kindergarten teacher, and *Junior* (1994), in which Schwarzenegger's character becomes pregnant. Reitman's attempt to transform Sylvester Stallone's image, by means of *Stop! Or My Mom Will Shoot* (1992), which Reitman produced but did not direct, ended distressfully for all of the principals.

In addition to his work with Schwarzenegger, Reitman directed *Ghostbusters II* (1989), a sequel to the 1984 hit, and *Dave* (1993), a lighthearted political satire, starring Kevin Kline and Sigourney Weaver, that involved a presidential doppelganger and an extralegal switcheroo. Both pictures did well commercially. As a producer, Reitman ventured into family comedy with *Beethoven* (1992) and *Beethoven's 2nd* (1993), movies about a lovable St. Bernard. The first film grossed more than $70 million. Critics praised *Beethoven's 2nd* for its restraint in not using voice-overs to communicate the thoughts of its canine characters; to serve the same purpose, the filmmakers employed a mood-specific soundtrack.

More recently, Reitman directed *Father's Day* (1997), a family comedy starring Robin Williams, Billy Crystal, Julia Louis-Dreyfus, and Nastassja Kinski, and *Six Days Seven Nights* (1998), a comedy–castaway-drama hybrid with Anne Heche and Harrison Ford. Like most of Reitman's work in the 1990s, those films tended to focus on the relationships between lead characters rather than on relatively isolated protagonists, as had been the case in his early work. Reitman attributed the shift to the growing importance of his own family in his life. "All those early films," he told Rothenberg, "were really about being in your 20's and being a teenager, as opposed to being in your 30's, 40's, and 50's and having children. . . . We really *were* saying, 'It just doesn't matter.' What we're saying right now is, 'It *does* matter.' You have to take responsibility for yourself, in your own little life and the life of your family. And then in the life of your country."

Road Trip (2000), for which Reitman served as co-executive producer, returned to *Animal House–*style campus comedy with a nod to the gross-out genre inaugurated by *There's Something About Mary.* "*Road Trip,*" Stephen Holden wrote for the *New York Times* (May 19, 2000), "is likely to inspire the usual puritanical hand-wringing about the foul state of movies and Hollywood's going to hell in a handbasket. But if you think back a few years, this movie is a lot funnier (and, dare I say, smarter) than the last cycle of gross-out movies initiated by *Porky's.* As we all know, bad taste is timeless. And sometimes it can be so funny that you can't help laughing." *Evolution* (2001), which Reitman directed and produced, likewise represented a return to tried-and-true themes: as a number of reviewers were quick to point out, *Evolution,* which pitted a team of scientists against the malign (and incontinent) alien spawn of a slime-oozing meteorite, was greatly indebted to *Ghostbusters* and its successors. "As the conclusion to a sunburned afternoon," Andrew O'Hehir wrote for *Salon.com,* "this loosey-goosey alien-attack shtick-fest makes perfectly acceptable entertainment. But it's not much more than fragments of other, some-

what better summer entertainments stitched together and whitewashed in the slapdash nonstyle of director Ivan Reitman."

Reitman lives in the Los Angeles area with his wife, Genevieve Robert, whom he married in 1976; a former actress, Robert directed the 1988 film *Casual Sex?* and has frequently worked with her husband on the set. The couple have three children—Jason, Catherine, and Caroline—all of whom have made cameo appearances in some of their father's films. — P.K.

Suggested Reading: *Chicago Tribune* XIII p24+ Nov. 27, 1994, with photos; *New York Times* H p15+ May 2, 1993, with photos; *Maclean's* p42+ June 9, 1986, with photos; *New York Times Magazine* p30+ June 15, 1986, with photos; *Newsweek* p59+ My 10 1993, with photo

Selected Films: *Cannibal Girls,* 1973; *Shivers,* 1975; *The House by the Lake,* 1977; *Rabid,* 1977; *National Lampoon's Animal House,* 1978; *Meatballs,* 1979; *Stripes,* 1981; *Ghostbusters,* 1984; *Legal Eagles,* 1986; *Twins,* 1988; *Ghostbusters 2,* 1989; *Kindergarten Cop,* 1990; *Beethoven,* 1991; *Stop! Or My Mom Will Shoot,* 1992; *Dave,* 1993; *Junior,* 1994; *Commandments,* 1996; *Father's Day,* 1997; *Six Days, Seven Nights,* 1998; *Road Trip,* 2000; *Evolution,* 2001

Rice, Condoleezza

Nov. 14, 1954– U.S. national security adviser; educator. Address: National Security Council, The White House, 1600 Pennsylvania Ave. N.W., Washington, DC 20500

Although many Americans have not yet learned to wrap their tongues around her silvery name, Condoleezza Rice, President George W. Bush's national security adviser, is not likely to remain obscure for long. A leading Soviet and Russian scholar, the youngest-ever provost at Stanford University, and an adviser in the presidential administration of Bush's father, George Herbert Walker Bush, Rice has already distinguished herself in the male-dominated worlds of political science and foreign policy. Named by her mother, a pianist, who was inspired by the Italian musical term *con dolcezza* (meaning "with sweetness"), Condoleezza Rice, according to many of her admirers, blends southern charm with a tough-as-nails intellect and steely confidence. "She's a steel magnolia," Coit Blacker, a colleague from Stanford, told James Robinson for the *Stanford Report* (June 9, 1999, on-line). She is also single, African-American, devoutly religious, and equal parts football fan and cultural sophisticate. Born in Jim Crow–era Alabama, Rice earned her Ph.D. at age 26 and worked in the White House

Archive Photos

before the age of 40; she has often described her personal and professional journeys, with modesty, as "a typical American story."

Condoleezza Rice was born on November 14, 1954 in Birmingham, Alabama, which was then still officially segregated. Growing up during the tumultuous days of the civil rights movement, Rice attended a segregated school in Birmingham and lived in a world inhabited almost exclusively by black people. On September 15, 1963 she was just a few miles away when a bomb planted in a Baptist church by white supremacists exploded, killing four black girls, one of whom was Rice's friend. Her father, an ordained Presbyterian minister and dean of Stillman College, a predominantly black school in Tuscaloosa, and her mother, an accomplished pianist and teacher of music and science, imparted to their only daughter the sense that—in spite of the racism all around her—she could do anything she desired with her life. "I remember it as a time when . . . my parents had to try to explain why we couldn't go to the circus, why we had to drive all the way to Washington, D.C., before we could stay in a hotel," Rice told George de Lama for the *Chicago Tribune* (August 15, 1993). "And they had to explain why I could not have a hamburger in a restaurant but I could be president anyway, which was the way they chose to handle the situation." Rice learned her parents' lesson well: according to a *Fox News* (August 2, 2000, on-line) reporter, during a family trip to Washington, D.C., the 10-year-old Condoleezza Rice stared at the White House through its gate and told her father, "One day, I'll be in that house."

When Rice's father became vice chancellor at the University of Denver, the family moved to Colorado, where Rice enrolled at an integrated Roman Catholic high school. Despite her high grades, a counselor there once told her that she was not "college material," but Rice was not discouraged by that assessment. Having skipped two grades (first and seventh), Rice became a freshman at the University of Denver at the age of 15. She had been playing piano since the age of three and intended to study music and become a concert pianist. After deciding, however, that she lacked the talent to make it to the top of the highly competitive world of classical music, she cast about for another course of study. She found a mentor in Professor Josef Korbel, a former Czech diplomat and refugee from Nazism and communism who was the head of Denver's international-relations program. Rice "adored" Korbel, she told Jay Nordlinger for the *National Review* (August 1, 2000, on-line). "He's the reason I'm in this field." In particular, Rice was influenced by Korbel's forthright and pragmatic approach to wielding political power. She frequently visited the Korbel home, where she met his daughter—the future Madeleine Albright, who would become U.S. secretary of state under President Bill Clinton. Many have remarked that, although the two women received early lessons in foreign policy from the same man, their thinking evolved in very different directions.

Rice graduated with a degree in international relations, in 1974, then entered the master's program in economics at the University of Notre Dame, in Indiana. She later returned to the University of Denver, where in 1981 she earned a Ph.D. in international studies, with a specialty in Soviet politics and culture. "I was attracted to the Byzantine nature of Soviet politics," she recalled to Nordlinger, "and by power: how it operates, how it's used." She became fluent in the Russian language and well versed in Russian culture and literature, preferring Dostoevsky to Tolstoy and Solzhenitsyn over all. (Dostoevsky "understood the dark side of Russia better than anyone else," she told Nordlinger. "Like most Russian novels, [his works offer] tragedy without redemption.") During her school years Rice also became a member of the Republican Party. As she explained in a speech at the 2000 Republican National Convention, her father had become a Republican by force of circumstance. "My father joined our party because the Democrats in Jim Crow Alabama of 1952 would not register him to vote. The Republicans did," she said, as quoted on the *Washington Post* Web site. Rice did not initially follow her father's political leanings; she voted for the Democrat Jimmy Carter in the presidential election of 1976. But after judging President Carter's response to the 1979 Soviet invasion of Afghanistan to be weak and naïve, she began to favor the Republicans' style of leadership, particularly as practiced by Carter's successor in the White House, Ronald Reagan.

In 1981 Rice became an assistant professor at Stanford University, in California. She has thus far spent her entire academic career there, an unusual figure in the school's Department of Political Science not only because she is black and female in a field that is predominantly white and male, but also because she is a political conservative on a campus that has historically been liberal. "We have jokes in the political science department," Rice told de Lama. "If the only two Republicans in the department aren't there, is there a quorum?" But Rice doesn't seem to mind being a trailblazer, even telling de Lama that she does not believe in the importance of role models: "Because if I'd been waiting to find a black female Soviet specialist, I'd still be waiting."

In the classroom, Rice has often employed what she terms "applied" teaching methods, including simulations of national-security crises in which students prepare strategic responses in real time. She is known as a demanding teacher, one who pushes her students to excel and encourages heated debate. "I tell my students, 'If you find yourself in the company of people who agree with you, you're in the wrong company,'" she told a reporter for the *New York Times* (June 23, 1993). Rice has won two of her department's highest honors—the 1984 Walter J. Gores Award for excellence in teaching and the 1993 School of Humanities and Sciences Dean's Award for Distinguished Teaching. She has written three books on the Cold War: *Un-*

certain Allegiance: The Soviet Union and the Czechoslovak Army (1984), *Germany Unified and Europe Transformed* (1995), with Philip Zelikow, and *The Gorbachev Era* (1986), with Alexander Dallin.

Rice made national headlines in 1993, when she was named Stanford's provost, or chief financial and academic officer, a powerful position that placed her second in rank to the university president. Rice was the youngest provost in the university's 103-year history, as well as the first woman and first African-American. During her six-year tenure, Rice successfully initiated a cost-saving program to eliminate the university's $43 million deficit and balance the billion-dollar budget. Inevitably, she stepped on some toes—in one case sparking protests and a hunger strike by a group of Chicano students after a Chicana administrator was let go as part of the restructuring. Rice also led a faculty reassessment of undergraduate education, a process that stimulated campus-wide debates over what should constitute the core of a liberal-arts education. In her interview with James Robinson, Rice admitted that she was personally divided over this issue. Though she criticized the practice of teaching courses on Western civilization without examining the other cultures that have informed it, she also dismissed what she called the "identity argument," or the "'I need to know about my culture'" stance, sometimes taken by minority students. "I think that you need to be able to cross cultural lines," she said, mentioning her own ability to "adopt" Russian culture. In the end, Stanford instituted a new "Introduction to Humanities" core, in which literature, art, history, and philosophy courses treated questions of cultural identity from many different perspectives. "I think that it is great that black history is being brought more into American history," Rice told Robinson, "because my view is that Africans and Europeans landed here together and built this country together, and the separation of African culture and African history from American culture and American history is just ahistorical. If you're going to read and understand Frederick Douglass, then you'd better understand Thomas Jefferson, because that is who he was referencing."

As an academic star and Soviet expert, Rice attracted the attention of Washington policymakers during the Cold War, and in 1986 she was awarded a fellowship from the Council on Foreign Relations to work on nuclear strategic planning with the director of the Joint Staff of the Joint Chiefs of Staff. After the election of George Herbert Walker Bush as president, in 1988, Rice accepted several concurrent, high-level appointments in Washington: director of Soviet and East European affairs with the National Security Council, special assistant to the president for national security affairs, and senior director for Soviet affairs. She arrived at an extraordinary moment in history: during her three years of service, the Berlin Wall, which had separated East and West Berlin since 1961 and had

come to symbolize the rift between the Western and Communist worlds, fell; Germany was reunified; the Soviet bloc collapsed; and—unthinkable only a few years earlier—the United States enlisted Russia as an ally in the war against Iraq in the Persian Gulf. Throughout this series of remarkable events, Rice was the only full-time Soviet specialist in the White House, and as such had a strong voice in shaping policy toward the new Europe. Rice attended three U.S.–Soviet summit meetings and served as a delegate to talks on German unification. In *Salon.com* (March 20, 2000), Steve Kettman recounted how then–president Bush introduced Rice to then–Soviet president Mikhail Gorbachev in 1989: "This is Condoleezza Rice," he said. "She tells me everything I know about the Soviet Union." Rice worked under Brent Scowcroft, Bush's national security adviser, and alongside Colin Powell, James Baker, and Richard B. ("Dick") Cheney—men whose names have again become familiar, with the new Bush administration. At the time, Rice told Nordlinger, she and her colleagues understood the "paradox" of the Soviet Union: that it was "weak and rotting" but "still exceedingly dangerous." Rice looks back on those "heady times," as she told de Lama, "with a real sense of amazement that it went as smoothly as it did." She cited, as examples of that smoothness, the peaceful withdrawal of Soviet forces from Germany and Eastern Europe and the entry of Germany into the North Atlantic Treaty Organization (NATO). But, alluding to the nationalist conflicts that have flared in the former Yugoslavia and elsewhere since the end of the Cold War, Rice added, "We're obviously paying some of the price now for what between '89 and '91 was an almost surreally smooth and amiable process of tumultuous change."

In 1991, more than a year before Bush's presidency ended, Rice returned to Stanford to resume life as an academic, though one with a higher profile than most. In an interview with Christopher Parkes for the *Financial Times* (December 28, 1995), Rice claimed not to suffer from "Potomac fever," or the feeling of those who have worked "inside the Beltway" in Washington, D.C., that they can never bring themselves to leave. "I ask myself if I would ever have that constellation of forces, events, and personalities again . . . a president I adored . . . George Bush, for whom the great issues at the end of the cold war were priority number one," she told Parkes.

Through her relationship with the former president, Rice developed a friendship with the Bush family. In July 2000, at George W. Bush's request, Rice took a leave of absence from Stanford to become chief foreign-policy adviser in his presidential campaign. She briefed him once a week on world developments, offering advice about situations likely to arise over the next few years. When asked her opinion of the qualifications of the younger George Bush, who has rarely traveled outside the U.S. and is often described as a foreign-policy neophyte, Rice has frequently mentioned his record as governor of Texas, a border state, and his ability to set an agenda and function as an effective leader.

Like Bush, Rice has identified herself as a new breed of Republican—an "all-over-the-map" Republican, as she told Nordlinger: "very conservative" with regard to foreign policy, but "moderate" on some issues and "almost shockingly libertarian" on others. Rice's foreign-policy views have often been described as tough or unsentimental, but she is also, in Nordlinger's words, "an unabashed believer in the American experiment, the United States as a model and force for good in the world." "I am a realist. Power matters. But there can be no absence of moral content in American foreign policy, and, furthermore, the American people wouldn't accept such an absence. Europeans giggle at this and say we're naive and so on, but we're not Europeans, we're Americans—and we have different principles." Nevertheless, Rice opposes peacekeeping efforts in such war-torn regions as Bosnia and Kosovo, "where all you can do is separate warring factions," because it "does not make you ready to fight big wars," she said during a speech in the summer of 2000, as quoted on the Stanford University Web site. One thing that makes the United States unique, Rice told Charlie Rose in an interview dated October 12, 2000 and archived on the Council of Foreign Relations Web site, is that it is the only country that has an army capable of deterring or winning a war of "global strategic significance." "To the degree that we're doing myriad peacekeeping operations around the world, we're not training for the one thing that only we can do. And I don't see that as a putdown or a condemnation of anyone else. I see it as a division of labor," she said. "[Bush] recognizes that the magnificent men and women of America's armed forces are not a global police force, they are not the world's 911," she said during her speech at the 2000 Republican National Convention. Still, she told Nordlinger, Bush knows that "the United States is *the* critical actor in international politics and has no choice but to been involved in the world." One of Bush's first acts as president-elect was his selection of Rice as his national security adviser, which made her part of a team that includes Colin Powell as secretary of state and Donald Rumsfeld as secretary of defense.

Now more than ever before, Rice is in the spotlight, as part of what has been touted as a notably diverse Republican administration. For years, Rice has been asked if her sex and skin color have hurt or helped her in her career. "I don't spend too much time thinking about it," she told Nordlinger, pointing out that she "can't go back and recreate [herself] as a white male" to test one theory or another. Nevertheless, she also said to Nordlinger that she wishes the "black middle class would spend less time thinking about itself and more time worrying about the witches' brew that is poverty and race. That is something that those of us who are black and privileged have a lot of responsibility

for." Rice is the co-founder of an organization in East Palo Alto, California, designed to help the neighborhood's poor, mostly minority youth. While she has acknowledged that many African-Americans are distrustful of the Republican Party (and, in fact, voted overwhelmingly for the Democrat Al Gore over Bush), Rice has said that, "for African Americans in particular, what I've been saying is just take another look," as she told Dan Balz for the *Washington Post* (August 1, 2000, on-line).

Nearly a year into her tenure as national security adviser, Rice has emerged as a powerful and highly visible figure in Washington. She is an aggressive advocate for the proposed national missile defense system, which would use ground and space-based technology to defend against long-range ballistic-missile attacks. In August 2001 Rice became the first high-level Bush official to visit Moscow, where she worked to overcome Russian president Vladimir Putin's concerns about the Bush administration's plans to abandon the 1972 Antiballistic Missile (ABM) Treaty in order to pursue missile defense. "Her mission to Moscow was unprecedented," Ivo Daalder, a Brookings Institution fellow, told Jane Perlez for the *New York Times* (August 19, 2001). "No national security adviser since [Henry A.] Kissinger has gone on a routine diplomatic mission to Moscow."

In the days following the terrorist attacks of September 11, 2001, President's Bush's security team quickly transformed itself into a war council. Along with Vice President Dick Cheney, Secretary of State Colin Powell, Defense Secretary Donald Rumsfeld, and others, Rice hastened to identify the enemy and to set into motion an appropriate response. Debates raged among the members of the war council: some called for a limited strike against the suspected organizers of the attack—the Al Qaeda network, led by Osama bin Laden—while others argued for a broad campaign against state sponsors of terrorism, including Iraq. According to many media accounts, Rice has been a pivotal figure in those debates, as well as a frequent presence at the president's side. "The outline of the war plan often emerges from the private conversations between two newcomers to the world of the battlefield, George W. Bush and Condoleezza Rice," David E. Sanger and Thom Shanker wrote for the *New York Times* (September 23, 2001). According to Sanger and Shanker, after hours of debate among his security advisers over the weekend following the attack, Bush called Rice to a private meeting and, instructing her to take notes, said, "Here's what I want to do."

Rice, who has claimed not to make career plans very far in advance, has nonetheless said that her dream job would be commissioner of the National Football League. Many, however, believe that she will go further in politics. Nordlinger predicted in 2000 that if Bush were elected and Rice signed on as part of his administration, she would become "rock-star big" and a "major cultural figure, adorning the bedroom walls of innumerable kids and the covers of innumerable magazines."

Called "Condy" by her friends and close associates, Rice has been a National Fellow at the Hoover Institute on War, Revolution, and Peace and has been awarded an honorary doctorate from the University of Notre Dame. She has never been married. — M.A.H.

Suggested Reading: *Chicago Tribune* VI p5 Aug. 15, 1993; *Financial Times* p8 Dec. 28, 1995; *National Review* (on-line) Aug. 1, 2000; *New York Times* B p7 June 23, 1993, A p10 Aug. 19, 2001, A p1+ Sep. 23, 2001; *Salon.com* Mar. 20, 2000; *Stanford Report* (on-line) June 9, 1999; *Washington Post* (on-line) Aug. 9, 2000; *Contemporary Authors* vol. 154, 1997

Selected Works: *Uncertain Allegiance: The Soviet Union and the Czechoslovak Army*, 1984; *The Gorbachev Era* (with Alexander Dallin), 1986; *Germany Unified and Europe Transformed* (with Philip Zelikow), 1995

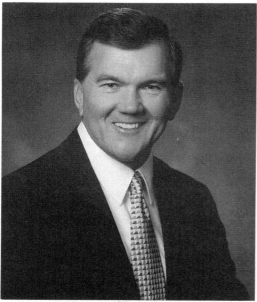

Courtesy of Pennsylvania governor's office

Ridge, Tom

Aug. 26, 1945– Director of the U.S. Office of Homeland Security; former governor of Pennsylvania. Address: Office of Homeland Security, The White House, 1600 Pennsylvania Ave., N.W., Washington, DC 20500

In his address to Congress nine days after the September 11, 2001 terrorist attacks on New York and Washington, D.C., President George W. Bush an-

nounced the creation of the new, Cabinet-level Office of Homeland Security, to be directed by Tom Ridge, who was then in his second term as governor of Pennsylvania. Bush praised Ridge, who is a Vietnam War veteran, as "a true patriot and a trusted friend," as Christopher Marquis reported for the *New York Times* (September 21, 2001). Ridge, Bush went on to explain, would be entrusted with a twofold task: "He will lead, oversee and coordinate a comprehensive national strategy to safeguard our country against terrorism and respond to any attacks that may come."

Like George W. Bush, who served as governor of Texas before becoming president, Tom Ridge was among the GOP politicians swept to power in the November 1994 elections, when the Republican Party captured both houses of Congress as well as a sizable majority of the nation's state governorships. According to conventional wisdom, the victorious GOP newcomers fell into two camps: the ideological firebrands in the Congress (commonly associated with then–House Speaker Newt Gingrich), and the more moderate, more pragmatically inclined GOP governors. Among the latter grouping, Ridge emerged as a rising star. He was mentioned as a possible presidential running mate for Bob Dole (in 1996) and George W. Bush (in 2000), and was likewise considered for secretary of defense in December 2000 by the incoming Bush administration. Conservative on some issues (he is, in the words of the *Economist* [December 11, 1999], "tough as old boots on crime") and liberal on others (he has proven himself consistently pro-choice), Ridge often built support for his policies across party lines, and was among the more popular Pennsylvania governors in recent history.

Thomas Joseph Ridge was born on August 26, 1945 in Munhall, Pennsylvania, into a working-class family. His father, also named Thomas, was a traveling salesman for the Armour Meat Co., and his mother, Laura, was a homemaker. Hearing-impaired at birth, Ridge grew up in Erie, a city in Pittsburgh's so-called Steel Valley. He attended the Cathedral Preparatory School, a Catholic high school in Erie, and performed well enough to win an academic scholarship to Harvard University, in Cambridge, Massachusetts. He graduated from Harvard in 1967, taking a bachelor's degree with honors in government studies, and then entered the Dickinson School of Law, in Carlisle, Pennsylvania. After his first year at Dickinson, Ridge's studies were interrupted: he was drafted into the U.S. Army and served from 1969 to 1970, as an infantry staff sergeant in the Vietnam War. During his tour of duty, Ridge received several military commendations, including a Bronze Star for Valor, the Vietnamese Cross of Gallantry, and the Combat Infantry Badge. (Combat duty worsened his hearing, and as a result he now wears a hearing aid.) He resumed his studies at Dickinson upon his return to the U.S. and completed his law degree in 1972.

For 10 years after graduating from law school, Ridge served as an assistant district attorney in Erie County. In 1982 he successfully ran for a seat in Congress, thus becoming the first enlisted Vietnam veteran to serve in the House of Representatives. Even at this early stage in his political career, Ridge proved adept at appealing to voters across party lines: although his district, the 21st Congressional District, had been largely and historically Democratic, he had run as a Republican. In office Ridge strove to maintain that bipartisan support, casting himself as a pro-business, tough-on-crime Republican who was nevertheless moderate on some social issues. He voted for the 1994 assault-weapons ban, for example, which was largely opposed by Republicans, and articulated a clear (if hardly activist) pro-choice stance on abortion. Ridge served six consecutive terms as a congressional representative, relinquishing the post only after his successful 1994 bid for the governorship of Pennsylvania.

That gubernatorial race was hotly contested. After capturing the GOP nomination in May by defining himself as an outsider and by distancing himself from the status quo in Harrisburg, the state capital (his principal opponent in the Republican primary, Ernest D. Preate, was the state attorney general), Ridge was pitted against the Democratic lieutenant governor, Mark S. Singel, in the November general election. (The Democratic governor, Robert P. Casey, had already served two terms and was prevented from seeking a third by Pennsylvania law.) Again, the campaign was pitched by Ridge and his supporters as a contest between an upright outsider intent on reform, on the one hand, and politics as usual, on the other: "I have not been part of the Harrisburg problem," Ridge told a crowd of well-wishers after capturing the GOP nomination, as quoted by Michael deCourcy Hinds in the *New York Times* (May 12, 1994), "but beginning tonight, you and I become part of the Harrisburg solution." For his part, Singel emphasized his experience in state government.

During the campaign, Ridge pledged to stimulate economic growth and create jobs by cutting corporate taxes and by reducing environmental regulations—which, he argued, were driving businesses out of the state. Until the final weeks of the contest, the two candidates were neck-and-neck: Singel, in an effort to capitalize on the nation's conservative mood, had sought to portray himself as a moderate—as opposed to a liberal—Democrat, with the result that the two would-be governors offered similar platforms. The race turned bitter in October, when a convicted murderer whom Singel had paroled was arrested in New York, accused of raping one woman and suspected of killing another. After the Ridge campaign ran ads accusing Singel of "bleeding heart stupidity" in the case of the parolee, who was black, Singel charged Ridge with playing the race card and attempting to "Willie Hortonize" the contest (a reference to a tactic used by George Bush in the 1988 presidential race). Soon, both candidates were bandying recrimina-

tions and striving to trump one another with tough-on-crime proposals, a development that led the *Philadelphia Inquirer*, as cited by Mimi Hall for *USA Today* (October 21, 1994), to brand the race a "my chest is hairier than yours" affair. Ridge pulled ahead in the final stretch. "In the end," Mimi Hall wrote for *USA Today* (November 10, 1994), "it may have been the convicted killer's release that gave Ridge the edge." On January 17, 1995 Ridge was sworn in as the state's 43d governor.

For the most part, Ridge has followed through on his campaign promises. In his first official act, the governor called the Pennsylvania General Assembly into a special session on crime, leading to a law that increased punishments for offenses against children and a "three-strikes" law, which requires mandatory sentencing for repeat offenders. The session also introduced measures for speeding executions, with the result that, under Ridge, Pennsylvania began employing capital punishment for the first time since 1962. As of late 1999 Ridge had signed more than 100 death warrants and had succeeded in implementing tough penalties for juvenile offenders. While Ridge and his supporters argue, as stated in the governor's biography on *www.state.pa.us*, that such measures have resulted in "an unprecedented elevation of victims' rights," critics point out that the tough new anticrime measures, including capital punishment, are applied disproportionately to African-Americans and Hispanics.

After taking the reins of government, Ridge also went about fulfilling his promise to stimulate the economy by cutting taxes. In his first year as governor, Ridge slashed taxes by $286 million—the second-largest tax cut in state history and the third-largest tax cut in the nation that decade—and he has continued to do so: since 1994, business taxes have been reduced by some $4 billion. In addition, the Ridge administration relaxed many government regulations (particularly environmental regulations) affecting companies that do business in Pennsylvania. As a direct result, Ridge and his supporters have argued, Pennsylvania has attracted 250,000 new jobs since January 1995. Others, however, give some of the credit for the state's job growth to Ridge's predecessors, as well as to a booming national economy. Terry Madonna, a political scientist at Millersville State University, said, as quoted by Jake Tapper in *Salon.com* (May 15, 2000), "He has had a set of fortuitous circumstances, the likes of which have never before been seen in Pennsylvania politics. He's the first governor in modern Pennsylvania to inherit hundreds of millions of dollars in budget surpluses."

Such large tax cuts necessitated reductions in government spending; under Ridge, that has meant cutbacks in welfare programs, especially Medicaid. Indeed, Ridge has been a prominent actor in the national trend toward welfare reform. In 1996 the governor signed into law a bill that required healthy welfare recipients without dependent children to work at least 100 hours per month; the bill also required young welfare parents to stay in school. In addition, Ridge moved to drop 220,000 Pennsylvanians from Medicaid programs. That measure in particular drew strong opposition: Ed Rendell, a Democratic former mayor of Philadelphia, took out a full-page ad in both the *Philadelphia Inquirer* and the *Philadelphia Daily* denouncing the cut as a "human and fiscal catastrophe," and Michael R. Veon, the Democratic whip in the Pennsylvania legislature, as cited by Tapper, objected that "the welfare reform wasn't innovative, like [what Governor] Tommy Thompson has done in Wisconsin. Tommy Thompson has done welfare reform the right way, and the harder way. By spending more money on welfare today. . . . Here, welfare reform essentially consisted of reducing the Medicaid rolls by cutting people off Medicaid." In response, Ridge spokesman Tim Reeves dismissed "the horror stories of what we were told would happen to Pennsylvania men and women if this were passed. If that were true, we'd be hearing from them." Nevertheless, Ridge has recently proposed returning 110,000 of the working poor to Medicaid coverage.

In the summer of 1996, Ridge briefly gained national prominence after Republican insiders let it be known that Senator Bob Dole, the Republican presidential nominee, was considering Ridge as his vice presidential running mate. Speculation about a possible Dole-Ridge ticket peaked in early summer, after a top Dole aide, as quoted by Kathryn Q. Seelye in the *New York Times* (July 26, 1996), pronounced Ridge "the top horse at the moment." However, Ridge's political star dimmed after the pro-life wing of the Republican Party objected vehemently to the Pennsylvania governor's support for abortion rights, and by July Ridge had more or less withdrawn himself from consideration. (The nod eventually went to Jack Kemp.) As Reeves told Seelye, "[Ridge] is flattered in the extreme, but he does not think he'll be asked. He thinks there are better people out there. And he's only been in office 18 months, and there is more to do here."

Ridge was quite popular in his home state at the conclusion of his first term, and on November 3, 1998 he was reelected with over 57 percent of the vote in a four-way race. He not only secured the widest margin of victory for a Republican governor in the state's history—he did so in a year in which the public, upset at the Republican-controlled Congress's efforts to impeach President Bill Clinton in connection with the Monica Lewinsky scandal, turned away from the Republican Party. Still, a number of observers suggested that Ridge's soaring popularity had more to do with good luck and a pleasant personality than with his governing skills. As state representative John Lawless, a conservative Republican from outside Philadelphia, told Tapper, "We've had six years of a great economy. I mean, I'm not ready to be governor, but I probably could have run the state, too. He's had a

great ride on the economy, all these guys have . . ." A correspondent for the *Economist* (December 11, 1999), on the other hand, attributed Ridge's political success to his "blurring of the [Republican] party's traditional division between social and economic conservatives, and the re-emergence of a Republican centre."

Whatever the reasons for Ridge's popularity, he was conspicuous enough during the early phase of the 2000 presidential campaign to attract the attention of George W. Bush, who was reported to have taken a long look at the Pennsylvania governor as a possible running mate. William Kristol, the editor and publisher of the conservative *Weekly Standard*, told Tapper in April of that year, "I think he's No. 1 on the short list." Ridge was attractive to Bush not only because of his image as a moderate in an election in which the Republicans strove to court the political center, but also because of the prediction that Pennsylvania would play a crucial role as a swing state in the November presidential election. (On Election Day, the state went to the Democratic nominee, Vice President Al Gore; its congressional delegation was split, with 11 Democrats and 10 Republicans elected or reelected.) Further, it was pointed out that Ridge, as a longtime friend of the U.S. senator and presidential candidate John McCain, might be able to smooth over the tensions that had emerged between the Bush and McCain camps during the Republican primaries. Ultimately, however, Ridge's pro-choice views appear to have kept him off the ticket, just as they had in 1996. As Dante Chinni speculated in the *Christian Science Monitor* (July 20, 2000), "Picking a pro-choice running mate would likely make Bush's abortion stance more of an issue, not less of one. Suddenly the questions about where exactly Bush draws the line on abortion get a lot tougher." While Ridge, as the governor of a battleground state, continued to play an important role in the election, he receded from the media spotlight with Bush's announcement that Dick Cheney was to be his running mate.

Speculation about Ridge's political future resurfaced in December 2000, as President-elect Bush indicated that he was considering naming Ridge secretary of defense. It was further reported that General Colin Powell, Bush's choice for secretary of state, supported the appointment of Ridge in that post. Ultimately, however, Ridge was passed over, in part because the Republican Party's ultra-conservative wing voiced strident opposition to him. While some, including the Reverend Jerry Falwell, took issue chiefly with Ridge's centrist stance on abortion, others on the right, among them John J. Miller and Ramesh Ponnuru of the *National Review* (December 20, 2000), objected to what Miller and Ponnuru identified as "a congressional voting record that included opposition to President Reagan's Strategic Defense Initiative, the MX missile, aid to the Nicaraguan contras, and nuclear testing, as well as support for the nuclear freeze."

Even after Ridge was sworn in as director of homeland security, on October 8, 2001, a number of questions remained as to the precise nature of his job and the precise extent of his powers. Indeed, Ridge himself seemed uncertain of his task; in a farewell news conference at the Pennsylvania State Capitol, in Harrisburg, he told reporters, according to Eric Pianin and Bradley Graham in the *Washington Post* (October 4, 2001), "There are so many laws and regulations that have to be sorted through to identify specifically what I can and cannot do in this position. But what I do know is this: The president has said, 'You'll have the authority and the personnel that you need to get the job done that I have asked you to do.'" Still, Ridge suggested that his job would consist chiefly of coordinating, rather than directing, the efforts of other agencies and subagencies involved in preventing and responding to terrorist attacks. "We've got a lot of good people, a lot of good assets; we just have to fine-tune how they operate with one another," he said. "I'm not running the Coast Guard; I'm not running FEMA; I'm not running the FBI."

Ridge and his wife, Michele, a former executive director of the Erie County, Pennsylvania, public library system, were married in 1979. The couple have two children, Leslie and Tommy, as well as three dogs: Molly, Allie, and Gus. — P.K.

Suggested Reading: *Economist* p31 Dec. 11, 1999; *New York Times* p25 Oct. 9, 1994, B p5 Sep. 21, 2001; *Salon.com* (on-line) May 15, 2000, with photo; *U.S. News & World Report* p30 Jan. 23, 1995; Washington Post A p24 Oct. 4, 2001

Courtesy of Quicksilver

Robbins, Tony

Feb. 29, 1960– Writer; motivational speaker.
Address: Anthony Robbins & Associates, 2698 Rte. 516, Suite E, Old Bridge, NJ 08857; Dreamlife, Inc., 425 W. 15th St., Suite #3R, New York, NY 10011

Ever since Benjamin Franklin extolled the virtues of industry and frugality in his *Poor Richard's Almanack* (1732), a host of inspirational writers, motivational speakers, and self-help gurus have appeared on the American cultural landscape to preach the gospel of success through optimism and self-reliance. Books such as the Horatio Alger novels, Dale Carnegie's *How to Win Friends and Influ-*ence People, Norman Vincent Peale's *The Power of Positive Thinking*, and Thomas A. Harris's *I'm OK, You're OK* have sold millions of copies and left their mark on the popular culture; their authors often doubled as public speakers, traveling around the nation to promote their messages in a style that borrowed equally from the evangelical preacher and the itinerant salesman. Tony Robbins, a writer and motivational speaker who has been called "America's results coach" and the "mahatma of motivation," is an heir to that tradition. Currently among the biggest names on the self-improvement circuit, Robbins inspires an enthusiasm among some of his disciples that borders on religious fervor. "I saw him as a powerful enlightened being who could bring light into anyone's life," Michael Bolduc, the former vice president of Anthony Robbins & Associates, wrote in the introduction to his biography of Robbins, as posted on *anthonyrobbinslifestory.com*. "I saw a light in this man, and it hasn't changed since the day I met him," the disc jockey Casey Kasem, a longtime Robbins fan, told Michael Walker for *Self* (August 1992).

In the past two decades, Robbins has written four motivational self-help books, which have been translated into 14 languages; has spread his message by computer software, late-night infomercials, and audio tapes (which include such titles as *How to Get What You Really Want*, *How to Shape Your Destiny Now*, and *How to Unleash the Financial Genius Within You* and which have sold more than 35 million copies); has advised Fortune 500 CEOs, members of two royal families, professional athletes, and former president Bill Clinton (while he was still in the White House); and has spoken before audiences at packed sports arenas and concert halls across the country. While he is tight-lipped about his precise income, many sources report that his books and seminars generate more than $50 million in annual revenue.

Tony Robbins was born Anthony J. Mahavorick on February 29, 1960 in Glendora, California, a suburb of Los Angeles. Early on, his father, an actor and parking-garage attendant named John Mahavorick, divorced his mother; Robbins took his surname from his mother's third husband, Jim Robbins. (His mother's second marriage was short-lived.) According to Bolduc, Robbins's mother had divorced and remarried three times by the time her son had finished grade school; Walker reported that she had divorced and remarried four times in that same period. While he was growing up, Robbins's family, which includes a sister, Taura Robbins, and a brother, Marcus Robbins, was often quite poor.

By all accounts, Robbins was an unhappy boy. In addition to the difficulties he experienced at home, he was overweight, which made him a frequent target of his classmates' jeers. Nonetheless, Robbins has said that he always harbored big plans for the future. "For most of my life I've had a sense of destiny," he told Bolduc. "I can remember at seven years old having images in my mind of reaching mass numbers of people and making a huge difference." He was an indifferent student until a high-school history teacher persuaded him that he had a gift for public speaking. "He pulled me aside and said, 'You are magical. You will be one of the best speakers who has ever spoken,'" Robbins recalled to Bolduc. With the teacher's encouragement, he memorized a speech entitled "The Will to Win" and presented it at a local public-speaking tournament, which he won.

According to Robbins, the content of that speech made a far greater impact on him than his victory. Inspired, he embarked on a regimen of study that entailed reading several hundred self-help books, and, as he recalled to Walker, he "got excited about human development. I started reading [Ralph Waldo] Emerson's essays, Dale Carnegie and all that stuff." Bolduc also mentioned Harry Lorayne's Secrets of Mind Power and Napoleon Hill's best-selling Think and Grow Rich as seminal early influences on Robbins. (Hill's Depression-era book teaches "how to recognize, relate, assimilate and apply principles whereby you can achieve any goal whatsoever that doesn't violate Universal Law," according to W. Clement Stone, the insurance magnate who chairs the Napoleon Hill Foundation, as quoted on amazon.com.)

After his high-school graduation, Robbins met Jim Rohn, a motivational speaker who ran seminars for companies and their employees. Robbins persuaded Rohn to hire him as a seminar promoter, a line of work at which he immediately excelled. Soon, other self-help gurus, such as Harvey and Marilyn Diamond, authors of the best-selling diet manual Fit for Life, were paying the young man to manage their seminars, too. Nevertheless, Robbins has said, he felt deeply unsatisfied. Then, one day, he had a revelation. As he recalled in his book Awaken the Giant Within: How to Take Immediate Control of Your Mental, Emotional, Physical and Financial Destiny! (1992), "I [remember] feeling like my life didn't matter, as if the events of the world were controlling me. I also remember the moment my life changed, the moment I finally said, 'I've had it! I know I'm much more than I'm demonstrating mentally, emotionally, and physically in my life.' I made a decision in that moment which was to alter my life forever. I decided to change virtually every aspect of my life. I decided I would never again settle for less than I could be."

Soon thereafter Robbins met John Grindler and Richard Bandler, psychologists associated with the University of California at Santa Cruz. From them, he learned a therapeutic technique called neuro-linguistic programming (NLP), which has roots in alternative therapy, linguistics, and hypnosis. (Adherents claim that NLP practitioners are able to duplicate the achievements of successful people by mimicking their subconscious habits.) By age 22 Robbins had begun to offer his own seminars—"Fear into Power" seminars, as he dubbed them—in which he taught NLP techniques. At one of his early seminars, one of the participants began challenging him belligerently. Robbins responded with a reference to "modeling," NLP jargon for emulating the behavior of a successful person. "I said to [the heckler], 'Look, you can do anything,'" he recalled to Walker. "I've 'modeled' a guy who walked on fire. You can do it, too. Tell you what, I've got this new seminar . . .' It was new because I was making it up while I was standing there. Then I had to figure out how to pull it off." Soon afterward Robbins successfully conducted a "fire walk," in which a group of people walked over hot coals. The stunt brought him widespread publicity, and the fire walk quickly became a centerpiece of every Robbins seminar. Thanks to the phenomenal popularity and profitability of his seminars, he earned his first million dollars before the age of 24.

Meanwhile, Robbins had begun committing his teachings to print. His first book, Unlimited Power, The New Science of Personal Achievement (1986), is characterized on the Web site of its publisher, Simon and Schuster, as "a guidebook to superior performance in an age of success" and "a revolutionary fitness book for the mind." In its first chapter, as reprinted on-line by Simon and Schuster, Robbins wrote, "The purpose of this book is to share with you what made the difference in changing my life for the better. . . . The power to magically transform our lives into our greatest dreams lies waiting within us all. It's time to unleash it!" Awaken the Giant Within, Robbins's next book, purported to offer, according to Simon and Schuster (on-line), "a step-by-step program teaching the fundamental lessons of self-mastery that will enable you to discover your true purpose, take control of your life and harness the forces that shape your destiny." "This is a giant book that you can use to produce giant results in your life . . . ," Robbins wrote in Awaken the Giant Within. "By consistently taking advantage of each of the chapters in this book, you'll ensure your ability to maximize your potential." Robbins's subsequent books, *Giant Steps* (1994) and *Notes from a Friend* (1995), further elaborated on his favorite themes—success, self-empowerment, and conquest of destiny. All his books have sold well, as have their audio versions. Robbins's forthcoming book, tentatively titled "The Driving Force," is scheduled for publication in 2001.

Many psychiatrists and health-care professionals have faulted Robbins for offering unrealistic, quick-fix solutions to difficult problems. Robbins has challenged such detractors to "find me somebody who's been to one of my seminars, or who's read my books, and says my message is simplistic and doesn't address the real problems," as Walker quoted him as saying. In an interview with David Abel for the *Boston Globe* (July 31, 2000), Robbins dismissed as "uneducated" the criticism of his approach as "simplistic solutions to lifelong problems," and he described the hypothetical criticizer as "some jerk who never took a risk." Robbins has also said that he doesn't think much of Freudian psychoanalysis, which he has derided for its "endless process of analyzing why things happen to us," as he told Walker. "Your past does not have to equal your future," he explained. Further, he is dismissive of rival self-help authors, such as John Bradshaw, who attribute emotional and psychological difficulties to "dysfunctional family" histories. "Everybody comes from a dysfunctional family," Robbins declared to Jeffry Scott for the *Atlanta Constitution* (October 17, 2000). "You can't use that excuse anymore. I hear people say, 'If God wanted me to be rich, I'd be rich.' Bull. You're broke because you're lazy and sit on your butt all day."

During his recent *Results 2000* tour, Robbins traveled the country spreading his message to audiences that occasionally exceeded 20,000 individuals, who paid upwards of $49 per ticket to hear him. He was joined by personalities who included (often via satellite) the radio and television talk-show host Larry King; the real-estate tycoon Donald Trump; the sales guru Brian Tracy; the lawyer, accountant, and tax expert Sanford C. Botkin, who is the founder of the Tax Reduction Institute; and the retired U.S. Army general H. Norman Schwarzkopf. Despite that celebrity roster, the main draw for most seminar-goers, according to most accounts, was Robbins, who earned as much as $125,000 for a one-day engagement.

A Tony Robbins seminar is a hybrid affair—part revival meeting, part group-therapy session, and part rock concert. Attired in a tailored black suit, Robbins restlessly paces the stage, giving high-fives, punching the air, and urging the audience to "quadruple the intensity!," "push beyond excellence to outstanding!," or shout "I'll do it!" Art Levine, writing for *U.S. News & World Report* (February 24, 1997), reported that on one occasion, Robbins instructed those in attendance to "close your eyes and make a picture in your mind of ecstasy. Now make it a sexual image . . . Breathe the way

you'd breathe if in ecstasy . . . make the sounds of ecstasy . . ."—to all of which the audience complied. In a typical show, his image is projected on giant video screens for the benefit of those seated far from the main stage, and he uses inspirational rock anthems (songs by Phil Collins and Michael Jackson are favorites), sophisticated concert lighting, and pyrotechnic effects.

A physically imposing man, the lantern-jawed Robbins stands six feet seven inches and wears size 16 shoes; his head, according to Janet Woolley in the *Washington Post* (February 12, 1995), "looks like something found on Easter Island." Industrious and driven, Robbins told a *New York Times Magazine* (May 11, 1997) interviewer that he sometimes goes "a whole week on three hours of sleep a night. I give 10,000 percent." According to Bolduc, he attracts admirers and autograph seekers with the frequency of a movie star. "Everyday, while going about his day-to-day activities, [Robbins] is stopped an average of 12 times by people who have been impacted tremendously by his teachings."

Robbins makes his home—several sources described it as a "castle"—in Del Mar, California, a suburb of San Diego, and often commutes to his seminars via private jet helicopter. In *Awaken the Giant Within*, Robbins noted that, during his commute, he enjoys watching the "dolphins playing with the surfers in the waves below. It's a sight that my wife, Becky, and I treasure as one of life's special gifts." As of April 2001, he and his wife, who has three children from a previous marriage, were reportedly filing for divorce. — P.K.

Suggested Reading: *New York Times Magazine* p17 May 11, 1997, with photos; *Self* p123+ Aug. 1992, with photos; *U.S. News & World Report* p53+ Feb. 24, 1997; *Washington Post* p12 Feb. 12, 1995

Selected Books: *Unlimited Power, The New Science of Personal Achievement*, 1986; *Awaken the Giant Within: How to Take Immediate Control of Your Mental, Emotional, Physical and Financial Destiny!*, 1992; *Giant Steps*, 1994; *Notes from a Friend*, 1995; *Driving Force*, 2001

Roberts, Nora

Oct. 10, 1950– Writer. Address: c/o Creative Promotions, 344 Cedar Ave., Ridgewood, NJ 07450

Every four minutes in the United States, someone buys a Nora Roberts romance novel. By the end of 2001, Roberts, whose first book appeared in 1981, will have published 142 novels. Her books are mainstays on best-seller lists—to date, 56 of them have been *New York Times* best-sellers, 14 in the

John Earle/Courtesy of Penguin Putnam Inc.
Nora Roberts

year 2000 alone. Since the 1990s she has also written under the name J. D. Robb. In 1986 Roberts was inducted into the Romance Writers of America Hall of Fame. According to her Web site in November 2001, more than 127 million copies of her books have been printed.

It was a dark and snowy night when Roberts started her writing career. A 29-year-old homemaker stuck inside her Silver Spring, Maryland, home during a fierce blizzard, she started writing in a spiral notebook. "I was snowbound with my then three and six-year-old sons. Can you possibly imagine the horror of this? Stuck, day after day, without four wheel drive transportation, without nearly enough chocolate to keep body and soul together, with two young boys bent on destruction and no morning kindergarten. We're all lucky to have survived. But out of it, my life changed when I decided to finally take one of the stories in my head and write it down on paper. I discovered the process of writing, and fell in love," she said in a 1998 interview for the *Book Report* (on-line).

The youngest of the five children—and only daughter—of Bernard Edward Robertson and the former Eleanor Harris, the writer was born Nora Robertson on October 10, 1950 in Washington, D.C. She attended Catholic schools in nearby Silver Spring. (She has never gone to college.) "I come from a family of readers," she said during the interview for the *Book Report*. "Books were always a part of our lives, our house, our day. I didn't realize until I was nearly an adult that there were people who didn't read for pleasure." She named Mary Stewart as one of "the authors I loved, still love, and consistently admire." In 1968, at age 17, she married her high-school sweetheart, Ronald Auf-

dem-Brinke, with whom she had two sons. The couple divorced in January 1985, and that July Roberts married a carpenter, Bruce Wilder, whom she had met when he was remodeling her house.

The book Roberts began writing during the blizzard of 1979, "Melodies of Love," was never published. "Editors rejected it soundly, for which I will always be grateful. There aren't words to describe how bad the book was. But it really taught me I could do it," Roberts told Nanci Hellmich for *USA Today* (March 7, 2000). With that experience under her belt, she continued to write. A casual acquaintance then told her about Silhouette, a publishing company originally set up to be the American counterpart of the Canadian-based Harlequin, a famous publisher of romances by which Roberts had already been rejected. Nancy Jackson, an acquisitions editor at Silhouette, found in the "slush pile" (submissions from authors without agents) Roberts's manuscript about a young Irish woman who falls in love with a horse breaker after she moves to the United States to work on her uncle's farm. The manuscript impressed Jackson. At this point Roberts followed a friend's recommendation and called Amy Berkower, a fledgling literary agent who was looking for clients. As a result, in 1981 Silhouette published the story Jackson had discovered—Roberts's first novel, *Irish Thoroughbred.*

Roberts has had great success in serializing her novels, exploring characters and entire families over the course of several books. Among her recurring characters are the O'Hurley triplets, the MacKades, and the Calhouns. Roberts's most popular series concerns the MacGregor clan; central to those books is Daniel MacGregor, the whimsical, matchmaking leader of the Scottish family. The first book in the series, *Playing the Odds*, centers on Serena MacGregor, a blackjack dealer on a cruise ship, who falls in love with Justin Blade, a savvy gambler. The series continued with *Tempting Fate* and *All the Possibilities*, novels in which Daniel MacGregor is a continual presence. The three books came out successively, in July, August, and September 1992. (The series' enormous popularity has inspired the manufacture and sale of a set of collectible porcelain dolls.)

It was Roberts's agent who suggested that the writer adopt a literary alter ego. The result was the pseudonym J. D. Robb, which Roberts has parlayed into another series of top-selling books. The Robb books are set in the year 2058 and focus on the lives of Eve Dallas, a police lieutenant in New York City, and her millionaire beau, Roarke. The franchise has been a phenomenal commercial success, spawning the hits *Naked in Death* (1995), *Glory in Death* (1995), *Rapture in Death* (1996), and *Ceremony in Death* (1997), among others.

Although she often incorporates mystery and suspense into her plots, central to all of Roberts's books are romance and relationships. Brokenhearted Irish glassblowers, losing themselves in their craft to avoid thinking about love, fall in love with

Dublin gallery owners; world-famous concert violinists, spurned by their conductor boyfriends, seek refuge in small towns and fall in love with murder suspects. Known for their wry humor and their alternating narrators, Roberts's books appeal to a large and varied readership. "There is no formula," she told Bobbie Battista for *CNN.com* (January 31, 1998). "There is a framework, as there is with any genre. If you are going to do romance, obviously, you have to have a love story. And that has to be the focus of the book. And in a romance, we want that love story to end happily. . . . There has to be conflict. There has to be emotional commitment. And there has to be sexual tension. That's it. Everything else is up to you, the writer. . . . It takes a good story teller, first and foremost. Romance writing isn't different from any other . . . sort of popular fiction in that—plot, narrative setting, dialogue—everything has to be there. You have to have good, interesting, strong characters. And for a romance, you have to have the dynamic between a man and a woman. You have to have a strong committed relationship and show that developing relationship throughout the book."

Roberts is quick to credit her strict Catholic upbringing when discussing her remarkable productivity. Her regimen consists of writing from 9 a.m. to 5 p.m. every day, and if she is very involved in a story, she will write more at night. "I have strong discipline, smacked into my head with the rulers of many of the nuns who educated me. There is no one more fierce than a nun. Bless them all. They also helped refine the guilt which is a strong motivator for doing your job. At least for me," she told the *Book Report*. Her method is to write a story quickly, then go back and flesh out characters and settings.

In 1997 Roberts filed a lawsuit against another romance writer, Janet Dailey, who admitted to having plagiarized Roberts's work in her novels *Aspen Gold* (1992), *Notorious* (1996), and "Scrooge Wore Spurs," which was eventually blocked from publication. The plagiarism was discovered when readers challenged Dailey about her texts during an online chat. Internet users then posted comparisons of the two writers' works, making clear what had occurred. Dailey claimed that when the copyright infringement took place, she had been suffering stress stemming from the cancer-related deaths of her two brothers, the lung-cancer surgery of her husband, and the death of the family dog. The suit was settled out of court, with Roberts receiving financial compensation, which she donated to Literacy Volunteers of America, the Authors Guild Foundation, and the Authors League Fund. Despite the settlement, the suit took a toll on Roberts, even forcing her to stop writing for a period.

Nonetheless, in 1998 Roberts notched some 11 novels on the *New York Times* best-seller list. Four of those books reached the number-one spot, and she won a lifetime achievement award from the Romance Writers of America that year. Fourteen of her novels made the *Times* best-seller list in 2000.

Her book *Sanctuary* was made into a CBS television movie, starring Melissa Gilbert, Costas Mandylor, and Kathy Baker, in 2001. The book and movie tell the story of JoEllen Hathaway, a professional photographer who is being stalked. "I was really, really happy with [the movie]," Roberts told *ET Television* (February 22, 2001, on-line). "It was just beautifully filmed. . . . It followed the book as much as it possibly could, and you don't always get that."

Roberts currently lives in Keedysville, Maryland, with her husband, Bruce Wilder. Wilder runs the Turn the Page Bookstore Cafe, in Boonsboro, Maryland, which specializes in books by Nora Roberts and other romance writers, science fiction, mysteries, and books about the Civil War. Items available for sale through Roberts's Web site include T-shirts, a book bag, and a wine glass imprinted with the words "The Villa." Offered free of charge is a bumper sticker that reads "I'd rather be reading a novel by Nora Roberts." — A.T.

Suggested Reading: *Book Report* (on-line) 1999; *CNN.com* (on-line) 1998; *ET Television* (on-line) 2001; Nora Roberts Web site; *Publishers Weekly* p18+ May 4, 1998; *Publishers Weekly* (on-line) 1998; *USA Today* D p1+ Mar. 7, 2000

Selected Books: *Irish Thoroughbred*, 1981; *Blithe Images*, 1982; *From This Day*, 1984; *Tempting Fate*, 1985; *All the Possibilities*, 1985; *The Art of Deception*, 1986; *Mind Over Matter*, 1987; *Irish Rose*, 1988; *Sweet Revenge*, 1989; *Taming Natasha*, 1990; *Luring a Lady*, 1991; *Unfinished Business*, 1992; *Hidden Riches*, 1994; *True Betrayals*, 1995; *Born in Shame*, 1996; *Sanctuary*, 1997; *Serena and Caine: The Mac-Gregors*, 1998; *River's End*, 1999; *Once Upon a Dream*, 2000; *The Villa*, 2001; *Midnight Bayou*, 2001; as J. D. Robb—*Naked in Death*, 1995; *Glory in Death*, 1995; *Rapture in Death*, 1996; *Ceremony in Death*, 1997; *Conspiracy in Death*, 1998; *Betrayal in Death*, 2001

Rodriguez, Arturo

June 23, 1949– President of United Farm Workers of America. Address: United Farm Workers of America, P.O. Box 62, Keene, CA 93531

Since he became its president, in 1993, Arturo Rodriguez has revitalized the United Farm Workers of America (UFW), the organization founded in 1962 by the charismatic Mexican-American labor leader Cesar Chavez. Rodriguez succeeded Chavez, who had been his father-in-law, soon after the older man's death, during a period when the UFW was experiencing a serious decline. Thanks to his vigorous organizing projects and other activities, Rodriguez has increased the union's profile and mem-

Jocelyn Sherman/Associated Press

Arturo Rodriguez

bership roles, and he has negotiated contracts that have significantly benefitted farm workers. His goal is to improve the quality of life of the millions of people, many of them Mexican immigrants, who do backbreaking farm labor for minimum wage in the U.S. "I think he's the Martin Luther King Jr. of this generation," Richard Bensinger, the director of organizing for the AFL-CIO, a federation of 68 American unions, told Steven Greenhouse for the *New York Times* (June 30, 1997), "in that he stands and fights and dedicates his life in a private way and public way to social justice. He sits on motel floors and speaks to workers. He doesn't do this just in public. He's the real thing. He has increased his union's membership by 25 percent in just a few years. He's a model for the rest of the labor movement to follow."

Arturo Rodriguez was born in San Antonio, Texas, on June 23, 1949. His father was a sheet-metal worker, and his mother a schoolteacher. One of his grandfathers raised cattle on a small farm outside San Antonio. Rodriguez attended Catholic elementary schools and graduated from La Salle High School, in San Antonio, in 1967. It was at La Salle that, through a parish priest, he first learned about the United Farm Workers and their iconic president, Cesar Chavez. Chavez had grown up on a small farm and was well aware of the injustices farmers and farm laborers faced. In 1962, with Dolores Huerto, family members, and others, he formed the National Farm Workers Union. (The name was later changed to United Farm Workers of America.) For the next three decades, he championed the rights of farm laborers, and through well-publicized marches, fasts, and boycotts, he succeeded in gaining better conditions for many workers and obtaining union contracts for them.

Rodriguez attended St. Mary's University, in San Antonio, where he became involved with the UFW boycott of grapes. The boycott had begun when grape growers refused to consider union demands for fair pay and better working conditions. After the workers went on strike, the growers brought in illegal workers to harvest the grapes. Rodriguez graduated from St. Mary's in 1971, with a B.A. degree in sociology. That summer he organized support for UFW boycotts. In the fall he entered the University of Michigan at Ann Arbor, where he pursued a master's degree in sociology. In 1972, while still a graduate student, he worked in Blissfield, Michigan, with a publicly funded antipoverty program that provided migrant workers in farm-labor camps with housing, sanitation services, and medical assistance. At around this time, through his own experiences and his reading of essays by Chavez, Rodriguez realized that changes in conditions for farm laborers could come only through collective bargaining.

After he earned his master's degree, in 1973, Rodriguez worked in support of UFW boycotts in Detroit. During that year he met Cesar Chavez and Chavez's daughter Linda, with whom he became romantically involved. He and Linda were married in March 1974 at the UFW's headquarters, in Keene, California. The couple then returned to Detroit, where they worked on boycotts. In 1975, with the pending implementation of the California Agricultural Labor Relations Act (ALRA), which protected the rights of farm workers to unionize and choose representatives, the Rodriguezes moved to California to help organize dozens of union-representation elections in the Salinas Valley. Their activities included the UFW campaign at Molera Packing Co.—an artichoke farm where the first election under the ALRA took place, on September 8, 1975. As a result of that balloting, the Teamsters Union, which had previously represented the workers, were voted out, 15–0, in favor of the UFW. In November 1975 Rodriguez followed the harvest to the Imperial Valley of California. There, he continued to organize union elections until January 1976, when the California Labor Relations Board shut down, after legislators refused to continue funding it. Rodriguez spent most of that year on two unsuccessful ventures: California governor Jerry Brown's campaign for the Democratic presidential nomination and the fight for passage of Proposition 14, a UFW-sponsored initiative that would have restored funding to the California Labor Relations Board. Although the proposition did not receive sufficient support from voters to pass, the publicity surrounding it spurred California lawmakers to vote for further funding for the board.

Over the next few years, Rodriguez was involved with organizing union elections in Imperial Valley vegetable fields and Ventura County citrus orchards. He also became the chief instructor at a school in California that had been founded by Chavez to provide formal training for union organizers.

In 1979 Rodriguez directed the UFW boycott in Michigan of Bruce Church Inc.'s Red Coach–brand lettuce, which would continue for many years. He returned to California the following year, to set up a union-sponsored service center in Ventura County that helped farm workers resolve grievances involving such issues as housing, education, and government services. He also coordinated UFW efforts in San Antonio, Texas, for Massachusetts senator Edward M. Kennedy's ultimately unsuccessful campaign for the Democratic presidential nomination.

In 1981 Rodriguez was elected to the UFW National Executive Board. During the next three years, he managed such union operations as organizing, negotiating, and administering contracts for the California table-grape, wine-grape, and tree-fruit industries. In 1984 he worked with Chavez on preparations for a new table-grape boycott; for the next two years, he focused largely on issues affecting grape workers and consumers. He also directed grape-boycott activities in the mid-Atlantic region. In 1988, when Chavez conducted his last major public fast, Rodriguez coordinated events in Delano, California, in which other people fasted as well. He then spent time in New York City, where he met with representatives of major East Coast supermarket chains in an effort to halt grape advertising and promotions. Following this, he headed the grape boycott in California.

From May to September 1992, Rodriguez coordinated UFW help for grape workers who were walking off their jobs in the largest Coachella Valley and San Joaquin Valley vineyard demonstrations since 1973. The workers were protesting poor working conditions and the failure of growers to increase their wages for eight years, among other grievances. The UFW organized thousands of workers at dozens of locations to participate in the walkouts. Thanks to these efforts an industry-wide increase in pay came about. From September to December 1992, Rodriguez led farm workers in a public-education drive to promote the New York grape boycott. Rodriguez was coordinating the grape boycott for the southern states when Chavez died, on April 23, 1993. Soon afterward Rodriguez was elected president of the UFW.

At the time that he ascended to the UFW presidency, conditions for farm workers were worse than they had been at any time since Chavez had gone on hunger strikes and protests in the 1960s and 1970s. Little publicity was being generated in connection with the UFW's grape protests, and sales of the fruit had actually reached new heights. Membership in the UFW was also at an all-time low—about 20,000, down from about 80,000 in the 1970s—and growers were refusing to renew contracts. Some members blamed Chavez for the decline of the UFW; responding to the atmosphere of hostility toward unions that existed in the Republican administrations of President Ronald Reagan and California governor George Deukmejian, Chavez had greatly reduced UFW field organizing in

recent years and at times had even relied on direct mail to recruit members. Nevertheless, stepping into the magnetic Chavez's shoes was no easy task, as Rodriguez was well aware. "I alone could never think of replacing Cesar Chavez," he told a writer for the New York Times (July 19, 1993). "He's just an extraordinary human being. But I have a great team of people to work with. The rest of the leadership of the organization is very dedicated, very committed to wanting to see Cesar's dreams come true." He also noted that, paradoxically, Chavez's death had actually helped the UFW, because it had spurred new interest in the union. "There's a tremendous rebirth taking place," he said. Miguel Contreras, a former UFW official who is currently executive secretary-treasurer of the Los Angeles County Federation of Labor, told Greenhouse, "Cesar had more charisma, but Artie's a better manager. Cesar was publicly perceived as more spiritual; Artie is more pragmatic. Cesar was never a fiery speaker and neither is Artie, but at a gut level, they both really connect when they speak to workers."

In April 1994, on the first anniversary of Chavez's death, Rodriguez led a 343-mile march from Delano to Sacramento, the California state capital, retracing Chavez's steps in 1966. As many as 20,000 farm workers and union supporters greeted the marchers at the capitol steps. The event marked the beginning of a highly successful UFW organizing and negotiating drive. Between 1994 and 1998, the UFW won 16 straight secret-ballot elections for union representation and concluded 21 new contracts with growers. Membership in the union grew by 6,000, to a total of more than 26,000 farm workers under UFW contract. The 16 election victories included votes conducted among rose, grape, mushroom, and strawberry field workers. After some mushroom workers were unionized, their wages jumped by 40 percent, to more than $12 an hour. According to the official National Farm Worker Ministry home page on the World Wide Web, the Wall Street Journal (December 19, 1995) quoted a top AFL-CIO official as stating, "The UFW has had the best record of organizing new members of any union [this year.]" John Sweeney, the president of the AFL-CIO, was quoted in the same article as saying that the UFW is "one of the few bright spots in the American labor movement today." That year, in recognition of his efforts with the UFW, Rodriguez was elected to the AFL-CIO's governing executive council.

In May 1996 the UFW and the Bruce Church Co. signed a work contract, after nearly 18 years of supermarket boycotts of lettuce, led by the UFW, and a series of lawsuits filed by both UFW and Bruce Church against each other. The agreement provided 450 workers with a 4 percent raise in the first year. In the New York Times (May 30, 1996), Carey Goldberg quoted Rodriguez as saying that the new contract was "a tremendous tribute to Cesar Chavez's life and work." Most recently, Rodriguez has led the UFW in what is currently the largest unionization drive in the nation—an effort directed at the 20,000 workers in California's $600 million strawberry industry. "We wanted to focus on a work force in desperate need. Their wages come out to $8,500 a year," Rodriguez told Greenhouse. "Even if families can afford a home, they often have to live two, three, four families together. We see our challenge as being out there to create a better life for these workers." In May 2000, after a drawn-out court case and battles with other unions that had sought to sign up the workers, the UFW won the right to represent 700 Ventura County strawberry workers. In March 2001 Coastal Berry, the world's largest grower of strawberries, signed a three-year contract according to which UFW became the representative of 750 of the company's Ventura County strawberry pickers. The contract, which also provided health-insurance coverage for all pickers who worked at least 60 hours a month, was the first-ever agreement between the UFW and a strawberry producer. Thanks to the agreement, the workers immediately received substantial wage increases.

On other fronts, in 1999 the mushroom producer Quincy Farms came to an agreement with the UFW, thus becoming the only farm in Florida whose workers were covered by union contract. The deal with the UFW promised profit-sharing for the workers—a benefit that is almost unheard-of on American farms. The accord gave the UFW hope for expanding into Florida, the second-largest agricultural state. The UFW also recently signed an agreement with Gallo, covering 450 workers at some or all of the wine maker's seven Sonoma Valley, California, vineyards. About 70 percent of mushroom workers on California's Central Coast are now protected by UFW contracts, as are more than half of Central Valley rose workers.

In November 2000 the UFW ended its 18-year-long boycott of grapes, citing the fact that some of the demands of workers in the industry had been met, such as the call for eliminating the use of harmful pesticides. Some observers noted, however, that many people, union members among them, had lost interest in the boycott, which, they claimed, had never had much of an effect anyway.

Rodriguez currently lives at the UFW headquarters in Keene, in the Tehachapi Mountains, about 80 miles north of Los Angeles. He has one son and two daughters. His wife, Linda, died in 2000, at the age of 49, from complications associated with scleroderma, a connective-tissue disorder that can affect both the skin and internal organs. Described as unassuming, tenacious, and dedicated, Rodriguez has earned only $6,362 annually for many years; he believes one must be poor to serve the poor. "Farm workers are so far behind other workers in terms of wages, health plans, the dignity and respect they don't get," Rodriguez told Greenhouse. "That's what drives us." — G.O.

Suggested Reading: National Farm Worker Ministry (on-line); *New York Times* A p12 July 19, 1993, with photo, A p16 May 30, 1996, with photo, A p8 June 30, 1997, A p14 July 21, 1999; *U. S. News & World Report* p36 Nov 17, 1997, with photo

---

Rollins, Edward J.

Mar. 19, 1943– Chairman of the Rollins Strategy Group; former political consultant. Address: c/o Speakers Platform, P.O. Box 21631, Santa Barbara, CA 93121

Edward J. Rollins has had several political lives. Over a 30-year career as a political consultant and campaign strategist, he helped to win many high-level campaigns, including President Ronald Reagan's landslide reelection victory, in 1984, and Christine Todd Whitman's come-from-behind gubernatorial win in New Jersey, in 1993. Shrewd, loyal, and possessed of sharp political instincts, Rollins is also outspoken and hubristic, qualities that have landed him in controversy after controversy. From his disparaging remarks about Reagan's daughter's political propsects, made while he was working at the Reagan White House, to his temporary switch of allegiance from the Republicans to Ross Perot's Reform Party, to his claim that he had paid members of the black clergy to suppress the black vote in a New Jersey gubernatorial race, to his use of an epithet to describe two Jewish congressmen, Rollins has spent much of his career in hot water. A communications and public-relations expert, specializing in image control and campaign-crisis management, Rollins has sometimes seemed surprisingly unable to manage himself. "Ed is the barber's son with a bad haircut, the cobbler's kid with no shoes," a former colleague of Rollins's told Randall Rothenberg for *Esquire* (December 1996). "He doesn't take his own advice; were he a candidate, he would shut up." Nonetheless, his record of victories is a testament to his strategic prowess. Currently Rollins serves as a frequent commentator on politics and as chairman of the Rollins Strategy Group, which advises corporate clients.

Edward J. Rollins was born on March 19, 1943 in Boston and was raised in Vallejo, California, a small town north of San Francisco. "It was a beautiful place to grow up, because there weren't any levels of society," Rollins told Elisabeth Bumiller in an interview for the *Washington Post* (December 19, 1983). "The only people who really had any money were the ones who had run the whorehouses and liquor establishments during [World War II]." Life in Vallejo revolved around the shipping yard, where Rollins's father worked as an

Edward J. Rollins

sultant studying management problems for government agencies—and managed congressional and state campaigns. In 1979 he married for the first time and returned to California to become staff director of the state assembly's Republican caucus. One year later his marriage broke up. After Reagan won the presidency, in 1980, Reagan's political aide Lyn Nofziger hired Rollins as his assistant. In 1982 Nofziger turned the job over to Rollins.

During his youth Rollins had been an amateur boxer with an impressive record of wins. Many observers have suggested that he approached his political career as a fighter; he is tenacious, aggressive, and determined to win. As Reagan's political aide he was an "enforcer" who believed in "protecting the president" and punishing disloyalty, according to Lou Cannon in the *Washington Post* (April 21, 1982). During the early, embattled years of Reagan's first term, Rollins concentrated on shoring up support for the president among moderate Republicans in Congress, occasionally cautioning some of them to toe the party line. "It's always going to be the role of this office and the person who sits in this office to be the political bad guy," Rollins was quoted as saying by Raines. During the 1982 midterm elections, Rollins demonstrated his skill as a grassroots campaign strategist. Traditionally, a presidential administration would lend its support to the campaigns of high-profile members of Congress, whether they needed it or not. Deeming that practice inefficient, Rollins instead drew up a list of 50 contests in which Republicans would face serious opposition and then devoted money, media attention, and the president's imprimatur to those races only. In this way, he successfully defended the Republican Party's base.

Even as Rollins displayed political acumen, he was also stirring up controversy, thus setting the pattern of success tainted by scandal that was to shape his career. During his first week on the job as political aide, he told reporters that he thought Reagan's daughter Maureen was sure to lose her run for the Republican nomination for a Senate seat in California, even offering a candid assessment of her faults. This loose talk earned Rollins a reprimand from his boss. A few months later, Rollins spoke at Georgetown University, in Washington, where he told a class how the administration had pressured a particular senator into voting to equip Saudi Arabia with an airborne warning and control system (AWACS) aircraft. "We just beat his brains out," Rollins was quoted as saying, according to Cannon. Such indiscretions prompted then–White House chief of staff James Baker to order Rollins to keep his opinions to himself, but they also earned Rollins a reputation in Washington as a refreshingly candid politician. After Baker's warning, "Unmuzzle Rollins" buttons appeared on the lapels of White House staff members, according to Bumiller.

On the evening of October 25, 1982, just one week before the midterm elections, Rollins suffered a severe stroke. "I was aware of being very

electrician. (Rollins's working-class background, he told Bumiller, distinguished him from the largely Ivy League set he encountered in the White House.) Rollins grew up in public housing and was educated in Catholic schools. He was among the first generation in his family to attend college, enrolling at San Jose State University, in California, where he was a star running back for the football team; after sustaining a serious injury, he transferred to California State University in Chico. In 1968 he worked for Senator Robert F. Kennedy's presidential campaign. While still in college Rollins switched from the Democratic to the Republican Party, in part because he was repelled by the student protests on campus in the late 1960s. "I had to work my way through school and I guess I sort of resented not being able to go to class. Ronald Reagan stood up for all that," he told Bumiller. Reagan, the Republican governor of California at the time and a former Democrat himself, vowed to keep the college campuses open and thereby earned Rollins's enduring respect. Rollins had trouble explaining this to his pro-union and Democratic father. "For a while he wouldn't talk to me," Rollins told Howell Raines for the *New York Times* (July 6, 1982). "We're a pretty political family."

After receiving a B.A. degree in political science, Rollins began a nomadic career in politics. His first job after college was as a staffer for Republican California assemblyman Ray Johnson. Rollins then worked for Assemblyman Robert Monagan, following him to Washington when Monagan became assistant transportation secretary under President Richard Nixon. In Washington Rollins worked for the administrations of Nixon and Gerald R. Ford—according to Bumiller, he was a con-

tired, but like most men in their late 30s and early 40s, I thought of myself as invincible," he told Garry Clifford for *People* (August 22, 1983). Doctors concluded that the stroke had been caused by damage to his right carotid artery from a blow taken years earlier, when Rollins was an amateur boxer, and that it had been triggered by the stresses of his job. While lying partially paralyzed on his hospital bed, Rollins realized that he had been working too hard and that the political process would continue with or without him. "Everything was put into perspective . . . ," he told Clifford. "The White House didn't miss a step. . . . For months I had thought I was the person making it happen, when the truth of it is that we all are just birds of passage. Life goes on." Rollins went back to work three months later, resuming his 14-hour days but also spending time at the White House gym, relieving stress by hitting punching bags. "I pretend the bags are Democrats who want to take the boss's job," he told Clifford.

In 1983 Rollins became executive director of Reagan's reelection campaign, dubbed "Morning in America" because it was designed to generate a sense of optimism and patriotism among voters. While other advisers worked on developing a winning theme, Rollins focused on the gristle of politics—the polls, the raw data, and the opinions of the proverbial man on the street. A consummate strategist, he created color-coded maps of the U.S., showing areas in which Catholics, Hispanics, blacks, single women, or senior citizens lived. According to Bumiller, Rollins knew how every state in the nation had voted since 1854. Over the protests of many of his fellow conservatives, he appointed a woman as co-chair of the election campaign in each state, as a way of appealing to women voters. In 1984 Reagan won a landslide victory, taking 49 states in the most successful presidential campaign in history.

After the election Rollins returned to his former position as a political aide, a move he likened to that of a one-star general who had run a military base coming back to the Pentagon. "There's a lot of one-star generals in the Pentagon," he told Bernard Weinraub for the *New York Times* (September 30, 1985), "and the two-star, three-star, and four-star generals are the ones with clout." Further disappointed that he was not rewarded with the Cabinet position of labor secretary, a job he coveted, Rollins left the White House in 1985 to become a political consultant for the firm Russo & Watts. As a consultant, working for individual candidates and lobbyists, Rollins would be able to earn much more money than he had at the White House, which he nonetheless left with some regrets. "What I'll miss is going out with the President on those domestic trips, seeing the people, seeing the country," Rollins told Weinraub. "I won't miss the security, the long hours. I won't miss the phone calls in the middle of the night."

In 1989 Rollins was hired by the National Republican Congressional Committee to direct a four-year effort aimed at regaining control of the House of Representatives. He thus became the first non-member of Congress to serve as the co-chairman and chief executive officer of the National Republican Congressional Committee. While Republican president George Bush played "good cop," working to make bipartisan deals with Democrats, Rollins had the role of "bad cop," by threatening to punish Democrats who voted for military cuts or tax increases, and by exposing any unethical behavior on their part. "My responsibility is not governing," Rollins told Robin Toner for the *New York Times* (February 23, 1989). "My responsibility is to go out and try to knock out as many Democrats as I can. . . . I promise you that I won't steal, murder, lie, cheat, or pillage, but other than that I think just about anything goes." Rollins and Bush, distrustful of each other since Rollins had helped Jack Kemp in his 1988 bid for the Republican presidential nomination, eventually clashed over Bush's decision to renege on his famous campaign promise not to raise taxes. In 1991 Rollins resigned from the Republican Committee, having failed to give the Republicans a majority in the House.

Meanwhile, in 1987, Rollins had married Sherrie Sandy. The couple had met while working on Reagan's presidential campaign in 1984, and by the early 1990s they had become one of Washington's well-known "power couples." Sherrie Rollins had built a successful career as a communications expert, and in 1992, the year Bush stood for reelection, she accepted a high-profile position in the White House as the assistant to the president for public liaison and intergovernmental affairs. That same year Rollins defected from the Republican Party, which he believed had lost its vision, and accepted a position as co-manager of the billionaire Ross Perot's third-party bid for the White House. By opposing Bush, Rollins was in effect also opposing his wife, and in doing so he set a political melodrama in motion within the Beltway. Even though President Bush came forward to offer conciliatory remarks to Sherrie Rollins, assuring her that she could keep her White House job, she resigned, arguing that she would be a "distraction" from Bush's reelection bid, as quoted by Richard L. Berke in the *New York Times* (June 16, 1992). For his part, Edward Rollins explained that he had urged his wife to keep her job—but that she couldn't live with the controversy. "There are warriors and there are healers," he told Berke. "I've always been a warrior. My wife is a healer." In the wake of that development, which outraged feminists and further polarized the political world with regard to Rollins, he left the Perot campaign after only six weeks on the job. He claimed to have "irreconcilable differences" with Perot, who refused to run television advertisements or release detailed policy statements.

In 1993, after his brief foray into third-party politics, Rollins became chief adviser to the New Jersey Republican gubernatorial candidate Christine Todd Whitman. Whitman was running against the incumbent, Governor Jim Florio. Florio's campaign manager was James Carville, a feisty political consultant from Louisiana, nicknamed the "Ragin' Cajun," who had helped bring Bill Clinton to the White House in 1992. The press frequently portrayed the election as being a contest as much between Rollins and Carville as between Whitman and Florio; Wayne King wrote in the *New York Times* (April 10, 1993) that the question was "not who's running, but who's running who's running."

Whitman won an upset victory over Florio, becoming the first person to defeat an incumbent governor in modern state history. Rollins was not able to relish the victory for very long, however. One week after the election, he attended a breakfast with reporters, who asked him about his campaign strategy. With little prompting, Rollins bragged that he had used $500,000 in "walking-around money" to bribe black ministers to suppress the African-American vote, which was presumed to be Democratic. Rollins recalled that after offering to help the churches with what he termed a "special project," he had said to black ministers, "Don't get up in the Sunday pulpits and preach. . . . Don't get up there and say, 'It's your moral obligation that you go on Tuesday to vote for Jim Florio,'" as quoted by Peggy Noonan in *Vanity Fair* (February 1994). As Noonan put it, "These words made that . . . breakfast the most famous political meal since President Bush threw up on the prime minister of Japan." "Walking-around money" is a term with a shady past, derived from the days when politicians could depend on local union leaders to deliver blocks of voters. It is now generally understood to mean money used legally for Election Day expenditures, from doughnuts to voter transportation. But Rollins's account of using walking-around money was interpreted as voter suppression and prompted—in addition to public outrage—a U.S. Justice Department investigation, a state investigation in New Jersey, and several lawsuits, including one filed by the Reverend Jesse Jackson and the Reverend Al Sharpton on behalf of black clergy.

Rollins testified under oath that he had made up the story in order to play "head games" with his archrival, Carville. This explanation rang true with many of Rollins's associates. "It is a shame for someone's ego and self-promotion to cast a cloud over such a wonderfully successful effort," Haley Barbour, chairman of the Republican National Committee, told Richard L. Berke for the *New York Times* (November 12, 1993). Members of the Whitman campaign vehemently denied the story, and many political consultants claimed that modern campaigns are fought and won on television and in the press, not with such tactics as Rollins had described. Yet Larry Sabato, a political scientist at the University of Washington, described Rollins's story as believable, since within the culture of politics, the architects of victory are not held to the same ethical standards as the candidates themselves. "They're expected to push the rules of the game to the absolute limit . . . ," Sabato told Michael Weisskopf for the *Washington Post* (October 10, 1994). "Winning on Election Day provides absolute absolution. It doesn't matter what techniques you used." Rollins himself took the matter seriously, speaking to reporters of his shame and his repentance for what he called his "sin of arrogance," which resulted in his return to the Catholic faith. The federal investigation eventually concluded that there was no substantial evidence to prove that Rollins or the Whitman campaign had broken any election laws.

That scandal proved to be the most far-reaching of Rollins's career; long considered a maverick, he now became, in the opinion of many observers, "radioactive" and "untouchable." Still, in Washington scandal can have a short shelf life, and within six months Rollins had returned to work as a political consultant. His reentry into politics took the form of an unpaid consultancy for Joseph Watkins, a black Philadelphia businessman and Baptist minister running for the Senate—a move on Rollins's part that many saw as an act of atonement. In 1994 Rollins had five political clients, and in 1995 he joined then-senator Bob Dole's ultimately unsuccessful presidential campaign. "Choosing a consultant is the first decision candidates make after they decide to run," Jay Severin, a Manhattan-based Republican consultant, told Iver Peterson for the *New York Times* (November 28, 1993). "They don't want to walk into a room and say, 'Hey, I got a great idea for a campaign commercial,' they want to say, 'I just hired Ed Rollins.'" For Rollins's clients, political expediency apparently trumped political legacy. But Rollins failed yet again to keep his tongue in check, sparking still another controversy by his use of a derogatory epithet during a dinner for California state assemblyman Willie Brown, who in 1995 was considering a run for mayor of San Francisco. In the speech that he made on that occasion, as quoted in the *New York Times* (May 29, 1995), Rollins referred to California Democratic congressmen Howard L. Berman and Henry A. Waxman and maintained that Brown actually wanted to be mayor of Los Angeles: "If elected mayor of L.A., [Brown] could show those Hymie boys, Berman and Waxman, who were always trying to make Willie feel inferior for not being Jewish." After resigning from the Dole campaign over this gaffe, Rollins decided to leave political consulting altogether.

Large and barrel-chested, "built like an amphibious landing craft," in the words of Elisabeth Bumiller, Rollins also has the white beard and intelligent eyes that fit the popular image of a sage. He and his wife adopted a child from China in 1995; they separated a few years later. In 1996 Rollins co-wrote, with Thomas M. DeFrank, a bestselling, tell-all book about his career, *Bare Knuckles and Back Rooms: My Life in American Politics.*

Involved with American politics mainly as a commentator for television and other media, Rollins now works as chairman of the Rollins Strategy Group, a communications and crisis-management firm with corporate and international clients. "I'm a strategist, a big-picture person, but unfortunately my legacy is probably tainted by controversies," he told Alex Tresniowski for *People* (September 26, 1996). "I think my legacy is that I played the game hard, I played it with the best, and I always tried to be honest about who I was." — M.A.H.

Suggested Reading: *New York Times* A p23 June 16, 1992, p21+ Apr. 10, 1993; *People* p55+ Aug. 22, 1983, with photo; *Vanity Fair* p83+ Feb. 1994, with photos; *Washington Post* p1+ Dec. 19, 1983, with photo; *Washington Post* A p6+ Oct. 10, 1994; Rollins, Ed, and Thomas M. DeFrank. *Bare Knuckles and Back Rooms: My Life in American Politics*, 1996

Selected Books: Rollins, Ed, and Thomas M. DeFrank. *Bare Knuckles and Back Rooms: My Life in American Politics*, 1996

Andrew Orth/Retna Ltd.

Rollins, Henry

Feb. 13, 1961– Singer; poet; actor; performer; producer; founder of 2.13.61 Publications.
Address: 2.13.61 Publications, P.O. Box 1910, Los Angeles, CA 90078

"I don't know what my appeal is—I never have," the multifaceted Henry Rollins told Anni Layne for *Rolling Stone* (August 18, 1998, on-line). "Maybe

it's just sitting in a seat and having someone else say that thing that you feel, very loud and in an unrestrained manner. Unrestraint is the American pastime." Rollins became a punk icon in the early 1980s, as the lead singer of the influential Los Angeles–based band Black Flag. In 1987 he formed the Rollins Band, which offered an aggressive blend of funk, blues, jazz, and hard-core rock. Since then, in addition to his work with the band, he has built a career as an actor, book publisher, spoken-word artist, and record producer. Rollins's spoken-word recordings include *The Boxed Life* (1993), *Think Tank* (1998), and *A Rollins in the Wry* (2001). His company, known as 2.13.61 (his date of birth), has published poetry and fiction by Henry Miller, Hubert Selby Jr., and Exene Cervenka (formerly of the band X), as well as collections of Rollins's essays and poems, among them *Black Coffee Blues* (1992), *Eye Scream* (1996), and *Solipsist* (1998); under the label 213CD, it has released albums by such jazz artists as the saxophonist Charles Gayle and the pianist Matthew Shipp. (Two additional record labels created by Rollins— Infinite Zero, a punk-reissue label that he cofounded with the producer Rick Rubin, and Human Pitbull—are now defunct.) He has had roles in more than a dozen films, including *The Chase* (1993), *Johnny Mnemonic* (1994), *Heat* (1995), *Lost Highway* (1996), and *Morgan's Ferry* (1998).

For most of the past decade, Rollins has spent nine to 11 months of each year on the road, touring with the Rollins Band or delivering spoken-word performances. "I am a workaholic, I freak out when I sit around," he told Greg Kot for the *Chicago Tribune* (April 12, 1992). "I don't have much talent. I can't play instruments or any of that, so I make up for that by working very hard on things. It's not much of a talent: You just apply yourself and work until you fall over." As a spoken-word artist, Rollins aims to empower his audiences by sharing tales of his own mistakes and insecurities. His performances are more humorous than his spoken-word recordings and reveal another side of him— that of a bemused observer.

An intense, imposing figure who expends enormous amounts of energy during his act, Rollins sings barefoot and shirtless, often leaning forward at the edge of the stage, the microphone cord wrapped around his hand. His work is confessional, fueled by rage and a lingering sense of worthlessness; according to some critics, the cathartic nature of his performances fosters an environment not unlike that of group therapy. "I'm not, nor do I want to be, 'the angriest young man in rock 'n' roll,'" Rollins told Kot. "I'm not angry, I'm just dealing with it. I've got the blues. . . . I'm not gonna go drinking, start fights and punch holes in the wall. I'm gonna make blistering music and straight-up writing that confronts, vanquishes and moves on toward daylight. I'm not into dwelling, I'm into moving on, cheering up and getting on with the show of life. . . . I'm moving, hopefully, forward and upward—that's the goal."

In 2000 *Henry Rollins: Live and Ripped in London*, his first television special, was broadcast on Comedy Central. Rollins has provided narration for such television series as *The Human Journey*, on the Discovery Channel, and an installment about the Doors for VH1's *Behind the Music*. He currently hosts the Fox network's weekly series *Night Visions*, which presents thrillers in the tradition of *The Twilight Zone* and *Tales from the Crypt*. Rollins has often publicly condemned racism and the sexual exploitation of women and has encouraged his fans to follow his example by abstaining from the use of drugs and alcohol. "The ultimate rebellion now," he told Paul Freeman for the *Chicago Tribune* (October 9, 1994), "is to get into art, higher learning, intensity and prolonging your life—at the expense of no one else."

Henry Rollins was born Henry Garfield on February 13, 1961 in Washington, D.C. He has claimed to have "no happy childhood memories," as he told William F. Powers for the *Washington Post* (August 21, 1994). After his parents divorced, when he was very young, he was raised by his mother in Glover Park, an upper-middle-class section of the nation's capital. Rollins has said that his mother, who worked for the U.S. Department of Education, encouraged his interests. Nevertheless, he felt close to neither her nor his father, whom he occasionally saw on weekends. (As a way of dissociating himself from his father, he changed his name later on.) During his early years he developed a sense of isolation, which was heightened as a result of harassment by classmates and physical abuse at the hands of one of his mother's boyfriends. He was also hyperactive, and for many years he took the drug Ritalin to control his behavior.

As a youngster Rollins did poorly in every subject in school except English. At the age of 12, he was enrolled at the Bullis School, which at that time was an all-boys military academy in Potomac, Maryland, about 30 minutes from his home. With the encouragement of his history teacher, a Vietnam veteran named Dennis Pepperman, he began lifting weights, an activity that marked "a major turning point in my life," as he recalled to Greg Kot. "When I was 14, I went from skinny, no presence, low self-opinion to someone who could actually feel his feet in his shoes. When I found I could actually lift something that six weeks before I could not lift, it was the first time in my life that I ever felt a sense of achievement." Rollins also benefitted from the encouragement of his English teacher, Mr. Clinger. "I had a 102 average," he told Murray Engleheart for his official DreamWorks Records biography. "I loved English. And I liked Mr. Clinger a lot. I'd write crazy, off-the-wall stuff, how I wanted to blow up the school and kill everybody. He'd read it and go: 'This is great. Don't show it to anybody, but this is good. Keep it up. You're writing outside of the established form.'"

As a teenager Rollins befriended Ian MacKaye, who shared his love for music and freestyle skateboarding. (MacKaye would later become a member of two influential punk groups, Minor Threat and Fugazi.) Invited to sing a few songs with MacKaye's band, the Teen Idles, while the lead singer was out of the room, Rollins "just went crazy," MacKaye recalled to Karen Schoemer for the *New York Times* (November 6, 1994). "I knew then that he wanted to be a singer." After he graduated from the Bullis School, in 1979, Rollins was kicked out of his mother's house. He lived in his car and then with MacKaye's family before finding his own apartment. He spent one semester at American University, in Washington, D.C., then worked as a manager of a Haagen-Dazs ice-cream store. He also sang with a straight-edge band known as State of Alert, or SOA. (Individuals who identify themselves as "straight-edge" vow to abstain from drugs, alcohol, and promiscuity.)

Rollins and MacKaye were fans of the Southern California punk-rock group Black Flag and attended a performance of the band in Washington during its first U.S. tour. Rollins soon became friends with the members of the group. In 1981, after sitting in with the band during a show in New York City, he was asked to audition for it. The Black Flag leader and guitarist, Greg Ginn, had had poor luck with a series of singers, and the lead vocalist, Dez Cadena, was eager to play rhythm guitar rather than sing. After passing the audition, Rollins immediately quit his job, sublet his apartment, sold most of his possessions, and moved to Los Angeles. "When I got into Black Flag," he told Paul Freeman, "I learned that music could be my steam valve, a way to vent." Before joining the group, he explained to Freeman, "I used to manifest my anger by hurting myself, mentally, physically, and spiritually." Members of the band as well as people in the audience often behaved violently during performances. "Black Flag shows were total craziness," MacKaye told Karen Schoemer. "Some would be so epiphanal; some would just be a bummer. I saw one show where Henry smashed this mirror, just hitting it with his face and arm. He had to be taken to a hospital. Those were rough shows. The violence that was going on then was very scary stuff."

After Black Flag disbanded, in 1986, Rollins began to attend open-microphone poetry readings. "I was doing the traditional reading thing," he told Karen Schoemer. "It never occurred to me that you could do whatever you want. So the first eight months I read things off paper, and while I was arranging the paper I'd tell some story." Before long he eliminated written material from his spoken-word performances. In 1987 Rollins formed the Rollins Band, with Andrew Weiss on bass, Chris Haskett on guitar, and Sim Cain on drums. The band's early releases included *Lifetime* (1987), *Do It* (1988), and *Hot Animal Machine* (1988), as well as some of Rollins's spoken-word material.

In 1991 the Rollins Band signed a record deal with a major label, Imago, and impressed audiences at the first annual Lollapalooza, an alternative-music festival founded by Perry Farrell, the front man of the rock band Jane's Addiction. The Rollins Band's first album for Imago, *The End of Silence* (1992), introduced the singer to a wider audience. The album features "Just Like You," an angry song that described Rollins's emotional reaction to seeing his father for the first time in nine years. "We talked [for] two minutes, and in watching his hands and the way he talked, I realized 'I'm just like him,'" Rollins told Greg Kot. "I walked away from that going, 'Damn, I'm that guy's son!' I was freaked inside my own skin." Rollins was also profoundly affected by the death of his best friend and roommate, Joe Cole, a member of Black Flag's road crew, who was shot in December 1991 during a robbery as he and Rollins were returning home from a grocery store in Venice, California.

The release of *Weight*, in 1993, brought the Rollins Band closer to mainstream success. By the time it came out, Andrew Weiss had been replaced by Melvin Gibbs, a New York–based bassist who had previously played with such jazz musicians as John Zorn and Sonny Sharrock. "There's definite differences between avant-garde jazz and what the Rollins Band does, but there's an emotional similarity," Gibbs told Karen Schoemer. "I didn't come up listening to this kind of music, but I came up pretty angry. That's the thread that runs through it." The following year the video for "Liar" (a song from *Weight*), directed by the Dutch photographer Anton Corbijn, was placed into heavy rotation on MTV, and Rollins appeared on the cover of *Details* magazine as the publication's "Man of the Year." Also in 1994 the Rollins Band was nominated for a Grammy Award for best metal performance and performed at Woodstock '94. That same year the company 2.13.61, which Rollins had founded in 1984, published the book *Get in the Van: On the Road with Black Flag*, a collection of photographs and journal entries that Rollins had written while touring with Black Flag. The hardcover edition sold 30,000 copies, an impressive number for a small-press publication.

Rollins spent 16 months working on the album *Come In & Burn* (1997), which received a less enthusiastic response than some of the band's earlier work. Following a tour in support of *Come In & Burn*, the singer decided to dissolve the Rollins Band. The split was amiable; on his official Web site, *two1361.com*, Rollins referred to his former bandmates as "some of the finest people I have ever met" and as "brilliant, hardworking, honest and 100 percent music." He continued, "We all have very different musical interests, though, and I don't think I can keep up with them. When we finished the last tour I gave the band, the guys and the music we made a lot of thought. I came to the conclusion that we had realized our potential [and decided] to leave it be and move on."

In 1998 Rollins produced an album entitled *Deep* for one of his favorite Los Angeles bands, Mother Superior. While in the studio he invited its members—guitarist Jim Wilson, bassist Marcus Blake, and drummer Jason Mackenroth—to write some songs with him. The four wrote three songs together and collaborated on the recording of *Get Some Go Again* (2000). The album was produced by Rollins and features Wayne Kramer, a former guitarist for the MC5, and Scott Gorham, of Thin Lizzy. Temporarily setting aside Mother Superior, Wilson, Blake, and Mackenroth became the new lineup for the Rollins Band. Rollins has credited Mother Superior with restoring his interest in making music. "I was tired of music right then," he wrote for his official Web site. "I figured I was done. But during the first night with those guys I thought, 'Oh yeah! I remember this!'"

For many years the heavily tattooed Rollins has worn the same pair of black shorts on stage. "I have to dunk them in water to get them to be cloth-like, 'cause otherwise they stand up straight," he told Bill Ribas for *NY Rock* (March 2000, on-line). "I can balance them on my outstretched palm. Sometime maybe someday they'll do the tour for me. My problem is Nike won't make those anymore. . . . They look like boxer shorts. And I really like them, and I wear these lycra leg-hugging bike pants underneath to keep my quads warm. And that's kind of been my gear, because I sweat a lot, and anything [that is] cloth rots. I've been using this setup for years. I just wring it out in the sink after the show. Hang it up in the bus to dry, and two hours later I'm ready to go again. That's why I stopped wearing shoes. I'd wear them out. . . . You know, the sweat eats rubber. So I just dispensed with all of that, 'cause it'd always be Lake Rollins, anyway, all around me. So I just went to what's functional." In 2001 Rollins gave spoken-word performances in Australia, New Zealand, Sweden, Denmark, Scotland, England, Germany, Belgium, and Holland; with the Rollins Band, he performed in half a dozen states.

In addition to his other pursuits, Rollins has appeared in ads for the Gap and the Macintosh Powerbook and lent his voice to commercials for GM trucks and Merrill Lynch, but he has denied accusations that he has sold out. "They're very commercial ventures, but it's not like I was coerced into it," he explained to Donna Freydkin for *CNN.com* (August 13, 1999). "I willingly went to the audition and with much jealousy I went after it. To me, the sell-out is when the record company tells you it wants you to put back-up chicks on a song. You don't want to, but you do it. That to me is selling out. Going after bigger game in the entertainment world—if I want to do it—is not selling out."

After several of 2.13.61's products failed to sell, among them an expensive, lavish collection of images of the band Led Zeppelin by the photographer Ross Halfin, the company returned to producing Rollins's work almost exclusively. Although Infinite Zero, his reissue label, no longer exists, Rollins has continued to buy and borrow old master tapes and bootleg tapes by such seminal bands as Bad Brains and Iggy Pop, which he then transfers onto compact discs and archives.

Rollins, who lives in Los Angeles, has compensated for what he sees as his relative lack of talent by working harder and with more determination than many other artists. "I've read really good books, so I know I'm not a good writer," he told Bill Ribas. "I have a lot of really good records, so I know I'm really not great at the music. But I also think there's something to be said for giving it all you've got." — C.L.

Suggested Reading: *Chicago Tribune* XIII p14+ Apr. 12, 1992, with photos, XIII p26+ Oct. 9, 1994; *New York Times Magazine* p38+ Nov. 6, 1994, with photos; *Washington Post* G p1+ Aug. 21, 1994, with photos; Vale, V. *Real Conversations, No. 1: Henry Rollins, Jello Biafra, Lawrence Ferlinghetti, Billy Childish*, 2001

Selected Recordings: with Black Flag—*Damaged*, 1981; *My War*, 1983; *Family Man*, 1984; *Slip It In*, 1984; *Live '84*, 1985; *In My Head*, 1985; with the Rollins Band—*Lifetime*, 1987; *Do It*, 1988; *Hard Volume*, 1989; *Turned On*, 1990; *The End of Silence*, 1992; *Electro Convulsive Therapy*, 1993; *Weight*, 1993; *Come In And Burn*, 1997; *Get Some Go Again*, 2000; as spoken-word artist—*Big Ugly Mouth*, 1987; *The Boxed Life*, 1993; *Get in the Van*, 1994; *Everything*, 1996; *Black Coffee Blues*, 1996; *Think Tank*, 1998; *A Rollins in the Wry*, 2001

Selected Books: *Black Coffee Blues*, 1992; *Get in the Van*, 1994; *Eye Scream*, 1996; *Do I Come Here Often? Black Coffee Blues, Part 2*, 1997; *The Portable Henry Rollins*, 1997; *Solipsist*, 1998; *Smile, You're Traveling: Black Coffee Blues, Part 3*, 2000

Selected Films: *The Chase*, 1993; *Johnny Mnemonic*, 1994; *Heat*, 1995; *Lost Highway*, 1996; *Frost*, 1998; *Morgan's Ferry*, 1998

Paul Elledge/Courtesy of University of Chicago

Rowley, Janet D.

(RAUW-lee)

Apr. 5, 1925– Molecular geneticist; physician. Address: University of Chicago, 5841 S. Maryland Ave. #2115, Chicago, IL 60637

The renowned molecular geneticist Janet D. Rowley made one of the key discoveries in the battle against cancer while sitting in her dining room. For two decades after she gave birth to the first of her four children, in 1952, Rowley pursued her career only part-time, so that she could devote herself as much as possible to parenting. In 1962, in the tiny laboratory space assigned to her at a University of Chicago cancer research center, she began conducting microscopic examinations of the chromosomes of leukemia patients; she sometimes worked at home, too, when her tasks did not require sophisticated equipment. Rowley—who began her professional life as a physician—told the geneticist Francis Collins in an interview for the Albert and Mary Lasker Foundation's *Living Library* (1998, on-line), "It was really almost ten years before I did anything that was noteworthy." Nevertheless, she persisted. The advent in 1970 of a new technique that enhanced the visibility of chromosome components in photographs marked a turning point for her. The far more detailed images that she could now obtain enabled her to pair up the 46 chromosomes present in human cells with great accuracy, by cutting each chromosome out of a photo and finding its match. "Her children often teased her about her 'puzzles' as she sat at their dining-room table," a University of Chicago Hospital and Health System press release (April 27, 1999, on-line) revealed. In 1972 she discovered that, in patients suffering from a particular form of leukemia, parts of two different chromosomes had broken off and exchanged places with each other—a phenomenon known as translocation. Rowley has since demonstrated the occurrence of translocation in several other forms of leukemia. Her discoveries have provided solid evidence that certain types of cancer are caused by particular chromosomal alterations.

For some years many other researchers questioned the link between translocations and cancer, but since the mid-1980s, Rowley's findings and their enormous significance have earned universal recognition. Rowley herself has received many honors for her achievements. The most prestigious include the National Medal of Science, bestowed by President Bill Clinton in 1998 for "revolutionizing" the diagnosis and treatment of cancer as well as for "her pioneering work on the relationship of prior treatment to recurring chromosome abnormalities," as the citation that accompanied the medal put it. She was also a co-winner of the 1998 Lasker Award for Clinical Science, which is widely considered the American equivalent of a Nobel Prize. A summary of her work that appeared on the Web site of the Lasker Foundation explained, "In addition to its implications for accurate cancer diagnosis, understanding . . . cancer at the level of chromosomes and genes is now opening the door to the design of drug and radiation therapy that encourages the hope that very specific therapies will be developed for specific diseases." Rowley—who, at 76 years of age, still does research—has since 1984 held the title of Blum-Riese distinguished service professor in the Department of Medicine and Department of Molecular Genetics and Cell Biology at the University of Chicago.

The only child of Hurford and Ethel (Ballantyne) Davison, Rowley was born Janet Davison on April 5, 1925 in New York City. Her father taught retail management on the college level; her mother taught high-school English before becoming a school librarian. "My parents were very encouraging of me in any kind of intellectual activity," she recalled to Collins. "My mother always hoped that I would be a doctor." Rowley attended a junior high in New Jersey rather than New York, because her mother felt she needed greater challenges than what her neighborhood school could offer. At the New Jersey school, her interest in science blossomed, and it continued to develop in high school.

An avid reader, Rowley excelled academically. At 15 she earned a scholarship to the "Four Year College," an elite University of Chicago program in which she completed the equivalent of the last two years of high school and first two years of college. Surrounded by bright peers in small classes, Rowley flourished. "We were really treated as though we were college students, even though we were 16 and 17, and given a great deal of responsibility and dealt with as adults," she told Collins. "It was an important experience for me because we were taught to question and to read primary materials, not just what you'd see in a textbook. So we had almost no textbooks to study." Rowley earned a bachelor of philosophy degree in 1944. That year she applied to the University of Chicago's medical school, but she was rejected, because the freshman-class quota of three women had been filled. "It was a time when female medical students were considered a bad investment. Why train someone who would never practice?" Anthony Colarossi

wrote for the *Chicago Tribune* (September 25, 1998), as reprinted on the Web site of the University of Chicago's Department of Human Genetics. The following year Rowley's medical-school application was accepted. Rowley has said that several professors under whom she studied, both male and female, influenced her significantly; among them was Charles B. Huggins, a cancer specialist who later won a Nobel Prize in medicine. While in medical school Rowley earned a B.S. degree, in 1946; she completed her M.D. degree in 1948.

On December 18 of that year, she married Donald Rowley, one of her fellow medical students. In 1949–50 she worked as a research assistant at the University of Chicago, and in 1950–51, as an intern at the Marine Hospital, a U.S. Public Health Service facility in Chicago. In 1952 her first son, Donald Jr., was born, and for the next two decades, she worked outside of her home only two or three days a week, "because I wanted to take care of my family," as she explained to Francis Collins. During that period her family grew to include three more sons: David, Robert, and Roger, who were born in 1954, 1960, and 1963, respectively. "I had a very rich, full life with my children and my husband," she told Collins. She regarded medicine, she told Colarossi, as a "hobby."

In 1953–54 Rowley worked part-time in infant- and prenatal-care clinics run by the Montgomery County, Maryland, Department of Public Health; from 1955 to 1961 she was a Levinson Foundation research fellow at the Cook County Hospital, in Chicago, where she treated retarded children, including some with Down syndrome; concurrently, from 1957 to 1961, she served as a clinical instructor of neurology at the University of Illinois School of Medicine, in Chicago.

Meanwhile, in 1959 researchers had discovered that the cells of Down syndrome sufferers contained an extra copy of chromosome number 21. The role of chromosomes in clinical abnormalities intrigued Rowley, and she soon got the chance to learn more about it. When her husband, an immunologist, chose to spend a sabbatical leave in England in 1961–62, she successfully applied for a U.S. Public Health Service fellowship from the National Institutes of Health and became a special trainee at the Radiobiology Laboratory of the Churchill Hospital at Oxford University; she worked there with Laslo Lajtha, whose research focused on DNA replication in normal and abnormal human chromosomes. She returned to the United States with a box of research slides and a determination to conduct scientific investigations.

Toward that end Rowley approached one of her medical-school professors, Leon Jacobson, the founder and head of the Argonne Cancer Research Hospital (now known as the Franklin McLean Memorial Research Institute), at the University of Chicago, with a request for lab space and a stipend to do research three days a week. "It seemed quite reasonable to me, but to any sensible person it would have been outrageous," she told Colarossi.

"I was going to be totally on my own. I was a novice." Widely known for his generosity in helping young researchers, Jacobson secured both space (three feet of a laboratory bench), funding ($5,000 a year), and an academic title—that of assistant professor at the Department of Medicine—for Rowley. (When Collins asked her "how likely would it be today" for an inexperienced researcher to make such an arrangement, she answered, "Not at all.")

Leon Jacobson was a hematologist—a specialist in blood, the blood-producing organs, and blood disorders, which include the variants of leukemia, which in turn is a category of cancer. At Argonne, where she began working in 1962, Rowley used a microscope to examine the chromosomes of Jacobson's leukemia patients in search of anything out of the ordinary. (Chromosomes are composed of genes, among them the genes that control the growth of cells. Cancer is a disorder in which certain cells become malignant and divide uncontrollably.) Although for years she found nothing significant, she did not feel discouraged. "The lab was a hobby," she told Collins. "The fact that it was going slowly . . . didn't bother me in the least. I never expected it to go anywhere anyhow."

Beginning in 1970 and continuing throughout that decade, Rowley's work benefitted greatly from rapid advances in a new technique called chromosome banding, in which staining the chromosomes with fluorescent chemicals creates visible bands; the pattern of the bands in each of the 23 chromosome pairs in human cells differs from that of every other pair. Working at Oxford again, in 1970–71, during another of her husband's sabbaticals, Rowley became proficient in chromosome-banding techniques and the use of the fluorescence microscope. Following her return to Chicago, Leon Jacobson "helped find the resources for me to buy a fluorescence microscope," as she recalled to Collins—an instrument that, Collins pointed out, was "not widely available to a lot of people at that point." With the aid of quinacrine and Giemsa stains, in mid-1972 she discovered that in people who suffer from acute myeloblastic leukemia (a disorder of the bone marrow, which produces blood cells), a small piece of chromosome 8 had swapped places with a small piece of chromosome 21; the pieces had broken off from their parent chromosomes and translocated. Her observation marked the first time that such a translocation was observed.

Rowley's next discovery, which she made in 1973, while working in Europe, ended a scientific hunt that had begun in 1960. In that year Peter C. Nowell and David A. Hungerford, doing research in Philadelphia, had reported the presence of a consistent chromosomal abnormality in the tumor cells of seven patients suffering from chronic myelogenous leukemia (CML). Specifically, they had found that in those patients, the long arm of chromosome 22—the Philadelphia chromosome, as it was dubbed—was abnormally small; apparently, a piece of it was missing. The reason for its truncated state was revealed when Rowley found its missing portion attached to chromosome 9—and a small bit from chromosome 9 attached to the long leg of chromosome 22.

By showing that specific translocations are associated with specific cancers—as was true in nearly all the cases of leukemia that she examined— Rowley provided evidence for the theory that when growth-controlling genes move, or translocate, from their "home" chromosome to a "foreign" chromosome, the mechanisms that control cell division are disrupted, and cancer may ensue. In a later study that Rowley conducted, translocations involving chromosomes 9 and 22 were found to have occurred in 92 percent of 1,129 CML patients, Jeff Lyon and Peter Gorner reported in the *Chicago Tribune* (March 9, 1986). Rowley told Lyon and Gorner that she was sure that the other 8 percent had been misdiagnosed and really suffered from a disease other than CML. In the mid-1980s other scientists pinpointed genes, called oncogenes, that can be adversely affected by translocations and can cause a normal cell to become cancerous. Speaking of an oncogene, known as *c-myc*, that is associated with lymphoma (a kind of blood cancer), Rowley explained to Lyon and Gorner, "*Myc* is one of the very early signals within a cell that tells the cell that it's going to undergo division. If there is some kind of derangement whereby *myc* is taken away from its normal regulator, and put next to a regulator that keeps it permanently switched on, it would forever be sending a signal to the cell, 'Get ready to divide.' So cells would keep dividing all the time, and the result would be cancer."

In subsequent research, Rowley and her collaborators found other translocations, which are associated with other malignancies. One such translocation involves chromosomes 14 and 18 and is seen in people suffering from follicular lymphoma; another, involving chromosomes 15 and 17, triggers the onset of acute promyelocytic leukemia. In the early 1990s Rowley discovered a reordering of chromosomal material that is exhibited in most instances of infant leukemia. Her research has also uncovered a possible link between infant or childhood leukemia and the consumption of heavy doses of some bioflavonoids (brightly colored chemicals that occur naturally in certain fruits and vegetables). In test-tube experiments conducted in her laboratory, Howard Wolinsky reported for *WebMD* (April 18, 2000, on-line), 10 bioflavonoids caused breaks in a gene that has been implicated in both infant and adult leukemia; the breaks occurred in a part of the gene that is associated specifically with the occurrence of the disease in infants rather than adults. "The public health message from this study is not yet clear," Rowley told Wolinsky. "The health benefits of a diet high in foods containing bioflavonoids, such as soybeans, citrus fruits and root vegetables, are unquestioned." Nevertheless, as a precaution, pregnant women have been advised to avoid taking supplements with high doses of bioflavonoids.

The first award that Rowley earned for her discoveries came in 1982—the Dameshek Prize (named for William Dameshek, a pioneer in the field of hematological oncology), the American Society of Hematology's highest honor. Her many other honors include, from Saudi Arabia, the King Faisal International Prize in Medicine (1988); from Canada, the Gairdner Foundation International Award (1996); and the Medal of Honor for Basic Research from the American Cancer Society (1996). She won Outstanding Investigator grants from the National Cancer Institute from 1986 through 1993. She was named Chicagoan of the Year by *Chicago* magazine in 1998 and has earned honorary doctor of science degrees from the University of Pennsylvania and four other institutions of higher learning. Along with the molecular geneticist Manuel O. Diaz, she holds a patent for methods of detecting gene rearrangements and translocations. She helped to organize the first five International Workshops on Chromosomes in Leukemia and other conferences, and is the co-founder and co-editor of the journal *Genes, Chromosomes and Cancer*. In 1995 the University of Chicago hosted an international symposium on cancer in honor of her 70th birthday. With John E. Ultmann, she edited the book *Chromosomes and Cancer: From Molecules to Man* (1983).

"I think there are at least two major unanswered questions," Rowley said to Collins during their 1998 conversation. "One is what causes chromosome translocations? . . . The second major goal, and this of course is dear to me as a physician, is trying to figure out how we can develop genotype-specific therapy"—that is, treatments that are specific for a particular genetic abnormality. Speaking of her long career to Collins, she cited as role models Charles B. Huggins, who was still working when he was in his 90s, and her husband, who does immunological research in a laboratory near hers at the University of Chicago. She also told Collins, "What has happened to me is totally unexpected. This is not something I strove for, was ever a goal, was ever anything I conceived of almost anytime in my life. Not until the last fifteen years or so, when it was clear that what I had done was important; then my view changed. But this was never anything that I really sought. What I think is important," she continued, "is that young people take a very long view of their life. Which implies that you're going to have good health, and I'm fortunate that that's the case with me. Don't be too impatient for things to all happen quickly. Or to think that by the time you're thirty-five and you haven't done much, that you're over the hill. . . . I was forty-seven years old before I did anything that people would really look at twice. So patience is certainly an important aspect of this."

Rowley and her husband live in the Hyde Park section of Chicago, where they maintain a flower and vegetable garden. Lovers of the outdoors, they often bike to work together. They have several grandchildren. — K.S.

Suggested Reading: Albert & Mary Lasker Foundation *Living Library* (on-line); *Chicago Tribune* III p7 Mar. 9, 1988; *Chicago Tribune* (on-line) Sep. 25, 1998; Grinstein, Louise S., Carol A. Biermann, and Rose K. Rose, eds. *Women in the Biological Sciences: A Bibliographic Sourcebook*, 1997; *Who's Who in America*, 2000

Rush

Rock band

Lee, Geddy
July 29, 1953–

Lifeson, Alex
Aug. 27, 1953–

Peart, Neil
Sep. 12, 1952–

Address: c/o Atlantic Records, 1290 Ave. of the Americas, New York, NY 10104

In the history of rock, few bands have endured for as long as Rush, and fewer still have displayed such vigor and inventiveness after recording and performing for more than a quarter-century. Once dismissed as musical dinosaurs mired in 1970s progressive rock, the Toronto-based Rush is now spoken of in almost reverential terms by fans, and such groups as Primus, Metallica, and Dream Theater have cited Rush among their most important influences. Rush's three members—bassist and vocalist Geddy Lee, guitarist Alex Lifeson, and drummer Neil Peart—who have played together since 1975, have all been recognized as masters of their instruments, and some high-school and college instructors have made teaching tools of Rush's songs, which contain abundant references to literary material, ranging from the Greek legend of Sisyphus to J.R.R. Tolkien's fantasy series *The Lord of the Rings*. They have also fashioned a reputation for being one of the top live acts in rock music, touring the world extensively and putting on shows that blend music and spectacle. "I think we've remained true to our own style, but [we've] not been so close-minded as to ignore new things that are going on in music that we respond to," Lee told *Current Biography*, when asked about Rush's longevity. "We love writing music together," Lifeson explained to Chris Gill for *guitarworld.com* in 1997. "We laugh a lot together. When we work we like to be secluded. We go away to a studio in the country and take the weekends off to go home. We're around each other all the time—having dinner, sitting around in the evening when we've finished working—and all we do is goof around and laugh. We've always done that. It's made us want to be together. In fact, we look forward to it."

The members of Rush (left to right): Alex Lifeson, Geddy Lee, and Neil Peart

Courtesy of Atlantic Records

Geddy Lee (born Gary Lee Weinrib on July 29, 1953 in Willowdale, Ontario, Canada) and Alex Lifeson (born on August 27, 1953 in British Columbia, Canada, with the surname Zivojinovich) met in Toronto as eighth-graders. Inspired by the then-recent invasion of British acts who blended blues with guitar-crunching hard rock, the boys began playing music together in their basements. "When we were growing up," Lee told Dan Nooger for *Circus* (April 27, 1976, on-line), "the big bands were [Led] Zeppelin and [Jeff] Beck. We used to do a lot of Zeppelin material before we started writing our own stuff and I used to have to scream to hit the high notes." After a while Lee and Lifeson hooked up with John Rutsey, a drummer, and formed Rush, a name suggested by a friend of theirs. Lee and Lifeson also adopted stage names ("Geddy" is how Lee's Polish-born mother pronounced "Gary"; "Lifeson" is the English translation of "Zivojinovich").

The band played their first gig at the Coffin, a makeshift club in the basement of a local Anglican church. There they met Ray Danniels, a high-school dropout with a keen head for business. Danniels made deals with club owners in and around Toronto, and soon Rush was getting engagements in clubs, school gyms, youth centers, and any other place that would take them. The pay was minimal, and more often than not, patrons paid no attention while the group performed, usually presenting songs written by others. By continuing to accept such gigs despite such undesirable conditions, the band developed a strong work ethic. "It was just persistence," Lee told Debra Frost for *Circus* (February 14, 1977, on-line). "We only did tunes that we liked, and we'd sneak in an original here and

there. Eventually we built up our own little following."

On the strength of that following, Rush recorded their first studio album—*Rush*, which Moon Records released in early 1974. The disc contained some songs that have become Rush chestnuts, among them "Finding My Way," "In the Mood," and "Working Man." Many critics dismissed *Rush* as a mediocre collection of Zeppelin-influenced blues-rock tunes, and it failed to generate much attention in either Canada or the U.S. The musicians were planning their first American tour, to support the album, when Rutsey announced that he was leaving the band. "It was obvious that his heart wasn't into it . . . ," Lee explained to Frost. "He just wasn't thinking the way Alex and I were and he decided it would be better for himself and for us if he left." After an extended search, Lee and Lifeson found a new drummer—Neil Peart (born on September 12, 1952 in Hamilton, Ontario). A self-educated high-school dropout who had spent a year in England playing with several bands, Peart impressed Lee and Lifeson with his powerful, intricate drumming, which favored syncopated beats over the straight-ahead rhythms used by most other percussionists at that time. Peart joined them on a tour of North America, during which they opened for such acts as Kiss, Uriah Heep, and ZZ Top, occasionally upstaging the headlining act. In the Midwest the trio discovered that Rush already had a fairly solid fan base, thanks in part to Donna Halper, a programmer at the Cleveland, Ohio, rock radio station WMMS, who had been inserting the Rush song "Working Man" into the station's daily rotation. During the tour, while the group's reputation as a top-shelf live act developed, sales of *Rush* began to rise, and Rush soon joined the roster of Mercury Records.

Meanwhile, Lee and Lifeson had discovered that Peart, an avid reader, could write lyrics. While still on the road, the band began writing songs for their next album, *Fly by Night*. Released in 1975, that record contains not only straightforward rockers, such as "Best I Can," but also epic-length pieces, with lyrics inspired by the writings of Tolkien, Ayn Rand, and Michael Moorcock. Fans' wildly enthusiastic responses to such songs as "Anthem," "Rivendell," and the seven-minute "By-Tor and the Snowdog," about a battle between an evil knight and a benevolent mythical beast, spurred the band to release another album, *Caress of Steel*, before the year was out. Two cuts from that disc, "Bastille Day" and "Lakeside Park," became staples of the band's live show, while "The Fountain of Lamneth," which took up one whole side of the album, demonstrated Rush's affinity for progressive rock. *Caress of Steel* struck critics as bloated and pretentious, and its sales lagged far behind those of its predecessor. Rush's subsequent live performances during the "Down the Tubes Tour," as they dubbed it, failed to generate much income; indeed, Lifeson, who had married and become a father by then, had to use the money remaining from his wedding gifts to support his family.

In the wake of the failure of *Caress of Steel*, Rush faced demands from their label to conform to a more mainstream sound. "There was a lot of pressure on us to be more accessible," Lee told *Current Biography*. "We responded with something that was even less accessible." Instead of a collection of three-minute pop songs, for *2112* (1976) Lee, Lifeson, and Peart produced a 20-minute title track, which told of how the discovery of a guitar by a young member of an oppressive futuristic society helped to free the minds of his compatriots. "We were kind of angry about how much pressure we were getting from everybody else to conform, and that whole album is about not conforming," Lee explained to *Current Biography*. "It's probably the most important record we ever did." With the liner notes from the album acknowledging "the genius of Ayn Rand," and with virtuoso playing by all three instrumentalists, *2112* catapulted Rush to official superstar status. Although, once again, they were an opening act, Rush's performances on their *2112* tour reinforced their standing as one of the premier rock acts of the late 1970s. Portions of the *2112* concerts were captured on the live collection *All the World's a Stage* (1976).

A Farewell to Kings (1977) features quieter songs, accompanied by classical guitar, synthesizers, and the temple blocks, chimes, and gong that Peart had acquired. In addition to such meditative reflections on the human condition as "Closer to the Heart," "Madrigal," and "Cinderella Man," the album includes the 11-minute "Cygnus X-1." Describing an astronaut's encounter with a black hole, the song was inspired by an article about black holes in *Time* magazine, and along with "Xanadu," a song based on Samuel Taylor Coleridge's poem "Kubla Khan," it established Rush as the thinking person's heavy-metal act. On their subsequent, seven-month "Drive Till You Die Tour," Rush was the headliner, and the band enhanced their show with rear-projected films (some of them made by Lee), laser effects, and an array of pyrotechnics. Taking advantage of the extra time allotted to them, they occasionally ended each show with a medley of songs, which they stitched together to form one long piece, and closed with a crowd-rousing explosion of fireworks and confetti. Lee explained to *Current Biography* that Rush's extravagant live show reflected concerts the musicians had seen while growing up, as well as experiences they had had as an opening act. "We opened for Kiss on our first couple of tours," he recalled. "And here we are, three Canadian musicians sitting on the side of the stage watching guys put makeup on and blow things up on stage. And, like their music or not, they worked really hard, and they tried to give an all-around performance and put on a show for their fans. So there was a work ethic that rubbed off on us, and we began to think, 'If we can play as well as we can, and add a show to that, that's gonna be kind of sensational.'"

A month after completing the tour, Rush released their sixth studio album, *Hemispheres* (1978), whose name refers to the left and right halves of the brain. Two concert tours and approximately 150 concerts later, the group made two albums that many casual admirers and die-hard fans consider to be their best—*Permanent Waves* (1980) and *Moving Pictures* (1981), for both of which the trio wrote shorter songs. Explaining Rush's reasons for this change, Lee told Howard Reich for the *Chicago Tribune* (November 14, 1982), "We got to a point where it was almost expected for us to do a 10- or 20-minute song on each album. It wasn't real challenging anymore, to be honest. It was like standing still. Sure, we could do another concept thing in a 20-minute piece, but that would really be like doing the same one again, except with different notes. It stopped becoming a challenge to write a tune that would be considered good simply because it lasted 10 minutes, and not good because it ran four minutes." "The Spirit of Radio" and "Free Will," from *Permanent Waves*, and "Tom Sawyer," from *Moving Pictures*, became radio hits. In addition, the instrumental "YYZ," from *Moving Pictures*, earned Rush their first Grammy nomination—for best instrumental—and the album itself went quadruple platinum. The live album *Exit . . . Stage Left* (1981) features highlights from the *Moving Pictures* tour.

In the next year Rush released *Signals*, a sleeker, more high-tech album that displayed Rush's continued interest in keyboard-driven rock. As he did for *Hemispheres*, whose songs examine the differences among people, Peart chose a theme for *Signals*—the idea of communication between people. The album generated the singles "Subdivisions," about suburban adolescents' isolation, and "New World Man," and also offered such songs as "The Analog Kid" and "Countdown," about the majesty of a shuttle launch.

Soon after the release of *Signals*, the band split from their longtime producer, Terry Brown. "For all intents and purposes, he was in the band; he was one of us, and that was great," Lee told Greg Armbruster for *Keyboard* (September 1984). "We made a lot of great albums together, but 10 records is a long time working with the same attitudes. Sometimes you have to have a radical change. Sometimes you have to shake yourself and make sure you're not falling asleep at the wheel, or falling into bad habits, or taking the easy way out every time." Working with the producer Peter Henderson, the group made the dark and introspective *Grace Under Pressure* (1984). That album includes "Afterimage," a tribute to the trio's friend Robbie Whelan, who had died in a car accident; "Between the Wheels," about what the group perceived as the decay of society; and "Red Sector A," which deals with the Holocaust. (Lee's parents survived incarceration in the Nazi concentration camp in Auschwitz, Poland.)

Rush left Henderson and linked up with the producer Peter Collins to make their next album, *Power Windows* (1985). An exploration of various forms of power, it includes such songs as "The Big Money," "Marathon," and "Manhattan Project," which deals with the aftereffects of the bombing of Hiroshima, Japan, in 1945. "When I started that song, I only wanted to dramatize the event itself," Peart told Ernie Welch for the *Boston Globe* (December 5, 1985). "But after doing so much research, I realized just what had happened and began to empathize with the people involved. They weren't heartless, crazy monsters, just regular, patriotic people caught up in the momentum of events." Employing strings, keyboards, and, on "Marathon," a full choir, *Power Windows* offers a more polished sound that previous Rush discs. The radio-friendly single "Mystic Rhythms" helped propel sales of the record to more than one million copies by the end of the year.

The lushly orchestrated, keyboard-heavy *Hold Your Fire* (1987), which is widely regarded as the band's strongest effort from this period, boasts a string of Rush classics, including "Force Ten," "Mission," and "Time Stand Still," the first Rush song to include an outsider (Aimee Mann) on backup vocals. Written by Peart, "Time Stand Still" reveals the musicians' desire to focus less on their careers and more on their personal lives; the lyrics include the lines, "I want to look around me now / See more of the people / And places that surround me now." "All through the 70s our lives were flying by; we spent so much time on the road that it became like a dark tunnel," Peart told Brett Milano for the *Boston Globe* (November 19, 1987). "You start to think about the people you're neglecting, friends and family. So the song is about stopping to enjoy that, with a warning against too much

looking back. Instead of getting nostalgic about the past, it's more a plea for the present."

Such sentiments notwithstanding, Rush spent eight months on a concert tour in support of *Hold Your Fire*. Afterward, Lee, Lifeson, and Peart took a break from performing and recording that lasted about two years. "Call it maturity, but we discovered that we didn't have to be obsessed about Rush 24 hours a day," Lee told Nicholas Jennings for *Macleans* (September 30, 1991). "It was just one of the things that we do."

In late 1989 Rush released their 13th studio album, *Presto*, the first recording to bear the band's own label, Anthem. Produced by Rupert Hine, it relies on basic rhythms from each instrumentalist rather than synthesized sound. "*Presto* is kind of a renewal to me," Lee told Nick Krewen for *Canadian Musician* (April 1990). "It's a renewal of energy and a positive outlook, in musical terms and in personal terms, both in my place in the band and my feeling about recording." Highlights of the album are "Show Don't Tell," which was inspired in part by the 1925 trial of John Scopes, a high-school teacher who broke Tennessee law by teaching the theory of evolution; "The Pass," which addresses suicide; and "Superconductor," about the vagaries of fame. The video for "Show Don't Tell," which aired repeatedly on the cable music channel MTV, raised the band's profile. It also introduced the band to a new generation of listeners, many of whom responded enthusiastically to Rush's next recording, *Roll the Bones* (1991). That album debuted at number three on the *Billboard* charts, and within a week of its release, its single "Dreamline" had become the most requested song on rock-oriented radio stations; within a month, the album had sold a half-million copies.

With *Counterparts* (1993), which is dominated by a hard-driving guitar, Rush reunited with Peter Collins. *Counterparts*, Lifeson told Andy Aledort for *Guitar World* (February, 1994), is "about the three of us playing together. There was something very satisfying about making this record. It took us back to what we've always been about as a three piece band." Another hiatus followed the release of *Counterparts*. "After 20 years, we needed to just explore ourselves as people," Lifeson told a reporter for *Billboard* (August 3, 1996). "Our lives had been centered around the band. When I think back over the last 20 years, I think in terms of tours, or where were we recording at any given time. My connection is always to the band, and we needed to break away from that." During this period Lee became a father for the second time and Lifeson released a solo album, *Victor* (1996). Peart engaged in various activities during his sabbatical: he produced and (along with several other drummers) performed on the two-volume *Burning for Buddy: A Tribute to the Music of Buddy Rich* (1994 and 1997, respectively); studied drum techniques with the renowned teacher Freddie Grubber; and wrote a book, *The Masked Rider* (1996), which describes his experiences while bicycling in West Africa.

Rush returned with *Test for Echo* (1996), their 16th studio effort. Centered on the concept of human interaction in a technological society, the album spawned two singles—the title track and the acoustic rocker "Half the World." "It was the most enjoyable [album] for us," Lifeson told Gerald Mizejewski for the *Washington Times* (November 7, 1996). "We were very unified in what the direction was. I think it shows on the album." *Test for Echo* debuted at number five on the *Billboard* charts, making Rush the only Canadian act with more than one *Billboard* Top 10 success. During the *Test for Echo* tour, the band performed for almost three hours without an opening act. "When you have 16 studio records out, we decided the only way we could do it is be so self-indulgent that we have the whole show to ourselves," Lee explained to Jancee Dunn for *Rolling Stone* (December 12, 1996). During their shows, Rush performed "2112" in its entirety, something they had never before done in concert.

In August 1997 Peart's only daughter, Selena, was killed in a car accident at the age of 19. Less than a year later, his wife, Jackie Taylor, an art dealer, succumbed to cancer. In the wake of these tragedies, the group took another extended break. "We're brothers," Lifeson explained to Tom Harrison for the Vancouver *Province* (November 10, 1998, on-line). "We feel for each other, especially in a time like this. We have a great relationship that's been strong since day one." To satisfy fans eager for something new, Rush released the triple album *Different Stages* (1998), a collection of highlights from their last few tours, as well as a rare recording of a 1976 concert at the Hammersmith Odeon, in London. On other fronts, Lee and Lifeson contributed a recording of "O Canada," the Canadian national anthem, to the soundtrack of the film *South Park: Bigger, Longer and Uncut* (1999).

Peart, who married Carrie Nuttall, a photographer, in 2000, has been traveling extensively. Lifeson's activities include managing his music club cum cocktail lounge, the Orbit Room, in Toronto. Lifeson and his wife, Charlene, are the parents of two sons, Justin and Adrian. Lee, who with his wife, Nancy, has one son, Julian, and one daughter, Kyla, took the time off to record a solo album, *My Favorite Headache*. "I was not interested in stepping out as a solo artist," Lee told *Current Biography*. "I've had enough attention to last me two lifetimes. And I have no frustration working with Alex and Neil. But [with *My Favorite Headache*], there was something different at work. I was expressing myself in a different way." *My Favorite Headache* was made in collaboration with the Canadian musician and producer Ben Mink, a longtime friend of Lee's. Lee began writing songs with Mink as a way to remain artistically engaged when not working with Rush. "But even before that Ben and I would always say 'We should write something together.' So basically we made a pact [in 1997] that we would write one song before the end of the year." That one song led to 10 more, and the result-

ing album, released in November 2000, has generated positive reviews and strong sales.

At the beginning of 2001, the members of Rush reunited and began working on their first new record in five years. "At present, Alex, Neil and I are just about approaching the end of our rather long and intensive writing sessions and have moved into the realm of album production," Lee wrote in a September 22, 2001 message on his Web site, *geddylee.net*. "Now I believe we are at the point where we are starting to feel pretty darn good about how we have spent the last 8 months, and what we have created."

The members of Rush have raised several million dollars for the United Way. In 1997 the group was awarded the Order of Canada, thus becoming the only rock act to be so honored. In 1999 they earned a star on the Canadian Walk of Fame, in Toronto. Also that year, in an on-line poll conducted by *JAM! Showbiz* (on-line), Rush was voted "Canada's most important musicians of all time." — J.K.B.

Suggested Reading: *Chicago Tribune* VI p11 Nov. 14, 1982; *Macleans* p66+ Sep. 30, 1991, with photos; *Rolling Stone* p33 Dec. 12, 1996, with photos; *Washington Post* p24 May 4, 1990, with photo

Selected Recordings: *Rush*, 1974; *Fly by Night*, 1975; *Caress of Steel*, 1975; *2112*, 1976; *All the World's a Stage*, 1976; *A Farewell to Kings*, 1977; *Hemispheres*, 1978; *Permanent Waves*, 1980; *Moving Pictures*, 1981; *Exit . . . Stage Left*, 1981; *Signals*, 1982; *Grace Under Pressure*, 1984; *Power Windows*, 1985; *Hold Your Fire*, 1987; *A Show of Hands*, 1989; *Presto*, 1989; *Roll the Bones*, 1991; *Counterparts*, 1993; *Test for Echo*, 1996; *Different Stages*, 1998; by Geddy Lee—*My Favorite Headache*, 2000

Ryan, George H.

Feb. 24, 1934– Governor of Illinois. Address: Governor's Office, 207 Statehouse, Springfield, IL 62706

On January 31, 2000 Governor George H. Ryan of Illinois made national headlines by announcing that he would halt all executions in his state until a government-appointed commission had determined whether the death penalty could be administered fairly. "I now favor a moratorium, because I have grave concerns about our state's shameful record of convicting innocent people and putting them on death row," Ryan, a Republican, said during a press conference, as quoted by Joseph P. Shapiro in *U.S. News & World Report*. As the governor pointed out, since Illinois reinstated capital punishment in 1977 (after the Supreme Court lifted a

Courtesy of Governor Ryan's office

George H. Ryan

to the *Economist*, 66 percent of adults support it); in the 2000 presidential election, both major candidates cast themselves as strong supporters of capital punishment. In light of such widely held approval for state executions, Ryan was praised for his moral courage in taking his stand. In an open letter to the governor, the human rights group Amnesty International stated, "We applaud your declaration of [a] moratorium as one of the most significant policies formulated by any state's Governor on this matter since the reinstatement of the death penalty in the US in 1976." "A moratorium provides a meeting ground between abolitionists and the conscience of the broader public," an editorialist for the *Nation* (March 6, 2000) wrote.

Still, Ryan's call for a moratorium did not come entirely out of the blue: by the time the governor had halted executions in Illinois, the serious defects in the state's death-penalty system had become evident to many, not least because of a series of investigative reports, published in the *Chicago Tribune*, that had exposed its flaws. Moreover, as Joshua Green pointed out in *American Prospect* (April 10, 2000), "Although Ryan has called for a task force to identify the system's shortcomings, his opposition is not to the death penalty in principle, but rather to how the system was working in practice." For such reasons, perhaps, Ryan's action encountered very little criticism. Even such staunch proponents of capital punishment as Mayor Richard Daley of Chicago, who as Cook County state's attorney during the 1980s prosecuted five of the cases in which convictions were later overturned, supported the moratorium. For supporters of capital punishment, the moratorium was simply a chance to repair the system. As Green wrote, Ryan's "continued support of capital punishment carries the implicit promise that one day he'll reinstate the death penalty."

The youngest of the three children of Thomas and Jeanette Ryan, George H. Ryan was born on February 24, 1934 in Manquoketa, Iowa. One year later Ryan's father, a pharmacist, took a job in Kankakee, Illinois, a small, staunchly Republican town some 60 miles south of Chicago. Ryan grew up in Kankakee and attended public schools there before serving in the U.S. Army in Korea. After his discharge from the military, Ryan studied pharmacy at Ferris State College (now Ferris State University), in Big Rapids, Michigan, where he received a bachelor's degree in 1961. Upon his graduation, he returned to Kankakee to work in the family pharmacy, which his father had founded in 1948. Ryan co-owned the pharmacy until 1990, when the business was sold to outsiders.

Ryan's first foray into politics came in 1962, when he served as the campaign manager for state senator Edward McBroom. Four years later he was appointed to the Kankakee County Board; in 1968 he was elected to the board. In 1972 he ran successfully for a seat in the Illinois House of Representatives, an office to which he was reelected four times. He rose to the position of Illinois House mi-

brief nationwide ban in 1976), the state had exonerated more death-row prisoners (13) than it had executed (12). Moreover, the process that had led to the overturning of the 13 convictions had uncovered fundamental flaws in the death-penalty system. In many cases, incompetent defense counsel, police errors, and dubious testimony had been instrumental in securing the convictions; African-Americans and the poor found it especially difficult to obtain good legal advice. And while the state was not known to have wrongly executed a prisoner, it had come dangerously close: in September 1998, 48 hours before a man named Anthony Porter was scheduled to be put to death, a university journalism class established his innocence. After reviewing these facts, Governor Ryan concluded, as quoted in *Commonweal* (February 25, 2000), "I cannot support a system which, in its administration, has proven so fraught with error and has come so close to the ultimate nightmare, the state's taking of innocent life. Until I can be sure that everyone sentenced to death in Illinois is truly guilty, until I can be sure with moral certainty that no innocent man or woman is facing a lethal injection, no one will meet that fate."

Illinois is not the only state with a history of wrongful convictions. Nationwide, according to the *Economist* (September 30, 2000), "82 prisoners have been released from death row after new evidence revealed their innocence." Nor does Illinois lead the nation in the number of death sentences that have been overturned: that distinction belongs to Florida, with 18 exonerations since 1976. Yet thus far, Illinois is the only state to have instituted a moratorium. As polls have shown, the death penalty remains popular among Americans (according

nority leader in 1977 and served as speaker of the House in 1981. As a legislator he acquired a reputation as a social conservative and a loyal member of the Republican Party. He generally opposed abortion-rights legislation, voted against or did not support bills that barred discrimination on the basis of sexual orientation, fought against the Equal Rights Amendment (which was eventually defeated in Illinois), and opposed gun control. Toward the end of his tenure in the state legislature, however, Ryan began to moderate several of these positions. For example, in 1982, according to Ray Long in the *Chicago Tribune* (Oct. 20, 1998), Ryan "made a critical ruling that effectively killed a bill prohibiting local governments from outlawing handguns. The ruling ensured the bill's failure—even though Ryan voted for it." More recently, as governor, Ryan added to his office's non-discrimination policy the category of sexual orientation.

When the office of lieutenant governor was vacated in late 1981 (the former occupant, Dave O'Neal, had forsaken it for a career in private business), Ryan successfully obtained his party's nomination for the position. In 1982 he was elected to the post, and he won reelection four years later; he served for those eight years under the Republican governor James R. Thompson. In 1990 Ryan successfully ran for Illinois secretary of state, an office that Jim Edgar, governor of Illinois from 1991 to 1998 and former Illinois secretary of state, characterized as "the greatest office in the United States," as Long quoted him as saying. "You don't have all that many problems. You don't get all that attention from the news media. For the most part, you don't make many people mad."

As secretary of state, Ryan channelled the greater part of his energies into uncontroversial administrative programs. For example, he helped draft and successfully lobbied for legislation to reduce the legal limit for drunk driving from a blood-alcohol content of .10 percent to .08 percent; introduced a zero-tolerance drunk-driving law for underage motorists; sponsored the creation of license plates stamped with the words "Prevent Violence"; supported various literacy campaigns; and helped raise public awareness of the need for organ donors.

Beyond contributing to the general welfare, these public-interest campaigns boosted Ryan's visibility among the electorate—which was beneficial, since he had begun to set his sights on the office of governor. On this point, Ryan drew fire from critics. Among the various promotional items bearing the secretary of state's name and official title were leaflets, refrigerator magnets, coasters for drinks, calendars, and coloring books. In response to those who charged that he had exploited state programs for political gain (*Chicago Magazine*, for example, ridiculed him "for charging taxpayers more than $1.3 billion to promote himself during his campaign"), Ryan pointed out that his office's printing budget had not increased during his tenure, and noted that other officials, such as Chicago

mayor Richard Daley, engaged in similar practices. "I think people are entitled to know who the secretary of state is," he told Long.

When Ryan declared his candidacy for the gubernatorial race in 1998, he had much greater statewide name recognition than did his Democratic rival, Congressman Glenn Poshard. Further aiding Ryan's campaign was the fact that Poshard hailed from southern Illinois, a region that R. Bruce Dold, writing for the *Chicago Tribune* (November 13, 1998), characterized as "closer to Memphis than it is to Chicago. Not just on the map. In the mind." A socially conservative populist who habitually exclaimed "Good gravy!" when exasperated, and whom John J. Miller, writing for the *National Review* (August 3, 1998), called "a dead ringer for Captain Kangaroo, the 1970s children's television personality," Poshard was wildly popular in the southern part of the state; in Chicago and its suburbs, however, which account for 40 percent of the statewide vote, he received a far cooler reception. Ryan, by contrast, had spent most of his life upstate. He had built an extensive regional support network over the years and was more popular than Poshard in the northern part of the state.

It was a contest largely without deep ideological differences; especially on social issues, both men espoused fairly conservative views. Indeed, the Democratic Poshard came down to the right of Ryan on several points: whereas both candidates opposed abortion, Ryan allowed for exceptions in cases of rape or incest; Poshard did not. Ryan further cast himself as an advocate of gun control: during the campaign he pledged to introduce tough penalties on crimes committed with guns, require child-proof locks on handguns, veto any bill that would allow Illinois residents to carry concealed weapons, and set a $1,000 fine for anyone failing to keep a handgun out of the reach of children. Poshard, for his part, received a strong rating from the National Rifle Association. Finally, while Ryan made overtures to gay voters and asked for the endorsement of the Illinois Federation of Human Rights, the largest political organization for gays in the Midwest, Poshard refused to meet with the group, prompting federation spokesperson Rick Garcia, as quoted by John J. Miller, to complain that Poshard's "voting record on gay issues is awful."

Garnering 51 percent of the ballots cast, Ryan won the election by a margin of nearly 120,000 votes and four percentage points. (Candidates other than Poshard gleaned the remaining 2 percent of the votes.) Aside from geography, Ryan's support of gun control proved decisive for the Republican victory. As R. Bruce Dold noted in an assessment of the election for the *Chicago Tribune* (November 13, 1998), "Ryan quickly defined Poshard as big on taxes and guns, and the election was over before Labor Day."

Since he instituted the moratorium on capital punishment, Ryan appears to have grown more skeptical regarding the ethical basis of the death penalty. He has said that he doubts that another execution will take place during his tenure, and has expressed the view that moral certainty is an impossibility in capital cases. Indeed, his skepticism about the fairness with which the death penalty is applied has extended to the criminal justice system as a whole, and he recently ordered an overhaul of the Illinois criminal code. Explaining his concerns, he told Bruce Shapiro for the *Nation* (January 8, 2001), "If innocent people are sentenced to death—cases that get all kinds of scrutiny—what does that say about invisible, low-level cases, drug cases and so on?"

Meanwhile, Ryan's popularity in Illinois took a dive after it was revealed that while he was Illinois secretary of state, inspectors in the state's driver-licensing office had fraudulently issued licenses to unqualified applicants in return for contributions to Ryan's campaign fund. Although Ryan, who was not charged with any crime, denied knowledge of the bribes, several of his associates, including a boyhood friend, were tried and convicted—circumstances that severely damaged the governor's reputation. (In early 2001 there were scattered calls for Ryan's resignation.) While the scandal appeared to have subsided to a degree by the summer of 2001, it continued to overshadow the governor's other accomplishments—which, in addition to the moratorium, included $1.1 billion tax-relief legislation, a $1 billion boost in education spending, the launching of a $12 billion public-works program, and the opening of a trade dialogue with Cuba.

On August 8, 2001 Ryan announced that he would not seek a second term. At the same time he attacked the "conservative, right-wing" elements in the GOP. "I worry for the Republican Party," Ryan said, according to Kevin McDermott in the *St. Louis Post-Dispatch* (August 10, 2001). Those statements, along with his subsequent actions as a lame-duck governor who was no longer forced to compromise with political opponents, conclusively demonstrated that Ryan's primary allegiance was to the moderate rather than the conservative wing of the GOP. In August he used an unusual "amendatory veto"—in Illinois, the governor is empowered to suggest changes to a bill before signing it—to insert gay-rights provisions into legislation originally designed to prevent discrimination against motorcyclists in public accommodations. "I favor equal and fair treatment for everyone, regardless of who they are as a person," the governor wrote, according to Kevin McDermott in the *St. Louis Post-Dispatch* (August 20, 2001), "whether they be a motorcyclist, an ethnic minority, a gay or a lesbian or even a gay or lesbian motorcyclist." Shortly thereafter, Ryan vetoed legislation that would have made it easier to sentence gang members to death. "I believe [the bill's] efforts are misdirected in light of existing laws, constitutional concerns and our past history of erroneously sentencing individuals to death," he said, as quoted by the Associated Press (August 18, 2001).

Ryan has been married to the former Lura Lynn Lowe since 1956. Together, they have one son, George; five daughters—Nancy, Lynda, Julie, Joanne, and Jeanette (the last three of whom are triplets); and 13 grandchildren. Ryan is active in such service organizations as the Elks, the Moose, and the Shriners. He is also a member of the Masonic Order; in 1992 he became a 33d degree Mason. — P.K.

Suggested Reading: *Chicago Tribune* p 1 Oct. 20, 1998, with photos, p 27 Nov. 13, 1998; *Nation* p3+ Mar. 6, 2000, p17 Jan. 8–15, 2001; *National Review* p24+ Aug. 3, 1998; *Time* p68 Feb. 14, 2000, with photos

© Jeffrey Kliman

Sánchez, David
(SAHN-chez, dah-VEED)

Sep. 1968– Jazz saxophonist. Address: c/o Sony Music Entertainment, 550 Madison Ave., 26th Fl., New York, NY 10022

The saxophonist David Sánchez is regarded by many critics as one of the most exciting and important young artists to emerge on the jazz scene in recent years. A native of Puerto Rico, Sánchez made his mark in Latin jazz with his first solo recording, *The Departure*, in 1994. Popularized by the trumpeter and bandleader Dizzy Gillespie, Latin jazz is known for its unique fusion of American jazz and the traditional, African-based music of South America and the Caribbean islands. Sánchez has transformed the music he heard as a child into a form that pushes the envelope of modern jazz interpretation. In the *New York Times* (June 26, 1996), Jon Pareles wrote, "Sánchez is carrying Latin jazz toward the millennium, testing new ways to integrate Caribbean rhythms and jazz swing." Sánchez has also demonstrated an appreciation for the historical precedents of his music. Commenting on his fifth album, *Melaza* (2000), Sánchez told Don Heckman for the *Los Angeles Times* (December 8, 2000), "What I was trying to do . . . was to basically take things that came from the folkloric traditions of Puerto Rico and combine them with jazz. Mix up loose rhythms and harmonies of jazz. . . . It was my way of paying a little tribute to the Puerto Rican people who developed the music that I inherited." Sánchez's saxophone playing has been featured on many albums, and he has appeared live, both as a headliner and an accompanying musician, at such prestigious events as the Montreal and San Francisco jazz festivals. Two of Sánchez's solo efforts, *Obsesión* (1998) and *Melaza*, were nominated for Grammy Awards.

David Sánchez was born in September 1968 in Guaynabo, a town of 100,000 on the outskirts of San Juan, Puerto Rico's capital. Inspired by his oldest brother, a percussionist in a band that included members of the legendary Rafael Cortijo Combo, Sánchez took up percussion at the age of eight. His father was a professional baseball player who was disappointed that his sons had decided to pursue musical careers rather than baseball. "I started playing on my brother's drum set and the conga," Sánchez told Isabelle Leymarie for the *Unesco Courier* (January 1997). "I had a particular liking for Cuban drummers such as Mongo Santamaria, Patato Valdes, Los Papines and El Nino, and jazzier groups such as Irakere." When Sánchez was 12 years old, his sister brought home a copy of the famed trumpeter Miles Davis's recording *Basic Miles*, an anthology that features John Coltrane on saxophone. "After I heard that record, I decided I would like to focus more on saxophone than on the [Latin] percussion I had been playing, and I decided I had to play this music, jazz," Sánchez told Howard Reich for the *Chicago Tribune* (March 26, 1995). When he was 14 Sánchez enrolled at La Escuela Libre de Musica (the Free School of Music) in San Juan. There, he began his formal classical training and concentrated on mastering the saxophone, while never completely abandoning percussion. Critics have noted the attention to rhythm that is evident in his music. "It is true, there is like a burst of rhythm, because when I grew up, that was my first instrument, percussion," Sánchez told Howard Reich for *Down Beat* (March 2001). "So when I play percussion in the band, I'm not doing it as just a show. Honestly, that's what I feel, that's what I hear." He also began playing with some of the local salsa bands, most notably Eddie Palmieri's group, which represented the vanguard of Latin jazz in Puerto Rico at the time. After he graduated from the Free School, he enrolled at the University of Puerto Rico, where he briefly considered abandoning music for a career in psychology. Fol-

lowing a year at the University of Puerto Rico, Sánchez won a scholarship to study jazz at Rutgers University in New Brunswick, New Jersey, a short distance from New York City, where members of his family lived.

Eddie Palmieri and his band had meanwhile moved to New York, and Sánchez soon began playing with them again. He also collaborated with the pianist Danilo Perez, the percussionist Giovanni Hidalgo, and the trumpeter Charlie Sepulveda, who were all students at Rutgers. In an interview quoted on the official Web site of B. H. Hopper Management, which represents him, Sánchez recalled that playing with Palmieri "was a great learning experience." Through Palmieri, Sánchez was introduced to many important musicians, among them Paquito D'Rivera, Claudio Roditi, and Dizzy Gillespie. Upon hearing the young saxophonist play, Gillespie invited Sánchez to join his Grammy Award–winning United Nations Orchestra. "There's a young tenor player from Puerto Rico," Gillespie announced, as quoted by *hoppermanagement.com*. "David Sánchez: good, very reserved mind, very old mind, knows his changes, knows where he's going and knows where he's coming from." Sánchez toured with Gillespie's ensemble from 1990 to 1992, when an illness forced Gillespie to retire from music. (He died in January 1993.) Sánchez then participated in the historic, month-long "Dizzy's Diamond Jubilee" at New York's Blue Note nightclub. He was also featured on the celebrated recording *To Bird with Love: Live at the Blue Note* (1992), a tribute to the jazz legend Charlie Parker. He spent the rest of 1992 performing in a series of concerts presented throughout Europe and the U.S. in honor of Gillespie's 75th birthday.

The following year Sánchez signed a deal with Columbia Records, and in 1994 he released his debut solo album, *The Departure*. Describing a live performance that Sánchez gave to promote the album, the *Chicago Tribune* (September 3, 1994) critic Howard Reich wrote, "Technically, tonally and creatively, [Sánchez] seems to have it all. His sound is never less than plush, his pitch is unerring, his rapid-fire playing is ravishing in its combination of speed, accuracy and utter evenness of tone. More important, Sánchez clearly commands the ability to create unconventional, unexpected melodic lines that consistently keep the listener on edge." *The Departure* featured an all-star cast of supporting musicians, among them Danilo Perez on piano, bassists Andy Gonzalez and Peter Washington, trumpeter Tom Harrell, drummer Leon Parker, and percussionist Milton Cardona. The album's blend of Caribbean and jazz sounds reflected Sánchez's musical upbringing. "The jazz tradition and the Afro-Cuban stuff . . . they're the same rhythms," he told Eugene Holley for *Down Beat* (August 1994). "That strong 6/8 thing with the triplet [feel]—that's a thing that we have in the Caribbean and Latin America, and the United States." That correlation was noted by several critics, and the album was widely praised. Don Heckman of the *Los Angeles Times* (October 7, 1994) wrote, "Several originals were based on Caribbean rhythms. One of the most impressive, the multimetric 'The Departure,' initially echoed the buoyant dance qualities of Rican bomba bands. But Sánchez's soloing . . . quickly moved into more exotic territory. His string of choruses—exploding with a collection of sounds that reached across the length and breadth of his instrument—provided the final evidence that Sánchez is quickly becoming a player to be reckoned with."

Sánchez next recorded *Sketches of Dreams* (1995), which inspired additional respect for his talents in both critics and peers. For that album he was joined by the musicians who had contributed to *The Departure* as well as by the percussionist Jerry Gonzalez and the pianist David Kikoksi. In a review of *Sketches of Dreams* for the *Washington Post* (May 19, 1995), Mike Joyce wrote, "What separates the young saxophonist David Sánchez from most of his peers is his musical conception, one in which cultural heritage outweighs the fashionable tenets of neo-traditionalism. . . . The tone of his tenor sax is full and robust, and he swings through the chord changes like someone . . . in love. His elliptical approach to Rodgers and Hart's 'It's Easy to Remember' is further proof of his unusual maturity." After the album's release Sánchez embarked on a nationwide tour, which also received rave reviews. After attending one of Sánchez's concerts, Howard Reich wrote for the *Chicago Tribune* (April 13, 1995), "Of all the splendid young tenor saxophonists emerging on the national stage, surely none has more smarts, more depth, more purpose or more savvy than David Sánchez. . . . As a performer, Sánchez seems to know precisely what he wants to achieve on stage and how to attain it, wasting no gestures in the process. . . . The intricacy of [his] melody lines and the exquisitely slow vibrato he produced reaffirmed that some of the most mature playing in jazz these days is coming from some of the youngest artists in the business."

In spite of a busy tour schedule, Sánchez found the time to record his third album, *Street Scenes* (1996). In *Billboard* (October 5, 1996), Paul Verna referred to it as a "compelling showcase for [Sánchez's] raw rich sax timbres and well-sculpted solos." Demonstrating his skill as a composer, Sánchez wrote all but one track (a piece by Thelonious Monk) on *Street Scenes*. In an assessment of *Street Scenes* for the *Washington Post* (November 22, 1996), Geoffrey Himes wrote, "Sánchez has a brawny tone on the tenor sax and an unusual, biting edge on the soprano horn, and he bulls his way through the chord changes toward strong, surprising solos. Yet he invents variations not only on the harmonies but on the syncopated Latin rhythms as well. . . . His striking compositions range widely from straight-ahead be-bop to breezy Brazilian romance to danceable salsa." "This new music challenges the cultural legacy of Europe in the Ameri-

cas," Peter Watrous wrote for the *New York Times* (December 22, 1996). "And with its polyglot way of thinking, [it] does everything it can to counter the magnetic pull of a Eurocentric way of hearing." Sánchez's Caribbean background has always been a primary source of inspiration. "I wanted to be in touch with my roots, which come from Latin America," he was quoted as saying by *hoppermanagement.com*. "I believe that Latin jazz was born in the U.S., but I also believe that we are really one: North America, South America, the Caribbean. There are native people in these places who are related to each other. I'm trying to put that together in my music, trying to get in touch with the unity of it all while I integrate the stylistic elements from the different regions." In his conversation with Isabelle Leymarie, he said, "In Puerto Rico, 90 per cent of the music has black roots. I'm thinking of bomba, of course, but also the more hybrid plena, which is played with tambourines and appeared after the First World War, and danza, which is orchestrated for European instruments. Danza comes from the old courtly dances like the minuet, and when it arrived in the Caribbean in the eighteenth century, it picked up African syncopation."

In his next offering, *Obsesión* (1998), Sánchez continued to provide listeners with his unique blend of Puerto Rican musical traditions and modern mainstream jazz. Co-produced with the saxophonist Branford Marsalis, the album ventured even deeper into Sánchez's past, evoking sounds enjoyed by his father and his grandfather. "*Obsesión* is a watershed album for Sánchez—a tribute to what he describes as the Cuban, Brazilian and Puerto Rican influences in his music," Don Heckman wrote for the *Los Angeles Times* (June 28, 1998). In *Hispanic* (October 1998), Mark Holston wrote, "On *Obsesión*, [Sánchez] reaches for an audience beyond the jazz crowd that he's successfully courted in recent years by recording a program of well-known romantic standards of decades past." As Bruce Handy pointed out for *Time* (May 18, 1998), Sánchez had tried to update and personalize the traditional Latin pieces that he chose to include on the album. "The tunes are Latin standards from Puerto Rico, Cuba and Brazil, and Sánchez delights in reversing fields on them, turning a gentle Antonio Carlos Jabim song, for instance, into a rowdy Caribbean parade," Handy wrote. *Obsesión* was nominated for a Grammy Award for best Latin jazz performance in 1999.

Sánchez's fifth album, released in 2000, is *Melaza*. The title, which is Spanish for "molasses," alludes to the connection between the labors of black sugarcane workers in the Caribbean and the process of making music. In the album's liner notes, Sánchez described the trials and tribulations of these workers, many of whom were slaves. (Slavery persisted on some Caribbean islands until the late 1880s.) "The end result of their backbreaking work, after the refining process, was sugar—sweet, with a rich taste," Sánchez wrote. "Despite suffering and deprivation, we celebrate the sweet and rich culture that is a vital part of our world." Many critics singled out *Melaza* as the highlight of Sánchez's career up to that point. In a review for *Down Beat* (March 2001), Howard Reich wrote that the album was Sánchez's "most accomplished recording to date," and one that "fearlessly merges various forms of jazz improvisation with the intricate Puerto Rican bomba and plena rhythms he grew up hearing. The result is a surprisingly fresh, dramatically charged music that's rhythmically more volatile, melodically more angular and harmonically more complex than most listeners are accustomed to hearing from less adventurous Latin jazz ensembles." "It's definitely a lot of stuff I put in that music," Sánchez told Reich, "and I don't blame some people if it takes them a minute to understand what we're doing. . . . For people who listen to the regular, straightahead Latin jazz, it's not going to be easy for them . . . but this is what I have to do now." *Melaza* garnered Sánchez another Grammy nomination for best Latin jazz performance, in 2001. "*Melaza* is a beginning," he was quoted as saying on the Web site for Sony Music, his current record label. "I'm excited because little by little I'm starting to find a voice, starting to hear something I didn't hear before. If I didn't hear it before, that means I'm starting to get close to finding something, some voice that hasn't been there before. That's the beauty of music for me."

October 2, 2001 marked the release of Sánchez's latest musical offering, *Travesía*. The musician's explanation for the title of the album appeared on Sony Music's Web site: "*Traversía* is a crossing—not really the journey itself, but the motion and the movement of it. It's part of life, it's living, moving forward." As of the end of October, little had been published about the album. In an unsigned, highly laudatory assessment for the *Washington Post* (October 12, 2001), the reviewer wrote, "Sánchez is able to communicate where he's coming from and where he's going with just a handful of notes. Yet it's not necessary to be familiar with his background to fall under the spell of his sensuous tone." Sánchez, who was the album's sole producer, enlisted the services of the alto saxophonist Miguel Zenón to accompany him on many of the album's tracks. The results, as reported by the *Washington Post* critic, "reveal by turns the impressive strides Sánchez has made as an interpreter and a composer."

Sánchez lives in the New York City borough of Brooklyn. — J.H.

Suggested Reading: *Billboard* p91 Oct. 5, 1996; *Calgary Sun* (on-line) June 23, 1998; *Chicago Tribune* I p29 Sep. 3, 1994, with photo; *Down Beat* p84 Oct. 2000, p46+ Mar. 2001, with photo; *Hispanic* p102 Oct. 1998; *Los Angeles Times* p10 Oct. 7, 1994, p66 June 28, 1998, F p23 Dec. 8, 2000, with photo; *New York Times* II p44 Dec. 22, 1996, with photo; *San Francisco Chronicle* E p3 Dec. 7, 2000, with photo; *Time* p97 May 18, 1998, with photo; *Unesco Courier* p48+ Jan. 1997; *Washington Post* N p14 Nov. 22, 1996

Selected Recordings: *The Departure*, 1994; *Sketches of Dreams*, 1995; *Street Scenes*, 1996; *Obsesión*, 1998; *Melaza*, 2000; *Travesía*, 2001

Sayles Belton, Sharon

May 13, 1951– Mayor of Minneapolis. Address: Office of the Mayor, 350 S. Fifth St., Minneapolis, MN 55415-1316

From her involvement in the civil rights movement to her efforts to combat sexual abuse and other crimes, Sharon Sayles Belton has dedicated her life to battling injustice and improving living conditions among the disadvantaged. A decade as a parole officer preceded her entry into politics. Sayles Belton has achieved several firsts in her career: she became the first African-American president of the Minneapolis City Council, established the city's first battered women's shelter, and, in 1993, became the first black woman to be elected mayor of Minneapolis. Through hard work and a gentle disposition that disarmed even her ideological enemies, Sayles Belton, in her eight years as mayor, contributed to Minneapolis's reputation as one of America's safest and most pleasant cities and one that boasts its lowest unemployment rate in 20 years. On November 7, 2001 she was defeated in her bid for a third term as mayor.

Sayles Belton was born Sharon Sayles on May 13, 1951 and grew up in St. Paul, Minnesota. Her mother was an evangelist and her father a car salesman. After her parents' divorce, she maintained a friendly relationship with her stepmother, who worked as a biostatistician. Sayles was a cheerleader in high school and gained her first volunteer experience as a candy striper at a local hospital.

Soon after entering Macalester College, in St. Paul, on a scholarship in 1969, Sayles joined in the struggle for civil rights, traveling to Jackson, Mississippi, to register black voters during what was referred to as the Freedom Summer campaign. "I became swept up in the call to fight injustice wherever it lay," she told R. Erica Doyle for *Ms.* (August/September 2000). During her senior year in college, Sayles gave birth to her daughter, Kilayna. When it was discovered that Kilayna suffered from brain damage and was severely disabled, Sayles's boyfriend left her to care for their daughter alone. At the time such children were usually institutionalized, but Sayles was determined to raise Kilayna

Courtesy of Mayor Sayles Belton's office

Sharon Sayles Belton

at home. Although she was forced to drop out of school temporarily, with her family's help Sayles was able to complete her education. In 1973 she entered the Minnesota Department of Corrections as a parole officer, raising her daughter on her own while fighting for access to important services such as child care and speech therapy. "In those early years, I always struggled with why—why was I chosen for this?" Sayles recalled to Joy Duckett Cain for *Essence* (June 1998). "There was a point in that first year and a half where it was really clear to me that I could get overwhelmed by Kilayna's disability. And what I remember is really feeling, like, if I didn't come to grips with it and figure out how I was going to cope with it and manage it, then it was going to manage me. And that really wouldn't be good for my daughter, and it wouldn't be good for me. If I wasn't going to be strong for her, she didn't have a chance. I had to figure out how to move on."

As assistant director of the Minnesota Program for Victims of Sexual Assault, Sayles established 26 centers for rape victims in Minneapolis. In 1978 she co-founded the Harriet Tubman Shelter for Battered Women, the first facility of its kind in the city of Minneapolis, and from 1981 to 1983 she served as the president of the National Coalition Against Sexual Assault. In 1981 Sayles married Steve Belton, an attorney, with whom she later had two children. She remained a parole officer until 1983, when she became the associate director of the Minnesota Program for Victims of Sexual Assault, a position she held for one year. In 1984 Sayles Belton was elected to the 8th Ward of the Minneapolis City Council, and in 1990 she became the council's first African-American president. Her

ability to defuse conflict earned her the respect of even those who did not share her views. While she was serving on the council, her sons, Jordan and Coleman, were born. Fellow council member Kathleen O'Brien recalled Sayles Belton's skillful balancing of motherhood and politics on one occasion when a budget meeting ran late. "Sharon and another council member, Steve Kramer, both had infants under a year old," O'Brien told Claire Safran for *Good Housekeeping* (November 1994), "and both had to leave the meeting to pick up their babies. 'Let's just bring them back with us,' Sharon suggested. So the rest of us took turns during that session, walking the babies. It seemed so appropriate. If we were spending money for parks and other kids' issues, it was good to have a couple of kids there to remind us what we were doing it for."

In 1993 Sayles Belton ran for mayor as a Democrat-Farm-Labor (DFL) candidate, promising to reduce crime by addressing the conditions that contribute to such behavior, such as insufficient education and job training. "My advisers thought the message was too complicated," she told Claire Safran, "but the people understood it." The campaign was difficult; she lost three campaign managers, who claimed to be disappointed by the political infighting that surrounded her campaign. In addition, Sayles Belton was hurt by the perception among some that her leadership style was too passive. Her Republican opponent in the general election, John Derus, relentlessly criticized her crime-prevention credentials, but during a televised debate Sayles Belton countered his accusations by citing her previous experience as a parole officer. "I don't know if anybody really made their decision by watching the debates," Sayles Belton's campaign manager, Mark Wallem, told David Brauer. "But I think Sharon did change because Derus made her mad. She got tired. The guy was always at her throat, in her face, and it finally made her angry. She showed passion." Many voters found Derus's bullying tactics distasteful, and perhaps as a result Sayles Belton became the first African-American woman to be elected mayor of Minneapolis, surprising to many in a city whose population is more than 80 percent white. During her tenure Sayles Belton worked to stimulate the economy, promote the interests of families and children, and improve education and public safety, building upon what she saw as the successful public policies implemented by her predecessor, Don Fraser. She hired more police, increased police presence in high-crime areas, and had success in creating programs to assist poor families in obtaining affordable housing.

Sayles Belton drew much of her inspiration from the feminist movement, whose leaders had discovered how to capitalize on "the power of the collective," as she told R. Erica Doyle. Sayles Belton owes much of her success to a broad base of support from women who represent a diverse assortment of backgrounds and ideologies. These women include a small group of politically connected women with whom she has vacationed each year in Acapulco, a popular Mexican resort. "These are DFL women, Republican women, liberals and moderates," Sayles Belton told David Brauer for *Mpls.St.Paul* magazine (March 1994, online). "I think what binds us is a commitment to fairness and justice. On the trips you've got to have fun; you can't come and do business. Well, maybe we have one dinner while we're there when we talk about serious stuff."

In 1997 Sayles Belton's position was challenged by City Council member Barbara Carlson, a radio talk-show host and the former wife of Minnesota governor Arne Carlson. One of the issues debated during the campaign was education; Sayles Belton hoped to facilitate a move toward the development of community schools—taxpayer-financed alternative schools that take advantage of an array of community assets—while Carlson was in favor of charter schools. Carlson accused Sayles Belton of not being aggressive enough on issues such as crime and education, but the incumbent mayor pointed to the fact that under her administration violent crime had decreased and more than 10,000 jobs had been created. Sayles Belton was elected to her second four-year term, defeating Carlson with 58 percent of the vote. The following year she established Mayor's Night In, a monthly event in which, in her office at City Hall, she made herself available for meetings with individual constituents. In 1998 she swore in 20 young people to serve on the inaugural Mayor's Youth Council.

Sayles Belton has co-founded several organizations, such as Way-To-Grow and the Minneapolis Initiative Against Racism, and has been asked to serve on boards of organizations including the Bush Foundation, the National Conference of Mayors, and President Clinton's Commission on Critical Infrastructure Protection. Her honors include the Rosa Parks Award, presented by the American Association for Affirmative Action in 1997; the Gertrude E. Rush Distinguished Service Award from the National Bar Association (1998); and the Harvey Milk Award, from GLBT [Gay, Lesbian, Bisexual and Transgender] Pride (1998). In 2000 Sayles Belton served as the co-chair, along with Dick Durbin of Illinois, of the Platform Committee for the Democratic National Convention.

In order to run in Minneapolis's 2001 general election, Sayles Belton needed to finish in one of the top two spots in the 22-candidate primary race, and she did so, coming in behind the Democrat R. T. Rybak. In the general election, held on November 6, Rybak was again victorious over Sayles Belton, winning the mayoral contest handily. (Unofficial returns on November 7 showed Rybak garnering 65 percent of the vote to Sayles Belton's 35 percent.) According to an editorial in the Minneapolis *Star-Tribune* (November 7, 2001, on-line), "Sayles Belton's quiet pursuit of the inside game left too many voters feeling outside the loop. It's not that her ideas were bad. . . . But she failed to sell her program, to take it to the street, to the media or

even down the corridor to City Council chambers to cajole her critics."

Sayles Belton lives in Minneapolis with her husband and three children. In her spare time she enjoys reading and cooking. — C.L.

Suggested Reading: *Essence* p84+ June 1998, with photos; *Good Housekeeping* p98+ Nov. 1994, with photos; *Minneapolis Star-Tribune* (on-line) Sep. 21, 1990, Nov. 7, 2001; *Mpls.St.Paul* (on-line) p36+ Mar. 1994, with photos; *New York Times* A p15 Sep. 4, 2001

Courtesy of Legacy Recordings

Schaap, Phil

Apr. 8, 1951– Disc jockey; jazz historian.
Address: WKCR, 490 Riverside Dr., New York, NY 10027

Phil Schaap, the curator, archivist, and disc jockey for WKCR, the radio station of Columbia University, is widely regarded as one of the most knowledgeable jazz historians alive. "There isn't anyone in the country who knows more about this music than he," the legendary drummer Max Roach told Corey Kilgannon for the *New York Times* (May 27, 2001). "He knows more about us than we know about ourselves." For more than 30 years, Schaap has taught thousands of students, scholars, and musicians—as well as those who tune in to any one of his three weekly radio programs—about America's indigenous music. He has also dedicated much of his time to restoring and reissuing classic recordings, work for which he has received seven Grammy Awards.

The only son of Walter Schaap, a jazz scholar, and Marjorie Schaap, a classically trained pianist, Philip Van Noorden Schaap was born in the New York City borough of Queens on April 8, 1951. Influenced by his parents' musical tastes—his mother was particularly fond of the Count Basie Orchestra—he began collecting jazz records at the age of six. Schaap's passion for jazz was further fueled by the fact that during the 1950s, a number of jazz musicians began to settle in Hollis, the Queens neighborhood where he grew up. While still a small child, Schaap would knock on the doors of musicians and introduce himself. Schaap's father, speaking with Kilgannon, recalled his surprise at his son's gumption: "When I started hearing that Phil was going around meeting all the jazz greats at the age of 6, I wondered if it was all fantasy." For his part, Phil Schaap remains puzzled at the warm reception he often got. "I don't know why they wanted to talk to me," he told Kilgannon. "Either I was just some cute kid, or maybe they saw it, even at my young age, as an investment in their legacy."

By the end of the 1950s, Schaap had acquainted himself with many of the jazz greats then living, including Louis Armstrong, Duke Ellington, Roy Eldridge, Charles Mingus, and Dizzy Gillespie. He became especially close to Papa Jo Jones, who played drums for Count Basie; the two often watched Bugs Bunny cartoons together. Schaap's enthusiasm for jazz history impressed the musicians he met, as did his eidetic memory. (Schaap is reportedly able to list the names of all the U.S. vice presidents, the full rosters of 1960s hockey teams, and the birthdays of all his thousands of acquaintances.) Indeed, many viewed Schaap, even at a young age, as a living repository of jazz history. Schaap related to Kilgannon how he was once "kidnapped" by Sun Ra, the jazz pianist who claimed to be from Saturn; en route to Boston, Kilgannon wrote, "Mr. Ra said he was lecturing at Harvard University the next day and needed a refresher about his tenure on Earth. Among other things, Mr. Schaap informed him that, according to his union application, he was born in Birmingham on May 22, 1914, a Friday, and that his favorite ice cream was banana-strawberry from Baskin-Robbins."

Schaap enrolled at Columbia University, in New York City, in about 1969. He already had a profound knowledge of jazz. James P. Shenton, a Columbia professor of history who has since retired, was so impressed with Schaap that he invited the young man—who was then only a sophomore—to deliver guest lectures to other students. "He had a passion for chronology and dates," Shenton told Kilgannon. "He was a bottomless pit of jazz knowledge, just awesome." While at Columbia, Schaap also volunteered at WKCR, the university radio station, as a disc jockey. He first went on the air at 7:00 p.m. on February 2, 1970, and has continued to broadcast on WKCR ever since. (The station officially hired him as a curator and archivist in 1977.)

Over the years Schaap has transformed WKCR into a world-renowned jazz archive. In addition to broadcasting three weekly shows—*Bird Flight*, which focuses on the music of Charlie "Bird" Parker; *Out to Lunch*, a general jazz program; and *Traditions in Swing*—Schaap has amassed a collection of reel-to-reel tapes containing an estimated 5,000 hours of interviews. The tapes are thought to be the largest archive of oral jazz history in the world.

In his work as an archivist and audio engineer, Schaap has remastered and reissued 16 recordings, including music by Miles Davis, Louis Armstrong, Billie Holiday, Charlie Parker, Benny Goodman, Duke Ellington, and Ella Fitzgerald, among others. To date, he has garnered seven Grammys for his recording work, including awards for audio engineering, best notes, and best historical album.

Schaap continues to deliver occasional lectures at Columbia, as well as at Princeton and Rutgers Universities and the Manhattan School of Music, and has inspired many students to pursue careers in jazz radio. According to Kilgannon, he expects his students, by the end of their semester with him, to be able to hear the difference between a Louis Armstrong solo and one by Bix Beiderbecke.

Schaap is separated from his wife. He makes his home in New York City. — P.K.

Suggested Reading: *Columbia University Record* (on-line) Feb. 10, 1995, with photo; *New York Times* XIV p1+ May 27, 2001, with photos

Selected Recordings: *Earl Warren: The Countsmen*, 1985; *Miles Davis: First Miles*, 1986; *Benny Waters: From Paradise (Smalls') To Shangrila*, 1987; *Ella Fitzgerald: Ella in Rome—The Birthday Concert*, 1988; *Stan Getz: The Complete Bossa Nova*, 1989; *Charlie Parker: The Complete Dean Benedetti Recordings of Charlie Parker*, 1990; *Teddy Wilson: Two Trios*, 1991; *Benny Carter: The Oscar Peterson Sessions*, 1992; *Doc Cheatham: The 87 Years Of Doc Cheatham*, 1993; *The Jazz Scene*, 1994; *Sarah Vaughn: In Hi-Fi*, 1995; *Billie Holiday: Lady in Satin*, 1996; *Miles Davis: The Complete Birth Of The Cool*, 1997; *Benny Goodman: The Famous 1938 Carnegie Hall Concert*, 1998; *Duke Ellington: Ellington At Newport*, 1999; *Louis Armstrong: The Complete Hot Fives & Seven*, 2000

Todd Warshaw/Allsport

Schilling, Curt

Nov. 14, 1966– Pitcher for the Arizona Diamondbacks. Address: Arizona Diamondbacks, 401 E. Jefferson St., Phoenix, AZ 85004-2438

Curt Schilling is an anomaly in the world of Major League Baseball: a three-time All-Star who has spent most of his career pitching for teams with losing records. Toiling away for the mediocre Philadelphia Phillies for much of the 1990s, Schilling was a largely underappreciated player until 2001, his first full season with the Arizona Diamondbacks, winners of the 2001 World Series. He is now widely recognized as being among the premier pitchers in the sport. Schilling is known for his fastball, which travels between 92 and 94 miles per hour, and also for his split-finger pitch and slider. His control of the ball allows him to throw a high percentage of strikes, which in turn lets him get away with comparatively few pitches per inning. A studious competitor, he often watches videos of hitters in order to figure out pitching advantages. Involved perhaps more than any other contemporary baseball player in charitable causes, Schilling has given millions of dollars to the fight against amyotrophic lateral sclerosis (ALS)—popularly known as Lou Gehrig's disease, for the baseball great who was its most famous victim.

Curtis Montague Schilling was born on November 14, 1966 in Anchorage, Alaska, to Cliff and Mary Schilling. He attended Shadow Mountain High School, in Phoenix, Arizona, where he played as a pitcher for the baseball team. Upon graduation, in 1985, he enrolled at Yavapai Junior College, in Prescott, Arizona, pitching there as well. In 1986 his team played in the Junior College

World Series. Selected by the Boston Red Sox in the second round of the 1986 draft, Schilling led his minor league in strikeouts in 1987 with 189. In 1988 he was traded to the Baltimore Orioles organization. "When I was actually with the Red Sox, the one thing I learned is, it's really important to have a pitching coach in the minor leagues," he told Bob Hohler for the *Boston Globe* (October 19, 2001, online). "I didn't have ny first true pitching coach until I was traded out of that organization." Called up to the major leagues in 1988, he pitched four games as a reliever for the Orioles, compiling a record of no wins and three losses with a 9.82 ERA. Schilling began the following season back in the minors, where he led the International League in innings pitched while tying for the lead in wins, starts, complete games, and shutouts. In September he was again called up to the Orioles as a reliever; in five games he completed a record of zero wins and one loss with an ERA of 6.23.

Although his brief appearances with the Orioles had not been stellar, the team's management had faith in the young pitcher, and in 1990 Schilling was used as a middle reliever in 35 games. In all he pitched 46 innings, striking out 32 batters and finishing with a commendable ERA of 2.54 on the fifth-place Baltimore team. At that time he wore a prominent earring and a mohawk hairdo and tinted his hair blue. "I was such a screwup when I got to the big leagues," he told Gerry Callahan for *Sports Illustrated* (February 2, 1998). "I was a total idiot. I ran the nightlife, I drank, I just acted crazy. I did all the stupid things you'd expect from a 21-year-old kid with money." The Orioles' manager, the baseball legend Frank Robinson, helped to turn the young righthander around. "He said to me, 'First of all, you don't throw an inning for me until that earring is gone. Second, when you get to the park tomorrow, I expect your hair to look professional,'" Schilling recalled to Callahan. "That was it for me. No more earring, no Mohawk."

Schilling was traded to the Houston Astros in time for the 1991 season, during which he appeared in 56 games, pitching more than 75 innings, striking out 71, and finishing the year with three wins, five losses, and eight saves. One day during the off-season, Roger Clemens, then the Boston Red Sox star pitcher, berated him about his attitude; sobered by Clemens's words, Schilling began to train harder and take the game more seriously. In April 1992 Schilling was traded to another struggling baseball club, the Philadelphia Phillies. During his first season with that team, the pitcher split his time between starting and relief work. Although the team managed only a sixth-place finish in the National League East, Schilling impressed fans and management alike by maintaining a 2.35 ERA and striking out 146 opposing batters. Schilling also pitched 10 complete games, and during one impressive stretch, he went for 29 consecutive innings without allowing a run. Opposing batters hit .201 against him—the lowest average in the major leagues.

The Phillies surprised everyone the following year, winning 97 games to capture the National League East Division title. Schilling, for his part, emerged as the ace of the team's pitching staff, compiling a record of 16 wins and seven losses with an ERA of 4.02 and 186 strikeouts. In the National League Championship series against the Atlanta Braves, Schilling started Game One and allowed only two runs in eight innings, but the game was ruled neither a win nor a loss for Schilling after the Phillies blew their lead in the ninth under a different pitcher. Game Five saw a similar scenario: Schilling held the Braves to no runs for eight innings and left the game with his team ahead, 3–0, only to watch as the Phillies allowed the Braves to score three runs in the ninth inning. Philadelphia went on, however, to win the game in the 10th inning, and then to triumph in the series, four games to two. In the World Series, against the Toronto Blue Jays, Schilling was not at his best in Game One, which the Phillies lost 8–5. Schilling pitched next in Game Five, with his team down three games to one and a single loss away from elimination. He allowed only five hits, and the Phillies won, 2–0. Following that feat, however, the Blue Jays won a dramatic ninth-inning victory in Game Six to take the series.

The Phillies were far from being pennant contenders in 1994, having won only 54 games and lost 61, when a players' strike brought the season to a close. For the first time in his career, Schilling went on the disabled list, due to a bone spur in his elbow; later in the season he suffered a knee injury. He ended the year with only two wins, compared with eight losses and an ERA of 4.48. The next season was not much better for the Phillies, who won 69 games and lost 75, finishing third in their division. Schilling won seven games and lost five, managing an ERA of 3.57 and 114 strikeouts, before a shoulder injury ended his season on August 23. Following shoulder surgery he spent the off-season in rehabilitation and started 1996 on the disabled list. After returning he won nine games and lost 10, compiling an ERA of 3.19 and 182 strikeouts. His efforts were not enough to save the team from another disappointing season, as the Phillies finished in fifth place. In 1997 the team topped that performance by only one win, with Schilling, once again, providing one of its few bright spots: that year he won a career-high 17 games against 11 losses, held an ERA of 2.97, and struck out 319 batters, also a career best—one that led the National League for the season and set a 20th-century league record for righthanders.

The following year the Phillies finally showed signs of improvement, finishing in third place in the National League East. Schilling was again outstanding, winning 15 games while putting together an ERA of 3.25 and a league-leading 300 strikeouts. In 1999 the Phillies won 77 games and again finished third. By this time, though, Schilling had become frustrated with what he saw as a lack of interest on the part of the Phillies' management in hav-

ing a winning team. That year the pitcher won 15 games against only six losses, struck out 152 batters, and held a 3.52 ERA. He was also the starting pitcher in his third All-Star Game. (The first two were in 1997 and 1998.) The game was held at Fenway Park, in Boston, the home of the Red Sox—the team that had drafted Schilling and then traded him away. "It was so early in my career," he said at a press conference after the game, as quoted on the official Boston Red Sox home page (on-line), "and being reminded of it the last couple of days, kind of ironic how it's come full circle and I get to start. And [former Red Sox executive] Ed Kenney came over and congratulated . . . me again, and apologized for making the deal again. No, they gave me a shot to be a professional baseball player, and for that I'm truly grateful, and a lot of good memories of the organization." In December 1999 Schilling fell prey to another shoulder injury; his rehabilitation took many months.

In 2000, after the Philadelphia Phillies once against started the season with a losing record, Schilling threatened to leave the city after his contract expired, in 2001. Wanting to get players in return for Schilling instead of losing him to free agency with no compensation, the Phillies traded him in 2000 to the Arizona Diamondbacks for Omar Daal, Travis Lee, Vicente Padilla, and Nelson Figueroa. Before being traded Schilling compiled a win–loss record of 6–6 with a 3.91 ERA and 96 strikeouts in 110 innings. In Arizona, a competitor for the National League West Division title, Schilling joined the pitching legend Randy Johnson. Schilling won four of his first five starts, but then lost five games in a row, and the team fell out of contention. His statistics with the Diamondbacks at year's end were five wins, six losses, 72 strikeouts, and a 3.69 ERA. Schilling then signed a three-year, $32 million contract extension with the team.

The Diamondbacks had high hopes for the 2001 season, and Schilling delivered, compiling a record of 22 wins and six losses with a 2.98 ERA and 293 strikeouts. In May he was named co-player of the month. The Diamondbacks went on to win their division with a record of 92–70. In the first round of the play-offs, Arizona faced the St. Louis Cardinals, the National League wild-card team. In game one Schilling pitched masterfully, outdueling Matt Morris to a 1–0 victory. Schilling allowed only three hits and struck out nine in nine innings. With the series later tied at two games apiece, Schilling started the deciding fifth game, once again against Matt Morris. In another spectacular outing, Schilling allowed six hits and one run in nine innings, striking out nine as the Diamondbacks won 2–1. They then faced the Atlanta Braves for the National League pennant. "It's a hairpulling, nail-biting, teeth-grinding experience," Schilling said, as quoted by an Associated Press reporter on *ESPN.com* (on-line). "We gave the fans everything they could want in this series. It was fitting that it would go down to the fifth game and the ninth inning." Schilling pitched only one game in the series against the Braves. In game three he went nine innings, allowing only one run on four hits while striking out 12 batters. The Diamondbacks captured that game by a score of 5–1 and won the series four games to one.

In the World Series the Diamondbacks faced the defending champions, the New York Yankees. Schilling started the first game of the series, which was held in Arizona. In another outstanding performance, he allowed only one run on three hits in seven innings and struck out eight, as the Diamondbacks cruised to a 9–1 victory. "It's just one inning, one out, one pitch at a time," Schilling said after the game, as quoted by an Associated Press reporter. "You're playing for all the marbles. . . . You just go hitter to hitter, pitch to pitch and just focus on what you're doing and your pitches." When Schilling next pitched, in game four, in New York City, his team was ahead two games to one. In his seven innings on the mound, he allowed only one run and three hits and struck out nine. He left the game with the teams tied at one run apiece. In a dramatic end to the game, the Yankees won in the 10th inning, 4–3. Schilling started in game seven, opposite the Yankees' ace pitcher Roger Clemens (who a decade earlier had inspired Schilling to take his work more seriously). Although there was some discussion before the game as to how well Schilling could pitch after so little rest, he showed few signs of weariness in his seven and one-third innings at the plate, striking out nine batters while allowing two runs and six hits. In one of the most sensational World Series wins in history, the Diamondbacks came back from a 2–1 deficit to win the game by a score of 3–2 in the ninth inning. Schilling and his fellow Diamondback Randy Johnson shared that year's World Series Most Valuable Player Award. He was runner-up for the 2001 Cy Young Award, the winner of which is chosen by 30 members of the Baseball Writers' Association of America. (The prize went to Randy Johnson.)

The right-handed Schilling is six feet four inches and 226 pounds. An avid collector of baseball and war memorabilia, he lives outside Philadelphia with his wife, Shonda, and three children, Gehrig, Grant, and Gabriella. As a member of the Phillies, he would often call in to sports talk shows and argue with the hosts and callers. "I tell people all the time that without the fans, I've got nothing," he explained to Callahan. "When I struck out five straight Braves in the [1993] playoffs, you know what made that special? Sixty-two thousand people on their feet cheering."

In 1993 Schilling, who is active in several charitable organizations, began Curt's Pitch for ALS, which makes annual donations to the Curt and Shonda Schilling ALS Research Fund; those contributions are supplemented by money brought in by his charity golf tournament. To date he has helped raise over $1.5 million for the fund. Explaining his interest in helping victims of ALS, he told Callahan, "I met a guy . . . who had been diagnosed with ALS; six months later I saw him again,

and he couldn't walk. I started thinking, What if that was my child or my wife, and I never got off my ass and did anything to help? How could I live with myself?" Since he arrived in Arizona, Schilling has donated $500,000 to the United Way and $250,000 each to the ALS chapters of Philadelphia and Phoenix. Schilling, who was named Baseball's Most Caring Athlete by *USA Today Weekend* in 1996, was the 2000 winner of the Philadelphia Sports Writers Association Humanitarian Award for his work in connection with ALS. Since 1997 the Schillings have sponsored a family from the People's Emergency Center, a social-service agency for homeless women and teenagers and their children. Schilling received the March of Dimes Phillie-of-the-Year honor for 1996 and was Philadelphia's True Value Roberto Clemente Award winner in 1997 and 1998. The three-time All-Star is also a history buff, with a particular interest in World War II. A fan of war-related games since he was 12, he currently serves as the president of Multi-Man Publishing, which produces war games for Hasbro. — G.O.

Suggested Reading: *ESPN* (on-line); *Sports Illustrated* p78+ Feb. 2, 1998, with photos, p75+ Aug. 14, 2000, with photos

---

Scottoline, Lisa

(scot-oh-LEEN-ee)

1955(?)– Writer. Address: c/o Author Mail, 7th Fl., HarperCollins Publishers, 10 E. 53d St., New York, NY 10022

The profile of Lisa Scottoline, a successful writer in the legal-thriller genre, rises with every book she produes. She is now eight novels into her second career—she was a practicing attorney in the 1980s—with books regularly appearing on the *New York Times* and *Publishers Weekly* best-seller lists. Asked by a participant in a Court TV on-line chat about the connection between practicing law and writing books, Scottoline replied, "I think that trial law is dramatic, the wins and losses, the money changing hands, or . . . a life sentence being levied. So if law is dramatic, then writing about law is dramatic if you do it right. . . . I also think there's a connection between the writing you do as a lawyer and the writing you do as a thriller writer in that both lawyers and thriller writers have to highlight the facts that are important and throw out the ones that are [irrelevant] and spin the story in a certain way." Dubbed by *People* magazine as "the female John Grisham," Scottoline is at home in courtrooms, partners' meetings, and in the streets and suburbs of Philadelphia, Pennsylvania, where she has lived her entire life.

Courtesy of John Earle

Lisa Scottoline

Lisa Scottoline was born in about 1955 in Philadelphia and raised in Bala Cynwyd, a suburb of the city. Her father was an architect, and her mother was a secretary; both were raised in Philadelphia, in separate Italian enclaves. "In Philadelphia," Scottoline explained to Melissa Dribben for the *Philadelphia Inquirer Sunday Magazine* (April 16, 2000), "if you're from South Philadelphia and your husband is from West Philadelphia, it's a mixed marriage. Even if you're both Italian." She has fond memories of girlhood visits to her mother's family in South Philadelphia, where one of her aunts owned a deli; she has often used the neighborhood as a backdrop for scenes in her novels. Not wanting to leave her hometown, Scottoline attended the University of Pennsylvania, where she majored in English, with a focus on the contemporary American novel; one of her instructors was the celebrated novelist Philip Roth. Unable to afford four years of tuition, she finished her bachelor's degree in three years. After two years of work as a paralegal, Scottoline went back to the University of Pennsylvania to study law, earning her degree in 1981.

Following her graduation Scottoline clerked for a Pennsylvania state appellate judge. She then became an associate at the Philadelphia law firm of Dechert, Price & Rhoads. There, she specialized in employment-discrimination law, which she thoroughly enjoyed. "I'd always wanted to be a lawyer," she told Melissa Dribben. "I was always as go-go as you could get. I was a cool, solvent lawyer." During this period she got married and had a daughter, and in spite of the fact that she loved her work, she decided to stay at home with her child. But six months after she became a mother, her marriage ended, and she was forced to find a source of income. Torn between her desire to be with her daughter and her need for a regular paycheck, she decided to gamble on becoming a fiction writer. "I loved being a lawyer," she revealed to Dribben. "But I loved being with this kid. It felt completely meaningful to me. I didn't want to leave her. I had to make a living." "I guess I originally went to law school with a secret wish to write a book," she explained during her on-line chat with Court TV. She added: "It took me until I got divorced and went broke to start the second career in writing and I'm really glad I did." Inspired by the success of other lawyers who had become novelists, such as John Grisham, she noted that there seemed to be no female lawyers-turned-writers on the publishing scene. "So, the impetus [to write] was seeing the genre explode, and understanding that there was a niche that wasn't being filled," she explained in an interview on *mysterynet.com*.

Scottoline spent the next few years taking care of her daughter, writing, and living in debt but surviving on credit cards. "I had five," she told Melissa Dribben, "each one with a $10,000 limit. I gave myself $50,000 to get published." But when she found herself $38,500 in the hole, her gamble began to frighten her. She applied successfully for a clerkship with Judge Dolores Sloviter, who was then the chief justice for the U.S. Court of Appeals, Third Circuit; Sloviter had a reputation for extending opportunities to women who had to balance their careers with family demands. When Scottoline was a week into her clerkship, she sold a novel to HarperCollins. (That sale represented her second attempt to publish a book. Nonetheless, with her first manuscript, which was not about the law and remains unpublished, she "was lucky enough to get the attention of a good agent," as she revealed in the Court TV chat.) *Everywhere that Mary Went*, which appeared in 1993, is a legal thriller based partially on Scottoline's experiences as a young attorney in a Philadelphia law firm. "The creative process as it applies to me is a complete mystery," she confessed to Martin Rapisarda for the *Pennsylvania Gazette* (July/August 1999), a publication of the University of Pennsylvania. "I can't really explain how things that are in your real life through some alchemical reaction bubble up to the surface in some other form. On the surface, I write about what I know—so I know Italian-American, I know women, I know law, I know Philly, I know Penn. I draw on what I live, but a lot of times I don't realize I'm doing that until a reader points it out to me." Initially published only in paperback (it was reissued in hardcover in 2000), *Everywhere that Mary Went*, which focuses on young law associate Mary DiNunzio as she is stalked and threatened from within her own firm, was nominated for a "Best First Novel" Edgar Award, the highest honor given by the Mystery Writers of America. *Publishers Weekly* called the book "an engaging, quick read, sprinkled with corny humor and melodrama in just the right proportions."

A year after her literary debut, Scottoline published *Final Appeal*, which won the 1994 Edgar Award for best original paperback. She gained a loyal following among mystery fans, prompting HarperCollins to issue her third novel, *Running from the Law* (1995), in hardcover. "Scottoline's writing style is sharp, intelligent, funny, and hip," Anita Manning wrote in a review for *USA Today* (December 2, 1999, on-line). "Her characters are blessed with believable personalities, carrying qualities both likeable and not. . . . She's a welcome addition to the mystery bookshelf."

Scottoline began producing books at the rate of about one a year. She has noted that it takes her about eight months to write a book from beginning to end—she writes without an outline—and approximately four months to revise it. "I just start with an idea and keep asking what would happen next each step of the way. It's really the stupidest and most anxiety producing way to pay your mortgage that you can imagine," she stated during an on-line chat for the Literary Guild (April 5, 2000). An important component of her writing is research; she does "tons" of it, she told *mysterynet.com*, in order to make her stories believable. The research varies, from taking boxing lessons to talking with homicide detectives to attempting to "escape" from an underground parking garage. "I also do a lot of research to help me flesh out my characters," she explained during an *iVillage.com* chat (March 19, 2001). "For example, I spent two weeks in a kosher butcher shop so I could write about a minor character who was a kosher butcher [who appears in *Running from the Law*]. It was invaluable." According to Melissa Dribben, Scottoline keeps her car stocked with paperback copies of her books, which she autographs to pacify security guards or to thank helpful strangers she talks to on the streets of Philadelphia. She also maintains a strict schedule. "I write early [in the] morning and most of the day," she told an interviewer for *amazon.com*. "Hard emotional scenes are reserved for late at night. Suspense for the morning, when all the cylinders are firing." "This is completely embarrassing to admit," she explained during her Literary Guild chat, "but I probably have about 3,041 odd little habits that I am convinced give me a fighting chance when I start to write," habits that involve eating (she always has spaghetti with Classico Four-Cheese pasta sauce for lunch) and television viewing (the set in her office is continually tuned to Court TV).

Scottoline's 1996 book, *Legal Tender*, introduced the gutsy, witty, sarcastic lawyer Bennie Rosato, who struck Molly Gorman, writing for *Library Journal* (August 1996), as an "irresistible protagonist" and a reviewer for *Publishers Weekly* (September 9, 1996) as a "delightful heroine." Rosato reappeared in the writer's sixth novel, *Mistaken Identity* (1999). Earlier, in 1997, Scottoline had published *Rough Justice*, her fifth book; in it, she explored a defense attorney's worst fear—a client who confesses after the jury has started to deliberate. *Kirkus Reviews* (June 15, 1997) hailed *Rough Justice* as a "gorgeously plotted novel"; Marilyn Stasio, in the *New York Times Book Review* (September 7, 1997), by contrast, complained that "the character growth is nil and the office jokes are wearing thin. So is the standard run-for-your-life plot." By this time Scottoline, with her personable manner and enthusiasm for her fans, had become a darling of HarperCollins book tours. "I know this sounds really hokey," she told Melissa Dribben, "but a book isn't really written until it's read."

Mistaken Identity (1999) became Scottoline's first *New York Times* best-seller, climbing to number five on the list. In that book, Bennie Rosato deals with surprises of a personal and professional nature; Alice Connolly, who claims to be her long-lost twin sister, asks Bennie to defend her in a murder trial. Scottoline herself had discovered as an adult that she had a half-sister, and she decided to make use of that experience in the novel. "Ironically, I had always wanted a sister, and it was a little startling to find out, past the age of thirty, that I had one," she explained for *mysterynet.com*. "She was searching for her birth parents, and that was how she found me. I mean, I thought I had known my family boundaries, and suddenly, here was this total stranger who looked a lot like me. So, questions obviously arose like where does she fit in, and how does it feel to have this person in my life? When something that cool happens to a writer, you have to use it!" "*Mistaken Identity* was definitely the hardest [book to write] because it involved all this Oprah type personal stuff and so it was more like therapy than a novel," Scottoline confessed during her Literary Guild chat.

Her seventh novel, *Moment of Truth*, hit the best-seller lists in 2000. Like its predecessors, that book featured a sharp female lawyer with a vexing problem: her client has confessed to a murder he didn't commit. In February 2001 her eighth book, *The Vendetta Defense*, made the *New York Times* hardcover best-seller list at the same time that *Moment of Truth*, having recently been reissued, occupied a spot on the paperback list. Scottoline remains grateful for her success and enthusiastic about the way her books are marketed—the first chapter of *Mistaken Identity*, for example, was distributed with packs of Diet Coke. "I think it's terrific," she told Hillel Italie for the Associated Press (February 2, 1999). "I think it's a very creative idea. I love being in grocery stores. I want to be in gas stations. My goal as an author is to be read."

Scottoline takes pains to maintain good ties with her fans. Her Web site (www.scottoline.com), designed by her second husband as a wedding gift, provides information about her books and tour dates, as well as an opportunity for fans to write to her or even watch her work, via the "LisaCam," a digital camera perched over her desk. She has posted the first chapters of some of her novels on her Web site, asking fans to make editorial comments. The response has been enthusiastic, and Scottoline incorporated a few of the suggestions into her final draft of *Mistaken Identity*. "It's hard to explain how flattered I am that people are out there reading me, that they take the time to give me a chance," she told John Knebels for *Book* magazine (March/April 2001). "Then they take the time to send me an e-mail, to ask me to sign something. Do you know how flattering that is?"

Scottoline, happily remarried, lives in Charlestown Township, a small community just west of Philadelphia. Her family includes her daughter, three stepchildren, a cat, three golden retrievers, and a poodle. — K.S.

Suggested Reading: Literary Guild (on-line)Apr. 5, 2000; *Pennsylvania Gazette* (on-line) July/Aug. 1999, with photo (on-line); *Philadelphia Inquirer Sunday Magazine* (on-line) Apr. 16, 2000, with photo

Selected Books: *Everywhere that Mary Went*, 1993; *Final Appeal*, 1994; *Running from the Law*, 1995; *Legal Tender*, 1996; *Rough Justice*, 1997; *Mistaken Identity*, 1999; *Moment of Truth*, 2000; *The Vendetta Defense*, 2001

Courtesy of the Los Angeles Dodgers

Scully, Vin

Nov. 29, 1927– Sportscaster for the Los Angeles Dodgers. Address: Los Angeles Dodgers, Dodger Stadium, 1000 Elysian Park Ave., Los Angeles, CA 90012

"The game is the thing, not me," Vin Scully, known as "the voice of the Dodgers," told Bill Plaschke for the *Los Angeles Times* (April 26,

1998). "I am just a conduit for the game. I am the guy between the expert and the fan. I am not the expert." Also called "the poet laureate of baseball," Vin Scully has worked as a sportscaster for the Dodgers since 1950, eight years before the team moved from Brooklyn, New York, to Los Angeles. He has thus served more consecutive years with a single team than any other broadcaster in Major League baseball. Celebrated for his fairness, accuracy, vivid, beautifully worded descriptions, and even-keeled delivery, he has witnessed and reported many historic moments in baseball. Among them are three of the sport's 15 perfect games: the ones pitched by Don Larsen, in the 1956 World Series, Sandy Koufax, in 1965, and Dennis Martinez, in 1991. Scully was also on hand for the pitcher Don Drysdale's streak of 58 scoreless innings in 1968 and the pitcher Orel Hershiser's new record of 59 scoreless innings in 1988. He was present at Atlanta's Fulton County Stadium on April 8, 1974 as Hank Aaron hit his 715th home run, thus breaking Babe Ruth's record for major-league homers. Scully has called 18 no-hitters and has been at the microphone during 12 All-Star Games, 25 World Series, and one Hollywood version of a baseball game: in the film *For the Love of the Game* (1999), directed by Sam Raimi and starring Kevin Costner, he played himself.

Scully has extended his expertise to other sports as well as baseball: he has narrated play-by-play for radio and television broadcasts of football and golf. Baseball, however, remains first in his affections, for reasons that he explained to Michael Arkush for the *Los Angeles Times* (April 5, 1994): "You don't lose sight of anybody. In football, the running back gets the ball and the next thing you know, there are 12 guys piled up and somewhere in there is your man. And there's symmetry and grace to baseball. The pace is relaxed, but it kind of builds. That's why I don't come on screaming and hollering to start a game. I say, 'Hi,' and hopefully, it builds and builds, and by the time you get to the last inning or two, the place is going wild. Another thing is that almost everyone has played some form of baseball. Put it all together, and it's love." Scully was inducted into the media section of the Baseball Hall of Fame in 1982, the Hall of Fame of the National Sportscasters and Sportswriters Association in 1991, and the Hall of Fame of the American Sportscasters Association in 1992.

Vincent Edward Scully was born to Irish immigrant parents on November 29, 1927 in the New York City borough of the Bronx. His father, Vincent Aloysius Scully, a silk salesman, died before Vin's fifth birthday. His mother, the former Bridget Freehill, later remarried, and the small family moved to a fifth-floor walk-up apartment in the Washington Heights section of Manhattan. From as far back as he can remember, Scully wanted to be a sportscaster. When he was about eight years old, as he told Michael Arkush, he wrote a composition for school that described a baseball game. He loved words, and he loved radio, too, as he recalled in a tribute to the renowned sportscaster Red Barber that he wrote for *Reader's Digest* (April 1993): "My family had one of those four-legged radio monsters that sat so high off the floor I could actually crawl under it. I'd lie there for hours with a box of saltines and a carton of milk, mesmerized by the play-by-play." Listening to broadcasts of college football games thrilled him; as he recalled to Arkush, "Something would happen, and the announcer would get excited. The crowd would roar, the sound would come out of that speaker like water out of a shower head, and it seemed to wash down on me, and I would get so excited and full of goose bumps, that I used to imagine being there and then I'd take it another step and imagine being the broadcaster." In his youth he enjoyed playing stickball on the streets of his neighborhood. His favorite baseball player was the New York Giants slugger Mel Ott.

Scully attended Catholic parochial schools. At Fordham Prep, a Jesuit boys' high school in the Bronx, he played on the baseball team. He honed his writing skills as sports editor for the school newspaper, and his speaking skills as a member of the debate team. After he completed high school, in 1944, he served in the U.S. Navy, gaining entry only by cheating on the color-blindness test. In 1945 he enrolled at Fordham University, in the Bronx, on a partial baseball scholarship. In addition to his athletic activities, he wrote for the campus newspaper and, as a stringer, for the *New York Times*. He also worked at the Fordham University radio station, calling school football, baseball, and basketball games, and sang in a barbershop quartet. He earned a B.A. degree from Fordham in 1949. That summer he worked as a replacement announcer for WTOP-AM, the CBS affiliate in Washington, D.C. "WTOP was huge," Scully told Lou Schwartz in a June 2, 2000 interview published on the Web site of the American Broadcasters Association. "I had sent in a letter to the station and they responded and asked me to send in an audition disk. I sent it in and soon after they called me and said they don't hire sight unseen. So I went down and auditioned and a few days later they told me I had the job. It was only when I started to work did I find out there were 52 other candidates for that one job. It was overwhelming since I never even thought about other people. Had I realized that so many people had auditioned, I might not have even gone down there because I would have been so intimidated."

In November 1949 Red Barber, the CBS sports director and, along with Connie Desmond, an announcer for the Brooklyn Dodgers, asked Scully to serve as the commentator at a football game between Boston University and the University of Maryland. (His mother took the message and, in conveying it to him, misidentified the caller as the comedian Red Skelton.) Portions of the game were to be broadcast from Boston on *The Saturday CBS Football Roundup*, a radio show that shifted from game to game, to focus on the most exciting mo-

ments. "I thought I'd be broadcasting from a booth," Scully recalled for *Reader's Digest*, "so I left my coat at the hotel. But when I got to Boston's Fenway Park, there was no booth. I went up on the roof with a microphone and 50 yards of cable. While I fought frostbite, Red switched network coverage from the 'big' game—Notre Dame's rout of North Carolina—to Fenway. Suddenly the whole country heard me." Scully's account modestly omitted the rest of the story, which Gary Kaufman (now known as King Kaufman) reported for *Salon.com* (October 12, 1999): "When Barber got a note from Fenway officials the next week, apologizing for not having a booth for his man on Saturday, he was shocked and impressed: Scully had never mentioned his plight on the air, had never grubbed for sympathy from the audience. Although Scully was sure he'd done a lousy job and blown his big chance, Barber soon offered him a job as No. 3 man in the Dodgers booth. He was 22 years old." "We just needed somebody to sort of take an inning here and there and just do little things," Barber said, as quoted by Kaufman. "As I put it, carry out briefcases if necessary. Scully was a very apt young man. And he took right over. He made the most of his opportunity."

Scully joined the Dodgers during their spring training, and he soon won the hearts of "Dem Bums," as the team was affectionately called. "To say I was in awe would be a huge understatement," he told Bill Dwyer for the *Los Angeles Times* (April 15, 1997). "They all treated me fine. . . . I was their 'little one' and they took care of me." His first broadcast for the Dodgers came on Opening Day 1950, at Ebbets Field. As Scully gained experience, Barber acted as his mentor and teacher. Indeed, as a Scully wrote for *Reader's Digest*, "Except for my mother, he was . . . the most influential person in my life. . . . Red became like a father to me in every way." Barber, whom Scully described as a "taskmaster, tough on himself and others," emphasized to him the importance of discipline, accuracy, objectivity, and knowledge. "One day I brought the batting lineup to Red," he recalled in *Reader's Digest*; "one of the Dodger sluggers, who batted third the day before, had been switched to fifth. Red asked why. I didn't know. That's the last time I said those words to The Ol' Redhead. Be prepared, he taught me."

Scully was a quick study; he rapidly developed his own style and a rapport with the radio audience. He guided listeners through the Dodgers' back-to-back National League pennant wins of 1952 and 1953 and then the 1953 World Series, in which the team lost to their crosstown rivals, the New York Yankees. (Barber had turned down the job after the Gillette Co., which sponsored the series, refused to negotiate his fee. In October of that year, he left the Dodgers to become a broadcaster for the Yankees.) When, almost 50 years later, Lou Schwartz asked Scully, "Is there anything you said on the air that you wish you could have taken back?," Scully recalled a moment from the 1953

World Series: "Someone on the Yankees hit a fly ball and Whitey Ford tagged up at third and without thinking I blurted out, 'He left third too soon.' [A player must not leave a base until the ball is caught.] He went about 25 or 30 feet down the line but he stopped and went back. After that game as I was driving home, I thought to myself, what would have happened if he scored had it been a one run game and I told the world he left too soon. That scared me to death." Scully was on the air in 1955 when Johnny Podres shut out every Yankee batter in Game Seven of World Series, and the Dodgers became the world champions for the first time in the team's history.

The first radio broadcast of a baseball game took place in 1921; the first televised baseball game aired in 1939 (with Barber at the mike). Scully has described calling a game on radio as being more challenging than doing the job for television; as he explained to Michael Arkush, "The best way to describe it is that on radio, the announcer can go in with a bucket of paint and a whole lot of brushes and an empty canvas, and he starts drawing thin lines and wide strokes, mixing colors, and at the end of three hours, he walks off and says, 'That's the best I can do.' In television, the picture's already there, so now he's trying to add footnotes, so there's a very big difference." According to Gary Kaufman, "Vin Scully has the most musical voice in baseball. . . . But even though he will occasionally toss off some verse (he's likely to find the lyrics of an old show tune more apt) or call a cheap base hit 'a humble thing, but thine own,' the real metaphor for Vin Scully isn't poetry, or even music: It's painting. Other radio announcers can tell you what's happening on the field, and you can imagine it. With Vin Scully, you can see it. His command of the language and the game is so masterful that he always has just the right words to describe what's going on." Kaufman quoted the celebrated sportscaster Dick Enberg as saying about Scully, "At times I'll be listening to him and I'll think, Oh, I wish I could call upon that expression the way he does. He paints the picture more beautifully than anyone who's ever called a baseball game." Kaufman also praised Scully for knowing when not to speak: "When Koufax struck out Harvey Kuenn to complete his perfect game, Scully stayed quiet for 38 seconds while the crowd roared. When Henry Aaron broke Babe Ruth's career home run record . . . , Scully said, 'It's gone!'—and then took off his headset and stood in the back of the booth so he wouldn't be tempted to ruin the moment by talking. When the Brooklyn Dodgers won their [first] World Series, in 1955, he said, simply, 'Ladies and gentlemen, the Brooklyn Dodgers are the champions of the world.' (He would later claim that he would have been unable to say more, for fear of bursting into tears.)"

During the winter of 1957–58, the Dodgers moved to Los Angeles. "My first feeling was of tremendous relief when [Walter O'Malley, the Dodgers' owner] told me I was in his plans to go to Los Angeles," Kaufman quoted Scully as saying to a *Los Angeles Daily News* reporter in 1997. "But I was saddened because being a New Yorker, everything I had and loved in the world was back there." Scully did the play-by-play during the Dodgers' first game in Los Angeles, at the Coliseum, on April 18, 1958. The team's change of venue coincided with the exploding popularity of the transistor radio; in Dodger Stadium, which opened in 1962, so many people in the stands would listen to Scully's broadcasts on their radios that even spectators without one could hear his commentary. In a 1997 interview that appears on Gary Semerjian's Web site, Scully recalled that he "tried very hard" to inform spectators and listeners about the players. "They might have known superstars, but they didn't know the rank and file players. . . . The advent of the transistor radio . . . helped us a great deal. . . . People . . . 70 rows away from the field . . . had the transistor radio, so I was able to talk directly to them."

In 1959 Scully received a TV award from *Look* magazine. In 1976 Dodger fans voted him the "most memorable personality" in the history of the team. In 1982 he earned the Ford C. Frick Award, which is presented annually to a broadcaster for "major contributions to baseball"; the recipient is automatically inducted into the Baseball Hall of Fame. Scully's many other honors, listed on the official Los Angeles Dodgers Web site in 2001, include being named Outstanding Sportscaster of the Year four times and California Sportscaster of the Year 22 times, both honors coming from the National Sportscasters and Sportswriters Association. In 1996 he earned the Lifetime Achievement Sports Emmy Award from the National Academy of Television Arts and Sciences, for his "distinguished and outstanding" work. In 2000 more than 500 members of the American Sportscasters Association named him the top sportscaster of the 20th century. At the beginning of the 2001 season, the Dodger franchise recognized Scully by naming the Dodger Stadium press box in his honor. The red-haired Dana Scully, one of the main characters on the television series *The X-Files* and the 1998 film spun off from it, was named for the sportscaster by the *X-Files*' creator, Chris Carter, a longtime Dodger fan.

In recent years the 73-year-old Scully has cut down on the number of games he narrates each season. Although he has not talked of retirement, by his choice his contracts with the Dodgers have extended only from one year to the next. He has consistently refused to appear on talk shows and has rarely given interviews, modestly insisting that he doesn't understand why he is so popular. "I know myself to be a very ordinary man, really I do," he told Bill Plaschke. Scully's family is his first priority. He and the former Joan Crawford (not the actress), whom he married in 1958, had three children together. In 1973, about two years after his first wife's death, he married the former Sandra Hunt; their daughter was born in 1975. (Their children also include Sandi Scully's two from a previous marriage.) Vin Scully's son Michael, an engineer, was killed in a helicopter crash in 1994, at the age of 33. Scully enjoys playing golf and reading and spending time with his family, which includes several grandchildren. "I have realized the most precious thing in the world you have is time," he explained to Plaschke. "I should be utilizing the time I have with the ones I love." — K.S.

Suggested Reading: *Houston Chronicle* (on-line) Aug. 6, 1995; Los Angeles Dodgers Web site; *Los Angeles Times* (on-line) Apr. 5, 1994, Apr. 26, 1998; *Reader's Digest* (on-line) Apr. 1993; *Salon.com* Oct. 12, 1999; *Who's Who in America 2001*

Selected Films: *For the Love of the Game*, 1999

Sears, Martha and William

Sears, William
Dec. 9, 1939– Pediatrician; writer; educator

Sears, Martha
Jan. 24, 1945– Nurse; writer; breastfeeding consultant

Address: Sears Family Pediatric Practice, 655 Camino de los Mares, Suite 117, San Clemente, CA 92672

The pediatrician William Sears and his wife, Martha Sears, a registered nurse and breastfeeding specialist, are the foremost proponents in the United States of a philosophy and approach to child rearing known as attachment parenting. The Searses maintain that through specific practices that, they believe, satisfy a child's physical and emotional needs more successfully than other methods, parents will form closer, more loving bonds with their children than would otherwise be possible; by so doing, they will help children develop self-esteem and the capacity for intimacy and compassion, which in turn will enable the children to form "secure, empathic, peaceful, and enduring relationships," as the Web site of Attachment Parenting International put it. (William Sears, who coined the term "attachment parenting," is a member of Attachment Parenting International's advisory board.)

William and Martha Sears have co-written nine books, among them *The Baby Book: Everything You Need to Know about Your Baby—From Birth to Age Two* (1993), *The Birth Book: Everything You Need to Know to Have a Safe and Satisfying Birth* (1994), *The Discipline Book: Everything You Need to Know to Have a Better-Behaved Child—From Birth to Age Ten* (1995), *The Complete Book of Christian Parenting and Childcare: A Medical &*

Moral Guide to Raising Happy, Healthy Children (1997), and *The Breastfeeding Book: Everything You Need to Know About Nursing Your Child from Birth through Weaning* (2000). As sole author, William Sears has also written *Nighttime Parenting: How to Get Your Baby and Child to Sleep* (1985), *Keys to Becoming a Father* (1999), and other books, and he has co-authored additional titles with people other than his wife. Besides maintaining a pediatric family practice with his wife and two of his sons (both of whom are pediatricians), Sears is an associate clinical professor of pediatrics at the School of Medicine of the University of California at Irvine.

William Sears was born on December 9, 1939 in Alton, Illinois. He was raised as a Roman Catholic and briefly considered becoming a priest. (He and his wife currently attend a Baptist church.) Sears received a B.S. degree from St. Louis University, in Missouri, in 1962, and earned an M.D. from the university's school of medicine four years later. He then completed an internship at the Children's Hospital Medical Center of Harvard Medical School, in Boston, Massachusetts. From 1967 to 1969 he worked for the U.S. Public Health Service at the National Institutes of Health in Bethesda, Maryland. Sears then spent three years in Canada, as a pediatric resident at the University of Toronto's Hospital for Sick Children, one of the largest children's hospitals in the world. While there he also received training in neonatology and cardiology. In 1972 he earned pediatric certification from Canada's Royal College of Physicians; in 1992 he became a fellow of the American Academy of Pediatrics.

Martha Sears was born Martha Vivian McMenamy on January 24, 1945 in St. Louis, Missouri. She received her license as a registered nurse (R.N.) from the DePaul School of Nursing, in St. Louis, in 1965, and then trained for a year on a postgraduate fellowship at St. Louis University. While working on a ward at the university hospital, she met her husband-to-be, at the bedside of a patient; the two married in 1966 and had their first child about a year later. Martha Sears later trained at the International Childbirth Education Association, in 1975, and in 1983 she received certification as a breastfeeding consultant from the Lactation Institute of Los Angeles, one of the largest such facilities in the country. Her advice to nursing mothers and mothers-to-be draws upon her 18 years of experience in breastfeeding. (She and her husband have seven biological children, all of whom she breastfed; their eighth child was adopted.) She directs the Breastfeeding Center in San Clemente, California, and is a leader in La Leche League International, an organization dedicated to promoting breastfeeding and assisting women who breastfeed. (La Leche League was founded in 1956; its name [pronounced LEH-chay], which means "the milk" in Spanish, was chosen at a time when breastfeeding was uncommon in the United States and many people felt uncomfortable about referring to breastfeeding in

Martha and William Sears   Leslie Byrd

public.) A popular lecturer, Martha Sears has identified herself as a "professional mother."

Attachment parenting, the approach to child-rearing that the Searses advocate, aims to foster intimacy between parent and child and help the child to feel that he or she is loved. Not a rigid system, it involves developing a closeness that will increase the parents' ability to intuit their child's specific needs. Toward that goal, some parents use what is known as a "baby sling," a carrying device, worn over the shoulder, that allows the infant to be physically close to his or her mother or father at all times. Some parents choose to sleep with their child in what they refer to as the "family bed." Sears has recommended that parents who wish to try this sleeping arrangement purchase a king-size bed. "The sleeping arrangement whereby all three of you (mother, father, and baby) sleep best is the right one for your individual family," he wrote in *Nighttime Parenting—How to Get Your Baby and Child to Sleep* (1985), as quoted on the Web. "Your baby trusts that you are open and receptive to the cues that he is giving you about where he needs to sleep. You are also trusting yourself to respond to your baby's needs for a certain sleeping arrangement even though this may not be in accordance with the norms of your neighborhood." He also wrote, "If sleeping with your baby feels right to you and is working, then it is okay. As with any feature of a parenting style, if it is not working and does not feel right, then drop it."

According to Sears, attachment parenting leads both parents and children to feel more secure, which ultimately helps children to become more independent than they might otherwise. "Parents who practice the attachment style of parenting know their child well," Sears wrote in *Nighttime*

Parenting. "They are observant of their infant's cues, respond to them intuitively, and are confident that their responses are appropriate. They have realistic expectations of their child's behavior at various stages of development, and they know how to convey expected behavior to their child. Their children are a source of joy. The feeling that the attachment style of parenting gives you and your child can be summed up in one word, harmony." The Searses have warned against "calendar parenting," or expecting—unrealistically—that all children will develop at the same pace and thus should be weaned or should sleep through the night by a certain age.

According to attachment-parenting proponents, mothers who adopt this approach produce more prolactin than other mothers; in *Nighttime Parenting*, Sears wrote that this hormone "may enhance a woman's ability to mother as well as create a feeling of calmness and well-being during trying times." He explained, "In experiments where this hormone is injected into male birds, they act like mothers. . . . Science is finally catching up to what intuitive mothers have known all along: Good things happen when mothers and babies spend more time with each other." William and Martha Sears contend that fussy children, whom they prefer to label "high need" children, are most in need of this style of parenting.

According to William Sears, attachment parenting leads both parents and children to feel more secure, which ultimately helps children to become more independent than they would otherwise be. In an article for *Baby Talk* (September 2000), he described studies conducted by doctors at Johns Hopkins University in the 1970s that showed that children who were raised this way "were able to crawl away from their mothers, play by themselves, and return to them less anxiously than infants who were less attached" and demonstrated that children who are raised to depend entirely on their parents in the earliest stages of development find it easier to make the transition to independence as they grow. Critics of attachment parenting have charged that the method results in uncontrollable behavior in children and ineffectuality in parents.

As a pediatrician with more than 30 years of experience, William Sears has noted that breastfed children are often healthier than children who have been fed formula or other forms of milk. "Mothers who breastfeed are more connected to their infants," he wrote for *Breastfeeding.com*. "Breastfeeding is an exercise in baby reading. Because breastfeeeding is such a social interaction, a mother gets to know her infant intimately, which sets her up to be a more effective disciplinarian." The Searses have often pointed to the more than 11 scientific studies that showed that breastfed babies grow to become healthier, smarter adults, in part because breast milk contains docosahexaenoic acid (DHA), a fatty acid that plays a crucial role in the development of an infant's brain (and is also necessary for the proper functioning of an adult's brain). William Sears has also noted that breastfed infants are generally less anxious than formula-fed babies. "I look upon breastfeeding as one of the best long-term investments that a parent can make," he wrote for *Breastfeeding.com*.

William and Martha Sears have co-written articles that appear regularly in the magazines *Baby Talk* and *Parenting*. William Sears has been a guest on more than 100 television talk or news shows, among them *20/20*, *Good Morning America*, *The Oprah Winfrey Show*, and *Dateline*. The couple share their child-rearing expertise on two Web sites, *Parenting.com* and *AskDrSears.com*. William Sears is the developer of the "Original Baby Sling," an infant carrier that received the 1989 Infant Product of the Year Award from the National Independent Nursery Furniture Retailers Association (NINFRA). He is a member of many organizations, including the American Academy of Pediatrics and the Orange County Pediatric Society. He is also a consultant for Arm's Reach, which manufactures cribs that allow babies and parents to have their own sleeping space yet still remain close enough to touch. In addition, he serves as a medical adviser to Martek Biosciences Corp., which makes nutritional products for pregnant and nursing women.

James and Robert Sears, the Searses' oldest sons, are now partners in the Sears family pediatric practice, in San Clemente, California; their third son, Peter, is currently a medical student. Their other children are Hayden, Erin, Matthew, Stephen (who was born with Down syndrome), and Lauren, the youngest, who was nine years old in early 2001. William and Martha Sears told *Current Biography* that their children make up "the cast of characters in The Sears Family Drama who provide much of the material for our books." — C.L.

Suggested Reading: *AskDrSears.com*; *Breastfeeding.com*; *Parenting.com*; *Contemporary Authors* vol. 160, 1998

Selected Books: by William and Martha Sears— *The Baby Book: Everything You Need To Know about Your Baby—From Birth to Age Two*, 1993; *The Birth Book: Everything You Need to Know To Have a Safe and Satisfying Birth*, 1994; *25 Things Every New Mother Should Know*, 1995; *The Discipline Book: Everything You Need to Know to Have a Better-Behaved Child—From Birth to Age Ten*, 1995; *Parenting the Fussy Baby and High Need Child*, 1996; *The Complete Book of Christian Parenting and Childcare: A Medical & Moral Guide to Raising Happy, Healthy Children*, 1997; *The Family Nutrition Book: Everything You Need To Know About Feeding Your Children—from Birth Through Adolescence*, 1999; *The Breastfeeding Book: Everything You Need to Know About Nursing Your Child from Birth Through Weaning*, 2000; by William Sears— *Nighttime Parenting: How to Get Your Baby and Child to Sleep*, 1985; *Keys to Becoming a Father*, 1999

Rick Stewart/Allsport USA

Seau, Junior
(Say-OW)

Jan. 19, 1969– Linebacker for the San Diego Chargers. Address: San Diego Chargers, P.O. Box 609609, San Diego, CA 92160-9609

Junior Seau, a linebacker for the San Diego Chargers football team, brings a wealth of gifts to the field. At six feet, three inches and approximately 255 pounds, he is bigger and stronger than many other linebackers; in fact, he can bench press 500 pounds and squat 670 pounds and has a 38-inch vertical leap. And for a man his size, he is astonishingly fast. Able to run the 40-yard dash in 4.5 seconds, he can chase down running backs and quarterbacks from nearly anywhere on the field. Seau possesses more than physical prowess, however; his tremendous drive and energy, in both games and practice workouts, are what make him a truly formidable presence on the football field. "There's not another linebacker who does the things he does," the quarterback Warren Moon said to Paul Attner for *Sporting News* (October 4, 1993). "But what really sets him apart is he plays with so much enthusiasm and emotion. That helps him get to the ball a little faster. It's almost like he plays possessed." That determination has not ebbed in Seau's 11 seasons in the National Football League (NFL). In 10 of them consecutively, Seau was voted to the Pro Bowl (making him one of only four players since 1970 to reach the Pro Bowl 10 times in a row), and he was named to the Pro Football Hall of Fame's All-Decade Team for the 1990s. As Michael Freeman wrote for the *New York Times* (August 12, 1994), "Seau is considered in a league of his own, the type of player who comes along every few decades and changes the way the position is played."

One of five children, Tiaina Seau Jr.—called Junior—was born on January 19, 1969 in Oceanside, California. In 1964 Seau's parents had immigrated from the Samoan island of Aunuu to San Diego, California, in search of medical treatment for their eldest son, David, who had developed a lung disease. Though neither of Seau's parents spoke English, his father, Tiaina Sr., found a job on an assembly line at a rubber factory, and his mother, Luisa, went to work in a Laundromat at the Camp Pendleton Marine Corps base. They soon earned enough money to pay for David's lung surgery. Money, however, was always scarce for the Seaus. Junior Seau slept on the concrete-floored garage of his parents' two-bedroom house, his bed crowded between a washer and dryer. The Seaus did their best to isolate their children from the violence of the gang-ridden slums of Oceanside. Tiaina Sr. adhered strictly to Samoan traditions, dressing his three sons in wraparound skirts called lavalalas. Luisa sewed long dresses called muumuus for the two girls. Because his parents spoke only Samoan in the house, Seau did not speak English until he was seven years old.

All of the Seau children were expected to get jobs to supplement the family income, but for Junior Seau the father made an exception. Though the other boys played sports, Tiaina Sr. could see that Junior Seau's talents in this area were extraordinary, and he slipped his son cash to reward him for his athletic victories. However, he also punished the boy for his losses. As Junior Seau's brother Sa-

vaii told Jill Lieber for *Sports Illustrated* (September 6, 1993), "If we lost, Dad acted like we were failures. He'd say, 'You're lazy.'" Seau's legendary work ethic thus began at an early age. He would often climb out of bed before his brothers were awake and lift dumbbells in front of a mirror. At the end of each day, he did hundreds of push-ups, and he practiced chin-ups on a branch of the backyard maple tree. The work paid off. As a senior at Oceanside High School, Seau led his football team to a City 2A Championship, even though the team had only 18 players. (Usually, there are at least 22 players—11 each on defense and offense.) As a linebacker he was named the defensive MVP (most valuable player) of San Diego County, and as a tight end he was named the offensive MVP of the Avocado League. In basketball he averaged 23 points per game and was named County Player of the Year.

Recruiters from most of the major college-football programs sought out Seau, and he won a scholarship to play for the Trojans of the University of Southern California (USC) at Los Angeles. There, he immediately suffered a setback, learning that while he had maintained a 3.6 GPA in high school and attained All-Academic status, his SAT score was 10 points below the minimum for NCAA (National Collegiate Athletic Association) freshman eligibility, and he would therefore have to sit on the bench his first year. "Everything I'd worked for, everything my family had stood for was gone," Seau told Lieber. "I was labeled a dumb jock." Seau took a special trip to Oceanside to apologize to his high-school coaches, and upon his return to Los Angeles he set to work. He maintained better-than-average grades during his freshman year, and despite being unable to play football, he impressed the Trojans when he beat the whole team in the annual Superman Contest of strength and speed. As a sophomore Seau injured his ankle during the preseason and was rendered ineffective as a player for most of the year. It was not until his junior year, in 1989, that he won a starting position on the team, and that was only after two Trojan starters were injured, vacating the outside-linebacker spot. Seau immediately dominated the league. He led USC to the Rose Bowl (where the team lost to Michigan State, 22–14) and was unanimously named first-team All-American and Pac-10 Defensive Player of the Year.

Seau left school early, and after only one full season of college football, he was recruited for the 1990 season by the San Diego Chargers, who gave him a $4.5 million contract. (He was a first-round draft pick for the Chargers and the fifth pick in the league overall.) He had an impressive rookie season, becoming the team's second-leading tackler, with 85. He was voted second alternate to the Pro Bowl and named to the *Football News* All-Rookie team.

In 1991 Seau started to emerge as a unique force in football. He had an impressive 129 tackles, including seven quarterback sacks, and was voted the American Football League's (AFL) top inside linebacker for the Pro Bowl. The following season, Seau plagued opposing NFL coaches with his great versatility. Though he remained an inside linebacker, he was allowed at various times to fill each of the seven defensive spots on the line of scrimmage. He led the Chargers that season with 108 tackles; made four and a half sacks, two interceptions, and one fumble recovery; defended 10 passes; and forced one fumble. The Chargers' defense was ranked second in the AFC and fourth in the NFL that year. The accolades poured in. Seau was the AFC's only unanimous choice to start in the Pro Bowl. He was named NFL Defensive Player of the Year by *Football Digest*, *Football News*, and the Newspaper Enterprise Association; he was also named AFC Defensive Player of the Year by United Press International and elected to the All-Pro teams of the Associated Press, *USA Today*, *Football Digest*, and *Sporting News*. Though the Chargers were demolished 31–0 by the Miami Dolphins in the AFC Divisional play-off game that season, Seau did everything humanly possible in his efforts to turn the game around, amassing an astounding 19 tackles.

His teammates were in awe of him. When Dave Sheinin asked several Charger players to relate their favorite stories about Seau for the *Washington Post* (January 9, 1993), the linebacker Gary Plummer recalled a spring practice in which he and another player were chasing a runner on their side of the field; suddenly, from the other side of the field, Seau sped by them and tackled the runner. "It was like the Coyote and the Road Runner," Plummer said. The guard David Richards described the time in practice when Seau creamed the running back at the line of scrimmage and realized only then that the running back didn't have the ball. Seau then ran down field and arrived in time to intercept the pass intended for the tight end. "One time in Denver," Charger Bob Gagliano explained, "[Seau] was shadowing [quarterback John] Elway and was about 10 yards away from him when Elway lets one rip like it was out of a cannon. But Junior's so quick, it was like it just stuck to him, and he intercepted it. Ten yards away."

Coaches around the league began to plan their offenses with Seau in mind when competing against the Chargers. "He can hurt you in more ways than any other defensive player in the league," the Houston offensive coordinator Kevin Gilbride said to Attner. "Not only can he be a significant force as a pass rusher, but he has tremendous range against the running game and he's very good on pass coverage." The now-retired Oakland Raider Howie Long told Lieber about Seau, "The guy's a buzz saw. . . . But mentally he's under control, and that's unusual for a young player."

Despite having won many fans, Seau was not content to sit back and enjoy the limelight. In 1992 he and his wife, Gina, established a youth-support organization called the Junior Seau Foundation. "Too many athletes are living in a tiny window," Seau told Lieber. "They have no vision for themselves—what they can be outside of football and what they can mean to a community. They just don't know any better. My hopes and dreams are unlimited." According to the Junior Seau Foundation's Web site, the organization's mission is "to educate and empower young people through the support of child abuse prevention efforts, drug and alcohol awareness, and anti-juvenile delinquency programs." Each year the foundation sponsors the TEAM Seau Dinner & Celebrity Golf Classic, which in 1993 raised $60,000. Seau designed and wrote the brochure for the event and held more than 40 meetings with business leaders to discuss sponsorship. Later, Seau also helped found both the Club 55 Teen Center, a fitness and education club for teens, and the Junior Seau Drug-Busters Basketball Team.

Seau soon faced a number of personal challenges. Just as he was working to help young people deal with the difficulties of growing up in poor, crime-ridden areas, his brother Tony became entangled in a San Diego–area gang. In 1993 Tony, armed with a baseball bat, participated in a gang war in which a member of the opposing gang was shot and seriously injured. Tony was charged with attempted murder and given a 10-year prison sentence. In the same year Seau's first child, a girl named Sydney Beau, was born two months prematurely and with underdeveloped lungs; she nearly died before gaining strength and health.

On the field, meanwhile, Seau was working as hard as ever. Even during the off-season, most of his days were structured around his workouts. His single-mindedness and determination manifested themselves even more spectacularly during games. "When I'm out there on the stage," Seau said to David Sheinin, referring to the football field, "all I care about is getting to the ball. It doesn't matter how I do it. If it takes going through somebody, I'll do it. If it takes going over somebody or around somebody, I'll do it. It doesn't matter how much is in front of me, I've got to get to that ball. I have to find a way." During the 1993 season Seau proved particularly adept at finding a way. He finished the season with 129 tackles and, for the third year in a row, was selected for the Pro Bowl. In a game against the Houston Oilers on September 19, Seau notched seven tackles and two defended passes and made two interceptions—both of which led to scores—as the Chargers beat the Oilers. He was selected as co-Most Valuable Player by his teammates and as NFL Player Association Linebacker of the Year by other NFL players. He was also named to the All-Pro teams of the Associated Press, *Football Digest*, the Pro Football Writers Association, *Sporting News*, *College & Pro Football Newsweekly*, and *Sports Illustrated*.

In 1994 Seau ushered the Chargers to the Super Bowl, compiling an incredible 155 tackles along the way—despite suffering from a pinched nerve that rendered one arm nearly immobile. In the AFC Championship game versus the Pittsburgh Steelers, he had brought his team to victory almost single-handedly, making 16 tackles, 12 of them unassisted. In the Super Bowl, in which the Chargers faced the San Francisco 49ers, however, Seau's menacing presence was not enough to subdue the NFL's best offense, and the Chargers lost, 49–26. Still, 1994 was another stellar year for Seau. He was selected for the Pro Bowl for the fourth consecutive year; he was also named the True Value Hardware NFL Man of the Year as well as the NFL's Linebacker of the Year. Additionally, he was named to the All-Pro first team by the Associated Press, *College & Pro Football Newsweekly*, *Football Digest*, Pro Football Weekly/Pro Football Writers of America, and *Sporting News*.

At the beginning of the 1995 season, Seau injured his right hamstring while playing against the Pittsburgh Steelers. That injury did not keep him from leading the Chargers in tackles for the fifth consecutive year, with 129, or from being named to his fifth consecutive Pro Bowl. Additional honors included being named to the All-Pro first team by the Associated Press and *Football Digest*, as well as to the All-Pro team of *Sporting News* and *USA Today*. In 1996 Seau continued to be plagued by the injury to his hamstring, but he had another great season, accomplishing what was becoming routine for him: he made 138 tackles and was named to his sixth consecutive Pro Bowl. The 1997 season was, by Seau's standards, a sub-par year, and proved to be a low point in general for the Chargers, whose record was 4–11. Seau began by tearing cartilage in his left knee during an exhibition game, and he missed the first game of the season while recovering from knee surgery. Still, he started in every game for the rest of the season, compiled 97 tackles, and was named to his seventh consecutive Pro Bowl. His teammates also voted him the Chargers' Most Valuable Player and Most Inspirational Player, in recognition of the fact that he had played through injuries all year and never allowed the team's losses to dampen his spirits or hamper his efforts on the field. After leading San Diego with 115 tackles in 1998, Seau was named to his eighth consecutive Pro Bowl and voted by his teammates as the Charger's Most Valuable Player and Defensive Player of the Year. The Chargers' defense was also ranked best defense in the NFL. Seau's national honors included being voted to the All-Pro first team by the Associated Press, *Pro Football Weekly*, and *Sporting News*.

In an off-season issue of *Sporting News* (June 7, 1999), Jay Paris wrote that Seau "remains one of the top linebackers in the NFL." Nonetheless, the 1999 season was Seau's 10th—a high number for an NFL linebacker, especially one who had played with such ferocity throughout his career. Although Seau played well and led the Chargers in tackles that season, with 98, he at first failed to make the Pro Bowl, for only the second time in his career and the first time in eight seasons. Seau and his teammates were outraged. "It's going to be a different approach next year," Seau told Bernie Wilson for the *Detroit News* (December 23, 1999, on-line).

The snub, he said, "started a war is what it did. It's a battle now, and coming into the next off-season, it is going to strike me even harder." The situation changed after legal difficulties made the Baltimore Raven linebacker Ray Lewis ineligible for the Pro Bowl, and Seau replaced him in that game.

The following summer Seau was named to the Pro Football Hall of Fame's All-Decade Team for the 1990s, thus becoming the third Charger in history to make an All-Decade team and confirming his place as one of the best linebackers ever to play the game. While the Chargers had a dismal 2000 season, with only one win and 15 losses, Seau performed admirably, compiling 123 tackles and earning a trip to his 10th consecutive Pro Bowl. The Chargers won five of their first seven games in the 2001 season, thanks in part to 33 tackles and an interception by Seau. He has averaged 118 tackles per season while starting 170 of 171 regular-season games for the Chargers. "When I leave the game, I want to be known as the greatest linebacker ever," he declared to Attner. "Why not want to be the best?"

In 1996 Seau opened the sports-themed Seau's The Restaurant, in San Diego. He and his wife have three children: Sydney, Jake, and Hunter. — P.G.H.

Suggested Reading: *Detroit News* (on-line) Dec. 23, 1999; *New York Times* B p11 Aug. 12, 1994; *San Diego Union-Tribune* D p4 July 26, 2000; *Sport* p22+ Oct. 1994, with photos, p100+ Nov. 1995, with photo; *Sporting News* p34+ Oct. 4, 1993; *Sports Illustrated* p64+ Sep. 6, 1993, with photos, p127 Dec. 22, 1997, p96+ Oct. 23, 2000, with photo; *Washington Post* D p5 Jan. 9, 1993

Seymour, Lesley Jane

Jan. 4, 1957– Editor of Marie Claire; *writer.*
Address: Marie Claire, 1790 Broadway, Third Fl., New York, NY 10019

"I'm a mom, I'm a workingwoman, and I'm a friend," Lesley Jane Seymour said during an on-line chat for *talkcity.com* on January 21, 1998, a few months after she became editor in chief of the women's magazine *Redbook*. "And that's the most important role—to be there with my readers and to explore with my readers the whole meaning of balancing this crazy life we lead." In June 2001 Seymour was named editor in chief of the United States edition of *Marie Claire*, one of the best-selling fashion magazines in the nation and one that Seymour believes "has clearly struck a chord with style-conscious, smart, and savvy American women," as she told *Fashion Wire Daily* (June 28, 2001). Seymour began her career in journalism in 1978, as a reporter for *Women's Wear Daily*. Subsequently, she worked in various capacities at *Vogue* and then, for more than 10 years, at *Glamour*,

Naomi Kaltman/Courtesy of Hearst Magazines

Lesley Jane Seymour

building a reputation as an expert in fashion and beauty and as a top-notch features editor. For a year and a half, in the late 1990s, she served as the editor in chief of *YM*, which is aimed at teenage girls. As the editor of *Redbook* for two and a half years, Seymour was credited with "break[ing] the matronly mold" of the nearly century-old magazine, as Brian Steinberg put it in the *Wall Street Journal* (February 16, 1999), and making it more appealing to young women who juggle marriage, motherhood, and jobs and try to schedule time for themselves as well. Articles by Seymour have been published in such magazines as *Harper's Bazaar*, the *New York Times Magazine*, and *Vanity Fair*, and she is the author of two books—*I Wish My Parents Understood: A Report on the Teenage Female* (1985), which she wrote as Lesley Jane Nonkin, and *On the Edge: 100 Years of Vogue* (1992), a collaborative effort of *Vogue* editors.

The daughter of a U.S. Navy physician, Lesley Jane Seymour was born on January 4, 1957 on the U.S. naval base in Puerto Rico. During the next dozen years, she lived in Florida, Missouri, New York, and New Jersey. At age 10 she started writing stories. By the time she was a sixth-grader, she told *Current Biography*, she had started associating events in her life with the clothes she was wearing at the time—"specific dresses I can remember to this day," she explained. "I've always had that awareness, of what I was wearing, of what others were wearing. . . . That combined with writing, it doesn't surprise me that I'm doing what I'm doing today." She also recalled that in sixth grade, she and a friend would read the August, "back-to-school" issue of *Seventeen* magazine together. "You were not allowed to open it until you were together, or you'd ruin the friendship," she said.

Seymour attended the Dana Hall School, a boarding and day school in Wellesley, Massachusetts, for girls in grades six through 12. After she completed high school, in 1974, she entered Duke University, in Durham, North Carolina, where she majored in English and minored in biology. As an undergraduate she wrote features as an intern with the *Durham Sun*, a daily newspaper. "I'd go into the student union and see the paper sitting there, and there's [President Jimmy] Carter and [the Soviet leader Leonid] Brezhnev shaking hands and then there on the right was my story about everyone's outraged downtown about the Christmas tree going up the day after Halloween. I was like: 'This is Hollywood, man,' I mean, who could ask for more than that? So I was set for journalism," she told *Current Biography*. Seymour, who is fluent in French, spent the spring term of 1977 taking courses in Strasbourg, France, under the auspices of Syracuse University, a school in New York State. During the summer preceding her senior year at Duke, she secured an internship at *Seventeen*, which is based in New York City. Although she spent most of her workday doing menial tasks, she gained useful knowledge as an intern, in part by reading the various trade magazines that arrived at the *Seventeen* offices. As the youngest person there at that time, she also received clothing and samples of makeup from other women on the staff. As a college senior she wrote freelance articles for *Women's Wear Daily*.

After she graduated from Duke, with a B.A. degree, in 1978, Seymour got a job as a reporter with *Women's Wear Daily*. Her beat included such nightclubs as Studio 54. "I'd walk past the big line of people, get in for free," she recalled to *Current Biography*. "I was covering things like Bianca Jagger coming out of the cake for Calvin Klein. I didn't know it at the time that these were some of the biggest moments in fashion in many ways. I had the time of my life. It was a great introduction." In mid-1980 Seymour left *Women's Wear Daily* to join the reportorial staff of "Tonight," a section of the New York *Daily News*, where she wrote about health, psychology, and fashion and interviewed celebrities. The following year she was hired by *Harper's Bazaar* as a copywriter. She wrote about sports from the perspective of good health and conducted interviews with the actress Liv Ullman and the singer Patty Lupone, among other performers.

Later in 1982 Seymour became a copywriter for the Condé Nast periodical *Vogue*. While with the magazine she transformed its "Women & Cars" column into one called "Driving Style," in which—practicing what would become her trademark—she increased coverage of hard news. She also wrote feature articles on beauty, fashion, travel, shopping, and the history of clothing. In 1987 her title changed to special-projects writer and co-editor of "Vogue's View." Three years later she was given full creative control of *Vogue*'s new popular-culture section, called "UpFront"; later renamed "People Are Talking About," it offered reports on trends in art, theater, music, and food. Not long afterward Seymour was promoted to features editor; that job involved assigning and editing articles about fashion and celebrities, among other topics. Working with a staff of five, each month she oversaw the preparation of copy for 85 pages, containing such regular features as "Talking Fashion," "Elements," "Last Look," and "Fashion Clips." She also wrote the monthly editorial column "Vogue's Point of View." For a short time Seymour worked as *Vogue*'s senior editor of books, a position in which she oversaw the *Vogue* book imprint. In about 1991 she began working out of her home more often, so as to be able to spend more time with her children. She also did freelance writing; her projects included feature articles about fashion and beauty.

In March 1993 Seymour left *Vogue* to become senior editor of beauty at another Condé Nast publication—*Glamour*, every issue of which typically contained about 26 pages devoted to personal beauty. With such columns as "Truth in Beauty," which provided information about the ingredients in and manufacture of various cosmetics and other products, Seymour helped *Glamour* develop a reputation for delivering hard-hitting copy. During her tenure as senior editor of beauty, readership of the magazine's beauty-related pages increased significantly.

In March 1997 Seymour again changed jobs, this time to become editor in chief of *YM* ("Young and Modern"), a magazine for teenage girls. When she arrived at *YM*, she told Jerry Schwartz for the Associated Press (June 27, 1998, on-line), she found "whole paragraphs" of the magazine incomprehensible to her because of the overabundance of young-teen slang in the copy. (She soon ordered a change in writing style.) Explaining to Schwartz that "there's no point in putting out a magazine that is not driven by readers," she had all mail from readers placed into categories according to topics (among them "breasts," "cannot find suitable lipstick," and various issues related to boyfriends), and then made sure that *YM*'s content addressed those subjects adequately. In response to complaints that *YM*'s treatment of sex-related matters was "age-inappropriate," as Paul Lochner, the Hauppauge, New York, superintendent of schools, put it to Schwartz, Seymour noted that the magazine had recently published articles with such titles as "21 Sexy Alternatives to Sex" and "Are You Sure You're Ready for Sex?" Other articles included "Love Clues: 15 Ways to Make Him Want You Bad," "Guys Confess Their Ultimate Dating Fears," and "Tragic Hair Transformed."

Seymour quit *YM* in November 1998 to assume the post of editor in chief at Hearst Magazines' *Redbook*. Along with *Better Homes & Gardens*, *Family Circle*, *Good Housekeeping*, *Ladies' Home Journal*, *Women's Day*, and *McCall's* (renamed *Rosie*, for the talk-show host Rosie O'Donnell, in 2000), *Redbook* was traditionally grouped with the mass-market women's magazines known as the Seven

Sisters. "When I arrived there was little to distinguish [*Redbook*] from *Good Housekeeping* or *Ladies' Home Journal*," Seymour told *Current Biography*. "They supposedly got younger readers, but if you ripped the cover off any of those magazines they were the same. Same layout, same stories, same feeling. So my mandate was to go in there and radically change it and that's what we did. . . . You just put it out on the newsstand and hope people notice it's different." In revamping *Redbook* to make it more attractive to "mothers and shakers," as the magazine called them, Seymour included more humor and increased the amount—and explicitness—of material on sex, and cut the number of pages devoted to such items as recipes. She also made it a policy, as she told *Current Biography*, to avoid publishing feature articles about anyone over 42. In addition, the photos and other design elements were changed, so as to give *Redbook* a jazzier appearance. While many readers over the age of 50 apparently reacted negatively to Seymour's reinvention of the magazine, causing *Redbook*'s circulation to drop by 12 percent (from 2.5 million in 1999 to 2.2 million in 2000), the number of female readers in the 30-to-39 age group reportedly jumped by more than 20 percent. Seymour also devoted much of her attention to *Redbook*'s Web site, which, in addition to text from the print magazine, offered interactive features created by *Women.com*, an i-Village site. A 1999 *Redbook* section on breast cancer, written by Susan Ince, was nominated for a 2000 National Magazine Award.

In June 2001 Hearst Magazines named Seymour editor in chief of the American edition of *Marie Claire*. She succeeded Glenda Bailey, who left *Marie Claire* to become editor in chief of *Harper's Bazaar*. Seymour's new job presents a different sort challenge for her, because *Marie Claire* is already hip and very successful. "It already has a great formula, and you don't need to do any surgery," Seymour told *Current Biography*. "If anything you want to avoid doing anything to it, you just want to keep it on that track and tweak it here and there. . . . I think I'm going to pep up the beauty visuals. I think the quality of writing could be improved, especially with the international stories. I want to put back in what I call 'The oh my god factor.'. . . In five years, hopefully the magazine will have evolved but you won't notice it. No magazine can stand still, people move, fashion moves. You have to feel it as you go."

Seymour lives in Larchmont, New York, a suburb of New York City, with her husband, Jeffrey, and their two children. In the 1998 on-line chat for *talkcity.com*, she said, "The most important event for my career was having my son, who was the best thing I would ever do in my life—and suddenly opened doors to all kinds of work I'd never thought of. It's hard to explain, but he gave me the security and the energy to pursue my dream. I am also lucky enough to have a husband who says, 'Go for it.' But if you believe in yourself and hang in there, you can achieve a lot." — A.T.

Suggested Reading: *Marie Claire* Web site; *Mediaweek* p6 Nov. 30, 1998, with photo; *New York Times* (on-line) June 29, 2001; *Redbook* Web site; *talkcity.com* Jan. 28, 1998; *Wall Street Journal* B p8 Feb. 16, 1999

Courtesy of Governor Shaheen's office

Shaheen, Jeanne

Jan. 28, 1947– Governor of New Hampshire. Address: Office of the Governor, State House, Rm. 208-214, Concord, NH 03301-4990

Since she was first elected to the office, in 1996, Governor Jeanne Shaheen—New Hampshire's first female chief executive—has pursued an agenda of reform focused on education, health care, and privatization of the state's electric utilities. Like one of her fellow Democrats, President Bill Clinton, to whom her Republican critics have often compared her, Shaheen has evinced a centrist, pro-business approach to economic issues and a more traditionally Democratic, liberal approach to social ones. Her most difficult and ongoing battles have been over the issue of imposing new taxes, a notoriously thorny subject in the fractious world of New Hampshire politics. Settled in the early 17th century, essentially as a business colony, that small but politically influential New England state has never levied a state income or general sales tax. Moreover, since before the Civil War, New Hampshire politics have been largely dominated by tax-wary Republicans.

Like Clinton, who carried New Hampshire by a margin of less than two percentage points over George Bush in the 1992 presidential election, Sha-

heen has often wrangled with a conservative, Republican-controlled legislature. Also like the embattled president, more often than not she has prevailed, impressing voters and foes alike with her strength and ability to ferry occasionally controversial initiatives through the legislative process. She easily won reelection in 1998. (New Hampshire's election cycle, established in 1784, is two years, for the governor and members of the bicameral state legislature.) A year later the national political stage beckoned: Shaheen was strongly considered as a running mate for Democratic presidential candidate Al Gore in 2000. Mindful, however, of the ambitious and important projects she had started but not yet finished as governor—and under pressure from local Democratic Party officials, who had trouble envisioning another gubernatorial candidate as electable as Shaheen—she made it known that she intended to remain in New Hampshire and seek another term as governor. In August 2001, seven months into her third term, Shaheen announced that she would be a candidate for U.S. senator in the 2002 election. According to an editorial in the *Concord [New Hampshire] Monitor* (August 23, 2001, on-line), "If Shaheen runs, she'll be by far [the state Democrats'] most accomplished candidate for the office in at least two decades."

Shaheen was born Jeanne Bowers on January 28, 1947 in St. Charles, Missouri, the second of the three daughters of Ivan and Belle Bowers. She has revealed little to the media about her upbringing. She earned a bachelor's degree in English from Shippensburg University, in Shippensburg, Pennsylvania, in 1969, and a master's degree in political science from the University of Mississippi, in 1973. In about 1970 she married William H. Shaheen, an attorney.

In the early 1970s Jeanne Shaheen worked as a high-school teacher in Mississippi and New Hampshire, and for a brief time she ran a small leather and silver-craft business with her husband. Her first experience in politics came when she worked on Jimmy Carter's successful 1976 presidential campaign. She managed victorious New Hampshire primary campaigns for President Carter in 1980 and Democratic presidential hopeful Gary Hart in 1984. In 1986 and 1988 she managed Paul McEachern's unsuccessful New Hampshire gubernatorial campaigns. Shaheen was elected to the New Hampshire state Senate in 1990, 1992, and 1994. As a state senator she sponsored legislation to curb abuses by health-insurance providers and worked on increasing funding for higher education and industrial research.

When, in 1995, Shaheen announced her plans to run for governor, the response from the nation's Democrats—including President Clinton—was enthusiastic. At a rally and press conference held in the parking lot of a Manchester, New Hampshire, restaurant on the eve of the election, the president called Shaheen "a diamond waiting to be discovered." Early in her campaign Shaheen promised that, if elected, she would not impose any broad-based taxes (such as a state income, property, or sales tax) during her term. This promise, known locally as the Pledge, had over the last few decades come to be expected of all candidates seeking statewide office in New Hampshire. Shaheen's brand of fiscal conservatism appealed to the same minority of independents and left-leaning Republicans who helped Clinton win in New Hampshire in 1996. On Election Day, Shaheen won in a landslide victory over her opponent, Ovide Lamontagne, the socially conservative chairman of the state Board of Education. Polls revealed that abortion, which Lamontagne ardently opposed but which Shaheen wanted to see legalized by the state legislature, had been a key issue for voters. On January 9, 1997 Shaheen took the oath of office, becoming not only the first woman governor in New Hampshire's history but only its fourth Democratic governor in 100 years.

As Shaheen began putting her education agenda in motion, expanding public kindergarten to every New Hampshire school district, the pledge not to enact broad-based taxes loomed as a possible trap. Traditionally, school funding was considered a local issue in New Hampshire, paid for with local property taxes augmented by income from the state lottery; but that was about to change. In the early 1990s, in what became known as the Claremont cases, several property-poor districts had sued the state, demanding equitable and adequate funding for education. In late 1993 the state Supreme Court ruled that New Hampshire must offer all children an adequate education, leaving the definition of "adequate" to the trial courts. After multiple lower-court decisions upheld the status quo, the Supreme Court ruled, in December 1997, that the state's extreme reliance on local property taxes was unconstitutional because it led to large disparities of funding among school districts. The Court imposed a deadline of April 1, 1999 for the state to develop a new solution to funding education.

That series of events, while adding up to a positive development for the state's long-neglected school system, presented Shaheen with a political dilemma. On one hand, as the state's newly elected chief executive, she was obligated to implement the Supreme Court's ruling; on the other, having achieved her office partly on the basis of an antitax pledge, she had effectively barred herself from taking the most direct route to aiding the schools and satisfying the Court.

At a corporate-sponsored Education Summit that she convened in October 1997, Shaheen raised the issue of alternative solutions, emphasizing the need for parents, teachers, businesses, community leaders, and government to work together to improve public education. In her keynote address, Shaheen iterated her unwavering support for public schools and stressed the need for "innovative" public/private partnerships to aid in preparing students for employment in a rapidly evolving job market. "Education is my top priority as governor because of its importance to the people of New Hampshire. But I also bring a very personal perspective to this issue," she stated, as quoted on the official Web site of the New Hampshire state government. "All three of my daughters attended public school in New Hampshire. . . . So I look at education not only from the perspective of a policy maker, but also as a parent, a taxpayer, a teacher, and a business person."

Education reform may have been the biggest issue facing Shaheen as she prepared for her 1998 re-election bid, but it was not the only one. While partisan debate over school funding raged in the media, she pursued her social agenda, shocking anti-abortion groups when, in 1997, she succeeded in striking down the 1848 law that had felonized abortion—making New Hampshire the only state in the Union that did not require parental consent for minors seeking abortions. She also backed the creation of a state holiday honoring slain civil-rights leader Martin Luther King Jr., a measure that had been rejected by the legislature every year since 1977. It failed by a single vote in 1997, but with Shaheen's continuous support it passed overwhelmingly two years later, making New Hampshire the last of the 50 states to adopt the King holiday. On other fronts in 1997, Shaheen signed a law giving military veterans priority in all state-operated job-training programs, as well as a law establishing a pilot needle-exchange program for drug addicts.

In 1998 Shaheen vetoed a Republican-sponsored bill calling for increased teacher tenure as a solution for troubled schools. She gave numerous speeches detailing her Best Schools Initiative, a comprehensive education-reform program involving tougher standards for teachers; report cards designed for parents to evaluate schools and teachers; a program to collect used computers from businesses and convert them for school use; increased funding for community and technical colleges; and a tax-deferred college savings plan for students. While the plan was well-received by parents, teachers, and many in the legislature, the question remained: how would the state raise the $825 million budgeted for education annually? (That amount reflected the anticipated cost of Shaheen's initiatives and took into account the state Supreme Court's ruling.) Pressed on all sides for a funding solution, Shaheen unveiled a controversial three-part plan in January 1998. The plan included a 23-cent "sin tax" on cigarettes, proposed the expansion of legal gambling in the state, and took the unpopular step of advocating a statewide property-tax rate.

In exchange for delaying debate on the politically touchy plan, the Republican-controlled legislature agreed to a $95 million increase in state aid to local school districts. Shaheen's three-part plan—or ABC plan, as it was called—was scuttled in June 1998, by a Republican-obtained state Supreme Court advisory ruling that declared the whole plan unconstitutional. Meanwhile, Republicans in the state Senate were clamoring—unsuccessfully—for a constitutional amendment overturning the Claremont ruling. Shaheen appealed to the federal government for stopgap aid, and by mid-1999 New Hampshire had received several million dollars in federal aid for school improvement, computer literacy, and other programs. While schools benefitted from the temporary largesse, little was accomplished in the way of finding a long-term solution to the basic funding problem. Eventually, the Court's April 1999 deadline passed, with no concrete plan in place for funding education.

New Hampshire's economy—which, after painful years in the 1970s and 1980s, had successfully made the transition from old-economy manufacturing and textiles to the highest concentration of high-technology workers in the country—gave Shaheen little cause to worry about the hopes of her Republican challenger in 1998, the businessman Jay Lucas. Without hesitation she took the Pledge on taxes again, assuaging some conservatives, who had been irked by her social policies and failed ABC plan. A successful trade mission to England and the Republic of Ireland in late 1997 resulted in the sale of more than $300 million in New Hampshire–produced goods and services to those countries, and contributed to the state's ranking third in the nation in international trade for 1998, with exports totaling almost $2 billion.

While Lucas and the Republicans focused, predictably, on Shaheen's perceived failure to propose a viable long-term solution to the school-funding problem, Shaheen shifted her focus to health-care issues, as well as the ongoing deregulation of New Hampshire's energy industry—a process designed to stimulate competition within the industry, thereby lowering consumer electric rates. In May 1998 Shaheen again demonstrated her commitment to New Hampshire's children, by instituting a program of low-cost, statewide children's health insurance. The program, created in partnership with the medical community and the federal government, became a model for other states. In October 1998, just weeks before the election, and with much fanfare, Shaheen announced the creation of a "Kids' Cabinet" composed of top state officials who would aid her in achieving "targeted outcomes for improving children's health and well-being."

After crushing Lucas by a margin of more than two to one in the November 3 election, Shaheen delivered an impassioned inaugural address that dealt with the ongoing funding debate but focused mainly on the booming economy and such issues as deregulation. In the same speech Shaheen tempered her renewed vigor on education reform with words intended to quell the concerns of those who, despite the Pledge, feared a coming state income tax: "Our challenge is to change the way we fund public education, without losing what is special about our schools and our state," she said.

Backed by the first Democratic majority elected to the state Senate since 1912, the increasingly powerful governor proposed a budget in February 1999 that included substantial monies for road and bridge repair; parks and historical landmark preservation; and promotion of tourism, New Hampshire's second-largest industry. In March, the latest attempt to solve the school-funding crisis—a state House-authored referendum offering the public a choice between two different income-tax schemes—was quashed by the state Supreme Court on constitutional grounds. (Shaheen had vowed to veto any income-tax proposal that might come across her desk.) In late April, facing impending school closures, the legislature approved an unpopular but allegedly temporary funding solution: a statewide property tax and other moderate tax increases—but no income tax—to be phased in over five years.

Bickering among legislators and political aspirants over a long-term solution to the education funding problem continued unabated—even as Shaheen enjoyed bipartisan support for her June 1999 signing of a law protecting the "first-in-the-nation" status of New Hampshire's presidential primary. Freshman state senator Mark Fernald weighed in early as a Democratic challenger to Shaheen in 2000, but as he strongly favored a flat income tax to fix the schools, he was given little hope of unseating the governor. Meanwhile, Shaheen's name was being added to the short list of Democrats to be considered as a running mate for Vice President Al Gore, the party's putative presidential nominee in 2000. Gore eventually chose Senator Joseph Lieberman of Connecticut, but by then Shaheen had taken herself out of the running.

In February 2000 Shaheen established the Information Technology Strategic Planning Commission, to advise the state on the use and application of technology in government. The same month she led a successful trade mission to Denmark and Germany. In March Shaheen's landmark HMO Accountability Act became law. An expanded version of the watchdog program that she had sponsored in the state Senate, the act outlawed common abuses and streamlined the grievance process, giving patients more control over decisions by their health-maintenance organizations. Another of Shaheen's health-care reforms, a law enabling small businesses to form purchasing alliances in order to buy health insurance for their employees at discount bulk rates, had passed the legislature in May 1999.

Just days after the HMO Accountability Act triumph, Shaheen suffered a defeat, when the 10-cent "sin tax" on cigarettes that she had supported to help fund education (and proposed this time without the other parts of the ABC plan) was rejected by the legislature. In early April Shaheen announced the formation of a Blue Ribbon Commission, to study New Hampshire's tax structure in depth and issue recommendations on how to solve the education-funding crisis. When it was announced that the commission's report was not expected until January 2001, her opponents—Fernald and a Republican gubernatorial candidate, former United States senator Gordon J. Humphrey—immediately cried foul. The timing of the report effectively relieved Shaheen of the obligation to disclose her school-funding plan prior to the November 7, 2000 election; she was attacked in the media for ostensibly "hiding behind" the commission.

In an apparent attempt to shore up the conservative part of her base, Shaheen shifted toward the right on a number of social issues in the spring of 2000. In April she spoke out against the legalization of homosexual marriage, in response to a recently passed Vermont law that accorded homosexual civil unions most of the legal benefits of marriage. (Her position came as an unwelcome surprise to some, since in 1997 Shaheen had been the first to add language on sexual preference to New Hampshire's antidiscrimination laws.) In May she overturned the legislature's historic repeal of New Hampshire's death penalty, saying in a message accompanying the veto, "I believe that there are murders that are so brutal and heinous that the death penalty is the only appropriate penalty."

Humphrey, a fierce political player who carried the endorsement of Warren Rudman, a popular former U.S. senator from New Hampshire, publicly suspected Shaheen of plotting an income tax. Lending some credence to his theory, in her formal announcement of her candidacy, at a May 30 campaign rally in Manchester, the governor stunned some supporters—and drew applause from others—when she announced that she would not make the Pledge on taxes a third time. She reiterated that message a few days later, on June 3, 2000, in her address to the Democratic State Convention in Concord, the state capital. She also brought up the idea, left over from the ABC plan, of using gambling revenues instead of an income tax to pay for education. Later that month she signed laws pertaining to gun safety and environmental placement of wireless communications towers, and in July 2000 she declared Disability Awareness Week in honor of the 10th anniversary of the Americans with Disabilities Act.

In a televised debate on October 2, with the election little more than a month away, Humphrey, now the Republican nominee and the most politically seasoned and formidable challenger Shaheen had encountered in a campaign to date, accused Shaheen of fundamental lack of action on school funding, as well as of secretly plotting an income tax. The two also tangled on the matter of judicial reform, Shaheen having earlier, in July, appointed the state's first Judicial Selection Commission, a move that Humphrey saw as a serious constitutional breach. The Humphrey campaign leveled accusations of illegal campaign money-laundering and influence-peddling at the Blue Ribbon Commission, but these latter charges were found to have little merit and were quickly squelched. Nevertheless, for the first time in her career, Shaheen had been put on the defensive by a political opponent. Public-opinion polls showed that her approval rating had slipped from 59 percent in December 1999 to 47 percent by September 2000. "Humphrey can

win this election, and I'm going to need all of your support in order to defeat him," Shaheen told the crowd at a campaign rally in Gilford on September 15. A preliminary report by the Blue Ribbon Commission in September 2000 indicated that a sales or income tax would most likely be required to meet the education budget. The report seemed to affirm Humphrey's assertion that New Hampshire's taxes were likely to rise if Shaheen stayed in office. The Republican continued to lobby for minor property-tax increases and a total freeze in education spending—a plan that Shaheen maintained was based on "creative math" and constituted "a recipe for two more years of stalemate" on the education issue. On November 7, 2000 Shaheen won a third term as governor with 49 percent of the vote, compared with Humphrey's 43 percent. (The independent candidate, Mary Brown, captured 6 percent.) She is only the fourth governor of the state to serve a third term.

In recognition of her efforts to improve New Hampshire's schools, Shaheen was elected chair of the Education Commission of the States, effective July 2000. She served as vice chair of the Economic Development Committee of the National Governors' Association (NGA) in the late 1990s, and in 2000 became a member of the NGA's Technology Task Force. In 1999 she was awarded an honorary doctorate of laws from New Hampshire College.

The governor's husband, William H. Shaheen, was United States district attorney for New Hampshire from 1977 to 1981 and was later appointed a judge. (In compliance with conflict-of-interest rules, he resigned the post and returned to private practice when his wife was elected governor.) The Shaheens, who have three daughters—Stefany, Stacey, and Molly—and one granddaughter, make their home in Madbury, in the southeastern part of New Hampshire, not far from Concord.

In the words of Democratic New Hampshire state senator Caroline McCarley, as quoted on the 2000 campaign Web site shaheen.org, "People don't realize that whenever the legislature confronted difficult, complex issues like electric rates and education funding, it was Governor Shaheen—late at night, on weekends, early in the morning—who made everyone sit down and stay at the table until we got the job done. That's leadership." In August 2001 the governor announced that she intended to run for one of New Hampshire's seats in the U.S. Senate in 2002. — G.K.R.

Suggested Reading: *Concord Monitor* (on-line) Dec. 30, 1999; Democratic Governors' Association Web site; Governor Jeanne Shaheen Campaign 2000 Web site; *Nashua Telegraph* (on-line), May 31, 2000; *New York Times* (on-line) Dec. 8, 1996; *Union Leader & Sunday News* (on-line), Oct. 3, 2000

Courtesy of Melanie Greene Management

Shearer, Harry

Dec. 23, 1943– Satirist; nonfiction writer; radio talk-show host; actor; director; musician; playwright. Address: c/o KCRW, 1900 Pico Blvd., Santa Monica, CA 90405

Harry Shearer is one of the most versatile people in show business. By trade, he is primarily a satirist, communicating his satire in various mediums—film, television, radio, theater, books, and magazines. He is best known as a member of the mock rock band Spinal Tap; as the provider of many of the voices on the popular television cartoon series *The Simpsons*; and as the writer, producer, and host of the National Public Radio series *Le Show*. "I am an entertainer," he told Jefferson Graham for *USA Today* (October 24, 1994). "My objective is to make people laugh." Although he has succeeded in triggering laughter in a great many people, Shearer rejects the label "comedian." "A comedian is someone who stands in front of a brick wall at a comedy club and says, 'Hey, how're you doing tonight?'" he told Dan Kening for the *Chicago Tribune* (March 11, 1994). "Not only do I not tell jokes, I don't even remember jokes." Shearer's books include *Man Bites Town: Notes from Someone Who Doesn't Take Notes* and *It's the Stupidity, Stupid: Why (Some) People Hate Clinton and Why the Rest of Us Have to Watch*. His CDs include *It Must Have Been Something I Said*, *J. Edgar!*, and *O.J. on Trial*.

Of Jewish descent, Harry Julius Shearer was born on December 23, 1943 in Los Angeles, California. His parents, Mack Shearer and the former Dora Kohn, emigrated separately from Europe to Havana, Cuba, during World War II to escape the Na-

zis. After meeting and marrying in Cuba, the Shearers settled in Los Angeles. Shearer's father ran a local gas station; he died when Harry was 12. His mother, who worked as a bookkeeper, later remarried. As a boy Shearer took piano lessons. His piano teacher, who was also a theatrical agent, recognized his talent for acting; with the teacher's encouragement, he began auditioning for roles in television and film when he was about seven. In the early 1950s he performed in several television series, among them *The Jack Benny Show*, *GE Theater*, and *Alfred Hitchcock Presents*. In 1953 he had an uncredited part in the film *Abbott and Costello Go to Mars*. Also that year he appeared in a small part in the biblical epic *The Robe*, which starred Richard Burton. In 1954 Shearer was cast in the pilot episode of the sitcom *Leave It to Beaver*. He played Eddie Haskell, the obsequious, scheming kid next door. (When the show was picked up as a series, he was replaced by Ken Osmond.)

Shearer then took a long break from performing. In 1960 he enrolled at the University of California at Los Angeles (UCLA), where he studied political science and drama. After he earned a B.A. degree, in 1964, he spent a year at Harvard University, in Cambridge, Massachusetts, doing postgraduate work in urban government. During that time *Newsweek* hired him as a reporter. He continued working for *Newsweek* after he returned to California. In 1965–66 he served as an intern in the California State Assembly, in Sacramento. Then, for two years, he taught high school in Compton, California. Meanwhile, In 1965, Shearer had joined the writing staff of KRLA, a popular Los Angeles radio station. In addition to playing rock music, the station offered comedy routines. In his occasional performances on air, Shearer imitated the voices of public figures, among them Richard M. Nixon.

After he quit his teaching job, in 1968, Shearer joined the station full-time. His first big break in radio came that same year, when he became a member of the Credibility Gap, a group that performed satiric newscasts and other comedic skits on radio. After some turnover in personnel, Credibility Gap came to include four permanent performers: Shearer, Michael McKean, Richard Beebe, and David L. Lander. Shearer also wrote material for the group and produced its radio shows. In 1970 Credibility Gap left KRLA and began broadcasting on other California radio stations. Developing a loyal following on the West Coast, the foursome often performed live shows at colleges and local clubs. The group released its best material on two albums: *A Great Gift Idea* (1974) and *The Bronze Age of Radio* (1975). Credibility Gap broke up in 1976, when McKean and Lander joined the cast of the ABC sitcom *Laverne and Shirley*. Shearer followed his friends to that show, to work as a writer. He did not enjoy the experience and left after 13 weeks. "I did it mainly out of curiosity," he recalled to Stan Berkowitz for the New York *Daily News* (June 23, 1985). "I wanted to see if the things they said about the TV business were true. And, by and large, they were."

In 1977 Shearer started writing for *Fernwood 2night*, a talk-show parody that aired daily in syndication. Although it was produced by the highly successful Norman Lear, who at that time was also producing the hit series *All in the Family*, *The Jeffersons*, *Maude*, and *Good Times*, and in spite of the fact that Shearer received an Emmy Award nomination for his efforts, *Fernwood 2night* was plagued by low ratings. The series returned for a second season with a new name—*America 2night*—and various other changes, but the overhaul did not attract more viewers, and it was canceled a short time later.

With Albert Brooks, Shearer co-wrote the film *Real Life* (1979), a spoof of the controversial PBS documentary *An American Family*, which had aired in 1973. In *Real Life*, a camera crew moves into a home in Phoenix, Arizona, to make a documentary of its residents' private lives. The family's personal secrets come to light, and chaos ensues. Brooks, who made his directorial debut with *Real Life*, also starred in it, as the documentary's director; Shearer played one of the cameramen. Also in 1979 Shearer joined NBC's hit series *Saturday Night Live*, as both an actor and a writer. Rejection of his ideas for skits soon led to his disillusionment with the show. "There's no percentage in being on national television and not being funny," he explained to Andy Meisler for the *New York Times* (March 6, 1994). "That resulted in my not being in very much stuff." When he was on camera, Shearer mainly did impressions of celebrities. He left *Saturday Night Live* after the season ended.

Shearer continued working in films, mostly in minor parts that attracted little attention. In 1983 he returned to radio, to produce, write, and host his own program, *Le Show*. Produced and distributed by KCRW and broadcast weekly from his own home, it has aired in syndication on National Public Radio (NPR) ever since; it is currently carried by about 65 stations. On *Le Show* Shearer offers satirical takes on politicians, sports figures, and other celebrities as well as offbeat commentary on current events. "I've never found anyplace else in the mass media that gives me as much freedom as *Le Show* does," he told Dan Kening. Shearer is not compensated financially for his work on *Le Show*; as he explained to William Booth for the *Washington Post* (July 30, 2000), "It occurred to me early on that the best protection from interference is to do the show for free."

Shearer's breakthrough on the silver screen came in 1984, when he teamed up with his Credibility Gap collaborator Michael McKean, the actor, scriptwriter, and comedian Christopher Guest, and the actor and director Rob Reiner to make the mock documentary *This Is Spinal Tap*; all four co-wrote the film, and Reiner directed it. Also referred to as a "mockumentary" and a "mock rockumentary," *This Is Spinal Tap* parodied Albert and David Maysles's *Gimme Shelter* (1970), about the Rolling Stones, Michael Wadleigh's *Woodstock* (1970), about the legendary 1969 music festival, and Mar-

tin Scorsese's musical documentary *The Last Waltz* (1976), which chronicled the alleged farewell concert of the Band. In addition to poking fun at well-known clichés of rock chronicles, *This Is Spinal Tap* satirized the music industry and skewered heavy-metal excesses. Reiner starred as a director named Marty DiBergi, who explains to the audience at the beginning of the film that he plans to record the American tour of his favorite rock band, Spinal Tap. Sporting long-haired wigs and adopting aristocratic British accents, McKean, Guest, and Shearer played the members of Spinal Tap, who claim to be the loudest band in England. (The amplifiers for their guitars reach sound levels of 11 rather than the standard 10.) Shearer was cast as the pipe-smoking Derek Smalls, a bass player. The soundtrack included songs that McKean, Guest, Reiner, and Shearer co-wrote and performed, among them "Listen to the Flower People," "Tonight I'm Gonna Rock You Tonight," "Stonehenge," "Hell Hole," and "Big Bottom." Although *This Is Spinal Tap* was not a commercial blockbuster, it received enthusiastic reviews and quickly acquired cult status. In his assessment for the *Chicago Sun-Times* (on-line), Roger Ebert wrote that the film "simply, slyly, destroys one level of rock pomposity after another" and was "one of the funniest, most intelligent, most original films" of 1984. The acting and performances were so convincing that many moviegoers believed that Spinal Tap was a real group. *The New Rolling Stone Encyclopedia of Rock and Roll* (1994) contains an entry on Spinal Tap, which it refers to as "the funniest inside joke in rock history."

In 1984 Shearer rejoined *Saturday Night Live*. During that year's Summer Olympics, he and his *Saturday Night Live* co-star Martin Short offered amusing portrayals of male synchronized swimmers. But Shearer again became dissatisfied with his situation and did not return after the end of the season. In their book *Saturday Night: A Backstage History of Saturday Night Live* (1986), Doug Hill and Jeff Weingrad—whom Frank Rich, in a review of the book for the *New Republic* (July 28, 1986), described as "thorough and non-partisan reporters" who "tr[ied] to be friendly"—described Shearer's battles with the show's producers and portrayed him as an uncooperative troublemaker whose co-stars disliked him.

In 1985 Shearer made his directorial debut, with his own mock documentary, *The History of White People in America, Vol. 1*, which aired on cable television. Narrated by the comedian Martin Mull, the movie presented supposed everyday customs of an average white American family, such as eating mayonnaise sandwiches. Its sequel, *The History of White People in America, Vol. 2* (1986), also directed by Shearer, discussed common stereotypes about whites. In 1988 Shearer directed his first feature film, *Portrait of a White Marriage*, a comedy, written by Mull and Allen Rucker, about a washed-up talk-show host who falls in love with a small-town homemaker. The picture, which starred Mull, attracted little attention.

In 1990 Shearer began doing voices for the Fox network's prime-time cartoon series *The Simpsons*. A spin-off from the *Tracy Ullman Show*, *The Simpsons* had become an immediate hit after its debut, in 1989. Since he joined the cast, Shearer has provided the voices for many of the show's supporting characters, among them the rich, nasty Montgomery Burns, who owns the nuclear power plant where Homer Simpson works; Burns's assistant, Waylon Smithers, a closet homosexual; Kent Brockman, an uptight newscaster; Seymour Skinner, a Vietnam veteran and school principal; Ned Flanders, the Christian do-gooder who lives next door to the Simpsons; Julius Hibert, an African-American doctor; Otto Mann, a spaced-out school-bus driver; and Rainer Wolfcastle, a hulking action-film star with a thick German accent. Shearer gives each of the characters a distinct voice and personality. In an interview for the *Chicago Tribune* (April 24, 1991), he said, "The show has a scope. It can move and go wherever the writers take it. There's something exhilarating about that as compared to these shows that just sit in the living room for 20 minutes. I think that makes for better writing and a funnier show."

In 1990 Shearer began writing a column entitled "Man Bites Town" for the *Los Angeles Times Magazine*. As with his radio show, he used the column as a platform for satire and parody; in this case, his target was life in Los Angeles. He approached the subject with affection as well as a keen sense of the ridiculous. "I do love this town," he told Rex Weiner for *Los Angeles* (January 1994). "It's my hometown, and I feel strongly about it. It's not an easy town for outsiders to get to know. I can't imagine anybody coming here as a tourist, because all of L.A.'s charms, aside from the weather, are very subtle. You have to approach it slowly, patiently. It's a Siamese cat of a city." On one occasion Shelby Coffey, the editor of the *Los Angeles Times*, refused to publish one of Shearer's pieces—a fictional letter of resignation written by the city's police chief at that time, Daryl F. Gates. Shearer wrote the letter after the televising of a videotape that showed Los Angeles police officers kicking and clubbing Rodney King, an African-American, after he had been stopped for speeding. In the storm of outrage that followed the airing of the tape, Gates was criticized for referring to the beating as an "aberration" and for refusing at first to criticize the officers, as well as for what many charged was a long-standing pattern of police brutality in Los Angeles. In a move that disturbed Coffey and others at the *Times*, Shearer succeeded in getting the rejected piece published in the *Los Angeles Reader*. In 1993 the *Los Angeles Times Magazine* stopped running Shearer's column. "Bret Israel called me up one day and said, 'Hi, I'm the new editor of the magazine. You know, I have to say, I haven't found your column consistently riveting,'" Shearer explained to Rex Weiner. "I resisted the temptation to say, if you want constant riveting, there are probably some workmen who'll agree to do that right outside your office." Shearer published a collection of his columns and the controversial Gates piece in his book *Man Bites Town: Notes from Someone Who Doesn't Take Notes* (1993).

In the 1990s, in addition to his work on *Le Show* and *The Simpsons*, Shearer had bit parts in many television shows and films; the latter included *Oscar* (1991), *The Fisher King* (1991), *Pure Luck* (1991), *A League of Their Own* (1992), *Wayne's World 2* (1993), *Little Giants* (1994), *Speechless* (1994), and *I'll Do Anything* (1994). In 1992 he teamed up with Christopher Guest and Michael McKean for an NBC special called *Spinal Tap: The 25th Anniversary London Sell-Out*, which was filmed at the Royal Albert Hall and aired on New Year's Eve. A new album, *Break Like the Wind*, was released concurrently. The band toured several cities and also performed at a London concert that paid tribute to Freddie Mercury, the lead singer of the group Queen, who died of AIDS in 1991.

In 1994 Shearer, the novelist Tom Leopold, and the composer and performer Peter Matz co-wrote *J. Edgar!*, a musical satire about J. Edgar Hoover, who, as head of the FBI from 1924 until his death, in 1972, was one of the most powerful and influential figures in the federal government. The work made use of material in a biography that had been published the previous year—*Official and Confidential: The Secret Life of J. Edgar Hoover*, by Anthony Summers, in which Summers wrote that Hoover had had a homosexual relationship with his longtime personal assistant, Clyde Tolson. *J. Edgar!* was broadcast on NPR in 1994 with Kelsey Grammar as Hoover, John Goodman as Tolson, and Shearer as the gossip columnist Walter Winchell; the musical is currently available on CD.

To celebrate the 10th anniversary of *Le Show*, Shearer issued a collection of the program's best pieces on a CD titled *It Must Have Been Something I Said* (1994). The presidency of Bill Clinton and the political ascendancy of the Georgia congressman Newt Gingrich, who served as Speaker of the House of Representatives from 1995 to 1999, provided Shearer with fresh material for *Le Show*. With his character Newtie, he satirized Gingrich, and with a segment called "Clintonsomething," he spoofed the president's troubles. In 1994 the cable channel Comedy Central contracted him to present his own show, *The News Hole*. He earned a CablACE Award for the series in 1995. That same year the show was canceled.

In the latter half of the 1990s, Shearer won more-visible roles on the big screen. He played a poetry reader in *My Best Friend's Wedding* (1997), an anchorman in *Godzilla* (1998), a television executive in *The Truman Show* (1998), a talk-show host in *EdTV* (1999), and G. Gordon Liddy, who figured in the 1970s Watergate scandal, in *Dick* (1999), a spoof of President Nixon. "My calculation was, I've got to raise my profile to get more strength in this town to get what I want to do done," Shearer said to Sean Mitchell for the *Los Angeles Times* (June 7, 1998). "It's not gonna happen through goodwill. . . . A lot of executives in this town tend to think of liking me as one of their refined tastes that they're not willing to share with the masses."

Shearer's second solo-written book, *It's the Stupidity, Stupid: Why (Some) People Hate Clinton and Why the Rest of Us Have to Watch*, came out in 1999. In it, he sought to explain why President Clinton, despite his superior intelligence and political skills, made the sorts of mistakes that nearly drove him from the White House and why he provoked such contempt among a significant minority of the population. In a review for *Time* (March 29, 1999), Richard Corliss described the book as a "brisk, witty, cheerfully dour screed" and "smart challenge to lazy thinking" in which Shearer "ladle[d] blame and caustic wit on the President, his G.O.P. posse and the moralizing TV newsies." Corliss also described Shearer as a "hidden national treasure of political common sense." Shearer wrote and directed the film *Teddy Bears' Picnic*, a spoof of elite men's clubs, which was screened at the U.S. Comedy Arts Festival in Aspen, Colorado, in March 2001.

Shearer's first marriage ended in divorce in 1977. He and his second wife, Judith Owen, a London-born singer-songwriter of Welsh descent, married in 1993. The couple live in Santa Monica, California. — D.C.

Suggested Reading: *Chicago Tribune* V p8 Apr. 24, 1991, V p3 Mar. 11, 1994, with photo; *Los Angeles* p28+ Jan. 1994, with photo; *Los Angeles Times* p5+ with photos Jun. 7, 1998; New York *Daily News* Leisure p3 June 23, 1985, with photo; *New York Times* II p39+ Mar. 6, 1994, with photos; *USA Today* D p3 Oct. 25, 1994; *Washington Post* G p1 July 20, 2000; *The New Rolling Stone Encyclopedia of Rock and Roll*, 1994; *Who's Who in America, 2001*

Selected Books: *Man Bites Town: Notes from Someone Who Doesn't Take Notes*, 1993; *It's the Stupidity, Stupid: Why (Some) People Hate Clinton and Why the Rest of Us Have to Watch*, 1999

Selected Films: as actor—*This Is Spinal Tap*, 1984; *Spinal Tap: The 25th Anniversary London Sell Out* (released on video as *The Return of Spinal Tap*), 1992; *Godzilla*, 1998; *The Truman Show*, 1998; *Dick*, 1999; *EdTV*, 1999; as director—*The History of White People in America, Vol. 1*, 1985; *The History of White People in America, Vol, 2*, 1986; *Portrait of a White Marriage*, 1988, *Call o' the Glen*, 2001; *Teddy Bears' Picnic*, 2001

Selected Plays: *J. Edgar*,1994

Selected Recordings: *A Great Gift Idea*, 1974 (with the Credibility Gap); *The Bronze Age of Radio*, 1975 (with the Credibility Gap); *This is Spinal Tap Soundtrack*,1984 (with Spinal Tap); *Break Like the Wind*, 1992 (with Spinal Tap); *It Must Have Been Something I Said*, 1994

Sissi

(see-SEE)

June 2, 1967– Soccer player. Address: Bay Area CyberRays, 1991 Park Ave., San Jose, CA 95126

In Brazil, where the soccer powerhouse Sissi grew up, soccer is a national passion, but fans' admiration has often been reserved for men's teams and male players. Sissi and the other members of the Brazilian women's team, which she joined in 1988, have struggled for acceptance in their home country as well as for recognition on the world stage. Armando Noguiera, a Brazilian sports commentator, told Larry Rohter for the *New York Times* (July 4, 1999), "Women's soccer still doesn't have a chance in Brazil. The best woman player in Brazil will never be as popular as the worst male player, and the main reason is that women have been idealized as delicate objects of desire, incapable of playing a physical-contact, body-to-body sport." Such attitudes notwithstanding, the Brazilian women's team rose from ninth place in the inaugural Women's World Cup, in 1991, to a bronze-medal finish at the third Women's World Cup, held in 1999. Sissi, who has been playing professionally since the age of 14, is known for her endurance as a midfielder and her uncanny prowess at left-footed free kicks. She has had a role in many international events, including each Women's World Cup, the 1996 and 2000 Olympic Games, and many South American competitions. In the spring of 2001, she began playing with the Bay Area CyberRays, one of eight teams in the Women's United Soccer Association (WUSA), a new professional women's soccer league.

Like most Brazilian soccer stars, Sissi uses only one name professionally. She was born Sisleide Lima do Amor on June 2, 1967 in Esplanada, Brazil. One of seven children of Antonio, a road-construction worker, and his wife, Vanilda, she grew up in Salvador, Brazil's third-largest city; also known as Bahia, it lies in the state of Bahia, along the Atlantic Ocean. At an early age she began to show an obsessive love of soccer; she would even remove her dolls' heads to use as soccer balls. "My father said to my mother, 'Buy her a soccer ball. That way, she'll leave the dolls alone,'" Sissi recalled, through an interpreter, to Bonnie DeSimone for the *Chicago Tribune* (July 3, 1999). The neighborhood boys were not especially eager to include her in their soccer games, but because she owned

Jamie Squire/Allsport

Sissi

similar to those of the 1991 competition, the team again finished ninth among 12 teams; still, during its three qualifying-round games, the team got three goals. Although Sissi played on both the 1991 and 1995 Women's World Cup teams, she did not any score goals or attract particular attention.

Thanks to corporate sponsorship from Nike, the Brazilian women's team became better organized, and its top players got salary increases. At the 1996 Olympics Games, in Atlanta, Georgia, the team placed fourth, losing to Norway, which came away with a bronze medal. Sissi had contributed her team's only goal in the quarterfinal match against Germany, which ended in a 1–1 tie and allowed Brazil to play in the semifinal round. The Brazilian team won the 1998 South American Women's Soccer Championships in grand fashion, outscoring their competitors 66–3 over the course of the tournament. Sissi, who had been named team captain, scored 12 goals, helping the team qualify for the 1999 Women's World Cup.

The team's most outstanding performance to date came during the 1999 Women's World Cup, hosted by the United States. The field for the Women's World Cup had been extended to 16 teams, up from 12 in 1991 and 1995. The Brazilian women opened the tournament with a 7–1 defeat of Mexico; Sissi scored three goals over the course of the game. In their next game, thanks to Sissi's two goals, Brazil delivered Italy a 2–0 loss. Sissi scored again during a game with Germany that resulted in a 3–3 draw, which allowed the Brazilian team to advance to the quarterfinal round. The quarterfinal game, against Nigeria, was dramatic; halfway through, the Brazilians had a 3–0 lead, with Sissi contributing two assists. But by the end of timed regulation play, the Nigerians had scored three goals and the teams were deadlocked. The game progressed into sudden-death overtime; a goal by either team would signal an instant win. In the 104th minute of play, Sissi blasted a 22-yard free kick (awarded to Brazil because of a Nigerian foul) over the heads of the opposition and into the corner of the net for a goal. In the *New York Times* (July 4, 1999), Jere Longman wrote, "This is [Sissi's] game, a rhythmic ebb and flow, moments of brilliance followed by long silences, followed by breathtaking re-emergence." Sissi called the feat her "golden goal"; she told Joseph White of the Associated Press, as reported in the *Boston Globe* (July 2, 1999), "Certainly, this is an extremely special goal, one that I will remember for the rest of my life." It was her seventh goal of the tournament and marked the first sudden-death overtime goal in Women's World Cup history. In the semifinals, the Brazilian team suffered a 2–0 loss against the American team, which went on to win the tournament. The game for the bronze medal, played against Norway, went 90 minutes with no score; the game was decided 5–4 in favor of the Brazilians after a penalty-kick shootout.

the ball, her status was assured among the ragtag group, which used oranges, balled-up socks, or any other vaguely circular object to practice their skills. Her brother Paolo was especially supportive of her soccer playing, she told Tim Nash for *womenssoccer.com* (February 25, 2001). "He is the one who believed in me when I was always practicing, and he is the one who I know helped to make me the player I am today," she said. "I am thankful that he always was there for me when I needed someone to believe in me."

At the age of 14, Sissi left home to play for a professional club, Flamengo of Feira de Santana. (Feira de Santana is a city near Salvador.) She spent four years there, living in dormitories provided by the team, before moving on to another club, Bahia F.C. In 1989 she switched to indoor soccer, and over the next seven seasons, she played for five different clubs in succession. Meanwhile, in 1988, Sissi had made her debut with the national women's team, which had recently been established and was struggling to gain respect in a culture that glorified men's soccer.

The Brazilian women's team won a spot in the first Women's World Cup, held in China in 1991, by winning the South American Women's Soccer Championships. The team did not play well in its debut on the world stage; it scored only once in its three tournament games and finished ninth among the 12 teams. Because women's soccer was not yet a medal sport during the 1992 Olympic Games, the next big year for the Brazilian team was 1995. Again qualifying for the Women's World Cup by becoming the South American Women's Soccer champions, the Brazilian team was disappointed during World Cup play in Sweden. With results

Sissi made an indelible impression over the course of the 1999 Women's World Cup. She was one of only 16 tournament players named to the Mastercard All-Star Team. She tied with China's Sun Wen for highest number of goals (seven) and assists (three), and she and Sun shared the Adidas Golden Boot for the highest scorer. In voting by journalists who had covered the event, Sissi was also awarded a Silver Ball as the second-most-valuable player. (None of the reporters were Brazilians; the Brazilian press, still having little regard for their women's team, had simply phoned the United States for the results of the women's matches.) Sissi was excited by her success, as well as the performance of her teammates. "I think now that I'm doing well, it is good not only for me but the entire team," she said, as reported by Bonnie DeSimone. "One of our goals is that people in society will accept that girls play soccer."

The 2000 Olympic Games, in Sydney, Australia, provided the Brazilian team with its next test. After two wins and one loss in the qualifying rounds, it lost to the United States in the semifinals and Germany in the bronze-medal game, thus finishing fourth. Sissi, who had been battling knee and ankle injuries for two years, did not score any goals. Nevertheless, in light of her significant contribution to international women's soccer, she was drafted to play with the Bay Area CyberRays, one of eight teams in a new U.S.-based women's professional soccer league, which launched its first season in the spring of 2001. "I cried when I was chosen to be part of this league," Sissi told Tim Nash. "When I first heard from my agent that there may be a women's professional league in the USA, I hoped to be part of it. I always wanted to have the opportunity to play with all of these spectacular players. It is a collection of the best players in the world." She added, "It's like living a dream. To be part of women's soccer growth and to help contribute to its growth both in the U.S. and Brazil is something that gives me great pride."

On August 25, 2001 the Bay Area CyberRays won the championship game of WUSA's inaugural season, defeating the Atlanta Beat in a penalty kick shootout after a 3–3 tie game. During the regular season the CyberRays had compiled a record of 11 wins, six losses, and four ties. Sissi, who was one of only two team members to play in all 21 games, finished the season with a total of one goal and 10 assists.

Sissi's long fascination with soccer continues to drive her. She wears the number 10 on her jersey, in honor of her Brazilian soccer hero Romario, whose jersey bears the same numerals. (The Brazilian soccer great Pelé also wore number 10.) To show alliance with Ronaldo, an enormously popular player on the Brazilian men's squad, she shaves her head. — K.S.

Suggested Reading: *Chicago Tribune* (on-line) July 3, 1999, with photo; *New York Times* IV p1 July 4, 1999, with photo, VIII p1 July 4, 1999, with photo

Reuters/Pierre Tostee/Hulton/Archive Photos

Slater, Kelly

Feb. 11, 1972– Surfer; actor; musician. Address: c/o Interactive Republic Corp., 1001 W. 17th St., Cosa Mesa, CA 92627-4512

Dubbed the "Michael Jordan of surfing," Kelly Slater is perhaps the sport's most prominent figure. During the 1990s he won the world title six times, setting records for number of wins and amazing observers and competitors alike with his moves. In 2000 and 2001 he remained a major presence in the world of surfing. While Slater has earned hundreds of thousands of dollars in prize money, he values those riches less than the satisfaction he finds in the act of surfing itself. "I make a good living," Slater told Brad Goldfarb for *Interview* (May 1996). "I make way more money than I ever thought I would, and I'm totally stoked with that. But I just wanna keep it in perspective. From the time we're born we're influenced to believe that money is the root of all happiness. And it's not. Happiness is all about being comfortable with yourself." Slater, who was a top student in high school and whose interests range from the environment to music, puts all other considerations aside when it comes to finding a perfect wave. "The joy of surfing is so many things combined," Slater told Goldfarb, "from the physical exertion of it, to the challenge of it, to the mental side of the sport. And there's a lot of solitude in surfing, time to be on your own and think."

Robert Kelly Slater was born on February 11, 1972 in Cocoa Beach, Florida. When he was very young, his mother, Judy, would take him and his brothers down to the beach to play. "As they got bigger, they got really bored," Judy Slater recalled to Franz Lidz and Shelley Smith for *Sports Illustrated* (April 22, 1991). "Their dad bought them [surf]boards, and that was that." Slater was soon surfing after school and, at the same time, excelling as a pitcher in Little League baseball. After parents and coaches of opposing players complained repeatedly that his pitches were too fast for the young batters to hit, Slater's mother, herself a Little League umpire, advised her son to give up baseball and concentrate on surfing. Slater also played other sports, including basketball and football, but surfing always came first; he would miss his practices in order to surf. "Growing up, I was always scared of surfing big waves, and many people doubted me," Slater recalled on his official Web site. "That's when my competitive desire took over, and then I learned to love the challenge and fear of big waves." Slater started competing when he was eight years old, winning his first contest, the Salick Brothers' National Kidney Foundation Event, in Cocoa Beach, that same year. When he was 10 he won the East Coast title in his age division, a feat he would accomplish for five straight additional years. At age 12 he won the U.S. title in his age group for the first of four consecutive times.

In 1982 Slater's parents separated. His father, Steven, who owned a bait-and-tackle shop, drank heavily, and as a result Slater resolved never to touch alcohol or drugs. "I can remember riding in a truck with my dad after he had been drinking," he told Lidz and Smith, "and seeing him just stop in the middle of the road and back up because he thought a car was coming at us. There was no car. We could have been killed." After the separation, Slater's mother held down several jobs in order to support the family, working as a firefighter, an emergency medical technician, a bartender, and a computer operator, as well as in other capacities, while moving the family from one rental house in Cocoa Beach to another before buying one.

Meanwhile, Slater and his older brother, Sean, also a surfer, were entering surfing competitions around the world, and Kelly Slater was building a considerable reputation for himself. He was ranked at number 240 among active surfers in 1989, and the following year he climbed to number 89. When he went pro, in 1990, the buzz surrounding him was so great that Quiksilver, a California-based surfing outfitter, signed him to a three-and-a-half-year endorsement deal worth almost $1 million. With scholarship and prize money coming his way as well, Slater helped pay off the mortgage that was still outstanding on his mother's house. His accomplishments were not limited to riding waves. He still found time for his studies, graduating from high school in 1991 with a 4.0 grade-point average. In the same year Slater improved his ranking to number 43 (one has to be in the top 44 to make the World Championship Tour for the next year), impressing the surfing world with moves said to be so innovative that few surfers have tried them even in practice. "Sometimes I don't even think," he told Lidz and Smith. "The moves just happen."

Three-time world champion Tom Current told Lidz and Smith in 1991, "Kelly has the highest technical talent I've ever seen for a surfer his age. Right now he is doing maneuvers that I can't do." Current added, no doubt meaning something different, "His limits seem endless." Shooting out of the water, Slater will execute such eye-popping stunts as a full 360-degree turn. Among his favorite surfing moves, known as "breaks," is the "backdoor," in which a surfer pulls into a tube (the usually cone-shaped hole created when the lip of a wave pitches out far and cleanly enough to form a space between the wave and the falls) from behind the peak of the wave. He prefers riding waves of six to eight feet and enjoys barreling—riding in the hollow of a wave that has arced but not yet collapsed.

Slater performed even more impressively in 1992, winning the first of 21 World Championship Tour (WCT) victories at Marui Masters and the Rip Curl Pro Landes. Since then he has also racked up two World Qualifying Series (WQS) victories. In January 1992 he won the Pro Junior at Narrabeen in New South Wales, Australia, becoming the first American to win the event. Over the course of the decade he became known as the world's greatest surfer, racking up a series of titles. From 1992 through 1998 he held the Association of Surfing Professionals (ASP) world title in the sport every year except for 1993, when he tied for fifth place. His six titles amount to a record, as does his feat of winning five years in a row. He considers his best year to be 1996, when he won seven of 14 events, including the Coke Surf Classic in Australia, the U.S. Open of Surfing, and the Rip Curl in France. During a break that he took from full-time professional surfing in 1999, he won his fifth straight Pipe Master's title at Pipeline, a pro event in Hawaii. In 2000 he appeared in the Olympic Games in Sydney, Australia; surfing was a demonstration sport that year. "I don't know when I'll do the tour again," Slater noted on his Web site, "but I love competing and I do the events with the best waves." In June 2001 Slater and a select group of other surfers traveled to a secret place along the Indian Ocean coast to seek out new spots for surfing. The event, called Kelly Slater Outside the Boundaries, was broadcast via the Internet.

Kelly Slater is five feet nine inches tall and weights 165 pounds. He currently lives in Cocoa Beach, Florida. His nickname is "Hell." "Many people think I'm the most competitive person they've ever met," he noted on his official Web site. Voted "most cute" in high school and chosen as one of the 50 most beautiful people of 1991 by *People* magazine, Slater has modeled for advertisements for Gianni Versace and Bruno Weber products. When not surfing, he enjoys reading and playing golf. Slater starred as Jimmy Slade on the television series *Baywatch* from 1992 to 1993. In 1994 he appeared in the surfing documentary *Endless Summer 2*. His surfing video, *Kelly Slater, in Black and White*, is the highest-selling surfing video of all time. In 1998 Slater, who has been practicing guitar for some time, released an album with his band, the Surfers, entitled *Songs from the Pipe*. The band members also include pro surfer Rob Macado and MTV host Peter King. "The music came out of the waiting," Slater told Sal Ruibal for *USA Today* (December 4, 1998). "On the tour, you travel by yourself. Playing the guitar is a good way to pass the time waiting for the waves." He has now begun to make guitars himself.

Slater, who is not married, has a daughter, Taylor, born on June 4, 1996. Her mother, with whom Slater is on good terms, has chief custody of the child. His younger brother, Stephen, was the East Coast junior longboard champion in 1996. "I think that the times when you really appreciate surfing are the times you're really sort of becoming one with nature," Slater told Goldfarb. "Surfing's as raw of a sport as it gets. I mean, you're riding a man-made thing, but you're riding it on top of nature, and nature is all around you." A surfing video game bearing Kelly Slater's name, which is being developed by Activision, will be sold starting in the fall of 2001. — G.O.

Suggested Reading: *Fortune* p50 Apr. 3, 2000, with photo; *Interview* p102+ May 1996; *Sports Illustrated* p86+ Apr. 2, 1991, with photo; *USA Today* C p22 Dec. 4, 1998

© 2000 Newsday Inc.

Smith, Elinor

Aug. 17, 1911– Aviator. Address: 402 Arroyo Seco, Santa Cruz, CA 95060-7359

Elinor Smith, who turned 90 in 2001, is one of the forgotten heroes of aviation history. In the late 1920s and early 1930s, Smith set many speed and endurance records: at the age of 15, she became the youngest woman to complete a solo flight, and two years later she earned the distinction of being the youngest person, male or female, ever to receive a pilot's license. Smith is also the only pilot in history to successfully fly a plane under all four bridges that cross New York City's East River. Dorothy Cochrane, a curator at the National Air and Space Museum, a division of the Smithsonian Institution, told Laura Muha for *Takeoff! How Long*

Island Inspired America to Fly (2000) that although Smith is "not a household word . . . she probably should be. She did some really significant flying." (Muha's profile of Smith appeared on the *LI History* Web site in early 2001.)

Elinor Smith was born Elinor Patricia Ward on August 17, 1911 in New York and grew up in Freeport, on Long Island, New York. Her father, Tom Ward, was a vaudeville comic and dancer who had adopted "Smith" as a stage surname. Tom Ward had an interest in airplanes, and he often took Elinor and her brother to Curtiss-Wright Airfield, in Mineola, where she went on her first flight at the age of six. "I could see out over the Atlantic Ocean, I could see the fields, I could see the [Long Island] Sound," she told Laura Muha. "And the clouds on that particular day had just broken open so there were these shafts of light coming down and lighting up this whole landscape in various greens and yellows." Smith took her first flying lesson when she was eight, and as a young girl she flew frequently. Curtiss test pilot Bert Acosta was so impressed with the assistance she provided on an occasion when his radiator burst that he agreed to mentor her training in aviation.

When Smith was 15 she became the youngest woman ever to complete a solo flight; although her father did not want her to fly solo until she was 18, her mother, Agnes, gave her permission to do so. The aviation pioneer Orville Wright, who then chaired the National Aeronautic Association (a private organization that has been in existence since 1922), initially refused to issue Elinor a pilot's license, because he thought she was too young, but he changed his mind after he met her. "I felt ridiculous, because he was old enough to be my grandfather," Smith told Laura Muha. "But I went to Washington, and as it turned out, he thought my parents were exploiting me. He had heard they were in the theatrical business and thought they were building me up to play Loews [Theater] on 34th Street. . . . If anything, I was exploiting my parents; they were kicking and screaming because they didn't want a daughter at 15 flying around."

Three days before her 17th birthday, Smith became the youngest person of either gender to receive a pilot's license. In October 1928, in response to a challenge by a male pilot, she flew under all four of the bridges that span the East River of Manhattan: the Queensboro, the Williamsburg, the Manhattan, and the Brooklyn Bridge. This amazing feat angered federal authorities, but luckily for Smith, New York mayor Jimmy Walker intervened on her behalf. To this day she is the only pilot who has accomplished that stunt. "The flight only lasted five minutes, yet when people referred to me in the later years, it was invariably [as] the girl who flew under the four East River bridges," she recalled to Laura Muha.

On January 31, 1929 Smith set the solo endurance record for women, when she piloted a Brunner Winkle Bird aircraft in a flight, mostly over Long Island, that lasted 13 hours, 16 minutes, and 45 seconds. (A picture of the Bird appeared on the Cradle of Aviation Museum Web site in early 2001.) The landing field was poorly lit and covered in ice, and flying above it just before midnight on January 30, she tried to figure out what to do. James H. ("Jimmy") Doolittle, a well-known army test pilot (and, later, World War II hero), came to her aid. Doolittle, who had been returning from a test flight to Philadelphia, Pennsylvania, had somehow sensed that Smith was in trouble—she had never landed a plane at night before—and he guided her by landing first. Frightened but relieved, she followed him in for a safe landing. "I just sat there for a minute and thanked God I was down," she told Laura Muha. "It was the worst flight of my life." Suffering from exhaustion, the young pilot had to be carried from the plane. In March 1929 Louise Thaden exceeded Smith's endurance record by nine hours; the next month Smith broke Thaden's record, with a flight of 26 hours, 23 minutes, and 16 seconds in a plane known as a Bellanca CH. Also in 1929 she became, at 18, the youngest person to receive a transport pilot's license and, in addition, became the first woman to pilot a military aircraft, when Admiral William Moffett of the U.S. Navy asked her to test one of his training planes in Hampton Bays, Long Island. She also became the first female executive pilot of the Irving Air Chute Co., which manufactured parachutes; in that capacity she traveled with a tour that staged parachuting demonstrations.

In November 1929 Smith teamed with Evelyn "Bobbi" Trout in an effort to set a new aviation endurance record for women. (Their two previous attempts to set such a record had failed.) Piloting a Sunbeam airplane, Smith and Trout alternated periods of sleeping and flying. They refueled twice a day, a process that required Trout to transfer 184 gallons of fuel (and a bag of food) from a Curtiss Carrier Pigeon plane to their own aircraft. The emergency landing of the refueling plane, after it began trailing smoke, soon forced the women to end their own flight, after running out of fuel at 3:47 a.m. The 42-hour, three-and-a-half-minute

journey set a new women's endurance record and also marked the first time that female pilots had refueled a plane in midair.

In 1930 Smith became the first woman test pilot for the Long Island–based Fairchild Aviation Corp. That same year, while working for Fairchild, she set a new altitude record for a female pilot—27,418 feet. She was also named the best female pilot in the country by the American Society for the Promotion of Aviation. "It was such an honor to know that my peers considered me the best," she told Laura Muha. In 1931 Smith became the first person of her gender to fly at an altitude exceeding 30,000 feet; during the flight she lost consciousness, after accidentally shutting off her oxygen while trying to restart the plane's dying engine, and her aircraft fell 23,000 feet. "When I came to, I was in a power dive right into the Hempstead Reservoir," she told Muha. Forced to land, she turned off the engine and hit the brakes, deliberately flipping the aircraft to prevent it from hitting two trees. The following week Smith broke her own record by flying at an altitude of 34,500 feet. In 1932 she set the straight-course speed record for women, clocking in at 229 miles per hour, as well as a record for the fastest trip between cities, when she made it from Philadelphia to a town on Long Island in 30 minutes. According to Muha, who described her as "among the flashiest and most colorful of early aviators," movie theaters nationwide showed newsreels of Smith's exploits, and "front-page headlines proclaimed her the 'youthful air queen.'" Muha added, "Many considered her more accomplished than [Amelia] Earhart," a reference to the celebrated American aviator whose disappearance over the Pacific Ocean in 1937, in the course of an attempted around-the-world flight, remains a mystery.

From 1930 to 1935 Smith served as an aviation commentator for NBC Radio. In 1931 she traveled to Albany to lobby the New York State legislature against allowing energy companies to place power lines adjacent to airports. Three years later she became the first woman whose image appeared on a box of Wheaties cereal; she endorsed other products as well, among them flight goggles and motor oil. During this period she also served as an adviser to the New York State Aviation Committee. Meanwhile, in 1933, she had married Patrick Sullivan, a lawyer and New York State aviation commissioner. At the age of 29, she learned that she was pregnant with her third child; one afternoon during her pregnancy, when she was flying a "balky aircraft," in Muha's words, she decided suddenly that she would retire. "It just struck me: This is not so smart," Smith recalled for Muha. "I've got two [children], and they need a mother more than I need to fly."

After her husband died, in 1956, Smith returned to work, writing and editing articles on aviation for several magazines. In 1960 she accepted an invitation from the United States Air Force to deliver a speech at Mitchel Field, in Garden City, New York, and consequently was invited to fly a T-33 jet training plane. "They didn't have to ask me twice," Smith told Muha. "Discovering the delights and differences between jet and propeller flying opened up a whole new world." She later flew the C-119 (nicknamed the "Flying Boxcar") in paratroop demonstrations for a group run by former World War II pilots.

At the age of 55, Smith retired again, so that she could be treated for cancer. Five years later she flew with the U.S. Naval Reserve Force in a successful effort to save Floyd Bennet Field, located in the New York city borough of Brooklyn, from developers. Currently, Smith lives in Santa Cruz, California; although impaired hearing prevents her from qualifying for a pilot's license, she occasionally flies with her son. Smith also enjoys piloting military flight simulators, such as the Challenger simulator, which the National Aeronautics and Space Administration (NASA) invited her to try in

March 2000. Smith's memoir of her life as a pilot, entitled *Aviatrix*, was published in 1981. She is represented at the 99s Museum of Women Pilots, at Will Rogers World Airport, in Oklahoma City, Oklahoma. The museum is a project of the Ninety-Nines, an international organization of licensed female pilots from 35 countries, which was founded in 1929. — C.L.

Suggested Reading: *LI History* (on-line); National Air and Space Museum (on-line); *New York Times* XIV p15 Aug. 16, 1998, with photos; *Newsday* B p6+ Nov. 14, 2000, with photos; *ninety-nines.org* (on-line); *Newsday* Books. *Takeoff! How Long Island Inspired America to Fly*, 2000; Smith, Elinor. *Aviatrix*, 1981

Selected Books: *Aviatrix*, 1981

Byron Holland/Courtesy of Warner Books

Sparks, Nicholas

Dec. 31, 1965– Novelist. Address: c/o Author Mail, Warner Books, 1271 Ave. of the Americas, New York, NY 10020

With the publication of his first, hugely popular novel, *The Notebook*, in 1996, Nicholas Sparks joined the small group of men who have gained enormous success as writers of romantic melodrama. Explaining to Jamie Kornegay for the *Daily Mississippian* (October 30, 1996, on-line), a University of Mississippi campus publication, how he came to choose the "love-story tragedy" genre, as

he has dubbed it, Sparks recalled, "There was a book that came out in 1972 called *Love Story* [by Erich Segal]. That book sold 25 million copies, and it was almost a short story. Then *Bridges [of Madison County*, by Robert James Waller,] comes along [in 1992] and sells 12 million hardcover, and you're like, 'Maybe there's something to these nice, well-written love stories that aren't romance novels that have a bittersweet attitude. Yeah, I want to do something like that.'" Sparks has since written three more best-sellers: *Message in a Bottle*, *A Walk to Remember*, and *The Rescue*. "A master at pulling heartstrings and bringing a tear to his readers' eyes," as Patty Engelmann wrote in an admiring review of *A Walk to Remember* for *Booklist* (August 19, 1999), Sparks has been chided by others for his "clumsy," "formulaic," "paint-by-numbers," "cliché-ridden" prose, treacly sentimentality, too-good-to-be-true characters, and absence of humor. But such criticism has not fazed him. "I made a choice to be mainstream," he told Jamie Kornegay. "I think it's a lot harder to be mainstream than it is to be literary. To be mainstream you're communicating with a great number of people. If you want to be literary, you only have to please one person, and that's you. So it's harder to be in the upper, excellent level of mainstream than to write word-smithy books where you have a tiny audience." His aim as a writer, he told an interviewer for the Doubleday Book Club (on-line) in 1999, is to produce "an easy-to-read, entertaining love story with a poignant ending. If I can do those things, the book accomplishes everything I hope for."

A middle child, Nicholas was born on New Year's Eve, 1965, in Omaha, Nebraska. After short spells in that state and Minnesota, his family settled in Fair Oaks, California. His mother and father had married at 20 and within a few years had become the parents of two sons and a daughter. Unable to support his wife and children as a student,

Sparks's father dropped out of college and took a job as a janitor. He eventually earned a bachelor's degree and later a Ph.D., and taught business on the college level. In an on-line Doubleday Book Club interview, Sparks described his parents as "great people"; in a *Reader's Digest Select Editions* on-line biography, he said that his mother and father "were in love and raised us with love."

In high school Sparks excelled academically and on the track; he was the valedictorian of his class and won an athletic scholarship to the University of Notre Dame, in Indiana. One summer during his undergraduate years, while nursing an injury to a tendon, he followed his mother's suggestion and tried writing a book. A horror novel that he called "The Passing," it took Sparks eight weeks to complete; although he did not try to get it published, the experience of writing the book "gave him . . . confidence" about "complet[ing] such an involved task" again some time, as Jamie Kornegay reported.

Sparks met his future wife, Cathy Cote, while on a spring break from college; during the next two months, he told Kim Hubbard for *People* (November 25, 1996), he sent her 150 love letters; the couple married in 1989. In the same year, he attempted to sell the manuscript for a mystery novel, "The Royal Murders," but it remains "in the attic, filled with rejection slips," as he noted in his on-line autobiography for Warner Books. During the next four years, his family grew to include two sons, and, having shelved as unpractical his dream of writing, he took a series of jobs—estate appraiser, waiter, telemarketer—before trying his hand at a business of his own and then, after he sold it, entering the field of pharmaceutical sales. With Billy Mills, a member of the Oglala Lakota Sioux who won the gold medal in the 10,000-meter race at the 1964 Tokyo Olympics (and whose daughter was one of Sparks's former girlfriends), he wrote *Wokini: A Lakota Journey to Happiness and Self-Understanding*, a spiritual parable. Published in 1994, it received scant publicity.

Meanwhile, the airing of the last episode of the long-running sitcom *Cheers*, in 1993, had inspired Sparks to reconsider the career path he was on. "When [*Cheers*] started, I was 16 years old," he told Jamie Kornegay. "At that time I wanted to be an Olympic runner, and I thought I could be a successful entrepreneur. Flash forward 12 years and I had a lot of great things—a great wife, great kids, a great job, a nice house on a river with a great view. It was nice to sit out there and say, 'This is what life's all about.' Then I asked myself, 'When did I fall into just doing life instead of chasing my dreams?' Twelve years ago I had a zillion dreams, and now my dreams are like, 'Well, maybe I'll get spaghetti tomorrow for dinner.'" He told Kim Hubbard, "I didn't want another 11 years to go by without chasing my dreams. I decided I'd give myself three more chances at writing."

It took Sparks just six months to write *The Notebook*. Inspired by the love between his wife's maternal grandparents, it tells the story of Noah and Allie, whose teenage love remains steadfast after a 14-year separation and whose mature love withstands the devastation caused after Alzheimer's disease strikes Allie. In the nursing home where the elderly Noah and Allie live in separate rooms, Noah reads daily to his wife from a notebook in which he has kept a journal of their lives; his words briefly draw Allie out of her Alzheimer-induced mental haze. Sparks found an agent, who soon sold the manuscript to Warner Books.

"So drenched with sentiment that Warner Books sends out Kleenex with its publicity kit," according to Kim Hubbard, *The Notebook* (1996) quickly became hugely popular, and, in hardcover and then paperback editions, it remained on the *New York Times* and other best-seller lists for over two years. Even many reviewers who found no literary merits in its prose acknowledged the allure of the novel. Joanne Wilkinson, for example, who assessed it for *Booklist* (August 1996), wrote, "This is well within the confines of the romance genre—love conquers all, even Alzheimer's, leaving the medical experts (and this reviewer) confounded. If you want to read a novel in which the romance is grounded in something real, and the magic is truly magical, read the work of Alice Hoffman. If you want to read an upscale Harlequin romance with great crossover appeal, then read *The Notebook*." A reviewer for *Amazon.com* described the novel as "a little glazed doughnut of a book: sticky-sweet, satisfying, not much nourishment," then added, "But who cares? Take an extra vitamin and indulge." Others found more to praise. In the *Christian Century* (December 17, 1997), for instance, Martha Hickman wrote, "This book has touched a nerve. . . . Perhaps that's because it is a story of fidelity and caring we would all like to experience. Is it possible that, despite the medical prognosis, love can redeem some hours for those afflicted with Alzheimer's? To the author's credit, he doesn't gloss over the confused cries, the terrors, the unknowing. A further appeal of the book is that the characters are such good people. . . . The book might be dismissed as old-fashioned and simplistic. No one engages in casual sex. People go to church. Relationships are honored, perhaps idealized. Noah and Allie seem never to have exchanged a cross word. But don't we sometimes long for such a world? And a peaceful beauty inhabits these pages."

When Jamie Kornegay asked Sparks to describe "the most appealing aspects" of *The Notebook*, he said, "It's a very universal story, something that appeals to a lot of different people. You've got young love—your first love gone away and reunited love. You deal with questions of 'What if I'd married someone else?' And toward the end of the book, you have real love. What is real love and how does it manifest itself? It's not necessarily a heavy, grinding passion. It's faithfulness, caring, holding and helping. Loving unconditionally. [That's] what love hopefully evolves to in everyone's life." New Line Cinema bought the film rights to *The Notebook* in 1996; a movie adaptation has not been made as yet.

For his next novel, *Message in a Bottle* (1998), Sparks again drew from a true story—in this case, his mother's sudden death, when she was in her mid-40s, and its impact on his father. The title refers to love letters that Garrett, a North Carolina boat-builder, writes to his dead wife and then tosses into the ocean. Theresa, a newspaper columnist and single mother, finds one of the messages and publishes it in one of her columns; after learning about other bottled messages from him that have washed ashore, she locates Garrett, and an ill-fated romance ensues. "I try to keep my men regular guys, doing regular things. Characters in love stories have to be in common settings, but have to meet in original ways and fall in love in original ways," Sparks told Martin Arnold for *the New York Times* (October 5, 2000), after noting, "A love story is a very tough genre to work in successfully." Gerald DiPego's adaptation of *Message in a Bottle* for the silver screen was released in 1999; starring Kevin Costner, Robin Wright Penn, and Paul Newman (as Garrett's father), it earned mostly thumbs-down reviews. Sparks did not write the filmscript because, as he told Christine Bielinski for TNT's *Roughcut* (February 11, 1999, on-line), "I just don't have the knack for [script writing]."

In Sparks's next novel, *A Walk to Remember* (1999), events lead Landon, an aimless 17-year-old boy from a privileged background, into a friendship with Jamie, a minister's daughter and do-gooder who carries a Bible along with her schoolbooks. (The inspiration for Jamie, Sparks has said, was his younger sister, Danielle.) Like his other novels, the book sold extremely well despite head-shaking from such critics as Susan Scribner, who reviewed it for *The Romance Reader* (on-line). Scribner, who had found much to like in *The Notebook*, labeled *A Walk to Remember* an "unremarkable, sketchy 200-page collection of clichés." "[Sparks's] plot has nothing new to offer," she complained. "It is such a calculated tear-jerker . . . that the emotions remain uninvolved. . . . When I think of all of the wonderful books I've read in the past year that are going unheralded, and then think of the millions of dollars that Nicholas Sparks must be realizing from the screenplay rights, I am more than a little mad." *Entertainment Weekly* on-line listed *A Walk to Remember* among the five worst books of 1999.

The Rescue, Sparks's fourth book, came out in the fall of 2000. Another exploration of the complexities of love, it focuses on Denise, a single mother whose four-year-old son, Kyle, has a severe learning disability, and Taylor, a contractor who serves as a volunteer fireman in the small town to which Denise has recently moved. Denise and Taylor meet when Taylor rescues Kyle after a car accident; later, Denise "rescues" Taylor from the psy-

chological demons that are preventing him from making an emotional commitment to her. The story struck a critic for *Kirkus Reviews*, as quoted on *Amazon.com* (on-line), as "more Hallmarkiana, from a shameless expert in the genre." But Patty Engelmann, who assessed the novel for *Booklist* (July 2000), enjoyed it: "All of Sparks' trademark elements—love, loss, and small-town life—are present in this terrific summer read," she declared. *The Rescue* quickly reached the *New York Times* best-seller list; as of December 24, 2000, it had spent 12 weeks there. "Women like reading love books by men because it makes them believe that men have a romantic side to them, or at least believe that some men understand women," Jaime Raab of Warner Books told Martin Arnold for the *New York Times* (October 5, 2000), to explain the popularity of Sparks's books among women. "When men write these books, it still seems a novelty to many women and that's another reason why they sell so well."

Sparks's latest novel was published in September 2001, just weeks after his wife gave birth to twins. Called *A Bend in the Road*, it serves up standard Sparks fare: love, death, and small-town charm. "Sweet, accessible, uplifting and predictable," a reviewer wrote for *Publishers Weekly*, as quoted on *Amazon.com*, "the latest love story from Sparks . . . leaves the reader with just one burning question: Why is this consummate beach book being published in the fall? The nearly thwarted but eventually triumphant romance of deputy sheriff Miles Ryan and second-grade teacher Sarah Andrews goes down as easily as marshmallow fluff and offers about as much real nourishment." Two weeks after *A Bend in the Road* reached bookstores, it appeared on the *Publishers Weekly* best-seller list at number four; it later rose to the second spot.

Although many critics and other readers have lumped his novels with those of Robert James Waller, Sparks is uncomfortable with the comparison; as a devout Catholic, he frowns on premarital and extramarital sex, which is often depicted in Waller's books. Referring to *A Walk to Remember* in an interview with Deirdre C. Mays for the *New Catholic Miscellany* (November 4, 1999, on-line), he said, "I did not want to write a book that includes premarital sex—that does not prove true love, and it is not where my moral underpinnings lie." According to Mays, Sparks "views novels with explicit sexual content as a lazy form of writing." (In *The Rescue*, however, the main characters do engage in sexual activity, although they are not married.)

In interviews Sparks has expressed pride in his novels. "I put out the best possible product," he said to Deirdre Donahue for *USA Today* (December 2, 1999, on-line). He told the Doubleday Book Club questioner that, although he can't name a favorite among his books, "there are sections [in each novel] that I find so incredibly strong, I'm amazed!" Sparks left his pharmaceutical-company job a few years ago. "Financial pressures have been replaced by performance pressures," he told Deirdre Donahue. While on the book tours that take him to dozens of cities, he writes love letters to his wife. (In one, which he showed to Kim Hubbard, he wrote, "When I think of you, I feel songs in my heart and I feel dreams before slumber . . .") His family now includes five children—Miles, Ryan, Landon, and the twins, Lexie and Savannah. — K.S.

Suggested Reading: *Daily Mississippian* (on-line) Oct. 30, 1996; *New Catholic Miscellany* (on-line) Nov. 4, 1999, with photo; *New York Times* E p3 Oct. 5, 2000; *People* p165+ Nov. 25, 1996, with photos; *Roughcut* (on-line) Feb. 11, 1999; *USA Today* (on-line) Dec. 2, 1999

Selected Books: *The Notebook: A Novel*, 1996; *Message in a Bottle*, 1998; *A Walk to Remember*, 1999; *The Rescue*, 2000; *A Bend in the Road*, 2001

Armando Gallo/Retna Ltd.

Spencer, John

Dec. 20, 1946– Actor. Address: The West Wing, Warner Bros. Television, 4000 Warner Blvd., Burbank, CA 91522

A veteran character actor with credits ranging from regional theater to Hollywood, John Spencer has spent much of his adult life before an audience. Acting has been his passion from the time he appeared on *The Patty Duke Show,* as a teenager, to his current assignment, as a cast member of the critically acclaimed and popular television show *The West Wing,* about the inner workings of a fic-

tional United States presidency. Spencer enjoyed success in Off-Broadway plays before making his way to the silver screen, in 1983. Guest television spots and supporting roles in such films as *Presumed Innocent* (1990) led to a starring role on the smash-hit TV series *L.A. Law,* in the early 1990s. More-prominent movie roles followed, with the actor winning parts in *The Rock* (1996) and *The Negotiator* (1998), among other motion pictures.

For his portrayal of the gruff White House chief of staff, Leo McGarry, Spencer earned an Emmy nomination as best supporting actor in a drama in *The West Wing*'s first season, in 1999–2000. By his own account, he feels completely at ease in the part of the prickly McGarry; in an interview with Ted Johnson for *TV Guide* (January 22, 2000), he compared the role to "a shirt that fits you perfectly." Noting the similarities between Spencer and his character, Johnson wrote, "Like McGarry, he's a devoted follower of politics; an Irish Democrat; a self-described workaholic; and a recovering alcoholic." Spencer himself told a reporter for the Associated Press, as quoted in the *New York Times* (October 3, 2000, on-line), "Like Leo, I've always been a workaholic, too. Through good times and bad, acting has been my escape, my joy, my nourishment."

The only child of John and Mildred Speshock, a truck driver and a waitress, respectively, John Spencer was born on December 20, 1946 in New York City. He grew up in New Jersey, in the town of Totowa (some sources say Paterson). As a child he tended a backyard vegetable garden, growing peas, beans, and Jersey tomatoes; his efforts earned him blue ribbons from the local 4-H Club. He spent his high-school years at the Professional Children's School, a nonprofit New York City school geared toward youngsters planning careers in the arts or competitive sports. As a student there he adopted "Spencer" as his stage surname. After his graduation he enrolled at Fairleigh Dickinson University, in New Jersey; he later transferred to New York University. Lured by the stage, which he felt would provide "an escape from his lower-middle-class upbringing," as Ted Johnson wrote, he left college without earning a degree.

Parts proved more scarce than he had hoped, and during the 1970s Spencer worked mostly as an understudy and in regional theaters; much of his income came from waiting tables. He has attributed his early difficulty in getting meaty roles to his youth; as he explained to Ted Johnson, "People don't know what to do with a character actor who is 20." Thanks to his father's support and encouragement, he stayed with acting. His fortunes improved in the 1980s. For his 1981 performance as Mark in John Byrne's play *Still Life*, Spencer won an Obie Award, Off-Broadway's highest honor. For his role in Emily Mann's courtroom drama *Execution of Justice* in 1986, he earned a Drama League Honor, and 1988 was capped with a nomination for a Drama Desk Award for his performance in the Manhattan Theater Club's production of *The Day*

Room, by the novelist Don DeLillo. Spencer also began appearing in films. In the popular movie *War Games* (1983), he landed the role of Captain Jerry Lawson, after the actor Kevin Costner asked to be released from filming that picture to appear in another one.

In *Presumed Innocent* (1990), an adaptation for the screen of Scott Turow's same-titled best-seller, Spencer was cast as Detective Dan Lipranzer, who helps the lead character, Rusty Sabich (played by Harrison Ford), prove his innocence in a murder case. After the release of *Presumed Innocent*, Spencer told Jason Lynch for *People* (July 6, 2000, online), his "life changed overnight." Most notably, the television writer/producer David E. Kelley selected him to play the maverick lawyer Tommy Mullaney in the hit series *L.A. Law*. Up to that time Spencer had had little television exposure, with only a guest spot on *Spencer: For Hire*, but *L.A. Law*'s casting director, Ronnie Yeskel, was seeking just such an actor. As Yeskel explained to Susan Lewin for *TV Guide* (May 11, 1991), "I look for faces that you don't see on television. I look for the-ater-trained actors. I love New York actors—actors who have studied, who can interpret a script, who can use their bodies, whose voices are trained. We want people who make choices and take risks, who are a little dangerous and have that edge to them. Actors who have only a television background just haven't had the opportunity to learn to do that."

An aspect of Spencer's history that might have been considered "dangerous" was his long addiction to alcohol (which he has attributed in part to his family history) and to drugs. On Memorial Day 1989 Spencer quit both. "I was disgusted with myself," he told Jason Lynch. "Suicide started to seem like some sort of option—that's how bad it was." With the help of his cousin, herself a recovering alcoholic, he enrolled in a detox program. The addiction had not interfered with his career, he told Ted Johnson; rather, "it was getting in the way of my life and my health." Spencer, who has been sober for 11 years, still regards his decision to give up drinking as momentous. "Quitting was the single best gift I ever gave myself—life," he told Lynch.

Spencer acted in *L.A. Law* for four years—1990 to 1994, when the show was canceled. Although he joined the series years after its premiere, in 1986, he had a voice in the development of his character, the fiery, witty Tommy. He and Cecil Hoffman, for example, who played Tommy's ex-wife, Zoey Clemmons, during the 1991–92 season, "decided Tommy was the cook," as he recalled to Ted Johnson. "Zoey would clean up after him. We invented a history for them." After awhile he began to feel like a real-life lawyer, and some other people, too, identified him as one, as he recalled to Margot Ebling for the *Village Voice* (March 11, 1997). "When I was shooting one episode, a background artist came over to me and said, 'Mr. Spencer, can I talk to you? My wife hurt herself at the workplace. How would you proceed *legally*?'"

After the run of *L.A. Law* ended, Spencer appeared with Billy Crystal in the film *Forget Paris* (1995); played the director of the FBI in the action thriller *The Rock* (1996), alongside Sean Connery, Ed Harris, and Nicolas Cage; and portrayed police chief Al Travis in *The Negotiator* (1998), a hostage drama that also starred Samuel L. Jackson, Kevin Spacey, David Morse, and Ron Rifkin. Earlier, in 1997, he had again played an attorney, this time on the New York stage: he was cast as Dennis, a once-fiery but now embittered civil-rights lawyer, in the Manhattan Class Company's production of Peter Hedges's *Good as New*. In *New York* (March 17, 1997), John Simon wrote, "Spencer plays Dennis with the right combination of bravado and contrition." In 1998 Spencer appeared in the short-lived television series *Trinity*, about an Irish-Catholic family in the Hell's Kitchen section of New York City. The next year he starred with David Schwimmer in a production of Warren Leight's play *The Glimmer Brothers*, at the Williamstown Theatre Festival, in Massachusetts. (In 2001 he reprised his role as Martin Glimmer in the play, the name of which was changed to *Glimmer, Glimmer and Shine*, in a Los Angeles mounting.)

Spencer hit it big with *The West Wing*, as did the other members of the show's ensemble cast: Dulé Hill, Allison Janney, Rob Lowe, Janel Moloney, Richard Schiff, Bradley Whitford, and Martin Sheen, who plays President Josiah Bartlet, a New Hampshire Democrat who is both idealistic and politically pragmatic. Written by Aaron Sorkin and lauded as a "tool for civic instruction," *The West Wing* has addressed such issues as school vouchers, capital punishment, the Pentagon's policy regarding homosexuals, and the controversial 2000 census. After its first season, in 1999–2000, the show garnered 18 Emmy nominations and won nine of those awards. It also captured three Viewers for Quality Television Awards, including one for Spencer as best supporting actor in a drama.

"From its beginning," according to the Associated Press reporter, "*The West Wing* has been fueled by the element of surprise, including the biggest surprise of all: that a weekly TV series about Washington politics could be funny, moving, smart, and inspirational. On the other hand, there could never have been any doubt that Spencer would prove as vital to the show as Leo McGarry to the Bartlet administration." President Bill Clinton's chief of staff, John Podesta, gave Spencer's portrayal of the fictional chief of staff a warm review. "John plays this role in a calm, thoughtful, kindhearted and loyal manner," Podesta told Jason Lynch. Spencer and Podesta met when the cast of *The West Wing* toured the White House. The performers also visited the 2000 Democratic National Convention, in Los Angeles. During the convention Jim Moret reported for CNN (August 29, 2000, online), "Spencer marveled at how his fictional TV politician connected with so many real-life politicos." "It's a little mind-boggling," Spencer told Moret. "The response of just walking up here tonight and the people in the hallways, and first and foremost, the appreciation of the show."

Spencer has claimed to "love politics," although, as he told Jason Lynch, he is "not nearly as political as Martin," referring to Sheen, who campaigned in character for Vice President Al Gore before the November 2000 presidential election. He told Moret that he is "a firm believer in no censorship at all" and expressed concerns about potential federal restrictions on the entertainment industry. "I feel I have a responsibility to the truth. I feel the artist's plight is to hold up a mirror to society," he declared. In 2000 he supported striking members of the Screen Actors Guild, during a dispute with the advertising industry over the issue of actors' earnings; along with several other *West Wing* cast members, he participated in protests and wore a gold ribbon of solidarity at various award ceremonies.

Spencer was married and divorced during the 1970s. His workaholic tendencies notwithstanding, he makes time for his favorite pastime—gardening. The Bel Air, California, home he shares with his longtime companion, Patti Mariano, an actress and choreographer, is filled with plants. For his outdoor gardens, he favors roses, hollyhocks, lilacs, and other species common in the Northeast rather than tropical Southern California species. "Gardening is the only thing that I know where the tapes in my head stop . . . ," he revealed to Ketzel Levine for the National Public Radio program *Morning Edition* (July 7, 2000, on-line). "Drinking alcohol used to be another way. . . . [When gardening] I can literally, almost transcendentally zone out." In the summer of 2000, Spencer cooked pasta Bolognese for the Food Network's TV series *Celebrity Dish*. Some time ago he quit smoking, a feat that he described to Ted Johnson as "hell on earth." "I've done very little in life that's been as challenging," he noted. — K.S.

Suggested Reading: *CNN Showbiz* (on-line) Aug. 29, 2000, with photos; *People* p115+ Apr. 29, 1991, with photos; *People* (on-line) July 6, 2000, with photos; *TV Guide* p4+ May 11–17, 1991, with photos, p48+ Jan. 22–28, 2000, with photos

Selected Films: *War Games*, 1983; *Presumed Innocent*, 1990; *Green Card*, 1990; *Forget Paris*, 1995; *The Rock*, 1996; *The Negotiator*, 1998

Selected Television Shows: *L.A. Law*, 1990–94; *Trinity*, 1998; *The West Wing*, 1999–

Selected Plays: *Still Life*, 1981; *Execution of Justice*, 1986; *Carousel*, 1987; *The Day Room*, 1988; *Good as New*, 1997; *The Glimmer Brothers*, 1999

Sprewell, Latrell

Sep. 8, 1970– Forward and guard for the New York Knicks. Address: New York Knicks, Madison Square Garden, 2 Penn Plaza, New York, NY 10121

Latrell Sprewell, a four-time National Basketball Association (NBA) All Star, has long been known for his power and fearlessness on the court. Able to charge his way to the basket, dunk over much taller players, and improvise when needed, he has been called one of the league's most talented and versatile members. At times, however, he has been noted as much for the volatility of his personality as for his prowess on the court. He was banned from playing in the NBA for an entire year, without pay, after physically assaulting the coach of his team, the Golden State Warriors, in 1997—the most severe punishment ever meted out by the league for a violation not related to drugs or gambling. Sprewell's four-year, $32 million contract with the Warriors was terminated in the wake of the incident, in which he choked, punched, and verbally threatened coach P. J. Carlesimo, and his endorsement deal with the athletic-shoe company Converse was swiftly canceled. Some sports commentators felt that the severity of the NBA's response was a signal that the league would no longer tolerate any type of bad behavior from its play-

Dana Belcher/Retna Ltd.

ers: the association's image had been greatly tarnished in recent years when, for example, Dennis Rodman of the Chicago Bulls had kicked a cameraman in the groin and the Houston Astros' Charles

Barkley had thrown a fan through a plate-glass window during a barroom fight. Others saw the punishment as racially motivated—a way for the NBA's predominately white management to remind the players, roughly 80 percent of whom are black, of who was in charge. No matter what the motivation for the league's actions, many observers saw the punishment as justified, and Sprewell was largely vilified in the media as a thug and a troublemaker, regardless of his assertions that Carlesimo's continual verbal abuse had provoked the attack. Despite his impressive average of 20.1 points scored per game, his career appeared to be irreparably damaged.

But in 1999, after his suspension was over, Sprewell—known to fans as Spree—was signed by the New York Knicks and gradually evolved into one of that team's most valuable members. Playing alternately as forward and guard, he is beloved by Knicks aficionados for his brash style of play, despite his ever-present scowl and aloof manner. When Sprewell donated $100,000 of his own money to a program for disadvantaged city youth in May 2000, his transformation from one of the most disparaged men in the NBA to one of the most celebrated seemed complete.

Latrell Sprewell was born on September 8, 1970 in Milwaukee, Wisconsin. He has said little in public about his early years. "I'm not into having people talking all about what I was like as a kid or what I did way back when," he told Phil Taylor for *Sports Illustrated* (December 15, 1997). "That's one of the things I always knew I wouldn't like about being in the public eye. I never asked to be famous." It is known that his father, Latoska Fields, left the family, which included two other siblings, when Sprewell was six years old. Sprewell divided his time between living in Milwaukee with his mother, Patricia Sprewell, who earned her living as a factory worker, and staying with Fields in Flint, Michigan. Sprewell preferred living with Fields, because Patricia Sprewell's boyfriend would sometimes beat him when he lived in Milwaukee. Fields was then selling marijuana for a living, and Sprewell fondly remembers not having to worry about food or clothing during his periods in Flint. In 1986 his father was arrested and sent to jail on a count of possession with intent to distribute. After that Sprewell returned to live with his mother permanently and seldom even visited Fields.

Sprewell attended Washington High in Milwaukee, and toward the end of his junior year he was approached by James Gordon, the school's basketball coach. "He was six-four already, 170 [pounds], and strong," Gordon recalled to Eric Konigsberg for *New York* (April 19, 1999). "I knew an athlete. Latrell had big, rawboned hands, and his biceps were all knots—knots upon knots." Sprewell agreed to play for Gordon his senior year, and under the coach's tutelage he averaged 28 points per game and made the All-City team. Through one of Gordon's connections, Sprewell was accepted at Three

Rivers Junior College, in Poplar Bluff, Missouri. Although he excelled on the school's basketball team, often proving to be the top scorer in games, he was less successful off the court, failing academic courses and once getting suspended for shoplifting batteries from a convenience store. In 1990 he received a basketball scholarship to the University of Alabama, where he spent his first summer making up course work and practicing his three-pointers. His teammates included the future pros Jason Caffey, Robert Horry, and James Robinson, but despite playing alongside people of that caliber, Sprewell shone. During his senior year he led the team in scoring—averaging 17.8 points, 5.2 rebounds, and 1.8 steals per game—and helping Alabama to the second round of the NCAAs.

Although he had begun to play basketball at a relatively advanced age and had rarely dreamed of a pro career, on June 24, 1992 Sprewell was the Golden State Warriors' 24th pick in the first round of the NBA draft. He would play five full seasons with the Warriors; while his own performance was consistently good, the team's overall record fluctuated during that period. During the 1992–93 season the Warriors lost 48 games, but Sprewell almost matched his college stats, averaging 15.4 points, 3.5 rebounds, and 1.6 steals and earning a place on the NBA All-Rookie Second Team. Sprewell became the first rookie in Warrior history to register at least 1,000 points, 250 rebounds, 250 assists, 100 steals, and 50 blocks in a season; only Michael Jordan and a handful of other players had reached such impressive milestones as rookies. During the 1993–94 season several of the Warriors' key players were sidelined by injuries—Tim Hardaway and Sarunas Marciulionis for the entire season and Chris Mullin for a portion of it. Don Nelson, then the Warriors' coach, often used Sprewell—who led the team in scoring with 21 points per game—as a replacement. During that season he played 3,533 minutes, more than any other player in the NBA.

Sprewell's next season was marked by turbulence. Several of the Warriors' key players were traded, including Chris Webber and Billy Owens, to whom Sprewell felt particularly close. (In protest he played much of the season with their numbers written on the backs of his shoes.) With so many changes in the team's roster, media attention focused increasingly on Sprewell as the Warriors' star, a situation he found distasteful; he often shunned requests for interviews. He began to feud with Nelson and was open in his disdain for teammate Hardaway, whom he considered Nelson's pet. During one practice Sprewell and fellow player Jerome Kersey began arguing during a scrimmage; sent from the court, Sprewell returned with a two-by-four board and attacked Kersey before being restrained by friends. He was suspended twice that season for conduct detrimental to the team and missed 13 games. Despite his troubles during 1994–95, that season Sprewell became the first Warriors guard in almost three decades to start in an All-Star game. When Rick Adelman replaced

Nelson as coach, he named Sprewell team captain. During the 1995–96 season Sprewell led the Warriors in both scoring, with an average of 18.9 points per game, and minutes played, an average of 39.3 per game. At season's end he was awarded a four-year, $32 million contract, which made him one of the highest-paid guards in the NBA.

In 1997 Adelman left the Warriors and was replaced by P. J. Carlesimo, who had worked with the Portland Trail Blazers and various college teams, including Seton Hall. Carlesimo had a reputation as a tough disciplinarian, often screaming and cursing at his players, and he and Sprewell clashed immediately. Sprewell was frequently embarrassed when Carlesimo berated him in front of his teammates, and he felt that the coach was blaming him alone when things went poorly for the Warriors—a situation that was occurring more and more. At the end of November 1997, the Warriors' record was a dismal 1–13. By December 1 of that year, the tension between the two men was at the breaking point. During practice that day Carlesimo exhorted Sprewell to improve his passes, and when Sprewell responded with an obscenity, Carlesimo ordered him off the court. Instead of leaving, Sprewell approached Carlesimo and grabbed him by the throat. Two assistant coaches managed to subdue him and lead him to the locker room, but Sprewell returned within moments and delivered an overhand punch to Carlesimo's face. A group of players and assistant coaches pulled him away, and this time Sprewell exited the gym, screaming his desire to be traded.

Sprewell quickly got his wish to be separated from the Warriors, although perhaps not in the way he had envisioned. Terminated by the team, and banned by the NBA for a full year as punishment for the attack, Sprewell became a media scapegoat for all that was wrong with the NBA. The African-American activist Jesse Jackson wrote for *Sports Illustrated* (December 22, 1997), "If the Sprewell episode has a larger implication, it is found in a sports-entertainment industry that tells athletes at a very young age that they may play by a different set of rules than their fellow students, that coddles them and spoils them and that showers them with rewards far out of proportion to their contributions to society." Sprewell's apparent lack of remorse only worsened public opinion of him. He was quoted by Mark Starr and Allison Samuels of *Newsweek* (December 15, 1997) as saying, "If I really went after P.J., he'd look a lot worse than he did on T.V." Some commentators were sympathetic to Sprewell, however, positing that Carlesimo's tirade had been racially motivated and that Sprewell had been justified in striking back. San Francisco mayor Willie Brown, an African-American, demanded that the National Association for the Advancement of Colored People (NAACP) investigate the incident, and Sprewell initiated a lawsuit against the NBA on the grounds that the league was not only depriving him of his livelihood and waging a campaign to tarnish his image but was doing

so for reasons directly related to his race. Pending the outcome of the suit, Sprewell returned to Milwaukee, where he spent much of his time with his young cousins and his own children. (He currently has five children, about whom he is characteristically taciturn.) He busied himself during the enforced hiatus by opening an auto-customizing shop. High-end custom cars had long been a passion for Sprewell, who owned several, although their use repeatedly earned him citations for reckless driving and speeding—and once for verbally threatening an officer who had stopped him.

On March 4, 1998 an arbitrator ruled that Sprewell's punishment was excessive and that the NBA suspension should end in July of that year, rather than December. He further ordered that the Warriors reinstate Sprewell's terminated contract, although it was evident to all concerned that a trade would be made as soon as possible. Vindicated, Sprewell found that several teams were vying for his talents, including the Indiana Pacers, Miami Heat, and San Antonio Spurs. An anonymous Western Conference coach explained to Jesse Barkin for the *Bergen* [County, New Jersey] *Record* (December 1, 1998, on-line), "He'll put it behind him. I think he's going to be absolutely straight down the line in terms of his behavior, and there are enough people in this league that understand that." In January 1999 Sprewell signed with the New York Knicks. The Warriors received John Starks, Chris Mills, and Terry Cummings in exchange. "Latrell is one of the top talents in the game, on both the offensive and defensive ends," Knicks club president Ernie Grunfeld was quoted as saying on the NBA Web site. "When you get the opportunity to improve your club with a three-time All-Star such as Latrell, you have to pursue it. We expect him to become an integral part of our team."

Sprewell's tenure with the Knicks got off to a rocky star, because he missed the first week of training camp, explaining only later that he had chosen to drive from his home to the camp rather than take a flight with the rest of the team. His prowess on the court, however, ensured that the small infraction was swiftly forgiven. During the 1999–2000 season he scored 30 points in a November win over Orlando and netted a season-high 33 points in March during a game in Washington. Sprewell, who had sporadically attended anger-management classes during his suspension, was reported to have undergone a personal transformation. "It's all about evolving," Knicks coach Jeff Van Gundy told Selena Roberts for the *New York Times* (April 2, 2000). "When you're part of an environment that places a standard on winning, your thinking changes. When you talk to Latrell now, he never talks about points or shots. All he talks about is team. He is completely unselfish. I couldn't be prouder of a guy's evolution." Sprewell has attributed the change to the fact that in New York he was finally surrounded by players of his own level of skill and did not have to carry the franchise alone, as he had often been required to do with the Warriors.

The Knicks made the NBA play-offs in 2000, sweeping the Toronto Raptors 3–0 in the Eastern Conference Quarterfinals and besting Miami 4–3 in the best-of-seven series. In the finals, against the Indiana Pacers, Sprewell averaged 19.67 points per game, scoring 32 points each in games three and six, but the Pacers nevertheless prevailed, winning the series 4–2. Earlier in the season, Sprewell had scored his 10,000th career point, made his 2,000th rebound, and logged his 20,000th minute of playing time.

Although his contract with Converse was never reinstated, the six-foot five-inch, 190-pound Sprewell was hired by a relatively young firm, And 1, to endorse their basketball products. In his first commercial for the company, Sprewell, shown having his hair braided while Jimi Hendrix's rendition of the national anthem plays in the background, declares to the camera, "I've made mistakes, but I don't let them keep me down. . . . I am the American Dream." He was chosen by the NBA to represent New York in promotional ads for the play-offs, and—judging from the many Sprewell quotes in the press—he has emerged as a frequent, albeit unofficial, spokesperson for the Knicks. "The image now, hopefully, is a positive one," he told Chris Broussard for the New York Times (May 4, 2000). He lives in Scarsdale, a suburb of New York City. — M.R.

Suggested Reading: CNN Web site (on-line); NBA Web site (on-line); New York p32+ Apr. 19, 1999, with photos; New York Times Magazine p40+ May 2, 1999, with photos; Newsweek p36+ Dec. 15, 1997, with photos; Sports Illustrated p60+ Dec. 15, 1997, with photos, p150 Dec. 22, 1997, with photo.

Jeff Gross/Allsport

Stackhouse, Jerry

Nov. 5, 1974– Forward and guard for the Detroit Pistons. Address: Detroit Pistons, The Palace of Auburn Hills, Two Championship Dr., Auburn Hills, MI 48326

By the time Jerry Stackhouse entered the National Basketball Association (NBA), in 1995, he had already drawn comparisons to the legendary Michael Jordan, and his impressive first-season performance—for which he was named to the All-Rookie team—seemed to justify such talk. Then, in his second season, he was joined by Allen Iverson, who is widely regarded as the league's best guard, and was no longer in the spotlight. After being traded to the Detroit Pistons, Stackhouse again found himself overshadowed, this time by the forward Grant Hill. Despite playing relatively well and being named to the All-Star Team in the 1999–2000 season, he did not reemerge as a superstar until the 2000–01 season, after Hill was traded. "O.K., I didn't like being second fiddle," Stackhouse admitted to L. Jon Wertheim for Sports Illustrated (January 22, 2001). "But to me that means I'm a competitor and I have confidence in my abilities. I can follow if I have to, but I'd rather lead." Feeling pressure to take up the slack after Hill's departure, Stackhouse responded to this self-imposed challenge by leading the league in total scoring and ranking second in average scoring per game (behind Allen Iverson). The six-foot six-inch, 218-pound guard-forward continued to dazzle with his authoritative dunks and blazing drives to the basket while also improving his outside shooting and passing skills. Now that he has approached his full potential, his biggest challenge lies in transforming the Detroit Pistons into a play-off–caliber team.

Jerry Stackhouse was born on November 5, 1974, the youngest of the 11 children of George Stackhouse, a sanitation-truck driver, and Minnie Stackhouse, a short-order cook and pastor of a chapel in Kinston, North Carolina. Stackhouse, who spent a lot of time in church as a boy, has credited his religious upbringing with instilling in him the work ethic and persistence that have led to his success in basketball. "The discipline my parents gave us came from our religion," he told Michael Sokolove for Sporting News (January 15, 1996). "Part of that discipline was: Do your best. Always. If things don't work out, fine. But the very worst thing you can do is not try. I know that sounds real corny, but I believe in it and try to live every day like that."

Stackhouse started playing basketball at a young age; in his senior year at Oak Hill Academy, a boarding school in Mouth of Wilson, Virginia, he helped his team win the High School National Championship title and was selected as the most valuable player (MVP) of the McDonald's High School All-America game. In 1993 Stackhouse enrolled at the University of North Carolina in Chapel Hill, where he was a second-string player, in keeping with the seniority-based system of the coach, Dean Smith. Nevertheless, when Smith unexpectedly let him play during the Atlantic Coast Conference (ACC) tournament finals in 1994, Stackhouse led the Tar Heels to victory and was named the ACC tournament MVP. As a sophomore he led the Tar Heels in scoring average (19.2 points per game), rebounding (8.2 per game), and total steals (50) and was named to the First Team All-American by the Associated Press. *Sports Illustrated* named him the College Player of the Year, and observers even began to compare him to Michael Jordan, who had also been a Tar Heel. "I don't want to make the comparison," Joe Nash, the Washington Bullets general manager, told the *Chicago Tribune* (June 11, 1995), "but at the same time, he is from North Carolina, and he did things that, at the same time in his career, Michael Jordan hadn't done yet. I'm not saying he's going to be a better player than Michael, but that's going to be the natural comparison."

Like Jordan, Stackhouse decided to leave college early (though temporarily, as it turned out) to join the NBA. He was drafted third overall by the Philadelphia 76ers in 1995 and given a three-year, $6.85 million contract. His NBA career began on an auspicious note when, in a game against the Washington Bullets, he scored 27 points—more than any rookie had scored in his opening game since Willie Anderson made 30 points in 1988. While the 76ers posted a poor record that season, Stackhouse went on to be the team's leading scorer, averaging 19.2 points per game (the most of any rookie that season) and setting a rookie franchise record for total points, with 1,384. He also had the most total assists on his team, with 278, and averaged 3.7 rebounds per game. His performance earned him a place on the All-Rookie Team, a chance to compete in the All-Star Slam Dunk contest, and a reported $3 million advertising contract with the FILA sneaker and clothing company, which was considered an unofficial confirmation of Stackhouse's place among the best of the NBA's rookie crop.

Stackhouse soon became known for his jumping ability and his knack for acrobatic dunks, skills on which he has continued to capitalize. In his first NBA game, he showed that he was unafraid of the big men in the middle of the court by jumping beyond the reach of the seven-foot seven-inch Gheorge Muresan and dropping a layup in the basket. In a game against the Los Angeles Lakers in the 1997–98 season, he jumped so high for an errant alley-

oop pass that he was still able to dunk the ball, after catching it off the backboard. (His soaring dunks show up regularly on highlight reels.)

In the 1996–97 season Stackhouse was joined on the 76ers by the point guard Allen Iverson, which made for a very exciting backcourt (which consists of the two guards of a team) and an optimistic attitude in Philadelphia. "I can honestly say there is no one else I'd rather be in the backcourt with," Stackhouse told Greg Boeck for *USA Today* (October 10, 1996). "We can really make our mark as 'us.' It doesn't have to be an individual thing. We can be 'The Backcourt' when people talk about backcourts in the league if we continue to work hard. We can be the standard. That's what we're trying to do." Stackhouse had another fine season, averaging 20.7 points per game and leading all NBA guards with 63 blocked shots. He was, however, somewhat overshadowed by Iverson, who averaged 23.5 points per game and won the Schick Rookie of the Year award.

The following season, on December 18, 1997, Stackhouse was traded to the Detroit Pistons in a deal that brought Theo Ratliff, Aaron McKie, and a first-round draft pick to Philadelphia. The 76ers' front office cited a lack of chemistry between Stackhouse and Iverson, as well as Stackhouse's own desire to be traded. Many speculated that Stackhouse had disliked playing second fiddle to Iverson; if so, matters did not improve in Detroit, where the superstar Grant Hill was the featured player. Stackhouse, perhaps eager to prove himself on his new team, seemed to force many shots—that is, to shoot when he was blocked or off-balance; as a result he suffered a decline in scoring, averaging only 15.7 points in his 57 outings in Detroit that season. Things got worse in the strike-shortened 1998–99 season, during which Stackhouse averaged 14.5 points per game and lost his starting position on some occasions to the veteran Joe Dumars and on others to Lindsey Hunter, considered only an average player. Dumars, known for his graciousness, publicly expressed appreciation for the tranquility with which Stackhouse relinquished his starting position. "I hope fans and everybody realizes he has made a sacrifice to come off the bench without complaining," he told Terry Foster for the *Detroit News* (May 16, 1999). "Here is a kid who has been a starter and a star all of his life and he has accepted a back-up role. People must realize it is a huge, huge adjustment."

The adjustment was indeed a significant one for Stackhouse, who is an exceptionally intense competitor. When double- or triple-teamed, he has been known to exhort his teammates to play harder by asking pointedly if they can score in a three-on-two or four-on-two scenario. Once, during an airplane flight with his teammates, he punched his fellow player Christian Laettner after a dispute involving a card game. After losses on the court, he often stews for hours over his missed shots and squandered opportunities; he sometimes lets off steam in late-night practice sessions.

Stackhouse's problems in the late 1990s extended beyond basketball. He had already lost a sister to diabetes not long before he was traded to Detroit, and a second sister died from the disease in February 1999. Both of his parents suffer from diabetes, and Stackhouse is tested regularly for it himself. With regard to basketball, Stackhouse, at the end of his difficult 1998–99 season, concluded that it was time to lift himself out of his doldrums. "It has been frustrating not to do as well as I would like to do," he told Foster. "But I kind of find some revelation or confidence in knowing there has been some things that have been beyond my control. I have learned to accept the things you can't control and that is what I have been doing. I just look at next year. Next year. It is all I can focus on. I just have to put in a lot of work to make sure I have myself ready and competing at the level I know I can."

During the off-season Stackhouse returned to Chapel Hill, where he worked out with a personal trainer and paid special attention to perfecting his jump shot. His performance improved dramatically in the 1999–2000 season: he averaged 23.6 points per game (eighth best in the league), led the league in free throws with 618, and had 4.5 assists per game, up from 2.8 per game the previous season. On the morning of December 19, 1999—a particularly memorable day for him—Stackhouse participated in graduation ceremonies at the University of North Carolina (he had been taking summer courses); later than day he scored 26 points to lead the Pistons to a 104–91 victory over his former team, the Philadelphia 76ers. On March 8, 2000 he scored a career-high 40 points in a 130–116 victory over the Denver Nuggets. He was voted to his first All-Star team, in which he scored 11 points despite sharing time with other All-Stars and placed fifth in the All-Star Slam Dunk competition.

Before the 2000–01 season, Grant Hill was traded by the Pistons to the Orlando Magic, making Stackhouse a team leader for the first time since his rookie season. He responded in spectacular fashion, racking up 2,380 total points (the highest in the NBA) and averaging 29.8 points per game (the second-highest average, behind Allen Iverson). He was elected to the All-Star team for the second straight season. On April 3, 2001 Stackhouse scored 57 points against the Chicago Bulls, the 19th-highest game total in history and the most by a guard since Michael Jordan scored 64 against the Orlando Magic in 1993. While some argued that he was being selfish with the ball, most, including his teammates, acknowledged that given the Pistons' modest talent, it was in the team's best interest for Stackhouse to take command. "He's putting up 30 shots because we need him to," Ben Wallace of the Pistons told Wertheim. "He's a great teammate and a great leader, not selfish at all." During the season Stackhouse even supplanted his former teammate Grant Hill to take third place among the Pistons' all-time leaders in scoring average. "Jerry Stackhouse is more of a leader now than Grant ever was," the Pistons' coach, George Irvine, told Wertheim. "Jerry's sure a lot more fiery and vocal."

Despite Stackhouse's impressive performances in the last two seasons, he remains a relatively low-paid player. His current contract was negotiated in 1998, while he was struggling to return to form, and in the 2000–01 season he earned $5.31 million, less than the earnings of many lesser-known players. But unlike many other athletes, who have attempted to renegotiate their contracts, Stackhouse is honoring his. "It was the best contract for me at the time," he told Terry Foster for the *Detroit News* (April 12, 2001). "It is no secret that I have been to the All-Star Game the last two years, but it doesn't matter. It was more than I thought I would be making anyway. My time will come."

On Christmas Eve of 2000, before 60 friends and relatives, Stackhouse got married in a ceremony in his living room. He and his wife, Ramirra, have two children, Jaye and Alexis. Stackhouse's 11,000-square-foot home in Orchard Lake, Michigan, features a three-story indoor palm tree; a gigantic hot tub; a basement recreation room with four big-screen TVs; a pool table; several full-sized arcade games; and a fish tank with six piranhas. He likes to entertain guests by feeding the fish live bait. — P.G.H.

Suggested Reading: *Chicago Tribune* III p11 June 11, 1995; *Detroit News* B p4 Jan. 6, 1998, E p4 Mar. 17, 1998, D p1 May 16, 1999, p2 Apr. 12, 2001, p2 Oct. 26, 2001; *Inside Sports* p44 July 1996; *New York Times* B p11 Feb. 15, 1995; *Sporting News* p34+ Jan. 15, 1996; *Sports Illustrated* p66+ Mar. 6, 1995, p98+ Apr. 27, 1998, p52+ Jan. 22, 2001; *USA Today* C p3 Oct. 10, 1996, C p4 Dec. 16, 1999; *Washington Post* D p6 June 26, 1995

Stanton, Bill

1964(?)– Private investigator. Address: Stanton & Maple P.I. Inc., 409A E. 88th St., New York, NY 10128

Bill Stanton is a "celebrity private eye," as Craig Horowitz described him in *New York* (January 10, 2001, on-line), using a label that might seem like a contradiction in terms. A one-time New York City police officer, Stanton has gained a reputation as an investigator for the rich and famous and others seeking help with high-profile cases. Since he co-founded the firm of Stanton & Maple, P.I., with Jack Maple, a former New York Police Department deputy commissioner, Stanton has worked for both individuals and Fortune 500 companies and has served as a consultant on security for the CNN and MSNBC networks. Cases on which he has worked include that of Charles Schwarz, who was among the New York City police officers accused in the brutal assault of Abner Louima in a police-station restroom; the high-profile divorce of the Wall

Bill Stanton

Courtesy of Bill Stanton

Street billionaire Carl Icahn and Liba Icahn; and the multimillion-dollar child-support battle between Patricia Duff and her former husband, the billionaire financier Ronald O. Perelman. "Billy is always my first call," Dominic Barbara, who gained prominence as the defense attorney for Joey Buttafuoco in the 1992 shooting of Buttafuoco's wife by his 17-year-old alleged lover, told Horowitz. "I've been doing this for 31 years, and he's the best I've ever seen. He always gets it done."

Born in about 1964 of mixed Polish and Puerto Rican ancestry, Bill Stanton grew up with his brother on City Island, in the New York City borough of the Bronx. His father was a cab driver, and his mother worked as a legal secretary. As a child he rarely traveled out of the Bronx. "It was like I lived in Mayberry and Manhattan was Mount Pilot," he said to Craig Horowitz, referring to the small town in which residents of the 1960s television sitcom *The Andy Griffith Show* lived, and the seldom-visited "big city" that was closest to Mayberry. Young Bill was a big fan of Sylvester Stallone, in particular of Stallone's *Rocky* and *Rambo* movies.

As far back as he can remember, Stanton wanted to become a police officer, and in about 1985 he began working for the New York City Police Department (NYPD) as a patrolman. He was assigned to the 40th Precinct, in the South Bronx, which covered what at that time was one of New York's roughest neighborhoods. After just two years on the job, Stanton suffered a debilitating injury: while chasing a fleeing robbery suspect, he leaped onto a railway bed, the depth of which he had underestimated in his haste. "As soon as I jumped," he recalled to Horowitz, "I knew I was in trouble.

I was in the air for too long." Landing on a pile of debris, Stanton severed a tendon in his right hand. Although he underwent several operations and extensive physical therapy, he never recovered the complete use of the hand. No longer able to pull the trigger on the standard-issue police firearm, he was forced to turn in his badge.

After leaving the NYPD, Stanton took a series of jobs as a bouncer and security guard. They helped him scrape by while he thought about other possible professions. The turning point came one night while he was guarding a construction site on the graveyard shift: "So I'm there, and this cop with a big gut shows up to work with me," he told Horowitz. "He's got his blanket and a little TV and his lunchbox, and he sets up his bed on the Sheetrock. I remember I just sat there all night freezing my ass off, listening to that fat, alcoholic [expletive] snore, and thinking about my life working for $12 an hour. As I watched him, I knew I was looking at the Ghost of Christmas Future."

Meanwhile, an acquaintance of his, who was a member of the security detail that guarded former secretary of state Henry Kissinger, had suggested to Stanton that he consider protecting celebrities and VIPs as his line of work. Attracted to the idea, Stanton enrolled at the Executive Protection Institute, in Bluemont, Virginia, a training facility for professional bodyguards. His classmates there included members of the FBI, CIA, and Secret Service, around whom, he has said, he felt intimidated. After completing the course, he went on to work for a series of high-profile figures, among them the king of Greece, members of the Rockefeller family, John F. Kennedy Jr., and Jacqueline Kennedy Onassis. In addition to swift reflexes and the ability to make split-second decisions regarding safety, Stanton has pointed out, the security professional must have a highly developed sense of decorum. "The clients wore us like they wore their jewelry, so the way you looked and behaved was important," he told Horowitz.

Stanton's career got a second boost thanks to another friend, through whom he got the job of handling security at the China Club, in Aspen, Colorado. The club, which had recently opened, had quickly become popular among celebrities and other wealthy people. In his new position Stanton developed ties to various Hollywood stars who regularly patronized the club, among them Sylvester Stallone and Bruce Willis. Stanton's acquaintance with Willis, a prominent Republican and outspoken supporter of law enforcement, proved especially useful: after persuading Willis to shoot a public-service commercial on behalf of the NYPD, Stanton introduced himself to William Bratton, who was then New York City's police commissioner. Soon afterward Bratton invited Stanton to dine with him at Elaine's, a New York restaurant popular with top law-enforcement officials and celebrity private investigators and their clientele. "Once I walked in there with [Bratton]," Stanton told Horowitz, "I was a made man."

Stanton has said that, aside from the necessary cultivation of his image on the New York social scene, most of his work involves routine surveillance. (To facilitate that activity, he has outfitted his maroon Durango with a two-way radio, a radar scrambler, a night-vision video camera, and a global positioning navigation system.) From time to time, though, he has received distinctly unusual assignments. "We handled a case where we were hired to protect the CEO of a pharmaceutical company," he recalled to Horowitz. "The company makes colored contact lenses, and believe it or not, one of these white-supremacist groups issued threats against him because he was enabling non-Aryan types to have blue eyes."

Stanton has said that a certain amount of self-promotion is crucial for a private investigator, and that Elaine's offers him the ideal forum in which to promote himself. "Remember," he told Horowitz, "perception is everything. I can bring my clients there, and I've met all kinds of important people in the corporate world and in law enforcement. It creates an aura of success. People say, 'Oh, who's that guy, I see him here all the time?' And it's like a subliminal sale. They think, 'Oh, if he's here all the time, he must be good.'"

When not on the job, Stanton leads a quiet domestic life. His wife of four years, Jane, is a chiropractor and nutritionist whom he has known since he was 19. — P.K.

Suggested Reading: *New York* (on-line) Jan. 10, 2001; *stantonandmaple.com*

Courtesy of Stanford University

Steele, Claude M.

Jan. 1, 1946– Psychologist; educator. Address: Dept. of Psychology, Jordan Hall Bldg. 420, Stanford University, Stanford, CA 94305-2130

Inevitably, the social psychologist and educator Claude M. Steele frequently finds himself compared with his twin brother, Shelby. The English professor and essayist whose 1990 book, *The Content of Our Character: A New Vision of Race in America*, won a National Book Critics Circle Award, Shelby Steele is often identified as a conservative for his emphasis on individual responsibility and his opposition to affirmative action. Like his brother, Claude Steele has since the early 1990s played a prominent role in the national debate on race. His studies of the ways in which racial and gender stereotypes affect academic performance are unconstrained by ideology and could, according to Ben Gose in the *Chronicle of Higher Education* (August 18, 1995), "provide fodder for both sides in the debate over affirmative action"—which, unlike his brother, Claude Steele supports. While the fact that twin brothers endorse opposite positions on such a divisive, emotionally charged issue is fascinating, the two men, understandably, refuse to comment publicly on each other's work. As Shelby Steele told Ethan Watters for the *New York Times Magazine* (September 17, 1995), "To be compared all your life to your twin is a form of existential Hell." Claude, too, has spoken of his "abhorrence of playing the brother-act sideshow." Both, perhaps, are chary of having their ideas subordinated to a simplistic image of the intractability of the race problem in the United States: if twin brothers raised in identical circumstances can't agree on race, what hope is there for the rest of the nation? Actually, though, the two agree on more than is commonly supposed. As Claude Steele told Ethan Watters, "I think of it as almost an unfortunate detail that we wound up following similar terrain and coming down on an issue like affirmative action on different sides. It suggests a bigger difference than there really is." Although it was Shelby who first attracted the media spotlight, there can be little doubt that Claude Steele's work on the psychological effects of social stigma is original and groundbreaking in its own right, and would have made an impact on the national debate even without his brother's prominence.

The son of Shelby Steele Jr., a black truck driver, and Ruth Steele, a white social worker, Claude Mason Steele was born on New Year's Day, 1946, in Chicago, Illinois, and grew up in nearby Phoenix, a working-class suburb of the city. Although his father never completed elementary school, Claude Steele recalled to Ethan Watters that his parents "were both very intellectual people," and added, "Our household was like a graduate school in race relations." Both parents were involved in the civil rights movement, and they raised their children—Claude, Shelby, and two daughters—to believe that they would succeed if they worked hard and got a good education.

Like his brother, Claude Steele took that advice to heart, and chose to pursue an academic career. After taking a B.A. in psychology from Hiram College, a small liberal-arts school outside Cleveland, Ohio, in 1967, Steele enrolled in a graduate program in social psychology at Ohio State University. He completed work on his M.A. degree in 1969 and his Ph.D. two years later. The time in graduate school was, for Steele, a period of transition, during which he came to feel more strongly about the work he had undertaken. Looking back, in a piece written for the Atlantic (April 1992), Steele revealed the roots of his professional interest in the relationship between identification with a field of study and academic performance in that field: "I remember conducting experiments with my research adviser early in graduate school and awaiting the results with only modest interest. The research enterprise—the core of what one does as a social psychologist—just wasn't ME yet. I was in school for other reasons—I wanted an advanced degree, I was vaguely ambitious for intellectual work, and being in graduate school made my parents proud of me. But as time passed, I began to like the work. . . . Gradually I began to think of myself as a social psychologist. With this change in self-concept came a new accountability; my self-esteem was affected now by what I did as a social psychologist, something that hadn't been true before. This added a new motivation to my work; self-respect, not just parental respect, was on the line."

After earning his Ph.D., Steele landed his first teaching job, as an assistant professor of psychology at the University of Utah. Meanwhile, his brother was finishing up his Ph.D. in English at the same university. Neither brother remained long in Utah: Shelby, upon completing his degree, took a job at San Jose State University, in California, while Claude relocated to the Seattle campus of the University of Washington, in 1973, again as an assistant professor of psychology. Claude Steele's research at this time focused primarily on processes of self-evaluation—in particular, on how a person copes with threats to his or her self-image. This work eventually culminated in a general theory of self-affirmation processes. A second interest was the relationship between the stress-reducing effects of alcohol and its addictive qualities.

The work for which Steele is best known grew out of his primary research on threats to self-image. In 1987, when he took a new position, in the Department of Psychology at the University of Michigan, Steele began to examine the relationship between self-image and academic achievement. He started by asking what effects negative stereotypes might have on the standardized-test scores and academic performance of black students. Steele was struck by the inability of established pedagogical theories—especially those that emphasized economic factors—to account for the academic difficulties of the brightest African-American students. Even when such students had middle-class advantages and resources, they were, according to university statistics, more likely to fall behind than equally qualified white students. "Black students with 1,300 SAT scores were going home from college with 2.4 GPA's," Steele told Ethan Watters. "When I realized that the smartest black students were having these terrible troubles, I figured something else was going on."

As Steele pointed out in his August 1999 article for the Atlantic, "SAT scores of black students . . . sometimes average 200 points below those of other students on the same campus." Further, the dropout rate for black college students hovers around 70 percent, as opposed to 40 percent for the general university population. There are two common explanations for such disparities. First, it is often argued that black students are generally handicapped by a lower level of academic preparation—a handicap that, in turn, results from socioeconomic discrimination and from unequal access to quality education. Second, some maintain that standardized tests are culturally biased in a way that is disadvantageous for blacks as well as other minority students. While Steele does not discount the influence of these two factors on academic performance and test results, his work has tended to focus on a third factor, namely, the psychological effects of social stigma in situations that make heavy demands on intellectual and cognitive abilities. "Like anyone," Steele wrote for the 1992 Atlantic article, "blacks risk devaluation for a particular incompetence, such as a failed test or a flubbed pronunciation. But they further risk that such performances will confirm the broader, racial inferiority they are suspected of."

In Steele's view, the fact that blacks are suspected of being inferior creates problems that extend beyond the province of individual agency. He wrote in the 1992 Atlantic article, "Because these images are conditioned in all of us, collectively held, they can spawn racial devaluation in all of us, not just in the strongly prejudiced. They can do this even in blacks themselves." However, while he does not deny its existence, Steele downplays the role of egregious or overt racism in this systematic devaluation. Instead, he speaks of "a devaluation that grows out of our images of society and the way those images catalogue people. The catalogue need never be taught. It is implied by all we see around us: the kinds of people revered in advertising . . . and movies . . . ; media discussions of whether a black can be President; invitation lists to junior high school birthday parties; school curricula; literary and musical canons. These details create an image of society in which black Americans simply do not fare well." To illustrate how such devaluation might operate, Steele, in a later article for the *Atlantic* (August 1999), asked his readers to imagine "a normally energetic black student who had broken up with his longtime girlfriend and had since learned that she, a Hispanic, was now dating a white student. This hit him hard. Not long after hearing about his girlfriend, he sat through an hour's discussion of *The Bell Curve* in his psychology class, during which the possible genetic inferiority of his race was openly considered. [*The Bell Curve*, the 1994 book by Richard J. Herrnstein and Charles Murray, was widely criticized as racist, arguing that differences in the standardized-test scores of various ethnic groups could be attributed to genetic factors.] Then he overheard students at lunch arguing that affirmative action allowed in too many underqualified blacks. By his own account, this young man had experienced very little of what he thought of as racial discrimination on campus. Still these were features of his world. Could they have a bearing on his academic life?"

The question is, of course, rhetorical; Steele felt quite strongly that the sum of such day-to-day experiences profoundly affects a student's academic life. But as a social scientist, he needed to confirm his suspicions experimentally. In order to do so, Steele and a colleague assembled a group of black and white Stanford undergraduates whose ability levels they had statistically matched, then asked the students to answer questions from a standard verbal assessment test. Since the test—the Graduate Record Examination (GRE) in literature—was designed to gauge the verbal ability of prospective graduate students, it was not easy for any of the testees, most of whom were sophomores; all the students were forced to confront the limits of their verbal skills. But the core of the experiment lay in the manner in which the test's ostensible purpose was represented to the student subjects. Some students were told that the test simply aimed to shed light on how certain problems were generally solved; others were informed that it intended to measure their cognitive ability. The results were striking. In the first instance, in which the subjects were led to believe that the test was a sort of laboratory task, the black students performed on a par with their white peers. By contrast, as Steele wrote in the *Atlantic* (August 1999), "when the difficult verbal test was presented as a test of ability, black students performed dramatically less well than white students."

Steele suspected that it was the fear of confirming a stereotype that lay at the root of this result, but he needed to make the connection between fear and poor performance more explicit. By administering a number of free-association exercises prior to the test, Steele determined not only that the black subjects were more mindful of race and racial stereotypes than their white peers, but that the black subjects' consciousness of race was heightened when they were told that the test was to be a measure of ability. He also found that a consciousness of racial or gender stereotypes affected the test results of other social groups. The performance of white males on a tough math test, for example, was adversely affected after the subjects were told that Asians generally did better on that particular test; in the absence of such preestablished expectations, whites and Asians achieved comparable results.

Further experimentation led Steele to conclude that it is precisely those students who are confident, well prepared, and—perhaps most important—who have identified with achievement in the past, who are most likely to be adversely affected by what he calls "stereotype threat." Paradoxical as this finding may at first appear, Steele explained that "a person has to care about a domain in order to be disturbed by the prospect of being stereotyped in it." Since strong, ambitious students have much at stake personally in an assessment of their abilities and prospects, they run an increased risk of succumbing to a crippling anxiety. For black students, the additional burden of having to contend with a negative stereotype can only compound the pressure to succeed, and is often, Steele argued, pivotal.

Steele's theory further departs from most established pedagogical models in that it does not assume that racial stigma is internalized. Belief in a negative stereotype, whether conscious or unconscious, is immaterial, Steele claims; rather, the knowledge of the stereotype is enough to depress performance in a taxing situation. Steele found, for example, that "black students taking the test under stereotype threat seemed to be trying too hard rather than not hard enough. They reread the questions, reread the multiple choices, rechecked their answers, more than when they were not under stereotype threat. The threat made them inefficient on a test that, like most standardized tests, is set up so that thinking long often means thinking wrong, especially on difficult items like the ones we used." In further defense of his theory, Steele has established that "the blood pressure of black students performing a difficult cognitive task under stereotype threat was elevated compared with that of black students not under stereotype threat or white students in either situation."

Steele's experimental research has encountered surprisingly little criticism from members of his profession and the broader audience of educators and policy makers. There are, of course, quibbles: some have suggested that Steele's emphasis on things psychological gives other factors, such as economic or cultural influences, short shrift. Still, the consensus is that Steele has achieved valuable, pathbreaking results. Even Charles Murray, co-author of *The Bell Curve*, conceded to Ethan Watters, "I think he probably has hold of something that might be one source of poor academic performance among blacks."

While much of Steele's work seeks to examine and quantify the effects of social stigma on standardized-test performance, he has also been involved in efforts to develop pedagogical models that would redress the inequities that his experimental research has uncovered. While at Michigan, Steele lobbied for and assisted in the creation of "The 21st Century Program," an integrated, dorm-based program for first-year University of Michigan students that aimed to bridge the academic gap between blacks and whites. Participants in the program, which began in 1991 and is still operating, were required to take a certain number of classes together and were encouraged to take part in weekly rap sessions about the personal side of university life. Central to the program, according to Steele, was a simple message: "You are valued in this program because of your academic potential—regardless of your current skill level. You have no more to fear than the next person, and since the work is difficult, success is a credit to your ability, and a setback is a reflection only of the challenge." By simultaneously reassuring and challenging students, the program attempted to counteract what Steele described as "the black students' double vulnerability around failure"—the fear not only that they lack ability (a fear Steele attributes to all students), but the additional dread that they will be stereotyped according to race.

Although some critics attacked the program as "assimilationist" (the position that African-Americans ought to give up their cultural identity in order to join the American mainstream), Steele and his supporters pronounced it a success: as he wrote in the *Atlantic*, "those [black students] in the program (about 15 percent of the entering class) got better first-year grades than black students outside the program, even after controlling for differences between these groups in the skills with which they entered college. . . . Black students in the program got first-year grades almost as high as those of white students in the general Michigan population who entered with comparable test scores." One reason for the program's success, Steele ventured, was that "when members of one racial group hear members of another racial group express the same concerns they have, the concerns seem less racial. Students may also learn that racial and gender stereotypes are either less at play than they might have feared or don't reflect the worse-feared prejudicial intent." He concluded that "even though the stereotypes held by the larger society may be difficult to change, it is possible to create niches in which negative stereotypes are not felt to apply."

In response to the charge of assimilationism, Steele has borrowed a line from the novelist and essayist Ralph Ellison, whom he quotes extensively in his own essays. Black Americans, Steele has maintained, already belong to the nation's cultural mainstream—and indeed, they have since the country's inception, so much so that the notion of a nonblack American culture is meaningless and self-abnegating. The problem for educators, according to Steele, is that many cultural institutions—schools among them—have persistently suppressed or distorted the reality of integration in American culture. As a result, "blacks have fallen victim to a collective self-deception, a society's allowing itself to assimilate like mad from its constituent groups while representing itself to itself as if the assimilation had never happened, as if progress and good were almost exclusively Western and white." Steele staunchly opposes this form of assimilation. On the other hand, he also feels that self-segregation—or, to use Steele's intentionally bland term, "disidentification"—is ultimately harmful to black students, since it effectively deprives them of part of their own cultural inheritance.

Still, Steele is not willing to place the burden of responsibility on the individual black student, and in this he differs from his brother, Shelby. Instead, he has said that the apparent rejection of the educational system by many black students is in fact only the final stage in a long process of vulnerability and struggle. "These kids want to make it," he told Ethan Watters. "These kids are in their dorm rooms confronting the beast of their deepest fears. Instead of telling them it is their responsibility to overcome the psychology that they are feeling in their gut, let's get rid of the beast." Claude Steele supports affirmative action, but his support is qualified; as he told Ben Gose, affirmative action "has so many meandering excesses that it makes it difficult for anyone to defend it." Further, he has agreed with critics of raced-based preferences that some affirmative action programs reinforce racial stereotyping. For Steele, affirmative action is best used in conjunction with programs, like the one at Michigan, that emphasize students' academic potential rather than their race. In this way, Watters noted, "any increase in vulnerability a black student feels for receiving admissions preference can be overcome when the student shows up on campus." In light of this supportive but highly qualified stance on affirmative action, and given his scrupulously dry rhetoric, which favors scientific terms ("stereotype vulnerability," "racial devaluation") over emotionally charged words ("racism"), Claude Steele seems intent on depolarizing the national debate on race. — P.K.

Suggested Reading: *Atlantic* p68+ Apr. 1992; *Atlantic* (on-line) Aug. 1999, with photos; *Chronicle of Higher Education* A p31 Aug. 18, 1995, with photo; *New York Times Magazine* p44+ Sep. 17, 1995, with photos

Walter McBride/Retna Ltd.

Stein, Benjamin J.

Nov. 25, 1944– Actor; writer; lawyer; economist; television game-show host. Address: c/o Paul Kohner, Inc., 9300 Wilshire Blvd., #555, Beverly Hills, CA 90202

"I think I've had the most diverse career of anyone in America," the actor, writer, lawyer, professor, and economist Benjamin J. Stein told Joe Garden in an interview posted on *theonionavclub.com*. Stein is known in disparate circles for wildly different achievements: he garnered recognition in the political realm for his work as a speechwriter for Presidents Richard Nixon and Gerald R. Ford; he became famous in the financial world for exposing the fraud perpetrated by the junk-bond king Michael Milken; and he has won fans among the general public with small but memorable roles in TV shows and movies, particularly the 1986 film *Ferris Bueller's Day Off*, in which he played a high-school teacher whose monotone lulls his class into unconsciousness. Stein has written columns for publications ranging from the *Wall Street Journal* to *E! Online*, and has also published screenplays, novels, and nonfiction books on topics including personal finance, Hollywood, drug use, and fatherhood. He is the host of a popular television game show, *Win Ben Stein's Money*, which pits him against guests in battles involving knowledge of trivia.

The second of the two children of Herbert Stein, an economist and writer, and Mildred Stein, a homemaker who often assisted her husband in research and writing, Benjamin Jeremy Stein was born on November 25, 1944 in Washington, D.C. He and his older sister, Rachel, grew up in Silver

Spring, Maryland, one of only a handful of suburban Washington neighborhoods in which Jews were then welcome. The family was close-knit, and Stein has pointed to both his parents as excellent role models. "They were both very successful, hard-working people who basically had come from a fairly modest background. . . . I was impressed by them and their achievements from day one, the first time I was conscious of their having achievements," he explained in an on-line chat with the Comedy Central cable network (June 15, 2000). He attended local public schools: Parkside Elementary School, which he has described in idyllic terms; Montgomery Hills Junior High School, where segregation ended in 1956, the year he enrolled, and where he regularly experienced fights and anti-Semitic epithets; and Montgomery Blair High School, "famous for its fine athletic teams and its great academics . . . ," as Stein, who was the editor of the school's paper and a member of the Latin Scrabble team, wrote in an article for *Washingtonian* magazine (May 1996). "To go there was to be the apple of the community's eye." A "wise guy in class" and a self-professed nerd, Stein attended classes with the future Hollywood stars Goldie Hawn and Sylvester Stallone. His childhood friends included the future journalist Carl Bernstein, who lived next door. Unlike many of his liberal neighbors in Silver Spring, the Stein family held conservative political views, voting Republican and supporting President Nixon, for whom Herbert Stein worked as a high-level policy maker, rising to the position of chairman of the Council of Economic Advisors.

Stein attended Columbia University, in New York City, graduating with honors and a bachelor's degree in economics in 1966. After spending a summer as a government intern in Washington, D.C., he enrolled at Yale Law School, in New Haven, Connecticut. Stein has recalled feeling "miserable and lonely" at Yale, where his professors were relentless in their use of the Socratic method, which relies on questioning students rather than simply feeding them facts. "I didn't like it," he wrote in a column for the *Washingtonian* (September 1996). "I don't like humiliation." The stress contributed to his developing colitis, and he left the school in November 1966. Returning to Washington, he worked as an economist for the U.S. Commerce Department for several months before deciding to renew his efforts toward a law degree. "When I returned to Yale in the fall of 1967, it was as if I had stepped through the looking glass," he explained in his September 1996 *Washingtonian* piece. "The class of 1969, my original cohort, was the last gasp of the 'silent generation,' the future men in gray flannel suits who would work hard, defer gratification, be self-effacing so that in some future era their children could have fun, fun, fun." As for the class of 1970, Stein's new affiliation, "we were the children," he continued, "and we were ready to party hearty. . . . Even though the party animals and rebels among us were a minority, we set the tone for the class and soon for the whole law school and then for the whole university." Stein remembers those days of rebelliousness—when he was thin and wore long hair—with fondness, even recalling that his mother, a devoted anti-Communist, packed him tuna sandwiches to eat at a rally held to protest the Vietnam War. (The U.S. had entered the war to contain the spread of communism.) Stein's classmates elected him valedictorian when he graduated, with a J.D. degree.

Stein put both his expertise in law and his knowledge of economics to use when he worked for the federal Office of Legal Services, specializing in poverty law. He left that job to work as a consumer lawyer at the Federal Trade Commission, a post he disliked intensely, in part because "[I] had my brains beat in by the far better lawyers arrayed against me," as he explained in his May 1996 *Washingtonian* article. Having pursued film studies as a sideline while at Yale, he began to teach evening classes in the subject at American University, in Washington. He then moved briefly to California, where he taught film studies at the University of California at Santa Cruz. While he enjoyed teaching, his return to conservative politics and support of President Nixon led him to feel isolated on the liberal campus. In 1973, through his father's connections in the Nixon administration, he became a junior speechwriter for the president—or "RN," as Stein has often referred to him—drafting discussions of economic policy. He held the job for a year; his time there coincided with the Watergate scandal, which involved a break-in at the Democratic National Committee headquarters and its subsequent cover-up, events that led to Nixon's leaving office in disgrace. Later in 1974 Stein went to New York and began an almost two-year stint as an editorial writer and columnist at the *Wall Street Journal*.

In the late 1970s Stein relocated to Los Angeles, hoping to further his writing career. "I moved out here because I wanted to write a book about the political and social and cultural content of prime time television . . . ," he explained in a conversation with Brian Lamb for the C-SPAN program *Booknotes* (January 31, 1993). "I had written a number of articles about how the political content of what's on prime time was dictated not by what the public was thinking, not by what the public was wanting, but by the mindset, the political views, of a very few dozen people who control prime time. . . . These people . . . [have] a kind of classic, liberal left viewpoint of the world. I interviewed several dozen of these people and found that their views coincided precisely with what was on TV." Stein's resulting book, *The View from Sunset Boulevard: America as Brought to You by the People Who Make Television*, was published in 1979. At the same time that Stein was casting an appraising eye on show business, however, he was becoming a part of it. Soon after he moved to California, he became a consultant to the influential producer Norman Lear, helping to create the television program

Fernwood 2Night, a mock talk show that took place in the fictional town of Fernwood, Ohio. Though it was hailed as quirky and funny, the show lasted less than two seasons.

Meanwhile, Stein had written or co-written a number of other books. He penned a futuristic political novel, *On the Brink*, with his father, Herbert Stein. In 1978 he produced a novel of his own, *The Croesus Conspiracy*, following it up with a personal-finance book he co-wrote with his father in 1979, entitled *Moneypower: How to Make Inflation Make You Rich*. Through the late 1980s he continued to write both fiction and finance-related nonfiction. He even delved into the world of illegal drugs, providing portraits of narcotics addicts in his 1982 book, *'Ludes, a Ballad of the Drug and the Dream*. (With Stein as a contributing screenwriter, *'Ludes* became a movie, entitled *The Boost*, in 1988.) While composing his longer works, Stein remained a frequent contributor to the *Wall Street Journal* and other publications, including the *Los Angeles Herald Examiner* (which folded in 1989). He also wrote screenplays and scripts for television programs. In addition, Stein published *Hollywood Days, Hollywood Nights: Diary of a Mad Screenwriter*, which covered aspects of show business ranging from screenwriting to auditioning for small parts. Neither Stein's works of fiction nor his Hollywood diary were well received by critics. In her *New York Times* (December 18, 1988) review of *Hollywood Days, Hollywood Nights*, Diane Jacobs called the book "turgid," and D. Keith Mano, critiquing Stein's novel *Her Only Sin* for the *National Review* (April 25, 1986), wrote, "There have been more offensive, worse written California novels, I'm sure. This book, though, is lacking a sense of the bizarre, of playful wildness. Almost as if Stein knew so much about his subject, was so concerned with authenticity, that he couldn't write fiction."

In the mid-1980s Stein's career took on yet another dimension. He began teaching undergraduate courses in securities law, libel, and other areas of the legal field at Pepperdine University, in Malibu, California, where he was an adjunct professor. In his first year there, he told Stephanie Dolgoff for the *New York Times* (August 21, 1994), he was voted "favorite teacher." At the same time he began acting in movies, with a bit part in *The Wild Life* (1984), which he followed up with his showstopping, ad-libbed turn as the droning high-school teacher in *Ferris Bueller's Day Off*. Michael Chinich, the casting agent who gave Stein the role, told Dolgoff, "Everyone has an image of a person in their past who you can just take a nap when they're talking to you. That's what Ben personifies." Having found a niche as an actor, he parlayed his success with *Ferris Bueller* into a recurring role as Mr. Cantwell, a dull junior-high-school teacher, on the hit sitcom *The Wonder Years*. "My voice, once my curse, now my fortune," he intoned to Joseph Hooper for the *New York Times* (February 20, 2000). Stein did not feel insulted at being typecast;

rather, he was happy that he had, by simply living his life, captured the essence of what directors wanted for specific parts. "They want me because I'm me," he explained to Dolgoff. "They say, 'We want a lawyer.' Well, I'm a lawyer. 'We want a teacher.' Well, I'm a teacher. I *am* that guy." Stein was able to appreciate his experiences on the sets of movies and television shows "because I have had some experience of what normal people's work lives are like," he told Garden. "Acting is bliss . . . ," he explained to Brian Lamb. "Reading long tomes about junk bond default rates, that's work. Acting is not work."

Still, while he was acting, Stein kept up with the financial world. Writing for the financial magazine *Barron's*, he uncovered and reported the junk-bond scheme run by Michael Milken, an executive at the investment-banking firm Drexel Burnham Lambert Inc. Milken, who was later arrested for racketeering and fraud, had practiced fraudulent bond pricing. "[Milken] would raise money for corporate borrowers, but because he could fix the market price at which the bonds were sold and because he could sell bonds that no one else could sell, he could capture a fantastic commission for underwriting these bonds," Stein explained to Brian Lamb. "The beauty of the Milken scheme and what made it so incredibly powerful was that Milken controlled both sides of the deal. He controlled both the lenders and the borrowers." Stein was appalled that Milken and Drexel Burnham Lambert had fooled so many people—journalists, financiers, and even the U.S. government's General Accounting Office—and thrust the burden of repaying their debts onto American taxpayers. "Everyone in America lost money—except for a few hundred or a thousand inside players—because 55 Drexel-controlled or -influenced [savings-and-loan institutions] failed. . . . The loss to taxpayers in making up the losses to the depositors was in excess of $10 billion, or at least roughly," Stein told Lamb. Stein published a book on the scandal, *A License to Steal: the Untold Story of Michael Milken and the Conspiracy to Bilk the Nation*, in 1992. The book received mixed notices, with reviewers praising the clarity of Stein's explanations of Wall Street activity but noting that his contempt for Milken had at times clouded his judgment.

In the early and mid-1990s, Stein continued to perform in movies, winning small parts in *Honeymoon in Vegas*, *Dave*, *North*, and *The Mask*, among others. Chuck Russell, who directed *The Mask*, allowed Stein to ad-lib his dialogue with Jim Carrey, the movie's star, and observed to Stephanie Dolgoff, "He has this . . . unique sense of humor. It's so dry it sucks the moisture right out of the air." Stein's voice was regularly featured on the cartoon *Duckman*, which ran for four seasons on the USA Network. He has also appeared in television commercials, most notably for Clear Eyes eye drops. In 1997 Stein became the host of his own game show on the Comedy Central cable network. Called *Win Ben Stein's Money*, the show is a trivia contest conducted by Stein and an assistant. (Stein's first assistant, Jimmy Kimmel, left the project to work on his own program and was replaced by Nancy Pimental.) The prize money is really his, he explained to Joe Garden, because "it is money that is put into a prize budget for me, and if I don't lose it, I get to keep it. By any arithmetic or ethical or economic standpoint, it is mine." Held on a funky set that includes a skeleton, many books, a portrait of Richard Nixon, spiffy lighting effects, and casts of the letters "B" and "S" (his initials), the show comprises three rounds. In the first, three contestants try to answer questions posed by Stein; in the second, the lowest-scoring player is eliminated, and Stein himself becomes a contestant; and in the final round, Stein and the higher-scoring of the two remaining contestants face off over a series of 10 questions composed by the show's writers and posed by Stein's assistant. If the contestant gives a greater number of correct answers, he or she wins the $5,000—and faces Stein's wrath. Stein hates to lose, and though he has won a majority of the face-offs, he "is tortured by his losses," as Joel Stein wrote for *Time* (December 6, 1999). "That mix of shock, disbelief and self-hatred isn't rehearsed; he says he sees a $250-an-hour psychiatrist to deal with his fear of losing." Despite—or because of—Stein's cagey on-screen personality, the Comedy Central audience has responded overwhelmingly positively, making *Win Ben Stein's Money* the highest-rated daily show on the network.

Win Ben Stein's Money has captured daytime Emmy Awards in the categories of writing, directing, outstanding game-show host, and outstanding game/audience participation show. Stein is proud of the program, which arrived on the air ahead of the prime-time quiz show *Who Wants to be a Millionaire?*, the ratings juggernaut broadcast on ABC and hosted by Regis Philbin. "I'm not even remotely outclassed by [Philbin]," Stein told John M. Higgins for *Broadcasting & Cable* (December 13, 1999). "He just has more money on the table. . . . My game show is by far the classiest, because it's funny and witty and involves having to think very fast."

Comedy Central allowed Stein to explore the medium of television even further; late in 1999 the network began broadcasting the weekly talk show *Turn Ben Stein On*. The half-hour format was envisioned as a cozy chat on a selected topic, held by Stein and two other celebrities. Although Comedy Central viewers kept the show afloat, *Turn Ben Stein On* received a cool critical reception. "Stein is a raconteur who moves best at a deliberate pace," Joseph Hooper wrote, "and he sometimes seemed rushed or distracted trying to fit two guests into a half-hour slot." *Turn Ben Stein On* has since been canceled.

Stein continues to write prolifically; his articles appear regularly in the *American Spectator*, *Brill's Content*, and *Los Angeles* magazine, and he posts a biweekly gossip column on *E! Online*, sharing the details of his Monday-night dinners at Morton's restaurant in Los Angeles. He maintains his conservative views, including his firm opposition to abortion. In his columns, he frequently railed against President Bill Clinton's administration, and he has invoked the memory and policies of President Nixon with admiration. In an on-line chat with AT&T Worldnet's Community Port (May 16, 2000), he named the arch-conservative Clarence Thomas as his favorite Supreme Court justice, with another conservative, Antonin Scalia, as runner-up. While conceding that such problems as racism continue to plague the U.S., Stein is an avowed lover of his country. "I am one hundred percent convinced that this country is the greatest event in the history of mankind," Stein stated during the Comedy Central chat.

Stein has twice married the entertainment lawyer Alexandra Denman; the couple have experienced a number of separations and reunions since their first date, in 1966. (A recent op-ed piece in the New York Times indicated that they are currently together.) Stein and Denman adopted a son, Tommy, in 1987. Fatherhood has provided a wealth of material for Stein, who often writes about Tommy ("my absolute reason for living," he said in his AT&T Worldnet chat) in his American Spectator diary and published the book Tommy and Me: The Making of a Dad in 1998. Stein has turned particularly introspective since the death of his parents, in the late 1990s, writing elegiac obituaries for both for the American Spectator. Summing up his outlook on life, he told Comedy Central, "I hardly know anyone in my whole life who's had more interesting things to do than I do or who is more

grateful for them. I am extremely, extremely, extremely grateful for everything that goes on in my life." An ardent dog lover, Stein told Comedy Central that his "favorite recreational activity" is "being with my dog. . . . I love going anywhere at all with my son—just going for walks with him or watching TV with him. I love having dinner with my wife and son. I have a boat on a lake in north Idaho, and I have a lot of fun on my boat. . . . My main recreation is just to be there with the people and dogs that I love." — K.S.

Suggested Reading: New York Times II p14 Aug. 21, 1994, with photo, II p39 Feb. 20, 2000, with photo, E-Commerce Part II p47, Sep. 20, 2000, with photo; People p85+ Sep. 29, 1997, with photos; Time p114+ Dec. 6, 1999, with photo; Washingtonian p72+ May 1996, with photos

Selected Television Series: Duckman; Win Ben Stein's Money; Turn Ben Stein On; The Wonder Years

Selected Films: Ferris Bueller's Day Off, 1986; Soapdish, 1991; Honeymoon in Vegas,1992; Dave, 1993; The Mask, 1994

Selected Books: Hollywood Days, Hollywood Nights: Diary of a Mad Screenwriter, 1988; A License to Steal: the Untold Story of Michael Milken and the Conspiracy to Bilk the Nation, 1992; Tommy and Me: The Making of a Dad, 1998

Stevens, Ted

Nov. 18, 1923–U.S. Senator from Alaska.
Address: 522 Hart Senate Office Bldg.,
Washington, DC 20510

On March 22, 2000 the Alaska state legislature joined with Alaskan of the Year Inc. in bestowing upon United States senator Ted Stevens, a prominent Republican, the title "Alaskan of the Century." The official proclamation (reprinted on the Web site of the Alaska Republican Party) read in part: "Senator Ted Stevens is . . . an asset to the United States and represents Alaska's finest contribution to our national leadership." That Stevens has exerted considerable influence in shaping modern-day Alaska is indisputable. As a member of the powerful Senate Committee on Appropriations since 1972 (he chaired it from late 1996 until mid-2001 and is now its ranking member), Stevens has also weathered criticism, most of it for fiscal decisions that have sometimes appeared to place the interests of his adopted home state above those of the country as a whole. As a champion of Alaska's booming oil industry and a known hawk on

defense matters, Stevens remains one of the most popular figures in Alaska's political history.

Theodore Fulton Stevens was born on November 18, 1923 in Indianapolis, Indiana. His parents, George and Gertrude Stevens, divorced at the start of the Great Depression. Stevens was sent to live with an aunt in Redondo Beach, California, where he took up surfing. After graduating from Redondo High School, in 1942, he attended Oregon State University, in Corvallis, and Montana State University, in Bozeman, before leaving college in 1943 to enter the Army Air Corps and World War II. Stevens spent the next three years in Asia, flying C-46 transport planes over the Himalayan "hump" and into China, in support of the Flying Tigers fighter squadron. In recognition of his bravery and dutiful service, he was awarded a Distinguished Flying Cross and an Air Medal. He left the military in 1946, having attained the rank of first lieutenant.

Stevens resumed his studies at the University of California at Los Angeles, obtaining a bachelor's degree in 1947. He then earned a law degree from Harvard Law School, in Cambridge, Massachusetts, in 1950. According to an article in the Anchorage, Alaska Daily News, cited by George Hager in Congressional Quarterly (December 14, 1996),

Courtesy of the U.S. Senate

Ted Stevens

Stevens paid his way through law school in part by selling his blood and working as a bartender.

Stevens joined the Washington, D.C., law firm of Northcutt Ely in 1950. Two years later he married the former Ann Cherrington, with whom he had five children. In 1953, at the age of 29, Stevens was recruited by a law firm in Fairbanks, Alaska, where he moved with his family. Within a few months he was appointed to the position of United States attorney, a job he held until 1956, when he returned to Washington to serve as legislative counsel for the U.S. Department of the Interior. He worked as an assistant to the secretary of the interior from 1958 to 1960, playing a key administrative role when Alaska achieved statehood, in 1959. In 1960 he became solicitor, or chief lawyer, for the Department of the Interior.

Stevens returned to Alaska, where he established the law firm of Stevens & Roderick, in Anchorage, in 1961. In the following year he gained the Republican Party's nomination for U.S. Senate, but he lost in the general election by some 10,000 votes to the Democratic incumbent, Ernest Gruening. Stevens was president of the Alaska Republican Club from 1961 to 1963 and served as the state chairman of Nelson Rockefeller's 1964 presidential campaign. Stevens ran for office again in 1964, winning a seat in the Alaska House of Representatives. In his second two-year term, he served as majority leader and Speaker Pro Tempore.

In 1968 huge oil reserves were discovered in Prudhoe Bay and the North Slope of Alaska, a finding that would reshape the Alaskan economy. Large-scale petroleum extraction promised enormous revenues that the state's traditional industries, such as wood products and the salmon fish-

ery, could not hope to match. Within a few years, Republicans—traditionally business-friendly—would come to dominate politics in Alaska, though Republicans and Democrats alike raced to align themselves with petroleum interests. In 1968 Stevens made another unsuccessful bid for the U.S. Senate, losing narrowly in the primary to the banker Elmer E. Rasmuson.

Stevens's political fortunes changed when, in December 1968, Alaska's popular Democratic U.S. senator, E. L. "Bob" Bartlett, died in office. Widely considered until his death to be Alaska's most powerful politician, Bartlett had served as the territorial delegate to Congress from 1945 to 1959 and was one of the chief architects of the Alaskan campaign for statehood. On December 24, 1968 Governor Walter J. Hickel, a Republican, chose Stevens to serve as Bartlett's replacement, until a special election could be called to fill the remainder of the late senator's term. A brief in *Newsweek* (January 6, 1969), announcing Stevens's appointment to the Senate, described the bespectacled freshman as "a 5-foot 6-inch cigar smoker who hunts moose and won a reputation as a scrapper in the Alaska House of Representatives."

In 1969 Stevens had the first of several skirmishes with environmentalists over the fate of Alaska's wilderness lands. Alaska, at 586,000 square miles—more than twice the area of Texas—is by far the largest state in the union and encompasses most of the country's remaining wilderness acreage. Much of Alaska's land is controlled by the federal government, which purchased the territory from Russia in 1867 for $7.2 million and has exercised authority in Alaskan affairs ever since. In a speech at the Alaska Science Conference, held at the University of Alaska at Fairbanks in August 1969, as reported by Lawrence E. Davies in the *New York Times* (August 31, 1969), Stevens complained that environmentalists were "coming out of the woodwork" in an attempt to prevent Alaska from opening more of its land to petroleum exploration. When another speaker at the conference, a University of Washington geographer, lamented Stevens's pro-oil views as "Neanderthal," Stevens's response reflected his thick skin concerning criticism from out-of-state: "As long as [the remark] wasn't made by an Alaskan, it doesn't bother me."

Recognizing the potential of the petroleum industry to bring much-needed money, jobs, and infrastructure (such as new rural roads and airstrips) to Alaska, Stevens emerged as a key ally of "big oil" in Congress, backing industry leaders in their efforts to gain access to wilderness land believed to contain deposits of oil and natural gas. Stevens also took a strong interest in native Alaskan issues; he played a key role in the passage of the Native Claims Settlement Act of 1971, which not only resolved the longstanding land-ownership dispute between Alaska's indigenous tribes and the federal government, but also cleared the way for the lease or sale to commercial interests of large tracts of federally controlled Alaskan land. In 1973 Stevens used his influence in the Senate to facilitate construction of the privately funded, 800-mile-long Trans-Alaska Pipeline, completed in 1977, which links the oil-producing region of Prudhoe Bay with the southern shipping port of Valdez.

Meanwhile, Stevens's victory over the Democrat Wendell P. Kay in the November 1970 special election entitled him to finish out the remainder of Bartlett's term. In 1971 Stevens made headlines when he co-sponsored an amendment to a Selective Service bill, pertaining to the war in Vietnam. The amendment set forth terms for the withdrawal of U.S. troops from the region, startling many party members who sided with the Republican president, Richard Nixon, in favor of continuing the war effort. The bill made it through Congress, but conditions governing the exchange of prisoners of war were not met, and U.S. involvement in the war continued until 1975. In 1972 Stevens sponsored successful legislation, known as Title IX, banning sex-based discrimination in federally funded educational institutions. That year he was named to the Senate Appropriations Committee, the powerful body that controls the spending of federal tax dollars. He was also named to the Appropriations Subcommittee on the Interior. In November 1972 Stevens was reelected to the Senate; he subsequently won reelection in 1978, 1984, 1990, and 1996. He was named to the Appropriations Subcommittee on Defense in 1975. Other committees on which Stevens has served, beginning in 1975, include the Committee on the Library of Congress and the Appropriations Subcommittee on Commerce, Justice, State, and the Judiciary. In 1977 the Republican Party, recognizing Stevens's growing influence in the Senate, appointed him to the influential position of assistant Republican leader, commonly known as the whip. His duties during the eight years he served as Republican whip included working with the members of his party to gain their understanding and support on key initiatives.

On December 4, 1978 the Lear jet carrying Stevens, his wife, and three other passengers crash-landed at Anchorage International Airport, en route from the capital city of Juneau, where they had attended the swearing-in ceremony of Republican governor Jay Hammond. Ann Stevens was killed in the crash, along with the pilot, the co-pilot, and two others. Stevens, then 55, suffered serious injuries. After spending several months recuperating from his injuries, Stevens made the news again in May 1979, when he changed his position on a national gasoline-rationing plan then being proposed by President Jimmy Carter to counteract the ongoing embargo against the United States by the Middle Eastern member nations of OPEC (the Organization of Petroleum Exporting Countries). Initially opposed to the Democratic plan, Stevens switched and offered his influential support for it in the Senate, in exchange for the adoption of his own guidelines as to when the rationing would take place. In addition to breaking legislative

gridlock in the midst of a national energy crisis, the move protected the interests of Stevens's Alaskan oil-producing constituents, whose profits were likely to diminish to a greater extent under Carter's original plan.

In the 1980s land-closure issues continued to dominate Alaska politics. ("Land closure" refers to the closure of land to commercial use, often by virtue of its being designated a state or national park.) After Alaskan U.S. senator Mike Gravel succeeded in blocking a popular land-closure bill, in 1978, Secretary of the Interior Cecil D. Andrus stepped in, using his executive powers to set aside millions of acres of federal parkland, part of which was designated as the Arctic National Wildlife Refuge (ANWR, pronounced "AN-wahr"). The issue of whether to permit drilling within ANWR, where good-sized petroleum deposits were thought to exist, was raised; in the ensuing debate, Stevens came out strongly in favor of allowing the drilling. (After years of squabbling between oil company advocates and environmental groups hoping to preserve one of the last remaining pristine wildernesses on Earth, the issue was thrust into the national spotlight in 2001, when President George W. Bush—himself a former oil executive—pushed for extraction of petroleum from ANWR as a means of avoiding another energy crisis.)

While still focused primarily on his Alaskan constituency, Stevens began asserting himself more forcefully on the national political stage. In January 1980 Stevens, with Republican representative John J. Rhodes of Arizona, co-delivered the Republican rebuttal to President Carter's State of the Union address. Supporting former California governor Ronald Reagan in his 1980 presidential bid, Stevens argued in favor of strengthening U.S. military defenses—an area that had not received sufficient attention under the Carter administration, in the opinion of the majority of Republicans. Stevens implied that Carter had acted irresponsibly by issuing a threat to use military force, if necessary, to deter a potential Soviet invasion of the oil-rich Persian Gulf region. (Such an invasion seemed a real possibility, as Soviet troops had only recently invaded nearby Afghanistan, igniting a 13-year war.) Claiming that U.S. forces in the region were ill-prepared to meet the challenge of armed conflict with the Soviets, Stevens warned that "the Persian Gulf is the worst place in the world to meet the Russians" (as reported by the Associated Press in the *New York Times*, January 29, 1980).

Following Reagan's victory at the polls, Stevens served on the president-elect's transition team. That same year he was appointed chair of the Appropriations Subcommittee on Defense. He was also named to the Committee on Commerce, Science and Transportation, as well as to subcommittees on aviation and communications. As the senior Republican on the Committee on Government Affairs, he worked to loosen restrictions on senators' outside earnings and to ensure free mailing privileges for senators. After enduring mild criticism for these self-serving initiatives, Stevens saw some of his legislation, including a large pay raise he had engineered for senators, rejected by the Senate. In the fall of 1982 and again in 1984, Stevens raised some Republicans' eyebrows when he advocated trimming Reagan's proposed military budget to comply with general budget guidelines. Stevens served as deputy majority leader of the Senate in 1982, but he failed in his 1984 bid to become majority leader, losing to Senator Robert Dole of Kansas.

By the early 1980s Stevens had been Alaska's senior senator for more than a decade, and his grasp on power was secure. While environmentalists continued to decry his coziness with the petroleum industry, his role in facilitating the unprecedented growth of the Alaskan economy could not be denied. Moreover, many in the largely conservative state had come to view Stevens's activities in the Senate as fundamental to their own economic well-being. As a high-ranking member of the Appropriations Committee, Stevens was able to funnel hundreds of millions of dollars in federal tax revenues directly to Alaskans, primarily through inserting spending provisions into existing bills just prior to Senate votes (thus usually avoiding debate, which might prove fatal to the last-minute insertions). Among the beneficiaries of this entirely legal fiscal maneuvering (known as "pork-barrel spending") were road-building and other regional infrastructure projects; rural and Native American medical clinics, museums, and historical societies; and small fishermen, craftspeople, and others in traditional occupations who struggled to make a living on the fringes of the oil boom. Stevens also dispensed money to fledgling defense contractors—for whom the next logical step, lucrative contracts with the Pentagon, might potentially result in hundreds or even thousands of jobs for Alaskans. The full scale of Stevens's power over Senate appropriations came to light in a *Washington Post* (December 28, 1986) article by William M. Arkin. Arkin detailed how, after the army had decided to commission a new infantry division, Stevens lobbied successfully to have the unit's base relocated to Alaska. "When it comes to pork-barrel politics," he wrote, "Ted Stevens is the master."

On March 24, 1989 the oil tanker *Exxon Valdez* struck Bligh Reef in Alaska's Prince William Sound, spilling more than 11 million gallons of crude oil that polluted beaches and resulted in the deaths of tens of thousands of birds, fish, and sea mammals. In the wake of that disaster, the largest oil spill in U.S. history, Stevens sponsored the Oil Pollution Act of 1990, which strengthened the regulations governing oil-tank owners and operators and provided financial compensation to Alaska for the extensive environmental damage caused by the spill. Following surgery for prostate cancer in 1991, Stevens turned his attention to one of his most beleaguered constituencies, Alaska's fishermen. For years, fishermen had watched their annual catch of salmon, cod, and pollack decline as the

result of decades of over-fishing, stiff competition from the Japanese, and environmental factors ranging from weather patterns to industrial pollution and oil spillage. Stevens worked in the 1990s to pass fishing legislation banning monofilament nets (which often trapped sea mammals and turtles, along with fish) and expanding Alaska's jurisdiction to include 200 miles of coastline. In 1998 he sponsored legislation banning factory ships more than 165 feet in length and requiring at least 75 percent U.S. ownership for all ships fishing in Alaskan waters. Stevens's efforts to help Alaska's fishermen culminated in the 2000 updating and reauthorizing of the Magnuson-Stevens Act, which he had co-authored in its original form, in 1976. That legislation reduced the maximum bycatch, among other measures aimed at stopping over-fishing and preserving fish stocks.

As a high-ranking Republican senator, Stevens had an ambivalent relationship with Democratic president Bill Clinton, elected in 1992. After lending support to Clinton's 1993 national service bill, Stevens turned to criticizing the president, mainly over matters of foreign policy. Stevens claimed that the president had weakened national defense by siphoning for peacekeeping missions in Bosnia, Somalia, and elsewhere money that might have been put toward the modernization of the U.S. military. When Clinton was impeached by the House of Representatives in late 1998 on counts of perjury, following the Monica Lewinsky sex scandal, Stevens led the cadre of Republicans who felt that Clinton's actions, while clearly wrong, were not the type of "high crimes and misdemeanors" that would warrant his removal from office by the Senate.

Stevens became chair of the Senate Appropriations Committee in late 1996. "Ted is very fierce," David R. Obey, a Democratic representative from Wisconsin and a ranking member of the House Appropriations Committee, commented to George Hager for the *Congressional Quarterly* (December 14, 1996). "It is going to be a much more confrontational situation [in Appropriations]. . . . Ted and I agree on issues [only] about three times a year, but I like him very much. There is not much guile there. It takes about eight-and-a-half seconds to figure out where he's coming from." Contrasting his style with that of his predecessor as Appropriations Committee chairman, Republican senator Mark Hatfield of Oregon, Stevens told the Freedom Channel (on-line), "Senator Hatfield had the patience of Job and the disposition of a saint. I don't. The watch has changed. I'm a mean, miserable SOB." In spite of controversy over the "pork" issue, which resurfaced in 1999 in connection with the presidential campaign of Republican senator John McCain of Arizona, Stevens received rave reviews from Democrats and Republicans alike for his efficiency in processing complex appropriations legislation. Stevens lost the committee chairmanship in June 2001, after Senator James Jeffords of Vermont changed his party affiliation from Republican to

Independent and the balance of power in the Senate switched to the Democrats.

Beginning in the mid-1990s, Stevens served on several other important Senate committees and subcommittees, including Oceans and Fisheries; Science, Technology, and Space; Surface Transportation and the Merchant Marine; the District of Columbia; Energy and Water Development; Foreign Operations; Labor, Health and Human Services, and Education; the Legislative Branch; Transportation; and Treasury, Postal Service, and General Government. In 1998 he created the Denali Commission to push for rural infrastructure in central Alaska. Stevens scored a record $300 million in federal appropriations for Alaska that year, including $50 million in disaster relief for salmon fishermen in the Kuskokwim River and Bristol Bay; $28 million for an elevated railway station at Anchorage International Airport to serve cruise-ship tourists; $60 million for highways and ferries; and $38 million for an airport road, medical clinic, doctor, and nurse for the tiny Aleutian village of King Cove. Stevens told Alan Fram for the Seattle, Washington *Post-Intelligencer* (December 27, 1999), "Alaska . . . has been left out of a lot of things. My job is to try to deal with some of these things." Also in 1999 he told the Freedom Channel Web site, "We ask for special consideration, because no one else is that far away, no one else has the problems that we have or the potential that we have, and no one else deals with the federal government day in and day out the way we do." In October of that year, as quoted in the *Congressional Record* (October 13, 1999, on-line), Stevens weighed in on the issue of a proposed worldwide ban on nuclear-weapons testing (known as the Comprehensive Nuclear-Test-Ban treaty), voicing the Senate majority opinion that while "a ban on testing under a fair treaty could be very much in our national interest . . . today we cannot indefinitely maintain with certainty the safety and reliability of our nuclear weapons. So . . . we are not yet prepared to assume the risks that would be imposed upon us if we give up the ability to test our own weapons."

On July 8, 2000 Stevens was honored at an official ceremony in which the Anchorage Airport was renamed Ted Stevens Anchorage International Airport. On hand was former governor Walter J. Hickel, who described to attendees the circumstances surrounding Stevens's appointment to the Senate, in 1968. Another speaker, Democratic senator Ernest Hollings of South Carolina, offered a toast (quoted on the Web site of the political group Commonwealth North): "[Stevens] is the epitome of public service. He knows where he's heading and he's not waiting on the polls. And he has a vision not just for America but particularly for your Alaska. . . . [President] Franklin Roosevelt years ago said where there's no vision the people perish. As long as Ted Stevens is in Washington the vision and interests of Alaska will never perish, but he won't do it quietly, I can tell you that. I'm ready

. . . to raise a toast to Alaska's man of the century, Ted Stevens."

Stevens married his second wife, Catherine Chandler, in 1980; they have one daughter. He received an honorary law degree from the University of Alaska in 1975, the same year he was named Man of the Year by the National Fisheries Institute. In 1997 he received the Harry S. Truman Award from the National Guard Association, and he was honored by the defense industry with the James Forrestal Memorial Award in 1998. Stevens maintains a residence in Girdwood, down the coast from Anchorage. One of his sons, Ben, is a lobbyist in Washington. — G.K.R.

Suggested Reading: Alaska Republican Party Web site; Commonwealth North Web site; *Congressional Quarterly* p2800 Sep. 16, 1995, with photo, p1859+ Aug. 2, 1997, with photo; *National Defense* p16+ May/June, 1998, with photos; *New York Times* p10 Dec. 24, 1968, with photo, p22 Aug. 31, 1969, A p20 Sep. 17, 1982; *Sierra* p50+ Nov. 1995, with photos; *Washington Post* D p1+ Dec. 28, 1986

Mike Blake/Archive Photos

Sun Wen
(soon wen)

Apr. 6, 1973– Soccer player. Address: Atlanta Beat, 1400 Lake Hearn Dr., Atlanta, GA 30319

Although she was raised in a society that shunned the notion of women playing team sports, in 1991 the 18-year-old soccer player Sun Wen joined the Chinese women's national team, which had been formed about seven years earlier. In time she gained recognition as one of the best offensive players in international competition. Her performance during the 1999 Women's World Cup competition raised her profile around the world, and in 2000 the Federation Internationale Football Association (FIFA), better known in the United States as the International Football Federation, named her one of the best female soccer players of the 20th century. She was the top draft pick for a new professional league, the Women's United Soccer Association (WUSA), which is based in the United States and was slated to begin competition in April 2001. Now a member of the Atlanta Beat, one of eight teams in the WUSA, Sun is a popular figure in her native land, particularly among her many young, female fans, who consider her a role model and eagerly seek her autograph.

The daughter of Sun Zhong Gao and his wife, Sun Wen was born in Shanghai, in eastern China, on April 6, 1973. Speaking of her early love for soccer, she told Jere Longman for the *New York Times* (July 7, 1999), "I was influenced by my father. He was a real soccer fan and he wanted me to play soccer." For a while Sun had to plead with neighborhood boys to allow her to play on their informal teams. When she was 13 she enrolled at a special sports school, in Shanghai, where she honed her soccer skills. In 1991 Sun joined the Chinese women's national team (formed in 1984) as a forward.

The first Women's World Cup, held in 1991, was hosted by China; nevertheless, the Chinese public largely ignored it. Sun later explained the prevailing Chinese attitude toward women's soccer for Brian Landman of the *St. Petersburg Times* (July 9, 1999, on-line): "Most of the families don't accept girls playing soccer. That is the tradition. Girls are supposed to be shy and not so active." The Chinese team finished fifth in the competition. "We had a big problem psychologically," Sun told Longman of that contest, speaking just before the final match of the 1999 Women's World Cup. "We hosted the tournament, but we didn't have enough international experience. Now we have better emotional control. We show more confidence."

Women's soccer was not an event in the 1992 Olympics, so the team's next major competition was the 1995 Women's World Cup; this time the Chinese team finished fourth. Sun was then studying the Mandarin language as a part-time student and writing poetry, some of which was published in Chinese newspapers. Most of her time was spent competing as a member of both the national team and her local club team, Shanghai TV. (Shanghai TV currently spends more than a million dollars annually to sponsor teams for girls 13 years old and up.)

Meanwhile, the Chinese women's national team, sometimes called the "Steel Roses" in the media, had been improving steadily, although it still did not enjoy the prominence or popularity of the Chinese men's team. That began to change during the 1996 Olympic Games, held in Atlanta,

Georgia, during which Sun's team took the silver medal in women's soccer. Sun scored the Chinese team's only goal in the gold-medal game, which the United States won, 2–1. She was also responsible for three assists during the Olympics. The women's team continued to do well during the rest of the 1990s, winning the 1998 Asian Games and finishing second to the Americans during the 1998 Goodwill Games, held in New York.

There was speculation that, in retaliation for the accidental bombing of the Chinese Embassy in Yugoslavia by North Atlantic Treaty Organization (NATO) forces on May 8, 1999, the Chinese government would withdraw the women's team from that year's Women's World Cup. But that did not happen—possibly, some commentators suggested, because Chinese officials considered women's soccer to be too unimportant to be used as a political tool. Sun told Jere Longman, "There was no fear of not coming. This is a sporting thing. We just play."

During the competition, held in the Rose Bowl stadium, in Pasadena, California, Sun received considerable media attention. An ad that was broadcast repeatedly by the Adidas shoe company showed her as a little girl heading (rather than catching) a ball tossed by her father. The recreation was "mostly true," she told Brian Landman, although—apparently unlike her father—the actor who portrayed him was "very handsome . . . like a movie star."

The American players who faced China in 1999 knew that Sun was a dangerous opponent. "She's gone up another level since the [1996] Olympics," Tony DiCicco, the head coach of the U.S. team, told Gary Davidson for *SoccerTimes* (July 9, 1999, on-line). "She was an excellent player in the Olympics, but now she's one of the best in the world. It's made everybody around her better." The U.S. team's star forward, Mia Hamm, who, like Sun, wears number 9, told Brian Landman, "She's an unbelievable player. The thing that she brings to their team is that player who with one touch of the ball can change the game for them. We've seen that throughout the tournament." When asked if Sun could be slowed down, Hamm joked that the only way to do so would be to "put her on the bench."

Over the course of the competition, Sun scored seven goals and had three assists. Although she did not score in China's opening-round 2–1 defeat of Sweden, she scored three goals in the second-round game, helping her teammates crush their Ghanaian opponents 7–0; she was named the Bud Light Player of the Game for her offensive showing. In the next round, in which China faced Australia, Sun's two goals contributed to China's 3–1 win. The team next defeated Russia in the quarterfinal round, 2–0, and routed the defending champions, Norway, in the semifinal, 5–0. Sun scored two of the goals in China's defeat of Norway, assuring that her team would meet the United States team, which had defeated Brazil in their semifinal match, in the World Cup final.

During the final China and the United States were locked in a scoreless tie after both regulation and overtime play. The championship was finally decided by a penalty-kick shoot-out, giving the win to the Americans, 5–4. The Chinese defeat did not signal the end of Sun's media reign. In voting by the 150 journalists covering the event, Sun was elected the winner of the Adidas Golden Ball, awarded to the tournament's outstanding player. She shared the Golden Shoe Award, for the competition's high-scoring player, with Brazil's Sissi (the nickname of Sisleide Lima do Amor), who had also accrued seven goals and three assists. In addition to her other accolades, Sun was named 1999's best women's soccer player by the Asian Football Confederation.

The 2000 Olympic Games, held in Sydney, Australia, were disappointing for the Chinese team; the players were getting older, and both the goalkeeper, Gao Hong, and Sun were battling injuries. (Sun later underwent knee surgery.) In the first round of the contest, the team beat Nigeria, 3–1, with Sun scoring two goals; they later tied the U.S., 1–1, in a game that featured a free-kick goal by Sun. Although Sun scored again against Norway, the Norwegian team upset the Chinese, 2–1, and eliminated them from the competition before the medal round. (The organizers of the event were criticized in some quarters for including China, the U.S., and Norway, considered the strongest teams, in the same group, thereby ensuring that one of those three countries would not be able to progress to medal contention.)

By her own account, Sun refused to view China's narrow losses in international competition as personal defeats. Seizing the opportunity to play professional soccer in a new United States–based league, she entered the WUSA draft late in 2000. Ranked number one in the draft, she was signed as a forward by the Atlanta Beat. "It's not for the money," she told Tim Nash. "In China, the money is similar." Instead, she revealed, she wanted to attend school in the U.S., with the goal of earning a master's degree in Chinese literature. (Her command of English is said to be improving, thanks in part to her love of karaoke.)

During the 2001 season Sun was hampered by knee and ankle injuries; as a result, she played in only five of the 21 regular-season games, scoring a total of one goal and making two assists. But her team did well, compiling a record of 10 wins, four losses, and seven ties, which left them in second place, behind the Bay Area CyberRays. In the championship game, held on August 25, 2001, the Beat succumbed to the CyberRays by losing a penalty-kick shootout after the score was tied 3–3.

Sun is keenly aware of her popularity and status in her native land. She would like to use her position to forge connections between youth soccer groups in China and the U.S. In China, which will host the Women's World Cup in 2003, women's soccer has been increasing in popularity, but the game is still not widely played there. (Currently, there are only 2,000 girls under 19 years of age registered in soccer clubs in China—roughly 1.3 million fewer than in the United States.) Sun told Tim Nash that she hoped to be "a model for a lot of Chinese youths. Right now, many of them want to become soccer players, but their parents are thinking that they might get hurt. There is not much support. I want to be able to show the young people—as well as the parents—that there is a future for them. They can follow the same steps and become soccer players." — K.S.

Suggested Reading: *New York Times* D p5 July 7, 1999, with photo, D p6 Aug. 25, 2001, with photo; *St. Petersburg* [Florida] *Times* C p1 July 9, 1999; *SoccerTimes* (on-line) July 9, 1999; *Womenssoccer.com* Dec. 6, 2000

Michel Euler/AP Photo

Swinton, Tilda

Nov. 5, 1960– Actress. Address: c/o Christian Hodell, Hamilton Asper Management, Ground Fl., 24 Hanway St., London W1T 1UH, England

"The second I found myself on a film set, I knew that was where I wanted to be," the actress Tilda Swinton told Peter Kobel for the *New York Times* (August 5, 2001). Often described as androgynous in appearance, Swinton captivated many critics and moviegoers with her performance as the title character—a man who becomes a woman—in Sally Potter's film *Orlando* (1992), an adaptation of Virginia Woolf's same-titled 1928 novel. A celebrated figure in the world of independent filmmaking, the Scottish actress made her cinematic debut in 1986, in the British director Derek Jarman's fanciful biopic *Caravaggio*. During the following seven years, she appeared in seven more Jarman films, all of which deal to some extent with blurred gender distinctions. In other explorations of androgyny, she portrayed Mozart in a 1988 theatrical production of Alexander Pushkin's *Mozart and Salieri* and starred as a woman who assumes the identity of her dead husband in stage and screen versions of Manfred Karge's drama *Man to Man*. In more conventional female roles, in 2000 she appeared in Danny Boyle's *The Beach*—her only big-budget Hollywood credit to date—and in 2001 in *The Deep End*, by the independent filmmakers Scott McGehee and David Siegel. "I get bored easily," she told John Clark for the *Los Angeles Times* (August 5, 2001, on-line). "I have to remain curious, and that means being in a dialogue with the people you're working with. I can't think of anything more boring than being given a task to achieve and then go home. It's just not what I'm in it for. And I've been very fortunate in continually meeting filmmakers who are in it for the same reason."

One of the four children of Major General Sir John Swinton and his wife, the former Judith Killen, Katherine Matilda Swinton was born on November 5, 1960 in London, England, into one of Scotland's historically most powerful and wealthy families. Her father served for a time as a commander of Queen Elizabeth II's household guards at Buckingham Palace, in London; he counts among his ancestors the novelist and poet Sir Walter Scott, who once proclaimed, according to Peter Kobel, that he was "honored to be a mere twig on the Swinton family tree."

During her early years Tilda Swinton and her three brothers were raised by a nanny in a castle in Berwickshire, Scotland, where the Swinton family has lived since the year 876. As a 10-year-old Swinton enrolled at West Heath, in Kent, England, a prestigious boarding school where one of her classmates was Diana Spencer, the future Princess of Wales. (The school closed in the late 1990s and then reopened as the New School at West Heath.) Swinton left West Heath in 1977 to enroll at Fettes College, a co-educational boarding school in Edinburgh, Scotland, for people up to age 18. "I think I was not so much shaped as paralysed by my seven years at boarding school," she told Peter Ross for the *Sunday Herald* (July 29, 2001, on-line), a Scottish publication. "Shut down, I would say. In some kind of internal holding pattern with my bearings lost, deadly shy and baffled." Asked to describe her younger self, she told Ross, "As a child—blithe. As a teenager—silent. And watchful, maybe. A natural punk, had I but known it."

Swinton next entered Cambridge University, in England, where she studied English literature and both social and political science. While at Cambridge she began acting in small stage productions—"serious political theatre," as Ross described them. She enjoyed acting, and after she earned a degree, in 1983, she joined the Traverse

Theatre Company, in Edinburgh, which specializes in productions of new plays. She also performed briefly with the Southampton Repertory and the renowned Royal Shakespeare Company. By her own account, she did not find stage acting sufficiently challenging, and, in addition, as she told Peter Kobel, she was "not gregarious enough to work with a bunch of actors in that way."

At around this time Swinton was introduced to the British painter turned film director and screenwriter Derek Jarman, whose goals and artistic vision, she discovered, closely matched her own. Jarman immediately cast the young actress in *Caravaggio* (1986), his highly imaginative rendering of the tumultuous life of the brilliant Italian artist Michelangelo Merisi da Caravaggio (1573–1610). Swinton played the part of Lena, a prostitute who is the lover of a favorite model of Caravaggio's. Having the opportunity to work with Jarman, she told Graham Fuller for *Interview* (August 2001), "was an extraordinary stroke of luck, because we made a kind of laboratory together. I sometimes wonder if I would have sustained my interest in film acting if I had only been allowed to exercise it in a more industrial environment"—that is, in a setting resembling Hollywood. "It would have alienated me, possibly. And so to have that apprenticeship with Derek was a miracle for me."

During the following years Swinton appeared in such little-noted films as *Egomania—Insel ohne Hoffnung* (Egomania—Island without Hope, 1986), directed by Christoph Schlingensief; the British director Peter Wollen's *Friendship's Death* (1987); and the British installation artist Cerith Wyn Evans's *Degrees of Blindness* (1988). She also performed in several uncelebrated films directed by Jarman, among them *The Last of England* (1987), *War Requiem* (1989), and *The Garden* (1990). In 1991 she took part in a project that received somewhat more attention, portraying the impetuous queen Isabella in Jarman's adaptation of Christopher Marlowe's 1590s tragedy *Edward II*, about the early-14th-century king of England, who was suspected of homosexuality. The film stars Steven Waddington as Edward and Andrew Tiernan as Piers Gaveston, the king's confidant. In the *San Francisco Chronicle* (March 27, 1992), Edward Guthmann wrote that Waddington and Tiernan "bring an impudence and passion to their roles as obsessed lovers, but it's Swinton . . . who steals the show with her camped-up Isabella. . . . Slinking about like a beady-eyed diva on a caffeine blast, her shoulders powered by unknown energy sources, Swinton's a mix of Evita Peron, Madame Duvalier of Haiti, Joan Crawford, Faye Dunaway playing Joan Crawford and any number of stylish despots." For her work in *Edward II*, Swinton won the Volpi Cup for best actress at the 1991 Venice Film Festival.

Swinton's close professional relationship with Jarman led some journalists to identify her as his muse—a label she has rejected. "I was a co-worker, friend and model," she told Kobel. "As a painter and filmmaker, he needed a model. Derek didn't really direct." Then, referring to the French film director Robert Bresson, she added, "It's like the Bressonian philosophy—the less acting the better." Swinton has often referred to herself as a performer rather than an actress. "I see acting as living on the stage," she explained to Kobel. "The truth is, I'm not interested in acting whatsoever. . . . You can't possibly describe me as an actor . . . because there ain't no acting going on." Similarly, she told Jonathan Romney for the London *Guardian* (March 5, 1993), "I don't know much about acting. . . . [I'm] not concerned with acting—at all."

Earlier, in 1988, Swinton had met the avant-garde filmmaker Sally Potter. In their first conversation, Swinton recalled to Matthew Gilbert for the *Boston Globe* (June 27, 1993), each learned that the other had for some time been considering making a film version of *Orlando*. Potter chose Swinton to play the title character because, as she explained to David Gritten for the *Los Angeles Times* (June 25, 1993), the actress "can really hold the screen. She knows how to work in a natural way with non-realism. And Tilda has a still quality, which I wanted, because we are in such a whirlwind of time travel with this story and we needed someone to be a constant." *Orlando* is based on a novel by Virginia Woolf that has been described as both a mock biography of Woolf's friend and lover Vita Sackville-West and a sort of love letter to Sackville-West. The plot spans 400 years, during which time the title character, who never ages, is transformed from a free-spirited Elizabethan nobleman to a liberated woman.

"I've been interested for quite a while in the idea of women playing men or men playing women," Swinton told Degen Pener for the *New York Times* (June 6, 1993). When Pener asked her if, like Sackville-West, she would rather have been a male, Swinton responded, "I've got no complaints, but I don't know that if someone came in now and shouted, 'All women leave the room,' if I would immediately leave. I would much rather say, 'Exempt!'" In a conversation with Gerard Raymond for the *Village Voice* (April 7, 1992), she said, "Somewhere there is a very deep taboo about gender that has to be cracked. It's interesting how worked up people get about it. Gender is the first set of limitations that are placed on a human being." Swinton told Matthew Gilbert that, in her view, immortality rather than androgyny is "the skewer to which all the other lesser themes [in *Orlando*] are attached. . . . There's the suggestion in the film that questions of gender are just distractions from the greater matters in life." But she also told Peter Kobel, "There's a gleeful sense of being able to travel in and out of identities. Androgyny—it's not anything, it's everything."

Critical reaction to *Orlando* and Swinton's work in it ranged from glowing to dismissive. In a positive review of the movie for *Rolling Stone* (June 24, 1993), Peter Travers wrote, "Tilda Swinton . . . is flat out amazing in a performance that is destined to become legendary." Similarly, in the *New York Times* (June 11, 1993), Vincent Canby wrote that the actress "has a sweetness, gravity and intelligence about her that make the more bizarre events [in the story] appear to be completely normal." In dissenting opinions, John Simon complained in the *National Review* (July 5, 1993), "Swinton . . . is neither believable as a man nor evocative as a woman," and Robin Morgan, in *Ms.* (July/August 1993), wrote that Swinton seemed "comatose." For her performance in *Orlando*, Swinton won the Golden Space Needle for best actress at the 1993 Seattle International Film Festival.

Swinton's next few films included two directed by Jarman. In the first, *Wittgenstein* (1993), which features Karl Johnson as the renowned Austrian-born philosopher, Swinton played Lady Ottoline Morrell, a prominent hostess who was a member of the Bloomsbury group, a literary clique that met in London in the early decades of the 20th century. The second was *Blue* (1993), Jarman's last film before his death, in 1994. In it, an unchanging blue background devoid of images is projected onto the screen; the soundtrack consists of music and readings, by Swinton and a few others, of poetry and excerpts from the diary in which Jarman recorded his struggle with AIDS. (Another film titled *Blue*, directed by Krzysztof Kieslowski and starring Juliet Binoche, was also released in 1993.) In 1994 Swinton appeared in John Maybury's unusual satirical comedy *Remembrance of Things Fast: True Stories Visual Lies*.

Taking a break from cinema, Swinton collaborated with the British sculptor and installation artist Cornelia Parker to create *The Maybe* (1995). In that live "performance," Swinton "slept" for eight consecutive hours in a glass case installed in the Serpentine Gallery, in London. Each day during the seven-day run of *The Maybe*, up to 3,000 people visited the gallery to view Swinton as she lay in bed. In a representative laudatory review, Waldemar Januszczak wrote for the London *Times* (September 10, 1995), "For Swinton this performance must feel like a caricature of her working life; *The Maybe* is a monument to every woman who has ever put herself on public display, and therefore to every actress." Soon afterward Swinton performed *The Maybe* in the Museo Barraceo in Rome, Italy. (About two years later she cancelled plans for a showing in Moscow, after learning that she was pregnant with twins.)

In 1996 Swinton appeared in the starring role in the American director Susan Streitfeld's debut feature film, *Female Perversions*—a "Freudian and feminist odyssey into the wilds of gender," as Brian D. Johnson described it in a review for *Maclean's* (July 7, 1997). The screenplay, which Streitfeld wrote, is based on the psychologist Louise J. Kaplan's same-titled study of female sexuality and the damage caused by gender divisions in society. In an undated interview with Jane Margetts for the Web site *This Swirling Sphere*, Streitfeld said, "The lead character had to be someone who appeared to be a winner in the perfection game. Someone we would all want to be: stunningly beautiful, brilliant, wildly erotic, with a powerful job and great lovers . . . but at the same time we're envying her, we would expose the Faustian bargains she's made to have the perfect life. There would . . . be some kind of unravelling of her psyche so that she too would be forced to confront her hidden demons. . . . The material needed someone who would plumb its depths. [Swinton] was that person."

Female Perversions focuses on Eve, a high-profile lawyer who loses her grip on her tightly controlled life in a crisis of self-esteem. Reviewers agreed that Swinton brilliantly captured Eve's desperate attempts to make order out of her emotional chaos. Among them was Stephen Holden, who wrote for the *New York Times* (April 25, 1997), "Swinton . . . imbues this character with an impetuous, high-strung hauteur that is both magnetic and infuriating. . . . As Eve swings from frantically obsessing about her image to dreaming of something more primitive, earthy and (by contemporary supermodel standards) androgynous, Ms. Swinton makes every zigzag ring psychologically true."

Swinton next appeared in a series of low-budget, independent films. In *Conceiving Ada* (1997), directed by the video and performance artist Lynn Hershman Leeson, she played Lady Ada King Lovelace (the daughter of the British poet Lord Byron), an amateur 19th-century mathematician who collaborated with Charles Babbage, the inventor of a "calculating machine" that is considered a precursor to the computer. Swinton played a London detective in *The Protagonists* (1998), directed by Luca Guadagnino, and a pregnant woman whose husband sexually abuses their teenage daughter in Tim Roth's *The War Zone* (1999).

In 2000 Swinton starred opposite Leonardo DiCaprio in Danny Boyle's *The Beach*. Based on a novel by Alex Garland, the picture focuses on a group of young Westerners who attempt, unsuccessfully, to maintain an anti-societal commune on a remote Thai island. The actress portrayed Sal, a domineering earth mother. "To me," Swinton told William Middleton for *Harper's Bazaar* (February 2000), *The Beach* "is my experimental film. To go and work with Leonardo DiCaprio for 20th Century Fox—it was an adventure." In part because it offered DiCaprio's first appearance in a feature film since the blockbuster *Titanic*, *The Beach* generated a great deal of publicity, thanks to which Swinton began to receive offers of parts in other big-budget films. She accepted a role in a more modest undertaking—the psychological thriller *The Deep End* (2001), co-written and -directed by Scott McGehee and David Siegel.

The Deep End, a critical though not a box-office success, is a remake of Max Ophuls's film noir *The Reckless Moment* (1949), which in turn is based on Elizabeth Sanxay Holding's story *The Blank Wall* (1947). The central character, Margaret Hall (Swinton), is a military wife and mother of three. After

learning that her teenage son (Jonathan Tucker) is gay, Margaret discovers the body of the boy's jilted lover (Josh Lucas) on the beach outside the family's lakefront home. Believing that her son is the killer and desperate to protect him from prosecution, she dumps the body in the lake; soon afterward she becomes the victim of an extortionist (Goran Visnjic), who has evidence that would weigh heavily against her son. "*The Deep End* thrives on the resolute Ms. Swinton, whose slender, finely drawn features can hold a position like a statue . . . ," Elvis Mitchell wrote for the *New York Times* (August 8, 2001). "The glory of the picture is the restraint of Ms. Swinton, which meshes with the underplayed malice of the directors. . . . Swinton's fixated intensity isn't ever remote; we're always aware of how deeply she's feeling. Her work is magnificent, an actress burrowing inside herself to play a woman doing the most horrible thing in the world to restore order to her life. The sadness is sealed by the recognition in her eyes that her life will never be orderly and clean again; her love for her family will have to be enough. It's [Swinton's] best and most memorable performance." Tom Long, in the *Detroit News* (August 22, 2001), described Swinton's performance as a "sure Oscar nomination" winner.

Upcoming movies in which Swinton will be seen include, in 2001, Cameron Crowe's romance *Vanilla Sky*, co-starring Tom Cruise, Penelope Cruz, Cameron Diaz, and Kurt Russell, and Lynn Hershman Leeson's futuristic *Teknolust*. In 2002 Swinton will appear in Spike Jonze's *Adaptation*, based on Susan Orlean's nonfiction book *The Orchid Thief* and co-starring Nicolas Cage and Meryl Streep, and *Young Adam*, the screenwriting and directorial debut of David McKenzie. Shot in Glasgow, Scotland, *Young Adam* is an adaptation of the Scottish writer Alexander Trocchi's same-titled 1954 novel; it will co-star Ewan McGregor.

Swinton's résumé also includes work on the stage, mostly during the 1980s, when, under the direction of Stephen Unwin, she appeared in Peter Arnott's *White Rose*, Bertold Brecht's *Die Massnahme*, and Manfred Karge's one-woman play *Man to Man* (the last of which John Marbury made into a 1992 movie, in which she again starred). In 1988 Karge directed her in Pushkin's *Mozart and Salieri*, in productions mounted in London, Vienna, Austria, and Berlin, Germany. Swinton's television credits include the leading role in the 1990 BBC-1 dramatic comedy serial *Your Cheatin' Heart*, written by her longtime companion John Byrne.

The tall, slender Swinton has extraordinarily pale, smooth skin and red hair that she cut short for her role in *The Deep End*, after letting it grow for 20 years. According to Jane Margetts, she is "beautifully androgynous and unearthly." In *Biennale News* (September 8, 1999), as quoted in *geocities.com*, Luca Guadagnino described her as "a surprising person, due to her almost unique mixture of craziness, naivete, sweetness and generosity, transcendence, charm and intelligence." "I don't know many people in film like her who are so natural and don't bother with appearances," Guadagnino added. She is a member of the Democratic Left, which she joined in 1983, when it was the Communist Party of Great Britain. "Capitalism never struck me as a system that worked or as a particularly rewarding way of putting one foot in front of the other," she said to Sarah Saffian for *US Weekly* (September 3, 2001). She and John Byrne, who is an artist as well as a writer, maintain a home in the Scottish Highlands, an hour north of Inverness. They have twin children, Honor and Xavier, who were three years old in 2001. When John Clark asked her their sexes, Swinton answered, "They are all variety of sexes. They have the full range." — J.H.

Suggested Reading: *Boston Globe* p87 June 27, 1993, with photo; *Harper's Bazaar* p161+ Feb. 2000, with photo; *Interview* p46+ Aug. 2001, with photos; *Los Angeles Times* p12 June 25, 1993, with photo; *Los Angeles Times* (on-line)

Aug. 5, 2001; *New York Times* IX p4 June 6, 1993, II p13+ Aug. 5, 2001, with photos; *Rolling Stone* p89 June 24, 1993, p111 Aug. 16, 2001, with photo; *US Weekly* p52+ Sep. 3, 2001, with photo; *Village Voice* p62 Apr. 7, 1992, with photo, p82 Apr. 29, 1997, with photo

Selected Films: *Caravaggio*, 1986; *Egomania—Insel ohne Hoffnung*, 1986; *Aria*, 1987; *Friendship's Death*, 1987; *The Last of England*, 1987;*Degrees of Blindness*, 1988; *Andere Ende der Welt*, 1988; *War Requiem*, 1989; *The Garden*, 1990; *The Party: Nature Morte*, 1991; *Edward II*, 1991; *Orlando*, 1992; *Man to Man*, 1992; *Blue*, 1993; *Wittgenstein*, 1993; *Remembrance of Things Fast: True Stories Visual Lies*, 1994; *Female Perversions*, 1996; *Conceiving Ada*, 1997; *Love Is the Devil*, 1998; *The Protagonists*, 1998; *The War Zone*, 1999; *The Beach*, 2000; *Possible Worlds*, 2000; *The Deep End*, 2001

Jenny Potter/Courtesy of New Press

Syal, Meera

1962(?)– Writer; actress; comedian. Address: c/o New Press, 450 W. 41st St., Sixth Fl., New York, NY 10036

When at first opportunity didn't come knocking on her door, Meera Syal went down the path to meet it. As a college student studying drama, Syal wrote a one-woman play to give herself the kind of meaty role she wasn't getting in her drama program. Since then, she has found success in the highly competitive fields of acting and writing. Syal has appeared in many plays and television shows, among them a hit comedy series, *Goodness Gracious Me*, in which she has a starring role; written an award-winning movie; and authored two critically acclaimed novels. An Asian native of Great Britain, Syal has translated her own experiences into art, finding rich, often comic material in the collision of cultures that defines contemporary British life.

Meera Syal was born to Indian immigrants in about 1962 in the British Midlands village of Essington. "People are often surprised when I say that I grew up in a place where some houses actually didn't have running water even, or none of the houses had inside toilets or bathrooms, that there was only one bus to town a day and if you missed it you had to walk," Syal told Griff Rhys Jones in an interview for the BBC's *Bookworm* program, archived briefly on-line. "And they go: 'Oh my god,' you know, 'where were you living, in the depths of the Punjab?' And I say: 'No, no, it was Wolverhampton, or pretty near there.'" Syal's parents came to Britain in the wake of India's independence and partitioning, in 1947. As a first-generation British Asian, Syal spent her childhood navigating the social currents of her small town and the "little India" that her parents preserved in their home.

Syal has cited the 1979 Southall uprising as the crystallizing event in the development of her own identity. The uprising was triggered when the National Front, a far-right, anti-immigration group, held a march through Southall, a West London neighborhood whose residents are mainly immigrants from Punjab, which straddles Pakistan and India. In the *World Press Review* (February 1995), Syal recalled that as a teenager, "watching news footage of Asian youths breaking down police barriers, Indian grannies throwing chili powder in police dogs' eyes, and the shocked faces of the National Front members who had thought marching over a few passive Pakis would be a doddle [meaning 'a very easy thing to do'], I knew for the first time I was not alone and I did belong." In an interview published in *New Statesman and Society* (April 19, 1996), Syal declared that for all British Asians, the event marked "the end of our image as victims, the beginning of a new pride in ourselves."

From the age of 11 through her graduation, Syal attended Queen Mary's High School for Girls, in Walsall, near Wolverhampton. She performed very well on the exams given in Great Britain to determine qualification for university admission—so well that she could have studied medicine, as her parents hoped, or attended Oxford University. Instead, Syal chose to enroll at Manchester University, in England, and major in English and drama. Her parents accepted her decision; at the same time, she recalled in an interview posted on *Caroline's Comedy Base* (on-line) in 2000, her father offered her some strong advice: "Whatever you do, be bloody good at it, better than the white person next to you," he told her. "That's the way it is."

Syal did not do much acting in college, because, she has said, she was rarely given good parts. Taking matters into her own hands, she created a role for herself, in the form of a one-woman monologue that she wrote with her friend Jacqui Shapiro. Called *One of Us*, the play is about a young Indian girl who runs away from home with the goal of becoming an actress. She rejects her Indian heritage and becomes obsessed with a white friend, Carol—an experience similar to what Syal herself had gone through earlier. "There was a long time that I wanted to have blonde hair, be called Tracey and go out with boys," she is quoted as saying on *Caroline's Comedy Base*. Syal's performances in *One of Us* on campus quickly attracted attention. The play won the National Student Drama Award, and Syal received a performance award from Yorkshire Television for "outstanding personal achievement." In 1984 Syal took *One of Us* to the Edinburgh Fringe Festival, in Scotland, where she won the Scottish Critics' Award for the most promising performance. A London theater director who saw Syal on stage offered her a professional acting job and, with it, a chance to earn membership in the actors' union. So, after she earned a bachelor's degree, with joint honors in English and drama, in 1984, Syal put aside her plans for graduate school and moved to London, where she began performing in the famously innovative works staged at the Royal Court Theatre. During the next seven years, Syal appeared in such contemporary works as the satirical play *Serious Money*, by Caryl Churchill, and the film *Sammy and Rosie Get Laid*, written by Hanif Kureishi and directed by Stephen Frears, as well as in such traditional works as Federico García Lorca's *Blood Wedding* and Henrik Ibsen's *Peer Gynt*.

Though Syal knew she was fortunate to be making a living as an actress, she soon began to have doubts about the politics of race in the theater. In a single week of auditioning, she recalled in an article for the London *Observer* (October 9, 1994) that was excerpted in *World Press Review* (February 1995), Syal had been asked to play "two victims of arranged marriage, three downtrodden shopkeepers' wives, four harassed National Health Service doctors, and a woman in an ad for a government retraining scheme," all stereotypical images of Asians in Britain. After this experience, Syal wrote, "the word tokenism began to flutter around my head." At a time in British society when issues of racism were coming to the forefront, and when British theater institutions were attempting to become more ethnically diverse, Syal knew that being an Asian female set her apart from most other young actresses looking for work. "I'd hate it if I was included in something because I was Indian rather than that I was good enough for the part," Syal told Carole Woddis for *Plays and Players* (March 1990). "But actually nobody has to do that now because there are so many good black and Asian performers around." Syal added that she thought most audience members would be willing to suspend their disbelief if faced with, say, an Asian Ophelia (a character from Shakespeare's drama *Hamlet*, which is set in Denmark). Nevertheless, Syal began to resent the "niggling whisper that 'you only got the job because you are Asian,'" as she wrote for the *World Press Review*. Moreover, she began to tire of the confining parts she was being offered. "Most of the roles were written with the noblest intentions, by white writers wanting to redress [Asians'] previous invisibility," Syal wrote. "But playing eternally noble, hard-done-by victims is somewhat limiting; rounded characters and real people have layers, make mistakes. . . . That is why I started writing."

In 1988, while out of work for nine months, Syal wrote three plays—*Black Silk*, *Citizens*, and *Tandoori Nights*. Then she was recruited by BBC producers who were seeking a new television script written by an Asian woman. The result was Syal's *My Sister Wife*, a three-part series that lampooned traditional and modern ideas of marriage. Syal acted in the lead role, and ever since she has been juggling careers as an actress, comedian, and writer. In an interview published on *Caroline's Comedy Base*, Syal said that she finds writing "lonely and hard" and acting, by comparison, "pure joy." But writing gives Syal a chance to overturn conventional views about a "typical" Asian woman's role. As she was quoted as saying on *Caroline's Comedy Base*, "The pleasure of writing as an Asian woman is the pleasure of exploding stereotypes."

Syal's next big project was writing the screenplay for *Bhaji on the Beach* (1993). The first feature film of both Syal and its director, Gurinder Chadha (an Englishwoman of Indian descent), *Bhaji on the Beach* follows nine Asian women from the working-class city of Birmingham in the course of a day's outing at a seaside resort. The women make discoveries about one another's lives—one woman has run away from her abusive husband, for example, and another is unexpectedly pregnant, by a black boyfriend. In the *New York Times* (May 22, 1994), Ann Hornaday described the movie as a hybrid of British and Asian culture, as is *bhaji*, an Indian snack food popular in Britain. The film, Hornaday wrote, is indebted both to the British social-realist tradition, which features working-class characters dealing with life's problems, and to the more allegorical, broad style of Indian storytelling. *Bhaji on the Beach* became a quiet hit after being shown at international film festivals, and it received an Evening Standard British Film Award nomination for best screenplay. Syal next wrote and starred in a short film, *It's Not Unusual* (1995), about a cab driver who is obsessed with the British rock star Tom Jones. *It's Not Unusual* won the 1995 award for best short film from the British Academy of Film and Television Arts.

Syal's first book, *Anita and Me*, was published in 1996. Like many first novels, it is loosely based on its author's childhood experiences. The story's narrator, Meena Kumar, is a daughter of Punjabi immigrants who live in a British mining town. At nine years of age, Meena is disdainful of her prim, obedient Indian cousins and longs to wear miniskirts and makeup, as her white friends do. Most of all, Meena wants to earn the respect of the white, 12-year-old Anita, the local wild child, a daughter of town outcasts and thus—like Meena—an outsider. Described by Sunil Iyengar in the *Washington Post* (April 6, 1997) as female counterparts of Tom Sawyer and Huckleberry Finn, respectively, Meena and Anita succeed in stirring up mischief and finding adventure in their small town. Their relationship changes after Anita hits puberty and takes up with the local bad boy, who is implicated in the beating of an Indian banker. Caught between her oppressive family ("I felt I was drowning in a sea of rustling saris, clinking gold jewelry and warm, brown, overpowering flesh," Syal has Meena complain, as quoted by Iyengar) and the emerging racism of the town's whites, Meena eventually finds her own path to maturity. *Anita and Me* was widely lauded as an impressive debut, winning the Betty Trask Award for fiction and making it to the short list for the London *Guardian*'s fiction prize. Syal, who has been commissioned to write a screenplay based on the book, has said that she has been approached by many British Asians who claim to recognize their own childhoods in Meena's. "It's like we were all going through it but nobody had actually sat down and talked about it and set it down," Syal told Rhys Jones.

Syal wrote her second novel, *Life Isn't All Ha Ha Hee Hee* (2000), while at home caring for her newborn daughter. The story is about three Indian women, friends since childhood, who, now in their late 20s, are grappling with questions of family, marriage, and career. The nice but homely Chila, to everyone's surprise, marries the most eligible bachelor around; Sunita, a former law student and activist, has become an overweight and underappreciated housewife and mother; Tania is a high-powered television executive with an English boyfriend. "I wanted to write a book about women of my age and my generation, the flip side of Bridget Jones—not young, free, and single, but in a long-term relationship, with kids," Syal told Fiona Morrow in an interview for the now-defunct on-line publication *NeonLit*, referring to the narrator of Helen Fielding's best-selling 1998 novel, *Bridget Jones's Diary*. "It's the compromises involved and whether the grass is greener—all the sort of stuff that everybody I knew was going through." The friendship of Sunita, Chila, and Tania is put to a test when Tania makes a documentary about her friends to illustrate aspects of contemporary Indian life. The documentary, and its production, exposes the stress fractures in all their lives, and Syal evoked the ensuing fallout with humor and compassion, according to the many laudatory reviews of the novel.

Syal is most famous for her appearances on the smash-hit British television comedy series *Goodness Gracious Me*. The show was the brainchild of the young producer Anil Gupta, who called upon Syal and other Asian actors and comedians to help him convince his boss that an all-Asian comedy show had merit; until then, Gupta told a reporter for the *Guardian* (February 20, 1999, on-line), the phrase "Asian comedy" was considered an oxymoron. Syal and her collaborators brainstormed to come up with a live test-performance in a London studio. "It didn't start out with an agenda to explain our culture, or to show people how funny Asians are," Syal said during the *Guardian* interview. "We didn't try to do things demographically. We wanted to do a show that made us laugh." Given the green light, *Goodness Gracious Me* aired first on radio, in 1996; it was launched as a television series the next season. Much of the comedy operates by inversion: for example, one famous sketch, "Going Out for an English," reverses features of the typically British activity of loading up on pints of beer and then "going out for an Indian [meal]" by portraying a group of drunken men from Bombay at an English restaurant, harassing the white waiter and boastfully ordering the blandest food on the menu; another, which pokes fun at the behavior of British tourists in India, depicts Indian students on holiday in London, where they complain about the beggars in the street and the bad food and insist that in order to see the "real England" you have to go to the villages. The comedy regards the foibles of British Asian society as fair game, too; one sketch, which mocked the holy fire at a Hindu wedding ceremony by calling it a "fondue," angered some Asian viewers. In her role as the Bollywood gossip columnist Smita Smitten, Showbiz Kitten, Syal has become known throughout Great Britain and has helped to make *Goodness Gracious Me* a mainstream hit among Asians and non-Asians alike. Many British commentators regard the series as a tool of social change—"the oil of race relations," as a headline in the London *Times* put it, as quoted by the *Guardian* reporter. The show's creators have said that they are not trying to be political but seek only to make people laugh; Syal, in her discussions about the program, focuses on Asian comedy as a sign of confidence and well-being. "I think being able to be humourous about who you are, and that dilemma, is a sign that you're at ease in the end with who you are," she told Rhys Jones. Ironically, starring in an Asian comedy show has made Syal more aware of her Britishness than ever before; she told the *Caroline's Comedy Base* interviewer, a "fantastic sense of humour and . . . irony" is the best thing that England has given her.

Currently, Syal is writing the book for Andrew Lloyd Webber's next musical project, tentatively called "Bombay Dreams." The constant support of her family, she has said, has enabled her to pursue her writing and acting careers. She told Carole Woddis, "The only reason I've been able to go out and make forays and be one of the few Asian women to do what I'm doing is because I've always had

people at home who say 'we believe in you, we love you.'" In 1998 she was named a Member of the Order of the British Empire (MBE) on Queen Elizabeth's annual birthday honors list. — M.A.H.

Suggested Reading: *Caroline's Comedy Base* (on-line), 2000; (London) *Guardian* (on-line) Feb. 20, 1999; *Plays & Players* p14+ Mar. 1990, with photos; *New Statesman & Society* p21 Apr. 19, 1996, with photo; *World Press Review* p56 Feb. 1995; *Contemporary Authors* vol. 160, 1998

Selected Written Works: Novels—*Anita and Me* (1996), *Life Isn't All Ha Ha Hee Hee* (2000); Screenplays—*Bhaji on the Beach* (1993), *It's Not Unusual* (1995); Television—*My Sister Wife* (1988)

Selected Acting Credits: Theater—*One of Us*, 1983–84; *Serious Money*, 1987; *Peer Gynt*, 1990; Television—*Absolutely Fabulous*, 1994; *Keeping Mum*, 1998; *Goodness Gracious Me*, 1996–99; Film—*Sammie and Rosie Get Laid*, 1987; *Beautiful Thing*, 1996; *Girls' Night*, 1997

Tajiri, Satoshi

Aug. 28, 1965– Video-game designer; creator of Pokémon. Address: c/o Nintendo of Japan, 60 Fukuine Kamitakamatsu-cho, Higashiyama-ku, Kyoto 605, Japan

"When you're a kid and get your first bike, you want to go somewhere you've never been before," the creator of the Pokémon video games, Satoshi Tajiri, remarked to Shuzo Ogushi for *Time Asia* (November 22, 1999, on-line). "That's like Pokémon. Everybody shares the same experience, but everybody wants to take it someplace else. And you can do that." Although the electronic-games manufacturer Nintendo agreed only reluctantly to release the first Pokémon (short for "Pocket Monsters") games—designed by Tajiri—in Japan in the mid-1990s, the games became an overwhelming success. It is now estimated that the Pokémon industry, which has come to include books, movies, card games, toys, and an animated TV series as well as video games, has generated over $5 billion in sales worldwide, more than the hugely profitable *Star Wars* films and their related products have earned in nearly 25 years. Based on real or legendary plants and animals, the Pokémon characters are cute in appearance but exist mainly to fight one another. The combination of those two qualities has been cited as part of the reason why children, especially boys ages five through 12, have become obsessed with the game and its various offshoots. Tajiri disagrees with those who argue that the Pokémon craze has succeeded in little

Shuzo Oguchi

more than luring kids into collecting merchandise. "I think a lot about kids and what they need and want to make their lives better," he told Ogushi. "You know, the cram school industry started when I was young. There was so little time to play. During school breaks, we'd run to the arcade to play games. Right now, there isn't much time for kids to relax. So I thought of games that could help kids fill in those five- or 10-minute gaps."

Satoshi Tajiri was born in Tokyo, Japan, on August 28, 1965. He grew up in Machida, a Tokyo suburb. "The place where I grew up . . . was still rural back then," he told Shuzo Ogushi. "There were rice paddies, rivers, forests. It was full of nature. Then development started taking place, and as it grew, all the insects were driven away. I was really interested in collecting insects. Every year they would cut down trees and the population of insects would decrease. The change was so dramatic. A fishing pond would become an arcade center." Tajiri became so intent on collecting insects that he acquired the nickname "Dr. Bug." "They fascinated me," Tajiri recalled to Ogushi about his passion for insects. "For one thing, they kind of moved funny. They were odd. Every time I found a new insect, it was mysterious to me. . . . I liked coming up with new ideas. Like how to catch beetles." By observing insects after he took them home or in their own habitats, he learned, for example, that beetles hid under stones during the day. Sometimes he would find beetles under stones that he himself had placed in strategic spots. "Tiny discoveries like that made me excited," Tajiri told Ogushi.

As he got older, and the rural area where he lived became increasingly suburbanized, Tajiri spent more and more time in the local video arcades playing such games as Space Invaders. In fact, he was seen playing that game so frequently that one arcade gave him a Space Invaders machine to take home with him. He especially liked playing Donkey Kong, designed by Shigeru Miyamoto. (Miyamoto joined Nintendo as the company's first staff designer in 1977. In addition to the immensely popular Donkey Kong, he created the phenomenally successful Super Mario Brothers. He was also responsible for such innovations as scrolling screens and hidden secrets within games. "He's always been my role model," Tajiri told Shuzo Ogushi. "He's a mentor for my heart.") Tajiri's father, a Nissan car salesman, was far from pleased by his son's interests, particularly when the boy started missing classes in high school to go to the arcade. Tajiri recalled to Ogushi that his parents wept over his all-encompassing love for video games and that they did not expect him to go far in life.

Refusing to enroll at a university, Tajiri studied electronics at the Tokyo National College of Technology. Even so, he later turned down his father's offer to find him a job as an electric-utility repairman. Instead, in a time when video games received little media attention, Tajiri and some of his friends founded *Game Freak* magazine. The earliest issues, dating from 1982, were assembled with a photocopier and a stapler. When sales increased, Tajiri took the magazine to a professional printer. He incorporated *Game Freak* in 1989, naming himself CEO. Earlier, in 1981, he had won first prize in the TV Game Idea Awards held by Sega Enterprises, a prominent maker of video games.

The more Tajiri learned about video games, the more frustrated he became with their widespread lack of quality. As a result, he decided to try designing his own game. He took apart the console from a Nintendo Entertainment System to see how it worked, and then, while continuing to write about games, he developed his own software. His first game was Quinty, created in 1987 for use in the Nintendo Entertainment System and released in the U.S. as Mendel Palace. The game's plot involves a young girl whose dolls have come to life in her dream and have taken her to Mendel Palace, in doll land, where she is held captive. The player controls the girl's best friend, Bon-Bon, the only one who can save her from the dream. Bon-Bon must search through eight dollhouses before arriving at Mendel Palace; there, he is attacked by dolls, which he can defeat with the use of movable tiles. Although designed for younger children, the game becomes increasingly difficult as the player progresses through its 50 levels; a bonus of an additional 50 levels is available to players who win the game.

In 1990 Tajiri published a novel, *Catch the Parkland*, for children fond of video games. Meanwhile, he had learned about the new Nintendo Game Boy, a portable video-game system on which two players competed by hooking each of their Game Boys to a cable over which data were exchanged. That system gave Tajiri the idea for what later became Pokémon. "In Tetris, [Game Boy's] first game, the cable transmitted information about moving blocks," he told Ogushi. "That cable really got me interested. I thought of actual living organisms moving back and forth across the cable." While he was developing what would be Pokémon, other of Tajiri's games went on the market. The year 1991 brought Jerry Boy, for the Super Nintendo Entertainment System, and Yoshi's Egg, for the Nintendo Game Boy. Jerry Boy won the Character Design Award in the Multimedia Grand Prix Video Game category. Yoshi's Egg, released in the U.S. as Yoshi, is a puzzle game featuring the dinosaur from one of the popular Super Mario Brothers games; in it, the player has to help the character Marko put Yoshi's eggshell together so that Yoshi can hatch. In 1992 Tajiri's Magical Tarurunto-kun was released for use with the Sega Megadrive system, followed by Mario and Wario (1993) for the Super Nintendo Entertainment System in Japan and Pulseman (1994) for the Sega Megadrive. In 1995 Tajiri published his second book, *New Games Designing*, a guide for neophyte video-game designers.

The year 1996 saw the release of Pocket Monsters for the Nintendo Game Boy in Japan. The game involves an unusual combination of role-playing and collecting. The player controls the character Satoshi (named for the game's creator but called Ash in the U.S. version), who has to travel the world with the goal of collecting 150 Pokémon. These creatures, with names such as Pikachu, Charmander, Bulbasaur, and Odish, can be captured only after being defeated in battle by other

Pokémon. Once caught, however, the Pocket Monsters will fight for the player and can evolve into more-powerful creatures. The game was released in two versions, Red and Green (Red and Blue in the U.S.), each of which contained its own set of characters; thus, in order to play the game fully, one had to trade Pocket Monsters with a player who had the cartridge for the game's other version. Pocket Monsters used Game Boy's cables; although Nintendo believed that the Game Boy, with its limited graphics capability, was becoming obsolete, they decided to release Pocket Monsters anyway. "They didn't expect much from the game," Tajiri told Ogushi. "Game Boy's popularity was declining. Just when I finished the game and took it to Nintendo, I felt like a baseball player who slides into second base even though you know you're going to be out—but then it turns out you are safe." The game slowly grew in popularity in Japan, where many video-game players did not have the money to buy expensive systems. When word got out that there was a 151st Pokémon hidden in some of the games, sales skyrocketed as players sought the character, called Mew. Unless one happened to purchase the games in which it had been hidden, "you [couldn't] ever get a Mew without trading for it," as Tajiri told Ogushi. "It created a myth about the game, that there was an invisible character out there. Someone gives me Mew, then I give Mew to you, then you pass it on. Introducing a new character like that created a lot of rumors and myths about the game. It kept the interest alive." The game won Tajiri the Japan Software Grand Prize as well as the CESA Award (given by the Computer Entertainment Software Association).

Sales of the Pocket Monsters soon led to the development of a Japanese animated TV series, plush dolls, and a series of trading cards that became as successful as the video games. The trading cards were part of an additional game system, in which players would pit the characters shown on their cards against one another, using an official set of rules. The phenomenon resulted in controversy when a December 17, 1999 episode of the animated television show featured a series of flashing lights that led to irritated eyes, vomiting, and convulsions in numerous viewers, more than 700 of whom were rushed to hospitals. That episode did little to curtail the popularity of Tajiri's creation, however, and in 1999 Pocket Monsters arrived in the United States—where it was marketed as Pokémon—setting off another wave of excitement. Sales of the video games were higher than anyone predicted, and analysts in the industry, in which trends come and go in a matter of months, were surprised when toy-store owners had difficulty keeping trading cards in stock almost a year after their initial release. Trading became such a popular pastime among young boys that fights sometimes broke out over cards, and some school administrators banned or restricted the use of the cards or the Game Boy cartridges on school grounds. Hasbro paid Nintendo $325 million for the rights to market the Pokémon toys in the U.S., and the slogan "Gotta Catch 'em All" increased the demand for the products. In its first weekend of release in the United States, Pokémon: The First Movie (1999) earned over $32.4 million; it had grossed over $85 million by the time it left theaters. Pikachu, the cute yellow mouse whose weapon is a strong electric charge, is the main character in the animated series (in which each Pokémon can say only one word—its name) and soon became the favorite with Pokémon fans. (A dubbed version of the show has aired in the United States since 1998.) Like those of all Pokémon, Pikachu's name comes from the Japanese language. As Tajiri told Ogushi, "'Pika' is the sound Japanese say an electric spark makes. And 'chu' is the sound a mouse makes. So Pikachu is like an electric mouse."

Tajiri strongly disagrees with the complaint from some groups, particularly in the United States, that the games are too violent for children. "I was really careful in making monsters faint rather than die," he explained to Ogushi. "I think that young people playing games have an abnormal concept about dying. They start to lose and say, 'I'm dying.' It's not right for kids to think about a concept of death that way. They need to treat death with more respect." Since the release of the Pokémon games in the U.S., Tajiri has been busy creating variations of them. "I sleep 12 hours and then work 24 hours," he told Ogushi in 1999. "I've worked those irregular hours for the past three years. It's better to stay up day and night to come up with ideas. I usually get inspiration for game designing by working this schedule." American additions to the Pokémon catalog include Pokémon Yellow, Pokémon Gold, and Pokémon Silver. The latter two both introduced the same additional 250 characters. For the Nintendo 64 video-game system, two Pokémon Stadium games have been released; players of those games can pit graphically enhanced versions of Pokémon against each other in an arena setting. In addition, the more relaxed Pokémon Snap, in which players attempt to take the best pictures of shy, wild Pokémon, became quite popular. The year 2001 saw the release of the first color Pokémon game for the Game Boy—Pokémon Crystal, which is a visually improved version of Pokémon Gold and Pokémon Silver, complete with new challenges. In Japan there is currently a game in which one can simply play with Pikachu or, with the help of a microphone, communicate with him.

Tajiri has been described as an unimposing, shy man with a soft voice. In Japan, where game designers are treated as celebrities, the Pokémon creator notoriously shuns media attention. In 1991 he was a guest speaker at the Vantan Design Institute, and in 1992 he became a judge at the Multimedia Grand Prix Video Game Section. Tajiri has said that if he had not succeeded as a game designer, he would have liked to work in animation. Although sales of Pokémon games have slowed since they were first introduced, they continue to sell well and have led to several similarly themed creations, such as Digimon. The latest Pokémon motion picture, *Pokémon 3: The Movie* (2001), grossed over $17 million in the United States alone. — G.O.

Suggested Reading: *Time* p80+ Nov. 22, 1999, with photos; *Time Asia* (on-line) Nov. 22, 1999

Rob Lewine/Outline Press

Tarter, Jill Cornell

Jan. 16, 1944– Astronomer; astrophysicist.
Address: SETI Institute, 2035 Landings Dr.,
Mountain View, CA 94043

Since the beginning of her education and throughout her career, the astronomer Jill Cornell Tarter has always taken the road less traveled. In high school she was the only female student to plow through upper-level science courses. At Cornell University in the early 1960s, she was the single female engineering student in her class of 2,000. Her graduate work in astrophysics at the University of California at Berkeley broke new ground in the study of "brown dwarfs" (a term she coined): small stars whose cores never reach a temperature that would permit nuclear fusion. Finally, as the director of, and principal investigator for, the Search for Extraterrestrial Intelligence (SETI) Institute, she is passionately committed to a question that the scientific community has largely dismissed: Are we alone in the universe? "This is the oldest unanswered question of the human species—I can't imagine anything more important than trying to do an experiment that might answer the question," Tarter said to an interviewer for the Web site of the

Jodrell Bank Observatory at the University of Manchester, in England. "We happen to live in the first era that can try the experiment."

Tarter's quest to find extraterrestrial intelligence has taken her to radio telescopes all over the world, from the Australian outback to Puerto Rico. The SETI program she directs, Project Phoenix, is designed to detect electromagnetic signals coming from an artificial source in outer space. Linda Grace-Kobas reported for the *Cornell Chronicle* (June 26, 1997) that Tarter described "SETI" as a "misnomer." "We can't find intelligence per se," Tarter explained, "but we can look for technology. If we can pick up radio signals, that remains the strongest argument for life on that planet." The current goal of Project Phoenix is to focus "on 1,000 sun-like stars in the Milky Way galaxy," as Irene Brown wrote for *Discovery* (September 9–17, 1998, on-line), referring to the huge assemblage of stars that contains the sun. "Stars that are too big, too hot, too young or too far away are easily eliminated. The cuts include most visible stars, which are typically white-hot distant stars or super-sized red giant stars that would consume any planetary companions." On the question of whether there is life elsewhere in the universe, Tarter told Irene Brown, "I can accept if the answer is no, that we are the only intelligent life forms. I just want to know what the answer is."

The only child of Betty and Richard Cornell, Tarter was born Jill Cornell on January 16, 1944 and grew up in Eastchester (some sources say New Rochelle), New York, a suburb of New York City. Tarter remembers stargazing with her father in the Florida Keys, where they visited her aunt and uncle, as she recalled to Bart Mills for *Biography* (July 2000): "When Dad and I walked on the beach at night, he taught me the constellations 'in case you ever have to find your way around the sky.'" At the age of eight, Tarter, a self-proclaimed tomboy who spent every weekend camping, hiking, and fishing with her father, balked at the idea of "learning to do what girls do," as she told Kenneth Chang for *ABCNews.com* (June 28, 2000). "I didn't see why you couldn't do both," she said to Bart Mills. "[My father] must have been startled, because he said, 'Of course, you can do anything you set your mind to, if you work hard enough.' That's when I announced I'd be an engineer. I knew it was a male profession held in high esteem." Tarter told the *Washington Post* in an on-line chat (March 24, 1999), "Both my mom and my dad encouraged me to try anything I was interested in doing," the only rule being "that I had to finish what I started." At age 12 she lost her father and his unswerving support. "After he died, I had one mindset," she recalled to Bart Mills: "[to] do things that would have made him proud."

Tarter began the "science track" of academic course work in elementary school, remaining on it through high school, even though she was the only girl to do so. (Because she was a drum majorette for her high school, she turned down the opportunity to take special Saturday science classes at Columbia University, in Manhattan.) In 1961 she matriculated at Cornell University, in Ithaca, New York, where she faced her first academic obstacle: she was denied the scholarship for descendants of Ezra Cornell, for whom the university was named, because of her gender. Fortunately, the Procter & Gamble Co. awarded her an engineering scholarship, making her the first woman to earn this honor. Tarter's years at Cornell often involved battling for respect in a male-dominated field; she was the only woman among 300 engineering students in her class. In her junior year she married Bruce Tarter, who had been her teaching assistant in freshman physics; they had a daughter, Shana, and later divorced. Procter & Gamble attempted without success to rescind their scholarship offer, claiming that as a married woman Tarter would never use her education.

The course at Cornell that determined the direction of her career was a graduate seminar in star formation, which was, as she related to Leigh Weimers for the *San Jose Mercury News* (January 3, 1999, on-line), "a kind of 'Eureka!' experience." As a result, she pursued graduate studies in astrophysics at the University of California at Berkeley. After earning a Ph.D. degree, she hoped to become an astronaut, but NASA (the National Aeronautics and Space Administration) rejected her application. "I thought I was a really good candidate," she told *ABCNews.com*, "but it may have had something to do with being a single mother and having a young daughter." She worked for NASA in a different capacity, by continuing her research on brown dwarfs at the Ames Research Center, in Moffett Field, California. She began work on SETI at the beginning of the project, which was then a very low-budget affair. Using Puerto Rico's Arecibo radio telescope from 1979 to 1981, Tarter listened for incoming signals from 200 stars similar to the sun, but she detected nothing unusual.

Why are Tarter and her colleagues convinced that other intelligent life exists somewhere in our galaxy? One reason is the Drake Equation, named after Frank Drake, who founded the SETI Institute with Tarter in 1984. In 1961 Drake formulated an equation to quantify the likelihood that there are other civilizations in the universe; the equation points overwhelmingly to that possibility. Despite heated controversy in the scientific community, Tarter and other physicists and astronomers, including her second husband, Jack Welch, have set out to prove the validity of the Drake Equation by finding an artificial signal from elsewhere in the universe, which would indicate the existence of extraterrestrial intelligence. In 1992 the SETI Institute was awarded a $12 million share of NASA's $14 billion budget to conduct a 10-year "targeted search," which involves listening for signals from neighboring stars as well as conducting an "all-sky" search of much wider scope. Tarter and her colleagues faced a challenge in 1993, when U.S. senator Richard Byran of Nevada achieved his goal of cutting funding for SETI. SETI supporters, caught off guard, had not had sufficient time to organize support in Congress, and as Andrew Chaikin reported in *Popular Science* (December 1995), some senators voting on the issue "had no idea what it was about." Chaikin quoted Senator Barbara Mikulski of Maryland, a longtime SETI supporter, as saying that the SETI cause had failed because of "the giggle factor." In one illustration of this, a press release from Bryan's office boasted that he had "single-handedly stopped 'the Great Martian Chase,'" as Chaikin wrote.

Undaunted, within a year the SETI Institute established Project Phoenix. (Previously, the project was known as the High Resolution Microwave Survey.) Named for the mythical bird that comes back to life after being burned to ashes, Project Phoenix was to be a private venture, backed by major figures in science and technology, among them William R. Hewlett and David Packard, co-founders of the computer company Hewlett Packard; Paul Allen, the co-founder of Microsoft; and Gordon Moore, the chairman of Intel. Hewlett-Packard's vice president for research, Bernard M. ("Barney") Oliver, also made a significant contribution, as a member of the institute's board of trustees and later, after his retirement from Hewlett-Packard, as the institute's chief engineer. In 1997, after Oliver's death, in recognition of her scientific achievements, Tarter became the first person to be appointed to an institute chair endowed in his name. Project Phoenix, which Tarter directs, has funded trips to listening outposts—in particular, the Parkes Radio Telescope, in Australia; the Jodrell Bank Observatory; and the Arecibo Observatory, in Puerto Rico. The group has also used telescopes in West Virginia and at the Very Large Array (VLA), a group of 27 huge antennas in New Mexico. Despite the change in funding sources, the SETI Institute's method of operation remains the same. As Tarter explained to *People* (November 16, 1997), rather than launching spacecraft to search for other intelligent life (a project for which the technology is not available, because of the great distances involved), "We're listening because electromagnetic signals travel at the speed of light, and this is the fastest you can go. . . . [We're listening] at microwave frequencies from about 1,000 to 10,000 megahertz. That is the band in which the background noise is the lowest, where from the surface of our planet we have the quietest window on the universe. Even so, the earth, with its airport radar, garage-door openers and cellular phones, for example, creates a lot of microwave noise. Soon we may not be able to hear above our own din."

SETI received renewed attention in 1997, with the release of the film *Contact*, based on the 1985 novel by Carl Sagan and starring Jodie Foster. Tarter was widely reported to be Sagan's model for Dr. Ellie Arroway, Foster's character. But, Bart Mills wrote, "unlike Jodie Foster in *Contact*, Tarter doesn't sit out among giant dishes with headphones listening to static. . . . She actually spends her time organizing and interpreting the tons of data that SETI collects [from its field sites]." In her interview with Andrew Chaikin, Tarter scoffed at any dreamy interpretations of what she does: "The romanticism went out of this, in some sense, a long time ago. This is hard work. . . . Tenaciousness is probably more the ingredient than romance." She has acknowledged, however, that she shares characteristics with the fictional Ellie Arroway: "Carl [Sagan] wrote a book about a woman who does what I do, not necessarily about me," she said on an *ABCNews.com* on-line chat (June 26, 1996). "The similarities result from the fact that women my age who managed to make it into a scientific field dominated by men often have very similar backgrounds."

Crucial to the SETI Institute's quest is the collection of evidence. Tarter has firmly denied that an extraterrestrial signal, if discovered, would be hidden from the public, as some have worried. In response to questions posed on *ABCNews.com* ("Why is SETI a more respectable endeavor than the study of abduction experiences and UFOs?" and "If a signal were to be detected signifying intelligent life elsewhere in the universe, do you think the public would ever learn of it?"), Tarter wrote, "The problem [with UFOs] is that there is no credible evidence. . . . As for SETI, we go to great lengths to be credible. We will seek an independent verification [from another site] of any signal we think might be real, and after an announcement we will make available all discovery records and data so that people can make their own analysis and decisions. . . . We are connected to the Internet for our observations, and there is no way to keep such information secret, nor would we want to. Our fear is the reverse—that it will leak out too fast, before we have had time to thoroughly check it out." An example of such a scenario, she wrote, occurred in 1997, when SETI's attention was caught by a signal that turned out to have emanated from a spacecraft of earthly origin. "We had a call from *The New York Times* while we were still doing confirmation procedures!" In collecting evidence, patience is vital. Tarter has spent almost her entire career listening for a sign from space, but, as she told Kenneth Chang, "I don't wake up and say I'm going to detect a signal today." "I am extremely optimistic that signals will be detected," she said to Donald L. Rheem for the *Christian Science Monitor* (June 3, 1986). "I am not sure that it will be in my lifetime." Nevertheless, a bottle of champagne is on hand wherever she listens to the sky.

The summer of 2000 brought promising news for the SETI Institute and its researchers. Paul Allen contributed $11.5 million to the institute so that it could build and use its own telescope array at Hat Creek Observatory, in California. Collectively, the hundreds of radio telescopes, organized in a grid, will be called the Allen Telescope Array, whose first project will extend through 2005. Tarter told Reuters, "We're overjoyed, and we're ready to move ahead."

Tarter's honors include two public service awards from NASA; a Lifetime Achievement Award from the organization Women in Aerospace, in 1989; the 1997 Person of the Year Award from the Chabot Observatory, in Oakland, California; and a 1998 Women of Achievement Award from the *San Jose Mercury News*/Women's Fund. In her leisure time, Tarter enjoys going dancing with her husband or piloting their small plane. "Her ultimate dream," William J. Broad reported in the *New York Times* (September 28, 1998), "is to build an observatory on the far side of the Moon, free of earthly interference, scanning the heavens for an unfamiliar hello. She wants to be there herself, at the controls." — K.S.

Suggested Reading: *Biography* p86+ July 2000, with photos; *People* p119+ Nov. 16, 1992, with photos; *Popular Science* p82+ Dec. 1995, with photos

Courtesy of the U.S. Congress

Tauscher, Ellen O.

Nov. 15, 1951– United States Representative from California. Address: 1122 Longworth House Office Bldg., Washington, DC 20515

"I grew up in a small town where my father managed a grocery store and my mother worked as a secretary," Ellen O. Tauscher, a Democrat who represents California's 10th Congressional District in the U.S. House of Representatives, wrote for *American Dreams* (on-line). "They taught me self-discipline, perseverance and dedication to the principle that individual responsibility must be accomplished by community concern and respect for others." The first member of her family to attend college, Tauscher has found success in areas where others saw only obstacles. At only 25 she became one of the first—and youngest—women to earn a seat on the New York Stock Exchange. After more than a decade in investment banking, she relocated to California and, spurred by her quest to find child care for her daughter, founded the ChildCare Registry, a national research service dedicated to assisting parents and child-care facilities in exploring the backgrounds of child-care workers prior to their being hired. Tauscher's involvement in California politics began when she worked as a co-chair of Dianne Feinstein's successful campaigns for the U.S. Senate in 1992 (in a special election) and 1994. At the urging of congressional Democrats George Miller and Anna Eshoo, Tauscher launched her own campaign for the U.S. House of Representatives in 1996, winning a seat in the district comprising the East Bay suburbs of San Francisco and Oakland. She was reelected to that position in 1998 and 2000. A centrist Democrat, Tauscher supports abortion rights, gun-safety laws, government-mandated environmental protection, and civil-rights legislation; she has also espoused fiscal caution and pushed for tax relief.

Tauscher was born Ellen O'Kane on November 15, 1951 in East Newark, New Jersey. Honoring a commitment to her family, who had made sacrifices to put aside money for her education, she attended Seton Hall University, a Catholic institution in South Orange, New Jersey. Although she received a B.S. degree in special education, in 1974, after graduation Tauscher went to New York City to work for Bache Securities, earning a seat on the New York Stock Exchange a short time later. During her 14 years on Wall Street, Tauscher was also employed by the firm Drexel Burnham Lambert, and she worked with Arthur Levitt Jr. to improve the American Stock Exchange during the period when he directed that association (1978–89). She married William Tauscher, a computer executive, in 1989, and the couple later moved to the San Francisco area. After the Tauschers' daughter, Katherine, was born, Ellen Tauscher applied her financial skills to the ChildCare Registry, Inc., the business she started in 1992 to provide background information on child-care workers; as Claire Collins wrote for the New York Times (March 17, 1994), Tauscher had been made uneasy by her own inability to obtain information about prospective nannies for her daughter. In 1996, as a resource for parents, Tauscher wrote with Kathleen Candy The ChildCare Sourcebook: The Complete Guide to Finding and Managing Nannies, Au Pairs, Babysitters, Day Care, and After-School Programs.

After twice helping to secure a Senate seat for Democrat Dianne Feinstein, Tauscher announced her candidacy for the congressional seat representing California's 10th District. In an upset victory, she narrowly defeated Bill Baker, a two-term Republican, using her own money to advertise her

commitment to fiscal responsibility, a balanced federal budget, and deficit reduction while also supporting traditionally Democratic causes such as abortion rights and environmental safety. The deciding factor in the Tauscher-Baker race, Congressional Quarterly (January 4, 1997) speculated, may have been the candidates' opposing views on gun control. Baker had voted against a ban on certain kinds of assault weapons, while Tauscher was in favor of such a ban; assault-style weapons had been used in a 1993 massacre in San Francisco, a tragedy whose impact was felt in the 10th District. Tauscher's own view of the race was that eschewing wasteful government spending while maintaining programs for senior citizens, children, and the environment was precisely the right approach in a bid to represent a well-to-do suburban electorate, and she was therefore not surprised by her election in a district that had formerly voted Republican. "They want [to have] their cake and eat it, too," she explained to Congressional Quarterly soon after her victory. "And they can have it with me." Tauscher's moderate approach proved popular in subsequent campaigns, and by the time those races occurred she had internalized her district's attitude toward government, as she explained on a BayArea.com chat (August 15, 2000): "My constituents are hard-working families who want a government that is out of their way, but on their side."

In January 1997 Tauscher took her pro-business, centrist-Democrat ideas to Washington, D.C., where she found she had company. She joined the Blue Dog Democrats, a small coalition of moderate-to-conservative members of her party who worked quietly to drum up bipartisan support for balanced-budget legislation and welfare reform. During her first term, three veteran members of Congress formed the New Democrat Coalition (NDC), which Tauscher joined as well. Like the Blue Dogs, the New Dogs—as the NDC came to be known—are moderate-to-conservative Democrats with an interest in fiscal restraint; the two groups parted ways, however, on other matters. As Peter Beinart noted in Time (November 24, 1997, on-line), the NDC members represent suburban rather than rural areas, so that whereas the Blue Dogs are advocates for more-traditional industry, the NDC members are concerned with high-tech issues and the "new" economy. Also, as Beinart observed, the NDC's constituents "are essentially contented, libertarian and relativistic." Tauscher and her New Democrat colleagues have supported legislation dealing with Internet privacy and high-tech export controls, among other issues.

Although Tauscher had hoped to put her business experience to use on the House Ways and Means Committee, she was instead assigned to the Armed Services Committee and the Transportation and Infrastructure Committee, on the latter of which she replaced her former opponent, Bill Baker. Through her work on the Transportation Committee, she helped her district and the larger San

Francisco area gain funds for needed highway and transit improvements; traffic and public transportation in her suburban, commuter-packed district has always been an important issue for her constituents. Tauscher's assignment to the Armed Services Committee has allowed her to pursue her interests in nuclear security and the Department of Energy's national laboratories, which conduct research in a wide range of areas. (California's 10th District is the only one in the U.S. that houses two such facilities.) She has worked for nuclear nonproliferation throughout her time in Congress and recently called for a moratorium on polygraph testing of employees at the nuclear laboratories—tests that she believes have been administered with insufficient discrimination. Tauscher has also pushed for greater efficiency with regard to spending and more-modern business practices, including the use of updated technology, within the armed forces. "As a member of the Military Personnel Subcommittee in the U.S. House of Representatives, I believe that we need to honor our commitment to our service men and women to provide top quality health care. But as a fiscal conservative and a former businesswoman, I know that we cannot just throw more money at Tricare [the military health-care plan] in hopes of solving the problem," she wrote for the San Ramon Valley Sentinel (May 2000, on-line). Outside her committee assignments, Tauscher has applied her education and business expertise to her legislation, securing funds for aging schools and libraries and ensuring affordable child care though the ACCESS plan. (ACCESS is the acronym for the Affordable Child Care, Education, Security, and Safety Act.) She has also favored the hiring of new teachers and teacher training.

Tauscher's priorities have not changed noticeably since she was first elected to Congress. An original co-sponsor of the bill to eliminate the "marriage penalty" (a tax disadvantage for married couples), Tauscher was upset that President Bill Clinton rejected the bill and promised to support an override of the veto. She also voted to repeal the estate tax and came out in favor of campaign-finance reform. Gun control has also been a key issue for Tauscher; she supported the banning of "cop killer" bullets and assault-style weapons and advocated waiting periods and background checks for gun purchases. While expressly supportive of the right to bear arms, she explained during her BayArea.com chat, "I strongly believe it is a lot easier to childproof a gun than it is to bulletproof a kid. We need to keep firearms out of the hands of criminals and children." Women's issues have also been part of the core of Tauscher's campaigns. She has supported funding for women's health initiatives, equal pay for women, and the elimination of "the glass ceiling that impedes women in the business world," as she told iVillage.com. She has also been a staunch backer of abortion rights, going so far as to identify then–presidential candidate George W. Bush as the biggest threat to Roe v. Wade

(the Supreme Court decision legalizing abortion) during her on-line chat with Planned Parenthood (March 23, 2000).

Immediately before she was reelected in 2000, Tauscher was praised by environmental groups for her voting record in Congress as well as for the bill she sponsored to protect the Bay Area's fish and wildlife; during her second term (1999–2001), she served on the Water Resources and Environment Committee. Garnering endorsements from groups as diverse as the Farmer's Union and the Chamber of Commerce and riding her wide appeal, Tauscher won easily over her Republican opponent, with 53 percent of the vote.

Tauscher is now divorced. She and her daughter divide their time between Washington and Alamo, California. — K.S.

Suggested Reading: Congressional Quarterly p49 Jan. 4, 1997, with photo; New York Times C p2 Mar. 17, 1994; Time (on-line) Nov. 24, 1997; Foerstal, Karen. Biographical Dictionary of Congressional Women, 1999

Selected Books: The ChildCare Sourcebook: The Complete Guide to Finding and Managing Nannies, Au Pairs, Babysitters, Day Care, and After-School Programs (with Kathleen Candy), 1996

Thomson, James A.

Dec. 20, 1958– Biologist. Address: Wisconsin Regional Primate Research Center, University of Wisconsin, 1220 Capitol Ct., Madison, WI 53715

"Imagine being able to reach into the freezer, take out a cell culture, treat it with growth factors, and produce almost any tissue in the human body. Sounds like science fiction? Today, it is," Eliot Marshall wrote for the November 6, 1998 issue of Science. "But the raw material for such human tissue engineering—in the form of a type of universal cell called a 'stem' cell—is now growing in the laboratory." In 1998 the biologist James Thomson, along with his team of researchers at the University of Wisconsin, became the first scientist to develop and isolate stem cells from human embryos and use them to produce "immortal" cell lines, which would reproduce without ever becoming specific types of cells, such as blood cells or liver cells. "What makes stem cells special is that they're immortal, and they can become anything they want to be," Thomson explained to Jenifer Joseph for ABCNews.com. "Our stem cells can give rise to potentially everything [in the human body], and they never die."

The discovery of the University of Wisconsin team placed Thomson, a shy, retiring researcher, in the thick of a political and ethical debate. In order

Jeff Miller/Courtesy of the University of Wisconsin, Madison

James A. Thomson

to conduct his experiments, he had removed cells from blastocysts (one-day-old human embryos) donated by women who had created them for purposes of in vitro fertilization but no longer needed them. The embryos had not yet reached the stage of development at which they could have been implanted in women's uteri. Theoretically, blastocysts removed from cold storage at a later stage can be implanted and develop into viable human beings. Since removing stem cells kills the blastocysts, and thus destroys their potential to become viable human beings, so-called right-to-lifers oppose stem-cell research. Those who support it maintain that stem cells hold the key to curing such disorders as juvenile diabetes, Parkinson's disease, and Alzheimer's disease, among many other maladies. Prohibited from using federal funds to perform research involving human embryos, Thomson's team was supported by grants from the Wisconsin Alumni Research Foundation and the Geron Corp., a private California biotechnology firm. Still, the creation of billions of potentially useful stem cells in the laboratory led officials of the United States government to reexamine the issue of using embryonic stem cells in federally funded projects. In August 2001 President George W. Bush announced that he had decided to permit limited stem-cell experimentation.

The son of a certified public accountant and a secretary, James A. Thomson was born on December 20, 1958 in Chicago, Illinois, and raised with at least one brother in the Chicago suburb of Oak Park. As a youngster, he was drawn to science. "I think most little kids want to be a scientist," he explained to Sheryl Gay Stolberg for the *New York Times* (July 10, 2001), revealing that he and his brother had a penchant for "blowing things up." When he was a bit more mature, he drew inspiration from an uncle who worked as a rocket scientist for the National Aeronautics and Space Administration (NASA). A National Merit scholar, Thomson graduated from high school in 1977 and enrolled at the University of Illinois at Urbana-Champaign. As a biophysics major there, he was captivated by embryonic development, especially how cells of a fertilized egg developed and differentiated into particular kinds of specialized cells. His interest in the subject took him to the University of Pennsylvania, where he earned a doctoral degree in veterinary medicine in 1985 and a Ph.D. in molecular biology in 1988.

The first stem-cell experiments had begun in about 1980, with cells extracted from mice. Starting in 1991, at the Wisconsin Regional Primate Research Center, in Madison, Thomson began the process of isolating stem cells of rhesus monkeys, a species much closer to humans. Uninterested in balancing professorial duties with research, Thomson joined the primate center as a staff scientist and hoped to shore up his job security by becoming a certified veterinary pathologist. By the mid-1990s he had isolated stem cells in monkeys and had published his findings; only days later Geron Corp. offered financial support for his quest to find human embryonic stem cells. (Using private funds would permit Thomson to experiment with human blastocysts donated through fertility clinics; U.S. government funding would not allow such experimentation.) Before deciding to explore the possibility of isolating human stem cells, however, Thomson seriously pondered the ethical implications of such work, both because his research would benefit from the discarding of human embryos and because it might contribute to the future cloning of humans, a practice he does not support. Thomson consulted with R. Alta Charo and Norman Fost, both bioethicists at the University of Wisconsin, before making up his mind to forge ahead. As he explained to Frederic Golden for *Time* (August 20, 2001), "I could not see that throwing them out was better." Fost told Sheryl Gay Stolberg: "[Thomson] has been fanatically attentive to the ethical issues. We are lucky that the guy who is the pioneer in all this is such a responsible, thoughtful person."

In 1998, with Joseph Itskovitz-Eldor and Sander S. Shapiro as co-authors, Thomson published a groundbreaking article in the journal *Science* describing the isolation and duplication of human embryonic stem cells, accomplished just ahead of John Gearhart, who had been doing similar work at Johns Hopkins University. Removing cells from blastocysts, Thomson succeeded in mixing them with growth-stimulating hormones—or growth factors—from mice, which led them to mature into stem cells. Caring for stem cells was delicate work, Thomson discovered, as he spent six months checking early every morning to make sure they were developing according to plan. "You have to watch them every day or they differentiate," he told Golden. Thomson and his team made it possible for the cells to multiply but did not allow them to mature to the point at which they would take on specific roles in the human body; this differentiation of cells would occur only when the growth factor was removed. "Right now, we don't know how to direct [stem cells] to become any specific cells," he admitted to Eliot Marshall in 1998. Six months after his successful generation of stem cells began, Thomson had cultured one trillion of them, in five independent cell lines, owned by Geron and the WiCell Research Institute, a subsidiary of the Wisconsin Alumni Research Fund. (As of August 2001, as the *New York Times* reported, about 30 private research groups had purchased embryonic stem cells, which sell for $5,000 for two vials, from Thomson's laboratory at WiCell, and about 60 applications to purchase the stem cells were pending.) For his unprecedented work, Thomson was honored with the 1999 American Academy of Achievement Golden Plate Award and was named a 1999 World Technology Finalist in Health and Medicine by the *Economist*.

Thomson's success temporarily upended his quiet, studious lifestyle. In an experience that "scared me to death," as he acknowledged to Frederic Golden, less than a month after his findings were published, he was called to testify before the U.S. Senate Subcommittee on Labor, Health, and Human Services, Education and Related Agencies on the importance of embryonic stem-cell research. Early in 1999 Tommy Thompson, then the governor of Wisconsin, angered the state's anti-abortion groups when he invited Thomson to be present for the state-of-the-state speech, thus indi-cating support of Thomson's research even though it used human embryos. In 2001, when Thompson became secretary of Health and Human Services under President Bush, the issue was brought to the forefront of the national consciousness, as Bush was called upon to decide whether federal funding would be made available for research using human stem cells. (Bush's predecessor in the White House, Bill Clinton, had supported stem-cell research; upon entering office, in 1993, he had overturned a ban issued by Bush's father, President George Herbert Walker Bush, on federal funding for research involving fetal tissue. Tommy Thompson had been firm in his support of stem-cell research since 1999, but President George W. Bush, when he first took office, was opposed to using human embryos for any research purposes.) Thomson, hoping to use the stem cells to test medicines in the short term and to replace diseased adult tissues in the long term, found himself in the middle of a fierce debate, along with the blastocysts. "The entities at the center of the controversy are the more than 150,000 embryos currently stored in liquid nitrogen at fertility clinics around the country," Arthur Allen wrote for *Salon.com* (December 29, 2000), "left there by parents who had their babies, or failed to get pregnant but moved on."

On August 9, 2001 President Bush announced that he would allow federal funding for limited stem-cell research that makes use of cell lines already in existence. Despite scientists' worries that the numbers of extant cell lines were extremely small, around the world there are said to be 64 such cell lines falling within Bush's restrictions; five of the 64 are at the WiCell labs. Within weeks of Bush's announcement, Thomson and Dan Kaufman, a hematologist visiting Thomson's lab, published a report stating that they had developed colonies of human stem cells that would produce human blood cells. They remain unsure of the signals that direct a stem cell to become one kind of cell instead of another, as Nicholas Wade reported for the *New York Times* (September 4, 2001, on-line): "They tricked the cells into choosing this fate by growing them in the presence of blood-forming cells derived from a mouse. Mice and people are so similar at the cellular level that the chemical signals released by the mouse blood cells were presumably recognized by the human embryonic stem cells and taken as a cue to morph into the blood-forming cells of the bone marrow." The team at the University of Wisconsin were further able to prepare the stem cells to become one of three types of human blood cell: oxygen-carrying red blood cells, disease-fighting white blood cells, and sticky, clot-forming platelets. Yet to be developed is the process through which blood-forming cells could function normally when grafted into bone marrow; if developed, the methodology could provide bone marrow and blood products for transplants that would pose very little risk of host rejection.

The recent acceleration of research in the arena of stem cells, and the attention surrounding it, may interfere with Thomson's two primary goals, which he identified for Frederic Golden as getting "back to work . . . [and] to obscurity." To preserve the normality of his life as much as possible, he grants interviews only rarely, and never to television reporters. "I don't own a television," he told Sheryl Gay Stolberg, "so why should I support a media I don't like very much?"

Thomson is currently an assistant professor of anatomy at the medical school of the University of Wisconsin–Madison; the chief pathologist at the

Wisconsin Regional Primate Research Center, which is part of the university's graduate school; and the scientific director of the WiCell Research Institute Inc. He is married to a scientist, with whom he has two young children. He often takes to the skies to relax, hang-gliding in the hills outside Madison or flying vintage 1930s and 1940s planes. — K.S.

Suggested Reading: *New York Times* A p1+ July 4, 2001, A p12 July 10, 2001, with photo, A p1+ Nov. 6, 1998; *Science* p1014+ Nov. 6, 1998; *Time* p26+ Aug. 20, 2001, with photo

---

Courtesy of Tigerman McCurry Architects

Tigerman, Stanley

Sep. 20, 1930– Architect; educator. Address: Tigerman McCurry Architects, 444 N. Wells St., Suite 206, Chicago, IL 60610

"I'm not interested in those who may see architecture as a way to make money," the architect Stanley Tigerman said to Mara Tapp for *New Art Examiner* (September 2000, on-line). "I hate that and I hate architects that do it and I'm very verbal about it." Using an archaic spelling of the word "complete," to mean highly skilled and accomplished in all aspects of an activity, Paul Gapp, in the *Chicago Tribune* (November 24, 1991), dubbed Tigerman "the Compleat Architect," noting the extraordinary stylistic variety and scope of the Chicago-based architect's designs. Many of those designs have been described as highly inventive and, in some cases, whimsical; they range from private houses and

apartment complexes to a church, a power station, a museum, a library for the blind and physically handicapped, an animal shelter, buildings that house institutions of higher learning, a café, a garage, and other commercial buildings large and small, as well as such merchandise as linens, dinnerware, and a "head-pointer," a device that enables victims of cerebral palsy to manipulate the keys of a computer. Tigerman launched his own design firm in 1962; since 1982 he has worked in partnership with his third wife, the architect Margaret McCurry. Individually or with McCurry, he has earned more than 110 awards for his designs; among the most recent is the 2000 Louis Sullivan Award for Architecture (named for a pioneering 19th–20th-century American architect whom Tigerman has cited as one of his heroes), from the International Union of Bricklayers and Allied Craftworkers.

Outside the studio, Tigerman has helped to organize several major exhibitions, served as a visiting professor or lecturer at many universities, and written several books, including *Versus: An American Architect's Alternatives* (1982), which discusses his life and philosophy. He directed the school of architecture at the University of Illinois–Chicago for eight years, until his ouster, in 1993, due to a perception of high-handedness on his part. Within a year of his dismissal, he co-founded a highly innovative, nonprofit, architectural think-tank, called Archeworks, which confers the equivalent of a one-year graduate degree; adopting a multidisciplinary approach, the school focuses on the design of buildings and other things for the homeless, the elderly, battered women, and AIDS patients, among other disadvantaged groups who normally do not benefit from architectural creativity. "Without morality and ethics, what is architecture? A profession? An art? A money-grubbing thing? Unless it has a moral root supporting its existence, it's of absolutely no interest. Not to me. Not at all," Tigerman declared to Mara Tapp. "How would you sustain an interest in one field for over a half-century unless there's a moral or ethical dimension? You can't do it just based on art. You surely can't do it based on professionalism and you certainly can't do it based on money. It would only be out of an ethical belief, by principled behavior. Now, there's always the question, of course, whose principle? Whose morality? It's a real question and it's an honest question but I'd rather argue and debate that question than not have any. At least it's the right question."

The only child of Samuel and Emma Tigerman, both of whom were Jewish immigrants from Hungary, Stanley Tigerman was born on September 20, 1930 in Chicago. At the age of 12, when he was in eighth grade, he read Ayn Rand's novel *The Fountainhead* (1943), about a stubbornly individualistic architectural genius who dynamites a housing project he has designed after bureaucrats adulterate the design. The novel, a rhapsody to the superior individual who successfully resists engulfment by the common herd, embodied Rand's philosophy, which, "in essence," as she herself described it, was "the concept of man as a heroic being, . . . with productive achievement as his noblest activity." "I read the book, put it down, and I was going to be an architect," Tigerman recalled to Mara Tapp. "Why? Because it was heroic. It was not about success. My parents were very poor, and my mother really envied her brother who was rich, as well as anybody else who was. . . . This was the way to reject my mother! To rebel against her was to not do something for success but to be heroic."

After he graduated from Senn High School, in Chicago, in 1948, Tigerman entered the architecture program at the Massachusettes Institute of Technology, in Cambridge, Massachusetts. He left the college after a year. "The official reason is because I met a girl. The real reason is because I wasn't smart enough to hack it," he told Eric Zorn for the *Chicago Tribune* (March 31, 1982). During the dozen years after his return to Chicago he was exposed to a wide range of architectural styles, through both schooling and employment. He studied at the Institute of Design for a year and also worked as an architect's apprentice, in the studio of George Fred Keck, an avant-garde modernist. In 1950 he enlisted in the U.S. Navy. During portions of his four-year military service, he worked at night as a draftsman and played piano in striptease clubs. For four years after his discharge, in 1954, he held a series of jobs, as a draftsman or designer, in such architectural firms as Skidmore, Owings and Merrill, in Chicago. After he learned that certain postgraduate architecture programs accepted students who lacked a bachelor's degree, he successfully applied to the one at the Yale University School of Architecture, in New Haven, Connecticut.

According to Tigerman, Paul M. Rudolph, who chaired the Department of Architecture at Yale at that time, was an unforgiving taskmaster who scared him and his fellow students into performing superlatively at all times; anything less—even a grade of 89 on one of Rudolph's weekly tests, as Tigerman once got—would trigger what amounted to a severe warning from Rudolph. "You [would]

go back and work your balls off, which is the whole point of it, right?" Tigerman told Mara Tapp. "I loved it, I thrived on it. Those of us who didn't end up on a shrink's couches—one kid committed suicide—did very well." Within two years he had earned both a bachelor's degree and a master's in architecture, in 1960 and 1961, respectively; in both years, he finished at the top of his class, and in 1961 he won the Alpha Rho Chi Bronze Medal, which is awarded at 100 schools to outstanding architecture students who also display exceptional leadership qualities and contribute to their communities.

While at Yale Tigerman served as a draftsman in Paul Rudolph's New Haven studio. He turned down the opportunity to work full-time for Rudolph, either in New Haven or in Rudolph's New York City office, after leaving Yale. "I said, 'Absolutely not,'" he told Mara Tapp; architects, he said, should build their careers "at home." "Always. I don't care if you're from Tupelo, Mississippi. If you stay in one place your whole life, you own it. It's yours. If you move around, you've got a problem. If you don't have longevity, what's the point?" He also told Tapp, explaining his love for Chicago, that the city has "an 'I will' spirit." "Chicago is the flame, the belief in modern architecture, in modernism—not meaning international style, . . . but in a sense of being modern and being of our time," he said.

In 1961 or 1962, after working for some months for another celebrated architect, Harry M. Weese, in Chicago, Tigerman opened a studio in partnership with Norman Koglin. Their projects included Chicago townhouses and the low-rise Woodlawn Gardens, a housing project for low-income residents on the city's South Side that offered a striking alternative to the dreary, towering structures that typified public housing erected during those years. In 1964 Tigerman established his own firm, Stanley Tigerman and Associates. Among its early designs was what he called a "visionary megastructure," or "instant city" (1965), conceived for a trade organization seeking a new urban plan that would accommodate the great increase in population projected for the country in the next two or three decades. His plan (which was never realized) called for pyramidal structures that would stand on stilts above expressways, to avoid destroying communities.

In the mid-1960s Tigerman was invited to what was then East Pakistan to design several schools devoted to technical subjects. He arrived during a period of growing turmoil, stemming from the East Pakistanis' demands for political and economic reforms. During the next decade a civil war broke out in East Pakistan, resulting in the creation of Bangladesh, in 1971. Despite this upheaval, construction of the Five Polytechnic Institutes, as they are known, was completed in 1975, each in a different Bangladeshi city. A photo of one of the institutes appeared on Tigerman's Web site in early 2001, along with pictures of other Tigerman or Tigerman-McCurry buildings. These include St. Benedict's Abbey Church, in southern Wisconsin (1971) and such one-family houses as Frog Hollow, in Berrian Springs, Michigan (1974); the Hot Dog House, in Harvard, Illinois (1975); the Glass and Metal House, in Glencoe, Illinois (1975); Animal Crackers, in Highland Park, Illinois (1978); and Urban Villa, in Berlin, Germany (1988), all of which look distinctly different. The Tigerman-McCurry Web site also shows photos of such multi-family dwellings as the Boardwalk Apartments (1974) and Pensacola Place (1981), both in Chicago, and the Momochi Residential Complex, in Fukuoka, Japan (1991), and such nonresidential structures as the Anti-Cruelty Society building (1978), the Juvenile Protective Association building (1984), the Hard Rock Café (1985), and the Early Childhood Educare Center (1999), all in Chicago. Also pictured are Tigerman-McCurry industrial designs, for such things as furniture, dinnerware, watches, fabrics, weathervanes, a cookie jar, and a mailbox—a galvanized-steel replica of the barn at the architects' weekend home, in Lakeside, Michigan.

For several years in the 1970s, Tigerman, along with a group of other architects, devoted a lot of time to arranging an exhibition to celebrate the works of such Chicago architects as George Fred Keck, Andrew Rebori, and David Adler and to demonstrate their influence. Tigerman and his collaborators, who were known briefly as the Chicago Four and then the Chicago Seven (their numbers eventually totaled 11), believed that the importance of those architects had not been recognized, in large part because historians and others were blinded by their adulation of Ludwig Mies van der Rohe; a pioneer of modern architecture who became famous as the designer of the first all-glass skyscraper, the German-born Mies had settled in Chicago after immigrating to the U.S.; in 1937. What prompted Tigerman and his colleagues to act was the mounting of a show in Munich, Germany, called *100 Years of Architecture in Chicago*, which was slated to come to Chicago's Museum of Contemporary Art in 1976 and which, they felt, exalted Mies (who had died in 1969) and some of his followers at the expense of his Chicago contemporaries. Although Tigerman has "severely criticized the impact of Mies," as John Zukowsky, the curator of architecture at the Art Institute of Chicago, wrote in a profile of Tigerman for *Contemporary Architects* (1994), he has also called Mies "a brilliant architect." "I've lived in a Mies building for 31 years," Tigerman told Mara Tapp. "You know why? So I always remember that I'm in the presence of greatness—lest I get out of control in my own head—in the presence of a challenge." The exhibition mounted by Tigerman and his associates, titled *Chicago Architects*, which opened in May 1976, ran concurrently with the *100 Years* show, and it drew national attention as well as large crowds. The exhibition triggered dialogue among "Miesian mainliners" and Tigerman and other "mavericks," as Paul Gapp wrote for the *Chicago*

Tribune (July 21, 1985), and it led to a series of gallery events and symposia with which Tigerman was involved. A high point of the new spirit of openness that was born was the revival, in 1979, of the Chicago Architectural Club, which had closed its doors in 1940. Three years later, in a conversation with Eric Zorn, the Chicago architect John F. "Jack" Hartray said of Tigerman, "He has been a great stimulant to us all; a refreshing disruptive influence."

Earlier, in 1975, Tigerman, together with Jerome R. Butler Jr., the Chicago city architect, had begun designing a new building for the Illinois Regional Library for the Blind and Physically Handicapped; construction was completed in the winter of 1977–78. Located in what Paul Goldberger, writing for the *New York Times* (August 9, 1978), described as a "desolate" section of Chicago, the library presents, on one side, a façade of bright red and bright yellow steel panels, thereby "provid[ing] library users who are not completely sightless with a strong visual experience" and "bring[ing] some liveliness into the drab neighborhood for the sighted," as Goldberger noted. The undulating window that stretches the length of another side of the building enables people in wheelchairs to get an uninterrupted view of the outdoors; the floor plans and furnishings, ranging from book-delivery areas to floor tiles, offer evidence, according to Goldberger, of "the intelligent decisions made throughout this building." "Tigerman was searching constantly for materials and form that would satisfy his own visual sense [of beauty]," Goldberger explained, "yet somehow convey the idea of beauty equally well to users who could understand it only through shape and texture." In Goldberger's view, the architect had succeeded in producing a "strong and handsome piece of design." A fivefold increase in walk-in patronage after the opening of the building, which also houses a branch of the city public library, testified to the wisdom of Tigerman's choices.

Also noteworthy among Tigerman's works from the mid-1970s are the Daisy House, in Porter, Indiana, which, when viewed from above, looks distinctly phallic; the man for whom it was designed was suffering from a fatal disease, and Tigerman's idea of amusing him produced the intended results. Another private home, the Animal Crackers house, in Highland Park, Illinois, "variously alludes to a box of cookies, a calliope, and a Volkswagen," according to Paul Gapp. The façade of the Anti-Cruelty Society building, in Chicago, is said to remind people of a basset hound's face. In 1976 Tigerman was among a dozen American architects who represented the United States at the Venice Biennale, one of the art world's most prestigious events; he participated in the show again in 1980.

In 1979 the twice-divorced Tigerman married Margaret I. McCurry, who had founded her own architectural firm in 1977, after working for Skidmore Owings and Merrill for 11 years. In 1982 Stanley Tigerman & Associates merged with Margaret I. McCurry Ltd. to form Tigerman McCurry Architects. That year the eminent Chicago architect Thomas Beeby, who was then the director of the School of Architecture at the University of Illinois at Chicago, said of Tigerman, as quoted by Zorn, "Overall, he has done some fabulous work. He's had a tremendous impact on the Chicago scene in the last 10 years and led a new generation of architects." "Tigerman is a thing unto himself," the New York Times architecture critic Paul Goldberger told Zorn. "Not part of any school, but highly personal, openly entertaining, and brash. He loves to play the bad boy and outsider, but no one has ever more wanted to be part of the establishment, if only the establishment will change to meet him."

Among the most prominent of the projects to emanate from the Tigerman-McCurry partnership is the 16-story Chicago Bar Association headquarters (1990), Tigerman's first office tower. Sitting harmoniously among its neighbors—including the 1920s-era buildings on either side of it—it incorporates an "amalgam of stylistic references," Paul Gapp noted in the Chicago Tribune (November 24, 1991), with some elements inspired by the Mies-designed Kluczynski Federal Building, located less than a block away. Another notable Tigerman-McCurry building is the Power House Energy Museum, in Zion, Illinois (1993), built for the Commonwealth Edison Electric Co. of Chicago. As with the couple's weekend house, constructed in 1984, Tigerman and McCurry designed the museum "to evoke both sacred imagery from its basilica form and everyday imagery of rural American structures," as John Zukowsky wrote; indeed, the building is reminiscent of both a barn and a church. Tigerman designed the museum's exhibition spaces and graphics as well as the theater, café, bookshop, offices, and library that are housed in the Power House. "This one building . . . ," Zukowsky wrote, "shows us Tigerman's fondness for layering imagery and meaning throughout his works, making them much richer than 'one liners' as his critics so often contend." In the Chicago Tribune (November 8, 1992), Blair Kamin wrote, "Power House is an exhibit in itself . . . [and] succeeds both as a . . . museum and as a work of art."

Tigerman served as the architect-in-residence at the American Academy in Rome, Italy, in 1980. He later served as a visiting professor or lecturer at several dozen universities, among them Washington University, in St. Louis; Northwestern University, in Evanston, Illinois; Cornell University, in Ithaca, New York; Harvard University, in Cambridge, Massachusetts; and the Cardiff College of Art, in Wales. In 1985 he was named director of the School of Architecture at the University of Illinois at Chicago (UIC). In the following years he attempted to "redirect" the school, as Blair Kamin put it, in part by hiring teachers whose philosophies some of the long-term faculty members considered highly unorthodox. Although, as Blair reported, "the school attained national visibility and an en-

hanced reputation" under his leadership, Tigerman's autocratic management style led to conflict between him and teachers; students, too, complained about his behavior. "I'm great with kids but I'm very tough," Tigerman told Mara Tapp. "During my tour of duty at UIC I was burned in effigy. . . . I had no problem with that because I was tough. I would take students' drawings if they were [not up to my standards] and tear them up. And boys—not just girls—I made cry. That's the way I was trained at Yale." Peter Eisenman, who held the title of Louis H. Sullivan research professor of architecture at the university, and other Tigerman supporters on the faculty mounted a campaign to block the administration's plan to fire him, but their efforts, which included securing letters on his behalf from developers, architects, and architectural historians nationwide, did not succeed, and his tenure ended in May 1993. "I feel it's a terrible tragedy," Eisenman, who resigned his professorship in protest, told Blair Kamin. "Stanley has taken a mediocre school and raised it to an international level in the true spirit of Chicago—cantankerous and unwieldy."

By the time he left the university, Tigerman and Eva Maddox, the president and creative director of an award-winning Chicago interior-design firm, were far along in their plans to open a think tank cum school that would provide students with "the knowledge and skills to develop design solutions for social needs," according to a bio of Maddox on the Web site of the University of Illinois at Urbana-Champaign, where she teaches. Called Archeworks (pronounced "AR-kee-works"), the school opened in 1994. Its students (numbering at most 25 a year), who specialize in such fields as engineering, architecture, and graphic design, work in teams to research the needs of disadvantaged segments of the population and develop ways to meet those needs. Projects have included improvements to an early-learning day-care center at a Chicago YWCA; a device that makes it easier for AIDS patients, many of whom must take two dozen or more pills a day, to take their medications at the proper times; the new head pointer for people with cerebral palsy; visual merchandizing techniques and concepts for women setting up independent businesses; a specialized Web site for a Chicago elementary school that is designed to improve communication among the students, teachers, parents, and other community members; and, in collaboration with the Illinois Department of Human Services, a model office designed "to motivate case workers and encourage self-esteem in people using the welfare system," according to archeworks.org (on-line). In 1997 the school moved into a new building; designed by Tigerman, its form is evocative of that of a locomotive, "to indicate that Archeworks is 'going places,' and represents a hands-on approach to education in a city known for industrious activity," according to archeworks.org, which added, "This is a school that makes things happen." To run the school, Tigerman and Maddox (who work there unsalaried) rely on grants, gifts from corporations and individuals, and tuition; there is "constant pressure to raise money every year," Tigerman told Tapp.

On his own or in partnership with Margaret Mc-Curry, Tigerman has earned seven national honor awards from the American Institute of Architects and dozens of professional and local awards for architecture and design excellence, among them *Architectural Record*'s Award of Excellence for Design, which he has received four times. Tigerman and McCurry were inducted into *Interior Design* magazine's Hall of Fame in 1990. In 1994 *A + U (Architecture and Urbanism)* magazine dedicated a special issue to the work of their firm; in 1998 the Archeworks building earned the Progressive Architecture Award from the magazine *Architecture*. In addition to *Versus*, Tigerman's books include *The Architecture of Exile* (1988), which discusses the relationship of architecture and Judeo-Christian traditions, among other subjects, and *Stanley Tigerman: Buildings and Projects, 1966–1989* (1989).

Tigerman has one son, Judson, and one daughter, Tracy, who wrote, with Margaret McCurry, the children's book *Dorothy in Dreamland* (1991), which Tigerman illustrated. Knowing that her husband's bluntness has offended many people, Mc-Curry has warned him, as he told Tapp, "They're going to find you face down in an alley one day. It'll take years to figure out who did it because the list is so long." "With civilians, I'm actually a very nice guy," Tigerman remarked to Tapp. "With architects, I'm brutal. I'm interested in excellence. I always have been. I always will be. Period." — M.H.

Suggested Reading: *archeworks.org* (on-line) with photo; *Architecture* p53+ Apr. 1998, with photo, p80+ July 2001, with photo; *Chicago Tribune* I p13+ Mar. 31, 1982, XIII p14+ July 21, 1985,with photos, II p1+ Jan. 26, 1993, C p1+ Mar. 2, 1994, with photo; *New Art Examiner* (on-line), Sep. 2000; Tigerman McCurry Architects Web site; Emanuel, Muriel, ed. *Contemporary Architects*, 1994

Selected Works: with Norman Koglin—Woodlawn Gardens, c. 1963; with Stanley Tigerman and Associates—St. Benedict's Abbey Church, Southern Wisconsin, 1971; Frog Hollow, Berrien Springs, Michigan, 1974; Boardwalk Apartments, Chicago, 1974; Hot Dog House, Harvard, Illinois, 1975; Glass & Metal House, Glencoe, Illinois, 1975; Five Polytechnic Institutes, Bangladesh, 1975; Anti-Cruelty Society, Chicago, 1978; Animal Crackers, Highland Park, Illinois 1978; Pensacola Place, Chicago, 1981; with Tigerman McCurry Architects—Juvenile Protective Association, Chicago 1984; Hard Rock Café, Chicago, 1985; Wit's End, Sawyer, Michigan, 1987; Urban Villa, Teglerhafen, Berlin, Germany, 1988; Chicago Bar

Association, Chicago, 1990; Powerhouse Edison Energy Museum, Zion, Illinois, 1993; Archeworks Design School, Chicago, 1996; Educare Center, Chicago, 1999; Burnham Station, Chicago, 2000; Children's Advocacy Center, Chicago, 2000

Selected Books: as author—*Versus, An American Architect's Alternatives*, 1983; *The Architecture of Exile*, 1988; *Buildings and Projects 1966–1989*, 1989; *Bruce Graham of SOM* (with Bruce Graham), 1989; as illustrator—*Dorothy in Dreamland* (by Tracy Tigerman and Margaret McCurry), 1991

Courtesy of the Embassy of Peru

Toledo, Alejandro
(toe-LAY-doe, ah-leh-HAHN-droe)

Mar. 28, 1946– President of Peru. Address: Palacio de Gobierno, Plaza de Armas, Lima, Peru

On July 28, 2001, after his successful, third attempt to win his nation's highest office, Alejandro Toledo, an American-educated economist, was sworn in as Peru's newest president. Known as "El Cholo"—"The Indian"—a racial epithet also used as a term of endearment among Central and South Americans of mixed or native blood, Toledo is the first Peruvian president of Indian descent. He assumed the leadership of a nation beset by poverty, guerrilla activity, drug trafficking, and political corruption. During his victory speech, as quoted by Alex Bellos in the London *Guardian* (June 5, 2001), Toledo proclaimed to a crowd of more than 10,000 supporters, "Together we share a dream that Peru be a more just country with more jobs, social justice and without corruption. I want to extend my hand to the unemployed, the peasants, the workers, the young students, the farmers, the incapacitated, the miners. I want to open my arms to all people of all bloods to construct a Peru for all."

Alejandro Toledo was born on March 28, 1946 in the village of Cabana, Peru, located in Ancash Province, in the Andean highlands. He was the eighth of 16 children born to his father, a sheepherder, and his mother, a washerwoman; seven of his siblings died in infancy. When Toledo was six years old, the family moved to the port town of Chimbote, on the Pacific coast of Peru. There, Toledo's father worked in the fishing industry, and young Alejandro shined shoes and sold lottery tickets and newspapers to help the family survive. The Toledos lived in a shack with no electricity or running water; right behind it was a large open sewer. Toledo attended grammar school in Chimbote. His education probably would have ended there had his teachers not noticed the boy's extraordinary intelligence and encouraged him to enroll in high school. While in high school he met two American Peace Corps volunteers, Joel Meister and Nancy Deeds, who, like his teachers, immediately recognized his academic talents. Toledo was awarded a scholarship to study in the United States, and Meister and Deeds, who hailed from the San Francisco Bay Area, steered him to the University of San Francisco. His scholarship covered only one year, so he tried out for the university soccer team with the hope of earning an athletic scholarship. Despite his slight build, he succeeded, and became the team's starting center forward. To supplement the partial athletic scholarship, Toledo worked as a gas-station attendant. In 1966 he was awarded a bachelor's degree in economics from the university. He then won a Ford Foundation fellowship, in a program designed to train Latin American students to be educators in their native countries, and enrolled at Stanford University, in Stanford, California. Martin Carnoy, his education professor and mentor at Stanford, recalled his first impressions of Toledo to Carl Nolte for the *San Francisco Chronicle* (May 31, 2001). "I saw this incredible burning determination. I [had seen] hundreds and thousands of students, but I [had] never met a person who was so focused." Carnoy arranged a full scholarship for Toledo, who earned master's degrees in both education and economics and a Ph.D. in the economics of human resources. (His doctoral thesis was on the effects of educational investment on income distribution.) While at Stanford Toledo met Eliane Karp, a Belgian-born graduate student in anthropology. In 1979 the two were married in Sunnyvale, California. Upon their graduation the couple moved to Washington, D.C., where Toledo accepted a position at the World Bank. In 1994, after successive stints at the United Nations and as a visiting scholar at Harvard University, in Cambridge, Massachusetts, Toledo moved back to Peru with his wife and his daughter, Chantal, who was then 11 years old.

Back in Peru Toledo formed a political party—the Peru Posible—and in 1995 staged a bid for the presidency against the incumbent, Alberto K. Fujimori. Toledo based his campaign almost solely on his Indian heritage, which he shares with more than 80 percent of Peru's 26 million citizens. During the campaign he called himself "El Cholo"; although it is used for anyone in Peru of Indian descent, "Cholo" most commonly refers to the millions of people who have migrated from the impoverished countryside to Peruvian cities during the last 50 years. Toledo, whose destitute childhood was similar to those of many other Peruvians, appealed to the masses through his call for a leader who would address their economic needs and revive the cultural traditions they had lost after leaving their rural homes. He lost the election resoundingly, winning only 4 percent of the vote; Fujimori was reelected easily. Both the Peruvian people and international observers viewed Fujimori's first five years in office favorably. After succeeding Alan García Pérez as president, Fujimori had stabilized the economy (under García, expenditures had exceeded revenues by three to one, and inflation had risen to 3,500 percent); he also attracted foreign investment and crushed two powerful guerrilla movements whose violent activities had plagued the country for years.

In 2000 Toledo, backed by the Peru Posible Party, again announced his candidacy for the presidency. His opponent was again Fujimori, who had persuaded the Peruvian Congress to change the nation's constitution so that he could run for a third time. While steadfastly calling attention to his pride in his Indian heritage, Toledo expanded his platform to make it appealing to people outside the peasant class as well. Fernando Tuesta, a Lima, Peru–based political analyst, told Anthony Faiola for the *Washington Post* (March 31, 2000), "Now [Toledo] has greatly strengthened his bid with an altered message that says, 'Hey, I look like you, and I'm proud, but I've also studied abroad and been accepted by the international community. Look, even my wife is white.'" Eliane Karp, who is Jewish, is an expert in the indigenous cultures of Peru. She is more fluent than her husband in Quechua, an Indian dialect that is one of Peru's two official languages. (The other is Spanish.) Karp often campaigned for her husband, speaking in Quechua to crowds of native South American and mixed-race Peruvians.

By March 2000 Toledo had gained a strong following. Polls conducted on the day of the election, April 9, showed him finishing second to Fujimori among the nine candidates in the first-round balloting—enough to prevent the incumbent president from gaining a majority and thus make necessary a runoff election the next month. Amid much questioning of the legitimacy of Fujimori's bid for a third term, international observers came to Peru to ensure the fairness and legality of the balloting. The observers soon noted irregularities. According to a writer for the *Economist* (April 15, 2000), "The

National Electoral Processes Office (ONPE), the supposedly independent electoral body set up under Mr. Fujimori's government, had promised a result within hours of the vote. But the collection of the ballots was chaotic. The computer system was not designed to allow monitoring of the count, and was vulnerable to outside interference." Although on the day after the election, most of the ONPE's computer centers were closed, ONPE declared that Fujimori had taken a decisive lead. Eduardo Stein, who headed a team of observers from the Organization of American States, complained that those results were "coming out of nowhere," as he was quoted as saying in the *Economist*. "Something very sinister is going on." Stein was also quoted in the *Los Angeles Times* (May 23, 2000) as saying, "[Fujimori and the ONPE] want to use our observation personnel to validate or endorse situations that . . . contradict what our own observers are reporting." In light of those reports, Toledo asked the Peruvian courts to grant a postponement of the May runoff election. His request was denied, and on May 23, five days before the scheduled election, Toledo officially withdrew from the race, on the grounds that Fujimori had rigged votes. He called on his supporters to boycott the election or write "No to fraud" on their ballots. That tactic failed, and Fujimori, running unopposed, won the election. Upon Fujimori's inauguration Toledo took his supporters to the streets in protest, and for the rest of the year 2000, Lima's Plaza de Armas, which runs in front of the presidential palace, was filled with protesters almost daily. Often the protesters, led by Toledo himself, were turned away by Peruvian military forces, who fired tear gas on the crowds.

In November 2000 a series of scandals in his government led Fujimori to leave Peru and take refuge in Japan, where his parents had lived before his birth. After learning that an international manhunt had been launched to find his intelligence chief, Vladimiro Montesinos, on charges of corruption, murder, and drug trafficking, Fujimori announced his resignation as president of Peru via fax from Japan. He subsequently renounced his Peruvian citizenship and assumed Japanese citizenship. (Toledo has tried in vain to have Fujimori extradited from Japan to stand trial in Peru on corruption charges.) After Fujimori's resignation an interim government was placed in charge of Peru, with Valentin Paniagua, the president of the nation's congress, at the helm. Formal presidential elections were set for April 2001. By then the Peruvian government, under the direction of Paniagua, had undergone a political purge. More than 200 people—including generals, former cabinet officials, and Supreme Court justices—had been placed under investigation by the Ministry of Justice for corruption, election rigging, and/or influence peddling. (Montesinos, who had been arrested, had disclosed the existence of thousands of secretly taped videos that implicated many members of the government in various crimes.) The presidential

candidates now included Alan García Pérez, who had led the country from 1985 to 1990. Known as the John F. Kennedy of Peru because of his youthful charisma, he had been living in exile in Colombia during Fujimori's years in office. Although initially considered an underdog, García won enough votes in the April balloting to deny Toledo a majority. In the six weeks leading up to the runoff election, the candidates attacked each other vigorously. Toledo continually reminded voters that during García's administration the country had suffered great turmoil and unrest. García, in turn, accused Toledo of pocketing campaign money, abandoning an illegitimate daughter, and using cocaine in 1998 while cavorting with three prostitutes in Lima. Toledo denied all of the accusations and claimed that he had tested positive for cocaine because he had been kidnapped and drugged by intelligence agents working for Fujimori. (He refused, however, to take a paternity test to determine the truth of the claims of the person claiming to be his daughter.) Toledo, who had been dubbed "Pachacutec" by his supporters, in reference to the 15th-century Inca emperor who ousted the Spanish invaders and restored the Inca empire, was now being linked with scandals rivaling those associated with Fujimori. Toledo's and García's campaigns both backfired, producing widespread apathy in Peruvian voters.

In the last days of the campaign, with the help of a series of televised debates in which he emphasized the need for a "market economy with a human face," Toledo won back a portion of his support. In the June 3, 2001 election, he captured 53 percent of the vote and was proclaimed president of Peru. The Peru Possible Party, however, won only 26 percent of the congressional seats, ensuring that Toledo's administration would face an opposition whose leaders include García.

Since his inauguration Toledo has promised to set up an agrarian bank, trim the budget deficit, fight corruption, and guarantee an independent judiciary. He is overseeing the construction of water and sewage systems and roads to serve the poorest areas of Peru, using $800 million that had been frozen during the Fujimori administration. He has stressed the importance of creating new jobs, and in early October 2001, he announced a $57 million short-term emergency program to develop almost 50,000 temporary positions. He also said that by the end of the year, he would launch a subsidized-housing construction program that would provide another 200,000 jobs. "The challenge I have set for the government is to make it so that the 54 percent of Peruvians who are sentenced to live below the poverty line, including the 17 percent in extreme poverty, can have the opportunity I had to move up, not as a statistical error but as a norm," Toledo told Lucy Conger for *Institutional Investor* (September 2001). "That is my dream."

Toledo currently resides in the presidential palace, in Lima, Peru, with his wife, Eliane Karp. (The two divorced amid reports that Karp had been the victim of domestic violence and abuse; they later remarried.) Their daughter, Chantal, is a student at the University of Toulouse, in France. Toledo, who has said that he loves eating McDonald's fast food and meeting celebrities, is reportedly able to sing a number of traditional Andean songs on request. "The challenge facing leaders today is to succeed in this competitive, globalized world without losing our identity," he told Joseph Contreras for *Newsweek* (August 13, 2001). "I see no contradiction between consuming the culture of CNN and the Internet and speaking Quechua." — J.H.

Suggested Reading: *Boston Globe* A p18 June 7, 2001; *Economist* p31+ Apr. 15, 2000, with photo; (London) *Guardian* p12 June 5, 2001; *Los Angeles Times* p4 May 23, 2000; *Nation* p4+ June 19, 2000; *New York Times* A p4 May 19, 2001, with photo, A p4 June 2, 2001, with photo; *San Francisco Chronicle* A p13 May 31, 2001, with photo; *Washington Post* A p1 Mar. 31, 2000

Piovanotto/Hulton/Archive

Tsui Hark
(choy hok)

Feb. 15(?), 1951 Producer; director; actor; screenwriter. Address: Film Workshop Co., Ltd., Unit 1375, 13/F, Hong Kong International Trade & Exhibition Centre, 1 Trademark Dr., Kowloon Bay, Kowloon, Hong Kong, China

In the 22 years since his name first appeared in credits on the big screen, the filmmaker Tsui Hark has served as director, producer, or screenwriter of, or actor in, more than 70 motion pictures; for most of them, he functioned in two or three of those capacities. Of Vietnamese ancestry, Tsui is among the best-known, most successful filmmakers in Hong Kong, where he founded his own production company, Film Workshop, in 1984, and where he has made most of his movies; in *Time* (May 14, 2001), the film critic Richard Corliss described him as "Hong Kong cinema's preeminent creative force." Tsui has tackled such genres as science fiction, fantasy, crime, and horror, usually in combination with comedy and romance and with the inclusion of much violence, and he is celebrated as a master choreographer of fights. "His best movies are made with such verve and craft that the viewer's head practically explodes with the concentration they require, the pleasure they bring," Corliss wrote. With such films as *Zu: Warriors from the Magic Mountain* and the *Swordsman*, *Once Upon a Time in China*, and *A Chinese Ghost Story* series, Tsui played a major role in reviving and popularizing the martial-arts genre of filmmaking. Markedly different from fare familiar to Western audiences, many of his pictures feature tortuously tangled stories and lightning-fast action sequences. Hal Hinson's description of the Tsui-directed and -produced *Peking Opera Blues* for the *Washington Post* (October 14, 1988) is representative of what other viewers have said about Tsui's works: "The plot is mind-bogglingly complex; your eyes cross just trying to figure it out. But even if you can't keep up, the visual exuberance is so entrancing that you don't mind feeling lost. . . . *Peking Opera Blues* is transcendent escapist entertainment." In an interview with Stephen Short for the Asia edition of *Time* (April 25, 2000, on-line), Tsui said, "I don't think Hong Kong people, or any people, go to a cinema to learn, unless in a practical sense, you go to watch a documentary. Cinema is first and foremost entertainment, and its purpose is to fill those gaps of human feeling when you're bored and frustrated with life and want to feel better."

The son of a pharmacist, Tsui Hark was born on February 15, 1951 in the part of Saigon, Vietnam, where many Chinese immigrants lived. (Some sources report his date of birth as January 2, 1951 and his father's occupation as acupuncturist.) According to most accounts, Tsui's family includes more than a dozen siblings from his father's three marriages. When he was 13 he made his first film, using an eight-millimeter camera to shoot a local magic show. At 14 he moved with his family to the British crown colony of Hong Kong (now part of China), where he attended high school. "Hong Kong was a totally different world," he recalled to Stephen Short. "It compared to nothing I'd seen in my life to that point." When he was about 15 years old, Tsui saw the Japanese director Akira Kurosawa's film *Yojimbo* (The Bodyguard, 1961), and Kurosawa became his "hero," as he told Stephen Short. "I never expected to see a Japanese film like that," he recalled to Short. "[Kurosawa] presented so many images, almost like one long montage of a movie. The more I watched his work the more I saw it was challenging, experimental and ground-breaking. As a director, you obviously don't want to be like anyone else. Almost nothing you do is new; it's all been done before and that's a personal and emotional challenge to overcome as a director."

With the goal of pursuing a career in film, Tsui applied for admission to universities in the United States. "There are two ways to get involved in the Chinese film industry," he explained to Craig D. Reid for *Film Quarterly* (Spring 1995). "Either you work hard as a continuity person, stunt man, or some sort of assistant in a studio here in Hong Kong or you go overseas to film school." During the height of the Vietnam War, Tsui attended the University of Texas, where he took courses in television and film. "When I went to Texas to study, everything was Saigon, Saigon, Saigon and Vietnam was the word on every American's lips," he continued. "I felt instantly more at home there than I ever did in Hong Kong." Tsui told Craig D. Reid, "My most prominent lesson in film-making occurred while studying television direction in the States. I was a cameraman filming a dance routine inside a studio. My professor told me not just to look in front of the camera but also behind the camera for something interesting. When I turned around, I saw shadows of the dancers. He taught me to always look for things that most people weren't looking for or at."

After he graduated from college, Tsui lived briefly in New York City, where, in 1976, he made a documentary about Chinese garment workers. (The title does not appear on Tsui filmographies.) He also worked as an editor for a Chinese-language newspaper. The next year he returned to Hong Kong and took a job as a producer and director for Hong Kong television, which was in a period of rapid growth. "It was easier to break into television [than film] and make those *lian xu zhu* TV miniseries [kung-fu soap operas]," Tsui told Reid. "It was easier to work with video from a filming, editing, and especially from a special-effects point of view. And I learned that I could change structure and tradition." In 1978 Tsui worked on the miniseries *The Gold Dagger Romance*.

Tsui's return to Hong Kong coincided with the arrival there of many other young, Western-educated Asian filmmakers seeking to launch their careers. The time was ripe for them to do so; as Pat Aufderheide reported in *Film Comment* (June 1998), "[Hong Kong] film studios were looking for new talent to replace a fading generation, [and] investment money was available." The first feature film that Tsui directed, *The Butterfly Murders*, was released in 1979; a mystery with lots of swordplay, it fared poorly at the box office. Next, inspired by Roman Polanski's satire *The Fearless Vampire Killers* (1966) and Roger Corman's horror flicks, Tsui directed *We're Going to Eat You* (1980), a film about cannibals; it, too, was a financial failure. *Dangerous Encounters of the First Kind* (1980), which Tsui wrote and acted in as well as directed,

underwent substantial cuts by local censors. When it arrived in theaters, it was no longer a bloody horror film involving slacker terrorists and a young woman who liked to drive pins through the heads of mice; rather, it had become an innocuous thriller, suitable for all ages. Although the public mostly stayed away, the critical praise Tsui's first three films earned in Hong Kong kept his career afloat.

The Hong Kong–based production company Cinema City hired Tsui to direct *All the Wrong Clues (For the Right Solution)*, which premiered in 1981. A parody of popular 1970s American gangster films, it was Tsui's first attempt at comedy and his first big success with audiences. For his work on that film, Tsui was named best director at the 1981 Golden Horse Awards ceremony, held in Taiwan. With the newfound clout that came in the wake of this honor, Tsui persuaded the production company Golden Harvest to hire some well-known American special-effects experts—among them Robert Blalack (*Star Wars*), Peter Kuran (*The Thing*), and John Scheele (*Tron*)—to collaborate with him on the epic kung-fu fantasy *Zu: Warriors from the Magic Mountain* (1983). In the opinion of Richard Corliss, *Zu* is a "pop masterpiece." Hong Kong's first special-effects extravaganza, the film solidified Tsui's reputation as a leader of Hong Kong cinema.

Tsui had a cameo role in Eric Tsang's *Aces Go Places 2* (1983) and served as an actor, producer, and production designer for Teddy Robin Kwan's *All the Wrong Spies* (1983). His next directorial effort was *Aces Go Places 3: Our Man from Bond Street* (1984); its box-office receipts—$30 million in Hong Kong (H.K.) dollars, or U.S. $3.8 million—made it the top-grossing film in Hong Kong up to that point. Meanwhile, however, Tsui had become increasingly unhappy with what he regarded as production companies' unjustified interference in the creation of his films. Soon after the completion of *Aces Go Places 3*, Tsui and his wife, the producer and production designer Nansun Shi, set up their own production company, Film Workshop, thinking it would function as a temporary solution to the problem of insufficient control. The first movie to emerge from Film Workshop was the romantic comedy *Shanghai Blues* (1984); like all of Tsui's classics, it includes kung-fu action sequences. "I have more affection for that film than any other . . . ," Tsui told Stephen Short. "I get very emotional when I watch it." *Shanghai Blues* was named one of the 10 best Chinese pictures of 1984 at the Hong Kong Film Festival, and Film Workshop became an overnight success—and a fixture of the Hong Kong film industry. When considering projects proposed to Film Workshop, Tsui told Craig D. Reid, his main criterion is that the film "appeal to the masses. A commercial film must be entertaining and make a person feel good. . . . The masses go to feel, not to understand."

Thanks to *Shanghai Blues*, offers from directors who wanted the chance to work with Tsui started to pour in to Film Workshop. One came from John Woo, who had fallen out of favor with audiences and Hong Kong production companies alike. Though Woo had been labeled box-office poison, Tsui teamed up with him to make *A Better Tomorrow* (1986), starring Chow Yun-Fat (seen most recently in the 2000 hit *Crouching Tiger, Hidden Dragon*). *A Better Tomorrow*, which explores questions of honor and friendship among cops and criminals, was a huge hit, setting a new box-office record by grossing H.K. $35.1 million (U.S. $4.5 million) and setting the standard for what was dubbed "the heroic bloodshed" genre, a mixture of pathos and gore.

During the filming of *A Better Tomorrow*, the relationship between Woo as director and Tsui as producer became strained. Woo later complained about Tsui's insistence on being involved in every shot, while Tsui expressed his unhappiness about Woo's refusal to accept his ideas. For example, Tsui wanted to cast only women in the film. In his conversation with Stephen Short, he said, "I remember clearly wanting Michelle Yeoh playing the Chow Yun-Fat role. Rather than examine the relationship between a group of men, I wanted the relationship to be between women. From very early on, I wanted to do movies without any guys." Despite such differences, Tsui and Woo made two more films together—*A Better Tomorrow 2* (1987) and *The Killer* (1989), both starring Chow Yun-Fat—before parting ways. (Woo has since gained success in the U.S., with such films as *Face/Off* and *Mission: Impossible II*.) "I was not a good producer," Tsui admitted to Corliss. "The roles of producer and director should be like coach and fighter: the coach has to tell the boxer he's strong on the left or right, that his eye's weakening, that it's time to call it quits. Back then, I got frustrated. I never learned the difference between producing and directing."

The year 1986 also saw the release of *Peking Opera Blues*, which Tsui produced and directed. Labeled "a masterpiece from the exuberant Hong Kong school of filmmaking" by David Denby in *New York* (February 6, 1989), *Peking Opera Blues* is set in 1913 China, two years after the Ch'ing dynasty—the Manchus, the last family to rule the country—was overthrown. The republic that was established soon turned into a dictatorship, and widespread fighting among competing warlords ensued. The film features three heroines: a guerrilla fighter, a thief, and a singer whose dream is to perform in the all-male Peking Opera. "The ambition of these women drives the plot, which is filled with scrambles, routs, escapes, confrontations, and satire," Denby wrote. Tsui told Pat Aufderheide, "The film clearly takes a poke at the audience, saying that the Chinese people do not know what democracy is. The first democratic revolution collapsed because of a power struggle. . . . The film also takes a sly poke at the current Government."

In an essay for *Subway Cinema* (2001, on-line), the screenwriter Lisa Morton described Tsui as "a thinking-man's filmmaker, with a clearly expressed political agenda that tends to pervade his films." Morton wrote, "He parodied or pilloried British colonialism (*Aces Go Places 3, Dangerous Encounter—1st Kind*) and Western imperialism (*Once Upon a Time in China*), he skewered communism (*We're Going to Eat You, A Better Tomorrow 3*), he was less than kind to the Japanese (*The Raid*)—but what shines through virtually every film is what Stephen Teo (in his book *Hong Kong Cinema: The Extra Dimensions*) calls Tsui's 'nationalism.' Tsui's cinema is nearly bursting with pride in Chinese tradition. . . . Over and over Tsui's films tell us that political institutions come and go, but his culture will last."

In 1987 Tsui, as producer, joined forces with the director Ching Sui-Tung to make *A Chinese Ghost Story*. Portraying the love between a man and ghost, the film was adapted from a short Chinese horror story written more than a thousand years ago. In his interview with Pat Aufderheide, Tsui described *A Chinese Ghost Story* as both an "historical film" and a "wild fantasy." He told Craig D. Reid, "I didn't want to imitate the American productions so I decided to make a horror film that a Chinese audience could relate to. . . . The problem was how to make a horror film *and* make it romantic. . . . I believe that romance is the key to all action films." There was some debate in film circles as to how much of the movie Ching had shot and how much was Tsui's work. Howard Hampton, for example, wrote for *Film Comment* (July/August 1997), "While producer Tsui may have applied structure to Ching's dazzling flights of fancy, the serenely lunatic vision is entirely Ching's." A writer for *Subway Cinema* (on-line), by contrast, declared, "It's accepted that the dramatic scenes may have been Tsui's work while Ching filmed the action and special effects sequences." In any event, *A Chinese Ghost Story* received wide critical acclaim: it won two awards at the Avoriaz Fantastic Film Festival, in France; was named best film at the 1988 Oporto Festival, in Portugal; earned four 1987 Golden Horse Awards, in Taiwan; and won five awards from the Hong Kong Directors Guild and three Hong Kong Film Awards. Tsui made two sequels to *A Chinese Ghost Story*, in 1990 and 1991, as well as an animated version of the tale, in 1997.

Tsui next tackled the popular story of the renowned Cantonese kung-fu master and healer Wong Fei-Hung (1847–1924), who supported opponents of the corrupt Chinese government and became a folk hero in his native land. *Once Upon a Time in China* (1991), which Tsui wrote, produced, and directed, is one of dozens of accounts of the exploits of Wong Fei-Hung. The film propelled the actor Jet Li, who portrayed Wong, to international superstardom. According to Kevin Thomas, writing for the *Los Angeles Times* (April 9, 1993) and referring to the pioneering American film director and producer Cecil B. DeMille, *Once Upon a Time in China* "has everything: a DeMillean sense of spectacle; dazzling displays of martial arts combat; handsome, meticulously detailed production design; superb color cinematography; a rousing score and an affable hero in Jet Li's Wong." Li portrayed Wong in the next two of the five sequels Tsui went on to make between 1992 and 1997, when *Once Upon a Time in China and America* was released. The *Once Upon a Time in China* series is unusual for martial-arts movies in that it touches upon political issues. As Kevin Thomas observed, "Wong and his rambunctious, rowdy band emerge as simple, uncomplicated men whose cause nevertheless raises complex, contradictory issues of national sovereignty and cultural identity that are as timely for China today as they were a century ago. . . . Hark evokes the notion of a China of necessity caught up in a perpetual balancing act, taking from the West whatever is beneficial yet striving to remain determinedly Chinese and assertively independent."

Working again with Ching Sui-Tung, who has become known as one of Hong Kong's premier action choreographers, Tsui produced *Swordsman* (1990), *Swordsman II* (1992), and *The East Is Red: Swordsman III* (1993), each of which offers nonstop action and a highly convoluted story. In the *Los Angeles Times* (May 20, 1994), Kevin Thomas described *Swordsman III* as "a dazzling yet poignant martial-arts period fantasy." "Emotion is the most essential element in my films," Tsui told Craig Reid, "even the *Swordsman* films, which are about hatred, conflict, and brotherhood. But mostly they're full of hope. . . . One always needs hope." He added, "The trilogy is a parody on the Cultural Revolution, reflecting the hatreds of splitting up but eventually getting back together."

Swordsman II introduced audiences to the character Asia the Invincible (portrayed by Brigitte Lin), a warrior who, in the third film, completes his transformation into a woman. "Tsui's specialty is turning traditionally male genres into showcases for beguiling actresses," Richard Corliss noted. In her on-line essay for *Subway Cinema*, Lisa Morton declared, "No one in history has made more interesting use of women on film" than Tsui. "In movie after movie . . . Tsui has explored feminine power. His women are never just girlfriends or wives or mothers or victims; they exist equally with their male counterparts or (as in *Swordsman 2* or *A Better Tomorrow 3*) plainly above them."

Shortly before the British relinquished control of Hong Kong to China, in mid-1997, Tsui came to the United States. (Many other Hong Kong filmmakers, fearing increased censorship under China's Communist rule, made similar moves.) For his first project in the U.S., Tsui directed *Double Team* (1997), starring the martial-arts legend Jean-Claude Van Damme as a counterterrorist agent, Mickey Rourke as a terrorist, and the basketball star Dennis Rodman as a weapons expert. While Tsui's devoted American fans had eagerly awaited its release,

few other Americans had ever heard of him, and *Double Team* attracted little interest. Janet Maslin, the reviewer for the *New York Times* (April 4, 1997), wrote, "Mr. Hark has the right energy level (excitable), but little interest in fine points. Sets are impersonal. Actors sleepwalk. Scenes don't end, they just stop. . . . The screenplay's only concern is for finding imaginative new settings where the actors can crash vehicles or open fire." Tsui's second made-in-the-U.S. directorial effort was *Knock Off* (1998), written by Steven E. De Souza, whose credits include *48 Hrs.* and *Die Hard.* The film features Van Damme as a fashion designer who teams up with a CIA agent to fight terrorists; Rob Schneider and Paul Sorvino co-starred. Like its predecessor, the picture was a critical and popular failure. "*Knock Off* deadens the brain with its convoluted plot, then tries to revive its victims with its stunts and shootouts," Lawrence van Gelder wrote for the *New York Times* (September 5, 1998).

In part because of his unhappiness with what he regarded as American studio executives' excessive interference during the shooting of *Double Team* and *Knock Off*, Tsui returned to Hong Kong and took a sabbatical from filmmaking. "Sometimes you have to take a long break," he explained to Stephen Short. "I had been working nonstop for so long, and I think you have to get away from what you do for a while and get a fresh perspective." Tsui directed and wrote the screenplay for his next movie, *Time and Tide* (2000). In that film the Hong Kong singing sensation Nicholas Tse co-starred with the Chinese rock star Wu Bai, the lead singer and guitarist for the band China Blue; portraying a clueless bodyguard and a gangster, respectively, they battle a South American drug cartel made up of beautiful young women. "*Time and Tide* . . . may have no meaning other than its own kinetic rush," Richard Corliss wrote, "but who cares? This is more than an exercise in style; it's a 113-minute Soloflex workout—the moviest movie of the year." In the *Houston Chronicle* (June 8, 2001), Louis B. Parks wrote that Tsui's "off-kilter camera setups and wild, digitally enhanced point-of-view-altering camera movements are incredibly creative and as intricately and lovingly choreographed as a Fred Astaire dance." In another highly favorable review, for *Film Comment* (May/June 2001), David Chute wrote, "For all its surface dazzle and fancy footwork, *Time and Tide* is refreshingly old-fashioned, even square in its underlying moral stance: this action fantasy about reckless youth advocates facing facts and the responsibilities that stem from them."

Tsui co-wrote and produced Yuen Woo-ping's *Iron Monkey* (2001), the original version of which premiered in Hong Kong in 1993. Yuen and Tsui worked closely with the production company Miramax to restore the film for its release in the U.S. Now subtitled, *Iron Monkey* chronicles the early life of Wong Fei-hung and his father, Wong Kei-ying, and their Robin Hoodesque adventures through 19th-century China. Tsui is currently completing a sequel to *Zu*. Another film, *Black Mask 2: City of Masks*, is in post-production; shot in Thailand, it is a sequel to Tsui's 1996 picture *Black Mask*. In the spring of 2001, retrospectives of Tsui's work were held at Anthology Film Archives, a New York City museum of film, and the Plaza Twin, a Brooklyn, New York, theater. (Poorly translated subtitles present problems for viewers of many of his films.) *The Cinema of Tsui Hark*, a book by Lisa Morton, was published in October 2001.

Tsui lives with his wife, Nansun Shi, in Hong Kong. — J.H.

Suggested Reading: *Film Comment* p42+ May/June 1988, with photos, p16+ July/Aug. 1997, with photos, p42+ June 1998, with photos, p28+ May/June 2001, with photos; *Film Quarterly* p34+ Spring 1995, with photos; *Houston Chronicle* p6 June 8, 2001; *Los Angeles Times* p6 April 9, 1993, p6 May 20, 1994, F p2 May 4, 2001, with photo; *New York Times* C p7 April 4, 1997, with photo, B p17 Sep. 5, 1998, with photo; *Time* p71 May 14, 2001, with photo; *Washington Post* B p7 Oct. 14, 1998; Morton, Lisa. *The Cinema of Tsui Hark*, 2001

Selected Films: as actor—*Aces Go Places 2*, 1983; as actor and director—*Zu: Warriors from the Magic Mountain*, 1983; as actor, director, and writer—*Dangerous Encounters of the First Kind*, 1980; as actor, producer, and production designer— *All the Wrong Spies*, 1983; as director—*The Butterfly Murders*, 1979; *We're Going to Eat You*, 1980; *All the Wrong Clues (For the Right Solution)*, 1981; *Aces Go Places 3*, 1984; *Shanghai Blues*, 1984; *Double Team*, 1997; *Knock Off*, 1998; as director, editor, and producer—*A Better Tomorrow 3*, 1989; as director and producer—*Peking Opera Blues*, 1986; *Swordsman*, 1990; as director and writer— *Once Upon a Time in China*, 1991; as director, producer, and writer—*Once Upon a Time in China 2*, 1992; *Once Upon a Time in China 3*, 1993; *Once Upon a Time in China 5*, 1994; *The Blade*, 1995; *Time and Tide*, 2000; as producer—*A Better Tomorrow*, 1986; *A Chinese Ghost Story*, 1987; *The Killer*, 1989; *A Chinese Ghost Story 2*, 1990; as producer and writer: *A Better Tomorrow 2*, 1987; *A Chinese Ghost Story 3*, 1991; *The Raid*, 1991; *Swordsman 2*, 1992; *East is Red: Swordsman 3*, 1993; *Black Mask*, 1996; *A Chinese Ghost Story—The Animation*, 1997; *Once Upon a Time in China and America*, 1997; *Iron Monkey*, 2001

Turre, Steve

(tuh-RAY)

Dec. 8, 1949– Trombonist. Address: c/o Telarc International, 23307 Commerce Park Rd., Cleveland, OH 44122

One of the most accomplished and well-rounded musicians currently working in any genre, Steve Turre has been the top jazz and freelance trombonist in New York City for more than a decade. Turre, who gained experience in the bands of Rahsaan Roland Kirk, Woody Shaw, Thad Jones/Mel Lewis, and Dizzy Gillespie (to name just a few musical giants), is known to television audiences for his longtime membership in the house band of the popular comedy show *Saturday Night Live*. Equally adept at muted and open-horn styles of jazz improvisation, Turre is a skilled composer, arranger, and jazz educator as well as an instrumentalist. Since the mid-1980s he has also led a seashell choir—an assemblage unprecedented in the history of jazz—in which the musicians use seashells as instruments, breathing new life into an ancient Mexican tradition.

Steve Turre was born on December 8, 1949 in Omaha, Nebraska. In early 1950 his father, a gynecologist, moved the family to San Francisco, California. His mother, a Mexican-American and former flamenco dancer, played the piano and castinets. As a child Turre expressed the desire to play

Sophie Le Roux/Retna Ltd.

the violin, but he was dissuaded from doing so by his father, who compared the sounds of that instrument in the hands of a beginner to "a cat in an alley," as Turre recalled to Bob Bernotas in a 1994 interview published in the *Online Trombone Journal*. Excited by the trombonists that he saw in a parade, Turre began studying the instrument, at about age 10. "The first time I played it, I liked it," he told Bernotas. By age 13 he was playing professional jobs with his older brother, Mike, a saxophonist.

In high school Turre joined the football team to avoid compulsory participation in the marching band. The summer after he graduated from high school, in 1968, he successfully "sat in" with the saxophonist and gifted multi-instrumentalist Rahsaan Roland Kirk at the Jazz Workshop in San Francisco. He told Bob Bernotas, "It felt like we had been playing together all our lives. It clicked immediately. We'd breathe in the same place. We would phrase the same, intuitively. I was just able to tap into his brain waves. . . . We really struck up a wonderful friendship, and every time he would come through San Francisco he would call me for the gig."

Having qualified for a football scholarship to Sacramento State University, in California, Turre was enrolled there briefly, in 1968. After a few months he transferred to North Texas State University, in Denton (now the University of North Texas), which had a respected jazz-education program. After encountering racism from other students because of his Hispanic ancestry, Turre became discouraged and dropped out. Returning to San Francisco in 1970, he rejoined Kirk for a weeklong engagement at the Both/And nightclub.

During the next year Turre worked and recorded with the Irish pop singer Van Morrison. In early 1972 he successfully auditioned in Los Angeles for the big band of the legendary rhythm-and-blues pianist and vocalist Ray Charles. Following a European tour with Charles, Turre returned to San Francisco in late 1972. The jazz trumpeter Woody Shaw, who had recently moved to that area, invited Turre to sit in with Art Blakey's Jazz Messengers at the Keystone Korner jazz club. Shaw was a member of that band, which had enjoyed a reputation since the 1950s as a finishing school for outstanding emerging jazz musicians. Despite being "scared to death," as he put it to Bernotas, Turre played well, and on the spot the eminent drummer and bandleader Blakey invited him to join the band. The next day Turre recorded several performances with the Jazz Messengers that were included on the albums *Anthenagin* and *Buhaina*, on the Prestige label. "Playing with Art Blakey, the things that he'd put on you musically would take you years to realize," Turre told Bernotas. "'Don't play everything you know in your first chorus. Take your time. Tell a story.' You know, all those kinds of things: how to build a solo, not just go out there and start playing. And so that was 'graduate school.' Art Blakey and the Jazz Messengers, that was a degree right there."

After fulfilling engagements in St. Louis, Missouri, and Chicago, Illinois, the band traveled to New York City, where they appeared at the Village Gate. There, Turre met and played alongside one of his key influences, Curtis Fuller, the original

Jazz Messengers' trombonist. Although Turre received job offers from the saxophonist Anthony Braxton and others during his first few months in New York, Turre told Bernotas in 1994, "I'm glad I didn't walk away from that school. I've been with everybody now and that training has served me in good stead all these years."

After he left Blakey, toward the end of 1973, Turre joined the Thad Jones–Mel Lewis Jazz Orchestra, the leading big band of the time, co-led by Jones, a trumpeter and composer, and Lewis, a drummer. In the trombone section Turre was seated next to Quentin "Butter" Jackson, who had formerly played with the Duke Ellington Orchestra and was a master of plunger-mute soloing. The plunger mute, used to create vocal effects from a trombone or trumpet, was popular early in jazz history. Its use declined in the bebop era, and by the 1970s, the plunger style was the province of only a few specialists; Jackson and the Count Basie Orchestra trombonist Al Grey chief among them. Turre continued to refine and modernize his plunger concept, and today he ranks with the trombonists Wycliffe Gordon and Art Baron as a leading plunger practitioner.

Although mainly influenced by the linear, melodic style of J.J. Johnson—who is generally considered the first bebop trombonist and who was Curtis Fuller's primary influence—Turre had become a student of the full jazz trombone lineage, having received encouragement from Kirk. "He turned me on to Vic Dickenson and Trummy Young and Dicky Wells and J. C. Higginbotham and Jack Teagarden—the guys from the swing period that were between J.J. and [the early jazz trombonist] Kid Ory," Turre told Bernotas. "You've got to build the house from the foundation on up. Rahsaan stressed this to me and I took it to heart." During the apprenticeship with Jackson, which lasted into early 1974, Turre went far in developing his vibrant, signature sound and perspicacious approach to the jazz trombone tradition.

In 1974 Turre joined Woody Shaw's septet, dubbed the Concert Ensemble. In December of that year, Shaw, with Turre, recorded *The Moontrane*, considered a classic of adventurous hard-bop writing and simpatico ensemble playing. In 1975 Shaw signed with Columbia Records, for which he recorded the critically acclaimed *Rosewood* (1978) and two other albums, all with Turre. The trombonist continued to play with the Concert Ensemble from time to time until 1981, when the group disbanded; it later re-formed as a quintet with Turre. Turre received much important musical and business guidance from Shaw, which served him well when he started his music publishing company, Fruit Tree Music (mainly, apparently, to maintain copyrights). From 1974 to 1976 Turre also played trombone and electric bass guitar with the drummer Chico Hamilton's quintet.

In 1976 Turre joined Rahsaan Roland Kirk's last group, the Vibration Society. After Kirk's death, from a stroke, in 1977, Turre played with the Collective Black Artists Ensemble, led by the trombonist and composer Slide Hampton—another prominent J.J. Johnson disciple who had a major stylistic influence on Turre. At about this time Turre worked in addition with the legendary tenor saxophonist Dexter Gordon. Gigs with the drummer Elvin Jones and the pianist Cedar Walton followed, in 1979. That year, after several years of course work, Turre earned a bachelor's degree from the University Without Walls, a division of the University of Massachusetts at Amherst.

The year 1980 saw Turre freelancing in the tenor saxophonist Archie Shepp's big band as well as with the bassist Reggie Workman and the trumpeters Lester Bowie and Jon Faddis. In 1981 Turre worked with Slide Hampton in Hampton's nine-trombone group, the World of Trombones, and with the tenor saxophonist Pharoah Sanders and the South African trumpeter Hugh Masakela. Performing from 1981 to 1987 with Shaw's quintet—an unusual group in that it had no saxophone in the front line—Turre displayed a powerful tone and sure sense of rhythm on such recordings as *Night Music* (1982) and *Imagination* (1987). In 1989 Shaw—widely considered the foremost jazz trumpeter of his generation—died, at the age of 44, two months after an accident in which he had fallen onto subway tracks and was hit by an oncoming train.

Throughout the 1980s Turre had freelanced extensively, deepening his involvement in New York City's Latin music scene. In 1982 he became a founding member of the trumpeter Jerry Gonzalez's progressive Afro-Cuban group, the Fort Apache Band. The next year he was a featured soloist in the Village Gate's "Salsa Meets Jazz" concert series, appearing with such Latin-music heavyweights as Tito Puente, Johnny Ventura, and Rubén Blades. In the mid-1980s he worked with, among others, Manny Oquendo & Libre, one of Turre's favorite groups, and the vocalists Celia Cruz and José Alberto. He also played in theater pit bands and in orchestras that backed such rhythm-and-blues singers as Lou Rawls and Gladys Knight. He became a member of Lester Bowie's Brass Fantasy in 1983, pianist McCoy Tyner's big band in 1984, and Cedar Walton's hard-bop sextet in 1985.

In 1986, benefitting from his reputation as a skilled and dependable freelancer, Turre was asked to join the house band for the NBC television network's long-running comedy series *Saturday Night Live*. His new salary was far greater than what he had previously earned as a jazz musician. ("I get more money doing that than playing with Dizzy [Gillespie]," he told Fred Jung for a 2000 interview published on the *Jazz Weekly* Web site. "That is a statement about America right there.") Thanks to his increased income, he moved with his wife, the cellist, composer, and conductor Akua Dixon, from New York City to a large house in suburban New Jersey. He also increased his activity as a bandleader: in addition to jazz groups of standard and not-so-standard instrumentation (some of the

latter included his wife and other string players), Turre began leading a unique seashell choir. Acting on an idea he had gotten from Rahsaan Roland Kirk in about 1970, he recruited several trombonists and trumpeters to play original compositions, jazz standards, and blues on giant conch shells. Using an ancient technique, he had cut and sanded each conch at one end to form a mouthpiece; with a hand inserted into the side opening of the shell, a player could produce a limited range of notes. "Rahsaan had a shell, and he would just blow one note, and he would do that circular breathing thing, and it would just mesmerize the audience," Turre recalled to Fred Jung. "After the gig I asked him, could I try, and he said, yeah. So I blew the shell, and oh, man, it got to me. . . . I just started experimenting with it, and one thing led to another." During a tour of Mexico with Shaw in 1978, Turre had been astonished to learn from relatives that his Aztec ancestors had made music using the same technique. "These ancient instruments are played the exact same way modern brass instruments are—by vibrating the lips, by blowing through a tube or chamber," he explained to Pat Cole for *Down Beat* (March 1993).

In 1987, at the age of 38, Turre released his first album as a leader, *Viewpoint*, on Stash, an independent label. That year he also won the *Down Beat* magazine critics' poll in the category "talent deserving wider recognition." Fast becoming a recognized presence on *Saturday Night Live*, thanks to his distinctive long braid and dark goatee, Turre released his sophomore Stash album, *Fire and Ice* (1988), to critical acclaim. Several tracks on that album feature the jazz string ensemble Quartette Indigo, of which his wife is a member. In the late 1980s Turre performed on trombone with the Art Farmer–Benny Golson Jazztet, and on trombone and seashell with Dizzy Gillespie's United Nations Orchestra. In the 1990 *Down Beat* readers' poll, he was named best trombonist, barely edging out J.J. Johnson. Thereafter, Turre has often ranked first or second among trombonists in the *Down Beat* and *JazzTimes* polls and has frequently topped the list of performers on "miscellaneous instruments" as well.

Meanwhile, with his job at *Saturday Night Live* providing a steady but musically unchallenging source of income, Turre had turned increasingly to recording as a means of self-expression. Together with the trombonist Robin Eubanks, he recorded *Dedication* for JMT, a German label, in 1989. In 1991 Turre signed with Antilles, a division of PolyGram. For the album *Right There* (1991), he assembled a sextet featuring his wife and the jazz violinist John Blake. He recorded the album *Sanctified Shells* (1993) for Antilles, with the shell choir and Dizzy Gillespie as a guest trumpeter. Turre's mother, Carmen, played castinets on the album. Supported by unusually vigorous promotion for a jazz album, *Sanctified Shells* was a modest commercial success. In 1993 and 1994 Turre recorded as a guest soloist on trombone with the Jamaican reggae pioneers the Skatalites.

Turre released a second shell-choir album, *The Rhythm Within*, in 1995. The album *Steve Turre*, recorded in 1996, includes shell music, but its main selling point was the contribution of J.J. Johnson on several tracks. (The following year Johnson featured Turre on his album *The Brass Orchestra*.) Ironically, although it had taken Turre years to persuade a label to approve of his making an entire album of shell music, Verve (a division of PolyGram) now pressed him to record more albums in the *Sanctified Shells* vein—simple melodies laid over hypnotic Latin grooves and spiced with hot jazz solos. His own idea, to further the trombone-and-strings concept explored on *Fire and Ice* and *Right There*, met with resistance from the label. When Turre finally succeeded in getting *Lotus Flower* made, in 1997, Verve delayed its release for more than a year. "They even went so far as to tell me that they thought the shell stuff was a gimmick they could make some money off," he told a writer for the *Jazz Report* (on-line). After *Lotus Flower*'s release, in 1999, the label dropped Turre, as he had requested.

Earlier, in 1995, Turre's shell choir had performed at the Monterey Jazz Festival, in California. The following year Turre wrote the score for a French film, *Anna Oz*, directed by Eric Rochant. In 1998 he appeared with Slide Hampton and Curtis Fuller at the Central Park Summerstage, in New York City. His album *In the Spur of the Moment* (2000) was released on Telarc, an independent label; the album features a reunion with Ray Charles, in a collaboration with Peter Turre, Steve's younger brother and Charles's drummer since the late 1970s. That summer Turre appeared on the National Public Radio series *Jazz at the Kennedy Center*, hosted by the pianist Billy Taylor, and he performed with Charles at the JVC Jazz Festival in New York City. In 2001 the trombonist marked his 15th season on *Saturday Night Live*. For his most recent album, *TNT* (2001)—the title is an acronym for "trombone 'n tenor"—Turre collaborated with the front-ranking tenor saxophonists David Sánchez, Dewey Redman, and James Carter. In a review of the record for *Amazon.com*, the jazz pianist Stuart Broomer wrote, "For all the variety, tenor fireworks, and input from two excellent rhythm sections, it's Turre who makes the strongest impression, imparting consistent musical and emotional focus. He's a consummate trombonist, from vocalic mute work to crisp bop articulation and warm balladry, and he feels his material, seemingly concentrating all his attention on the phrase at hand."

In addition to his concertizing and recording activity, Turre has taught at some of the nation's top schools of jazz, including the Manhattan School of Music, in New York City; the Berklee College of Music, in Boston, Massachusetts; the University of Hartford, in Connecticut; and William Paterson University, in New Jersey.

"I feel very, very lucky and blessed to be able to make a living playing this music that I love so much," Turre told Bob Bernotas. "It's truly America's classical music and even though we haven't gotten full respect at home, I feel it's coming. And in the meantime, I'm still able to grow and be around people that share the same interest and inspiration and goals as myself. A musician's like a doctor, you're supposed to heal people. You make them feel better. As long as I can keep doing that, I'm a happy man." — G.K.R.

Suggested Reading: *All About Jazz* (on-line); *Chicago Tribune* Arts p14+ Apr. 29, 1990, with photos; *Down Beat* p28+ Dec. 1987, with photos, p21+ Mar. 1993, with photos, p34+ Aug. 2000, with photo; *Down Beat Jazz Weekly* (on-line); *Unesco Courier* p44 Dec. 1997, with photo

Selected Recordings: as leader—*Viewpoint*, 1987; *Fire and Ice*, 1988; *Right There*, 1991; *Sanctified Shells*, 1993; *The Rhythm Within*, 1995; *Steve Turre*, 1996; *Lotus Flower*, 1999; *In the Spur of the Moment*, 2000; *TNT*, 2001; with Art Blakey and the Jazz Messengers—*Anthenagin*, 1973; *Buhaina*, 1973; with Woody Shaw—*The Moontrane*, 1974; *Rosewood*, 1978; *Night Music* 1982; *Imagination*, 1987; with Robin Eubanks—*Dedication*, 1989

Tyson, John H.

1954– Chairman, president, and CEO of Tyson Foods Inc. Address: Tyson Foods Inc., P.O. Box 2020, Springdale, AR 72765

In 1998 John H. Tyson became the chairman of Tyson Foods Inc., the poultry and prepared-foods conglomerate founded by his grandfather John W. Tyson. His ascension to the chairmanship was followed by his appointment as president and chief executive officer (CEO), in April 2000, after the retirement of Wayne Britt, a development that shifted the executive powers of the company fully into the hands of the founding family. Since its establishment, in the 1930s, the Tyson business has expanded from the hauling of chickens to include the hatching, feeding, raising, processing, and distributing of poultry; in addition, the company has had holdings in the fish, pork, beef, and baked-goods industries. Although much of the company's voting power remains with John W. Tyson's son Donald J. Tyson, who retired from the posts of chairman, president, and CEO in 1995 to become senior chairman, Don Tyson has endorsed his own son as a worthy successor—this despite John H. Tyson's struggles with alcohol and drugs and his mediocre job performance in the 1970s and 1980s. "Within the past years, [John has] stepped forward and proven himself a serious business person," Don

Courtesy of Tyson Foods Inc.

John H. Tyson

Tyson told David Barboza for the *New York Times* (March 4, 2001). "I am really proud of what he's done since assuming the role of chairman in 1998. The way our company has operated in the face of very difficult circumstances in our industry is a testament to John and his entire management team." (According to Barboza, "That Mr. Tyson got to the top, despite abusing drugs and sometimes acting cavalierly on the job, illustrates just how much power the Tyson family retains in what is, after all, a public company. Family members own less than a majority of the outstanding shares, yet they control 90 percent of its votes.") After facing scandals ranging from the alleged giving of illegal gifts to former United States secretary of agriculture Mike Espy to illegal handling of waste at farms in Maryland, Tyson Foods Inc. is hoping for stability.

The company that has come to dominate the poultry-processing market had humble beginnings. During the Great Depression, John W. Tyson, a produce hauler from Missouri, moved to the neighboring state of Arkansas, settling in the small town of Springdale with his wife, Helen, and infant son, Don. There, he opened a small hauling business, transporting hay, fruit from nearby orchards, and chickens from hatcheries to local markets. In the mid-1930s Tyson extended his routes and began delivering chickens to Kansas City and St. Louis; when that venture proved successful, he expanded further, finding buyers in Chicago in 1936 and in Houston, Cincinnati, Detroit, Cleveland, and Memphis over the next few years, according to the company's Web site. In the mid-1940s the business was threatened by a chick shortage. To defend himself against similar shortages in the future, Ty-

son imported New Hampshire Red Christy chickens and began to breed them himself. A chicken-feed shortage in 1947 prompted him to start producing his own chicken feed; livestock and pet feed remain important parts of the business. Incorporated in 1947, the Tyson Feed and Hatchery now oversaw chickens from egg to market; the company's slogan, featured in its advertisements and painted on its trucks, was, "When better chicks are hatched, we will hatch them!"

In 1952, while struggling to deal with low chicken prices, diseases that affected the chickens, and increasing competition—more than a dozen companies in northwestern Arkansas were involved in poultry—John W. Tyson refused a buyout offer from the Swanson Co. Hurriedly recruiting his son Donald, who had not yet finished his agriculture studies at the University of Arkansas, Tyson weathered the 1950s and expanded even further, opening a chicken-processing plant in about 1958. In 1961 the father-and-son team began commercially producing eggs. Two years later the company went public, as Tyson's Foods, and began to expand by purchasing other outlets; its first acquisition was the Garnett Poultry Co., in nearby Rogers, Arkansas. Don Tyson started to take the reins from his father, introducing Rock Cornish game hens in 1965. (The Rock Cornish hens, crossbreeds of two kinds of chickens, were sold at a fixed price, 50 cents initially, to avoid market fluctuations. Tyson Foods' market share of this product is more than 50 percent today, according to the company's Web site.)

Don Tyson became the president of Tyson's Foods in 1966 and was named chairman of the company the following January, after his father and stepmother were killed by a train that struck their car. Under his leadership Tyson's Foods (renamed Tyson Foods Inc. in 1971) continued to grow and diversify. One of his crowning achievements, in the late 1960s and early 1970s, stemmed from his decision to have chickens prepared and cooked in Tyson's factories and then sold at a higher price as "heat and eat" convenience food. As Thomas Heath wrote for the *Washington Post* (July 23, 1995), "Tyson's timing couldn't have been better. American women were beginning to move into the work force in large numbers, and the fast-food industry was ready to expand beyond burgers and fries." Tyson Foods became the purveyor of frozen, prepared chicken products to both individual and corporate consumers. Don Tyson also expanded into pork, beef, and seafood production, through acquiring small companies in those areas, and he also negotiated the purchase of the Mexican Original brand, which makes flour and corn tortillas and other food products. John H. Tyson has said that he plans to follow in his father's footsteps, by making chicken and other meat products ever more convenient for consumers while maintaining the high quality of Tyson foods.

The oldest of the three children—and only son—of Don Tyson and his wife, the former Twila Jean Womochil (called Jean), John H. Tyson was born in 1954 in Springdale, Arkansas, a small town in the northwestern corner of the state. He went to local public schools, where he was a good student; while at Springdale High School, he was active on the student council and in several sports. During his years at a succession of universities—the University of Arkansas at Fayetteville, the University of Southern California, and Southern Methodist University—in the early 1970s, he began drinking and using drugs, stumbling into an addiction that would plague him for nearly two decades. During this period he abandoned his Methodist roots. "I didn't stay on the path," he explained to David Barboza. "I was wandering around." Tyson graduated from Southern Methodist University with a degree in business in 1975 and spent a year in law school at the University of Arkansas before joining the family firm.

When John H. Tyson became an employee of Tyson Foods, the company was emerging as the leader in poultry farming and processing, incorporating factory-farming methods into the hatching and raising of chickens to ensure quality and consistency. In about 1977 the new father-and-son Tyson team took a big step in terms of diversification, purchasing hog-production facilities in North Carolina. John Tyson was sent to oversee the operation, and two years later the company was the largest hog producer in the United States. It is possible that the venture was successful despite, rather than because of, the son's efforts; over the next decade, during which John Tyson was shifted among various divisions within Tyson Foods, he was continually hampered by his addictions. "Everything was foggy," he admitted to David Barboza. (During a trial related to the investigation of former U.S. secretary of agriculture Mike Espy, Tyson testified, as quoted by Barboza, "I can tell you the only reason I was on the payroll is because I was the son of the boss. Any other corporation, I would have been thrown to the wolves.") He ultimately undertook treatment, devoting himself to the 12-step recovery programs of Alcoholics Anonymous and Narcotics Anonymous. Tyson has said that he took his last drink in November 1990, according to Barboza, who quoted him as saying, "I count my birth date as December 1, 1990. Since then, I've been headed in the right direction."

For Tyson, the 1990s represented a time for healing his relationships with the people in his life and improving his business acumen. He smoothed over differences with his father, with whom he had barely been on speaking terms, and in 1990 he was awarded a vice chairmanship of the company, albeit one that involved few responsibilities and little influence. Three years later he became president of the beef and pork division, which at that time was beginning to experience a slowdown. He was then made chief of the international division, which opened a plant in Russia in the mid-1990s,

only to watch it suffer because of the instabilities of the Russian economy. Industry analysts were critical of the actions John Tyson took during this period. "One could argue that he's never been given the best hand to play," John McMillin, a Prudential Securities analyst, told David Barboza. "But I don't think he did much with the cards he had." Tyson's on-the-job training experiences were interrupted by the investigation of Mike Espy for illegal acceptance of gifts; Tyson Foods was under suspicion for directing gifts to Espy at a time when the Agriculture Department was considering new regulations for food labeling that would have introduced extra costs into the industry. Tyson Foods paid a $6 million fine in 1997, and Don and John Tyson were granted immunity from prosecution in exchange for their testimony. Other company employees were ultimately indicted for their roles in the scandal. (Espy was acquitted of illegally accepting gifts, and the Tyson Foods employees were pardoned by Bill Clinton during his presidency.) The company was later fined when two Maryland farms contracted to breed Tyson Foods chickens were found to be in violation of environmental and sanitary regulations.

During the transitional period, from 1998 to 2000—when John H. Tyson was the chairman but not yet president and CEO of the company—several small processing units for seafood, beef, and pork, products with which the company had limited experience, were eliminated in order to redouble the effort to promote chicken products. The undisputed champion of poultry production in the United States, Tyson Foods has the capacity to slaughter and prepare 45 million chickens per week in its 66 processing plants. Capitalizing on the fact that his company was the industry leader, Tyson, in one of his first moves after being anointed president and CEO, forged a partnership with Share Our Strength, a charitable organization that stocks food banks in the United States. Tyson Foods has made a commitment to donate 6.5 million pounds of chicken to Share Our Strength by 2003. Late in 2000 Tyson decided to renew the company's efforts to produce and market other meats. Working from the egg-shaped office that had been his father's, Tyson maneuvered to outbid Smithfield Farms to purchase IBP, a beef and pork producer. Tyson attempted to allay fears that he would apply chicken-farming methods to beef and pork production. "Our expertise is on marketing and convenience items and taking them to the next level," he explained to David Barboza. "We want to spend our money on marketing." "To hit a home run, we have to move IBP into being a branded deal," Tyson told Scott Kilman for the *Wall Street Journal* (January 10, 2001), seeking to counter the current trend of delivering many beef and pork products anonymously—that is, without a brand label—to consumers. Late in March 2001, however, Tyson Foods terminated the merger with IBP, citing "misleading" accounting information given by an IBP subsidiary, DFG Foods, which was itself being investigated by the Securities and Exchange Commission. (Even before the accounting irregularities were made public, some industry insiders speculated that Tyson would back out of the deal. The financial analyst John McMillin explained to Sam Jaffe for *Business Week Online* [March 12, 2001], "Part of me thinks they will chicken out. They have to have a lot of guts to buy a beef company in the midst of mad cow, foot and mouth, and declining beef consumption.") IBP has sued Tyson Foods to force the completion of the buyout, valued at $3.2 billion.

Although Tyson is still learning the ropes, in terms of politics, finance, and the labor market, he pointedly told David Barboza, "If I wasn't qualified, I wouldn't have this job." The company has faced a number of difficulties in the last several years, both internal and external. In 1999 it was forced to negotiate with workers at an Indiana processing plant who went on strike after Tyson tried to eliminate work breaks; after nearly three months, the workers signed a three-year contract that gradually phased out the break in exchange for increases in hourly wages. Also that year, the company experienced seven work-related deaths. Tyson Foods was fined by the Labor Cabinet of Kentucky for delinquency in paying back wages and by Maryland safety inspectors for violations at company-owned farms. Along with another Arkansas-based giant, Wal-Mart, Tyson successfully pushed for the construction of the Northwest Arkansas Regional Airport; completed in late 1998, the aiport is served by five carriers.

Carol Marie Cropper noted in the *New York Times* (November 8, 1998) that John H. Tyson has a "charmingly boyish manner." Tyson married the former Kimberly McCoy in 1987; the couple divorced in 1998 and share custody of their two children, John and Olivia. Since he has been in recovery from alcoholism, Tyson has renewed his religious faith, and he participates in Bible classes. He gives lectures in prisons and schools on conquering addictions. — K.S.

Suggested Reading: *New York Times* III p1+ Mar. 4, 2001, with photo; *Wall Street Journal* B p1 Jan 10, 2001; *Washington Post* H p1 July 23, 1995

Courtesy of the Jet's Gym

Urquidez, Benny

(ur-KEE-dez)

1952(?)– Martial artist; film choreographer.

Address: The Jet's Gym, 6247 Laurel Canyon Blvd., North Hollywood, CA 91606

The fight sequences in many high-profile movies owe their authenticity to the guiding hand of Benny "The Jet" Urquidez. From the 1970s to the 1990s, Urquidez dominated the world of kick boxing, amassing six world titles in five weight classes and losing—according to official records—only once in approximately 60 bouts. While he stands about five feet seven inches tall and weighs 145 pounds, at his peak as a kick boxer Urquidez possessed such speed and control, and proved so relentless a fighter, that he was consistently able to subdue larger men. "The Jet" takes his nickname from his trademark flying back-kick and from his habit of performing a back flip after each victory. He has developed his own martial-arts technique, Ukidokan (a Japanese term meaning "a way of life"), about which he has written several books. "Control is the key to understanding," Urquidez told Steve Henson for the *Los Angeles Times* (August 17, 1985). "Control of the body, of the mind, of the spirit and of the heart. I don't fight out of anger. I am a sportsman. Through my sport I have learned self-respect and discipline." In the early 1980s Urquidez began appearing in minor roles in action films. Since he retired from kick boxing, in 1989 (with the exception of his brief, successful comeback in the mid-1990s), Urquidez has turned his enormous energy to training other martial artists and to choreographing combat scenes for movies and TV. His most recent film work was on *Pearl Harbor* (2001), for which he coached the actor Cuba Gooding Jr. in the combat sequences. Numerous other stars have sought out Urquidez as a personal trainer.

Of Spanish-Mexican descent, Benny Urquidez was born in Tarzana, California, in about 1952 and grew up in the San Fernando Valley. He came from a family of fighters: his grandmother rode with the Mexican revolutionary Pancho Villa; his father, who left the family when Urquidez was eight, was a professional boxer; and his mother was a professional wrestler who supported her eight children (four boys and four girls) by wrestling at such venues as the Olympic Auditorium in Los Angeles. Most of Urquidez's siblings participated in martial-arts competitions; his older sister Lilly was a world-championship bantamweight kick boxer. "My oldest brother, Arnold, would send the family out to seek new fighting techniques," Urquidez told Henson. "We would return and share our knowledge with the others. Judo, karate, kick-boxing, western boxing—we blended them into a family style." During Urquidez's youth, he and his brothers and sisters roamed the streets of San Fernando, often getting into fights. "When we fought in the street, we fought for real," Urquidez told Henson. "We didn't believe in leaving the other guy standing because he might come back with a 2-by-4 and cave in our skulls. We owned the valley. We would walk the streets and a hundred kids would follow behind."

Urquidez started boxing at age three, and by the time he was five, he was competing in the pee-wee division at the Olympic Auditorium, the same venue where his mother sometimes wrestled. At age seven he began to study karate and judo; he earned a black belt at the extremely young age of 14. Urquidez attended Grant High School in Van Nuys and Polytechnic High School in Long Beach (where he was on the wrestling team) before graduating, in 1969, from North Hollywood High School. There, he played defensive back for the football team and specialized in laying hits on opposing offensive players.

Urquidez continued to practice martial arts after high school. When he was 22 he accepted an invitation from the karate champion and action-film star Chuck Norris, who had begun the National Karate League (NKL), to join his team, the Los Angeles Stars. (Urquidez's brothers Adam and Manuel were alternates on the team.) Later in the same year Urquidez made his mark on the world of full-contact fighting when he participated in the World Series of Martial Arts, a two-day event held in Honolulu, Hawaii. Even though there were no weight divisions in the full-contact tournament, the lightweight Urquidez won his first four fights by knockout. "After the first day, everybody was in slings and casts," Urquidez told Jim Coleman for *Black Belt Magazine* (December 1985, on-line). "Only 15 showed up the next day." His fifth fight, for the championship, was against the six-foot one-inch, 225-pound heavyweight kick-boxing champion Dana Goodson. Against the expectations of most, Urquidez scored a third-round knockout. "I attacked him like a leech sucking blood," Urquidez told Henson, recalling his victory. "I am a stone survivor and that day I proved it to the martial arts world."

Also in 1975 Urquidez won the NKL lightweight title. In the following year he captured a title from the Professional Karate Association (PKA), a sanctioning body that forbade kicking below the waist. Urquidez continued to steamroll his opponents during the remainder of the 1970s, winning most of his fights by knockout. He made his debut in Japan in the summer of 1977, against the lightweight champion Katsuyuki Suzuki—who absorbed relentless punishment from Urquidez before being knocked out in the sixth round. Seeing one of his country's most admired kick boxers so handily beaten provoked the former Japanese lightweight champion Kunimatsu Okao to come out of retirement for a November 1977 bout with Urquidez. Okao gave Urquidez far more trouble than Suzuki had. In the second round Okao knocked Urquidez down with a bludgeoning overhand right. Urquidez continued to struggle in the third. "I was shocked," Urquidez told Coleman. "He had a cocky look like 'You're fighting against the best.' It was a matter of honor." In the fourth round Urquidez summoned his energy, unleashing an uninterrupted barrage of punches and kicks that culminated in a knockout victory. Urquidez had beaten one of Japan's most celebrated fighters and won legendary status for himself. Word went around Japan that Urquidez was half Japanese, and soon the *Benny The Jet* comic book appeared, which featured Urquidez as a superhero.

The one loss that appears on Urquidez's record, according to the Standardized Tournaments and Ratings Service (STAR), occurred in August 1980 before a crowd of 6,000 in West Palm Beach, Florida. His opponent was a relatively unknown fighter named Billye Jackson. Accounts of the episode differ; Urquidez has maintained that before the bout, he thought he was scheduled to fight an unofficial exhibition match against Glen Mehiman. He was then informed that Mehiman had backed out and that he would instead take on Jackson. Urquidez was next told that Jackson would not fight unless the judge forbade kicks to the legs, one of Urquidez's strengths. During the seven-round match, Jackson wore a set of boxing gloves that were heavier than Urquidez's, which enhanced Jackson's ability to deliver knockout-strength blows. Howard Hanson, the president of the World Karate Association (WKA), which sanctioned the fight, has said that Urquidez was aware that the bout was not an exhibition. He has agreed, however, with the other elements of Urquidez's version of events. "If Benny had had the same gloves," he told Coleman, "he would've torn [Jackson's] head off." Instead, Jackson dominated the early rounds and at one point knocked Urquidez down. Urquidez began to surge back in the late rounds, but by then it was too late. "Once Benny figured out what he could do without the leg kicks," Hanson told Coleman, "he went after the guy and beat the crap out of him. If it had been a nine-round fight, he would've knocked him out."

Urquidez also lost, according to some sources, to Prayoud Sittiboonlert, a practitioner of Thailand's Muay Thai technique, which uses kicks to the legs, knee thrusts, and clinching. Those reports indicate that Urquidez's corner threw in the towel after the second round, judging their fighter to be too battered to continue. In the U.S. the bout was scored as a "no contest" and did not show up on Urquidez's record.

Urquidez's most unnerving fight occurred in November 1980, when he was in Hong Kong to promote a movie. He was being interviewed on a talk show when a man in the audience stood up and began yelling at Urquidez. As the translator explained, the man said that Urquidez was not a real fighter but an actor, and he challenged Urquidez to a fight to the death. Urquidez accepted, and after the show a promoter approached him, asking for his terms. Urquidez, not believing that his demands would be met, asked for $20,000 and a mink coat. The next morning the money and the coat were delivered to his hotel. Urquidez then learned that his opponent was a Chinese champion and that the fight was scheduled for the next day. The venue was dark and smoky, with a small, square ring surrounded by old wooden benches. Hundreds crowded into the small space, and as the bell rang, signaling the start of the first round, the Chinese fighter raised his fists in the air and yelled, "To the death!" Fueled by fear when he heard the words, Urquidez went on the attack. He battered his opponent for three rounds, which did not stop the other fighter from yelling "To the death!" at the beginning of each. "In the fourth round," Urquidez recalled to Coleman, "he went down and the people gave the thumbs down sign. They expected me to kill the guy. It was to the point where he was down and barely breathing, and blood everywhere, and they wanted me to kill him. They told me later they had to fuse his nose, jaw and cheekbone. So I did a backflip in the middle of the ring and ran out. The security people locked me in the locker room for four hours because they were rioting outside. I've had a lot of experience with different things, but this was one . . . I don't like to talk about. It bothered me for the longest time."

In 1981 Urquidez appeared in the movie *Force Five*, in which he played Billy, one of the five heroes who try to rescue a young girl who has been kidnapped by a cult leader. Urquidez appeared in a number of other films in the 1980s and 1990s, playing mostly minor roles. His acting credits include *Wheels on Meals* (1984), *The Kick Fighter* (1987), *Dragons Forever* (1987), *Down the Drain* (1990), *Bloodmatch* (1991), *Diggstown* (1992), *Deathmatch* (1994), *Grosse Point Blank* (1997), and *Enter the Eagles* (1998). The final battle scene of *Dragons Forever*, which starred the action-movie superstar Jackie Chan, features a match between Chan and Urquidez. Chan has referred to it as his finest fight sequence on film.

In 1983 Urquidez opened a martial-arts academy in Van Nuys, California, called the Jet Center, which also serves as the headquarters for Project Heavy and the Knockdown Dropout Academy, programs to help local youths employ the discipline of martial arts in dealing with the challenges of growing up. The Jet Center specializes in Urquidez's Ukidokan system, about which he has written several books: *Training and Fighting Skills* (1980), *Karate Dynamics: The Ukidokan System* (1991), *King of the Ring: How to Use Your Gym Equipment and Other Tricks of the Trade* (1995), and *Practical Kick Boxing: Strategy in Training and Technique* (1998).

Urquidez continued to fight without a loss during the rest of the 1980s. He retired in about 1989, the year that he began working as a fight and stunt choreographer for movies. He coordinated fight scenes for *Road House* (1989) and trained the movie's star, Patrick Swayze. Urquidez has also coordinated fight scenes for the feature films *Tango and Cash* (1989), *Batman II* (1992), *Natural Born Killers* (1994), *Con Air* (1996), and *The Big Hit* (1998), among others. Because of his intensive work with movie stars, he became a much sought-after personal trainer with a reputation for toughness. He has worked with such actresses and actors as Juliette Lewis, Nicole Kidman, John Cusack, Michelle Pfeiffer, and Louis Gossett Jr., as well as the musicians Duff McKagan (formerly of Guns 'n' Roses) and David Lee Roth. Cusack, whose character in *Grosse Point Blank* fights a hit man played by Urquidez, told an interviewer for *People* (October 16, 1995), "I don't know any other workout this hard."

In Las Vegas on December 4, 1993, Urquidez came out of retirement to fight for the world light-middleweight crown. His opponent was Yoshihisa Tagami, the 25-year-old undefeated Japanese WKA welterweight champion. It had been four and a half years since the 41-year-old Urquidez had fought in the ring, and in the early rounds the effects of the hiatus showed: Tagami landed punches and kicks repeatedly, sending Urquidez to the mat in the second round with a right-hand blow. Urquidez rallied in the late rounds, however, landing solid blows of his own. At the end of the scheduled 12 rounds, with both fighters still standing, two of the three judges awarded the fight to Urquidez. The victory marked his sixth world championship. Shortly after that, he retired again.

Urquidez continues to train students in his Ukidokan system at the Jet Center. He lives with his wife, Sara, in North Hollywood, California. The couple have a daughter, Monique, who is a kick boxer and model. — P.G.H.

Suggested Reading: *Black Belt Magazine* (on-line) Dec. 1985; *Los Angeles Times* p16+ Aug. 17, 1985, p17 Aug. 17, 1985, p1 Nov. 30, 1993, p14 Dec. 5, 1993; *People* p81+ Oct. 16, 1995

Selected Books: *Training and Fighting Skills*, 1980; *Karate Dynamics: The Ukidokan System*, 1991; *King of the Ring: How to Use Your Gym Equipment and Other Tricks of the Trade*, 1995; *Practical Kick Boxing: Strategy in Training and Technique*, 1998

Keibun Miyamoto/Retna Ltd.

Valentine, Bobby

May 13, 1950– Manager of the New York Mets. Address: New York Mets, Shea Stadium, 123-01 Roosevelt Ave., Flushing, NY 11368

Bobby Valentine, the manager of the New York Mets, is known for his unparalleled baseball acumen. "You could take the most knowledgeable baseball writer there is, and when you compare what he knows to what Bobby knows, you'd have the difference between someone in kindergarten and someone going for their Ph.D.," Tom Grieve, the general manager of the Texas Rangers, with whom Valentine worked for seven and a half years, told Michael Knisley for the *Sporting News* (September 21, 1999, on-line). Valentine's expertise has won him a devoted following of fans, baseball experts, and players. At the same time, his tendency to flaunt his knowledge and his occasional combativeness have enraged some of his peers and people in the media. Valentine, who sometimes refers to himself as "the most hated man in baseball," has rarely apologized for his behavior. "I don't need my competition to like me," he told S. L. Price for *Sports Illustrated* (October 11, 1999). "But a lot of them just absolutely fear that someday they're going to have to be on a panel with me or something,

and they'll just be exposed. . . . People say I'm arrogant when someone who's a newspaperman or sportscaster or someone in uniform says something really dumb, and I'm supposed to accept it? I don't accept that." When Valentine managed the Texas Rangers, his detractors cited the team's mediocre record as evidence that he was full of hot air. As the manager of the Mets, he led the team to the World Series in 2000, and by the end of that season he had compiled the second-best record (379–301) of any Mets manager—successes that have left his critics with little ammunition.

Robert John Valentine was born on May 13, 1950 in Stamford, Connecticut. At the age of seven, he acquired a coloring book that depicted many of baseball's Hall of Fame players, and he resolved to join their ranks someday. An outgoing boy, he loved to organize neighborhood baseball games. "I was the kid who got everyone to come out and play," he told Leigh Montville for *Sports Illustrated* (April 6, 1992). "I was the one outside the window yelling, 'Hey, Joey, let's play baseball.' I think I read the rule book for the first time when I was 13, and I have read it every year of my life ever since."

Valentine played Little League baseball throughout his youth, and by the time he was a teenager, he had become something of a celebrity in Stamford. At 14 he won a regional championship ballroom-dancing competition. At Rippowam High School he was elected president of the student council and played a leading role in the school production of the comedy *Teahouse of the August Moon*. At age 18 he won a pancake-eating contest. The source of his greatest local fame, however, was his athleticism; indeed, he is still widely considered the greatest all-around high-school sports star in Connecticut history. Valentine was an All-State player in football, baseball, and track and field. He held the student record for the 60-yard dash and, as a football running back, for the most career touchdowns. In his sophomore year he led his football team to a 9–0 record and a state championship. As a senior he sneaked into the pep rally of an opposing team and discovered that its members had hung an effigy of him. The next day he avenged himself by scoring six touchdowns before his removal from the game in the second half.

Among the many college scouts who expressed interest in Valentine was John McKay, the football coach of the University of Southern California (USC) in Los Angeles, who needed someone to replace his former running back O. J. Simpson. On his subsequent visit to USC, Valentine met the former Los Angeles Dodgers manager Tommy Lasorda; soon afterward Valentine decided to join the Dodgers. Drafted as the fifth overall pick in 1968, he received a $70,000 bonus from the Dodgers and went to play for their minor-league team in Ogden, Utah. According to John Altavilla, writing for the *Hartford Courant* (October 19, 2000, on-line), the Dodgers' scouting director, Al Campanis, told Valentine he had the potential to be the best baseball player in the U.S.

Valentine was a league most-valuable-player (MVP) both at Ogden, where he played under Tommy Lasorda, and at a Triple A minor-league team in Spokane, Washington. But from the outset of his professional baseball career, he repeatedly behaved recklessly. Thanks to his brazenness, in 1969 he broke his jaw, and in 1970 he tore his knee, significantly reducing his running speed. Valentine's outspokenness also worked against him. For example, he openly campaigned to replace the Dodgers' manager, Walter Alston, with Lasorda; that conduct, in part, led to his being traded to the California Angels in 1973. He had achieved a batting average of .300 when, later that year, while running at full speed in an effort to catch what turned out to be a home run, he crashed into the outfield wall and shattered his right leg in two places. Incorrectly set, the leg threw him off his stride so badly during his attempted comeback that he sometimes fell while running toward first base. (His right calf is now permanently atrophied, and a baseball-sized mass of bone protrudes from his shin.)

After playing for the Angels in 1974 and part of 1975, Valentine was traded to the San Diego Padres. In 1976 he was traded to the New York Mets; he finished that season and the next with the Padres. In 1978 he returned to the Mets and compiled a batting average of .269 in 69 games. When the Mets failed to extend his contract, Valentine scrambled to get signed with another team. "I didn't have any alternatives, but I wasn't going to stand for it," he told Barry Shapiro for *Sport* (August 1987). "I became a madman. I called every team. I begged people, 'Just let me try out.' I was so naive. I thought I could walk into any camp and outplay someone else. I kept thinking my leg was going to get better, or at least well enough for me to be better than other people." In 1979 the Seattle Mariners, in great need of a third baseman, signed Valentine. He hit .276 that year and then retired, with a career batting average of .260.

In need of a second career, the 29-year-old Valentine opened a restaurant, Bobby Valentine's Sports Gallery Cafe, in Stamford. Working 17-hour days, he expanded his business into a profitable chain of restaurants, in Texas and Rhode Island as well as Connecticut. (Currently, there are three cafés, in Arlington, Texas, Stamford, and Norfolk, Connecticut.) In the early 1980s he also coached in the minor leagues. After three years he was hired by the Mets as a third-base coach. He spent two years with the Mets before Tom Grieve offered him the position of manager of the Texas Rangers. "I'd roomed with him with the Mets [in 1977]," Grieve told Montville. "I guess we sat on the bench a lot together, too. His passion in life was baseball. His goal was to be a big league manager. He was the only guy on the team who never missed a pitch." On May 16, 1985 Valentine was hired to replace the Rangers' manager, Doug Rader, who had led his team to nine wins and 23 losses so far that season. Plagued by mediocre personnel and bad trade decisions, the Rangers had not had a single winning season since 1979 and had become the laughingstock of the American League. "I took the job because of the challenge it presented," Valentine told Phil Rogers for the *Sporting News* (March 6, 1989). "I don't think I'll ever have as great a challenge again. It's going to be tough to find a team as down as the Texas Rangers."

In 1985 Valentine guided the Rangers to a record of 53–76. The team started the next season with a pitching staff composed of five rookies. To improve the combined major-league career record (36–64) of the previous year's pitching starters and strengthen their arms, Valentine and his pitching coach ordered the men to throw footballs before games. Although that season every active Ranger except two infielders missed at least one game because of injury, the team finished in second place in the American League West, with a record of 87–75. In recognition of that achievement, United Press International named Valentine the American League Manager of the Year. Referring to his boldness in starting rookie pitchers, Valentine told Shapiro, "I take calculated risks. I try to do a risk/reward ration. A lot of times, it's my risk and the players' reward, you know. That's been bassackwards with a lot of managers in the past. They take a low personal risk and put the player out in the field. Then [when he doesn't perform], they badmouth him in the lounge and I don't particularly like to do it that way."

For the most part Valentine saved his badmouthing for umpires and opposing teams. He soon earned himself the nickname "Front Step," for his habit of standing at the top of the dugout stairs and, with his trademark fixed smile, unleashing a stream of remarks toward the field. In the 1986 and 1987 seasons, umpires threw him out of a total of 12 games to punish him for what they regarded as unacceptable behavior. Accusations flew that Valentine would stop at nothing to win. Some contended that he had shortened the distance between the mound and home plate in the Rangers' visitors' bullpen so that opposing pitchers would be forced to make adjustments when they pitched on the field. Others charged that Valentine purposely boosted the air conditioning in the visitors' locker rooms to make the opposing team feel the Texas heat on the field more intensely. Conversely, he was blamed when the air conditioning in the visitors' locker rooms broke down while the home locker rooms remained cool.

The Rangers finished the 1987 season in sixth place in the division, with 75 wins and 87 losses. The following year the team again finished sixth, with 70 wins and 91 losses. In 1989 and 1990 the Rangers' record improved, to 83–79 in both years, but they still placed only fourth and third, respectively. In 1991 the Rangers went 85–77. While they scored the most runs in baseball that year, the chronically weak pitching staff gave up the most runs. "If I had the same record in New York that I have here, I'd have been fired after my third year managing," Valentine told Montville. As it happened, he was fired during his eighth year, on July 9, 1992, after the Rangers had compiled a record of 45–41.

The next season Valentine found work with the Cincinnati Reds, first as a scout and then as a third-base coach. In 1993 he managed a Mets Triple A club in Norfolk, Virginia. In 1994 Tatsuro Hirooka, the new general manager of the Chiba Lotte Marines in Japan, asked him to manage that team. The Marines had not won in their division in 20 years and had placed fifth in eight of the previous nine years. Hirooka was hoping for a big change, and Valentine, with his aggressive American-style managing approach, seemed the perfect choice. By accepting the offer, Valentine became the first person to manage in the major leagues in both Japan and the U.S. When Jim Reeves, writing for the *Sporting News* (February 20, 1995), asked Valentine whether he thought his managing techniques would be accepted in Japan, where strategy is generally more conservative than in the U.S., he said, "I suspect it's just like in the U.S. If you win, you're a genius. If you don't . . . well, we know what happens then." This standard apparently did not apply in Japan: although Valentine led the Marines to their best record ever, Hirooka fired him, citing philosophical differences.

In 1996 Valentine returned to the Mets Triple A Norfolk club. On August 26 of that year, Mets officials announced that Valentine was replacing the team's dismissed manager, Dallas Green, to finish out the season with the struggling club. From 1990 to 1996 the Mets had posted the worst seven-year record in baseball. Valentine was unable to reverse that trend during the 31 games he managed in 1996 (the Mets finished 71–91), but the following season he helped the team improve vastly. Under his tutelage the Mets became one of the best-fielding teams in baseball. Valentine rotated his lineup constantly in order to keep his players fresh and arrange matchups with members of opposing teams that—based on the voluminous scouting reports that he continually perused—he felt would be most advantageous to the Mets. "This team is amazing," Carlos Baerga, a Mets second baseman, said to Tom Verducci for *Sports Illustrated* (August 4, 1997). "It's a different guy every night helping us win. We never get down." The Mets finished the 1997 season at 88–74—not good enough to get to the play-offs but good enough to regain respect in the league.

In 1998, after keeping up a similar pace, the Mets lost their final five games of the season and thus failed to make the play-offs—an outcome for which Valentine was blamed. Critics noted that only two men had managed more major-league games than Valentine without taking their teams to the play-offs. "You judge a manager on how he wins, and the talent he has to win," the Astros' hitting coach, Tom McCraw, told Michael Knisley. "So the question in my mind is, 'Has he won?' He has not. And he's had talent. But to me, it's not even about the ballgame. You don't manage a ballgame. You manage people. If you want to be a successful manager, that's the key. So I don't see [any] successful manager[s] who [don't] handle people very well. And I think Bobby Valentine is very short there."

Valentine was also derided for "micromanaging"—getting bogged down in the details of the game, the scouting reports, and strategic minutiae. Sometimes Valentine's micromanagement has indeed been counterproductive. With a 1–1 count in a game against the Houston Astros, for instance, Valentine had his pitcher throw a pitchout, because he knew that four out of seven times that season the Astros had attempted squeeze bunts at that count. But the pitchout was wasted, because this time the Astros' manager waited until the count was 2–1. Sometimes, however, Valentine's obsessive attention to detail has paid off. In a game against the Baltimore Orioles, for example, Valentine noticed an Orioles runner on second base shift his foot toward third base, so he instructed his pitcher to throw to second; as he had foreseen, the runner was tagged out. At Wrigley Field, in Chicago, Valentine noticed that the shadows cast by the Cubs' catcher revealed where he was positioning himself to receive each pitch, thus giving the Mets' batters clues as to what pitches might be expected.

In 1999 Valentine continued to take calculated risks with the Mets and act bizarrely at times both on and off the field. On June 9, for example, after being ejected from a game against the Toronto Bluejays, Valentine was caught on camera in the dugout wearing a black hat, a black shirt, a pair of sunglasses, and an obviously fake mustache (possibly just a piece of black tape). The rules of baseball prohibit an ejected player from reentering the dugout, so the crudely disguised Valentine was fined and suspended for two games. "Let's not kid anyone," Valentine told Murray Chass for the *New York Times* (June 13, 1999). "I knew where the camera was. If I thought this was punishable by death, the camera never would have seen me. I didn't think it was that big a deal. But again, I was incorrect." Commenting on the mustache incident and the widespread criticism it provoked, T. J. Quinn noted in the *Bergen Record* (August 10, 1999, on-line), a New Jersey newspaper, "If the Braves' beloved Bobby Cox had worn a mustache and shades, he wouldn't have been ridiculed for not taking the game seriously, he would have been called a cutup. But Cox has won seven straight division titles, four pennants, and a World Series, so he has some slack. Valentine has never been popular in baseball, and he has never been to the play-offs, so his strange stunts set off red flags."

Earlier, on June 5, 1999, in the midst of an eight-game losing streak (which brought the Mets to 27–28), Valentine had read in a newspaper that the Mets' general manager, Steve Phillips, had fired the team's pitching coach, Bob Apodaca. Valentine denied the report, only to soon learn that not only Apodaca but his hitting coach, Tom Robson, and his bullpen coach, Randy Niemann, had been dismissed. Managers traditionally choose their own coaches, and Valentine viewed the firings as a grave insult. Many commentators suggested that Phillips's move had been an indirect attempt to push Valentine to resign. The next day Valentine issued a statement in which he declared, as quoted in the *New York Times* (August 7, 1999), "I believe within the next 55 games if we're not better, I shouldn't be the manager." Perhaps in response to this apparent call to arms, the team won 40 of the next 55 games and moved from third to first place in the National League East division. (Valentine later claimed that he had predicted that the Mets would chalk up exactly 40 wins and 15 losses during that period.) In September 1999 the Mets went into another late-season slump. After their fifth consecutive loss, on September 25 in a contest with the Philadelphia Phillies, Valentine astounded those present at a press conference by saying, as quoted in the *Atlanta Journal-Constitution* (September 26, 1999), "I shouldn't come back next year if we don't go to the playoffs." Having lost eight of their last nine contests, the Mets needed to win all three of the games in their final series with the Pittsburgh Pirates to get to the play-offs—and they succeeded. The third game ended dramatically: in the ninth inning, with the Pirates and Mets tied, 1–1, the Mets had the bases loaded with Pirate pitcher Brad Clontz on the mound. As Clontz went into his delivery, Valentine yelled to his base runners to watch for the wild pitch. Sure enough, Clontz bounced the ball into the backstop, and the Mets scored the winning run. "I do it every time a guy's on third," Valentine later told Price. "And I do it so the pitcher hears me." Thus, after one of the most trying seasons of his career, Valentine had finally led his team to the play-offs. "I've never seen a man take as much heat in one season," the veteran Mets pitcher Orel Hershiser said to Steve Campbell for the Albany, New York *Times Union* (October 4, 1999). The Mets went on to beat the Arizona Diamondbacks in the National League division series. Facing the Atlanta Braves in the National League Championship Series (NLCS), the Mets lost the first three games, won the next two, and then lost the sixth. Valentine subsequently earned the 1999 New York Athletic Club's Manager of the Year award.

Early in the 2000 season, Valentine said to Bill Altman for the *Village Voice* (June 20, 2000), "I'm sure there's not a person in the Mets organization who would be disappointed if we got to the World Series and the [New York] Yankees weren't there. But if we had to write the perfect postseason, I think everyone in the organization would have the opponent be from the Bronx [the site of Yankee Stadium]." For a while the Mets held first place in the National League East. Then, for the third season in a row, the team went into a September slump. They lost six of 12 games during the first three weeks of the month, dropping into second place behind the Atlanta Braves. But they captured

the National League wildcard spot and then beat the San Francisco Giants in the league's division series. During that series Valentine made several notable managing decisions. In the first game he replaced the injured Mets right fielder Derek Bell with a rookie, Timo Perez, instead of with the relatively experienced Bubba Trammell. Perez performed well in the game and went on to bat .304 and score a record-tying eight runs in the NLCS against the St. Louis Cardinals. Valentine's lineup maneuvers helped keep the Cardinal slugger Mark McGwire (relegated to the position of designated hitter because of an injury) from being a big factor in the series. The Mets beat the Cardinals and thus won a trip to the World Series against the New York Yankees.

The Mets lost the first two games of the 2000 series to the formidable Yankees, who thereby extended their World Series winning streak to 12 games. The Yanks' string of successes ended with Game 3, in which Valentine used four pitchers, while the Yankees' manager, Joe Torre, retained the celebrated Orlando Hernandez into the eighth inning. Valentine's tactics paid off, as the Mets got some runs off the flagging Hernandez in the eighth inning. "Joe Torre was outmanaged . . . ," Bill Plaschke wrote for the *Los Angeles Times* (October 25, 2000). "Torre was too liberal with his starting pitcher, too conservative with his offense, and too apathetic [overall]. Valentine was bolder and smarter and as consistent as his grin. Torre, a man whom even [the Yankees' owner] George Steinbrenner cannot fire, worked the game as if he was afraid to lose his job. Valentine, a man whose contract expires any minute now, worked the game as if he has a lifetime contract." But that win was the only one that Valentine and the Mets could manage against the Yankees: the Bronx Bombers clinched the series in Game 5. In the top of the ninth of that game, with the score tied 2–2 and with two outs, the Mets' starting pitcher, Al Leiter, remained on the mound. Leiter then gave up a single and a walk, enabling Yankees runners to reach first base and third. Even though Leiter had hurled more than 140 pitches, Valentine left him in the game as Luis Sojo came to bat. Sojo dribbled a weak ground ball just past Leiter. Center fielder Jay Payton's throw to home hit Jorge Posada as he was sliding onto the plate, allowing both runners to score and giving the Yankees the World Series championship. After the game Gordon Edes, a *Boston Globe* (October 27, 2000) reporter, questioned Torre about Valentine's controversial decision to leave Leiter in the game. "Just like the way I felt about Hernandez the other day," Torre responded, "he pitched well enough to get the win or loss at that point. I thought Bobby made the right choice. That's an emotional choice that nobody should second-guess. He put his blood and guts into that."

On October 31, 2000 the Mets extended Valentine's contract for three years, for a total of approximately $7.5 million. In the first three-quarters of the 2001 season, the injury-plagued Mets underperformed. During the final weeks of the season, when they went 25–6, it seemed as though the team might surge into the play-offs. But after the Mets' reliever Armando Benitez squandered ninth-inning leads of 4–1 and 5–1 in two games against the first-place Atlanta Braves, the Mets' play-offs hopes died. They finished the season at 82–80.

Valentine earned the William A. Shea Distinguished Little League Graduate Award in 1987, the year that Little League Baseball established that honor. In 1990 he was inducted into the Italian American Sports Hall of Fame. He and his wife, the former Mary Branca, have been married since 1977. They have one child, Robert John Valentine Jr. — P.G.H.

Suggested Reading: New York *Daily News* p69 July 20, 1986, with photo; *New York Times* D p1 Sep. 23, 1998, VIII p7 June 13, 1999, D p12 Oct. 2, 2001; *Newsday* p82 Sep. 2, 1986, with photo; *Sport* p23+ Aug. 1987, with photo; *Sport* (on-line) Sep. 21, 1999; *Sporting News* p10+ Mar. 6, 1989, with photo, p10+ Feb. 20, 1995, with photos; *Sports Illustrated* p26+ June 30, 1986, with photos, p42+ Apr. 6, 1992, with photos, p30+ Aug. 4, 1997, with photos, p62+ Aug. 9, 1999, p68+ Oct. 11, 1999

Jonathan Daniel/Allsport

Van Gundy, Jeff

Jan. 19, 1962– Head coach of the New York Knicks. Address: New York Knickerbockers, Madison Square Garden, 2 Penn Plaza, New York, NY 10121

"Winning drives me," Jeff Van Gundy, the head coach for the New York Knicks basketball team, told the New Jersey *Bergen Record* (November 2, 1999, on-line). "You can't put a price on winning, and you can't be paid enough to lose." A former point guard, Van Gundy comes from a family of coaches: his father, Bill Van Gundy, and his brother, Stan Van Gundy, have led teams, and his brother is currently the assistant coach for the Miami Heat, which is headed by Jeff Van Gundy's one-time mentor, Pat Riley. Van Gundy, who is the youngest coach in the National Basketball Associa-

tion (NBA), stresses teamwork and a positive attitude and endeavors to "be direct and honest and open to suggestions," as he told Ira Berkow for the *New York Times* (March 13, 1996). As of March 2001 Van Gundy's career average stood at .596; Pat Riley, with .680, is the only coach in the Knicks' history with a higher career average. Unlike many of his colleagues, Van Gundy eschews designer clothes and expensive cars. At five feet nine inches, he is far shorter than the average basketball player, and sports journalists have occasionally described him as resembling a businessman or an accountant. "He may be small in stature, but he has a big heart, and a strong mind," Knicks shooting guard John Starks told S. L. Price for *Sports Illustrated* (May 11, 1998). "Players see that, and they respect that." Dave Checketts, the CEO and president of Madison Square Garden (the parent organization of the Knicks franchise), believes that Van Gundy is a better coach than Pat Riley. "I've worked with both of them, and so much of what Pat does is to maintain Pat's image, and it takes away from his ability to focus on coaching," Checketts told Price. "Jeff is consumed with getting his players to play in a way that will help him win. He's the perfect coach for New York."

A son of Bill Van Gundy and his wife, Cindy, Jeff Van Gundy was born on January 19, 1962 in Hemet, in Southern California. As an eighth grader he began playing basketball with his brother, Stan, who was then a high-school basketball star. During Van Gundy's boyhood the family moved to New York State. His father was working as a coach at Brockport State College, in New York, when Jeff started college there; he became the school's star point guard. Van Gundy later transferred to Nazareth College of Rochester, near Brockport, where he went on to lead the school's basketball team to the NCAA Division III Eastern Regional title in 1984. After he graduated from Nazareth, in 1985, Van Gundy spent one year as the head coach at McQuaid Jesuit High School, in Rochester. The following season he became an assistant to Rick Pitino, the head coach at Providence College, in Rhode Island. He worked long hours to guide the

Providence team through their Final Four run in the National Collegiate Athletic Association (NCAA) in the 1986–87 season. After Pitino left for the NBA, Van Gundy assisted his replacement, Gordon Chiesa. He left Providence to serve, during the 1988–89 season, as assistant coach to Bob Wenzel at Rutgers University in New Brunswick, New Jersey.

The following season the New York Knicks' head coach, Stu Jackson, hired Van Gundy as an assistant coach. Van Gundy later worked under Jackson's successors, John MacLeod, Pat Riley, and Don Nelson. The Knicks excelled during Riley's tenure, then faltered under Nelson's direction, in spite of the presence of the same core group of players. (Earlier, when Pat Riley had left New York to coach the Miami Heat, in 1995, he had invited Van Gundy to accompany him. The Knicks had refused to release Van Gundy from his contract, so Riley had hired Stan Van Gundy instead.) In March 1996 Nelson was dismissed (because of his inability to communicate with the players and his tendency to make what were viewed as unjustifiable tactical decisions), and Jeff Van Gundy was hired as his temporary replacement. Firing Nelson "was very difficult," Ernie Grunfeld, who was then the Knicks' president, told Jackie MacMullan for *Sports Illustrated* (March 18, 1996), "but the players were not responding. We take a lot of pride in our work ethic, and for some reason that was slipping away from us."

Van Gundy's debut game as head coach ended with an embarrassing 100–92 loss to the Philadelphia 76ers. In the next game the Knicks beat the Chicago Bulls, 104–72. That contest also marked the triumphant return of center Patrick Ewing and point guard Derek Harper, both of whom had recently suffered from slumps. After the game Harper demonstrated his respect and support for Van Gundy by presenting him with the ball used in the game. Emulating Pat Riley, Van Gundy emphasized teamwork and a positive attitude and worked with the team to build a strong defense. He also rotated the line-up more frequently than Nelson had, thus allowing underused players, such as point guard Charlie Ward, more time on the court and bringing the team closer together. In the 1995–96 play-offs, the Knicks swept Cleveland, 3–0, before being defeated by the Chicago Bulls, who won the best-of-seven series in five games. Van Gundy's position became permanent after the play-offs.

The Knicks entered the 1996–97 season with a number of new players, among them Larry Johnson, Allan Houston, and Chris Childs, who joined such Knicks veterans as Patrick Ewing, John Starks, and Charles Oakley. By the end of Van Gundy's first full season as head coach for the Knicks, the team had 57 wins and 25 losses. Five members of the Knicks were suspended for the last two games of the first round of the 1997 play-offs, against the Miami Heat, after leaving the bench when a fight broke out between Miami forward P.J. Brown and New York's Charlie Ward. Van Gundy

accepted responsibility for his players' poor judgment, as well as their loss of the play-off series.

The final seconds of the fourth game of the 1997–98 play-offs—in which the Knicks faced the Heat again and won, 90–85—were marred by a brawl between the Heats' center Alonzo Mourning and the Knicks' Larry Johnson. The two players, who had been teammates on the Charlotte Hornets from 1992 to 1995, tangled after Johnson slammed Mourning in the face with his forearm. Mourning threw several punches, none of which landed; Van Gundy ran from the bench and tried to stop the fight by wrapping his arms around Mourning's leg. Mourning, who is much larger than Van Gundy, shook his leg in an effort to force the coach to release it. "I looked like a fool," Van Gundy admitted to S. L. Price. Riley later accused Van Gundy of provoking the incident by encouraging Johnson to poke Mourning in the face and criticized Van Gundy's decision to restrain Mourning rather than his own player. He also ridiculed Van Gundy's receding hairline and declared that he wished that Mourning's swing had connected with its intended target. "There comes a point where a man takes a stand," Riley told Charlie Nobles for the *New York Times* (May 3, 1998), defending Mourning's actions. "You haven't been in [Mourning's] shoes for eight games against the Knicks. . . . You haven't been hit with the elbows, double-teamed, smacked in the face." Van Gundy responded to the criticism diplomatically, with words of praise for his former mentor. "Coach Riley has done a lot for me and my family," he told reporters, according to Mike Lurie in *CBS SportsLine* (May 3, 1998, on–line). "I worked for him for four years. I learned a lot from him as a coach. I respect him greatly. His opinion has obviously changed of me. But that won't change my opinion of him." Riley and Van Gundy later attended a meeting with the NBA commissioner, David Stern, in an effort to find a way to curb violence in professional basketball and diminish the "trash talk" and excessive physical aggressiveness with which it had increasingly become associated.

The 1998–99 season, which was shortened because of a dispute between players and team owners over salaries and pensions, was particularly difficult for Van Gundy. He was nearly dismissed over differences with Ernie Grunfeld, who by then had been demoted to general manager; he also clashed with forward Marcus Camby, who felt that the coach was underutilizing him, and guard Latrell Sprewell, whom he had forced to accept a sixth-man role that the player felt was beneath him. Sprewell had been absent from league play for 14 months before the 1998–99 season, following his suspension from the Golden State Warriors for choking P.J. Carlesimo, the Warriors' coach; Van Gundy was disheartened by Sprewell's reluctance to change his aggressive playing and adopt the team spirit he had tried to foster in the Knicks. He expressed his disappointment over Sprewell's behavior to Selena Roberts for the *New York Times*

(March 28, 1999): "If I had my druthers, would I have him say: 'The Knicks brought me here. They have a lot of faith in me, and I'll do whatever they say to help us win'? Yes, that's what I'd rather hear him say. And not just say it, but believe it in his heart. But this is the NBA. So I'm not sure that's necessarily going to happen or is realistic." Although at the beginning of the season, Van Gundy had been reluctant to use Camby and Sprewell, who had been acquired by Grunfeld in a trade that had sent the core of Van Gundy's team to other franchises, both players proved instrumental in bringing the team out of an early-season slump to reach the finals. In April 1999 Madison Square Garden president Dave Checketts fired Grunfeld and replaced him with Scott Layden, formerly of the Utah Jazz.

After winning six of their final eight games of the regular season and finishing with a record of 27–23, the Knicks beat Miami, the Atlanta Hawks, and the Indiana Pacers before losing to the San Antonio Spurs 4–1 in the finals. The Knicks won 12 out of the 15 games needed to win the NBA championship and were the first eighth-seeded team to make it to the finals in the history of professional basketball. After Patrick Ewing was injured in a game against the Pacers in the Eastern Conference finals in the spring of 1999, other top players, such as Camby, Sprewell, and Allan Houston, began to receive more media attention. (For a long while sportswriters had tended to focus on Ewing, one of the Knicks' strongest players, at the expense of the rest of the team.) By the end of the season, Camby and Sprewell had come to praise Van Gundy's coaching abilities and seemed happy to be playing for a winning team. "We're playing together more," Camby told William C. Rhoden for the *New York Times* (May 10, 1999). "The ball's being swung around; we don't have any egos; everyone wants to share the spotlight. When different guys are scoring and passing like that, it makes the game fun." Dave Checketts refused to discuss Van Gundy's status publicly until the season had ended, and rumors spread that Van Gundy would not be asked back; in mid-April Checketts had courted former Chicago Bulls coach Phil Jackson, who turned him down to sign with the Los Angeles Lakers. In July Van Gundy received a contract extension good through the 2002–03 season, a deal reported to be worth between $10 million and $14 million.

The Knicks began the 1999–2000 season as one of the smallest teams in the league, with both Ewing and Chris Dudley out with injuries. (Ewing would be traded to the Seattle Supersonics in September 2000.) Latrell Sprewell skipped training camp, and the season began with a series of losses. Still, the Knicks beat the Toronto Raptors and the Miami Heat to go to the finals, where the Indiana Pacers defeated them four games to two. The following season Van Gundy publicly agreed with critics who had claimed that the Knicks were not playing hard enough. "I just want us to be a special team," he explained to Ursula Reel for the *New York Post* (November 27, 2000, on-line). "Really, all that's asked of you is that you come on time, be ready to play, play hard, and play to win. I think we have to look ourselves in the eye and ask, 'Are we doing that?' To me, the answer is no, not enough people.'" According to the *New York Post* (December 19, 2000), the players disagreed with his assessment and later asked Van Gundy to keep future discussions of their abilities private.

In January 2001 Van Gundy once again found himself in the middle of an altercation on the basketball court, when he attempted to stop Camby from hitting forward Danny Ferry of the San Antonio Spurs. Camby swung at Ferry just as the latter was being removed for hitting Camby moments earlier in the game. As Van Gundy jumped in, his head slammed into Camby's, resulting in an injury that required more than a dozen stitches over the coach's left eye. "He got the shot in that every one of our players would like to do to me," Van Gundy joked later, according to Mike Kahn for *CBS SportsLine* (January 17, 2001, on-line). "He just got a free one." Both Camby and Ferry were fined; in addition, Camby received a five-game and Ferry a one-game suspension. While the incident was cited in the media as another example of the diminishing level of civility in the NBA, Van Gundy's players applauded him for his demonstration of loyalty. "It shows that our coach will stick his neck out and put it on the line for his players," Kurt Thomas told John Brennan for the *Bergen Record* (January 16, 2001, on-line). "But Jeff needs to let the bigger guys break it up. . . . Still, Jeff is going to do whatever it takes to protect his players."

In early March Van Gundy exceeded Pat Riley's record of 223 victories, thus boosting him to third place on the Knicks' career-victory list, after Red Holzman (613) and Joe Lapchick (326). In May the Knicks were defeated by the Toronto Raptors in the fifth game of the first round of the play-offs, by a score of 93–89. It was the first time that the team had lost the opening round since 1991. As the 2000–01 season came to an end, Van Gundy's career win–loss record stood at 238–163.

Although the players do not always agree with his decisions, Jeff Van Gundy believes that tension serves the team well. "The good part about coaching here—there's always unrest," he told Dave D'Allessandro for the Newark, New Jersey *Star-Ledger* (November 2, 1999, on-line). "The names change, and the stories remain the same: It's going to be me and somebody not being on the same page, or player-to-player [conflict], whatever that is. That's what you have to fight through. It's good—to a point. I think you do perform better when it's not easy." Van Gundy makes no effort to disguise his displeasure when games go badly. "Losing has an unbelievably negative impact on me," he told S. L. Price. "I read somewhere that failure is an event, not a person, but I never feel that way. It's who I am."

According to Bill Van Gundy, both his sons have become "better coaches than me," as he told George Vecsey for the *New York Times* (March 10, 1996). "I wouldn't say that I pointed them into coaching, but they definitely were raised around basketball. . . . I don't recall either of them, after junior high school, ever saying they were going to do anything else." The brothers often argue about basketball and have agreed not to speak to each other during play-offs. Jeff Van Gundy has expressed his desire to coach alongside his brother, but Stan has no interest in playing a supporting role. "I'm used to being on even ground in arguments," Stan Van Gundy told S. L. Price. "I'm as convinced that my side's right as he is, and I always will be."

Jeff Van Gundy lives in Chappaqua, New York, with his wife, Kim, and their daughter, Mattie. — C.L.

Suggested Reading: *CBS SportsLine* (on-line) May 3, 1998, Jan. 17, 2001; *New York Times* VIII p1 Mar. 10, 1996, with photo, B p11 Mar. 13, 1996, with photo, VIII p6 May 3, 1998, with photo, VIII p7 Mar. 28, 1999, D p3 May 10, 1999, with photo, VIII p1+ Mar. 11, 2001, with photos, VIII p1+ May 6, 2001, with photos; *Sports Illustrated* p34+ Mar. 18, 1996, with photos, p54+ May 11, 1998, with photos, p102+ Oct. 30, 2000, with photos

---

Alex Wong/Getty Images/Archive Photos

Walsh, John

Dec. 26, 1945– Host of America's Most Wanted; *victims' rights advocate. Address: National Center for Missing and Exploited Children, Charles B. Wang International Children's Bldg., 699 Prince St., Alexandria, VA 22314*

The career of John Walsh, who hosts the television series *America's Most Wanted*, was shaped by a personal tragedy: the abduction and murder of his son Adam in Florida in 1981. Appalled by the meagerness of the resources that law-enforcement agencies had brought to bear in the disappearance of their son—and their discovery that many other parents of missing children had had similar experiences—Walsh and his wife, Revé, began a crusade

to connect the federal justice system, local police departments, and the public in cases involving missing children. His efforts in Washington, D.C., helped to forge two pieces of legislation: the Missing Children's Act of 1982 and the National Missing Children's Assistance Act of 1984, the latter of which led to the founding of the National Center for Missing and Exploited Children. Since 1988 Walsh has hosted the weekly television series *America's Most Wanted*, which profiles some of the country's most notorious suspected criminals and fugitives from justice and encourages the public to call in with tips for the police. *America's Most Wanted* became an overnight success, logging its first "capture" four days after its premiere, and it quickly earned the support of the Federal Bureau of Investigation (FBI), police departments, and lawmakers. By October 2001 more than 680 suspected criminals and escaped convicts had been apprehended as a result of tips from viewers, among them a dozen whose names had appeared on the FBI's "Ten Most Wanted Fugitives" list. "I get great satisfaction when we take somebody really dangerous off the streets," Walsh told Macon Morehouse for *People* (March 3, 1998). The program has also been credited in the rescue of 26 abducted children. Walsh has received threats on his life and for years has relied on the protection of bodyguards; nevertheless, he said in a *Fox.com* on-line chat (May 13, 2000), "I love [hosting the show]. I've often said during the week that it's the worst job on television because I see the worst of American society: child molesters, serial killers, cop killers, the worst of the worst. But on Saturday night we catch the worst of the worst. The American public is our partner. . . . And when we catch a child molester or a brutal murderer on a Saturday night, it's the best job on TV, and I love it."

Since 1995 Walsh has also hosted *America's Most Wanted: Final Justice*, which airs on Court TV. In addition, he travels extensively to lobby state governments and speak at colleges and other venues about "anything that has to do with children's rights, victims' rights, [and] repeat-offender statutes for hard-core criminals," as he told Mervyn Rothstein for *Cigar Aficionado* (August/September 2000, on-line). He has also published two books: the first, written with Susan Schindehette, is *Tears of Rage: From Grieving Father to Crusader for Justice: The Untold Story of the Adam Walsh Case* (1997); the second, written with Philip Lerman, is *No Mercy: The Host of America's Most Wanted Hunts the Worst Criminals of Our Time—In Shattering True Crime Cases* (1998). In recognition of his efforts and achievements, Walsh has been honored by the FBI, the United States Marshals Service, and—in ceremonies held in the Rose Garden of the White House—three presidents: Ronald Reagan, George H. W. Bush, and Bill Clinton. He is the only private American citizen to receive a Special Recognition Award from the U.S. attorney general.

The oldest son of Jack Walsh and his wife, John Walsh was born on December 26, 1945. He and his brothers, Jimmy and Joe, and sister, Jane, were raised in a traditional Irish-Catholic household in Auburn, New York, a small town in the Finger Lakes region of New York State. An athlete and daredevil, as a boy he often got into fistfights, and he later took up spear fishing and free diving (in which one descends to unusual depths wearing only a face mask and fins). He attended Catholic parochial schools before enrolling at Auburn Community College and then the University of Buffalo. In college he majored in history and played soccer; during summers he worked in construction. After earning a bachelor's degree, in about 1967, he settled in Florida with some friends of his. He got a job as a cabana boy at a hotel; in his free time he became an accomplished scuba and deep-sea diver. One day he rescued the son of John Monahan, a hotel executive, by pulling the boy out from under a drainage pipe in the ocean, where the youngster had gotten stuck as the tide was coming in. The grateful Monahan offered him a job in hotel management, and during the next few years, Walsh learned the hotel business. Eventually, he started his own hotel management and development firm, which focused on expanding the tourist trade into the outer islands of the Bahamas. Meanwhile, in 1971, Walsh had married his college girlfriend, Revé Drew; their first child, Adam, was born in 1974.

On July 27, 1981 Revé Walsh took the six-year-old Adam to a Florida shopping mall. She agreed to let the boy play video games while she shopped for a lamp a few aisles away. During the short time that passed before she went to retrieve him, Adam disappeared. Certain that he had not run away or wandered off, the Walshes were left with the terrifying suspicion that Adam had been kidnapped. To their great distress, the Hollywood, Florida, police department moved very slowly to spread information about Adam's disappearance. "At the time," Walsh told Jane Marion for *TV Guide*

(March 18, 1989), "70 percent of the police agencies in the state of Florida didn't know Adam was missing." Moreover, according to some sources, the Hollywood police refused to ask the FBI to get involved in the case. (Other sources reported that the FBI refused to step in without concrete evidence of a kidnapping or indications that state lines had been crossed in the commission of the crime.) Walsh recalled to Ronald Laney for the *Juvenile Justice Journal* (May 1998), "We were left to our own devices to figure out what to do and where to turn. We felt alone and isolated. We began beating on doors asking for help. We called anyone and everyone. We often felt as if we were in charge of the investigation. While we feared for our son's safety, we were also angry at the system that was supposed to protect our son and help us." Enlisting friends and colleagues, Walsh formed his own search party, distributed flyers, and made announcements on local radio and television stations. Two weeks after Adam's disappearance, the Walshes went to New York City to appear on *Good Morning America* and display Adam's picture to a nationwide audience. That same day the Hollywood police department notified them that fishermen in Vero Beach, Florida, more than 100 miles north of Hollywood, had found Adam's head in a canal. (The rest of his remains have never been found.) "I went down. Right onto the floor," Walsh recalled in his book *Tears of Rage*. "It felt like somebody took a huge wooden stake and shoved it into the wall of my chest. . . . Death would have hurt me so much less." He told Marianne Szegedy-Maszak for *Biography* (May 1997), "I could deal with my father's death. But children are your immortality. You don't bury your children."

In the months following Adam's murder, Walsh was consumed by grief and contemplated suicide. Unable to concentrate on his work (his management company was building a luxury resort in the Bahamas—a project that, before his son's death, he had relished as the biggest coup in his burgeoning career), he was forced to abandon his job. His house soon teetered on the edge of foreclosure, and his marriage became severely strained. Meanwhile, thousands of letters were flooding the Walshes' mailbox, many of them from parents who, like them, had experienced the loss of a child to an act of violence. Over the next year he channeled his grief into a determination to force law-enforcement agencies to improve their methods of locating and recovering missing children—something that had not happened despite the national media coverage, two years earlier, of the disappearance of a six-year-old New York City boy named Etan Patz, last seen walking to school.

In October 1981 Walsh and his wife testified before a congressional committee in support of a bill that became the Missing Children's Act of 1982. The first legislation to address the problem of missing children, it stipulated that all information gathered in such cases be entered in the U.S. Justice Department's central computer file and made available to parents. "I became almost totally obsessed with trying to get this Missing Children's Bill passed," Walsh confessed to Diane Bartley for the *Saturday Evening Post* (April 1990). President Ronald Reagan signed the bill into law in October 1982. Walsh also lobbied successfully for the passage of the National Missing Children's Assistance Act of 1984, which allocated federal funding for the National Center for Missing and Exploited Children (NCMEC), a private, nonprofit organization that provides assistance in cases of missing children (including children abducted by family members or others, runaways, and youngsters who have disappeared for any other reason). Now based in Alexandria, Virginia, and funded by businesses and individuals as well as the federal government, the center uses the latest technology to find missing children, including a computer program that shows how an individual's facial features might have changed with the passage of time; it also maintains a 24-hour missing-children hotline and a data bank of missing children, and publishes educational materials, such as booklets that provide young people with suggestions for getting to and from school safely. According to its Web site in May 2001, "To date, NCMEC has worked on 66,350 cases, helped recover 47,284 children, and raised its recovery rate from 60 percent in the 1980s to 93 percent today."

A year after Adam's death, Revé Walsh gave birth to a daughter, named Meghan. "What saved us from terrible, terrible, unbearable grief was the fact that we had this beautiful little girl we had to take care of," John Walsh told Szegedy-Maszak. Two years later the Walshes' son Callahan was born. In about 1985 the couple founded the Adam Walsh Children's Fund and opened the first Adam Walsh Outreach Center, a storehouse of information about cases of missing children. (A total of seven such centers were established; later, they merged with the National Center for Missing and Exploited Children.) *Adam*, a made-for-television movie about the Walshes' ordeal, with Daniel J. Travanti and JoBeth Williams as John and Revé Walsh, aired in 1983. At the end of the film, the faces of 55 missing children appeared; in the following weeks, 13 of them were found. After each of two subsequent reruns of *Adam*, and after the airing of *Adam: His Song Continues*, in 1986, others among the missing children were located. In total, 65 children were reunited with their families. In collaboration with Travanti, Walsh made the documentary *How to Raise a Street-Smart Child*, which aired on HBO in 1987. During this period Walsh traveled to almost every U.S. state to lobby for stricter laws against crimes that targeted children and for measures to ensure victims' rights. As a salaried consultant to the Justice Department, he pleaded with representatives of local, state, and federal law-enforcement agencies to work together to find missing children, and he strived to increase the prominence of the National Center for Missing and Exploited Children.

In 1987 the upstart Fox Broadcasting Co. developed a true-crime show that featured profiles of wanted criminals, along with reenactments of the crimes they had committed, a presentation of clues, and an 800 number that viewers could call to give the police or FBI tips about the whereabouts of the perpetrators. As a possible host for the show, called *America's Most Wanted*, its executive producer, Michael Linder, considered John Walsh. "He looks right for the part," Linder explained to Diane Bartley, "[and] he has a voice that's compelling. But more than that, he's a living metaphor for what we're trying to do." Walsh pondered the offer for six months before he accepted the job; as he explained to John Stanley for the *San Francisco Chronicle* (March 12, 1989), "I had some concern at first about the exploitative aspects of it. Sometimes this new 'reality TV' goes too far, and I didn't want to have that happen. I wanted the anonymity of the callers respected, I didn't want to give out any awards or act like we were bounty hunters, I didn't want to give running tallies on callers as if we were a telethon." He made up his mind to do the show after he was told that the first installment would profile David James Roberts, a multiple murderer who had escaped from prison while serving six life sentences. The first installment of *America's Most Wanted* aired in February 1988, and though only a handful of Fox affiliate stations had carried it, within a week Roberts was arrested after a tip from a viewer. Two months later the show premiered nationally, on all Fox stations, and it quickly became a Saturday night institution. Thanks to information from viewers, captures of criminals occurred almost weekly; those caught even included people on the FBI's "Ten Most Wanted Fugitives" list. Regarded with suspicion at first by those who felt that its reenactments were unnecessarily grisly and who questioned the fairness of including among the "most wanted" a few individuals whose guilt had not yet been established, the show earned the support of governmental agencies, politicians, and people who felt that the program was helping to make their neighborhoods safer.

By mid-1996, Lawrie Mifflin reported in the *New York Times* (September 7, 1996), information revealed on *America's Most Wanted* had led to the capture of more than 400 criminals. Nevertheless, that year, because of the series' increasingly disappointing ratings, Fox decided to cancel it. In what he thought would be the final installment, Walsh aired a segment about Adam's murder, having kept alive the hope that someday he would learn who had killed his son. (A drifter named Ottis Toole, whom Walsh regarded as the most likely suspect, had confessed to the murder twice but had twice recanted. A blood-stained mat taken from his car by the Hollywood police was later lost, before the development of DNA technology that could have determined whether the blood was Adam's. At about the time of what was thought to be the last *America's Most Wanted* installment, Toole died in prison, where he had been serving time for other crimes.) But Fox executives apparently had not realized the intensity of the attachment that those who still tuned in to the show felt toward it. More than 85,000 letters—200,000, according to Walsh in his conversation with Mervyn Rothstein—arrived at Fox's studios from viewers protesting the cancellation. In addition, more than 30 governors, 40 members of Congress, and ranking officials in the FBI, the Drug Enforcement Agency, and the Bureau of Alcohol, Tobacco, and Firearms urged Fox to keep *America's Most Wanted* on the air. Three days after the "final" broadcast, Fox announced that the show would be revived six weeks later, with the name *America's Most Wanted: America Fights Back*. According to Rothstein, "It was the shortest cancellation . . . in the history of network television."

Walsh has played himself in the television movies *If Looks Could Kill* (1996), which he executive produced, and *Safety Patrol* (1998). His cinematic credits also include appearances in the little-noticed feature films *Jesuit Joe* (1990), *Wrongfully Accused* (1998), *Grey Owl* (1999), and *Press Run* (1999). He devotes half of every week to scripting and producing *America's Most Wanted*. Since 1995 he has also hosted the Court TV spin-off *America's Most Wanted: Final Justice*, each half-hour installment of which tracks two criminals after their capture following an episode of the original series. *Final Justice* emanates from Straight Shooter, a production company that Walsh set up in partnership with Lance Heflin, the executive producer of *America's Most Wanted*. He often makes public appearances as a representative of the National Center for Missing and Exploited Children, which boasts a recovery rate of over 90 percent. "My life is now one thing: seeking justice for Adam and all the other Adams out there," he told John Stanley. "We all have the right to seek justice from the system, and I believe that criminals should be held responsible for their actions. Do crime, do time." But, he added: "I'm not a fanatic. I don't believe in public executions. Let's not start witch hunts or turn to vigilantism." Within days of the September 11, 2001 terrorist attacks on New York City and Washington, D.C., Walsh and *America's Most Wanted* began producing shows about the hijackers of the planes used in the attacks. The shows highlighted Osama bin Laden and other terrorists suspected of operating from Al Qaeda–connected cells in the United States or abroad.

"You learn through all kinds of things—through experience, through meeting the parents of murdered children—that you take life one day at a time," Walsh said to Mervyn Rothstein. "I'm the perfect example that no matter how prepared you are, or how goal-oriented you are, no matter what your dreams and aspirations are, one day, one event can change your life forever." According to Rothstein, Walsh's "once-dark hair is more than slightly salted with white, and his craggy good

looks are a little withered from time. . . . [He] looks charismatic and debonair, but also a bit foreboding. His demeanor almost shouts, 'Wrongdoers, beware!'" His recreational activities include water sports—scuba diving, jet skiing, surfing, and snorkeling; riding his motorcycles; and collecting fine wines. In addition to Meghan and Callahan, he and his wife are the parents of Hayden, a son. "I want to be the best father, a world-class father," he told Diane Bartley. But Adam is constantly in his thoughts, he added. "I'll always be the father of a murdered child. I imagine I'll be fighting back until the day I die." — K.S.

Suggested Reading: *America's Most Wanted* Web site; *Biography* p28+ May 1997, with photos; *Cigar Aficionado* (on-line) Aug./Sep. 2000; *Los Angeles Times* E p1 Feb. 6, 2001, with photo; *People* p111+ Feb. 5, 1996, with photos; *Saturday Evening Post* p44+ Apr. 1990, with photos; *TV Guide* p22+ Mar. 18, 1989, with photo, p42+ Feb. 24–Mar. 2, 2001, with photos

Selected Television Shows: *How to Raise a Street Smart Child*, *America's Most Wanted*, *America's Most Wanted: America Fights Back*, *America's Most Wanted: Final Justice*

Selected Books: *Tears of Rage* (with Susan Shindehette), 1997; *No Mercy* (with Philip Lerman), 1998

Wayans, Shawn and Marlon

Shawn Wayans:
Jan. 19, 1971– Actor; comedian; screen-writer; film producer

Marlon Wayans:
July 23, 1972– Actor; comedian; screen- writer; television producer

Address: c/o United Talent Agency, 9560 Wilshire Blvd. #500, Beverly Hills, CA 90212

The press has often cast Shawn and Marlon Wayans in the shadows of their celebrated older brothers, the comedians Damon and Keenen Ivory Wayans. Recently, though, Shawn and Marlon have come into their own, as the screenwriters and stars of *Scary Movie* (2000), a parody of teen slasher films that became the highest-grossing African-American–produced film in motion-picture history. After spending several seasons in the early 1990s in Keenen Ivory Wayans's sketch-comedy show *In Living Color*, Shawn and Marlon developed their own television series, *The Wayans Brothers*, for the fledgling Warner Bros. (WB) Network. While producing, writing, and starring in that program, they appeared in leading roles in

Steve Granitz/Retna

Shawn (left) and Marlon Wayans

the film *Star 80* (1983) before working with Robert Townsend on *Hollywood Shuffle* (1987), which he co-wrote and starred in. Damon also enjoyed some success during this period, as a cast member of *Saturday Night Live* (1985–86) and then with a role in *Hollywood Shuffle*.

Whenever Keenen returned to New York to visit his family, Shawn and Marlon would pressure him to watch them act out skits that they had written. Class clowns, they hoped that such performances would inspire him to bring them to Hollywood. They made it there when Keenen gave them bit parts in his movie *I'm Gonna Get You Sucka* (1988), which lampooned 1970s blaxploitation films. *I'm Gonna Get You Sucka* so impressed Fox Broadcasting executives that they offered Keenen his own television show. The result, *In Living Color*, written by Keenen and Damon, debuted in April 1990 with a cast that included Damon, Shawn, and their sister Kim. Marlon, who studied at the film school of Howard University, in Washington, D.C., after graduating from New York City's famous High School of Performing Arts, joined the cast two years later. *In Living Color*, which showcased the comedic abilities of Marlon and Shawn as well as those of their siblings, pushed the television-comedy envelope and thereby challenged the writers of other shows—notably *Saturday Night Live*—to do the same.

In 1992 Marlon Wayans appeared in Peter MacDonald's action comedy *Mo' Money*, as the younger brother of the main character, a small-time con artist played by Damon Wayans (who also wrote the screenplay). The following year Marlon Wayans left *In Living Color*. He won a role in Jeff Pollack's *Above the Rim* (1994), a basketball movie that starred Tupac Shakur. Meanwhile, he and Shawn were developing a new television show; *The Wayans Brothers*, as it was called, premiered on the brand-new WB Network in January 1995. In addition to writing and producing the series, Shawn and Marlon starred as two brothers who share an apartment after being thrown out of their house. The serious brother, named Shawn, works as a driver for a delivery service; the happy-go-lucky Marlon, as the other brother is called, works in their father's diner. Although the show was among the most popular in WB's lineup, it never achieved high Nielsen ratings and was canceled in May 1999, after some 100 installments.

While *The Wayans Brothers* was still in production, Marlon and Shawn wrote, produced, and starred in *Don't Be a Menace to South Central While Drinking Your Juice in the Hood* (1996), a send-up of such sober, issue-oriented movies as Ernest Dickerson's *Juice*, Steve Anderson's *South Central*, John Singleton's *Boyz N the Hood*, Allen and Albert Hughes's *Menace II Society*, and Mario Van Peebles's *New Jack City*. In *Don't Be a Menace*, Shawn played Ashtray and Marlon portrayed Loc Dog, two "homeboys" whose adventures are supposed to reveal the reality of living in South Central Los Angeles, an area that includes the Watts

some feature films, both individually and as a team. They also co-wrote, produced, and starred in *Don't Be a Menace to South Central While Drinking Your Juice in the Hood,* a 1996 film that spoofed early 1990s inner-city gangster films. On the heels of their success with *Scary Movie*, they co-hosted the MTV Video Music Awards 2000. Also in 2000 Shawn performed for the film *Open Mic* (2000), while Marlon had roles in *The Tangerine Bear* and *Dungeons and Dragons* and impressed critics with his acting in *Requiem for a Dream*, a disturbing depiction of addiction. In their most recent collaboration, the brothers co-wrote, co-executive produced, and co-starred in *Scary Movie 2* (2001), directed by Keenen Ivory Wayans.

Shawn Wayans was born on January 19, 1971 and Marlon Wayans on July 23, 1972, both in New York City. They are the two youngest of the 10 children of Howell and Elvira Wayans. With so many siblings, Shawn Wayans told Terry Lawson for the *News-Times* (July 7, 2000, on-line), a Connecticut daily, "in that house you had to fight for everything: attention, food, whatever. It was competitive, but in a good way. We all got our sense of humor from our mother, but our father was pretty funny, too. I mean, the man sold condoms for a living, and he's got ten kids. That's pretty amusing in itself." Howell and Elvira Wayans often looked to Keenen to help keep the younger children from misbehaving; in *People* (November 15, 1999, online), Shawn called Keenen "the assistant parent." He also gave him credit for being the first in the family to try to make it in Hollywood: "I admire Keenen's strength. When I think of Keenen, I think of that arm on the baking-soda box. To me, he's that arm. He's strong." Keenen won a featured role in

neighborhood. "Outrageous is the key here," Esther Iverem noted in a review of the film for the *Washington Post* (January 15, 1996). "In many successful scenes the Wayans[es] deftly play on our assumptions and cliches. They catch the viewer sleeping and deliver deadly punches: A gray-haired grandmother who is not sweet and, instead, uses the trendiest 'hood profanity, smokes blunts of marijuana and out-dances Rosie Perez. . . . Ashtray's big love scene, rather than tender and romantic, becomes the funniest moment in the whole movie. Let's just say that it involves Kool Aid, hot dogs, and hot sauce."

Later in the 1990s the Wayanses appeared in movies separately. In Randall Miller's comedy *The Sixth Man* (1997), Marlon was cast as a basketball player whose deceased older brother returns as a ghost to help his sibling's team win the championship. In Penelope Spheeris's *Senseless* (1998), Marlon played a financially strapped Ivy League college student who, after becoming a human guinea pig for a drug company as a way to earn enough money to pay his own expenses and provide for his mother and siblings, finds his senses extraordinarily heightened. Although the films were moderately popular, they did little to advance Marlon's career. Shawn was featured in Michael Hurst's small-time-gangster drama *New Blood* (1999), which attracted scant attention and was of little professional benefit to the actor.

The brothers' true breakthrough came with *Scary Movie* (2000), written by Marlon and Shawn and directed by Keenen. Developed from an idea that the three brothers bandied about after seeing a number of teen horror films, *Scary Movie* used extreme gross-out humor in parodying such slasher pictures as the *Scream* and *I Know What You Did Last Summer* series and mocking more serious films, such as *The Sixth Sense*, *The Blair Witch Project*, and *Matrix*. "This movie is different because it's not a black film," Marlon said in an interview with Steven Sato for *Channel6000.com* (on-line). "It's just a movie. Hopefully, this will help black filmmakers in doing movies that can gross big money and attract a broad audience, because that's what we're trying to do." Costing just $19 million to produce, *Scary Movie* brought in more than $42 million at the box office in its first weekend and went on to gross almost $157 million in the United States alone. Critical reaction to the film, however, was mixed. Michael Atkinson, for example, writing for the *Village Voice* (July 12–18, 2000), argued, "If you accept that many original slasher movies already began with a clear idea of how absurd they were, then the Wayans boys . . . are working at several removes from their proposed ground." Roger Ebert, by contrast, in a review for the *Chicago Sun-Times* (on-line), noted the difficulty of assessing parodies and then wrote of *Scary Movie*, "The bottom line in reviewing a movie like this is, does it work? Is it funny? Yes, it is."

Also in 2000 Marlon Wayans earned praise for his dramatic turn in Darren Aronofsky's harrowing tale of addiction, *Requiem for a Dream*, an adaptation by Aronofsky and Hubert Selby of Selby's same-named, 1978 novel. In the course of the film, Wayans's character, Tyrone, Tyrone's best friend, Harry, and Harry's girlfriend destroy their lives after obtaining a pound of pure cocaine to sell on the street and sampling it themselves; meanwhile, Harry's mother suffers a similarly awful fate after becoming addicted to diet pills. In a review for *Variety* (May 22, 2000), Todd McCarthy wrote, "Wayans comes across as appealing and natural in his first dramatic role." James Berardinelli offered his assessment of *Requiem for a Dream* on *Reelviews* (on-line): "Every actor with a major role—Ellen Burstyn, Jennifer Connelly, Jared Leto, and Marlan Wayans—should be commended not only for their strength of performance but for the courage they exhibit in putting themselves on the line the way Aronofsky requires. They are artists in the truest sense of the word, sublimating their egos and committing themselves fully to the needs of the project. . . . They are depicted doing the kinds of things that many higher profile celebrities would not permit."

Shawn and Marlon Wayans's most recent cinematic project, *Scary Movie 2*, was released in 2001. Like its predecessor, the film received mixed reviews but was a solid box-office success. — C.M.

Suggested Reading: (Connecticut) *News-Times* (on-line); *Jet* p60+ Feb. 12, 1996, with photo, p56+ Jan. 19, 1998, with photos, p32+ Feb. 23, 1998, with photo; *People* p78 Feb. 16, 1998, with photo; *People* (on-line), with photo; *Rolling Stone* p147 Sep. 14, 2000, with photo; *'Teen* p56 Feb. 1998, with photo; *TV Guide* p20+ Aug. 26–Sep. 1, 2000, with photo

Selected Television Shows: Shawn Wayans—*In Living Color*, 1990–93; Marlon Wayans—*In Living Color*, 1992–93; Shawn and Marlon—*The Wayans Brothers*, 1995–99

Selected Films: Shawn Wayans—as actor: *New Blood*, 1999; *Open Mic*, 2000; Marlon Wayans—as actor: *Above the Rim*, 1994; *The Sixth Man*, 1997; *Senseless*, 1998; *The Tangerine Bear*, 2000; *Dungeons and Dragons*, 2000; *Requiem for a Dream*, 2000; Shawn and Marlon—as actors: *I'm Gonna Get You Sucka*, 1988; as actors and screenwriters: *Scary Movie*, 2000; as screenwriters, producers, and actors: *Don't Be A Menace to South Central While Drinking Your Juice in the Hood*, 1996; *Scary Movie 2*, 2001

Reuters/Sue Ogrocki/Hulton/Archive

Webb, Karrie
(KAHR-ree)

Dec. 21, 1974– Golfer. Address: c/o LPGA Tour, 100 International Dr., Daytona Beach, FL 32124-1092

Karrie Webb's dominance on the Ladies Professional Golf Association (LPGA) Tour for the past six seasons has largely sneaked under public radar. While many aficionados of the sport agree that she is one of the greatest golfers—male or female—ever to play the game, the fact that she is a woman in an age of such international male superstars as Tiger Woods and Sergio Garcia has robbed her of the widespread recognition that her accomplishments on the course would otherwise command. Lisa D. Mickey wrote for *Golf World* (September 15, 2000), "Webb could win every tournament for the rest of the LPGA's schedule, break her own scoring records . . . win every available year-end honor—and still barely make the front page of the sports section." Since her debut on the LPGA Tour, in October 1995, Webb has won 25 times, including five major victories. In 1996 she won Rookie of the Year honors and became the first woman ever to win $1 million on the LPGA Tour. (She was the first golfer on any tour to take home that amount as a rookie.) By the end of her 2000 season, Webb had surpassed the $6 million mark in career earnings faster than any LPGA player before her. Peter Thomson, whom many consider to be Australia's greatest contribution to the world of golf, has himself conceded that distinction to Webb, telling David Davies for the London *Guardian* (March 8, 2001), "Karrie Webb is now the best golfer, man or woman, in the world. And without any doubt she

is the best golfer Australia has ever produced." On June 3, 2001 Webb took her second consecutive U.S. Women's Open title in record fashion, eclipsing her nearest competitor by eight strokes. With her $520,000 Open paycheck, she accumulated at least $7 million in career earnings in record time— five years, four months, and 22 days. Three weeks later she captured her first McDonald's LPGA Championship title, thus completing her career Grand Slam (all four major events on the LPGA Tour). Only four other women have completed this feat, and none as quickly as Webb.

Karrie Webb was born on December 21, 1974 in Ayr, Queensland, Australia. She began playing golf at the age of eight and has credited her parents, Evelyn and Robert, as well as her longtime coach, Kelvin Haller, with having the greatest influence on her career choice. In an interview with Tom Callahan for *Golf Digest* (January 2001), Webb recalled her early exposure to Haller's brand of golf fundamentalism. "I was 11 or 12," she said. "[Haller would] get me to hit 9-irons. Just 9-irons. 'Repeating is the key,' he'd say. 'If you can't repeat it with a 9-iron, you can't with anything else.' I'd be there all day hitting that 9-iron. Picking up the balls and hitting them again. The other kids would be hitting drivers." (A 9-iron, the face of which usually slants backward 40 to 43 degrees, is used for shorter golf shots and is much easier to control than a driver, which usually slants backward 9 to 12 degrees and is designed to hit a golf ball farther than any other club. A 9-iron is also much shorter than a driver, adding to its manageability. The distance gained by hitting a driver, many golfers believe, is among the most enjoyable aspects of the sport.) While Haller's regimen contributed to her success, Webb's own drive and dedication proved to be her greatest assets. Haller, in the same *Golf Digest* article, explained what it was like to work with a young Karrie Webb. "She had the most guts," he told Callahan. "When it came to little tournaments, going off by herself, she loved it. . . . The little trips hardened her up. She always knew there was a big journey ahead."

Physically, at least, Haller would not be able to join Webb on that journey. When Webb was 16 Haller suffered a work accident that has confined him to a wheelchair. Although a quadriplegic, he is able to move his right arm in a six-inch arc, which mirrors the motion of an ideal golf swing; thanks to that ability, he has been able to remain Webb's golf teacher. Through a custom-designed computer program, Webb also E-mails to Haller videos of her swing, which they then discuss by telephone to correct any flaws he sees or implement any improvements he feels are necessary. Webb trusts Haller completely and has eschewed suggestions by Haller himself that she employ a new, more celebrated coach. "I'm not Butch Harmon," Haller admitted, referring to Tiger Woods's famous instructor. "And, anyway, I'm not the one who made Karrie the competitor she is. . . . All of the really important things, she taught herself."

But Webb was reluctant to allow Haller such modesty. She explained to Callahan, "There's a reason I play so well at the start of the year. It's because I've been home and have just seen Kel in person. It's because he's sat there for two or three hours five days in a row watching me hit balls."

Readily available sources do not provide information about Webb's academic schooling. Presumably, she was still in high school when, in 1991, she won a Greg Norman Junior Golf Foundation tournament and was invited, along with the other divisional winners, to Norman's estate in Hobe Sound, Florida. Norman, himself a world-renowned professional golfer, recognized the immense talent of his fellow Australian and encouraged Webb to pursue a career in golf. After she returned home, she began competing in international amateur contests, and in 1994 she won the Australian Stroke Play championship. Later that year Webb turned professional, playing on the Futures Tour as well as the Women Professional Golfers' European Tour (WPGET). In her fourth tournament on the Futures Tour, Webb broke through with her first professional victory. While that win did not bring Webb recognition among those playing on the more prestigious and more lucrative LPGA Tour, it allowed her the opportunity to play in the 1995 Women's British Open, a chance she seized with vigor. Virtually unknown, she shot a quiet 69 in the first round, held on a Thursday, which garnered her a fifth-place tie. She followed that round with a three-under-par 70 on Friday and then went on to shoot another 69 on Saturday, taking the surprise lead going into Sunday's final round. Facing two of the world's best female golfers—Annika Sorenstam and Jill McGill—Webb played an inspired final round of 70, which placed her atop the leaderboard, six shots clear of her veteran competitors. "I knew she was good," Haller explained to Callahan following Webb's triumph, "but I didn't really have any idea. None of us did. . . . When Karrie played in that first British Open, and—bang!—she won it, I guess we all started to catch on." Her British Open victory and subsequent WPGET Rookie of the Year honors gave Webb the opportunity to take her game to the next level. In October 1995 she qualified for the LPGA Tour on her first try, by finishing second in the LPGA Final Qualifying Tournament—while playing with a broken wrist.

Beginning in January of every year, the LPGA Tour makes "tour stops" at golf courses around the world. There is a tournament almost every week, Thursday through Sunday, with 18 holes played on each day. The golfer whose cumulative score is the lowest after the fourth round wins that tournament. The season ends in mid-December, after 40 tournaments; many players enter only some of the 40. Webb announced her tour presence quickly and with authority. After a second-place finish in the first tournament of 1996, Webb continued her strong play at the HealthSouth Inaugural by beating out Jane Geddes and Martha Nause in a three-

way play-off, thus capturing her first LPGA title. She followed her win with top-10 finishes in each of the next three tournaments, and only six tournaments into her rookie season, Webb stood atop the LPGA earnings list. She went on to win three other tournaments that year: the Sprint Titleholders Championship, the Safeco Classic, and the ITT LPGA Tour Championship.

Webb might be said to have picked the wrong year to make her debut. In 1996 the focus of the golfing world was Tiger Woods's phenomenal rookie season on the PGA Tour. Still, Webb managed to share a portion, however small, of the spotlight. While Woods stole the show for male honors, Webb was awarded a 1996 ESPY as the Female Golfer of the Year. During the next two years, she continued to ascend higher and higher up the ranks of the LPGA Tour. In 1997 she notched three victories, winning at the Susan G. Komen International and successfully defending both her Safeco Classic title and her Weetabix Women's British Open crown. Perhaps more impressive during the season was Webb's consistency. In 25 events she finished out of the top 20 only twice and out of the top 10 only four times. Her season scoring average was 70.00, which proved good enough to win her the esteemed Vare Trophy, awarded to the player with the lowest season scoring average. In February 1998, after only two years as an LPGA touring pro, Webb surpassed $2 million in earnings, thus crossing that mark faster than any other LPGA player. She went on to win two tournaments during the 1998 season, first taking the prestigious Australian Ladies Masters and then capturing the City of Hope Myrtle Beach Classic. Again, consistency was the key, as Webb recorded 20 top-20 finishes in only 23 starts.

Her momentum increased in 1999. In only her third tournament of the year, Webb captured the Office Depot crown, marking her 10th career LPGA Tour victory. In 25 starts Webb would win six times, including her first major championship, at the du Maurier Classic. Along with her six wins, Webb recorded 22 top-10 finishes, topping off one of the most impressive seasons in golf history. Her 26-under-par (262) performance at the Australian Ladies Masters set what was then an all-time record for lowest 72-hole score in relation to par. Her $1,591,959 in earnings established an LPGA single-season earnings record. In addition, Webb's 69.43 season-scoring average was an all-time record and earned her a second Vare Trophy. And to complete the sweep, Webb earned her first Rolex Player of the Year award. But again, much of the attention during her stellar season went to Tiger Woods, who finished the year with four consecutive wins. In a teleconference interview with *golf.com* (March 14, 2000), Webb was asked whether Woods's "steal[ing] some of the thunder" had bothered her. "The only thing that annoys me about that," Webb answered, "is just that the LPGA really hasn't had as much publicity from it as they probably should have and that is just a little disappointing. . . . We are great players and we have just as good a show as the PGA Tour does and when stuff like that happens, it just sets us back a little bit." LPGA Tour Hall of Famer Juli Inkster agreed with Webb, telling Doug Ferguson for *nandotimes.com* (March 14, 2000), "Karrie has done as well or better than Tiger. She just doesn't have the TV support or media to have what Tiger has."

In 2000, coming off one of the best golf seasons ever, Webb faced the challenge of topping what appeared untoppable—and that is exactly what she did. She ended the 2000 season with seven victories under her belt—one more than in 1999—including two more majors (the Nabisco Championship and the U.S. Women's Open). She also eclipsed her own single-season earnings record, by taking home $1,876,853. At the Oldsmobile Classic, her sixth win of the year, she tied or rewrote several LPGA scoring records (most of them her own), including 36-hole and 54-hole records of 127 (–17) and 193 (–23), respectively. (The 54-hole record was the only one that still stood as of the end of October 2001.) Webb won three international titles that year in addition to her seven LPGA wins, bringing her professional total for the year into the double digits. She won another Rolex Play-

er of the Year award as well as her third Vare Trophy, with a 70.05 season-scoring average. Perhaps Webb's most impressive accomplishment during the season, though, was her win at the U.S. Women's Open: her five-stroke victory gave her the 27 points she needed to qualify for the LPGA Tour Hall of Fame. Webb now lacks only the 10-year LPGA membership requirement, which means that she will automatically be inducted at the conclusion of the 2005 season. Speaking about Karrie Webb's career, Louise Suggs, who helped found the LPGA and has 58 career wins to her credit, told Dave Anderson for the *New York Times* (March 31, 2000), "If she doesn't get hurt, she'll break every record in the book."

Webb currently resides in Boynton Beach, Florida. — J.H.

Suggested Reading: *Golf Digest* p92+ Jan. 2001, with photos; *Golf Magazine* p70+ Aug. 1996, with photo, p128+ Aug. 2000, with photo; (London) *Guardian* p33+ Mar. 8, 2001, with photo; *People* p68 Apr. 28, 1997, with photo; *Sports Illustrated* p68+ May 12, 1997, with photos, p46+ Mar. 13, 2000, with photo

---

Wek, Alek

(uh-LEK)

1977– Model; social activist. Address: c/o IMG Models, 304 Park Ave. S., New York, NY 10010-5339

Since 1996 the fashion model Alek Wek has been turning heads on catwalks and attracting notice internationally through the images of her in advertisements for cosmetics and clothing. A member of the Dinka tribe, Wek is a native of Sudan, in northeastern Africa. After fleeing the Sudanese civil war, she won asylum in Great Britain, where a modeling agent discovered her on a London street in the mid-1990s. The five-foot 11-inch Wek made waves in the fashion world with her dazzling, slightly uneven smile and distinctly African looks: dark skin, closely cropped hair, wide nose, and full lips. Although she did not intend to be a role model for black women, Wek has quietly become an antidote to the dominance of European standards of beauty. As a member of the U.S. Committee for Refugees, a nonprofit organization that strives to defend the rights of refugees and asylum seekers, she has capitalized on her visibility to bring attention to the human misery spawned by the civil unrest in her native land. Currently, she serves on the committee's Advisory Council.

The seventh of nine children, Alek Wek was born in 1977 in the southern Sudanese village of Wau. Her father, a teacher, and her mother, a social worker, were both Dinkas. Wek remembers her life

with her four sisters and four brothers as being happy until she reached the age of about five. At that time Sudan became disrupted by a civil war that pitted the national government, dominated by Arab Muslims in the north, against southern rebels, most of them Christians or animists. (Fighting had actually erupted in 1955, the year before Sudan gained independence from Great Britain, because of the southerners' fear of Muslim rule. Hostilities intensified in 1983, when the then-president, Colonel Jaafar Muhammad al-Numeiry, revised the Sudanese penal code to link it "organically and spiritually," as he put it, with Islamic law.) "It was such a nice household and a beautiful little town," Wek said in a conversation with the Somali supermodel Iman for *i-iman.com*. "But once the war broke out everything changed." Education and other services ended abruptly. "Suddenly the taps would be shut off, the electricity gone, and the schools and businesses closed," she explained in an interview posted on the Web site of the U.S. Committee for Refugees.

In 1989, after the Wek family made several abortive attempts to escape to Khartoum, the capital of Sudan, a neighbor took the 12-year-old Wek, at her mother's request, to the home of an uncle who lived in Khartoum. The rest of the family arrived there months later. More hardships followed after her father received improper treatment during an illness and died. "Things became very difficult after my father died," Wek told Iman. "He and my mum had always been there for us. When he passed away, my mum said to us, 'I have to do what

Alek Wek

STR/Archive Photos

your father would have done for you. I want to take you somewhere where you can be safe, wake up every morning and go to school.'" In 1991 Alek and her younger sister Atheng were granted asylum in England, where their older sister Ajok had lived with her husband since before the outbreak of the Sudanese civil war. "I had never been away from home before," Wek told Iman. "I really thought that I would see my mum a month or so after we arrived. But I didn't get to see her until two years later, because she was rejected from the Home Office three times." (The Home Office regulates the entry and settlement of foreign nationals in Great Britain.) In 1993 her mother and two more of her siblings obtained permission to immigrate to England; her remaining siblings were forced to seek asylum elsewhere.

In England Wek quickly mastered English and adjusted to her new life. At the Catholic high school that she attended, she was subjected to teasing from other students, but in time, she told Nick Charles for *People* (February 2, 1998), "they got used to me." After she completed high school, she enrolled at the London College of Fashion, where she planned to major in business and fashion technology. Soon afterward, in the summer of 1995, Fiona Ellis, of Models 1, a London agency, noticed Wek at a London street fair and asked her if she had ever considered modeling. Wek never had, but she eagerly had some photos taken and realized that she loved the idea. As she told Charles, she recalled thinking, "Oh, my God, this is me! This is what I do!" After persuading her mother to allow her to pursue modeling rather than a college degree, as her mother had hoped, Wek signed a contract with Ford Models. She was then cast in a Tina

Turner music video and sent on photo shoots for Spanish and British magazines.

In 1996 Wek left Ford for the IMG modeling agency and moved to New York City. She was photographed by Steve Meisel, an influential fashion photographer, and got runway work with the fashion houses Chanel and Ralph Lauren. She became increasingly sought-after, much to her delight—and occasional confusion. "My mother has never painted her nails or worn makeup. No one grows up hearing the word 'beautiful' in Sudan," she explained to a reporter for *People* (May 10, 1999), which listed her among the 50 most beautiful people in the world in 1999. She added, "In Sudan, we would never go on about beauty and body parts and proportions."

In New York Wek discovered that she had become a role model to the many African-American women who had longed to see someone resembling themselves in the pages of *Elle* and *Vogue*. "I didn't get all the 'sister' stuff I kept hearing," she confessed to *People*. "I didn't understand what my modeling meant to some people." She has shied away from being a black icon. "I'm not just wrapped in a black color," she told Nick Charles. "I'm Alek. I'm a person."

Continuing to expand her modeling portfolio, Wek participated in runway shows mounted by the designers Todd Oldham, Donna Karan, and Isaac Mizrachi, among others. She signed contracts to model Moschino clothes and—to the surprise of some in the fashion industry—to appear in advertisements for Clinique cosmetics. "People [had] said I was too black and I'd never get makeup work," she explained to Constance C. R. White for *Essence* (September 2000). Wek has also done advertisements for Revlon and modeled for the high-profile fashion makeup artist François Nars. She has made it a policy to refuse auditions that request black models. "Why bring it all down to being black?" she said to Constance C. R. White during an interview for the *New York Times* (November 16, 1997).

Wek has worked in Milan, Italy, as well as in London, Paris, and the U.S. She is the only member of her family who, as an adult, has seen all of her siblings, who are now scattered in far-flung parts of the world. (Some have had their travel restricted by the countries where they live.) "For me, the most important thing is my family," she told Nick Charles. Wek won the modeling industry's Venus de la Mode Award in 1997, and she has been honored for her modeling by MTV and *i-D* magazine. She has appeared in music videos with Janet Jackson and Busta Rhymes.

International recognition, which grew after her image appeared on the cover of *Elle* in November 1997, and a high income have enabled Wek to work toward heightening public awareness of the plight of the Sudanese. An estimated one and a half to two million Sudanese have died of starvation and other war-related causes since 1983, and millions more have become refugees within or outside Sudan. The ruling military government has often prevented food and other essential supplies from reaching people who need them. After becoming active on the U.S. Committee for Refugees, Wek joined the group's Advisory Council. In 1998, to celebrate her 21st birthday, she hosted a benefit for the organization. "It is very important to me to raise awareness for those people who—unlike me—are unable to escape the brutality of war in Sudan," she explained in a press conference on April 16, 1998. "When I think about how bad it was then, and how much worse it must be now . . . it must be a wreck! That's why I'm trying to give back to the people who are still living in Sudan—those who are refugees, those who are enslaved, and those who are starving. If nobody had saved me, I would have died too! When you've been through something like this, you do not forget," she explained in an interview posted on the U.S. Committee for Refugees Web site.

"You've got to make yourself happy," Wek said to Constance C. R. White for the *New York Times.* Following her own advice, Wek surrounds herself with friends at her Brooklyn, New York, brownstone, and she cooks familiar foods, such as okra and *fufu* (an African dish made with cassava or yams), as her mother taught her. A vegetarian who neither drinks nor smokes, she shuns the junk food available backstage during runway shows. "I believe in home-cooked food. That's what I always eat. People shouldn't diet because it's not good for the body," she said in an on-line interview with Great Day America. Wek is reportedly writing her autobiography. She enjoys in-line skating, sewing, and restoring antiques, and she takes advantage of New York's club scene. She has expressed the fervent wish that her appearance will remain in vogue. As she told Nick Charles, "I hope people don't think I'm just a look for the moment." — K.S.

Suggested Reading: *Essence* Sep. 2000; *New York Times* IX p2 Nov. 16, 1997, with photo; *People* p120+ Feb. 2, 1998, with photos, p136+ May10, 1999, with photo; U.S. Committee for Refugees Web site; *Vibe* p186 Sep. 1999, with photo

Courtesy of Alabama Music Hall of Fame

Wexler, Jerry

1917– Record producer; former recording-industry executive. Address: c/o Blues Foundation, 40 Union Ave., Memphis, TN 38103-2492

Jerry Wexler, a former producer and partner at Atlantic Records, has presided over the creation of some of the most memorable and vibrant music to come out of the post–World War II United States. Over the course of a career that has lasted almost half a century, Wexler has worked with such seminal American musical figures as Ray Charles, Joe Turner, Otis Redding, Aretha Franklin, Willie Nelson, and Bob Dylan. In the process, he has helped to define such musical genres as soul and R&B (rhythm and blues). Although Wexler, as an industry executive, has necessarily approached the music from a business perspective, he has remained first and foremost a loyal fan, whose dedication to and love of the music he produces are acknowledged even by those who have complained about his habit of aggressive self-promotion and occasional nastiness. As Alex Halberstadt recently observed in *Salon.com*, "Even as the music business . . . moves towards ever-greater corporate consolidation, Wexler remains an uncomfortable reminder of an individual's—and an organization's—ability to champion the most vulnerable and profound expressions of our culture, and in the process reconfigure society around it. Along with Sam Phillips [who produced the work of, among others, Elvis Presley, B.B. King, Jerry Lee Lewis, and Johnny Cash], he remains the epitome of that potential." In 1995 the Memphis, Tennessee–based Blues Foundation honored Wexler with its first Lifetime Achievement Award.

The son of Jewish emigrés, Jerry Wexler was born in 1917 in Washington Heights, a section of Manhattan directly north of Harlem; especially in the first half of the 20th century, the area was home to a large Jewish population. His father, Harry, who arrived in New York from Poland at the age of 19, worked all his life as a window washer. As Wexler later recalled in his memoir *Rhythm and the Blues*

(1993), his father's resignation about his humble lot in life was a source of shame for his son. (However, as Tom Graves noted in the *Washington Post* [June 23, 1993], Wexler has recalled elsewhere that his father brought home about $200 a week during the 1930s Depression, a sum that, in the American South in that decade, for example, "was literally enough to feed and clothe an entire family for a year." A new car, to offer another comparison, cost an average of $1,000 in those years.) Wexler's mother, who was of German-Jewish extraction, doted on her son and had very specific plans for him: she wanted him to become a writer. After spending hours on the streets of Harlem selling copies of the left-wing newspaper the *Daily Worker* (published by the American Communist Party), she would bring home copies of the works of Shakespeare, Molière, Havelock Ellis, and Theodore Dreiser for young Jerry, to inspire him.

By his own account, Wexler never liked school. As an adolescent he would cut classes regularly, spending his truant afternoons hustling in the local pool halls. When he was in his teens, the music scene in Harlem was flourishing, and he developed an abiding passion for jazz and blues. By day he would scavenge through secondhand shops and old furniture stores for cast-off records. In the evenings he and his friends frequented Harlem jazz clubs. Meanwhile, Wexler's mother, disappointed by his ne'er-do-well conduct, had concluded that drastic measures were needed to whip her son into shape. Reasoning that there could be no improvement as long as he remained among the temptations of New York, in 1936 she enrolled him at Kansas State University, in Manhattan, Kansas. There, Wexler opted to study journalism. Before long, though, he discovered the thriving music scene centered on Kansas City's famous 12th Street, and he began making the hundred-mile trip to the Missouri border regularly, to catch performances by the likes of Count Basie, Bennie Moten, and Joe Turner. Again, Wexler began to neglect his schoolwork, and within two years of his arrival at the university, his grades had plummeted to such dismal levels that his mother ordered him back to New York.

For several years after his return to the city, Wexler drifted aimlessly. Sometimes he would accompany his father on his window-washing rounds; he would spend nights and weekends at nightclubs in Harlem or around 52d Street, which from the mid-1930s to the mid-1940s was a nucleus of jazz. Among the now-legendary names that performed in such venues as the Apollo and the Savoy Ballroom were Billie Holiday, Ella Fitzgerald, and Roy Eldridge. Wexler remembers the time as one of easy pleasure; as he told Alex Halberstadt, speaking of a famous trumpeter and a well-known night spot, "Nothing would make me happier than to share a joint with Max Kaminsky in the basement of Jimmy Ryan's."

Wexler's idyllic existence ended abruptly when the United States entered World War II, in December 1941. Within days he was drafted into the army, and although he was never sent overseas to fight—he spent the war stationed in Texas and Florida—his experience in the military seems to have accomplished what his mother couldn't: it fired his ambition. While still in the service, Wexler enrolled in correspondence courses; after his military discharge he returned to Kansas to complete his schooling. After earning a bachelor's degree in journalism, in 1947, Wexler returned to New York and began casting about for a job as a reporter, but he was repeatedly rejected by the big New York dailies. Rather serendipitously, he found a position as a cub reporter for *Billboard* magazine, where his love of jazz and blues stood him in good stead. In 1949 he coined the term "rhythm and blues" (or "R&B") for *Billboard*'s black-music chart, which had previously borne the title "Race Records." The many interviews he conducted with music publishers, record-label owners, composers, and song pluggers provided him with an extensive network of industry contacts that would later prove invaluable.

Among the business insiders whom Wexler befriended at the time was Ahmet Ertegun, a co-founder of Atlantic Records, then a small R&B label in New York. While the urbane Ertegun, the younger son of Turkey's wartime ambassador to the United States, might have seemed an unlikely associate for Wexler, the enthusiasm for jazz and blues that the two shared proved stronger than their differences. Soon Wexler and Ertegun, together with Herb Abramson, Atlantic's other co-founder, were vacationing together on Fire Island, New York, and in 1952, Ertegun and Abramson invited Wexler to join their firm. They withdrew the offer when, to their amazement, Wexler responded with the demand that he be made a full partner. Then, one year later, Abramson departed for a two-year stint in the military, and Wexler was asked to fill in as provisional co-director of Atlantic.

Atlantic had already launched a number of hits prior to Wexler's arrival. Artists including Ruth Brown, Stick McGhee, and Joe Turner had all done well on the R&B charts, and the label had just signed the as-yet-unknown singer Ray Charles. But after Wexler joined the firm, things began to pick up steam. In 1954, a year after his arrival, Big Joe Turner's rowdy "Shake, Rattle and Roll" helped inaugurate the rock-and-roll revolution. That hit was one of the first to demonstrate widespread crossover appeal, and white teenagers snapped it up in droves. Their elders' outrage about the lyrics' lewd insinuations probably only magnified the song's appeal. That same year Ray Charles cut "I've Got a Woman," which redefined R&B by blending the ecstatic, abandoned vocals typical of gospel with a traditional blues rhythm. Not only was the song a smash hit, it also laid the groundwork for the development of soul music. Indeed, "I've Got a Woman" proved so influential that it earned Charles the title "the Father of Soul" (not to be confused with that of James Brown, the "Godfather of Soul"). Later, the vocal group the Coasters scored many hits for Atlantic, including "Yakety Yak," a jaunty ballad that concealed sharp racial satire beneath a buoyant chorus of saxophones and a veneer of 1950s-style suburban domesticity. During Wexler's first two years with Atlantic, no fewer than 30 of the label's singles made it to the R&B Top 10.

In coming to Atlantic when he did, Wexler had the good fortune to be in the right place at the right time. Speaking with Thomas Calvin for the *New York Times* (December 12, 1993), Wexler recalled the dynamic Zeitgeist of the era: "That time in the early '50s was the crucible. Rhythm and Blues was taking off. Rock and Roll was lurking in the wings. Things were ready to explode. . . . The timing was right. People were coming back from [World War II], ready to try new things. Before the war all the streams and tributaries that go into Rock and Roll existed in parochial settings. Mississippi blues stayed down there. Rockabilly was Appalachian music that had stayed in the hills. Delta blues stayed down in the deep Delta area. But with World War II communications opened up. More people were getting together, and a lot of back pressure built up." At the same time, the era of the big bands was ending, and radio stations were looking about for a fresh sound. Record labels like Atlantic formed a conduit between radio broadcasters eager for new music with which to fill the airwaves and figures connected with local music scenes, which were bubbling with creativity. And finally, the fledgling civil rights movement had begun to challenge the institution of segregation, in the music industry as well as in other spheres of American life. Integrated musical ensembles gained wider acceptance, and white teenagers, while perhaps not fully grasping the racial issues involved, were more open to black music than their elders had ever been.

Wexler himself made a significant contribution to Atlantic's success. Since Ertegun preferred what Alex Halberstadt euphemistically called "the more bohemian aspects of making records," most of the nitty-gritty involved in running the business fell to Wexler. He worked the phones, hired musicians, hobnobbed with disc jockeys and distributors, and even composed music and lyrics for performers. He also testified during the Manhattan district attorney's 1959 probe into payola. (At the time, it was common for record companies to offer disc jockeys payola—illicit payments—in return for promotion of particular songs and albums.) But it was in the studio, as a producer, that Wexler proved most successful. He was unusually skilled in managing sessions and delegating responsibilities among musicians and technicians; he also knew when to let well enough alone. Most notably, he showed a knack for coaxing memorable performances out of the singers and instrumentalists he worked with. Sometimes he would exercise charm to persuade a musician to give his or her best for

a track; at other times he would be aggressive, even abrasive. As the studio musician Jim Dickinson recalled to Alex Halberstadt, "Jerry will get up in the bass player's face, so you could smell his breath, and sing a bass part. He may not necessarily want the bass player to play what he's singing, he just wants him to play something different."

Among the R&B greats whose records Wexler produced in the 1950s and 1960s were Wilson Pickett, Percy Sledge, and Otis Redding. All of those performers were commercially successful as well as critically respected, and thanks to his work with them, as well as with Ray Charles, he gained a reputation as one of the foremost producers in the business. A high point of his career came in 1967, when Aretha Franklin (the "Queen of Soul") broke with Columbia Records and signed with Atlantic. By his own account, Wexler had been trying to lure Franklin to his label ever since he heard a recording of the singer performing with her father's gospel choir. Franklin, in turn, was eager to launch a pop career after years of languishing on the so-called chitlin' circuit of small, predominantly black nightclubs. In recordings she made before coming to Atlantic, bland melodies and insipid strings often detracted from Franklin's extraordinary voice. Wexler encouraged the singer to avoid musical frills; as he recalled to Leo Sacks for the *New York Times Book Review* (August 29, 1993), "I urged Aretha to be Aretha." He told Halberstadt, "I was cutting basic R&B and blues. All I had to do was drop her into the context." Many of Franklin's songs on *I Never Loved a Man the Way I Love You* (1967), the first album she cut with Wexler, were R&B standards; one, "Respect," an Otis Redding number that Redding had recorded earlier for Atlantic, sold more than a million copies and became her first international hit. Franklin later told Timothy White for *Rolling Stone* (November 27, 1980), "My sessions with Jerry Wexler are among my favorite sessions. I feel the things we did together were dynamite, and I would also say they were some of the finest records of the Sixties and early Seventies."

Also in 1967 Wexler persuaded Ertegun to sell Atlantic to Warner Bros. for $17.5 million—in retrospect, a steal for the buyer. The two men continued to administer Atlantic. But in the wake of the sale, unexpressed tensions between them became manifest, and they began to go their separate ways. In the late 1960s and early 1970s, Ertegun cultivated big-name rock acts, among them the Rolling Stones, AC/DC, Foreigner, Yes, and Led Zeppelin, while Wexler chiefly worked with southern musicians—Duane Allman, Dr. John, and Delaney & Bonnie, as well as the country singer Willie Nelson. Although these artists were far from unsuccessful, they did not dominate the market as Led Zeppelin and the Rolling Stones did. Consequently, Wexler began to feel increasingly alienated at Atlantic. In 1975 he resigned from the company to work as a freelance producer—a move that some feel marked the beginning of a period of decline in his career. As Tom Graves wrote years later for the *Washington Post* (June 23, 1993), "Although Wexler doesn't want to admit it, as the '70s wound to a close he had all but lost his ability to pick hits." For his part, Wexler has insisted that he simply didn't care for the popular music of the time—in particular, rock and roll. (When Elizabeth Renzetti, writing for the Toronto *Globe and Mail* [April 8, 1995], asked him to consider the role of genius in modern American music, for example, Wexler replied, "This is purely subjective, . . . but you begin by dismissing rock 'n' roll.")

Nevertheless, Wexler was soon to affiliate himself with a musician who had virtually epitomized rock music in the mid-1960s (while also transcending that genre): Bob Dylan. Wexler's first chance to work with Dylan came in 1979, the year Dylan announced that he had become a born-again Christian. Although Dylan's religious zeal turned off many of his fans, a number of critics greeted with enthusiasm the album he released that year, *Slow Train Coming*, a strong work of gospel rock that contained the hit single "You Gotta Serve Somebody." Wexler, too, earned praise: "Like Dylan," Jann Wenner wrote for *Rolling Stone*, as quoted on the Web site *there1.com*, "Wexler has his finest LP since those fabulous Sixties, one that ranks with his greatest achievements." (Wexler has often said that although he has worked with a number of great talents in his career, he has collaborated with only three "geniuses": Ray Charles, Aretha Franklin, and Bob Dylan.)

As a freelancer in the 1980s, Wexler also worked with such well-known artists as Dire Straits, Carlos Santana, and George Michael. Toward the end of the decade, he began to slow down (he turned 70 in 1987), and while he continued to produce, his name is associated with no landmark recordings after the mid-1980s. Starting around then, he began to channel part of his energies into writing his memoir, with the help of David Ritz. The result, *Rhythm and the Blues: A Life in American Music* (1993), provides a wealth of first-hand tales about the music icons Wexler knew and worked with. It also offers a brutally frank account of Wexler's personal life, including discussions of his marital infidelity and the death of his daughter Anita from AIDS. *Rhythm and the Blues* won the 1993 Ralph J. Gleason Music Book Award, which is co-sponsored by New York University, BMI (Broadcast Music Inc.), and *Rolling Stone* and is named for one of *Rolling Stone*'s co-founders.

Wexler has two surviving children from his first marriage, to Shirley Kampf, which ended in divorce (as did his second marriage, to Renee Pappas). He maintains waterside homes in Florida and Long Island, New York, where he lives with his third wife. (Her name has appeared variously as Jean Arthur and Jean Martin.) While he is no longer one of the music industry's movers and shakers, he has expressed confidence that his contribution to music history will be of lasting import. As he expressed it to Elizabeth Renzetti, "You know we're

going to be listening to Dylan and Ray Charles and Aretha as far as the mind can project." — P.K.

Suggested Reading: *New York Times Book Review* p17 Aug. 29, 1993; *Rolling Stone* p49+ Nov. 27, 1980; *Salon.com* (on-line), with photo; (Toronto) *Globe and Mail* C p3 Apr. 8, 1995; *Washington Post* C p1 June 23, 1993; Wexler, Jerry, and David Ritz. *Rhythm and the Blues: A Life in American Music*, 1993

Natasha Stovall/Courtesy of Doubleday

Whitehead, Colson

1969– Writer. Address: c/o Bantam Doubleday, 1540 Broadway, New York, NY 10036

After the publication of his first novel, *The Intuitionist* (1999), Colson Whitehead was heralded as the most exciting African-American voice of his generation and drew comparisons to such celebrated authors as Ralph Ellison. The story of a black elevator inspector turned sleuth, *The Intuitionist* received so much critical acclaim that it left many pundits wondering if Whitehead could possibly top his debut. Yet he did just that with *John Henry Days* (2001), an encyclopedic look at the modern era through the eyes of a young freelance journalist who finds himself on the same ill-fated course as the mythic railroad laborer John Henry, who died trying to outperform a steam engine in the Industrial Age.

Colson Whitehead was born in 1969 in New York City. As a child and teenager he was obsessed with pop culture—everything from television sitcoms to action movies to Marvel Comics. He also had an early interest in writing and attended Harvard University, in Cambridge, Massachusetts, with the intention of enrolling in creative-writing classes. Because he was not accepted into the writing seminars he wanted to take, he studied English and comparative literature instead, earning a degree in those subjects, in 1991. Shortly after his graduation Whitehead secured a job with the literary supplement of the *Village Voice*, as an editorial assistant. At the time he wanted to become a pop-culture critic and quickly found himself writing music, television, and book reviews. He was eventually promoted to the position of TV editor, and he wrote a regular column that gave him some sense of satisfaction. "All my wasted time as a child and teenager [was] now actually income-generating and [paid] my rent," he remarked to Kevin Larimer for *Poets and Writers* magazine (July/August 2001).

During his time at the *Village Voice*, Whitehead wrote his first novel. "It was a kind of pop-culture-heavy book about a child-genius cherub, Michael Jackson-Gary Coleman type," Whitehead told Logan Hill for *New York* (May 7, 2001). "He's not a midget, but he gets plugged into all sorts of stereotypical black roles until he becomes a sort of super-bad-ass Shaft character." The book was turned down by almost 25 publishing houses. Six months later his agent dropped him. In an interview with the author Walter Mosley for *Book* (May/June 2001), Whitehead reflected on the loss of his agent. "It was [depressing], because you have all these rejection letters and the person who you thought was your one ally is like, 'So where do we send these manuscripts? Put them in the garbage? You want them back?' I think being dumped by the agent was actually beneficial because it was like, no one gives a crap, no one cares. I had to keep doing it, though no one cared except me."

One night in 1996, while watching a television segment on defective escalators, Whitehead stumbled on the inspiration for his next book. He changed the focus from escalators to elevators and wrote a detective novel, a genre that had recently begun to fascinate him. The result was *The Intuitionist*.

In the novel, Lila Mae Watson, one of the few black elevator inspectors in an unnamed city, has become the scapegoat in a political tug-of-war between two main factions in the Department of Elevator Inspectors: the Empiricists and the Intuitionists. (An Empiricist solves elevator problems through an exhaustive understanding of mechanical details; an Intuitionist, such as Lila Mae, solves problems through instinct and meditation.) After the crash of an elevator she has inspected, the Empiricists, who control the department, try to use the accident to stop the spread of their rivals. In order to save herself, as well as the Intuitionists, from being run out of the department, Lila Mae must find the missing blueprints for the "black box," a cutting-edge elevator design.

"In *The Intuitionist*," Brian Gilmore wrote for the *Washington Post* (June 21, 1999), "Whitehead somehow accomplishes two completely unrelated things: He educates the reader in some of the specifics of elevator technology and carves out an exclusive space for himself in America's literary canon." Writing for *Booklist* (December 1998), Donna Seaman cheered: "The story is mesmerizing, but it is Whitehead's shrewd and sardonic humor and agile explications of the insidiousness of racism and the eternal conflict between the material and the spiritual that make this such a trenchant and accomplished novel." In *Time* (January 25, 1999), Walter Kirn commented: "The invention of rich, new literary metaphors is difficult enough. When the subject is race in America, however, it's almost impossible. In his first novel, Whitehead has solved the problem, coming up with the freshest racial allegory since Ralph Ellison's *Invisible Man* and Toni Morrison's *The Bluest Eye*." *The Intuitionist* won the Quality Paperback Book Club's New Voices Award, in 1999, and a Whiting Writer's Award, in 2000.

For his next novel, *John Henry Days*, Whitehead used the legend of the folk hero John Henry—who died beating a steam engine in a race to cut a tunnel through a mountain—to reflect on the modern American obsession with popular culture. John Henry's legend is compared to the life of J. Sutter, a black freelance journalist trying to beat the record for most consecutive days covering staged events—including the unveiling of a commemorative stamp in John Henry's honor—on someone else's bill.

Most reviewers had only mild criticisms of the novel. In *Time* (May 21, 2001), Paul Gray noted: "*John Henry Days* is a narrative tour de force that astonishes on almost every page, but it generates more glitter and brilliance than warmth." In *Newsweek* (May 21, 2001), Malcolm Jones remarked on how Whitehead "extends his narrative every which way with little vignettes that use the John Henry legend as a jumping off point—a touchstone—to explore how pop culture subverts and destroys legitimate myths. . . . The amazing thing is, he nearly pulls it off. There's no way he could, of course. But if this novel is a mess, it's a grand mess, one of those stories where the getting there is all the fun." Though noting that *John Henry Days* has "encyclopedic aspirations," and includes many sections that have little direct impact on the central story, Jonathan Franzen, in the *New York Times Book Review* (May 13, 2001), nevertheless praised the work: "Again and again, you hit passages of wry and largehearted descriptive prose that are the clearest measure of Whitehead's achievement and promise as a writer."

Colson Whitehead is married to Natasha Stovall, a photographer he met while working at the *Village Voice*. He lives in the New York City borough of Brooklyn and is currently at work on a novel about Band-Aids. — C.M.

Suggested Reading: *Book* p44+ May/June 2001; *Booklist* p651 Dec. 1, 1998; *New York* p38+ May 7, 2001; *New York Times Book Review* p8+ May 13, 2001; *Newsweek* p59 May 21, 2001; *Poets and Writers* p20+ July/Aug. 2001; *Time* p78 Jan. 25, 1999, p91 May 21, 2001; *Washington Post* C p3 June 21, 1999

Selected Works: *The Intuitionist*, 1999; *John Henry Days*, 2001

Courtesy of Flossie Wong-Staal

Wong-Staal, Flossie

Aug. 27, 1946– Director of the Center for AIDS Research at the University of California at San Diego; virologist. Address: University of California at San Diego, Dept. of Medicine 06655, 9500 Gilman Dr., La Jolla, CA 92093-5003

The virologist Flossie Wong-Staal has been at the forefront of AIDS research for almost two decades. She is a co-discoverer of HIV—human immunodeficiency virus, the virus that causes AIDS (acquired immune deficiency syndrome); she was the first researcher to clone the HIV virus; and currently, she is involved in efforts to develop an HIV vaccine and long-term therapies for HIV-positive patients. In 1990 the Institute for Scientific Information named Wong-Staal the top woman scientist of the 1980s and ranked her among the top scientists under the age of 45. In 1994 she was elected to the prestigious Institute of Medicine, one of the U.S.'s four National Academies.

The daughter of Sueh-fung Wang, a textile importer-exporter, and his wife, a homemaker, Flossie Wong-Staal was born Yee Ching Wong in Guangzhou (Canton), China, on August 27, 1946. In 1952, about three years after the Communists under Mao Zedong formally established the People's Republic of China, the family fled to Hong Kong, which was then under British control. There, Wong-Staal was enrolled in a Catholic school. When the school's American nuns asked the students' parents to select English names for their children, Wong-Staal's father, who spoke no English, chose "Flossie," the moniker given to a typhoon that had struck Hong Kong the previous week. "I used to be embarrassed by [the name]," Wong-Staal told Yvonne Baskin for *Discover* (December 1991). "Now I'm trying to change the image of the name." Wong-Staal showed an aptitude for math and science, and by the time she graduated from the Catholic school, she had decided to pursue scientific study in the U.S. That decision was unprecedented in her family; as she later explained, as quoted by *writetools.com*, "I did not really have a role model in my family when I was growing up. All the women in the family were full-time housewives. Most of the men were in business and few had pursued higher education." Nevertheless, Wong-Staal's family supported her in her aspirations. Moreover, as Wong-Staal recalled for *Asian American Biography*, as quoted by *gale.com*, "surprisingly, my being female was not an issue with them."

In 1965 Wong-Staal enrolled at the University of California at Los Angeles (UCLA), where she majored in molecular biology. The field was both relatively new and extraordinarily exciting then, thanks to James Watson and Francis Crick's discovery, in 1953, of the helical structure of DNA, the molecule that carries each cell's genetic information and serves as a kind of blueprint for every individual organism. Among the most important scientific breakthroughs of the 20th century, Watson and Crick's discovery had opened the door to vast, uncharted terrain for researchers in the biological sciences. Wong-Staal found the excitement catching, and after receiving a B.A. degree, magna cum laude, in 1968, she continued to study molecular biology at UCLA at the graduate level. In 1971 she married a UCLA medical student, Steven Staal, and appended his surname to her own. (Their marriage, which produced two daughters, ended in divorce.) While pursuing her Ph.D., Wong-Staal worked as both a teaching assistant and a research assistant at UCLA. She earned the degree in 1972.

After a brief stint as a postdoctoral fellow at the University of California, San Diego, Wong-Staal relocated to Bethesda, Maryland, outside Washington, D.C., where she began working in a National Cancer Institute laboratory under the well-known medical researcher Robert Gallo. Her research involved retroviruses, a family of viruses about which little was known at the time. Her painstaking, analytical approach to laboratory work proved invaluable in unraveling the genome, or genetic fingerprint, of particular viruses; it also complemented Gallo's research style, which Wong-Staal, speaking with Baskin, characterized as "flamboyant and creative." Gallo, as quoted in Lisa Yount's *A to Z of Women in Science and Math* (1999), later wrote that Wong-Staal "evolve[d] into one of the major players in my group. Because of her insight and leadership qualities, she gradually assumed a supervisory role."

In the early 1980s Wong-Staal's research group achieved a number of scientific breakthroughs. In 1981 the researchers identified a retrovirus that causes cancer in humans; they labeled it human T-cell leukemia virus (HTLV). (While scientists had previously suspected that some retroviruses cause human cancer, this was the first time such a virus had been isolated in the lab.) Later, Wong-Staal and her colleagues identified a similar virus, which they named HTLV-2. The team's most important finding, however, came in late 1983. While investigating the possibility that either HTLV or HTLV-2 might be the agent responsible for the AIDS epidemic then sweeping large cities, Gallo and Wong-Staal identified a third (and previously unknown) retrovirus, which they called HTLV-3. HTLV-3, which eventually became known as HIV, turned out to be the pathogen researchers had been searching for. For their work, Gallo and Wong-Staal (together with French scientists who independently isolated the virus at about the same time) were credited as co-discoverers of the HIV virus.

Gallo and Wong-Staal next turned to the full-time study of the HIV virus. In 1984 Wong-Staal became the first researcher to successfully clone the HIV virus and the first to genetically map it. That work led to the development of tests to determine the presence of the HIV virus in blood; the tests are used to identify people who are infected and to screen donated blood. In the succeeding years Wong-Staal authored or co-authored a number of books and papers on the HIV virus. According to a 1990 survey conducted by the Philadelphia-based Institute of Scientific Information, in the 1980s papers by Wong-Staal were cited more often than those of any other female scientist.

In 1990 Wong-Staal left the National Cancer Institute to accept a professorship at the University of California at San Diego (UCSD) and to direct the Center for AIDS Research there. This position has allowed Wong-Staal to concentrate on translating the often highly theoretical aspects of AIDS research into concrete medical applications. As she told Baskin, "I consider it necessary, almost an obligation on our part, to put the knowledge we've gained to use." Wong-Staal's work at UCSD has focused mainly on developing a vaccine that would immunize uninfected people against the HIV virus. She has also continued to investigate procedures such as gene therapy, which would benefit those already infected. Explaining why a multipronged approach to AIDS prevention and treatment is nec-

essary, she told Baskin, "It's a question of trial and error, and we can't afford to wait until one thing fails to try another."

The effort to develop an effective HIV vaccine is fraught with difficulties. Chief among them is the virus's mutability. Like most viruses, HIV reproduces by invading the DNA of a host cell and then converting the host into a factory for manufacturing copies of itself. Sometimes, as happens in the reproduction of all organisms, errors or mutations lead to differences between one generation and the next. After a series of mutations over many generations, a particular organism may bear little resemblance to a distant ancestor. (Indeed, the accumulation of reproductive mutations is what drives the process of evolution.) Because the HIV virus reproduces so rapidly—in an infected person, Wong-Staal has shown, it produces as many as a trillion copies of itself daily—and because its rate of mutation is high, it tends to evolve relatively quickly. Thus, the virus is like a moving target, making it very difficult to develop an effective HIV vaccine: even if a particular vaccine proves effective against one strain of the virus, the vaccine will most likely prove useless against other, newly evolved strains.

Vaccines work by triggering the body's own immune response without actually infecting the host—or, more precisely, without infecting the host with a fully virulent pathogen. The challenge for researchers is to alter the virus so that it is too weak to cause an infection but can still set the body's own defenses in motion. Speaking of the quest for an HIV vaccine, Wong-Staal explained to Baskin, "Our goal is to make a virus as similar to the real one as possible, but to make sure there's no risk of introducing its dangerous genes into an uninfected population." To date, weakening the HIV virus properly has proved to be extremely difficult. That problem is another formidable barrier to the development of an HIV vaccine.

Gene therapy, in contrast to vaccination, focuses on treatment rather than prevention. Essentially, gene therapy aims to weaken a virus that has already infected a host, thus giving the body's immune system an edge. Recently, Wong-Staal has been working on drugs that aim to short-circuit the virus's reproductive cycle. The hope is that, with sufficient advantage, the immune system will be able to rid the body of the virus. Before that becomes a possibility, more detailed knowledge of the HIV virus is needed, since it is difficult to generate drugs that can distinguish viral processes from cellular processes. — P.K.

Suggested Reading: *Discover* p16+ Dec. 1991, with photo; *National Geographic World* p25+ June 1993, with photos; *Time* p73 Dec. 30, 1996, with photo; Yount, Lisa. *A to Z of Women in Science and Math*, 1999

Charles Hopkinson/Retna

Zaillian, Steven

Jan. 30, 1953– Screenwriter; film director.
Address: c/o Writers Guild of America, 7000 W.
Third St., Los Angeles, CA 90048-4329

"There are so many stories of screenwriters who write a script and sell it for a million dollars, and people think those are the ones who lead charmed lives," Steven Zaillian told Bernard Weinraub for the *New York Times* (August 9, 1993). "I feel I've led a charmed life in a way because I've worked on things I've really liked." Zaillian's screenwriting credits include the films *The Falcon and the Snowman*, *Awakenings*, *Jack the Bear*, *Clear and Present Danger*, *Mission: Impossible*, and *Hannibal*; *Searching for Bobby Fischer* and *A Civil Action*, which he also directed; and *Schindler's List*, for which he won an Academy Award for best adapted screenplay. All of his screenplays are based on novels or books of nonfiction. Zaillian has been successful in building his career largely on his own terms. "I know there are a lot of people who are successful by giving the public what they want or giving the producers what they want," he told Alan Waldman in the late 1990s during an interview for the Writer's Guild of America (on-line). "I think that's a mistake for the soul. I think that the best films are those that are written by people who care about what they write and who aren't trying to figure out what it is that people want to see. They're not trying to second-guess what an audience wants to see. The truly great films are those that are original and can't be second-guessed or predicted." He added, "That's a very long-winded way of saying that I think you should write about what you care about."

Steven Zaillian was born in California on January 30, 1953. His father was a radio news reporter in Los Angeles. In 1975 Zaillian graduated from San Francisco State University. He began his film career as an assistant editor on such B movies as the Chuck Norris vehicle *Breaker! Breaker!* (1977) and *Kingdom of the Spiders* (1977), starring William Shatner. Within the next several years, he sold his first script, "Bad Manners," to the producer Ray Stark. The screenplay, a coming-of-age story about a group of boys in the final days before their high-school graduation, caught the attention of people of influence in the movie industry. "Even though the film wasn't made, the phone began ringing off the hook," Zaillian's agent at that time, Harold Greene, told Bernard Weinraub. "Everybody wanted to hire this guy. He was very young, sort of monosyllabic. We began setting up meetings for Steven, but after a few days he came in and closed the door to my office and asked me to stop the lunches and meetings. I told him that's the way things are done here. And he said, 'I'm not interested in having them find out the way my head works, and I'm not interested in the way their head works.' People all over town couldn't believe it. They thought it was some kind of ploy."

Zaillian's first screenwriting credit was the script for *The Falcon and the Snowman* (1985). An adaptation of a nonfiction book by the *New York Times* reporter Robert Lindsey, it is about two young California men from upper-middle-class families—Christopher Boyce, a low-level CIA employee, and Daulton Lee, a small-time drug dealer—who became spies for the Soviet Union in the 1970s. The film, directed by John Schlesinger and starring Timothy Hutton and Sean Penn, earned mostly mixed reviews; many critics faulted the story for failing to present well-developed characters or to offer a credible motive for Boyce's treasonous behavior.

Zaillian's screenplay for the film *Awakenings* (1990), directed by Penny Marshall, was based on the same-titled nonfiction book by the neurologist Oliver Sacks. It focuses on patients (mainly, a man portrayed by Robert De Niro) in a long-term-care facility who, decades before, had entered catatonic states after suffering a form of encephalitis. After the Sacks character (called Malcolm Sayer and played by Robin Williams) gives them the newly discovered drug L-dopa, many of the patients regain near normalcy, only to revert before long to their earlier condition. Although some reviewers disliked what struck them as Hollywood clichés in the script and criticized the film's oversimplification of its subject, Zaillian earned an Academy Award nomination for his script. The film and Robert De Niro also received Oscar nominations. Zaillian's next effort, *Jack the Bear* (1993), was based on Dan McCall's novel about an alcoholic widower and his two sons; directed by Marshall Herskovitz and starring Danny De Vito, it received mostly thumbs-down reviews.

Earlier, the producer Edgar Scherick, who had expressed interest in "Bad Manners," had introduced Zaillian to Scott Rudin, the producer of *Flatliners* (1990) and *The Addams Family* (1991), among other films. Having noted the cinematic qualities of Zaillian's writing, Rudin began to encourage him to direct. "Steve's scripts read like movies," the producer told Weinraub. "He writes like a director. His writing is so specific and carefully wrought, all you need to do is follow what he has on the page and you'll end up with a wonderful scene." Rudin produced Zaillian's directorial debut, *Searching for Bobby Fischer* (1993), for which Zaillian also wrote the script, based on the memoir of the same name by the sportswriter Fred Waitzkin. The book's title refers to the player who, in 1958, at the age of 15, became the youngest international grand master of chess in the history of the game; the book and film chronicle the experiences of Waitzkin's seven-year-old son, Josh, after the boy's phenomenal aptitude for chess becomes apparent. The role of Josh was played by eight-year-old Max Pomeranc, one of the top 100 U.S. chess contenders among children in his age group. "We interviewed hundreds of kids," Zaillian told Bernard Weinraub. "And Max just seemed so normal. He had composure and confidence, and he was totally unintimidated, and he had holes in his jeans and his hair was messed up. He had no acting experience, but we decided to gamble. It turned out that he was so natural that he's incapable of a false moment." The film also starred Joe Mantegna, as Josh's father, whose dream that his son will turn into the next Bobby Fischer leads him to push the boy to succeed; Joan Allen, as the boy's mother, who is determined to let Josh lead a normal life; and Laurence Fishburne and Ben Kingsley, as chess experts whose approaches to mentoring the boy differ markedly. The film opened to glowing reviews, and Conrad L. Hall won an Academy Award nomination for his cinematography. Still, *Searching for Bobby Fischer* suffered from a lack of interest-generating publicity (ads did not adequately convey the fact that a knowledge of chess was not required to enjoy the story), and it fared poorly at the box office. "I can't agonize over what's done when the film is made," Zaillian told Max Alexander for *Variety* (January 3–9, 1994). "What can you do but make the best movie you can?"

By his own account, Zaillian prefers to write about subjects about which, initially, he has little knowledge. "Having an outsider's view allows me to discover it in a way that I can write about it with some enthusiasm," he explained to an interviewer for *Entertainment Weekly* (June 27, 1997). While reading a book that is to be adapted for the big screen, "I try to create a bit of a road map as I go along," he told John Horn for *Premiere* (December 1998). "Often, I turn out to be wrong." He admitted to Max Alexander, "I hate the actual writing of scripts. Halfway through, I just want to throw them in the trash. So when someone pays me to adapt

something, I take the money and spend it right away; then I have to finish the job." In an interview with Christopher Probst for *American Cinematographer* (January 1999), he said, "When I'm writing a script, I cannot help but visualize it in my head. In fact, I can't write it if I can't see it. In a way, I've already directed the film just by writing it. It's then a matter of either trying to capture what I imagined, or being open to another idea that's better. Since *Bobby Fischer* was my first film, I was literally terrified and planned a lot of it out. I actually sat down and wrote up shot lists and my own little storyboards. I could only get through the first two weeks of shooting, however, because I was too overwhelmed to think beyond all that. Then when I showed up the first day with all of these storyboards. . . [Hall] didn't want to have anything to do with them! He just wanted to know what I felt the scene was about. . . . Somehow, while we discussed a scene, we would arrive at some way of shooting it. He taught me not to be too set in what I thought a scene should look like until after I had seen a rehearsal." This method of working is conducive to what Zaillian has referred to as "happy accidents."

Zaillian devoted the better part of three years to writing the screenplay for *Schindler's List* (1993). An adaptation of Thomas Kenneally's nonfiction novel *Schindler's Ark*, the film depicted the rescue of more than 1,100 Jews by the German-born, Catholic industrialist Oskar Schindler during World War II. During the course of the film, Schindler opens a factory in Poland with the goal of increasing his wealth; he later uses his own money—and risks his life—to prevent the deaths of his workers at the hands of the Nazis. The movie starred Liam Neeson as Schindler, Ben Kingsley as Schindler's accountant, Itzhak Stern, and Ralph Fiennes as Amon Goeth, the commandant of a concentration camp. Almost universally hailed for "its poetic visual sense, intelligent grasp of history, and profound sense of humanity," as Julie Salamon put it in a review for *Harper's Bazaar* (February 1994), the film was nominated for a dozen Oscars and won seven, including those for best film and best adapted screenplay. Zaillian's script for *Schindler's List* also received a Golden Globe Award in 1993.

Along with John Milius and Donald Stewart, Zaillian wrote the screenplay for *Clear and Present Danger* (1994); adapted from a novel by Tom Clancy, the plot centers on Jack Ryan, a CIA operative (played by Harrison Ford) who must engineer the rescue of U.S. infantrymen whose drug-related mission in Colombia has gone awry. Zaillian is credited along with Bruce Geller and David Koepp with co-wroting the story for *Mission: Impossible* (1996), directed by Brian De Palma and starring Tom Cruise. He worked on the screenplay for Steven Spielberg's *Amistad* (1997), about the 1839 shipboard mutiny of a group of African captives led by Joseph Cinqué and the subsequent trial that led to their freedom, but only David Franzoni was credited for the script.

Zaillian wrote, directed, and executive produced *A Civil Action* (1998), a courtoom drama based on a book by Jonathan Harr. The best-selling book tells the true story of a group of families in Woburn, Massachusetts, who sued two huge corporations whose questionable environmental practices, they believed, had led to the deaths of seven of their children from leukemia. (All told, there had been 28 cases of childhood leukemia in the Woburn area, with 16 deaths.) *A Civil Action* depicts the effects of the case on the plaintiffs' attorney, Jan Schlichtman (John Travolta), who devoted several years to gathering evidence for the families' lawsuit; in the process, he gained compassion and self-knowledge and abandoned his flashy lifestyle while bankrupting himself financially. "From the beginning, I insisted we find a movie star for the role because Jan was a bit of a movie star in his profession," Zaillian told Louis B. Hobson for the *Calgary Sun*, in an article reprinted on *Jam!* (January 5, 1999, on-line). "Both Jan and John are very charismatic and they're self-possessed and a bit vain. It's why they're successful and why people like them so much." He also explained to Hobson that he "concentrated on the lawyers"—those who represented the two corporations as well as Schlichtman—rather than on the parents of the victims, because "after a great deal of consideration, I decided I only needed one major scene to establish the shared pain of those families." In a conversation with Hobson, John Travolta commented on Zaillian's meticulous attention to detail: "Steve is a perfectionist whose vision is everything. We would do dozens of extra takes of each scene after the actors felt we'd achieved what we needed to. Steve would move an ashtray on a desk and then start over again. I'd definitely work with Steve again but not for awhile. I need to do a few films my way before going back to his way. It's just too emotionally and physically exhausting. Steve liked what I was doing. He just wanted me to do it too often for my liking."

Most of the outdoor scenes in *A Civil Action* take place in cold temperatures under overcast skies. Zaillian and Conrad Hall, the cinematographer, used images of water as a reminder that the plaintiffs' case hinged on the question of the safety of the town's water supply. "If you look closely, there's a glass [of water] in almost every shot . . . ," Zaillian told Christopher Probst. "For the same reason, there's a lot of rain in the movie. If you go too far with a visual symbol it can become obnoxious, so we tried to be as subtle as possible. But water is the opening image of the film, and that's what the story is really about—the [Aberjona] river [which runs through east Woburn], and the drinking water. The sickness and the death in the story is all tied to water."

Zaillian wrote the screenplay for the director Ridley Scott's *Hannibal* (2000), a sequel to the highly successful psychological thriller *Silence of the Lambs* (1991). Both films are adaptations of novels in a trilogy by Thomas Harris that feature Hannibal Lecter, a cannibalistic serial killer. Zaillian shared the screenwriting credit with the renowned dramatist and motion-picture writer and director David Mamet, whose earlier draft had been rejected by Universal Studios. Zaillian had no desire to rewrite Mamet's screenplay; instead, he worked closely with Harris and the screenwriter Hossein Amini to create a new screenplay that was faithful to the spirit of the novels. Together with Jay Cocks, Kenneth Lonergan, and Martin Scorsese, Zaillian co-wrote the screenplay to Scorsese's film *Gangs of New York*, which is set in the mid-1800s and is based on Herbert Asbury's 1928 nonfiction account, subtitled "An Informal History of the Underworld." Starring Leonardo DiCaprio, Cameron Diaz, and Willem Dafoe, *Gangs of New York* is scheduled to premiere in 2002. Zaillian, Stephen Gaghan, Ken Nolan and three others cowrote the screenplay for Ridley Scott's *Black Hawk Down*, a film based on Mark Bowden's 1999 book about the Battle of Mogadishu, the October 1993 conflict in which 18 Americans died while fighting forces in Somalia in an attempt to end a famine stemming from that nation's civil war. The release of *Black Hawk Down* is set for 2002.

While working on a screenplay, Zaillian told the *Entertainment Weekly* reporter, "I actually avoid everything. I stop reading, stop going to movies, and I try not to be influenced by anything." In his interview with Alan Waldman, he said that, for him, the greatest moments in film were "visual moments, not moments of dialogue." "They were pictures," he explained. "One of them comes at the end of *The 400 Blows*, as the boy is wandering around the beach not knowing which way to turn. . . . Another is the moment in *To Kill a Mockingbird* when Scout is sitting on the porch with Boo Radley. The things that I really feel in movies—and that I think that most people really feel—are often visual moments. So I believe that it's very important for screenwriters to think visually and to tell their stories as visually as they can." Zaillian's honors include Scripter Awards for both *Schindler's List* and *A Civil Action*; bestowed annually by the Friends of the University of Southern California Libraries, the award recognizes "the best realization of a book adapted to film." — C.L.

Suggested Reading: *American Cinematographer* p48+ Jan. 1999, with photos; *New York Times* C p11+ Aug. 9, 1993, with photo; *Premiere* p90+ Dec. 1998, with photos; *Variety* p4 Jan. 3–9, 1994, with photo

Selected Films: as screenwriter—*The Falcon and the Snowman*, 1985; *Awakenings*, 1990; *Schindler's List*, 1993; *Clear and Present Danger* (with John Milius and Donald E. Stewart), 1994; *Hannibal* (with David Mamet), 2000; as director and screenwriter—*Searching for Bobby Fischer*, 1993; as executive producer, director, and screenwriter—*A Civil Action*, 1998

Paula Bronstein/Getty Images/Archive Photos

Zhu Rongji

Oct. 1, 1928– Premier of China. Address: Office of the Premier, State Council Secretariat, Zhong Nan Hai, Beijing, China

Known as the third-most-powerful man in China (behind President Jiang Zemin and Li Peng, the second-most-powerful member of the Chinese Communist Party), Premier Zhu Rongji, the head of China's State Council, has been responsible for much of the nation's economic policy for the last 10 years. Twice purged from the government in past decades for being a "rightist," Zhu later initiated mass reforms, first as a vice premier of China and then as governor of the national bank. By untangling enormous webs of debt and using tough macroeconomic measures, Zhu managed to stabilize China's currency, increase investment from overseas, and lower inflation while also keeping the economy growing at a steady rate. While much of the East Asian economy fell on hard times in the mid-1990s, thanks to Zhu's efforts the Chinese economy continued to prosper. Considered until recently to be a developing nation, China today stands poised to become an economic powerhouse. For his efforts, Zhu has been hailed as both the "Gorbachev of China," for opening up his nation's economy as the political reformer Mikhail Gorbachev did in the Soviet Union when he was its president, and the "Alan Greenspan of China," in reference to the highly regarded chairman of the United States' Federal Reserve Board. The latter label is perhaps more apt, for while Zhu has encouraged increased privatization of China's industries and the opening of the Chinese market, he has not been a reformer in terms of the nation's stance toward

human rights, its foreign policy, or its efforts to maintain control over Tibet and regain jurisdiction over Taiwan.

Zhu Rongji was born on October 1, 1928 in Changsha, the capital of China's Hunan Province. Although his ancestors were wealthy landowners, the death of his father before Zhu's birth impoverished his mother, who died while Zhu was young. Thereafter, the boy was raised by an uncle, who, when Zhu reached college age, gave his nephew 100 pieces of silver to help pay for a university education. Zhu, who had educated himself up to that point, attended Qinghua University in the nation's capital, Beijing, where he studied engineering in the Electrical Machinery Department. While in school he joined the New Democratic Youth Alliance, and in October 1949, the same month that the People's Republic of China was formed under Communist rule, he became a member of the Communist Party of China. Zhu graduated from Qinghua in 1951 and was then hired by the Northeast China Ministry of Industries as deputy head of its Production Planning Office. In 1952 Zhu began work at the State Planning Commission, serving first as section chief at the Bureau of Fuel and Power Industry, Comprehensive Planning, and then deputy division chief of the Minister's Office and Comprehensive Division of the Bureau of Machine-building. Although highly regarded there for his knowledge of economics, he was purged by the state for criticizing the government's economic policy during China's "Hundred Flowers" campaign, the brief period when the nation's then-leader, Mao Zedong, encouraged intellectual and political debate—a practice that was followed by recriminations against those who had criticized the state. Demoted, Zhu worked as a teacher at a so-called spare-time school (a facility where youths who had dropped out of school could resume their studies) run by the State Planning Commission. In 1962 he was "rehabilitated" (in other words, the government officially forgave him) and went to work as an engineer at the Comprehensive Bureau of National Economy of the State Planning Commission.

During China's Cultural Revolution, a 10-year attempt (beginning in 1966) to repress all thought and action contrary to those sanctioned by the state, Zhu was again purged for his rightist views and in 1970 was sent to work at a May Seventh Cadre School, a "reeducation" center in the Chinese countryside. Asked at his first news conference as premier about this experience, Zhu stated, as quoted by Reuters (March 19, 1998), "I learned deeply from it. It was not a happy experience. I do not want to talk about it." According to various sources, during his political exile in the country, Zhu was forced to herd cattle, feed pigs, and clean toilets. Although not officially rehabilitated, Zhu returned to Communist Party work in 1975 as deputy director and deputy chief engineer of the Power and Communication Engineering Company, under the Bureau of Pipeline Construction of the Ministry of the Petroleum Industry. At the same time he also worked as division chief of the Institute of Industrial Economics of the Chinese Academy of Social Sciences. In the late 1970s he briefly served as a professor at Qinghua University's Institute for Economics and Management. There, he taught classes on economic management, actively supervising graduate students.

In 1978 Zhu was officially rehabilitated by Deng Xiaoping, who, as chief of staff of the army, vice premier, and vice chairman of the Communist Party, was then China's most powerful political figure. Deng was seeking the help of economic advisers interested in reform; Zhu, who was known mainly for his being purged for his rightist inclinations, was appointed the division chief at the Bureau of Fuel and Power Industry and deputy director of the Comprehensive Bureau at the State Economic Commission (SEC). Zhu rose through the ranks of the commission, becoming director of the SEC's Bureau of Technical Transformation in 1982, and was promoted the following year to the position of vice minister of the Leading Group of the SEC. In addition to that title, he was named deputy secretary of the SEC in 1985.

In 1987 Zhu was appointed mayor of Shanghai, which, in spite of being the industrial and financial capital of China, was ailing economically. Zhu turned the city's fortunes around, overseeing development in the telecommunication, urban construction, and transport sectors. He was also responsible for investing a great deal of money in the transformation of Pudong, the district between downtown Shanghai and the East China Sea, into a high-tech industrial area. He invited financial investment from abroad and made trips to other provinces in China to ask for coal and other fuels when Shanghai was short of raw materials to run its factories.

In 1989 residents of Shanghai held mass protests in sympathy with those who had been gunned down in Tiananmen Square, in Beijing, for demanding political reform. Instead of using military force to dispel the protestors, Zhu made a nationally televised speech calling for stability and allowed the protests to peter out on their own. His handling of the conflict brought him praise from both party leaders and citizens of the city.

In 1991, in recognition of his great success in Shanghai, Zhu was appointed a vice premier of the State Council and head of its Production Office. Almost immediately, Zhu formed the State Council's Economic and Trade Commission to make policy regarding such matters as trade, energy, technology, and state-enterprise reform. At the time he took office, many provinces were involved in public-works projects, thus driving up the price of materials. Exacerbating the problem, the municipal governments were paying for their projects through what is known in China as "triangular debt," in which borrowers are unable to repay loans to lenders who are similarly unable to repay their own loans; these debts were devaluing the national currency and using up revenues needed to buy summer crops from farmers, meet factory payrolls, and pay for essential transportation and energy projects. As one of his first acts, Zhu untangled the staggering "debt chains" among state-owned companies (so called because no companies could repay their debts) and cut government spending by 20 percent by reducing the scope of public-works projects. Zhu also eliminated IOUs in state purchases of grain, making sure that farmers were paid right away for their harvests. In 1992 he instituted a series of tough macroeconomic control measures designed to address the excessive investment in machinery and other fixed assets, the rampant inflation, and the nation's excess money supply. Zhu's measures also included backing projects in transport, energy, and agriculture, among other sectors that had potentially bright prospects for economic growth. "Many people abroad confuse China's macro-control measures with tightening credit," he told Tony Walker and Peter Montagnon for the *Financial Times* (November 13, 1995). "This is not correct. We are not excessively tightening credit. To put it more correctly, we are readjusting the direction of our investment." Also in 1992, Zhu became a full member of the Fourteenth Chinese Communist Party (CCP) Central Committee as well as a member of the highest decision-making body in the nation, the Standing Committee of the Politburo.

Appointing himself governor of the People's Bank of China in 1993, when the country's economy began to become overheated (because of an epidemic of entrepreneurialism, which had led to high inflation and debt), Zhu implemented an austerity program that by the spring of 1996 had stabilized the economy. Specifically, he raised interest rates, reformed taxes, devalued China's currency, and significantly curbed bank lending in order to halt inflation, which had reached a rate of 24 percent. By the time he stepped down as governor of the bank, in 1995, inflation had fallen to 17.6 percent, and China's financial sector was far more organized. Meanwhile, the economy of the country as a whole continued to grow at a rate of over 10 percent a year.

Zhu's reforms were nonetheless criticized by hard-liners, who wanted to see interest rates lowered and who resented Zhu's streamlining of the state. The reforms also met with some restlessness on the part of Chinese citizens, who suddenly found their pay docked, as Zhu brought back the mandatory purchasing of government bonds in order to promote long-term investment. Finally, Zhu made enemies of provincial leaders with his heavy tax plan and his decision to discontinue provincial subsidies for various projects. As a result of his measures, however, new retail and distribution channels were opened, and state-owned enterprises that had previously stored tons of aging products in warehouses, and sold them at fixed prices, cut prices to win consumers. With the country's economy more secure, foreign investors were able to move in and compete with domestic businesses, lowering prices. During the East Asian financial crisis in the mid-1990s, Zhu decided not to devalue China's currency, instead helping those countries hardest hit by the crisis, in the belief that the economic stability of the larger region was essential to China's well-being. Meanwhile, China rapidly built up its foreign reserves, which grew from $20 billion in 1993 to nearly $140 billion by the end of 1997. Such funds were vital in defending China from speculators hoping to turn the weakness of the nation's currency to their advantage.

Having weathered both favor and disfavor among the Chinese political elite, with the rate of consumer inflation at barely 3 percent in 1997 and the economy continuing to grow even during the East Asian financial crisis, Zhu was nominated by one of his strongest supporters, President Jiang Zemin, for the office of premier of the People's Republic of China. In March 1998 his nomination was confirmed by the National People's Congress, China's national legislature, with an overwhelming vote of 2,890 in favor to 60 "no" votes or abstentions. As premier, Zhu turned his focus to reforming state enterprises and agricultural policies and running a tight financial ship. His economic plans for China also called for achieving moderate growth of the economy—at a rate of about 8 percent per year—while keeping inflation at 3 percent and ensuring the stability of the national currency. Among Zhu's long-term goals was the privatization and consolidation of large sections of the state-owned sector, which would involve selling off, merging, or phasing out the majority of the nation's approximately 300,000 government-controlled enterprises. Zhu also decided to reform the nation's bloated and often corrupt bureaucracy by cutting the number of government workers by half. As a precursor to that move, he reduced the number of ministries from 40 to 29. Amalgamating several departments, Zhu also cut the State Planning Commission, the center of China's economic planning and his former employer. By the end of 1998, the reforms had sparked rising unemployment, social unrest, and major losses in profitability in the state sector. As retail prices continued to fall, China's state-run businesses were having great difficulty making profits—a situation made worse by the fear of unemployment among many Chinese, which in turn made them nervous about spending. International investment remained lackluster, and there were rumors that Zhu would lose his position. Nevertheless, Zhu stuck by his reforms, believing that in the long term the measures would improve life for a majority of Chinese. Indeed, many government workers who had been laid off soon found work in the private sector or began receiving state support. Zhu continued to work hard at luring Western investment and increasing market competition to force Chinese firms to become more efficient and upgrade their technology. In 1999, in order to continue the 8 percent economic growth,

Zhu called for spending on infrastructure and other areas, which would increase the country's budget deficit by over 50 percent. Reaction to his plan was so negative that there were again rumors that Zhu was on his way out as premier.

Such speculation increased during Zhu's trip to the United States in April of that year. After having agreed to what some Chinese thought of as humiliating concessions so that China could join the World Trade Organization (WTO) and circumvent the trade barriers between itself and several other nations, Zhu made the first official visit of a Chinese leader to Washington, D.C., in 15 years, seeking necessary U.S. approval for its WTO membership. Relations between the two countries had been tense in recent months, following the NATO bombing of the former Yugoslavia, which the Chinese had opposed on the grounds that it constituted interference in a sovereign nation's internal affairs. Many in the West viewed China's position as being based on its wish to avoid foreign interference with its desired retaking of the island of Taiwan, the breakaway republic that formed in 1949, after the Communists took control of the mainland. Zhu was also confronted with anti-Chinese sentiments in the United States over the suspected theft of nuclear secrets by an alleged Chinese spy. Worried that the time was wrong to advocate China's entry into the WTO, U.S. president Bill Clinton refused to do so. That decision came as a major blow to Zhu and his standing in China, and even though he was able to make important business connections in the U.S., Zhu returned to China disgraced by his failure. Responding to what he saw as many Americans' fear of the Chinese, he asked PBS news anchor Jim Lehrer, as quoted on *Online NewHour*, "What are [Americans] afraid of? President Clinton said the United States has about 6,000 nuclear warheads and that China has 20 or 30 of them. . . . So my question would be, what are you afraid of? China cannot possibly constitute a threat. And if you mean should you fear China as an economic competitor, then I should say your economy is 10 times the size of our economy. Your per capita income is 10 times our per capita income, and it would take a very, very long time for China to yet become even relatively a major economic power. And besides, even if China were to become an economic power, why should the United States fear it, because the stronger that China becomes, the bigger the market for the Americans?"

For the next few months, Zhu maintained a low political profile, amid a few reports that he had offered his resignation but had been refused by President Jiang. After making a successful visit to Europe in the fall of 1999, however, Zhu succeeded in reaching an agreement with the U.S. that would result in China's entry into the WTO in November 1999. As its part of the deal, China cut its tariffs to levels below those of most of America's other trade partners and agreed to end export subsidies; give American exporters the right to distribute goods in China; and open up Chinese markets to American farms, banks, and insurance, telecommunications, and Internet companies. Although some saw the agreement as far from beneficial to China, Zhu insisted that any short-term problems would be outweighed by the long-term benefits. Further, he felt that with international law now on the side of China because of its membership in the WTO, the opportunities for increased business competition within his country, which would lead to a stronger economy, seemed bright.

In March 2000 Zhu opened the session of the national legislature by promising tougher penalties for corrupt government officials. Zhu had been pushing anticorruption measures for years, helped by the fact that he was not associated with any particular political faction in the government. "Honesty in the performance of official duties is the minimum requirement for people at all levels," Zhu was quoted as saying by the *Times of India* (March 6, 2000, on-line). "We still fall far short of what the central authorities require of us and what the people expect of us." The speech came at a time when the country faced a host of corruption scandals, which resulted in the trials of about 200 officials and the execution of 11 others, all of whom were implicated in a multibillion-dollar smuggling scheme. In his speech to the legislature, Zhu also promised a third year of deficit spending to help stimulate growth. He supported a buildup of the military and stated that more money should be channeled to poor Chinese and to less-developed western China. In October he visited China's estranged neighbor, Japan, in the hope of establishing greater trust and closer cooperation between the two nations. Although the visit was seen as a success, Zhu faced negative public opinion at home for not forcing the Japanese government to apologize for atrocities committed against China during World War II. Meanwhile, official figures published in China showed that the remaining state-owned enterprises had reduced their losses the previous year, suggesting that they might break even during the next. U.S.-China relations continued to be tense, however, as the United States began to explore an antimissile shield. Realizing that such a shield might protect Taiwan, Zhu adamantly opposed the project as unjust U.S. interference in the region.

In 2001, in his annual address to the National People's Congress, Zhu predicted that China's economy would strengthen significantly over the next 10 years. He set a target growth rate of roughly 7 percent per year and noted that reform of the ailing state-run industries was essential to achieving this goal. At a summit of the Association of Southeast Asian Nations, held in Singapore, Zhu remarked that it was time to begin considering the establishment of a free-trade zone in East Asia, encompassing the majority of the Pacific Rim nations. Currently, Zhu faces a host of problems, including the short-term negative consequences of joining the World Trade Organization (such as the depressing effect on domestic markets of the arriv-

al of foreign-made products), growing unemployment, water and gasoline shortages, and a surplus of substandard agricultural products. Although relations between the U.S. and China were further strained by the Chinese capture of a U.S. spy plane and its crew in the spring of 2001, following a mid-air collision with a Chinese fighter plane and the presumed death of the Chinese pilot, Zhu remained publicly silent on the subject.

Zhu grappled with a widespread public outcry in March 2001, after a schoolhouse explosion in Jiangxi Province killed 38 children between the ages of nine and 11 and four adults. Parents of the victims attributed the disaster to the youngsters' assemblage of fireworks in a forced "work-study" program—an activity that, although illegal, is apparently common in rural China, as sale of the fireworks is a way of generating income for local schools. Zhu, however, maintained that the incident was caused by a deranged suicide bomber. Nine days later, after the tragedy had become major international news and anger among the Chinese populace had increased, Zhu—in a move highly unusual for a Chinese leader—apologized publicly. As reported by Craig S. Smith for the *New York Times* (March 16, 2001), he said that the State Council (a body analogous to the U.S. president's Cabinet), which he heads, bore "unshirkable responsibility" for what had happened. He also said that he had ordered a full-scale investigation. The explosion called attention to the financial crisis that had left many rural villages without money to operate schools and clinics. Soon afterward Zhu announced that China would cut local government staffs, end special tax levies imposed by rural officials, and allocate up to $3.6 billion a year in subsidies to local governments, both to compensate for the losses incurred and to pay for school-related expenses. He reassured the nation that if such an incident happened again, everyone from the town chief to the provincial governor would face punishment.

Zhu Rongji is known for being a strict, short-tempered administrator who is a stickler for integrity and efficiency. According to one story, when a department head had to turn to one of his underlings for information to supply to Zhu at a meeting, the premier promptly ordered the two men to switch jobs. Despite his seriousness, Zhu is said to have a sense of humor, and he is a fan of Peking Opera. He has a strong command of English and is known for his eloquent speeches. Zhu is married to Lo An, a former vice chair of the board of directors of China International Engineering and Consulting Corp. The couple have a son and a daughter. While admitting that China has a tarnished human-rights record, he has criticized the U.S. for not working sufficiently to solve its own troubles with regard to race and poverty. Answering a human-rights-related question after a speech at the Massachusetts Institute of Technology (MIT), he stated, as quoted on the MIT Web site, "Human rights in China have been improving from one day to the next, and I think it's fair to say that the degree of human rights being enjoyed by the Chinese people is unprecedented in China's history. We acknowledge that we still have shortcomings, and these shortcomings are ones which we are still working hard to address." Zhu is scheduled to retire from his post in 2002. — G.O.

Suggested Reading: *Contemporary Review* p291+ June 1998; *Financial Times* Nov. 18, 1993, p 15 Apr. 26, 1994, with photo, p19 Nov. 13, 1995, with photo; *Institutional Investor* p91+ Apr. 1998; *New Statesman* p30+ Mar. 13, 1998; *New York Times* A p3 July 23, 1993; *Time* p38+ Mar. 16, 1998, p61+ Apr. 12, 1999; *Washington Post* A p1 Aug. 21, 1997

OBITUARIES

Written by Kieran Dugan

ADAMS, DOUGLAS Mar. 11, 1952–May 11, 2001 British author; comic novelist; scriptwriter; with fecund wit, whimsical imagination, and a stream-of-consciousness style, borrowed from the devices of science fiction to lampoon contemporary culture, most famously in the picaresque adventures of the space travelers in his best-selling novel *The Hitchhiker's Guide to the Galaxy* and its four sequels (1980–92), which had originated as a 12-part BBC radio series in 1978 and was later reincarnated as a BBC television program, a record album, and stage productions; created the psychic private investigator Dirk Gently, the protagonist of his comic mystery novels *Dirk Gently's Holistic Detective Agency* (1987) and *The Long Dark Tea-Time of the Soul* (1988); co-wrote two mock dictionaries of British place names, *The Meaning of Liff* (1983) and *The Deeper Meaning of Liff* (1990); on the more serious side, with the zoologist Mark Cowardine, engaged in a year-long (1988–89) international search for endangered animal species, an expedition that resulted in a BBC radio series and the book *Last Chance to See* (1990); became a popular lecturer and commentator on science and technology issues; founded a multimedia company, the Digital Village; wrote an array of sophisticated computer games, including an interactive novel based on the *Hitchhiker* books; in 1983, worked in Hollywood on an abortive project aimed at a screen version of the *Hitchhiker* story; settled in California with his wife and young daughter in 1999; died in Santa Barbara, California. See *Current Biography* (July) 1993.

Obituary *New York Times* A p23 May 15, 2001

ADLER, LARRY Feb. 10, 1914–Aug. 7, 2001 Musician; raised the harmonica (which he insisted on calling the "mouth organ") to the level of a virtuoso's instrument, played by him in philharmonic, jazz, modern-music, and stage-musical contexts as well as solo concert performances; included in his repertoire music ranging from Gershwin to Bach, Mozart, and the classical romantics; in childhood, taught himself to play the piano as well as the harmonica by ear and from memory; after finally learning to read music, at age 27, had many works composed for him by the likes of Ralph Vaughan Williams and Darius Milhaud; in 1928, ran away from home (in Baltimore) to seek his fortune in New York City, where Rudy Vallee hired him for his Heigh-Ho Club and got him a job playing the harmonica for animated-movie cartoons; subsequently, performed as an harmonica-playing urchin in two Broadway revues and with a vaudeville unit; during the 1930s, was cast in five motion pictures, including *The Big Broadcast of 1937* (1936); made his adult stage debut in a booking at the Palace Theater in Manhattan in 1934, which led to a succession of lucrative engagements in London, including a revue built around him, *Tune Inn* (1937), and tours of South Africa and Australia; dur-

ing World War II, devoted himself chiefly to performing in USO tours of American military bases around the world in partnership with the dancer Paul Draper; after being blacklisted as an alleged Communist sympathizer by the Un-American Activities Committee of the U.S. House of Representatives in the late 1940s, established permanent residence in London; performed there regularly; made many recordings of classical and popular music; in addition to concert pieces, composed scores for television, children's records, and many motion pictures, including *Genevieve* (1953); wrote several books, among them *How I Play* (1937) and his autobiography, *It Ain't Necessarily So* (1985); died in London. See *Current Biography* (February) 1944.

Obituary *New York Times* A p15 Aug. 8, 2001

ADLER, MORTIMER J. Dec. 28, 1902–June 28, 2001 Philosopher; education reformer; author; editor; against the tide of relativism and multiculturalism in American education and intellectual life, helped to lead a return to the classic texts of Western literature; in particular, championed the Aristotelian-Thomist view that there are universal, absolute, unchanging truths and values; for the masses, created the Great Books program; at 15, dropped out of public high school in New York City after a dispute with the principal led to his suspension from the school newspaper; became secretary to the editor of the *New York Sun* newspaper; at 17, upon reading Plato's *Dialogues*, decided to become a philosopher instead of a journalist; as a scholarship student at Columbia College, Columbia University, became a protégé of John Erskine, a pioneering promoter of classics-based education; would become the nemesis of another of his teachers, the pragmatist John Dewey, who introduced a shifting, situational value system into American education; finished first in his class at Columbia but refused to fulfill physical-education requirements mandatory for a B.A. degree; became an instructor in psychology at Columbia in 1923; five years later, upon acceptance of a dissertation titled "An Experimental Approach to the Measurement of Music Appreciation," was awarded a Ph.D. degree by the university; at the invitation of Robert Maynard Hutchins, president of the University of Chicago, joined the faculty of that university as an associate professor of the philosophy of law in 1930; became full professor in 1942; helped Hutchins to revise the Chicago curriculum to stress broad training in the humanities, grounded in an undergraduate seminar in the classics; participated in the creation of a similar curriculum at St. John's University in Annapolis, Maryland, where he had become a visiting lecturer in 1937; in 1946, launched for the general public the Great Books program, a classics-based plan in accordance with which hundreds of reading-and-discussion groups for people from all walks of life were organized in numerous cities; arranged for the publication by the Encyclopaedia Britannica Inc. of *Great Books of the Western World*, comprising 443 books by 74 authors (from Homer through John Locke and John Stuart Mill to Marx and Freud) in a 54-volume set, completed in 1952; directed a staff of 90 in compiling *The Syntopicon* ("a synthesis of topics"), a two-volume index to, or concordance of, 102 main ideas (such as "induction" and "God") in the collection; in 1952, left the University of Chicago to found, in San Francisco, the Institute for Philosophical Research, a think tank devoted to discussion and analysis of the great ideas and the generation of such works as the two-volume *The Idea of Freedom* (1958, 1961); moved the institute to Chicago in 1963; at the institute in 1984, created the Paedelia Project, aimed at providing public-school pupils with a traditional humanist education; from 1988 to 1991 was a professor at the University of North Carolina at Chapel Hill; with Max Weismann, founded the Center for the Study of Great Ideas in Chicago in 1990; as chairman of the board of editors of Encyclopaedia Britannica Inc., was instrumental in forging a radical, tripartite revision of the encyclopedia, introduced in 1974 in the form of an introductory volume (the propaedia), a 10-volume ready-reference dictionary (the micropedia), and a 19-volume in-depth encyclopedia (the macropedia); published his best-known work, the best-seller *How to Read a Book; the Art of Getting a Liberal Education*, in 1940; among dozens of other books, wrote *Art and Prudence* (1937), *How to Think About War and Peace* (1944), *Aristotle for Everybody* (1978), *How to Think About God: A Guide for the 20th Century Pagan* (1980), and two volumes of memoirs, *An Intellectual Autobiography* (1977) and *A Second Look in the Rearview Mirror* (1992); died at his home in San Mateo, California. See *Current Biography* (September) 1952.

Obituary *New York Times* B p8 June 29, 2001

AILES, STEPHEN Mar. 25, 1912–June 30, 2001 Lawyer; government official; began practicing law in West Virginia in 1937; taught law at the University of West Virginia from 1937 to 1940; during World War II, worked on the legal staff of the Office of Price Administration; in 1946, joined the Washington, D.C., law firm of Steptoe & Johnson, where he worked primarily as an antitrust litigator; remained with the firm for 39 years, marked by leaves of absence for public service; served as counsel to the U.S. Economic Mission to Greece in 1947 and legal consultant to the director of the Office of Price Stabilization in 1951; assisted Defense Secretary Robert McNamara in reorganizing and increasing the efficiency of the U.S. military establishment in the early years of the U.S.–Vietnam conflict, first as undersecretary of the army (1961–64) and finally as secretary of the army (1964–65); on another leave of absence from Steptoe & Johnson, served as president of the Association of American Railroads from 1971 to 1977; during the administration of President Gerald R. Ford, was a member of the chief executive's Foreign Intelligence Advisory Board; contributed to the writing of the charter of the Corporation for Public Broadcasting; died at his home in Bethesda, Maryland. See *Current Biography* (January) 1965.

Obituary *New York Times* A p11 July 7, 2001

ALLEN, STEVE Dec. 26, 1921–Oct. 30, 2000 Comedian; actor; self-taught pianist; singer; composer; prolific author; a multitalented television entertainer known for his natural amiability and a bent for spontaneous low-brow comedy (accompanied by his own chuckles, giggles, and belly laughs) that was as irrepressible as his liberal social conscience; in the course of a busy television career, hosted (live, not on tape) the prototype of the *Tonight Show*, the weekday late-night talk/variety program, television's most profitable long-term series; was the son of two vaudeville comedians; began his career on radio in the early 1940s, in Phoenix, Arizona, and Los Angeles, successively; as a disc jockey at a CBS Hollywood affiliate on Saturday nights in the late 1940s, introduced the musical improvisations at the piano and the spontaneous comic chatter, often in rapport with random audience members as well as celebrity guests, that he would carry over to television; in 1950, broadcast on a CBS national radio hookup; later that year, moved to Manhattan to inaugurate *The Steve Allen Show*, a half-hour television version of the radio program, which ran on the CBS television network until 1952; a year later, took his show to NBC's New York flagship station, where it was revamped into the *Tonight* format under the supervision of NBC executive Sylvester "Pat" Weaver; in that format (a relaxed experimental variety/talk laboratory open to outlandish comic stunts), found foils for his inspired ad-libbing not only in cast and audience members but even in passersby on the street outside the studio; hosted the show (then called *Tonight!*) on the NBC network from 1954 to 1957; on NBC from 1956 to 1960, under the revived title *The Steve Allen Show*, hosted a prime-time comedy/variety program that was initially NBC's challenge to CBS's *The Ed Sullivan Show* on Sunday nights; for that program, recruited a company of previously unknown or little-known improvisational comedians; gave exposure to jazzmen and many other underappreciated musicians; during the 1960s, taped weekly 90-minute shows for syndication; later hosted *The Steve Allen Comedy Hour*, first on CBS and then on NBC; as panelist or moderator, participated in such shows as the quiz/audience participation program *I've Got a Secret*, which he moderated from 1964 to 1967; created and hosted *Meeting of the Minds*, a series of imagined philosophical debates between historical figures (played by actors, including his second wife, Jayne Meadows) presented on PBS from 1977 to 1981; had a number of motion-picture credits, including the title role in *The Benny Goodman Story* (1955); wrote the lyrics for the title ballads of several films, including *Picnic*; on Broadway, had a leading role in *The Pink Elephant* (1953) and wrote the music and lyrics for the musical *Sophie* (1963); wrote the book, music, and lyrics for the musical-comedy revue *Seymour Glick Is Alive But Sick* (1982); composed at the piano, facilely, producing thousands of songs, including "This Could Be the Start of Something Big," "An Old Piano Plays the Blues," "Let's Go to Church Next Sunday," "Impossible," and "Gravy Waltz"; recorded the two-volume *Steve Allen's All-Star Jazz Concert* and such other albums as *Allen Plays Allen* and *Steve Sings*; delineated his political position in debate format in *Dialogues in Americanism* (1964); presented a selection of his humor, with autobiographical commentary, in the book *Bigger Than a Breadbox* (1967); expressed his concern about the state of the nation and the world in such books as *The Ground Is Our Table* (1966), about migrant farm workers, *Ripoff: A Report on Moral Collapse and Corruption in America* (1979), about white-collar crime and malfeasance, from petty to corporate, *"Explaining China"* (1980), a sympathetic book about the Communist nation, and *Vulgarians at the Gate*, about the rising tide of "filth, vulgarity, sex and violence" on television, which he was completing at the time of his death; wrote (by dictation into a pocket tape recorder) more than 50 books, including two loosely autobiographical novels, a collection of short stories, and surveys of humor; campaigned for nuclear disarmament, world peace, and a halt to capital punishment; died in Los Angeles. See *Current Biography* (March) 1982.

Obituary *New York Times* B p13 Nov. 1, 2000

AMADO, JORGE Aug. 10, 1912–Aug. 6, 2001 Brazilian writer; his country's all-time best-selling author; with particular empathy for the underprivileged, wrote socially conscious and insightful novels about the people of his native Bahia, Brazil's most colorful, racially and culturally mixed state; had a flair for the ribald and the humorous that became more evident the more he progressed beyond the Marxist class-struggle didacticism that freighted his early work; began to become aware of social inequality and injustice while growing up on his family's cacao plantation in Bahia; revealed his incipient commitment to a socialistic ideal in his first book, the autobiographically based coming-of-age novel *O país do carnaval* (The Land of Carnival, 1932); while working for a doctorate in law during the 1930s, secretly joined the Communist Party and began engaging in agitprop, which was reflected in his early series of proletarian novels: *Cacáu* (1933), which dealt with the exploitation of plantation workers by the cocoa "colonels" of southern Bahia, *Suar* (Sweat, 1934), in which he sketched the lives of deprived black tenement dwellers in Salvador, the capital of Bahia, *Jubiabá* (1935), about the venerable leader of an African religious cult in Salvador and a street urchin who becomes a labor leader, *Mar morto* (Dead Sea, 1936), about sailors of small boats in the port of Salvador, and *Capitães sa areia* (The Beach Waifs, 1937), his angriest work, a virtual jeremiad about the plight of homeless young men and boys in Salvador's slums and on its beaches; was forced by right-wing dictatorships to spend most of the period from 1938 to 1942 in exile, in Mexico, the U.S., Uruguay, and Argentina; in 1943 published what many critics have regarded as his masterpiece, the novel later translated from the Portuguese as *The Violent Land* (1945), a panoramic cocoa-plantation epic; was elected to Brazil's National Constituent Assembly on an overtly Communist ticket in 1946; was again forced into exile from 1948 to 1952, when he lived chiefly in France and Communist Eastern Europe, where he was lionized; received the Stalin Peace Prize in 1951; subsequently, seemed to distance himself from communism, calling himself a "utopian socialist"; returned to the writing of fiction with a new set of beliefs and interests; explored the "good and

bad in everyone," rich or poor, the subversive uses of laughter against oppression, and the importance of dreams in surviving adversity; gave expression to his new perspective in the 1956 picaresque novel later translated as *Gabriella, Clove and Cinnamon*, about an Arab immigrant's love for his "cinnamon-colored" housekeeper, as well as in the 1969 comic novel about a sensual woman translated as *Dona Flor and Her Two Husbands* (1969) and in two comic novels about prostitutes published in the 1970s and translated as *Tereza Batista Home from the Wars* and *Tieta the Goat Girl*; achieved his greatest international popularity with *Gabriella* and *Dona Flor*, both of which were made into motion pictures as well as soap operas that enjoyed a mass *succès de fou* in Brazil and Portugal; wrote a total of 32 novels (translated into a total of four dozen languages), including those translated as *Tent of Miracles* (1971), about a mulatto practitioner of the Afro-Bahaian faith, and *War of the Saints* (1993), another comic novel with an unconventional female protagonist; died in Salvador. See *Current Biography* (March) 1986.

Obituary *New York Times* B p7 Aug. 7, 2001

AMICHAI, YEHUDA May 3, 1924–Sep. 22, 2000 German-born Israeli poet; a benign blasphemer who sought in his poetry, as in making love, a substitute for the religious orthodoxy he rejected, an antidote to war and history (which he connected), and an imagined permanence and tranquility amidst the flux and conflicts of human life; did so in a personal, sometimes confessional, mode; wrote in modern Hebrew, subsequently translated into English by many hands, including his own (in collaboration with Ted Hughes); created poetry rich in metaphor, wordplay, allusion, and ironic wit, as exemplified in such poems as "Jerusalem Is Full of Used Jews," "The Hand of God in the World" ("like the hand of my mother in the entrails of the slaughtered chicken"), "From Man Thou Art, and Unto Man Shalt Thou Return," "Gods Come and Go, Prayers Remain Forever," and the title poem in the collection *Even a Fist Was Once an Open Palm with Fingers* (1989); with his parents, who were Orthodox Jews and supporters of Zionism, moved from Nazi Germany to Palestine in 1936; served with a Jewish brigade in the British army in World War II; subsequently, was a commando in the Haganah, an underground military organization; in 1948, fought in the first Arab-Israeli war, which led to the formal establishment of the state of Israel; after the war, attended the Hebrew University in Jerusalem, taught school, and began to submit his poems to magazines; explained that, as a participant in two wars, he needed the words of his poetry "to achieve peace with myself"; later fought in the Arab-Israeli wars of 1956 and 1973; in 1955, published the first of his numerous volumes of poetry, *Akhshav u-veyamin Aherim*, which included the well-known poem later translated as "God Has Pity on Kindergarten Children," seemingly suggesting that God is real only to the immature; began to receive international attention in 1968, when his 1963 novel, *Lo me-Akhshav, lo-mi-Kan*, regarded by some as the first important novel by an Israeli dealing with the Holocaust, was published in English under the title *Not of This Time*; realized the first book-length translation of his poetry, *Poems*, in 1969; in 1971, published a second novel, *Mi yitneni malon* ("O That I Had a Lodging"), about an Israeli poet living in New York; published a collection of his short fiction, *The World Is a Room and Other Stories*, in 1984; wrote several plays and books for children; published a succession of definitive collections of his verse, including *Yehuda Amichai: A Life of Poetry 1948–1994* (1995); not long before his death, published a book of new poems, including one in which he said, "God is change and Death is his prophet"; died in Jerusalem. See *Current Biography* (February) 1998.

Obituary *New York Times* A p14 Sep. 23, 2000

AMMONS, A. R. Feb. 18, 1926–Feb. 25, 2001 Poet; professor emeritus, Cornell University; a nature poet in the transcendental tradition; in poems inspired by such natural surroundings as the North Carolina back country and New Jersey's tidal marshes and southern seashore, sought to link "the cell to the cosmos," to rise above sensory bonds and embrace what Ralph Waldo Emerson called "the World-Soul" or "the Real"; could be moved to poetic meditation by anything that came within his ken, including McDonald's fast-food restaurants and a waste dump alongside Interstate 95 in Florida; constructed a poetry of intellectual depth and complexity with simple, clear language and a conversational style; was favorably compared to Robert Frost and William Carlos Williams; more than any other poet of his time, succeeded in connecting "the intricacies of science to the mystery of human nature" and what he perceived to be "the high design of God," as A. T. Baker observed; was born in a farmhouse in North Carolina; originally aspired to be a physician; started writing poetry while serving aboard a U.S. Navy destroyer escort during World War II; in his development as a poet, was influenced by the lyrical prose of the Old Testament, Emerson's philosophy, Robert Browning's poetic monologues, Walt Whitman's unconventional free verse, and the poetry of Samuel Taylor Coleridge and Emily Dickinson; under the G.I. Bill, majored in biology as an undergraduate at Wake Forest College; later studied English for three semesters at the University of California, Berkeley; early in his career, was a shipyard worker, an executive with a glassware-manufacturing company, an elementary-school principal, and a real-estate salesman; began contributing poems to the *Hudson Review* in 1953; two years later published his first book, *Ommateum, with Doxology*, at his own expense; won National Book Awards for *Collected Poems 1951–1971* (1973) and *Garbage* (1993), the Bollingen Prize for *Sphere: The Form of a Motion* (1974), and a National Book Critics Award for *A Coast of Trees* (1981); in all, published well over a score of books of poetry, including *Expressions of Sea Level* (1964), *Carson's Inlet* (1965), *Selected Longer Poems* (1990), and *Glare* (1997), his last; began teaching creative writing at Cornell University in 1964; was named Goldwin professor of poetry at Cornell in 1973; retired in 1998; died at his home in Ithaca, New York. See *Current Biography* (February) 1982.

Obituary *New York Times* B p7 Feb. 27, 2001

ANDERSON, CONSTANCE May 19, 1898–Jan. 31, 2001 President of the national board of the Young Women's Christian Associations of the USA (1946–52); a longtime volunteer with and board member of the New York City YWCA; helped to found the United Service Organizations; served on the board of the U.S. Committee for UNICEF and the board of deacons of Manhattan's Riverside Church; died in Kennett Square, Pennsylvania. See *Current Biography* (May) 1948.

Obituary *New York Times* B p7 Feb. 3, 2001

ARMSTRONG, J. SINCLAIR Oct. 15, 1913–Nov. 5, 2000 Lawyer; banker; former U.S. government official; began practicing law with the Chicago firm of Isham, Lincoln & Beale in 1941; as a partner in the firm, beginning in 1950, specialized in corporation law and finance, including municipal finance; joined the Securities and Exchange Commission in 1953; was chairman of the commission from 1955 to 1957; as assistant secretary of the U.S. Navy for financial management (1957–59), tried to tighten cost controls while the navy was in transition, acquiring missiles, rockets, and nuclear power; upon leaving government, joined the United States Trust Co. of New York as executive vice president; subsequently became a partner in (and, still later, counsel to) the law firm of Whitnam, Breed, Abbott & Morgan, where he was concerned with historic preservation law (his passionate cause) in addition to securities and banking law; during the 1980s was a leader in the effort to block the plan of the rector and church-wardens of Manhattan's St. Bartholomew's Episcopal Church (where he had been baptized in 1916) to build a 59-story skyscraper on parish property, next to the church; in court, successfully argued that the church was a landmark building and the property was therefore subject to New York City landmark preservation laws; died in Manhattan. See *Current Biography* (March) 1958.

Obituary *New York Times* D p8 Nov. 9, 2000

ATKINS, CHET June 20, 1924–June 30, 2001 Guitarist; record producer; songwriter; arranger; was, in his own words, a creator (along with the Decca Records producer Owen Bradley) of the smooth "countrypolitan" Nashville sound, which "took the twang out" of country music and enabled it to cross over into the pop market; as a guitarist, had a distinctive style, marked by thumb-and-three-finger (rather than standard-pick) plucking and simultaneous playing of melody and rhythm; was born into a musically inclined family on his grandfather's mountain dirt farm in southeastern Tennessee; before mastering the guitar, played the fiddle at pass-the-hat hoedowns, with his brother Tommy on guitar; as a teenager, lived with his father and stepmother in Georgia; listening to southern country music on a crystal radio set, was heavily influenced by the guitarist Merle Travis's finger-picking style; after leaving high school, in 1941, performed with a series of groups, including staff bands at a succession of country-music radio stations, before joining the Carter Sisters and Mother Maybelle on radio in Knoxville, Tennessee, and on tour; with the Carter Sisters, in 1950 became a regular featured performer on the weekly radio show Grand Ole Opry, a country-music show-case broadcast nationally from Nashville; mean-while, had recorded his first hit single, "Galloping Guitars," in 1947; in 1951, recorded two albums on the RCA Victor label, *Chet Atkins Plays Guitar* and *Chet Atkins in Three Dimensions*; cut the signature single "Country Gentleman" in 1953 and the hit "Mr. Sandman" in 1955; later recorded "Yakety Axe," his first Top Five hit; at RCA, worked as a session side-man with the likes of Porter Wagoner, Faron Young, Kitty Wells, Webb Pierce, Hank Williams, Elvis Pres-ley, and the Everly Brothers; in 1957, left the Carter Sisters and the Grand Ole Opry to manage RCA re-cording operations in Nashville; persuaded RCA to set up its own Studio B on Nashville's Music Row; began his career as a talent scout and producer there auspiciously, with the signing of Don Gibson, who scored a smash hit with "Oh, Lonesome Me" (1958); subsequently, launched or escalated the recording careers of Roger Miller, Charley Pride, Waylon Jen-nings, Willie Nelson, Jessi Colter, Charlie Rich, Roy Orbison, Floyd Cramer, and many others; realized some of his biggest successes as a producer with the recordings of Jim Reeves, one of the artists whom he often accompanied; also produced recordings by Eddy Arnold, Dottie West, the Browns, Homer & Jethro, and Hank Snow, among others; in 1966, recorded the album *Chet Atkins Picks on the Beatles*; in 1968, was promoted by RCA to the position of di-vision vice president in charge of country music; in 1970 and 1971, produced two crossover hits by Jerry Reid; in 1976 signed his last RCA protégé, the consis-tent hit maker Steve Wariner; six years later, left RCA to record on the Columbia label, where he was allowed to experiment more freely with elements of jazz, rock, gospel, and classical music; returned to the charts with his 1985 album *Stay Tuned*; recorded a total of approximately 100 albums, including duets with Jerry Reed, Merle Travis, Les Paul, Suzy Bog-guss, Mark Knopfler, Steve Wariner, and others; recorded the solo album *Almost Alone* in 1996; won 14 Grammy Awards; wrote the autobiography *Coun-try Gentleman* (1974); died at his home in Nashville. See *Current Biography* (January) 1975.

Obituary *New York Times* B p8 July 2, 2001

BALTHUS Feb. 29, 1908–Feb. 18, 2001 Artist; a French painter who was paternally of Polish de-scent; a School of Paris realist who never capitulated to the hegemony of passing abstractionist fads; exe-cuted approximately 300 figurative canvases (some representing years of perfectionist revision), includ-ing dreamlike Parisian cityscapes, landscapes in the tradition of Courbet, still lifes and interiors reminis-cent of Cézanne and Matisse, portraits of André De-rain and Joan Miró, among others, and, most notably, such controversial studies of nymphets in erotically suggestive poses as *Alice*, *Toilette de Cathy*, and *La Jeune Fille au Chat* (in which there is a tantalizing glimpse of the reclining maiden's virginal, plain white panties); in some paintings, incorporated styl-ized hints of the sinister and perverse, reflecting sur-realist influences, especially that of his friend An-tonin Artaud, the promoter of a "theater of cruelty"; invited publicity by the very intensity with which he guarded his privacy; was born Balthazar Klossowski,

the second son of artistic and scholarly parents who gave him entrée to a childhood of upper-class vaga-bondage throughout Western Europe and introduced him to such friends of theirs as the painter Pierre Bonnard and the poet Rainer Maria Rilke, who be-came his mentor; in his early reading, was perhaps most influenced by Lewis Carroll's *Alice* books as il-lustrated by John Tenniel and the sometimes grue-some German children's books of Heinrich Hoff-mann; hinted at the obsessive themes of his adult oeuvre in the 40 ink drawings published (with text by Rilke) as *Mitsou* (1921), named after his lost cat; beginning at age 16, taught himself painting by copy-ing old masters, especially Piero della Francesca; at that time, found a patron in André Gide; in his first one-man show, in Paris in 1934, impressed Albert Camus (among others) with *La Rue*, a dreamlike street scene in which the people appear "petrified by some kind of enchantment"; in the same show, creat-ed a *succès de scandale* with *The Guitar Lesson*, the only one of his paintings that he avowed to be delib-erately shocking in its barely disguised pornogra-phy; later in the same decade, did a series of draw-ings inspired by Emily Brontë's *Wuthering Heights* and painted *Les Enfants* (which was bought by Pablo Picasso) and *The Mountain*, the best known of his landscapes, a Swiss alpine scene with three day-dreaming young people in the foreground; in the 1940s executed such paintings as *The Living Room*, *Gotteron Landscape*, and *Golden Days*, in which a sensuous adolescent female provocatively languish-es on a chaise longue; in *The Room* (1952–54), de-picted a pubescent girl sprawled suggestively on a chair, flooded with light from a window whose cur-tains are being drawn by a wicked-looking dwarf; be-tween 1954 and 1961 produced 61 paintings, includ-ing *Collette in Profile*, *Girl in White*, and *Bouquet of Roses on a Window Sill*; was influenced by Heinrich Hoffmann's *Struwelpeter* fantasies in painting *L'Enfant aux Pigeons* (1960); subsequently painted *The Turkish Room*, *Nude in Front of the Mantle*, and *The Dream*; until the 1960s, painted with oil or wa-tercolor; while serving as director of the Académie de France in Rome, from 1961 to 1977, worked for the first time with casein tempera; during a sojourn in Japan in 1962, steeped himself in that country's language and culture; met a young woman named Setsuko Ideta, who became his favorite model and, in 1967, his second wife; worked for six years (1968–73) on *The Card Game*, a painting of two opposing players, a male and a female, uncanny in its commu-nication of seething hatred and threat of violence; af-ter leaving Rome, retired, with Setsuko and their daughter, to a chalet in La Rossinière, near Gstaad, Switzerland; died in the chalet. See *Current Biogra-phy* (November) 1979.

Obituary *New York Times* B p8 Feb. 19, 2001

BANDARANAIKE, SIRIMAVO Apr. 17, 1916–Oct. 10, 2000 Former prime minister of Sri Lanka (former-ly Ceylon, which achieved dominion status in the British Commonwealth of Nations in 1948); as such, was the world's first female principal minister and head of government in a nation with a parliamentary system; was born into Ceylon's Ratwatte family, a dynasty of Buddhist Sinhalese aristocrats, when the country was still a British crown colony; in 1940, married Solomon W. R. D. Bandaranaike, a nationalist politician who founded the Sri Lanka Freedom party, in 1951, and, three years later, became prime minister, pledged to a Socialist program and an independent foreign policy; following the assassination of her husband, in 1959, served her first two terms as prime minister (1960–65, 1970–77); began to implement her agenda for nationalization early in her first term, by exerting state control over newspapers and private schools; in 1961, replaced English with Sinhalese as the official national language; by that act, slighted the country's predominantly Hindu Tamil minority; by subsequent acts (including changes in university admissions policy detrimental to the Tamils), further inflamed the ethnic tensions that would erupt into the violent rebellion of Tamil separatists in the early 1980s; directed the framing of the new constitution under which Ceylon became the Republic of Sri Lanka in 1972; in the early 1970s, was challenged by a national economic crisis, accompanied by terrorism by ultra-leftists (thousands of whom were executed); in the following years, instituted massive land reform and nationalized many local economic enterprises and foreign-owned plantations; was again prime minister, this time in a largely ceremonial mode, under the presidency of her daughter Chandrika Kumaratunga, who, after taking office in 1994, moved away from state socialism, toward a market-oriented economy, and sought reconciliation (not successfully) with the Tamil rebels; retained her seat in Parliament after resigning as prime minister in mid- 2000; died in Colombo, Sri Lanka. See *Current Biography* (May) 1961.

Obituary *New York Times* A p33 Oct. 11, 2000

BARNARD, CHRISTIAAN N. Nov. 8, 1922–Sep. 2, 2001 South African surgeon; author; the foremost pioneer in heart transplantation, now a fairly standard, albeit not routine, medical operation; also contributed to the advancement of techniques in operating on children with abnormal hearts; was an Afrikaner who often transgressed the racial barriers in place in apartheid-era South Africa; was assisted by so-called colored nurses in treating and operating on white as well as nonwhite patients; in one operation, replaced the failing heart of a black man with the healthy heart of a white woman; as a research fellow at the University of Cape Town Medical School (his alma mater) in the early 1950s, studied gastrointestinal birth defects; trained in heart surgery in the U.S. (1955–61), chiefly at the University of Minnesota; became director of cardiothoracic surgery at the University of Cape Town Medical School in 1961; for many years, did experimental heart transplants on animals; performed the first successful human heart transplant in medical history at Groote Schuur Hospital, in Cape Town, on December 3, 1967, when he implanted the heart of Denise Darvall, a brain-dead automobile-accident victim, in the chest of Louis Washkansky, who died of pneumonia 18 days later; performed a second such operation on January 2, 1968, when he placed the heart of Clive Haupt, a mixed-race stroke victim, in the chest of the white dentist Philip Blaiberg, who survived 19 and a half months; with the development of anti-rejection

drugs, saw longer survival rates in subsequent transplant patients; in 1973, performed a transplant operation on Dick van Zyt, who went on to live for 23 more years; continued to perform surgery until the mid-1980s, when rheumatoid arthritis forced him to retire; after retiring, raised sheep in his native Cape Province, South Africa; established a game preserve; became a jet-set celebrity; was married thrice, the third time to Karen Setzkom, a model 41 years his junior; while continuing to travel the world, established his permanent residence in Vienna, Austria; wrote a number of books in the fields of medicine and health, including *Hartaanval Alle Hoop Op Lewe* (*Heart Attack: You Don't Have to Die*, 1971), *Good Life, Good Death: A Doctor's Case for Euthanasia and Suicide* (1980), and, with Peter Evans, *Christiaan Barnard's Program for Living with Arthritis* (1984); also wrote several novels and co-wrote the autobiography *Christiaan Barnard: One Life* (1969); through the Christiaan Barnard Foundation, provided financial support for pediatric medicine in developing countries; died (apparently of a heart attack precipitated by an asthma attack) while vacationing in Papros, Cyprus. See *Current Biography* (May) 1968.

Obituary *New York Times* p1+ Sep. 3, 2001

BARNOUW, ERIK June 23, 1908–July 19, 2001 Dutch-born dean of American media historians; veteran radio and television writer and producer; documentarian; professor emeritus of dramatic arts at Columbia University, where he founded and was first chairman of the film, radio, and television department; author of the authoritative trilogy *The History of Broadcasting in the United States* (1966–70) and *Media Marathon: A Twentieth-Century Memoir* (1996); also wrote, among other books, *Handbook of Radio Writing* (1939), *Documentary: A History of the Non-Fiction Film* (1974), *The Magic and the Cinema* (1981), a study of early motion pictures; in collaboration with S. Krishnaswamy, wrote *Indian Film* (1963); as an undergraduate at Princeton University, wrote the play *Open Collars*, a comedy, and lyrics for musicals; after graduating from Princeton, in 1929, briefly pursued a career in acting and spent nine years writing and directing radio commercials and programs for General Foods, Camel cigarettes, and *True Story* and *Liberty* magazines, among other sponsors; for a year (1936–37), wrote the NBC serial *The Honeymooners*; joined the Columbia University faculty in 1937; subsequently was a writer and editor for the CBS and NBC radio networks; in 1944, won a Peabody Award for the radio series *Words at War*; in 1970, produced the television documentary *Hiroshima-Nagasaki, August 1945*; retired as professor at Columbia University in 1973; from 1978 to 1981, served as first chief of the division of motion pictures, broadcasting, and recorded sound at the Library of Congress; published *Migrations*, a family chronicle, in 2000 and *Media Lost and Found*, in 2001; died in Fair Haven, Vermont. See *Current Biography* (November) 1940.

Obituary *New York Times* B p9 July 26, 2001

BEAME, ABRAHAM D. Mar. 20, 1906–Feb. 10, 2001 Democratic mayor of New York City (1974–78); majored in accounting at the City College of New York; after earning his B.B.A. degree, in 1928, co-founded the small accounting firm of Beame & Greidinger; taught accounting in public high schools in Brooklyn and Queens until 1946; helped to found the Haddingway Democratic Club in Brooklyn; in the early 1940s, served as legislative representative of the Joint Committee of Teachers Organizations; joined New York City's bureau of the budget as assistant director in 1946; was director of the bureau from 1952 to 1961; was elected city comptroller in 1961; as the Democratic candidate for mayor in 1965, lost to fusion (Republican-Liberal) candidate John V. Lindsay; returning to private life, founded Abraham D. Beame Associates, an investment counseling firm; running as an independent, was again elected comptroller in 1969; taking office as mayor following his victory in the 1973 election, faced a host of municipal problems, including a wave of terrorist bombings in Manhattan and the "Son of Sam" serial murders in several boroughs; in addition, had to cope with the gravest fiscal crisis in the city's history, a state of affairs that had been building for 15 years—the result of reckless spending and borrowing policies, to some extent in the administration of Mayor Robert Wagner and to a greater extent during Mayor Lindsay's two terms—and that began to be resolved only after the de facto takeover of the city's finances by New York State regulators in 1975; helped in that resolution by his decision not to defer payment on city notes; was widely praised for his frugal and fair allocation of the city's diminished revenues; was defeated by Edward I. Koch in the 1977 Democratic mayoral primary election; died in Manhattan. See *Current Biography* (July) 1974.

Obituary *New York Times* p1+ Feb. 11, 2001

BEBEY, FRANCIS July 15, 1929–May 28, 2001 Cameroon-born musician; ethno-musicologist; composer; singer; novelist; broadcast journalist; studied English at the University of Paris and radio and mass communications at New York University; in the early 1960s, became known to African radio listeners as the host of music and cultural interview programs broadcast by Radiodiffusion Outre-Mer, the French overseas radio system; during the 1960s, was a program specialist with UNESCO's information services in Paris, for which he organized concerts and conferences (including colloquiums on African traditional music) and produced films; headed the music section of UNESCO's cultural department from 1969 to 1974; during 13 years with UNESCO, traveled widely in Africa, becoming exposed to its many cultural traditions; was especially influenced by the West African griots, bards who recite the lore of their peoples to the accompaniment of traditional stringed instruments; as a musician, first concentrated almost exclusively on the classical guitar, for which he wrote and performed such pieces as *Lake Michigan Summer* (1958), his first substantial composition, and *Concert pour un vieux masque* (circa 1964), his first with an African subtext; later "Africanized" his guitar playing, as he himself observed, "particularly with the introduction of new techniques such as us-

ing the box as a percussion instrument, or making strings rattle"; on his album *African Sanza* (1982), used for the first time a traditional African instrument, the sanza, or thumb piano; on *Akwaaba* (1985), paired the sanza with the two-note Pygmy flute (together with electric bass and percussion); continued to combine Western and African instruments on subsequent recordings, including "Lambarene Schweitzer," on which he played the balafon, or African xylophone, Pygmy flute, sanza, acoustic piano, and synthesizer; included a wide range of international styles (including Latin-American rhythms and Texan folk singing) on the album *Django Préface* (1992), dedicated to the memory of the Belgian Gypsy jazz guitarist Django Reinhardt; as a singer, delivered lullaby-like songs of his own composition in a soothing baritone voice; sang in French, English, and Douala; maintained a busy international concert schedule; often performed with his son Toups, a multi-instrumentalist; between 1967 and 1991 published six novels—including those translated as *Agnes Moudio's Son*, *The Ashanti Doll*, and *King Albert*—in which he tried, sometimes satirically, "to convey the message of . . . not just an African but a man living within the human community"; also published collections of novellas, short stories, and poetry and the acclaimed work of nonfiction translated into English as *African Music: A People's Art* (1975); died in Paris. See *Current Biography* (April) 1994.

Obituary *New York Times* p31 June 7, 2001

BIRENDRA BIR BIKRAM SHAH DEV, KING OF NEPAL Dec. 28, 1945–June 1, 2001 Ruler of the world's only Hindu kingdom, the Himalayan region's most popular tourist attraction; was the 10th in a succession of kings of the Shah Dev dynasty, a royal family, descended from Gurkha warriors, whose history has been replete with palace intrigue and bloodshed; was crowned king in 1972; at the beginning of his reign, wielded virtually absolute power in keeping with Nepal's complex panchayat system of partyless government; following student riots protesting the system in 1979, permitted a modification of the system to allow for a spectrum of political parties, the final result of which was rampant fractiousness (which abetted a Maoist insurgency) rather than true democracy; was shot to death in the royal palace in Katmandu, in a massacre, allegedly perpetrated by his son Crown Prince Dipendra, that left 10 dead, including Dipendra's mother, brother, sister, aunt, and uncle and Dipendra himself (by an allegedly self-inflicted pistol shot to the left temple). See *Current Biography* (August) 1975.

Obituary *New York Times* A p1+ June 2, 2001

BORGE, VICTOR Jan. 3, 1909–Dec. 23, 2000 Danish-born pianist; comedian; conductor; an elegant but droll, at times even slapstick, classical pianist who succeeded in appealing to the risibilities of both musical sophisticates and people not musically oriented; as a prodigy, made his concert debut in Copenhagen when he was three; to release nervous tension, began to introduce improvised, lighthearted banter into his performances when he was 23; soon, added musical impersonations and parodies and even such physical jokes as falling off his piano bench; as his own writer, incorporated his ad-libs into continually reworked scripts; by 1937 was a top-ranked entertainer on Danish stage, screen, and radio; when the Nazi Germans invaded Denmark, in 1940, was performing in Sweden; imperiled, as a Jew, fled to the U.S. via Finland; first attracted a national following in the U.S. as a regular member (for a year and a half) of the cast of the popular radio musical variety program *Kraft Music Hall*; subsequently, was heard on other radio programs, including the *Victor Borge Show* (in the summer of 1945); took his "Concert with Comedy" act from Carnegie Hall and the elegant Wedgwood Room of the Waldorf-Astoria Hotel in Manhattan to concert halls, auditoriums, and other venues across the U.S.; made the first of his many appearances on Ed Sullivan's television show (then called *Talk of the Town*) in 1949; starred on Broadway in his one-man show *Comedy in Music*, for a three-year run beginning in 1953 and in revivals in 1964 and 1977; meanwhile, was touring Europe and Asia as well as the U.S.; conducted major orchestras in such cities as New York, Philadelphia, London, Amsterdam, and Copenhagen; was managed by one of his sons; died at his home in Greenwich, Connecticut. See *Current Biography* (May) 1993.

Obituary *New York Times* B p7 Dec. 25, 2000

BOUDREAU, LOU July 17, 1917–Aug. 10, 2001 Baseball player-manager; playing with the Cleveland Indians from 1940 through 1950, was third in the lineup (the designated power slot), seldom struck out, and was almost flawless at shortstop; was voted the American League's most valuable player in 1948; as Cleveland's manager from 1942 through 1950, had a record of 728 wins and 649 losses; in his overall major-league career, batted .295, led the American League in doubles three times, and tallied a managerial record of 1,162–1,223; had an uncanny anticipation for, or seeming prescience of, the moves of opponents; at the University of Illinois, was captain of the baseball and basketball teams; began playing professional baseball in the Cleveland farm system in 1938; two years later, in his first season with the Indians, led American League shortstops in fielding, as he would in seven subsequent seasons, and was an All Star, as he would be in six subsequent years; in a game against the New York Yankees on July 17, 1944, caught barehanded a ball hit by Joe DiMaggio and thereby started a double play that brought DiMaggio's historic 56-game hitting streak to an end; four months later, signed the contract that made him the youngest full-time manager in major-league history; in 1944, had the best batting average in the American League, with .357; in 1948, batted .355, hit 18 homers, drove in 206 runs, and struck out just nine times in 560 at-bats; in the middle of the 1948 season, with Cleveland second baseman Joe Gordon, made up the first double-play combination to start in an All-Star game; in the 155-game 1948 season, guided the Indians to 97 victories and a tie with the Boston Red Sox for the league pennant; in a one-game play-off, had four hits (including two home runs) in four times at bat as Cleveland defeated Boston 8–3; in the subsequent six-game World Series against the Boston Braves, led the Indians to the world champi-

onship; as a defense against the left-hand pull-hitting Red Sox slugger Ted Williams, introduced (in 1948) the much copied Williams shift, in which all four infielders were positioned to the right of second base and the center fielder was moved into right field; with the Boston Red Sox, played shortstop in 1951, was player-manager in 1952, and manager in 1953 and 1954; managed the Kansas City Athletics from 1955 to 1957; was radio and television broadcaster for Chicago Cubs games from 1957 through 1959; was field manager of the Cubs in 1960; returned to the Chicago broadcasting booth in 1961 and remained there through 1988; was inducted into the Baseball Hall of Fame in 1970; died in Olympia Fields, Illinois. See *Current Biography* (August) 1942.

Obituary *New York Times* A p13 Aug. 11, 2001

BROOKS, GWENDOLYN June 7, 1917–Dec. 3, 2000 African-American poet; a lifelong inhabitant of Chicago whose work focused on life in that city's black South Side ("Bronzeville"), on its "people and their concerns, their troubles as well as their joys"; wrote, in her words, about what she "saw and heard in the street"; did so with both a knowledge of colloquial language and a mastery of a range of poetic form, from free verse to more-controlled arrangements of meter and rhyme, including an experimental combination of sonnet and ballad; published her first collection of poetry, *A Street in Bronzeville*, in 1945; won a Pulitzer Prize (1950) for her second book, *Annie Allen* (1949), a sequence of poems tracing a Bronzeville girl's progress to womanly maturity; plumbed often painful emotional and psychological depths both in that work and in her coming-of-age novel *Maud Martha* (1953); widened her perspective to include national civil rights themes (in an integrationist mode) in some of the verse in *The Bean Eaters* (1956); for the first time, showed influence by the militant black power and self-reliance movements in poems in the volume *In the Mecca* (1968); in keeping with her "transformation," left Harper & Row to publish subsequent books of verse—including *Family Pictures* (1970), *Aloneness* (1971), and *Beckonings* (1975)—under the imprint of the Broadside Press, a small African-American–owned publishing house; directed such Broadside publications as *A Capsule Course in Black Poetry Writing* (1975); among numerous other honors, had a chair in black literature and creative writing named for her at Chicago's Columbia College, where she taught for six years in the 1960s; was named poet laureate of Illinois in 1968; was consultant in poetry to the Library of Congress (1985–86); conducted poetry and creative writing workshops for college students and, on Chicago's South Side, for young people; sponsored and judged poetry writing contests for school-age children; wrote many poems for children; published two autobiographical volumes, *Report from Part One* (1972) and *Report from Part Two* (1995); died at her home in Chicago. See *Current Biography* (July) 1977.

Obituary *New York Times* C p22 Dec. 5, 2000

BROWER, DAVID July 1, 1912–Nov. 5, 2000 Radical environmentalist; was the principal activist in campaigns that preserved for posterity a significant number of irreplaceable resources of wildlife and wilderness in the U.S.; later concentrated on global environmental projects; in the then-wild hills surrounding his childhood home in Berkeley, California, became so intimate with nature that he could identify species of butterflies in flight; during six years (1935–41) with the National Park Service in Yosemite National Park, in California, made the first of his 33 ascents of peaks in the Sierra Nevada; during World War II, served as an instructor with an army mountain division; was an editor at the University of California Press until 1952, when he became executive director of the Sierra Club; in the latter position, initiated the publication of a series of 20 handsome coffee-table books containing photographs by Ansel Adams and others of American landscapes, from the Maine islands to the Sierra Nevada mountain range; at the same time, steered the previously benign conservation organization on a new militant course that put fear into the hearts of the timber, mining, and utility lobbyists and infuriated federal dam-builders; with his vigilantes, successfully agitated for passage of the Wilderness Act, the Wild Rivers Act, and laws establishing Redwoods National Park and other parklands; blocked the building of environment-threatening dams on the Green River in Utah and in the Grand Canyon; was instrumental in saving for future generations the Central Great Smokies, Kentucky's Red River Gorge, Maine's Allagash Wilderness, New York's Storm King Mountain, the Florida Everglades, and Utah's Dinosaur National Monument, among other preserves; successfully lobbied for the creation of North Cascades National Park, Canyonlands in Utah, and national seashores on Cape Cod, Massachusetts, and at Point Reyes, California; by politicizing the Sierra Club, caused the organization to lose its tax-exempt status; alienated the club's moderate members, who forced him to resign in 1969; immediately created two complementary organizations, the educational John Muir Institute for Environmental Studies and the political-activist Friends of the Earth; was president of the latter until 1979 and chairman of the Friends of the Earth Foundation until 1984; meanwhile, in 1982, founded the Earth Island Institute, a San Francisco–based organization devoted to promoting conservation projects in countries around the world; in addition to his Sierra Club series of books, designed and oversaw the editing of two Friends of the Earth series, the 10-volume *The Earth's Wild Places* (1970–71) and the three-volume *Celebrating the Earth* (1972–73); edited a number of other books; wrote an autobiography in two volumes, *For Earth's Sake* (1990) and *Work in Progress* (1991); after reconciling with the Sierra Club, was its honorary vice president for many years (until recently, when he again became estranged from the organization); died at his home in Berkeley, California. See *Current Biography* (June) 1973.

Obituary *New York Times* C p22 Nov. 7, 2000

BROWN, ROBERT McAFEE May 28, 1920–Sep. 4, 2001 Presbyterian clergyman; liberal theologian; university professor; author of books generally addressed to the lay reader; an activist in such causes as civil rights, social justice, antiwar causes, liberation theology, and ecumenism; was a preeminent

leader in initiating interfaith dialogue and cooperation, especially between Protestants and Catholics; held degrees from Amherst College, Union Theological Seminary, and Columbia University, where he received his Ph.D. degree in the philosophy of religion in 1951; while completing the requirements for his doctorate at Columbia, was an instructor of the philosophy of religion and systematic theology at Union Theological Seminary; from 1951 to 1953, was professor of religion and head of the Department of Religion at Macalester College, in St. Paul, Minnesota; subsequently served on the faculties of Union Theological Seminary (1953–62), Stanford University (beginning in 1962), and the Pacific School of Religion, in Berkeley, California (1975–85); began his work in ecumenism when, while at Macalester College, he was stunned and appalled at outbursts of Protestant bigotry directed against Democratic U.S. representative (later senator) Eugene J. McCarthy, a Roman Catholic; later helped to quell Protestant worries about presidential candidate John F. Kennedy's possible ties to the Vatican; at the successive invitations of Pope John XXIII and Pope Paul VI, was an official observer at the second session of Vatican Council II, in 1963 and 1964; wrote the 38-page manifesto of Clergy and Laity Concerned About Vietnam, issued in 1965; published 28 books, including *The Bible Speaks to You* (1955), *The Spirit of Protestantism* (1961), *The Ecumenical Revolution* (1967), *Elie Wiesel, Messenger to All Humanity* (1983), and *Gustavo Gutierrez: An Introduction to Liberation Theology* (1990); poked satirical fun at matters theological and ecclesiastical in the essays in *The Collect'd Writings of St. Hereticus* (1964); with Gustave Weigel, wrote *An American Dialogue: A Protestant Looks at Catholicism and a Catholic Looks at Protestantism* (1960); with Daniel Ellsberg in 1997, fasted and demonstrated at the United Nations in a protest against nuclear weapons; died in Greenfield, Massachusetts. See *Current Biography* (May) 1956.

Obituary *New York Times* B p13 Sep. 7, 2001

BUNDY, WILLIAM P. Sep. 24, 1917–Oct. 6, 2000 U.S. government official; lawyer; a Boston blueblood who, with his better-known brother McGeorge Bundy (national security assistant to presidents John F. Kennedy and Lyndon B. Johnson), was, in the words of David Halberstam, one of those "best and brightest" centrally implicated in the ill-starred strategy for America's tragic war in Vietnam; after serving for 10 years on the Central Intelligence Agency's Board of National Estimates, joined the incoming Kennedy administration in January 1961 as deputy to Paul H. Nitze, assistant secretary of defense in charge of international security affairs; succeeded to Nitze's post in October 1963; in 1964 was named by President Johnson assistant secretary of state for Far Eastern affairs, a position described by David Halberstam as "the pivot" of the State Department's Vietnam policy; after leaving government, in 1969, taught at the Center for International Studies at the Massachusetts Institute of Technology; became editor of *Foreign Affairs* in 1972; later did research and taught part-time at Princeton University; in 1998 published the book *A Tangled Web: The Making of Foreign Policy in the*

Nixon Presidency; died at his home in Princeton, New Jersey. See *Current Biography* (January) 1964.

Obituary *New York Times* A p13 Oct. 7, 2000

CARAS, ROGER A. May 24, 1928–Feb. 18, 2001 Nature writer; broadcast journalist; advocate for companion animals, wildlife, and the environment; as president of the American Society for the Prevention of Cruelty to Animals (ASPCA) from 1991 to 1999, promoted, with considerable success, spaying and neutering rather than euthanasia as a solution to the overpopulation of dogs and cats; oversaw the development of the first poison-control center for animals in the U.S.; grew up surrounded by a wide variety of pets, including snakes, turtles, and birds, in the then-rural town of Methuen, Massachusetts, as he recounted in his books *A Celebration of Dogs* (1982) and *A Celebration of Cats* (1986); as a schoolboy, worked as a kennel aide at the Methuen SPCA; after earning a degree in cinema at the University of Southern California, directed animation for Michael Myerberg Productions in New York City (1952–53); subsequently, worked for a decade with the Columbia Pictures Corp. in New York, first as a press agent and then, concurrently, as assistant to the vice president and director of merchandising for the U.S. and Canada; as vice president of Polaris Productions (New York) and Hawk Films (London) from 1965 to 1968, was involved in the making of the motion picture *2001: A Space Odyssey*; was a producer with Ivan Tors Films (1964–65); starting in 1964, appeared regularly for about a decade as the "house naturalist" on the NBC television network's morning *Today* show; in 1975 joined the ABC network, where he was animals and environment correspondent for news productions; was seen on a number of PBS television specials; made several hundred guest appearances on national television; for two decades, beginning in 1969, gave a series of three-minute talks titled *Pets and Wildlife* on the CBS radio network; in 1973 conducted the radio program *Report from the World of Animals* on NBC; in 1981 became a news correspondent for ABC radio; on ABC, presented the radio program *The Living World* from 1981 to 1983; served as adjunct professor of English at Southampton College on Long Island and adjunct professor of animal ecology at the University of Pennsylvania's School of Veterinary Medicine; for many years, through 2000, was the announcer at the Westminster Kennel Club's annual dog show; contributed widely to print media; wrote several newspaper and magazine columns, including the syndicated weekly column "Our Only World"; published his first book, *Antarctica: Land of Frozen Time*, in 1962; never wrote about a place or animal without first-hand experience; with cameras and notepad, stalked the Kodiak bear in Alaska to write the fictionalized biography *Monarch of Deadman Bay: The Life and Death of a Kodiak Bear* (1969); subsequently published similar biographies of a Custer wolf (a so-called outlaw wolf) of South Dakota, a California condor, a Pacific sockeye salmon, an African lion, and a panther as well as such nonfictionalized studies of animals in their natural habitats as *North American Mammals* (1967), *Venomous Animals of the World* (1974), and *Animals in Their Places* (1987); wrote a

total of more than 70 books, including handbooks on domestic animals, eloquent essays on the interrelationship of myriad species of trees, plants, and animals, children's books, and impassioned pleas for the protection of endangered species; published his last book, *Out of the Blue*, about show dogs and dog shows, a few days before his death; lived on his farm in Freeland, Maryland; died in nearby Towson, Maryland. See *Current Biography* (April) 1988.

Obituary *New York Times* B p9 Feb. 20, 2001

CARROLL-ABBING, J. PATRICK Aug. 11, 1912–July 9, 2001 Irish-born Roman Catholic monsignor; social worker; founder and president of Boys' Towns and Girls' Towns of Italy Inc.; was ordained a priest in Rome in 1936; the following year, entered the Vatican's diplomatic service; during and immediately after World War II, was involved in numerous Vatican mercy missions, at first to wounded Italian soldiers in military hospitals and later, after the Allied landing at Anzio, to civilians caught in the military crossfire; was instrumental in setting up refugee camps and first-aid stations for displaced persons and in channeling medicine, food, and other supplies to them; of all the innocent victims of the war, was most moved by the plight of the thousands of children left orphaned or homeless; organized his first boys' refuge, a "Shoeshine Hotel" in Rome, in 1944; over the following quarter-century, with money raised for the most part in the U.S., expanded his work throughout Italy, founding nine self-governing Boys' Towns, a Girls' Town, and 31 day-care centers; also led church relief projects for victims of floods and earthquakes in Italy; told the story of his work with children in two books of nonfiction, *A Chance to Live* (1952) and *But for the Grace of God* (1965), and one novel, *Journey to Somewhere* (1955); was active in his charities until shortly before his death, at Boys' Town of Rome. See *Current Biography* (July) 1967.

Obituary *New York Times* B p9 July 11, 2001

CAVANNA, BETTY June 24, 1909–Aug. 13, 2001 Writer; an author chiefly of novels for a young readership; created protagonists with whom juveniles, especially teenage girls, could identify; majored in journalism at the New Jersey College for Women, where she was managing editor of the *Campus News*; after taking her degree, in 1929, did newspaper editorial work, held a job in advertising and a post as art director for a publishing house, and wrote radio scripts and short stories; published her first book-length story, *Puppy Stakes,* in 1943, and her second, *The Black Spaniel Mystery,* in 1945; began to write of the joys and aches of growing up in *Going on Sixteen* (1946) and *Spurs for Suzanna* (1947); studied aviation for the writing of *A Girl Can Dream* (1948); in creating the character Kate in *Paintbox Summer* (1949), set in a village on Cape Cod, hoped that "through Kate, girls may get a little perspective on their own problems and their own romances"; in a change of pace, wrote the mystery *Secret Passage* (1947); for younger teens, wrote *A Date for Diane, Take a Call, Topsy,* and *She's My Girl*; brought together her favorite dog stories in *Pick of the Litter* (1955); subsequently published *The Boy Next Door*

(1955), *Stars in Her Eyes* (1958), *Accent on April* (1960), *A Time for Tenderness* (1962), and *Jenny Kimura* (1964); also wrote the nonfictional *The First Book of Sea Shells* (1955), *Touch of Magic* (1961), a biography of Anne Sullivan Macy, Helen Keller's teacher, and, with her first husband, Edward T. Headley, *The First Book of Wool* (1966); wrote two runners-up for the Edgar Allan Poe Award: *Spice Island Mystery* (1970) and *The Ghost of Ballyhooly* (1972); with her second husband, George Russell Harrison, traveled widely in Europe, South America, Africa, Asia, and elsewhere, meeting with many young people as she did so; with grist from her travels, wrote a series of nonfiction books called Around the World; wrote a total of more than 80 books, the last of which, *Banner Year*, was published in 1987; sometimes wrote under the names Betsy Allen and Elizabeth Headley; died at her home in Vézelay, France. See *Current Biography* (Yearbook) 1950.

Obituary *New York Times* C p15 Aug. 16, 2001

CHABAN-DELMAS, JACQUES Mar. 7, 1915–Nov. 10, 2000 French government official; former prime minister; a leader of the left wing of the Gaullist party; held the rank of brigadier general in the French Resistance during the German occupation of France (1940–44); in the postwar provisional government, was secretary general in the Ministry of Information; was elected to the National Assembly as a Radical Socialist in 1946; the following year, joined General Charles de Gaulle's Rally of the French People, which subsequently became the Social Republican Party; became chairman of the Social Republicans in 1953; in a succession of Fourth Republic governments, was minister of public works (1954–55), minister of state (1956–57), and defense minister (1957–58); as prime minister under President Georges Pompidou in 1969, pushed for "a new society" in France, against the grain of his more conservative fellows, who regarded the proposal as dangerously socialistic; in 1972, was forced to resign by Pompidou; in 1974, ran for president, unsuccessfully; was president of the National Assembly for several terms, the last from 1986 to 1988; was mayor of Bordeaux from 1947 to 1995; wrote several books, including a biography of Charles de Gaulle and an account of the liberation of France in 1944; died in Paris, France. See *Current Biography* (July) 1958.

Obituary *New York Times* B p7 Nov. 13, 2000

CHANDRASEKHAR, SRIPATI Nov. 22, 1918–June 14, 2001 Demographer; a crusader for population control, especially in his native India, whose population has grown from 340 million in 1947—the year the country won its independence from Britain—to more than a billion; after graduating from Madras Presidency College, studied at New York University, where he received his Ph.D. degree in sociology, with a dissertation on India's population problems; during the following scholastic year, lectured on Indian social and economic problems at the University of Pennsylvania; in the waning months of World War II, worked for the U.S. Office of Strategic Services as an expert on Indian demography; after the war, traveled across the U.S. speaking in behalf of an India on the threshold of political independence; between

1947 and 1955, was back in India, heading the economics departments at, successively, the universities of Annamalai and Baroda; directed demographic research for UNESCO in 1948; from 1956 to 1967, directed the Indian Institute for Population Studies at Madras; in March 1967, was named minister of health and family planning in the cabinet of Indian prime minister Indira Gandhi; launched a massive campaign to make Indians aware of the desirability of smaller families and of the means to achieve that goal; used every available means of communication, including radio and sound trucks, to carry into 566,000 Indian villages his message that "the simple sex act must be a responsible act, an act where the consequences are controlled in the interests of . . . our children, . . . our wives and families, . . . and the social progress of our country"; arranged for the mass distribution of contraceptives; established family-planning centers and mobile units; instituted incentive programs for voluntary vasectomies and insertions of contraceptive loops; fought the custom of early marriage for women; to enable him to concentrate on the family-planning program, was moved from the cabinet to the position of state minister in the Ministry of Health, Family Planning, and Urban Development in November 1967; saw the average number of children born per woman in India decline from six to three, a population trend nullified by longer life spans; during the last three decades of his life, traveled the world, teaching, participating in conferences on population control, and heading efforts to set up voluntary sterilization programs in underdeveloped countries; wrote hundreds of articles and more than 30 books and monographs, including *Hungry Peoples and Empty Lands* (1955), *Infant Mortality in India, 1901–55* (1959), and *American Aid and India's Economic Development* (1965); moved between homes in La Jolla, California, and southern India; died in San Diego, California. See *Current Biography* (October) 1969.

Obituary *New York Times* A p11 June 23, 2001

COCA, IMOGENE Nov. 18, 1908–June 2, 2001 Comic actress; brought a vaudevillian's broad style—typified by histrionic mugging, pantomimic gesticulation, and high-pitched articulation—to the live sketch comedy (including spoofs of popular motion pictures and marital relations) for which she and Sid Caesar became famous during television's so-called golden age; was born to theater professionals in Philadelphia, where she made her debut as a vaudeville song-and-dance girl; in her mid-teens, began performing in musical revues in New York; joined Leonard Sillman as his dancing partner in a vaudeville act; after Sillman turned to producing, was cast by him in *New Faces of 1934*; subsequently had featured spots in seven more Sillman productions, including *New Faces of 1936* and *New Faces of 1937* and in Max Liebman's Broadway production *Straw Hat Revue* (1939), among other musical/variety stage productions; during the 1940s, attracted a small but faithful following with her appearances in such nightclubs as the Blue Angel and Café Society Uptown; did not gain wide recognition until her arrival on television; was first teamed with Sid Caesar in Max Liebman's weekly variety hour *The Admiral*

Broadway Revue, televised simultaneously on the NBC and Dumont networks from January to June 1949; was second banana to Caesar on Liebman's *Your Show of Shows*, a 90-minute variety show televised on NBC from 1950 to 1954; received an Emmy Award for best television actress of 1951; had her own half-hour program, *The Imogene Coca Show*, on NBC during the 1954–55 season; was reunited with Caesar on a program that ran on the ABC network for 18 weeks in 1958; on CBS, was seen in the *The Sid Caesar, Imogene Coca, Carl Reiner, Howard Morris Special*, which was awarded the Emmy for outstanding variety special of the 1966–67 season; performed in regional theater with King Donovan, her second husband; starred with Jack Lemmon in the motion picture *Under the Yum Yum Tree* (1963); died at her home in Westport, Connecticut. See *Current Biography* (April) 1951.

Obituary *New York Times* p32 June 3, 2001

COMO, PERRY May 18, 1912–May 12, 2001 Singer; a popular crooner with a smooth baritone voice and a studied casual style; rode the crest of easy-listening sound's dominance of the jukeboxes and airwaves from the 1940s to the 1960s; became known for his renditions of songs ranging from "Don't Let the Stars Get in Your Eyes," "Wanted," and "Papa Loves Mambo" to a string of novelty ditties, including the huge hit "Hot Diggity"; began his career as a barber in Canonsburg, Pennsylvania; toured the Midwest as featured singer with Frankie Carlone's band from 1934 to 1937; sang with the Ted Weems orchestra for six years thereafter; in 1943 began singing on the CBS radio network and performing in such upscale venues as Manhattan's Copacabana nightclub and Paramount Theater; signed a contract with RCA Victor, which released his first disk, "Goodbye Sue" (with "There'll Soon Be a Rainbow" on the flip side) in August 1943; in the mid-1940s topped the charts with his recordings "If I Loved You" and "Till the End of Time" and nudged the top with "I'm Always Chasing Rainbows"; had singing roles in several motion pictures, including *Doll Face* (1945) and *Words and Music* (1948); in 1948 moved from network radio to network television, where he remained for 15 years, reaching the height of his popularity as the host of the prime-time Emmy Award–winning CBS weekly variety hour *The Perry Como Show* (1955–63); in 1958 won the Grammy Award for best recording artist with "Catch a Falling Star"; by the 1980s had accumulated total record sales of almost 100 million; was married to the former Roselle Belline from 1933 until her death, in 1998; died at his home in Jupiter, Florida. See *Current Biography* (April) 1947.

Obituary *New York Times* B p7 May 14, 2001

CONNOR, JOHN T. Nov. 3, 1914–Oct. 6, 2000 Former U.S. government official; retired banker and corporate executive; lawyer; early in his career, successively practiced law with a Manhattan firm, was general counsel for the federal Office of Scientific Research and Development, an agency in operation during World War II, and served as an intelligence officer in the U.S. Marines; was a special assistant to Secretary of the Navy James V. Forrestal from 1945

to 1947, when he became general attorney with Merck & Co., a major pharmaceutical manufacturer; served as president and chief executive officer of Merck from 1955 to 1965; as U.S. secretary of commerce in the administration of President Lyndon B. Johnson beginning in 1965, did his best to keep inflation under control during the escalation of the Vietnam War; in protest of war policy, left government in 1967; joined the Allied Chemical Corp. as president (1967–68); later was chief executive officer (1968–79) and chairman (1969–79) of Allied Chemical; after leaving Allied Chemical, was nonexecutive chairman of the New York City operation of Schroders Inc., the London-based merchant banking firm, for eight years; died in Boston, Massachusetts. See *Current Biography* (April) 1961.

Obituary *New York Times* B p10 Oct. 10, 2000

CRANSTON, ALAN June 19, 1914–Dec. 31, 2000 Liberal Democratic U.S. senator from California (1969–93); was an International News Service correspondent in England, Germany, Italy, and Ethiopia from 1936 to 1939; in the latter year, published an abridged translation of *Mein Kampf* with anti-Nazi explanatory notes; from 1939 to 1941 was a Washington lobbyist for the Common Council for American Unity, an organization whose aim was to exercise a liberalizing influence on legislation affecting the foreign born; during World War II, was chief of the foreign-language division of the Office of War Information (1942–44); as an enlisted man, edited *Army Talk* (1944–45); in the postwar years, was a leader in the world federalist movement; wrote the book *The Killing of the Peace* (1945), an account of the events from 1916 to 1923 that led to the defeat of the League of Nations; for the purpose of revitalizing the California Democratic Party, co-founded the California Democratic Council, in 1953; was elected to a four-year term as controller of the state of California in 1958 and to a second term in 1962; ran for the U.S. Senate, as he said, "because there I can work on the issues of war and peace, and the environment, and justice and opportunity"; was elected to the first of his four six-year terms in the U.S. Senate in 1968; became Senate majority leader in 1977; with his constant note-taking and calculator-like brain, was uncanny in his ability to predict Senate votes; described the Senate as the place where he kept his commitment to "get us out of the tragic war in Vietnam . . . where one act of mine helped to keep us out of war in Angola . . . where I'm doing the utmost to dispel the threat of nuclear war"; unsuccessfully sought the Democratic nomination for president in 1984; was the most seriously charged of the "Keating Five," five senators tainted by association with the savings-and-loan executive Charles H. Keating Jr., who had been indicted on securities fraud charges; for seeking to influence federal regulators on Keating's behalf, after receiving $1.2 million in political contributions from Keating, was formally reprimanded by his Senate peers in 1991; had already announced his decision not to seek a fifth term in the Senate; in 1996 became chairman of the Global Security Institute, founded in San Francisco by former Soviet president Mikhail S. Gorbachev for the promotion of world peace and disarmament; died at his home in Los Altos, California. See *Current Biography* (October) 1969.

Obituary *New York Times* B p6 Jan. 1, 2001

DE VALOIS, NINETTE June 6, 1898–Mar. 8, 2001 Anglo-Irish ballet director; choreographer; teacher; a prime force in transforming Continental classical ballet through the prism of British culture and establishing and nurturing a distinctive, sustained ballet tradition in the United Kingdom; founded the Royal Ballet (now state-subsidized), one of the top five classical-ballet ensembles in the world, and the Royal Ballet School; directed the troupe until 1963 and headed the school until 1970; fostered choreographic themes drawn from British literature, music, and painting; made her debut as a principal dancer in a pantomime at the Lyceum Theatre in London in 1914; over the following 12 years, danced only in pantomime and music-hall variety acts because, as she once explained, "there was no ballet group then"; toured Europe with Sergei Diaghilev's Ballets Russes for three years (1923–26); in 1926 opened the Academy of Choreographic Art in London; in the late 1920s was choreographic director for several theaters, including the Old Vic, and a charter choreographer with the Camargo Society, formed to produce dance dramas with British talent; in 1931 became director of ballet performances at the Sadler's Wells Theatre; organized the ballet school and dance group that developed into the Sadler's Wells Ballet during the 1930s and that was renamed the Royal Ballet when it received a royal charter in 1956; also founded the Sadler's Wells Theatre Ballet, the forerunner of the Birmingham Royal Ballet; in 1947 took time out from her work in Britain to found Turkey's National School of Ballet; created such choreographic works as *Job* (1931), *The Rake's Progress* (1935), and *The Prospect Before Us* (1940); published two books on dance, *Invitation to the Ballet* (1937) and *Step by Step* (1997), the autobiography *Come Dance with Me* (1957), and the poetry collection *The Cycle* (1985); died at her home in Barnes, southwest London. See *Current Biography* (December) 1949.

Obituary *New York Times* B p8 Mar. 9, 2001

ETHERINGTON, EDWIN D. Dec. 25, 1924–Jan. 8, 2001 Former president of the American Stock Exchange; former president of Wesleyan University, his alma mater; after majoring in English and creative writing at Wesleyan, earned a law degree at the Yale University Law School; as an assistant with a Wall Street law firm from 1954 to 1956, became familiar with the legal affairs of the New York Stock Exchange; joined that exchange as assistant secretary in 1956; rose to secretary within the same year and to vice president in charge of civic and governmental affairs in 1958; left the New York Stock Exchange to join the brokerage firm of Pershing and Co. in January 1961; 14 months later, in March 1962, was chosen president of the American Stock Exchange (second only to the New York Stock Exchange among U.S. exchanges), which had been charged by the U.S. Securities and Exchange Commission with "manifold and prolonged abuses"; directed a reformation and rejuvenation program that restored public confidence in the American Stock Exchange; expanded

career opportunities for women and minorities at the exchange; was president of Wesleyan University, in Middletown, Connecticut, from 1967 to 1970, a period of nationwide campus unrest fueled by Vietnam War protests and such other issues as racial and gender discrimination; kept tensions at Wesleyan to a relative minimum; opened the university to women for the first time, and to a larger number of minority students; was instrumental in the creation of the Center for African American Studies (originally known as the African American Institute), a multibuilding Center for the Arts, and a scholarship program for Connecticut community-college graduates; died at his home on Jupiter Island, Florida. See *Current Biography* (April) 1966.

Obituary *New York Times* B p7 Jan. 15, 2001

EVANS, DALE Oct.31, 1912–Feb. 7, 2001 Actress; singer; composer; recording artist; author; evangelist manqué; "Queen of the West"; the wife and showbusiness partner of the late Roy Rogers, who vied with Gene Autry for the title of "king of the singing cowboys"; co-starred with her husband in motion pictures, rodeos, and road shows and on television and recordings; wrote 25 songs, including "Will You Marry Me, Mr. Laramie," "The Bible Tells Me So," "Happy Birthday, Gentle Savior," "Aha, San Antone," and the duo's theme song, "Happy Trails to You" (on which Roy collaborated, according to some sources); began her career singing on radio; made her screen debut in a minor role in *Orchestra Wives* (1942); subsequently had supporting roles in such films as the John Wayne vehicle *In Old Oklahoma* (1943); appeared with Roy Rogers for the first time in *The Cowboy and the Senorita* (1944); later co-starred with him in more than 30 Westerns, including *Don't Fence Me In* (1945), *Utah* (1945), *Apache Rose* (1947), and *Pals of the Golden West* (1951); on network television, co-starred with Roy Rogers in 102 half-hour Western dramas on the *Roy Rogers Show* (1951–57); also on network television, co-hosted the weekly musical/variety hour *Roy Rogers and Dale Evans Show* (September–December 1962); in Victorville, California, seven miles from their ranch in Apple Valley, founded the Roy Rogers and Dale Evans Museum, where the most popular attractions are the stuffed remains of Rogers's palomino, Trigger, and Evans's buckskin horse, Buttermilk; in the 1950s, made appearances at some of the Christian revival meetings of the Reverend Billy Graham; also gave witness to unquestioning religious faith in the books *Angel Unaware* (1953), inspired by the life and early death of her daughter Robin Elizabeth, a Down syndrome child, and *My Spiritual Diary* (1955); following the death (in 1964, at age 18) of one of her several adopted children, John David ("Sandy") Rogers, wrote the book *Salute to Sandy*; hosted a weekly show on a Christian broadcasting network; died in Apple Valley, California. See *Current Biography* (September) 1956.

Obituary *New York Times* A p28 Feb. 8, 2001

EYTAN, WALTER July 24, 1910–May 23, 2001 German-born, British-bred Israeli government official; read medieval and modern languages at Queens College, Oxford University; lectured in German at the college from 1934 to 1946, when he settled in Palestine; in behalf of the Jewish Agency, the Zionist government in the making, founded a public-service college in anticipation of the founding of the state of Israel, which was realized in 1948; in that year, became the founding director general of Israel's foreign service, a post he held for 10 years; subsequently served for a decade as Israel's ambassador to Paris; chaired the Israel Broadcasting Authority from 1972 to 1978; wrote the book *The First Ten Years: A Diplomatic History of Israel* (1958); died in Jerusalem. See *Current Biography* (October) 1958.

Obituary *New York Times* A p14 May 26, 2001

FRANCIS, ARLENE Oct. 20, 1907–May 31, 2001 Actress; television personality; for 25 years, was a witty and good-natured panelist on *What's My Line?*, the longest-running game show in the history of prime-time television; made her debut on the New York stage in 1932; had her first major role on Broadway in *All That Glitters* (1938); had featured roles in Orson Welles's Mercury Theater production of *Danton's Death* (1938) and Maxwell Anderson's *Journey to Jerusalem* (1940); realized her greatest Broadway success as Natalia in *The Doughgirls* (1942–43); accrued subsequent Broadway credits in *The Overtons* (1945), *The French Touch* (1945), *The Little Blue Light* (1951), *Late Show* (1953), and *Once More with Feeling* (1958); on radio in the 1940s had roles in several dramatic series, including *Portia Blake* and *Mr. District Attorney*, and hosted the audience-participation show *Blind Date*, on which servicemen competed for blind dates; on the CBS television network's popular Sunday-night quiz program *What's My Line* (1950–67), based on a 20-questions format, joined such other celebrity panelists as Bennett Cerf and Dorothy Kilgallen in trying to guess the occupations of guests; remained with that show after it went into syndication (1968–75); on the NBC television network, hosted *Home*, a weekday women's show with a magazine format, from 1954 to 1957; had roles in the motion pictures *Murders in the Rue Morgue* (1932), *Stage Door Canteen* (1943), *All My Sons* (1948), *One, Two, Three* (1961), and *The Thrill of It All* (1963); died in San Francisco, California. See *Current Biography* (May) 1956.

Obituary *New York Times* B p7 June 2, 2001

GEBEL-WILLIAMS, GUNTHER Sep. 12, 1934–July 19, 2001 Silesian-born circus-animal trainer; one of the first to use positive reinforcement with performing animals; departing from the macho "animal tamer" tradition, had a quiet (albeit hard-won) rapport with his menagerie and a dazzling effect on his audiences; for more than three decades, captivated those audiences with the glamorous image (enhanced by flowing bleached-blond hair, sequined and rhinestoned costumes, and a boyish grin) and casual daring he brought to his athletic, almost balletic performances, which required extraordinary stamina; as the stellar attraction of the Ringling Bros.–Barnum & Bailey Circus from 1969 to 1990, was that traveling big top's highest-paid performer; at age 12, began his career as an acrobat with the German one-ring Circus Williams, whose owners, Harry and Carola Williams, became his foster parents; managed the Circus

Williams after the death of Harry Williams; in training animals, advanced gradually from the bareback and Roman post riding of horses to the handling of elephants, tigers, panthers, and other animals, preferably ones born in the wild; in his autobiography, *Untamed* (1991), written with Tony Reinhold, explained, "I built a world around the animals with whom I worked, and in it I was their father and they were my children. . . . [Mutual] respect is the foundation of my training style"; learned to control his animals without snapping a whip or brandishing a blank pistol, a water hose, or a chair; communicated commands by gesture, touch, or gentle voice; trained tigers to drape themselves on his shoulders and to ride on the backs of horses and elephants; spent years perfecting his pyramid act, in which a tiger would jump on an elephant's back and he himself would then climb up the elephant and straddle the tiger; sustained numerous deep scars and other injuries, many resulting from his attempts to break up scraps between his animals; toured Europe with Circus Williams until Ringling Bros.–Barnum & Bailey acquired him by buying Circus Williams, in 1968; enjoyed the advantage of three rings after moving to the U.S.; put his elephants and tigers through their paces in the center ring while his horses pranced at the same time in the side rings; in Manhattan's Madison Square Garden alone, performed approximately 1,190 times; after retiring as a performer, became a part owner of Ringling Bros.–Barnum & Bailey and the circus's vice president for animal welfare; died in Venice, Florida. See *Current Biography* (December) 1971.

Obituary *New York Times* B p7 July 20, 2001

GEIS, BERNARD Aug. 30, 1909–Jan. 8, 2001 Publisher; as founder and director of Bernard Geis Associates, sought out potentially sensational books and aggressively promoted them to best-sellerdom; "made authors into celebrities and celebrities into authors," as Letty Cottin Pogrebin, his head of publicity, once observed; early in his career, edited *Apparel Arts*, *Esquire*, and *Coronet* magazines; became editor in chief at the publishing company Grosset & Dunlap in 1945; from 1956 to 1958 was an editor at Prentice-Hall, where he was the power behind the publication of Art Linkletter's *Kids Say the Darndest Things*; founded Bernard Geis Associates in 1959; did so in partnership with numerous persons in television and magazine publishing whose informal plugging of books contributed to the immediate success of the enterprise; relied heavily on appearances of his authors on television talk shows; scored his first phenomenal success with *Valley of the Dolls*, Jacqueline Susann's novel about drug-addicted Hollywood actresses, which remained on the *New York Times* best-seller list for 65 weeks; followed that up with Helen Gurley Brown's nonfiction blockbuster *Sex and the Single Girl*; later published the sexy novels of the Catholic priest Andrew Greeley; also published books by such authors as Harry S. Truman and Groucho and Harpo Marx; in protest of some of the sexually oriented material he was publishing, especially in books with characters resembling real celebrities, lost many of his partners in 1967; soon thereafter, lost Random House as his distributor;

subsequently issued his imprint through other publishers; published his last book in 1995; died in New York City. See *Current Biography* (September) 1960.

Obituary *New York Times* C p15 Jan. 10, 2001

GENNARO, PETER Nov. 23, 1919–Sep. 28, 2000 Dancer; choreographer; a master of modern jazz movement in dance; was one of the busiest and most visible creators and performers of dance on Broadway and television in the 1950s and 1960s; received a Tony Award for his choreography for the 1977 musical *Annie*; in his studio or at production sites, taught dance to numerous well-known actors; directed his own ensembles; when serving in the U.S. Army's Ordnance Air Corps during World War II, was recruited to dance with a military entertainment troupe in India; after the war, studied dance at the American Theater Wing and the Katherine Dunham School; in 1947, toured with the ballet chorus of the Chicago-based San Carlo Ballet Opera Company; in 1948, began dancing in the choruses of musical comedies; first caught the attention of Broadway critics with his dancing of the "Steam Heat" number (choreographed by Bob Fosse) with Carol Haney in *Pajama Game* (1954); had a leading dance role in *Bells Are Ringing* (1956); was the co-choreographer of *West Side Story* (1957) and the choreographer of *Fiorello!* (1959), *The Unsinkable Molly Brown* (1960), *Mr. President* (1962), *Bajour* (1964), and *Jimmy* (1969); choreographed and performed on numerous network television shows in the 1950s and 1960s; became well-known nationally through his performances in dance routines (created by him) with the Peter Gennaro Dancers on Perry Como's weekly television show *Kraft Music Hall* from 1960 to 1963; in addition, coached guests on the show in dance; adapted his stage choreography for the screen version of *The Unsinkable Molly Brown* (1965). See *Current Biography* (June) 1964.

Obituary *New York Times* A p18 Sep. 30, 2000

GIEREK, EDWARD Jan. 16, 1913–July 29, 2001 Former Polish Communist leader; as first secretary of the Polish United Workers Party, headed the government of Poland for eight years beginning in early 1971; was the first Communist leader in Eastern Europe not to have been subjected to Stalinist indoctrination in the Soviet Union; "opened up Poland to the world," as Lech Walesa observed, "but at the same time threw the country into terrible debt" (more than $25 billion); by his failure, helped to spawn Walesa's pro-democracy Solidarity movement; in his youth, worked as a coal miner in France; in 1937, after helping to organize the first sit-down strike in French history, was deported back to Poland; in 1937, emigrated again, to northeastern Belgium, where he worked in collieries and engaged in Communist activism; after returning to Poland in 1948, earned a degree in mining engineering and became a functionary with the Polish United Workers Party in his native province of Katowice, also known as Silesia, where he built his political power base; in 1954, joined the party's Central Committee as head of the department of heavy industry; in 1956, was selected for membership in the committee's nine-man Politburo; beginning in 1957, was a deputy in the

Sejm, the national Parliament; served for many years as a member of the Sejm's presidium; after 40 people, while rioting in protest of rising food prices, were shot to death on Poland's Baltic coast in December 1970, was chosen by the Central Committee to succeed First Secretary Wladyslaw Gomulka; brought a new, more relaxed and accessible presence to Poland's Communist leadership; sought to improve the living conditions of the average citizen; was credited with instrumentality in the building of 2.5 million apartments and the creation of three million new jobs; introduced Poland to Western consumerism, freer travel, more social amenities, and greater cultural diversity; above all, invested lavishly in heavy industry, including coal mines and steel furnaces in Silesia; saw his economic strategy begin to fail when a recession hit Poland in the mid-1970s, and later watched it collapse completely under the weight of his massive borrowing of foreign capital; was swept out of office in a bloodless coup in 1980; under the regime of General Wojciech Jaruzelski, who imposed martial law in 1981 in an effort to squash Solidarity, was expelled from the Polish United Workers Party and interned for a year, after which he retired to the life of a virtual recluse in Katowice; published his best-selling memoirs in the 1990s; died in Cieszyn, Katowice. See *Current Biography* (May) 1977.

Obituary *New York Times* B p6 July 30, 2001

GILBRETH, FRANK B. JR. Mar. 17, 1911–Feb. 18, 2001 Author; journalist; was the eldest of six sons among the 12 children of two time-and-motion efficiency experts who applied their professional expertise to the raising of their offspring; with his older sister Elizabeth Gilbreth Carey, described the resultant odd family experience in the nonfiction bestseller *Cheaper by the Dozen* (1949) and its sequel, *Belles on Their Toes* (1950), both of which were made into motion pictures; subsequently published *Held's Angels* (1952), a novel spoofing the Roaring '20s, illustrated by the cartoonist John Held Jr.; wrote a total of 10 books, including *Inside Nantucket* (1954), about a family-operated rooming house, *Of Whales and Women: One Man's View of Nantucket History* (1957), *He's My Boy* (1962), about his young son, and *Time Out for Happiness* (1962), about his parents; early in his career as a journalist, was a police reporter with the Charleston, South Carolina, *News and Gazette* (now the *Post and Gazette*); became an editorial writer with that newspaper in 1947; for decades, until 1993, wrote the column "Doing the Charleston" under the pseudonym Ashley Cooper; maintained homes in Nantucket, Massachusetts, and Charleston; died in Charleston. See *Current Biography* (May) 1949.

Obituary *New York Times* B p8 Feb. 20, 2001

GOLDOVSKY, BORIS June 7, 1908–Feb. 15, 2001 Opera conductor; impresario; pianist; lecturer; author; for half a century, was known to a national radio audience as intermission commentator during broadcasts of Saturday matinee performances of the Metropolitan Opera; was born into a musical family in Russia; studied piano in Moscow, Berlin, Paris, and Budapest; made his professional debut as a pianist in Berlin when he was 13; after immigrating to the U.S., in 1930, studied at the Curtis Institute of Music, in Philadelphia, where his mother, a concert violinist, had joined the faculty; there, became a conducting pupil of Fritz Reiner; after graduating, in 1932, remained at Curtis as an assistant to Reiner; while coaching opera at Curtis, was also an assistant conductor with the Philadelphia Grand Opera Company and the Philadelphia Orchestra; in 1936 moved to Cleveland, Ohio; for six years was head of the opera department at the Cleveland Institute of Music and chorus master and opera coach with the Cleveland Orchestra; in 1942 joined the faculty of the New England Conservatory of Music, in Boston, as head of its opera department; in 1946 added to his responsibilities the direction of the opera workshop at the Berkshire Music Center, in Lenox, Massachusetts; for a score of years, directed operatic fare at the Berkshire Music Festival that was innovative, daring in its scope, and often provocative; presented the first American productions of Mozart's *Idomeneo* and Benjamin Britten's *Peter Grimes* and *Albert Herring*; had a revolutionary approach to opera, the aim of which was simply to give the audience a good show—a theatrical experience they could understand and enjoy "as they would television or movies"; to that end, presented the operas in English; in 1946 founded the Goldovsky Institute (originally called the New England Opera Theater), where he offered Bostonians quality opera at reasonable prices; without neglecting the warhorses, continued in his theatrical venturesomeness in staging such operas as Berlioz's *The Trojans* (which is rarely produced because of its length and complexities), which he modified and presented in 1955; further demonstrated his willingness to take risks by means of the Goldovsky Grand Opera, the touring contingent of his Boston company; as a pianist, toured the U.S. giving concerts and recitals as a soloist or with his mother or other relatives; wrote *Bringing Opera to Life* (1968) and *My Road to Opera* (1979), among other books; died in Brookline, Massachusetts. See *Current Biography* (December) 1966.

Obituary *New York Times* p41 Feb. 18, 2001

GONZALEZ, HENRY May 3, 1916–Nov. 28, 2000 The first Latino from Texas to serve in the U.S. Congress; a first-generation Mexican-American who, as a crusading Democratic representative from the greater San Antonio area for 37 years, lost not an iota of his hero status with his constituency while establishing in Washington a reputation for obstinate honesty and independence, even to the point of estrangement from the Congressional Hispanic Caucus; a champion of the downtrodden and foe of government abuse; early in his career in San Antonio, was, successively, chief probation officer and deputy director of family relocation during slum clearance; as a city councilman in the mid-1950s, won passage of an ordinance desegregating city facilities; as a state senator in the late 1950s, successfully filibustered against a set of bills designed to keep public schools racially segregated; headed the Viva Kennedy Committee in John F. Kennedy's campaign for the presidency in 1960; was first elected to Congress from Texas's 20th Congressional District (which at that time comprised all of Bexar County) to finish the unexpired term of Paul J. Kilday in 1961; was elected to the first of his 18 full two-year terms in 1962; in Congress, was a stalwart of the Kennedy and Johnson administrations; drafted a bill to end poll taxes (which discriminated against the poor and minorities), which became part of the Civil Rights Act of 1965; in 1977 was assigned to chair a House select committee investigating the assassinations of President Kennedy and Martin Luther King Jr.; left the committee in shambles when he walked out, charging that organized criminal elements had succeeded in undermining the investigation; over the next several years, repeatedly charged that members of organized crime had been involved in the murder of Judge John W. Wood in San Antonio; felt vindicated when, in 1982, five men were indicted for the murder; as chairman of a subcommittee on housing of the House Committee on Banking, Finance, and Urban Affairs, beginning in 1981, fought ferociously for more federal low-income housing programs at a time when the Reagan administration was dismantling housing programs already in place; as chairman of the Banking Committee, conducted an investigation into the collapse of a number of savings and loan associations, especially in the Southwest, after real-estate values plummeted and many borrowers defaulted; exposed the fraud and lax regulation that contributed to the scandal; oversaw the drafting of a comprehensive savings-and-loan bailout law, which included a tightening of lending, accounting, and regulating procedures; also exposed the case of the so-called Keating Five (involving Charles H. Keating Jr., a savings-and-loan executive accused of attempting to buy influence on Capitol Hill, and five U.S. senators accused of improperly using their influence with regulators on Keating's behalf), a case subsequently investigated by the Senate Ethics Committee; introduced resolutions of impeachment against President Ronald Reagan twice, in 1983 for the invasion of Grenada and in 1987 for the Iran-Contra affair; in 1991, introduced an impeachment resolution against President George Bush for Bush's initiation of the Persian Gulf War against Iraq over the fate of Kuwait without seeking a declaration of war from Congress and for having helped Iraq build up its arsenal on the very eve of the war; won passage of the Affordable Housing Act in 1990; served in Congress through 1998, when his son Charlie won the campaign to succeed him in the San Antonio seat; died in San Antonio. See *Current Biography* (February) 1993.

Obituary *New York Times* A p33 Nov. 29, 2000

GORDON, CYRUS H. June 29, 1908–Mar. 30, 2001 Orientalist; university professor; in his study of ancient languages, dramatically challenged the conventional wisdom in biblical and classical scholarship by asserting that the Greek and Hebrew civilizations had a common origin in the Semitic culture of the Minoan era; as an undergraduate at the University of Pennsylvania, majored in Hebrew and minored in Greek; for his doctorate in Semitics at Pennsylvania, wrote the thesis published as Rabbinic Exegesis in the Vulgate of Proverbs (1930); did archaeological research in Palestine, Iraq, Egypt, Crete, and elsewhere in the Near East from 1931 to 1935; over the following seven years, served, successively, on the faculties of Johns Hopkins University, Smith College, and the Institute for Advanced Study, in Princeton, New Jersey; was a U.S. Army Signal Corps technical adviser in Arab countries during World War II; was professor of Assyriology and Egyptology at Dropsie College, in Philadelphia, from 1946 to 1956; in 1940 published *Ugaritic Grammar* (1940), the first of the several books establishing his reputation as an authority on Ugaritic, one of the members of the Semitic family of languages, dating to ancient coastal Syria; subsequently published, among other books, *Lands of the Cross and Crescent* (1948), *Introduction to Old Testament Times* (1953), and *Adventures in the Nearest East* (1957); as early as 1931, believed that "solving the inscriptions of Minoan Crete" was the most important problem facing orientalists; spent three decades tracking down linguistic evidence to support his hypothesis of a common origin of the Greek and Hebrew heroic ages; clinched his theory in 1961, when he was able to pinpoint the Minoan language of the early Cretans as Northwest Semitic or, broadly speaking, Phoenician, a Semitic language similar to the Akkadian tongue that had been his "working hypothesis" for several years; first published his decipherment of Eteocretan (pure Cretan) tomb inscriptions and Minoan pictographs and syllabic signs in the Journal of Near Eastern Studies in 1962; presented a comprehensive exposition of his linguistic findings in the book *Before the Bible: The Common Background of Greek and Hebrew Civilizations* (1963); was professor of Near Eastern Studies at Brandeis University from 1956 to 1973; chaired the Department of Mediterranean Studies at Brandeis from 1958 to 1973; was professor of Hebrew studies at New York University from 1973 to 1989; wrote the autobiography *A Scholar's Odyssey* (2000); died at his home in Brookline, Massachusetts. See *Current Biography* (May) 1963.

Obituary *New York Times* B p6 Apr. 9, 2001

GOTTLIEB, MELVIN B. May 25, 1917–Dec. 1, 2000 Plasma physicist; a preeminent figure in the effort to find in fusion a cleaner alternative to fission in the controlled generation of thermonuclear energy for peaceful purposes; as director (1961–80) of the Plasma Physics Laboratory at Princeton University, was responsible for the building of the Tokamak Fusion Test Reactor (TFTR), which reached an annual production rate of 11 megawatts of fusion energy—a record, but still not enough for cost-effectiveness and commercial feasibility; earned a B.S. degree in mathematics and a doctorate in physics at the University of Chicago, where he did research in cosmic-ray physics in the late 1940s; in 1950 became an assistant professor at Iowa State University; there, during the early 1950s, worked with the astronomer James A. Van Allen, using rocket-launched ion chambers to study nuclear interactions of high-energy particles at high altitudes; in 1954, joined the staff of the Plasma Physics Laboratory at Princeton University as a research associate on Matterhorn, a then-secret fusion research-and-development project funded for the most part by the U.S. Atomic Energy Commission; after the project was declassified, in 1958, traveled

to the Soviet Union to begin sharing information with scientists there; during his early years as director of the laboratory, in the 1960s, oversaw experiments in generating energy by forcing the collision and fusion of atomic nuclei in hot electrified gases (plasmas) in a vessel invented by Lyman Spitzer Jr.; in 1969, learned of the Soviet invention of a superior "magnetic bottle" for controlled fusion, called the tokamak; after verifying the effectiveness of the new reactor, initiated a program at Princeton that culminated in the construction (1977–82) of the TFTR, which, after 15 years of operation, was shut down for budgetary reasons, in 1997; died in Haverford, Pennsylvania. See *Current Biography* (January) 1974.

Obituary *New York Times* B p12 Dec. 14, 2000

GRAHAM, KATHARINE June 16, 1917–July 17, 2001 Newspaper executive; former publisher of the *Washington Post*; former chair and chief executive officer of the Washington Post Co., which owns, in addition to the *Post*, *Newsweek* magazine, and several television stations, and co-owns the International *Herald Tribune* with the *New York Times*; with Benjamin C. Bradlee, the editor she chose to manage the *Post*'s newsroom during her tenure, guided the paper in the 1970s to a stature comparable to that of the *New York Times*, previously unrivaled as America's national newspaper of record; helped the *Post* accomplish this through its daring publication of the Pentagon Papers (classified documents revealing the history of U.S. government policy in Vietnam) and its singular cracking of the Watergate scandal (culminating in the resignation of President Richard M. Nixon), as well as its successful emergence from a bitter conflict with the printers' and pressmen's unions over the issue of automation; on the business side, with the help of the investor Warren Buffet, led the Post Co. into the ranks of the Fortune 500; was a daughter of Eugene Meyer, a banker, who bought the *Washington Post* in 1933; after earning a B.A. degree at the University of Chicago and working briefly as a reporter for the San Francisco *News*, joined the *Post*'s staff as a handler of letters to the editor in 1939; was employed in the editorial and circulation departments of the newspaper's Sunday edition from 1939 to 1945; in 1940, married Philip L. Graham, who became publisher of the *Post* in 1946 and president of the Washington Post Co. in 1948; following the suicide of her husband, in 1963, succeeded to the presidency of the Post Co.; later became publisher of the *Post* as well; turned over the position of publisher to her son Donald in 1979; stepped down as CEO in 1991 and as chair in 1993; spent 10 years writing (in longhand on legal pads) her autobiography, *Personal History* (1997), which won the Pulitzer Prize for biography; died in Boise, Idaho. See *Current Biography* (January) 1971.

Obituary *New York Times* A p1+ July 18, 2001

GRAVES, MORRIS Aug. 28, 1910–May 5, 2001 Artist; the last of a group of four regional painters (including Mark Tobey, Guy Anderson, and Kenneth Callahan) known as the "Northwest Mystics," who combined belief in Zen Buddhism and other transcendental philosophies with gentle appreciation for the natural world; working as a seaman after dropping out of high school, visited Japan and China twice; painted his early oils in a rough, bold style, with heavy impasto, and employed a rich, dark color scheme; for his first major work, *Moor Swan*, won the first purchase prize at the Seattle Art Museum's Annual in 1933; at the same museum, had his first one-man show in 1936; in that same year, joined the WPA's (Works Projects Administration) Federal Arts Project in Seattle; influenced by Mark Tobey and his use of Chinese brush painting and calligraphy in semiautomatic "white writing," turned from oil to tempera and gouache, applied in delicate washes and subtle tonal harmonies to thin Chinese paper, as in *Bird Singing in the Moonlight* (1939), *Blind Bird* (1940), and *Little-Known Bird of the Inner Eye* (1941); during a sojourn in Puerto Rico in 1938 and 1939, painted his "Purification" series of nine temperas of amorphous rocks in which the image of a chalice figured prominently; had 31 of his works included in the *Americans 1942* exhibition at the Museum of Modern Art in New York City; in 1943, painted *Young Rabbit and Fox Fire*, among other monochromatic temperas; over the following several years, executed his *Joyous Pines* series and *Wounded Birds* series, along with seven kakemonos, paintings mounted on vertical scrolls in the Oriental tradition; in the early 1950s, returned to oil in such large canvases as *Ecstatic Gander* while continuing also to work in tempera and with ink on Chinese paper; lived in Ireland from 1954 to 1956; in 1964, settled near the town of Loleta in northern California, where he bought 25 acres of old-growth redwood forest and created Japanese-style gardens; subsequently turned from his emotional (albeit mutedly so) images of small animals and birds toward softly lighted depictions of flowers, vegetables, Chinese ritual bowls, and other still lifes; died at his home near Loleta. See *Current Biography* (July) 1956.

Obituary *New York Times* B p9 May 8, 2001

GRECO, JOSÉ Dec. 23, 1918–Dec. 31, 2000 Dancer; choreographer; a leading exponent of the Spanish dance; was born in Italy to an Italian father and a Spanish mother; lived with his mother's relatives in Spain from 1926 to 1928, when his father, who was by then in the U.S., sent for his family; attended public elementary schools in Brooklyn, New York; after dropping out of high school, studied art before deciding to pursue a career in Spanish dancing; following two years of training, made his first professional appearance in the incidental dances for *Carmen* in a 1937 production of the opera by the New York Hippodrome Opera Company; beginning in 1942 toured the U.S. with the celebrated Spanish dance stylist La Argentinita and her ensemble with productions that included ballets by Ravel and de Falla; following La Argentinita's death, in September 1945, went to Spain and danced there with, and did choreography for, the company of La Argentinita's sister, Pilar López; while in Spain, in 1948, was the choreographer of, and principal dancer in, a 10-minute dance sequence for *Manolete*, a motion picture about bullfighters; organized his own troupe, which gave its first public performance in Barcelona in January 1949 and subsequently toured Europe for more than two years; on Broadway in October 1951, launched

an American tour in which he and his Spanish Ballet (consisting of 20 dancers, a small orchestra, several instrumental soloists, and a singer) performed Spanish ballets and dances of classic, folk, flamenco, and modern derivation; at that time, was observed by the dance critic John Martin to have "brilliant" footwork, "elegance" of movement, and a style "more of silk . . . than of steel"; over the following years, became known to a wider audience through frequent appearances on popular network television variety shows as well as tours; with his company, performed in the motion pictures *Around the World in 80 Days* (1956) and *Ship of Fools* (1965); officially retired as a performer in 1974, but later performed on stage with his children numerous times; saw his choreography (including *El Cortijo*, in which zapateados, or heel work, suggested the galloping rhythm of horse hoofs) carried forward in performances by his son José Greco II's troupe; died at his home in Lancaster, Pennsylvania. See *Current Biography* (March) 1952.

Obituary *New York Times* B p8 Jan. 4, 2001

GUERARD, ALBERT J. Nov. 2, 1914–Nov. 9, 2000 Novelist; critical essayist; professor emeritus of literature at Stanford University; wrote complex experimental novels in which psychosexual obsessions (especially oedipal) and political trauma are handled with inventive but controlled fantasy; was the son of Albert L. Guerard, a professor of general literature at Stanford and an authority on French literature and history; began teaching English at Harvard University in 1938; as a technical sergeant in the U.S. Army's psychological warfare branch during World War II, worked closely with the French underground; in the years following his return to Harvard, advanced to a full professorship; moved to Stanford University in 1961; at Stanford, was Albert L. Guerard professor of literature from 1965 to 1985; described the delicate, differing relationships between a boy and his mother and father in his first novel, *The Past Must Alter* (1937); in his second, *The Hunted* (1944), explored the psyche of a waitress unhappily married to a neurotic college English professor in a small New England town; in his third, *Maquisard: A Christmas Tale* (1945), left readers with a warm record of comradeship in the French underground at the time of the Battle of the Bulge; in his most ambitious novel, *Night Journey* (1950), a work compared by many to George Orwell's *1984*, presented a surreal and frightening view of the postwar, Cold War world; in that novel, internalized the destructive political and moral ambiguities of the undeclared American-Soviet war in the protagonist, Paul Haldan, and particularized them in the middle European city of his childhood that Haldan returns to, a place "disrupted by the two great powers and betrayed by both"; pursued the theme of "romantic love vitiated by immaturity and regression" in several novels, including *The Bystander* (1958) and *Christine/Annette* (1985), in each of which an innocent young man is erotically drawn to a mature actress (who, in *Christine/Annette*, turns out to be his mother); wrote a total of nine novels, including *The Exiles* (1963) and *The Hotel in the Jungle* (1996); in addition, wrote the book *Triumph of the Novel: Dickens, Dostoevsky, Faulkner* (1976), critical volumes on

Robert Bridges, Joseph Conrad, Thomas Hardy, and Andre Gide, and the memoir *The Touch of Time: Myth, Memory, and the Self* (1980); died at his home on the Stanford University campus in Palo Alto, California. See *Current Biography* (Yearbook) 1946.

Obituary *New York Times* A p17 Nov. 18, 2000

HALL, GUS Oct. 8, 1910–Oct. 13, 2000 General secretary of the Communist Party U.S.A.; was born in Minnesota to immigrant Finnish parents, who were Communists; became a member of the national committee of the Young Communist League as a teenager; trained at the Lenin Institute in Moscow from 1930 to 1933; after returning to the U.S., devoted himself to union organizing and labor agitation; in 1937, became a section organizer, his first salaried position in the Communist Party; after service with the U.S. Navy in World War II, became the party's general secretary in Ohio; was named national secretary (the number-two leadership position in the party) in 1950; meanwhile, in 1949, with several other party leaders, was found guilty in federal court of conspiring to teach and advocate the violent overthrow of the U.S. government in violation of the Alien Registration Act; when the conviction was upheld by the U.S. Supreme Court, in 1951, jumped bail; was captured in Mexico while attempting to flee to Moscow; was imprisoned for five and a half years, until 1957; promising to "Americanize" the party, succeeded Eugene Dennis as general secretary in 1959; in the early 1960s, disobeyed, and successfully challenged in the courts, the registration requirements of the Subversive Activities Control Act; was the Communist nominee for U.S. president in 1972, 1976, 1980, and 1984; lived in Yonkers, New York; died in Manhattan. See *Current Biography* (May) 1973.

Obituary *New York Times* B p11 Oct. 17, 2000

HANNA, WILLIAM July 14, 1910–Mar. 21, 2001 Animated-film producer; with his longtime partner, the writer and animator Joseph R. Barbera, was a prodigious creator of popular cartoon characters, including Tom and Jerry for the motion-picture screen and the Flintstones, Yogi Bear, Huckleberry Hound, and myriad others for television; began his career in the entertainment industry in a menial job with Pacific Art and Title, Leon Schlesinger's Hollywood cartoon production company; in 1930, joined the story department at Harmon-Ising Studios, the animation company that created the Looney Tunes and Merrie Melodies cartoon series; in 1937, left Harmon-Ising to become an animation director and idea man at MGM Studios in Culver City, California; during a score of years at MGM, worked side by side on cartoons with Barbera (who was responsible for the storyboards, while Hanna concentrated on the technical aspects of production); with Barbera, created the battling cartoon characters Tom (a bullying cat) and Jerry (a spunky mouse), the antagonists in 113 MGM animated shorts, 12 of which were nominated for Academy Awards and seven of which won Oscars; moved to television after co-founding Hanna-Barbera Productions, in 1957; in 1958, launched into national syndication the half-hour *Huckleberry Hound Show*, which became the first television car-

toon series to win an Emmy Award (the first of a total of eight garnered by Hanna-Barbera), in 1960; subsequently introduced the syndicated shows *Quick Draw McGraw* (1959–62) and Yogi Bear (1961–63); with the ABC network show *The Flintstones* (1960–66), a series set in the Stone Age, realized the first animated situation comedy to be broadcast in prime time; also on ABC, introduced *Top Cat* (1961– 62), another prime-time entry, and *The Jetsons* (the space-age counterpart of *The Flintstones*), which ran in the network's evening schedule for one season (1962–63) before moving to Saturday mornings, where it ran on a succession of networks for more than a decade; during the 1960s contributed to television's daytime roster a menagerie of anthropomorphic animals, including the protagonists of *Peter Potamus* (1963–67) and *Secret Squirrel* (1965–67); to meet increased demand beginning in the late 1960s, created a host of new programs and produced numerous spin-offs and specials of *The Flintstones* and other Hanna-Barbera classics; during the 1970s and 1980s, turned out some 100 cartoon and live-action series for Saturday morning consumption; died at his home in the North Hollywood section of Los Angeles, California. See *Current Biography* (July) 1983.

Obituary *New York Times* C p13 Mar. 22, 2001

HENDERSON, JOE Apr. 24, 1937–June 30, 2001 Jazz musician; an inventive tenor saxophonist with a lyrical, wailing blueslike style often compared to that of Stan Getz; was known as a "long-distance improviser"; as one of 15 siblings growing up in a musically oriented family in Lima, Ohio, played makeshift drums and the clarinet before turning to the saxophone; at 14, composed his first tune, "Recordame," which would later become a staple in his repertoire, along with "Inner Urge" and others of his compositions as well as covers of "Invitation," "Lush Life," and "Round Midnight," and other classics; studied music at Kentucky State University, in Frankfort, and Wayne State University, in Detroit; in Detroit, played nightclub gigs with such musicians as Donald Byrd and Sonny Stitt and briefly fronted his own band; in the U.S. Army (1960–62), toured military bases with a musical revue; after his discharge from the military, moved to New York City, where he became an associate and friend of the trumpeter Kenny Dorham, a talent scout for Blue Note Records; began recording on the Blue Note label, at first as a sideman on recordings of Dorham, Lee Morgan, and others and then, in the mid-1960s, in his own right, with the albums *Page One*, *Inner Urge*, and *In 'n' Out* (on which Dorham accompanied him); later recorded on the Milestone label the albums *The Kicker*, *Tetragon*, *Power to the People*, *Joe Henderson in Japan*, *Black Is the Color*, *The Elements*, *Black Miracle*, and *Black Narcissus*; during the 1960s, played under the leadership of Horace Silver, Miles Davis, and Herbie Hancock; in the late 1960s, co-led the hard-bop Jazz Communicators, the first of several collaborations with Freddie Hubbard, and performed and recorded with Paul Chambers, Jimmy Cobb, and Wynton Kelly; during the 1970s, played briefly with the popular mainstream jazz-rock group Blood, Sweat and Tears before teaming up with Chick Corea (one of his accompanists on the 1980 album *Mirror Mirror*); during the 1980s, recorded live at the Village Vanguard in Manhattan the two-volume *The State of the Tenor*; did not achieve due recognition until 1992, with the great critical and commercial success of his Verve album *Lush Life* (1992), a tribute to the music composed by Billy Strayhorn that brought him his first Grammy Award; followed that up with *So Near, So Far* (1993), an homage to Miles Davis, for which he won Grammys for best jazz instrumental album and best instrumental solo ("Miles Ahead"); breathed new life into old jazz standards on the album *The Standard Joe* (1992); saw *Joe Henderson: The Milestone Years*, a selection of his recordings from 1967 to 1976, released by Verve in 1994; on *Double Rainbow* (1995), paid homage to the music of Antonio Carlos Jobim; on some of his latter-day Verve recordings, was accompanied by such well-regarded young musicians as Christian McBride and Wynton Marsalis and was reunited with Herbie Hancock; died in San Francisco, California, where he had been living since 1972. See *Current Biography* (June) 1996.

Obituary *New York Times* A p15 July 3, 2001

HOOKER, JOHN LEE Aug. 22, 1917(?)–June 21, 2001 Legendary Mississippi Delta–born blues guitarist; singer; performed and recorded songs of his own making, in a percussive style uniquely his; created the boogie, a straight-from-the-soul brooding narrative song of woe, with ominous free-verse lyrics that he delivered with a deep growl, redolent with age-old hurt and heartbreak, to the prolonged one-chord sound of his guitar and a hypnotic chugging rhythm, accented by the relentless stomp of his right foot; viewed the blues positively, as a lift to the troubled spirit, "not a let-down"; was born into a family of cotton sharecroppers in Clarksdale, Mississippi; learned his guitar style from his stepfather; migrated northward when he was a teenager; in Cincinnati, worked with the Delta Big Four and other gospel groups; in Detroit in the 1940s, abandoned the acoustic guitar for an electric one; when performing on Hastings Street in Detroit in 1948, was discovered and signed to a contract by Saul and Jules Bihari of Modern Records; debuted on the Modern label with his song "Boogie Chillen," which quickly climbed to number one on the blues charts and sold a million copies; subsequently, recorded such Modern hits as "I'm in the Mood" (another million seller), "Crawlin' Kingsnake," and "Hobo Blues"; later recorded such well-known songs of his own as "Boom Boom," "Burnin' Hell," and "I'll Never Get Out of These Blues Alive"; between 1949 and 1953, using a variety of pseudonyms, cut scores of records on more than 20 other labels; after several years in the doldrums, recorded "Dimples" (1956), which became a major hit in the United Kingdom in 1958; when the folk movement gained momentum in the late 1950s and the 1960s, toned down the amplification on his electric guitar or, alternatively, played his acoustic guitar; attracted a new following among white music lovers, at the New Port Jazz Festival, on the college and coffeehouse circuits, and in tours of Europe; had an influence on rock music acknowledged by such musicians or groups as Eric Clapton, Pete Townshend, Bob Dylan, the Doors, Bruce Springsteen, ZZ

Top, the Rolling Stones, and Led Zeppelin; released a total number of LPs estimated at well over 100, including those comprising *John Lee Hooker: The Ultimate Collection 1948–1990* (1991); collaborated with Canned Heat on *Hooker N' Heat* (1987); struck international gold with the 1989 album *The Healer*, which included collaborations with Carlos Santana and Robert Cray, among others; for his duet with Bonnie Raitt for the cut "I'm in the Mood" from *The Healer*, received the first of his several Grammy Awards, in 1990; collaborated with the singer Van Morrison and the musician and producer Los Lobos for the album *Don't Look Back* (1997); was inducted into both the Blues Hall of Fame and the Rock and Roll Hall of Fame; in his last years, performed regularly at his club in San Francisco, the Boom Boom Room; was always nattily dressed, and often wore sunglasses; was married four times; died at his home in Los Altos, California. See *Current Biography* (November) 1992.

Obituary *New York Times* B p7 June 22, 2001

HORWICH, FRANCES July 16, 1908–July 25, 2001 Educator; a pioneer in television programming for preschool children; as host of her half-hour daily show, *Ding Dong School*, from 1952 to 1959, set the template for such successors as *Romper Room*, *Sesame Street*, and *Mr. Rogers' Neighborhood*; earned a Ph.D. degree at Northwestern University; began her career in education as a first-grade teacher in Evanston, Illinois, in 1929; over the following two decades, held such positions as supervisor of nursery schools in Chicago, director of kindergartens in Winnetka, Illinois, school principal, counselor of student teachers at one teachers' college, and dean of education at another; was a visiting professor of education at the University of North Carolina from 1947 to 1949, when she became professor of education at Roosevelt College (now Roosevelt University), in Chicago; introduced *Ding Dong School* on October 3, 1952 as a local show on WNBQ-TV, the NBC network's Chicago affiliate; took the show national two months later; in addition to hosting *Ding Dong School*, was the network's director of children's programming until 1959, when she and NBC parted ways; thereafter, hosted the program in syndication out of Los Angeles; on the show, spoke directly to her preschool viewers, read them stories, and led them in song and in exercises involving paper, scissors, paste, clay, finger paint, and other standard preschool materials; as props, had two animal puppets and three goldfish; enjoyed large sales of high-quality, affordable "Ding Dong School" brand supplies; died in Scottsdale, Arizona. See *Current Biography* (October) 1953.

Obituary *New York Times* B p9 July 26, 2001

HUNTER, KERMIT Oct. 3, 1910–Apr. 11, 2001 Playwright; composer; wrote historical plays for presentation in outdoor theaters; composed incidental music for those productions; was educated at the Juilliard School of Music and the University of North Carolina, where his mentor was Paul Green, widely regarded as the founder of the outdoor historical theater movement, a largely southern summertime art form; as his M.A. thesis at the University of North

Carolina, wrote *Unto These Hills* (1950), a dramatization of the "trail of tears" experienced by the Cherokee Indians who were forcibly moved from North Carolina to Oklahoma in the second quarter of the 19th century; in *Forever This Land* (1951), commissioned by the New Salem Lincoln League, dramatized Abraham Lincoln's growth to young manhood in New Salem, Illinois; told the story of Daniel Boone in *Horn in the West* (1952), commissioned by the Southern Appalachian Historical Association; dealt with the life of Father Eusebio Francisco Kino, the Jesuit missionary explorer of the Southwest, in *The Bell and the Plow* (1954), with Florida history in *Voices in the Wind* (1955), with John Sevier, the first governor of Tennessee, in *Chucky Jack* (1956), with President Woodrow Wilson in *The Eleventh Hour* (1956), and with St. Paul the Apostle in *Thy Kingdom Come* (1957), his eighth play; wrote a total of 42 plays, some of which are still presented annually in outdoor theaters in such places as Boone, North Carolina, and Beckley, West Virginia (where his *Honey in the Rock* has been performed since 1959); died in Dallas, Texas. See *Current Biography* (May) 1959.

Obituary *New York Times* C p17 Apr. 26, 2001

KAEL, PAULINE June 19, 1919–Sep. 3, 2001 Film critic; an irreverent, often rude, contrarian with a lively, hyperbolic yet conversational prose style who delighted in writing reviews of movies (the term she preferred) that were pointedly provocative as well as insightful and funny; during a 38-year career, most of it with the *New Yorker*, established herself, in the words of Louis Menand, as "the most brilliantly ad hoc critic of her time," the inventor of "the manner of appreciation" that "has become the standard manner of popular culture criticism in America"; "shaped American film criticism for generations to come and, more important, the national understanding of the movies," as David Remnick, the current editor of the *New Yorker,* has observed; considered herself, in her words, "a film critic the way somebody might write poetry, for fun or love"; was passionate in championing what she liked, especially when it challenged the initial critical consensus (for example, the motion pictures *Bonnie and Clyde* and *Last Tango in Paris*); could be stingingly acerbic in her put-downs (for example, judged *Rain Man* to be a "wet piece of kitsch" and *Dances with Wolves* to be a "nature-boy movie"; wrote of a celebrated actress, "She makes a career of seeming to overcome being miscast," and of a popular young male star, "His knowing that a camera is on him produces only fraudulence"); targeted the pompous, the pretentious, and the self-indulgent; studied philosophy at the University of California at Berkeley, without taking a degree; a late bloomer, was 35 years old when she wrote her first review (of *Limelight*, which she dismissed as "Slimelight"), published in the little San Francisco magazine *City Lights*; subsequently contributed to *Film Quarterly* and *Partisan Review*, among other publications, and broadcast her film criticism without pay on Berkeley's listener-supported radio station KPFA; from 1955 into the 1960s, managed (and wrote the program notes for) a two-screen art cinema in Berkeley; in 1965, with her young daughter, Gina, moved to the East Coast; began contributing to such mass circulation magazines as *Life* and *Mademoiselle*; was the regular film critic for *McCall's* (until she mocked *The Sound of Music)* in 1966 and the *New Republic* in 1967; began her association with the *New Yorker* in 1968; during the first 11 years of that association, published weekly reviews during the six autumn and winter months; was spelled by Penelope Gilliatt during the other six months; during a hiatus from the *New Yorker* in 1979 and early 1980, worked in Hollywood as a production executive for Warren Beatty and a consultant and scout for Paramount Pictures; upon her retirement, in March 1991, received a farewell "appreciation" from Tom Carson in *Entertainment Weekly*: "Since the days of James Agee—whom Kael surpassed—no other critic has ever had her brains, her humor, her enthusiasm, or her influence. . . . This woman . . . wrote like she took the world on for breakfast every morning. . . . She'd always seen culture as one way the world talked about itself. From the late '60s through the mid-'70s movies mattered more that way than they have since, and Kael was at her influential peak. . . . Single-handedly, Kael changed the way her readers thought about the movies, and pop, and how the shoddiness or electricity of art underpins everyone's life"; published her first collection of reviews, *I Lost It at the Movies*, in 1965, and her second, *Kiss Kiss Bang Bang* in 1968; in *Going Steady* (1970), included her essay "Trash, Art, and the Movies," in which she defined movies as "a tawdry corrupt art for a tawdry corrupt world" and explained: "Movies took their impetus not from the desiccated, imitation European high culture but from the peep show, the Wild West show, the music hall, the comic strip—from what was coarse and common"; published a total of 10 collections of her reviews and essays, including *Reeling* (1976), *When the Lights Go Down* (1980), *Hooked* (1989), and *Movie Love* (1984); won a National Book Award with *Deeper into Movies* (1973); brought together the best of her writings from 1961 to 1991 in the 1,250-page volume *For Keeps* (1964), of which Mark Harris wrote: "You can cherish *For Keeps* . . . as the evolution of an influential style of argumentative writing, and as a topography of American culture as seen through its most popular art. Or you can just enjoy the free-swinging wit of some of the smartest movie reviews ever written. . . . [Kael's] writing is sparked by the searching, intuitive connections she makes between movies and painting, literature, opera, theater, politics, and . . . sex"; deplored the decline in the quality of movies, an effect of the hegemony of television combined with the commercial deals "prearranged and anticipated" by movie producers, as she explained in her 1980 essay "Why Are Movies So Bad? Or, the Numbers"; died at her home in Great Barrington, Massachusetts. See *Current Biography* (March) 1974.

Obituary *New York Times* C p12 Sep. 4, 2001

KAINEN, JACOB Dec. 2, 1909–Mar. 19, 2001 Artist; painter; printmaker; print curator; one of the pioneers of color lithography as an art form; was depicted in Ad Reinhardt's famous newspaper cartoon "Tree of American Art" (1946) on the same branch as the painters Mark Rothko, Adolph Gottlieb, Morris Graces, and Loren MacIver; later, was sometimes associated with the branch of color-field painting known as the Washington color school; in reality, tended to be an artistic contrarian; with the Federal Arts Project in New York in the 1930s, made etchings and such lithographs as *Cafeteria* when most federally supported artists were painting murals; after moving to Washington, D.C., as a curator at the Smithsonian Institution, painted cityscapes in oils and made woodcuts of monumental figures when the trend in Washington color painting favored hard-edge abstract acrylics; when figuration made a comeback among younger painters from 1969 through the 1970s, began creating serene geometric abstractions in oil, such as *Escape Artist* and *Elisa*, albeit with figurative implications, as if, as one critic observed, the abstractions were somehow "inhabited"; in the 1980s created larger canvases with geometric or biomorphic forms; in such paintings as those in his Dabronsky series, applied layer upon layer of paint; joined the Smithsonian's U.S. National Museum (now the National Museum of American History) as assistant curator of the division of graphic arts in 1944 and became curator in 1946; was credited with building and organizing the museum's print collection virtually from scratch; retired from his post at the Smithsonian after three decades of service; subsequently, worked part-time as curator at the National Collection of Fine Arts, now known as the Smithsonian American Art Museum; earlier, had taught printmaking at the Washington Workshop Center for the Arts (1947–54); died at his home in Chevy Chase, Maryland. See *Current Biography* (February) 1987.

Obituary *New York Times* C p13 Mar. 23, 2001

KETCHAM, HANK Mar. 14, 1920–June 1, 2001 Cartoonist; creator of the popular comic strip *Dennis the Menace*, which chronicles the inadvertent but constant mischief wrought by a lovable little scamp, whose main victim is his grumpy neighbor Mr. Wilson; began his career in Hollywood in 1938 as an animator for Walter Lantz, the creator of the screen cartoon character Woody Woodpecker; subsequently worked for Walt Disney on the animated feature films *Fantasia* (1940), *Pinocchio* (1940), and *Bambi* (1942) as well as Donald Duck shorts; began contributing cartoons to the *Saturday Evening Post* and other popular magazines in 1942; enlisted his art in the promotional service of the U.S. Navy during World War II; in October 1950, was inspired by the antics of his first child, Dennis, then four and a half years old, to conceive his masterpiece cartoon character; in March 1951, launched *Dennis the Menace* as a black-and-white comic strip in 15 daily newspapers served by the Post Hall Syndicate; expanded into full color in the Sunday funny pages in January 1952; by May 1953, was reaching an estimated 30 million readers of 193 newspapers in the U.S. and 52 abroad; ultimately, was syndicated to approximately 1,000 newspapers in 19 languages in 48 countries; turned over to younger hands (Marcus Hamilton and Ronald Ferdinand) the drawing of the Sunday panels in the mid-1980s and the dailies in 1994; oversaw Hamilton and Ferdinand's work by fax, while otherwise devoting himself to painting oils and watercolors of such subjects as golf scenes and portraits of women,

other cartoonists, and jazz musicians; published several collections of his comic strips; saw his major creation spun off into a motion picture, a television show, and a stage musical; wrote an autobiography, *The Merchant of Dennis the Menace* (1990); died at his home in Carmel, California. See *Current Biography* (January) 1956.

Obituary *New York Times* B p7 June 2, 2001

KLAUS, JOSEF Aug. 15, 1910–July 26, 2001 Former chancellor of the Republic of Austria (1964–70); a leader of the right-of-center People's Party; after obtaining a doctorate in law, in 1934, worked in various positions in law, business, and public service; was provincial governor of Salzburg from 1949 to 1961; was minister of finance in the cabinet of Chancellor Alfons Gorbach from April 1961 to November 1962; as chancellor from 1964 to 1966, headed a People's Party–Social Democrat coalition government; from 1966 to 1970, headed Austria's first post-war single-party government; after leaving office, retired from politics; was seldom seen at public events during the long subsequent period of Socialist dominance; died in Vienna. See *Current Biography* (January) 1965.

Obituary *New York Times* C p15 July 28, 2001

KONER, PAULINE 1912–Feb. 8, 2001 Dancer; choreographer; a widely eclectic stylist, New York–based but internationally influenced, who eluded simple "modern dance" categorization; was especially noted for fiery solos in both her choreography and her performances; when she was 13 and 14, received a thorough training in classical ballet under Michel Fokine, who remarked, "In her, the soul dances"; subsequently, studied Spanish dance with Angel Cansino; at 16, learned Asian dance from Michio Ito; in 1930, gave dance recitals with Yeichi Nimura; gave her first solo performance at the Guild Theater (which would become the ANTA) in December 1930; performed in Prokofiev's ballet *Angel of Steel* at the Metropolitan Opera House in 1931; in the same year, signed with Columbia Concerts for a series of solo performances that took her across the U.S.; in the early and middle 1930s, studied the history and development of Egyptian dance in Cairo, gave recitals in Palestine and elsewhere in the Near East, and made approximately 100 concert appearances in various parts of the Soviet Union; in the late 1930s and early 1940s, staged and performed dances at the Roxy Theater; with Kitty Doner, choreographed for the *Holiday on Ice* revue; for a pioneering CBS television program in 1945–46, choreographed and danced 10 ballets; for almost 15 years (1946–60), was a leading guest artist with the José Limón Dance Company, of which Doris Humphrey was artistic director until her death in 1958; under Humphrey's guidance, emerged as a dancer of recognized genius; with the Limón company, created a number of memorable roles in such productions as *La Malinche*, *The Moor's Pavanne*, *There Is a Time*, and *Ruins and Visions*; at the American Dance Festival in New London, Connecticut, in 1953, danced Cassandra, choreographed by herself to music by Aaron Copland and John Butler; during her association with the Limón company, established her own company, the

Pauline Koner Dance Company, in 1949; for her troupe, created such works as *The Visit, Amorous Adventure,* and *The Shining Dark* (her homage to Helen Keller); in 1962 danced the premiere of *The Last Farewell,* her tribute to Doris Humphrey, a brilliant fusion of motion and emotion, set to music by Gustav Mahler; from 1976 to 1982, headed the Pauline Koner Dance Consort; wrote the autobiography *Solitary Song* (1989); died at her home in Manhattan. See *Current Biography* (October) 1964.

Obituary *New York Times* C p11 Feb. 9, 2001

KRAMER, STANLEY Sep. 29, 1913–Feb. 19, 2001 Motion-picture producer and director; as a pioneer independent filmmaker in the late 1940s and the 1950s, helped Hollywood break away from the formulaic thinking of the old studios and renew its vitality; also demonstrated that quality films could be made economically; throughout a career spanning more than three decades, tried to make "strong" films that were also "exciting"; often addressed liberal social concerns—including racial inequality, juvenile delinquency, and the threat of nuclear holocaust— without sacrificing dramatic form or clear narrative trajectory; arrived in Hollywood as an aspiring writer in 1933; subsequently worked at various studios as a back-lot laborer, set dresser, researcher, and film cutter and editor as well as staff writer, before becoming an associate producer; made training films with the U.S. Army Signal Corps during World War II; after the war, in collaboration with others, independently produced several low-budget films, beginning with the quirky comedy *So This Is New York* (1948) and including the prestigious "message" movies *Champion* (1949), *Home of the Brave* (1949), and *The Men* (1950); in 1951 brought the Stanley Kramer Co. as an autonomous unit under the aegis of Columbia Pictures; at Columbia, produced on relatively frugal budgets such films as *Death of a Salesman* (1951), *High Noon* (nominated for the Oscar for best picture of 1952), *Member of the Wedding* (1952), *The Wild One* (1954), and *The Caine Mutiny* (nominated for best picture, 1954); formed the Stanley Kramer Pictures Corp. in 1954; was credited as director for the first time with the release of *Not As a Stranger* (1955), which he also produced, as he would all of his subsequent directorial efforts; as both producer and director, was nominated for Academy Awards for *The Defiant Ones* (1954), *Judgment at Nuremberg* (1958), and *Guess Who's Coming to Dinner* (1967); drew another Academy Award nomination with *Ship of Fools* (for best picture, 1965); in 1961 received a special Oscar, the Irving Thalberg Award, for "consistently high quality in filmmaking"; in a change of pace from his heavily serious output, produced and directed the star-studded slapstick comedy *It's a Mad, Mad, Mad, Mad World* (1963); in the 1950s, while serving in a way as a still-working voice in cinema for those silenced by the "blacklist" of that era, was criticized by some radical leftists for being too oblique in his political statements; was sometimes faulted by others for what they perceived to be lapses into didacticism and sentimentality; later conceded, in retrospect, that he sometimes "oversimplified" issues, particularly racism; in the 1960s, distanced himself from insurgent directors whom he viewed as deceptive exploiters of technique—"the nouvelle vague, the neo-realists, and the angry young men [who] have opened the gates to interrupted dialogue, mismatching, jump cuts, . . . split screens, and the camera as primary weapons in the director's bag"; as producer or producer/director, made a total of 35 films, including *Cyrano de Bergerac* (1950), *The Sniper* (1952), *The Four Poster* (1952), *The Juggler* (1953), *On the Beach* (1959), *Inherit the Wind* (1960), *R.P.M.* (1970), *The Domino Principle* (1977), and his last, *The Runner Stumbles* (1979); died in the Woodland Hills section of Los Angeles. See *Current Biography* (May) 1951.

Obituary *New York Times* A p1+ Feb. 21, 2001

LACY, DAN Feb. 28, 1914–Apr. 17, 2001 Librarian; publishing executive; expert on copyright law; served on the National Advisory Commission on Libraries and Information under President Lyndon B. Johnson and on the National Commission on New Technological Uses of Copyrighted Works under President Gerald R. Ford; began his career as a teaching fellow and then instructor in history at the University of North Carolina; in 1936, left his teaching post to join the federal WPA's (Works Projects Administration) Historical Record Survey, in which he rose to the position of assistant national director; in the early 1940s, was director of operations of the National Archives; in 1947, joined the staff of the Library of Congress, where he rose to the position of deputy chief assistant librarian; directed the U.S. State Department's overseas library and book activities from 1951 to 1953, when he became managing director of the American Book Publishers Council; in 1965 joined the McGraw-Hill Book Co. as senior vice president; subsequently served as senior vice president and executive assistant to the president of McGraw-Hill; after retiring from McGraw-Hill, served as vice president and director of the Business Council for Effective Literacy; died in Durham, North Carolina. See *Current Biography* (November) 1954.

Obituary *New York Times* p46 Apr. 29, 2001

LAPIDUS, MORRIS Nov. 25, 1902–Jan. 18, 2001 Russian-born architect; interior designer; an unorthodox and flamboyant virtuoso showman of his craft; an architectural postmodernist well ahead of his time; after an early grounding in the imaginative design of attractive retail shops, devoted himself to the creation of sensuously lavish, fun-indulgent "livingspace," most prominently in the form of swank resort hotels in south Florida, including the mock-French Fontainebleau, which he unabashedly acknowledged to be "the world's most pretentious hotel"; in the mid-20th century, against the tide of Bauhaus modernism (with its functional austerity and bare, angular, boxlike structures), introduced opulent and curvaceous designs, free of corners, with sweeping lines, splashes of color, and unusual use of light and new materials; was for many years dismissed by the architectural establishment as a renegade perpetrator of vulgar, glitzy "palaces of kitsch," but lived to see his dramatic innovations become staples of American design, most conspicuous perhaps in the architecture of today's Las Vegas; self-effacingly, thought of himself as "just an architect who happened to be carried away by his emotions"; confessed that he "never outgrew" the "emotional surge" he experienced when, as an immigrant boy of six, he first saw the nighttime illumination of Luna Park, the Coney Island amusement park; originally aspired to a career in art or theater, perhaps as a stage designer; after earning a degree in architecture at Columbia University on the eve of the Depression, found employment with a succession of architectural firms; in 1930, became the architect with the contracting firm Ross-Frankel, which became Ross-Frankel, Morris Lapidus Associates; during some 13 years with that firm and afterwards as head of his own office, designed and supervised the construction of more than 500 shops, storefronts, and showrooms for retail chains; became known for his experimental use of combinations of metals, glass, plastics, and fabrics in retail-space decoration; during World War II, joined his father and brothers at the family-owned company U.S. Metal Products, which designed and manufactured the signaling searchlight that was used for all landings in the European and Pacific theaters of operation; in 1949, was commissioned to design the interior of the Miami Beach resort hotel the Sans Souci; on the strength of that stunning overstatement in decor, earned commissions as associate architect of several other Miami Beach hotels; realized his first design of a whole hotel with the 14-story, 560-room Fontainbleau, completed in 1956; with that Miami Beach landmark, established such of his signature features as a whiplash-shaped façade and an opulent lobby leading the visitor to the vista of a multilevel, multicolored interior traversed by the swath of a flyaway "staircase to nowhere"; subsequently designed the faux-Italian Eden Roc, also in Miami Beach; just to the north, in Bal Harbour, borrowed a variety of motifs from the countries comprising the Americas in designing the Americana (later renamed the Sheraton Bal Harbour), completed in 1956 at a cost of $17 million; provided that building's Aztec-inspired lobby with a gigantic terrarium that he stocked with live alligators; also designed resort hotels in New Jersey, New York, and several foreign locations; in the 1960s, designed four non-resort hotels in New York City: the $25 million, 21-story, 800-room Summit (later renamed the Loews New York and soon to be renamed the Metropolitan), the Sheraton Center, Howard Johnson's Motor Lodge, and Loew's Motor Inn; also in New York, designed or contributed to the design of the Edgerton (in Queens), Fairfield Towers (in Brooklyn), Presidential Towers (in Manhattan), Trump Village, and Cadmon Plaza apartments; in Washington, D.C., designed two non-resort hotels, two urban redevelopment projects, and a large office building; between 1943 (when he became an independent architect) and 1984 (when he retired), designed hundreds of buildings, including several synagogues, some 200 hotels, and more than 100 condominiums, most of them in Florida; wrote the autobiography *Too Much Is Never Enough* (1994); died at his home in Miami Beach, an apartment in one of the high-rise buildings he designed. See *Current Biography* (April) 1966.

Obituary *New York Times* C p11 Jan. 19, 2001

LARDNER, RING JR. Aug. 19, 1915–Oct. 31, 2000 Screenwriter; the last surviving member of the "Hollywood 10," the group of motion-picture writers, directors, and producers who refused to answer questions about their political affiliations put to them by the House Un-American Activities Committee (HUAC) in 1947 and who were subsequently imprisoned for contempt of Congress and blacklisted; was a son of Ring Lardner Sr., the celebrated sports writer, short-story writer, and humorist; in the summer of 1934, following his sophomore (and last) year at Princeton University, traveled to the Soviet Union and attended the University of Moscow's Anglo-American Institute; after his return to the U.S., worked as a reporter for the New York *Daily Mirror* for 10 months; in 1935, began his Hollywood career in the public-relations department of Selznick International Pictures; in 1937, was assigned some work as a script doctor by Selznick; subsequently sought more regular screenwriting assignments at other studios; realized his first on-screen credits as co-writer of the films *Meet Dr. Christian* (1939) and *The Courageous Dr. Christian* (1940); shared an Academy Award with Michael Kanin for the story and scenario for *Woman of the Year* (1942); collaborated on the screenplays for *The Cross of Lorraine* (1944), again with Kanin, *Tomorow the World* (1944), with Leopold Atlas, *Cloak and Dagger* (1946), with Albert Maltz, and *Forever Amber* (1947), with Philip Dunne; meanwhile, had joined the Hollywood cell of the Communist Party U.S.A. soon after his arrival in the movie capital; for his refusal to cooperate with HUAC, was sentenced to a year in prison; thereafter, had to work underground for more than a decade; without credit, re-wrote the dialogue for *Four Days Leave* (1950) and co-wrote the scenarios for *The Big Night* (1951), *A Breath of Scandal* (1960), and *The Cardinal* (1963); co-wrote the screenplay for *Virgin Island* (1959) under a pseudonym; in the late 1950s and early 1960s, co-wrote several television series, including the British-produced *The Adventures of Robin Hood*; in 1965, emerged from anonymity on the silver screen as the credited co-writer (with Terry Southern) of *The Cincinnati Kid*; won his second Oscar for his screenplay for *M*A*S*H* (1970), an irreverent black comedy about a medical unit in the Korean War; in his last film effort, wrote the scenario for *The Greatest* (1977); displayed originality, wit, and a dazzling style in his first novel, *The Ecstasy of Owen Muir* (1955); combined science fiction with social satire in his second novel, *All for Love* (1985); wrote the family memoir *The Lardners* (1976); died at his home in Manhattan. See *Current Biography* (July) 1987.

Obituary *New York Times* C p23 Nov. 2, 2000

LE CLERCQ, TANAQUIL Oct. 2, 1929–Dec. 31, 2000 Ballerina; a svelte and long-limbed dancer who, in a brilliant, tragically abbreviated career, combined energy with elegance and dramatically projected pathos and comedy with equal luminosity; was, in the words of Lincoln Kirstein, "the epitome" of choreographer George Balanchine's modernized and "lyrically athletic American criterion"; entered Kirstein and Balanchine's School of American Ballet on a scholarship when she was 11; became a principal dancer with Ballet Society, which Balanchine and Kirstein founded in 1946 and which evolved two years later into the New York City Ballet, a company devoted, like its precursor, chiefly to new works; became identified with the roles Balanchine wrote for her in such ballets as *Triumph of Bacchus and Ariadne*, *Symphony in C*, *Bourrée Fantasque*, and *La Valse* (a neoromantic work, set to music by Ravel, in which the heroine feverishly dances herself to death); graduated to prima ballerina with the City Ballet when she replaced Maria Tallchief, Balanchine's fourth wife, in the leading role in *Swan Lake* in February 1952; the following December, became Balanchine's fifth wife; in 1954 created the role of the dance-hall girl in *Western Symphony*, which Balanchine set to cowboy music; with Ballet Society and the New York City Ballet, created a total of 32 roles, including the sensuous young woman in Jerome Robbins's *Afternoon of a Faun* and the comic heroine in Robbins's *The Concert*; performed in the premiere of the latter in 1956; within the same year, contracted polio, which left her permanently paralyzed from the waist down; later became a teacher at Dance Theater in Harlem; wrote two books; was divorced from Balanchine in 1969; died in Manhattan. See *Current Biography* (July) 1953.

Obituary *New York Times* B p7 Jan. 1, 2001

LEMMON, JACK Feb. 8, 1925–June 27, 2001 Actor; the silver screen's anxious urban Everyman next door; in a distinguished motion-picture career spanning half a century, explored the comic and tragic aspects of American life; was, in his words, "attracted to contemporary characters" because he understood "them and their frustrations"; deftly conveyed those frustrations in gestures and facial expressions, sometimes exaggerated, sometimes nuanced; a year after he arrived in Hollywood, found the template for his screen persona in his Academy Award–winning supporting role as Ensign Pulver in the shipboard comedy-drama *Mister Roberts* (1955)—a scheming, obsequious nice guy with a skewed but ultimately correct moral code; was directed by Billy Wilder in seven of his screen roles, beginning with that of a musician who, while fleeing the mob, disguises himself as a woman, in the outrageous farce *Some Like It Hot* (1959), and including that of the office worker currying favor by lending his apartment key to executives for extramarital trysts, in *The Apartment* (1960); turned in his first great tragic performance as the alcoholic husband of an alcoholic wife in *Days of Wine and Roses* (1962); as Harry Hinkle, co-starred in *The Fortune Cookie* (1966) with Walter Matthau, an inspired pairing that would be repeated in many films over three decades; had another happy collaboration with the playwright Neil Simon, several of whose neurotic protagonists he brought to life on the screen, including the obsessively fastidious Felix Ungar in *The Odd Couple* (1968); won the Academy Award for best actor for his portrayal of Harry Stoner, the desperate garment manufacturer who resorts to arson, in *Save the Tiger* (1973); was powerful in portrayals of quiet conformists who become radicalized when their illusions are shattered, such as the nuclear-plant manager Jack Godell in *The China Syndrome* (1979) and, in *Missing* (1982),

Ed Horman, the conservative American businessman who comes up against U.S. embassy stonewalling when searching for his son in a politically volatile Latin American country; gave a riveting performance as Shelley Levene, a pathetic, superannuated Willie Loman–like real-estate salesman, in *Glengarry Glen Ross* (1992); had a total of approximately 60 film credits, including roles in *Short Cuts* (1993), *Grumpy Old Men* (1993), *Grumpier Old Men* (1995), *The Grass Harp* (1995), and several made-for-TV movies; after graduating from Phillips Andover Academy and Harvard University and serving in the U.S. Navy, began his career on the Off-Broadway stage in 1947; in 1948, obtained a part on a radio soap opera; over the following five years, had roles in several hundred live television dramas, including episodes of a number of situation comedies that he produced with Cynthia Stone (the first of his two wives); made his Broadway debut as Leo Davis in a revival of *Room Service* in 1953; returned to Broadway as the idealistic lawyer in *The Face of a Hero* in 1960, as the dying press agent in *Tribute* in 1978, and as James Tyrone in a revival of *Long Day's Journey into Night* in 1986; died in Los Angeles, California. See *Current Biography* (August) 1988.

Obituary *New York Times* p1+ June 29, 2001

LEWIS, JOHN May 3, 1920–Mar. 29, 2001 Pianist; composer; arranger; conductor; created what Gunther Schuller, his mentor at the Manhattan College of Music, called "third stream music," an elegant fusion of classical counterpoint and polyphony (including fugues) with jazz and blues; as the driving force behind the sophisticated, tuxedo-clad Modern Jazz Quartet (originally composed of veterans of Dizzy Gillespie's bebop band), elevated a genre traditionally associated with jam sessions in smoky nightclubs to a concert-hall art form; to that unique ensemble's performing and recording repertoire, contributed such compositions as "Afternoon in Paris," "Two Degrees East, Three Degrees West," and "Django," his tribute to the legendary Belgian Gypsy jazz guitarist Django Reinhardt; began learning to play the piano and the violin when he was seven; studied anthropology as well as music at the University of New Mexico; while serving in the musical branch of the U.S. Army's Special Services in World War II, met the drummer Kenny Clarke, a bebop pioneer; after his discharge from the army, in 1945, moved to New York City, where Dizzy Gillespie was forming a big band with Clarke as his drummer; while studying classical theory, advanced orchestration, and composition at the Manhattan School of Music (where he would receive a master's degree in 1953), made such arrangements for Gillespie as "Two Bass Hit," "Emanon," "Stay on It," and "Minor Walk"; composed his first major work, Toccata for Trumpet and Orchestra, in 1947; after touring Europe with the Gillespie band, played with Illinois Jacquet's band for eight months in 1948 and 1949; subsequently recorded with Lester Young and Charlie Parker; worked as soloist and arranger on the influential chamber-jazz recordings that Miles Davis made for Capitol Records in 1949 and 1950; for Davis, did the arrangements for "Move," "Budo," and "Rogue"; later accompanied the singer Ella Fitzgerald on a national tour; joined with vibraphonist Milt Jackson, bassist Percy Heath, and Kenny Clarke (later replaced by Connie Kay) to form the Modern Jazz Quartet (first known as the Milt Jackson Quartet), which began recording in 1952 and giving public performances two years later; performed with the quartet until 1974, when it temporarily disbanded, and again from 1983 into the 1990s (with Percy Heath's younger brother Albert replacing the deceased Connie Kay in 1994); aside from the quartet, was musical director of the Monterey Jazz Festival (1958–82), a leader of the Orchestra U.S.A. (1962–65), and musical director of the American Jazz Orchestra (1985–92); was a founder of the Lenox (Massachusetts) School of Jazz; taught music at the Manhattan School of Music, Harvard University, and the City College of New York; in 1999 recorded a solo recital, *Evolution*, released, as most of the Modern Jazz Quartet's albums had been, on the Atlantic label; with the quartet, recorded his final album, *Evolution II* (2001); died at his home in Manhattan. See *Current Biography* (January) 1962.

Obituary *New York Times* B p9 Mar. 31, 2001

LINDBERGH, ANNE MORROW June 22, 1906–Feb. 7, 2001 Aviator; author; widow of the aviator Charles A. Lindbergh, celebrated as the "lone eagle" and the "last hero," who died in 1974; brought to her writings, including her autobiographical contributions to aeronautical history, the touch of "a poet, an artist," as the critic Lewis Gannett observed; produced a phenomenal best-seller in her book of philosophical meditations *Gift from the Sea*, the title of which was inspired by the "bare beauty" of seashells; was the daughter of Elizabeth Reeve Morrow, a poet and educator who served briefly as acting president of Smith College, and Dwight W. Morrow, a noted lawyer, banker, and diplomat; was in her junior year as an English major at Smith College when Charles A. Lindbergh made his historic flight from New York to Paris in May 1927; the following Christmas, met Lindbergh at the U.S. Embassy in Mexico City, where her father was ambassador; married Lindbergh in 1929; was co-pilot and navigator when she and her husband broke the transcontinental speed record in 1930; the following year, accompanied him on a pioneering survey flight to the Far East by way of the Arctic; in March 1932, suffered the kidnapping (from the nursery in their home in Hopewell, New Jersey) and murder of their 20-month-old son, Charles A. Lindbergh Jr., a crime for which Bruno Richard Hauptmann was convicted and executed; gave birth to a second son, Jon Morrow Lindbergh, in August 1932; later gave birth to two more sons and two daughters; with her husband, spent five and a half months surveying transatlantic air routes in 1933; left the U.S. in 1935, taking up residence first in England and later in France; returned to the U.S. in 1939; published her first book, *North to the Orient*, an account of her 1931 Arctic-Asia flight, in 1935; in *Listen the Wind* (1938), described 10 days of the 1933 transatlantic survey flights; in the controversial manifesto *The Wave of the Future* (1940), encouraged the isolationist sentiment dominant in the U.S. at the time, calling for "reform at home rather than crusade abroad"; in writing *The Steep Ascent*

(1944), a fictional story about a young couple's hazardous flight over the Alps, was inspired by an experience that had occurred during a flight by the Lindberghs to India in 1937; in the eight essays in *Gift from the Sea* (1955), reflected on such subjects as love and marriage, possessions, youth, and aging and underscored the necessity for a wife and mother occasionally to retreat from her busy life and find in solitude the refreshment vital for self-fulfillment; the following year, published *The Unicorn and Other Poems, 1935–1955*; subsequently published, among other books, volumes of excerpts from her diaries and letters spanning her life back to adolescence, including *Bring Me a Unicorn* (1972), *Hour of Gold, Hour of Lead* (1973), and *Locked Rooms and Open Doors* (1974); because of their differing personalities, derived from her complex marriage to Charles A. Lindbergh (who abhorred any display of emotion) some joy, but also experienced depression and, sometimes, rage; reportedly fell in love with at least two other men (including, early on, the French author and aviator Antoine de Saint-Exupéry), but resisted the temptation to leave her husband; died at her home in Passumpsic, Vermont. See *Current Biography* (June) 1976.

Obituary *New York Times* A p29 Feb. 8, 2001

LINDSAY, JOHN V. Nov. 24, 1921–Dec. 19, 2000 Former two-term mayor of New York City; former four-term U.S. congressman; lawyer; an ostensible political outsider who was adept at fashioning his own political power bases; to his first inauguration as mayor, on January 1, 1966, brought a handsome presence, a fresh and energetic spirit, and a patrician dedication to public service; attracted to City Hall a team of political neophytes (the likes of Leon Panetta, Sid Davidoff, Samuel R. ["Sandy"] Berger, and Ken Auletta) brimming with ideas for progressive municipal planning; was mayor of New York from 1966 to 1974, a period of tumultuous change marked by strikes and other disruptive job actions by teachers, transit workers, and other municipal unions, by a cyclical police corruption scandal, and by racial unrest, which he calmed with greater success than most other big-city mayors at that time; emerged with a divided reputation, generally positive with inner-city minorities, who benefitted from his administration's antipoverty and other high-budgeted social programs, and negative with middle- and working-class residents in the outer boroughs, who regarded him as an elitist "limousine liberal"; was charged by his critics with bequeathing to his successor in the mayor's office, Abraham Beame—through the combination of financial concessions to unions, a more than doubling of the city's welfare rolls, and the flight of the city's tax base to the suburbs—a severe fiscal crisis, resolved only by the de facto takeover of New York City's finances by New York State regulators in 1975; in 1958, running on the Republican ticket, was elected U.S. representative from New York's 17th ("Silk Stocking") Congressional District, which included the wealthy residential areas on Manhattan's Upper East Side; was reelected in 1960, 1962, and 1964; ran as a Republican in his first mayoral campaign and as a Liberal-Independent fusion candidate in his second;

switched his enrollment to the Democratic Party in 1971; unsuccessfully sought the Democratic nomination for U.S. president in 1972 and U.S. senator in 1980; wrote a novel, *The Edge* (1976), and two autobiographical volumes, *Journey into Politics* (1967) and *The City* (1969); was chairman of the Lincoln Center Theater from 1984 to 1991; practiced law (with two Manhattan firms, successively) until 1995; later was special counsel to the New York City Commission for the U.N.; died near his home on Hilton Head Island, South Carolina. See *Current Biography* (November) 1962.

Obituary *New York Times* A p1+ Dec. 21, 2000

LINK, O. WINSTON Dec. 16, 1914–Jan. 30, 2001 Photographer; recorded the last years of American steam railroading in dramatic photographs composed with an artist's eye, chiefly black-and-white pictures, typically of locomotives belching plumes of smoke into nighttime skies; in so doing, also documented a vanished era of American small-town life, relatively innocent in retrospect; became fascinated with pre-diesel railroad locomotives as a boy growing up in Brooklyn, New York; began familiarizing himself with the camera and the darkroom as a teenager; earned a degree in civil engineering at the Polytechnic Institute of Brooklyn; became a commercial photographer specializing in industrial subjects for such clients as New York City's Triboro Bridge and Tunnel Authority, the Ethyl Corp., Freeport Sulphur, Alcoa Aluminum, B. F. Goodrich, and Texaco; also carried out assignments for advertising agencies, newspapers, and fashion houses; in 1955, began to record on film the activities of the Norfolk & Western (N&W) Railway, a freight and passenger line, the last major American railroad to operate exclusively with steam power; to that task, brought an old-fashioned box camera on a tripod and a unique, complex synchronized flash system involving reflectors, miles of cable, and the equivalent of 300,000 60-watt light bulbs, which enabled him to capture, in the pitch black of night, striking images, with shining contrast and great depth of field; through elaborate preparation, achieved effects of seeming spontaneity; in the five and a half years ending in May 1960 (when the N&W's last steam engine was retired), took 2,400 photographs (including some shot in daylight and about 200 in color) of the railroad's 450 locomotives, its trainmen, and the waning culture of the people living in the towns along the road's 2,500-mile right-of-way through the Appalachian Mountains and the Shenandoah Valley; was unrecognized by the world of art until 1976, when the Museum of Modern Art in Manhattan became the first of several museums to buy some of his N&W pictures; following the appearance of an article about him in *American Photographer* magazine in 1982, began to exhibit his work, chiefly at the Manhattan gallery of Robert Mann; published two collections of the N&W photographs: *Steam, Steel & Stars* (1987) and *The Last Steam Railroad in America* (1995); was the subject of the British TV documentary *Trains That Passed in the Night* (1990); in August 2000, launched a traveling exhibition of 79 of his photographs, also titled *Trains That Passed in the Night*; was twice married and divorced; brought court action against his second wife, Conchita Mendoza Link, who in 1996 was convicted of stealing 1,400 of his photos, valued at an estimated $1.6 million, and sentenced to a prison term of six and a third to 20 years; lived in South Salem, New York; died in nearby Katonah, New York. See *Current Biography* (June) 1995.

Obituary *New York Times* C p13 Feb. 2, 2001

LONDON, JULIE Sep. 26, 1926–Oct. 18, 2000 Singer; actress; as a nightclub and supper-club singer, was widely perceived to be "sultry"; specialized in blues and torch songs, which she delivered in a small voice, breathy and intimate, best appreciated when amplified; was most closely identified with her recording of the lament "Cry Me a River" (written by Arthur Hamilton), which reached number 16 on the pop charts in 1955, becoming her sole million-selling single; began her Hollywood career in bit parts in the early 1940s; progressed to a supporting role in the melodrama *The Red House* (1947) and the female lead in the Western *Return of the Frontiersman* (1950), among other credits; in 1947 married the actor Jack Webb, by whom she had two daughters; withdrew from show business in 1950; after her divorce from Webb, in 1953, returned to her career despite sagging self-confidence; did so with the encouragement of the songwriter and jazz musician Bobby Troup (whom she would marry in 1959); included "Cry Me a River" on her popular album *Julie Is Her Name* (1956) and sang it in the film *The Girl Can't Help It* (1956); reached the peak of her film career with her starring performance as a beloved television singer whose dark side is revealed after her death, in the motion picture *The Great Man* (1956); between 1956 and 1961 was cast in some dozen screen roles, including those of a secret alcoholic in *Drango* (1957), a worldly dance-hall singer in *Man of the West* (1958), the wife of a sterile husband opposed to her wish for artificial insemination in *A Question of Adultery* (1958), and the suffering wife of an alcoholic in *Voice in the Mirror* (1958), for which she composed the title song; in appearances on network-television variety shows in the middle and late 1950s, sang or lip-synched her recorded songs; on the NBC network from 1972 to 1977, played the Los Angeles emergency-room nurse Dixie McCall (while Bobby Troup played Dr. Joe Early) in the weekly faux-documentary dramatic series *Emergency!*; had three children by Troup, who died in 1999; recorded more than 30 albums, including *In Person at the Americana* (1964) and the compilations *Julie's Golden Greats* (1963) and *The Best of Julie London* (1984); lived in California's San Fernando Valley; died at the Encino-Tarzana Regional Medical Center, northwest of central Los Angeles. See *Current Biography* (May) 1960.

Obituary *New York Times* C p20 Oct. 19, 2000

LUDLUM, ROBERT May 25, 1927–Mar. 12, 2001 Novelist; perhaps taking a cue, in part, from the blockbuster success of Ken Deighton's *The Ipcress File* (1962), became, beginning in 1971, a major progenitor of a genre of best-selling espionage thrillers that have been described as "pseudo-objective"; originally pursued a career in theater; began acting while in prep school; played Sterling Brown in *Jun-*

ior Miss on Broadway in 1943; was subsequently cast as Haskell Cummings in the national touring-company production of the same play; after service in the U.S. Marine Corps, majored in theater at Wesleyan University, where he received a B.A. degree in fine arts in 1951; during the 1950s accumulated a few acting credits in New York and summer stock and many on network television, chiefly in productions of the dramatic anthologies *Studio One, Kraft Television Theater, Danger, Suspense,* and *Robert Montgomery Presents;* in 1957 became producer at the North Jersey Playhouse in Fort Lee, New Jersey; in 1960, with his wife, Mary (Ryducha) Ludlum, founded the Playhouse-on-the-Mall in Paramus, New Jersey, a year-round legitimate theater that flourished throughout the 1960s; in 1971 published his first novel, *The Scarlatti Inheritance,* in which an American intelligence officer investigates an international conspiracy of businessmen and financiers who surreptitiously bankrolled the rise of Adolf Hitler in Germany and may continue to exert a nefarious influence in world affairs; in *The Osterman Weekend* (1972), began with the assumption of a Soviet plan to destroy the U.S. economy, a premise that was turned on its head in the ensuing labyrinthine plot; in *The Rhineman Exchange* (1974), set in the final days of World War II, imagined a top-secret exchange of military matériel between the Germans and the Allies; in the view of aficionados, achieved his masterwork with *The Gemini Contenders* (1976), a controversial novel about the origins of Christianity; through the last three decades of the 20th century, published on average one novel every year and a half; in one of his most popular series, created the protagonist Jason Bourne, an amnesiac spy hunted by assassins; died in Naples, Florida. See *Current Biography* (November) 1982.

Obituary *New York Times* B p9 Mar. 13, 2001

MAGLOIRE, PAUL E. July 19, 1907–July 12, 2001 Former president of Haiti; rose to power through the ranks of the military; became president following a military coup in 1950; six years later, was himself ousted by another military coup, which ushered in the brutal successive dictatorships of François "Papa Doc" Duvalier and Papa Doc's son, Jean-Claude ("Baby Doc"); lived in exile in the U.S. until Baby Doc was driven from power, in 1986; was an adviser to Lieutenant General Henry Namphy, who was president briefly in 1988; died in Port-au-Prince, Haiti; See *Current Biography* (February) 1952.

Obituary *New York* Times B p7 July 16, 2001

MASTERS, WILLIAM H. Dec. 17, 1915–Feb. 16, 2001 Physician; gynecologist; sex researcher; counselor; sexual-dysfunction therapist; founder of the Reproductive Biology Research Foundation and co-founder of the Masters and Johnson Institute; building on the earlier, secondhand work of Alfred Kinsey, devoted himself to direct, definitive laboratory studies of the physiology of sexual activity using scientific instruments; after taking his M.D. degree, in 1943, served internships and residencies in obstetrics and gynecology as well as internships in internal medicine and pathology at various hospitals in St. Louis; in 1947 joined the faculty of the Washington University School of Medicine, where he advanced over the years from instructor to associate professor of clinical obstetrics and gynecology; began his work in sexology in 1954; two years later hired the psychologist Virginia E. Johnson (who would become the second of his three wives) to assist him in interviewing and screening volunteers to be monitored while engaged in coitus and/or masturbation; over a period of 11 years, thus monitored 382 men and 312 women, using color film along with electrocardiographs and electroencephalographs; with technological advances in the miniaturization of cameras and electronic devices, was able to record (by means of a plastic phallus) changes within the vagina during orgasm; did follow-up consultations for as long as five years; in 1969 abandoned the use of prostitutes as sexual surrogates with sexual partners suffering impotence or frigidity; with Johnson, published accounts of their laboratory work in the books *Human Sexual Response* (1966) and *Human Sexual Inadequacy* (1970), which were written especially for physicians but became best-sellers; again with Johnson, wrote the book *The Pleasure Bond* (1975), for a general readership, and reported his and Johnson's treatment of 84 dysfunctional homosexual men and women in *Homosexuality in Perspective* (1979); in collaboration with Johnson and Robert Kolodny, wrote *Crisis: Heterosexual Behavior in the Age of AIDS* (1988), a book that drew criticism from U.S. surgeon general C. Everett Koop and others who viewed it as irresponsibly alarmist in its assertion that AIDS could be transmitted by casual contamination and would soon attack the general population "at a frightening pace"; retired in 1994; died in Tucson, Arizona. See *Current Biography* (November) 1968.

Obituary *New York Times* B p7 Feb. 19, 2001

McGRAW, ELOISE JARVIS Dec. 9, 1915–Nov. 30, 2000 Best-selling author of action-packed novels for young people; artist; did the cover art for many of her books, including *The Moorchild,* a medieval fantasy that was a 1996 Newbery Honor book; had garnered previous Newbery honors, including one for *The Golden Goblet,* and an Edgar Award from the Mystery Writers of America for *A Really Weird Summer;* was born into a family steeped in the experience of the opening of America's Western frontier; began publishing short stories for children while living with her husband, a newspaperman, and their son and daughter in San Diego, California, in the late 1940s; moved with her family to a filbert farm in Sherwood, Oregon (where she had spent summers as a child) in 1950; in that year, published her first novel, *Sawdust in His Shoes,* a story (for ages 12 to 16) about circus folk, some with farming backgrounds; subsequently published *Crown Fire* (1951), a timber-country story filled with authentic and colorful logging details, and *Moccasin Trail* (1952), another Newbery Honor winner, about a white boy adopted by Crow Indians; departing from type, wrote *Mara, Daughter of the Nile* (1952), for teens; died in Oswego Lake, Oregon. See *Current Biography* (Yearbook) 1955.

Obituary *New York Times* C p23 Dec. 5, 2000

McGUIRE, DOROTHY June 14, 1918–Sep. 14, 2001 Actress; a gentle and sensitive but strong leading lady of American stage and film; arrived in Hollywood in 1943 to reprise on screen the title role of the girlish young wife who develops an adult maturity at an accelerated pace in the warm comedy *Claudia*, a characterization she had created with radiant charm on Broadway in 1941; went on to give such memorable motion-picture portrayals as Katie Nolan, the mother, in *A Tree Grows in Brooklyn* (1945), the mute servant in the thriller *The Spiral Staircase* (1946), and the wife and mother in the Quaker family in *Friendly Persuasion* (1956); made her stage debut playing the lead in *A Kiss for Cinderella* at the Omaha (Nebraska) Little Theater when she was 12; subsequently acted in student productions at a convent school in Indianapolis, Indiana, and at Pine Manor Junior College, in Wellesley, Massachusetts; made her Broadway debut in 1938 as Martha Scott's understudy in *Our Town*; before her stage triumph in *Claudia*, had roles in summer stock and in the road company of *My Dear Children*, among other stage productions; went on tour with *Claudia* in the summer of 1942; in Hollywood, carried her role in the film *Claudia* over into its sequel *Claudia and David* (1946); meanwhile, appeared on the screen as the plain young woman who finds mutual happiness with a disfigured man in *The Enchanted Cottage* (1945); played the troubled war widow in *Till the End of Time* (1946); was nominated for an Academy Award for her role opposite Gregory Peck in *Gentleman's Agreement* (1947); had roles in well over a score of motion pictures, including *Mister 880* (1950), *Invitation* (1952), *Three Coins in the Fountain* (1954), *Trial* (1955), *A Summer Place* (1959), *The Dark at the Top of the Stairs* (1960), *Swiss Family Robinson* (1960), *Susan Slade* (1961), *Summer Magic* (1963), and *Flight of the Doves* (1971); was cast as the Virgin Mary in *The Greatest Story Ever Told* (1965); in returns to the stage, toured with the La Jolla Players in *Summer and Smoke* in 1950 and appeared on Broadway opposite Richard Burton in *Legend of Lovers* in 1951; acted in television dramas in such formats as the Hallmark Theater; died in Santa Monica, California. See *Current Biography* (September) 1941.

Obituary *New York Times* B p7 Sep. 15, 2001

McINTOSH, MILLICENT CAREY Nov. 30, 1898–Jan. 3, 2001 Educator; the first president of Barnard College; in 1926 joined the faculty of Bryn Mawr College as an instructor in English; in addition, was dean of freshmen at Bryn Mawr (1928–29); in 1929 was named assistant in English and acting dean of the college; was headmistress of the Brearley School, a college-preparatory school for girls in Manhattan, from 1930 to 1947; in July of the latter year, took over the administration of Barnard College, the women's undergraduate school of Columbia University; did so with the title of dean, which was upgraded to president when Barnard became autonomous, in 1952; taught classes in English and modern living at Barnard; oversaw a campaign that raised $10 million in development funds, $1 million of which was contributed by John D. Rockefeller Jr. because of, in his words, his "confidence in the excep-

tional vision and leadership" she was bringing to the college; stepped down as president of Barnard in 1962; retired to a farm in Tyringham, Massachusetts, with her husband, Rustin McIntosh, a pediatrician, who died in 1986; died at the farm in Tyringham. See *Current Biography* (July) 1947.

Obituary *New York Times* B p9 Jan. 5, 2001

McKINNEY, ROBERT Aug. 28, 1910–June 24, 2001 Owner and publisher of the Santa Fe daily *New Mexican*; former government official; early in his career, was a Wall Street financial-investment analyst, chairman of a farm-machinery company, and a board member of the Rock Island Railroad and several major corporations; bought the *New Mexican* (along with its weekly Spanish version, the *El Nuevo Mexicano*) in 1948; later acquired two other newspapers in New Mexico and one in Colorado; meanwhile, served as assistant secretary of the interior under President Harry S. Truman, ambassador to Switzerland under President John F. Kennedy, and in Treasury Department posts in the Johnson and Nixon administrations; sold the *New Mexican* to the Gannett newspaper chain in 1976, with the stipulation that he would continue to have editorial and managerial control; two years later, sued Gannett for breach of contract; won a favorable court ruling in 1980; after further court procedures, was restored as publisher of the *New Mexican* in 1987; two years later, bought the paper back in exchange for his Gannett stock, then worth approximately $33 million; remained publisher until his death, when his daughter, Robin, succeeded him; died in New York City, where he also maintained a residence. See *Current Biography* (January) 1957.

Obituary *New York Times* B p8 June 28, 2001

MEYER, CORD JR. Nov. 10, 1920–Mar. 13, 2001 Former U.S. Central Intelligence Agency official; during a quarter century (1951–77) with the CIA, played key roles in the collecting of foreign intelligence and counterintelligence and the planning and implementation of America's covert efforts to counter and contain the worldwide influence of Soviet communism during the Cold War; as the CIA's associate deputy director for plans (1967–73), was second in command of such efforts; was responsible for the secret subsidization of labor and student groups (including the National Student Association) and such enterprises as the once highly respected literary journal *Encounter*; also oversaw the operations of Radio Free Europe and Radio Liberty, which beamed their broadcasts to audiences in Eastern Europe; came from a privileged background; majored in literature and philosophy at Yale University; served as a Marine Corps officer in the Pacific during World War II; in combat on the island of Guam in 1944, suffered the loss of his left eye; from the war front, wrote a series of letters that were published in the *Atlantic Monthly*; also wrote a short story based on his experiences in combat, "Waves of Darkness," which won the O. Henry Prize for best first-published short story in 1946; was an aide to Harold Stassen in the American delegation to the 1945 conference in San Francisco at which the United Nations charter was drafted; in essays published in the *Atlantic Monthly*, set forth what he saw as weaknesses in the U.N. as organized in San Francisco, including the "unfettered license" enjoyed by major powers vis-à-vis lesser countries; co-founded the United World Federalists, "primarily to strengthen the United Nations into a world government of limited powers adequate to prevent war"; served as first president of that organization, from 1947 to 1949; was recruited into the CIA in 1951 by Allen Dulles, who later became director of the agency; at the time of his resignation from the CIA, in 1977, was chief of the agency's London station; in 1980 published the memoir *Facing Reality: From World Federalism to the CIA*; lectured at Georgetown University from 1982 to 1988; died in Washington, D.C. See *Current Biography* (March) 1948.

Obituary *New York Times* A p17 Mar. 16, 2001

MILLER, JASON Apr. 22, 1939–May 13, 2001 Playwright; actor; as a playwright, won a Tony Award and Pulitzer Prize for best Broadway play of 1972–73 with *That Championship Season*, a tragicomedy about the reunion in middle age of the members of a winning high-school basketball team; was nominated for an Academy Award for best actor for his performance as Father Damien Karras in the motion picture *The Exorcist* (1973); began acting and writing for the theater as a student at the Jesuit-run University of Scranton; subsequently studied drama at the Catholic University of America; married a fellow student at Catholic University, Linda Gleason, a daughter of the comedian Jackie Gleason; garnered early acting credits with regional acting companies; subsequently sought his fortune as an actor and playwright in New York City; after having several of his one-act plays, including *Lou Gehrig Did Not Die of Cancer*, produced Off-Off-Broadway, moved to Off-Broadway in 1970 with his full-length play *Nobody Hears a Broken Drum*, based on the rebellion in the 1860s and 1870s of the oppressed Irish immigrant Pennsylvania coal miners known as the "Molly Maguires"; on television, played the title role in *F. Scott Fitzgerald in Hollywood* (1976); reprised his role as Father Karras in the motion picture *The Exorcist III* (1990); died in Scranton, Pennsylvania. See *Current Biography* (January) 1974.

Obituary *New York Times* A p22 May 15, 2001

NARAYAN, R. K. Oct. 10, 1906–May 13, 2001 Indian novelist; was credited with raising the genre of Indo-English fiction to its highest level of perfection; with grace and wit, wrote in English as an insider about life in a small city in southern India, fictionalized under the name Malgudi; in doing so, created a literary microcosm comparable in its richness and diversity of characterization to William Faulkner's Yoknapatawpha County or Thomas Hardy's Wessex; worked as a schoolteacher and journalist before devoting himself to the full-time writing of fiction; drew heavily on his own experience in his first novel, *Swami and Friends*, which was published by Hamish Hamilton in 1935 on Graham Greene's recommendation; completed a loosely autobiographical trilogy with the novels *The Bachelor of Arts* (1937) and *The Dark Room* (1938); after the death of his wife, Rajam, in 1935, was severely depressed and

wrote virtually nothing for five years; made his grief the grist for his fourth novel, *The English Teacher* (1945), which was published in the U.S. with the title *Grateful to Life and Death* (1953); in the three novels of his "middle period"—*Mr. Sampath* (1949), *The Financial Expert* (1952), and *Waiting for the Mahatma* (1953)—traced the character Sampath's difficult search for "true identity" in a time of cultural disintegration; achieved what is widely regarded as his masterpiece in *The Guide* (1958), in which Raju, a former food vendor turned tourist guide, finds his true vocation as a mahatma, or spiritual adviser; expanded life in Malgudi in such novels as *The Man-Eater of Malgudi* (1961), *The Vendor of Sweets* (1967), *A Tiger for Malgudi* (1983), and *Talkative Man* (1987); in addition to 34 novels, published several collections of short stories and such works of nonfiction as *Next Sunday: Sketches and Essays* (1960) and *My Days: A Memoir* (1974); died in Madras, India. See *Current Biography* (September) 1987.

Obituary *New York Times* B p6 May 14, 2001

NATHAN, ROBERT R. Dec. 25, 1908–Sep. 4, 2001 Economist; former government official; consultant; at the Wharton School of Business at the University of Pennsylvania, received a B.S. degree in 1931 and an M.S. degree in 1933; during the 1930s, worked in income and unemployment research with the Pennsylvania state government and the U.S. Department of Commerce, where he became chief of the national income division in 1939; the following year, when the administration of President Franklin Delano Roosevelt began accelerating its defense buildup, including support for Britain's war effort, was appointed, with no formal title, to coordinate for a national defense commission studies of prospective military and nonmilitary needs and the nation's capacity to meet those needs; in that task, found that, in his words, "one must vary from being an expert statistician and economist at one moment to being a commodity expert or industrial authority the next"; in 1942, after the U.S. entered World War II, became chairman of the War Production Board's planning committee; after the war, founded Robert R. Nathan Associates, an economic consulting firm that has had as clients U.S. government agencies, industrial and other private-sector associations, and a number of foreign governments, including those of Vietnam, Israel, and Salvador; served a term as chairman of Americans for Democratic Action in the 1950s; was an adviser to Democratic candidate Hubert H. Humphrey's presidential campaign in 1968; chaired Robert R. Nathan Associates until August 2001; died in Bethesda, Maryland. See *Current Biography* (September) 1941.

Obituary *New York Times* A p27 Sep. 10, 2001

O'CONNOR, CARROLL Aug. 2, 1924–June 21, 2001 Actor; after years of yeoman character acting on stage, screen, and television, achieved the status of pop-culture icon in the role of the narrow-minded and irascible but somehow likable Archie Bunker—a caricature of a bigoted blue-collar WASP mossback given to ethnic and racial slurs—in the groundbreaking TV situation comedy *All in the Family*, which, with its taboo-shattering confrontation of controversial political and social issues and its spawning of spin-offs, was among the most influential such programs in the history of broadcasting; grew up in the New York City boroughs of the Bronx and Queens (the latter being the locus of *All in the Family*); sailed the North Atlantic as a merchant seaman during World War II; studied for a while at Wake Forest University; began acting as a student at the University of Montana; after completing his undergraduate studies, at University College, in Dublin, Ireland, remained in Ireland and the United Kingdom for approximately two years, as an actor at the Gate Theatre in Dublin, the Edinburgh Festival, and other venues; after returning to the U.S., in the mid-1950s, earned an M.A. degree at the University of Montana, with a pageant about the history of Montana as his thesis, and taught English in public high schools in Manhattan; on the Off-Broadway stage in the late 1950s, played Buck Mulligan in *Ulysses in Nighttown* and Marcus Huff in *The Big Knife*; beginning at about the same time and through the 1960s, was regularly employed on television, in roles in dramatic anthologies and in such series as *Naked City*, *Gunsmoke*, *The Fugitive*, and *Ben Casey*; later starred in a television adaptation of the musical *Of Thee I Sing* and the political drama *The Last Hurrah* (which he scripted); made his motion-picture debut as Matt Keegan in *Fever in the Blood* (1961); during the following decade, had supporting roles in more than a score of films, including *Lonely Are the Brave*, *Cleopatra*, *Point Blank*, *Kelly's Heroes*, and *Death of a Gunfighter*; co-starred (as a New York City auxiliary policeman) in the screen comedy *Law and Disorder* (1974); meanwhile, as the army general in the film *What Did You Do in the War, Daddy?* (1966), displayed the right "combination of bombast and sweetness" that Norman Lear, the producer-writer of *All in the Family* (modeled after the BBC series *'Til Death Do Us Part*), was looking for in the character Archie Bunker; played Archie in *All in the Family* from 1971 to 1979 and in its sequel, *Archie Bunker's Place*, from 1979 to 1983; won four Emmy Awards as Archie; received a fifth Emmy for his performance in the more politically correct role of Bill Gillespie, the gruff but liberal small-town Mississippi police chief in the comedy-drama series *In the Heat of the Night* (1988–94), loosely based on the same-named 1967 film; wrote and starred (as a New York City chief of detective) in the TV movie *Brass* (1985); in the mid-1990s, had a guest role in the situation comedy *Mad About You*; on the stage, directed himself in the Broadway flop *Brothers* (1983) and wrote and starred in *A Certain Labor Day* (1995); following the suicide of his cocaine-addicted, adopted son, Hugh, in 1995, devoted most of his energy to anti-drug activism; made his last motion-picture appearance in *Return to Me* (2000); wrote the memoir *I Think I'm Out of Here* (1998); with his wife, Nancy, funded the foundation of the Center for the Rocky Mountain West at the University of Montana; died in Culver City, California. See *Current Biography* (July) 1972.

Obituary *New York Times* B p8 June 22, 2001

O'HAIR, MADALYN MURRAY Apr. 13, 1919–1995 The most famous American atheist of her time; founder of the Freethought Society of America, American Atheists, United Secularists of America, the Society of Separationists, and the monthly newsletter *American Atheist*; was best known for launching the legal suit that culminated in the U.S. Supreme Court decision declaring prayer in public schools to be unconstitutional; before her two marriages, had the maiden name Madalyn Mays; in World War II was a cryptographer in the Women's Army Corps; studied at a succession of colleges and universities, including the South Texas College of Law, where she earned a law degree, and Howard University, where she studied social work for two years; was employed as a casework supervisor in the department of public welfare in Baltimore, Maryland, when, in 1960, she filed a legal suit against "sectarian opening exercises" in public schools on behalf of her son William Murray, who was then a student in a city junior high school; pursued the case, *Murray v. Curlett*, up to the Supreme Court, which, ruling by a vote of eight to one in favor of Murray in 1963, outlawed prayer in public schools; in a later suit (which ended unsuccessfully in the Supreme Court in 1979), sought the removal of the motto "In God We Trust" from U.S. coinage; also campaigned against the tax-exempt status of churches; in 1965 settled in Austin, Texas, where she opened the American Atheist Center and established the American Atheist Press to publish such works as *Why I Am an Atheist* (1965), *An Atheist Epic* (1970), and *Atheist Heroes and Heroines* (1992); lectured widely; in 1995, along with the younger of her two sons, Jon Garth Murray, and her granddaughter, Robin Murray O'Hair (the daughter of her son William), was abducted from her Austin home, robbed of more than $500,000 in gold coins, and murdered—a series of events shrouded in mystery for more than five years, until the mastermind of the crime (which had begun as an extortion plot), David Roland Waters, her former office manager, led FBI agents to the dismembered and burnt remains in a shallow grave on a cattle ranch in Real County, Texas; on March 23, 2001 was given a proper burial (but one that was nonreligious, in deference to her wishes) at an undisclosed cemetery in Austin by her long-estranged son William, who is now a fundamentalist-Christian minister. See *Current Biography* (January) 1977.

Obituary *New York Times* A p10 Mar. 16, 2001

PAZ ESTENSSORO, VICTOR Oct. 2, 1907–June 7, 2001 The most influential Bolivian politician of the 20th century; leader of the Movimiento Nacionalista Revolucionario (MNR); served as president of Bolivia four times, for a total of more than a dozen years spanning four decades (1952–89); between terms, wielded power as a gray eminence; coming from a land-owning family, always remained at heart less radical than the typical MNR member; over the course of his career, was able to move from left to right of center, as pragmatism demanded; was trained in law and economics; early in his career, worked as a financial expert in both government and the private sector; with others, founded the MRA party in the early 1940s; attracted support from workers in Bolivia's tin-mine industry (then largely controlled by three families) and from the Aymara and Quechua Indians (who comprise a majority of the Bolivian population but were then second-class citizens in both the feudal countryside and urban centers such as La Paz); during his first term as president (1952–56), embarked on a sweeping program of political, labor, and agrarian reform; nationalized the tin-mining industry; extended suffrage universally, to include the Indians; redistributed land, to the benefit of the Indians; served two brief presidential terms in the 1960s; began his last term (a four-year tenure) as president in 1985, when political instability, poor economic management, and collapsing tin prices on the world market had led Bolivia to the brink of bankruptcy, with an inflation rate of 23,000 percent and rising; brought inflation under control and restored economic stability only by a drastic reversal of policies he had instituted in his first presidency; with Decree 21,060, turned Bolivia away from statism, onto a free-market course; slashed public spending, lifted price controls, and invited the infusion of foreign capital; shut down many tin mines and privatized the rest; over the years, held diplomatic posts, including that of ambassador to Britain (1956–59); taught economics at London University (1966); died in Tarija, Bolivia. See *Current Biography* (May) 1953.

Obituary *New York Times* A p13 June 9, 2001

PERKINS, CHARLES June 16, 1936–Oct. 18, 2000 Australian civil rights activist; social-welfare director; was born to "half-caste" parents on a reservation in Australia's Northern Territory; as a young man, was a star soccer player in Australia and, for a period, in England; subsequently, in 1966, became the first person of Aboriginal descent to receive a university degree; while earning a B.A. degree in government and anthropology at the University of Sydney, was the leader of Student Action for Aborigines; in 1965, led 30 white students on a 10-day "Freedom Ride" by bus through northern New South Wales to challenge and call attention to blatant discrimination against Aborigines in many Outback towns; evoked much sympathy among white Australians, but drew criticism even from moderates in the Aboriginal community for some of his militant language and actions; in August 1965, to protest and publicize Australia's racially discriminatory immigration policies, temporarily "abducted" a six-year-old Fijian girl of Indian background who was about to be deported as an illegal alien; in 1966, became full-time manager of the Foundation for Aboriginal Affairs, devoted to helping urban Aborigines solve some of their problems in such areas as housing, employment, health, and education; died in Sydney. See *Current Biography* (January) 1969.

Obituary *New York Times* B p11 Oct. 25, 2000

PIERCE, SAMUEL R. JR. Sep. 8, 1922–Oct. 31, 2000 Former government official; lawyer; banker; a fiscally conservative and socially liberal Republican who had positions in three Republican presidential administrations; was secretary of the Department of Housing and Urban Development (HUD) from 1981 to 1989; was a star halfback in football at Cornell

University, where he received a B.A. degree after serving with a criminal investigation division of the U.S. Army during World War II; in the early 1950s, earned law degrees at Cornell and New York universities; subsequently, worked as an assistant district attorney and assistant U.S. attorney; first went to Washington in 1955, as assistant to the undersecretary of labor in the administration of President Dwight D. Eisenhower; in 1955 and 1960, was appointed by New York governor Nelson E. Rockefeller to fill vacancies on New York County's Court of General Sessions; became the first black partner in a major New York law firm when he joined Battle, Fowler, Stokes & Kheel in 1961; specialized in labor, tax, and antitrust law; served on the New York State banking board from 1961 to 1970; beginning in 1961, successfully helped to defend the Reverend Martin Luther King Jr. and others in a landmark U.S. Supreme Court libel case; became the first black director of a Fortune 500 company when he was chosen to sit on the board of U.S. Industries in 1964; during that year, co-founded the Freedom National Bank, the first predominantly black-managed bank in New York State; co-chaired a fund to back loans to black businessmen; was involved in the leadership of other projects aimed at helping minorities to enter various occupations and professions; during the administration of President Richard Nixon, was general counsel to the Department of the Treasury (1970–73); returned to his law firm as a name partner in 1973; as Secretary of HUD during President Ronald Reagan's two terms in office, broadly accepted the sharp budget cuts the administration imposed on his department; at the same time, fought to preserve several key programs for promoting rehabilitation in housing and urban neighborhood projects; after leaving office, was a target of a criminal investigation into allegations that HUD, during his tenure there, had distributed millions of dollars in housing subsidies (under the guise of consultant fees) to well-known Republicans; saw several of his former aides go to prison, but was himself never charged with a crime; died in a hospital in a suburb of Washington, D.C. See *Current Biography* (November) 1982.

Obituary *New York Times* B p13 Nov. 3, 2000

POMEROY, WARDELL B. Dec. 6, 1913–Sep. 6, 2001 Psychologist; psychotherapist; a senior research associate of the late Alfred C. Kinsey, the famed surveyor of the sexual practices of Americans; was co-author of the so-called Kinsey Reports, landmark best-sellers that professed to indicate much more varied patterns of sexual behavior than commonly assumed; also wrote *Dr. Kinsey and the Institute for Sex Research* (1972), an intimate account of Kinsey and his work, and wrote or co-wrote for children and their parents several controversial books on sex; while pursuing his graduate studies at Indiana University in Bloomington, Indiana, worked as a clinical psychologist with the city welfare department in South Bend, Indiana, and at the state penitentiary in Pendleton, Indiana; took his M.S. degree at the university in 1941 with a thesis titled "Personality Factors in Mentally Superior Felons"; later earned his doctorate in psychology at Columbia University, in New York City, with a dissertation titled "Sex Before and After Psychosurgery"; as a graduate student at Indiana University, became acquainted with Kinsey, a biology professor who was then beginning to organize his sex-study team; in 1941, joined the Kinsey team, which was formally incorporated as the Institute for Sex Research in 1947; during his years with Kinsey, shared with him the responsibility for the bulk of the in-depth sample interviewing of volunteer subjects across the U.S.; conducted approximately 8,000 of the 18,000 interviews ultimately recorded; with Kinsey and Clyde E. Martin, wrote the first of the two Kinsey Reports, *Sexual Behavior in the Human Male* (1948), based on the sexual histories of 5,300 white males; with Kinsey, Martin, and Paul H. Gephard, wrote the second report, *Sexual Behavior of the Human Female* (1947), based on the sexual histories of 5,940 white women; with Gephard, reorganized the Institute for Sex Research after Kinsey's death, in 1956; became the institute's field director, while Gephard assumed the post of executive director; with Gephard and others, prepared the institute's statistical studies *Pregnancy, Birth and Abortion* (1958) and *Sex Offenders: An Analysis of Types* (1965); in 1963, left the institute and, with his wife, moved to New York City; established a psychotherapy and marriage-counseling practice on Manhattan's Upper East Side; with Cornelia V. Christenson, wrote *Characteristics of Male and Female Sexual Responses* (1968); with the professional writer John Tebbel, wrote *Boys and Sex* (1968) and *Girls and Sex* (1970); later wrote *Your Child and Sex* (1974) and *Taking a Sex History: Interviewing and Recording* (1982); died in Bloomington, Indiana. See *Current Biography* (July) 1974.

Obituary *New York Times* C p14 Sep. 12, 2001

QUINE, W. V. June 25, 1908–Dec. 25, 2000 Philosopher; Pierce professor of philosophy emeritus, Harvard University; a mathematical logician who built a philosophical system in which the analytical and the empirical were unified; addressed metaphysical questions, concerned with the ultimate nature of reality and how human beings relate to it, in terms of language, symbolic logic, and mathematics; rephrased the fundamental question of epistemology, "How do we acquire our theory of the world?" to read, "How do we acquire our talk about the world?"; as an undergraduate at Oberlin College, majored in mathematics; as a graduate student, studied at Harvard University under Alfred North Whitehead, an eminent pioneer in the philosophy of science, and in Prague under Rudolf Carnap, a leading exponent of logical positivism; laid out his system of mathematical logic (based on a "natural deduction" method, leaner and more efficient than the axiom-laden method advanced by Whitehead and Bertrand Russell) in such books as *A System of Logistic* (1934), *Mathematical Logic* (1940), *Set Theory and Its Logic* (1963), and *The Logic of Sequences* (1990); established the complex relationship between his philosophy and logical positivism in his seminal paper "Two Dogmas of Empiricism" (1951), which was reprinted in his book *From a Logical Point of View* (1953); in that paper, repudiated an opposition or boundary between purely analytic thought (received, or a priori) and synthetic knowledge (ac-

quired empirically, or a posteriori); espoused "a more thorough pragmatism," in which a human being's "scientific heritage" is rationally warped to fit his or her "continuing barrage of sensory stimulation"; in his magnum opus, *Word and Object* (1960), wrote about two language-problem theses: "indeterminacy of translation" and "uncertainty of reference" between a word and the object to which it refers; published a total of 20 books, including two books of essays, *The Ways of Paradox* (1966) and *Ontological Relativity* (1969), an autobiography, *The Time of My Life* (1985), and a casual tour de force in wit and word play, *Quiddities: An Intermittently Philosophical Dictionary* (1987); taught philosophy at Harvard from 1936 until 1978; died in Boston, Massachusetts. See *Current Biography* (November) 1999.

Obituary *New York Times* C p11 Dec. 29, 2000

QUINN, ANTHONY Apr. 21. 1915– June 3, 2001 Mexican-born character actor; a larger-than-life motion-picture screen presence, with an earthy persona; in more than 130 films, portrayed an extraordinary range of ethnicities, from Inuit to Arab; projected a vital charisma and a robust masculinity; won two Academy Awards for best supporting actor, for his performances as the cynical brother of the Mexican revolutionary Emelio Zapata in *Viva Zapata!* (1952) and the painter Paul Gauguin in *Lust for Life* (1956); achieved international stardom as Zampano, the traveling carnival strongman, in *La Strada* (1954); is perhaps best remembered for his vibrant personification of Dionysian joie de vivre in the role of the peasant Zorba in *Zorba the Greek* (1964); was the son of an Irish father and a Mexican mother of Aztec ancestry, who immigrated to the U.S. with him when he was an infant; at first aspiring to a career in architecture, became an apprentice to Frank Lloyd Wright, who sent him to a voice teacher (to cure a speech impediment), who in turn directed him to a career in acting; following a stint with the Federal Theater Project, won a leading role in Mae West's play *Clean Beds* (1936); after a nonspeaking part in the movie *Parole* (1936), was cast in several film roles a year, including that of a Cheyenne in *The Plainsman* (1936), Captain Ricardo Alvarez in *Last Train from Madrid* (1937), Mamoulian in *Blood and Sand* (1941), Chief Crazy Horse in *They Died with Their Boots On* (1941), a North African sheik in *The Road to Morocco* (1942), a Mexican in *The Ox-Bow Incident* (1943), a Mexican-American Marine in *Guadalcanal Diary* (1943), a Filipino guerrilla in *Back to Bataan* (1945), Charley Eagle, a Native American oil millionaire, in *Black Gold* (1947), Quasimodo in *The Hunchback of Notre Dame* (1956), the title role in *Barabbas* (1962), the pathetic aging prizefighter in *Requiem for a Heavyweight* (1962), the fierce Bedouin leader Auda Abu Tayi in *Lawrence of Arabia* (1962), the Russian pope in *Shoes of the Fisherman* (1968), Theo Tomasis in *The Greek Tycoon* (1978), Omar Mukhtar in *Lion of the Desert* (1981), Lou Carbone in *Jungle Fever* (1991), and Don Pedro Aragon, the patriarch of a vineyard-owning family in California, in *A Walk in the Clouds* (1995); during the last three decades of his career, increasingly worked less on the big screen and more on television, where he had begun acting in dramatic anthologies and series in the 1950s; played Thomas Jefferson Alcala, the ruggedly independent mayor of a southwestern city, in the hour-long weekly network dramatic series *The Man and the City* (1971–72); hosted and narrated *Ten Who Dared* (1977), a syndicated documentary series on great explorers; often appeared as Zeus in the syndicated series *Hercules— The Legendary Journeys* (1995); had roles in a number of made-for-TV movies, including Michael Reyman in *This Can't Be Love* (1994) and a mobster in *Gotti* (1996); made his Broadway debut in the title role in *The Gentleman from Greece* in 1947; returned to Broadway as Henry II in *Beckett* (1960) and as the male lead in the romantic fantasy *Tchin-Tchin* (1962–63); played Zorba in a revival of *Zorba!*, the musical adaptation of *Zorba the Greek*, which he took on a national tour (1982–85) that included a stop on Broadway (1983); wrote two autobiographies, *The Original Sin* (1972) and, with Daniel Paisner, *One Man Tango* (1995); in addition to acting, was a visual artist whose paintings and sculptures have been exhibited internationally; was married three times and divorced twice; fathered 13 children by five women; died in Boston, Massachusetts. See *Current Biography* (December) 1957.

Obituary *New York Times* B p6 June 4, 2001

RHODES, JAMES A. Sep. 13, 1909–Mar. 4, 2001 Four-term Republican governor of Ohio (1963–71, 1975–83); had previously served as mayor of Columbus, Ohio, and Ohio state auditor; as governor, was appreciated in Ohio for attracting industry to the state, substantially lowering its unemployment rate, and building up its infrastructure (including highways and airports) and university and vocational-education systems; nationally, was chiefly remembered for his role in the Kent State University massacre of May 4, 1970; on that day, with the aim of quelling antiwar disturbances prompted by the American invasion of Cambodia, ordered to the Kent State campus National Guard troops, some of whom opened fire on student demonstrators and other students, killing four and wounding nine; collaborated with R. Dean Jauchius, an aide and speechwriter, in the writing of three historical novels: *Johnny Shiloh* (1959), *The Trial of Mary Todd Lincoln* (1959), and *The Court-martial of Commodore Perry* (1961); died in Columbus, Ohio. See *Current Biography* (April) 1976.

Obituary *New York Times* A p19 Mar. 6, 2001

RICHLER, MORDECAI Jan. 27, 1931–July 3, 2001 Canadian novelist, essayist, and motion-picture and television scenarist; a deliberately provocative curmudgeon who offended myriad targets of his scathing wit, from feminists and French separatists to fellow Jews, with his sometimes nasty, always forthright, social criticism; set most of his novels in the place and time in which he grew up—the working-class Jewish ghetto on and around St. Urbain Street in Montreal in the 1930s and 1940s; throughout his career, contributed articles regularly to *Maclean's* magazine; directly in his nonfiction and more archly in his often ribald fiction, mocked "Canada's artistic elites, 'fatted' on subsidized Canadian nationalism

. . . the scratch-my-back world of Canadian literary politics, and the deadly world of political correctness," as Barbara Amiel, contributing editor of *Maclean's*, observed; was "fearless, and fun [to read]"; rejected his father's religious orthodoxy; out of contrariness, joined the Zionist Habonim when he was 17; at 19, dropped out of college and went to continental Europe, where he "wandered" (his word) for two years; subsequently lived in England (where he supported himself by writing for television and motion pictures) for 18 years, keeping in touch with Canada by returning there twice a year; had not yet found his own voice when he wrote his first novel, *The Acrobats* (1954), set in Spain; first evoked life in Montreal's Old World quarter in *Son of a Smaller Hero* (1955); did so most famously in the coming-of-age comedy-drama *The Apprenticeship of Duddy Kravitz* (1959), in which he created the ruthlessly ambitious young underclass street hustler of the title, along with such supporting characters as Rabbi Harvey Goldstone, a caricatured representative of trendy Reform Judaism, and Virgil, an unsophisticated epileptic who is outrageously exploited by the manipulative Duddy; wrote the screenplay for the 1974 motion-picture adaptation of that novel; in 1957, published *A Choice of Enemies*, a novel about blacklisted Canadian and American screenwriters living and working in exile in England; subsequently published the comic novels *Stick Your Neck Out* (1963) and *Cocksure* (1968); spent five years writing *St. Urbain's Horseman* (1971), which he regarded as his best novel; in it, interwove threads from his early life, his mature perspective on life in Canada, and his experience in British television and film; with his second wife and children, moved back to Canada in 1972, but continued thereafter to spend part of each year in England; in 1980, published *Joshua Then and Now*, a novel (about a young Canadian Jewish writer whose father, a small-time gangster, marries into a socially prominent WASP family) that was made into a 1985 feature film; was inspired by the history of the Bronfmans, Canada's richest family, and Seagram's, their whiskey empire, and influenced by the magic realism of Gabriel García Márquez in writing the novel *Solomon Gursky Was Here* (1990); wrote 10 novels, ending with *Barney's Version* (1998), and several books of fiction for children about a boy named Jacob Two-Two, who has to say everything twice to be understood by adults; expanded a 31-page *New Yorker* article ridiculing the de jure suppression of public use of English in the predominantly French province of Quebec into the book *Oh Canada! Oh Canada!: Lament for a Divided Canada* (1992); collected other pieces of nonfiction in *Broadsides: Reviews and Opinions* (1990) and *Essays, Reports, and Opinions* (1998); edited the book *The Best of Modern Humor* (1983); died in Montreal. See *Current Biography* (May) 1975.

Obituary *New York Times* A p13 July 4, 2001

RIPLEY, S. DILLON Sep. 20, 1913–Mar. 12, 2001 Museum director; biologist; zoologist; ecologist; ornithologist; former secretary [a title equivalent to chief executive officer] of the Smithsonian Institution in Washington, D.C.—the largest museum complex in the world, in part a gigantic warehouse of memorabilia popularly known as "the nation's attic"; directed the Smithsonian during its most spectacular period of growth as a dynamic national center for education and research in the sciences, arts, and humanities; held a B.A. degree from Yale University and a Ph.D. from Harvard; in the late 1930s participated in zoological expeditions to New Guinea and Sumatra sponsored by the Philadelphia Academy of Natural Sciences; was assistant curator of birds at the Smithsonian Institution in 1942; from 1942 to 1945, served with the Office of Strategic Services, the forerunner of the Central Intelligence Agency, in Ceylon, Burma, and India; before taking direction of the Smithsonian, was a member of the faculty of Yale (1946–64), where he taught zoology and biology and was curator of the Peabody Museum of Natural History; wrote a number of books, including *Search for the Spiny Babbler* (1952) and, with Salim Ali, the 10-volume *Handbook of the Birds of India and Pakistan*; died in Washington, D.C. See *Current Biography* (October) 1966.

Obituary *New York Times* B p9 Mar. 13, 2001

ROBARDS, JASON JR. July 26, 1922–Dec. 26, 2000 Actor; in a long and illustrious career on stage and in film, brought authenticity to a range of challenging roles; was a definitive interpreter of the playwright Eugene O'Neill, whose darker, most serious works he was instrumental in immortalizing; was most closely identified with his intense portrayals of two O'Neill characters: the desperate soul searcher Hickey, from *The Iceman Cometh*, and the beguiling failure James Tyrone Jr., from *Long Day's Journey Into Night* and *A Moon for the Misbegotten*; grew up in Hollywood, where his father, an actor, appeared in approximately 175 movies; after naval service in World War II, studied at the American Academy of Dramatic Arts in New York City; Off-Broadway, under the direction of José Quintero, attracted some attention in the role of Ed Moody in Victor Wolfson's *American Gothic*, in 1953, and gained overnight recognition with his stunning performance as the tragic hero Hickey in the 1956 revival of *The Iceman Cometh*; again under Quintero's direction, played James Tyrone Jr. in the Broadway premiere (1956–58) of O'Neill's autobiographical *Long Day's Journey into Night* (which the playwright had not allowed to be staged during his lifetime); on Broadway in 1958–59, won a Tony Award for his performance as Manley Halliday in Budd Schulberg and Harvey Breit's *The Disenchanted* (in which his father had a minor role); among other Broadway assignments in the early 1960s, starred in Herb Gardner's warm comedy *A Thousand Clowns* as Murray Burns, a role he would reprise in a 1965 film; in the mid-1960s had roles in several Lincoln Center Repertory Theater productions, including that of the character representing the playwright in Arthur Miller's *After the Fall* and Eerie Smith in O'Neill's *Hughie*; subsequently had roles in Joseph Heller's *We Bombed in New Haven* and a revival of Clifford Odets's *The Country Girl*, among other theatrical productions; on Broadway in the 1973–74 season, played James Tyrone Jr. in O'Neill's *A Moon for the Misbegotten*; in his motion-picture debut, played the Hungarian freedom-fighter Paul Kedes in *The Journey* (1959); in the 1960s was

cast in some 14 screen roles, including those of Julius Penrose in *By Love Possessed*, Dick Diver in *Tender Is the Night*, George S. Kaufman in *Act One*, Nelson Downes in *Divorce American Style*, Al Capone in *The St. Valentine's Day Massacre*, and reprises of his roles in *The Iceman Cometh*, *Long Day's Journey into Night*, and *A Moon for the Misbegotten*; in the 1970s had a score of screen roles, including Lew Wallace in *Pat Garrett and Billy the Kid*, Ewing in *Comes a Horseman*, and Will Varner, the father, in the made-for-television film *The Long Hot Summer*; won Academy Awards for best supporting actor for his performances as Ben Bradlee in *All the President's Men* (1976) and Dashiell Hammett in *Julia* (1977); was outstanding as the grizzled, eccentric Howard Hughes in *Melvin and Howard* (1980) and the derelict father making lavish amends in the sweet Neil Simon comedy *Max Dugan Returns* (1983); maintained his pace in screen work (including made-for-TV movies) into the 1990s, when his roles included Charles Wheeler in *Philadelphia* and Graham Keighley in *The Paper*; in his last film, *Magnolia* (1999), played a dying television executive; was married four times, most famously to the actress Lauren Bacall (1961–73); lived in Southport, Connecticut; died in Bridgeport, Connecticut. See *Current Biography* (October) 1959.

Obituary *New York Times* A p1+ Dec. 27, 2000

ROGERS, WILLIAM P. June 23, 1913–Jan. 2, 2001 Lawyer; government official; served as attorney general in the presidential administration of Dwight D. Eisenhower and secretary of state in that of Richard M. Nixon; was assistant district attorney of New York County from 1938 to 1947, with a four-year interruption for navy service in World War II; between 1947 and 1950 was chief counsel to two U.S. Senate committees investigating malfeasance in the arranging of federal contracts with private firms; at that time, began his association with Nixon, then a congressman; advised Nixon to pursue the investigation that led to the perjury conviction of Alger Hiss, a former State Department official accused of passing classified documents to Soviet agents; in 1950 joined the Washington office of the New York law firm of Dwight, Royall, Harris, Koegel & Caskey; worked closely with Nixon in the successful 1952 presidential election campaign in which Nixon was the vice-presidential candidate on the ticket headed by Eisenhower; when, during that campaign, Nixon's candidacy was threatened by the revelation of a "slush fund" raised for him by a group of California businessmen, advised Nixon to stand firm and helped him prepare a public explanation (the nationally televised "Checkers speech"); under President Eisenhower, was deputy attorney general (1953–57) and attorney general (1957–61); returned to the private practice of law in 1961; in a Supreme Court libel case in 1964, filed a friend-of-the-court brief (on behalf of the *Washington Post*), the thrust of which was accepted by the Court in a landmark decision affirming wide protection for journalists under the First Amendment; at the U.N., was a member of the U.S. delegation to the 20th session of the General Assembly, in 1965, and a delegate to an ad hoc committee on Southwest Africa, in 1967; as President Nixon's secretary of state, beginning in 1969, was disappointed to find the role he expected to play in foreign policy assigned in actual practice to Henry A. Kissinger, the president's chief national security adviser; early in Nixon's second term, in 1973, resigned at the request of the president, who then appointed Kissinger secretary of state in name as well as in fact; after leaving government, practiced law in the Washington office of the firm of Clifford Chance Rogers & Wells; in 1986, at President Ronald Reagan's request, headed a special commission that investigated the explosion of the space shuttle *Challenger* and issued a report more critical of the National Aeronautics and Space Administration than Reagan had anticipated; died in Bethesda, Maryland. See *Current Biography* (September) 1969.

Obituary *New York Times* B p7 Jan. 4, 2001

ROWAN, CARL T. Aug. 11, 1925–Sep. 23, 2000 Journalist; author; described his political stance as "independent non-Republican"; grew up disadvantaged in the Jim Crow–era South; scrubbed porches to earn tuition money for admission to Tennessee Agricultural and Industrial State College, where he joined the U.S. Navy's World War II V-12 officer-training program; in 1944 became one of the first 15 African-Americans to be commissioned navy officers; served as a communications officer on two ships in the Atlantic; after the war, used the G.I. Bill of Rights in earning a B.A. degree in mathematics at Oberlin College and an M.A. degree in journalism at the University of Minnesota; after writing for several black newspapers, joined the Minneapolis *Tribune* as a copyreader; became a general assignment reporter at the *Tribune* in 1950; traveled South to report on the condition of black people at that time in a series of articles published in the *Tribune* under the title "How Far from Slavery?," the basis for his book *South of Freedom* (1952); reported on landmark events in the civil rights struggle, including the U.S. Supreme Court's 1954 school desegregation decision; under the auspices of the U.S. Department of State, spent nearly a year lecturing in India, Pakistan, and Southeast Asia; recorded observations made during that experience in the book *The Pitiful and the Proud* (1956), portions of which first appeared in the Minneapolis *Tribune* and were widely syndicated; in an article in 1957, warned that the thousands of blacks ("potential voters") migrating from the South to the industrial North could be a "responsible source" of "civic growth" or "a new pocket of corruption to be exploited by selfish men"; during 1957, wrote a series of articles on the American Indians ("the forgotten people . . . who forgot to vanish") for the *Tribune*; published the book *Go South in Sorrow*, based on a second investigative tour of the South, in 1957; was a deputy assistant secretary of state and a delegate to the U.N. in the administration of President John F. Kennedy and director of the U.S. Information Agency in that of President Lyndon B. Johnson; as a conspicuous advocate of handgun control, was embarrassed at one point in the 1980s to be charged with shooting and wounding an intruder in his backyard with an unregistered pistol; was often seen as a panelist on television public-affairs programs; wrote three newspaper columns a week, syndicated nationally by King Features; with a series of columns in 1997, contributed to a reform in the leadership of the NAACP; wrote a total of eight books, including an autobiography, biographies of Jackie Robinson and Thurgood Marshall, and *The Coming Race War in America* (1996); died in Washington, D.C. See *Current Biography* (January) 1958.

Obituary *New York Times* p54 Sep. 24, 2000

SCAMMON, RICHARD M. July 17, 1915–Apr. 27, 2001 Statistician; political scientist; elections analyst; was educated at the University of Minnesota, the University of Michigan, and the London School of Economics; in 1955, became the first director of the nonprofit, foundation-supported Elections Research Center in Washington, D.C.; without resigning that position, served as director of the federal Bureau of the Budget from 1961 to 1965; was a political consultant to *Newsweek* magazine and to the NBC News elections unit; lectured widely; co-wrote the books *This U.S.A.* (1960) and *The Real Majority* (1970); died in Gaithersburg, Maryland. See *Current Biography* (March) 1971.

Obituary *New York Times* p46 Apr. 29, 2001

SCHINDLER, ALEXANDER M Oct. 4, 1925–Oct. 15, 2000 German-born rabbi; was president of the Union of American Hebrew Congregations (UAHC), the governing body of Reform Judaism in the U.S. and Canada, from 1973 to 1996; departed from Orthodoxy in treating Jewish law, *halakhah*, as flexible rather than rigid, regarding it as a guideline for "a living faith, constantly evolving"; was unafraid to take controversial stands, in favor of the validation of Jewishness through paternal (rather than solely maternal) descent, the ordination of women and avowed homosexuals to the rabbinate, and outreach to intermarried couples and their children and to non-Jews open to conversion to Judaism; on the other hand, encouraged Reform Jews to greater adherence to classical Jewish tradition, including domestic observance as well as public worship on the Sabbath and on holy days; deplored organized American Jewry's "flirtation with the Christian right"; championed a host of liberal causes; with his Yiddish-speaking parents, emigrated from Germany to the U.S. via Italy and France in the 1930s; served in combat with the U.S. Army in Europe in World War II; subsequently earned degrees at the Community College of New York and the Hebrew Union College-Jewish Institute of Religion; after his ordination as a rabbi, in 1953, was attached to Temple Emanuel in Worcester, Massachusetts, until 1959, when he became council director of the Federation of Reform Temples of UAHC for the six-state New England region; from 1963 to 1967 was director of education for UAHC at its New York City headquarters; as such, headed UAHC's publications department; also headed the Joint Commission on Jewish Education of UAHC and the Central Conference of American Rabbis; was vice president of UAHC for six years before becoming president; since 1957, was also a member of the board of the Conference of Presidents of Major American Jewish Organizations; chaired the board from 1976 to 1978; died at his home in Westport,

Connecticut. See *Current Biography* (September) 1987.

Obituary *New York Times* B p13 Oct. 16, 2000

SCHULTES, RICHARD EVANS Jan. 12, 1915–Apr. 10, 2001 Botanist; professor emeritus of natural sciences and botany at Harvard University; called himself "just a jungle botanist"; actually, was the leading figure in the development of ethnobotany, the study of the medicinal and cultural use of plants among indigenous peoples; began his research in the U.S. and Mexico; for a dozen years in the 1940s and early 1950s, and in regular visits thereafter, lived in the Amazon Basin among Indians, including the Yukuna of Colombia; learned to speak at least two Indian dialects, Witoto and Makuma; collected specimens of thousands of species of flora, including hundreds used by *curanderos* (medicine men, or healers) for treating disorders or injuries and inducing visions; anticipated by decades the contemporary environmental movement's concern for the preservation of what is now known as the rainforest; inadvertently, sparked the countercultural pursuit of psychedelia led by Gordon Wasson, Timothy Leary, William S. Burroughs, and Allen Ginsberg, among others; modeled his career on that of Richard Spruce, with whose book *Notes of a Botanist on the Amazon and Andes* (1909) he became acquainted through his parents when he was a child; at Harvard University, found a mentor in Oakes Ames, the director of the Harvard Botanical Museum; for his B.A. thesis, spent a month in Oklahoma with the Kiowa Indians and wrote about their use of the hallucinogen peyote, derived from the mescal cactus; later became an influential defender of the legality of the sacramental use of peyote by American Indians; for his doctorate at Harvard (received in 1941), spent time with medicine men in the Mexican state of Oaxaca and wrote about their use of the psychedelic mushroom teonanácatl and the psychoactive vineyard seed ololiuqui, among other plants, in his dissertation, "Economic Aspects of the Flora of Northeastern Oaxaca"; became a research associate of the Harvard Botanical Museum and a fellow of the National Research Council in 1941; in his first project among the Indians of Amazonia, in 1941 and 1942, identified the many species of plants (within the genera Strychnos and Chondodendron) providing the resins the shamans mixed in varying compounds of curare, a muscle relaxant and neurological cure that can also cause paralysis and death (as, for example, when used in a mixture applied to the heads of arrows and darts); during World War II, when the Japanese cut off American access to the British and Dutch rubber plantations in Southeast Asia, found wild rubber trees in Amazonia and taught Indians how to extract the latex; following the war, found new species of rubber trees in Ceylon (now Sri Lanka) and Malaysia; after returning to the Harvard Botanical Museum, in 1953, served as curator of the orchid herbarium, curator of economic botany, and, for many years, director of the museum; became a professor in 1973; retired in 1985; in his field explorations, took the photographs—among a total of approximately 8,000— that profusely illustrated some of his 10 books, including *Where the Gods Reign* (1987); with Albert Hoffman, the Swiss chemist who discovered and synthesized LSD, wrote *The Botany and Chemistry of Hallucinogens* (1968) and *Plants of the Gods* (1979); with others, wrote *Plants and Human Affairs* (1960), *The Healing Forest* (1990), and *Vine of the Soul: Medicine Men of the Colombian Amazon— Their Plants and Rituals* (1992); was honored by the naming after him of many orchids as well as medicinal plants and the Sector Schultes, a 2.2 million–acre jungle preserve in Colombia; died in Boston, Massachusetts. See *Current Biography* (March) 1995.

Obituary *New York Times* D p11 Apr. 13, 2001

SHAPIRO, IRVING S. July 15, 1916–Sep. 13, 2001 Lawyer; corporate executive; from 1974 to 1981 was chairman of the board and chief executive officer of E. I. DuPont de Nemours & Co., the giant, Delaware-based manufacturer of petrochemical products, synthetic chemicals, and plastics; in 1941, graduated from the University of Minnesota and passed the Minnesota bar; the following year, joined the wartime Office of Price Administration in Washington, D.C.; in 1943, moved to the Department of Justice; for eight years, argued the government's position in cases before various circuit courts of appeal and the U.S. Supreme Court; in 1949 and 1950, was a member of the victorious five-man prosecution team in the trial in New York City of 11 leaders of the Communist Party accused of violating the Smith Act; rose to the post of executive assistant to the assistant attorney general for the Justice Department's criminal division; in 1951, left government service to join the DuPont Co.'s legal department, an aggregation of 130 lawyers; played a major role in the protracted antitrust case that culminated in 1957 in a Supreme Court decision requiring the company to divest itself of its stock in the General Motors Corp. (estimated to be between one quarter and one third of GM's total shares); subsequently masterminded a plan for spinning off the GM stock to DuPont stockholders without their incurring too great a tax liability; implemented that plan through further court action and a tax-relief bill that he maneuvered through Congress in 1962; became a vice president of DuPont in 1970, a senior vice president in 1972, and vice chairman of the executive board in 1973; took the helm of the company the following year, during an unprecedented national energy crisis; established the company's first energy department and set up energy conservation programs; as chairman and CEO, divested DuPont of a number of unprofitable divisions and invested millions of dollars in the development of new chemicals and plastics, including synthetic substitutes for oil and gas; streamlined the company's bureaucracy; regularly consulted with the division vice presidents, as a president might with his cabinet; at a time when corporations in general were increasingly viewed with animosity by environmentalists and others, became a spokesman for corporate America; on television talk shows, before congressional committees, and in other forums, decried excessive governmental regulation, including "the banning of useful products," and called for a more positive relationship between government and business and industry; from 1976 to 1978, chaired the Business

Roundtable, a group of prominent corporate executives often consulted by Congress and the White House; was a personal adviser to President Jimmy Carter; after leaving DuPont, joined the Washington office of the law firm of Skadden, Arps, Slate, Meagher & Flom; died in Washington, D.C. See *Current Biography* (November) 1976.

Obituary *New York Times* B p7 Sep. 15, 2001

SIMON, HERBERT A. June 15, 1916–Feb. 9, 2001 Interdisciplinary social scientist; Richard King Mellon professor of computer science and psychology at Carnegie-Mellon University, in Pittsburgh; a leading pioneer in the development of behavioral economics and the cognitive sciences; with Allen Newell in 1955, invented the first "thinking machine," a computer that simulated human information processing and decision making and was capable of proving the theorems presented by Bertrand Russell and Alfred North Whitehead in their classic work *Principia Mathematica* (1910–13); in 1978 was awarded the Nobel Prize in economic science for his pioneering research into the decision-making process in economic organizations; earned B.A. and Ph.D. degrees in political science at the University of Chicago; published his doctoral dissertation under the title *Administrative Behavior: A Study of Decision-Making Processes in Administrative Organizations* (1947) and subsequently revised it three times; after serving on the political-science faculty at the Illinois Institute of Technology for seven years, in 1949 became a professor in the graduate school of business administration at the Carnegie Institute of Technology, which later became Carnegie-Mellon University; with his associates at Carnegie-Mellon, spent a decade doing field studies into decision making in some 10 companies; concluded that the construct of the omniscient decision maker known as "economic man" was unrealistic, and offered in its stead what he called "administrative man," who "looks for a course of action that is satisfactory or 'good enough'"; published a total of 27 books, including *The New Science of Management* (1977), *Sciences of the Artificial* (1996), *Models of Bounded Rationality* (1997), and his autobiography, *Models of My Life* (1991); died in Pittsburgh, Pennsylvania. See *Current Biography* (June) 1979.

Obituary *New York Times* A p13 Feb. 10, 2001

SINOPOLI, GIUSEPPE Nov. 2, 1946–Apr. 20, 2001 Italian conductor; composer; was also a trained physician and psychiatrist; studied music at the Venice Conservatory and, out of deference to the wishes of his father, medicine at the University of Padua; decided to forego a potentially lucrative career in medicine to concentrate on music; in Vienna, studied conducting under Hans Swarowsky; to support himself, returned regularly to Venice to teach advanced composition at the conservatory, where he was professor of contemporary and electronic music; began his career as a composer in the late 1960s; turned to conducting after founding the Bruno Maderna Ensemble, a contemporary-music group, in 1975; over the following years, took on increasingly challenging guest-conducting roles with many of the world's top orchestras, including the Philharmonia in London,

which named him its music director in 1987; as a conductor, became known especially for his absorbing if idiosyncratic readings of Mahler, Brahms, Bruckner, and other German Romantic and post-Romantic composers, whose lushly orchestrated scores he refreshed with his "psychodramatic" approach, and for his daringly original interpretations of Italian operas, which appealed to him because of the psychological complexity of the characters; tended to be impassioned in his conducting, concerned with "the visceral rhythmic definition that serves . . . to clarify structure," as the critic John Rockwell observed; recorded extensively with the Philharmonia, the New York Philharmonic, and the Berlin Philharmonic, among other orchestras; composed, among other major works, *Numquid et unum*, for harpsichord and flute (1970), the massive *Symphonie imaginaire*, for three solo voices, children's choir, three choruses, and three orchestras (1972–73), *Souvenirs à la mémoire*, for two sopranos, countertenor, and orchestra (1973–74), and the expressionistic opera *Lou Salomé* (1981); in 1990, went to Berlin, Germany, to lead the Deutsche Oper; in 1992, became musical director of the Staatskapelle orchestra in Dresden; died after collapsing on the podium during a performance of Verdi's *Aida* in Berlin. See *Current Biography* (March) 1991.

Obituary *New York Times* B p7 Apr. 23, 2001

SOTHERN, ANN Jan. 22, 1909–Mar. 15, 2001 Actress; singer; dancer; television producer; in an acting career that included performances in more than 60 motion pictures and 175 television episodes, projected charm, warmth, and vitality as well as a beautiful image; starred in the network television situation comedies *Private Secretary* (1953–57), as Susie McNamara, the busybody aide to a talent agent, and *The Ann Sothern Show* (1958–61), as Katy O'Connor, the problem-beset assistant manager of a plush Manhattan hotel; had earlier risen to fame in motion pictures, chiefly with her portrayal of Maisie Ravier, a sassy platinum-blond showgirl from Brooklyn, the protagonist in a series of comedy/adventures; was trained as a vocalist by her mother, a concert soprano who became a diction and singing coach in Hollywood; under her real name, Harriette Lake, began her career in bit parts in several movies in 1929 and 1930; in the latter year, ventured onto the musical stage; on Broadway, was the ingenue in *Everybody's Welcome* (1931) and the female lead in *Of Thee I Sing* (1933); back in Hollywood, over the following several years had featured or starring roles in a score of pictures, including such musicals, comedies with music, and grade B comedy-dramas as *Kid Millions* (1934), *Let's Fall in Love* (1934), *The Girl Friend* (1935), *Folies Bergère* (1935), *Hooray for Love* (1935), *Fifty Roads to Town* (1937), *Dangerous Number*, (1937), and *Danger, Love at Work* (1937); following her marriage to the actor/bandleader Roger Pryor (the first of her two husbands), in 1936, traveled as a singer with Pryor and his band; returned to the screen impressively in the fourth-billed role of Jean Livingstone, the ostensibly "dumb," manipulative detective's stenographer, in the grade A comedy/drama/mystery *Trade Winds* (1938); over a period of eight years, made 10 "Maisie" films, including *Maisie* (1939), *Congo Maisie* (1940), *Swing Shift Maisie* (1943), *Maisie Goes to Reno* (1944), and *Undercover Maisie* (1947); later played Maisie in a radio series; during the eight-year Maisie period in Hollywood, garnered some half-dozen other screen credits, including the supporting female role in *Brother Orchid* (1940), top billing in the musicals *Lady Be Good* (1941) and *Panama Hattie* (1942), and the leading role of a nurse on Bataan in the World War II melodrama *Cry Havoc* (1943); gave what was probably her best dramatic performance as Rita Phipps in *Letter to Three Wives* (1949); in her last regular role on television, supplied the tart/sweet voice of the automobile in the farfetched situation comedy *My Mother the Car* (1965–66); rarely appeared in films during her television career; following an absence of more than 20 years from the motion-picture screen, was nominated for an Academy Award for her supporting performance as the upbeat neighbor and friend of one of the protagonists (Lillian Gish) in *The Whales of August* (1987); died at her home in Ketchum, Idaho. See *Current Biography* (December) 1956.

Obituary *New York Times* C p17 Mar. 17, 2001

SPENCE, HARTZELL Feb. 15, 1908–May 9, 2001 Author; was the elder son of an itinerant Methodist minister, about whom he would write in his best-seller *One Foot in Heaven: The Life of a Practical Parson* (1940); after receiving a B.A. degree in English at Iowa State University, in 1930, joined United Press as its Iowa bureau manager; later moved to New York to supervise the wire news agency's special services; after 10 years with United Press, left to concentrate on his freelance writing; co-wrote the screenplay for the motion-picture adaptation of *One Foot in Heaven*, released by Warner Bros. in 1941; in the same year, published his second book, *Radio City*, a novel reflecting his experiences with advertising agencies and radio production; in 1942, published *Get Thee Behind Me: My Life as a Preacher's Son*, a memoir of his growing up in a series of parishes in Iowa and Colorado; as a U.S. Army captain during World War II, was executive editor of *Yank*, a weekly newspaper written by and for military servicemen, in which he introduced, among other regular features, glamorous photographs of attractive female movie stars wearing lingerie or swimsuits, whom he called pinups, a usage of that term that he is widely credited with inventing; later contributed some 200 articles to the *Saturday Evening Post* and other popular magazines; wrote historical novels, the biography *Marcos of the Philippines* (1964), and, in collaboration with the veteran ringmaster Fred Bradna, a book on the circus; died at his home in Essex, Connecticut. See *Current Biography* (October) 1942.

Obituary *New York Times* B p8 May 25, 2001

STARGELL, WILLIE Mar. 6, 1940–Apr. 9, 2001 Baseball player; former team captain with the Pittsburgh Pirates; a free-swinging left-handed slugger who often struck out but just as often came through with power hits in the clutch; signed with the Pirates in 1959; after almost four years in the minor leagues, was called up to Pittsburgh toward the end of the 1962 season; during most of his career, played left field, until sore knees slowed him down and he switched to first base; in 1971 (when the Pirates won the National League pennant and the world championship), led the league in home runs, with 48, and drove in 125 runs; scored the winning run in Game Seven of the 1971 World Series, in which the Pirates defeated the Baltimore Orioles; led the National League in home runs in 1971 and 1973; succeeded Roberto Clemente as Pittsburgh's field leader after Clemente died in a plane crash, in December 1972; rallied the Pirates to another league pennant and world championship in 1979; was voted Most Valuable Player in the 1979 World Series (again against the Orioles), in which he had a .400 batting average, drove in seven runs, and hit three homers and four doubles; retired after the 1982 season, with a career batting average of .282 and career totals of 2,232 hits, 475 home runs, and 1,540 runs batted in; was runner-up for the National League record for career strikeouts, with 1,936; died in Wilmington, North Carolina. See *Current Biography* (June) 1980.

Obituary *New York Times* B p8 Apr. 10, 2001

STASSEN, HAROLD E. Apr; 13, 1907–Mar. 4, 2001 Former governor of Minnesota; presidential aide; diplomat; university president; perennial presidential candidate; lawyer; a liberal, internationalist Republican; was elected governor of Minnesota in 1938 (thus becoming that state's youngest governor) and reelected in 1940 and 1942; in 1943, four months into his third term, joined the wartime U.S. Navy as a commissioned officer; served as chief of staff to Admiral William F. Halsey in the Pacific; as a delegate to the founding conference of the United Nations in San Francisco in 1945, was one of the eight American signers of the U.N. charter; was president of the University of Pennsylvania from 1948 through 1952; when President Dwight D. Eisenhower assumed office in 1953, became the president's assistant in overseeing foreign-aid programs; was special assistant to the president on disarmament matters, with Cabinet rank, from 1955 to 1958; unsuccessfully campaigned for the Republican nomination in every presidential election year but one from 1948 to 1992; died in Bloomington, Minnesota. See *Current Biography* (May) 1948.

Obituary *New York Times* B p6 Mar. 5, 2001

STORR, ANTHONY May 18, 1920–Mar. 17, 2001 British psychiatrist; psychotherapist; had a passionate concern for mental suffering, rooted in his own lifelong bouts with depression, experiences that convinced him of the creative possibilities inherent in coping with mental problems; began trying to explain human cruelty when he was overwhelmed by newsreel footage of the British liberation of a Nazi concentration camp; rejected Freud's theory that violence is a result of sexual frustration; concluded that aggressiveness is a given in human nature but that it can be channeled into positive attitudes and actions; was educated at Christ College, Cambridge University (where he found a mentor, patron, and friend in C. P. Snow) and Westminster Hospital Medical School in London; trained in psychoanalysis and psychotherapy while working as a physician at Runwell Mental Hospital and Maudsley Hospital; at first, called himself a Jungian, but soon developed his own dynamic approach to psychoanalysis; challenged the conventional wisdom that interpersonal relationships are essential to mental health; strove "to show that the dividing lines between sanity and mental illness have been drawn in the wrong places," that "the sane are madder than we think, the mad saner"; asserted that "it's not psychopathology that matters," but "what you do with it"; was in private practice as a psychotherapist for 22 years; in 1974 left his highly successful practice to return to the mainstream of psychiatry as a consultant in Oxford, England, and a teacher at Oxford University; in 1960, when it was revealed that British psychiatrists had used psychological torture in the interrogation of prisoners during World War II, published "Torture without Violence," an angry magazine article that caused repercussions in high places and led to further revelations about such subjects as drug-induced hypnosis; testified on psychiatric responsibility before a government committee that subsequently issued rules against psychological brutality; between 1960 and 1984 published the books *The Integrity of the Personality, Sexual Deviation, Human Aggression, Human Destructiveness, The Dynamics of Creation, Jung, The Art of Psychotherapy,* and *Churchill's Dog and Other Phenomena of the Human Mind*; retired from teaching in 1984; subsequently published the books *Solitude: A Return to the Self* (1988), *Freud* (1989), and *Music and the Mind* (1992); became a familiar figure as a commentator on British television; wrote and spoke on deep and complex psychological subjects simply and lucidly, with sharp insight and in an elegant and enthralling style; died in Oxford, England. See *Current Biography* (June) 1994.

Obituary *New York Times* C p21 Mar. 21, 2001

STRATTON, WILLIAM G. Feb. 26, 1914–Mar. 2, 2001 Two-term Republican governor of Illinois (1953–61); had previously served two terms as U.S. congressman at large from Illinois (1941–43 and 1947–49) and two terms as state treasurer (1943–45 and 1951–53); during the closing months of World War II, served as a commissioned officer with the U.S. Navy in the Pacific; ran unsuccessfully for Illinois secretary of state in 1948; went to the U.S. House of Representatives as an anti–New Deal isolationist; on returning to Congress after the war, brought "a resolute isolationism and conservatism back into the House," as a Capitol Hill observer wrote at the time in *U.S. News & World Report*; as governor, numbered among his proudest achievements the completion of the first 200 miles of the Illinois tollway system; was the first Illinois governor to appoint a woman and a black to his cabinet; died in Chicago. See *Current Biography* (April) 1953.

Obituary *New York Times* B p6 Mar. 5, 2001

SUCKSDORFF, ARNE Feb. 3, 1917–May 4, 2001 Swedish documentary filmmaker whose work included such short subjects as *Hunter and the Forest—A Story without Words* (1956), *Shadow of the Hunter* (1957), and *Struggle for Survival* (1959); approached his subjects, especially nature, with a poet's touch; during the 1940s and early 1950s, filmed short documentaries in India, Lapland, and elsewhere for the major Swedish film studio Svensk Filmindustri; in 1949, won a Hollywood Academy Award for best short subject for *Symphony of a City*, an impressionistic study of his native city, Stockholm; in partnership with Niles Gustav Orn, formed an independent company in 1953; in the acclaimed feature film *The Great Adventure* (1953), photographed wildlife in and around a Swedish farm, focusing on the story of two young brothers who rescue, tame, and shelter an otter surreptitiously, hiding the fact from their parents; invested the profits from *The Great Adventure* in a less successful feature, *The Boy in the Tree*; left Sweden, moving first to Sardinia and then to Brazil, where he lived for three decades; in Brazil, taught documentary filmmaking for UNESCO; made the film *My Home Is Copacabana* (1965), about the plight of derelict children in Brazil's urban slums; returned to Sweden in the early 1990s; died in Stockholm. See *Current Biography* (April) 1956.

Obituary *New York Times* p34 May 13, 2001

SULLIVAN, LEON H. Oct. 16, 1922–Apr. 25, 2001 Baptist clergyman; social activist; a leader in bootstrap black entrepreneurship and capital investment; was a protégé of Adam Clayton Powell; served as an assistant at Powell's church in Harlem while studying theology at Union Theological Seminary and sociology at Columbia University; after completing his studies, was pastor of the First Baptist Church in South Orange, New Jersey; in 1950, became pastor of Zion Baptist Church in the inner city of North Philadelphia; there, set about countering juvenile delinquency and unemployment; organized boycotts of Philadelphia businesses that did not hire blacks; set up job training programs with generous support from several major corporations, foundations, and labor unions as well as the federal government; in 1964, opened in North Philadelphia the first of a number of facilities of his Opportunities Industrialization Center (OIC), offering courses in such trades as electronics, power sewing, drafting, cabinetmaking, cooking and other restaurant services, welding, retail sales, and dry cleaning and laundry work; over a period of five years, trained 6,000 workers (not counting thousands more enrolled in OIC branches in other cities) and placed 5,000 in jobs; in 1962, founded Zion Investments Associates; sold shares to his parishioners on easy installment plans of $10 a week; through the investment firm, financed an apartment complex, a garment-manufacturing company, a shopping center, and an aerospace-parts subcontracting company; in his parish, established an employment agency, a family counseling service, a day-care center, a community center, a home for the aged, and athletic teams; saw the membership of his congregation grow from 600, when he arrived, to 5,000; in 1971, joined the board of directors of the General Motors Corp.; was instrumental in expanding black employment in the corporation and black auto dealerships; after visiting South Africa in 1974, helped organize and wrote the guidelines for boycotts by American companies that contributed to the eventual demise of apartheid; concentrated on the antiapartheid campaign after retiring as pastor of Zion Baptist Church, in 1988; died in Scottsdale, Arizona. See *Current Biography* (March) 1969.

Obituary *New York Times* C p17 Apr. 26, 2001

THOMSON, MELDRIM JR. Mar. 8, 1912–Apr. 19, 2001 Three-term Republican governor of New Hampshire (1973–79); a conservative constitutionalist who, as he wrote in his book *Live Free or Die* (1979), was proud of having "fought the holy cause of liberty against the sinister encroachments of the federal government"; was fierce and fiery in campaigning for states' rights, Second Amendment rights, and voluntary prayer in public schools and against income and sales taxes; began his career practicing law in Florida; subsequently worked in legal publishing in Brooklyn and Stony Brook, New York; in the mid-1950s, moved with his wife to Oxford, New Hampshire, where they established the Equity Publishing Co. and began maple-sugar farming; founded a group called the Taxfighters; after leaving the governor's mansion, continued maple-sugar farming and became a columnist for the *Manchester Union Leader*; died at his home in Oxford, New Hampshire. See *Current Biography* (October) 1978.

Obituary *New York Times* B p9 Apr. 20, 2001

TITOV, GHERMAN Sep. 11, 1935–Sep. 20, 2000 Russian cosmonaut; was the second person (after fellow cosmonaut Yuri Gagarin) to orbit Earth; began his training as a Soviet military pilot in 1953; graduated from the Stalingrad Flying Academy in 1957; began training for space flight in 1950; in the spaceship *Vostok II* on August 6 and 7, 1961 (four months after Gagarin's one-orbit trip), circled Earth 17 times during a journey of 24 hours and 11 minutes; later was a senior officer in the design department of the Soviet air force's space program; rose to the rank of colonel-general in the Soviet air force (1988–92); as an unreconstructed Communist, was elected to the post–Soviet Russian Parliament in 1995; wrote five books about space travel, some autobiographical; died in Moscow. See *Current Biography* (December) 1962.

Obituary *New York Times* A p25 Sep. 22, 2000

TRENET, CHARLES May 18, 1913–Feb. 18, 2001 French popular singer; songwriter; a legendary progenitor of the contemporary *chanson française*; a sometimes playful master at combining catchy melodies and inventive rhythms with poetic and often surreal lyrics, ranging from ebullient to melancholy; won the hearts of French audiences with his songs, including the swinging dance number "Le Soleil et la lune" and the sentimental patriotic anthem "Douce France"; scored internationally as well with such hits as the hauntingly romantic "La Mer" (popularized in the U.S. as "Beyond the Sea") and the lament "Que reste-t'il de nos amours" ("I Wish You Love"); wrote hundreds of songs, including "J'ai ta main," "Il pleut dans ma chambre," "Fleur bleue," and "Route Nationale 7"; inspired generations of French music-hall and cabaret singers and songwriters; was born and grew up near the Spanish border in southern France; as a teenager drawn to painting,

music, and poetry, was encouraged by the Catalan painter Fons-Godail and the Catalan journalist and poet Albert Bausil; at 17 moved to Paris; became a grip at the Joinville film studios; collaborated on the musical score for the motion picture *Bariole*; published poetry in periodicals; found a patron in the avant-garde painter and poet Max Jacob; in the cafés and cabarets of Montparnasse, made friends with the likes of the writer and filmmaker Jean Cocteau (who dubbed him "the last of the troubadours") and the young piano player Johnny Hess; collaborated with Hess in composing songs ranging from clever tongue-twisters to "Vous qui passez sans me voir," a poignant song of heartbroken love; from 1933 to 1936 performed on stage and radio with Hess under the billing Charles et Johnny; in 1937 realized hits with "Je chante" and "Y'a d'la joie" (which was popularized by Maurice Chevalier); honed his solo act in a piano bar in a Marseilles hotel while doing military service there; in March 1938 took the act into a Paris music hall, wearing the blue suit and shirt, white tie and carnation, and floppy felt hair that would remain his trademarks; in 1938 composed "Boum," an onomatopoetic ditty with jazz-like phrasing, including scat-like riffs; scripted and starred in the romantic musical films *La Route enchantée* (The Enchanted Road, 1938) and *Je chante* (I'm Singing, 1938), vehicles for him and his hit songs; during the Nazi occupation of the World War II years, wrote the songs "Bonsoir jolie Madame" and "La Romance de Paris"; for six years following the war, when he was out of favor in France, lived in the U.S. and toured other countries in the Americas; returned to France in 1951; toured in Europe, the U.S., and the Soviet Union in the early 1960s; in 1963 was arrested and jailed in a homosexual scandal; wrote several novels, including *Un Noir éblouissant* (1965) and *Pierre, Juliette, and l'automate* (1983), and a memoir, *Mes jeunes années racontées par ma mère et moi-même* (1979); recorded new songs for the album *Les Poètes descendant dans la rue* (1999); died in the Paris suburb of Creteil. See *Current Biography* (February) 1989.

Obituary *New York Times* B p9 Feb. 20, 2001

TRENKLER, FREDDIE 1913(?)–May 21, 2000 Austrian-born ice skater; one of the 20th century's great on-ice comics; "the Bouncing Ball of the Ice"; a diminutive, prankish clown whose costume consisted of tattered clothes and a battered hat; performed mock pratfalls and other slapstick stunts with a slick, deceptive artlessness possible only to a master of basic athletic, even acrobatic skating; as a juvenile in Vienna, became a junior figure-skating champion, but was more interested in free skating; was in his early 20s when he introduced his clown act; after touring with amateur ice carnivals in Austria and several neighboring countries, made his first trip to the United States, in 1937; in December of that year, appeared professionally in a show called *Gay Blades* at Madison Square Garden, in New York City; subsequently, made professional appearances in London, England; in 1940, returned to the U.S. to join the figure skater and movie star Sonja Henie's *Hollywood Ice Revue*; skated with that troupe for 15 years; also performed in other shows produced by Henie and

Arthur Wirtz; appeared in the motion picture *The Countess of Monte Cristo* (1948), a Henie vehicle; after the *Hollywood Ice Revue* disbanded, toured with the *Ice Capades* until his retirement, in 1981; died in Los Angeles. See *Current Biography* (June) 1971.

Obituary *New York Times* p33 June 3, 2001

TROUT, ROBERT Oct. 15, 1909–Nov. 14, 2000 Broadcast journalist; during a career spanning seven decades, chiefly with the CBS network, regularly covered such national and world events as political party conventions and campaigns, floods, the Kentucky Derby, the 1939 New York World's Fair, the opening of Boulder Dam, New Year's Eve celebrations at Times Square, navy maneuvers, and coronations and marriages of British royalty; most memorably, was one of Edward R. Murrow's colleagues at CBS's London bureau during World War II; in reporting the Allied invasion of France to the American radio audience, manned the microphone many times, including one unbroken stretch of seven hours and 18 minutes; possessed a deep and dulcet baritone voice, precise and polished elocution, and a ready facility with words; early in his radio days, was dubbed "the iron man" by his peers, for his aplomb in handling breaking news and his stamina in ad-libbing through long stretches of non-breaking news; was eulogized by his fellow broadcast journalist and friend Andy Rooney for being "fastidious with the facts" and "perspicacious with their presentation"; began broadcasting at radio station WJSV in Mount Vernon Hills, Virginia, during his early 20s; in 1932, when WJSV joined the then-nascent Columbia Broadcasting System, moved with the station (as staff reporter) to Washington, D.C., where its call letters were changed to WTOP; broadcast President Herbert Hoover's lighting of the White House Christmas tree in December 1932 and President Franklin D. Roosevelt's first inauguration, in March 1933; coined the term "fireside chats" when introducing FDR's informal radio talks to the nation; joined the CBS news and public-affairs staff in New York in 1935; was sent to London in 1941; after World War II, anchored the daily CBS radio program *Robert Trout with the News Till Now*; as TV grew in popularity, had some assignments on that medium, including a daily newscast at one point; in 1965 served CBS in Europe as a special roving correspondent; in his last years, until shortly before his death, delivered oral essays (often relating to persons and events he had covered years before) on the National Public Radio program *All Things Considered*; maintained homes in Manhattan and Madrid, Spain (to and from which he traveled by ship, because he refused to fly); lived mainly in Madrid for two decades, until the death of his wife; died in Manhattan. See *Current Biography* (October) 1965.

Obituary *New York Times* B p14 Nov. 15, 2000

TRUDEAU, PIERRE ELLIOTT Oct. 18, 1919–Sep. 28, 2000 Former prime minister of Canada; a bilingual Québecois who brought to the Canadian national leadership an unprecedented cosmopolitan panache; staving off the insurgent French secessionist movement in Quebec, his native province, realized his federalist vision of a united, multicultural Canada; cut a dashing figure on the international scene, where he was a somewhat quixotic champion of world peace and nuclear disarmament; in the course of his international education in law and political science in the 1940s, came under the influence of the Marxist theorist Harold Laski at the London School of Economics; early on, dedicated himself to the pursuit of a "just society" for Canada; began that pursuit in the 1950s on the provincial level, in Quebec, through *Cité Libre*, a leftist intellectual quarterly that he co-founded, through a pro bono law office (heavily concerned with labor cases), and through Rassemblement, a short-lived political movement that he co-founded; taught classes in constitutional law and civil liberties at the University of Montreal from 1961 to 1965; was elected to Parliament as a "new age" Liberal in 1965; was parliamentary secretary (1966–67) to Prime Minister Lester Pearson (1966–67) and minister of justice and attorney general in Pearson's cabinet (1967–68); in the Ministry of Justice as in the House of Commons, worked effectively for the expansion of social-welfare programs, gun control, and the liberalization of laws relating to gambling, divorce, abortion, and homosexuality; in 1968, became leader of the Liberal Party and prime minister; as prime minister, took tough, effective measures against French-Canadian separatist terrorists in Quebec; thereby temporarily projected what was perceived in western Canadian provinces to be a move to federal encroachment on provincial authority; was turned out of office when the Liberals lost their majority to the Progressive Conservatives in May 1979; was returned to the prime ministership in March 1980; led a successful challenge to a Parti Québecois secessionist referendum, defeated by the electorate in May 1980; two years later, persuaded the British Parliament to turn control of Canada's constitution over to the Canadian Parliament; was instrumental in liberalizing Canada's immigration policy, to the end of diversifying the country's ethnic constituency; realized a long-term goal when French became an official language across Canada, alongside English, in 1984; left office in 1984; from 1971 until their divorce in 1984, was married to Margaret Sinclair, 30 years his junior, who embarrassed him with her gallivanting with rock musicians; wrote some eight books, including *Canadian Dualism/La dualité Canadienne* (1960), *Federalism and the French Canadians* (1968), and *Memoirs* (1993); died in Montreal. See *Current Biography* (November) 1968.

Obituary *New York Times* A p1+ Sep. 29, 2000

VERDON, GWEN Jan. 13, 1925–Oct. 18, 2000 Dancer; singer; actress; one of the brightest stars in the firmament of the American musical theater; on Broadway during the 1950s, created roles in four musical comedies—*Can-Can*, *Damn Yankees*, *New Girl in Town*, and *Redhead*—that earned her Tony Awards; at that time, was described by critics as an "alluring" and "vivacious" redhead who performed with an "athletic ebullience" infused with "a delicacy of spirit"; was the daughter of Gertrude (Standring) Verdon, a member of the modern-dance troupe Denishawn; in early childhood, wore knee-high orthopedic boots to support and correct legs bent by infant disease; began taking dancing lessons at age two; was tap-dancing in theaters in Los Angeles at six; as a teenager, danced in chorus lines in nightclubs; behind the scenes, was an assistant to dance director Jack Cole at several Hollywood studios in the late 1940s and early 1950s; did some specialty dancing on screen; danced with Betty Grable in *The Farmer Takes a Wife* (1953); in 1950, was one of Cole's dancers in the short-lived Broadway musical *Alive and Kicking*; when *Can-Can* opened, in May 1953, stole the show and attained instant stardom with her explosive performances of two specialty numbers, including a sizzling Apache dance; starred as Lola, the devil's seductive disciple and agent, in the Faustian musical comedy *Damn Yankees* (choreographed by Bob Fosse), which began its long run in 1955; developed a close, long-term personal and professional relationship with Fosse, who would become her second husband, in 1960; gave a moving performance in the title role of the wretched but redeemed prostitute in the musical *New Girl in Town* (1957), for which she shared a Tony Award with her co-star, Thelma Ritter; reprised her interpretation of Lola in the movie version of *Damn Yankees* (1958); found her best vehicle in the role of Essie Whimple, a timid London waxworks-museum worker turned music-hall dancer in the musical murder mystery *Redhead* (1959), directed and choreographed by Fosse; starred as the good-hearted dance-hall hostess in *Sweet Charity* (also directed and choreographed by Fosse), which began a two-year run on Broadway in 1966; remained close to Fosse after her legal separation from him, in 1971 (and was with him at his death, in 1987); gave her farewell Broadway performance as Roxie in Fosse's musical *Chicago* (1975); made many dramatic appearances on television, most notably in the network daytime serial *All My Children*; on the silver screen, was one of the lauded cast of senior citizens in *Cocoon* (1985); died in Woodstock, New York. See *Current Biography* (October) 1960.

Obituary *New York Times* C p21 Oct. 19, 2000

WAUGH, AUBERON Nov. 17, 1939–Jan. 16, 2001 British writer; a social critic, known for his outrageous satirical vitriol, who was too anarchistic by temperament to be politically pigeonholed; as the second child (among seven) and eldest son of the novelist and essayist Evelyn Waugh, seemed to have inherited a well-born sense of social hierarchy; wrote five comic novels, in the earlier of which, he conceded, he "used the same sort of jokes" that his father had in his novels; was better known as a curmudgeonly journalist, in particular a columnist who devoted himself to "cultivating the vituperative arts"; while privately a kind and gentle person of old-fashioned civility, established a public persona as "the rudest man on Fleet Street"; was regarded by his enemies as an elitist reactionary, "a public-school snob" perpetuating "the myth of the superior cultured English gent" who represented "an upper-class yesterday" and viewed by his admirers as a "contemporary equivalent of Jonathan Swift" whose mordantly witty and rhetorically energetic fulminations constituted "a brilliant portrait of a world unraveling"; in *Another Voice: An Alternative Anatomy of Britain* (1986), a collection of 83 of the col-

umns he wrote over a 10-year period for the London *Spectator*, a conservative weekly journal, presented, in his words, a "grisly spectre of modern Britain, now reduced by over-emphasis on social welfare and workers' rights to a nation of unemployable, semi-imbecile football hooligans"; in conjuring up that "spectre," savaged organized religion, the press, social engineers, Cabinet ministers, so-called New Brits, importers of America's fast-food culture, and a variety of others he viewed as social parasites, predators, fools, louts, practitioners of sham, cant, and pomposity, and authoritarians of all stripes; was educated at elite Roman Catholic primary and prep schools (All Hallows and Downside, respectively); after graduating from Downside, did his military service as a second lieutenant with the Old Horse Guards; was seriously injured by accidental machine-gun fire during a training exercise; subsequently studied for a year at Christ Church College, Oxford University; in 1960 published his first novel, *The Foxglove Saga*, partly inspired by his own experiences; in it, attacked the shallowness and hidebound hypocrisy of various traditional British institutions; in his second novel, *Path of Dalliance* (1963), which viewed academic and intellectual life at Oxford through the eyes of two undergraduates, punctured what he perceived to be the pretensions and excesses of the political left as he satirized the students' efforts in behalf of such causes as civil rights and nuclear disarmament; in *Where Are the Violets Now?* (1965), created the protagonist Arthur Friendship, a pseudonymous, friendless writer of insipid articles for women's magazines, who is drawn into a rather sinister organization named the International Peace Movement, headed by a man who turns out to be a Nazi war criminal; realized what he and most critics regarded as his best novel in *Consider the Lilies* (1968), an attack on religious hypocrisy for which he made his faithless protagonist an Anglican rather than a Roman Catholic clergyman only because he needed him to be a married man; in his fifth, and last, novel, *A Bed of Flowers* (1972), used the plot of Shakespeare's *As You Like It* (reworked and updated) as a device for splenetic assaults on some of his favorite targets, including certain types of ambition-driven journalists and ecumenical clergy; meanwhile, in the early 1960s, had begun his career in journalism as an editorial writer for the *London Daily Telegraph*; in the late 1960s, as chief political correspondent for the *Spectator*, covered the civil war (which involved genocide) between Nigeria, a former British colony, and the secessionist state of Biafra; co-wrote the book *Biafra: Britain's Shame* (1969); later, was chief fiction reviewer for, successively, the *Spectator*, the London *Evening Standard*, and the London *Daily Mail*; in 1970 began a 16-year association with the magazine *Private Eye*, for which he wrote a spoof diary, fizzing with surreal comic mixtures of fact and fantasy, later collected in the books *Four Crowded Years* (1976) and *A Turbulent Decade* (1985); made the history of a notorious court case splendidly readable in *The Last Word: The Trial of Jeremy Thorpe* (1980); was the charter editor (1986– 2000) of the monthly *Literary Review*, in which he promoted such causes as the Common Reader and repudiated such literary practices as verse that did not scan or rhyme; established the review's annual Bad Sex Awards for the most egregious purple passages in "serious" novels; for a decade (ending in December 2000), wrote the "Way of the World" column for the *Daily Telegraph*; died in Taunton in his native Somerset, England. See *Current Biography* (May) 1990.

Obituary *New York Times* B p11 Jan. 18, 2001

WELTY, EUDORA Apr. 13, 1909–July 23, 2001 Author; a regional storyteller, commonly identified with the Southern School, who combined her strong sense of place with universal relevance to human nature; in short stories and novels (extended short stories, for the most part), set in rural and small-town Mississippi, wrote lovingly but realistically, and in low-keyed lyric prose, of the characters she created and their interior lives; left her native Mississippi to earn a B.A. degree at the University of Wisconsin (1929) and do postgraduate work at Columbia University, in New York City (1930–31); during the Depression of the 1930s, traveled throughout Mississippi as a publicist for the federal Works Progress Administration (later renamed the Work Projects Administration), armed with a simple Kodak camera, taking gritty photographs of ordinary people in their daily routines; exhibited the photographs at a Manhattan gallery in 1936 and published them in a volume titled *One Time, One Place* (1971); from her Depression experiences, drew the inspiration for many of her early short stories, including the first, "Death of a Traveling Salesman," published in the little magazine *Manuscript* in 1936; subsequently, contributed stories to the *Southern Review*, the *Atlantic Monthly*, and the *New Yorker*, among other magazines; in the volume *A Curtain of Green* (1941), brought together 17 of her early pieces of short fiction, including her most humorous story, "Why I Live at the P.O.," the ironic story "The Petrified Man," and "A Worn Path," about an old black woman walking miles to obtain an antidote for her grandson's ingestion of lye, the first of six of her stories to win an O. Henry Memorial Contest award; in 1942, published the novella *The Robber Bridegroom*, a fantasy tour de force set in the Natchez Trace that was later adapted for the musical stage; in her first full-length novel, *Delta Wedding* (1946), focused on the complex but basically loving interplay of members of a prosperous plantation family whose way of life is fading away; wrote about characters in a fictional Mississippi Delta small town in the interrelated stories in *The Golden Apples* (1949); created the garrulous character Edna Earle Ponder as the monologist narrating the humorous story of her eccentric Uncle Daniel Ponder in *The Ponder Heart* (1954), a stage adaptation of which was produced on Broadway in 1956; for 15 years, wrote and published little because she, an unmarried woman, was preoccupied with caring for her terminally ill mother, her two ill brothers, and the children of one of the brothers; in 1970, published her longest novel, *Losing Battles*, a 436-page epic dramatic comedy about a reunion of the members of a proud, impoverished family in Depression-era rural northeastern Mississippi; brought direct autobiographical information into her fiction for the first time in *The Optimist's Daughter* (1972), for which she received a Pulitzer Prize; published

eight collections of short stories, including *The Wide Net* (1943), *The Bride of Innisfallen* (1953), and *The Collected Stories* (1980), and several collections of essays and book reviews, including *One Writer's Beginnings* (1984), comprising three autobiographical pieces; in 1998, was gratified to see a two-volume compilation of her work issued by the Library of America; died in Jackson, Mississippi. See *Current Biography* (October) 1975.

Obituary *New York Times* p1+ July 24, 2001

WIGGINS, JAMES RUSSELL Dec. 4, 1903–Nov. 19, 2000 Journalist; former diplomat; as an editor, was instrumental in building the *Washington Post* from a small, struggling capital-city daily into a leading national voice; in the words of Chalmers M. Roberts, one of his colleagues at the *Post*, "gave its news pages tone and integrity and . . . gave passion to the editorial page as well"; began his career with newspapers in Minnesota, as a reporter, editor, publisher, and Washington correspondent; was assistant to the publisher of the *New York Times* (1946–47); joined the *Washington Post* as managing editor in 1947; six years later, acquired the additional title of vice president; in 1955, when the *Post* absorbed the *Washington Times Herald*, became vice president and executive editor of the expanded enterprise, which was known as the *Washington Post and Times Herald* for five years thereafter; out of concern over "national security" policies inimical to freedom of the press, wrote the book *Freedom and Secrecy* (1956); as editor and executive vice president of the *Post* from 1960 to 1968, was credited with helping to steer the newspaper on a generally interventionist liberal editorial course; supported President Lyndon B. Johnson's domestic "Great Society" programs and, with some reservations, the Americanization of the war in Vietnam; in 1968, was named U.S. ambassador to the United Nations by Johnson; served four months in the U.N. post; in 1969 settled in Maine as owner and editor of the Ellsworth (Maine) *American*; remained editor and publisher of the *American* after selling the weekly newspaper in 1991; died at his home in Brooklin, Maine. See *Current Biography* (November) 1969.

Obituary *New York Times* B p10 Nov. 21, 2000

WOODCOCK, LEONARD Feb 15, 1911–Jan. 16, 2001 President of the United Auto Workers (UAW), formally the United Automobile, Aerospace and Agricultural Implement Workers of America (1970–77); U.S. ambassador to the People's Republic of China during the administration of President Jimmy Carter; as the son of a British father, received his early education in British schools; while working as a machine assembler in Detroit, Michigan, in the early 1930s, joined an American Federation of Labor union that subsequently became a UAW local; was on the staff of the UAW's regional office in Grand Rapids, Michigan from 1940 to 1944; in 1946 was appointed administrative assistant to UAW president Walter Reuther; the next year, was elected a Michigan UAW regional director; was a UAW vice president, responsible for negotiating with General Motors and the aerospace industry, from 1955 to 1970, when he succeeded to the presidency, after Reuther's death; as president, oversaw a strike against General Motors that resulted in wage increases and cost-of-living protection, albeit at a sizable cost to the union and its members and an escalation in consumer car prices; also oversaw a strategic series of strikes that thwarted General Motors's plans to establish nonunion supply plants in the South; dealt with the threat of foreign auto-company competition by pressing, not for quotas, but for domestic content guidelines (which would preserve American jobs by causing Japanese and Korean auto manufacturers to move some of their plants to the U.S.); was an influential supporter of Democratic candidate Jimmy Carter in his successful campaign for the presidency in 1976; after Carter took office, in 1977, was selected by him to lead a commission to Vietnam and Laos to try to determine the fate of Americans missing in action in the Vietnam War; later in 1977, became chief of the U.S. mission in Beijing, China; after negotiating a normalization of diplomatic relations with China, in 1979, acquired the title of ambassador, which he retained until 1981; in the 1990s, departed from standard labor policy in favoring the granting to China of permanent "most favored nation" trading status with the U.S. and admission to the World Trade Organization; died at his home in Ann Arbor, Michigan. See *Current Biography* (November) 1970.

Obituary *New York Times* B p12 Jan. 18, 2001

WOODS, DONALD Dec. 15, 1933–Aug. 19, 2001 Expatriate South African journalist; in print and lectures, contributed to the toppling of the Afrikaner government that oppressed South Africa's black majority with its apartheid laws for more than four decades; as the son of a white trader in the region of southeastern South Africa now known as the Eastern Cape, was the only white child growing up among thousands of Bonvana tribesmen, whose language, Xhosa, he learned to speak fluently; at first aspired, ambivalently, to a career in law; studied law for three years at the University of Cape Town; clerked in law for two years; incrementally, shed his own inbred racist attitudes; in 1957, became a cub reporter with the East London, South Africa, *Daily Dispatch*; on leave from that newspaper, traveled abroad from 1958 to 1959; interned with newspapers in Britain and North America; became deputy editor of the *Daily Dispatch* in 1963 and editor in 1965; stepped up the newspaper's criticism of the Afrikaner government and apartheid; also voiced such criticism in a syndicated column that ran in six South African newspapers; considered himself a moderate liberal until 1973, when he met Stephen Biko, the leader of South Africa's Black Consciousness movement; led a public outcry when Biko died under suspicious circumstances while in security police custody on September 12, 1977 (a death later revealed as a murder); on October 19, 1977, was placed under a five-year "ban" silencing him as a journalist and severely restricting even his private speech and movements; when his family was threatened, fled South Africa in the dark of night on December 29, 1977; settled with his wife and children in England; wrote and lectured against apartheid in Europe and the U.S.; wrote the biography *Biko* (1978) and the autobiography *Asking for Trouble* (1981), books that provided the director

David Attenborough with the grist for his motion picture *Cry Freedom* (1987), in which Kevin Klein was cast as Woods; between 1990 and 2001, revisited South Africa three times; died in Sutton, Surrey, England. See *Current Biography* (February) 1982.

Obituary *New York Times* B p6 Aug. 20, 2001

WOODWARD, ROBERT F. Oct. 1, 1908–May 18, 2001 Career foreign-service officer; expert on Latin American affairs; joined the U.S. Foreign Service in December 1931; over the following two decades, was assigned to various consular posts, chiefly in South America; at the State Department in the early 1950s, was, in turn, chief of the division of Foreign Service personnel and deputy assistant secretary of state for Inter-American Affairs; was given his first ambassadorial assignment in 1954, to Costa Rica; presented his credentials as ambassador to Uruguay in 1958 and Chile in 1961; following a stint as assistant secretary of state for Latin American affairs, was ambassador to Spain, from 1962 to 1965; in his last foreign-service assignments, was an adviser in Panama Canal treaty negotiations and U.S. representative to a conference drafting amendments to the charter of the Organization of American States (OAS); retired from the foreign service in 1968; in retirement, worked as a consultant; briefly, was acting provost of Elbert Covell College at the University of the Pacific; for four years, was a member of the OAS Inter-American Commission on Human Rights; died at his home in Washington, D.C. See *Current Biography* (December) 1962.

Obituary *New York Times* C p18 May 22, 2001

XENAKIS, IANNIS May 29, 1922–Feb. 4, 2001 Greek-French composer; architect; using models drawn from science and math, including game theory and the laws of numbers (because of his interest in groups of sounds), ventured into highly innovative explorations in musical composition; studied engineering at the Athens Polytechnic Institute; fighting with the Greek Resistance during World War II, suffered wounds that left him with a scarred face and only one eye; in 1947, emigrated to France, where he became an apprentice of the Swiss architect Le Corbusier; worked with Le Corbusier for 12 years; was a principal architect of such projects as the Philips electronics company's pavilion at the Brussels World's Fair and the Convent of St. Mary at La Tourette; meanwhile, in music, sought the guidance of Olivier Messiaen, who advised him, at his age, not to "try to catch up on harmony and counterpoint," but to build on his "grasp of math and architecture"; in some of his architectural plans, started with a mathematical concept and from it plotted a graph; using the same approach, created his first acknowledged musical composition, *Metastasis* (1954), an eight-minute piece for 61 players that builds on glissandos—rapid slides up and down the scale—that gradually increase in volume; thus, rather than using the orchestra to carry related individual lines (as in the classical tradition) or isolated notes (as in serial music), used it to form blocks or clusters of sound going in different directions; in *Pithoprakta* (1955–56), his first mature musical work, formalized the masses of sound into "stochastic" music (a term based on the Greek word for "goal," *stochos*), in which seemingly random sounds may lead toward a state of stability; further explored the probabilities of behavior of sound clusters in such stochastic compositions as *ST/10-1.080262* (1957–62) and *Eonta* (1963), in which a piano solo is followed by two trumpeters and three trombonists marching back and forth across the stage, an example of his interest in visual aesthetics; achieved his most unusual work in *Stratégie* (1959–62), which incorporates mathematical game theory into a concert setting; for the Montreal Expo (1966), created his first "polytope," a music-and-light show in a space he himself designed; to promote the use of electronic tools in musical endeavors, established in Paris in 1966 the Centre d'Études Mathématique et Automatique Musicales; in the 1970s turned to other scientific models to suggest musical processes—to fractal theory with *Mikka* (1971), for example, and to dendritic forms with *Erikthon* (1977); in the mid-1970s invented a computerized composing machine, the UPIC; in the 1980s and 1990s, was one of the most-performed composers of new music; died at his home in Paris. See *Current Biography* (September) 1974.

Obituary *New York Times* B p7 Feb. 5, 2001

YATES, ELIZABETH Dec. 6, 1905–July 29, 2001 Author; wrote more than 50 books of fiction or nonfiction, chiefly for children, and most illustrated by Nora S. Unwin; received the Newbery Medal for *Amos Fortune, Free Man* (1950), a biography, based on painstaking original research, about an African-American slave who bought his freedom and became a successful weaver and tanner in New Hampshire; following a private-school education in the U.S. and abroad, began doing freelance writing and book reviewing; in 1929, married William McGreal, whose business took them to England for the next 10 years; wrote travel articles for American newspapers; published her first book, *High Holiday*, in 1938; from the notebooks of Enys Tregarthen, put together a volume of Cornish folk tales, *Piskey Folk* (1941), as well as *The Doll Who Came Alive* (1942); after returning to the U.S. and settling on a farm outside Peterborough, New Hampshire, wrote *Patterns on the Wall* (1943), a biography of Jared Austin, a 19th-century New Hampshire journeyman painter, and *Mountain Born* (1943), about a farm boy and his pet lamb; for younger children, wrote *Under the Little Fir* (1947), six short stories set in times past, and *Once in the Year* (1947), a New England Christmas tale; later wrote the biography *Prudence Crandall* (1955), about a Connecticut schoolteacher who challenged a state law in 1833 by opening a racially integrated private girls' school; also wrote, among other books, *Carolina's Courage* (1964), *Up the Golden Stair* (1966), *Sara Whitcher's Story* (1971), *Skeezer, Dog with a Mission* (1972), *Call It Zest: The Vital Ingredient After Seventy* (1977), and three autobiographical books; with *The Road Through Sandwich Notch* (1972), aided opposition to the commercial development of a White Mountains site and spurred its being classified a national forest; donated her farm to the state of New Hampshire and the Society for the Protection of New Hampshire Forests; died in Concord, New Hampshire. See *Current Biography* (Yearbook) 1948.

Obituary *New York Times* A p19 Aug. 2, 2001

YATES, SIDNEY R. Aug. 27, 1909–Oct. 5, 2000 Former Democratic congressman from Illinois; lawyer; an unswerving liberal throughout his long tenure in the U.S. House of Representatives; was first elected in 1948; was victorious in every subsequent biennial congressional election through 1960; ran for the U.S. Senate, unsuccessfully, in 1962; returned to the House in January 1965 and remained there through 1998; as a senior member of the House Appropriations Committee, had privileged influence in the molding of the federal budget; as chairman of the committee's Subcommittee on the Department of the Interior and Related Agencies, was a dauntless and powerful champion of funding for the national endowments of the arts and the humanities; died in Washington, D.C. See *Current Biography* (August) 1993.

Obituary *New York Times* p46 Oct. 8, 2000

ZATOPEK, EMIL Sep. 19, 1922–Nov. 22, 2000 Czechoslovakian runner; army officer; a world-champion runner with a deceptively ungainly, agonized-looking style; was regarded by his peer Roger Bannister as "the greatest athlete of the postwar world"; set 18 world records during his 17-year career; was the first runner to clock 10,000 meters in less than 29 minutes; in winning three gold medals at Helsinki in 1952 (in the 5,000 meters, the 10,000 meters, and the marathon), scored an achievement unmatched in Olympic history; developed incremental "interval" training, now standard among the best 10,000-meter runners; with the Czech Olympic team in London in 1948 (the year in which a Moscow-controlled Communist regime took power in Czechoslovakia), won a gold medal with a record clocking of 29:59.6 in the 10,000-meter event; also won a silver medal in the 5,000 meters; in the 1952 Olympics, again won the gold medal in the 10,000 meters, bettering his record by 42.6 seconds; also won gold medals and set new Olympic records in the 5,000 meters and the full marathon (26 miles, 385 yards, which he clocked in two hours, 23 minutes 3.2 seconds, an improvement of 6:16 minutes over the previous record); between 1948 and 1954, garnered an unprecedented total of 38 first-place finishes in 10,000-meter races; retired from track competition in 1958; at that time, held the rank of major in the Czech army; participated in the anti-Stalinist democratic reform movement that swept Czechoslovakia in 1968 but was crushed by an invasion of Warsaw Pact armies; in punishment, lost his high military position and was reduced to making a living as a garbage collector and street cleaner, a plight that served only to solidify his cult status with the Czech public; after political rehabilitation, was given a position with the national sports ministry; there, used his multilingual talent (he spoke nine languages) to cull from foreign sports journals information useful to Czech coaches; died in Prague, Czechoslovakia. See *Current Biography* (April) 1953.

Obituary *New York Times* C p11 Nov. 23, 2000

CLASSIFICATION BY PROFESSION—2001

AERONAUTICS
Ericsson-Jackson, Aprille J.

AGRICULTURE
Boyd, John W.
Rodriguez, Arturo

ARCHITECTURE
Maki, Fumihiko
Piano, Renzo
Tigerman, Stanley

ART
Abakanowicz, Magdalena
Calle, Sophie
DeCarlo, Dan
Ferrer, Rafael
Golden, Thelma
Gorman, R. C.
Hinojosa, Maria
Kcho
Kentridge, William
McGruder, Aaron

ASTRONOMY
Tarter, Jill Cornell

AVIATION
Smith, Elinor

BUSINESS
Arnesen, Liv
Bethune, Gordon M.
Brin, Sergey, and Page,
  Larry
Burnett, Mark
Bush, George W.
Calderón, Sila M.
Cuban, Mark
Daft, Douglas N.
Djerassi, Carl
Djukanovic, Milo
Evanovich, Janet
Evans, Donald L.
Fox Quesada, Vicente
Gary, Willie E.
Good, Mary L.
Greenberg, Jack M.

Johnson, Eddie Bernice
Kelleher, Herb
Kid Rock
Marcinko, Richard
McCaw, Craig
Middelhoff, Thomas
Nasser, Jacques
O'Neill, Paul H.
Osbourne, Sharon
Phillips, Sam
Popeil, Ron
Reid, L. A.
Robbins, Tony
Ryan, George H.
Sparks, Nicholas
Stanton, Bill
Tajiri, Satoshi
Tyson, John H.
Walsh, John
Wexler, Jerry

CONSERVATION
Fay, J. Michael

ECONOMICS
Krugman, Paul

EDUCATION
Arnesen, Liv
Blackburn, Elizabeth H.
Bond, Julian
Bush, Laura
Canin, Ethan
Clyburn, James E.
Epstein, Samuel S.
Ericsson-Jackson, Aprille J.
Evans, Donald L.
Ferrer, Rafael
Fukuyama, Francis
Gaubatz, Lynn
Goff, M. Lee
Goldsmith, Jerry
Good, Mary L.
Harjo, Joy
Hass, Robert
Konaré, Alpha Oumar
Krugman, Paul
Lewis, David Levering

Maki, Fumihiko
McLean, Jackie
Morella, Constance A.
Paige, Roderick R.
Rice, Condoleezza
Schaap, Phil
Sears, William and Martha
Steele, Claude M.
Stein, Benjamin J.
Tigerman, Stanley
Turre, Steve
Wong-Staal, Flossie

FASHION
Farhi, Nicole
Seymour, Lesley Jane
Wek, Alek

FILM
Beckinsale, Kate
Björk
Blakemore, Michael
Chase, David
Columbus, Chris
Cruz, Penelope
Deakins, Roger
Del Toro, Benicio
Dunst, Kirsten
Farrelly, Peter and Bobby
Fraser, Brendan
Goldberg, Bill
Goldsmith, Jerry
Googoosh
Harden, Marcia Gay
Harjo, Joy
Hoffman, Philip Seymour
Kani, John
Kentridge, William
Li, Jet
Lindo, Delroy
Menken, Alan
Miyazaki, Hayao
Morris, Errol
Osawa, Sandra Sunrising
Petersen, Wolfgang
Pierce, David Hyde
Reitman, Ivan

Kid Rock
Lynne, Shelby
Mahal, Taj
McLean, Jackie
Menken, Alan
Moby
Osbourne, Sharon
Phillips, Sam
Radiohead
Reid, L. A.
Rollins, Henry
Rush
Sánchez, David
Schaap, Phil
Shearer, Harry
Slater, Kelly
Turre, Steve
Wexler, Jerry

NONFICTION
Arnesen, Liv
Bennett, Lerone
Bond, Julian
Burnett, Mark
de la Rúa, Fernando
Djerassi, Carl
Douglas, John E.
Edwards, Bob
Ferris, Timothy
Foley, Mick
Fong-Torres, Ben
Fukuyama, Francis
Gaskin, Ina May
Goff, M. Lee
Gruber, Ruth
Hendrickson, Sue
Hinojosa, Maria
Jakes, T.D.
Krugman, Paul
Lewis, David Levering
Lupica, Mike
Marcinko, Richard
Rice, Condoleezza
Robbins, Tony
Rollins, Henry
Sears, William and Martha
Seymour, Lesley Jane
Shearer, Harry
Stein, Benjamin J.
Tigerman, Stanley
Wong-Staal, Flossie

ORGANIZATIONS
Bond, Julian
Boyd, John W.
Brueggemann, Ingar
Bush, Laura
Chao, Elaine L.
Gandy, Kim
Gary, Willie E.
Gaskin, Ina May
Goldberg, Bill
McDonald, Gabrielle Kirk
Rodriguez, Arturo
Tauscher, Ellen O.
Wek, Alek

PHOTOGRAPHY
Calle, Sophie
Gruber, Ruth
Gursky, Andreas

PUBLISHING
Bailey, Glenda
Friedman, Jane
Middelhoff, Thomas
Rollins, Henry
Seymour, Lesley Jane

RADIO
Burnett, Mark
Edwards, Bob
Fong-Torres, Ben
Goldsmith, Jerry
Googoosh
Hinojosa, Maria
Schaap, Phil
Scully, Vin
Shearer, Harry

RELIGION
Egan, Edward M.
Jakes, T.D.

ROYALTY
Rania

SCIENCE
Benzer, Seymour
Blackburn, Elizabeth H.
Djerassi, Carl
Ericsson-Jackson, Aprille J.
Fay, J. Michael
Goff, M. Lee
Good, Mary L.
Gowers, Timothy

Hendrickson, Sue
Konaré, Alpha Oumar
Rowley, Janet D.
Tarter, Jill Cornell
Thomson, James A.
Wong-Staal, Flossie

SOCIAL ACTIVISM
Bond, Julian
Boyd, John W.
Clyburn, James E.
Epstein, Samuel S.
Francisco, Don
Gandy, Kim
Gary, Willie E.
Goldberg, Bill
Green, Darrell
Gruber, Ruth
Jakes, T.D.
McDonald, Gabrielle Kirk
Rania
Rodriguez, Arturo
Sayles Belton, Sharon
Sears, William and Martha
Walsh, John
Wek, Alek

SOCIAL SCIENCES
Brueggemann, Ingar
Douglas, John E.
Fukuyama, Francis
Lewis, David Levering
Steele, Claude M.
Toledo, Alejandro

SPORTS
Arnesen, Liv
Austin, "Stone Cold" Steve
Baker, Dusty
Burnett, Mark
Bush, George W.
Capriati, Jennifer
Cuban, Mark
Elliott, Sean
Foley, Mick
Garcia, Sergio
Goldberg, Bill
Green, Darrell
Harrison, Marvin
Jones, Chipper
Lara, Brian
Li, Jet
Martin, Mark
Martinez, Pedro

2001 INDEX

This is the index to the January 2001–November 2001 issues. For the index to the 1940–2000 biographies, see *Current Biography: Cumulated Index 1940–2000*.

Gaskin, Ina May May 2001
Gaubatz, Lynn Feb 2001
Gebel-Williams, Gunther obit Oct 2001
Geis, Bernard obit Mar 2001
Gennaro, Peter obit Feb 2001
Gierek, Edward obit Oct 2001
Gilbreth, Frank B. Jr. obit Jul 2001
Gilmore, James S. III Jun 2001
Goff, M. Lee Jun 2001
Goldberg, Bill Apr 2001
Golden, Thelma Sep 2001
Goldovsky, Boris obit Aug 2001
Goldsmith, Jerry May 2001
Gonzalez, Henry obit Feb 2001
Good, Mary L. Sep 2001
Googoosh May 2001
Gordon, Cyrus H. obit Aug 2001
Gorman, R. C. Jan 2001
Gottlieb, Melvin B. obit Mar 2001
Gowers, Timothy Jan 2001
Gowers, William Timothy see Gowers, Timothy
Graham, Katharine obit Oct 2001
Graves, Morris obit Sep 2001
Greco, José obit Mar 2001
Green, Darrell Jan 2001
Greenberg, Jack M. Nov 2001
Greenwood, Colin see Radiohead
Greenwood, Jonny see Radiohead
Gruber, Ruth Jun 2001
Gudmundsdottir, Björk see Björk
Guerard, Albert J. obit Mar 2001
Gursky, Andreas Jul 2001

Hall, Gus obit Jan 2001
Hall, Richard Melville see Moby
Hall, Steffie see Evanovich, Janet
Hanna, William obit Sep 2001
Harden, Marcia Gay Sep 2001
Harjo, Joy Aug 2001
Harrison, Marvin Aug 2001
Hass, Robert Feb 2001
Headley, Elizabeth see Cavanna, Betty
Henderson, Joe obit Oct 2001
Hendrickson, Sue Oct 2001
Hill, Faith Mar 2001
Hinojosa, Maria Feb 2001
Hoffman, Philip Seymour May 2001

Hooker, John Lee obit Sep 2001
Horwich, Frances obit Oct 2001
Hughes, Karen Oct 2001
Hunter, Kermit obit Sep 2001

Jackson, Thomas Penfield Jun 2001
Jakes, T.D. Jun 2001
Jeffords, James Sep 2001
Jet see Urquidez, Benny
Johnson, Eddie Bernice Jul 2001
Jones, Chipper May 2001
Jones, Larry Wayne Jr. see Jones, Chipper

Kabila, Joseph Sep 2001
Kael, Pauline obit Nov 2001
Kainen, Jacob obit Aug 2001
Kani, John Jun 2001
Karbo, Karen May 2001
Katsav, Moshe Feb 2001
Kcho Aug 2001
Kelleher, Herb Jan 2001
Kentridge, William Oct 2001
Ketcham, Hank obit Sep 2001
Kid Rock Oct 2001
Klaus, Josef obit Oct 2001
Knowles, Beyoncé see Destiny's Child
Konaré, Alpha Oumar Oct 2001
Koner, Pauline obit Apr 2001
Kostunica, Vojislav Jan 2001
Kramer, Stanley obit May 2001
Kreutzberger, Mario see Francisco, Don
Krugman, Paul Aug 2001

Lacy, Dan obit Nov 2001
Lapidus, Morris obit Apr 2001
Lara, Brian Feb 2001
Lardner, Ring Jr. obit Feb 2001
Le Clercq, Tanaquil obit Mar 2001
Lee, Geddy see Rush
Lemmon, Jack obit Oct 2001
Lewis, David Levering May 2001
Lewis, John obit Jun 2001
Li, Jet Jun 2001
Li Lian Jie see Li, Jet
Lifeson, Alex see Rush
Lima do Amor, Sisleide see Sissi
Lindbergh, Anne Morrow obit Apr 2001

Lindo, Delroy Mar 2001
Lindsay, John V. obit Mar 2001
Link, O. Winston obit Apr 2001
London, Julie obit Feb 2001
Ludlum, Robert obit Jul 2001
Lupica, Mike Mar 2001
Lynne, Shelby Jul 2001

Machado, Alexis Leyva see Kcho
Magloire, Paul E. obit Nov 2001
Mahal, Taj Nov 2001
Maki, Fumihiko Jul 2001
Maloney, Carolyn B. Apr 2001
Mankind see Foley, Mick
Marcinko, Richard Mar 2001
Martin, Mark Mar 2001
Martinez, Pedro Jun 2001
Masters, William H. obit May 2001
Mathers, Marshall see Eminem
McCaw, Craig Sep 2001
McDonald, Gabrielle Kirk Oct 2001
McGraw, Eloise Jarvis obit Mar 2001
McGreal, Elizabeth see Yates, Elizabeth
McGruder, Aaron Sep 2001
McGuire, Dorothy obit Nov 2001
McIntosh, Millicent Carey obit Mar 2001
McKinney, Robert obit Yrbk 2001
McLean, Jackie Mar 2001
McLean, John Lenwood see McLean, Jackie
Menken, Alan Jan 2001
Meyer, Cord Jr. obit Aug 2001
Middelhoff, Thomas Feb 2001
Miller, Jason obit Yrbk 2001
Minner, Ruth Ann Aug 2001
Miyazaki, Hayao Apr 2001
Moby Apr 2001
Morella, Constance A. Feb 2001
Morris, Errol Feb 2001
Mosley, Sugar Shane Jan 2001
Musharraf, Pervaiz see Musharraf, Pervez
Musharraf, Pervez Mar 2001

Narayan, R. K. obit Jul 2001
Nasser, Jacques Apr 2001
Nathan, Robert R. obit Nov 2001

Nixon, Agnes Apr 2001
Norton, Gale A. Jun 2001

O'Brien, Ed *see* Radiohead
O'Connor, Carroll obit Sep 2001
O'Hair, Madalyn Murray obit Jun 2001
O'Neill, Paul H. Jul 2001
Osawa, Sandra Sunrising Jan 2001
Osbourne, Sharon Jan 2001

Page, Larry *see* Brin, Sergey, and Page, Larry
Paige, Roderick R. Jul 2001
Palmeiro, Rafael Aug 2001
Paz Estenssoro, Victor obit Sep 2001
Peart, Neil *see* Rush
Perkins, Charles obit Feb 2001
Petersen, Wolfgang Jul 2001
Phillips, Sam Apr 2001
Piano, Renzo Apr 2001
Pierce, David Hyde Apr 2001
Pierce, Samuel R. Jr. obit Feb 2001
Pincay, Laffit Sep 2001
Pomeroy, Wardell B. obit Yrbk 2001
Popeil, Ron Mar 2001
Powell, Colin L. Nov 2001

Quine, W. V. obit Mar 2001
Quine, Willard Van Orman *see* Quine, W. V.
Quinn, Anthony obit Sep 2001

Radiohead Jun 2001
Ralston, Joseph W. Jan 2001
Rania Feb 2001
Reeves, Dan Oct 2001
Reid, Antonio *see* Reid, L. A.
Reid, L. A. Aug 2001
Reitman, Ivan Mar 2001
Rhodes, James A. obit Jul 2001
Rice, Condoleezza Apr 2001
Richler, Mordecai obit Oct 2001
Ridge, Tom Feb 2001
Ripley, S. Dillon obit Aug 2001
Ritchie, Robert James *see* Kid Rock
Robards, Jason Jr. obit Mar 2001
Robb, J. D. *see* Roberts, Nora

Robbins, Anthony *see* Robbins, Tony
Robbins, Tony Jul 2001
Roberts, Nora Sep 2001
Rodriguez, Arturo Mar 2001
Rogers, William P. obit Mar 2001
Rollins, Edward J. Mar 2001
Rollins, Henry Sep 2001
Rowan, Carl T. obit Jan 2001
Rowland, Kelly *see* Destiny's Child
Rowley, Janet D. Mar 2001
Rush Feb 2001
Ryan, George H. Sep 2001
Ryder, Jonathan *see* Ludlum, Robert
Ryer, Jonathan *see* Ludlum, Robert

Sánchez, David Nov 2001
Sayles Belton, Sharon Jan 2001
Scammon, Richard M. obit Sep 2001
Schaap, Phil Sep 2001
Schilling, Curt Oct 2001
Schindler, Alexander M. obit Feb 2001
Schultes, Richard Evans obit Sep 2001
Scott, George *see* Blind Boys of Alabama
Scottoline, Lisa Jul 2001
Scully, Vin Oct 2001
Sears, Martha *see* Sears, William and Martha
Sears, William and Martha Aug 2001
Seau, Junior Sep 2001
Selway, Phil *see* Radiohead
Seymour, Lesley Jane Nov 2001
Shaheen, Jeanne Jan 2001
Shapiro, Irving S. obit Nov 2001
Shearer, Harry Jun 2001
Shepherd, Michael *see* Ludlum, Robert
Simon, Herbert A. obit May 2001
Sinopoli, Giuseppe obit Sep 2001
Sissi Jun 2001
Slater, Kelly Jul 2001
Smith, Elinor Mar 2001
Sothern, Ann obit Aug 2001
Sparks, Nicholas Feb 2001
Spence, Hartzell obit Yrbk 2001
Spencer, John Jan 2001
Sprewell, Latrell Feb 2001
Stackhouse, Jerry Nov 2001

Stanton, Bill May 2001
Stargell, Willie obit Sep 2001
Stassen, Harold E. obit May 2001
Steele, Claude M. Feb 2001
Stein, Benjamin J. Sep 2001
Stevens, Ted Oct 2001
Storr, Anthony obit Sep 2001
Stratton, William G. obit Aug 2001
Sucksdorff, Arne obit Sep 2001
Sullivan, Leon H. obit Sep 2001
Sun Wen Apr 2001
Swinton, Tilda Nov 2001
Syal, Meera Feb 2001

Tajiri, Satoshi Nov 2001
Tarter, Jill Cornell Feb 2001
Tauscher, Ellen O. Mar 2001
Thomson, James A. Nov 2001
Thomson, Meldrim Jr. obit Sep 2001
Tigerman, Stanley Feb 2001
Titov, Gherman obit Jan 2001
Toledo, Alejandro Nov 2001
Trenet, Charles obit Sep 2001
Trenkler, Freddie obit Yrbk 2001
Trout, Robert obit Jan 2001
Trudeau, Pierre Elliott obit Jan 2001
Tsui Hark Oct 2001
Turre, Steve Apr 2001
Tyson, John H. Aug 2001

Urquidez, Benny Nov 2001

Valentine, Bobby Jul 2001
Van Gundy, Jeff May 2001
Verdon, Gwen obit Jan 2001

Walsh, John Jul 2001
Waugh, Auberon obit May 2001
Wayans, Marlon *see* Wayans, Shawn and Marlon
Wayans, Shawn and Marlon May 2001
Weinrig, Gary Lee *see* Rush
Wek, Alek Jun 2001
Welty, Eudora obit Nov 2001
Wexler, Jerry Jan 2001
Whitehead, Colson Nov 2001
Wiggins, James Russell obit Mar 2001
Williams, Michelle *see* Destiny's Child
Wong-Staal, Flossie Apr 2001

Woodcock, Leonard obit Apr
  2001
Woods, Donald obit Nov 2001
Woodward, Robert F. obit
  Yrbk 2001

Xenakis, Iannis obit Jul 2001

Yates, Elizabeth obit Nov
  2001
Yates, Sidney R. obit Jan 2001
Yorke, Thom *see* Radiohead

Zaillian, Steven Oct 2001
Zatopek, Emil obit Feb 2001
Zhu Rongji Jul 2001
Zivojinovich, Alex *see* Rush